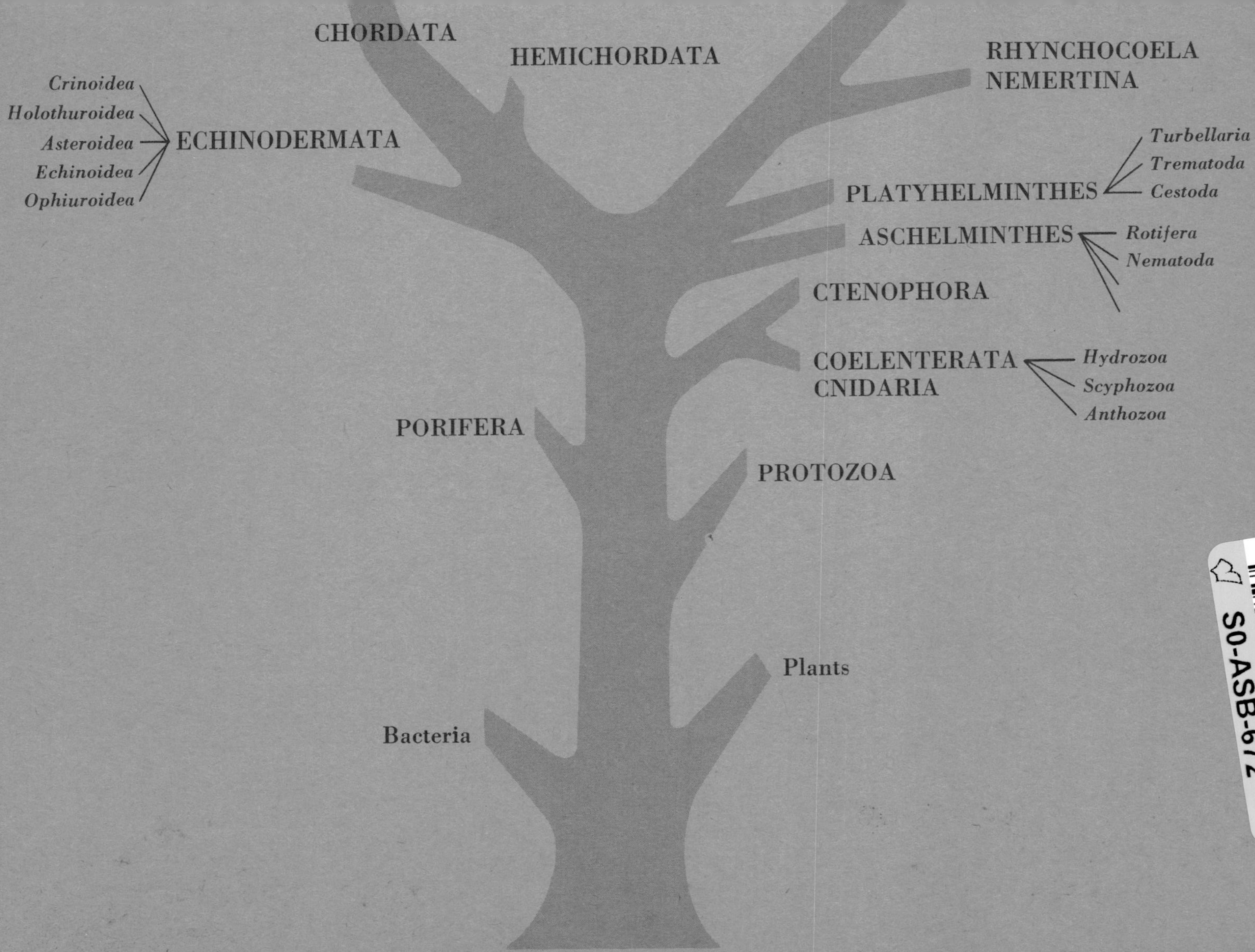
CHORDATA
HEMICHORDATA
RHYNCHOCOELA
NEMERTINA
Crinoidea
Holothuroidea
Asteroidea
Echinoidea
Ophiuroidea
ECHINODERMATA
Turbellaria
Trematoda
Cestoda
PLATYHELMINTHES
ASCHELMINTHES
Rotifera
Nematoda
CTENOPHORA
COELENTERATA
CNIDARIA
Hydrozoa
Scyphozoa
Anthozoa
PORIFERA
PROTOZOA
Plants
Bacteria

Prentice-Hall Biological Science Series

William D. McElroy and Carl P. Swanson
Editors

*Biochemical Systematics,** RALPH E. ALSTON AND B. L. TURNER
Classic Papers in Genetics, JAMES A. PETERS
Experimental Biology, RICHARD W. VAN NORMAN
Foundations of Experimental Embryology, BENJAMIN H. WILLIER AND JANE M. OPPENHEIMER
General and Comparative Physiology, WILLIAM S. HOAR
Mechanisms of Body Functions, DEXTER M. EASTON
Milestones in Microbiology, THOMAS D. BROCK
Papers on Human Genetics, SAMUEL H. BOYER, IV
Poisonous Plants of the United States and Canada, JOHN M. KINGSBURY
Principles of Biology, NEAL D. BUFFALOE
Radiotracer Methodology in Biological Science, C. H. WANG AND DAVID L. WILLIS
Selected Botanical Papers, IRVING W. KNOBLOCH
Selected Papers on Virology, NICHOLAS HAHON
A Synthesis of Evolutionary Theory, HERBERT H. ROSS

CONCEPTS OF MODERN BIOLOGY SERIES

*Behavioral Aspects of Ecology,** PETER H. KLOPFER
Molecular Biology: Genes and Chemical Control of Living Cells, J. M. BARRY
Process of Organic Evolution G. LEDYARD STEBBINS

FOUNDATIONS OF MODERN BIOLOGY SERIES

Adaptation, 2nd ed., BRUCE WALLACE AND A. M. SRB
Animal Behavior, 2nd ed., VINCENT DETHIER AND ELIOT STELLAR
Animal Diversity, 2nd ed., EARL D. HANSON
Animal Physiology, 2nd ed., KNUT SCHMIDT-NEILSEN
The Cell, 2nd ed., CARL P. SWANSON
Cell Physiology and Biochemistry, 2nd ed., WILLIAM D. MCELROY
Chemical Background for the Biological Sciences, EMIL H. WHITE
Growth and Development, 2nd ed., MAURICE SUSSMAN
Heredity, 2nd ed., DAVID M. BONNER AND STANLEY E. MILLS
The Life of the Green Plant, 2nd ed., ARTHUR W. GALSTON
Man in Nature, 2nd ed., MARSTON BATES
The Plant Kingdom, 2nd ed., HAROLD C. BOLD

*These titles are also in the PRENTICE-HALL INTERNATIONAL SERIES IN BIOLOGICAL SCIENCE. Prentice-Hall, Inc., Prentice-Hall International, United Kingdom and Eire; Prentice-Hall of Canada, Ltd., Canada.

General and Comparative

Prentice-Hall, Inc. / Englewood Cliffs, New Jersey

PHYSIOLOGY

WILLIAM S. HOAR

Department of Zoology
The University of British Columbia
Vancouver, Canada

PRENTICE-HALL INTERNATIONAL, INC., *London*
PRENTICE-HALL OF AUSTRALIA, PTY., LTD., *Sydney*
PRENTICE-HALL OF CANADA, LTD., *Toronto*
PRENTICE-HALL OF INDIA (PRIVATE) LTD., *New Delhi*
PRENTICE-HALL OF JAPAN, INC., *Tokyo*

GENERAL AND COMPARATIVE PHYSIOLOGY
by William S. Hoar

Current printing (last digit):
10 9 8 7 6 5 4 3

Library of Congress Catalog Card Number 65–22254

Printed in the United States of America

C–34770

TO MY STUDENTS

Past

Present

and

Future

Preface

Physiological literature is now rich in details pertaining to every major group in the animal kingdom. Zoologists, who must acquire a working knowledge of this information, are faced with the difficult task of remembering diverse facts and incorporating them into a meaningful scheme. The details often seem isolated or pertinent to only one animal and, although they may have real meaning for the specialist, the beginner frequently finds little interest in them. Yet the numerous facts of comparative physiology are not really unrelated. They are all a part of the story of evolution. The processes have been discovered and recorded as isolated facts, but they came into existence and acquired meaning as steps and stages in the progressive adaptation of animal life to varied habitats and changing environments. They are historical details in the organization of protoplasm for the varied activities of animal life.

This book is written with the conviction that a story of phylogeny in animal functions can now be sketched and that this will provide a framework into which the many details of physiology can be interestingly fitted. It is written for students who must acquire a working knowledge of functional biology whether their special field is to be animal physiology or any one of the many other branches of zoology.

No attempt has been made to write a detailed treatise. A wealth of well-established information—related particularly to human, medical and cellular physiology—is not included. These topics are comprehensively covered in many excellent texts. Likewise, numerous monographs on the different animal groups provide a ready source of detailed physiological information. What seems to be less generally available is a synthesis of the major trends in physiological adaptation. This has been attempted here. It is hoped that the student will find it a structure into which the accumulated and ever-increasing body of facts concerning animal physiology can be easily and interestingly fitted.

The bibliography will direct the alert student to many experimental details and additional evidence to support the factual statements and hypotheses. Because science is a cooperative venture, neither the writer nor the student can afford to disregard the achievements of his predecessors. I have found three groups of scientists while writing this book. Most numerous are those who year after year accumulate facts pertaining to their own particular field of interest and in this way lay the foundations and assemble the materials from which a true understanding evolves. Their names do not often appear in my bibliography but their contribution is acknowledged none the less; they have provided most of the facts of comparative physiology. Less numerous are those who, through superior abilities, unusually productive environments, or sheer accident, make the more fundamental discoveries. They alter the direction of our thoughts, initiate great new lines of research and provide the significant landmarks in the progress of physiological understanding. I have tried to include some of their names for they are often lost in the flood of work designed to test their findings or theories. Lastly, there are the reviewers and coordinators of symposia who, at irregular intervals, bring the scattered literature together and provide the detailed bibliographies of that large first group of workers. Their efforts are most useful to the textbook writer and invaluable to the student or research worker attempting to grasp a particular segment of knowledge. They are most frequently quoted in the pages which follow since, through this channel, students can most speedily locate the many pertinent original references.

Some familiarity with animal phylogeny and taxonomy is assumed throughout the text and both common and scientific names are often used without reference to their taxonomic position. Since this assumption may not always be justified, all scientific names have been identified to major taxonomic groups in the index and these groups are shown on a phylogenetic tree at the front of the book. In this way it is hoped to orient the reader with limited background in systematic zoology and make the discussion more meaningful.

It is only possible to acknowledge the assistance of a few of those who have contributed to this book through advice on factual matters or by their encouragement during its production. The uncompromising criticisms of my wife improved the manuscript at every stage. She read the early drafts and checked all the typescripts and proofs. I could not have finished the task without this cheerful support and cooperation on the home front. Mary Needler Arai read most of the manuscript and made numerous helpful comments. In addition, the following specialists have offered advice on specific points or checked bulky sections of the manuscript:

M. A. Ali, E. C. Black, J. J. R. Campbell, P. A. Dehnel, F. E. J. Fry, C. P. Hickman, Jr., W. N. Holmes and D. J. Randall. I am most grateful to them all.

William S. Hoar

Contents

Sources of Energy and its Distribution

1 The Origin Of Animals And Their Environment

The Russian biochemist Oparin, about 1923, first developed those ideas which have become basic to the modern concepts of the origin of life. Oparin (1953) emphasized two alternatives. One might postulate that life arose in a world much like ours, or one might assume that it originated under very different conditions. Until about a generation ago only the first alternative seemed likely. Oparin argued that all the evidence pointed to the second alternative and that the earth, in its youth, was probably very different. He maintained that, although spontaneous generation is now impossible, it might well have been inevitable in the earth which knew no life. The living environment has evolved with living organisms. They are inseparable, and our present world, filled with so much life, precludes a spontaneous generation.

This argument now seems sound, and it is likely that the world and the animals which live in it have evolved together. Geochemists and biologists agree that there has been a series of irreversible steps while the earth cooled, generated an atmosphere rich in hydrogen and produced the first simple organic compounds which gradually increased in complexity and formed the self-duplicating living systems (Calvin, 1962; Fox, 1960; Gaffron, 1960*a* and *b*). Each step has changed conditions and reduced the likelihood of a repetition of earlier events. Darwinian evolution has been documented by convincing facts for over a hundred years, but it is only in the last twenty-five years that scientists have found evidence for the evolution of the organic from the inorganic, the biochemical from the organic, and the living from the biochemical.

The duration of the prebiologic period is incomprehensible. Gaffron (1960*a*) suggests that it required three billion years for the development of the first cells and that Darwinian evolution, by comparison, has lasted only about a third as long. Estimates by other writers are shorter, but there is no real agreement on this point. Scientists, however, are unanimous that the early evolutionary period was longer than that with which Darwin was concerned. Three major stages are thought to have preceded conditions suitable for the life of our familiar plants and animals (Gaffron, 1960*a* and *b*). These were probably anaerobic or nearly so.

Anaerobic Stages in Terrestrial Evolution

ERA OF EXCESS HYDROGEN

Life had its origin in highly reducing conditions. The prebiologic atmosphere contained water, hydrogen, ammonia and methane in unknown amounts and proportions (Fig. 1.1). Small amounts of carbon dioxide may have been present, but methane and not carbon dioxide furnished the carbon for the first organic compounds. Hydrogen was abundant; free oxygen was absent. The primary source of energy for organic syntheses in the beginning was, as now, the sun. The photochemical and ionizing radiation and the heat were intense and electrical storms frequent. These were the conditions which favored the first fortuitous combinations of carbon, hydrogen, oxygen and nitrogen.

This hypothesis is now supported by many exciting experiments (Ponnamperuma *et al*, 1963). Mixtures of gases, such as those present in the earth's first atmosphere, when subjected to ionizing or short ultraviolet radiation at temperatures of 80° to 90°C yield small amounts of familiar organic compounds in great variety (Fig. 1.1). Although the quantities formed are minute, they may be readily identified by chromatographic techniques. Organic acids of low molecular weight, such as formic, acetic, succinic and lactic acids are common. The amino acids glycine and alanine, urea, adenine and some simple sugars such as ribose have been identified. Acetic acid and glycine occur frequently, and these are primary building blocks for many of the important living compounds.

Life is much more than a solution of simple amino and aliphatic acids, and the chemist has now been able to show that sources of energy which must have been present during this era will also produce complex polymers and aggregates. Under appropriate conditions heat alone will form stable macromolecules (polypeptides) from a mixture of simple amino acids (Fox, 1960; Calvin, 1962). These peptide-linked amino acids have a tendency to coil and produce well-defined structures which favor the further accumulation of similar molecules. Stability of such aggregates is greater in either pure D- or L-type polymers than in the racemic

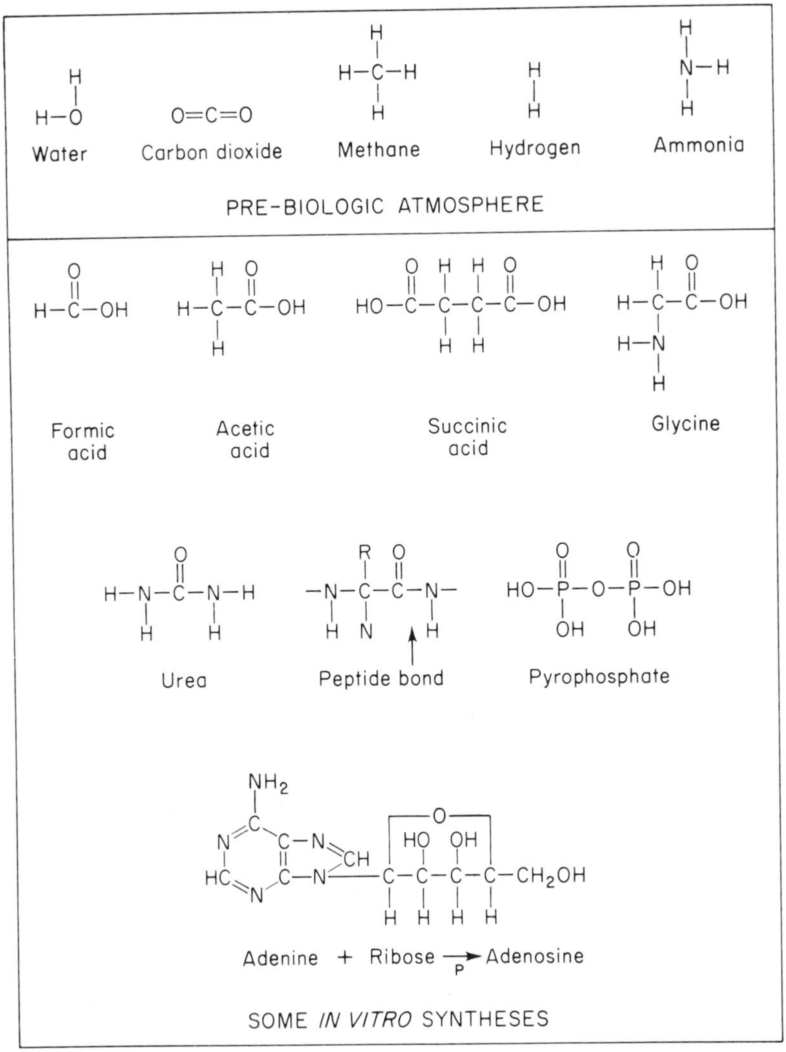

Fig. 1.1. The prebiologic atmosphere and some likely prebiological compounds. Combinations shown in lower group have been identified in *in vitro* systems.

(D-L) mixtures, and this may be the basis of the almost universal occurrence of one type of optical activity in living material (Gaffron, 1960*a*).

More complex biochemical units have not yet been identified in these organic mixtures. However, *in vitro* systems frequently yield many of their "building blocks" and chemists can often suggest logical synthetic pathways. The porphyrins (page 173), for example, are key substances in a multitude of electron transfers associated with photosynthesis and respiration, and they can be synthesized from glycine and acetate or succinate. It is now apparent that random processes could have produced the essentials of such vital compounds as chlorophyll, hemoglobin, the cytochromes and the nucleosides. Oparin postulated an immensely long period for these random syntheses before living material appeared and before the photosynthetic activities of plants filled the air with oxygen and the evolving animals began to oxidize plant materials as a source of energy. The oceans became a thick brew of organic material. Urey (1952) calculates that the primitive oceans may have been a 10 per cent solution of organic compounds.

CHANGING PREBIOLOGIC ATMOSPHERE

Conditions during the second stage remained essentially anaerobic, although the atmosphere was gradually changing. Progressively more hydrogen escaped from the earth, and traces of oxygen began to accumulate from the direct decomposition of water and, later, from the action of living organisms. The ozone, formed from the oxygen by the intense ultraviolet radiation, gradually escaped into the upper atmosphere to form a thickening curtain between the short-wave ultraviolet and the earth. Under this ozone blanket organic compounds became more diversified and complex. The direct formation of the amino and aliphatic acids from methane and ammonia would decline, but the more elaborate and complex organic materials, for example, the nucleosides, porphyrins and polypeptides, often decomposed by intense ultraviolet radiation, could persist. The details are unknown; but certain classes of organic compound must have appeared since this stage is thought to have terminated with the appearance of life in the true sense of the word.

In particular, this stage was probably marked by an increasing utilization of chemical energy through the rearrangement of the more complex molecules formed during the earlier stages. A large and varied group of ENZYMES must have preceded the first truly living units. The enzymes are organic catalysts which permit life processes to proceed at low temperatures and release energy in a controlled manner. They are either simple proteins or proteins combined with complex non-protein groups (prosthetic groups). Many of the enzymes concerned with the transfer of energy are of the complex type; the prosthetic group is characterized by the presence of a metallic element. Their properties are adequately described in many excellent textbooks, and it is only emphasized here that a varied array was essential for the utilization of chemical energy by the first living materials.

In the present world, living organisms utilize chemical energy through a group of high-energy phosphate compounds, the most important of which is ADENOSINE TRIPHOSPHATE, usually referred to as ATP (Chapter 7). The important components of this compound have also appeared in laboratory experiments under conditions which simulated those that might have preceded life. The structure of ATP (Fig. 7.1) and many details pertaining to the transformation of energy in living systems will be summarized in Chapter 7. At this point in the discussion, it is noted that the hydrolysis of the terminal phosphate bond of ATP is associated with the exchange of about 8500 calories of free energy per mole; ADENOSINE DIPHOSPHATE (ADP) is formed by the reaction. Much of the chemistry of life has to do with the formation of these high-energy phosphate bonds of ATP from low energy bonds (such as carbon-carbon, carbon-hydrogen or carbon-oxygen) and subsequently with the utilization of this high energy phosphate to do work. ATP is like a fully-charged storage battery whose energy can be transformed into mechanical work, light or heat; when a muscle contracts or a gland secretes, or when chemical syntheses are performed, the source of energy is usually the pyrophosphate bond of ATP. The universality of the ATP/ADP mechanism suggests that these compounds appeared early in the prebiologic world. It seems reasonably clear that the storing, transforming and mobilizing of energy by the phosphate bond of the ATP/ADP system and the associated heavy metal electron transfer enzyme systems are older than life itself and have persisted, relatively unchanged, for a billion years or more.

EMERGENCE OF LIVING SYSTEMS

During the third stage the early anaerobic systems took full advantage of the preformed organic compounds. The tempo of evolution increased with the appearance of chemical machinery for self-duplication. The second stage, referred to above, may be looked on as a network of interlocking chemical loops, changing shape and absorbing ever greater quantities of the raw material until the more rapid and more efficient reactions came to dominate the field. The third stage is characterized by the presence of substances which have the property of self-reproduction. Again, it is a phosphorus compound (deoxyribonucleic acid, DNA) which has this property of self-duplication and the ability to provide a specific code for the assembling of the individual units of complex molecules such as the proteins.

DNA and its closely related co-worker, ribonucleic acid (RNA), are chain compounds composed of four nitrogenous "bases," pentose sugar and phosphate groups (Fig. 22.1). These are strung together in definite ways to form a code for the duplication of complex organic compounds. The presence of the DNA/RNA machinery removed the haphazard development of organic systems. When superior units appeared with the power of self-duplication, their advantage would be tremendous. Many of the characteristics of living systems probably preceded cellular organization and were present in self-duplicating macromolecules.

The first living organisms must have been small and simple in structure. They may have been of bacterial size but less rigidly organized; if the assumptions concerning the atmosphere are correct, all of them were anaerobic. Present-day anaerobic organisms can liberate energy in many ways. The alcoholic fermentation of sugar by yeasts or bacteria is a familiar but not a simple process. It must have developed after many experiments in biochemical evolution. A dozen major reactions with as many enzymes and coenzymes or activators are involved. Energy transfer involving ATP and ADP occurs at four stages, and there is a net gain of two ATP molecules for each molecule of sugar fermented (Fig. 7.3). In contrast, the aerobic breakdown of glucose yields 38 high-energy phosphate bonds. Only about 5 per cent of the total energy available by aerobic oxidation is obtained in the alcoholic fermentation process. Even so, alcoholic fermentation is a relatively efficient anaerobic reaction, and some other fermentations yield much less energy (as little as 2.5 per cent of the energy that is available). Butyric acid fermentation is considered a particularly primitive reaction. It often occurs in the decomposition of organic material in bogs and swamps. Such processes are assumed to have occurred also in the primitive anaerobic world.

The energy for life in this phase may not have been entirely chemical. Solar radiation may have been vital, even before the chlorophyll-containing organisms made use of it for synthetic purposes. As Gaffron and others have emphasized, the rate of evolution would have slowed down considerably during this stage if it had depended alone on the energy stored in organic compounds. Although the action of the short, more energetic components of solar radiation was greatly reduced, photochemical energy could have been abundantly available through various pigmented compounds. Iron and copper salts and many well known dyes produce photochemical effects by absorption of energy in the visible spectrum. Transfer of hydrogen and varied oxidation reactions can be greatly accelerated by light-excited dyes. The porphyrin compounds, all of which are colored, may have played a vital part in photochemical reactions before one of them (the magnesium porphyrin, chlorophyll) initiated the era of photosynthesis.

Photosynthesis and the Origin of an Aerobic World

The advent of photosynthesis marked the beginning of the fourth and final stage in the evolution of life—the stage with which we are primarily concerned in comparative animal physiology. In this, plants utilize radiant energy to produce ATP and then to synthesize carbon compounds and store chemical energy for themselves and for the animals which feed on them. "Each year the plants of the earth combine about 150 billion tons of carbon with 25 billion tons of hydrogen, and set free 400 billion tons of oxygen" (Rabinowitch, 1948). This liberation of oxygen gradually converted an anaerobic world into an aerobic world and set the stage for Darwinian evolution.

Photosynthesis, however, like other biological processes, evolved gradually, and it is unlikely that there was ever a sharp break between the non-photosynthetic and the photosynthetic world, between the anaerobic and the aerobic. Photosynthesis depends not only on the chlorophyll molecule but also on an associated light-trapping machine (the chloroplasts or their counterparts) and on many of the same electron carriers and enzymes concerned with tissue respiration. The essential new trick is the conversion of radiant energy into chemical energy in the form of the reactive bond of adenosine triphosphate. This is done not in one way but through at least three somewhat different reactions, two of which are anaerobic and might have preceded the third during phylogeny (Arnon, 1960, 1962).

SYNTHESIS OF PHOSPHATE BONDS AND REDUCED PYRIDINE NUCLEOTIDE

The photosynthetic processes are complex and not yet completely understood. During the past two decades, however, since the advent of radiochemical and chromatographic techniques, it has been possible to discard many of the old ideas and fit together some of the larger pieces of the puzzle.

A direct cyclical photophosphorylation mechanism is suggestive of the first step in the evolution of the photosynthetic machinery (Fig. 1.2*a*). If so, it could have supplied abundant active phosphate during the later anaerobic era of evolution. In this process the photons of radiant energy excite the chlorophyll molecule to send electrons into a high-energy state. They are captured by complex electron transport compounds, and as they are passed from one of these to another and drop to a lower energy state, ADP molecules are changed into ATP. In another anaerobic process (Fig. 1.2*b*) electrons are donated by compounds such as thiosulfate, and again ATP is formed. However this process is non-cyclical, and the H^+ may be used to reduce several important compounds. One of these is triphosphopyridine nucleotide (TPN), a universal spoke in several of

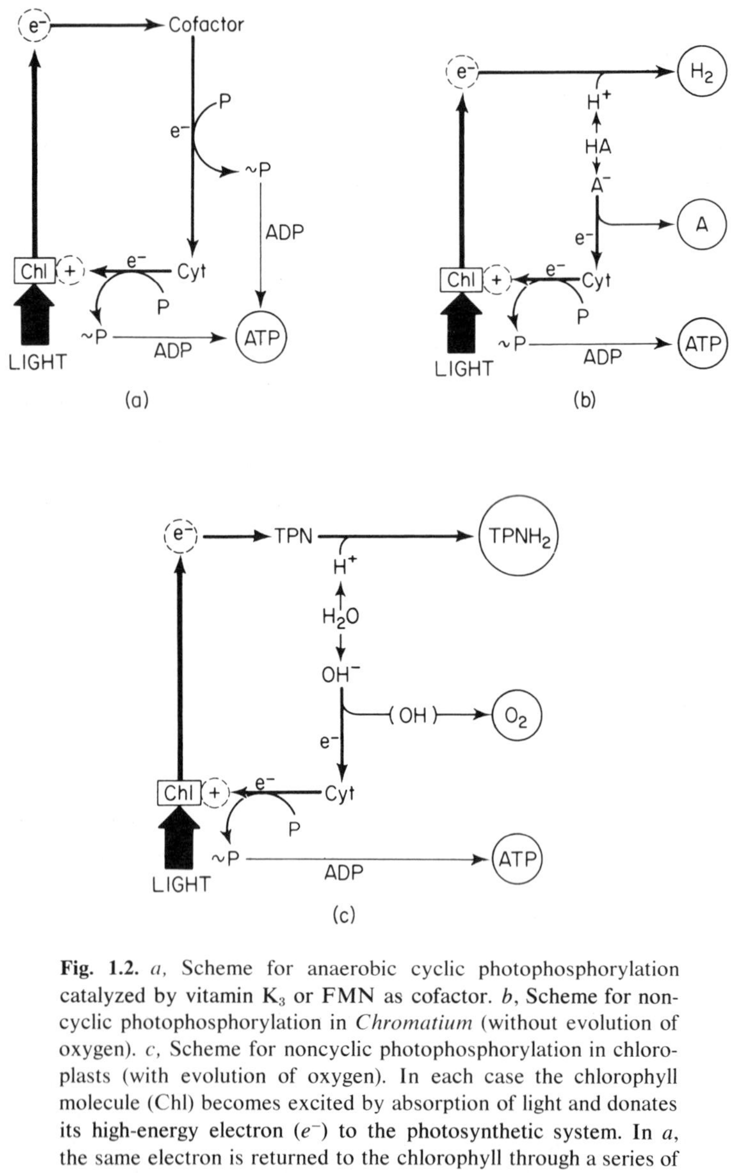

Fig. 1.2. *a*, Scheme for anaerobic cyclic photophosphorylation catalyzed by vitamin K_3 or FMN as cofactor. *b*, Scheme for non-cyclic photophosphorylation in *Chromatium* (without evolution of oxygen). *c*, Scheme for noncyclic photophosphorylation in chloroplasts (with evolution of oxygen). In each case the chlorophyll molecule (Chl) becomes excited by absorption of light and donates its high-energy electron (e^-) to the photosynthetic system. In *a*, the same electron is returned to the chlorophyll through a series of carriers; in *b* and *c*, it is used to reduce TPN and replaced in the chlorophyll by an electron from an electron donor (thiosulphate, succinate, water). [Arnon in McElroy and Glass (1961).]

life's biochemical wheels. In the third process (Fig. 1.2*c*) water becomes the electron donor, reduced pyridine nucleotide compounds and ATP are formed but—of paramount importance from the standpoint of animal evolution—oxygen is at last liberated in large quantities, and the evolution of an aerobic world becomes possible.

FIXATION OF CARBON

There are actually two parts to the photosynthetic production of organic compounds by plants. In the first of these which has just been sketched, the energy-rich bonds of ATP are generated through the action of sunlight. In the second, this ATP energy is utilized to reduce atmospheric carbon dioxide and then, to synthesize the carbohydrates, fats and proteins characteristic of plant protoplasm. This second system is an enzyme-operated process which does not require sunlight but can proceed just as well in the dark. These two systems—one dependent on light and the other independent of it—must have evolved separately and then interlocked fortuitously (Calvin, 1962).

The important steps in carbon fixation are summarized in Fig. 1.3, but the details will be more meaningful when the section on tissue respiration has been studied in Chapter 7. At this point it should be noted that carbon dioxide, water, phosphate in the form of ATP and hydrogen in reduced pyridine nucleotide are fed into an enzyme pool which synthesizes a three-carbon compound (glyceraldehyde-3-phosphate or PGAL). The cycle of chemical changes may be considered to start and end with ribulose-5-phosphate, and with each turn of the "wheel" one unit of this three-carbon compound, PGAL, is synthesized from inorganic sources. In Chapter 7 it will become evident that the PGAL thus synthesized enters into other enzyme pools which lead directly to complex carbohydrates, fats and proteins and that the compounds and the enzymes (with two exceptions) which form the carbon dioxide fixation cycle (Fig. 1.3) are also present in tissue respiration. In general, the carbon dioxide fixation cycle elaborates the carbon compounds, and tissue respiration breaks them down in reversed reactions.

AUTOTROPHIC AND HETEROTROPHIC WAYS OF LIFE

In our world, two main streams of life are quite distinct. The plants (AUTOTROPHIC or self-nourishing organisms) utilize inorganic materials to elaborate a great variety of organic compounds; the animals (HETEROTROPHIC organisms) exploit the organic compounds elaborated by the plants. The distinction is not so sharp among the more primitive forms of life and must have been even less evident during early periods of

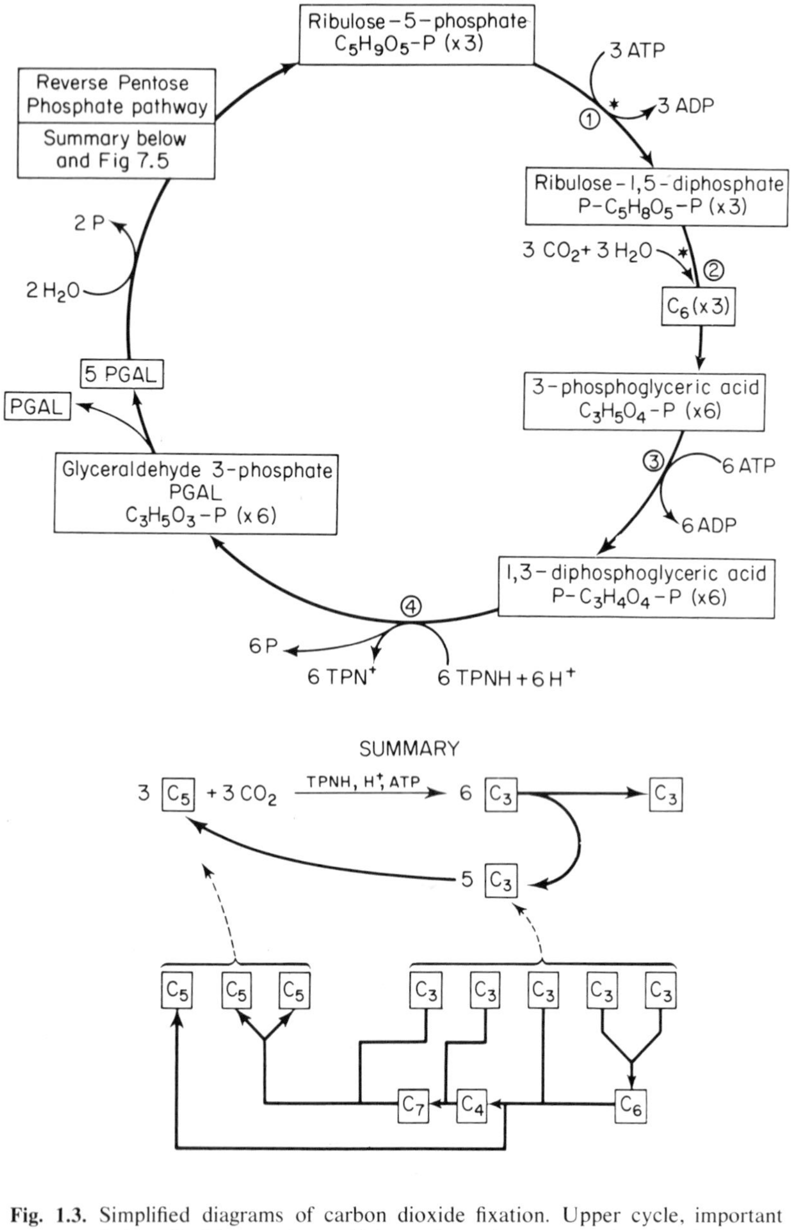

Fig. 1.3. Simplified diagrams of carbon dioxide fixation. Upper cycle, important compounds identified in reactions which produce triose sugar, showing three units of an unidentified 6-carbon compound between ribulose diphosphate and phosphoglyceric acid. Lower diagrams summarize carbon dioxide fixation with the formation of triose and (at the bottom) the reverse pentose shunt which generates pentose and hexose from triose. Asterisk, reactions peculiar to photosynthesis while others are also found in tissue respiration. ENZYMES: 1, phosphoribulokinase and Mg^{++}; 2, ribulose diphosphate carboxylase or carboxydismutase; 3, 3-phosphoglycerate-l-kinase and Mg^{++}; 4, glyceraldehyde-3-phosphate dehydrogenase. [Based on Fruton and Simmonds (1958) and Karlson (1963).]

evolution. A great range of metabolic machinery has been found in present day bacteria; investigations of their metabolism first provided useful clues to biochemical evolution (van Niel, 1935, 1943; Starkey, 1962).

Chemosynthetic bacteria. These are forms which derive their primary energy from the oxidation of inorganic compounds rather than from sunlight. The oxidizable materials include sulfur, hydrogen sulfide, thiosulfate, ferrous and manganous salts, methane, hydrogen gas, ammonia and nitrite. The energy yields are small (of the order of 25 to 120 kilocalories per mole) but sufficient to elaborate the familiar carbon compounds of protoplasm from carbon dioxide, ammonia or other nitrogen source and water. In all probability the energy is channelled through the ATP/ADP machinery. Bacterial protoplasm is organized much like that of other living organisms, but in the chemosynthetic forms the enzyme cycles are operated by energy derived from the oxidation of inorganic compounds (Fromageot and Senez, 1960; Starkey, 1962).

Photosynthetic bacteria. The photosynthetic bacteria are particularly interesting since they contain pigments (chlorophylls, carotenoids) and make direct use of the sunlight as well as of a variety of oxidizable materials, including inorganic substances such as the sulfur compounds. Van Niel (1935, 1943 and in "Gabriel and Fogel," 1955) has presented acceptable arguments for the evolution of photosynthesis and carbon dioxide fixation, based largely on studies of the chemoautotrophic and photosynthetic bacteria.

There are several groups of these photosynthetic bacteria showing a range in metabolism from that of the colorless chemosynthetic sulfur bacteria mentioned above to forms which depend entirely on photochemical reactions for their primary energy (Thimann, 1963). The GREEN SULFUR BACTERIA (*Chlorobacteriaceae*) reduce CO_2 and oxidize H_2S to form sugars, depositing sulfur granules (generally outside the cells) according to the following scheme:

$$CO_2 + H_2S \xrightarrow[\text{light}]{} (CH_2O) + H_2O + 2S$$

These are obligate photosynthetic and strictly anaerobic organisms; they might have existed at an early stage in the origination of life. Their metabolism may be even more primitive than that of the colorless sulfur bacteria which require oxygen.

The purple to red *Thiorhodaceae* can perform the above reaction but may go further and convert the sulfur granules into sulfate as follows:

$$2CO_2 + H_2S + 2H_2O \xrightarrow[\text{light}]{} 2(CH_2O) + H_2SO_4$$

In addition, the *Thiorhodaceae* can utilize hydrogen directly or obtain it from a variety of hydrogen donors such as the simple organic acids:

$$CO_2 + 2H_2 \xrightarrow[\text{light}]{} (CH_2O) + H_2O$$

or

$$H_2A + CO_2 \xrightarrow[\text{light}]{} 2A + (CH_2O) + H_2O$$

where H_2A represents a simple organic acid such as acetic or butyric acid.

Finally, the purple bacteria *Athiorhodaceae* are mainly non-sulfur organisms requiring organic compounds as hydrogen donors and certain growth factors (vitamins) for their metabolism. They are particularly interesting since they live aerobically in the dark and oxidize a variety of organic materials; in the light they utilize radiant energy and synthesize organic compounds photochemically. They obtain hydrogen from different hydrogen donors such as acetate, propionate or butyrate (Thimann, 1963; Hill and Wittingham, 1957). These photochemical reactions are referred to as PHOTOREDUCTIONS to distinguish them from typical photosyntheses where the H_2A in the above reaction would correspond to H_2O and oxygen would be liberated. The "photosynthetic bacteria" do not liberate oxygen like typical green plants. They seem to operate according to the anaerobic noncyclical scheme shown in Fig. 1.2*b*.

Photoreduction to photosynthesis. Metabolic machinery, such as that studied in the single-celled green alga *Scenedesmus*, may bridge the step from photoreduction to photosynthesis (Hill and Wittingham, 1957). *Scenedesmus* performs typical photosynthesis in light and releases oxygen into the atmosphere (Fig. 1.2*c*). In the dark, however, it becomes chemoautotrophic; like the bacterium *Bacillus pycnoticus* or *Hydrogenomonas*, it may reduce carbon dioxide in the presence of hydrogen and oxygen.

$$6H_2 + CO_2 + 2O_2 \longrightarrow CH_2O + 5H_2O$$

Scenedesmus can also perform photoreduction, at least experimentally. If the algae are preadapted in the dark under anaerobic conditions with an atmosphere of hydrogen, they will absorb hydrogen and, following this preadaptation, photoreduction occurs directly in the light without a preliminary formation of hydrogen from water by photolysis (Hill and Whittingham, 1957). *Scenedesmus* in this way combines the mechanisms of the chemosynthetic bacteria, the photosynthetic bacteria which depend on photoreduction (Fig. 1.2*b*) and the green plants which perform typical photosyntheses.

Van Niel (1935) emphasized the generalized nature of the light reaction in all of these photochemical reactions. The process may be represented by an oxidation-reduction reaction as follows, where *A* represents oxygen in the green plants, while it (*A*) represents other substances such as sulfur or organic groups in the photosynthetic bacteria.

$$CO_2 + 2H_2A \longrightarrow (CH_2O) + H_2O + 2A$$

This concept has been amply confirmed through tracer carbon techniques with a chromatographic identification of the intermediate products (Arnon, 1960). There is still speculation about biochemical details, but the major events have been outlined. For the animal physiologist, the most significant of the processes is that in which solar energy liberates oxygen from water into the atmosphere and passes the hydrogen ions and electrons to a series of carriers, thus forming reduced pyridine compounds and some ATP. This process permitted the evolution not only of animals but also of the environment in which they live.

The Animal and its Environment

The animal and its environment have evolved together. Before any animals appeared an atmosphere of H_2, NH_3, and CH_4 was converted into one of N_2, CO_2 and O_2, and a planet of bare rock was gradually covered with thick layers of pulverized earth, rich in soluble nitrates, sulfates, phosphates and organic materials. Then the developing cover of green plants provided oxygen for respiration and shelters for the animals. The waters were filled with oxidized materials, both animate and inanimate, and the air became a transport medium for bacteria, seeds, and spores, and a highway for insects, birds and some mammals. The animal, in its evolution as in its daily living, is inseparable from the environment.

The physiologist may look at animals in many ways. In one sense, they are biochemical machines, acquiring elements from the environment and arranging these in a series of electron transfers to provide the necessary energy for the operation of their machinery. They must acquire fuel, distribute it, burn it and remove the waste. These problems are considered in Part I of this book. An animal usually operates in an oscillating environment. Cold periods are followed by warmer periods, day is followed by night, and the organism is geared to adjust and to regulate, to tolerate and to resist these changes. The mechanisms related to these environmental compensations are discussed in Part II. To the layman, perhaps, the most characteristic thing about animals is the way in which they move and behave, the manner in which they see and hear and react to other animals or to objects in their environment. These activities depend on a battery of sensitive receptors, a group of specialized effector organs and an elaborate integrating nervous system. The physiology related more specifically to animal activity is dealt with in Part III. Finally, life is constant renewal; the old must be replaced by the new. Only through replacement by a somewhat variable progeny has an evolutionary change been made possible and the formation of increasingly more complex and specialized animals become a reality. The physiology of reproduction and development is considered in the final section.

Any of these topics might be treated in various ways. One might emphasize the many functional differences or stress the similarities in patterns of metabolism and machinery. Superficially, the differences are more evident, and the pioneers in comparative physiology were particularly concerned with their tabulation and description. However, with the accumulation of information it has become evident that there are many fundamental similarities in metabolism and that the basic life processes are essentially the same wherever they are found.

Regulatory Mechanisms 2

Comparative physiology owes one of its most basic concepts to the renowned French physiologist of the nineteenth century, Claude Bernard. As early as 1859 he pointed out that complex organisms live in two environments—an external environment which is the same for both animate and inanimate objects and an internal fluid environment which surrounds the cells and tissues of the body, is characteristic of the animal species and remains relatively constant. Claude Bernard argued that the animal did not really live in the *milieu extérieur* but in the liquid *milieu intérieur*—which bathes the tissues and serves as a medium for the exchange of foods and wastes and for the distribution of chemical messengers of many kinds.

Bernard made many contributions to physiology, but the outstanding one was his appreciation of the vital role of this internal environment. He wrote, "It is the fixity of the '*milieu intérieur*' which is the condition of free and independent life," and, "All the vital mechanisms, however varied they may be, have only one object, that of preserving constant the conditions of life in the internal environment." (Bernard, 1957; Cannon, 1929, 1939). The individual cells and tissues of the complex organisms exist in a remarkably constant environment and, during the hundred years since Bernard, it has become evident that many of the familiar physiological phenomena are essentially mechanisms directed to the maintenance of this steady state. W. B. Cannon (1939) applied the term "homeostatic" to these coordinated physiological processes which maintain steady states. By HOMEOSTASIS, Cannon did not mean a static or stagnant condition, but one which varied only within narrow and precise limits. These limits of variability and the means of regulation form a large part of the classical physiology with which Bernard and Cannon and a host of other investigators have been concerned.

Concepts of the internal environment and homeostasis were first developed by mammalian physiologists with particular reference to the autonomic nervous system and the hormones which regulate metabolism (Adolph, 1961). Comparable controls have now been studied in the lower vertebrates and in many of the invertebrates and, although the variability is regularly greater in the lower forms, it is characteristic of all physiological processes to operate within definite limits. Rates of metabolism, blood sugars, moisture, electrolyte content and many other factors show relatively minor fluctuations. This concept of the regulated physiological rate can be extended to the cellular and enzyme level, for it is just as characteristic of the enzyme reactions as it is of the complex processes which ultimately depend on them. The genetic system preserves a constancy in the lines of protoplasm, and this is expressed in the physiology and biochemistry as well as in the morphology. It extends from the enzymatic to the cellular level and from the cell to the organ-system and on to the social level of organization.

Prosser (1955) has made a useful distinction between physiological adjustment or conformity and physiological regulation. This distinction, developed in connection with an organism's responses to altered environmental conditions, is also valuable in a discussion of homeostatic mechanisms. The less specialized animals operate over a much wider range of internal environmental conditions than the more complex ones. Blood sugars are more variable; the buffering action of the blood is less; the osmotic value of body fluids varies, and temperatures change with those of the environment. Here ADJUSTMENTS of the internal environment occur, and the tissues function over wide ranges. The internal environment, in contrast, is stable in the higher vertebrates with an almost constant temperature and with the blood sugar, electrolytes and other constituents precisely REGULATED. The evolution of large, active and more specialized animals has been associated with a phylogeny in regulatory mechanisms, from simple adjustments to precise regulations. There are, nevertheless, limitations in these adaptive processes for the animal which adjusts as there are for the animal that regulates. At the molecular level, the most frequent limitation is probably in the range of enzyme activity. In unicellular forms the metabolic controls are entirely adjustments within a complex system of interconnected enzyme reactions; in multicellular animals, the many organs and organ-systems are integrated through nervous and endocrine mechanisms, although these too are limited by enzyme-controlled processes.

Factors Regulating Enzyme Activity

Even the simplest manifestations of life involve a great complexity of enzymatic reactions. The fermentation of sugar (glucose), for example, requires a dozen well known enzymes with associated coenzymes and activators (Chapter 7). These catalysts are highly specific, and the reactions always occur in orderly sequence. Characteristically, the control which they exercise is not on the nature of the reaction but on its rate. The kinetics of enzyme activity are discussed in textbooks of biochemistry and enzymology, and only a brief summary of the major rate-controlling factors is attempted here.

ENZYME-SUBSTRATE COMPLEX

To begin with, enzymes are simple proteins or proteins associated with a complex organic group (prosthetic group). They associate themselves reversibly with the materials on which they act (substrates) in a relationship (the enzyme-substrate complex) which is intimate and specific. It may involve both the protein portion and its prosthetic group. This union is so intimate and specific that it is often likened to a complex lock and its individual key. While in this association, the substrate is in some manner activated, subjected to molecular strain or otherwise altered, so that the reaction path is smoothed and the end-products form rapidly. Thus, the enzyme does not contribute energy; it activates the substrate.

The hypothesis of an enzyme-substrate combination has long been supported by an impressive amount of biochemical data, and more recently it has been possible to identify certain intermediate compounds and demonstrate the reality of the complex (Fruton and Simmonds, 1958). Biochemists agree that the enzyme-substrate complex is an essential first step in enzyme action; this means that reactions of this sort are strictly limited by the amount of enzyme present or, to put it another way, by the specific amount of reacting enzyme surface. When these enzyme surfaces, or their reactive centers, are tied up with substrate, reaction velocity will decline.

It is important to understand that these active enzyme centers may also be tied up by compounds similar in structure to a substrate but incapable of forming the end-products. In this manner, essential reactions may be blocked. The phenomenon, known as COMPETITIVE ENZYME INHIBITION is extremely important, both theoretically and practically. Theoretically, it has been used to investigate the elusive enzyme-substrate complex since some of the enzyme-inhibitor complexes are more readily isolated and identified than the normal substrate products (Baldwin, 1963). Practically, a multitude of important metabolic poisons which work on this principle are now used in medicine, in insect toxicology and in research (Adams, 1959). Two examples will suffice at this point. The sulfa drugs bear a marked structural similarity to an important biochemical, *p*-aminobenzoic acid (P.B.A.) . So similar are they that in the presence of sulfanilamide and related compounds, bacteria (which require P.B.A. for their metabolism) may fail to obtain sufficient P.B.A. for growth. Their multiplication is thereby checked to the benefit of the sufferer with certain infectious diseases. Other interesting examples are found in some of the nerve poisons. Transmission of nerve impulses at many synapses and myoneural junctions is dependent on the release of acetylcholine. Only a brief period is required for stimulation, and the acetylcholine is then destroyed by the enzyme cholinesterase. If acetylcholine accumulates through failure of the cholinesterase mechanism, a continual stimulation with serious consequences may be expected. This is precisely what takes place when physostigmine, a poison once used in West African ordeal trials, is present in the system. Physostigmine, and the synthetic substitute neostigmine, combine with cholinesterase about 10,000 times more readily than acetylcholine and thus form competitive inhibitors of the enzyme cholinesterase.

KINETICS OF ENZYME ACTION

Since the enzyme-substrate combination is essential for enzyme activity, relative amounts of the two substances forming the complex are of major significance in the reaction kinetics. Figure 2.1 is based on data from the hydrolysis of soluble starch (substrate) in reaction mixtures containing pancreatic amylase. Enzyme activity is expressed as mg of reducing sugar produced from the starch. When the amount of enzyme is constant (Fig. 2.1*a*), activity increases regularly with additional amounts of substrate up to a maximum where all the enzyme is (at that moment) associated with substrate. This is the sort of relation expected if an enzyme-substrate combination is requisite to the hydrolysis of starch by amylase. When the amounts of enzyme are varied, in the presence of excess substrate (Fig. 2.1*b*), activity rises in direct relation to the available enzyme, again in accordance with the enzyme-substrate concept.

Temperature and pH also modify these rates. Enzyme reactions, like other chemical activities, depend on molecular motion and this is, in part, temperature controlled. There is usually a well marked optimum. Further, enzymes are proteins, and proteins because of their amino and carboxyl groups, are amphoteric electrolytes (ampholytes) which dissociate either as acids or bases, depending on the pH of the solution.

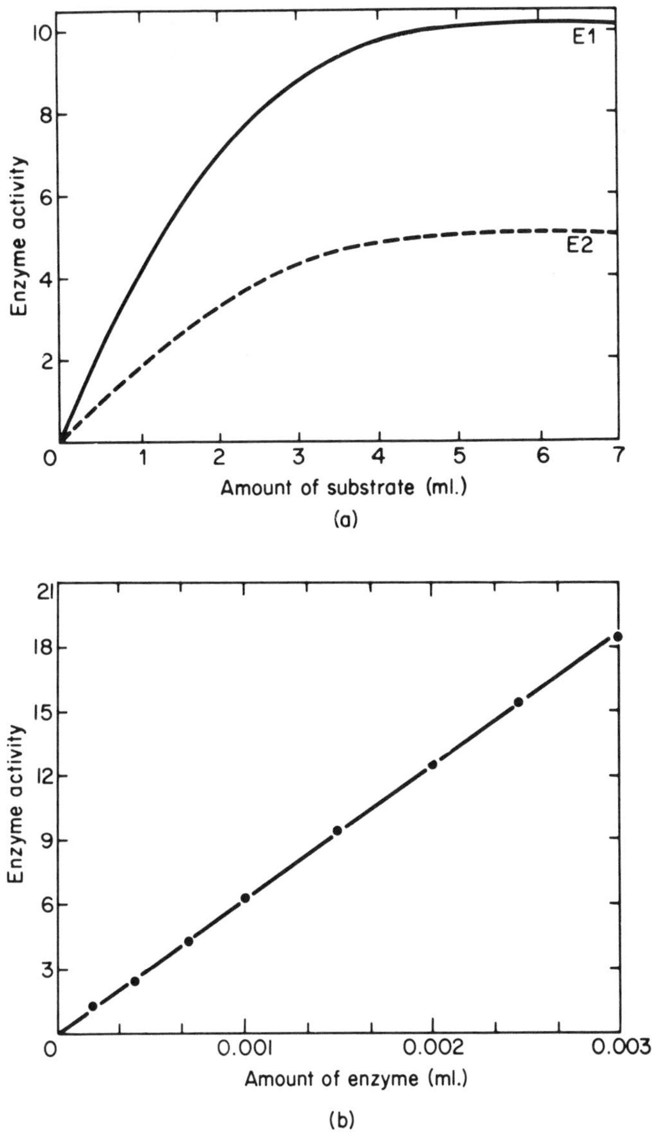

Fig. 2.1. Some factors controlling the rates of starch digestion by pancreatic amylase. Enzyme activity measured as mg reducing sugar formed. *a*, Amount of substrate varied with constant amounts of enzyme-E1 (upper) and E2 (lower). *b*, optimum amount of substrate and variable amounts of enzyme. The substrate was 1% soluble starch; the enzyme was a sample of duodenal contents at optimum pH and chloride. [Myers and Free (1943).]

Consequently, the chemical properties of the enzyme and its ability to form reactive enzyme-substrate complexes, may be expected to vary over a range of pH with the development of a well marked optimum (Fig. 2.2).

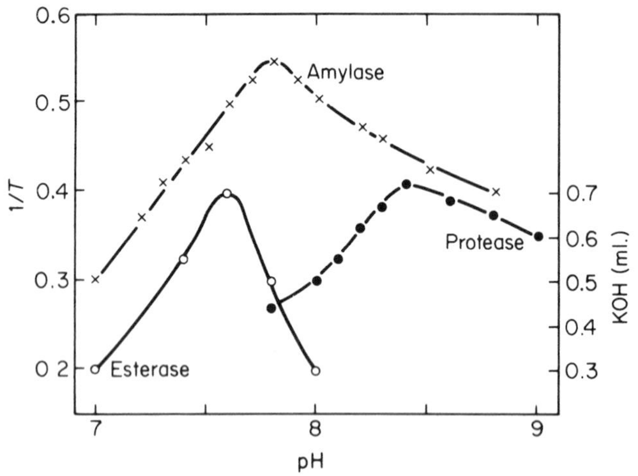

Fig. 2.2. Effects of pH on the action of the digestive enzymes in the midgut of an echiuroid *Ochetostoma erythrogrammon*. $1/T$, the reciprocal of time taken by the amylase-starch mixture to become colorless with iodine; ml KOH, titer of 0.01N KOH per 0.1 ml digest of protease-gelatine and per ml digest of esterase-benzyl *n*-butyrate. [Chuang (1963).]

Under natural conditions, these optima may have real meaning only in relation to an appropriate time-scale. Berrill's (1929) studies of digestion in an ascidian, *Tethyum*, illustrate this beautifully (Fig. 2.3.). When *in vitro* tests of hydrolytic activity were carried out for only a short 3-hour period, the optimum temperature for the formation of reaction products was as high as 45°C. If, however, the *in vitro* tests were run for 50 hours then the maximum development of reaction products occurred at 25°C. Since it requires about 50 hours for the food to pass through this animal's gut, the biological optimum for digestion is, in fact, 25°C and not 45°C.

In addition to these quantitative relations between enzyme and substrate, rates are also modified by the concentration of reaction products. Many enzyme reactions are reversible, and the equilibrium between reacting compounds and end-products depends on the law of mass action. The hydrolysis of fats by lipase is a familiar example. If a fat such as triolein is incubated with lipase, fatty acids and glycerol are formed; but presently the rate of reaction declines and an equilibrium is attained. This equilibrium will be the same if one starts with fatty acid and glycerol (plus enzyme) and measures the synthesis of triolein. There is a balance between hydrolysis and synthesis in accordance with the law of mass

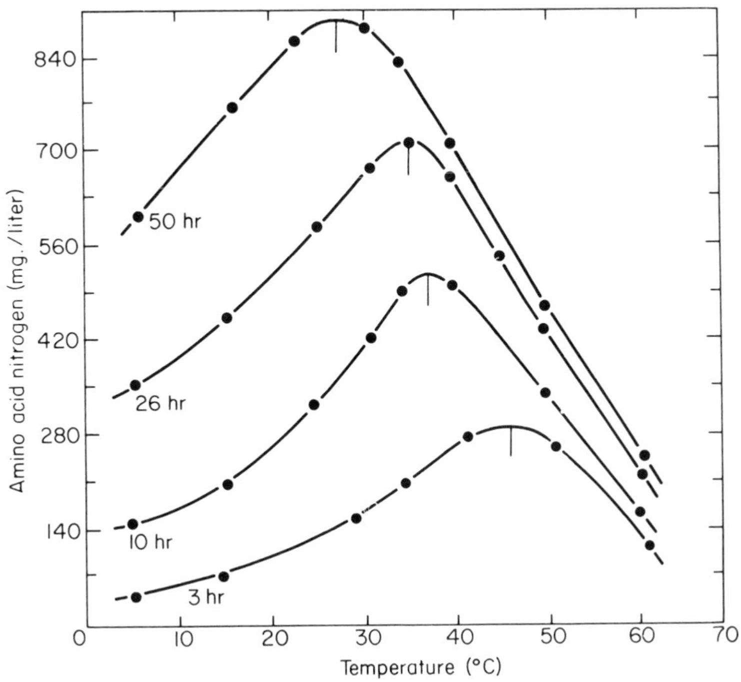

Fig. 2.3. Influence of temperature on the digestion of gelatin by proteinases of the ascidian *Tethyum*. Further description in the text. [Berrill (1929).]

action. Enzyme-catalyzed reactions may also be retarded by the accumulation of certain types of end-products which in some way combine with the enzyme or inhibit its further reactivity. Hence, reaction products, in one way or another, can serve as a "feed-back system" to regulate enzyme processes.

These, then, are the familiar controls of enzyme reactions. Regulation of life processes at the cellular level depends on variable amounts of enzymes, substrates, activators, inhibitors and by-products, reacting under the modifying influence of temperature and pH. No one factor can be singled out as of prime importance, but in living systems the regulation very often seems to depend on quantitative changes in the enzyme concentration. Reserves of inactive enzyme molecules (pro-enzymes) may be present, awaiting some form of activation. For example, the protein splitting enzyme produced by the vertebrate gastric mucosa is secreted as the pro-enzyme pepsinogen; this is activated, in the first instance, by the hydrochloric acid in gastric juice. This process is referred to as UNMASKING, and involves the removal of a polypeptide, leaving the active protease, pepsin. Several similar examples will be given in the discussion of digestive enzymes. Proenzymes may be present intracellularly as well as in the digestive juices. This is one of the important ways in which stores of enzymes are maintained.

Similarly, reserves of enzymes may be brought into action through the removal of inhibitors or by the existence of coenzyme mechanisms or specific activating ions. Such activators sometimes appear in the reaction system through biochemical rearrangements and chain reactions, or through a modification of cell permeability associated with the changing metabolism of the cell. Phosphate, (– SH) and other groups, released in one reaction, may activate or form part of another enzyme system.

The variety, complexity and precision of enzyme control mechanisms is currently a subject of active biochemical research (Davis, 1961*a*). The regulation is achieved not only through the feed-back controls on the catalytic reactions as just described, but also through more complex mechanisms involving INDUCTION or complete REPRESSION of certain enzyme systems. In short, organisms possess a multitude of CONSTITUTIVE enzyme systems which are always present and demonstrable but, at the same time, may show the capacity to develop appropriate enzyme systems after the addition of a substrate. Enzyme induction is evidently a widespread phenomenon; it has now been intensively investigated in bacteria and in mammals (Hogness, 1959; Prosser, 1958).

ENZYME INDUCTION

These processes of induction and repression can play a very significant role in metabolic regulation. In cultures of bacteria it is sometimes difficult to determine whether the observed changes are at the genetic or cellular level. However, several cases of enzyme induction have now been described, and it is evident that populations of primitive organisms such as bacteria, yeasts and protozoa may respond to a new substrate by developing the necessary enzyme as an INDUCIBLE ENZYME. Some of the better known examples are discussed in the Cold Spring Harbor Symposia on Quantitative Biology (vol. 26, 1961) and in the Symposium edited by Prosser (1958). Only a few are mentioned here.

Yeast, for instance, normally metabolizes little galactose, but if grown in a galactose medium develops sufficient enzyme to effect ready metabolism of this compound. This is true even in cases where the development of mutant stocks—with different genetic potentialities for the production of this enzyme— has been ruled out. However, it is not certain whether the enzyme develops *de novo* or from minute amounts already present in the cell, or from some precursor whose activity is stimulated by a shift in the reaction equilibrium. In any case, a regulation at the enzyme level has taken place.

Further interesting examples are found in the feed-back mechanisms which control the biosynthesis of many important cellular constituents such as the amino acids, purines, or pyrimidines. For example, in some bacteria the accumulation of these compounds inhibits their further synthesis. Thus, when tryptophan is added to the culture medium of *Escherichia coli*, the endogenous synthesis of this particular amino acid ceases. This is not merely an equilibrium attained in a reversible reaction, since a great many chains of enzymatically controlled processes are involved in such a synthesis. Formation of other amino acids (methionine, proline, arginine) has been repressed in a similar way. In certain cases, inhibition seems to be due to an interruption of enzyme formation. Regulatory mechanisms of this type keep the different enzyme systems of a cell in step with one another. In an organism such as *E. coli,* which can synthesize a variety of amino acids, the accumulation and wasting of important compounds is avoided, and a balanced enzyme production maintains a steady or constant biochemical make-up. The enzymatic constitution is regulated according to demand. Similar phenomena have been demonstrated for the catabolic as well as the anabolic enzymes in bacteria.

Enzyme induction has also been studied in the higher animals. One of the best known examples is the induction of tryptophan pyrrolase (tryptophan peroxidase) in the liver of the rat (Knox, 1951). The activity in this enzyme may increase by as much as ten-fold in 5 to 6 hours following a dose of tryptophan equivalent to about twice that consumed in the normal daily diet of the rat. The substrate tryptophan is, in this case, the inducer. The enzyme may also be induced by an injection of the adrenocortical hormone, hydrocortisone. This hormone as an inducer can produce a three-fold increase within the same time period. This is a significant demonstration of regulatory processes operating in a higher animal by way of enzyme induction.

Regulation at the Organ-System Level

The complex multicellular organism is more than a collection of enzyme-regulating cells. The grouping of specialized cells into tissues, each adapted for a particular job, the association of tissues into organs designed to perform the major functions, and the arrangement of organs into a whole and unified animal require a different type of integration. For this, intercellular communication is essential. In final analysis, this too depends on enzyme reactions within individual cells but at a different level: it involves feed-back mechanisms from metabolizing tissues, specialized coordinating chemical materials (hormones and pheromones), communication by circulating fluids and the transmission of nerve impulses.

Throughout the animal kingdom a measure of regulation is achieved by feed-back stimuli from tissue metabolites. Carbon dioxide, one of the universal by-products of metabolism, is the most important of these metabolites. It acts directly on the cardiac and vasomotor centers in the vertebrate medulla to participate in the control of breathing and blood pressure. Comparable regulation occurs in many invertebrate animals. The respiratory activities of the annelid *Tubifex,* breathing movements of the pulmonate gastropods, the ventilation of the *Octopus* and the pumping movements of crustacea may be cited as examples of complex activities which are adjusted in part by the level of carbon dioxide.

In addition to feed-back stimuli from tissue metabolites, the multicellular organisms possess an integrating nervous system, and most of them also have masses of specialized secreting cells (the endocrine glands) whose sole function it is to elaborate regulatory compounds. The line of separation between the integrating (autonomic) nervous system and the endocrine system is not always very distinct. In both cases, the action is mediated through chemicals, and many of the endocrine tissues actually develop from modified nerve cells.

Welsh (1957, 1959) recognizes two groups of neuroendocrine substances. The NEUROHUMORS are produced in nerve cells relatively unspecialized for secretory purposes. They are released at the ends of the fibers, travel only very short distances before being enzymatically destroyed and act on other neurons, muscles or glands in intimate contact with the nerve endings (Fig. 2.4). They are, then, short-range and short-lived materials. Acetylcholine, adrenaline and noradrenaline are well recognized members of this group. In addition, there is circumstantial evidence for a similar action by a few other chemicals, such as 5-hydroxytryptamine and gamma-aminobutyric acid, which are widely distributed in nervous tissues.

NEUROSECRETORY SUBSTANCES, on the other hand, are produced by neurons which are specialized for secretion. The endings are associated with special storage centers called NEUROHEMAL ORGANS. The chemicals are released from the storage centers; they are relatively stable and act at greater distances and over longer periods (Fig. 2.5).

They may control such phenomena as molting and chromatophore activity in arthropods, or may be associated with water balance and urine production in the vertebrates.

Florey (1962*a*) uses the term TRANSMITTER SUBSTANCE rather than neurohumor for the chemicals which mediate synaptic transmission; he restricts the usage of neurohormone to the hormones released by the neurosecretory cells. He emphasizes the differences rather than the similarities and draws a sharp line between transmitter substance and

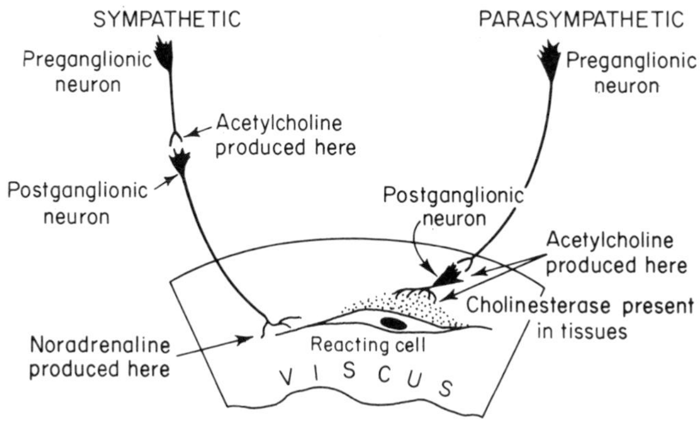

Fig. 2.4. Diagram showing the arrangement of the vertebrate autonomic fibers. [Bard (1961) after Meyerson (1938).]

neurosecretions. Thus, the micromorphology of the synapse (Chapter 21) shows that chemical transmission at this point is by way of specialized passages and bears no relation to blood transport, a characteristic of the classical concept of endocrines. Further, there is no clear evidence for a phylogeny of one group of chemicals from the other. Rather, they represent two different ways in which protoplasm has specialized to produce integrating chemicals and use them in the regulatory mechanisms of higher animals.

In the majority of animals the endocrine system also includes glands of a non-nervous origin which may or may not be controlled by the neurosecretory materials. A distinction between the autonomic nervous system and the endocrine system is convenient for descriptive purposes, but it should be appreciated that the integrative homeostatic mechanisms are neuroendocrine and the nervous and endocrine systems are intimately related and often interdependent.

Autonomic Nervous System

The concept of an autonomic nervous system was introduced by Langley in 1921. Langley was concerned only with the mammal. The autonomic, as he described it, was the system of nerves controlling the

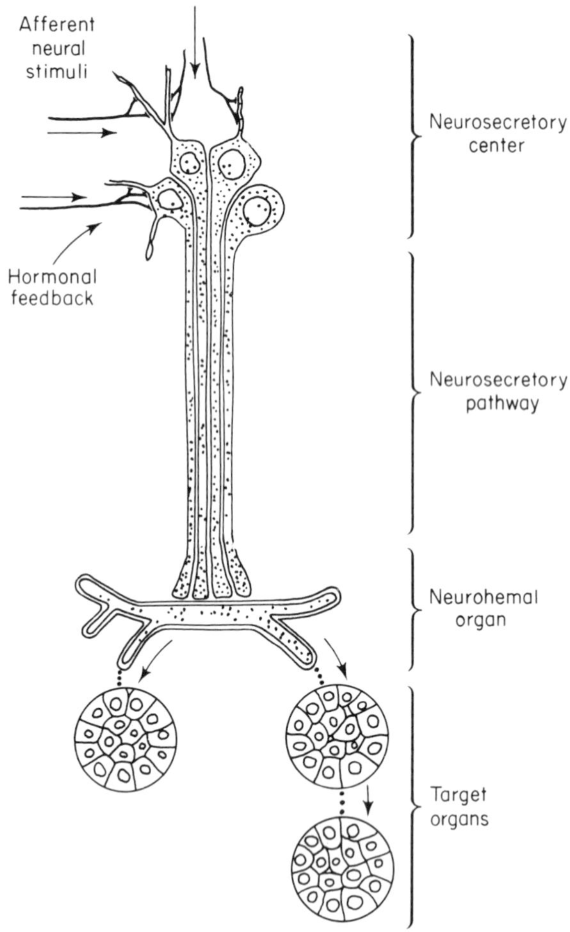

Fig. 2.5. Generalized diagram of the neurosecretory system applicable both to invertebrates and vertebrates. [Scharrer and Scharrer (1963).]

visceral effectors for digestion, circulation, excretion and other more or less involuntary functions; more precisely, it was the motor innervation of smooth muscle, cardiac muscle, and glands. He distinguished two divisions of the vertebrate autonomic—the SYMPATHETIC and the PARASYMPATHETIC nervous systems.

In the mammal these two divisions are distinct anatomically, physiologically and pharmacologically. The sympathetic arises from the thoracico-lumbar regions of the central nervous system, the parasympathetic from the cranio-sacral regions (Fig. 2.6). Typically, each visceral organ receives both sympathetic and parasympathetic fibers; one is excitatory while the other is inhibitory. Pharmacologically, excitation is mediated through two different transmitters—the sympathetic effects usually by adrenaline (adrenergic nerves) and the parasympathetic effects by acetylcholine (cholinergic nerves). The exceptions with respect to the sympathetic include the preganglionics of all the sympathetics, the postganglionics to the sweat glands, vasodilators to skeletal muscles and preganglionics to the adrenal medulla—all of which are cholinergic.

The presence of ganglia provided another basic feature in Langley's description of the autonomic nervous system. Whereas the motor fibers associated with the voluntary muscles have their cells located in the central nervous system, those associated with the autonomic have their cell bodies in ganglia located at some distance from the central nervous system. These ganglia are in turn connected by nerve fibers to the central nervous system. Thus, a PREGANGLIONIC FIBER arising in the central nervous system forms a synapse in a ganglion with the POSTGANGLIONIC FIBER, which is in contact with the visceral effector organ (Figs. 2.4 and 2.6).

VISCERAL NERVOUS SYSTEM OF INVERTEBRATES

The mammalian autonomic nervous system described by Langley is highly specialized and must have had a long phylogenetic history. Comparable controls of visceral function are efficiently organized in the lower vertebrates; many of the invertebrates show suggestive anatomical and physiological parallels in the arrangements for the regulation of visceral functions. It seems reasonable to extend this concept of the autonomic nervous system to the lower phylogenetic groups but preferable to term it the VISCERAL NERVOUS SYSTEM.

The most primitive anatomical arrangement of nervous elements is that of a net of synaptically joined fibers. These nerve nets are often regulated by concentrated masses of nerve cells in the form of ganglia, while more rapid transmission from one point to another is attained by means of bundles of long nerve fibers or particularly large conducting fibers within the net. Such arrangements are present in the submuscular plexus and other plexuses of the flatworm and in the well-developed nerve nets of the pharynx and copulatory organs of the same group.

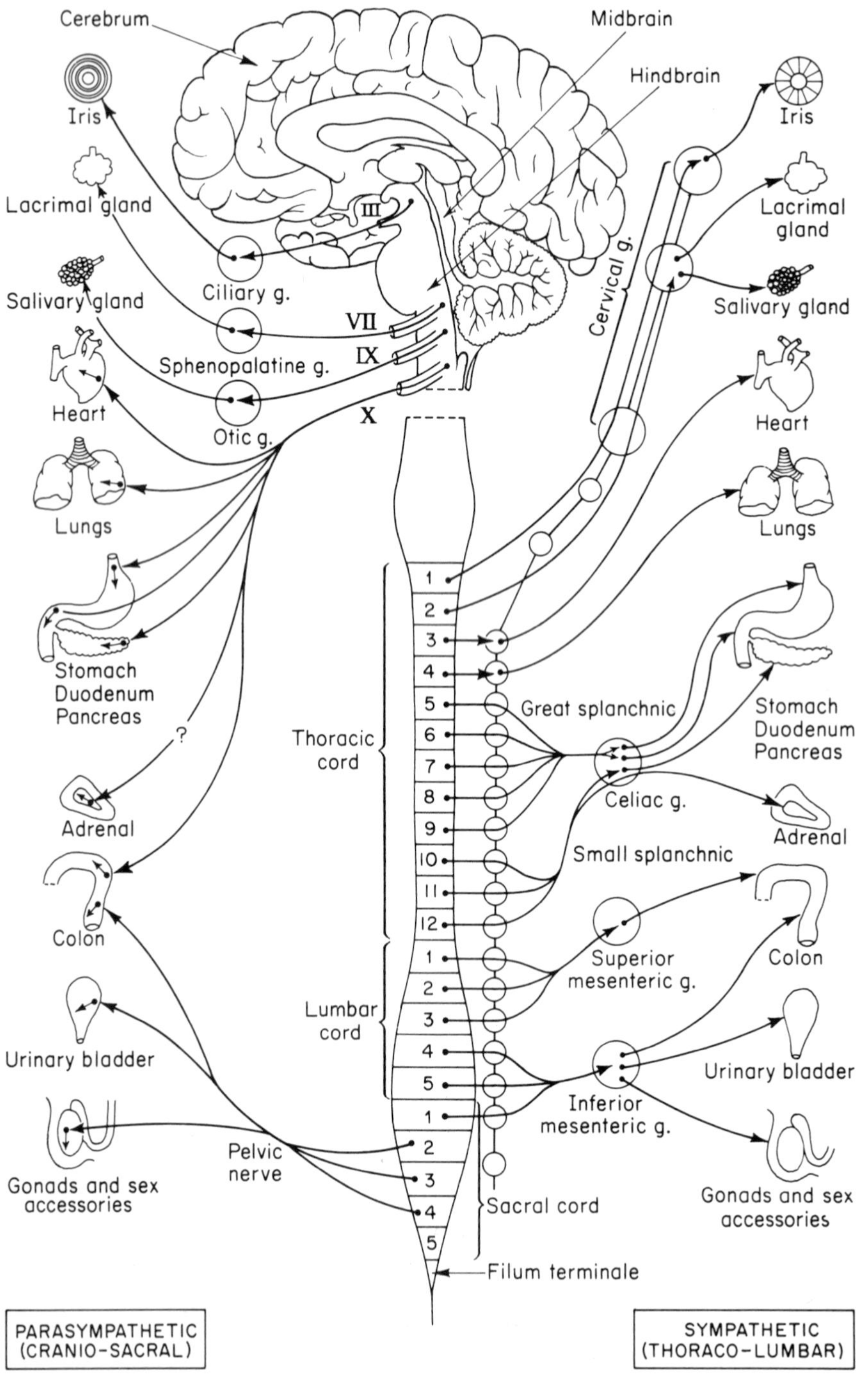

Fig. 2.6. Diagram of the mammalian autonomic nervous system. [Turner (1960).]

Distinct visceral plexuses of this type are present in the pharynx and rectum of the nematode, in the gut of the annelid, in the proboscis, pharynx, gut and heart of the balanoglossids and in comparable locations in other phylogenetic groups (Hyman, 1951, 1959; Nicol, 1952, 1960*a*). Their first function in animal phylogeny was to regulate the visceral musculature. Other effectors, such as glands and chromatophores came under autonomic control much later. This pattern of a nerve net associated with the visceral effectors is basic to both invertebrates and vertebrates and represents an anatomical constancy throughout the animal kingdom.

Physiological similarities are also found. The neurohumoral control is sometimes a double one, with excitation and inhibition by different fibers associated with characteristic neurohumors. Even more universal is the widespread distribution of relatively few transmitter materials. Acetylcholine (ACh) occurs in relatively high concentrations in nervous tissues of molluscs and arthropods and in lesser amounts in several other invertebrate groups (Florey, 1963). Adrenaline and noradrenaline seem to be less common among the invertebrates but have been identified in annelids, molluscs and arthropods. Another amine of very widespread distribution is 5-hydroxytryptamine (5HT or serotonin), identified in several groups ranging from the coelenterates to the vertebrates. These three substances – ACh, the catechol amines and 5HT – are common from the flatworms to men (Welsh, 1959; Prosser and Brown, 1961) and have been experimentally shown to affect visceral functions in a number of representative invertebrates as well as in the vertebrates. Evidence for a transmitter action under physiological conditions among the invertebrates is less satisfactory (Florey, 1963).

The physiological details of visceral control in animals near the base of the phylogenetic tree are not well known, but in the more complex invertebrates the organization seems to be based on a system of balanced excitation and inhibition. The situation in the different groups of animals, however, is variable. The cardiac activity of many molluscs is depressed by acetylcholine and excited by 5-hydroxytryptamine, but in at least one mollusc (*Mytilus californianus*) the heart is excited by both neurohumors. Again, adrenaline generally has an excitatory action on the invertebrate heart but is without effect on the heart of *Nereis*, *Artemia* and *Ciona* (Prosser and Brown, 1961; Welsh, 1957). In *Aplysia* ganglia, ACh acts like an inhibitory transmitter on some and like an excitatory transmitter on other ganglion cells (Florey, 1963). In most of the vertebrates acetylcholine inhibits the heart, while adrenaline excites it; but the heart of *Myxine* does not respond to ACh or adrenaline and in the teleost fishes adrenaline is apparently without effect. Thus, these neurohumors have different effects in various species. However, the principle of a control based on separate excitatory and inhibitory materials seems to have

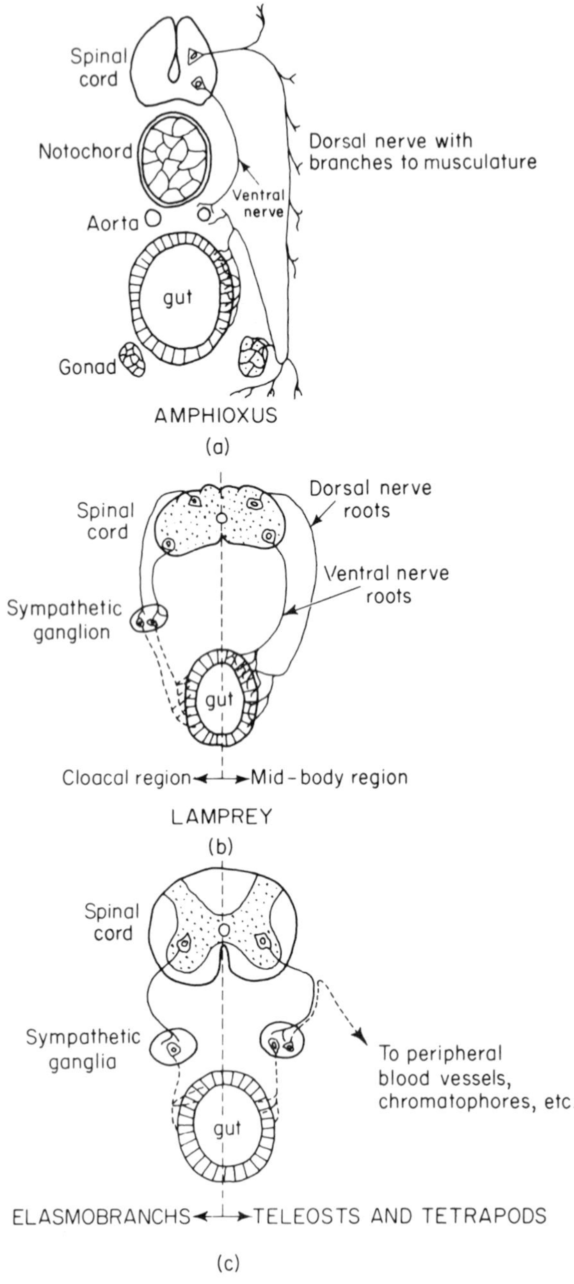

Fig. 2.7. Diagrammatic cross section through the nerve cord of representative chordates to show the pattern of the autonomic sympathetic system. Preganglionic fibers shown as continuous lines; postganglionics as broken lines. A nerve plexus in the wall of the gut is associated with the preganglionics which pass directly to its wall (parasympathetics in the higher forms). Some of the fibers to the cloacal region of the cyclostome are preganglionics like those of the mid-body region.

been established early in animal organization and to have persisted throughout its evolution.

The sympathetic nervous system of *Amphioxus* (Nicol, 1952), is representative of the autonomic nervous system of many prevertebrate groups (Fig. 2.7*a*). The nerve plexuses of the visceral organs receive motor fibers from the central nervous system (spinal cord). The fibers in the spinal cord of *Amphioxus* or in the ganglionic concentrations of the invertebrate may be considered preganglionic, while the cells of the nerve net itself are the postganglionic fibers (terminal ganglia arranged as in the parasympathetic system of vertebrates). *Amphioxus* lacks a brain and there is thus no division into sympathetic and parasympathetic components. Further, there is no supply to the skin or its blood vessels, hence no proximal ganglia (Fig. 2.7). Whether *Amphioxus* depends on one or more types of neurohumor remains to be demonstrated.

VERTEBRATE AUTONOMIC NERVOUS SYSTEM

The cyclostomes are the most primitive of living vertebrates, and for this reason they occupy a critical position in discussions of phylogeny. The fragmentary information on the autonomic nervous system is particularly interesting. The parasympathetic system is probably represented only by the vagus. In the hagfish *Myxine*, the vagus has a strong effect on the gall bladder and intestine, but the sympathetic system is so poorly developed that its presence has been questioned. However, recent work reveals segmental visceral or spinal sympathetic fibers arising ventrally which seem to exercise a vasomotor control. No ganglia have been identified (Fänge *et al*, 1963). The absence of cardiac nerves is particularly interesting.

The pattern of the parasympathetic is similar in the lamprey *Lampetra* with the addition of vagal fibers to the heart (Johnels, 1956*a*); the sympathetic component is much more prominent with fibers emerging from dorsal as well as ventral spinal roots (Fig. 2.7*b*). In this latter feature it is similar to *Amphioxus* but differs from *Myxine* and all gnathostomes which show only the ventral emergence (Fig. 2.7*c*). The vertebral ganglia characteristic of the sympathetic system of higher vertebrates are diffuse, scattered and not united into a chain. The autonomic supply to the relatively undifferentiated gut is particularly feeble, consisting mainly of vagal fibers to the anterior and posterior ends. Comparative data for cyclostomes and other vertebrates are summarized in Table 2.1.

The autonomic nervous system of elasmobranch and teleost fishes is more elaborate than that of the cyclostomes and presents many of the features of the mammalian system. In fishes, however, it is always less complete anatomically, while physiologically its two components fail to show the dual actions of excitation and inhibition with respect to many of the organs. There is no sacral parasympathetic division in any of the fishes. The cranial division of the parasympathetic receives contributions from the III, VII, IX and X cranial nerves in the elasmobranchs as in

TABLE 2.1.

SUMMARY OF ANATOMICAL ORGANIZATION OF VERTEBRATE AUTONOMIC NERVOUS SYSTEM. ROMAN NUMERALS, CRANIAL NERVES; +, COMPONENT OR INNERVATION PRESENT; —, ABSENT.

Animal or Group	*Parasympathetic*		*Sympathetic*					
	Cranial	*Sacral*	*Origin Dorsal or ventral root*	*Ganglia* *Chain*	*Ganglia* *Prevertebral*	*Gray rami*	*Heart*	*Gut*
Amphioxus	absent		Dorsal	—	—	—	+	Feeble
Hagfish	X	—	Ventral	—	—	—	—	Feeble
Lamprey	X	—	Dorsal & Ventral	Scattered	—	—	+	Feeble
Elasmobranch	III, VII IX, X	—	Ventral	loose connections	—	—	+	Incomplete double control
Teleost	III, X	—	Ventral	+	—	+	+	Incomplete double control
Anura	III, VII IX, X	+	Ventral	+	+	+	+	Double control well-defined
Amniota	III, VII IX, X	+	Ventral	+	+	+	+	Double control well-defined

the higher vertebrates, but the teleosts apparently lack the components from VII and IX. The elasmobranchs have no sympathetic supply to the head or to the skin. The teleosts possess a well developed supply to both regions. The chromatophores of the teleost, but not those of the cyclostome or elasmobranch, are usually under autonomic control. The gut and viscera receive both sympathetic and parasympathetic fibers, but both pharmacological and physiological studies fail to show the clear-cut division between adrenergic and cholinergic controls. Physiologically, the sharp division between sympathetic and parasympathetic systems is a feature of the higher vertebrates (Barrington, 1957; Nicol, 1952).

The familiar tetrapod pattern of the autonomic system is established in the Amphibia. The sacral parasympathetic division appears in this group with a clearly marked double innervation to the esophagus, the stomach, the rectum, the bladder and the heart. A prevertebral ganglion (coeliac plexus) is found in the Anura.

The more detailed arrangement of the autonomic system of the tetrapod is shown in Fig. 2.6. Three groups of ganglion cells may be conveniently distinguished. The well-marked chains of VERTEBRAL GANGLIA on either side of the spinal cord are sympathetic; these are the loci of synapses between pre- and postganglionic fibers supplying the iris, salivary glands, sweat glands, blood vessels, heart and respiratory organs. The gut, from the stomach to the rectum, as well as the genital organs are innervated by postganglionic sympathetic fibers which arise in the PREVERTEBRAL or COLLATERAL GANGLIA. These collateral ganglia may be looked upon as vertebral ganglia moved into closer relationship with the viscera which they innervate. Finally, TERMINAL GANGLIA, associated with the parasympathetic system, are located within the organs involved. The nerve plexuses of the digestive tract are familiar examples. It will be noted that, in the mammal, the preganglionics are frequently very long in the parasympathetic division (the vagus nerve, for example), and the postganglionics very short, while the reverse is true of the corresponding sympathetic components. This, however, is not true of the lower vertebrates. Sympathetic fibers to portions of the digestive tract and bladder of fish and some amphibians synapse with plexuses of terminal fibers in the viscera concerned after the manner of the mammalian parasympathetic fibers.

Endocrine System

Hormones are special chemicals which are elaborated in restricted areas of the organism. They diffuse or are transported over variable distances to adjust metabolism, control remote effectors or regulate morphogenesis. They are effective in minute quantities. Their regulatory action is sometimes one of excitation and sometimes one of inhibition; consequently the word *hormone,* which comes from the Greek root meaning "to excite" is really a misnomer. The term endocrine (*endon,* within and *krinen,* to separate) was likewise coined before the true significance of this group of chemical co-ordinators was known. Vertebrate physiologists first recognized the endocrine gland as a ductless organ which discharged its secretions directly into the blood. Particular emphasis was placed on the vascularity and specialized anatomy. Now, however, endocrines are known to occur in animals with scanty circulating fluids, while very vascular organs such as the brain and the intestinal wall not only produce hormones but at the same time perform quite different physiological activities. As a matter of fact, the first internal secretion conclusively demonstrated was the hormone SECRETIN produced by the wall of the gut, and discovered in 1902 by the celebrated British physiologists Bayliss and Starling (Gabriel and Fogel, 1955). Since 1902 a host of chemicals have been added to the list of hormones.

The classical methods of investigation have been: removal of the endocrine tissue, either by surgical or chemical techniques, the study of the resulting disturbances in metabolism, and the restoration of the animal to normal physiological state by replacement of the endocrine tissue or the administration of tissue extracts (Figs. 23.6 and 23.7). Histophysiological studies have also contributed much, and the biochemist has now added substantially to the physiology by purifying or synthesizing many of the better known hormones. Several excellent texts of general and comparative endocrinology are available (Barrington, 1963; von Euler and Heller, 1963; Gorbman and Bern, 1962; Turner, 1960; Williams, 1962).

INVERTEBRATE ENDOCRINE TISSUES

Neurosecretory substances are the main source of hormones in the lower invertebrates. These are elaborated in specialized nerve cells with glandular functions. Histochemical methods have revealed characteristic neurosecretory granules in all groups of multicellular animals, including the coelenterate *Hydra*, several of the polycladian turbellarians and the nemerteans (Gilbert, 1963; Knowles, 1963; Gabe *et al.*, 1964). Although hormonal functions are yet to be demonstrated for these cells in the lower invertebrates, it can be assumed that endocrine regulation is phylogenetically based on the primitive nervous system.

Sometimes these neurosecretions are discharged directly into the vascular or tissue fluids while in other cases storage depots (neurohemal organs) are present, and the hormones accumulate in these prior to their discharge in response to appropriate stimuli (Fig. 2.5). No storage organs are known in lower forms such as the Platyhelminthes, but they are well developed in the more complex invertebrates and seem to make their first appearance as simple structures among the annelids (Knowles, 1963).

In phylogeny, the first functions to come under endocrine control were probably those concerned with the timing of reproduction and the regulation of growth. This can be logically argued from the seasonal nature and precise timing of reproductive processes. The nervous system receives information of seasonally changing environmental conditions by way of light or temperature stimuli and regulates the physiology of the animal in an adaptive manner through its specialized neurosecretions. In annelids, the most primitive group in which neurosecretory phenomena have been precisely associated with physiology, the endocrine system is clearly regulating reproduction and growth through mechanisms comparable to those in higher forms (Durchon, 1962; Heller and Clark, 1962). It is probably only a matter of time until similar evidence is found in the more primitive worms.

The physiology associated with reproduction and growth involves many different metabolic pathways. In suggesting that the hormonal regulation of these phenomena is phylogenetically primitive, there is the implication that endocrines influenced metabolic processes at an early stage. In higher forms the hormonal regulation of metabolism and processes associated with reproduction has been extended to general metabolism, water and electrolyte balance and behavior. Such an extension of these controls is evident in the Mollusca and the Arthropoda and may also occur in lower groups, although there is at present little relevant information.

Neurosecretions form only part of a large endocrine complex. In all the more specialized animals, invertebrate as well as vertebrate, hormones are also produced in varied tissues of non-nervous origin. These endocrine glands of non-nervous origin become conspicuous in the arthropods and the vertebrates, although a number of comparable tissues of suspected hormonal activity are known among the lower invertebrates—for example, the internephridial organs of the *Physcosoma* (Scharrer, 1955) and the salivary glands of the cephalopods (Jenkin, 1962). Among the arthropods intensive research has demonstrated endocrine tissues arising from the non-nervous ectoderm (*Y*-organ of crustaceans, prothoracic glands and corpora allata of the insects) and from the mesoderm (androgenic glands and the gonads of crustacea). In the vertebrates endocrine tissues also arise from the endoderm (thyroid, parathyroid, Islets of Langerhans, gut epithelia), but none of the invertebrate structures has, as yet, been traced to this germ layer (Jenkin, 1962). Thus, it appears that, during phylogeny, hormones first made their appearance as secretions of nerve cells. In the most primitive condition, these may have been used as they were produced, but later their secretions passed by axon transport to special receiving structures where they might accumulate to meet urgent demands more effectively. Subsequently, with increasing complexity of physiological organization, regulating glands developed in several other places.

Hormones in crustaceans. The endocrine system of the crustacean is illustrated in Fig. 2.8. Its neurosecretory portion, located in the head and thorax, consists of three major components (Carlisle and Knowles,

1959). The SINUS GLAND, in the eye stalk, is a storage center for secretions produced in neurons with cell bodies in the brain (supraesophageal ganglion), in the ganglionic *X*-organ and neighboring optic ganglia and, perhaps also, in the ventral ganglia. The *X*-organ terminology is still unsettled (Carlisle and Knowles, 1959; Passano, 1960). In addition to the sinus gland many of the higher Crustacea also have POSTCOMMISSURE ORGANS, located just behind the esophagus as paired extensions of the epineurium of the postesophageal commissure and serving as centers for storage and release of secretions arising in the posterior portion of the brain (tritocerebrum). Finally, in addition to these neurosecretory systems in the head and thorax, the Crustacea possess PERICARDIAL ORGANS, glandular masses of variable anatomy on the wall of the pericardium. Their probable activity in heart regulation is discussed in a later chapter. Besides these three neurosecretory components there is a paired *Y*-organ, concerned with molting and located in the antennary or maxillary segment (Chapter 24), while reproductive controls depend in part on the ovary in the female and the androgenic gland (an outgrowth of the vas deferens) or the testes in the male (Chapter 23).

Hormones in insects. The morphology of the insect endocrine system is somewhat parallel to that of the crustaceans. Groups of nerve cells in the brain elaborate substances which pass by axon transport to the corpus

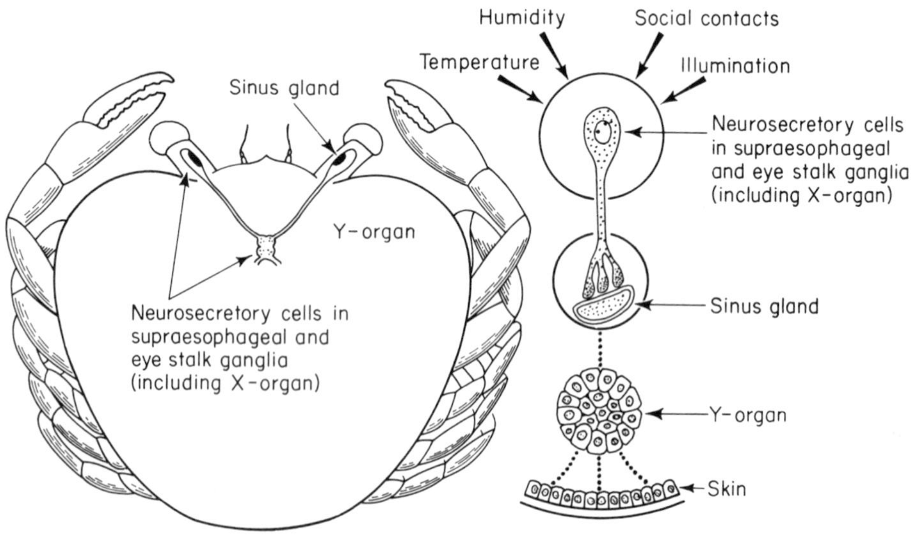

Fig. 2.8. Endocrine system of a crustacean. [Scharrer in Gorbman (1959).]

cardiacum in most species (Fig. 24.2). The hormone(s) stored here activates the prothoracic (ecdysial) gland to produce a well recognized substance (ecdysone) concerned with molting. The corpus allatum, anatomically closely associated with the corpus cardiacum, is of non-nervous origin and produces several different hormones—one of them, the juvenile hormone, acting with ecdysone to control the molt (Chapter 24). Anatomical details show considerable variation in the different groups of insects, and in some forms (Diptera) the corpora cardiaca and corpora allata are fused into a single organ, the ring gland. This system is discussed in the chapters concerned with reproduction and development (Part IV).

VERTEBRATE ENDOCRINE ORGANS

The vertebrate hormones are much more completely known than those of the invertebrates. In several cases their biochemical structure has been determined and their role established at the molecular level. Present indications are that the actual number of hormones is greater and the controls more rigid in the vertebrates, but this may be due to rather limited knowledge of the metabolism of the invertebrates. On the other hand, this difference may be a real one since vertebrate homeostatic mechanisms—particularly among the homeotherms—are much more precise and consequently may require a more complex and varied chemical system for integration. The morphology of the glands and the major activities of the hormones are described in textbooks of general zoology and will not be repeated here. More detailed discussion is reserved for the appropriate sections on metabolism, reproduction and development. Several topics of general interest, however, seem appropriate at this point.

Neurosecretions may have provided the main source of integrating hormones in the ancestral vertebrates. It is of interest, in line with arguments for a phylogenetic antiquity of this part of the endocrine system, that neurosecretory cells are widespread in the central nervous system of the more primitive groups of vertebrates. In higher forms they become restricted to the head region in association with increasing encephalization, but among the fishes they are often prominent in the posterior region of the spinal cord. In teleosts the secretions of this caudal neurosecretory system pass into a neurohemal organ (UROHYPOPHYSIS), forming a morphological arrangement similar to the neurohypophysis in the hypothalamic region of the brain (Fig. 2.9). The urohypophysis seems to be concerned with osmoregulation in some fishes, but its hormones and functions are not yet established. The epithalamic region of the diencephalon (pineal-parietal complex) forms a second region of neurosecretory activity. Although its place in the endocrine system is not yet definitely settled, there is some evidence that it produces secretions concerned with metabolism (Gorbman and Bern, 1962) and the control of chromatophores (Chapter 20). The third and dominant region of neurosecretory activity is the hypothalamic region of the forebrain. Neurons, with cell bodies located in several different hypothalamic nuclei (supraoptic and paraventricular in mammals, preoptic in lower forms) elaborate

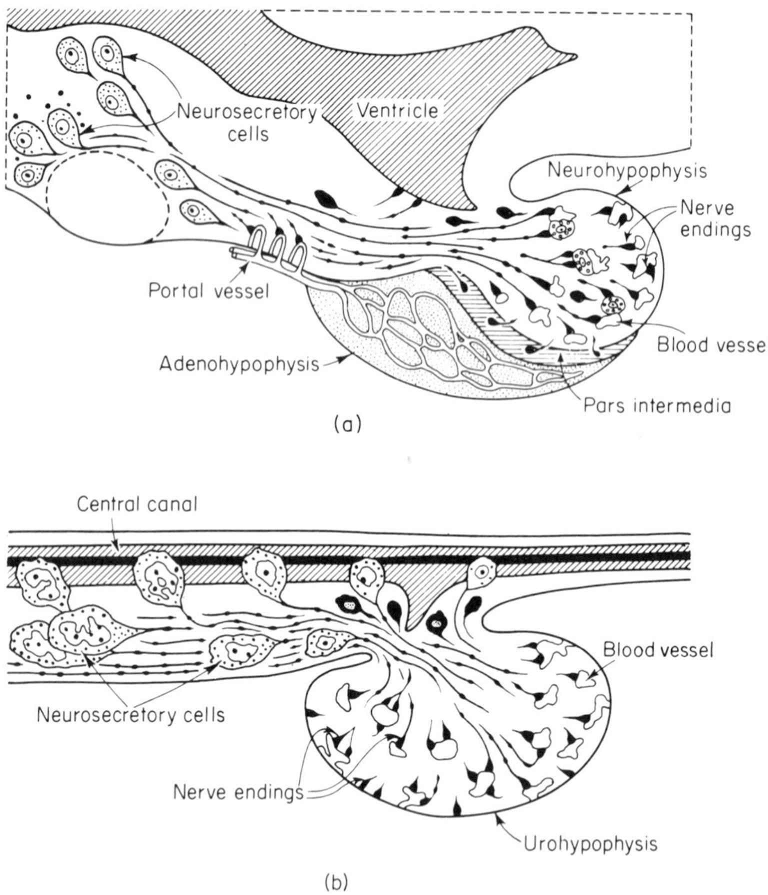

Fig. 2.9. Comparison of the organization of the hypothalamo-hypophyseal system of a mammal (above) with the caudal neurosecretory system of a fish (below). [Enami in Gorbman (1959).]

substances which control the activities of the adenohypophysis (anterior pituitary) and are also stored in a neurohemal organ, the neurohypophysis or posterior lobe, to be released in the regulation of varied activities such as water balance and lactation.

Two other anatomical regions, besides the nervous system, make contributions to the vertebrate endocrine system. One of these is the anterior part of the gut and stomodaeum and the other is the nephrogenic mesodermal tissues associated with the urogenital organs. The adenohypophysis, thyroid, parathyroid, Islets of Langerhans and parts of the intestinal epithelium belong to the first group; endocrine tissues of the gonads and the adrenal cortex belong to the second.

Hormones produced by the derivatives of the primitive gut are proteinaceous and may have become differentiated phylogenetically from the copious mucoid secretions characteristic of this region of the digestive system in primitive vertebrate filter-feeders. If this hypothesis is valid, then several regions such as the hypophyseal pouch (Hatschek's pit of *Amphioxus*, Barrington, 1963), the endostyle, gill pouch epithelium and some of the intestinal cells must have specialized to produce proteins of a regulatory nature. These first biosyntheses and associations with metabolic regulation were fortuitous, and the products were discharged into the gut. Later specializations led to vascular transport and, in the case of the adenohypophysis, a direct linking of this system with the neurosecretory centers. The phylogeny of the thyroid from the endostyle is suggestive and will be described in a later section. Other significant evidence is found in the anatomical relationships of the pituitary in the Chondrostei. *Calamoichthys*, for example, retains an open ciliated hypophyseal duct which connects with the pharynx (Dodd and Kerr, 1963) and might retain an exocrine function along with its endocrine activities.

The second group of hormones, arising from the nephrogenic tissues, are steroids. Those synthesized in the gonads coordinate a variety of reproductive functions; those formed in the adrenal tissues seem to have been phylogenetically first concerned with electrolyte regulation in the nearby nephric tissues but have assumed additional functions in the higher vertebrates. Both groups of tissues are regulated from the neurosecretory centers by way of the trophic hormones of the adenohypophysis; in turn, they regulate the activities of the neural centers through the feed-back of information.

Neurohypophysis. Several biochemically distinct octapeptides from the neurohypophysis have now been identified; additional ones may be expected when more groups of animals have been examined (Heller, 1963; Perks and Dodd, 1963). The biochemical similarities and taxonomic distribution of several of these are shown in Fig. 2.10 and Table 2.2. The phylogeny is still uncertain. Physiologically, their most consistent action throughout the vertebrates is on the control of water and salt metabolism. In the primitive groups sodium regulation seems more important, while water regulation assumes greater significance in the terrestrial animals (Heller, 1963). This meager physiological evidence suggests that the neurohypophyseal octapeptides were first concerned with the regulation of electrolytes.

A somewhat different hypothesis for their phylogeny is based on the comparative anatomy of the pituitary and the difficulty of assigning pre-

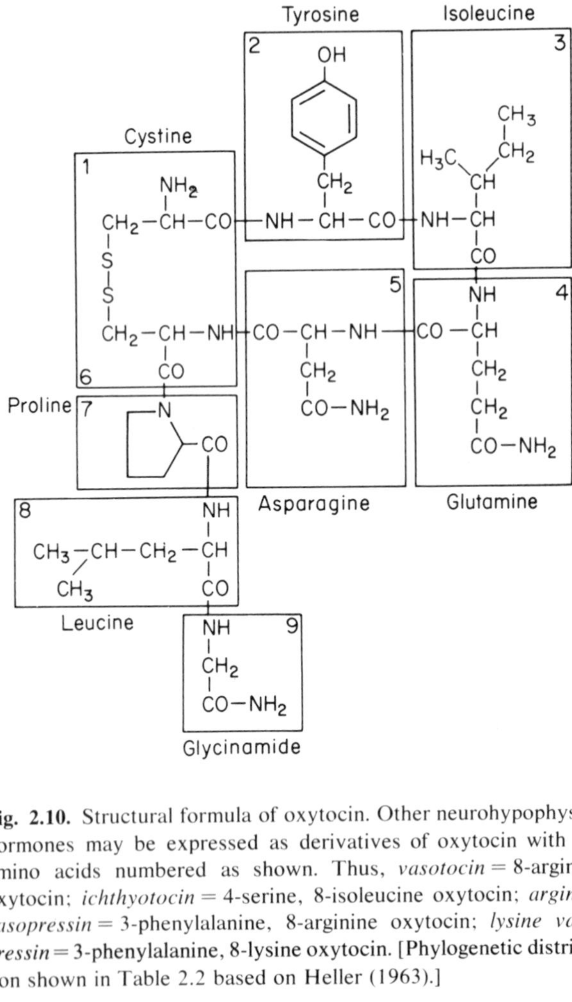

Fig. 2.10. Structural formula of oxytocin. Other neurohypophyseal hormones may be expressed as derivatives of oxytocin with the amino acids numbered as shown. Thus, *vasotocin* = 8-arginine oxytocin; *ichthyotocin* = 4-serine, 8-isoleucine oxytocin; *arginine vasopressin* = 3-phenylalanine, 8-arginine oxytocin; *lysine vasopressin* = 3-phenylalanine, 8-lysine oxytocin. [Phylogenetic distribution shown in Table 2.2 based on Heller (1963).]

cise roles to the octapeptides in the aquatic vertebrates (Sawyer *et al*, 1960). This theory suggests that the octapeptides first formed a chemical link between the brain and the adenohypophysis or anterior pituitary gland. Among the fishes the neurohypophysis is broadly connected with the adenohypophysis, frequently digitating into it; the anatomical arrangements are thus appropriate for a direct delivery of information from the brain (Fig. 2.11). Several of the activities of the adenohypophysis, such as the timing of reproduction, are regulated by environmental changes acting through sensory organs and the hypothalamic neurosecretory pathways.

TABLE 2.2

TENTATIVE SCHEME OF DISTRIBUTION OF NEUROHYPOPHYSEAL HORMONES. SYMBOLS: +, PRESENCE DEMONSTRATED; −, NOT FOUND. BASED ON HELLER (1963)

	Vasotocin (8-arginine oxytocin	*Ichthyotocin (4-serine, 8-isoleucine oxytocin)*	*Oxytocin*	*Vasopressin*[1]
Agnatha	+	?	−	−
Elasmobranchii[2]	−	?	−	−
Teleostei	+	+	−	−
Dipnoi	+	−	?	−
Amphibia	+	−	?	−
Reptilia	+	−	?	−
Aves	+	−	+	?
Mammalia[1]	−	−	+	+

[1]Arginine vasopressin (3-phenylalanine, 8-arginine oxytocin) has been demonstrated in all mammals investigated. The Suiformes have 8-lysine vasopressin in addition.

[2]A peptide with oxytocic properties has been described in elasmobranch pituitaries and identified chemically as 3-serine, 8-isoleucine oxytocin (Perks and Sawyer, 1964).

Among the tetrapods the neurohypophysis forms a distinct neural lobe, the pars nervosa, containing the terminations of many hypothalamic neurosecretory fibers and serving as a storage area (neurohemal organ) for their secretions (Fig. 2.11). The evolution of a distinct neural lobe is thought to be related to the water balance demands of terrestrial living even though a number of very different activities (lactation, for example) have evidently come under its control. It should be noted that the vascular relationships of the tetrapod pituitary are such that the adenohypophysis receives chemical information from the hypothalamic nuclei (via the portal vessels, Fig. 2. 11) even after the establishment of a neural lobe. Thus, in the higher vertebrates, secretions from the hypothalamic

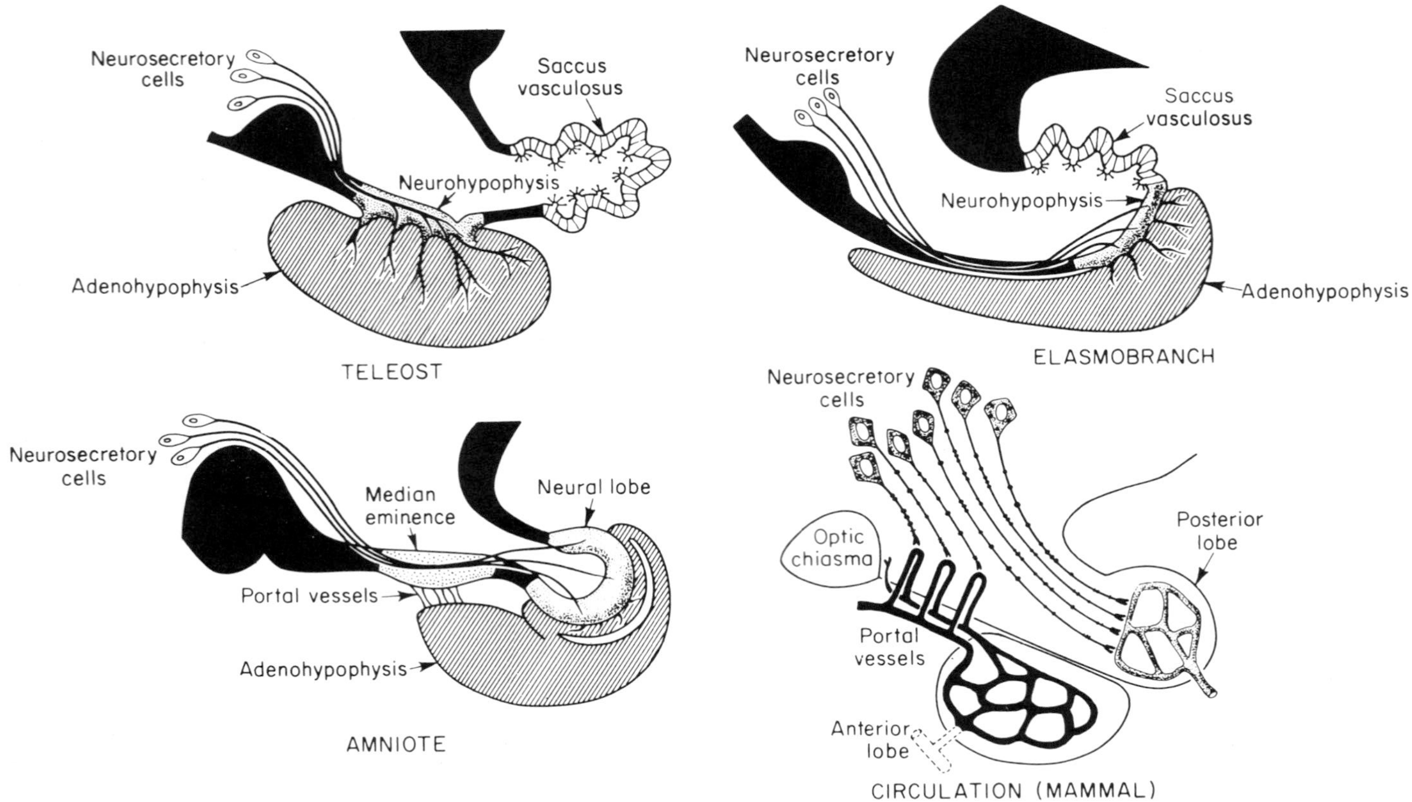

Fig. 2.11. Diagrams of median sagittal sections of the pituitary of a teleost, *Anguilla;* an elasmobranch, *Scylliorhinus;* an amniote; and the circulatory pattern and distribution of neurosecretory fibers in mammal. [Wingstrand in Gorbman (1959) and Scharrer in Gorbman (1959).]

nuclei control the adenohypophysis locally and exercise a more remote control over distant organs by neurosecretions which may be stored in the neural lobe prior to release into the blood (Figs. 2.9 and 2.11). At present there is only scanty information concerning the nature of the biochemical links between hypothalamus and adenohypophysis. The corticotropin-releasing factor seems to be closely allied to the neurohypophyseal hormones (Jorgensen and Larsen, 1963), but this is probably not true for some of the other factors (the thyrotropin-releasing factor, for example).

These two lines of argument concerning the phylogeny of the neurohypophyseal hormones are not mutually exclusive. At a very early stage in vertebrate evolution, the neurosecretory cells of the hypothalamus may have assumed a control of the adenohypophysis but at the same time acquired some responsibilities for electrolyte balance. At any rate, in modern fishes both functions seem to be controlled from the neurohypophysis (Maetz, 1963; Heller, 1963). It may be pertinent that the posterior neurosecretory system of fishes (urohypophysis) also seems to be concerned with electrolyte balance.

Adenohypophysis. This part of the pituitary secretes six or more protein hormones, each apparently elaborated by a different type of cell. Since these hormones are proteins it is not surprising that they often show considerable species specificity. Although interspecific testing with pituitary fractions usually elicits some response, the efficacy is much greater in closely related species. Size and complexity of the protein molecule are probably responsible for the observed differences. Thus, beef thyrotropin with a relatively small molecule (about 10,000 molecular weight) elicits responses in thyroidal cells of all groups of vertebrates from the cyclostomes to the mammals, but the beef gonadotropins with molecular weights four to ten times greater are often relatively ineffective in lower vertebrates. The biochemistry of the pituitary hormones is a subject of much interest and in some of them—the melanophore stimulating hormone, for example—the amino acid sequences are now known (Geschwind, 1959).

The growth promoting hormone SOMATOTROPIN (STH) has been studied in different vertebrates from fish to man and has displayed both metabolic and morphogenetic activities. The former are discussed in Chapter 7 and the latter in Chapter 24. The thyroid stimulating hormone or THYROTROPIN (TSH) regulates iodine metabolism by way of its action on the thyroid gland. The ADRENOCORTICOTROPHIC HORMONE or CORTICOTROPIN (ACTH) plays a comparable role with respect to the adrenal cortex. The melanophore stimulating hormone, INTERMEDIN, (MSH) and the melanophore concentrating hormones (MCH) are considered with chromatophores in Chapter 20. The GONADOTROPINS, the follicle stimulating hormone (FSH) and the luteinizing hormone (LH), as well as the LUTEOTROPIC HORMONE or LACTOGENIC HORMONE PROLACTIN (LTH) are discussed with reproduction in Chapter 23.

The activities of the various cells of the adenohypophysis are mainly controlled by the hypothalamus. The hypothalamus obtains its information from the external environment (seasonal cycles and the temperature controlling the gonads and growth), from stimulation of peripheral sense organs (suckling of the mammary glands leading to lactation, action of radiant energy on the retina) and by a feed-back of information from changing levels of hormones in the blood (level of thyroxine and the control of TSH secretion, the level of gonadal steroids and the production of gonadotropins). Thus, there is a regular flow of information to the hypophysis, both by nervous and chemical routes, and in this way the many activities of the anterior pituitary are adjusted to the demands of the organism.

Thyroid hormone. Iodine combines readily with the amino acid tyrosine to form a series of iodinated compounds as shown in Fig. 2.12. The first of these to be described in natural materials was 3,5-diiodotyrosine, named iodogorgoic acid by Drechsel, its discoverer, when he found it in the gorgonian corals in 1896. Iodoproteins are widely distributed, and at least one of the iodinated amino acids has now been identified in every major group of animals—except the Protozoa and the Echinodermata—and in a number of marine plants (Gorbman and Bern, 1962). Bromine, iodine's nearest relative in the halogen series, also forms a tyrosine compound in some of the corals.

Iodination of protein occurs readily under certain *in vitro* conditions. Casein, for example, when incubated with iodine yields monoiodotyrosine (MIT), diiodotyrosine (DIT) and thyroxine (Tx or T_4). Some proteins, because of their tyrosine content—perhaps also because of the structure of their molecules—have greater affinities than others for iodine. In nature, some nonthyroidal tissues are particularly rich in iodoproteins—for example, the notochord, the tunic of tunicates, the radula of molluscs, the jaws of polychaetes. Since iodoproteins evidently form easily in some kinds of protein, their presence in such locations as tunic, jaws, radula and notochord might be purely fortuitous and of no physiological significance.

Gorbman, following this line of argument, postulates that at some point in evolution these iodinated amino acids—which occurred at first by chance—gradually assumed an indispensable role as one of the vertebrate hormones (Gorbman and Bern, 1962). Iodine trapping cells became specialized and eventually formed an organ for the synthesis, storage and regulated delivery of the hormone in accordance with the demands of the organism. The ubiquity of the iodoproteins, the failure to demonstrate any function for them in the invertebrates, the phylogeny

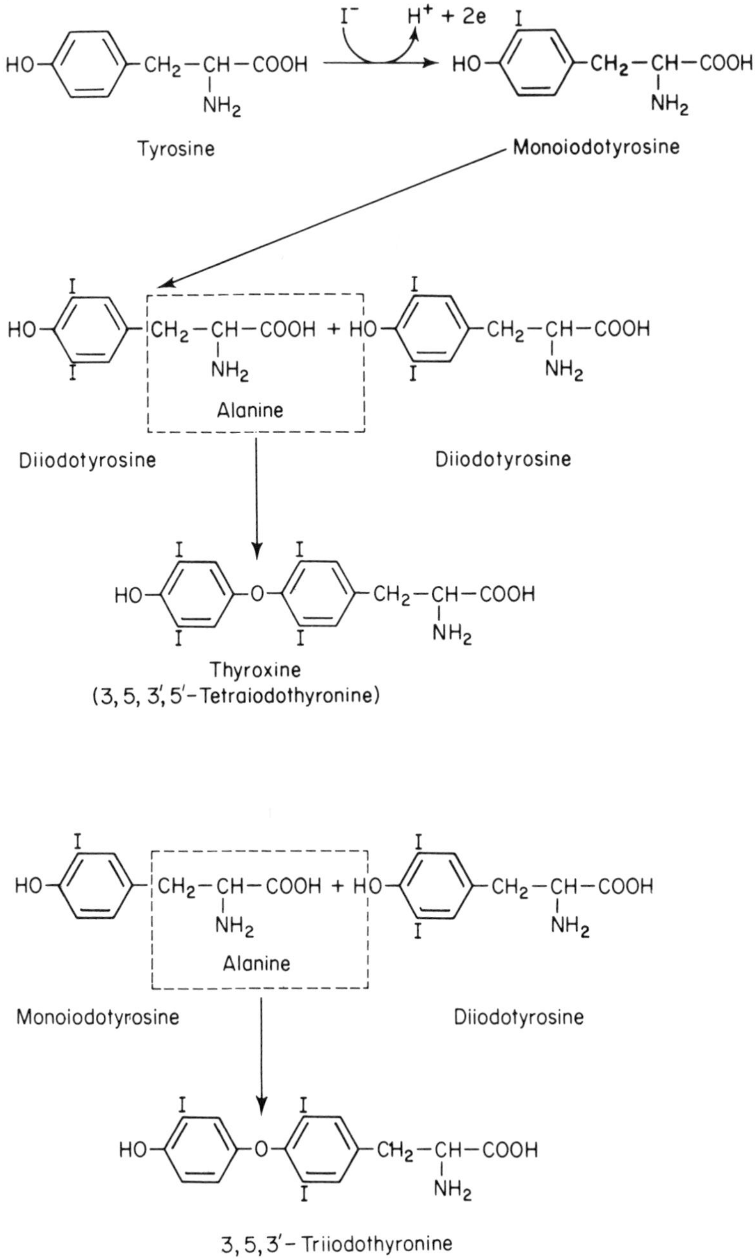

Fig. 2.12. Biosynthetic pathways for the thyroid hormones. [Turner (1960).]

of the gland in the lower vertebrates and its increasing importance in the higher vertebrates all give strong support to this hypothesis.

The phylogeny of the thyroid forms one of the most convincing pieces of this evidence. Barrington (1959) has identified special iodine-binding cells in the endostyle (ventral pharyngeal groove) of the protochordate which secrete iodoprotein (not definitely categorized biochemically). This presumably passes back with the mucus and food particles into the digestive tract where the proteolytic enzymes of the gut release the iodinated amino acids. In the ammocoetes (larval lamprey), the endostyle (actually a pouch-shaped subpharyngeal gland) also contains special iodine metabolizing cells, and these have been shown to form thyroid follicles when the endostyle disappears at metamorphosis (Olsson, 1963). Thus, in the lamprey, cells which at one stage in life (ammocoete) secrete directly into the digestive canal are later, in the adult, converted into an endocrine gland which discharges into the blood. The follicular cycle of iodine binding and subsequent release of thyroxine into the blood of the adult reflects this phylogeny since it involves a production of protein bound material (thyroglobulin) and its proteolysis or digestion WITHIN the follicle before release to the blood; the steps are at least superficially similar in the endostyle-gut sequence and in the thyroid follicle-blood sequence.

The thyroid physiologist has now traced many of the steps by which iodine is incorporated into the proteins of the follicular colloid and then converted into the hormone thyroxine and released into the blood. His task has been greatly aided by three techniques. Standard histological methods, the oldest of these, are particularly useful; the height of the follicular epithelium and the staining characteristics of the colloid reflect rather faithfully the functional condition of the gland. Radiochemical techniques have also been valuable since radioiodine is relatively inexpensive, safe and easy to use. Several components of iodine metabolism can be precisely traced in this way. The technique is rapid and shows a good correlation with the histology. Finally, there are several chemicals (goitrogens or antithyroid substances) which block specific steps in the iodine cycle and have been especially valuable in studying animals, such as the teleost fishes, where the thyroid is diffuse and cannot be removed surgically.

The follicular epithelium either secretes or pumps iodides and other essential compounds, such as amino acids, into the follicle. Within the follicular colloid, the iodide is then oxidized to iodine – probably enzymatically. This is followed by an iodination of the tyrosine or thyroglobulin, again presumably by enzyme action although the precise steps are unknown. Antithyroid drugs such as thiocyanate, perchlorates and iodates block the iodide uptake, while substances such as the thiocarbamides (thiourea, thiouracil and others) block the iodination of tyrosine; but the precise mechanism, at the molecular level, is not understood in either case.

This biosynthesis leads to the formation of a protein thyroglobulin with a molecular weight of about 700,000. The hormone which circulates in the blood is almost entirely L-thyroxine with only traces of triiodothyronine. This is released in accordance with the demands of the animal through the digestion of the thyroglobulin by proteases produced by the follicular cells. The thyroid stimulating hormone (TSH) forms the link between the central nervous system and the thyroid. Stimuli from the external or the internal environment, including the "feed-back" control from thyroxine itself, regulate the production of TSH. TSH, in turn, increases both the production and the secretion of thyroid hormones. This hypophyseal-pituitary control is probably an old one phylogenetically since the iodine accumulating cells of the endostyle of the ammocoete seem to be responsive to TSH (Gorbman and Bern, 1962).

Thyroidectomy, either surgical or chemical, and thyroid therapy of many different kinds is followed by a variety of disturbances in metabolism, development and growth. There is no lack of evidence for important activities of thyroid hormones—both metabolic and metamorphic—throughout the vertebrates, and many of these will be referred to at appropriate points in later chapters. However, in spite of this vast body of literature there is not yet a clear understanding of the essential biochemical role of the hormone. The current research in this field is active and centers around studies of the oxidative enzymes, phosphorylation and the control of mitochondrial permeability (Gorbman and Bern, 1962; Pitt-Rivers and Tata, 1959).

Parathyroid gland. The pharyngeal endoderm is the embryological source not only of the thyroid but also of the parathyroid glands. The latter develop as epithelial buds, usually from the third and fourth pairs of gill pouches.

The thymus and the ultimobranchial bodies also originate from pharyngeal endoderm, but they have not yet been shown to possess endocrine activity. The parathyroids, however, have been recognized as indispensable to some animals since the end of the nineteenth century when the lethal effects of "thyroidectomy" in cats and dogs were traced to the removal of the parathyroids and not the thyroid; they have had a firm place in the endocrine society since Collip (1925) prepared a proteinaceous extract—parathormone, parathyroid hormone (PTH)—which counteracted the symptoms of parathyroidectomy. Collip's hormone remained the only parathyroid hormone for almost forty years until a second fraction (calcitonin) with opposite effects was demonstrated in

1962 (Copp, 1964). The role of calcitonin is still speculative but the over-all function of the parathyroid glands is clearly to maintain the balance between the levels of soluble calcium and phosphorus in the blood and the reservoirs of these elements in the bones.

The embryology shows that these mineral-regulating tissues are derived from the gill pouch endoderm, and since the parathyroids are unknown among the fishes and first appear in the tetrapods it is possible that the phylogeny is associated with the loss of gills and the assumption of the terrestrial condition. Biologists, however, have not agreed on the physiological significance of this phylogeny. It is of interest and may be significant that epithelial cells at the base of the gills of fishes are concerned with electrolyte balance and that, when gills are lost in phylogeny, epithelial cells from this area produce the parathyroid glands concerned with calcium-phosphorus regulation.

There are other tantalizing problems in parathyroid physiology. One of these is the indispensable character of the gland in some animals and its apparent unimportance in others. In outline, our present knowledge is that in some vertebrates, parathyroidectomy is followed by a disastrous fall in the blood calcium and a rise in the inorganic phosphorus and that these changes are reversed by extracts from the gland. The immediate cause of death from parathyroidectomy is the low blood calcium which leads to hyperexcitability of muscles and eventually spasms of essential groups of muscles such as those involved in respiration. Collip's hormone, PTH, regulates the levels of both calcium and phosphorus, but the mechanisms are rather different for the two ions. Calcium levels are at least in part controlled through the action of PTH on the osteoclastic cells which remove bone spicules. The number of osteoclasts increases in response to PTH; these cells, in turn, digest and absorb the bone to release calcium and phosphate into the body fluids. The kidney is also influenced by PTH so that phosphate absorption by the renal tubules is decreased when the blood levels of PTH are elevated. In this way phosphate excretion rises. Secretion of parathyroid hormone seems to be directly regulated by the blood calcium, low serum calcium stimulating and high serum calcium suppressing the activity of the glands. Phosphate levels may also regulate gland activity, but the evidence is not as clear as is that for calcium.

It is strange that this regulation whose vital importance is readily demonstrated in some tetrapods is evidently of little or no significance in others. Much of the information is based on the dog which is particularly responsive. Likewise, the cat is a good subject but the white rat shows little response. A similar situation is found among the birds. Ducks and pigeons respond promptly to removal of the parathyroid but chickens show little change. A similar generalization may be made for Amphibia where parathyroidectomy of the bullfrog (*Rana catesbeiana*) produced low blood calcium; but a similar operation in several other species of Amphibia was without effect (Gorbman and Bern, 1962). Greep's (1963) review is the best source of comparative data.

ENDOCRINE TISSUES OF THE GASTRO-INTESTINAL ENDODERM

The lining of the gut and its derivatives secrete a variety of hormones concerned with the regulation of digestive activities and carbohydrate metabolism. Those connected with digestion proper—usually called the GASTROINTESTINAL HORMONES—are elaborated by mucosal cells in the wall of the stomach and intestine and, passing by way of the blood, act on the stomach, intestine, pancreas, gall bladder and liver. The hormone secreting cells have not been identified, but it is evident that they are scattered in the mucosa and are never organized into compact glandular masses. Most of the information comes from studies of the higher vertebrates, and this is summarized with the physiology of digestion in Chapter 3.

Embryologically, the pancreas and liver develop as evaginations of the gut endoderm; their epithelia may be thought of as extensions of that of the gut. Both of these glands elaborate secretions concerned with digestion, and these activities are regulated by the gastrointestinal hormones. In addition, the liver plays a major role in metabolism. It is strategically located to receive blood loaded with nutritive molecules from the digested food. These it metabolizes, stores and delivers on demand to the tissues of the body. Glucose is one of the key metabolites, and its movements and transformations are in large measure controlled by endocrine tissues—the FOLLICLES or ISLETS OF LANGERHANS—which also develop as specialized outgrowths of the gut endoderm. This region of the digestive tube, together with its complex endocrine controls, must have evolved as a unit.

The embryology seems to reflect the phylogeny (Barrington, 1962; Gorbman and Bern, 1962; Houssay, 1959). In the larval lampreys (ammocoetes), distinct Follicles of Langerhans are embedded in the submucosa of the anterior intestine. Ducts are not present, and the secretions pass directly into the blood. Barrington (1942) has shown that these follicles are concerned with carbohydrate metabolism and comparable to the Islets of other vertebrates where the cells are arranged in nests—the Islets of Langerhans. In some teleost fishes and in a few snakes they are grouped in several small but distinct globular masses (principal islets) in the region of the gall bladder, but in most vertebrates they are scattered throughout the exocrine tissue of the pancreas.

Islet tissues contain two types of cells and produce two different protein secretions. The α-cells secrete GLUCAGON with a hyperglycemic effect; the β-cells secrete INSULIN with a hypoglycemic effect. The proportions of the cell types differ in various groups of animals, and α-cells sometimes seem to be absent (urodele amphibians). These differences are probably related to dietary and metabolic demands, but there is at present insufficient information for generalizations. Since the two cell types are intimately associated in small cellular masses it is fortunate for the physiologist that they respond differently to certain chemical agents and can be selectively eliminated. The β-cells, for instance, are readily destroyed by alloxan and the α-cells by cobaltous chloride. This differential reaction has been most useful in the study of their functions.

The islet hormones pass by way of the blood to the liver, and this is probably the major target of their physiological activity. The enzyme insulinase is particularly abundant in liver tissues and leads to rapid inactivation of insulin. Thus, although insulin has marked *in vitro* activity on some other tissues such as muscle, its major action—at least phylogenetically—seems to be on glucose metabolism in the liver. Glucagon also loses its biological activity when it passes through the liver (Turner, 1960).

The action of insulin was first demonstrated in 1921 by Banting and Best (Best, 1959). It is interesting that, after more than forty years of active research, there is still uncertainty about its action at the cellular level. At the moment, the weight of evidence is in favor of a TRANSPORT HYPOTHESIS which attributes the major action of insulin to its ability to stimulate the movement of glucose across cell membranes. A second popular theory is the INTRACELLULAR ENZYME HYPOTHESIS which attributes the effect of insulin to some as yet unexplained action on the hexose kinase enzyme system or the pathways of oxidative phosphorylation (Chapter 7). Although the transport hypothesis has more support at the present time, the evidence is still incomplete. The two theories may not be mutually exclusive. Some unpublished work on frog muscle by J. E. Manery indicates that neither of these theories, developed for mammalian tissues, may be appropriate for some other vertebrates. Frog muscle, unlike mammalian muscle, in the presence of insulin shows an increased uptake of potassium and a markedly stimulated oxidation of lactic acid. Further, glucose uptake, which is sharply elevated by insulin in mammalian muscle, is only slightly increased by this treatment in frog muscle, and the effect varies with the season.

There is considerably more agreement concerning the action of glucagon. It stimulates glycogenolysis, acting on the liver phosphorylase system whereby glucose-1-phosphate is formed from glycogen (Turner, 1960). Further discussion of the action of these hormones is reserved for Chapter 7.

Chromaffin tissues and the adrenal medulla. These tissues are a part of the autonomic sympathetic as well as of the endocrine system. Morphologically, the chromaffin cells, like the sympathetic ganglia, arise from the neural crests and are, in fact, postganglionic neurons which have lost (or almost lost) their fibers. They discharge their secretions directly into the blood instead of passing them along axons to the effector organs as in the neurohumors of the autonomic nervous system proper. In the most primitive of the vertebrates (cyclostomes) numerous small masses of these chromaffin cells (paraganglia) are scattered, in close proximity to the cardinal veins, in every segment of the body from the second branchial to near the end of the postanal region (Chester Jones, 1957). The number is reduced and the masses become progressively larger and more compact in higher vertebrates. In the elasmobranchs there is still a paired, distinct chain of paraganglia; but in the teleosts and higher forms they become associated with, and embedded in, the cortical tissues until, in the mammals, the chromaffin tissue forms a distinct and readily separable mass (the adrenal medulla) within the adrenal cortex. Nevertheless, it retains its preganglionic sympathetic nerve fiber connections. In this it is exceptional among the vertebrate endocrine glands. In general, the vertebrate endocrine glands are activated chemically, but the adrenal medulla receives its cues from the sympathetic nerves.

Histochemically, the granules in these cells become brown when treated with certain oxidizing agents; chromium salts are most frequently used, and for this reason, the tissues are called "chromaffin." This term is the preferred one for the lower vertebrates while the same tissues in the higher vertebrates—particularly the mammals—are usually called "medullary." The chrome reaction is another mark of the relation between these cells and the autonomic ganglia which show the same staining. In both cases the reaction is due to the presence of certain catecholamines. There are two of these—noradrenaline and adrenaline, also called norepinephrine and epinephrine. The cells which produce them may be cytochemically separated by appropriate staining methods. Within the medullary tissues, the cells have been shown to be separately innervated and responsive to different types of stimuli (Bard, 1961; Gorbman and Bern, 1962).

The biosynthesis of these two important amines is shown in Fig. 2.13. The neurohumor of the postganglionic sympathetic nerve fibers is mostly noradrenaline (Turner, 1960). The chromaffin or medullary tissues produce varying amounts of both amines in different animals. In most mammals, adrenaline seems to predominate, but there are many exceptions, and as much as 80 per cent noradrenaline is sometimes found (whales). In the lower vertebrates the proportions are more equal (Gorbman and Bern, 1962). Since noradrenaline is a precursor of adrenaline this is not an unexpected finding; the actual analyses of medullary tissues may give different results depending on physiological conditions. The nature of the physiological product of the tissue is another question. It has been suggested that noradrenaline is the "tonus" hormone for circulatory regulation and adrenaline the "emergency" hormone released during excitement or excessive activity, acting to meet sudden metabolic demands for glucose and to make appropriate circulatory adjustments. Further discussion of the physiology of the catecholamines is found in connection with the processes which they regulate.

It should be added that adrenaline and noradrenaline are of widespread occurrence in the animal kingdom. Chromaffin cells are found in the nervous system of many invertebrates (annelids, molluscs, arthropods), and both adrenaline and noradrenaline have been identified (Prosser and Brown, 1962; Gorbman and Bern, 1962). These amines

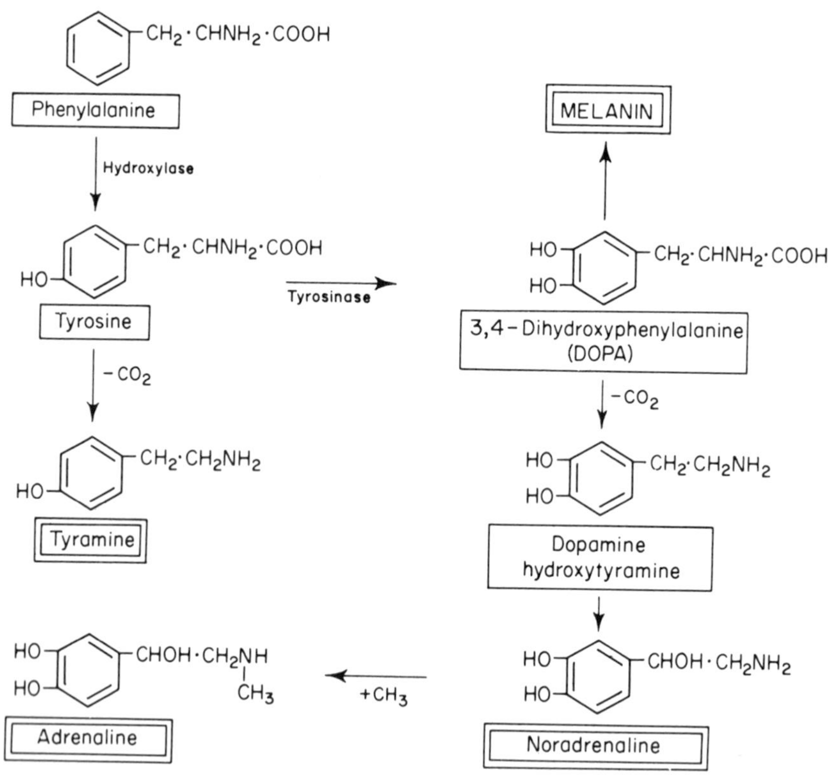

Fig. 2.13. Some of the metabolic pathways of phenylalanine and tyrosine, the source of adrenaline, noradrenaline, tyramine and melanin.

have also been isolated from non-nervous tissues such as the salivary glands of vertebrates and the *Octopus* (Gorbman and Bern, 1962).

Interrenal gland and the adrenal cortex. The mesoderm of the roof of the coelom has an interesting history. Laterally, the nephrogenic tissue gives rise to the tubules and ducts of the excretory system; medially, as the genital ridge, it produces the gonads. Between these two areas strands of cells are budded off to form the adrenal or interrenal cortical tissues essential to the life of vertebrate animals. In the cyclostomes these buds of cells retain their scattered distribution in the tissues around the cardinal vein, along most of its length (Chester Jones, 1957). In the elasmobranchs they form compact structures of variable shape between the kidneys where they were quite appropriately named the "interrenals" in early descriptions. The progressively more intimate association which occurs between these and the chromaffin tissues in vertebrate phylogeny was mentioned in the previous section. No special physiological significance has as yet been ascribed to this association.

Physiologically, the cortical tissue suggests affinities with the organs which develop from neighboring anlagen. On the one hand, hormones produced by both the gonads and interrenals belong to the same biochemical group (steroid hormones) and show many common biosynthetic pathways. In fact, several of the same steroids may be isolated from both organs. On the other hand, with respect to the nephric anlage, it has been suggested that the interrenal gland may have been developed as a response (evolutionary) to the demands for ionic regulation by the kidney (Chester Jones and Phillips, 1960). It has been argued that ionic regulation is one of the primary functions of the vertebrate kidney. It is now known that cortical steroids are concerned with electrolyte balance in vertebrates ranging from fish to men. There is a suggestive connection, and the speculation may be extended to bring the corticosteroids into the group of materials essential for the evolution of the vertebrates.

The cortical tissues are centers for the manufacture of steroids; about fifty different variations of this molecule have been identified in the mammalian adrenal. Not all are hormones. Many represent biochemical steps in the synthesis of the active hormones (Figs. 2.14 and 23.5). Closely related steroids often have similar physiological activities, and it is not surprising that the proportions of the different fractions vary in different groups of animals—perhaps in accordance with metabolic demands (Dorfman, 1959). There is, however, a definite pattern and some of the best known steroids have now been identified throughout the phylogenetic series (Chester Jones and Phillips, 1960; Holmes *et al*, 1962).

It has been possible to block the biosynthetic pathways in the adrenal cortex by the use of chemicals (amphenone, for example). The technique has the same experimental potentialities as chemical thyroidec-

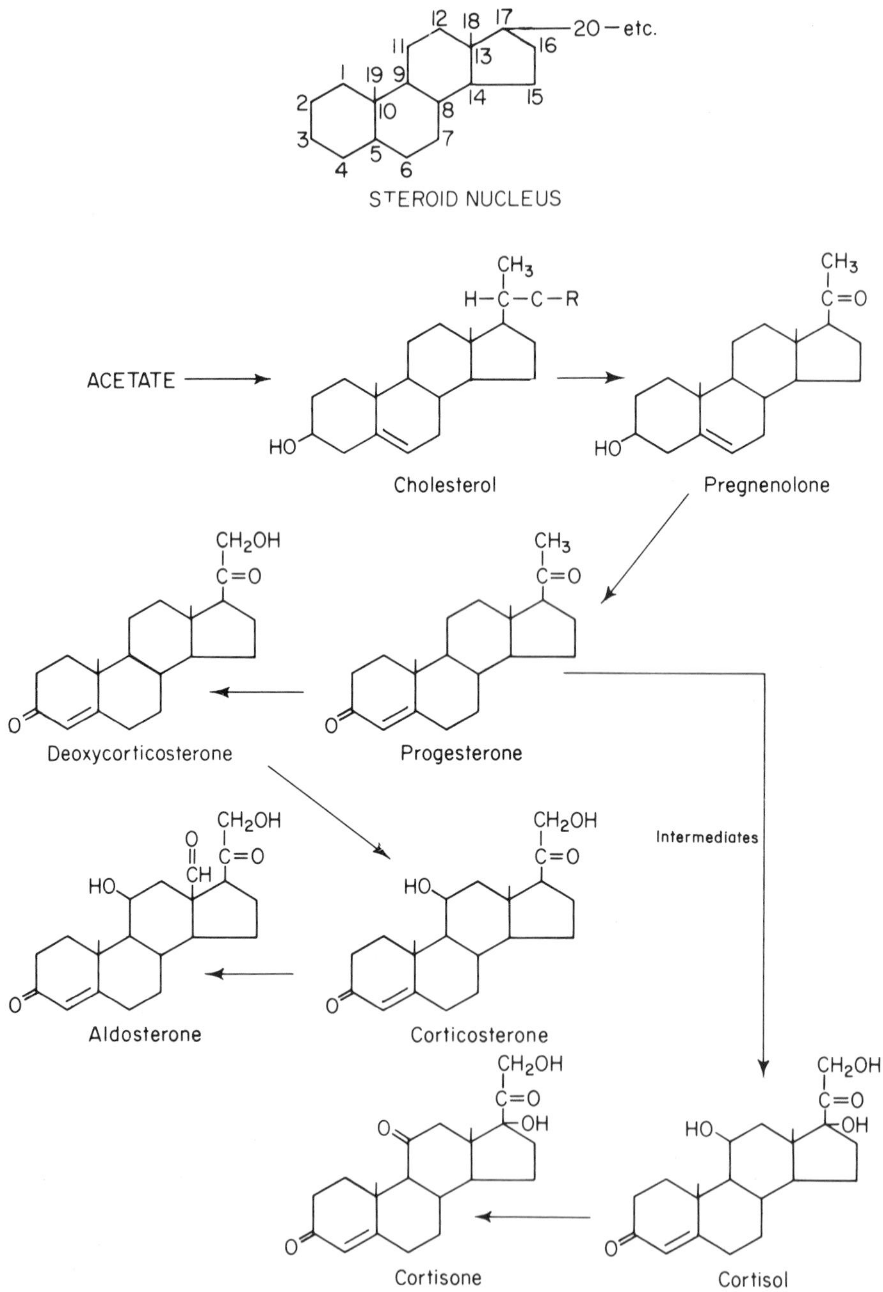

Fig. 2.14. The steroid nucleus with several of the suggested steps in biosynthesis of the most active adrenal steroids. Aldosterone exists also in the 11-hemiacetyl forms.

tomy in studies of the thyroid or the production of diabetes with alloxan. It has been particularly useful in the lower forms where the cortical tissues are diffuse and cannot be removed surgically (van Overbeeke, 1960). It has also been used to inhibit adrenal activity in clinical work (Williams, 1962).

Two major physiological groups of corticosteriods are recognized—one concerned with gluconeogenesis or the formation of glucose from protein and fat (GLUCOCORTICOIDS) and the other with a primary action on electrolyte balance (MINERALOCORTICOIDS). This dichotomy into gluco- and mineralocorticoids is not a sharp one biochemically; compounds which are most active in gluconeogenesis may have some electrolyte effect, and vice versa. In mammals, cortisol (hydrocortisone) is by far the most active of the glucocorticoids although cortisone and corticosterone are also well known representatives of this group. These compounds occur throughout the vertebrate series (Chester Jones and Phillips, 1960). Aldosterone, the most active of the mineralocorticoids, is also of wide occurence, although it has not yet been identified in the most primitive of the vertebrates (Chester Jones *et al.*, 1962). Deoxycorticosterone (DOC) is likewise active in electrolyte regulation but much less potent than aldosterone. Little is known of the cellular mechanisms by which these hormones control metabolism, although it is suspected that their action is, in many cases, a general one rather than an operation on specific target organs. Further discussion of the activities of corticosteroids is reserved for the chapters on metabolism, excretion and osmoregulation.

Two distinct and rather complex mechanisms control secretion by the cortical tissues. The adrenocorticotrophic hormone (ACTH) of the anterior pituitary is the prime regulator of glucocorticoid production, although there is also a mild effect on the secretion of mineralocorticoids. In the zonated mammalian gland, ACTH has its greatest action on the zona fasciculata and reticularis, but in other vertebrates, where zonation is largely absent, the effects are not localized. At the next higher level of integration ACTH is liberated in response to the hypothalamus, and this in turn is directly responsible to the body as a whole. The link between the hypothalamus and the adenohypophysis (ACTH) is chemical and involves a distinct humoral factor (CRF— the corticotrophin release factor). The hypothalamus receives its cues from the changing levels of glucocorticoids in the blood and is also activated by a variety of situations known collectively as "stress" (Selye, 1961), which call forth adrenaline as discussed in the next section. Thus, the glucocorticoids are secreted in accordance with the changing needs of the animal through the integrative activities of the hypothalamic-pituitary system.

Mineralocorticoid production, on the other hand, is independent of this axis (Fig. 11.10). Experimental evidence based almost entirely on the mammal is far from complete, but there is now an accumulating evidence for renal and perhaps also epithalamic control. An altered electrolyte and water balance activate the kidney epithelium of the dog to secrete a "renal factor" with a direct action on aldosterone output. Present indications are that this factor is the renin-hypertensin mechanism of the kidney (Chapter 5 and literature in v. Euler and Heller, 1963). In addition, the dorsal area of the diencephalon (pineal) seems to be activated by low extracellular sodium, high extracellular potassium or a low extracellular fluid volume to secrete a hormonal factor (glomerulotropin or adrenoglomerulotropin) which is extremely potent in the regulation of aldosterone. The evidence comes from classical types of endocrinological experiment involving pinealectomy of the dog, perfusion and injection of extracts. These controls of aldosterone output are still not well understood and are under intensive study. The comparative physiologist has scarcely entered the field.

A Coordinated System of Regulation

For descriptive purposes it has been necessary to dissect the regulatory machinery of animals and separate out the various parts—enzymes, neurons, glands—for examination and study. Actually, enzymes, transmitter substances, neurosecretory substances and the hormones operate as an integrated group of chemicals. In addition, there are several substances which act like hormones but differ in their mode of formation or distribution. These are the metabolites such as carbon dioxide which regulates the breathing centers of the brain, the secretagogues important in digestion and other metabolic products such as histamine. These are usually called PARAHORMONES. The PHEROMONES (Karlson, 1960) also form a part of this chemical interrelation; unlike the hormones proper which operate within the animal which produces them, these work on other members of the same species. They have been called "social hormones" and include substances responsible for olfactory attraction between the sexes, alarm substances which warn other members of the species of dangers (Pfeiffer, 1962), and some of the "markers" used to establish territories and trails or to mark rich sources of food. The extent and details of this broad system of chemical integration are only beginning to emerge. It is an exciting area for productive research.

In the last few pages on vertebrate hormones the discussion has turned again and again to the hypothalamic control of endocrine secretion. Although this is a relatively recent subject of study, it is now certain that the activities of the vertebrate endocrine glands are controlled from centers in the brain, and the evidence is just as convincing for a parallel control among the invertebrates (Scharrer, 1959). This is a neuroendocrine system, and in the vertebrates the hypothalamus is only one of the centers involved in this coordination. The epithalamus or pineal has now been implicated in the control of chromatophores of lower vertebrates, in the regulation of the sexual cycles of higher vertebrates (Wurtman and Axelrod, 1965) and perhaps also in adrenal activity. The urohypophysis in the tail of fishes is also a part of the neuroendocrine system of vertebrates.

This neuroendocrine relationship is basic to the physiology of most animals and important both in the integration of the metabolism of the animal through the various feed-back mechanisms and in the interplay between the animal and its oscillating and changing environment. Seasonally altering photoperiods and temperatures act through the neuroendocrine system to trigger reproduction, growth and other physiological phenomena at the most appropriate time for reproduction and success of the species. Many fruitful areas of research await the interested investigator.

There is much less information at the next level of integration—the connection between the hormone and the enzyme system of the effector organ. Knowledge of the connecting links between enzyme and gene is even scantier. However, the field has been pioneered, and present results support the belief that an understanding will emerge. The insect molting hormone, ecdyson—now isolated and purified by Karlson and his associates—seems to activate a gene which controls the synthesis of an enzyme which regulates tyrosine formation (Karlson, 1962). Again, the action of glucagon in carbohydrate metabolism seems to be at the enzyme level but, with relatively few exceptions, physiologists have not yet probed to the molecular levels of regulation. Interest is now high and exciting findings can be expected.

3 *Nutrition*

The term nutrition, as used here, includes most of the many processes involved in nourishing the individual animal cells. It is sometimes used in a more restricted sense as synonymous with food or nutriment, but the older definition of the word, which implies also the processes of feeding, digestion and assimilation, is more appropriate for the comparative animal physiologist. In final analysis, it is the individual cell which requires for its nourishment a steady flow of energy-rich materials from the environment.

Living organisms may be loosely classified as AUTOTROPHIC or HETEROTROPHIC. The autotrophic organisms are able to synthesize all essential organic compounds from inorganic mineral sources. They include the chemosynthetic bacteria (CHEMOTROPHS) and the chlorophyll-bearing green plants (PHOTOTROPHS). The heterotrophic organisms, on the other hand, require organic substances as food and have limited synthesizing abilities. However, it has already been pointed out that there is a range of living forms with numerous examples of intermediate modes of metabolism between that of the typical chemotroph and the typical phototroph, and between the strictly autotrophic and the strictly heterotrophic individuals. Some of the chlorophyll-bearing Euglenae, for example, can elaborate many of the essential organic compounds but require certain growth factors or vitamins to do so. They are not independent of organic sources of food and have been called MESOTROPHIC. An elaborate terminology has been developed to describe the different intermediate conditions (Lwoff, 1951), but it is not particularly pertinent to the present discussion. Almost all animals are heterotrophic and obtain energy for their life processes and the materials necessary for growth, repair and manufacture of essential secretions by swallowing, devouring or engulfing other animals and plants, and breaking down the complex organic compounds which they contain through hydrolytic or other processes. A much smaller group of animals, including many parasitic forms, are saprozoic and absorb relatively complex organic compounds through their body surfaces. This is considered a secondary method of nutrition, although, at one stage in evolution, the "soaking up" of organic compounds from the environment probably preceded the nutritional arrangements which are now found in animals and plants.

Nutritive Requirements

The holophytic (photosynthetic) mode of nutrition, although found only in a small group of animals (the mastigophoran Protozoa) is of particular interest to the comparative physiologist because of its supposed phylogenetic antiquity. There are several theoretical possibilities for the phylogeny of the holozoic condition which depends on devouring other organisms. It might be assumed that the first living organisms had a complete range of synthesizing abilities and that, as living material increased in quantity and variety, some forms began to absorb materials from other organisms or from the dissolved residues of their disintegrating bodies. Thus, the ability to manufacture food may have been gradually lost as some of the evolving species became dependent on others. On the other hand, one might assume that the first units which could be truly called living cells required a complete range of preformed materials from their environment, that they absorbed these essential constituents in a strictly saprophytic manner and that photosynthesis and the ability to lead a purely autotrophic existence was secondary. The latter view is probably closer to the truth, although it is also possible that both of these situations occurred as steps in evolution. In any case, as far as animal life is concerned, the advent of photosynthesis either initiated its phylogeny or marked an entirely new stage in it. The photoautotrophic organisms changed the anaerobic world to the aerobic world and permitted the evolution of animal life which is strictly dependent on the synthetic activities of plants. The suggestion is that animal phylogeny has been from primitive plant to animal and from holophytic to holozoic nutrition. This view is consistent with the greater synthesizing abilities of the simpler forms of animal life. With increasing complexity, there is increasing dependence on special nutritive factors in the form of vitamins, essential amino acids and other complex organic groups.

GENETICS AND NUTRITIONAL DEMANDS

Synthesizing abilities are controlled by genes, and a failure to manufacture any compound must depend on changes in the genetic material. This was first convincingly demonstrated by Beadle and Tatum (1941) in classical experiments on the genetic control of biosyntheses in the bread mold *Neurospora* (Fig. 3.1). This fungus has two distinct advantages for such a study. In the first place, its life cycle is short, requiring ten days for a generation; secondly, the cells of the mycelia are haploid and thus contain only one set of genes for any particular character. The haploid mycelia which grow vegetatively during asexual reproduction are of two mating types, each with seven chromosomes. During sexual reproduction cross fertilization takes place between the two types, their haploid nuclei fuse within a common cytoplasm to form a diploid zygote with seven pairs of chromosomes. These chromosomes replicate and undergo two meiotic divisions to give four haploid nuclei, each with a single set of seven chromosomes; these then divide mitotically to yield eight ascospores within a sac from which they can be readily dissected under the microscope and grown separately in culture tubes (Anfinsen, 1959). In this way rapidly maturing individuals with single genes for particular characters are obtained. The genetics is reduced to simple terms. For example, if a yellow and a white strain of bread mold are crossed and the resulting spores cultured separately, half of them will give white and half of them yellow molds. There are no dominant and recessive individuals to be sorted out in back crosses.

The red bread mold proved especially suitable for these experiments; it can be grown in pure cultures on a medium of nitrate, sulfate, phosphate and various other inorganic substances together with some sugar and biotin (minimal medium, Fig. 3.1). From these simple starting materials, the mold synthesizes about 20 amino acids, 9 water-soluble vitamins of the B-complex and other equally elaborate groups. Every so often a mutant spore appears which is incapable of growing in the medium of salt, sugar and biotin but will grow on the addition of a mixture of complex organic compounds such as occur in an extract of yeast. The ability to synthesize one or more of these complex molecules has evidently been lost. Beadle (1948) increased the rate of mutation by using X-rays or other mutagenic agents, and isolated strains which were unable to synthesize certain particular molecules. These isolations were made by patiently testing strains which failed to grow in the salt-sugar-biotin medium with media which had been supplemented by a single purified chemical such as one of the B-vitamins or an amino acid. A study of the genetics of these mutant strains then provided clear evidence for the genetic control of the biosyntheses. For example, when a strain

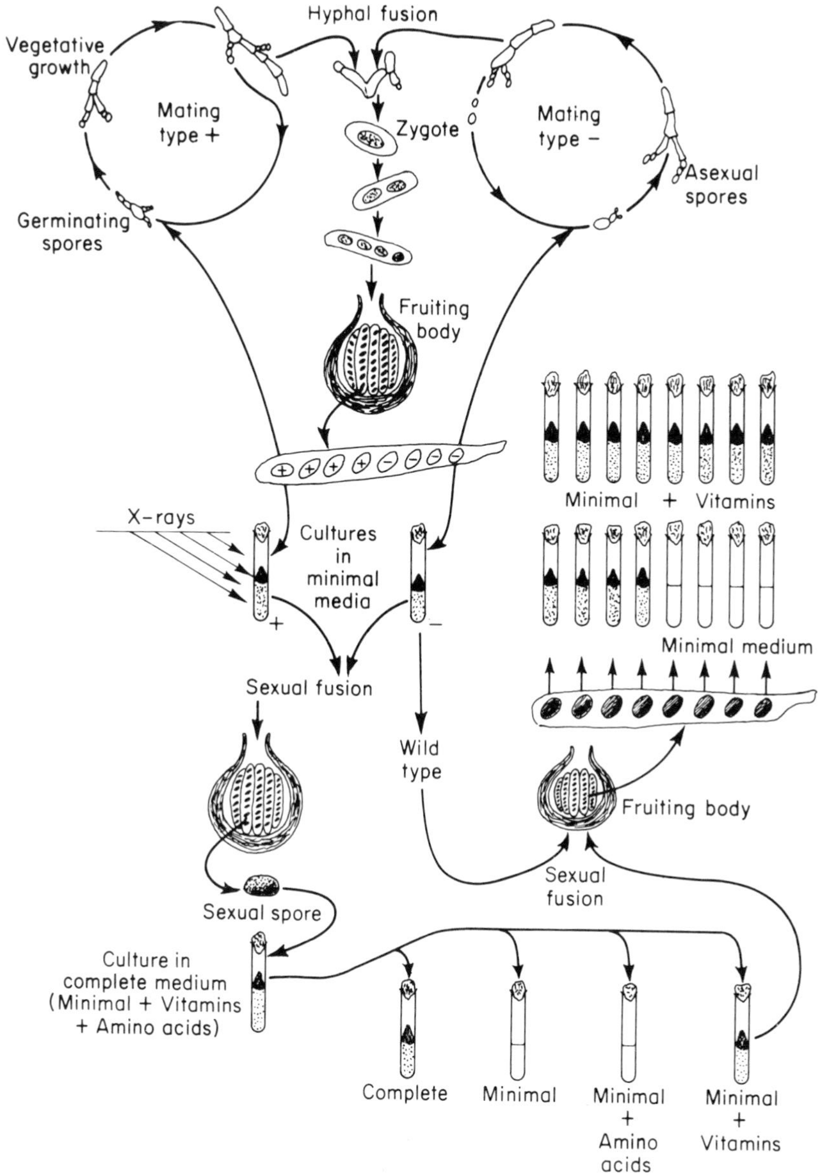

Fig. 3.1. The life cycle of *Neurospora* and a diagrammatic representation of the classical experiments which demonstrated the genetics of its vitamin requirements.

which grows only if pyridoxine is added to the salt-sugar-biotin mixture is crossed with the wild type, it is found that half of the resulting spores can manufacture pyridoxine and half of them cannot. These experiments support the theory that the ability to synthesize materials such as pyridoxine is controlled by single genes. The techniques are summarized diagrammatically in Fig. 3.1.

The evolution of animal life involved not only the loss of chlorophyll and the photosynthetic ability, but also a loss of the biochemical machinery for the manufacture of many essential enzymes. It is assumed that organisms growing in nutritively rich media occasionally produced mutants lacking the genes required for the production of certain enzymes. These mutants could survive and compete with other individuals if they lived in environments capable of supplying the missing enzyme. The protozoa provide many examples of closely related species with nutritive requirements which vary in accordance with the materials available to them in their environments.

NUTRITION AMONG THE EUGLENOIDINA

Among the euglenoid Mastigophora, there is an almost continuous series from obligate photoautotrophs to obligate heterotrophs, with some strains capable of shifting back and forth from one mode of nutrition to the other (Hall, 1953; Hutner and Lwoff, 1955). *Euglena anabaena* is claimed to be photoautotrophic and able to manufacture all the compounds essential to its life, while some other Euglenae require certain growth factors even though they can elaborate such compounds as carbohydrates and proteins. *E. gracilis typica* requires the pyrimidine and *E. klebsii* the thiazole as well as the pyrimidine component of thiamine (Scheer, 1963). In the dark, some of the Euglenae (*E. gracilis*, for example) may lose their chlorophyll and become saprozoic. Related genera likewise show variable modes of nutrition. *Polytoma* is a colorless and purely saprozoic flagellate; *Monas* lacks the colored pigments but possesses a pit or gullet for the entrance of food into the body and thus exemplifies the holozoic condition. Some of the colored forms also possess gullets and may combine the holozoic and the holophytic methods. *Ochromonas* (and perhaps many other flagellates) combines all three modes of nutrition. All of the known methods of nutrition are evidently exploited by these primitive animals. With the loss of photosynthesis and a definite commitment to the holozoic way of life, there is a progressive loss of synthesizing abilities and a trend toward the obligate heterotroph.

There are many interesting differences in the capacity of the phytoflagellates to utilize inorganic nitrogen. *Euglena stellata* can satisfy its nitrogen requirements with nitrate, and this is considered primitive (Lwoff, 1951). *E. gracilis*, on the other hand, cannot use NO_3 but must obtain nitrogen from ammonia or an amino acid. Other species may require complex organic groups such as amino acids (*E. deses*) or peptones (*E. pisciformis*) and cannot make use of either NO_3 or NH_3 (Scheer, 1948, 1963). Amino acid requirements are also variable; some forms are able to grow on a single amino acid, while others may require as many as a dozen different ones (Hall, 1953). In their phylogeny, these organisms seem to have become progressively more dependent on the complex organic nitrogen compounds, and many forms require a rather specific group of ESSENTIAL AMINO ACIDS just like the higher vertebrates. They have become specialized to exploit an environment which regularly contains these food factors and have lost the ability to manufacture them.

Many similar examples are now known, and one more will be mentioned here. Thiamine, sometimes called vitamin B_1, is a coenzyme for decarboxylation and transketolation. It enters into a chain of biochemical reactions which is a part of all life. It seems likely that animals, specializing in holozoic ways of nourishment, lost the ability to form this molecule at an early stage in evolution. Structurally, thiamine is a combination of two biochemical units, the pyrimidine ring and the thiazole ring (Fig. 7.6). The construction of each ring presents distinct biochemical problems and, although some protozoa can manufacture the completed thiamine unit, others must be provided with either the pyrimidine or the thiazole; still others must find both in their food (Scheer, 1963). Thus, thiamine is a vitamin or essential accessory food factor for two subspecies of *Euglena gracilis* but not for *Euglena stellata* which can synthesize all of these thiamine factors. Pyrimidine is a vitamin for *Euglena pisciformis* and thiazole a vitamin for *Polytoma caudatum*, while *Polytomella caecae* requires two vitamins (pyrimidine and thiazole) to perform the same task. It is not surprising to find that the natural habitats of the different species provide an adequate supply of these accessory food factors. *Polytoma* and *Polytomella* live in stagnant water where there is an abundance of organic material, while *Leptomonas*, which must have thiamine as such, is an animal parasite. The mutations which give rise to forms incapable of manufacturing these essential enzyme groups would be lethal, unless they occurred in environments containing an abundance of them. Once the mutant is established as a new species it is chained forever to such an environment and has a vitamin requirement as part of its genetic constitution.

COMPONENTS OF AN ADEQUATE DIET

There is a constant exchange of materials between living organisms and their nonliving environment. In animal life this involves, among other things, the acquisition of varied complex organic molecules. The energy requirements are met through oxidation of a series of carbon compounds—particularly the carbohydrates, fats and proteins. Growth, tissue repair and the synthesis of various secretions demand the amino acid units of protein. A number of the enzymes responsible for the catalysis of both the catabolic energy-yielding and the anabolic growth-promoting reactions cannot be manufactured by animals and must be obtained from outside sources. These dietary supplements are referred to as the vitamins. Finally, life demands a diversified group of minerals for the regulation of osmotic pressure and acid-base balance, the formation of skeletal materials, and the activation of numerous enzyme reactions.

THE SOURCES OF ENERGY

Carbohydrate usually forms the major source of energy. In the well balanced human diet, 55 per cent to 70 per cent of the calories are derived from carbohydrate. However, all animals may utilize other compounds as energy sources. Some green flagellates, which depend largely on photosynthesis, metabolize simple organic compounds such as acetate or butyrate. These animals are said to be FACULTATIVE because they can utilize a variety of organic acids when these are available. There is considerable variation in facultative abilities among different forms. Simple carbon groups, such as acetate, can probably be used by most animals. Fats and proteins are also sources of energy and may replace carbohydrate in the diet. Fats are stored when food is abundant, but when required they are readily converted into energy, and many animals (the migrating salmon, for example) can live for months on reserves of accumulated fat.

Biochemically, the basic energy-yielding units of carbohydrate, fat and protein are readily interconverted (Chapter 7). Variations in the ability to use some of the complex carbohydrates, fats and proteins as foods are correlated with the complement of digestive enzymes. The essential materials for animal tissues are the monosaccharides, simple triglycerides and a variety of amino acids. The metabolic machinery can readily shuffle these groups to obtain energy from any one of them, or to store them in the form of fat (Chapter 7).

ESSENTIAL AMINO ACIDS

A minimal amount of protein is imperative, since its structural units, the amino acids, are required for the construction of new tissues and the repair of old ones. Moreover, the amino acid requirements are usually very specific because of genetic limitations in the abilities to synthesize these complex molecules. The genetical work on *Neurospora* has shown that in this organism the synthesis of amino acids such as lysine, tryptophan or proline depends on a single gene. Nutritional studies of several species of protozoa suggest that primitive animals lost the ability to synthesize these groups through random mutations in suitable environments.

All multicellular animals and most protozoa require some specific amino acids as dietary factors. These are referred to as ESSENTIAL AMINO ACIDS, and some of them are probably required by all animals. Rose (1938) did much of the pioneer work on the rat and later (1949) showed that adult men could remain in nitrogen balance only if the following amino acids were included in their diets: lysine, trytophan, phenylalanine, threonine, valine, methionine, leucine and isoleucine. The same acids are required by mice, chickens, the ciliate protozoan *Tetrahymena* and the insect *Tribolium confusum*. Many other animals are known to have similar requirements, and it is probable that all animals must obtain some preformed amino acids from their environment. They are the fundamental building blocks of animal tissues, and the enzyme systems required for their manufacture occur only in the plant world. Davis (1961*a*) points out that the number of enzymatic reactions involved in the biosynthesis of these essential amino acids is relatively large. Thus, acids such as alanine or glycine have only one enzyme in the main anabolic pathway while essential acids such as threonine or arginine require six or seven, and the most complex ones (tryptophan, phenylalanine, isoleucine) have ten to fifteen such enzymatic pathways in their biosynthesis.

Essential lipids. All animal tissues contain some fat or lipid material. In addition to that present as depot or reserve energy material, there are lipids in every cell, forming essential components of the plasma membrane and such important cytoplasmic constituents as the mitochondria. Animals can readily synthesize fats from carbohydrates or proteins but, as in the case of the amino acids, there are limitations with respect to certain chemical units. This is particularly true of certain unsaturated fatty acids and the more complex lipid materials such as cholesterol.

The rat is unable to synthesize linoleic, linolenic and arachidonic acids. These are all polyunsaturated fatty acids in which the location and configuration of the double bonds is evidently of the utmost importance. A similar fatty acid requirement has been demonstrated for several other mammals, for some birds and certain insects. The moth *Ephestia*, for example, is unable to synthesize linoleic acid while the mealworm *Tenebrio* can live on diets without this fatty acid (Roeder, 1953; Aaes–Jorgensen, 1961). Many of the protozoa can grow without lipid supplements. Although relatively few animals have as yet been investigated, it seems that the ability to synthesize the necessary lipids is much more widespread than the ability to form the necessary proteins. This seems to be related to differences in biochemical complexity of the two classes of compounds.

The steroids are more complex biochemically than the unsaturated fatty acids. There is now some information on the dietary requirements for steroids and other complex lipoidal materials. The cholesterol molecule (Fig. 2.14), is ubiquitous as a constituent of cell membranes; its four-ring nucleus forms the skeleton of such important compounds as the vertebrate sex hormones and adrenocortical hormones.

Although the higher vertebrates can synthesize cholesterol from acetic acid or its active derivatives, this is not true of all animals. Many insects, perhaps all, require dietary supplements of cholesterol or a related sterol. They are evidently unable to construct the phenanthrene nucleus. The crab *Cancer pagurus* also lacks the ability to synthesize cholesterol (van den Oord, 1964) and it seems possible that the cholesterol found in all arthropods is of dietary origin. Some protozoans, but by no means all of them, likewise require preformed cholesterol. The flagellate *Trichomonas* requires cholesterol or something close to it, and Lwoff (1951) has shown that substitutes for cholesterol must meet rather rigid specifications. The OH in position 3 (Fig. 2.14), for example, is essential. If this is not present, the molecule no longer meets the animal's dietary requirements.

The vitamins. The story of the vitamins is one of the most interesting chapters in the history of medicine and biochemistry. Much of it is written around two of the ancient scourges of mankind, scurvy and beri-beri. Scurvy was all too well known to the Crusaders of the thirteenth century and probably to generations of men from the beginning of human history. Wherever men must exist for prolonged periods without fresh fruits and vegetables, widespread small hemorrhages develop, the joints become swollen, the teeth loosen in their sockets, bones break easily and wounds fail to heal. Death is the inevitable result. In times of war and famine, on lengthy sea voyages, and in institutions with restricted diet, men and women were familiar with the symptoms long before an Austrian physician, Kramer, recommended citrus fruit for a prophylaxis in 1520. Another 200 years or more were to pass before James Lind in 1753 produced his classic report on this disease and presented such forceful evidence for the efficacy of citrus fruits that the British Navy introduced limes and lemons into their rations (1795). Thus, their sailors earned the name "limey," and their ships were rid of scurvy (Drummond and Wilbraham, 1939). The wharf area of London became "Limehouse," but the physiology of the disease was really no better understood than in the days of the Crusades.

In 1928 the active component of the citrus fruit juice (ascorbic acid) was isolated by Szent-Györgyi, to be followed by its crystallization in 1932. By this time it was clearly recognized that ascorbic acid is essential for the formation of the intercellular cement, and that without it the defective connective tissues fail to support bones, joints and teeth, while the ruptured capillary walls produce hemorrhages and the other characteristic pathologies of scurvy. It is still not known why the cementing substance is imperfectly formed, although the lack of an essential enzyme is suspected. The final chapter remains to be written.

At present the history of beri-beri has a somewhat more satisfactory conclusion, since the identification of the missing dietary factor (thiamine) was followed by the demonstration of its role as a coenzyme involved in the oxidation of pyruvate. Without thiamine, the chain of reactions in carbohydrate oxidation stops at the pyruvic acid stage and this material accumulates. Carbohydrate metabolism is depressed; fat metabolism is accentuated. The nervous tissues suffer most; neuritis develops and leads to a paralytic condition and also to gastrointestinal and cardiovascular symptoms which, if not relieved, are fatal. Beri-beri was best known in the Orient where constant diets of polished rice prevailed. The polishing and preparation of the cereal remove a compound which, in nature, is formed only by plants. In 1882, Takaki reduced the incidence of the disease in the Japanese Navy by varying the diets, but it remained for a Dutch investigator, Eijkman in 1897, to show that the disease could be produced experimentally in chickens and cured with a water-soluble extract of rice polishings. Thiamine was crystallized in 1926, and its role as cocarboxylase recognized in 1937 (Gabriel and Fogel, 1955).

The discovery and identification of many of the other food factors is just as interesting as that of ascorbic acid and thiamine. Intense research during the first forty years of the present century has explained the functions of many of these accessory food factors. Discussions of their chemistry and place in animal physiology can be found in texts of biochemistry (Fruton and Simmonds, 1958). Our knowledge is primarily based on the higher vertebrates. There is really little information for the majority of animals, but enough to show that the vitamin concept extends through all groups from the unicellular to the most complex multicellular forms. Thiamine and many other accessory food factors are just as truly "vitamins" for the protozoa as they are for man. There are, however, many variations in nutritional requirements. Ascorbic acid, for example, although a dietary requirement for man, is not necessary for the rat nor for some protozoans. This probably also applies to some other animals and thus raises the question of a definition.

The term does not refer to compounds with biochemical similarities but to a group of substances with similar general functions in metabolism. Vitamins are organic compounds, required in catalytic amounts by animal tissues. The organism cannot synthesize them and requires a constant supply; the ultimate source is the plant or bacterial world. Vitamins are obtained in food or supplied as by-products of intestinal bacteria. Strictly speaking, any particular compound—ascorbic acid for example—may or may not be a vitamin depending on the synthesizing abilities of the particular animal concerned. Certain amino and fatty acids have already been mentioned as dietary essentials. These are not vitamins, however, since they usually enter into the construction of tissues or form building blocks in secretions and other essential biochemical entities. Vitamins, on the other hand, act as catalysts. This, at any rate, is true of those which are best understood, although this distinction is not so satisfactory for some of the lipid materials such as the sterols. The group of sterols known as vitamin D have long been recognized as essential for mammalian bone formation and the proper utilization of calcium and phosphorus. Insects and some protozoa require cholesterol and cannot use other sterols such as vitamin D (calciferol). Cholesterol is sometimes classed as an insect vitamin, but whether it is structural or catalytic in action, or both, is not yet known.

On the basis of their solubility, vitamins are usually considered in two groups, and in general these two groups discharge rather different functions. Most of the water-soluble factors are universally vitamins since they perform the same functions wherever they occur; they are catalytic factors and, in consequence, form vital links in the chains of biochemical reactions characteristic of all life. Thiamine, for example, is required wherever sugars are oxidized aerobically to release energy. The fat-soluble vitamins, on the other hand, play more specialized roles in certain groups of animals and in particular types of activities. They function in the formation of a blood-clotting factor in the vertebrates (vitamin K), the absorption of calcium and phosphorus from the vertebrate intestine (vitamin D), or in the formation of a visual pigment (vitamin A). Thus, most of the water-soluble vitamins are a part of all metabolizing tissue, but the fat-soluble ones are involved in particular tissues and special physiological activities.

Minerals. In Table 3.1 the elements have been listed in the approximate order of their abundance in living tissues. The first four (oxygen, carbon, hydrogen and nitrogen) form more than 95 per cent of protoplasm. Appropriately combined, they are the structural basis of living material. The element carbon unites readily with itself and with other members of this quartet to form the long chains and the complex rings which are the molecular framework of protoplasm. Carbon has been referred to as "the great juggler of matter" (Ducrocq, 1957), and no other element produces such an infinite variety of complex organic groupings. Hydrogen and oxygen, combined as water, form 70 per cent or more of active tissue;

TABLE 3.1.

COMPOSITION OF ANIMAL TISSUES
(Compiled from Hawk *et al*, 1954, and Underwood, 1962)

Elements	Group	Essential for higher animals / Perhaps required by higher animals	Essential for higher Plants	Per cent *In man*	Per cent *In tissues generally*
Oxygen				65.0	> 1.0
Carbon	Major elements Always present and essential			18.0	> 1.0
Hydrogen	Major elements Always present and essential			10.0	> 1.0
Nitrogen	Major elements Always present and essential			3.0	> 1.0

Phosphorus	Major elements Always present and essential			1.0	> 1.0
Calcium	Major elements Always present and essential			1.5	0.05 to 1.0
Potassium	Major elements Always present and essential			0.35	0.05 to 1.0
Sulphur	Major elements Always present and essential			0.25	0.05 to 1.0
Sodium	Major elements Always present and essential			0.15	0.05 to 1.0
Chlorine				0.15	0.05 to 1.0

Magnesium				0.05	0.05 to 1.0
Iron	Trace elements (always present)		←	0.004	

Manganese	Trace elements (always present)	← Essential for higher animals	←	0.0003	<0.005
Copper	Trace elements (always present)	← Essential for higher animals	←	0.0002	<0.005
Iodine	Trace elements (always present)	← Essential for higher animals		0.00004	<0.005
Cobalt	Trace elements (always present)	← Essential for higher animals			
Zinc	Trace elements (always present)	← Essential for higher animals	←		
Selenium	Trace elements (always present)	← Essential for higher animals			
Molybdenum	Trace elements (always present)	← Essential for higher animals	←		
Boron	Trace elements (always present)		←		
Silicon	Trace elements (always present)	← Perhaps required by higher animals	←		
Nickel	Trace elements (always present)				
Aluminum	Trace elements (always present)				
Fluorine	Trace elements (always present)	← Perhaps required by higher animals			
Barium	Trace elements (always present)	← Perhaps required by higher animals			
Strontium	Trace elements (always present)	← Perhaps required by higher animals			
Chromium	Trace elements (always present)				
Tin	Trace elements (always present)				
Lead	Trace elements (always present)				
Titanium	Trace elements (always present)				
Rubidium	Trace elements (always present)				
Lithium	Trace elements (always present)				
Arsenic	Trace elements (always present)				
Bromine	Trace elements (always present)				
Vanadium	Occasionally present				
Silver	Occasionally present				
Gold	Occasionally present				
Cerium	Occasionally present				
etc.	Occasionally present				

water is the most plentiful single compound of protoplasm. Nitrogen, in the NH_2 group attached to a carbon atom, characterizes the amino acids which are the structural units of protein and one of life's most abundant and specific biochemical entities.

The next seven elements in Table 3.1 are also included in those referred to as "major." They justify this title because of their occurrence in relatively high percentages (usually more than 0.1 per cent), and also because most of their activities are concerned with processes which are widespread or universal in living material. Phosphorus, through its high energy bonds, is involved in all major energy exchanges of life. It is also a constituent of the phospholipids which are a part of cell membranes and certain other equally indispensable structures. Further, in many animals phosphorus is a component of the skeleton and an important part of the phosphate buffer system. Calcium is associated with phosphorus in several of these activities but, in addition, discharges its own special functions in clotting reactions (blood clotting, milk coagulation and cell surface precipitation reactions) and in numerous enzyme activities. The movements of sodium and potassium ions through cell membranes are constant features of the stimulus response phenomena (Chapter 15); sodium chloride is the most important single compound in the control of osmotic phenomena. Sulfur forms a part of the essential amino acids cystine and methionine and also has a number of special functions in the $-SH$ group. This is by no means a complete catalogue of the duties of the major elements. It does, however, emphasize their ubiquitous distribution and the type of role which they play in the universal construction and functioning of tissues.

Magnesium and iron are sometimes placed in a group with the major, and sometimes with the minor constituents. Quantitively, they are much less abundant than those at the top of the list but far more abundant than those usually grouped as trace elements. Their activities are both structural and catalytic. Structurally, they are components of such universal and indispensable materials as chlorophyll (magnesium) and hemoglobin (iron); catalytically, like the trace elements, they are active in numerous enzyme systems.

Many of the trace elements are now known to be as essential to life and as universally distributed as the major elements. Like the vitamins they are not placed together because of chemical affinities but because they are all required in such minute amounts and because they are usually concerned with specific biochemical compounds and physiological activities.

The list of essential trace elements will probably grow as research continues. One of the more recent additions to the list is cobalt, now known to be a part of vitamin B_{12} or cyanocobalamine. This material is required by many animals ranging from certain of the protozoa (Lwoff, 1951) to the vertebrates (Underwood, 1962). It may be universally required. It is interesting that this cobalt-containing compound, unlike other members of the B-vitamin complex, is not manufactured by the higher plants nor by yeasts. It is synthesized only by bacteria, and in some way the higher animals have become dependent on bacteria for it. Without B_{12}, blood formation is impossible in the higher vertebrates.

As components of enzyme systems, the trace elements are involved in two somewhat different ways. Many of them form an actual part of the structure of the enzyme—or more particularly, its prosthetic group. For example, xanthine oxidase is a molybdo-flavoprotein, and the prosthetic group of catalase is an iron porphyrin compound. On the other hand, the trace elements may activate enzyme systems in some manner not well understood. In the latter type of relationship the metallic ions are readily removed by dialysis. Aminopeptidases and dipeptidases, for example, are activated by traces of specific metals such as Mn, Zn or Mg, and enzyme activity is lost following dialysis (Baldwin, 1963). However, where the trace element enters into the structure of the enzyme there is no loss of activity with dialysis.

Finally, it should be emphasized that these elements are often physiologically interrelated, and this interaction is such that the functions of one cannot be divorced from one or more of the others. This is not surprising if it is remembered that life consists of interrelated chains of highly specific enzymatic reactions and that this specificity extends also to their prosthetic groups and activators.

These interactions may occur in a variety of ways. Molybdenum may not be excreted sufficiently if dietary copper and sulfate are low. Cattle on forage rich in molybdenum then develop a severe diarrhea ("peat scours"), and grazing lands which appear rich and luxuriant may in this way be lethal. Soil rich in selenium may produce a different but equally serious condition called "alkali disease" or "blind staggers" in livestock. In this case the sulfur of the two essential amino acids cystine and methionine is partially replaced by selenium, and certain enzyme systems (succinic dehydrogenase) are also inactivated, perhaps through the removal of sulfhydryl groups (Underwood, 1962). Selenium is physiologically indispensable to higher animals. The structure and role of the selenium factor (Factor 3-selenium) has not been determined, but the element, in large amounts, evidently travels with sulfur and tends to replace it in metabolism (Schwarz, 1961). In the vertebrates iron-deficient diets lead to a condition of anemia; but even if the dietary iron is abundant, blood formation does not occur normally in the absence of minute amounts of copper. Enzymes containing copper are probably involved in the synthesis of the hemoglobin units.

The list could be extended. Bone formation depends on an appropriate calcium/phosphorus ratio; diets high in potassium create extra demands for sodium in mammals (sodium chloride hunger); excess magnesium may produce narcosis, and an appropriate balance of anions and cations (ion antagonism) is essential for the integrity and normal responsiveness of all tissues (Heilbrunn, 1952). These examples will suffice to illustrate the intricacies of the interactions and to emphasize that physiological investigation of one element may require the simultaneous study of several others. A study of copper requirements, for example, is of little value without a knowledge of molybdenum metabolism in the ruminant or without an understanding of the zinc metabolism of the rat (Underwood, 1962). Since the biochemistry is most likely to be explained in terms of interacting systems of enzymes, similar interlocking relationships may be expected in all forms of life.

Collection of Food

Only plants and saprophytic animals such as intestinal and blood parasites can soak up or directly absorb the materials necessary for their life processes. The active procurement of food is basic to animal life, and much of animal evolution in terms of specialized anatomy and physiology is an adaptation for the capture of different kinds of food and its preparation for the cells of the body.

Yonge (1928), in a classical paper published many years ago, grouped feeding mechanisms into three major categories according to the type of food utilized: 1. MECHANISMS FOR DEALING WITH SMALL PARTICLES (pseudopodia, cilia, tentacles, mucus, setae, muscles); 2. MECHANISMS FOR DEALING WITH LARGE PARTICLES OR MASSES (swallowing inactive food, scraping, boring, seizing the prey and then swallowing or chewing it or digesting it externally); and 3. MECHANISMS FOR TAKING IN FLUIDS OR SOFT TISSUES (piercing and sucking, sucking only, absorption through the body surface). His article provides a detailed and well illustrated description of the feeding mechanisms of the invertebrates. Nicol (1960*a*) has dealt in a similar way with both the vertebrates and the invertebrates. Yonge's classification, based on food size and feeding structures, is instructive; but the emphasis might equally well be placed on the animal and its physiological ecology.

FILTER FEEDING

In general, the sessile animals and sedentary feeders such as a bivalve mollusc, an *Amphioxus* or ammocoete larva, depend on a varied group of filtering and trapping devices. Cilia and setae create complex water currents which bring particles of food onto the feeding surfaces where the particles are trapped in mucus. A moving belt or cord of mucus, propelled by cilia, carries the food particles into the digestive tract. These feeding currents may be elaborate and the structures may be highly specialized. Tentacles often form trapping organs. In some of the sea cucumbers, the sticky tentacles which trap small organisms are one by one thrust into the pharynx to wipe off the food (Hyman, 1955). Hydra, and some other coelenterates, also make use of a tentacle trap; in this case the trailing appendages are armed with nematocysts and these are discharged by tactile and chemical stimuli to pierce, poison and hold the prey (Lenhoff, 1961).

Filter feeding, although characteristic of sessile and sedentary animals, is by no means confined to this way of life. Small active copepods are filter feeders as well as the sockeye salmon (*Oncorhynchus nerka*), the huge basking shark (*Ceteorhinus*) and the whalebone whale (Mysticeti). Feeding and digestive processes show many convergent adaptations (Morton, 1960); there is no particular phylogenetic trend in filter feeding mechanisms among the more specialized animal groups where it is exceptional and always a secondary modification.

Among the lower groups of animals, where filter feeding is widespread, the most prevalent technique is the ciliated mucus field (Morton, 1960). The secretion of mucus, its circulation onto an external surface, its movement back into the body and finally its partial disintegration or digestion for reutilization require work. But this is a price of living just as certainly as are the muscular efforts of those animals which actively search for their daily requirements. Morton (1960) has described the details in a systematic way. Usually the mucus in the esophagus forms a cord which is gradually rotated through the gut. While it moves along as a firm rotating rod or food string, viscosity changes (dependent on the pH) release particles to be taken up by phagocytes or digested extracellularly in the intestine. These mechanisms reach their greatest complexity in the molluscs, even though the most primitive members of the phylum browse on algae by means of a radula (Morton, 1960).

Feeding mechanisms are also conveniently grouped into the nonselective and the selective. Filter feeders are rather nonselective and must take what comes to them. They can control the situation only by operating or ceasing to operate the filter, and many of them are receptive to chemicals or other stimuli which warn them when filtering conditions are hazardous. Another type of nonselective feeder is the animal which passes the external medium through its body and takes from it whatever can be digested and absorbed. Many of the annelids, some of the echinoderms and the hemichordates feed in this way. The environment must be rich in nutritive material, and it seems likely that these forms absorb some part of the food directly in a saprophytic manner. These nonselective feeders are omnivorous and take whatever comes their way, provided it is sufficiently small to be caught in their filters or traps. Grinding organs may be present internally, but the piercing and cutting mouth parts characteristic of the selective feeders are absent.

SELECTIVE FEEDERS

Selective feeders have varied techniques for the capture and utilization of bulky foods or for the removal of juices from the bodies of animals and plants. The phylogeny which permitted the exploitation of varied sources of food has shaped the anatomy of many structures and altered the physiology as well. Mammalian feeding mechanisms provide an interesting example of the former (Davis, 1961*b*). Mammals have the unique ability to masticate food and reduce large objects to sizes readily managed by the digestive system. The jaws of the reptilian ancestors were primarily organs of prehension, and the evolution of efficient mastication involved not only changes in bones and muscles but also in the air passages to the lungs. Breathing must continue during mastication, and the air passages are separated and guarded by the soft palate, epiglottis and palatopharyngeal folds—characteristic mammalian structures. Such radical differences in cranial and buccal architecture are apparently directly related to these changes in feeding habits.

The emphasis on special types of foods may produce changes not only in the physiology of digestion and nutrition but also in such different functions as sexual maturation and social behavior. Many of the insects, for example, depend on only one specific type of food. The female mosquito must have a meal of blood and the number of eggs produced sometimes depends both on the amount of blood and the kind of blood (Roeder, 1953). *Culex pipiens* is reported to lay twice as many eggs per mg of canary blood as per mg human blood. The reproductive cycle of the rabbit flea *Spilopsyllus cuniculi* is directly controlled by its host's reproductive hormones which it obtains through feeding on breeding or pregnant rabbits (Rothschild and Ford, 1964). Nutrition in the honey bee determines whether the female larvae will develop into sterile workers or sexually perfect queens. There are many such curious adaptations.

Neurosensory and neuromuscular specializations are also associated with selective feeding. The evolution of an active animal, with the phylogeny of a complex nervous system and a battery of sense organs, is both directly and indirectly related to the struggle for food. The location and capture of particular foods depend on sensory organs and the animal's ability to become conditioned to visual, chemical and other stimuli. Simple learning phenomena such as conditioning and the evolution of many other capacities of the central nervous system are, in a very real way, responses to the pressures for food and the specialization of the selective feeder.

Digestion

The word DIGESTION comes from two Latin words meaning "to carry" (*gerere*) and "apart" or "asunder" (*dis*). In this process complex foods are broken down into the monosaccharides, amino acids, fatty acids, glycerol and several other constituents. Only these much simpler units can be utilized by cells or incorporated into living protoplasm. Digestion is an essential physiological activity in all animals, whether they feed on minute food particles (microphagous) or on large plants and animals (macrophagous). Some of the internal body parasites, such as the tapeworms, can dispense with a digestive system and absorb food predigested by their hosts. However, these parasitic conditions are secondary and not particularly relevant in the evolution of physiological processes.

In the macrophagous animal digestive processes are both mechanical and chemical. Mechanical difficulties are substantial when animals utilize the higher plants with heavy cellulose walls or prey on animals with hard exoskeletons. The final processes of digestion are always chemical, but there is frequently an essential pretreatment of the food, either before or after it is taken into the body.

MECHANICAL TREATMENT

The biochemical disintegration of the cellulose molecule evidently presents difficulties. In most animals cellulose passes directly through the digestive canal, and only the noncellulose portions of the plant tissue are digested and utilized. This means that cellulose walls must be crushed or otherwise broken in preparation for the enzymatic treatment of the cell contents.

Three groups of animals, with three different sorts of machines, are responsible for the primary utilization of most of the bulky plant material (Ramsay, 1952). The amphineuran and gastropod molluscs form one of the three groups. With their ribbon or strap-like radulae, set with numerous chitinized and readily replaceable teeth, they scrape away small particles of food from larger plants. The radula operates like a rasp or file and is moved to and fro with a set of special muscles. Insects such as the locusts with their grinding and cutting mandibles form a second great group of plant feeders; the herbivorous mammals with their corrugated and grinding molar teeth form the third. Radulae, insect mandibles and molar teeth are all highly specialized for the mechanical destruction of cellulose plant walls.

There are several other structures concerned with cellulose disruption, but they turn over a relatively small amount of plant material. The valves of the mollusc have been modified to pulverize cellulose in the wood borers (*Teredo*). The insect mouth parts form stylets in plant bugs which puncture cell walls and suck out the contents. The Lantern of Aristotle in the Echinoidea is an effective crushing organ, and some sea urchins are mainly herbivorous, chewing algae and scraping seaweeds from the rocks with Aristotle's Lantern (Hyman, 1955).

The mechanical treatment of the food continues within the bodies of many animals. Practically all digestive systems have gut musculature and often it is highly specialized. Heavily developed areas of muscle are sometimes assisted in their action by hardened surfaces. In certain forms these hardened surfaces are the stones or grit taken in with the food (gizzards of earthworms, some birds and reptiles); in other cases, concretions of calcium salts develop in the stomach to serve a similar purpose (gastroliths of crayfish); or chitinized lining areas may develop in the anterior part of the gut (gastric mill of crayfish and comparable structures in some molluscs).

MOVEMENTS OF THE GUT CONTENTS

Digestion and absorption take place while the food is slowly moved through the gut. The propulsive force is almost always provided by cilia or a special gut musculature; sometimes both cilia and gut musculature cooperate in this activity. The Nemathelminthes are exceptional and depend on the somatic musculature, both for locomotion and the maintenance of the activities of the digestive tract; cilia are absent in this group and visceral musculature either completely or almost completely lacking (Hyman, 1951).

Muscular action usually plays a subsidiary part in the ciliary feeders (Morton, 1960). Transport of food particles takes place in a mucus rod or cord (ERGATULA). The cilia which rotate this food string are localized in one area of the gut, and in this way other areas are free to perform different functions such as the sorting of different sized food particles (molluscan stomach) or digesting them (molluscan intestine). The rotating movement itself provides an important stirring and circulating action in the gut. The rotating style as a propulsive force in the movement of the gut contents is most highly developed in the Mollusca but is also a characteristic feature of most other ciliary feeders, both invertebrate and vertebrate. Some of the sedentary polychaete annelids, however, provide exceptions. Within the gut cilia are short or absent, and the propulsive force is provided by the contractions of both visceral and somatic musculature. Ciliary feeding in these animals is regarded as secondary in their phylogeny (Morton, 1960).

Cilia would be of little use when the food is bulky or hard; animals which live on such diets depend on well developed layers of visceral muscle. This includes all the arthropods and vertebrates except the larval lampreys and anuran tadpoles. Arrangements of the gut musculature are extremely variable. Throughout the vertebrates there is a thick inner circular and an outer longitudinal layer in the main wall of the tube with thinner layers, similarly arranged, just beneath the mucosa. The situation is less uniform among the invertebrates. In many of them the main inner layer is longitudinal and the outer layer circular (squid, sea cucumber, some insects), but in some (Oligochaetes, certain insects) the disposition of the layers is like that of the vertebrate. Circular muscle may predominate with little or no longitudinal muscle (*Aplysia*); an oblique layer may also be present (squid stomach); or the muscle may be striated rather than smooth (arthropods). These isolated examples testify to the variability in muscle arrangement but do not exhaust the patterns which the invertebrates have attained (Andrew, 1959).

The type of muscular activity most characteristic of the hollow viscera is referred to as PERISTALSIS. Peristalsis has long been defined as a wave of contraction preceded by a wave of relaxation. In reality the relaxation is often inconspicuous, and peristalsis appears as a wave of contraction in the circular muscle which sweeps along the hollow viscus for a certain distance before dying out. Such a wave is easily initiated experimentally by mechanical stimulation. It may start at any point and proceeds for variable distances.

In addition to peristalsis there are several other movements of the vertebrate visceral musculature. A TONUS RHYTHM in the various muscular layers produces slow alterations in the size of the gut. Superimposed on the tonus rhythm a strong RHYTHMIC SEGMENTATION is sometimes seen—most frequently in the duodenum and jejunum—and is essentially a mixing process. PENDULAR MOVEMENTS, involving the longitudinal as well as the circular musculature, produce rhythmic to and fro movements of a loop of digestive tube and tend to force the food from one end of the loop to the other, creating a rapid mixing. The activity of the vertebrate muscularis mucosa may also be important in mixing and transporting food, but in the small intestine it probably serves especially to move the villi about in the food.

CHEMICAL ACTION

In the body of an animal, as in the laboratory, a successful chemical reaction depends both on the characteristics of the reaction vessel and the nature of the chemical reagents. The locus of enzyme activity will be considered prior to a discussion of the chemical reactions.

Intracellular digestion. Digestion is intracellular in the protozoa, and this was presumably the situation in the most primitive animals. The protoplasm of the single-celled animal captures its food, digests it in a food vacuole, discharges wastes and incorporates the simple sugars, amino acids and other molecules. It is still not clear just how the digestive enzymes enter the food vacuoles (Barrington, 1962). The hydrolytic enzymes of a cell are thought to be contained in special packages called LYSOSOMES (de Duve, 1963). These are surrounded by membranes which separate them from the cytoplasm in the living cell to prevent the auto-digestion which occurs so quickly after death. Presumably, during intracellular digestion, the lysosomes are in some manner discharged into the food vacuoles.

Digestion is wholly intracellular only in the Protozoa and the Porifera (Barrington, 1962). In other phyla an extracellular digestion either supplements the intracellular mechanisms or completely replaces them. Many different variations in this combination of processes have been described. Yonge's (1937) review should be consulted for a wealth of detail; Nicol (1960*a*) and Barrington (1962) have also provided valuable summaries.

Only a very few broad generalizations can be made, and the notes which follow are mostly from Barrington (1962). The phylogenetic trend is toward the extracellular process; the most highly organized of the invertebrates, such as the cephalopods among the molluscs and the insects among the arthropods, rely entirely on this mode of digestion. Intracellular digestion, with supplementary extracellular processes, is characteristic of the Coelenterata, Platyhelminthes, Nemertea, Annelida, Mollusca and some of the minor phyla. With few exceptions, such as protein digestion in the arachnids, digestion is entirely extracellular in the Arthropoda, the Nematoda and the Echinodermata; in the latter group it is probably strongly aided by phagocytic amebocytes. The intracellular process is clearly the phylogenetically primitive one, and some of the simple multicellular forms, such as the acoelan worm *Convoluta* depend entirely on it. However, it seems to be a short step from digestion within ameboid cells to the release of enzymes from them into a space or onto a surface; such a simply organized animal as *Hydra* carries out a preliminary hydrolysis of its food before taking up the macerated remains in the phagocytic cells which line the gastrovascular cavity. Size of food may not always be an obstacle to intracellular digestion. The land planarian *Orthodemus terrestris* feeds on slugs by protruding its pharynx and disintegrating the body of its prey with a strong sucking action, aided by proteases secreted by the acidophilic gland cells of the pharynx. The tiny food particles eroded in this manner are sucked into the gut and taken up by phagocytosis (Jennings, 1962). *Polycelsis cornuta*, a freshwater triclad, attacks large items of food in the same manner. Extraintestinal digestion is also found in some other invertebrate phyla and may be combined with intracellular or a mixture of intra- and extracellular digestive processes. Some of the arachnids, for example, exude proteases onto their prey and suck up the semidigested material for further digestion which is partially intracellular. Some of the echinoderms and insects such as the water beetle *Dytiscus* also rely on extraintestinal digestion, but in these animals the later stages, which take place within the body, are also extracellular.

As a group, the molluscs provide the most varied array in combinations of intracellular and extracellular processes. Two specializations are of particular interest. The first of these is the digestive gland, made up of branched glandular follicles which communicate with the stomach by a system of ciliated ducts (Fig. 3.2). In some groups the epithelial cells are phagocytic and digestion is intracellular; in at least one group, the Nuculidae, it seems to be entirely extracellular with enzymes secreted into the lumen (Owen, 1956); in many forms there is a combination of the two processes. A curious process in connection with the intracellular digestive activities of the epithelial cells is a fragmentation of the outer border of the cell to form spheres containing the food vacuoles together with waste products and some enzymes. These then pass into the stomach and may be the source of some of the enzymes there (Owen, 1955, 1956). The second of these special features is the crystalline style, most characteristic of the lamellibranchs, but also found in the more advanced herbivorous gastropods. The evolution of the style sac in connection with ciliary feeding is discussed by Morton (1958, 1960). To the physiologist it is a thick gelatinous rod loaded with enzymes and rotated by strong cilia which force it gradually into the stomach where it rubs against the horny gastric shield to release its enzymes and to stir up the stomach contents. Amylases are the most abundant enzymes in the crystalline style, but lipases seem also to be present.

In a few animals intracellular digestion is partially dependent on an extensive phagocytosis. A host of wandering amebocytes or phagocytic cells procure food particles, digest them and pass their products to the other cells of the body. The lamellibranchs and the echinoderms provide the best examples (Yonge, 1937; Nicol, 1960*a*). In the lamellibranchs, amebocytes have been observed to pass both into the digestive tract and into the mantle cavity where they capture food particles and transport them back into the body of the animal while digesting them. The three major classes of enzymes (carbohydrate, fat and protein-splitting) have been identified in these amebocytes (Yonge, 1937). Amebocytes or

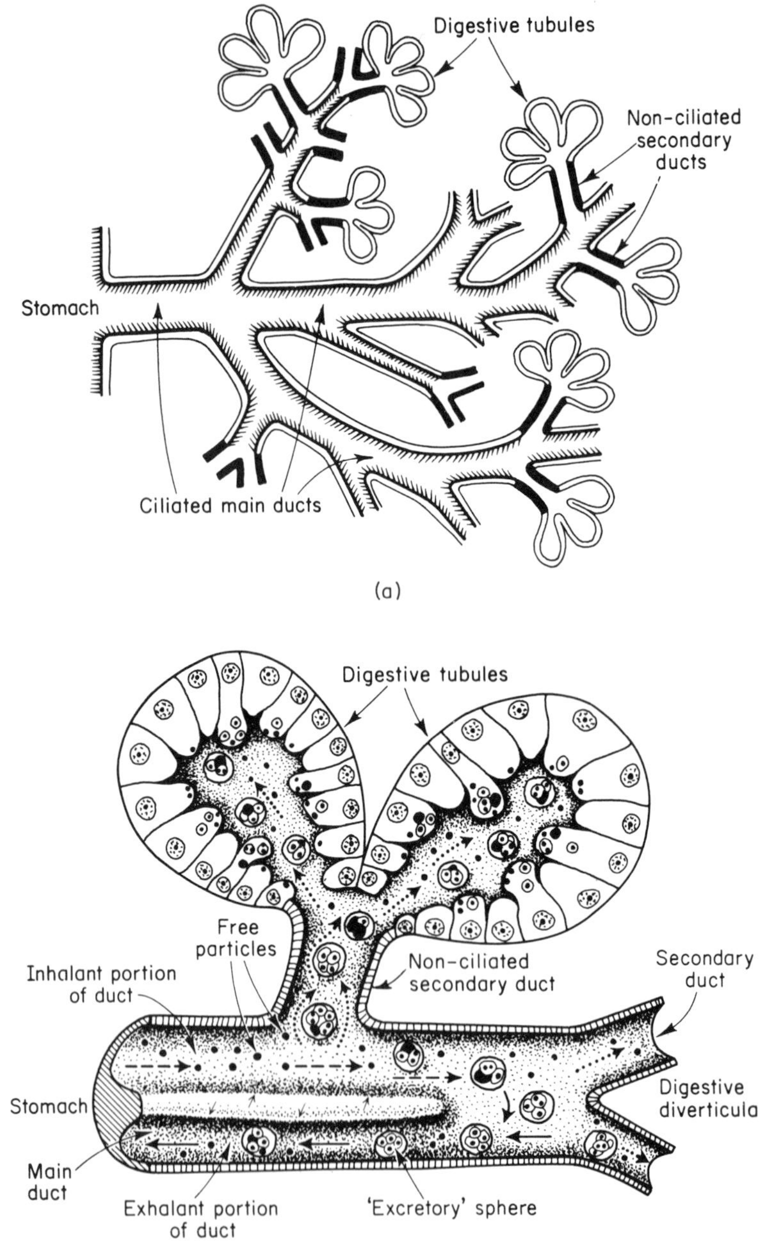

Fig. 3.2. The digestive diverticula of the Anisomyaria and Eulamellibranchia. Upper, the arrangement of ducts and tubules; lower, the probable circulation of particles. Unbroken arrows, exhalant ciliary currents: broken arrows, non-ciliary, inhalant, counterpart currents; dotted arrows, movement due to absorption by cells of the tubules. [Owen (1955).]

phagocytes, with their varied digesting enzymes, operate in the higher animals also but as part of the defense against foreign bodies and not as a major organ of digestion.

Extracellular digestion. Many new avenues of evolution were open to the first organisms which secreted some of their digestive juices onto larger and more complex items of food. Such organisms were not only able to utilize bulky foods but could devote fewer cells to digestive processes and specialize in producing enzymes suitable for peculiar food substances. Digestion could be carried out more rapidly and less time had to be devoted to the actual business of feeding. It seems likely, however, that most of the advantages could not have been realized without the essential anatomical development of a tubular digestive tract, open at both ends. Animals such as the coelenterates and the flatworms, which lack an anus, have not evolved separate areas for storage, digestion and absorption of food nor for the separation and discharge of those portions of the food which are not usable. Likewise, animals which depend almost entirely on intracellular processes have only achieved a modest specialization in cell types. Their digesting cells usually contain all the different types of enzymes and there are no particular masses of cells (glands) devoted specifically to the digestion of starch, protein or other types of food.

The digestive tract and its "enzyme chain," Yonge (1937) described five regions of the digestive system of the metazoan: (*a*) reception, (*b*) conduction and storage, (*c*) digestion and internal triturition, (*d*) absorption, (*e*) conduction and formation of feces.

This arrangement has permitted numerous anatomical specializations with concomitant physiological advantages. The region for reception is often associated with devices for food maceration (teeth), for paralyzing struggling prey (salivary toxic enzymes) for initiating digestion (salivary enzymes) or for lubricating the food (mucus-secreting buccal glands). Buccal glands may have more specialized functions in some groups. The bloodsucking insects and leeches produce an anticoagulant. Some of the carnivorous gastropods secrete a strong acid which dissolves calcareous shells. All those animals which carry on extraintestinal digestion produce proteolytic enzymes for the hydrolysis of connective tissue to produce the fluid material which they suck into their digestive tracts.

A separate region for storage has been even more important phylogenetically, since this permits the utilization of foods which are not continuously available. The leech may take several months to digest a single meal of blood. The herbivorous animal spends many hours masticating the food which it gathers hurriedly and stores temporarily in its stomach. The production of acid in this region of the vertebrate gut may have arisen as an adaptation for killing prey and for checking bacterial activity (Barrington, 1957); the production of an enzyme (pepsin) which is active in acid medium may have followed later. The special storage region also permits the gradual release of macerated and partially digested food into the main area of digestion.

In the third region the enzymes rapidly reduce the food to an absorbable form. The terminal regions of the gut also present a number of specialized features; several of these which are related to absorption will be considered below. In some herbivorous animals such as the rabbit, there are colonies of symbiotic bacteria which provide vitamins as by-products of their metabolism and assist digestion through fermentation processes.

Vonk (1937) has discussed the "enzyme chain" in vertebrate digestion and stressed its physiological significance. In general, digestion occurs in only one area of the invertebrate gut, while among the vertebrates there is a localization of at least some enzyme activities. In certain mammals (man, monkey, pig) carbohydrate digestion may start in the mouth by the salivary amylases or ptyalin. In all vertebrates the pancreas splits starches into oligosaccharides in the anterior part of the duodenum. In subsequent steps these are hydrolyzed by oligosaccharases and maltases, mostly secreted by the gut lining. Here then is a chain of carbohydrases starting in the mouth and continuing into the intestine. Similarly, gastric or pancreatic enzymes initiate the protein hydrolysis, but the final separation of the dipeptide links occurs farther along the duodenum through the action of dipeptidases formed by the intestinal cells. Vonk suggests that this localization of enzymes in the vertebrates is associated with a more intense metabolism and a greater sensitivity to changes in blood sugar or amino acid levels. In this way food products enter the blood gradually and the animal is not inundated after a meal. This may or may not be a significant point. The greater efficiency provided by groups of cells devoted to the production of one or a few enzymes may be important, and this could work more easily if those promoting the hydrolysis of the major links were placed anterior to those concerned with the final cleavage.

In contrast to the vertebrates, the secretion of enzymes is more localized in the invertebrates. Moreover, the same glandular areas produce a mixture of the different kinds of enzymes, and the digestive epithelia are usually absorptive as well as secretory. The hepatopancreas of the crustacean provides a good example. This diverticulum from the mid-gut secretes enzymes, absorbs digested food and stores fats, carbohydrates, probably proteins and minerals. The epithelia of the coelenterate enteron or the turbellarian gut, the pyloric caecae of the starfish, the digestive caecum of *Amphioxus* and some of the glands of the mollusc are equally versatile. In many cases the same cells seem to be capable of performing these multiple activities (Barrington, 1962).

Some of the more specialized invertebrates (insects and cephalopods) have achieved a partial separation of functional areas for the secretion of different enzymes and the absorption of digestive products. The octopus and the squid provide the best known examples (Florkin, 1949; Barrington, 1962). The digestive glands are separated into two parts which discharge their secretions in different regions so that food is first acted on by one and then by the other. In *Loligo*, but not in *Octopus*, absorption seems to have been completely separated from the digestive glands. In comparison with the other invertebrates, digestive processes are extremely rapid in the predacious cephalopods and seem to approach those of the vertebrates in their efficiency.

In the higher vertebrates, each area of the gut is concerned with a special activity. Digestive enzymes are produced in discrete glands as well as in the wall of the gut; absorption occurs predominantly in certain areas of the intestine, and a special organ (the liver) takes over the job of storing food materials. This is a decidedly more efficient arrangement, since larger animals require more food and a more precise homeostatic control over metabolic processes.

DIGESTIVE ENZYMES

The actual enzymes concerned with digestion are conveniently considered according to the three major food items: carbohydrases or glycosidases acting on carbohydrates, lipases and esterases acting on fatty materials, and proteinases concerned with proteins.

Carbohydrases. Dietary carbohydrates are potential sources of the simple hexose sugar glucose, which plays the key role in metabolism and is the direct source of much of the energy in all animals. Both plant and animal foods may contain free glucose, but most of the dietary carbohydrate is in a complex form and consists of numerous glucose or similar units joined by a condensation reaction, with the elimination of one water molecule for each linkage formed. Before these hexose units can be incorporated into the body the glycosidic bonds (Fig. 3.3) must be hydrolyzed, and this reaction is catalyzed by a family of highly specific and varied enzymes, the carbohydrases or glycosidases.

Many different carbohydrases have been reported from animal tissues (Prosser and Brown, 1961; Barrington, 1962). The key to this complex situation is the structure of the carbohydrate molecule itself, as is readily apparent from the architecture of glucose (Fig. 3.3). This molecule has a skeleton of six carbon atoms and, because 4 of these are asymmetrical, there is potentially a family of 16 isomers (8 belonging to

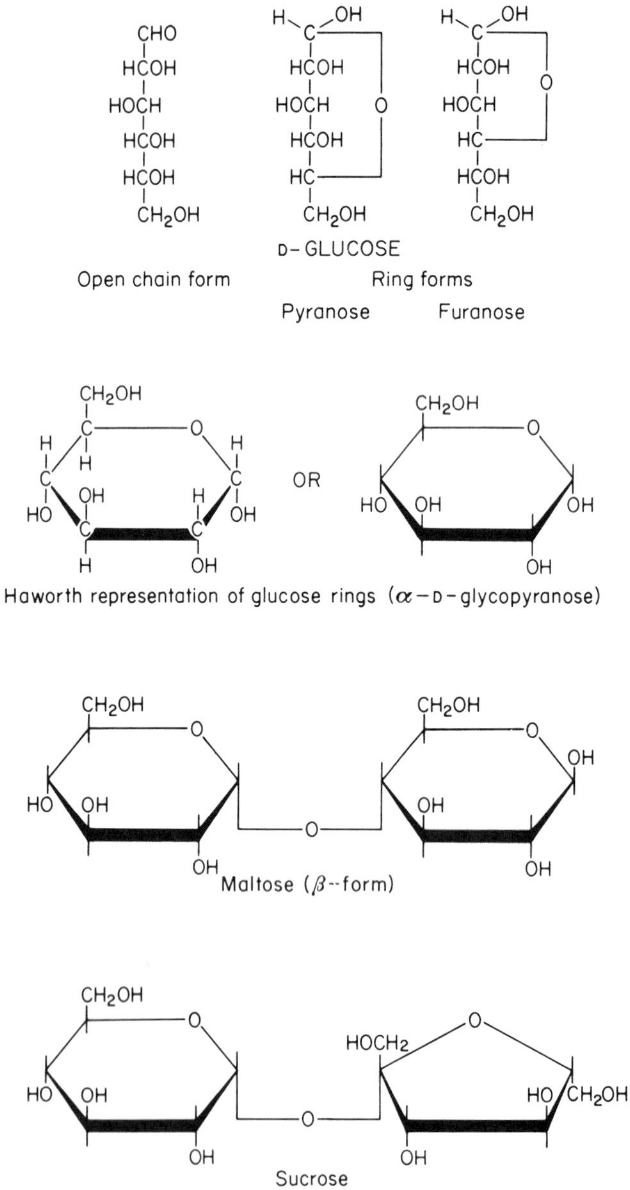

Fig. 3.3. The structure of carbohydrates. Above, several methods of representing the glucose molecule; below, the glycosidic linkage in a disaccharide, represented by the general formula R-CH-OR. [For further details, see Fruton and Simmonds (1958).]

the D-series and 8 to the L-series). Actually, the open-chain form occurs only in traces; the ring forms are the active units, and these may be linked into molecules ranging from disaccharide size (sucrose with a molecular weight of 342) to the starches with molecular weights up to 500,000 (rice starch) and cellulose with even larger particles (Fruton and Simmonds, 1958). Thus a potentially great variety of slightly different molecules are possible, and many different ones do occur in biological systems. The carbohydrases, as a group, are all concerned with the hydrolysis of the glycosidic bond between the different monosaccharide units, but the isomeric arrangements are often sufficiently different to require specific enzymes; this accounts for the variety of these catalysts found in nature. Bernfeld (1962) reviews their distribution in both plants and animals.

TABLE 3.2.
SOME CARBOHYDRATES OF INTEREST IN ANIMAL PHYSIOLOGY

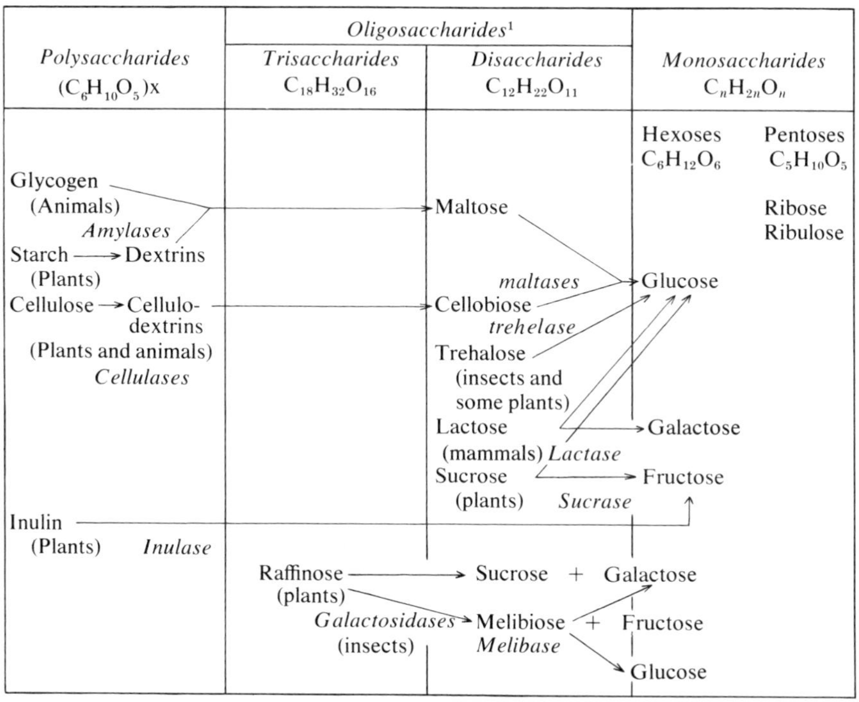

[1]The root *oligo-* means "few" and there is no sharp point of division between the oligosaccharides and polysaccharides

The carbohydrates of particular interest in animal nutrition, together with their associated enzymes, are listed in Table 3.2. More precise classifications of the enzymes, based on the structural arrangements of the hydrolyzed linkages, are found in texts of biochemistry and enzymology (Fruton and Simmonds, 1958). Many of the enzymes listed in Table 3.2 are not, in reality, single protein molecules but classes or families of enzymes. This is particularly true of the amylases and polysaccharases. Several different amylases, for example, are now well known chemically (Baldwin, 1963).

Phylogenetic trends in the distribution of carbohydrases are usually said to be absent. It is possible that the most primitive animals could digest a variety of carbohydrates and that enzymes were lost as the animals specialized on foods which did not require them. On the other hand, it is equally likely that the variety of naturally occurring carbohydrates has increased immensely since the dawn of animal life and that animals which have evolved with the plants have, through mutation, acquired enzymes appropriate to the utilization of the more varied plant foods. Thus, some of the present-day protozoa possess all the major groups of carbohydrases listed in Table 3. 2 while others are much more restricted in their digesting abilities. The same is true among the metazoans. The correlations are most often with the diet of the animal and not with its phyletic position.

Amylases and maltases are evidently ubiquitous, but the cellulases, inulases, raffinases, lactases, trehalases and sucrases are less frequently found. Inulases may not occur in the animal world (Bernfeld, 1962); trehalases have been found in some terrestrial isopods and insects. Some of the earlier reports of polysaccharases are now known to be based on the activities of associated cellulolytic bacteria. The occurrence of cellulases has, however, been established in some representatives of all phyla except the Chordata. The molluscs and arthropods in particular, have many cellulose-digesting species. In contrast, cellulases are extremely rare among echinoderms and seem to be entirely absent in the protochordates and the vertebrates. Yokoe and Yasumasu (1964) argue that the distribution of cellulases is more closely correlated with phylogenetic position than feeding habits, contrary to the usual concept for distribution of digestive enzymes (Baldwin, 1964). Lichenases and xylanases are present in several invertebrates which feed on polyglucosans (Bernfeld, 1962). Sucrases are more widely distributed than trehalases or lactases and are found in some species at all the different levels of organization (Prosser and Brown, 1961; Barrington, 1962).

The vertebrates possess a more limited group of carbohydrases than the invertebrates. However, it should be emphasized that relatively few animals have been examined carefully for all types of digestive enzymes, and there may be many exceptions to these broad generalizations. For example, it is claimed that certain species of teleost fish can digest hemicelluloses as well as xylan and algin (Barrington, 1957). These substances are probably enzymatically broken down by several invertebrates (Nicol, 1960*a*; Prosser and Brown, 1961).

The utilization of cellulose by animals merits an additional comment. It does form an important item in many diets, but its digestion is usually by symbiotic organisms rather than by a specialized system of digestive enzymes. Many insects feed on woody plants, and this group of animals has found a variety of ways to deal with the complex carbohydrate molecules. In some cases the plant cells are pulverized and the starches and sugars which they contain are digested, but the cellulose is of no nutritive value (powder post beetles, Lyctidae); in other groups of insects, hemicellulases (bark beetles, Scolytidae) and cellulases (wood-boring beetles, Cerambycidae and Anobiidae) are actually present and the woody plant material is enzymatically hydrolyzed; in still others (termites and roaches) symbiotic bacteria and flagellate protozoans find shelter and an abundance of macerated cellulose in the digestive tract of the insect and in return release products of their anaerobic metabolism or fermentation (mainly lower fatty acids) which serve the insect as an energy source.

The stomach of the ruminant is the most specialized organ for the digestion of plant material. The anterior division forms a huge fermentation chamber within which bacteria, yeasts and protozoa reduce cellulose and related carbohydrate to a usable form (Annison and Lewis, 1959; Barnett and Reid, 1961). The cellulolytic bacteria are the most important, and the role of the protozoa is either insignificant or secondary. These bacteria are anaerobes or facultative anaerobes and release a variety of fatty acids (formic, acetic, propionic, butyric, succinic, lactic), depending on the cellulose and associated starches and sugars in the diet. These acids are absorbed directly from the rumen and enter immediately into various metabolic pathways. Considerable amounts of carbon dioxide and methane are produced by the fermentation. Most of this gas is eructed but some is passed via the lungs. The operation of this complicated fermentation chamber involves several specializations of the gut and is dependent on the maintenance of a constant and suitable environment for the bacteria. A very copious supply of saliva, rich in bicarbonate, maintains the fluid content and pH. The rapid absorption of the fatty acids is also important and prevents their accumulation which would inhibit the activities of the bacteria. The volume is regulated by the passage of the semifluid material into the omasum at intervals. Gastric juice is secreted in the abomasum, and here the animal's own digestive enzymes come into play. The rumen and its microbial population is important in the utilization and metabolism of protein as well as carbohydrate and will be referred to again.

Lipases and esterases. The lipids or fatty substances are a varied group of organic compounds, utilizable by living organisms and characterized by their insolubility in water, their solubility in certain organic solvents and the ester linkage which is actual or potential in all of them (Fig. 3.4). The enzymes which hydrolyze lipids are actually esterases since it is the ester linkage which is broken to produce acids and alcohols. It is customary, however, to refer to the enzymes concerned with the triglycerides (esters of fatty acids and glycerol) as LIPASES while the term ESTERASES is reserved for enzymes which act on compounds such as ethyl butyrate (simple esterases) and more complex lipids such as the phospholipids, cholesterol and waxes, where the linkages require more specific enzymes (cholesterol esterase, for example).

The lipases seem to be less varied than the carbohydrases and proteinases, perhaps because they are concerned with the hydrolysis of only one or two types of linkage. Two enzymes are thought to be active in pancreatic lipase as indicated in Fig. 3.4, where RCOOH represents some long chain fatty acid, such as palmitic acid with sixteen carbon atoms or oleic acid with eighteen.

Lipases have been identified in many groups of animals from the protozoa to the vertebrates but may not be as universally present as the carbohydrases and the proteinases (Vonk, 1937). Perhaps finely emulsified fats are directly absorbed by many animals as they evidently are, to some extent, by the mammals (Baldwin, 1963; Davson, 1959) and insects (Yonge, 1937; Roeder, 1953). In the vertebrate, emulsification of fat by the bile salts from the liver is extremely important in connection with its digestion and absorption. The finely emulsified lipid presents a larger surface for enzyme action, and if the droplets are fine enough (0.5 μ or less and negatively charged) they may pass directly into the intestinal cells and into the circulation. Bile salts alone do not produce this degree of emulsification, but in association with fatty acid and monoglyceride (from the enzymatic hydrolysis of the neutral fat) such a degree of dispersion is attained.

The direct absorption of emulsified fat may also occur in the lower vertebrates and the invertebrates, but this does not seem to have been carefully investigated. Where intracellular digestion takes place fats are presumably taken into the cell by phagocytosis. However, this does not explain how they are passed on to other tissues or into the vascular fluids or made available for metabolism. Presumably lipases must be at work. Fat droplets are commonly seen in the intestinal epithelia and other cells of the lower invertebrates so that an active metabolism of fat is indicated. Surface tension lowering compounds with an emulsifying action like bile have been identified in the digestive fluids of representative invertebrates including sea cucumbers, crabs, molluscs and annelids (Vonk, 1962).

The digestion of the more complex esters, such as those of the compound lipids (phospholipids and cerebrosides), the derived lipids (sterols,

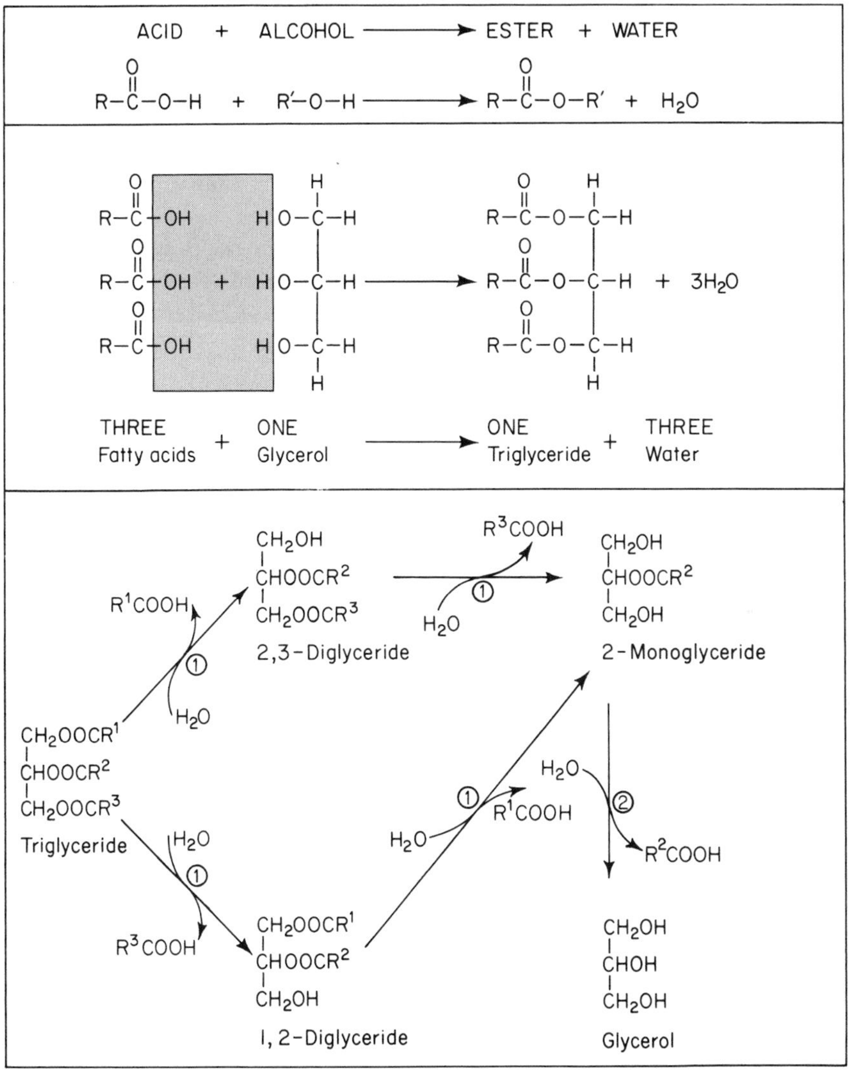

Fig. 3.4. Structure of a triglyceride (above) and the probable reaction sequence in its hydrolysis by pancreatic lipase (below). Enzymes operating in positions 1 and 2 are probably different. [Fruton and Simmonds (1958).]

etc.) and waxes (esters of fatty acids with alcohols other than glycerol) has been demonstrated in many groups of animals. The wax moth,

Galleria, is said to utilize beeswax, probably through a combination of bacterial and enzymatic action in the digestive tract (Roeder, 1953). This same animal has a cholesterase which converts cholesterol into its fatty acid esters. Lecithinases are common in many kinds of tissues, including the digestive mucosa of some animals. The presence of curious enzymes, such as cerase, in association with the digestion of unusual foods has often been considered evidence of the ready production of adaptive hydrolases by animals. However, careful investigation has frequently shown symbiotic microorganisms rather than digestive hydrolases, and physiologists are now more cautious in proclaiming the presence of cellulases, cerases and chitinases in multicellular animals (Florkin, 1952; Barrington, 1962). An example of this is the honey guide (genus *Indicator*), a small African bird which has the curious behavior of leading men and other animals to the nests of bees. This they do by very noisy activities which may attract animals from considerable distances. When the bees' nest has been destroyed by the cooperative mammals the honey guides then gorge themselves on the wax, but it is an intestinal microflora which hydrolyzes the wax and not enzymes produced by the bird itself (Friedmann and Kern, 1956).

Although the digestive lipases seem more conservative than the carbohydrases or proteinases, this is probably because they have a simpler task and is not due to any inability on the part of protoplasm to deal with lipid materials. Actually, the esterases emphasize again the resourcefulness of protoplasm. Organisms exhibit a marked potential for the development of adaptive enzymes, and where an animal exploits an unusual diet such as beeswax, enzymes for its digestion are occasionally found.

Esterases from the digestive epithelium have sometimes been adapted to nondigestive functions. The salivary or buccal glands provide an interesting example. These organs, derived from gut epithelium, may produce amylases, proteases, or lipases. They play a minor part in digestion. Even among mammals, where amylases occur regularly, the digestion which takes place in the mouth is preliminary and often nonessential; the lubricating mucus of the saliva is more important than its enzymes. Lipases and proteinases, when found in buccal gland secretions, often serve specialized nondigestive functions. In some of the reptiles they are potent constituents of venom. Some of the snake venoms contain a phospholipase capable of hydrolyzing lecithin to produce a powerful hemolytic agent, lysolecithin; others produce proteolytic enzymes which act as thromboplastic materials capable of inducing extensive intravascular blood clotting. Venoms often contain a mixture of toxic materials, including many enzymes which are not associated with digestive processes (hyaluronidase, phosphatases, etc.) and other compounds (proteins, amines, etc.) which are not enzymatic in nature (Buckley and Porges, 1956; Jimenez-Porras, 1961). The buccal glands of some amphibians and some reptiles produce several of these toxic materials. Some of the same substances are found in scorpion venoms and insect poisons. In these animals, buccal gland secretions are important in paralyzing the prey and sometimes also in initiating an extra-intestinal digestion.

Proteinases. Proteins are organic substances of high molecular weight, composed of numerous amino acids united by the peptide linkage. On hydrolysis the SIMPLE PROTEINS yield only amino acids while the conjugated proteins yield, in addition, nonamino groups. The nonprotein portion of the conjugated protein is called the prosthetic group. A peptide linkage between two simple amino acids is shown in Fig. 3.5. During digestion the peptide links are hydrolyzed one by one to split off amino acids or groups of amino acids.

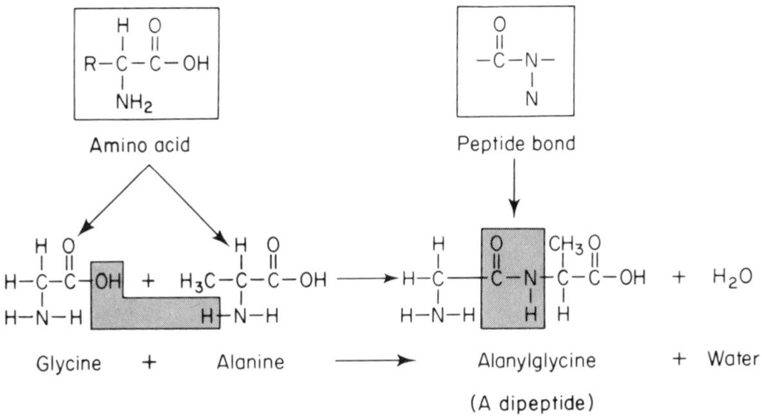

Fig. 3.5. Two amino acids unite through a peptide bond to form a dipeptide.

The most familiar proteolytic enzymes are shown in Table 3.3. They are highly specific and should be thought of as groups or families of enzymes rather than as specific chemical entities. There is no single pepsin molecule in the same sense as a NaCl or HCl molecule. The specificity is of three sorts. Like all proteins, these enzymes show species specificity, and it has been demonstrated that pepsins from various species of vertebrates, for example, act differently on certain substrates and have different reaction optima (Prosser and Brown, 1961). In addition, the proteases show a marked preference for particular peptide links. The presence of particular groups in the vicinity of the peptide bond makes it sensitive to the catalytic activity of only one of the proteases (Fig. 3.6.). Finally, there is a stereospecificity, and the enzymes listed in Table 3.3 are specific for only the L-form of the amino acids.

TABLE 3.3

PROTEIN DIGESTING ENZYMES OF ANIMALS. FURTHER DETAILS OF SPECIFICITY ARE GIVEN IN FIG. 3.5; I–IV, CATHEPSINS OF SOME TEXTS; *A–C*, CATHEPSINS NOW CHARACTERIZED (FRUTON AND SIMMONDS, 1958).

		"*Zymogen*" $\xrightarrow[\textit{Autocatalyst}]{\textit{Activator}}$ *Enzyme*	*Preferred peptide link*
Endopeptidases (proteinases)	I — — *A*	Pepsinogen $\xrightarrow[\text{Pepsin}]{\text{HCl}}$ Pepsin	Carboxyl group of dicarboxylic amino acid *to* amino group of aromatic amino acid
	II — — *B*	Trypsinogen $\xrightarrow[\text{Trypsin}]{\text{Enterokinase}}$ Trypsin	Carboxyl groups of arginine or lysine
	C	Chymotrypsinogen $\xrightarrow{\text{Trypsin}}$ Chymotrypsin	Carboxyl group of aromatic amino acids (side opposite pepsin)
Exopeptidases (peptidases)	III	Aminopeptidase (Mn, Mg, Zn)	Terminal amino acid with free amino group
	IV	Carboxypeptidase (Zn)	Terminal amino acid with free carboxyl group
		Tripeptidase	Tripeptides
		Dipeptidase (Mn, Mg, Zn)	Dipeptides

The digestive proteases may be broadly grouped into ENDOPEPTIDASES and EXOPEPTIDASES (Table 3.3). The former, usually referred to as PROTEINASES in older literature, are concerned with the hydrolysis of very specific and central peptide links of the protein molecule (Fig. 3.6); the latter, often called PEPTIDASES in older literature, catalyze the removal of terminal amino acids. Endopeptidases and exopeptidases occur both as intracellular and extracellular enzymes. The three intracellular endopeptidases—Cathepsin *A*, *B* and *C*—are the counterparts of pepsin, trypsin and chymotrypsin in the exopeptidase group. In addition, cells contain intracellular exopeptidases corresponding to the four major groups of extracellular exopeptidases listed in Table 3.3. It should be emphasized that these intracellular enzymes have not yet been crystallized and are recognized only as broad groups (Fruton and Simmonds, 1958).

All animals probably have at least the minimum protease complement necessary to dismantle a protein molecule. An endopeptidase of the trypsin type, an aminopeptidase and a carboxypeptidase have now been

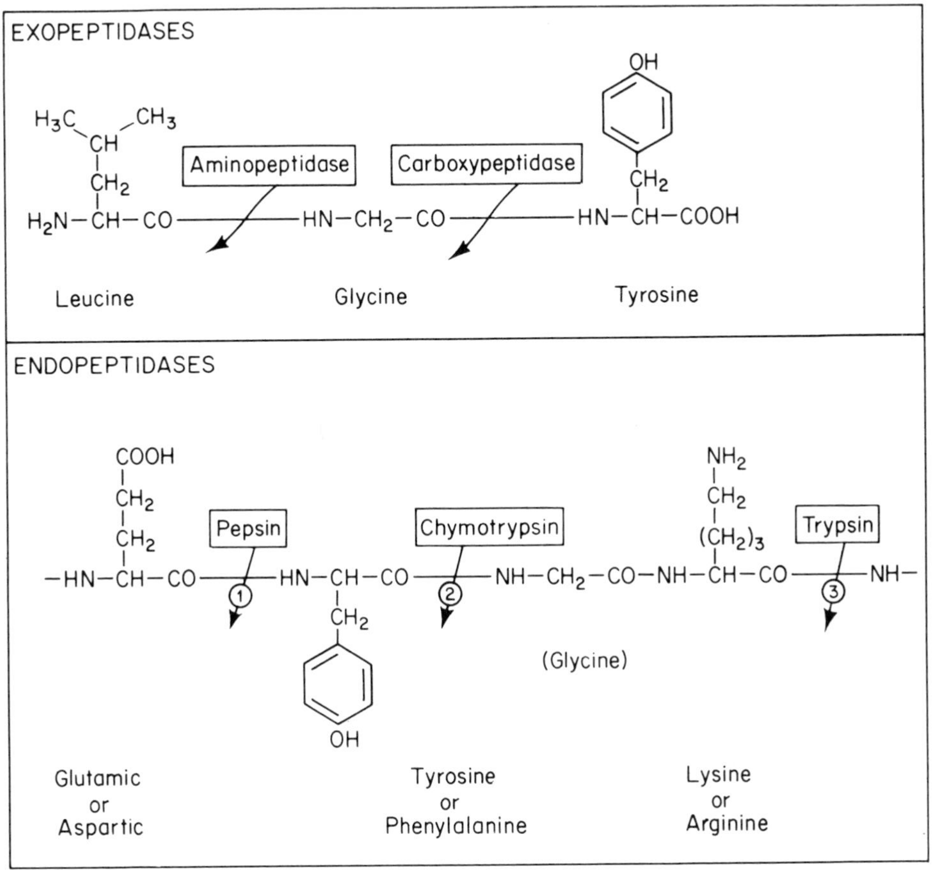

Fig. 3.6. The specific peptide bonds associated with activities of different proteases. 1, Pepsin acts at links between the carboxyl of a dicarboxylic acid and the amino group of an aromatic amino acid. 2, Chymotrypsin acts on the carboxyl group of an aromatic amino acid (tyrosine or phenylalanine). 3, Trypsin acts on the carboxyl of lysine or arginine.

identified in all groups where careful investigations have been carried out. These three enzymes would be adequate for the digestion of proteins, although the process might not be as rapid or as complete as the vertebrate digestive process with additional specific enzymes. However, even the lower invertebrates usually have more than these three kinds of proteolytic enzymes, and further research may reveal the presence of all the major groups of both endo- and exopeptidases in most animals.

Endopeptidases, active in acid as well as in more alkaline media, are found among the intracellular digestive enzymes as well as in the vertebrate extracellular digestive fluids. In the ciliate *Glaucoma pyriformis* an endopeptidase is active in the pH range of 2.2 to 9.6, with an optimum at about pH 6.0 (Hall, 1953). If the intracellular digestive endopeptidases of primitive animals had similar characteristics, the step to extracellular enzymes of the peptic type, (active at a very low pH—about 2.0) or the tryptic type (active in alkaline medium) should not be a difficult adaptation. Pepsin itself is found only in the vertebrates with a stomach, and it has already been suggested that this organ, with its very acid content, may sometimes be important in killing and sterilizing foods as well as in serving the storage and digestive functions.

Extracellular digestive enzymes, in contrast to the intracellular ones, usually require an activator—either in the form of another enzyme, an inorganic compound or an ion (Table 3.3). This is a part of the homeostatic or control mechanism of extracellular digestion. Enterokinase, for example, triggers a series of reactions when it promotes the change of trypsinogen to trypsin, since trypsin is not only a proteinase but also an activator for trypsinogen, chymotrypsinogen and carboxypeptidase. Homeostasis is discussed in more detail below.

The digestion of the very hard, resistant scleroproteins such as collagen (connective tissue), keratin (wool) and the fibrous protein (silk) presents a special challenge which only the insects in the animal world seem to have met (Barrington, 1962). A keratinase, capable of digesting wool, is found in several insects and is well known in the clothes moth. Silk too can be utilized by the clothes moth and certain dermestids, but the mechanism has not been investigated (Roder, 1953). A collagenase has been reported in the blow-fly larva *Lucilia* (Wigglesworth, 1942).

Other digestive enzymes. Various other molecules which are not pure carbohydrate, lipid, or protein, are present in any varied diet and are digested by some animals. Chitin, for example, is a hexoseamine containing amino groups in addition to hexose sugar. Several molluscs, arthropods and insect eating vertebrates are said to have chitinases (Jeuniaux, 1961). Other hexoseamines are chondroitin in cartilage and the constituents of mucoproteins. Conjugated proteins such as the nucleoproteins (Chapter 22) have several specific enzymes associated with their digestion in the vertebrates, and other animals may be expected to have comparable catalysts.

Absorption

The monosaccharides, amino acids and other products of digestion, whether arising in a food vacuole or in a complex digestive tube, must be passed on to the tissues before they can perform essential cell functions. The process by which they are transferred from the locus of digestion is referred to as absorption. In the higher animals this is essentially a transfer from the digestive tract to the circulatory fluids. Similar mechanisms may be involved in the transfer from blood to the metabolizing cell, but this is not usually included in a discussion of absorption.

Two distinct questions have been investigated, viz., the locus of absorptive activity and the mechanics of transferring molecules through cells and cell membranes.

LOCUS OF TRANSFER

In intracellular digestion the same cells are obviously concerned with digestion and absorption if, in fact, the latter is considered to operate. With the development of extracellular digestive enzymes and one way traffic through a tubular gut, separate areas are often devoted to absorption and are specialized accordingly. This is particularly true in the vertebrates. Among the invertebrates, enzyme secreting and absorbing cells are often in close proximity, and the same areas of epithelium are often concerned with both processes. With finely divided or liquid foods this is not an unreasonable arrangement. In some of the invertebrates (crustaceans and insects, for example) the same cells have been shown to operate in cycles, at one time secreting enzymes and at another absorbing digested foods (Yonge, 1937; Barrington, 1962).

In many of the larger invertebrates such as the Mollusca, Arthropoda and Echinodermata, there is an extensive series of diverticulae or caecae from the stomach or mid-gut region—the digestive gland or so-called "liver" of the mollusc (Fig. 3.2), the hepatopancreas of the crustacean and the pyloric caecae of the starfish. These glandular developments greatly increase the available surfaces and serve a combined function of secreting and absorbing. Digestion within these structures is often both intracellular and extracellular. Food, which is reduced to particulate size in the anterior gut or stomach region, is moved into the tubules of these glands where final digestion occurs and the absorption of digested materials takes place. The circulation of food within the diverticula is maintained by cilia or muscle fibers or both (Yonge, 1937). In the Crustacea the contraction of the circular muscles of the diverticula forces digestive juices from the diverticula into the stomach; their relaxation and the contraction of the longitudinal muscles draws digested or partially digested material into the diverticula—sometimes after a preliminary sorting or straining. In the lamellibranch or the starfish the exchange of materials between the gut and the digestive gland depends entirely on the activity of long cilia.

Among the invertebrates, several of the molluscs show a strong tendency to localize absorptive activities and, thus, to separate them from enzyme secretion. Although absorption is usually confined to the mid-gut glands, in at least one group of lamellibranchs (Nuculidae) it seems to have been entirely relegated to the stomach and intestine while the gut diverticulae operate as an extracellular digestive organ (Owen, 1956). Similar trends are evident in the gastropods, but some of the cephalopods have made the greatest strides toward a separation of digestive and absorptive activities (Morton, 1958; Barrington, 1962). Cephalopod digestion shows many of the advances found in the vertebrates; in consequence, they achieve a rapid and efficient flow of nutrients to the body tissues.

The diverticular glands of the invertebrate gut are often concerned with storage of reserve food as well as with digestion and absorption. The hepatopancreas of the crustacean (Vonk, 1960) and the pyloric caecae of the starfish (Hyman, 1955) have been shown to store reserves of carbohydrate and fat which disappear during starvation. In the vertebrates, the liver which develops as a diverticulum of the gut is a major organ of food storage and has no capacities for digestive enzyme production. In most of the higher invertebrates, one and the same gland secretes enzymes, absorbs digested foods and stores the body reserves.

In the vertebrates, a portion of the wall of the small intestine is concerned with absorption. Again, this is not an exclusive property of a single area and some absorption may occur at almost all points in the gut. The teleost fish usually have an elaborate development of pyloric caecae which are comparable physiologically and anatomically to the digestive glands of some of the invertebrates, since they are concerned both with the secretion of enzymes and the absorption of digested foods (Barrington, 1957). Food storage, however, seems unlikely in pyloric caecae; this occurs in liver and body fat as in other vertebrates.

The wall of the vertebrate intestine is variously folded and ridged to provide an extensive surface for absorption. The "spiral valve" of some cyclostomes, the elasmobranchs and certain other groups of fish is an elaborate series of folds which seems to have arisen phylogenetically from a single longitudinal ridge or typhlosole like that of the earthworm or the ammocoete larva. Among other fishes (teleosts), amphibia and reptiles an intricate network of ridges, often bounding deep tubular crypts, adds greatly to the absorptive area of the intestine. In the birds and mammals, comparable ridges are covered with a velvet-like pile of minute absorptive villi. These are highly specialized absorptive organs with a core containing a network of capillaries derived from blood vessels in the wall of the gut. Each also contains a central lymph capillary or LACTEAL which begins blindly under the epithelium at the tip of the villus and drains into the main lymphatic channels of the gut wall. The consensus is that lipids pass primarily into the lacteals while the sugars and amino acids are absorbed directly into the capillary blood. Both the villus and the intestinal fold contain smooth muscle, and the rhythmic movements thus produced are important in bringing the villi into contact with the intestinal contents and in maintaining circulation in the lacteals, lymphatics and small blood vessels.

MECHANICS OF TRANSFER

Three main processes are involved in the transfer of digested food to the circulation of the neighboring tissues, (*a*) transfer by phagocytes, (*b*) passive diffusion and (*c*) active transport.

Phagocytosis. Phagocytic amebocytes may pick up particles of food from the digestive tract or elsewhere (mantle cavity in some bivalves) and then digest and transport the remnants to various tissues of the body. This process is particularly conspicuous in some of the Lamellibranchiata and the Echinodermata (Yonge, 1937; Wagge, 1955) and permits the digestion of food particles (diatoms, for example) which may be too large to enter the tubules of the digestive diverticula. Yonge (1937) suggests that this may account for the fact that a highly specialized group such as the Lamellibranchiata has evolved so successfully with only a limited degree of extracellular digestion.

Diffusion. In PASSIVE TRANSPORT materials move through cells, membranes and intercellular spaces because of differences in the concentration gradient. The substances are in aqueous solution, and their migration is the result of the random motion of solute molecules. Most living membranes have very special permeability properties which restrict the movements of many molecules and ions; consequently, a study of diffusion through living cells involves not only the concentration gradients or physical forces of diffusion but also the osmotic properties of the cell membranes or tissues. In some cases, however, the cell membranes and tissues SEEM TO have little effect on the migration of the molecules, and absorption is primarily due to concentration gradients. Passive diffusion is admittedly a somewhat artificial concept since living cell membranes probably always exert some control. However, the distinction between this and active transport is valid. The extent of "passive" transport varies with the type of cell, its physiological condition and the properties of the penetrating molecule. With these reservations, the absorption of quite a variety of materials may be said to depend on passive transport or diffusion (Holter, 1961).

Many drugs, poisons, alcohols, acid amides and other extraneous substances which pass from the digestive tract into the blood, do so in accordance with their concentration and show no evidence of active transport. Absorption of water may also be largely passive although, in some cases, there is a physiological control (Davson, 1959). Most of the digested foods, on the other hand, are actively transported—at least in the mammal—and enter the blood against a concentration gradient. One of the interesting exceptions to this rule is the absorption of volatile fatty acids from the stomach of the ruminant. It has already been pointed out that the fermentation processes in the rumen produce large amounts of volatile fatty acids and ammonia and that the ready and rapid absorption of these materials is essential to the maintenance of constant conditions of pH, ions and other ecological factors of importance to the rumen flora. There is no evidence of active transport. Volatile fatty acids and ammonia diffuse readily into the blood capillaries and are quickly metabolized so that the diffusion gradient is continuously steep (Annison and Lewis, 1959).

The invertebrates show two specialized anatomical developments for direct diffusion of materials from the absorptive regions of the gut. These are essentially molecular strainers. The gut of *Helix* is in part an absorption membrane which allows even disaccharides to pass directly through it (Yonge, 1937). The PERITROPHIC MEMBRANE of many insects (and some polychaetes) is a thin membranous sleeve, lining the mid-gut and anterior part of the hind-gut, and separating the gut epithelium from the mass of digesting food. It is an extremely delicate structure (0.5 μ or less in thickness) composed of chitin with a small amount of protein. Colloidal particles are unable to penetrate, but the digestive enzymes, the digested food and the simpler molecules of partly digested food pass freely through it (Andrew, 1959; Roeder, 1953). It protects the delicate epithelium of the gut from the abrasive action of hard foods. Many animals achieve a similar protection through copious secretions of thick mucus.

Active transport. During ACTIVE TRANSPORT, molecules may pass from the gut against a diffusion gradient. In other words, glucose, amino acids and other substances may move from very dilute solutions through the intestinal cells and membranes into more concentrated body fluids. Active metabolic work is required. Neither the transport mechanism nor the coupling of this with the energy generator of the cell is as yet understood (Holter, 1961). Current theories assume the activity of special carrier molecules which form a complex with the transported material on one side of the membrane and release it on the other (Andersen and Ussing, 1960; Holter, 1961).

Glucose transport from the gut has been intensively investigated

(Crane, 1960). For a long time phosphorylation was considered an essential step, but physiologists are no longer satisfied with this concept. The movement of glucose against a concentration gradient seems to involve its conversion into some complex (phosphate sugar? disaccharide?) within the absorptive cells. This complex subsequently dissociates on the serosal side of the cell. The nature of the complex or complexes is in question; a coupling of sugar absorption with sodium transport has been suggested (Crane, 1960). Proteins are normally absorbed actively as amino acids, but again the mechanisms are not established. There are marked differences in the absorption rates of different amino acids and sugars.

Fat absorption is also an active process. In birds and mammals most of the products of fat digestion pass into the lacteals, although there is some absorption, particularly of the shorter chain fatty acids, directly into the capillaries; in the invertebrates and probably the lower vertebrates absorption is directly into the circulation. The glycerol and fatty acids of the hydrolyzed fats seem to form complexes with the bile salts in the mammal and are then built into phospholipids or neutral fats in the intestinal mucosa. These then pass into the lymph. The detailed mechanisms are not known. At least a part of the highly emulsified (but not digested) fat is directly absorbed into the cells of the gut wall and thence passed to the lacteals. Almost all the investigations have been conducted on the mammal.

Several factors are known to regulate absorption in the mammal. The action of bile salts in lipid absorption has been mentioned. The D-vitamins stimulate the uptake of calcium ions from the intestinal tract; the level of mucosal ferritin controls the uptake of iron. These mechanisms are detailed in textbooks of human and medical physiology.

Coordination of Digestive Activities

The regulated passage of food through the gut provides sufficient time for effective enzyme action and proper absorption before the wastes (feces) are discharged. The necessary coordinating mechanisms are much less elaborate in the continuous feeder than in the periodic feeder. In many of the invertebrates and particularly in the filter feeders, there is normally a continual flow of food particles into the body, a constant secretion of enzymes, with incessant digestion and absorption. The continuous feeder thus avoids the problems of storage between meals and the potential hazards of fluctuations in the blood levels of digested foods. A periodic feeder, on the other hand, may obtain large volumes of food during a relatively brief period, and these must be digested, absorbed, and stored to avoid excessive flooding of the tissues with nutrients. At the upper level of phylogeny, a complex interaction of the autonomic nervous system and endocrines initiates enzyme secretion, regulates the discharge of accumulated juices and governs the motility of the gut and the passage of food through it. Even the filter feeder, however, may face periods of starvation and, although the controls are less elaborate, digestive activity varies somewhat in accordance with demands at all levels in phylogeny. For example, in a filter feeder such as the bivalve mollusc, the crystalline style (source of amylases) may actually disappear during periods of starvation; in *Helix* the digestive gland cells show a secretion cycle which operates at varying speeds according to demand (Scheer, 1948); at the coelenterate level of organization, extracellular protease secretion has been shown to be stimulated by the presence of food and depressed by its absence.

Both humoral and neural mechanisms are active in the coordination of digestive functions, but the relative importance of the two varies in different animals. Primitive forms are often continuous feeders, and the enzyme producing cells secrete constantly or are cyclically active in accordance with the supply of food or in response to secretagogues in the form of partially digested food. It would appear that the neuromuscular control necessary to mix and move the food through the gut and to discharge the wastes is a more acute problem in these lower forms than the problem of regulating enzyme secretion.

THE VISCERAL AUTONOMIC SYSTEM

Characteristic of the digestive canal of the higher invertebrates and the vertebrates is the presence of one or more nerve nets. In the vertebrates a MYENTERIC PLEXUS OF AUERBACH between the two thick layers of smooth muscle is primarily responsible for the movements of the gut, while MEISSNER'S PLEXUS in the submucosa controls the activities of the enzyme producing glands. In the decapod crustacean there is one well developed nerve plexus resembling that of Auerbach (Vonk, 1960), and similar nerve nets have been described in many other arthropods, in the annelids and the molluscs (Hyman, 1951). Other phyla of invertebrates lack the special nerve nets of the visceral sympathetic or enteric system. There are, however, definite nerves to the specialized muscular areas such as the pharynx, stomach, and rectum. A circumenteric nerve ring anteriorly, and sometimes also posteriorly, with branching nerves is a rather constant feature (Hyman, 1951–59). In the more primitive groups these may be thought of as nerve nets which have been concentrated into circumenteric nerve cords.

Among the invertebrates, the enteric, somatogastric or sympathetic supply is primarily motor to the muscle of the gut. The earthworm seems to be an exception in that secretion of proteolytic enzymes follows stimulation of the enteric nerves. On the other hand, nervous control of gut secretion does not exist in insects (Roeder, 1953; Barrington, 1962), and similarly, in the crustaceans stimulation of the ventral nerve cord initiates peristalsis and other motor activities but produces no effect on the glands (Vonk, 1960). In *Arenicola,* a rhythmically spontaneous activity of the gut musculature (especially the proboscis and esophagus) is associated with a burrowing life in soft mud (Wells, 1950). This rhythm depends only on pacemakers in the enteric net and is quite independent of the central nervous control. Spontaneous activity is probably present in other invertebrates as well.

The vertebrate autonomic nervous supply to the gut is typically double with parasympathetic and sympathetic fibers responsible for opposing activities. In the bird and mammal, stimulation of the vagus nerve (parasympathetic) increases enzyme secretion (especially in the salivary glands and stomach) and heightens gut motility while the sympathetic effect is inhibitory. Normally, a balance between the two systems maintains proper muscle tone and glandular activity (anteriorly) in relation to feeding. The pattern differs in the lower vertebrates, and either the sympathetic or the parasympathetic supply may be absent (Table 2.2). Thus in the elasmobranch, the vagus has no action on the gut and the sympathetics are excitatory to muscle, but the glands appear to be independent of any autonomic influence (Nicol, 1952; Healey, 1957). The teleost stomach, on the other hand, receives a motor supply from the vagus nerve; stimulation of sympathetics produces different effects in various species. Nervous control of digestive secretion has not been demonstrated in the lower vertebrates and, as in the invertebrates, the autonomic control of the muscle is the more constant feature of the visceral system. Actually, even in the mammal there are variations in the different regions of the gut; a double balanced innervation is characteristic, but it is not safe to go beyond this in generalizing.

GASTROINTESTINAL HORMONES

Vertebrate physiologists have described a series of hormones produced by the gastrointestinal epithelium and concerned with the regulation of the secretions of the digestive glands. A comparable system has not been found in the invertebrates and may well be absent. Among the invertebrates, a chemical regulation of feeding and digestive activities is often evident, but this depends on the presence of food or partially digested food products (secretagogues) and not on chemical messengers produced by the animal itself. In *Hydra,* for example, the presence of glutathione released from injured prey induces an elaborate series of feeding activities (Lenhoff, 1961). Even in the most complex invertebrates, processes of digestion, secretion and storage take place side by side, and a nervous control of gut motility with some direct response of the enzyme secreting cells to the presence of food (secretagogues) is evidently adequate. The vertebrates, on the other hand, must mobilize a series of digestive juices and regulate the passage of food through several different areas at rates which permit sufficient time for the appropriate enzymes to act and for the digested foods to be absorbed. The demands on particular enzyme secreting tissues vary in accordance with the type of food eaten. To meet this complexity of demands, the vertebrate has a series of hormones (Fig. 3.7) as well as a highly organized autonomic control.

The first of the gastrointestinal hormones to be discovered was SECRETIN. Actually, secretin, isolated from the intestine by Bayliss and Starling (1902) was the first substance to which the term "hormone" was applied. These investigators showed that the presence of HCl stimulated the intestinal mucosa to liberate into the blood a compound (secretin) which initiated the release of pancreatic juices. They showed later (1903) that a similar mechanism existed among the lower vertebrates. In 1906, Edkins suggested that the stomach might also be responsible for the elaboration of a hormone and, since that time, no less than seven distinct gastrointestinal hormones have been described in the mammal (Turner, 1960; Gorbman and Bern, 1962). The comparative physiology of most of these factors has not been investigated, and the description which follows is based on the mammal.

GASTRIN, secreted by the gastric mucosa, is responsible for the balanced production of HCl in the stomach. Local nervous mechanisms, initiated by the presence of food, cause gastrin production, and this in turn stimulates the parietal cells. The gastrin mechanism is responsible for the control of the volume of HCl; the presence of HCl itself serves as a feedback to inhibit gastrin secretion. Thus, the first link in the hormonal control of digestive activity provides a proper concentration of acid for peptic activity within the stomach.

Intestinal hormones are involved in the control of the stomach, the pancreas, the gall bladder and the intestinal mucosa itself (Fig. 3.7). ENTEROGASTRONE is liberated into the blood when fats enter the intestine and serves to inhibit the secretion of the gastric juice—especially HCl. In this way the presence of partly digested food in the intestine gradually slows down the activity of the stomach.

The endocrine control of the pancreas has now been found to be more complicated than visualized by Bayliss and Starling in 1902.

Instead of one hormone, secretin, there are two–SECRETIN and PANCREOZYMIN. Secretin which is released under stimulus of low pH (HCl), digested fat or bile, initiates the production of a copious pancreatic juice; this juice is low in enzymes but rich in salts which may be important

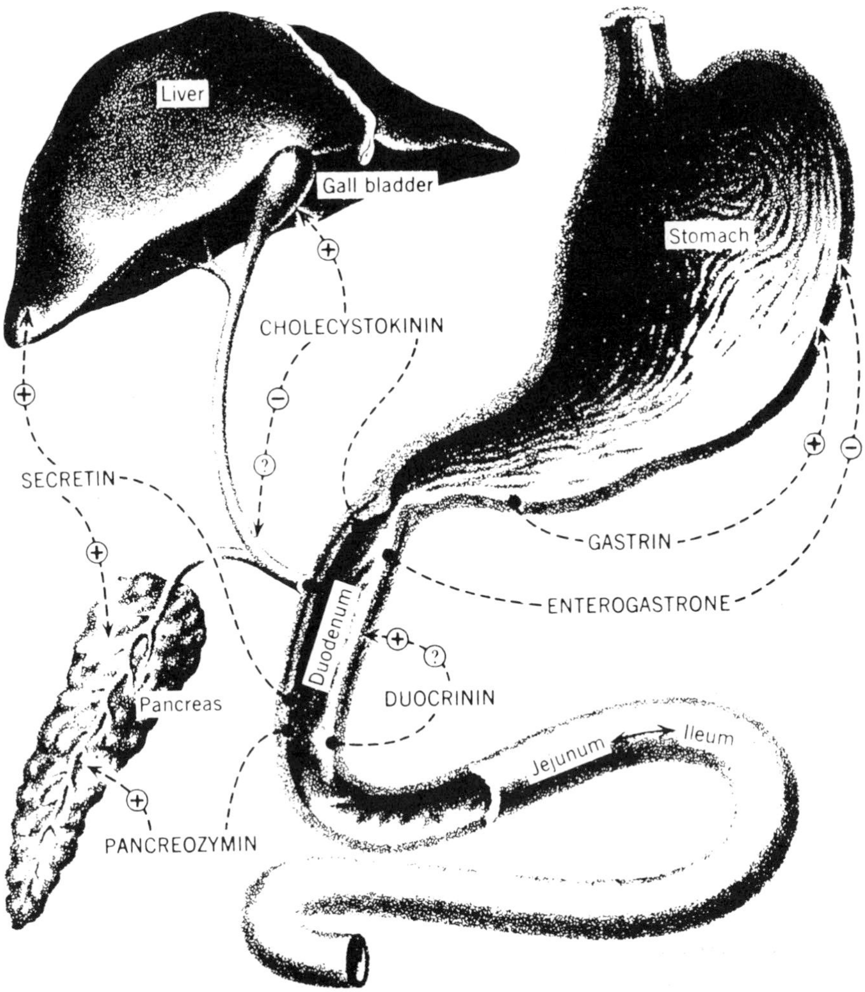

Fig. 3.7. Six gastrointestinal hormones. The places of origin and actions of each are entirely within the digestive tract but they are carried from one place to another by the systemic circulation. A stimulatory action is indicated by a plus sign; an inhibitory action is indicated by a minus sign. [Gorbman and Bern (1962).]

in neutralizing the acid chyme. Pancreozymin, secreted under the stimulation of partially digested protein (HCl to a lesser extent), induces the flow of an enzyme-rich secretion. Thus, the partially digested food from the stomach triggers the release of fluid, but the important proteolytic enzymes are only produced when they are required by the presence of peptone and proteoses.

The rapid hydrolysis of fats depends on their prior emulsification by the bile salts and secretions of the liver. The arrival of fat from the stomach initiates the release of CHOLECYSTOKININ by the intestinal mucosa, and this hormone elicits contraction of the gall bladder. In this way, an accumulated store of bile is promptly added to the intestinal content in response to the fat which requires it for digestion. Secretion of bile by the hepatic cells depends on a different set of stimuli. The hormone secretin and the bile salts themselves, when reabsorbed into the blood, are responsible for this activity.

The presence of a gall bladder permits an animal to meet a sudden demand for large amounts of bile, and its anatomical development probably bears some relation to the diet. It is sometimes absent. Among mammals, the horse, deer and rat lack a gall bladder while in the giraffe it is said to be sometimes present and sometimes absent (Dukes, 1955).

It has been claimed that the stomach chyme in the upper intestine stimulates the release of additional hormones which activate mechanisms further down the intestine in preparation for the food which has entered its upper end. Evidence for these claims is still rather incomplete. ENTEROKININ and DUOCRININ are said to release enzymes at different points in the small intestine; a hormone VILLIKININ seems to stimulate the motility of the absorptive villi.

In the intestine the control is entirely humoral; at the level of the salivary glands it is entirely nervous. The presence of food and the acts of feeding promptly activate nervous mechanisms for the immediate initiation of digestion, but as the food progresses along the gut, more slowly operating humoral controls regulate the different digestive glands in accordance with the foods eaten and their passage from one area to another. The interplay of nervous and humoral mechanisms—basic to most homeostatic regulation—is beautifully shown in the coordination of all the activities of the alimentary canal.

The Exchange of Gases

4

Aerobic life, characteristic of animals, demands a steady flow of oxygen into the cells and a ready removal of the carbon dioxide which arises from their metabolism. At the cellular level, physical forces of diffusion alone effect these exchanges. No convincing evidence has ever been presented for active transport or secretion of either oxygen or carbon dioxide by cells. Diffusion is quite adequate, but in a large multicellular animal this is only possible because of a number of special adaptations—some respiratory and some circulatory.

Two main factors have shaped the structures and refined the processes of gaseous exchange. The first of these is associated with the increasing size of animals during phylogeny. Since rates of diffusion are relatively slow and since in many environments the oxygen supply is marginal, greatly extended surfaces for diffusion are usually required. These respiratory appendages are variously modified in relation to the habitat. The extent of the surface may be enormous in proportion to the mass of the organ. It has been calculated that the human lungs have a surface area of from 50 to 90 square meters (Bard, 1961), somewhere between thirty and fifty times the external surface area of the body.

The second major factor is due to terrestrial life and aerial respiration. Soft protoplasmic extensions which characterize the respiratory organs of aquatic animals collapse and dry out in air. The evolution and success of terrestrial forms have, in part, depended on the development of respiratory surfaces inside the moist bodies of the animals. These surfaces are perpetually wet. Whether the animal is aquatic and extends its branchial membranes into the water, or terrestrial with internal gas-filled cavities, oxygen and carbon dioxide are always dissolved in a water layer at the surface of the cell. Although the thickness of the water layer varies, respiration is, in a sense, aquatic in both cases.

Unless gases are piped to the individual cells, as they are in the tracheates, mere extension of surfaces could never solve the problem of gas exchange for a bulky animal. Diffusion of gases in protoplasm is slow, and a constant movement of the external environment over the outer surface of these membranes (ventilation) must be coupled with an equally efficient and continuous movement of gases inside the membranes. Thus, the evolution of organs for ventilation and a blood circulatory system have accompanied the expansion and elaboration of the respiratory epithelium. The continuous circulation of gases – both on the inside and outside of the respiratory epithelium – is indispensable to a system which depends on concentration gradients and convection currents. The varied pigments involved in gas transport are discussed in Chapter 6. The machinery responsible for ventilation, as well as the respiratory membranes themselves, will be considered here. Krogh's (1941) monograph, published more than twenty years ago, remains an excellent summary of the pertinent information.

Integumentary Respiration

Gases move slowly through protoplasm. Calculations based on the metabolic demands of animals and on rates of diffusion of gases in protoplasm show that simple diffusion cannot satisfy the oxygen demands of organisms much larger than 1 mm in diameter (Krogh, 1941). The precise size limits depend not only on the rate of metabolism but also on the shape of the animal; any departure from the spherical will increase the surface area relative to the mass. Thus, a number of the smaller metozoa and the larvae of much larger ones exceed the 1 mm diameter range. Giant land planarians (Terricola) may be 50 cm long, but their flat elongated bodies result in very large surfaces in relation to the mass. Coelenterates and sponges often reach even larger sizes with modest metabolic demands and relatively short diffusion distances. A jellyfish is largely water with only about 1 per cent organic dry material; a sponge maintains a circulation of water by cilia over the surfaces of cells which line an intricate series of canals and spaces; tissues of some of the coelenterates have been shown to operate at very low oxygen tensions. Modifications such as these permit relatively large animals to effect sufficient exchange of gases without gas-transport pigments or specialized areas of respiratory epithelia.

Theoretically, the addition of an efficient circulatory system should allow adequate gaseous exchange through the integument. Metabolism is nearly proportional to body surface (Chapter 7), and if the surfaces are readily permeable and vascular they alone should suffice. The earthworm, the leech and some larval fishes are among the many animals which meet their oxygen demands in this way. Oligochaetes, for example, may reach much larger sizes than the 50 cm turbellarians referred to in the last paragraph; it seems likely that the circulation of hemoglobin through a highly vascular hypodermis is one reason for the difference (Carter, 1931). Even larger animals, such as amphibians and fish, may rely on cutaneous respiration during emergencies or use it continuously as a supplement to gills or lungs. The eel can exchange 60 per cent of its respiratory gases through a highly vascular skin, and this is enough to permit prolonged activity in moist air at temperatures of 15°C or less (Carter, 1961). Cutaneous respiration is adequate for an animal submerged in water if metabolic demands are not elevated by temperature or excessive activity. In air also frogs normally exchange large amounts of oxygen and carbon dioxide through the skin. Cutaneous respiration is important in all amphibians. In *Ambystoma,* approximately 80 per cent of the carbon dioxide is released through the skin at all temperatures above 5°C; below this temperature the lung and buccopharyngeal exchange of carbon dioxide is too small to be measured. The cutaneous oxygen consumption in this salamander increases with temperature in a linear manner to about 50 per cent of the total at 15°C and then declines to about 35 per cent of the peak value at 30°C (Whitford and Hutchinson, 1963). Foxon (1964) tabulates comparative values of relative capillary area in lungs, skin and buccal cavity as a measure of the contribution of each of these to respiratory exchange. The buccal cavity is apparently of minor importance since the capillary surface is always small, ranging from less than 1 per cent to 3 per cent. In a number of species the capillary areas are about equal in lungs and skin, but there is considerable variation, and the integumentary contribution ranges from as low as 20 per cent in dry-skinned forms, such as some toads, to about 76 per cent in the urodele *Triturus alpestris.*

Cutaneous respiration can only be successful, however, if the surfaces are moist, thin and readily permeable. This imposes a serious restriction in many habitats. Soft coverings are vulnerable to predators and prone to abrasion. Problems of electrolyte and water balance are magnified in proportion to the extent of permeable surface. The hazards of desiccation in the terrestrial environment are obvious. The addition of chitin to the cuticle, for example, drastically reduces the cutaneous exchange of gases, and none of the Crustacea which rely on cutaneous respiration have reached the size of the nonchitinized annelids. The compromise between moist, readily permeable surfaces and a protective impermeable outer covering has been met by the development of body surface extensions in the form of gills or lungs—usually housed in moist chambers specialized for this particular purpose.

Branchial Respiration

Any appendage of the body primarily concerned with the exchange of gases may be called a gill. Gills are typically the respiratory organs of aquatic animals and range from cirri and simple epithelial extensions, which only supplement cutaneous respiration, to elaborate structures consisting of thousands of highly specialized lamellae, enclosed in a gill cavity which is ventilated by a continuous flow of water.

EXTERNAL GILLS

External gills are phylogenetically more primitive. There is a multitude of structural variations, and only a few examples from this vast array will be included here. The echinoderms, like other major groups of invertebrates, have experimented with a variety of gill structures. The body of the asteroid is rather uniformly clothed with hollow, papillate, body-wall extensions from the coelom (papulae), while in most echinoids five pairs of small branched structures (the gills) surround the peristomial region. In both cases, exchange of gases through these structures is supplementary to the exchange which occurs through the tube feet or podia. Among the annelids the locomotory appendages often supplement the integument to meet the respiratory demands (*Nereis*); or there may be paired, segmentally arranged branchial tufts along the sides of the body (as in the burrowing polychaete, *Arenicola*); or the branchial tufts may be developed only anteriorly (as in the tubulous polychaetes) where they appear as plumes and feather-like structures or masses of tangled filaments.

Among some of the amphibia the length of the external gill filaments has been shown to change with the oxygen content of the water. A functional response to low oxygen tensions has been reported for both *Salamandra* and *Rana* (Krogh, 1941). In some fishes (Elasmobranchii, Dipnoi, Polypteridae) external gills are present only in the larvae and precede the development of the adult branchial apparatus. In the male lungfish, *Lepidosiren,* masses of filamentous respiratory appendages grow on the pelvic fins at the time of reproduction when the male attends the nest. He makes periodic excursions to the surface, fully aerates his blood by the lung, and returns to supply oxygen to the developing eggs and larvae in the nest by way of the highly vascular external pelvic gills. There are many other curious examples of external gills. They attest the primitive nature and varied form of this method of gaseous exchange.

INTERNAL GILLS

Exposed gills have several obvious disadvantages. In some habitats delicate appendages are subject to abrasion and may attract predators; they also increase resistance to locomotion. Further, the movement of water over their surfaces is intermittent, depending on the gentle movements of the appendages or on the water currents in their surroundings. The withdrawal of gills into a cavity permits the streamlining of the body, provides maximum protection for the delicate epithelia and favors the specialization of a pumping system for their ventilation. Internal gills are found in some members of all the groups of large aquatic animals—whether sessile or active. Their many forms are described in textbooks of general zoology, and only the principles associated with their phylogeny and operation will be considered here.

In evolution there seems to have been a compromise between the attainment of a sufficiently large respiratory surface and the housing of this in limited spaces. To meet these demands a continuous flow of water is maintained through the branchial apparatus at rates which depend on the demand for oxygen. In addition, the flow of water and the circulation of blood are in opposite directions (counter current principle) and thus create maximum gradients between the external and the internal environments. Further refinements in efficiency involve variations in the number of gills and in the transport capacities of the blood pigments. Adaptations, both morphologically and physiologically, meet the demands of varied habitats.

Among sessile animals, such as bivalves, tunicates and some of the echinoderms, the circulation of water through the branchial chamber often depends on ciliary activity. A supply of food particles as well as oxygen is carried by this gentle stream. On the other hand, active, free living forms as well as many tube-dwelling and semisessile animals depend on muscular activity and frequently combine ventilation with locomotion—sometimes also with feeding. The coordinated action of many groups of muscles periodically aerates the branchial chambers or constantly pumps water through them. Integration depends on ganglionic and brain centers and may include a sensory system with specialized mechano- and chemoreceptors. Several examples will illustrate the trends in specialization.

The rhythmic ventilation of the *Arenicola* burrow exemplifies a relatively simple situation found in some marine burrowing forms. Van

Dam studied *Arenicola* many years ago by placing worms in U-shaped tubes and measuring the rate of flow of water through the tubes (Krogh, 1941). Wells (1949) traced the rhythmic activities of these animals in

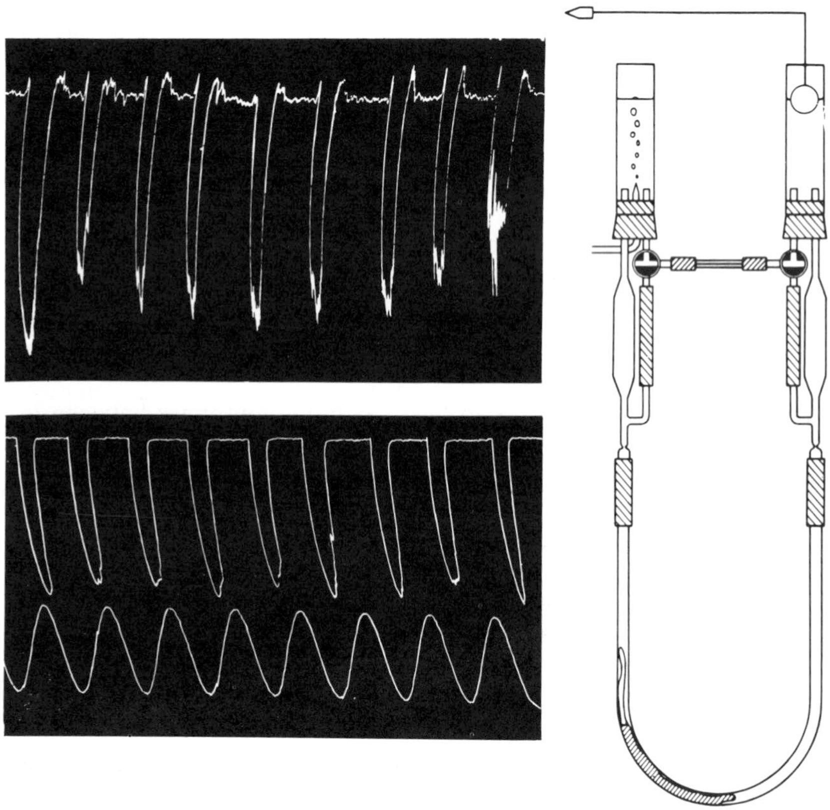

Fig. 4.1. Respiratory movements of *Arenicola*. Right, apparatus used by Wells (1949) to record irrigation cycles; internal diameter of U-tube is 0.75 cm. Left upper, three phase irrigation cycle; middle, cycle with first and third phase inconspicuous. In both traces the head of the worm is towards float. Bottom record, time trace. Upper trace, about two cycles per hour; middle trace, one cycle per hour; traces read from left to right. [Wells (1949).]

U-tubes of sea water by a float connected with a writing lever (Fig. 4.1.). The irrigation of the burrow is due to the wave movements in the musculature of the trunk, and Wells also recorded rhythmic contractions in isolated preparations of the body wall. These experiments established the presence of a pacemaking system in the ventral nerve cord, responsible for the rhythmic irrigation and other activities of the worm in its burrow. The pacemaker may be set at different rates in accordance with circumstances (Wells, 1949, 1950).

A highly successful group, such as the Crustacea, displays a variety of gills ranging from an exposed series of relatively simple leaflets to masses of intricately divided filaments housed in regularly ventilated chambers; in some small forms and in larvae, integumentary respiration suffices and respiratory appendages are absent (Wolvekamp and Waterman, 1960). The more primitive gilled species, such as the fairy shrimp *Branchipus* or the brine shrimp *Artemia,* have vascularized lamellae on the eleven or more pairs of thoracic appendages. These appendages are also equipped with a brush of filtering hairs, and the currents which they maintain supply food as well as oxygen. In the Anostraca, these lamellate gills are fully exposed, while they are covered by a carapace in other orders of the Branchipoda. In the Decapoda, among more specialized crustaceans, the gills are housed in a branchial chamber which, in forms such as the crab, communicates with the external environment only through small slits (one above each leg) and a main inhalant and exhalant passage on each side. The exhalant passage is the largest and is situated in front of the mouth where the scaphognathite (of the second maxilla)

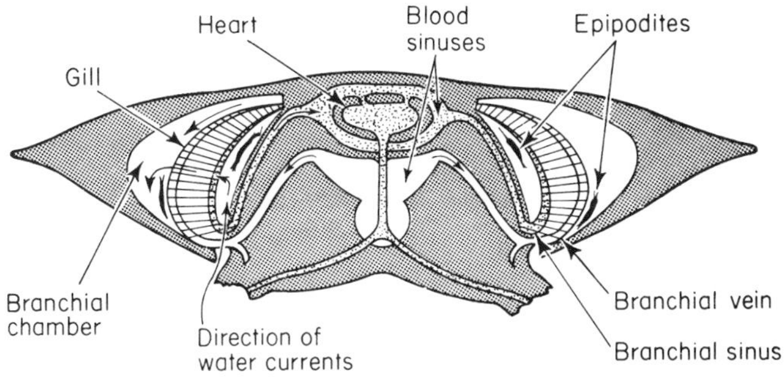

Fig. 4.2. Branchial chambers and the blood supply of the gills in *Cancer pagurus* (diagrammatic cross section). Arrows indicate directions of water currents and blood flow [Waterman (1960).]

moves to and fro as a bailer to draw water out of the exhalant passage and thus create currents over the gills. The mechanics of circulation in the chamber are such that the gills are thoroughly bathed, and water is brought close to the blood (Fig. 4.2). The gill surface is extensive and, in addition to the podobranchiae arising from the epipodites of the thoracic appendages, there are also filaments from the articular membranes connecting the limbs with the trunk (arthrobranchiae) and from the lateral walls of the thorax (pleurobranchiae). The extent of gill epithelium is related to habitat and respiratory demands (Gray, 1957 and Chapter 12).

The gills of the mollusc are organs of the mantle cavity and this space provides ready-made housing for them. In the sessile and relatively inactive forms, ventilation of the mantle depends on cilia, but in the active cephalopods the respiratory currents are created by muscles and ventilation is combined with locomotion. In species which lack a shell (*Octopus* and squid), two sets of opposing muscles (the longitudinal and circular) alternately expand and constrict the mantle. As the mantle space enlarges, water is drawn in around the edges of the mantle and circulates over the gills. Contraction of the circular muscles first constricts the edges of the mantle around the neck and then forces the water out in a jet from the funnel. In the Shelled *Nautilus* the flow of water and somewhat gentler swimming movements depend only on contractions of the funnel—a modified foot. Perhaps because of the less vigorous means of ventilation, the *Nautilus* has four pairs of gills while the more active forms operate with two pairs.

Branchial respiration attains its greatest efficiency in the aquatic vertebrates. Hughes and Shelton (1962) have critically reviewed the available information. Only the teleost fish is considered here. Its branchial apparatus exemplifies the specialized features of a highly efficient gill system: extensive and protected respiratory surfaces, a continuous circulation of water over them, and a counter current flow of oxygenated water and deoxygenated blood.

A series of gill filaments is spread like a curtain to separate two chambers, the oral cavity and the opercular cavity (Fig. 4.3). While a fish is breathing quietly, the tips of the hemibranchs on neighboring gill arches meet as shown in Fig. 4.3 to form a complete screen through which water flows from the oral to the opercular cavity. During activity, delicate muscles move the paired filaments on the branchial arches rhythmically and permit some of the water to bypass the interlamellar septa and flow more freely from one chamber to the other; in this way resistance is decreased and damage to the delicate filaments is avoided (Saunders, 1961). The movement of the gill filaments may be especially important during swimming when the mouth is open and water flows directly through it. Some fish (mackerel, for example) do not actively ventilate the gill chamber but, by continuously swimming, maintain a steady current over the gills. In fact, this may be a most efficient means of gas exchange since a constant rate of flow can be maintained over the gills by the degree to which the mouth is opened and since no energy is required to operate respiratory muscles.

The mackerel and its allies are exceptions; branchial irrigation normally depends on the skeletal muscle of the jaws, gill arches and

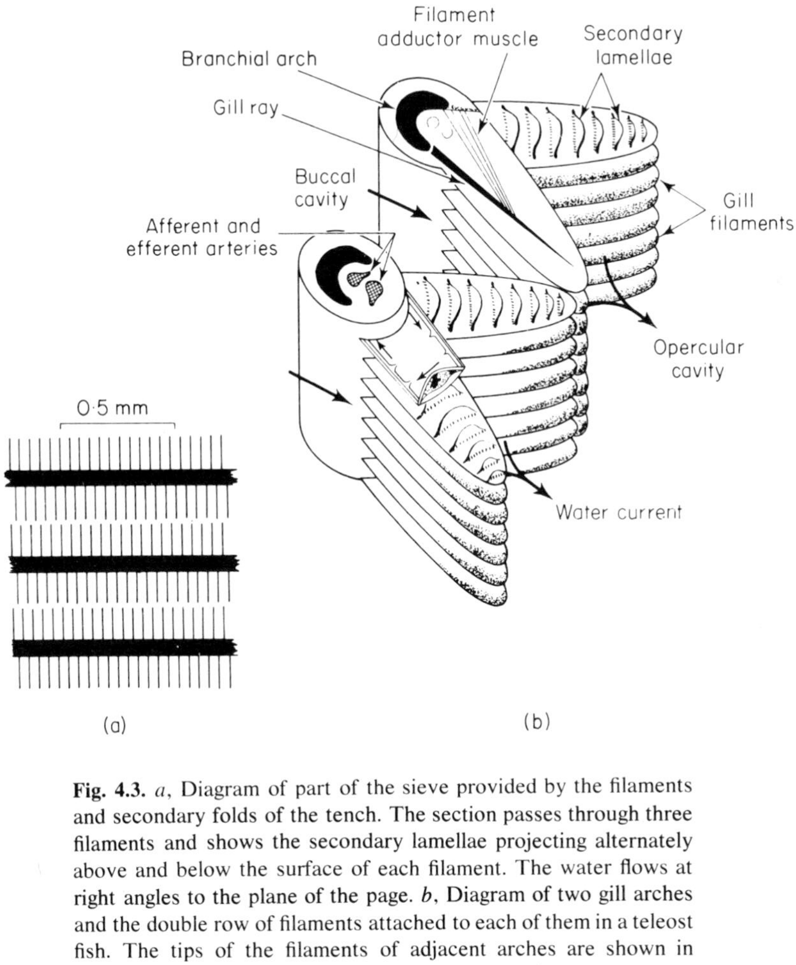

Fig. 4.3. *a*, Diagram of part of the sieve provided by the filaments and secondary folds of the tench. The section passes through three filaments and shows the secondary lamellae projecting alternately above and below the surface of each filament. The water flows at right angles to the plane of the page. *b*, Diagram of two gill arches and the double row of filaments attached to each of them in a teleost fish. The tips of the filaments of adjacent arches are shown in contact with one another. [Hughes and Shelton (1962).]

operculum. The mechanics may be explained in terms of two pumps: a pressure pump in the oral cavity pushing water through the gills and a suction pump posteriorly drawing water over them (Fig. 4.4). As the mouth closes in the breathing rhythm, folds of mucous membrane on the inner surface of the jaws (the oral valves) come into position to prevent an outflow of water anteriorly. Pressure in the oral cavity rises, and as the space is constricted the water is forced back over the gills into the opercular cavity. This is the action of the pressure pump. Opercular movements are also involved. First, the abduction of the opercula takes place while the branchiostegal membranes are closed and thus prevent the entrance of water posteriorly. In this way water is drawn from the oral into the opercular cavity (the suction pump). Then, with the adduction of the opercula, the branchiostegal valves open and the water flows out posteriorly.

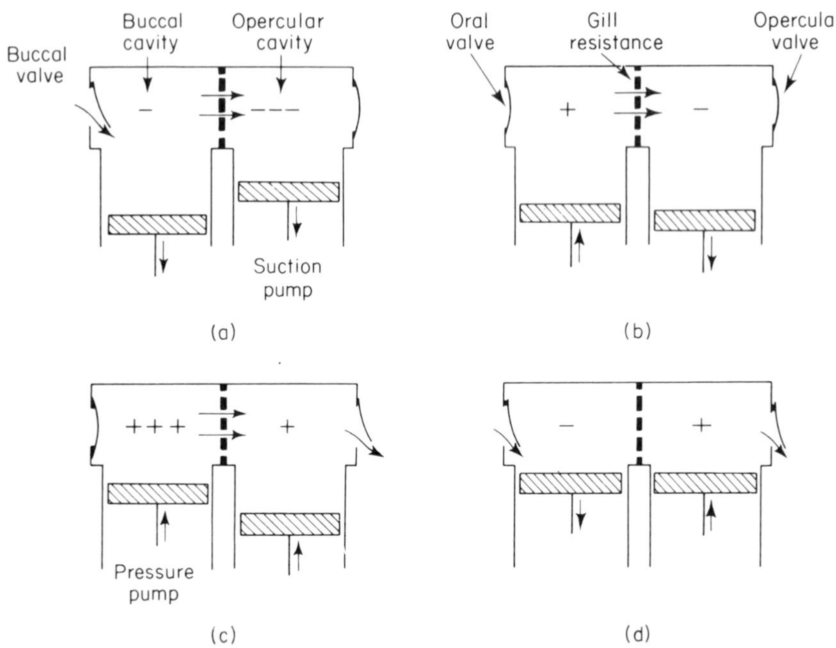

Fig. 4.4 Diagram to illustrate the double pumping mechanism for ventilating the gills of fishes. The two major phases of the cycle are *a* in which the suction pumps are predominant and *c* when the buccal pressure pump forces water across the gills. The two transition phases *b* and *d* each take up only one-tenth of the whole cycle. [Hughes and Shelton (1962).]

Saunders (1961) measured the associated hydrostatic pressure changes by introducing polythene cannulae attached to manometers into the two areas of the branchial pump. His records (Fig. 4.5) show that the pressure in the oral cavity is higher for all, or almost all, of the breathing cycle. Thus, although breathing is rhythmical, there is a continuous flow of water over the gills. These findings are in agreement with those of Hughes and Shelton (1962). Gaseous exchange is still further improved

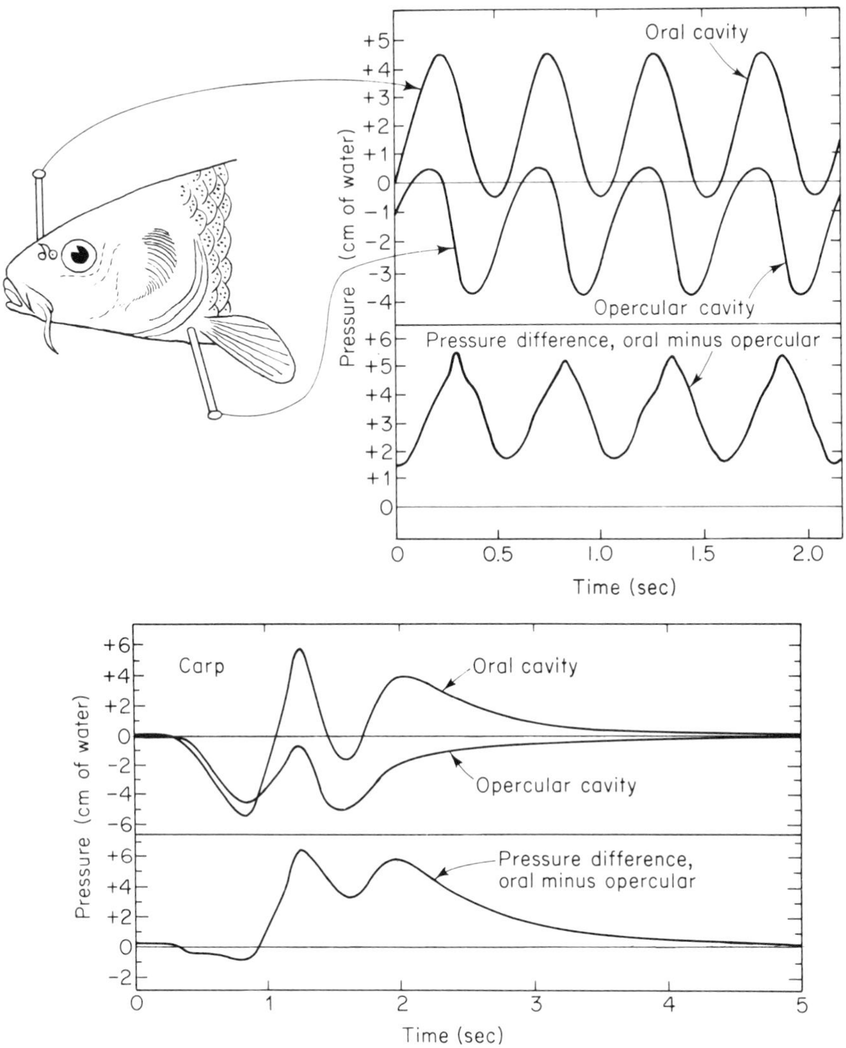

Fig. 4.5. Recordings of the pressures in the oral and opercular cavities of a carp through polythene tubes inserted into these two chambers. Upper graph, when fish was induced to breathe heavily by increasing the ambient carbon dioxide; lower graph, during quiet breathing. [Based on Saunders (1961).]

by the counter current flow of oxygenated water and deoxygenated blood.

Counter current exchangers find a use in several physiological operations and are also well known to engineers and laboratory workers. The principle is simple. Two channels in close proximity carry fluids in opposite directions. If the channel walls are freely permeable to any particular material and if the channels are long enough, equilibria will be established in the concentration of the permeable materials. The diagram in Figure 4.6 shows a hypothetical situation in which the numbers may

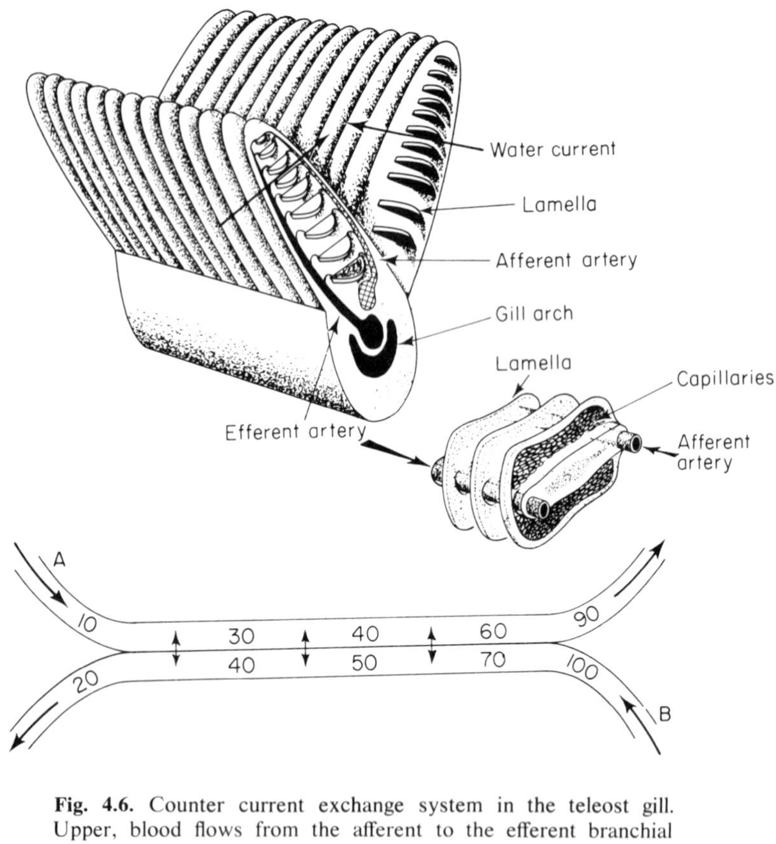

Fig. 4.6. Counter current exchange system in the teleost gill. Upper, blood flows from the afferent to the efferent branchial arteries through the minute vessels in the secondary lamellae; arrows show the direction of water current flowing between the lamellae; lower, diagram of a counter current exchanger.

represent concentrations of oxygen, sodium chloride, temperature or some other identity which moves freely through the wall. If deoxygenated blood were travelling in tube *A* and oxygenated water in tube *B*, then the maximum exchange of oxygen might be expected, and this is precisely the arrangement which occurs in the gills of fishes (Fig. 4.6). The system is extremely efficient, and in some teleosts 85 per cent of the oxygen may be extracted from the water passing over the gills (Saunders, 1962). Exchangers of this type are found in the temperature control system of Arctic animals, in the swim bladder of fishes, in the placenta and in the kidney. They will be referred to again when the physiology of these structures is considered. The principle is the same in each case.

In many teleosts, the efficiency of gaseous exchange can be modified by vascular responses in the gill filaments (Steen and Kruysse, 1964). Two functionally different circulatory paths have been described in the gills of several teleosts; the species represented are so widely separated taxonomically as to suggest that this is a universal feature of the teleost gill. In addition to the respiratory route whereby blood flows through the lamellae, there is also a system of nonrespiratory vessels in the central portion of the filament. The distribution of blood can be altered from one route to the other. Adrenaline favors circulation through the lamellae and, consequently, increases the oxygenation of the blood; acetylcholine has the opposite effect.

The oxygen uptake capacity of the gills differs in various species of fish and in relation to such factors as gill area, rate of ventilation and the oxygen-carrying capacities of the blood and water. Hughes and Shelton (1962) discuss these factors, and further comment is given in Chapter 12.

From Aquatic To Aerial Breathing

The aquatic environment was the first habitat of animal life. The more primitive members of all phyla are aquatic, and several phyla have no truly terrestrial representatives. However, all major phyla—including the purely aquatic ones such as the coelenterates and echinoderms—have representatives which use atmospheric air, even though they do so by way of their aquatic breathing organs (Carter, 1931). Air is the superior source of oxygen (210 ml per liter as compared to 5 to 10 ml per liter in fresh water), and if the additional hazards of terrestrial life (a much less stable environment, subject to desiccation) can be met, the potentialities of active life and aerobic living can be more completely realized. Carter (1931), in an outstanding review, finds that the evolutionary migration from water to land has occurred many times—more frequently than any other change which requires such profound modifications in animal organization. He describes the modes of aerial respiration in the different groups of animals and stresses the evolutionary trends.

There are two aquatic habitats where the ability to utilize atmospheric oxygen has distinct advantages, and these have probably been the geographic points of origin for the major terrestrial groups. One of these is the littoral area which is subject to periodic fluctuations in water level, through either tidal rhythms or seasonal droughts. The other is the area of stagnant water, especially the swampy, shallow tropical bogs and pools where water stagnates and where the dissolved oxygen reaches a low level. It is this latter environment which Carter believes was most forceful in the evolution of terrestrial groups.

Many animals make use of atmospheric oxygen and yet operate an aquatic mode of breathing. This may be done by living near the surface where there is relatively more dissolved oxygen; or the animal may actually come out into the moist air and still rely on cutaneous or gill respiration. Air may also be taken into a body cavity and mixed with the water circulating around the respiratory epithelia. For example, the sea cucumber *Holothuria tubulosa,* which is the only known echinoderm using atmospheric air, rises to the surface (when in stagnant water) and draws air into the rectum where it is used to oxygenate the water in the respiratory tubes. A few of the crustaceans and fishes rely on comparable mechanisms, and from this it is a short step to the development of a moist, vascular respiratory epithelium—usually in some area of the branchial cavity. The mantle of the gastropod, the epithelia of the branchial chambers of crustaceans and fishes, and parts of the gut may thus operate in the exchange of oxygen. These accessory developments are often elaborate and associated with distinctly altered mechanisms for ventilation. For example, in the swamp dwelling teleost, *Pseudapocryptes,* the walls of the oral and branchial chambers are richly vascularized; during ventilation the operculum remains closed and the cavities alternately expand and contract to draw air into and expel it from the mouth (Krogh, 1941).

Cutaneous respiration, the oxygenation of water surrounding the gills, and the special adaptations of gills and gill chambers have never led to marked evolutionary advances in the air breathing machinery. With the possible exception of the gastropod mantle, it may be argued that the evolution of the advanced terrestrial groups has depended on the innovation of special air sacs (lungs) and air tubes (trachea). These are basic to the colonization of the land by the vertebrates and the insects.

Lungs

A lung is a vascularized air sac. The exchange of gases between the environment and the body tissues depends on an intermediate circulating fluid. Morphologically, there is slight distinction between minute tubular lungs, such as the book lung of a spider or the tracheal lung of the chilopod *Scutigera*, and the tracheae of insects; but the gaseous exchange mechanisms are different, since oxygen is transported from lungs by a circulating fluid while it is piped directly to the tissues through tracheal tubes.

Lungs, thus defined, are found in several of the terrestrial invertebrate groups: pulmonate snails, scorpions and some of the spiders, chilopods and isopods. The efficiency of these lungs is restricted by the lack of a ventilating system; the to and fro movements of gases depend only on diffusion. In some forms the size of the lung aperture is altered in relation to activity, temperature and environmental carbon dioxide, but this provides the only control on the system. The movement of fresh air at any distance from the lung opening is slight, and none of the larger terrestrial animals, with their high rates of metabolism, depends on the diffusion type of lung.

VENTILATION LUNGS

Ventilation lungs are characteristic of the terrestrial vertebrates. Coordinated muscle movements create a rhythmic exchange of air, so that gradients remain relatively high in the air spaces even at considerable distances from the external environment. Embryologically, the vertebrate lungs arise from a median groove in the floor of the pharynx. Their morphological phylogeny is "none too certain" (Romer, 1955). Any sacculation of vascular epithelium, open to the air, would be useful to the emerging terrestrial vertebrates. It is probable that primitive fishes experimented with a variety of such structures. Among the present day forms, highly vascular mucous membranes of the mouth and anterior gut, outpocketings and elaborate convolutions of the branchial cavities and sacs which may open dorsally, laterally or ventrally into the gut, suggest something of the varied nature of this experimentation.

In a physiological sense, the phylogeny seems more evident. The amphibian lung, for example, merely supplements the cutaneous and oral exchange of gases, and the respiratory physiology of the successful terrestrial vertebrates has evidently evolved from this sort of beginning. Three interconnected trends are evident: progressive enlargement of the respiratory epithelium, specializations in the machinery for ventilation and the provision of an efficient circulation. These trends reach a somewhat different climax in the birds and mammals.

Surfaces have increased through extensive alveolation. This tendency reaches a climax in the mammals, with limitations set by the bulk of the lungs and the presence of dead air spaces in the minute alveoli. In the human lung, the alveolar carbon dioxide tension reaches about 40 mm Hg, and this is greater than usually found in the most stagnant pond waters. The birds reduced the bulk of the lungs and eliminated the dead air spaces with the evolution of a special system of air sacs.

The bird lung. Like several other avian structures, the lung of the bird is the most specialized organ of its type. Maximum differences in gas tension can never be achieved with the closed alveolar system of mammals. In the bird lung, the alveoli are replaced by air capillaries through which it is theoretically possible to circulate almost fully charged atmospheric air. The operation of this system depends on the presence of nonrespiratory air sacs, connected with the lungs and serving as reservoirs or bellows. About 75 per cent of the inspired air (Krogh, 1941) passes directly into the air sacs, so that the air capillaries are connected by only short distances to tubes containing fully oxygenated air. The morphological phylogeny of the air sacs can be traced from thin-walled, nonrespiratory areas in the lungs of some reptiles. Their significance in the reptiles is unknown, but in the birds they have provided the basis for the evolution of the highly efficient respiratory system required in a flying homeotherm.

The physiological unit of the bird lung is a five- or six-sided cylinder about 1.0 mm in diameter, containing a central air passage—the parabronchus—with numerous radiating tubes—the air capillaries (Fig. 4.7). These minute air capillaries (about 10 μ in diameter) coil and branch in intimate contact with the blood capillaries. In species with high respiratory demands, the air capillaries of one unit anastomose with those of other units; thus the many different units may be interconnected. In less active species connections are absent (Salt and Zeuthen, 1960), but even when absent, the maximum diffusion distances from the parabronchi are not more than 0.3 to 0.4 mm. At both ends the parabronchi join the larger bronchial tubes, and these in turn connect with the air sacs or the outside world through the trachea (Fig. 4.7).

Attempts have been made to measure the flow of air through the parabronchi. This is difficult (Salt and Zeuthen, 1960) and probably varies in different species. The important point is that a flow does occur. The direction of flow may possibly change during the respiratory cycle. Moreover, pulsations have been described in the parabronchi, and these would also serve to ventilate at least a part of the air capillaries in an active manner.

Many of the details of air circulation have not yet been fully described; but it is evident that such a system is extremely efficient and flexible. Bird lungs are small and compact; this economy has been achieved through efficiency in ventilation. Rhythmic movements of the ribs, sternum and associated structures alternately enlarge and restrict the thoracic dimensions to effect inspiration and expiration in a manner comparable to that described below for the mammals. In the birds, however, the action is largely on the air sacs—particularly the thoracic and abdominal sacs. While flying, these movements may be supplemented by the action of the flight muscles on the thin-walled air sacs. Species variations have been described, and the contribution of the flight action to the respiratory demands (indeed, whether it is at all necessary) has not been fully established. This and the problem of temperature regulation and water demands during flight are discussed by Salt and Zeuthen (1960). As one might anticipate in such a highly successful group, the extent of the air sacs and their associated machinery shows many curious modifications related to habitat and behavior.

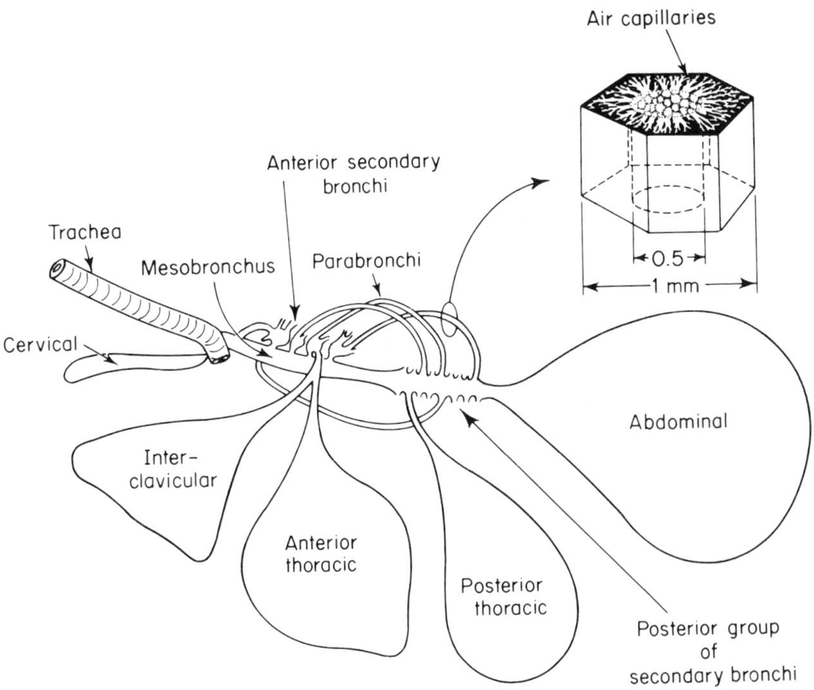

Fig. 4.7. Diagram of one of the units of the bird lung showing the central parabronchus and the net of air capillaries which radiate from it. [Based on Hughes (1963).]

Mechanics of ventilation. Another trend in the evolution of respiratory efficiency among the terrestrial vertebrates is a progressive change in the structures associated with lung ventilation. A frog makes rhythmic movements of the floor of the mouth which only ventilate the moist, vascular epithelium of the buccopharyngeal cavity. At much less frequent intervals, air is swallowed (nares closed, glottis open) and the lungs filled by positive pressure action (force pump). In expiration, the elastic recoil of the lungs, the contraction of the flanks and the lowering of the floor of the mouth with nares closed, forces air out when the glottis is open.

The physiological significance of the buccopharyngeal oscillations has been questioned but it is apparent that this is sometimes quite significant at higher temperatures (Whitford and Hutchinson, 1963). In *Ambystoma*, the volume of air moved through the lungs increases about three-fold between 10° and 25°C, while that moved through the buccopharyngeal cavity increases twenty-five-fold. If the air moved by the buccopharyngeal oscillations were excluded from respiration, the efficiency of the lungs would have to double to account for the increased oxygen consumption at 25°C.

In the higher vertebrates the breathing action is that of a suction pump (negative pressure mechanism) rather than a force pump. The situation is best illustrated by the mammal where the lungs are enclosed in the pleural cavities bounded by the thoracic cage and the dome-shaped diaphragm posteriorly. Inspiration is the active process. Impulses originating in the respiratory center activate the intercostal muscles and the diaphragm. The dome-shaped diaphragm flattens, the ribs are elevated, the space is enlarged and air flows into the lungs. As the muscles relax and the space is restricted, the elastic recoil of the lungs results in a passive expiration of the air.

Circulation combined with ventilation. In birds and mammals a double heart provides for a complete pulmonary as well as a complete systemic circulation of the blood. In this way fully oxygenated blood is supplied to the tissues. The branchial system of fishes also provides fully oxygenated blood to the tissues but, with only a single pump for both respiratory organs and body tissues, the pressures are greatly reduced in the oxygenated supply lines. The comparative anatomy again suggests that the evolving terrestrial forms tried several arrangements before the appearance of the double heart. In a few species (*Saccobranchus*, Fig. 4.8) the air-breathing organs are in parallel with the gills. In theory, this should be quite satisfactory for the amphibious way of life if there is a suitable mechanism for changing from one scheme to the other in association with the habitat. In most fishes, the blood supply to the air bladder is the same as that to the digestive tract from which the air bladder develops. In the lungfishes, an almost completely double circulation is established with two atria, an interventricular septum and a twisted valve in the conus (Foxon, 1955; Hughes, 1963). The evolution of the double circuit in birds and mammals is probably based on the dipnoan heart

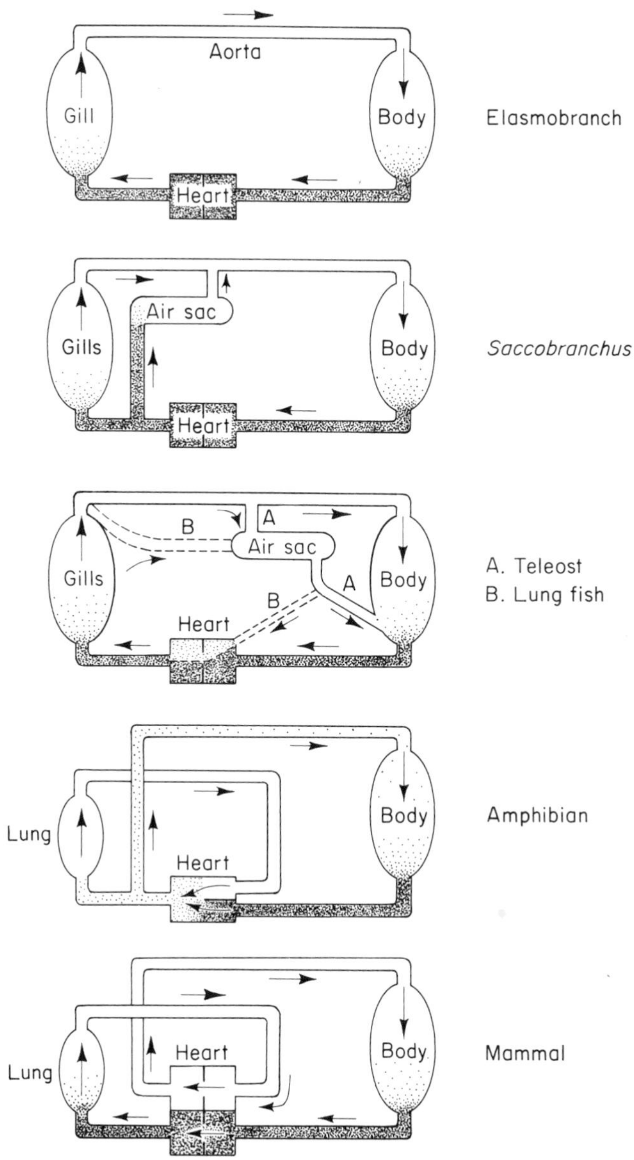

Fig. 4.8. Diagrams of circulation in several different groups of vertebrates.

rather than that of the amphibians (Fig. 4.8). The latter is considered specialized for the reception and distribution of oxygenated blood, both from the lungs and the cutaneous organs of respiration (Foxon, 1964; Chapter 5).

Tracheae

Carter (1961) draws a parallel between the tracheal system of the terrestrial arthropods and a highly divided lung, a lung in which the alveoli have extended throughout the intercellular spaces as a ramiform network of tubes. It serves the dual functions of bringing air into the body and distributing it to the cells; consequently, the respiratory functions of the transport system are no longer required. The pattern of tracheae and air capillaries (tracheoles) is similar to the pattern of blood vessels in other highly successful groups of animals; although, of course, there is not a complete circuit within the system of air tubes.

Air enters the tracheal system through the spiracles. In primitive tracheates (*Peripatus,* some Apterygota), the apertures are permanently open, and there is no control of the movement of air through them. In most forms, however, the spiracles are provided with valves of one type or another, operated by muscles and sometimes provided with filters (Snodgrass, 1935).

The tracheal tubes which lead from the spiracles develop as invaginations of the body surface, and their walls have the general structure of the integument. In the larger tracheae, thickenings (taenidia) in the cuticular layers form a chitinized spiral which permits a stretching of the tubes but prevents their collapse; taenidial support is also present in the smaller tubes although complete helices are absent. The walls of the tracheae become progressively thinner as the tubes become smaller. At a diameter of 2 to 5 μ, the tracheae pass into the air capillaries or tracheoles. These minute channels, less than 1 μ in diameter, are the physiologically important units in gas exchange, even though it seems unlikely that this process is confined entirely to them. Wigglesworth (1942) described a to and fro movement of fluid in the terminal tracheoles, associated with the activity of the organs which they supply (Fig. 4.9). His observation has often been confirmed, although the precise mechanism is still debated. Wigglesworth ascribed it to the formation of tissue metabolites during activity and the withdrawal of water osmotically from the tubes into the interstitial spaces. These minute air capillaries make numerous and intimate contacts with the cells. Contrary to older views, they do not enter the cells but only indent or sink into the plasma membranes of cells with high oxygen demands (Miller, 1964).

The phylogeny of the tracheae is no more certain than that of the lungs. In this case also it is probable that the emerging terrestrial forms experimented with several simple arrangements of air sacs and tubes. Living forms testify to the probable variety. In *Peripatus,* spiracles

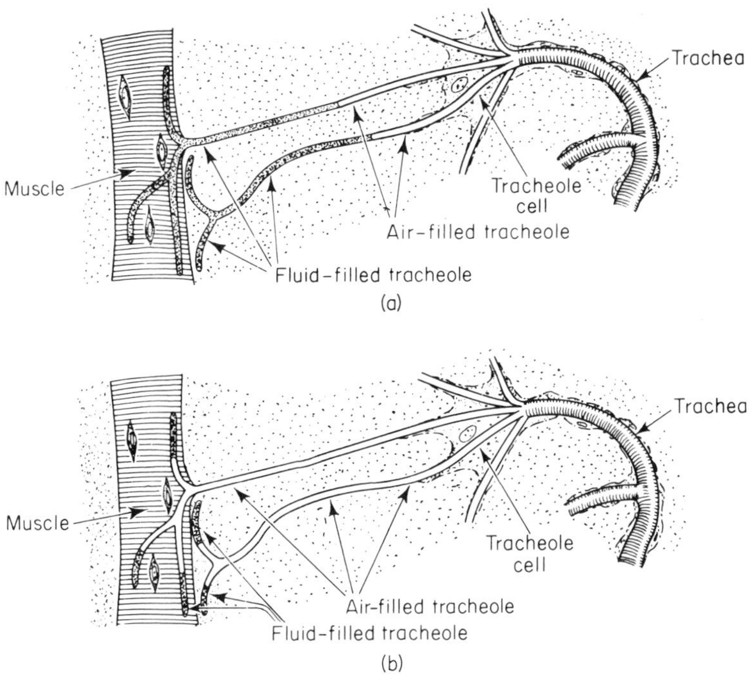

Fig. 4.9. Diagram of movement of liquid in the tracheoles. *a*, Resting. *b*, Active. [Wigglesworth (1930).]

which are permanently open, lead into pits which communicate with bundles of minute tracheae. In some of the terrestrial isopods (*Porcellio, Armadillidium*) tuft-like invaginations of the integument of the exopodites of the pleopods form branching air tubes known as pseudotracheae. Among the arachnids a series of forms suggests an evolution of lung books in the terrestrial scorpions and some spiders from the gill books of the aquatic arachnids (*Limulus*), and subsequently a replacement of the lung books by tracheae. Almost every combination of lung books and tracheae is found among the spiders, from species which depend on lung books to species entirely dependent on tracheae (Kerkut, 1958). However, even among the arachnids some groups (Acarina) are not in this series and show a different kind of tracheal system, while among the insects, where the tracheal system attains its most complete development, there is no evidence of an evolution by way of the lung books. It appears that ectodermal invaginations have formed air tubes in many different anatomical locations, and the segmental ones of the evolving insects were most adaptable.

There is no active ventilation in many of the tracheates. The Onychophora, Myriapoda, tracheate Arachnoidea and the larvae and pupae of all insects depend on simple diffusion for the exchange of gases in the air tubes (Krogh, 1941). Calculations have shown that this is adequate in small and less active forms. However, in the adult insects which sometimes have very high rates of metabolism, there is ventilation of the system and control of the volume of air and the direction of its flow through the system. Three specializations will be considered: the spiracular control, the unidirectional flow of air and the action of air sacs.

Spiracular control is usually present even when there is no ventilation. The hazard of a fully open system of spiracles is evident in *Peripatus*. Although this animal has a dry and much less permeable skin than the earthworm, it loses moisture twice as fast due to the open spiracles scattered over the surface of the body—several in each segment (Kerkut, 1958). Moreover, *Peripatus* loses water forty times as fast as a caterpillar which is also unable to ventilate its tracheae but is able to control its spiracles. A DIFFUSION CONTROL of respiration by the opening and closing of the spiracles is thus effective in the important compromises between water loss and the requirements for air. Wigglesworth (1942) described it in the flea. At rest only two pairs of spiracles operate. They open and close rhythmically at rates which depend on the temperature. If the animal is active, eight pairs of thoracic spiracles remain open until the activity has ceased and the metabolism returns to the resting condition. With a less forceful stimulation of the metabolism, such as occurs during digestion or while the eggs are ripening, the two pairs of spiracles may remain continuously open and the others may rhythmically open and close or, if metabolism so demands, remain open all the time. Thus, although this animal is unable to ventilate its system, there is an adequate control for the conservation of water and the regulation of the air supply in accordance with the demands.

VENTILATION OF THE TRACHEAL SYSTEM

Active ventilation is brought about through movements of the body wall which rhythmically compress the air spaces and force the air out of them. There are several different kinds of movement but the most common are the dorsoventral flattening of the abdomen (grasshoppers, beetles) and the telescoping movements of the abdominal segments (bees and flies). In the insects, contrary to the vertebrates, expiration is the active process; as the terga and sterna are pulled together or the segments are telescoped, the pressure of the rigid exoskeleton on the soft organs of the body forces air from the tracheal system. With the reverse movement, air again flows into the system.

In many forms the flow of air is unidirectional and thus the dead air space is reduced to a minimum. In the grasshopper, for example, it has been demonstrated that the thoracic spiracles are used primarily for inspiration while the air flows out through the abdominal spiracles. However, whether the flow is tidal or streams through the system, only the larger trunks are actively ventilated, and the smaller branches always depend on diffusion and the movements of fluids in the tracheoles.

The efficiency of ventilation is greatly improved in some species by the air sacs. These are balloon-like dilations of the trachea which range in size from tiny vesicles among the leg muscles of some insects to huge sacs in the main air tubes of the Hymenoptera. Their importance in ventilation is unquestioned. As in the birds, air sacs in the insects may serve functions other than respiration, but their primary activity is associated with ventilation (Roeder, 1953; McCutcheon, 1940).

Regulating Mechanisms

Sluggish and sedentary animals may temporarily suspend gaseous exchange and live anaerobically. Their rates of metabolism are low and their tissues capable of tolerating high concentrations of acid metabolites. Bivalves, tube-dwelling worms and a host of invertebrates which live along the sea shores have margins of safety and discontinue the exchange of gases at low tide. Ventilation may be elevated for three or four hours after the flood while waste metabolites are eliminated and a supply of oxygen is accumulated for the next emergency (Chapter 5 and 12). In contrast, active animals such as the vertebrates, many of the arthropods and the cephalopods, cannot withstand anoxia for even a brief period and have special machinery to insure a steady flow of water or air over the respiratory epithelium.

It has already been emphasized that the flow of gases THROUGH the epithelia is a matter of simple diffusion and depends on rapid distribution to the tissues from the internal surface and steady renewal of the air or water on the external surface. Regulation on the tissue side is considered in later chapters. The control of ventilation is discussed here.

Respiratory currents depend on either cilia or skeletal muscles. The former, when used for ventilation, operate mechanisms which provide food as well as oxygen. Unless conditions become intolerable and the animal suspends most of its activities, they work continuously and automatically. A nervous control of ciliated epithelia has been described in several organs (Chapter 19), and the activities of these cilia-driven respiratory currents may also be under nervous control. Their responsiveness to transmitter substances such as acetylcholine and 5-hydroxytryptamine suggests this (Gosselin, 1961). However, a large element of automaticity is certainly present, as evidenced by prolonged and continuous activity of small pieces of ciliated epithelium (lamellibranch gill) when removed from the animal and completely divorced from central nervous control.

The situation is quite different when ventilation depends on skeletal muscle. Whether the animal combines the activities of feeding and ventilation by creating water currents with its appendages (*Branchipus*, *Daphnia*), ventilates a tube or burrow (*Arenicola*), pumps water over gills or moves air into lungs or tracheal tubes, the muscles involved lack automaticity and depend on a flow of impulses from neurons in central ganglia or nerve cords. The phylogeny of oscillatory activity in central neurons which control the respiratory muscles seems to be fundamental to all these controls. Such pacemaking systems have been described in many different animals.

THE PACEMAKERS OF VENTILATION

The pacemaking system in the ventral cord of *Arenicola* has already been mentioned (Fig. 4.1). Wells (1950) removed intact worms from their tubes, pinned them on cork plates submerged in sea water and recorded the worm's movements by a hook passing under the middle of the body and attached to a light lever. Bursts of activity corresponded to the irrigation cycles. Similar results were obtained with longitudinal strips of the body wall containing the ventral nerve cord; the brain was not necessary. Wells concluded that there is a pacemaker in the ventral nerve cord and that this controls the rhythm, although its action can be modified, like that of the heart, by a number of conditions.

In the insects also, physiologists have obtained evidence for pacemaking neurons concerned with the rhythm of ventilation. Inhibition of specific breathing movements occurs when certain nerve ganglia are sectioned; stimulation of specific ganglia modifies breathing, while the rhythmic changes in action potentials of certain ganglia correspond to the respiratory activities. Experiments of this sort with several species of insects have shown the presence of a segmental control of the spiracles and respiratory rhythm with higher coordinating centers in the thoracic ganglia. It has also been shown that the isolated nerve cord of the praying mantis produces rhythmic bursts of action potentials which occur with the same frequency as the normal resting movements of ventilation (Roeder, 1953).

It has long been known that the hind brain of the vertebrate contains groups of neurons which are required for rhythmical breathing. Lesions in various parts of the brain show that the breathing centers are located in the medulla. In the skate, for example, only the medulla is involved in the motor control. There are bilateral groups of neurons; the two sides operate independently with control for the spiracle and first gill arch clearly separated from that which regulates the last four gill arches (Healey, 1957). Similarly, in the mammal there are several centers or subcenters in the hind brain (the pneumotaxic and apneustic center in the pons and the medullary centers) concerned with ventilation (Ruch and Fulton, 1960). Lesions in these different areas show that their neurons are concerned with the regulation of breathing.

Further evidence for centrally located pacemakers of respiration is found in the electrical activity associated with these neurons. More than thirty years ago, Adrian recorded rhythmic action potentials from the isolated hind brain of the goldfish and found that this corresponded to respiratory movements (Adrian and Buytendijk, 1931). In anaesthetized fish it has also been possible to insert microelectrodes and record oscillating potentials which correspond to breathing movements. These early experiments have been carefully repeated in recent years, and the results are consistent with the earlier findings of an autonomous activity in the respiratory center of teleost fishes (Healey, 1957; Hughes and Shelton, 1962). Numerous experiments of the same sort have been carried out on the higher vertebrates.

Thus, evidence from several lines and many different groups of animals indicates that ventilation depends on autonomous pacemakers in groups of central neurons. The mechanism which generates this rhythmic respiratory activity is unknown although several theories have been considered (Ruch and Fulton, 1960; Hughes and Shelton, 1962).

The activities of these pacemakers are modified by reflexes, set in action by sensory impulses arising primarily from chemical and pressure stimuli. In addition, both pacemakers and the effector organs of ventilation (cilia or muscles) sometimes show direct responses to thermal or chemical changes in their surroundings.

CHEMICAL REGULATION OF RESPIRATION

Structures concerned with ventilation have evolved in response to the demands for oxygen and the necessity of removing waste metabolites, particularly carbon dioxide. It follows then that levels of oxygen and carbon dioxide (through feedback mechanisms) provide reliable cues for the regulation of ventilation. This has been abundantly demonstrated in a wide variety of animals at many different levels in phylogeny. Only a few examples can be given here.

Tubifex, a minute, thread-like oligochaete worm, shows a series of interesting behavioral responses to changes in the gas tensions of its environment (Krogh, 1941). These small animals and some of their immediate relatives live in the mud at the bottom of stagnant pools. With a depletion of the oxygen they extend their bodies by more than ten times and, by wriggling, improve the circulation of the surrounding water. Some species avoid asphyxiation in extreme conditions by swimming toward the surface. Many other animals make equally effective responses. The bivalve pumps more water through its mantle cavity; the movement of the respiratory appendages of the crustacean is more rapid; the pumping action is augmented in the tracheal system of the insect; ventilation of the gills of fishes and the rate of breathing of birds and mammals have all been shown to change in relation to the oxygen and carbon dioxide tensions of the environment. Many curious examples are known. The male three-spined stickleback (*Gasterosteus aculeatus*) for example, incubates the eggs by creating a water current through his nest with a rapid movement of the pectoral fins (fanning) and the intensity of this fanning activity is dependent on the CO_2 produced by the developing embryos.

These varied responses are appropriate to the life of the animal but, in detail, may be quite different even in closely related species. Thus, although carbon dioxide frequently stimulates respiratory activities, it may be without any effect as in some of the crustaceans (Prosser and Brown, 1961), or it may depress respiratory activity. When the bivalve is forced to close its shell and when acid metabolites accumulate in the tissues, the cilia–on which respiration depends–become inactive. This is a characteristic response of cilia to lowered pH and provides an appropriate adjustment in an animal which must conserve energy when its filtering machinery is not operating. Again, terrestrial birds respond to elevated carbon dioxide by more rapid ventilation; but diving birds, most appropriately, show apnea (cessation of respiratory movements) under similar conditions of CO_2 stimulation. In this way, the respiratory center is not excited when the birds are gathering food under water and the carbon dioxide accumulates in the respiratory passages (Salt and Zeuthen, 1960).

Even in the same animal entirely different reflexes may sometimes appear with changes in tensions of the same gas. *Erythrinus unitaeniatus,* a fresh-water fish found in swamps of northern South America, provides an interesting example (Carter, 1957). This animal depends on its gills when the water is well-oxygenated but can use its air-bladder as a lung and breathe at the surface when the water is stagnant. Its complete oxygen demand may be met from the air or the water, but under certain conditions both sources of oxygen are used, and the animals make periodic excursions to the surface so that the air sac supplements the gills (intermediate respiration). Willmer (1934) was able to modify the breathing behavior experimentally. If the oxygen of the water fell below 1.5 ml per liter the gill opening closed and the animal became a terrestrial breather; this same response was obtained when the CO_2 was elevated above 35 ml per liter. These reactions are obviously appropriate but Willmer also found that the animal closed its gill openings and breathed air when the CO_2 tension fell below 5 ml per liter. He concluded that a certain minimum level of CO_2 was necessary for activity of the respiratory center (as it is in the mammal) and that if the blood becomes too alkaline there is no excitation of the branchial breathing apparatus and the animal uses air. Thus, it is evident that the changing levels of CO_2 in the blood of this animal not only control the rate of respiration but also control a series of reflexes which signal gill breathing at certain levels and lung ventilation at others.

The carotid and aortic bodies. Although the responses to changes in oxygen and CO_2 are well known, the details of the controls have not often been analyzed. For example, it is frequently not known whether the effective stimulus is elevated CO_2 or depressed pH or lack of oxygen, while the precise receptor cells and details of the reflexes have rarely been described. These controls are best understood in the mammal, but even here there are still some uncertainties after years of careful study.

If one rebreathes a small volume of air by holding a tight rubber bag around the mouth and nose, ventilation is soon noticeably accelerated. When the CO_2 rises to 3–5 per cent and the O_2 falls to about 17 per cent this increase is marked. If the expired CO_2 is absorbed by some agent such as soda lime, then the effects are not noted until the O_2 falls to about 14 per cent; if the oxygen tension is kept at the normal level of 21 per cent or higher but CO_2 is permitted to accumulate, then hyperpnea air. Simple experiments such as these long ago demonstrated the excita- (increased ventilation) again develops as in the rebreathing of normal tory nature of CO_2 on the rate of breathing, and it was concluded that this response was of more significance in removing excess CO_2 than it was in meeting an oxygen emergency (Haldane, 1927; Haldane and Priestley, 1935). The importance of oxygen in the regulation of respiration was not fully appreciated until the classical experiments of Heymans and his associates focussed attention on the carotid and aortic bodies as chemical receptor areas of great significance, not only in ventilation but also in cardiovascular responses (Heymans and Neil, 1958). In 1938, Heymans was awarded a Nobel prize for these discoveries.

The carotid bodies of the mammal are small nodules of vascular and neurosensory tissue (diameter, 2–5 mm in the human adult) lying near the fork of the common carotid, supplied by carotid blood and receiving fibers from the cervical sympathetic, the glossopharyngeal and vagus nerves. The aortic body situated near the arch of the aorta is similar in structure and function. These bodies have not been found in the fishes and amphibia, but homologous cells have been described in some reptiles; the carotid body is well known in birds although its location differs slightly from that of the mammal (Adams, 1958). Embryologically these tissues arise from the aortic arches and their functional phylogeny may be based on chemoreceptors in the branchial vessels of fishes.

If the carotid and aortic bodies are perfused with a physiological saline solution, predictable effects are noted with alterations in the oxygen and carbon dioxide tensions or in the pH of the perfusion fluid. Ventilation increases markedly with lowered oxygen tension and, to a lesser degree, with elevated CO_2 and depressed pH. These responses disappear with denervation of the perfused bodies, thus indicating the reflex nature of the respiratory responses. This is also evidenced in the changing pattern of action potentials of the intact nerves in response to alterations in the perfusate. The receptors are particularly sensitive to oxygen, and although responses to elevated CO_2 and depressed pH can be demonstrated, this is only possible at relatively high levels of acidity. Whereas the respiratory centers of the mammal often respond to CO_2 changes of as little as 1 mm Hg partial pressure or even less, it requires something of the order of 10 mm to excite the centers by way of the peripheral chemoreceptor system. Thus, in the intact animal, the carotid and aortic bodies contain the important receptor cells for lowered oxygen, while the effects of elevated bicarbonate ion and other acid metabolites are directly on the centers in the medulla (Ruch and Fulton, 1960).

Peripheral chemoreceptors have been described in other groups of vertebrates, but in no case are the details well known. In several fishes increased respiration has been recorded when the CO_2 rises or the O_2 decreases in the water flowing over the gills; but neither the peripheral receptors nor the reflex pathways have been identified. The literature has been reviewed and the problem carefully discussed by Hughes and Shelton (1962). The evidence for chemosensitive cells in the medulla of fishes is good. In birds, the excitability of the medullary respiratory centers to CO_2 is well known and in addition, CO_2 receptors are recognized in the lungs and upper respiratory passages; but changes in response to lowered oxygen in the bird's blood are said to be slight (Salt and Zeuthen, 1960).

PRESSORECEPTORS AND VENTILATION REFLEXES

In 1868, Hering and Breuer, two Austrian scientists, reported an inhibition of respiration with distension of the lungs. This reflex, called the Hering–Breuer reflex, was carefully analyzed a few years later by Head, using a slip of rabbit diaphragm which can be freed sufficiently to record its contractions without disturbing the circulation or innervation (Bard, 1961). His experiment is interesting. It will be recalled that ventilation in the mammal consists of an inspiration involving contraction (hence posterior movement) of the dome shaped diaphragm and an elevation of the ribs to enlarge the thoracic cavity; air flows into the lungs. Head found that the contractions of the strips of rabbit diaphragm were inhibited by distension of the lungs; alternatively, as long as the lungs were collapsed the diaphragm muscle remained contracted. In short, there is a reflex control of breathing which depends on stretch receptors in the lung alveoli; when stimulated, these discharge volleys of vagal impulses to the inspiratory centers of the medulla, and inspiration is inhibited. Action potentials in the vagus have been recorded in relation to this stretching of the lung alveoli. A rhythmic control is maintained with an excitation of the respiratory muscles which are periodically inhibited by the Hering–Breuer reflex. In addition to the pressoreceptors of the lungs, there is a system of stretch receptors in the adventitia of the aorta, common carotids and carotid sinus which plays a prominent part in the regulation of blood pressure but also modifies respiratory rhythm. The carotid sinus system is discussed with the control of mammalian circulation in the next chapter. Here it is noted that respiration is adjusted with blood pressure by means of this system of tension receptors.

Such detailed investigations have not yet been carried out on other animals, but there is evidence for comparable mechanisms in several different groups. The effects of altered CO_2 and oxygen were mentioned earlier, and this seems to form a part of many self-regulating respiratory mechanisms. Pressure receptors, associated with the Hering–Breuer type of reflex, have also been described in some fishes and higher invertebrates. Recent work on the dogfish indicates that the inflation of the pharynx reflexly inhibits inspiration. The experimental evidence comes from sectioning or stimulating the IX, X and prespiracular branch of the VII cranial nerves, from inflation of air-filled balloons in the pharynx and from the recording of action potentials from the branchial nerves (Satchell, 1959; Satchell and Way, 1962). Fingerlike (branchial) processes lining the internal openings of the gill pouches are richly supplied with proprioceptors responsible for the sensory discharge via the vagus to inhibit respiration. Satchell (1960) also described a coordination of the respiratory and cardiac rhythms (branchiocardiac reflex) which seems to adjust the flow of blood in the gills so as to effect maximum oxygenation. A similar relationship has been described in the teleost (Shelton and Randall, 1962). Hughes and Shelton (1962) discuss the physiological significance of this reflex.

Ventilation of the mantle cavity of the cephalopod is also a highly coordinated process depending on rhythmic contractions of skeletal muscle. Neurons are located in the pleurovisceral ganglia and a well-defined giant fiber system controls the contractions of the mantle. The anatomy has been carefully described and a Hering-Breuer type of reflex assumed to operate but the details remain to be established (Kerkut, 1958; Morton, 1958).

In summary, more than a hundred years of careful study of mammalian ventilation has demonstrated a series of pacemaking neurons in the hind brain which are indispensable to breathing. These generate oscillating volleys of impulses which, in turn, rhythmically stimulate the diaphragm and intercostal muscles. A series of interlocking and stabilizing mechanisms control the rate and precision of oscillation through information arising in effector organs (stretch receptors in the lungs) and in the blood (oxygen, carbon dioxide and the acid metabolites). The comparative physiologist finds equivalent pacemaking neurons and rhythmically controlled reflexes in the lower vertebrates and the more specialized invertebrates. Rhythmic movements of ventilation seem to be regulated by similar machinery at different levels in phylogeny from the polychaete worms to the mammals.

5

The Internal Fluid Environment and its Circulation

In many small animals the nutritive molecules, respiratory gases and waste metabolites diffuse readily through the intercellular spaces. No special arrangements are required for their transport. Likewise, some rather large animals because of their primitive organization or low rates of metabolism lack a circulatory system. The coelenterates and flatworms have achieved considerable size and complexity with little more than a highly branched and ramifying gut or gastrovascular cavity which combines some of the functions of a circulatory system with the digestive machinery; the echinoderms have such a low rate of metabolism that an active circulation does not appear to be essential. However, the majority of multicellular animals because of bulk, activity and the associated metabolic demands require a continuous and reliable circulation of body fluids which are specialized to transport nutrients and gases to tissues located remotely from the source of supply. The coelenterate or platyhelminth plan would never suffice for an elaborate organ such as the vertebrate eye or kidney. At any rate, it is hard to imagine how such specialized cells and tissues could be associated with masses of closely applied gastrovascular tubes to form an efficient photoreceptor or compact excretory organ. The evolution of a transport system was essential to the phylogeny of the highly complex organ-systems of the higher animals.

Vascular Channels

Embryologically, the hemal channels appear first as a series of spaces in the mesenchymal tissue. These coalesce, extend and gradually differentiate into the vascular system characteristic of any particular species. Mesenchymal cells included in these spaces and channels become the first blood cells. Phylogenetically, the primitive vascular system must have become organized in a similar manner. Many of the present-day flatworms do not possess vascular channels or even sinuses and lacunae in the mesoderm but transfer nutrients, respiratory gases and wastes by simple diffusion. In others, however, a definite system is present, consisting of several longitudinal tubes on each side of the body which give off blind branches to the intestinal crura, the reproductive organs and the suckers (Fig. 5.1). These tubes are lined with

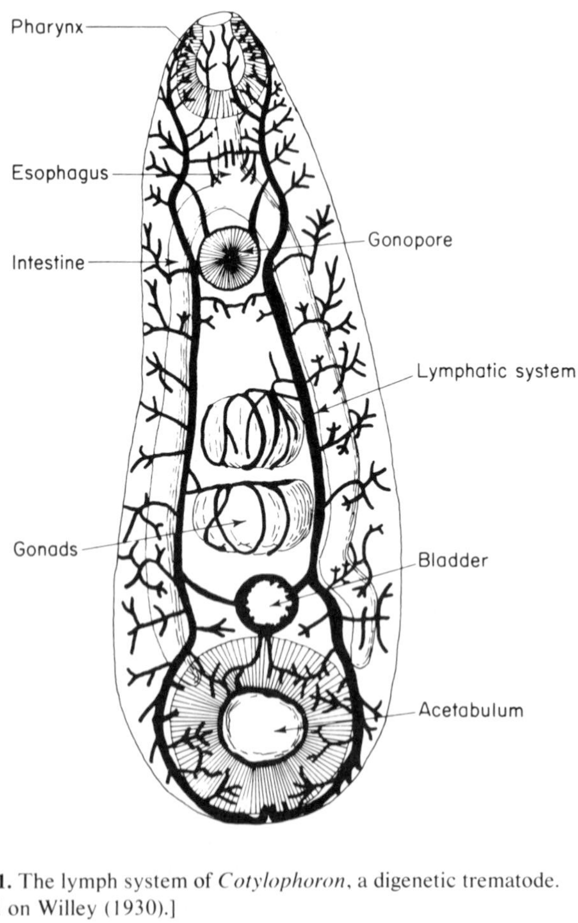

Fig. 5.1. The lymph system of *Cotylophoron*, a digenetic trematode. [Based on Willey (1930).]

flattened mesenchyme and contain a lymph with some cellular elements arising from the neighboring mesenchyme. There is no special means of circulating the fluid, but it moves gently to and fro with the activities of the animal and thus expedites the diffusion of food, gases, and excretory products.

Hemal spaces and channels are not the only mesodermal cavities of the multicellular animal. Within the massive layers of mesoderm a series of spaces are necessary, not only for the circulation of fluids, the distribution of fuel and gases and the removal of wastes, but also to provide space within which large visceral organs can achieve an independence of movement and through which excretory products and genital cells may find ready exits. These spaces or body cavities are related in one way or another to the vascular channels. Two patterns are found in the animal kingdom. In one, the major perivisceral space—referred to as the PRIMARY BODY CAVITY—is, in fact, a persistent blastocoel which has not been obliterated by the expanding mesoderm. This space, in an animal such as the arthropod, becomes an enlarged blood sinus, the hemocoel. The coelomic spaces proper (cavities in the mesoderm) are restricted to the gonads and excretory organs (Fig. 5.2). In the second pattern, an extensive SECONDARY BODY CAVITY (true COELOM) develops between two layers of mesoderm (mesothelium) and expands to obliterate the primary body cavity or blastocoel (Fig. 5.2). The coelomic spaces thus formed are only indirectly connected with the vascular channels and are intimately related to the urogenital drainage systems (Chapter 8). In animals belonging to this second group, hemal channels are organized in the mesoderm as a system of continuously connected closed channels.

Thus, two distinct arrangements of circulatory channels characterize the highly organized groups of animals. Arthropods, most molluscs and several groups of lesser animals have an OPEN SYSTEM in which there are no small blood vessels or capillaries connecting the arteries with the veins. Nets of minute sinuses or capillaries are found in some places such as the wings of insects or the gills of crayfish. However, these are interposed at some point in a blood sinus (insect wing) or located at the ends of arteries (cerebral ganglion and green gland of crayfish) or along certain veins (Fig. 4.2). They do not form a closed network between arteries and veins, and the arterial blood, sooner or later, passes into sinuses (large spaces) or lacunae (small spaces), so that the circulating fluids bathe the major organs and tissues. From these tissue spaces the fluids slowly work their way back into the open ends of the veins or the ostia opening into the heart. In these open systems the organs lie directly in the blood-filled hemocoel or in a primary body cavity. In the second type of system the animals (vertebrates, annelids and a few other groups of invertebrates) have a completely CLOSED SYSTEM of blood channels.

A continuous network of minute capillaries unites the smaller arteries with the veins. Fluids filter through the walls of the capillaries into the tissue spaces and thus transfer nutrients to the cells (Fig. 5.3 and 5.8).

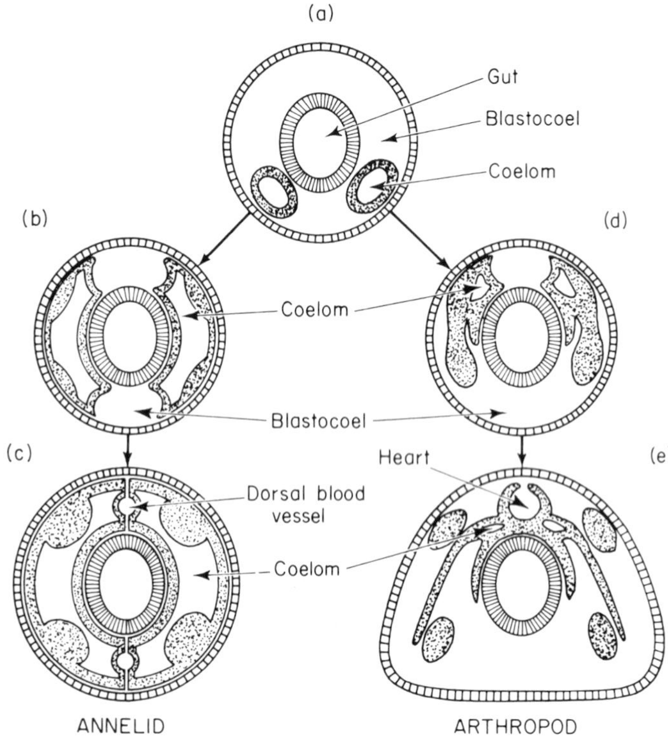

Fig. 5.2. Cross-sectional diagrams to show the relations of the body cavities in annelids and arthropods. *a*, Early embryonic condition. *b* and *c*, The blastocoel persists only in the dorsal and ventral blood vessels and the coelom becomes the secondary body cavity. *d* and *e*, The coelom remains small and the blastocoel persists as the hemocoel or primary body cavity. [Ramsay (1952).]

Vascular Fluids

In this discussion the body fluids will be referred to as TISSUE FLUIDS or LYMPH, BLOOD and HEMOLYMPH. Invertebrates which lack a circulatory system possess tissue fluids or lymph (Latin, *lympha*—clear water) surrounding their cells and forming minute lakes of watery solution with relatively low protein content, some salts, nutritive materials and wastes.

Primitive blood cells (largely phagocytic in nature) float in this lymph or move through the tissue spaces. Animals with a closed circulatory system maintain a distinct separation between the blood (a tissue composed of cells and fluid plasma) and the tissue fluids. The latter are formed by filtration through the walls of the capillaries into the intercellular spaces

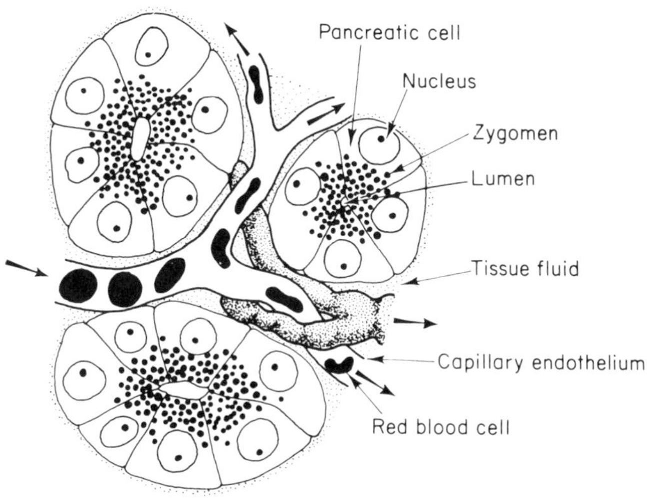

Fig. 5.3. The interrelations of the three vascular fluids in most vertebrates. Fine stipple, tissue fluid; clear, blood; close stipple, lymph as seen in a section of pancreas. [Cowdry (1950).]

under hydrostatic pressures. The filtrate is essentially noncolloidal (about 0.85 per cent protein content in man) and is in part returned to the circulatory system by a special system of channels, the lymphatics. In the higher vertebrates, these lymphatics commence blindly in the tissues and empty into the veins. Thus, a distinct separation between the interstitial fluids and the contents of the lymphatics (lymph) is maintained (Fig. 5.3). The invertebrates and fishes other than the teleosts lack proper lymphatics, although sinuses in the tissues may connect with the veins and foreshadow the development of this system. Some of the teleosts and amphibians exemplify intermediate conditions with many of the terminal lymphatics arising from tissue spaces (Young, 1962). In these animals tissue fluids and lymph proper are sometimes in direct continuity.

These varied arrangements make it illogical for the comparative physiologist to maintain a rigid distinction between tissue fluid and lymph. In all cases the lymph is derived from tissue fluids, whether it enters the lymphatics by diffusing through their walls or flows in through terminal openings. Further, in the open circulatory system, the distinction between blood and lymph or tissue fluid breaks down completely. The same fluids move through vascular channels and tissue spaces, and the term hemolymph seems justified. Hyman (1951), however, refers to this also as lymph and includes the coelomic fluids and contents of other fluid spaces under the same term. In this book the terms blood, hemolymph, tissue fluid and lymph will be retained as useful terms for somewhat different body fluids.

The morphology of blood cells is described in textbooks of comparative histology and anatomy; the composition of the fluids can be found in reference books of biochemistry. These topics will not be considered here; mechanisms concerned with the circulation of the fluids will be outlined in this chapter and several specialized characteristics of vascular fluids in the next.

Hemodynamics

Hemodynamics is the study of blood flow and blood pressure. Many of the principles involved are the purely physical principles of the movement of viscous fluids (water, plasma, lymph) or "plastic" fluids (blood, a suspension of cells) through tubular channels. These physical principles are elaborated in textbooks of mammalian physiology. Here the concern is less with the fluid and how its physical properties affect the flow but more with the specializations of the tubular system and the various ways in which it has been modified to meet the demands of an efficient circulation.

Locomotion and the associated movements of the body provide sufficient agitation of the body fluids in a coelenterate, a flatworm and some of the small animals in more advanced phyla. It is also the main propulsive force in some relatively large animals (certain leeches and echinoderms); the pressure in the body cavity of a holothurian increases from a low of about 1 mm Hg to a high of 25 or 30 mm Hg during activity (Table 5.1). Moreover, at all stages in phylogeny, locomotion is an important adjunct in hemodynamics; the massaging action of muscles on thin-walled veins and lymphatics is essential to the venous return in the appendages of higher vertebrates.

In most animals, locomotion is only subsidiary to a group of mechanisms which actively force the blood through special channels. A gentle stirring of fluids in a series of diffuse channels would be wholly inadequate to maintain the necessary exchanges in a bulky animal depending on different kinds of highly specialized tissues. From the nemertean worm to the vertebrate animal, the blood vessels are usually reinforced with muscle. In the primitive circulation, widespread propulsive force, due to the peristaltic activity of these muscles, moves the blood in a rather haphazard manner through its vascular channels. In a specialized circulation, the contractile force is localized in one or more rhythmically pulsating areas (hearts); the flow is directed throughout the system by a series of valves, and the pressures are steadily maintained (both during cardiac contraction and relaxation) by the operation of the pumps in a closed series of highly elastic tubes.

Physically, the movement of viscous fluids through extremely small and lengthy tubes requires considerable force. Frictional resistance increases with the length and the complexity of the tubular net. Pressure is also essential in the discharge of several associated physiological demands. For example, kidneys usually operate partly as filters; it is the high pressure in the vascular channels which forces the noncolloidal molecules through the lining of the blood vessels and associated membranes into the capsular spaces (Fig. 8.13). Likewise, the intercellular fluids, which ultimately carry the nutritive molecules to the cells, are driven through the capillary endothelia by the hydrostatic pressures in the blood channels (Fig. 5.8). These demands have become progressively more acute in the evolution of large active animals such as the cephalopod molluscs among the invertebrates and the birds and mammals among the vertebrates. The phylogenetic trend is toward mechanisms which provide a continuous blood flow at constant high pressures. Elaborate controls are necessary for the coordination of many interrelated physiological events.

PERISTALSIS AND "THE EBBING AND FLOWING" OF VASCULAR FLUIDS

Galen (A.D. 131–201) the towering biological authority of antiquity, failed to understand a circulation of the blood. He visualized an ebbing and flowing in the great blood vessels of the body—between the heart and the viscera where NATURAL SPIRITS were formed; between the heart and the brain which was the locus of ANIMAL SPIRIT formation: and between the heart and the VITAL SPIRITS which came from the outside world through the windpipe and the lungs (Singer, 1959). Fourteen centuries passed before William Harvey (1578–1657), using simple demonstrations and logical arguments, corrected these ideas and proved the existence of a completely closed circulation. Harvey argued from his observations of the beating heart, from simple experiments on the direction of the flow of blood in the veins and from calculations of the volume of blood ejected from the left ventricle, that a closed and complete circulation was logical even though he could not see the connecting links.

He drew on his knowledge of the lower vertebrates with a single ventricle (fish, frog) to support his assumption that blood is transferred from veins to arteries by the heartbeat. Thus, he combined comparative anatomical and physiological observation and used quantitative data to test the validity of his hypothesis (Bard, 1961). His book, published in 1628, remains one of the outstanding scientific contributions of all time and a landmark in comparative as well as in medical physiology.

Since Harvey's time the circulation of the blood has not been seriously questioned in most animals. However, the ebbing and flowing of blood does occur in some of the more primitive forms, and a discussion of hemodynamics can be conveniently introduced with a cursory description of the circulation in the annelid *Nereis* which shows a somewhat Galenic circulation, at least in its parapodia (Ramsay, 1952).

Peristalsis is the most primitive mechanism for the movement of the contents of tubular organs. A wave of muscle contraction, sometimes preceded by a wave of relaxation, progresses for variable distances along the tube and slowly forces the contents in the direction of the wave; activity in the embryonic vertebrate heart starts in this way. In *Nereis*, long peristaltic waves, involving the entire length of the dorsal blood vessel, squeeze the blood forward dorsally while waves in the connecting segmental vessels drive it ventrally into an intestinal network (Fig. 5.4). It finds its way by a rather haphazard course into the noncontractile ventral vessel which carries it passively backward. In each segment there is a rich supply of blood to the parapodia which are important

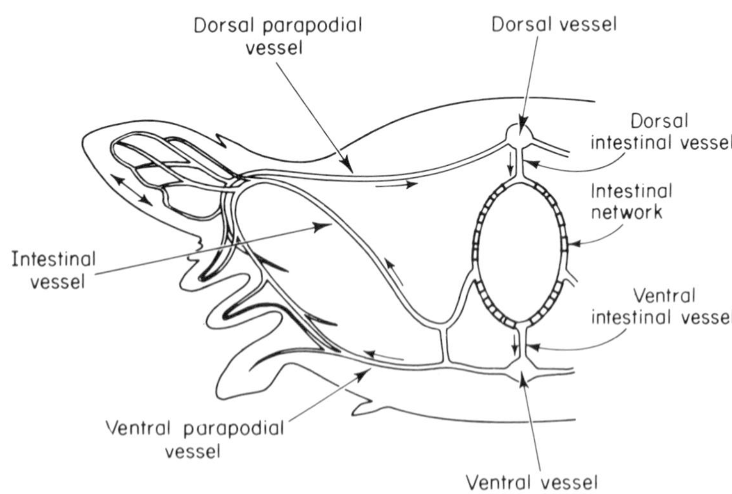

Fig. 5.4. Cross section through *Nereis* at the level of a parapodium to show the arrangement of the major blood vessels. [Ramsay (1952).]

organs of gaseous exchange. This parapodial circulation also links ventral with dorsal channels. A ventral parapodial and an intestinal vessel move the blood outward from the intestinal network while a dorsal parapodial vessel returns it to the dorsal aorta. Peristaltic waves in these main vessels carry the blood in the appropriate direction. Within the highly vascularized parapodia, however, there is no definite direction to the circulation. On the contrary, alternating contractions and relaxations result in an "ebbing and flowing" of the fluids much as Galen had postulated for the mammal. In *Nereis*, the blood does regularly flow forward in the dorsal vessel and backward in the ventral vessel, but beyond this the pattern is ill defined and in the parapodia results in an "ebb and flow" rather than a circulation.

VASCULAR PUMPS

As in any physical system, so also in the animal body, the efficient circulation of fluid through a series of pipes depends in large measure on the pumping arrangements. In both cases there are obvious advantages with larger pumps for more elaborate and longer systems and in the use of centralized pumping stations with auxiliary pumps at strategic points where additional flow or more reliable control is required. The annelid worms provide a primitive example. In the earthworm *Lumbricus* the peristaltic activity of the dorsal valvular vessel carries the blood forward as in *Nereis*, but a series of five specialized pairs of anterior segmental vessels (hearts) connect the dorsal to the ventral vessel in the esophageal region. These are rhythmically contractile and provide the main propulsive force of the entire circulation.

The hearts of arthropods. The arthropods show a high level of organization in which circulation is maintained in an open system. Some of the smaller representatives (*Cyclops*, for example) do not possess a heart or a proper circulation of the blood. The hemolymph is only gently stirred by the movements of the gut and body musculature. The majority of the arthropods, however, depend on the rhythmical contractions of the dorsal blood vessel or a heart which is a specialized area of the dorsal vessel. These hearts are single chambers with heavily reinforced walls containing striated muscle (Fig. 5.5). They may be tubular and extend for a considerable length of the body (*Branchipus, Artemia*, Insecta) or pulsating muscular sacs as in the crustaceans (Maynard, 1960). In any case, the major artery is directed anteriorly and carries the hemolymph forward; it returns through lateral ostia and sometimes posterior veins (Fig. 5.6).

Auxiliary hearts are often present in the arthropods. These differ from the auxiliary hearts of the molluscs and the vertebrates (except

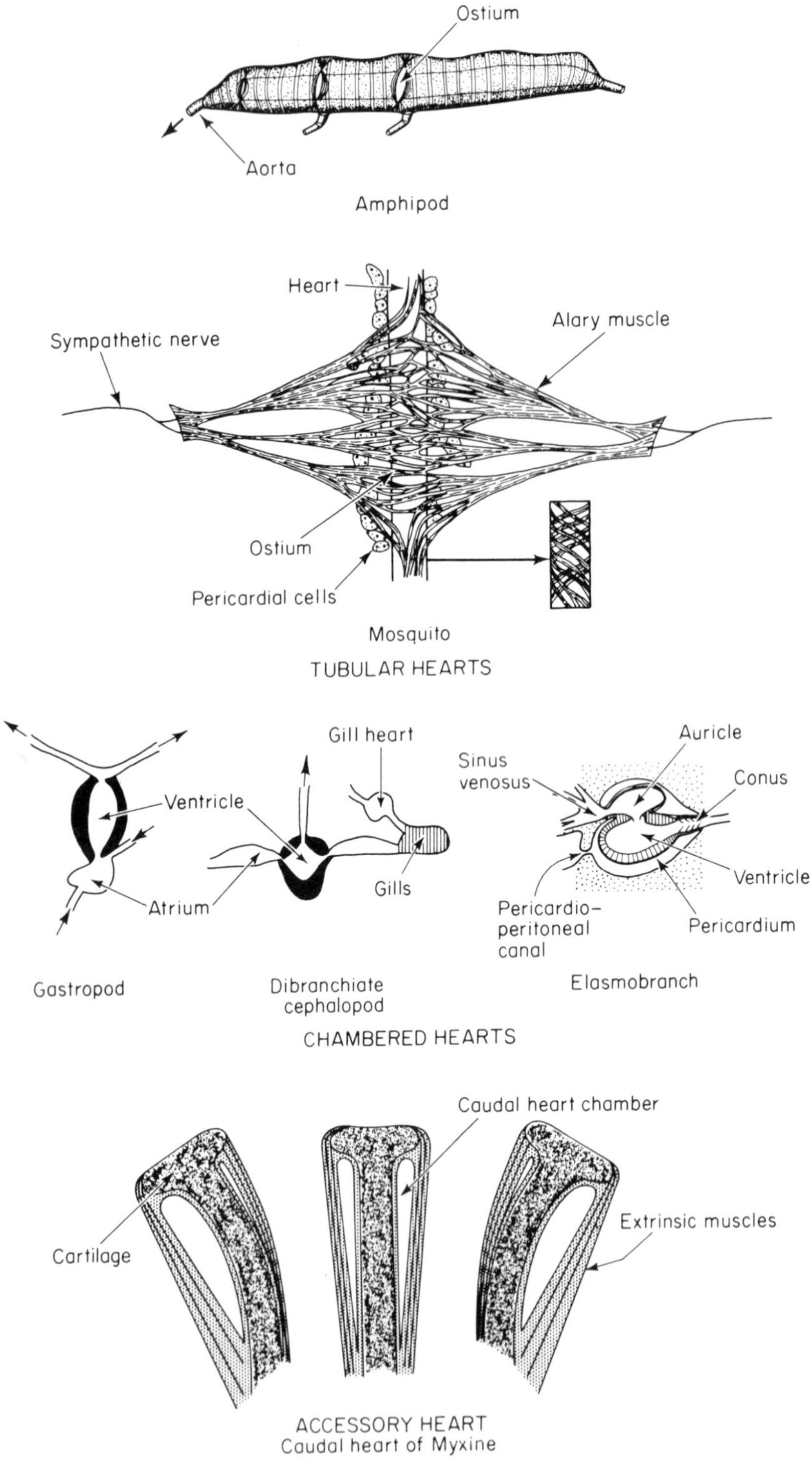

Fig. 5.5 Several morphological kinds of hearts.

Myxine, Fig. 5.5) in that their activity usually depends on specialized extrinsic muscles rather than on an intrinsic cardiac musculature. In some Crustacea for example, there are marked local distensions of the blood vessels, called blood pumps; these are compressed by contractions

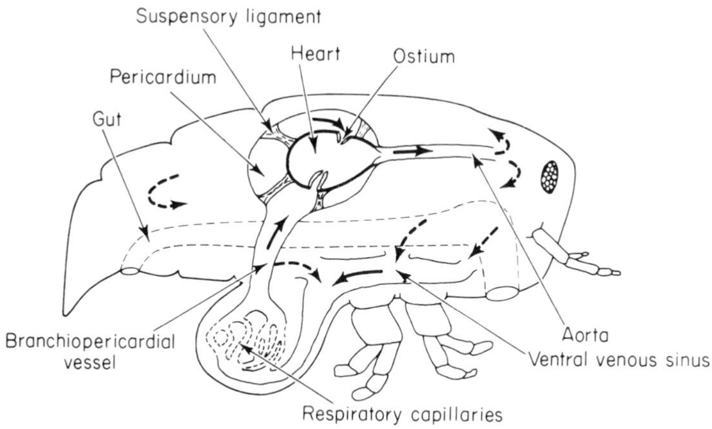

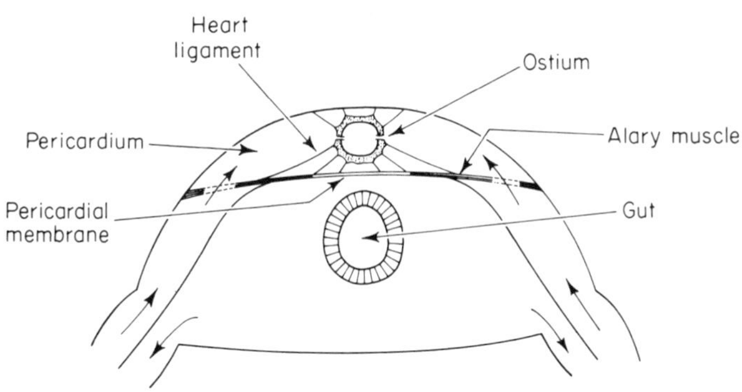

Fig. 5.6. Diagrams of the crustacean circulation. Solid arrows (upper figure), hemolymph flow in vessels; broken arrows, flow in unbounded sinuses. [Upper, logitudinal section from Waterman (1960). Lower, cross section from Ramsay (1952).]

of somatic muscles which have their origins and insertions outside the heart and run through the heart or its wall or lie in close proximity to it. These somatic muscles are secondarily adapted to the problems of circulation; in some cases they contract rhythmically (Maynard, 1960).

Accessory pulsatile ampullar organs are rather common in some groups of insects. They have been described in connection with the circulation in the wings (Diptera, Odonata), the antennae (Orthoptera) and the legs (Hemiptera). In some cases their musculature is intrinsic; in other cases it is extrinsic. Their rhythm is independent of the main heart and sometimes also varies in the several accessory hearts (Roeder, 1953).

The main dorsal heart is suspended in a fluid-filled pericardial sinus. Its hemodynamics require the filling of a perforated bag with fluid from the container which houses it. The mechanisms are entirely different from those which operate in chambered hearts. The arthropod heart is suspended by a series of elastic ligaments or striated muscle fibers which are attached to the exoskeleton and to a heavy pericardial septum bounding the pericardial space ventral to the heart (Fig. 5.6). This septum is a tough connective tissue membrane; it may contain some muscle (alary muscle). The contraction of the heart places these elastic ligaments and muscles under considerable tension. As the heart relaxes in diastole the tension of the ligaments pulls the ostia open and stretches out the walls of the heart so that the hemolymph flows into the organ. The rhythmic contraction of the myocardial muscle is associated with a passive filling during relaxation when the organ is stretched open by these elastic suspensory ligaments.

Chambered hearts. These are characteristic of most of the molluscs and the chordates. Some members of these phyla maintain an efficient circulation with a single heart while others have several vascular pumps (Fig. 5.5). The snail and the mussel operate an open system and fishes (other than the hagfishes) a closed one with a single vascular pump. The octopus and its allies, on the other hand, utilize two auxiliary pumps (branchial pumps) to insure the circulation of the blood through the gills (Fig. 5.7); the primitive cyclostome *Myxine* has a portal, a cardinal and a caudal heart in addition to the systemic pump and also depends on contractions of the gill musculature to keep the blood moving in a partially open, very low pressure system (Johansen, 1960, 1963). The frog requires several additional pumps (lymph hearts) to return the lymph to the venous system while the bird and the mammal operate two strong pumps in a central pumping station—one for the systemic circulation and the other for the pulmonary circuit (Fig. 4.8).

The chambered heart is potentially a much more efficient pump than the pulsating ampullar chambers of the arthropods and many other invertebrate animals. Widely scattered accessory hearts are less common, and the pumping station is central in large and active animals. Birds and mammals maintain a continuous circulation of their body fluids at high pressures with a strongly muscular double pump.

The continuous output of blood at high pressure can best be achieved by increasing the thickness of the muscular cardiac walls. These thick walls, however, must be stretched somewhat when the organ is filled; this in itself creates a mechanical problem which is solved by coupling a thinner walled receiving chamber (atrium) with a thicker walled systemic

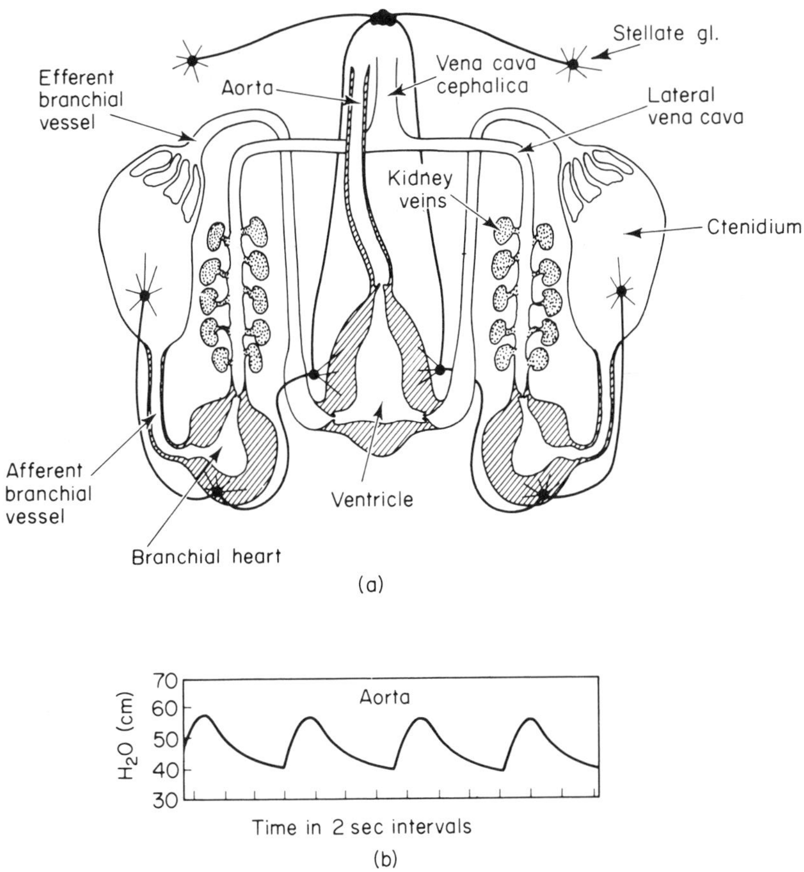

Fig. 5.7. Diagram of the central vascular system in the octopus (above) and a pressure record from the aorta cephalica with time marks at 2 sec. (below). [Johansen and Martin (1962).]

pumping chamber (the ventricle). A sinus venosus may also be present, as in the frog or fish, and the pressure filling of the ventricle carried out in two stages. A system of valves prevents backflow; the ventricle is put under considerable tension in filling, and this improves the efficiency of the contracting muscle (see below). The coupling of a thin-walled primer pump with a thicker-walled pumping chamber is characteristic of both the molluscs and the vertebrates.

A pericardium is another characteristic structure of physiological significance in the operation of chambered hearts. The pericardial space, a special chamber of the coelom, bounded by a tough connective tissue membrane, seems to contribute to the action of filling the thin-walled receiving chambers of the pump (Krijgsman and Divaris, 1955; Ramsay, 1952). The expulsion of the blood from the ventricle during contraction (systole) may be expected to create a negative pressure within the pericardium which will favor the filling of the thin-walled sinus and atrium during the subsequent period of relaxation (diastole).

The lymphatic circulation. In the vertebrates, with their closed systems of vascular channels, the return of the lymph to the main circulation may require special assistance. The problem can be presented most easily by reference to Starling's classical hypothesis summarized in Figure 5.8.

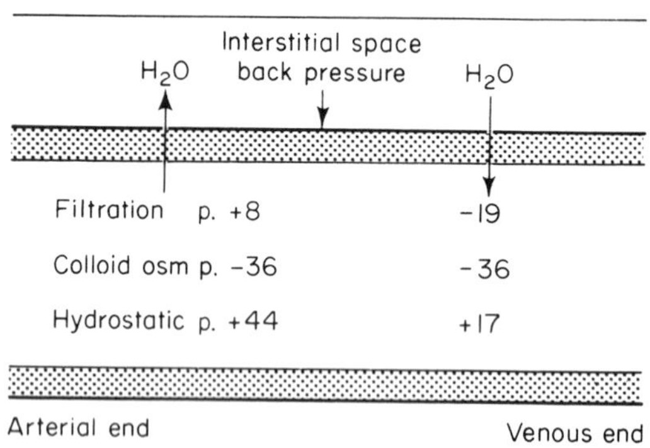

Fig. 5.8. Diagram of fluid exchange across the wall of a capillary. [Young (1957) after Davson (1951).]

The osmotic content of the blood is always greater than that of the tissue fluids and produces a colloidal osmotic pressure of about 36 cm H_2O. At the arterial end of the capillary the hydrostatic pressure, which depends on the cardiac pump, is 44 cm H_2O, and this results in a net filtration pressure of 8 cm H_2O. At the venous end of the capillary the hydrostatic pressure is much lower (17 cm H_2O), and the net pressure of 19 cm is in the reverse direction and returns fluid to the capillary. In addition, there is a certain mechanical resistance (tissue pressure) to the flow of fluids from the capillaries into the tissue spaces. This diagram emphasizes the significance of blood pressure (cardiac pump), osmotic content of the fluids and tissue pressures which may depend somewhat on the activity of the muscles. In some vertebrates these forces alone provide for the fluid exchanges between capillaries and tissue spaces, but in most vertebrates a lymphatic system is also required. Lymphatics are absent in the cyclostomes and the elasmobranchs but present in the bony fishes and tetrapods (Romer, 1955). A few of the fishes (eels and *Silurus*), all of the amphibians and reptiles, all bird embryos and some adult birds have lymph hearts which improve the circulation of the lymph and aid its return to the venous channels. Vertebrates with elaborate lymphatic systems, such as the mammals, depend on the massaging action of muscles and the pressure of neighboring pulsating arteries and other organs. This massaging of thin-walled vessels provided with numerous valves to direct the flow, constitutes the so-called "lymphatic pump" of the mammal.

The hagfishes show a unique condition among vertebrates with arterial blood actually flowing into tissue spaces ("red lymphatics") from vascular papillae on the branchial and carotid arteries (Brodal and Fänge, 1963). The several accessory hearts mentioned previously are essential to the circulation in this semiclosed system.

VALVES AND STOPCOCKS

An intricate system for the circulation of fluids will require valves at appropriate points to direct the flow and stopcocks to control its volume. The vascular channels of all animals with a true circulation are generously supplied with these; they become particularly vital to the maintenance of the sustained high pressures and continuous flows of vertebrate animals. Among the invertebrates, valves are common in the region of the heart. In an annelid, flap-like valves ensure the forward movement of the fluids in the long dorsal vessel and prevent its reversal where the noncontractile vessels enter the dorsal vessel. Several types of valves have been described in the crustaceans (Maynard, 1960) and are found where arteries arise from the heart as well as in the arteries and venous sinuses. Semilunar valves, consisting of two membranous flaps are common. These flaps when stretched form pockets. Reversal of flow fills the pockets and expands them so that the two components come together and close the vessel. Single flap-like valves are also present. In these, the reversal of blood flow stretches the flap to close the lumen of a small vessel.

Chambered hearts, whether vertebrate or invertebrate, possess valves as an essential feature of the primer pump arrangement. The semilunar type of valve attains a high degree of development in the vertebrate heart where two or three such pockets guard the atrioventricular openings, and the flaps of tissue are supported by fibers of muscle (papillary muscle) and connective tissue (chordae tendineae). Paired flap-like pocket valves in many of the veins and in the lymphatics of the vertebrates are essential to the movement of their fluids. Valves are essential features of hemodynamics in all circulatory systems.

Several devices operate as stopcocks in circulation. The ostia of an "open heart" such as that of the crustacean are controlled by special sphincter-like valvular arrangements. Arterioles also control blood flow by sphincter-like muscle in their walls. Although some muscle is characteristic of many blood vessels from the level of the nemertean up the phylogenetic series, it is in the vertebrates that the development becomes marked in the smaller peripheral vessels and functions as an efficient stopcock arrangement to control the flow to different parts of the capillary bed. The muscle of the arterioles is actively controlled by both nervous and chemical factors to meet the variable circulatory demands of the tissues. These arteriolar stopcocks control the peripheral resistance and thus become one of the major factors in the maintenance of the high and constant blood pressures of the vertebrates.

ELASTICITY OF BLOOD VESSELS AND A SUSTAINED PRESSURE

Fluid flow depends on the construction of the pipes as well as on the nature of the pump and the valves in the system. If the walls are rigid, fluids move through the system in accordance with the action of the pump; if forced in as a series of jets, the fluids emerge in the same way. On the other hand, elastic tubes which are stretched under pressure recoil when that pressure is released and exert a continued force on the fluid during the interval between the strokes of the pump. In this way, a sustained and continuous flow is maintained even though the fluid enters the tubes as a series of jets. Such a mechanism can operate efficiently only in a closed system and the sustained high pressures of the vertebrates depend on the marked elasticity of the main arteries as well as the peripheral resistance, referred to above, and the action of the pump. In an open circulation there is practically no peripheral resistance. Flows tend to be intermittent; the pressures are variable and low (Table 5.1).

RÉSUMÉ

Throughout the animal kingdom, the contractions of the somatic musculature play an indispensable part in the circulation of the body fluids. In higher forms, locomotion is an adjunct to other hemodynamic mechanisms; in many primitive animals, the intermittent movements of

TABLE 5.1
BLOOD VOLUMES AND PRESSURES OF REPRESENTATIVE ANIMALS. PRESSURES EXPRESSED AS SYSTOLIC/DIASTOLIC (E.G. 120/80); OR LIMITS OF SYSTOLIC (90–100); OR MEAN PRESSURES.
Data from Prosser and Brown (1961).

Species	*Blood volume*[1] % body weight (dye method)	*Blood pressure*	
		Vessel	Pressure mm Hg
Vertebrata			
Man	8.0	radial artery	120/80
Dog	8.0	femoral artery	110
Rabbit	6.5	femoral artery	90–100
Frog	8.0	dorsal aorta	22/11
Eel, *Anguilla*	2.9	ventral aorta	25–60[2]
Ray, *Raja*	4.6	ventral aorta	16/7.4
Dogfish, *Squalus*	8.7	ventral aorta	32/16
		dorsal aorta	16/10
Annelida			
Earthworm at rest		body cavity	1.5
Earthworm active		body cavity	10
Arenicola at rest		body cavity	9.0
Arenicola active		body cavity	26.4
Mollusca			
Fresh water mussel	9.0	heart	4.4
Octopus	5.8	aorta	40/60
		gill veins	5–6
Arthropoda			
Lobster at rest	17	ventricle	13/1
Lobster active		ventricle	27/13
Carcinus	37	sternal artery	9.6
Crayfish	25.1	cheliped sinus	7.4
Cockroach	19.5		
Dragonfly nymph		abdominal hemocoel	33
Echinodermata			
Sea cucumber (*Thyone*) at rest / active		body cavity	0–1.8 to 27.1

[1]Blood volumes recorded in the literature vary with the technique used for determination. There are also marked differences in closely related groups of animals (for example, in four species of marine elasmobranchs – Thorson, 1958).

[2]Unpublished values obtained by D. J. Randall for free swimming trout (no anaesthetic) are 38–40 in the dorsal aorta and 70–80 in the ventral aorta.

the lymph and the variable blood pressures are entirely dependent on it.

A continuous circulation and sustained blood pressure require a constant pumping of the fluids through a system of tubes or spaces. In a few forms, this pumping depends on widespread peristalsis in the tubes but, almost universally, specialized contractile areas of the tubes (hearts) provide the major hemodynamic force. Increasing animal size, high levels of activity and steady metabolic rates become possible only when the tissues are constantly perfused with nutrients and when the important capillary nets responsible for gaseous exchange and the removal of wastes are continuously serviced. The open plan of circulation does not permit such high and continuous pressures as the closed type and, partly for this reason, animals with open systems are limited in their size and/or activity. The *Octopus,* a large and active representative of the Mollusca (a phylum characterized by an open circulation), has an essentially closed circulation; the circulation in the intricate capillary net of the insect wing depends on special booster pumps.

The chambered heart is a feature of most circulations of the closed type and is primarily responsible for the high pressures attained. In the chambered heart, one or more thinner-walled receiving chambers serve as booster pumps to fill the thick-walled ventricle which provides the main pumping force. The closed pericardium is an important adjunct to this pump.

The higher vertebrates exemplify the climax in circulatory efficiency. Separate pumps for the respiratory and systemic capillary nets insure high and continuous pressures in all parts of the system. By contrast, a single pump in the fishes must force blood through both sets of capillaries. The high systemic pressures, associated with the double circulation, insure steady perfusion of tissue juices into the intercellular spaces while a system of lymphatics (characteristic of animals with higher pressures) assists in the return of the lymph to the main circulation. Diastolic pressures are maintained by the elasticity of the vessels, and the relatively high pressures throughout the cardiac cycle permit a continuous operation of such vital functions as respiratory exchange and kidney filtration.

Homeostasis and the Circulation of the Body Fluids

To meet the requirements of active cells, located far away from sources of fuel and points of waste disposal, the transport system must not only operate continuously but must be capable of adjustments in accordance with variable demands. This is achieved through the constant, but rate-variable, activity of the pump (SUSTAINED CARDIAC OUTPUT) and the adjustments of stopcocks in the blood vessels (PERIPHERAL RESISTANCE). Homeostatic mechanisms for the operation of the pump appeared early in animal phylogeny, but the precise control of peripheral resistance became essential and was established only in the vertebrates (particularly the homeothermic members of this group) and in the largest and most active of the invertebrates.

CARDIAC RHYTHM

Peristaltic activity, characteristic of smooth muscle in the larger vessels of embryonic and phylogenetically primitive circulations, is succeeded by more localized pacemaking areas in the heart. Groups of specialized muscle or nerve cells control the rhythmic activity of the muscle and are the centers through which temperature, neurohumors and other factors operate to vary the cardiac output. Although such pacemakers are conspicuous in most hearts, it should be remembered that the rhythm is inherent in the cardiac muscle and that the pacemaking areas are established during differentiation. This fact was not always appreciated; for many years the origin of the heartbeat (whether myogenic or neurogenic) was a topic of intensive research and prolonged arguments.

Both types of control are now recognized. All of the vertebrates have myogenic hearts; but one cannot so easily generalize for the invertebrates. Even within the different invertebrate phyla there may be little uniformity. The majority of crustaceans and insects have neurogenic hearts, but in some representatives ganglia are absent and the control is wholly dependent on the muscle. Molluscan hearts are myogenic. Several of the annelid hearts have been shown to be neurogenic. The ascidian heart—particularly interesting because of its regularly reversing beat—has a pacemaker at each end, but it is still not clear whether this is myogenic or neurogenic (Krijgsman, 1956; Krijgsman and Krijgsman, 1957).

PACEMAKERS OF MYOGENIC HEARTS

In the myogenic hearts of birds and mammals pacemaking activity resides in a system of specialized muscle cells. These impulse-conducting cells are histologically different from the general cardiac muscle fibers. Davies and Francis (1946) considered them neomorphic, but Prakash (1957), in a long series of researches, finds histologically distinct impulse-conducting tissues in teleost fishes, amphibia and reptiles as well as in the birds and the mammals. These different views have still not been reconciled (Bourne, 1960). Whatever the phylogenetic status of the impulse-conducting fibers of the homeotherms, cardiac rhythm is evident in both the myogenic invertebrate hearts and in embryonic vertebrate hearts, neither of which contains histologically distinct impulse-conducting cells. An autonomous rhythm is characteristic of cardiac

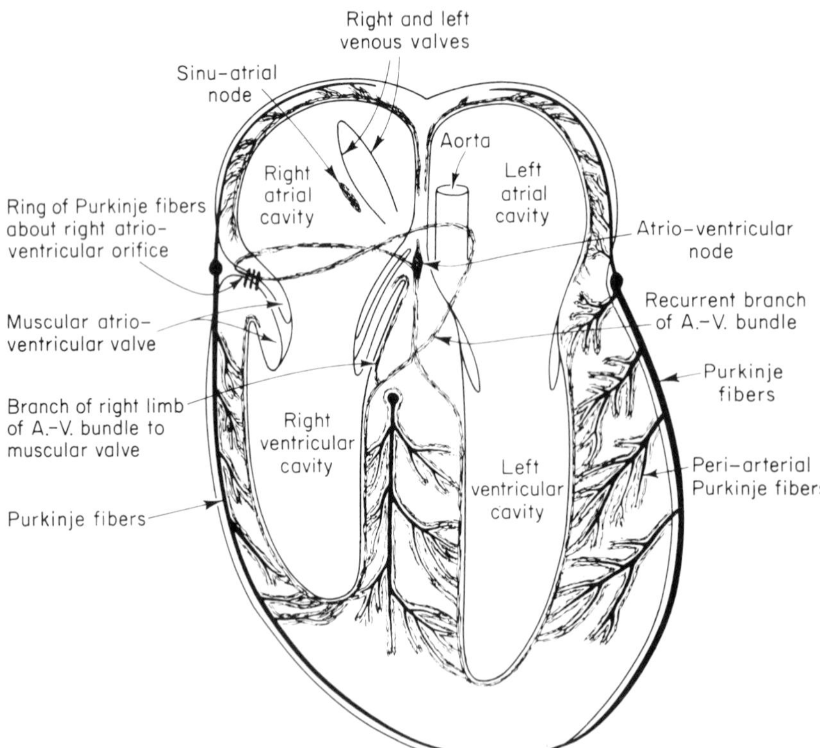

Fig. 5.9. Diagram of the impulse conducting system of the avian heart. [After Davies (1930) in Marshall (1961).]

muscle at all levels in phylogeny. A coordinating pacemaker is present in the complex pumps of higher vertebrates.

In the bird or mammal, pacemaking impulses arise in the sinuatrial node (S–A node), a small mass of specialized cells measuring about 2 cm by 2 mm in man and located in the right atrium near the entrance of the great veins. This is the true pacemaker of the heart; localized changes in temperature, surgical manipulations and electrical stimulations have shown that the wave of excitation associated with cardiac activity spreads from this point. It is picked up by a similar mass of tissue (the atrioventricular node or A–V node) situated in the right atrium of the mammal near the ventral part of the interatrial septum. Thence, excitation spreads along the atrioventricular bundle into the right and left bundle branches of the ventricles and from these, by fine ramifications (the Purkinje fibers), into the mass of cardiac tissue. The system is similar in the bird, except for the extensive development of conducting fibers in the left as well as in the right atrium (Fig. 5.9).

It is assumed that the cardiac pacemaking system of the homeotherm has, during phylogeny, been derived from the sinus venosus. This hypothesis is supported by the embryology and by the presence of pacemaking tissue in the sinus venosus of many poikilotherms. Embryologically, the sinuatrial node is derived from the primordial sinus venosus; physiologically, it can be demonstrated that the sinus venosus of amphibians and reptiles (frog or turtle) is the area from which excitation spreads throughout the entire organ. Even though the cardiac muscle of the frog or turtle will show rhythmic contractions when divorced from the sinus venosus, under normal conditions excitation, as measured by electrocardiograms, spreads from the sinus; experimental manipulations, such as altered temperatures or stimulation of this area, will affect the entire organ.

However, the sinus venosus and the sinuatrial node are not the only pacemakers of vertebrate hearts. In teleost fishes the floor of the atrium and the atrioventricular junction usually contain the pacemaking cells, although in the eel the sinus venosus is also involved. In the elasmobranchs, the sinus venosus, the atrioventricular junction and truncus arteriosus all show pacemaking activity (Mott, 1957).

No distinct areas of pacemaking cells have been described in the myogenic hearts of the invertebrates where rhythmic activity is assumed to be an inherent property of the cardiac muscle (Krijgsman and Divaris, 1955).

THE RHYTHM OF NEUROGENIC HEARTS

Classical studies of the pacemaking activity of a neurogenic heart were performed on *Limulus* by A. J. Carlson, about 60 years ago (Krijgsman, 1952). At that time, this heart seemed almost to have been designed to decide the controversy which was current between myogenic and neurogenic theories for cardiac rhythm. A series of ganglia on its dorsal surface can readily be removed without destroying the cardiac muscle. By appropriate experiments Carlson showed that the rhythm of the adult heart resided in these ganglia and that changes in temperature, stimulation of inhibitory nerves and other manipulations would modify the muscular rhythm through their effects on these pacemaking ganglia. Comparable pacemaking ganglia have now been studied in some other neurogenic hearts (Maynard, 1960), but demonstrations of their activities are more difficult because of the anatomical distribution of the ganglia. Krijgsman in his 1952 review concluded that *Limulus* was the only arthropod in which the heart mechanism was clearly understood.

ELECTROCARDIOGRAMS

The spread of excitation and the rhythmic activity of the heart creates an orderly sequence of changes in electric potential. Kolliker and Johannes Müller (1858) first demonstrated electrical activity in the beating heart (Fulton, 1955). They were able to detect movements in the crude coil-type galvanometer available at that time but depended on a biological experiment for proof of "animal electricity." The sciatic nerve of a frog gastrocnemius nerve-muscle preparation was looped around the ventricle of the frog, and two contractions of the gastrocnemius were noted with each heartbeat. It remained for Einthoven (1903), a Leiden professor, to develop the first suitable electrocardiograph for the measurement of these changes in electric potential. Einthoven's instrument is now superseded by precise electronic recording devices which have become indispensable for research and for clinical diagnosis of cardiac pathology. The records (electrocardiograms, ECG or EKG in German terminology) show consistent variations from the normal pattern in association with a variety of experimentally induced or naturally occurring pathological states.

Understanding of bioelectric phenomena has come a long way since Galvani (1737–98) first demonstrated the presence of "animal electricity" in his pioneer experiments with the gastrocnemius-sciatic nerve preparations of the frog (Verworn, 1899). It is now known that the ECG depends on one of the fundamental properties of living cells. Each and every cell, as long as it is alive, shows an electric potential difference across the surface membrane. This transmembrane potential depends on active metabolic processes which create an unequal distribution of ions between the interior and exterior of the cell. Its genesis will be considered in Chapter 15. At this point it is noted that the "resting" cardiac muscle cell of the vertebrate maintains a transmembrane potential of between 70 and 100 mv and that stimulation is associated with a drop in this potential to zero and then a momentary reversal in the sign to about 20 mv in the opposite direction. Thus, the rhythmically contracting muscle cells show an oscillation in the depolarization and repolarization of their surface membranes; the synchronous activity of many cells in a beating heart produces quite sizeable potentials which can be recorded on the surface of the animal's body.

Each type of pulsating heart produces a characteristic pattern of electric potentials (Fig. 5.10). The myogenic heart of the bivalve mollusc shows a fast component associated with the spread of excitation and a slow wave during contraction. The form varies considerably in different

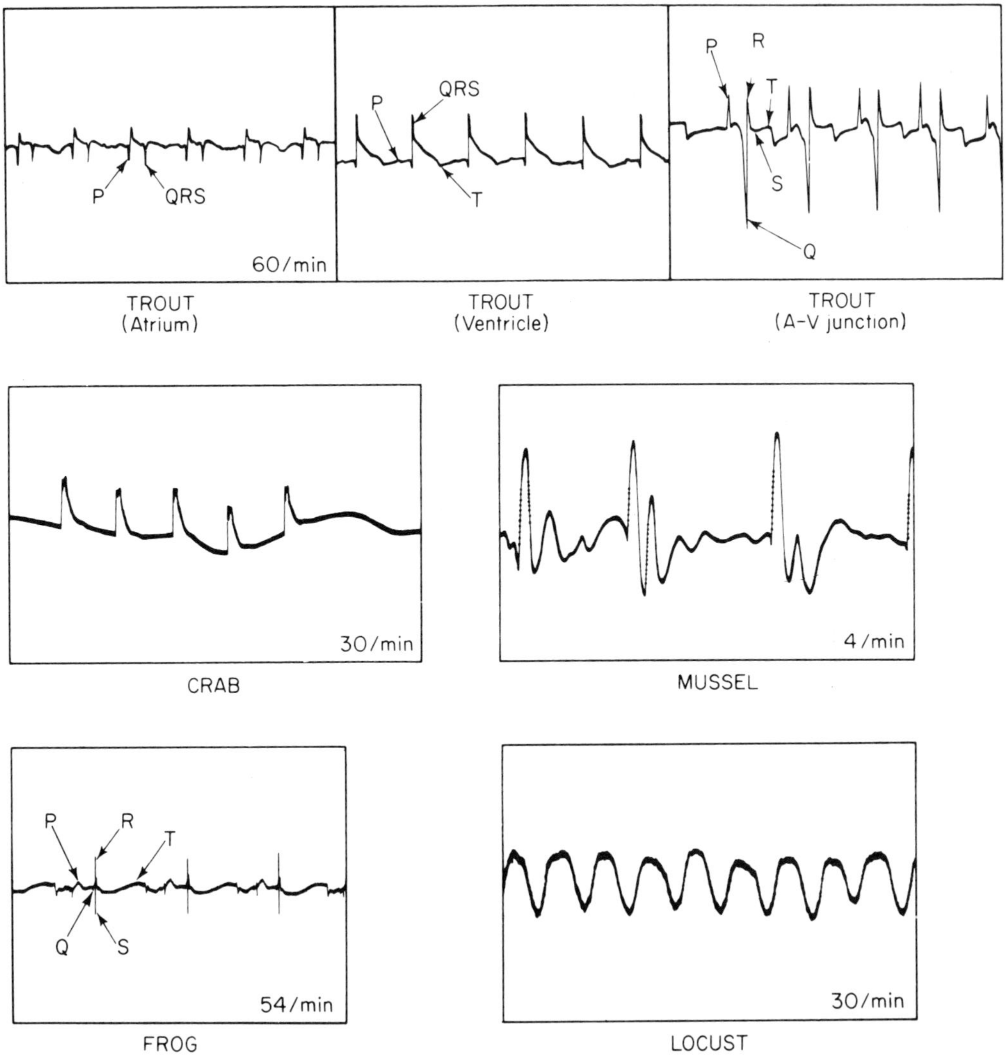

Fig. 5.10 Examples of electrocardiograms. Note *V* wave (associated with sinus venosus) which precedes the *P* wave in frog and trout atrium. *B* wave not evident in these records. Records from Comparative Physiology Laboratory, D. J. Randall.

species and under different conditions. The neurogenic hearts of arthropods create a continuous series of rapidly (tenths of millisecond) oscillating waves superimposed on a series of slower waves. The rapid oscillations are due to the discharge of the neurogenic pacemaker system, and their presence is considered evidence of the neurogenic type of heart. In both decapods and insects these oscillations may disappear and reappear under experimental conditions (Roeder, 1953; Maynard, 1960). Again, the spread of excitation is associated with the "fast" waves while the "slow" waves occur with the contraction of the heart.

The chambered hearts of vertebrates show a regular series of characteristic potentials as the different chambers contract. The fish heart produces a pattern of potential changes which can be related to the activity in the sinus venosus (*V* wave) the atrium (*P* wave) the ventricle (*R* wave) and the conus (*B* wave). In the double heart of the mammal the atria contract together, as do also the ventricles, so that only two major components are associated with the cardiac contractions. These waves are, by convention, labelled *P*, *Q*, *R*, *S*, and *T*. The *P* wave and the *QRS* complex are caused by the depolarization of the muscle in the atria and the ventricles respectively. These waves of depolarization precede the contraction of the chambers. The *T* wave is a repolarization wave of the ventricle and marks the end of ventricular systole. The *P–R* interval represents the time required for excitation to spread from the pacemaker to the ventricle. The *QRS* wave associated with the spread of depolarization over the ventricle is a complex, dependent on numerous electrical changes impinging on the surface from the intricate arrangement of muscular units. The intervals and patterns of waves may be altered in a predictable manner by different experimental procedures and in various cardiac pathologies.

FACTORS MODIFYING CARDIAC RHYTHM

Several factors are known to modify the rate and force of the heart either through an action on the pacemakers or on the cardiac muscle itself. The human heart may contract at anywhere from about 50 to 130 or more times per minute, depending on the age, health, activity or emotions of the individual. Factors which modify cardiac rhythm may be conveniently grouped as chemical, mechanical, thermal and nervous.

Chemical control. A consideration of the effects of the mineral environment should certainly begin with a description of Sydney Ringer's classical experiments on the influence of inorganic constituents of the blood on ventricular contraction. These were recorded in a series of papers published between 1880 and 1886 in the Journal of Physiology (particularly Volume 4) and are summarized in many textbooks of vertebrate physiology. Bayliss (1920) reproduced some of the original records.

Ringer perfused the frog heart with an isotonic solution of sodium chloride and found that it ceased beating after a short time and came to rest in a relaxed condition (diastole). If a small amount of calcium was then added the beat was temporarily restored, but with excess calcium the heart was gradually arrested in a contracted condition (calcium rigor). Traces of potassium abolished the toxic action of calcium without destroying its ability to "neutralize" the sodium effect. By itself, the action of potassium chloride was like sodium chloride and favored relaxation. A balanced solution containing these three ions was thus shown necessary to maintain a rhythmic activity for any length of time. Ringer seems to have been the first to note that single ion solutions are extremely toxic.

We know that Ringer made a fundamental physiological discovery and that the activity of all tissues and cells is dependent, not only on the osmotic content of the medium but also on its specific ions. Single ion solutions are always toxic. A balance is required. This is the phenomenon of ION ANTAGONISM and may be demonstrated with many different tissues. Ringer's specific findings for the frog heart are in general true for other vertebrates, but many differences will be found in the effects of the particular ions if hearts of invertebrate animals are compared. For example, although high potassium favors a diastolic arrest and high calcium a systolic arrest in the frog heart, the reverse is true in many invertebrates, while the sodium effects are frequently, although not always, the same in both vertebrates and invertebrates (Prosser and Brown, 1961). The general rule is that a balance of monovalent and divalent ions is as essential to the heart as it is to other types of tissue; if certain ions are present in excess or not properly antagonized by other ions the rhythm will be affected.

The pH may also be important. In general, acid metabolites and a low pH favor relaxation and are stimulating to the cardiac muscle while the reverse is true of alkalis. Marked changes in pH destroy the rhythm. However, the heart, whether vertebrate or invertebrate, is often rather insensitive to experimental changes in the alkalinity or the acidity of the medium. This can probably be attributed to the slow penetration of hydrogen or hydroxyl ions into cells (Heilbrunn, 1952).

In addition to the mineral constituents there are many organic substances, both natural and synthetic, which modify cardiac activity. Several of the naturally occurring ones are considered with the transmitter substances in the discussion of nervous control.

Mechanical effects. Muscle cells contract more forcefully when partially stretched. The improved performance of the distended heart is a reflection of this general property of muscle cells—whether they be smooth, skeletal or cardiac; adequate filling is an essential requisite to effective cardiac output. Starling (1918) first emphasized this in his studies of the vertebrate heart and expressed it as the oft-quoted "law of the heart." Textbooks of physiology since Starling's time have expressed the law in different ways, but it means simply that, within physiological limits, the output per beat is directly proportional to the diastolic filling. The greater the volume of blood in the heart at the beginning of systole, the greater the amount of blood ejected per beat, although beyond a certain critical stretch the contractions will become weaker (Fig. 5. 11).

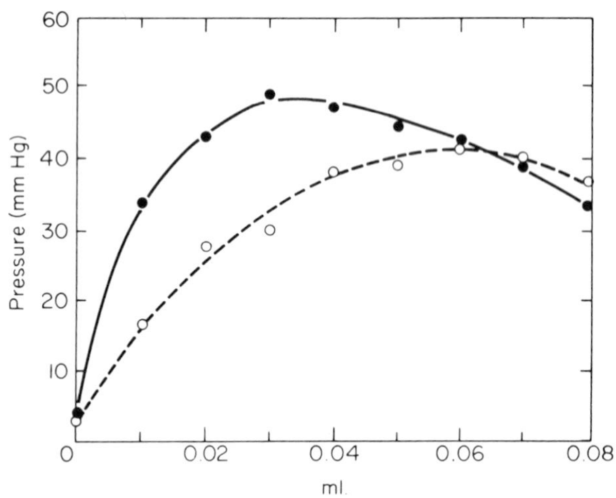

Fig. 5.11. Relation between tension developed by a frog heart contracting isometrically and its initial contained volume. Solid line, at 5°C; broken line, at 15°C. [Doi (1920).]

In some kinds of hearts the degree of inflation affects the frequency as well as the amplitude of the contraction (Fig. 5. 12). In crustaceans the stretching of the cardiac tissues probably stimulates the ganglionic neurons in the organ, and these operate reflexly to control the frequency. In this case the inflation of the organ not only stretches the muscle and thus directly modifies its contractility but also activates ganglionic neurons which initiate the contraction phase. The crustacean heart and other neurogenic hearts of this type usually cease to beat and become quite unresponsive when isolated and empty. In all kinds of hearts stretching has an action on the muscle fibers; in the neurogenic heart the rhythm may be set by the stretch reflex developed in the filling process.

Temperature has the expected action on cardiac frequency (Fig. 10.2) and Q_{10} values of about 2.0 have often been recorded for both poikilotherms and homeotherms. However, force of contraction as well as frequency is important in cardiac output and, in the frog and dog (heart-lung preparation) increasing frequency is associated with a diminished force. The diastolic filling is less complete, and the reduced tension on the fibers results in a less forceful contraction as discussed above. If in the frog the rate is kept constant, contractions are more forceful at higher temperatures (Bard, 1961). At higher temperatures the optimal fiber length is greater for the development of the maximum tension (Fig. 5.11).

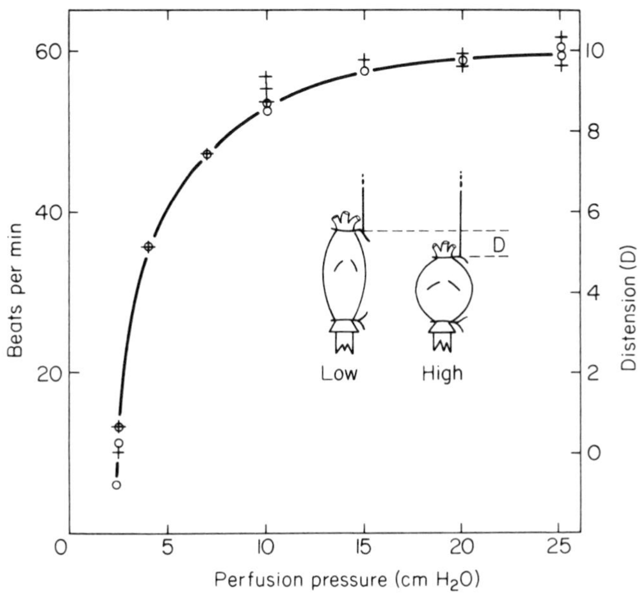

Fig. 5.12. Distension and heart rate in a malacostracan. Abscissa, perfusion pressure; left ordinate and open circles, heart rate; right ordinate and crosses, arbitrary measure (shown in insert) of distension (*D*) of heart resulting from perfusion pressure. [Waterman (1960).]

Nervous regulation. The visceral nervous system often plays an important role in cardiac activity. The intrinsic rhythm resides in the pump, and this pump often continues its regular pulsations when isolated from the nervous system. But in the living and intact animal the rate and force of the contraction are modified in accordance with the demands of the organism through a series of well defined cardiac reflexes. Sensory afferent nerves, stimulated through pressure and chemical receptors, feed information into the cardiac centers. The efferent or motor fibers arising in these centers modify the activities of the cardiac muscle either directly, or indirectly through the pacemakers. The link between motor nerves and cardiac tissues is by way of the accelerating or inhibiting transmitter substances. Thus, as in any reflex system, the cardiac reflexes are based on three components: sensory nerves, cardiac nervous centers and efferent cardio-regulatory nerves.

Experimental evidence indicates that the most likely transmitter substances are acetylcholine, adrenaline, noradrenaline, and 5-hydroxytryptamine. Acetylcholine accelerates neurogenic hearts but inhibits the myogenic ones. Adrenaline, noradrenaline and 5-hydroxytryptamine (serotonin) usually excite the heart but have no effect in some animals. These generalizations are not without exception, and sometimes effects vary or may even be reversed with an alteration of the concentration of the drug (Roeder, 1953).

It is important to note that a pharmacological response to these chemicals does not necessarily mean that they are naturally occurring transmitter substances. Acetylcholine, adrenaline and noradrenaline are recognized in all of the vertebrates. The hearts of the higher vertebrates show adrenaline and acetylcholine-mediated cardiac effects, but the teleost heart is unresponsive to adrenaline although inhibited by acetylcholine. Again, adrenaline, noradrenaline, dopamine and acetylcholine have been identified in the insects (Welsh, 1957), but there has been no certain demonstration as to which of these, if any, may be the natural neurohumors.

Special organs for the accumulation and storage of neurohumors or neurosecretory substances are well known in the animal kingdom. The pericardial organs of the Malacostraca are probably structures of this kind (Carlisle and Knowles, 1959). First described in *Squilla*, they have now been identified in many of the Malacostraca and may be a general feature of the anatomy of this group. The pericardial organs differ somewhat morphologically and geographically in various genera. Essentially they are masses of interlacing nerve fibers forming a network through which must pass the blood returning to the pericardium from the gills. The location of the nerve cell bodies has not been determined, but it has been suggested that the neurons arise in the ventral thoracic ganglion (Maynard, 1960). Extracts of the pericardial organs always increase the amplitude of the heart beat, but frequency may be increased in some species and decreased in others. The chemical mediator has an action almost indistinguishable from 5-hydroxytryptamine (Carlisle and

Knowles, 1959).

The CARDIAC REGULATING CENTERS have been localized in several groups of animals. In the vertebrates, both cardio-accelerator and cardio-inhibitor centers are functionally independent although closely associated morphologically in the floor of the fourth ventricle. Definite ganglia and nerves have been associated with cardio-acceleration or inhibition or both in many of the molluscs. The pleural ganglion has been implicated in several of the gastropods and the visceral ganglion in several of the pelecypods and the cephalopods. However, it is not possible to go far in generalization since the pleural ganglion may be fused with the cerebral ganglion (for example, in all of the lamellibranchs except the Protobranchiata); many other modifications occur in this group which probably explain differences observed in nervous control. In the Malacostraca cardio-inhibitory fibers arise in the subesophageal ganglion and acceleratory fibers in the region of the third maxilliped and fourth walking leg (Maynard, 1960). Cardiac inhibition (but not acceleration) has been observed following stimulation of the back part of the cerebral ganglion of *Limulus*. It is evident that in many of the invertebrates cardiac rhythm is modified by nervous reflexes; but in some cases only inhibitory fibers have been found and in others only accelerators. Some, such as the ascidians, apparently lack nervous reflexes.

The AFFERENT SENSORY LIMB of the reflex is excited by a variety of stimuli. Pressure receptors are located at strategic points in the vascular channels while chemical receptors, responsive to variations in carbon dioxide or pH and perhaps oxygen tensions, may be located either in blood vessels or central nervous tissue; these ensure appropriate changes in pumping action. In addition, many receptor organs associated with protective reflexes alter the activity of the cardiac centers, and in the higher vertebrates cerebral processes, quite divorced from peripheral stimulation, often have a significant effect.

A branchial depressor reflex is well known in the teleosts and elasmobranchs. Elevation in the branchial blood pressure brings about a reflex slowing of the heart (Mott, 1957). This might protect the delicate gill capillaries. The branchial reflex is evidently homologous with the aortic depressor and carotid sinus reflexes in the terrestrial vertebrate. These reflexes have been carefully investigated in the mammal. Stretch receptors in the wall of the aorta, the root of the innominate and the carotid sinus respond to pressure changes. Under "normal" conditions a flow of tonic impulses along the aortic branches of the vagi and the sinus branches of the glossopharyngeal nerves reaches the cardiac centers in the medulla and maintains a continued vagal restraint on the heart. Elevations in the pressure augment the flow of impulses and increase tne vagal inhibition, while a decrease in the pressure has the reverse effect. These reflexes in the higher vertebrates are associated with other pressure reflexes originating in the roots of the great veins and the right

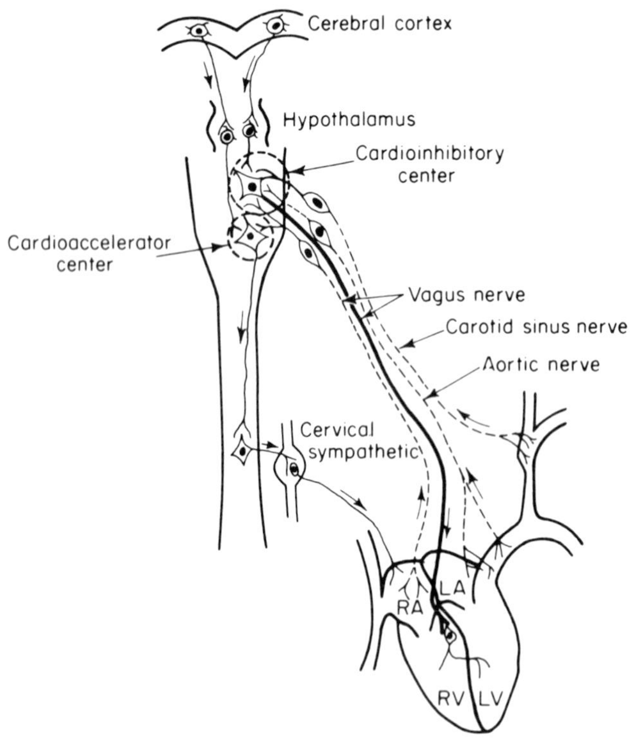

Fig. 5.13. The cardiac reflexes. Afferents from the carotid sinus and aortic arch are excited by changing tension (blood pressure) and reflexly control the efferent vagal neurons of the cardio-inhibitory center so that increased blood pressure in the aorta and carotid sinus slows the heart (parasympathetic control); vagal afferents from the right atrial region synapse in both the inhibitory center and the accelerator center to decrease the inhibition and increase the acceleration; thus, increased pressure in the great veins and the right side of the heart causes cardiac acceleration. The efferent pathways for acceleration are the sympathetics. A parallel system of reflexes alters blood pressure through the vasomotor centers and the vasoconstrictors and dilators of the arterioles. *RA* and *LA*, right and left atria; *RV* and *LV*, right and left ventricles.

auricle. Stretching of these tissues which form the receiving chambers of the heart increases the flow of impulses via afferents to the medulla and results in cardio-acceleration through decreased vagal inhibition and increased sympathetic acceleration. These important reflexes provide a nice control of cardiac activity in accordance with the variations in blood pressure (Fig. 5.13). Similar reflexes may exist in the lower vertebrates and invertebrates but have not been convincingly demonstrated. In the poikilothermous tetrapods, structures homologous with the carotid sinus are anatomically well known but have not been studied physiologically. The carotid labyrinth of amphibians, for example, appears considerably more complex than the carotid sinus of other groups of land vertebrates (Adams, 1958). Its functions await careful study.

Chemoreceptors sensitive to changes in carbon dioxide (in reality changes in pH) and oxygen tensions of the blood modify the cardiac rhythm of higher vertebrates. The carotid and aortic bodies contain such receptors and operate to increase cardiac activity when the blood becomes more acid and anoxic. Alterations in blood pH may also act directly on the cardio-accelerator center of the hind brain. The aortic and carotid bodies are phylogenetically derived from the branchial vessels of the lower vertebrates; several unsuccessful attempts have been made to demonstrate comparable chemoreceptors in the gill regions of fishes (Hughes and Shelton, 1962).

Bradycardia associated with vagal inhibition and the development of a marked synchrony between cardiac and respiratory rhythms follows the passage of deoxygenated water over the gills of a teleost, but it is not known whether this is initiated by peripheral reflexes or centrally, through the oxygen tension of the blood (Randall and Shelton, 1963).

Chemoreceptors involved in cardiac reflexes have not been demonstrated in the invertebrates. However, variations in the carbon dioxide and oxygen tensions of the surroundings alter cardiac activity in *Daphnia* (Maynard, 1960) and probably in other invertebrates, and this action could be a direct one on the heart or its pacemaking system. On the other hand, it could operate indirectly on these tissues through cardiac reflexes.

Sensory stimulation, particularly stimuli eliciting protective reflexes, often activates the cardiac reflexes. In man, an inhalation of irritating vapors or stimulation of the integumentary pain receptors act in this manner. Mechanical stimulation of the skin and abdominal viscera of the skate (*Raia* sp.) likewise alters the heart rate and raises the blood pressure. In the decapods, removal of a leg or placing foreign materials in the mouth have also been shown to activate cardiac reflexes (Maynard, 1960). This type of protective reflex is widespread among animals.

BLOOD PRESSURES AND THE CONTROL OF PERIPHERAL RESISTANCE

Several functions of the circulatory system depend on high and relatively constant pressures. Food and oxygen requirements of dense masses of active tissue require the flow of blood through minute channels, and this creates considerable frictional resistance. In fact, the high blood pressures found in the vertebrates and in a large invertebrate such as the octopus are primarily due to this peripheral resistance.

Adequate blood pressures may also be essential for reasons other than the maintenance of flow through the capillaries. The filtration processes of the kidney and the transfer of nutritive fluids from the capillaries into the tissues are dependent on blood pressures. Locomotion in many invertebrates is contingent upon pressures developed in fluid-filled spaces. The erectile tissue in the copulatory organs of the vertebrates also depends on local accumulations of blood under pressure. This mechanism is found in several places in the animal body where turgidity is required.

Among the vertebrates the control of peripheral resistance is by the smooth muscle of the arterioles. A group of vasomotor reflexes operate to vary the caliber of these vessels and thus control the blood pressure and the flow to different areas. The finest of the arterioles (metarterioles) constitute precapillary sphincters or stopcocks, and their contractions can effectively stop the circulation into an area of the capillary bed. In many places, arteriovenous anastomoses (thoroughfare channels) can shunt the blood directly from arterioles to venules and thus bypass an area of the capillary bed. The vasomotor reflexes which control the smallest of the blood vessels are well defined and have been carefully studied in the higher vertebrates.

These reflexes parallel those already described for the heart which, in a sense, is only a specialized region of the vascular channels. The vasomotor centers, like the cardiac centers, are located in the floor of the medulla. Functionally, if not anatomically, a distinct vasoconstrictor and vasodilator region may be distinguished. The vasoconstrictor center, in particular, exhibits a constant tonic action on the arterioles. As in the case of the cardiac centers, a group of reflexes activated by pressure changes in the great veins and right auricle of the heart (vasopressor or McDowall reflex) and in the aortic and carotid bodies leads to appropriate adjustments in blood pressure by a modification of the peripheral resistance at the level of the precapillary sphincters. Pain and temperature receptors as well as receptors in the peritoneum and viscera may also activate the vasopressor reflexes. The chemoreceptors in the carotid and aortic bodies act on the peripheral resistance in a manner comparable to the cardiac reflexes already described. In addition, chemicals, such as carbon dioxide, adrenaline, noradrenaline, histamine and others can modify the tone of these small vessels directly so that strictly local adjustments in circulation may occur.

Vasomotor control and peripheral resistance of the type found in the vertebrates is not found in most of the invertebrates. Even the larger representatives have relatively low blood pressures (Table 5.1) which vary greatly with activity. In fact, pressure changes which accompany locomotion in many of the invertebrates may be considerably greater than those which follow cardiac and other vascular stimulation. The octopus and its allies, however, have an essentially closed circulation and a blood pressure which is comparable to that of some of the vertebrates (Table 5.1). Changes in the caliber of the blood vessels follow stimulation or sectioning of nerves and indicate the presence of vasomotor reflexes in this animal.

The fluid skeleton. Many of the invertebrates rely on a hydrostatic skeleton. This skeleton, like the more familiar skeleton of the vertebrates, depends on the action of antagonistic groups of muscles; these operate, not on hard skeletal parts but on a volume of fluid in a fixed space. The rise in pressure of the coelomic fluid of many invertebrates when they become active (Table 5.1) is the reflection of the operation of this fluid skeleton. Chapman (1958) discusses its physiology in many animals ranging from the ameba to the higher invertebrates. Nicol (1960*a*) also describes many examples. The best known are among the worms, molluscs and echinoderms.

The body of the annelid operates on a fluid skeleton. Its length and diameter are altered through the alternate contraction of longitudinal and circular muscles acting against a cylindrical tube which contains an almost constant volume of fluid. The molluscs also make extensive use of hydrostatic skeletons. In the bivalves, burrowing and locomotion depend on the turgidity developed in the foot through the movement of hemolymph into extensive connective tissue spaces. In some forms, *Ensis* for example, burrowing is extremely rapid. The extension of the foot is associated with a relaxation of the pedal muscles and the flow of hemolymph to the foot. The tip of the foot swells into a bulbous anchor; when the pedal muscles contract and the fluid is forced back into the mantle spaces, the animal moves quickly forward. Extensions of the siphon in the lamellibranchs is likewise by the movements of fluid into tissue spaces, while the gastropod foot can be greatly expanded by locking the hemolymph in the pedal sinuses.

In cephalopods the hemal skeleton as a part of the locomotory machinery, is reduced or completely lost. The activities and high rate of metabolism of these creatures demand a closed circulation, and large volumes of hemolymph can no longer be locked up in sinuses to provide a skeleton. Locomotion is by pallial jet propulsion, and the arms and mantle are operated by an interplay of muscles. The body space is no longer a hemocoel but a true body cavity developed independently in this group of molluscs as an extension of the pericardium around the rest of the viscera (Morton, 1958).

Erectile tissues of the vertebrates also operate through the accumulation of vascular fluids in blood spaces. The mammalian penis is the most developed example. In this case the pressure is generated by the heart and not through muscular action on fluids in a closed space. The penis contains a sponge-like system of irregular vascular spaces between the arteries and veins (the corpora cavernosa penis). These are greatly distended when filled with blood under pressure. Stimulation of the parasympathetic produces dilation of the arterioles and blood flows into these spaces. Venous return is then restricted through pressure of the thin-walled veins, and the organ becomes turgid with pressures equivalent to those in the carotid artery. Valves have been described in the larger veins. Constriction of the arteries (sympathetic stimulation) leads to a gradual escape of blood from the spongy tissue, and during the flaccid condition flow into this tissue is further restricted by longitudinal ridges in the intima of the arteries (Ruch and Fulton, 1960).

The Laws of Circulation

In summary, the circulation of the blood and the pressures within the vascular channels depend on three major factors. The first of these is the GENERAL ACTIVITY OF THE ANIMAL. In small and primitive organisms this is the only force involved and it is still an important factor in the maintenance of flow in certain areas of the most highly organized animals—lymphatics and small veins of birds and mammals, for example. The second is the CARDIAC OUTPUT. The amount of blood pumped in a unit time is a function of the blood volume as well as of the force of the heart. Both the blood volume and the force of the heart are subject to considerable variation. The third factor is the PERIPHERAL RESISTANCE which depends on the total frictional surface of the vascular tubes. This third factor is of major significance only in the vertebrates and larger invertebrates with closed circulations. In these, the velocity and pressure within different areas of the system follow familiar physical laws. From the arteries to the capillaries and on to the veins there is first a gradual widening of the total cross sectional area of the system—to a maximum in the capillaries—and thence a narrowing as the veins come together in the heart. The pressure falls throughout the system, and the velocity varies inversely with the cross sectional area of the stream. These relationships are shown in Fig. 5.14. They are familiar to anyone who has watched a turbulent river widen and discharge its waters into a placid lake; as the water flows from the lake it gains velocity once more while it moves on downstream to the ocean.

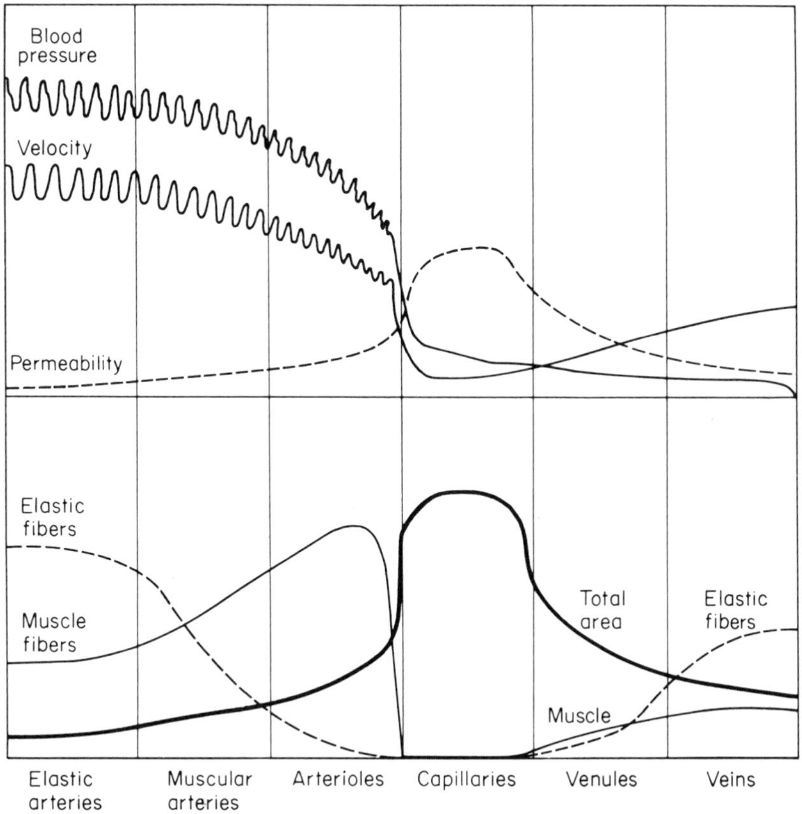

Fig. 5.14. Graph showing some of the changes in structure (below) and function (above) of vessels in the direction of blood flow from ventricle to atrium. [Cowdry (1950).]

6 *The Vascular Fluids*

At the lowest levels of phylogeny the functions of the interstitial fluids or lymph are essentially trophic. At the highest levels the vascular fluids have assumed several additional roles and, as a consequence, have changed both biochemically and morphologically. At all levels the nutritive or trophic functions depend on aqueous solutions of sugars, amino acids and other readily dissolving molecules, together with colloidal droplets of fatty substances. The respiratory gases, on the other hand, are insufficiently soluble to be carried in adequate amounts by simple solution. The phylogeny of a gaseous transport system depends on a group of special proteins (chromoproteins) and becomes one of the major events in the evolution of larger and more specialized animals. Certain other functions which are largely absent in the simpler forms depend on the phylogeny of the albumins and globulins. The albumins play an important part in the distribution of body water because of their colloidal osmotic pressure. The globulins are active factors in an elaborate defense against disease and foreign materials; blood cells are also involved in this activity. Another group of plasma proteins is concerned with blood clotting mechanisms and the preservation of the fluids themselves. The very existence of the higher animal is so dependent on the continuous flow of blood at high pressures that intricate mechanisms become associated with hemostasis and the clotting processes which occur following injury to the vascular channels. These several specialized activities of the vascular fluids (gaseous transport, the regulation of fluid volume, defense mechanisms and hemostasis) are discussed in this chapter.

The Transport of Oxygen

Water in equilibrium with atmospheric air at 37°C dissolves about 0.46 volumes per cent of oxygen, and this is adequate only for tissues with low rates of metabolism. Only about 1 per cent of man's total oxygen requirement can be transported in this way. Human blood in equilibrium with alveolar air combines with about 20.0 volumes per cent of oxygen. It is worth noting, however, that the small amounts of oxygen which can be carried in simple solution serve the needs of many invertebrates and some curious vertebrates living a sluggish existence in extremely cold waters. Rudd (1954) first described three fishes (Chaenichthyidae) from Antarctica which lack special transport pigments and have vascular fluids with oxygen-combining capacities only slightly greater than those of water (0.54 to 0.90 vol per cent). The Leptocephalus larvae of the eel also lack transport pigments, and several other fish (goldfish, carp, pike) may, if they are not forced into any activity, live for hours after their transport pigments have been tied up with carbon monoxide (Anthony, 1961). This suggests that the specialized transport mechanisms became necessary with increasing activity and high rates of animal metabolism. Evidence from a study of the many different respiratory pigments supports this hypothesis and suggests further that a storage function probably preceded a transport function in the evolution of the respiratory proteins.

The storage and transport of oxygen is achieved by a group of colored proteins capable of forming loose combinations with oxygen when exposed to it at high tensions, and of releasing the gas readily at the lower tensions which prevail in the tissues. They are quite different biochemically in the various phyla. Even in the same phylum there may be several distinct pigments, and more than one pigment may even exist in the same animal (Fox and Vevers, 1960; Manwell, 1960). One can only generalize by saying that they are colored proteins (chromoproteins) which contain a metallic atom in their constitution and have the property of forming loose combinations with oxygen and sometimes with carbon dioxide. Table 6.1 lists the known pigments together with their distribution and some of their properties.

HEMOGLOBIN

Hemoglobin is the most familiar, the most widespread and the most efficient of the respiratory pigments. It is most familiar because of its presence in human blood, but it occurs also in the plant world, in some protozoa and in most of the major animal phyla (Fox and Vevers, 1960; Gratzer and Allison, 1960). As indicated in Table 6.1, the most efficient of the hemoglobins combine with far greater amounts of oxygen than any of the other pigments.

Hemoglobin is made up of an iron porphyrin compound, HEME,

TABLE 6.1.
OXYGEN CAPACITIES OF SOME DIFFERENT BLOODS.
Values selected from Nicol (1960a) and Prosser and Brown (1961).

Pigment	*Color*	*Site*	*Animal*	*Oxygen Vol. per cent*
Hemoglobin	Red	Corpuscles	Mammals	15–30
			Birds	20–25
			Reptiles	7–12
			Amphibians	3–10
			Fishes	4–20
		Plasma	Annelids	1–10
			Molluscs	1–6
Hemocyanin	Blue	Plasma	Molluscs	
			Gastropods	1–3
			Cephalopods	3–5
			Crustaceans	1–4
Chlorocruorin	Green	Plasma	Annelids	9
Hemerythrin	Red	Corpuscles	Annelids	2

associated with a protein GLOBIN. Heme is a metalloporphyrin. It is composed of four pyrrole rings joined with methene groups to form a super-ring with an atom of ferrous iron in the center attached to the pyrrole nitrogens (Fig. 6.1). This heme component of the molecule is a constant feature of all hemoglobins, but the globin portion varies in different species. In addition, varying numbers of these basic hemoglobin units may unite to form polymers of different size. For example, the muscle hemoglobin of all vertebrates (myoglobin) and the blood hemoglobin of the lamprey correspond to one unit with a molecular weight of 16,500 to 17,000. Two basic units (mol wt 34,000) are united in the hemoglobin of the polychaete worms *Glycera* and *Notomastus* and the insect *Gastrophilus*. The molecular weight of the hemoglobin of the blood of most vertebrates corresponds to four units (mol wt about 67,000), while in some of the annelids (*Arenicola* and *Lumbricus*) the molecule

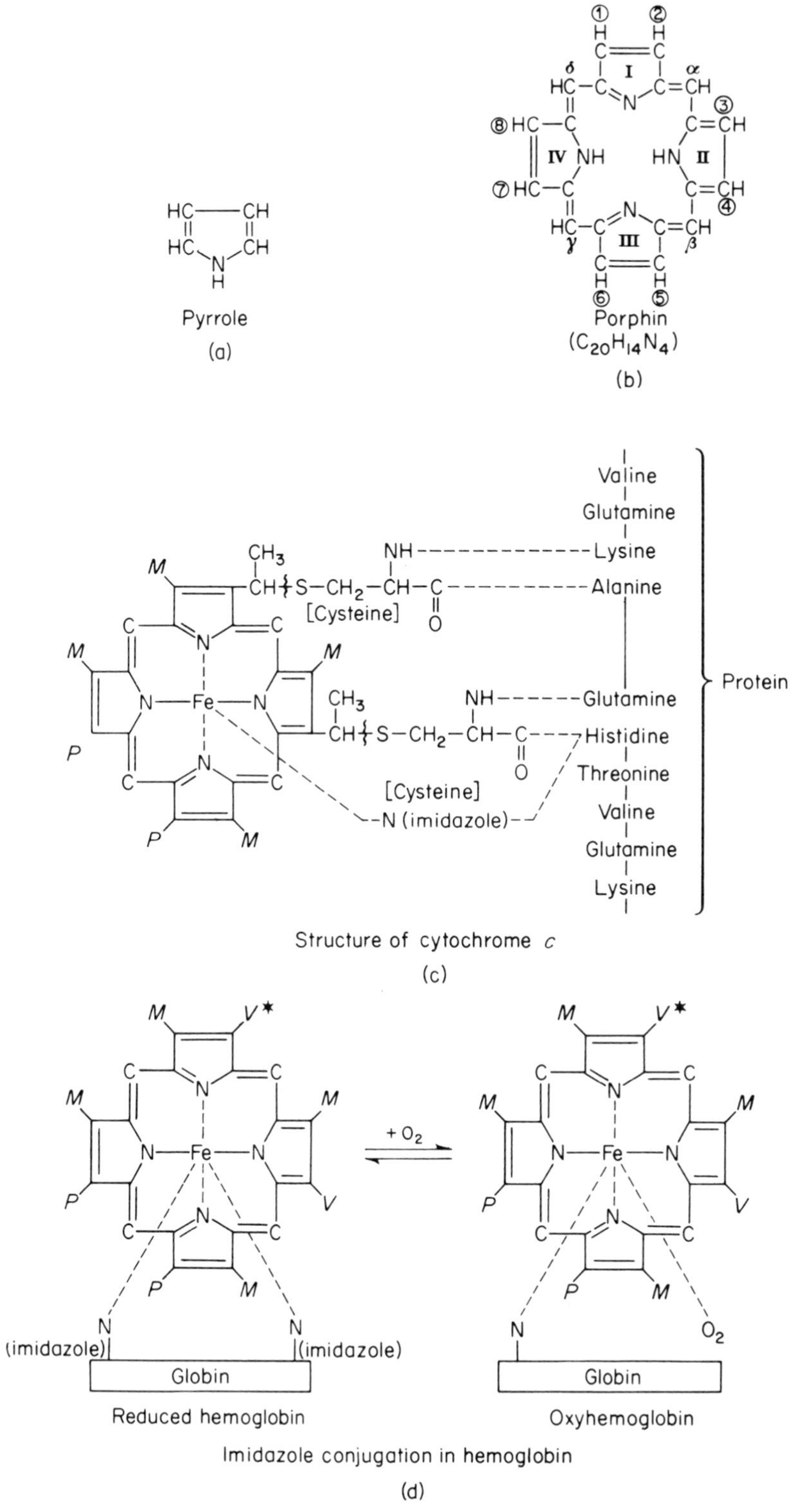

Fig. 6.1. Porphyrins. Upper, the skeletal structure of the porphyrin molecule (tetrapyrrole ring) with the conventional numbering of positions and rings; middle, the structure of cytochrome *c*; lower, imidazole conjugation in hemoglobin. *M*, the methyl group $—CH_3$; *V*, the vinyl group $—CH{=}CH_2$; *P*, propionic $—CH_2—CH_2—COOH$. In chlorocruorin, position 2 (marked with an asterisk in hemoglobin) is filled by the formyl group $O{=}CH$.

may correspond to 180 units or a weight of 3,000,000. To repeat, no matter what the variability in molecular weight and protein structure, the heme portion of the molecule is the same. This portion belongs to a phylogenetically ancient group of biochemicals, the metalloporphyrins, and the machinery necessary for their synthesis seems to be universal.

The metalloporphyrins were encountered in Chapter 1. It was pointed out that animal life only became possible when chlorophyll and the cytochromes became a part of the photosynthetic processes which transformed an anaerobic into an aerobic world, and when the cytochrome carriers permitted the release of large amounts of energy in aerobic respiration. All animals possess the biochemical machinery for the manufacture of cytochrome and, as indicated in Figure 6.1, these materials are structurally very similar to hemoglobin. Cytochrome oxidase is present, whether or not an animal possesses hemoglobin, and all animals are thus familiar with biochemical combinations of oxygen and a metalloporphyrin compound. In view of the close relation between hemoglobin and the cytochromes and the widespread occurrence of hemoglobin in many different animal groups it seems likely that, phylogenetically, it is a very ancient respiratory pigment (Gratzer and Allison, 1960).

The many different hemoglobins vary in oxygen-combining capacities (Table 6.1). This variation in oxygen capacity is a property of the total molecule and does not depend on basic differences or changes in the metalloporphyrin component. In all cases the atom of ferrous iron (heme unit) is associated with one molecule of oxygen to form oxyhemoglobin. The reaction is readily reversible; the unoxygenated compound is referred to as deoxyhemoglobin or less accurately as reduced hemoglobin. These are not enzymatic reactions; whether or not the heme unit combines with oxygen depends not only on the availability of the oxygen but on the pH and ionic content of the solution as well as on the construction of the total hemoglobin molecule. In contrast, the change of cytochrome from an oxygen-poor to an oxygen-rich state involves a valence change of the iron from the ferrous to the ferric state and is governed by specific enzymes (Chapter 7).

Even in the same species of animal there may be marked differences in properties of the hemoglobin, depending on small variations in the protein component of the molecule. The difference between sickle-cell and normal hemoglobin is a difference in only one of the amino acids which make up the side chain and depends on the presence of a single mutant gene (Anfinsen, 1959). Again, maternal and fetal hemoglobins have quite different properties adapted to the oxygen transport problems of the two environments. These relationships and comparisons can be better understood by an analysis of the OXYGEN EQUILIBRIUM CURVES (also called OXYGEN DISSOCIATION CURVES).

Oxygen equilibrium curves. These curves are developed by determining the amount of oxygen which combines with blood exposed to oxygen at a series of pressures. The amount of gas combined with the

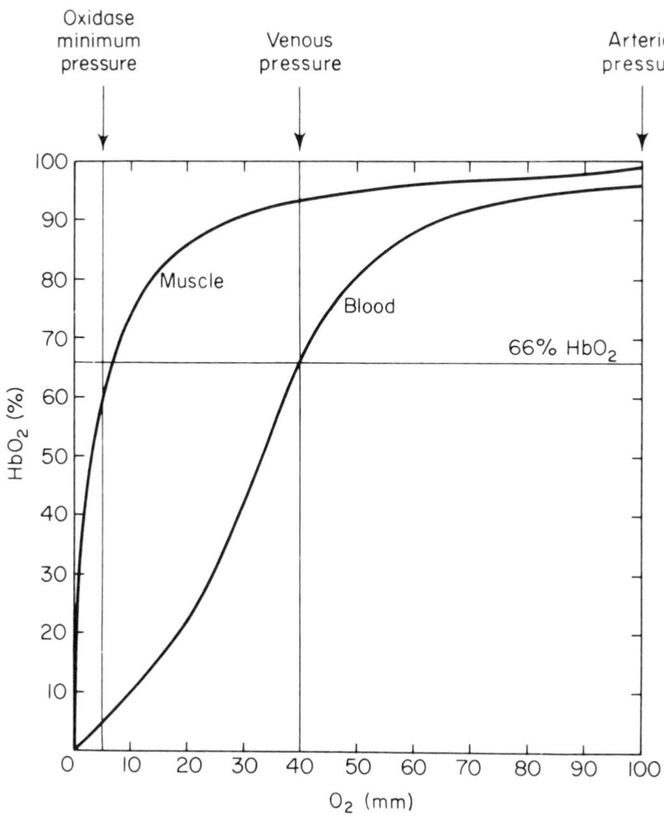

Fig. 6.2. Oxygen equilibrium curves of mammalian myoglobin and hemoglobin measured at body temperature and neutral reaction. The vertical line at the left indicates the oxygen pressure at which the rate of tissue respiration first begins to decline; presumably it represents the pressure at which the cytochrome oxidase system is just saturated with oxygen. The oxygen affinity of myoglobin lies between those of hemoglobin and the cellular oxidase system. The result is that myoglobin readily takes up oxygen from the blood and gives it up to the tissues. [Wald (1952). Graph from Hill (1936).]

blood at equilibrium is expressed as a per cent of the amount when saturated. The equilibrium curve for mammalian blood is sigmoid. It is evident (Fig. 6.2) that almost complete saturation occurs at the tensions of oxygen found in the lungs (about 95 mm Hg) and that the oxygen is very quickly lost at the tensions normally found in the tissues (about 40 mm). In this way, there is an efficient transport and a rapid unloading where required.

The curve for muscle hemoglobin or myoglobin, in marked contrast, is hyperbolic, and the unloading occurs only at very low tensions (about 5 mm). Myoglobin is a storage pigment. The red muscles are thus able to hold considerable amounts of oxygen and supply this to the cells when they are thrown into activity which overtaxes the regular delivery service. The oxygen debt is less than it would otherwise be. In the case of myoglobin the pigment is probably something more than the kind of store house which is exploited only in emergencies. As indicated in Fig. 6.2, the oxygen affinity of myoglobin lies between that of the blood hemoglobin and the oxygen tension at which the cytochrome oxidase system is just saturated with oxygen. Consequently, myoglobin will readily pick up oxygen from the blood and deliver it to appropriate enzyme systems of the tissues (Wald, 1952). The hemoglobins may come into the oxygen transfer systems at several different levels.

Phylogeny of efficient oxygen transport. The evolution of the highly efficient oxygen transport system of the higher vertebrates has involved changes related both to the biochemistry of the hemoglobin molecule and to the morphology of the cellular constituents. The most significant of the biochemical events have been (1) the establishment of an oxygen combining dependence on pH (Bohr effect) and (2) a change in the shape of the oxygen equilibrium curve from the hyperbolic to the sigmoid (Wald, 1952). The biochemical details are not entirely clear; the first of these events appears to be related to the presence of free sulfhydryl groups in the molecule and the second to the heme-heme interactions which develop through the association of units of molecular weight of about 17,000 into aggregates of four units (Gratzer and Allison, 1960; Manwell, 1960).

The tendency of the oxygen tension of the blood to be dependent on the pH facilitates the liberation of oxygen to the tissues (Fig. 6.4). Increasing acidity, which in life follows the accumulation of carbon dioxide and other metabolites, brings about a more ready release of oxygen at comparable pressures. The equilibrium curve is shifted to the right, a phenomenon first described by the Danish scientist C. Bohr (1909) and called after him, the "Bohr Effect." Most of the invertebrate hemoglobins have little or no Bohr effect while the homeothermic vertebrates have a very definite one. This relationship between oxygen equilibrium and pH varies greatly in the different species of cold-blooded vertebrates and is clearly related to their ecology and the necessary adjustments of loading and unloading oxygen under different environmental conditions. Since temperature also affects the equilibrium curve (Fig.

12.2), this factor may be balanced against the pH to utilize the oxygen resources of the environment maximally. These problems will be considered in Chapter 12.

The second significant step in the biochemical evolution of hemoglobin is related to the formation of multi-heme units and results in a sigmoid equilibrium curve. Most animals contain not one but several slightly different hemoglobins; it is evident that mutations in the genetic system responsible for their synthesis are common and have provided abundant material for the evolution of transport pigments nicely adapted to environmental conditions (Ingram, 1961). At the oxygen tensions of the animal's environment, any useful transport pigment should take up a full load of oxygen; but the efficiency of the pigment in transport will depend on its ability to unload the oxygen quickly at the oxygen levels of the tissues. Bloods characterized by *S*-shaped equilibrium curves have a relatively low affinity for oxygen at these intermediate tensions. For a given fall in oxygen tension the sigmoid curve discharges much more of its load than the hyperbolic one (Fig. 6.2).

The biochemical details of the heme-heme interaction are gradually being elucidated (Perutz, 1964) and it now seems that the tetra-heme unit is so organized that it tends to carry either four molecules of oxygen or none. In theory, each of the iron atoms might be expected to combine with one molecule of oxygen but heme alone does not combine with oxygen at all. It requires the associated protein. Each of the four amino acid chains (two alpha and two beta chains) of the tetra-heme unit enfolds one heme group. They work together as a physiological unit so that the coupling of any three of them with oxygen accelerates the fourth combination by several hundred times. The change from the deoxygenated to the oxygenated state occurs rapidly after three of the four iron atoms have combined with oxygen. The oxygen equilibrium curve owes its sigmoid form to the molecular architecture of the tetra-heme unit.

The cyclostome hemoglobins are suggestive of early stages in the biochemical phylogeny of the oxygen transport. Lamprey (*Lampetra*) hemoglobin, like that of many invertebrates, has a molecular weight of about 17,000, corresponding to one of the basic units; the oxygen equilibrium curve (like that of all invertebrates) is hyperbolic and there is, of course, no heme-heme interaction. This blood, however, has a marked Bohr effect which may be related to the presence of one free sulfhydryl group per molecule. The hagfishes also have hyperbolic equilibrium curves, but the Pacific genus *Polistotrema* has no Bohr effect; the Atlantic genus *Myxine* is said to have a mixture of hemoglobin units of molecular weight 17,000 and 34,000, marking a possible step in heme-heme interaction. The high oxygen affinity and absence of a Bohr effect in the hagfishes correlates with their habits of going inside their host, while the lower oxygen capacity and marked Bohr effect in the lampreys is more appropriate to life in the open water.

Many adjustments in the shape of the equilibrium curves have evidently been made during phylogeny. Changes also occur during ontogeny (Wald, 1963). Developing animals often live in environments of relatively low oxygen tension. The amphibian tadpole in its aquatic habitat has much less oxygen available than the terrestrial adult. Tadpole blood has a much more rectangular equilibrium curve than frog blood (Frieden, 1963) and consequently binds a maximum of oxygen in fresh waters which

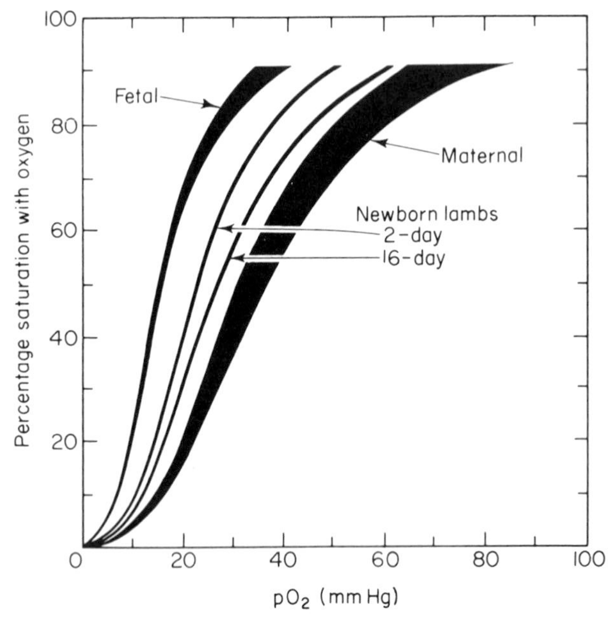

Fig. 6.3. Oxygen equilibrium curves at 38°C and pH 7.4 of fetal, newborn and maternal sheep blood. For fetuses and adults the area is indicated within which the individual curves fall. [Meschia *et al.* (1961).]

always contain much less oxygen than air. Frog hemoglobin, on the other hand, displays a sigmoid equilibrium curve, binds oxygen less tightly and delivers it more readily to tissues of the more active land animal. Further, frog hemoglobin has a marked Bohr effect which is absent in the tadpole. It is of interest that the amino acid cysteine which contains a SH group, appears in frog hemoglobin at metamorphosis and thus supports the theory that the Bohr effect is related to free SH groups.

The equilibrium curves of the avian embryo in its shell and the mammalian fetus in the uterus are likewise adjusted to their environmental limitations. In the case of the viviparous species, this permits an easy unloading of oxygen from maternal to fetal bloods (Fig. 6.3).

Florkin (1949) describes another step in the phylogeny of efficient transport fluids. This one is, in part, morphological. Carrying capacity will depend on the actual amount of hemoglobin being circulated as well as on the biochemical characteristics of the pigment. Thus, any increase in the quantity of hemoglobin will improve the ability of the blood to transport gases. This, however, soon creates a hazard by raising the osmotic content of the circulating fluids. In phylogeny two quite different physiological mechanisms have appeared in response to this dilemma. In many invertebrates larger quantities of soluble chromoprotein have been incorporated into the circulating fluids by increasing

TABLE 6.2.
SIZE AND NUMBER OF ERYTHROCYTES IN A SERIES OF REPRESENTATIVE VERTEBRATES
(From Herter, 1947).

Kind of Animal	*Diameter in Microns*	*Number of Cells in Millions per cu mm*
Proteus anguinus	58.2×33.7	0 .036
Lacerta agilis	15.9×9.9	1.42
Columba domestica	13.7×6.8	2.40
Canis familiaris	7–8	6.65
Homo sapiens ♂	6.6–9.2	5.00
Homo sapiens ♀	6.6–9.2	4.50

the size of the molecules. Since osmotic phenomena depend on the actual number of particles (molecules or ions) and not on their size, this is sometimes an adequate solution to the problem. *Lumbricus*, and some of its relatives, with hemoglobin molecular weights in the vicinity of 3,000,000, seem to represent the extreme in this direction of specialization.

The presence of extremely large polymers is at best a partial answer to the increasing oxygen demand. Not only do the very large protein molecules increase viscosity, but they seem to be less active in oxygen transport than the four-heme unit which is common in the most efficient hemoglobins. The vertebrates retained the advantages of the four-heme unit, kept the viscosity at a minimum and increased the quantity of hemoglobin tremendously by putting it in small packages, the erythrocytes.

In this way the pigment was actually removed from the vascular fluids. Subsequent improvements in transport efficiency were achieved through specialization of the erythrocytes—in particular, through the loss of the nucleus and the decrease in the size of the cell to produce a maximum of surface per unit volume (Table 6.2). A single human red blood corpuscle contains about 280 million molecules of hemoglobin (Perutz, 1964).

CHLOROCRUORIN

Chlorocruorin is also a metalloporphyrin compound (Fig. 6.1) closely allied to hemoglobin and the cytochromes. Its prosthetic group is the same as that of cytochrome *A* (Baldwin, 1963). Chlorocruorin is restricted in its distribution to four families of polychaete annelids (Manwell, 1960). It is never found in the cells; but as a plasma chromoprotein it has as great an oxygen-combining power as the comparable hemoglobins (Table 6.1). This is not surprising since the two pigments are so similar biochemically. Clearly, its phylogeny is also by way of the cytochromes. It is interesting that within the same family of worms (Sabellidae, Serpulidae and Ampharetidae) some species have chlorocruorin while others have hemoglobin. Further, in one genus *Serpula* both of the pigments are present in the blood, and the relative amounts vary with the age. Younger individuals have more of the hemoglobin. In the sabellid *Potamilla*, chlorocruorin is the blood pigment but the muscles contain hemoglobin. These various facts suggest that a genetic mutation produced the chlorocruorin molecule in a world which already knew hemoglobin and that the mutation was, for some reason, preserved (Fox and Vevers, 1960).

OTHER RESPIRATORY PIGMENTS

The remaining respiratory pigments lack the porphyrin nucleus; although they go by the names hemocyanin, hemerythrin and sometimes hemovanadium, there is in fact, no heme component. Hemocyanin is of wide occurrence and discharges those functions already discussed for hemoglobin. Hemerythrin occurs only in a few groups of animals and is probably not concerned with the transport of oxygen although the storage function is present. Hemovanadium can now be removed from the list of respiratory pigments (Manwell, 1960).

Hemocyanin is the only one of the non-heme respiratory pigments which is at all abundant in the animal kingdom. Redfield (1934) did much of the pioneer work on this pigment, and his reviews should be consulted for the early literature. Hemocyanin occurs in many of the molluscs and arthropods and is the blood pigment of the largest and most active representatives of these phyla. However, it is not considered to be a phylogenetically primitive pigment, and some of the more lowly members of these two phyla possess hemoglobin (the mollusc *Arca* and the crustacean *Daphnia,* for example). Further, the gastropod *Buccinum* and a few other invertebrates possess hemoglobin in the muscles and hemocyanin in the blood. Although the hemocyanin molecule seems to be biochemically simpler than hemoglobin, the phylogenetic distribution does not argue for a greater evolutionary antiquity.

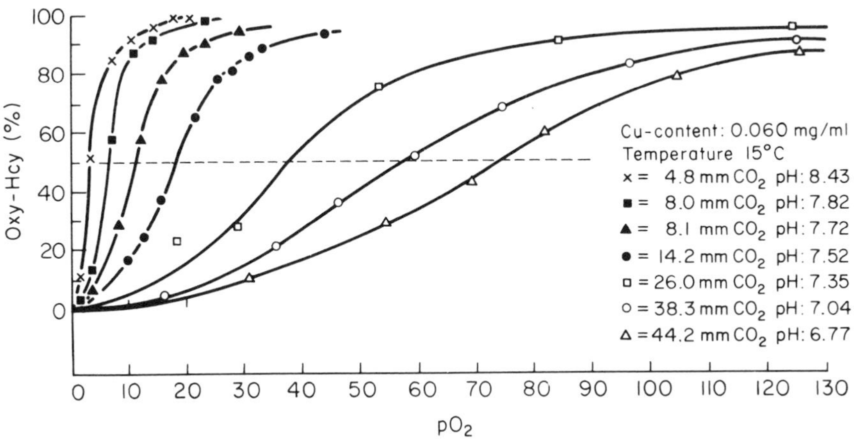

Fig. 6.4. Oxygen equilibrium curves for the blood of *Homarus gammarus* (pO_2 in mm Hg). [Waterman (1960).]

The copper containing chemical group of hemocyanin has not been characterized beyond the fact that it is a polypeptide. In deoxyhemocyanin the copper exists in the cuprous condition, but it is partially changed to the cupric state in oxyhemocyanin. Two copper atoms are required to hold one oxygen molecule, and the indications are that one of these atoms is in the cuprous and one in the cupric condition when the blood is oxygenated and changes from almost colorless to blue. Although this molecule with two copper atoms (mol wt 50,000 to 74,000) is theoretically the minimum sized oxygen combining unit, some polymerization is probably universal. Hemocyanin never occurs in blood cells, and the quantity of pigment can only be increased by forming giant molecules. In the spiny lobster (*Palinurus*) the molecular weight is 447,000; in *Octopus vulgaris* it is 2,785,000 and in the snail *Helix pomatia* 6,650,000 (Fox and Vevers, 1960).

The pigment clearly functions in transport as well as storage. In some of the cephalopods the oxygen capacity compares with that of the less efficient hemoglobins although it is always much lower than the vertebrate hemoglobins (Table 6.1). The equilibrium curves are rather rectangular, but the shapes depend markedly on the pH (Fig. 6.4) and the temperature (Fig. 6.5). In some species they depend also on Ca^{++} (Fig. 6.6), a fact which may be of significance during molting when calcium levels are markedly altered (Chapter 24).

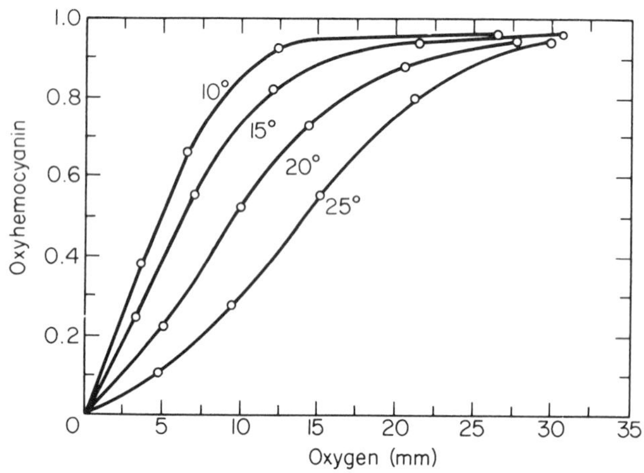

Fig. 6.5. Oxygen equilibrium curves of *Panulirus interruptus* hemocyanin at various temperatures (pH 7.53). [Waterman (1960).]

Hemerythrin has been considered a close relative of hemocyanin although the biochemistry of neither is established. It is only known that in both the metallic atom is held, in some way, by the protein and not in a special prosthetic group. Hemerythrin contains iron, and it appears that three atoms of the iron are necessary to form combinations with an oxygen molecule. In oxyhemerythrin the three atoms of iron are in the ferric state; in the deoxy- condition two of these revert to the ferrous state while the other remains in the ferric condition (Fox and Vevers, 1960). The pigment was first discovered in the ancient brachiopod *Lingula* and has been found in only a few other animals (the sipunculids, the priapulids and one polychaete annelid, *Magelona*). It may occur in cells (coelomic corpuscles of *Sipunculus*) but is usually in plasma solution. Its function as a storage pigment is indicated, and it could be an oxygen transporter in *Magelona* (Fox and Vevers, 1960). Molecular weights of 66,000 and 120,000 have been recorded for different hemerythrins (Manwell, 1960).

Several other compounds, at one time thought to be respiratory pigments, have now been removed from the list, either because more refined techniques have failed to show any capacity for the formation of reversible compounds with oxygen (the vanadium chromogens) or

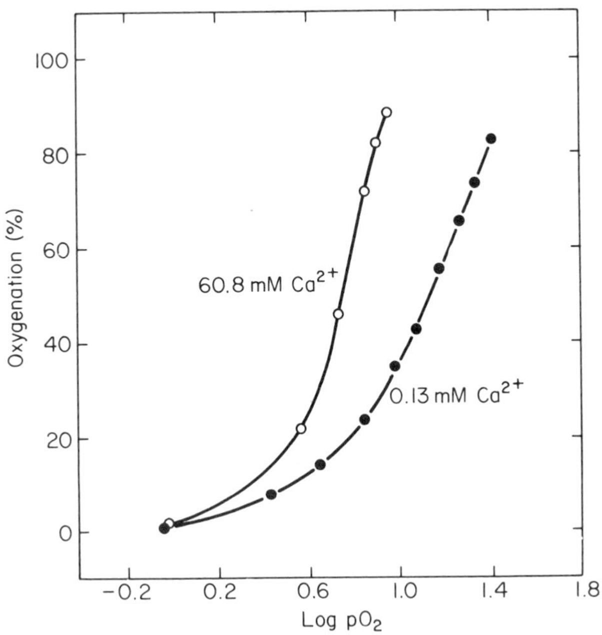

Fig. 6.6. Effect of calcium on the oxygen equilibrium curve of crayfish hemocyanin at pH 7.6. Note that Ca^{++} increases the oxygen affinity and that this effect increases with degree of oxygenation. [Larimer and Riggs (1964).]

because the identification of the compound as a chromoprotein was probably mistaken (the manganese pigment, pinnaglobin and the zinc compound, hemosycotypin). Vanadium chromogen (hemovanadium) remains interesting, however, for it is present in the blood cells (vanadocytes) of several families of ascidians and in the plasma of some others (Nicol, 1960*a*). The compound contains pyrrole rings but not the porphyrin complex. It has been suggested that these rings form a chain as in the bilins (Fox and Vevers, 1960). It may be concerned with oxidation-reduction, but its function has not been established.

The Transport of Carbon Dioxide

Although the solubility of carbon dioxide in water is much greater than that of oxygen, the amounts which can be carried in simple solution are totally inadequate for most animals. A transport based on solubility would take care of less than one tenth of the requirements of a mammal. Carbon dioxide, like oxygen, is carried in a chemical combination of a highly specialized nature as indicated by Fig. 6.7.

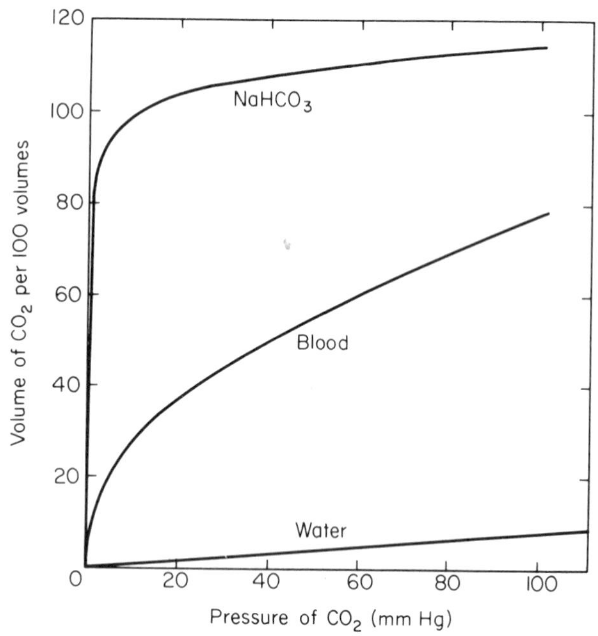

Fig. 6.7. Comparison between the carbon dioxide equilibrium curves of blood and sodium bicarbonate solution of a concentration 0.0484*N*. The amounts of CO_2 held in physical solution in water are shown in the lowest line. [Evans (1956).]

The relatively small amounts held in simple solution depend on the pressure (and temperature) but do not exceed about 5 volumes per cent. Sea water, with its excess of strong cations, forms carbonates and hence has a greater capacity than fresh water. A bicarbonate solution contains much CO_2, but in forming this combination the chemical reaction is rapid and complete at relatively low pressures. It is further evident from the equilibrium reaction:

$$2NaHCO_3 \rightleftharpoons Na_2CO_3 + CO_2 + H_2O$$

that under vacuum only half of this carbon dioxide of a bicarbonate solution will be discharged. Acid must be added to evolve the other half.

Blood does not behave in this way at all. As indicated in the middle curve of Fig. 6.7, blood combines with carbon dioxide rapidly at first and then more slowly; but even at the highest pressures shown there is still a reserve capacity for the transport of this gas. Neither a simple solution nor a bicarbonate compound would satisfy the transport problems of a large active invertebrate or a vertebrate.

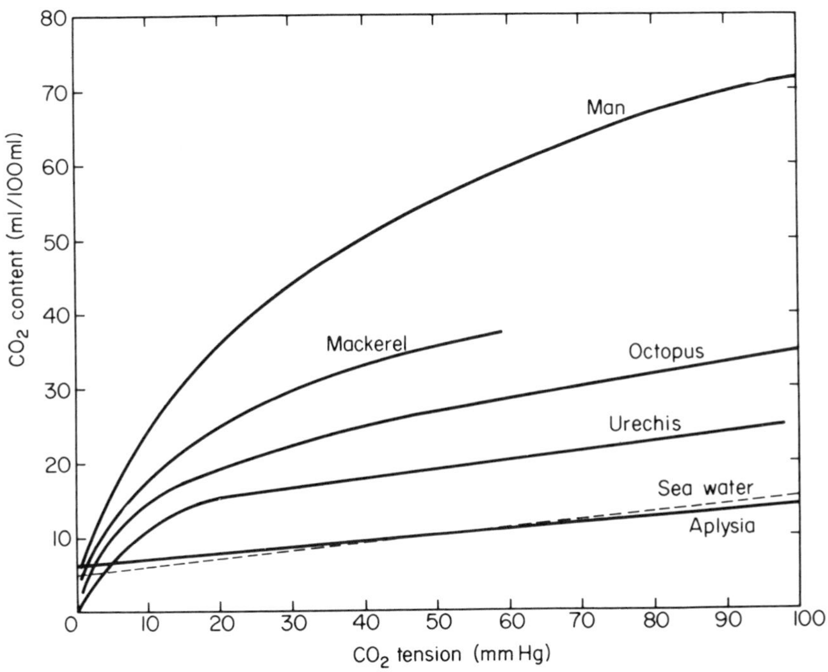

Fig. 6.8. A family of CO_2 equilibrium curves for bloods compared with sea water (broken line). [Data from Parsons and Parsons (1923) and Florkin (1934).]

Although this is true for many animals, there are some species which do depend on these ordinary chemical mechanisms. This is only possible if they are relatively sedentary or have low rates of metabolism. A group of carbon dioxide dissociation curves is shown in Fig. 6.8. The hemolymph of *Aplysia* or an ascidian has no special transport materials, and the amounts held in the body fluids are essentially the same as those dissolved or in other ways held by the buffers of sea water. The blood of *Urechis*, on the other hand, shows an additional capacity for CO_2 (in the form of organic buffers), but this is quickly reached at about 20 mm Hg; thereafter the curve parallels that of sea water. Finally, the hemolymph of the octopus or the blood of man takes up more and more CO_2 over the entire range and has evidently some additional capacity at the upper limits shown on the graph. At 100 mm Hg mammalian blood holds about 10 times more carbon dioxide than the blood of the sedentary tunicate or the nudibranch. What are the CO_2 transport peculiarities of these more highly specialized bloods?

Three major factors account for the high carbon dioxide capacities of bloods and hemolymphs. The first of these is the same chromoprotein material involved in oxygen transport. Although other proteins of blood may have a certain buffering capacity, the chromoproteins form the major protein constituent and hence are the main chemicals for the FORMATION OF BICARBONATE COMPOUNDS. Hemoglobin is a potassium salt and will combine with carbonic acid as follows:

$$KHb + H_2CO_3 \rightleftharpoons KHCO_3 + HHb$$

Similarly, hemocyanin and the other respiratory pigments can buffer the carbonic acid. In some bloods there are also inorganic buffer systems. In mammalian blood, for example, the phosphate buffers of the plasma (sodium salts) and the corpuscles (potassium salts) will also take up carbonate. Thus, the reaction:

$$Na_2HPO_4 + H_2CO_3 \rightleftharpoons NaH_2PO_4 + NaHCO_3$$

accounts for some of the combination, but this is a minor factor in comparison with the blood proteins. As a matter of fact, it has been shown that if hemocyanin is deproteinized it will then combine with no more CO_2 than will sea water.

In the second place, some of the chromoproteins are also able to form DIRECT COMBINATIONS WITH CARBON DIOXIDE. In hemoglobin solutions carbon dioxide forms direct links with amino groups in the protein portion of the molecule as follows:

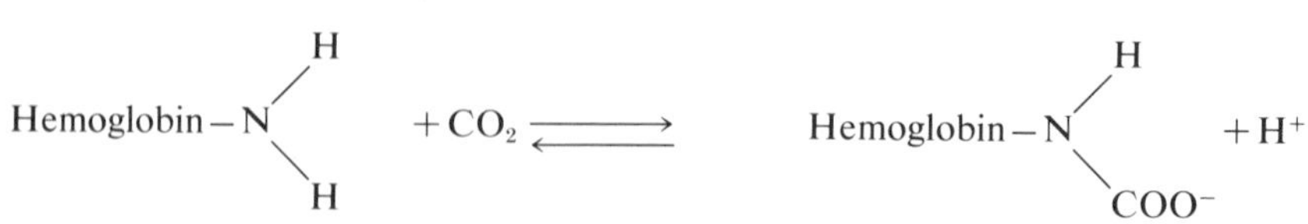

The carbamino compounds so formed constitute only a small factor (2 to 10 per cent) in the transport but are particularly significant because of the rapidity with which the combination occurs. Other chromoproteins may form similar linkages, but CO_2 transport in the invertebrates is considered to depend primarily on the buffers.

A third important factor in efficient CO_2 transport mechanisms is the presence of the zinc-containing enzyme carbonic anhydrase which promotes the reaction between water and carbon dioxide.

$$H_2O + CO_2 \underset{}{\overset{\text{carbonic anhydrase}}{\rightleftarrows}} H_2CO_3 \rightleftarrows H^+ + HCO_3^-$$

This enzyme is always found in cells and is known to play a part in the ion movements which occur in several tissues (kidney, gastric mucosa, pancreas) as well as in blood. Its significance in the transport of CO_2 by the invertebrates is speculative, but its presence in gills is suggestive. It might be concerned with the release of CO_2 from gill epithelium, since the enzyme catalyzes the reaction in both directions. It is also abundant in some muscles and glands of the invertebrates (Wolvekamp and Waterman, 1960) and might serve to accelerate the removal of carbon dioxide from actively metabolizing cells and bring it more quickly into the hemolymph. This is speculation. Its established function in CO_2 transport has been demonstrated only in the vertebrates where, as a blood constituent, it is confined to the corpuscles. The CO_2 passing from the tissues into the capillaries diffuses quickly into the corpuscles and is held largely as carbonate. Without carbonic anhydrase the reaction is so slow that only small amounts are probably combined directly with water in the plasma. This does not mean that the carbonate formed within the red cell is entirely transported in this structure since it can readily diffuse into the plasma. The point emphasized here is that the initial combination occurs almost entirely in the cell (85 to 90 per cent in the mammal).

The details of CO_2 transport in the vertebrate are summarized in Table 6.3. Small amounts of CO_2 entering the plasma dissolve as such or form carbonic acid (line *a*), but almost all of it diffuses directly into the corpuscle and forms carbamino groups (line *b*) or is converted into carbonic acid by the special enzyme system (line *c*). Some of this carbonic acid may diffuse back into the plasma (line *d*1), but the bulk of it is tied up by the hemoglobin reaction as bicarbonate (line *d*2). In the plasma, the carbonic acid (from whatever source) unites with plasma proteins (NaPr) or inorganic buffers (Na_2HPO_4) as shown in lines *e*1 and *e*2. In the corpuscle the ionized potassium bicarbonate provides bicarbonate ions which can exchange with the chloride ions in the plasma in a Donnan equilibrium shift (Davson, 1959) as shown in lines *f*1 and *f*2. This is the so-called chloride or Hamburger shift. The net result is that, although most of the CO_2 is first combined with hemoglobin in the corpuscle, a very considerable portion of this is, in reality, transported as carbonate in the plasma.

TABLE 6.3.
CARBON DIOXIDE TRANSPORT IN VERTEBRATES
(Modified from Harper, 1963).

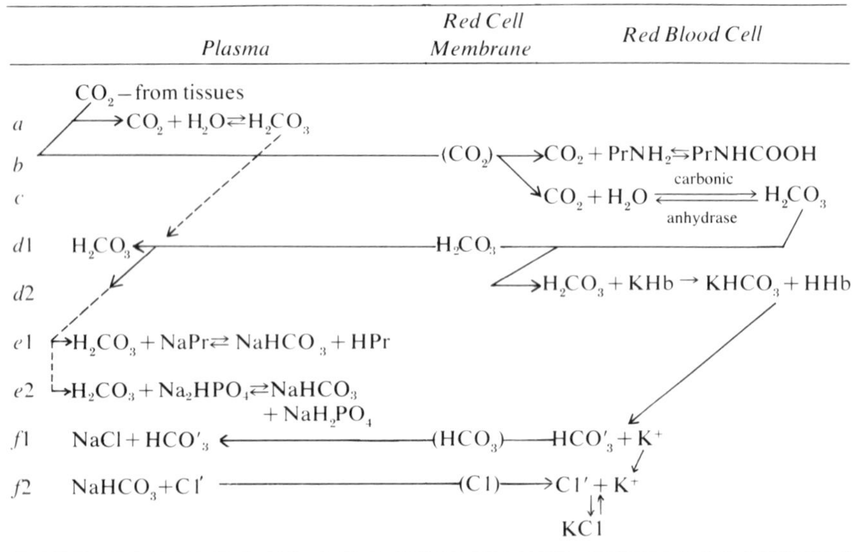

It is emphasized that the CO_2-combining powers of hemoglobin and hemocyanin (and perhaps of other chromoproteins) depend to some extent on their state of oxygenation (Bard, 1961; Wolvekamp and Waterman, 1960). Oxyhemoglobin is relatively acid, and deoxyhemoglobin is relatively alkaline. With the discharge of oxygen in the tissues, the hemoglobin becomes more alkaline and will combine with increasing amounts of carbonic acid. Thus, the horizontal distance between the titration curves of Fig. 6.9 shows the pH shift which occurs when hemoglobin is oxygenated or deoxygenated; the vertical distance is a measure of the buffering capacity and shows how much H^+ can be added without a shift in pH. This amounts to 0.7 millimole of hydrogen ions taken up by hemoglobin when 1 millimole of oxygen is given off. The calculations have been summarized in a lucid manner by Davenport (1958). The mechanisms are reversed in the lungs and the CO_2 is readily discharged into the atmosphere.

Finally, the blood is not the only material which will combine with carbon dioxide to form carbonates. Shells, chitin and skeletal materials usually have a high carbonate content. Under acid conditions produced

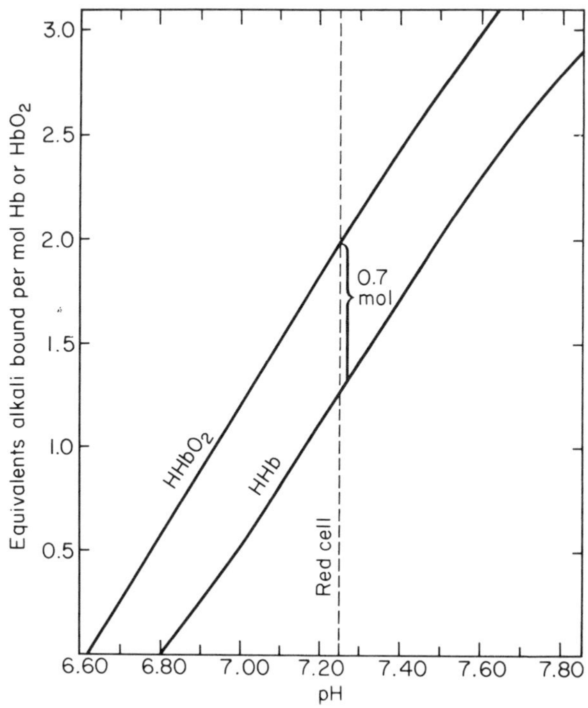

Fig. 6.9. Influence of pH on equivalents of alkali bound per mole of oxygenated ($HHbO_2$) or deoxygenated (HHb) hemoglobin. Note that the titration curves for the two hemoglobins are parallel. At any pH (e.g., the 7.25 pH within the erythrocytes) the oxyhemoglobin binds 0.7 equivalents more base than does the deoxyhemoglobin. Hence, for each mole of O_2 released from oxyhemoglobin in the tissues, 0.7 *M* of H^+ formed by release of CO_2 can be neutralized by the deoxyhemoglobin without altering the pH. [Based on Bard (1961) after Peters and Van Slyke (1931).]

by anaerobic metabolism during anoxia, such structures may be an important means of CO_2 elimination. This has been demonstrated in some of the bivalve molluscs (Dugal, 1939).

Plasma Proteins and Regulation of Fluid Volume

The plasma volume of an animal with a closed circulatory system depends on a balance between the rate of filtration from the capillaries into the tissue spaces and the rate of reabsorption of this filtrate (Fig. 5.8). The blood pressure creates the driving force for filtration, while the osmotic pressure of the plasma operates in the reverse direction. The plasma proteins are responsible for a large part of this osmotically active material.

Osmotic forces are also important in the fluid balance of invertebrate animals with open circulatory systems. Those which operate with a fluid skeleton develop relatively high internal hydrostatic pressures during movement, and these pressures could force fluids from the animals through permeable membranes even though these fluids are isotonic with the environments. Preservation of the body fluids depends on the permeability of the surface membranes and colloidal osmotic pressures of the body fluids.

Prosser and Brown (1961) tabulate the protein content of body fluids in representative animals from different phyla; these show a range from about 0.2 to 1.0 mg/ml in lower forms to about 35 to 65 mg/ml in many arthropods and vertebrates. In the higher vertebrates the albumin fraction amounts to about 55 per cent of the total plasma protein (mammals) and is primarily responsible for maintenance of plasma volume. It is readily separated electrophoretically because of the mobility of the relatively highly charged small molecules (mol wt about 69,000 as against 170,000 for other plasma proteins). This technique has now been applied to many animals and the albumins have been shown to be characteristic only of the bloods of the higher vertebrates with their more refined homeostatic controls. An electrophoretic analysis of the serum proteins of 26 species of fish (representing 14 families) from the Gulf of Mexico provides an interesting example of the phylogenetic trends (Gunter *et al*, 1961). Representatives from the elasmobranchs, holosteans (gar pike) and teleosts were included. The total plasma protein was lower than in the mammals and showed a general increase from primitive to more specialized groups. The elasmobranchs, the gars and about half of the Clupeidae (relatively primitive teleosts) lacked the albumin fraction. The correlation between albumin and phyletic position was not perfect since two of the perciform species (relatively advanced teleosts) also lacked albumin. There was, however, a definite increase in complexity of plasma proteins in the more advanced groups, and this was reflected in the globulin fractions as well as in the albumins.

The phylogenetic significance of the serum proteins may have been particularly great in the evolution of terrestrial life with the acute problem of maintaining fluids within the vascular system in the face of desiccation and preserving a balance between the blood and the fluids of the tissue spaces. Several studies of metamorphosing amphibians support this argument (Frieden, 1963). Tadpoles contain little or no serum albumin; virtually all the plasma proteins are globulins. At metamorphosis there is a steady increase both in the amount of serum protein and in the proportion of albumin to a maximum of about 50 per cent of the serum protein. Albumin because of its large electrical charge binds smaller organic molecules and salts and is particularly important osmotically.

Phagocytosis, the Reticulo-Endothelial System and Immune Reactions

PHAGOCYTIC CELLS

Ameboid phagocytic cells are found in the tissues of all multicellular animals (Wagge, 1955). They occur in the circulating fluids, in body spaces such as the coelom and in the tissues generally. In some of the primitive invertebrates, ameboid phagocytes are the only blood cells; they arise from mesenchymal cells included in the differentiating spaces which form the blood channels. Among the invertebrates these cells perform a variety of functions—digestion, excretion, regeneration and repair. At the lower phylogenetic levels they have two main capacities in the defense mechanisms of the animal: engulfing foreign material and migrating into an injured area to initiate the processes of repair. At the higher phylogenetic levels the system is more elaborate as these cells have acquired additional capacities in reactions to foreign materials.

In many groups of animals, from nematodes through the phylogenetic series, some of the phagocytic cells are organized into distinct organs. Huff (1940) describes three different arrangements among the invertebrates. LYMPHOGENOUS ORGANS are made up of masses of primitive blood cells grouped in nodules and held together by connective tissue. They are found in blood sinuses and have been described in annelids, scorpions, cephalopods, and in a few insects and crustaceans. NEPHROPHAGOCYTES, with a dual function of excretion and phagocytosis occur separately or as masses of cells scattered through the tissues of many animals from annelids through echinoderms. The PHAGOCYTIC ORGANS, consisting of a reticular network filled with phagocytes, are usually situated in the pericardial space where blood must pass over them to reach the heart. They are best known in the insects but have also been described in nematodes, some annelids, crustaceans and molluscs. In some species of midge several stages have been described in the ontogeny of phagocytic organs from the phagocytic hemocytes of the blood (Roeder, 1953). A parallel in phylogeny is suggested.

Among the vertebrates the phagocytic system (usually referred to as the reticulo-endothelial system or the macrophage system) is highly organized with circulating leucocytes, ameboid tissue cells and extensive reticular nets. Some writers include both wandering and sessile phagocytic cells in this system, while others restrict the term "reticulo-endothelial (R-E) system" to the fixed reticulum of phagocytic organs (Ham and Leeson, 1961). In any case, wandering and fixed cells operate together to remove the debris from worn-out or injured cells and to maintain the defenses of the body against invading organisms. In the mammal these phagocytic activities depend on the blood neutrophils and monocytes, tissue histocytes or macrophages, the microglial cells of the central nervous system and the sessile reticulum cells of the liver (Kupffer cells), bone marrow, spleen, lymph nodes and other sinusoidal tissues of the body. In some cases, such as the lymph nodes (found only in birds and mammals—Young, 1957) the tissues form a compact filter, placed strategically in the lymph drainage system. The phagocytic system, whether composed of wandering or sessile cells, performs the important function of disposing of waste or foreign matter.

ANTIGEN-ANTIBODY REACTIONS AND THE IMMUNE PROCESS

Many animals have acquired special capacities for the removal or inactivation of bacteria, viruses and large organic molecules. This ability depends on the elaboration of specific proteins which agglutinate, precipitate, neutralize or dissolve the foreign organisms and materials. Foreign material which evokes such a response in an organism is called an ANTIGEN, while the material elaborated to counteract its presence is an ANTIBODY. The process is sometimes referred to as the IMMUNE PROCESS or reaction, sometimes as an ANTIGEN-ANTIBODY REACTION.

Although the immune response is usually evoked by proteins, it may develop with other large molecules (mol wt 10,000 or more) such as some of the polysaccharides. The antigenic material is often a part of foreign cells or bacteria, but it may be a protein in solution. A PRIMARY RESPONSE is induced by the first injection. This normally passes unnoticed, but at the tissue level it promotes the elaboration of the antibodies (proteins of the gamma globulin type). When a second injection is made the violent reaction of antigen and antibody produces a variety of symptoms in the animal and may lead to death. Basically, the antibody molecules seem to act as bridges between the foreign particles, linking them together in large clumps which may later dissolve or be phagocytized. These reactions are markedly specific in mammals. As yet it is not clearly understood how an antigen stimulates cells (in the mammal these are the plasma cells) to elaborate antibodies. Several theories have been proposed, and details may be found in textbooks and monographs devoted to immunology (Burnet, 1959; Najjar, 1963).

Immune reactions are observed in the invertebrates as well as in the vertebrates (Bang, 1962; Cushing, 1962; Huff, 1940). Although they seem to be less intense and of lower specificity among the poikilotherms, there are still insufficient comparative data to draw firm conclusions. Much of the published work is devoted to the homeotherms; since temperature has a definite effect on the immune reaction, some of the observed differences between poikilotherms and homeotherms may be due to temperature rather than to the genetic capacities to develop immunity. It has, for example, been shown that the antibody response of the toad *Xenopus* takes place in two stages and that one of these is so highly temperature-dependent that the entire process can be masked at lower temperatures. FORMATION of antibodies occurs at lower temperatures, down to 8°C, but RELEASE into the circulation occurs only at 20°C or higher (Elek *et al.*, 1962). Such findings argue for caution in making general comparisons between poikilotherms and homeotherms.

Blood groups. There are many NATURALLY-OCCURRING antigens and antibodies in addition to those which may be INDUCED in response to foreign substances. These have now been detected at several different levels in phylogeny. The hemerythrocytes of the sipunculid worm *Dendrostomum* has antigens which react with human anti-A and anti-B serum; the serum of the spiny lobster *Panulirus* contains a substance which agglutinates erythrocytes from whale species belonging to the *Ju*2 blood types (Cushing *et al.*, 1963); the Atlantic lobster has a factor in its serum which clumps the red cells of the herring (Sinderman and Mairs, 1959); seminal fluids of many animals contain natural antibodies which clump sperm or cells of other species (Metz, 1957; Metz and Kohler, 1960; Kohler and Metz, 1960). The literature contains many other examples. These reactions depend on highly specific proteins whose syntheses are genetically controlled. In some cases the interactions are probably fortuitous and of no particular biological significance; the interactions between sipunculid blood cells and human blood sera would seem to be of this sort. In other cases these reactions are highly important to the species; the chemicals which control the interactions between eggs and sperm must certainly be in this class (Raven, 1959).

The human blood group system is one of the best known of the naturally-occurring immune reactions. Landsteiner described the ABO system in 1900; excerpts from his and several other classical papers on human blood groups have been reproduced in Boyer (1963). Human erythrocytes may carry one or the other, both or neither of two antigens A and B; the blood plasma may carry corresponding antibodies as indicated in Table 6.4. The proportions of the genotypes (Table 6.4) vary signifi-

TABLE 6.4.
HUMAN BLOOD GROUPS
(Boyd, 1950).

A. *The blood groups*

Blood group		*Agglutinogen in corpuscle*	*Agglutinin in serum*
Phenotype	Genotype		
O	OO	O	Anti-A + Anti-B
A	AA AO	A	Anti-B
B	BB BO	B	Anti-A
AB	AB	A + B	–

B. *Determination of human blood groups with two test sera, Anti-A and Anti-B.*

	Known serum Anti-A	*Known serum Anti-B*	*Group*
Agglutination of unknown blood corpuscles	–	–	O
	+	–	A
	–	+	B
	+	+	AB

cantly in different races. In Western races the O group forms about 50 per cent; A, 40 per cent; B, 8 per cent; and AB, 2 per cent; but in the pure North American Indians (except for one or two tribes) group AB is unknown, and group B is very rare. In Siam, group B (relatively uncommon in some Western races) occurs to the extent of 35 per cent. Boyd (1950) provides detailed tables of the frequencies of these groups. There are many other naturally-occurring antigens in human blood; these were not recognized as early as the AB antigens because there are no corresponding antibodies. They can, however, be readily demonstrated by inducing specific antigens for them in another animal; they are often induced in man through blood transfusions or some other association with the particular antigen. A full discussion of the human blood groups is given in textbooks of medical physiology.

For many years it was tacitly agreed that man was unique in the possession of distinct blood groups. However, first dogs and chickens, then many other groups of animals have been shown to have systems of this nature (Swisher and Young, 1961). Blood groups now seem to be demonstrated wherever a careful search is made. The dogfish *Squalus acanthias* in the Gulf of Maine has four groups with a clear-cut genetic system (Sinderman and Mairs, 1961); sockeye salmon *Oncorhynchus nerka* are of at least eight different antigenic types or combinations of types, and the frequency of these different types varies in different geographical races (Ridgway and Klontz, 1960). Many other examples will be found in the literature cited above.

Serology as a tool in taxonomy. Several of these antigenic differences in blood proteins have been used in taxonomy as adjuncts to gross morphological characters. There seems to be no convincing evidence that the blood proteins are generally superior to the morphological characters for taxonomic purposes, but they do frequently provide useful additional evidence. Boyden (1942, 1963) and his associates have made extensive use of precipitin testing in which antibodies are induced (usually in rabbits), and these antisera then mixed with sera from the same and other species. The strongest reaction (agglutination or protein precipitation) is given with the homologous serum, the intensity of reaction decreasing with distance in phyletic position (heterologous sera). Other workers have used naturally-occurring antigens and antibodies such as those which are demonstrated by mixing lobster serum with herring erythrocytes. In these tests, mentioned above (page 193), two distinct groups of Atlantic herring were noted, one in which the cells were clumped at dilutions of 1 : 128 and another in which they clump at 1 : 4. Other blood tests of a comparable nature include the direct electrophoretic separation of plasma proteins and the rates of hemolysis of erythrocytes suspended in a series of hemolysins (Jacobs *et al*, 1950). These different blood tests add a number of useful characters for the taxonomist who must make difficult decisions on animal relationships.

Hemostasis and the Coagulation of Blood

Loss of body fluids becomes a progressively greater hazard as the circulating fluids assume more functions and as specialized physiological mechanisms become dependent on the continuous flow of blood at high pressures. The dangers are probably also greater for aquatic organisms in the fresh water habitat (markedly hypotonic) than in the ocean where the invertebrates and some of the vertebrates live in an isosmotic medium. Phylogenetically more advanced animals have a group of safeguards which restrict the loss of fluid in bleeding hazards from the trauma of blood vessels. Grégoire and Tagnon (1962) have summarized the available information in tabular form.

HEMOSTASIS WITHOUT PLASMA CLOTTING

The most primitive arrangement depends only on the contractility of body musculature and blood vessels. In many of the soft-bodied invertebrates this may be the sole hemostatic mechanism. Spasms of blood vessels and contractions of the body wall have been noted among marine worms and sea cucumbers, and in some of the annelids nothing more complex may be required. Such devices, however, would be inadequate for hard-bodied animals such as the arthropods, many echinoderms and molluscs or for the soft-bodied animals with even moderate blood pressures. In these forms the vascular fluids contain cellular elements and special jelling proteins which form plugs at the site of injury. Although most groups of animals have not yet been carefully studied, there is now enough information based on careful studies of the echinoderms (Boolootian and Giese, 1959), the arthropods (Florkin, 1960) and the vertebrates (Fulton, 1955) to draw some general conclusions (Grégoire and Tagnon, 1962).

In the more primitive groups of animals only blood cells are involved in clot formation. In several of the echinoderms (the crinoid, *Heliometra,* the ophiuroid, *Gorgonocephalus* and the echinoid, *Dendraster*) the blood cells, following injury, show a temporary agglutination but do not lose their identity. This may also happen in some of the arthropods and molluscs. But usually in these groups, and also in the asteroids among the echinoderms, the cell agglutination is followed by plasmodium formation in which the protoplasm of the agglutinated cells fuses and the cells lose their identity. In the next step, the cells produce a fibrous protein material which serves to entangle other cells and increase the size and strength of the cell coagulum. This phenomenon was carefully studied by Loeb, many years ago, in *Limulus.* The fibrous material produced by the cells was called CELL FIBRIN but is not biochemically similar to the fibrins of the plasma clots. Similar processes of cell coagulation have been described in several groups of spiders and in some crustaceans such as the edible crab *Cancer* (Grégoire and Tagnon, 1962).

PARTICIPATION OF THE PLASMA PROTEINS

In many of the arthropods, and in all of the vertebrates, blood clots are primarily composed of tangled protein fibers which develop from a plasma protein, fibrinogen. The conversion of fibrinogen to fibrin is an enzymatic reaction which is initiated by material released from injured cells. Among the invertebrates and the lower vertebrates the thromboplastic activity responsible for the transformation of fibrinogen to fibrin is either completely or almost completely contained in cells and released only when they rupture. In the higher vertebrates several thromboplastic factors (along with anti-thromboplastic elements) are also found in the plasma.

The crustaceans and insects exemplify the simpler situation. In many species, islands of coagulation develop around agglutinations of blood cells, and then the coagulation extends through the hemolymph. The speed of clotting varies in different species, and several different categories of coagulation are recognized (Florkin, 1960; Grégoire and Tagnon, 1962). Highly specialized fragile blood cells associated with the clotting mechanisms are called Hardy's explosive cells in the crustaceans and coagulocytes in the insects.

The formation of the mammalian blood clot is controlled by several different factors. Intensive medical research has demonstrated a dozen or more distinct factors in the plasma, with an initial activation of the plasma system by factors from damaged cells. These mechanisms are detailed in textbooks of medical physiology and in the review already cited. The following is a somewhat simplified scheme for fibrin formation in mammalian blood:

$$\text{Platelets} + \text{antihemophilic globulin} \xrightarrow[\text{(Factor IX)}]{\text{Christmas factor}} \text{Product I}$$

$$\underset{}{\text{Product I}} + \underset{\text{(Factor V)}}{\text{Proaccelerin}} \xrightarrow[\text{(Factor VII)}]{\text{Proconvertin, } Ca^{++}} \text{Thromboplastin}$$

$$\text{Prothrombin} \xrightarrow[Ca^{++}]{\text{Thromboplastin}} \text{Thrombin}$$

$$\text{Fibrinogen} \xrightarrow{\text{Thrombin}} \text{Fibrin}$$

Thus, cell injury (rupture of mammalian platelets) initiates a chain of reactions in the plasma. Cells, other than blood platelets, may also contain clotting factors, and an injury to certain tissues releases substances similar to Product I; these initiate the reaction sequence at this point.

Blood clotting in the lower vertebrates depends much more on cellular factors. The thrombocytes of fishes and amphibians seem to provide all of the thromboplastic factors shown in the first two lines above (Doolittle and Surgenov, 1962). Reptiles and birds are also deficient in the plasma thromboplastic components; they seem to rely more on vasoconstriction and the rapid liberation of TISSUE THROMBOPLASTIN (Fantl, 1961). The trend in the higher vertebrates has been an extension into the extracellular plasma of mechanisms primitively confined to the intracellular medium. The initial steps always depend on cellular elements, but the presence of abundant clotting factors in the plasma provides for the production of a more permanent type of hemostasis (Grégoire and Tagnon, 1962).

Several anticoagulants in mammalian plasma provide safeguards in this clotting system which is so effective and necessary in trauma, but a potential hazard if activated within the vascular channels. There is enough clotting enzyme in 10 ml of human blood to coagulate all the blood in the human body. An albuminoid material, antithrombin, is believed to neutralize some of the clotting factors, thereby preventing the formation of dangerous intravascular clots. Heparin, a mucopolysaccharide, is a powerful anticoagulant, perhaps acting as a cofactor with antithrombin. Additional safeguards may be present.

Besides these anticoagulants produced as protective compounds in the animal's blood, there are materials of similar nature which enable predacious species to take vertebrate blood without troublesome clottings. The leech produces an antithrombin (hirudin) which permits the removal and storage of blood in the fluid condition. Blood-sucking insects inject anticoagulants when they puncture vertebrate skin in feeding. Predators have exploited thromboplastins as well as anticoagulants; the venom of the viper contains a powerful proteolytic enzyme which causes disastrous intravascular clots when injected into an unlucky mammal.

The Transformation of Energy

7

Energy necessary for the varied activities of life is generated in a series of chemical reactions, collectively referred to as cellular metabolism or respiration. The term METABOLISM is universally used to describe the many chemical reactions which take place in the living organism whether these are constructive (ANABOLISM) or destructive (CATABOLISM). The term RESPIRATION, on the other hand, has several different usages. The Latin word, from which it is derived, means "to breathe" or "exhale" and, in this sense, respiration was originally applied to the exchange of gases between an organism and its environment. It referred to the obvious activities of breathing or their equivalent. As the years went by, it became apparent that the really fundamental exchanges were occurring at the cellular level, and the term INTERNAL RESPIRATION was often applied to this phase of gaseous exchange. At present, the adjective "internal" has been dropped, and respiration is frequently applied to cellular processes. Some writers restrict it to those which involve the uptake of gaseous oxygen, while others use it more generally for all of the energy-yielding reactions of the cell. In this book it will be used in the latter sense. Those activities of an animal which involve an exchange of gases between the organism and its environment will be referred to as VENTILATION. The term INTERMEDIARY METABOLISM is synonymous with cellular metabolism as used here.

Energy-Producing Reactions

OXIDATION AND REDUCTION

The energy exchanges of life center around the transfer of electrons. When electrons are removed from a substance it is said to be oxidized; when they are added to atoms or groups of atoms these atoms are said to be reduced. As one substance is oxidized through the removal of electrons, another substance which picks up the electrons is thereby reduced. Thus, when the ferrous ion is oxidized to the ferric state, an electron is released. The reversibility of such an oxidation-reduction is thus indicated:

$$Fe^{++} \underset{\text{reduction}}{\overset{\text{oxidation}}{\rightleftharpoons}} Fe^{+++} + e$$

Very often, and this is true of many biological reactions, the electron travels with a proton as a part of the hydrogen atom. In this case the oxidation is a dehydrogenation and the reduction a hydrogenation. Two familiar biochemical reactions of this sort are:

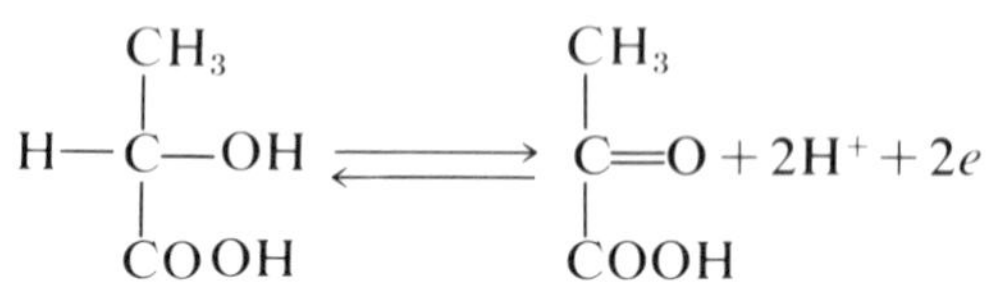

LACTIC ACID   PYRUVIC ACID

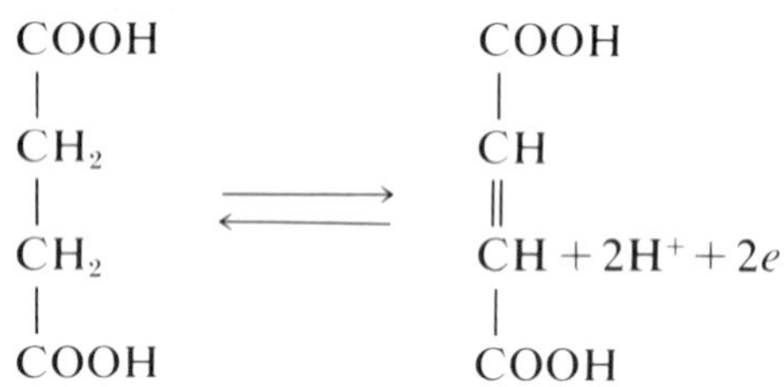

SUCCINIC ACID   FUMARIC ACID

Exchanges of electrons are almost always accompanied by the release or the absorption of energy. The cellular work necessary for life depends on an intricate series of such electron exchanges or oxidation-reduction reactions. Details of the energetics will be found in textbooks of biochemistry and cell physiology. Only the general principles will be emphasized here.

THE EXCHANGE OF ENERGY

Several generalizations, necessary for an understanding of the metabolic pathways in tissue respiration, concern relative amounts of energy associated with different biochemical reactions. Some of the reactions of life are accompanied by only minor redistributions of energy; others proceed only when supplied with energy from outside sources; a relatively small number are associated with the release of very large amounts of free energy. This last group of reactions involves a series of biochemicals, collectively referred to as the energy-rich compounds. One of them, adenosine triphosphate or ATP, was identified in the introductory chapter.

The situation may be visualized by referring to the familiar hexose sugar, glucose. The blood of a fasting man contains 80 to 120 mg of this sugar per 100 ml. It is a rich potential source of energy for all sorts of animal activities and may be used for this purpose or stored in the form or glycogen or fat. However, the glucose molecule is at a very low free energy level and cannot be directly utilized for energy purposes; first its energy relationships must be altered through a priming reaction in which it captures free energy through the hexokinase reaction. The scheme may be summarized as follows (Baldwin, 1963):

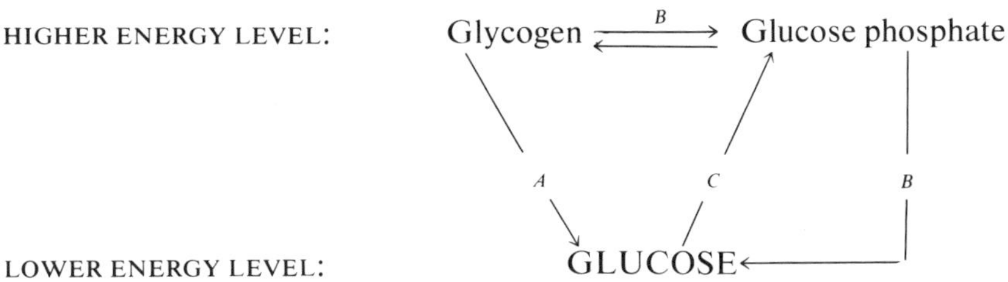

Thus, when starch or glycogen is hydrolyzed to glucose, either through digestion (*A*) or by the enzyme systems of the liver (*B*), there is a decrease in free energy (exergonic reactions); the pathways are "down-hill" and irreversible. The glucose molecule must have its energy relations changed through the incorporation of free energy from an energy-rich compound (*C*) before it can combine with other glucose units to form glycogen, or before it can be metabolized to provide energy for the life processes. The glucose priming reaction (endergonic reaction), by which the free energy level is raised, depends on the enzyme HEXOKINASE and the energy-rich compound ATP. The reaction is typical of many biological reactions, both in the nature of the priming process and in the "detonating action" provided by the enzyme hexokinase.

ENERGY-RICH COMPOUNDS

In cellular work, the most conspicuous energy-rich bond is the terminal one of adenosine triphosphate (Fig. 7.1). Adenosine triphosphate

(ATP) is a combination of three common biochemical materials: the purine base adenine (6-aminopurine), the 5-carbon pentose sugar (ribose) and phosphoric acid. A unit composed of adenine and the pentose forms a combination known as adenosine (a NUCLEOSIDE). This, when associated with one phosphate unit, forms adenosine monophosphate (AMP), also called adenylic acid and known as a NUCLEOTIDE. Two more units of phosphate may also be added as shown in Fig. 7.1 to form the diphosphate (ADP) and the triphosphate (ATP).

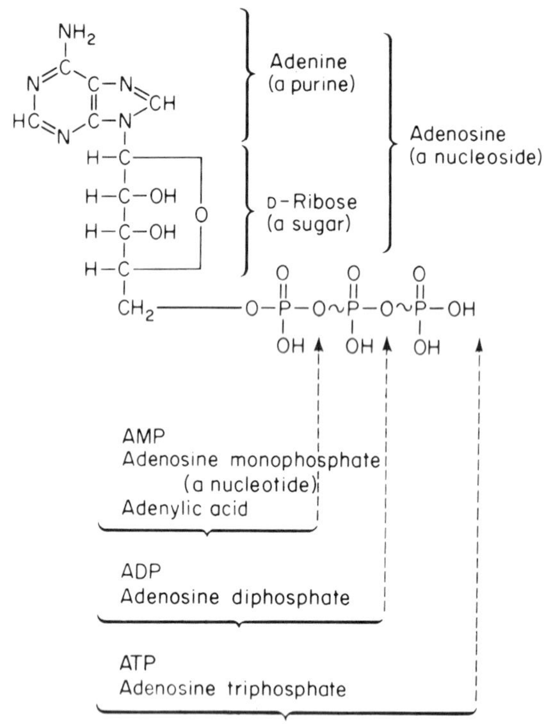

Fig. 7.1. Structure of adenosine triphosphate.

The energy relationships of the terminal monophosphate bond and those of the diphosphate and triphosphate bonds are quite different. Hydrolyses of the latter are associated with the release of large amounts of free energy—approximately 8000 cal/mole (Fruton and Simmonds, 1958), while the phosphate bond of adenylic acid is associated with only 1000 or 2000 cal/mole. Low-energy phosphate bonds are ester linkages between phosphoric acid and the alcohol group of a sugar; like other organic esters, they are resistant to hydrolysis and yield comparatively small amounts of energy. High-energy phosphate bonds are normally anhydride linkages between two molecules of phosphoric acid or between a molecule of phosphoric acid and a carboxylic acid. These bonds are relatively unstable and on hydrolysis release large amounts of energy. The high energy bonds, symbolized by the "swing dash" or "tilde" in Fig. 7.1, are the important energy "accumulators." Most of the specific tasks of the animal cell, such as contraction or secretion, depend directly on the energy of these ATP bonds.

Thus, at one level of thinking, cellular metabolism is a matter of capturing, or of transforming the low-energy bonds of many different carbon compounds into the high-energy pyrophosphate bond. In tissue respiration, numerous reactions involving small energy changes lead step by step to a major energy-yielding reaction in which large amounts of free energy are made available for cell work. In these metabolic chains, electrons and hydrogen ions are passed along by a series of compounds, and at certain points ATP molecules appear. In most animals, the final stages require oxygen for the burning or oxidation of hydrogen, and in this series of reactions the greatest amount of ATP is generated (oxidative phosphorylation).

In a sense, this reaction whereby hydrogen combines with oxygen, is the same reaction which is familiar to every student in general chemistry. As has so often been demonstrated in the high school laboratory, it may occur with explosive violence. In the living cell, however, a series of enzymes operates an extended chain of reactions, and the low-energy bonds are transformed or "stored" in pyrophosphate bonds of ATP. Unlike the mistimed laboratory experiment, the energy never appears suddenly with an explosive production of heat. The energy transformations of life are remarkably efficient. The overall thermodynamic efficiency for the conversion of food energy into pyrophosphate bond energy is 60 to 70 per cent (Krebs and Kornberg, 1957).

Biological classes of energy-rich compounds. Although ATP is a member of a select group, it is by no means the only energy-rich compound. Energy-rich compounds as they are known to the biochemist are of two types: derivatives of phosphoric acid and derivatives of carboxylic acid (Huennekens and Whiteley, 1960). In the first group, energy is released in the hydrolytic split of the bond joining phosphoric acid to the rest of the molecule; in the second group, carboxylic acid is hydrolytically split from its derivative. These reactions may be shown as follows:

$$\text{(1)}\quad \mathrm{HO{-}}\overset{\displaystyle \mathrm{O} \atop \displaystyle \|}{\underset{\displaystyle | \atop \displaystyle \mathrm{OH}}{\mathrm{P}}}\mathrm{{-}}X + \mathrm{H_2O} \rightleftharpoons \mathrm{H}X + \mathrm{HO{-}}\overset{\displaystyle \mathrm{O} \atop \displaystyle \|}{\underset{\displaystyle | \atop \displaystyle \mathrm{OH}}{\mathrm{P}}}\mathrm{{-}OH} + \text{Energy}$$

$$(2)\quad R{-}\overset{\overset{\displaystyle O}{\|}}{C}{-}X' + H_2O \rightleftharpoons HX' + R{-}\overset{\overset{\displaystyle O}{\|}}{C}{-}OH + \text{Energy}$$

In the first reaction, X represents ADP (in ATP) or phosphate (in the polyphosphates) or the guanidino group (in creatine phosphate). In the second reaction, R represents the acetyl group and X' represents coenzyme A in the energy-rich bonds of acetyl CoA. These compounds will be identified in subsequent sections. They are introduced here to exemplify the two biochemical groups of energy-rich bonds.

From a functional standpoint, the energy-rich compounds fall into three major groups. ATP and the other nucleoside polyphosphates are the PRIMARY PHOSPHORYLATING AGENTS responsible for the energy transfers associated with the important animal activities of muscle contraction and protein synthesis. A second group acts as TRANSIENT INTERMEDIATES in phosphorylating reactions and is concerned with the synthesis of the primary phosphorylating agents. Some of these (acetyl CoA, phosphoenolpyruvate and glycerylphosphate) appear to be universal, while others may be more restricted in their distribution. The third group consists of the highly important ENERGY RESERVOIRS. The quantity of primary phosphorylating agent in the tissues is usually rather small; where demands are likely to be sudden and of considerable magnitude the tissues store energy-rich bonds for the rapid regeneration of the primary phosphorylating agents. In the plant world the inorganic polyphosphates discharge a similar function. The primary phosphorylating agent, ATP, is evidently universally distributed in living materials, but the energy reservoirs are quite different in the animal and the plant worlds.

The energy reservoirs. The amidine phosphates (also called the guanidine phosphates or the phosphagens) are the important muscle reservoirs of high-energy phosphate. Their discovery and the recognition of their significance forms an interesting chapter in the history of physiological chemistry (Baldwin, 1963).

In 1907, Fletcher and Hopkins, using improved techniques, had focussed attention on lactic acid as a key substance in muscle biochemistry. Their analyses of isolated and electrically stimulated frog muscle demonstrated the formation of lactic acid in both an anaerobic and an aerobic environment. They showed further that fatigue appeared sooner and more lactic acid accumulated in the anaerobic environment, and that as lactic acid disappeared carbon dioxide was produced. These studies were followed by those of Meyerhof who proved that glycogen was the source of lactate. Within the next few years a ratio was established between the work done, glycogen used, and lactic acid formed, and the chemical events associated with muscle contraction were explained in terms of the metabolism of carbohydrate.

Lundsgaard in 1930 made the significant discovery that muscles poisoned with iodoacetate could no longer form lactic acid but could still contract anaerobically. This quickly shifted biochemical interest from the carbohydrates to the organic phosphates as the primary source of energy. Further work showed that creatine phosphate (phosphagen) was breaking down to form creatine when the iodoacetate-poisoned muscle was activated and that the work done by the muscle was equivalent to the breakdown of phosphagen. Creatine phosphate had been isolated from vertebrate muscle in 1927 and the presence of unidentified organic phosphates had been recognized earlier. However, their true significance was not recognized until after Lohmann, in 1934, showed that the phosphagen changes in contracting muscle depended on the presence of ATP. In 1937 he suggested a scheme of reactions which has now been generally accepted by physiologists.

In Lohmann's scheme the primary source of energy is provided by the hydrolysis of ATP to ADP and inorganic phosphate (P); the creatine phosphate forms a reservoir of high-energy phosphate which is used to regenerate the stores of ATP. The glycogen-lactic acid changes, studied first during the history of muscle biochemistry, are concerned with the regeneration of creatine phosphate (CP) from creatine (C). Thus:

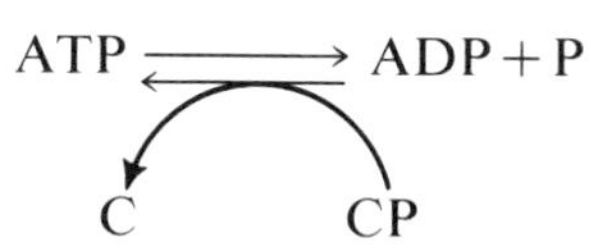

The regeneration of the creatine phosphate is indirect by way of the ATP formed in muscle glycolysis and oxidative phosphorylation.

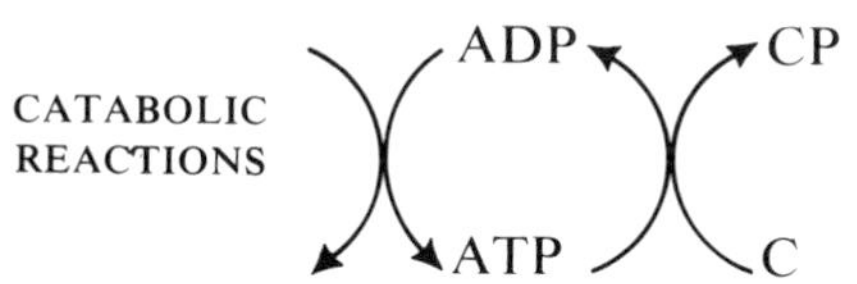

Although the muscles of all vertebrate animals contain creatine phosphate, those of the majority of the invertebrates contain arginine phosphate. When it was discovered that the major exceptions to this general rule are found among the echinoderms and the protochordates, the phosphagens very naturally became prominent in discussions of biochemical evolution. Both arginine phosphate and creatine phosphate are found among the echinoderms and protochordates, and this seemed to be in agreement with speculated lines of evolution which suggest a common ancestry for the echinoderms and the chordates. The formulas of these two common phosphagens are as follows:

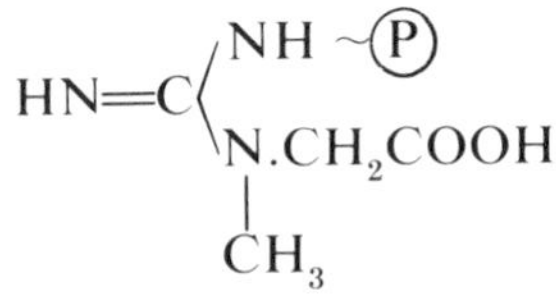

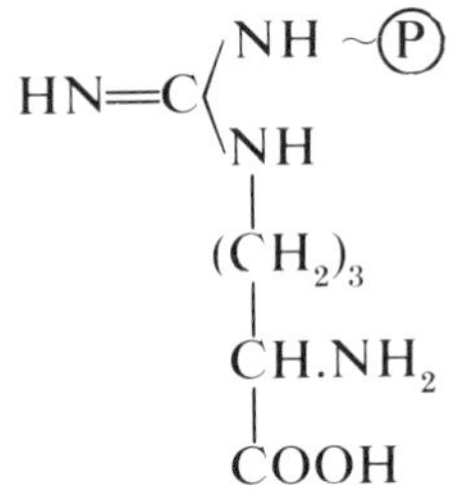

CREATINE PHOSPHATE ARGININE PHOSPHATE

The earlier data have now been greatly amplified; it is apparent that creatine phosphate is not confined to the echinoderms and protochordates among the invertebrates but is also found in at least one sponge (*Thetia lyncurium*), a coelenterate (*Anemonia sulcata*), a sipunculoid (*Sipunculus nudis*) and several of the annelids (Huennekens and Whiteley, 1960 and Prosser and Brown, 1961). Moreover, three other phosphagens, peculiar to the annelids, nemerteans and sipunculoids have been isolated and studied. These are also characterized by the presence of the amidine group $(HN{=}\underset{|}{C}{-}NH_2)$ as shown by the following formulas:

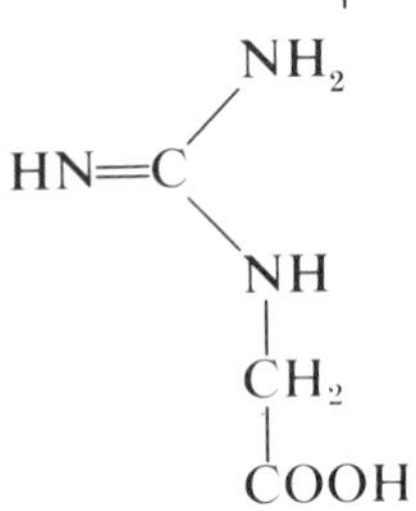

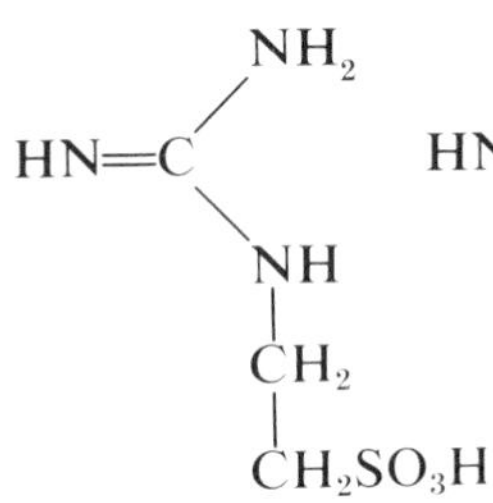

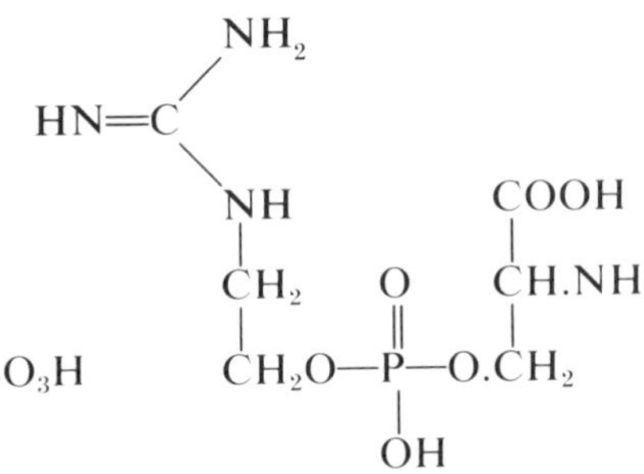

GLYCOCYAMINE TAUROCYAMINE LOMBRICINE

In spite of these exceptions the earlier broad generalization remains. The vertebrates do utilize only phosphocreatine; the majority of the invertebrates rely on phosphoarginine, while different members of the echinoderms and protochordates are about equally divided in the nature of their phosphagen. Thinking must, however, be adjusted concerning the phylogenetic antiquity of phosphocreatine. Enzymes and compounds essential for its formation are found in the most primitive multicellular organisms. Moreover, several different, although apparently rare, mutations have given rise to other phosphagens as exemplified by the annelids.

Arginine was probably the starting point in the biochemical evolution of the storage system of amidine phosphates. It is a ubiquitous amino acid and enters into the composition of the protoplasm of animals of all kinds. The guanidino group of the arginine molecule which couples with phosphoric acid to form the high-energy bond of phosphoarginine is common to the other phosphagens and is the functioning portion of all these molecules. Creatine is formed from arginine, glycine and methionine. The enzymes involved in biosynthesis have been studied in mammalian kidney and liver, and ATP energy is required in some of the steps. In the first step, arginine and glycine react to form glycocyamine (guanidinoacetic acid) and ornithine. This is methylated in a second reaction involving methionine to form creatine. In some of the worms, however, the glycocyamine is directly phosphorylated to form a phosphagen. The taurocyamine molecule is only slightly different; the lombricine molecule contains D-serine linked by phosphoric acid to guanidinoethanol. The guanidino group is common to all these phosphagens.

Animals at almost every stage in phylogeny seem to have experimented with phosphocreatine, and several phyla tried other guanidine phosphates as well before the evolving chordates made the irrevocable decision to use only creatine phosphate in their muscle machinery. This may have been a purely fortuitous "decision"; or phosphocreatine may be superior for the purposes of muscle contraction in the vertebrates. This and many other problems (Huennekens and Whiteley, 1960) associated with the evolution of the phosphagens await further investigation.

Pathways of Cellular Metabolism

Animal evolution is founded on the products of photosynthesis. During the phylogeny of the photosynthetic mechanisms protoplasm became associated with most of the organic compounds, enzymes and reactions involved in the respiration of animal cells. The process of photosynthesis provided the carbon compounds required for the heterotrophic way of life and, at the same time, generated the oxygen atmosphere necessary for high-energy aerobic reactions. Before the Darwinian evolution of animals was possible, the biochemical compounds, the enzymes necessary for their metabolism and the fundamental energy exchanges of life were operating universally in living protoplasm.

It is not then surprising that the production of energy follows the same general pathways in bacteria and plants and in animals at different stages of phylogeny. These universal processes will be outlined first. Energy released in these processes is utilized to do special kinds of work which may be peculiar to certain types of cells and may depend on the way of life of the particular animal. Although these special energy exchanges—whereby a muscle contracts, a gland secretes or a cell produces light—also depend on familiar compounds and reactions, they are, in a sense, more distinctively related to animal life and its phylogeny. They will be considered later.

PRODUCTION OF ENERGY FROM FOOD

Only the simple building blocks of the complex foods can serve as fuel for cellular respiration. Carbohydrates are utilized within the cell as monosaccharides, proteins as amino acids and fats as fatty acids and glycerol. Through a series of reactions the monosaccharides, the fats and many of the amino acids are oxidized (with a relatively small release of energy) to the familiar two-carbon compound, acetic acid—actually combined in the cell with coenzyme A in an especially reactive form known as ACETYL CoA or ACTIVE ACETATE. Active acetate (along with two other residues from certain amino acids) may then enter an enzymatic pool (the citric acid or tricarboxylic acid cycle) which generates hydrogen for the reduction of gaseous oxygen and the production of ATP chemical energy. These events are outlined in Table 7.1 and Fig. 7.2. Although some energy is released in the pre-acetate steps (phase II of Table 7.1), the bulk of the ATP energy is liberated after the active acetate enters the citric acid cycle. Of the three phases of energy production shown in Table 7.1, the third is responsible for about 65 per cent of the total energy liberated, while the first produces less than 1 per cent (Krebs and Kornberg, 1957). The overall thermodynamic efficiency of these processes is high (of the order of 60 to 70 per cent) and, to a very large degree, this depends on the citric acid cycle and the aerobic processes of respiration. The different steps in energy production will now be described in more detail.

Monosaccharides to pyruvic acid. A fundamental chain of biochemical reactions, known as the "Embden-Meyerhof" sequence was the first series of energy-yielding reactions to be worked out in detail. This is a pathway of glycogen or glucose metabolism. Since animals usually depend on carbohydrate for much of their energy, it forms one of the important sequences of their cellular metabolism. Its elucidation occupied the minds of many other biochemists during the first half of the present century even though the names of Embden and Meyerhof are usually attached to it. This is now known to be the major route in the metabolism of carbohydrate, whether the sugars are being utilized in the contraction of muscle (glycolysis) or whether they are fermented by microorganisms in the production of alcohol. The important steps are outlined in Fig. 7.3.

A comprehensive discussion of this sequence would require many pages. The enzymes, the energetics and the molecular arrangements

TABLE 7.1

THE THREE MAIN PHASES OF ENERGY PRODUCTION FROM FOODSTUFFS
(Krebs and Kornberg, 1957)

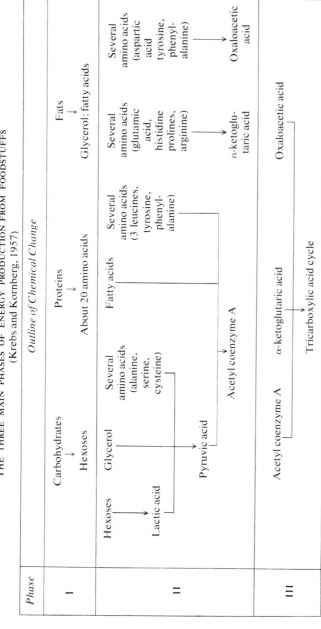

Phase	*Outline of Chemical Change*
I	Carbohydrates → Hexoses; Proteins → About 20 amino acids; Fats → Glycerol; fatty acids
II	Hexoses → Lactic acid; Glycerol, Lactic acid, Several amino acids (alanine, serine, cysteine) → Pyruvic acid; Pyruvic acid, Fatty acids, Several amino acids (3 leucines, tyrosine, phenyl-alanine) → Acetyl coenzyme A; Several amino acids (glutamic acid, histidine prolines, arginine) → α-ketoglu-taric acid; Several amino acids (aspartic acid tyrosine, phenyl-alanine) → Oxaloacetic acid
III	Acetyl coenzyme A, α-ketoglutaric acid, Oxaloacetic acid → Tricarboxylic acid cycle

will be found in textbooks of biochemistry. Here, the general nature of the processes is emphasized and attention is directed to the important energy-transferring compounds, ATP and DPN. The first of these has already been described (Fig. 7.1).

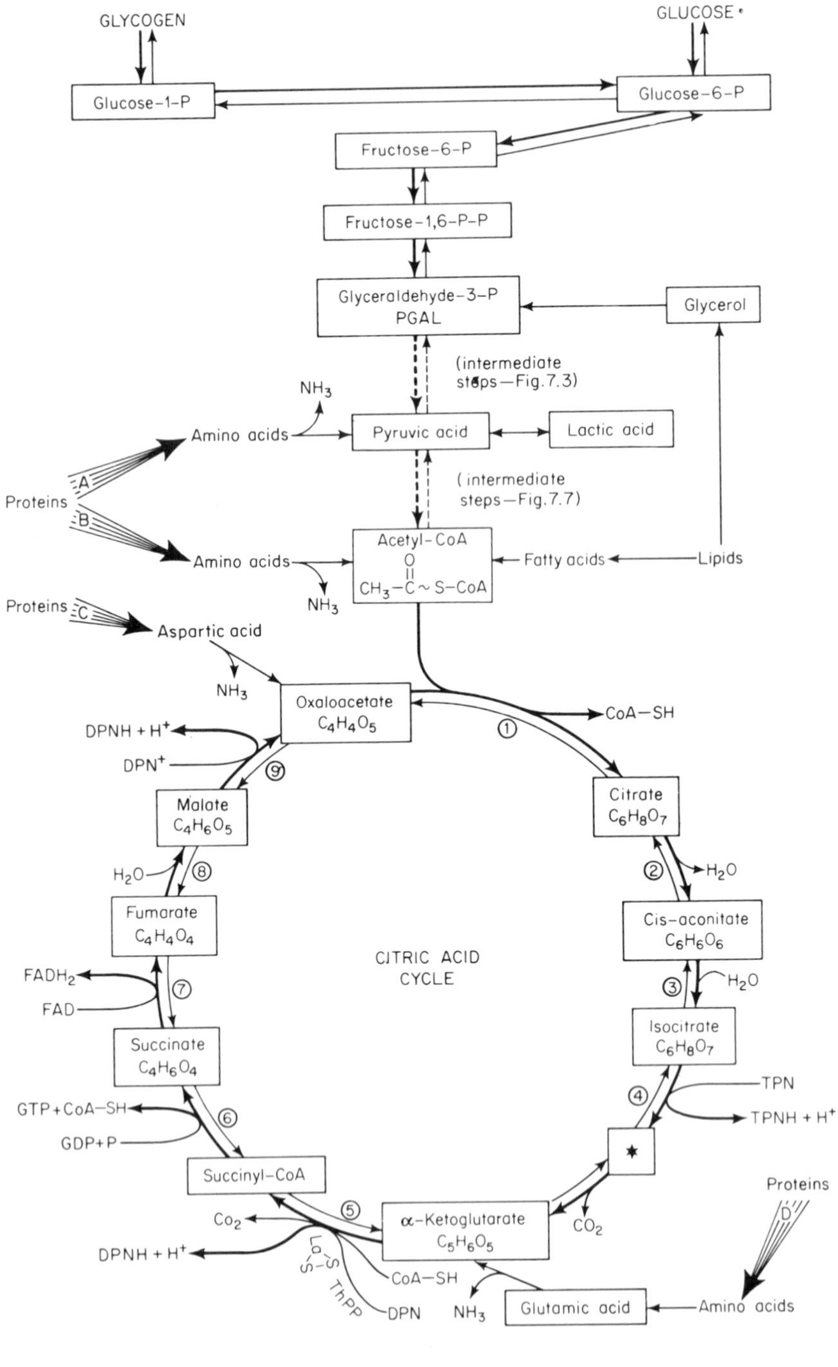

Fig. 7.2. Summary of metabolic pathways for the different foods. AMINO ACID GROUPS A, Glucogenic series: alanine, glycine, serine, threonine, methionine, cysteine, valine. B, Ketogenic series: leucine, isoleucine, phenylalanine, tyrosine. C, Aspartic acid. D, Glutamic acid itself or derived from arginine, proline, hydroxyproline, histidine, ornithine. ENZYMES OF THE CITRIC ACID CYCLE. 1, condensing enzyme 2, Aconitase (inhibited by fluorocitrate). 3, Aconitase. 4, Isocitric dehydrogenase and Mn^{++} (inhibited by anaerobiosis). 5, α-ketoglutarate dehydrogenase with thyamine pyrophosphate, lipoic acid and *CoA*. 6, Succinyl *CoA* synthetase with Mg^{++} (inhibited by arsenite). 7, Succinic dehydrogenase (inhibited by malonate). 8, Fumarase. 9, Malic dehydrogenase. Asterisk, Oxalosuccinate ($C_6H_6O_7$) if formed is firmly bound to the enzyme and hence not shown as an intermediary. [Sallach and McGilvery (1963).]

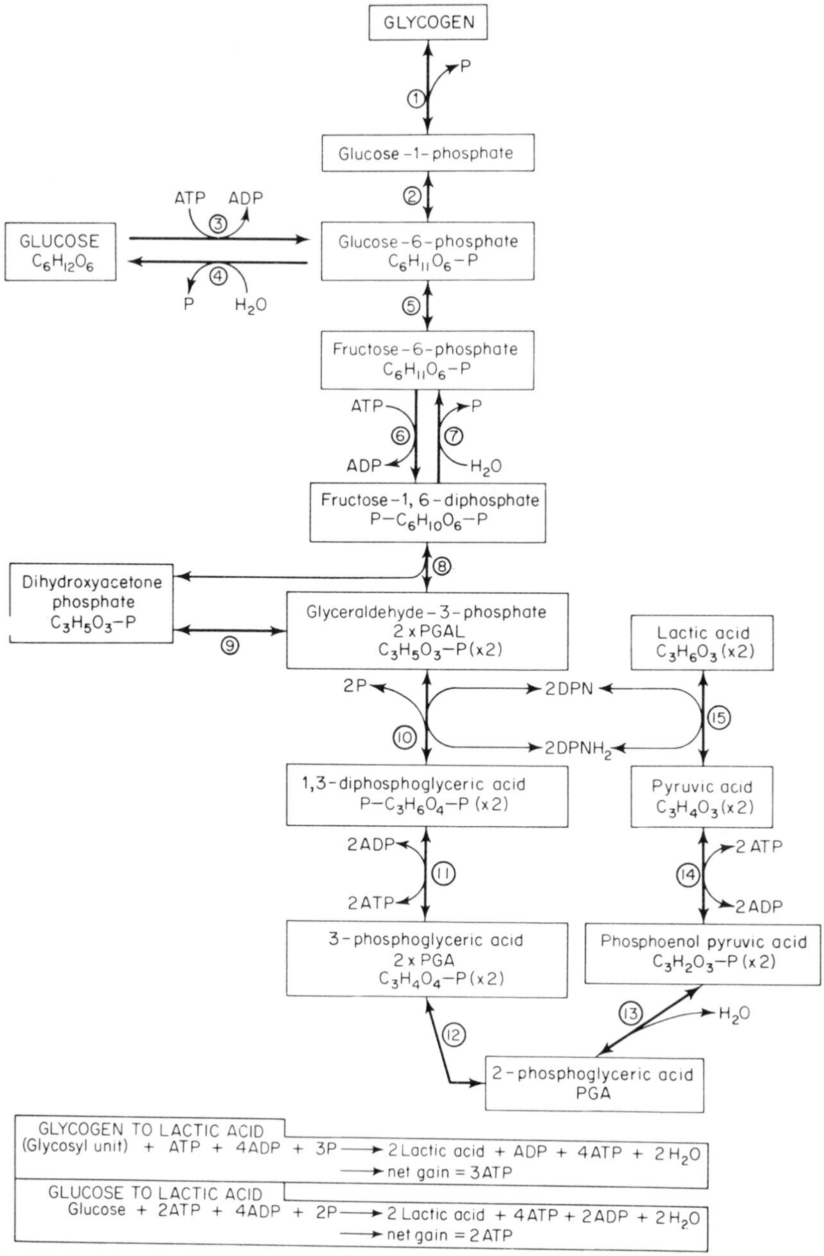

Fig. 7.3 Embden-Meyerhof sequence for the metabolism of glucose or the glycosyl units of glycogen to pyruvic or lactic acid. Enzymes indicated by numbers as follows: 1, Phosphorylase (inhibited by phlorizin). 2, Phosphoglucomutase and Mg^{++}. 3, Hexokinase and Mg^{++}. 4, Glucose-6-phosphatase. 5, Phosphohexoisomerase. 6, Phosphofructo-1-kinase. 7, Fructose-1, 6-diphosphatase. 8, Fructoaldolase. 9, Triose isomerase. 10, Glyceraldehyde-3-phosphate dehydrogenase (inhibited by iodoacetate). 11, 3-phosphoglyceric-1-kinase and Mg^{++}. 12, Phosphoglyceromutase and Mg^{++}. 13, Enolase and Mg^{++} (inhibited by fluoride). 14, Pyruvic kinase and Mg^{++}. 15, Lactic dehydrogenase and Zn^{++}. [Sallach and McGilvery (1960).]

The second is DIPHOSPHOPYRIDINE NUCLEOTIDE (DPN). This compound discharges its important cellular function by transferring hydrogen. It is readily reduced to DPNH and then oxidized to DPN. Thus, it transports much of the hydrogen to the carrier system where it is combined with oxygen to form water and release ATP energy. Biochemically, DPN, like ATP, contains a unit of adenylic acid (Fig. 7.4). This is combined through a pyrophosphate link to another pentose unit which is

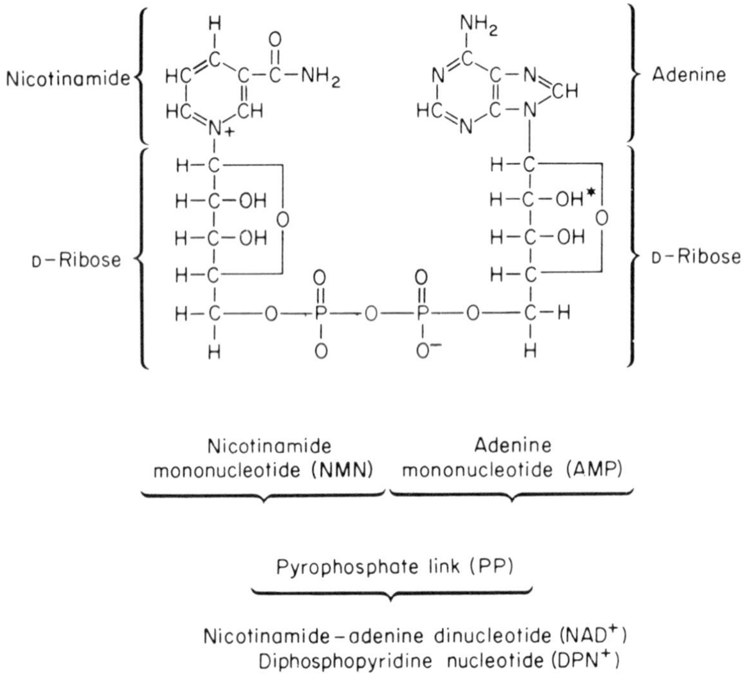

Fig. 7.4. Structure of diphosphopyridine nucleotide, DPN. An additional phosphate in the 2 position of the pentose of the nucleoside portion of the molecule produces triphosphopyridine nucleotide, TPN. The Commission on Enzymes of the International Union of Biochemistry has recommended "nicotinamide-adenine dinucleotide" (NAD) and "nicotinamide-adenine dinucleotide phosphate" (NADP) for DPN and TPN respectively; the older terminology has been retained in this book.

attached—not to a purine as in the adenylic acid unit—but to a pyridine ring which forms a reactive group and can accept two electrons and a proton as follows:

$$DPN^+ + 2H^+ + 2e \rightleftharpoons DPNH + H^+$$

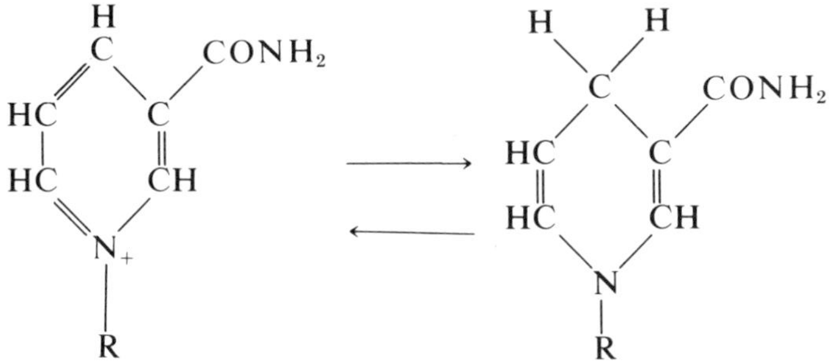

DPN DPNH
REDUCED DPN

The reactions outlined in Fig. 7.3 may now be examined in more detail. It will be noted that oxidation (dehydrogenation) and the generation of ATP are preceded by several preparatory reactions. Glucose, as previously mentioned, is in a low-energy state when it enters the cell and must have its energy relations changed through phosphorylation by ATP. The formation of the glucose-6-phosphate in the Embden-Meyerhof sequence is followed by a molecular rearrangement of the sugar, and another priming reaction with a second unit of ATP to form a diphosphate sugar (fructose-1, 6-diphosphate). Enzymatic reactions then split this 6-carbon diphosphate compound into two 3-carbon units with no particular change in the energy values of the phosphate bonds. Particular attention is drawn to this 3-carbon unit, D-glyceraldehyde-3-phosphate, also called phosphoglyceraldehyde or PGAL for short, since it is the primary carbon compound produced by carbon dioxide fixation in the photosynthetic process (Fig. 1.3). As indicated in Fig. 7.2, PGAL forms a meeting place in carbohydrate metabolism and photosynthesis as well as in the metabolism of glycerol arising from the lipids.

The formation of the PGAL is followed by a coupled reaction in which it is oxidized in the presence of inorganic phosphate to form a diphosphate, and this reacts with ADP in a transphosphorylation to form 3-phosphoglyceric acid (PGA) and a unit of ATP. In this way, the two molecules of PGAL which came from the single molecule of glucose pay back the two ATP molecules which were required for the priming reactions. In the next series of enzymatic reactions the two units of PGA release the other phosphate to ADP, and there is thus a net gain of two ATP molecules for each glucose unit metabolized to pyruvic acid. This sequence of reactions has also produced two units of reduced DPN ($DPNH + H^+$), but this can only be turned into high-energy phosphate

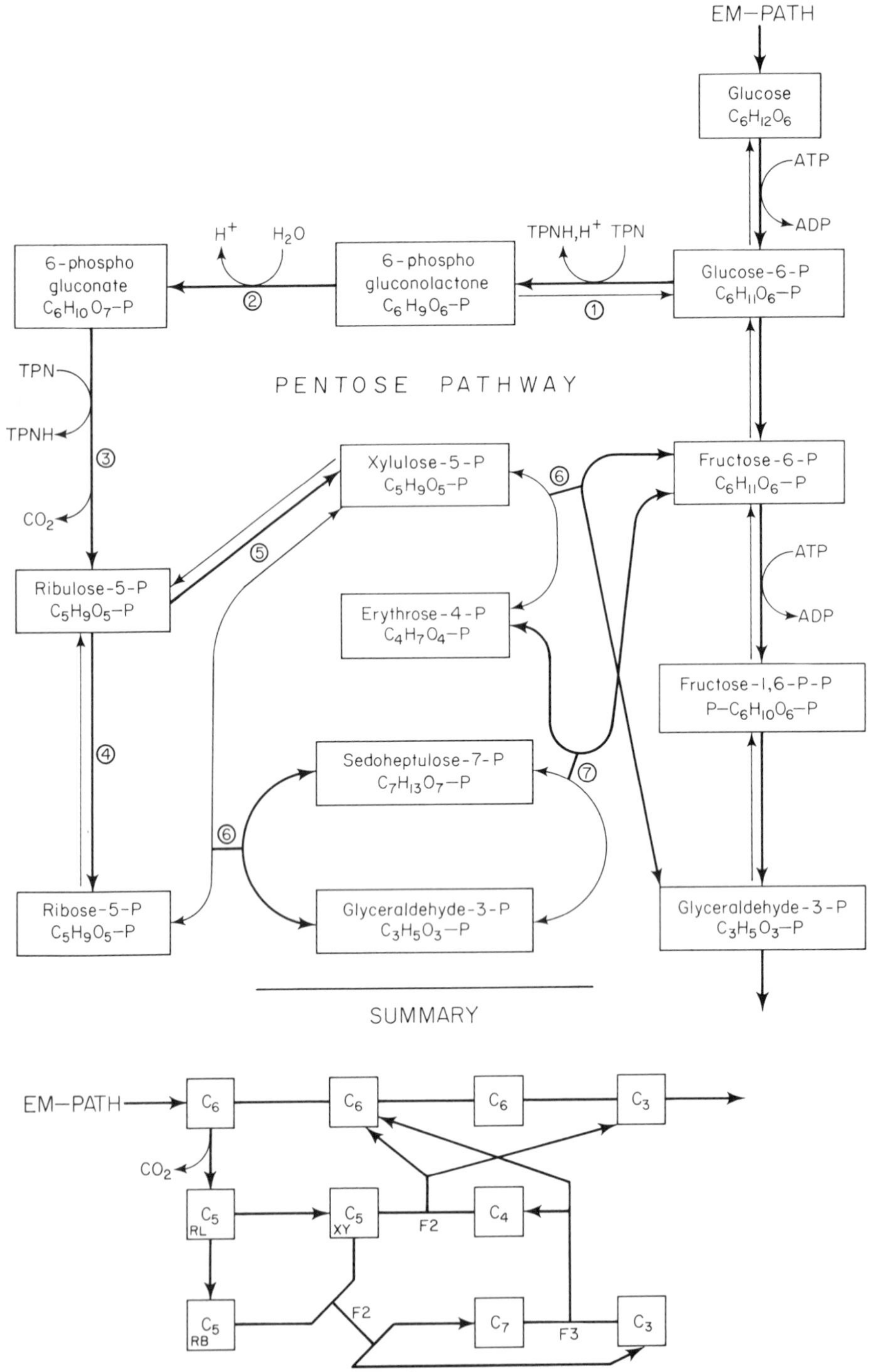

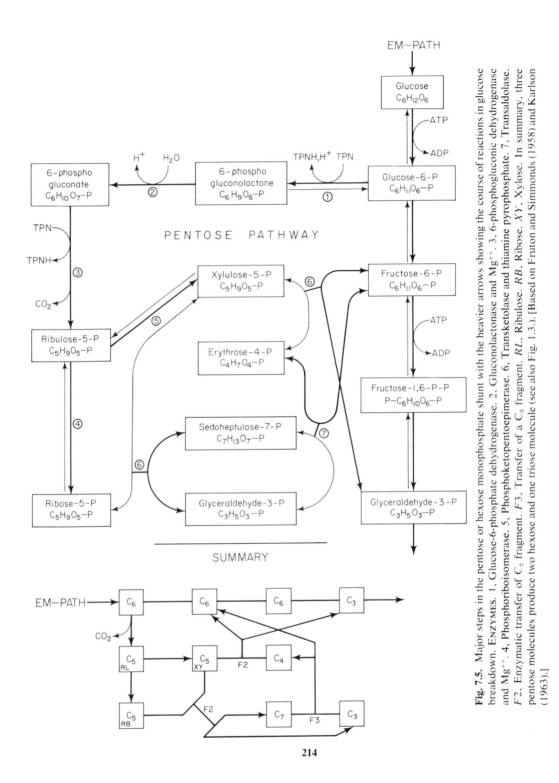

Fig. 7.5. Major steps in the pentose or hexose monophosphate shunt with the heavier arrows showing the course of reactions in glucose breakdown. ENZYMES. 1, Glucose-6-phosphate dehydrogenase. 2, Gluconolactonase and Mg^{++}. 3, 6-phosphogluconic dehydrogenase and Mg^{++}. 4, Phosphoriboisomerase. 5, Phosphoketopentoepimerase. 6, Transketolase and thiamine pyrophosphate. 7, Transaldolase. *F*2, Enzymatic transfer of C_2 fragment. *F*3, Transfer of a C_3 fragment. *RL*, Ribulose. *RB*, Ribose. *XY*, Xylose. In summary, three pentose molecules produce two hexose and one triose molecule (see also Fig. 1.3.). [Based on Fruton and Simmonds (1958) and Karlson (1963).]

bonds if oxygen becomes available, as described below for the aerobic respiratory chain of oxidative phosphorylation. Otherwise, the DPNH + H^+ enters into the oxidation-reduction reactions of anaerobic glycolysis (Fig. 7.3).

The pentose phosphate pathway. The widespread occurrence of the enzymes and compounds involved in the Embden-Meyerhof sequence might suggest that it is the universal and obligatory pathway for carbohydrate respiration in all animals. It has been followed in biochemical studies of many vertebrate and insect tissues as well as in some of the protozoans, parasitic worms and other invertebrates. However, enzymes are known to exist (glucose oxidase in the liver, for example) which could directly oxidize the carbohydrate, and several alternative pathways involving phosphate have been discovered in bacteria. The appropriate enzymes and compounds for metabolism by these routes have been shown to exist in some animals. One of these, the pentose phosphate pathway—also called the "Warburg-Dickens pathway" or the "hexose monophosphate (HMP) oxidation shunt"—is outlined in Fig. 7.5.

As indicated in this figure, the pentose pathway or cycle may be thought of as an enzymatic pool in which 6-carbon sugars (glucose and fructose) are converted into 5-carbon sugars with the formation of carbon dioxide. Two 5-carbon units may then be converted into a 7-carbon and a 3-carbon unit (PGAL); the 7-carbon and the 3-carbon unit may be further rearranged into a 6-carbon unit (fructose) and a 4-carbon unit; the 4-carbon sugar and a 5-carbon sugar can then produce a hexose and a triose (PGAL). The reactions are reversible, and this enzyme pool provides the important machinery for rearranging varied monosaccharides. In the overall reaction, every three units of 6-carbon sugar which enter the pool will return two of these units and form one unit of triose phosphate (PGAL) and three molecules of CO_2. In the course of these reactions the 6-carbon sugars are first condensed to 5-carbon sugars, and the hydrogen transfers are made through TPN. It is noted that this scheme requires TPN instead of DPN, that it generates PGAL which can be added to the pyruvate pool or combined again into hexose, and that pentose compounds appear.

The pentose cycle is an essential adjunct to the normal function of aerobic metabolism. It occurs almost universally in living organisms and has been identified in many, but not all bacteria, in plants, and in animals from flatworms to mammals. As a biochemical process, it may be phylogenetically older than photosynthesis (Krebs and Kornberg, 1957). Fermentation processes, as exemplified by the Embden-Meyerhof (EM) pathway, were probably responsible for the release of energy during the evolutionary stages when preformed compounds of many kinds were abundant. Later, however, before the advent of photosynthesis, the dwindling supplies of key substances may have limited energy exchanges, growth and reproduction. The pentose pathway generates the 5-carbon sugars which are essential building blocks in the electron transport system, the genetic material and in synthetic processes. It also provides TPNH which is required for carbon dioxide fixation, for fatty acid synthesis and other synthetic reactions (Horecker, 1962). It also results in the formation of tetroses and C_7 compounds such as sedoheptulose-7-phosphate whose significance is not yet fully understood. Although this is not an energy-yielding sequence, it is none the less important to life and might have provided many important metabolic compounds prior to photosynthesis.

Tracer techniques with C^{14} provide a means of comparing the relative contributions of the EM and the HMP pathways in the metabolism of glucose. In the former, glucose-1-C^{14} and glucose-6-C^{14} are metabolized in the same manner, but in the HMP shunt they are handled differently, and the $C^{14}O_2$ is preferentially liberated from the first carbon atom. These techniques have shown the pentose pathway to be more active in some animals than in others and, within any particular animal, to be more conspicuous in certain tissues. It is said to be a major pathway in some insects (Chefurka, 1958*a*), to be active in mammalian liver but absent in mammalian muscle (Fruton and Simmonds, 1958), to operate in the hepatopancreas of the crayfish during intermolt but not during the later stages of premolt (McWhinnie and Corkill, 1964), and to play a greater part in the metabolism of fish acclimatized to very low temperatures (Hochachka and Hayes, 1962). The significance of some of these facts is obscure.

Metabolism of pyruvic acid. Pyruvic acid or its fermentation products are "dead ends" as far as animal evolution is concerned. They still contain a large part of the potential energy of the original glucose molecule. The evolution of active animals could never have taken place if biochemical evolution had stopped at this point; their many ways of life depend on the release of this additional energy. This is effected through a series of aerobic metabolic processes which involve an additional array of enzymes and electron transport systems and which can be conveniently described as three interlocking sequences. IN THE FIRST SEQUENCE an oxidative decarboxylation and molecular activation converts the pyruvic acid into "active acetate" or acetyl CoA. IN THE SECOND, the 2-carbon units of active acetate are fed into an enzymatic cycle where each such fragment unites with a 4-carbon compound (oxaloacetic acid) to form a 6-carbon unit (citric acid); as the cycle revolves through eight major transformations, the 6-carbon citric acid unit reverts to the 4-carbon unit of oxaloacetic acid by releasing two molecules of carbon dioxide and eight hydrogens (Fig. 7.2). The latter are passed to the pyridine nucleotide and other carriers. This fundamental and important cycle is sometimes called the "Krebs cycle" after the famous biochemist who did much toward its elucidation. Since the name of Krebs is also associated with other chemical sequences it is better to call it the "citric acid cycle" or the "tricarboxylic acid (TCA) cycle." IN THE THIRD SEQUENCE OF REACTIONS the electrons released in the citric acid cycle are picked up and passed along a series of electron carriers; hydrogen eventually combines with oxygen to form water; and three units of ADP are changed to ATP for each two hydrogens passed down the chain. In this way each turn of the citric acid wheel (which produces eight hydrogens) may be thought of as generating twelve high-energy phosphate bonds in the form of ATP. It should be remembered that these three sequences are interlocked in cellular metabolism and are separately discussed here only for convenience.

Pyruvic acid to active acetate and acetic acid. This is an oxidative decarboxylation in which the 3-C pyruvic acid reacts with water to become a 2-C acetic acid compound, releasing carbon dioxide as a waste product of metabolism and supplying two hydrogens to the DPN carrier system. Arithmetically, these changes can be summarized as follows:

$$\underset{\text{PYRUVIC ACID}}{C_3H_4O_3} + H_2O \longrightarrow \underset{\text{ACETIC ACID}}{C_2H_4O_2} + 2H + CO_2$$

The acetic acid, however, does not exist as such. It forms a highly reactive combination with the sulfur atom of coenzyme A. Reference to Fig. 7.6 will show that the complex molecule, known as coenzyme A, or more frequently as CoA, is based on the purine, ribose and phosphate combinations already described as a nucleotide (Fig. 7.1). In CoA there is an attachment to a unit of pantothenic acid and one of β-mercaptoethanolamine with its reactive SH group at one end in Fig. 7.6.

The reaction whereby an acetyl is attached to some other molecule (acetylation), is relatively common; in this case it constitutes a priming reaction required before further respiration of the carbon units is possible. Acetyl CoA is also an intermediary in the formation of acetic acid from higher fatty acids and forms a meeting place in several metabolic pathways (Fig. 7.2). The activation of the acetyl group is required for its transfer. Just as the phosphorylated group can be transferred from ATP to other compounds, so also can the acetyl group be transferred from acetyl CoA.

This particular acetylation is summarized in Fig. 7.7. At the end of the sequence the acetyl CoA may transfer acetate to the citric acid cycle or provide the energy necessary to add inorganic phosphate to ADP. In the first case C_2 units are provided for the operation of the TCA cycle. In the second, high energy ATP is generated and acetic acid added

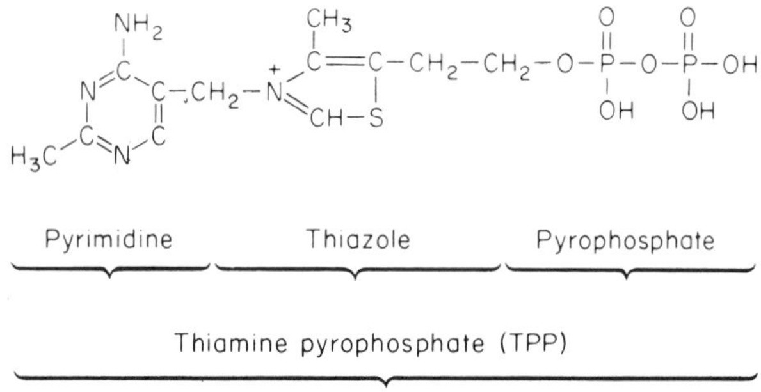

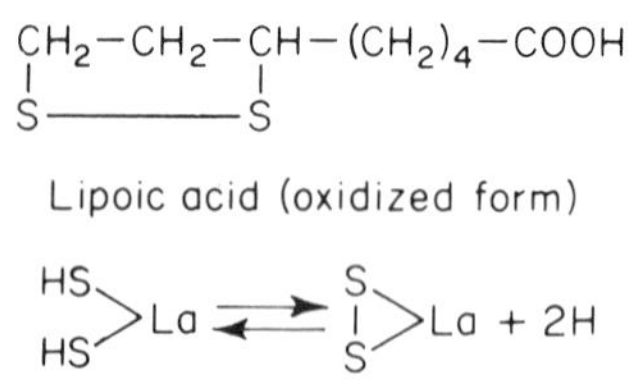

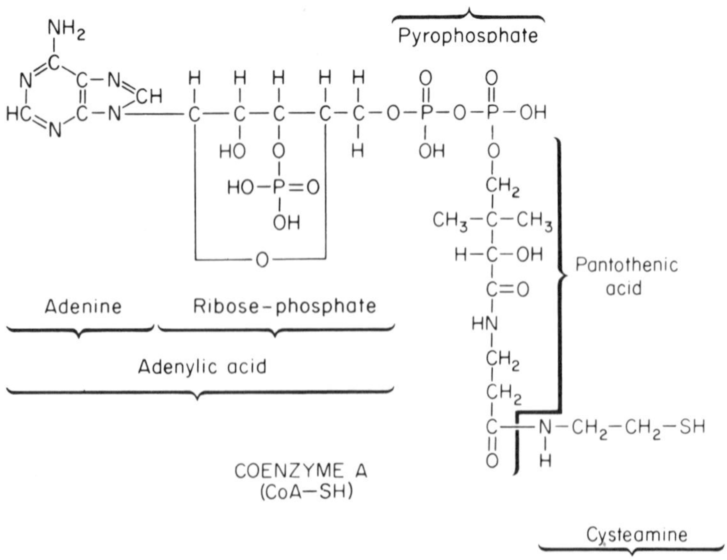

Fig. 7.6 Three important transfer molecules in the metabolism of pyruvic acid to acetic acid.

to the system. In both cases CoA has discharged its function and is available for further transfers.

For the animal physiologist, one additional point of interest in this conversion is the array of coenzymes and activator factors involved.

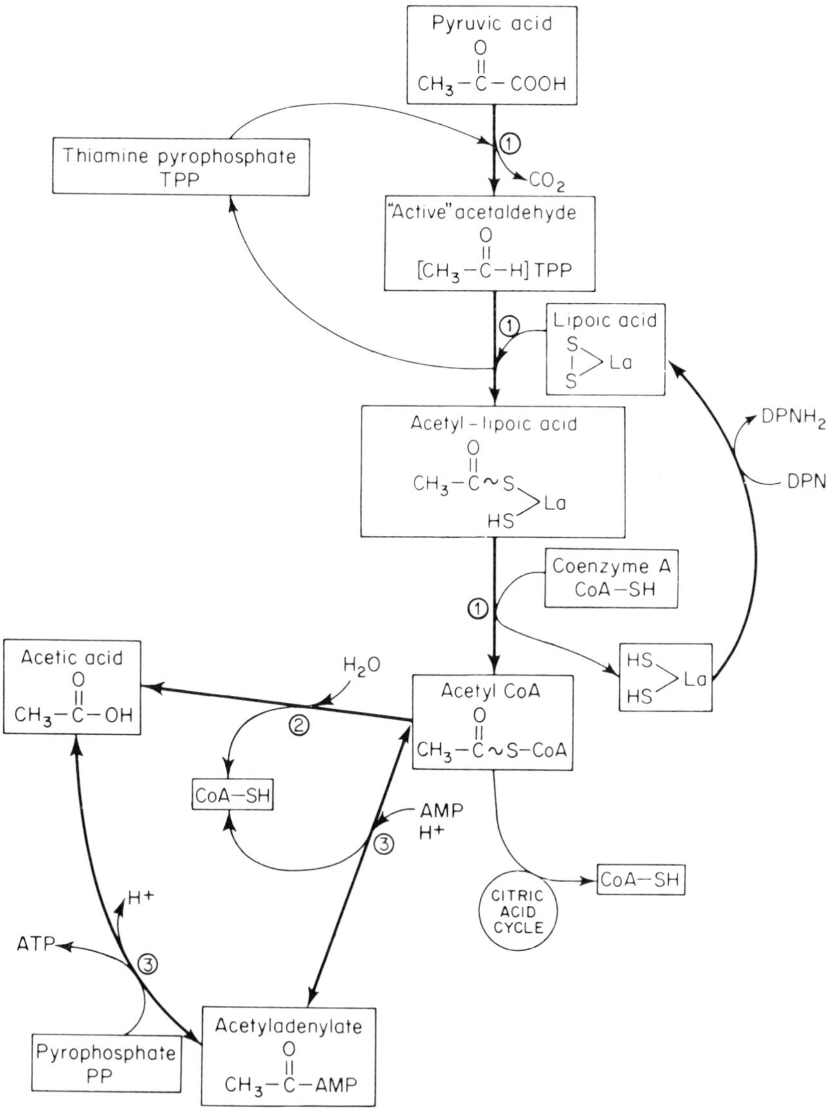

Fig. 7.7. Metabolism of pyruvic acid to acetyl CoA and acetic acid. ENZYMES. 1, Pyruvic dehydrogenase. 2, Acetyl CoA deacylase. 3, Acetic thiokinase.

Three vitamins—thiamine, lipoic acid and pantothenic acid (Fig. 7.6) (as well as magnesium ions, DPN and ATP)—are required to effect this decarboxylation and acetylation. The majority of animals are unable to synthesize these coenzymes and depend on plants for their manufacture.

THE CITRIC ACID CYCLE

This cycle is a common terminal pathway for the oxidation of foodstuffs and almost universal in aerobic energy-yielding mechanisms. Some animals have modified it to meet the demands of unusual habitats, such as those associated with parasitism, but it has remained dominant in the main stream of animal phylogeny. In the complete cycle one acetic acid equivalent is "burned" to CO_2 and H_2O, while a series of di- and tri-carboxylic acids appear as intermediaries (Fig. 7.2). Most writers show the cycle as producing CO_2 and releasing hydrogen which is then picked up by a group of special carriers. These carriers pass the hydrogen to molecular oxygen in a series of oxidation-reduction reactions which actually generate the pyrophosphate bonds (OXIDATIVE PHOSPHORYLATION). It should be remembered, however, that the dehydrogenase and other enzymes of the cycle proper and those which pick up the electrons and shuttle them along to oxygen in the process of oxidative phosphorylation are components of one system. Although the many enzymes are evidently localized in a rather precise and definite manner on the membranes and within the matrix of the mitochondria (Green, 1962), they function as a unit. The processes are only described separately as a matter of convenience.

The sequence of compounds and reactions in Fig. 7.2 shows the points where carbon dioxide and water are released as direct metabolites and where hydrogen is delivered to the special transport system involved in oxidative phosphorylation. Attention is directed to four major points: (A) acetate is not the only carbon compound regularly delivered to and incorporated in the chain; (B) the cycle is not only the prime source of ATP energy in animals but also supplies carbon skeletons for the manufacture of many of the constituents of protoplasm; (C) three compounds are actually concerned with the pickup and transfer of electrons to the cytochrome chain and, finally (D) the energy associated with this portion of tissue respiration forms a major parcel of the total released to the animal.

The process by which glutamate and aspartate are relieved of their amino nitrogen and incorporated in the chain as α-ketoglutarate and oxaloacetate respectively will be considered with the metabolism of the amino acids. It should be emphasized here that the reactions of the

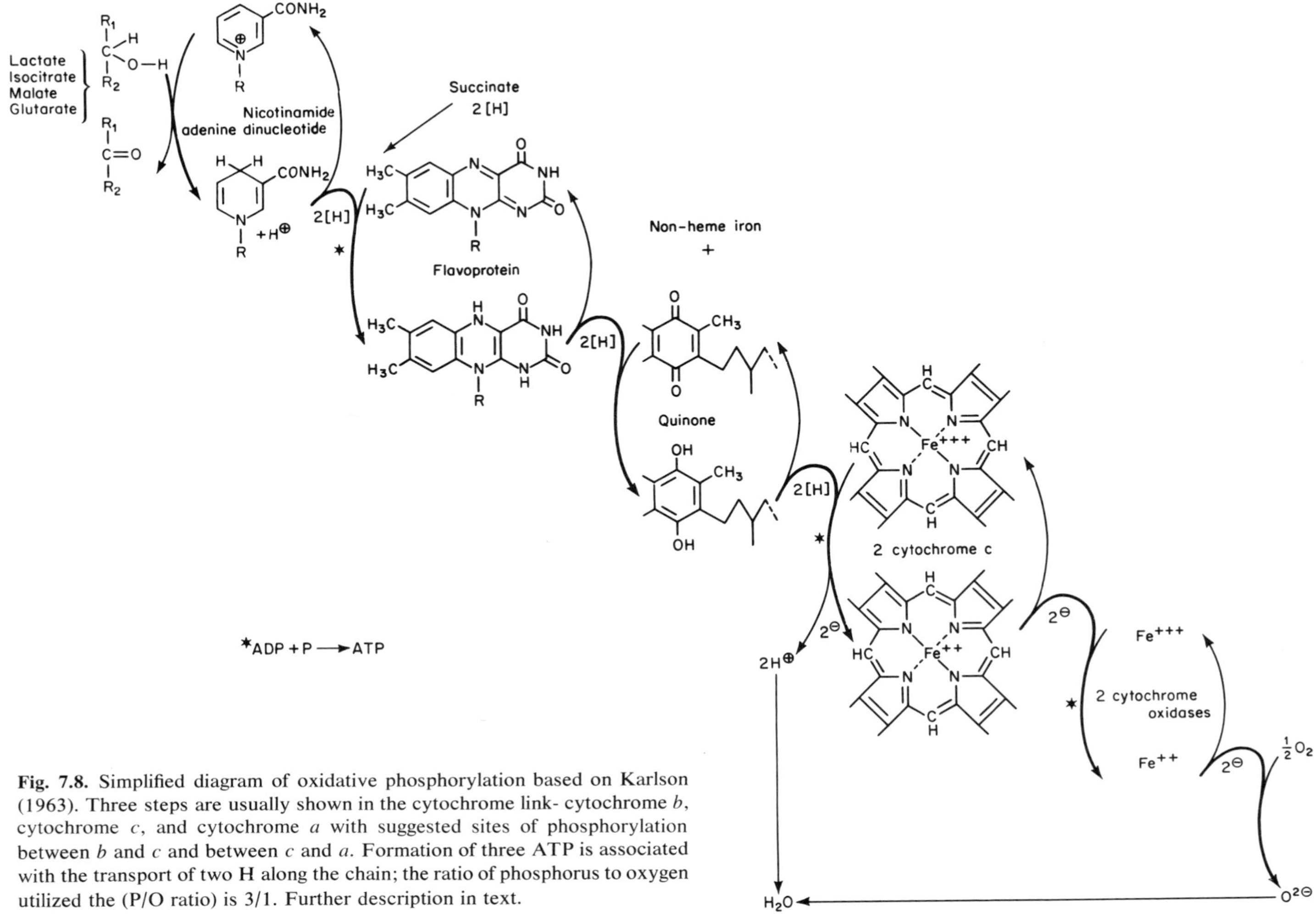

Fig. 7.8. Simplified diagram of oxidative phosphorylation based on Karlson (1963). Three steps are usually shown in the cytochrome link- cytochrome *b*, cytochrome *c*, and cytochrome *a* with suggested sites of phosphorylation between *b* and *c* and between *c* and *a*. Formation of three ATP is associated with the transport of two H along the chain; the ratio of phosphorus to oxygen utilized the (P/O ratio) is 3/1. Further description in text.

citric acid cycle are reversible (Fig. 7.2). This means that several different carbon skeletons maintain its structure; on the other hand, the cycle can supply different carbon fragments for the synthesis of other compounds. This reversibility of reactions also suggests that carbon dioxide may be used directly to increase the lengths of the carbon chains. This has indeed been shown to occur in mammalian liver; carbon dioxide fixation is a recognized cellular activity in animals as well as in the photosynthetic processes of plants. Other reactions have been studied whereby microorganisms may synthesize C_4 dicarboxylic acids from acetate via the glyoxalate cycle and thus permit the formation of the necessary carbon compounds of the citric acid sequence and its operation when the organism has only acetate or such highly oxidized compounds as glycolate or oxalate at its disposal. As emphasized by Krebs (Krebs and Kornberg, 1957), the citric acid cycle performs two major functions: the supply of chemical energy in the form of ATP and the formation of C_4, C_5, C_6 skeletons for the synthesis of many different cell constituents.

OXIDATIVE PHOSPHORYLATION

The release of electrons (hydrogen) at many points in the metabolic pathways has been noted. In the specialized "terminal transport system" of aerobic metabolism, these are passed to a series of carriers which are successively reduced and then oxidized as the electrons move along it until they reach the final cytochrome link (Fig. 7.8); here the enzyme, cytochrome oxidase, catalyzes the reduction of molecular oxygen to form water.

Most of the links in the chain have now probably been identified, although there are many puzzling details still to be explained. In the first steps, electrons from the citric acid pool are picked up by the flavoproteins. This seems to be a direct transfer for those coming from succinate (f_s, below), while those released at other points in the cycle are picked up by the pyridine nucleotides and then passed to the flavoproteins (f_D, below). At this point in the transport chain, Green (1962) describes two parallel paths which probably fuse as the electrons move along a common series of cytochrome carriers. Non-heme iron (Fe_{NH}) and coenzyme Q are active in passing the electrons from the flavoproteins to the cytochromes; Cu^{++} is essential in the final cytochrome link. Green (1962) shows the sequence as follows:

$$\begin{array}{lllllllll} \text{Succinate} & \rightarrow f_s\text{- Fe}_{NH} & \rightarrow & Q & \rightarrow b \rightarrow c_1 \rightarrow & c & \rightarrow (a\text{-Cu})_2 \\ & & & | & & | & \\ \text{DPNH, H}^+ & \rightarrow f_D\text{- Fe}_{NH} & \rightarrow & Q & \rightarrow b \rightarrow c_1 \rightarrow & c & \rightarrow (a\text{-Cu})_2 \end{array}$$

He suggests that the flavoprotein-Fe_{NH} section, the $b \rightarrow c_1$ cytochrome section and the *a*-Cu cytochrome sections are fixed while coenzyme Q and cytochrome *c* form mobile links between them.

At three points in the chain there is a release of energy through the coupling of inorganic phosphate with ADP. Probable sites of phosphorylation are indicated in Fig. 7.8. To the physiologist, this is the really significant event in oxidative phosphorylation since it provides the major parcel of energy in the aerobic processes of animal life; in this way the mitochondria, through the citric acid enzymes and those involved in oxidative phosphorylations, generate twenty-four units of ATP for each unit of glucose metabolized. Thus, there is a net gain of thirty-eight units of ATP for each unit of glucose completely oxidized and the balance sheet may be written as follows:

$$\text{1 Glucose Unit} \xrightarrow{\text{E-M Path}} \text{2 Pyruvate Units} + 2\text{ATP} + 4\text{H}$$

$$\text{2 Pyruvate Units} \xrightarrow{\text{oxidation}} \text{2 Acetyl CoA Units} + 2\text{CO}_2 + 4\text{H}$$

$$\text{2 Acetyl CoA Units} \xrightarrow{\text{TCA Cycle}} 4\text{CO}_2 + 16\text{H}$$

$$24\text{H} \xrightarrow{\text{oxidative phosphorylation}} 36\text{ATP}$$

$$\text{Summary}\quad \text{C}_6\text{H}_{12}\text{0}_6 + 6\text{0}_2 \longrightarrow 6\text{C0}_2 + 6\text{H}_2\text{0} + 38\text{ATP}$$

The structure of the pyridine nucleotides (Fig. 7.4) and the cytochromes (Fig. 6.1) has already been shown; the important flavoproteins and coenzyme Q are given in Fig. 7.9. The flavin component contains the familiar adenylic acid coupled with riboflavin phosphate (an isoalloxazine ring attached to a C_5 sugar) which is another of the important vitamins; most animals depend on plants or bacteria for their supply of it. Coenzyme Q is a tetrasubstituted benzoquinone with a side chain containing ten isoprenoid units. It is capable of being reversibly oxidized and reduced as indicated in Fig. 7.9 and in this way links the flavoproteins with the cytochromes.

Alternate terminal pathways. The cytochrome system is the predominant terminal pathway in aerobic respiration. It is probably the only one in the free-living animals. However, cytochrome oxidase is not the only enzyme capable of catalyzing reactions involving molecular oxygen; studies of alternative terminal oxidases have been particularly numerous in the field of plant biochemistry. To be of significance, such systems must participate in the oxidation of reduced pyridine nucleotides and flavoproteins. Simultaneously, these oxidations must be coupled with the formation of ATP.

Two possible alternative respiratory pathways are those involving phenol oxidase and those involving ascorbic acid oxidase (Fruton and Simmonds, 1958). These are copper-containing enzymes. The first (also called polyphenol oxidase, phenolase and tyrosinsase) occurs widely in both plant and animal tissues. Ascorbic acid is particularly abundant in some plants and of vital importance in their respiration. It is also an essential vitamin for higher animals, but although the scorbutic effects associated with its deficiency in man have been known for centuries, its essential role is still not satisfactorily explained. It is certainly involved in important oxidation-reduction reactions both in the higher plants and animals, but its association with phosphorylation is questionable.

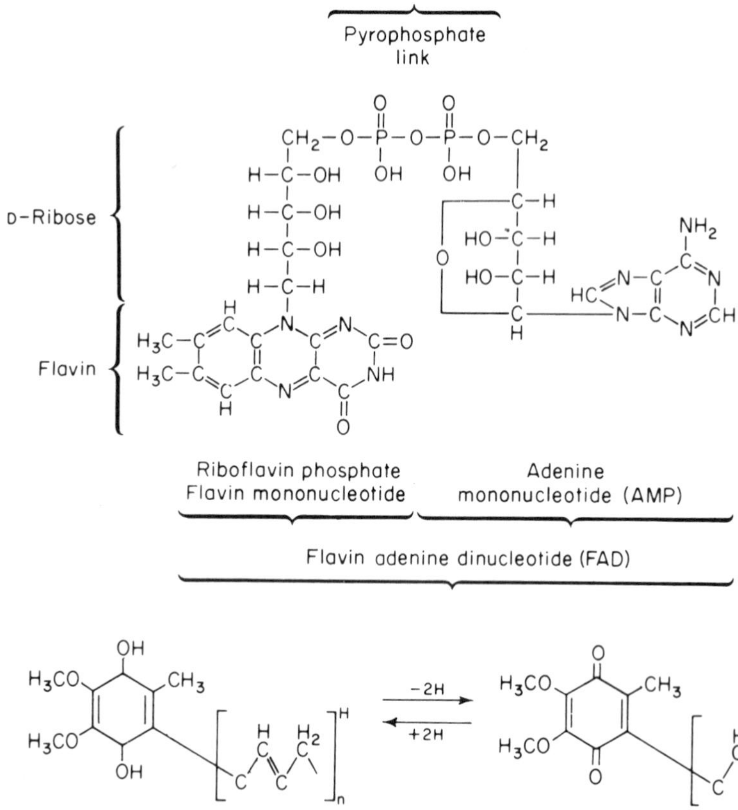

Fig. 7.9. Structure of flavin adenine dinucleotide (above) and the Coenzyme *Q* oxidation-reduction system—ubihydroquinone to ubiquinone (below).

Insect physiologists have devoted considerable attention to tyrosinase as an oxidase of the terminal respiratory transport system. It is particularly active at the time of pupation when the cytochrome system may be undergoing changes. However, no really good evidence exists that the phenolases serve as alternates for the cytochromes in insects or even in plants where these enzymes are very active. The high phenolase activity associated with insect pupation seems to be specifically related to the synthesis of quinones which are active in the tanning of the cuticular protein (Gilmour, 1961).

On the whole, an increasing body of evidence from animals at all levels in phylogeny supports the view that oxidative phosphorylation involving the cytochrome system forms a common denominator in the release of energy in the world of the free-living animals.

INTERMEDIARY METABOLISM OF ANAEROBIC ANIMALS

Exceptions to these generalizations for free-living animals are now well documented in several parasitic species. Trematodes, cestodes and nematodes have been sufficiently studied to show that, although their biochemical machinery is based on the fundamental pathways described for the free-living forms, there are many short-cuts and variations, with end-products quite different from carbon dioxide and water. This is still a most fruitful field of research in intermediary metabolism. Several reviews are available (Fairbairn, 1957; Read, 1961; Bueding, 1962). The Embden-Meyerhof sequence and the pentose shunt have been found in parasitic worms, but pyruvate frequently gives rise to higher acids (valeric, caproic, propionic) rather than to acetic and lactic acids. The Krebs citric acid cycle is present but probably considerably altered. Marked modifications are found in the terminal mechanisms of oxidative phosphorylation, and this might be expected of tissues operating in an oxygen-deficient environment. In some cases no activity has been found in the cytochrome systems, although the enzymes are present. Even if oxygen is added to, and taken up by, these systems, it does not significantly displace the hydrogen acceptors which normally operate in the absence of oxygen. The details have not been worked out, but possible schemes for electron transport have been proposed (Kikuchi *et al.* 1959).

Read (1961), in summarizing some of the recent literature, comments on the adaptive significance of the observed differences. In general, carbohydrate is metabolized at a high rate. However, it is not oxidized to carbon dioxide and water but incompletely metabolized to a variety of fatty acids, leaving a considerable store of potential energy still locked in the C-H-O bonds. This seems wasteful and inefficient; but Read argues that, when food is abundant and the animal has been freed of the problem of locating a source of energy, there may be a distinct advantage in reducing the number of chemical processes. It is important to extract all of the energy from the glucose molecule if glucose molecules are in short supply.

This, in itself, however, requires energy; if the organism is relieved of the problem of obtaining the molecules it can afford to live a lazy life of luxury and reduce the number of biochemical steps to a minimum. This may be an advantage. The fact remains that oxidative phosphorylation is impossible in the anaerobic world, and life in this environment demands alternatives.

At present, the only animal with a predominantly aerobic metabolism that is known to lack several of the common enzymes of the citric acid cycle (and, possibly also of the electron transport system) is the vinegar eel, *Tubatrix aceti* (Ells and Read, 1961). However, such generalizations must be made with considerable caution until more species of animals have been carefully studied. Knowledge of the intermediary metabolism of invertebrates is particularly fragmentary. The insects are the best known; they have now been investigated for many years, yet it was not until 1957 that the major blood sugar in the circulating hemolymph was shown to be the disaccharide trehalose and not glucose which is characteristic of the vertebrates (Wyatt, 1961; Gilmour, 1961). Monosaccharides absorbed in the mid-gut as well as the energy reserves in the fat gland are converted to trehalose and circulate as such in the hemolymph. At the point of carbohydrate utilization, the trehalose is converted to glucose and follows the pathways already outlined. Trehalose is also the important blood sugar in several other invertebrate groups (Gilmour, 1961).

METABOLISM OF FAT

Lipid substances form an essential component of all protoplasm (CONSTANT ELEMENT) and even during extreme starvation considerable amounts can be extracted from the tissues. In addition, however, fat forms an important fuel reserve (VARIABLE ELEMENT) and is often stored in large quantities. The present discussion is confined to a consideration of fats as fuel for the production of ATP energy.

Many animals live for a long time almost exclusively on the fat reserves. Atlantic salmon enter fresh water, cease feeding and live an active life, sometimes for as long as a year, while they utilize stored fat (Greene, 1926). During this time blood sugars and liver glycogen remain essentially unaltered, indicating that the fat is readily converted into these essential carbohydrates in addition to being used directly as a source of energy.

The neutral fats which form the main source of lipid energy are esters of glycerol and the long chain fatty acids with an even number of carbon atoms. Many cells contain lipolytic enzymes which readily hydrolyze these triglycerides into their constituent fatty acids and glycerol. This is the first preparatory step in their metabolism (Fig. 7.2).

The glycerol, through an enzymatic priming reaction with ATP, is converted into glycerolphosphate. There follows an oxidation (dehydrogenation) in which hydrogen passes to the DPN carrier system and a triosephosphate (PGAL) is formed. This compound has already been identified in the Embden-Meyerhof sequence at the cross-roads of several metabolic paths. From PGAL the products of glycerol may be synthesized to carbohydrate or further oxidized through acetate and the citric acid cycle (Fig. 7.2).

Fatty acids are usually oxidized by a process referred to as β-oxidation. In this, two carbon units are progressively removed from the carboxyl end of the carbon chain to yield acetate equivalents which can then be completely metabolized via the citric acid cycle or, alternatively, built up into glucose and more complex carbohydrate units if the demands are for these substances (Fig. 7.2). Since the majority of the naturally occurring fats contain even numbers of carbon atoms, oxidation at the β-position is always possible. Several of the important steps in this oxidation are indicated in Fig. 7.10.

The reaction sequence commences with an ATP-CoA priming. A fatty acid-CoA derivative results, and this is then desaturated between the α and β carbon positions. In the mammal, enzymes capable of performing this desaturation have been found in the liver, and the hydrogen released in this way is first passed to the flavin hydrogen carriers. It may then proceed along the aerobic oxidative phosphorylation chain, yielding ATP energy. The α, β unsaturated fatty acid CoA compound now undergoes hydration and dehydrogenation with the reduction of DPN, and more fuel is added to the hydrogen carrier chain. At this point a further enzymatic reaction splits off acetyl CoA and leaves a residual fatty acid CoA compound which can likewise cycle the desaturation, hydration and dehydrogenation series. The process is repeated until the long chain fatty acid is completely metabolized (Fig. 7.10).

The acetyl CoA fragments can, of course, enter the citric acid cycle by familiar routes or be synthesized into complex carbon compounds (Fig. 7.2). They may, however, have quite a different fate. Under certain conditions two fragments combine to form acetoacetate. In some animals (man, for example) this seems to happen if large amounts of fat are being metabolized and there is insufficient utilization of carbohydrate, with a deficit of compounds which provide the essential components of the citric acid cycle. Thus, in man diabetes produces a characteristic ketosis in which ketones (acetone, acetoacetic acid and β-hydroxybutyric acid) accumulate in the blood.

Animals vary considerably in their tendency to form ketone bodies.

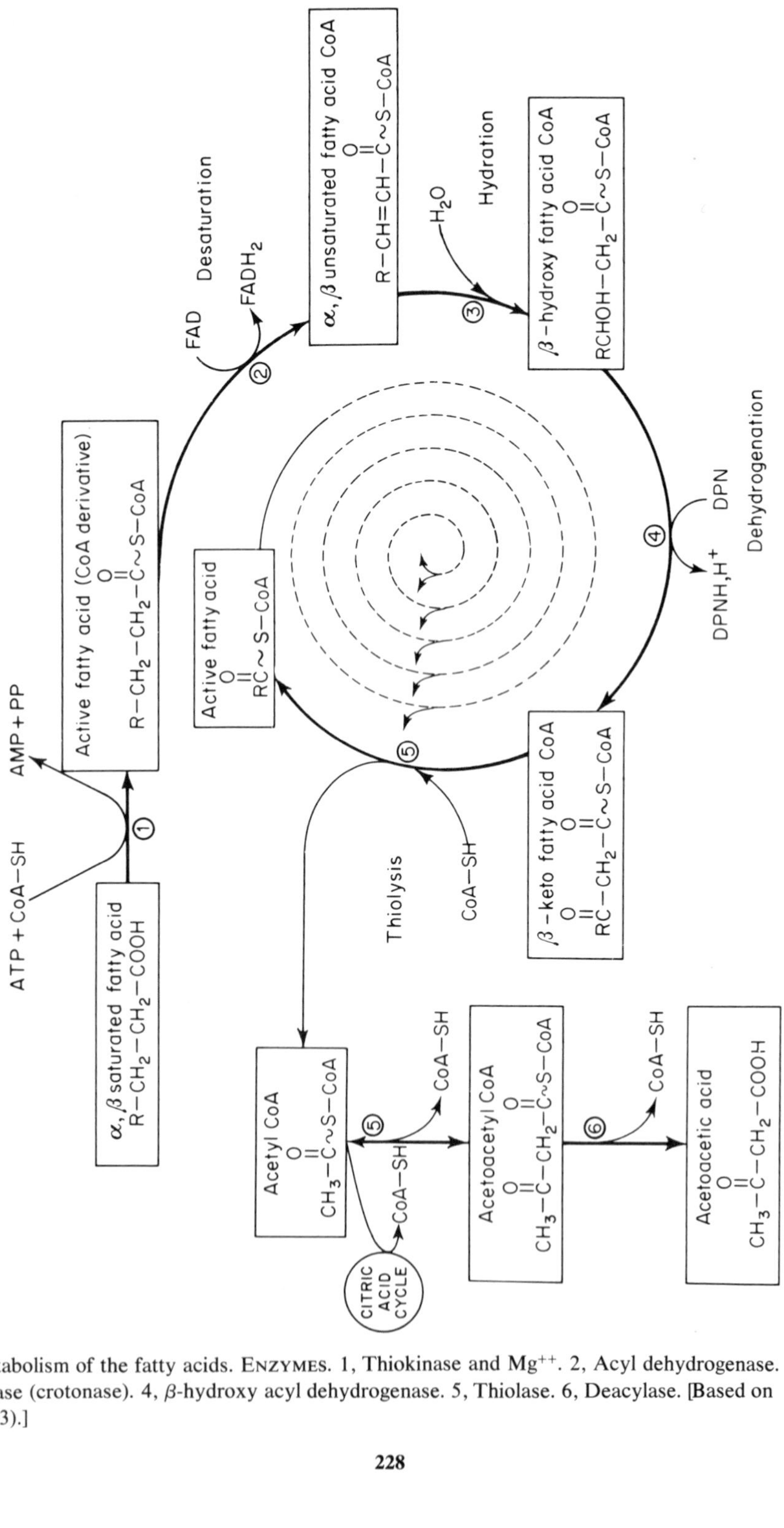

Fig. 7.10. Metabolism of the fatty acids. ENZYMES. 1, Thiokinase and Mg^{++}. 2, Acyl dehydrogenase. 3, Enol hydrase (crotonase). 4, β-hydroxy acyl dehydrogenase. 5, Thiolase. 6, Deacylase. [Based on Baldwin (1963).]

As already indicated, some fishes may, for prolonged periods, metabolize fats almost to the exclusion of other foods. Similarly, a chick embryo during development, depends almost entirely on fats for its energy, and the same is true of many other animals. Variations are common among the mammals and even in the different species of the same genus. It is, for example, difficult to induce a starvation ketosis in the rat, while among different races of men, the Eskimo diet is notoriously rich in fat.

The energetics of fat metabolism are interesting. Although the glycerol molecule must be primed with one ATP, there is a return of some twenty units of ATP when the glycerol unit is completely oxidized through the citric acid cycle and the associated oxidative phosphorylations. Further, each step in the β-oxidation of fatty acids requires a priming of ATP but yields about eighteen ATP units. Since the common fatty acids of animal cells—palmitic and stearic—contain sixteen and eighteen carbon atoms respectively, it is apparent that fatty acids are rich sources of ATP energy.

AMINO ACID METABOLISM

Amino acids, derived from the digestion of protein, pass into the fuel system if they are not required for growth, tissue repair or the construction of important secretions and enzymes. Their fate depends on the amount of protein in the diet, the age of the animal and the other sources of fuel available to it. In emergencies, amino acids may be withdrawn from the protoplasm of the cell, and thus during starvation the cellular protein content declines. This is true even though protein is not stored in the same sense that carbohydrate and fat are stored in special organs and depots. The protein reserve of the cell forms an active, although partially expendable, portion of its protoplasm.

Deamination. Before entering the fuel system, nitrogen (also sulfur and iodine if present) must be removed from the amino acid molecule. Deamination, the process by which the amino groups are split off, is one of the conspicuous removal processes. More than a quarter of a century ago Krebs (1935) showed that slices of kidney and liver from many animals, when incubated with amino acids, took up oxygen and produced ammonia; further, that approximately one mole of oxygen was used for every two moles of ammonia formed. A family of enzymes, the amino acid oxidases, catalyzes these oxidative deamination reactions. Several steps are now known, with flavin compounds acting as intermediary hydrogen acceptors. The overall reaction may be written as follows:

$$\underset{\alpha\text{-AMINO ACID}}{R \cdot CHNH_2 \cdot COOH} + \tfrac{1}{2}O_2 \longrightarrow \underset{\alpha\text{-KETO ACID}}{R \cdot \overset{\overset{O}{\|}}{C} \cdot COOH} + NH_3$$

Oxidative deamination, although prominent in tissues, is by no means the only way in which amino groups are removed. A series of non-oxidative deamination enzymes are associated with certain specific amino acids such as the hydroxy amino acids (dehydrases), the sulfur-containing amino acids (desulfhydrases), histidine (histidase), tryptophan (tryptophanase) and others.

In general these reactions lead to one or the other of two familiar residues, pyruvate or acetate. Dietary experiments with individually labelled amino acids have shown that in mammals the non-essential amino acids usually produce a pyruvate residue (GLUCOGENIC AMINO ACIDS), while most of the essential amino acids form an acetate residue (KETOGENIC AMINO ACIDS). The significance of the terms glucogenic and ketogenic is obvious. The first group of amino acids in large quantities leads to the production and storage of carbohydrate, while fat metabolism is emphasized in the case of the ketogenic group. Through deamination at least half of the common amino acids are reduced to these two familiar carbon residues, and from this point, as acetyl CoA, they can enter the energy-yielding reactions of the citric acid cycle (Fig. 7.2).

Ammonia metabolism. The production of deaminated carbon residues for the citric acid cycle was emphasized in the previous section. This is only a small part of the story of nitrogen metabolism. There are several other ways in which NH_2 groups may be moved about and, although sometimes excreted, they more frequently enter an extremely labile nitrogen pool and become part of the synthetic and regulatory machinery. The importance and lability of the amino nitrogen will now be considered. Its excretion as a waste product is described in Chapter 8.

Through TRANSAMINATION, a family of enzymes (the transaminases associated with pyridoxal phosphate as a cofactor) transfer amino groups of various amino acids to keto or other organic acids (Fig. 7.11). At transfer point *A* (Fig. 7.11) the amino group moves from glutamic to pyruvic acid and thus forms the amino acid alanine and α-keto glutaric acid. The transfer point *B* shows a particularly important molecular rearrangement in which amino acids are linked with the citric acid cycle at two points (the oxaloacetic and α-ketoglutaric links). Through deaminations or transaminations involving glutamic and aspartic acids, α-ketoglutaric and oxaloacetic acids respectively may be added to the citric acid cycle. Conversely, the appropriate carbon skeletons may be picked up from the cycle and coupled with the amino nitrogen for the synthesis of protein. In this way, the metabolism of the proteins is connected with the metabolism of the carbohydrates and the fats. Carbon fragments from the latter two may turn up in the proteins through the oxaloacetic and the α-ketoglutaric links. Alternatively, deaminated amino acids may become a part of the carbohydrates and the fats.

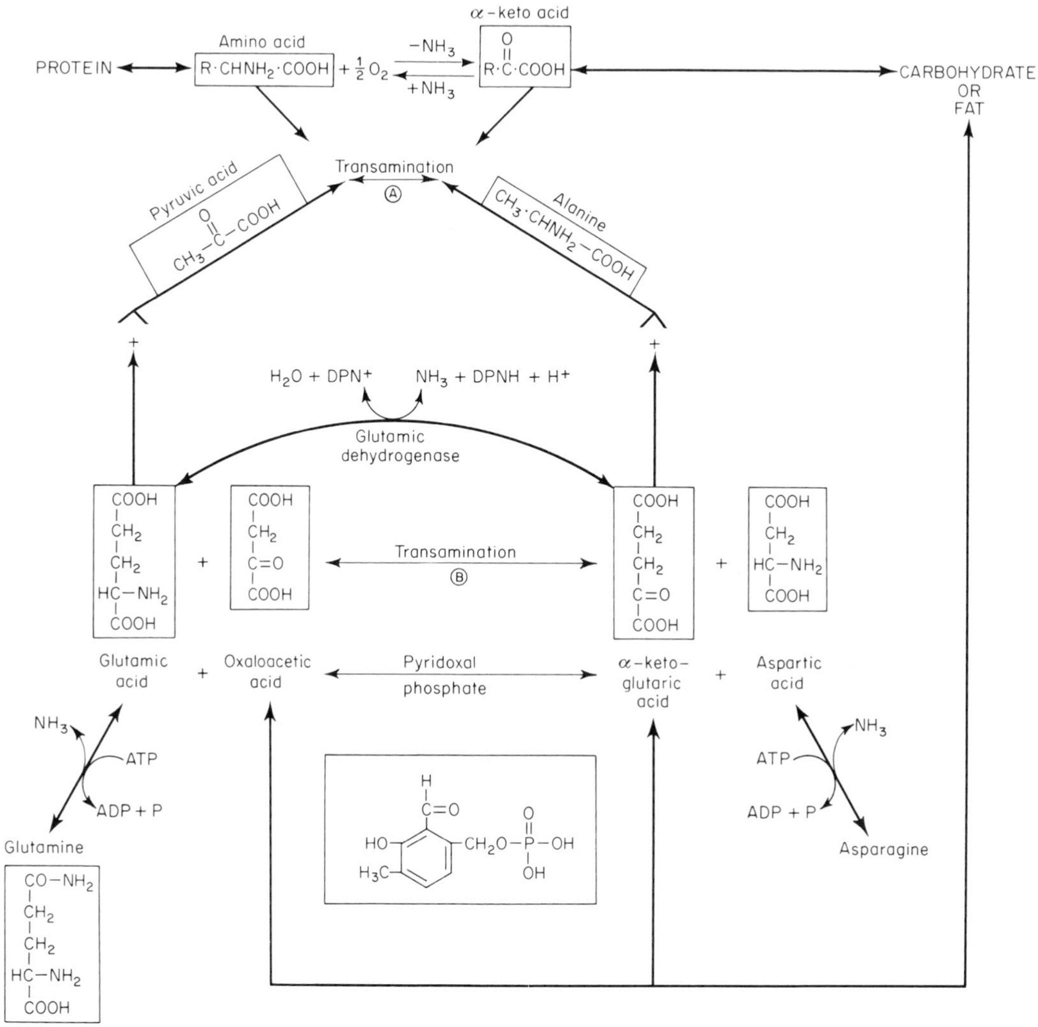

Fig. 7.11. Transamination and some metabolic paths connecting proteins with carbohydrate and fat. Description in text.

In addition to transamination, there are several AMINATION reactions through which amino groups may be coupled with organic acids and other compounds. Two of these are illustrated in Fig. 7.11. At the center of the diagram, glutamic dehydrogenase (in a process of reductive amination requiring energy from reduced pyridine nucleotide) incorporates ammonia into α-ketoglutaric acid to form glutamic acid. In the reversed reaction a deamination occurs. The second amination process is shown where the amides of glutamic and aspartic acids (glutamine and asparagine respectively) are formed through energy derived from ATP.

The ammonia used in these various reactions may be derived from deaminations but can also be obtained from inorganic sources. Although animals are unable to utilize most forms of inorganic nitrogen, they can probably all derive some from ammonia. It has, for example, been shown that rats fed a diet containing N^{15} ammonium citrate will later contain radioactive amino acids (Fruton and Simmonds, 1958). Intestinal bacteria produce ammonia and this, as well as that derived from the dietary ammonium salts, will enter the circulation and be incorporated into metabolically important nitrogen compounds or form nitrogenous wastes such as urea. The ammonium ion itself is rather toxic (Chapter 8) and never occurs as such in significant amounts in animal tissues. However, the nitrogen is indispensable for life and occurs largely as amino (NH_2) or imino (NH) nitrogen, in which forms it is transported and stored.

Energetics of ammonia formation. Most deamination reactions produce a certain amount of heat, but there is no gain in ATP. In poikilotherms the production of heat may be thought of as a useless by-product of metabolism. Useful energy appears in other forms, particularly as in the pyrophosphate bond of ATP. It has been suggested that a coupling of the glutamic acid dehydrogenase reaction with the transaminase systems may be of considerable importance in the production of ATP from protein (Cohen and Brown, 1960). These enzymes are found everywhere in the living world, and glutamic acid dehydrogenase requires DPN or TPN which, when reduced, can enter the chain of oxidative phosphorylation (Fig. 7.12).

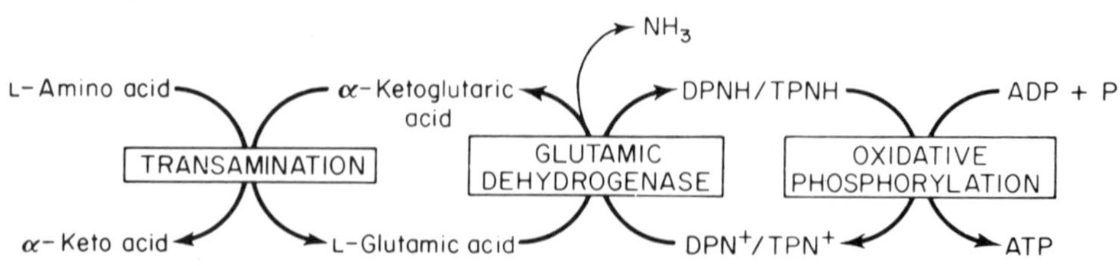

Fig. 7.12. Scheme for deamination of amino acids via coupled transaminase(s) and glutamic dehydrogenase. [Based on Cohen and Brown (1960).]

Storage of amino groups. Glutamine forms an important store of amino groups in the animal body. About one fifth of all the amino acid nitrogen in human blood is contained in glutamine and glutamic acid. In plants, asparagine as well as glutamine stores nitrogen. The reactions (Fig. 7.11) whereby these mono-amides of glutamic and aspartic acids are formed require ATP energy and an appropriate enzyme (glutamine synthetase for glutamine), but the resulting compounds form an indispensable reservoir of amino nitrogen. Specific enzymes remove the amino groups to form glutamic and α-ketoglutaric acids or transfer them in various ways during the synthesis of purines, amino sugars (glucosamine) and numerous amino acids. Thus, glutamine and asparagine (plants) play a central role not only in the storage of amino groups but also in their utilization.

EVOLUTION OF ENERGY-TRANSFORMING MECHANISMS

The general processes of energy transformation will not be followed further. Those so far discussed seem to be universal in living tissues. Their relatively small number suggests that they are of great phylogenetic antiquity and that life itself is founded upon them. Krebs and Kornberg (1957), in an outstanding summary of the energy transformations of living matter, suggested the following evolutionary sequence: ANAEROBIC FERMENTATION (glycolytic enzymes, ATP and pyridine nucleotide), PENTOSE PHOSPHATE CYCLE, PHOTOSYNTHESIS (metalloporphyrins), and CELL RESPIRATION (including the citric acid cycle, the cytochrome system and oxidative phosphorylation).

It seems logical, both on biochemical and geochemical grounds, to place the anaerobic fermentation type of reaction in the basal position. These reactions are the most widespread of biochemical activities and, as discussed in Chapter 1, there is now general agreement that life originated under anaerobic conditions. The evolutionary position of the pentose cycle is more speculative, but pentoses are found in several ubiquitous and indispensable molecules, and a supplementary supply may have been required before photosynthesis provided the conditions essential to the evolution of the plants and animals. If this were the sequence, the development of the pentose cycle could have provided several additional biochemical reactions which were later associated with photosynthesis. Given the pentose shunt and fermentation, only two more reactions (Fig. 1.3) would have been required in the carbon pathways of photosynthesis itself (Krebs and Kornberg, 1957). Photosynthesis then provided oxygen for aerobic respiration and energy stores for the evolution of an animal world.

Even in the most primitive present-day plants and animals, these fundamental energy-generating reactions are only known to operate in orderly sequences within the architecture of living cells. Cellular morphology probably evolved in association with the biochemical reactions which are a part of it. Some minimum organization of cellular structure must have preceded the familiar processes of Darwinian evolution. Enzymes and compounds responsible for the release of energy (largely in the form of the pyrophosphate bond) are not distributed uniformly throughout the protoplasm but are arranged in an orderly way on a special fabric of cytoplasmic structures (Green, 1962). They have been localized through electron microscope examinations of ultrastructure and special cytochemical staining techniques and through the isolation and chemical analysis of different cellular constituents such as the mitochondria and microsomes. The metabolic requirements of the various cellular constituents have been determined by providing organisms and cells with isotopically labelled compounds.

Such studies show that the Embden-Meyerhof system and the enzymes required to form pyruvate, acetate and other residues necessary for the citric acid cycle, are located in the cytoplasmic matrix or hyaloplasm. The citric acid cycle itself is largely operated in the matrix of the mitochondria, while the electron transport system of oxidative phosphorylation is spread out in a very definite and organized way (Lehninger, 1960; Green, 1962) on the mitochondrial membranes (cristae). Mitochondria are mainly responsible for the liberation of ATP energy and are integral parts of all the cells of plants and animals. Their evolution would seem to have been associated with the phylogeny of efficient aerobic tissue respiration.

Energy-Utilizing Processes of Animal Life

The ATP energy, liberated through tissue respiration, is transformed in various ways into characteristic animal activities. The links are graphically depicted in Lipmann's (1941) "energy dynamo" (Fig. 7.13). The catabolic transformations from the food or fuel and the amidine phosphate storage systems have been outlined in previous sections. The transformers which convert the pyrophosphate energy into animal work are less well known. There is, for example, little doubt that ATP provides energy for the operation of the contractile machinery, but the molecular details of the coupling are matters of speculation. Again, the activation of molecules in synthetic processes, such as those involved in the coupling of the amino acids to form protein, is recognized; but the molecular details are still subjects of intensive investigation.

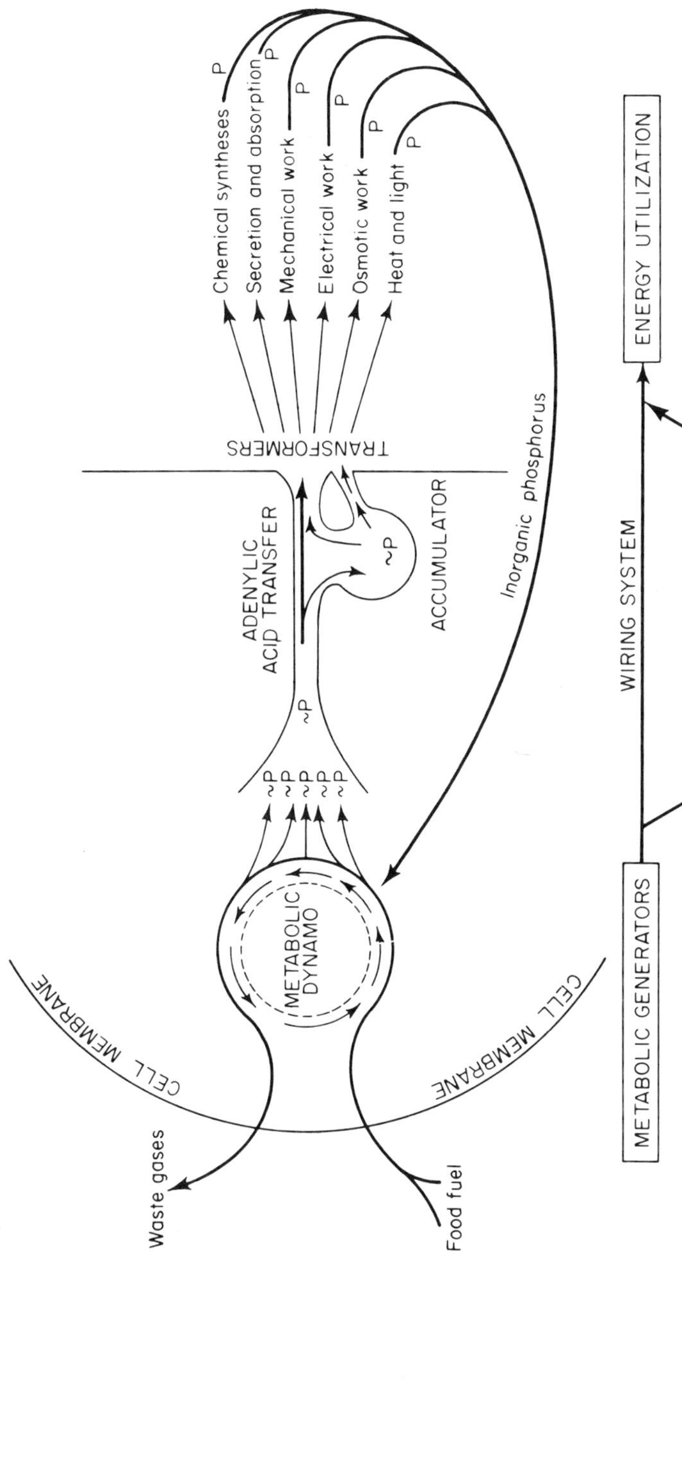

Fig. 7.13. The "Energy Dynamo". [Based on Lipmann (1941).]

Active transport of materials across the cell or through its membrane, the maintenance of bioelectric potentials and the excitation processes in nervous tissue are likewise incompletely understood at the molecular level. Heat and light may be regarded as by-products of metabolism. Natural selection has taken advantage of both of these energy by-products and adapted them in varied ways. Many details concerning the utilization of free energy to support varied animal functions are compiled in Volume 2 of a comprehensive treatise on comparative biochemistry edited by Florkin and Mason (1960).

The Rate of Metabolism

Lavoisier, in the latter part of the eighteenth century, first examined living systems thermodynamically and established relationships between the energy liberated in the form of heat and that which entered the animal as food. In 1780, in association with his colleague Laplace, he put a guinea pig in a closed box surrounded by ice and recorded the melting of 341 g of ice in a 10-hour period. These workers also measured the carbon dioxide production of a guinea pig of similar size during a 10-hour period and calculated that the burning of carbon to form this amount of gas would generate enough heat to melt 326.7 g of ice. The agreement was remarkably good; animal respiration was equated to the combustion of carbon compounds. At that time Lavoisier did not have the information necessary to appreciate the differences between the burning of food and the burning of carbon. He concluded that animal heat is due to the transformation of carbon to carbon dioxide during respiration. In 1781 Cavendish described the oxidation of hydrogen to form water, and in 1785 Lavoisier recognized the probable significance of this reaction in animal respiration and noted that he had been incorrect in assuming that only carbon was oxidized in animal respiration. These pioneer experiments are outlined in several familiar textbooks (Brody, 1945; Gabriel and Fogel, 1955; Kleiber, 1961).

HEAT PRODUCTION

To the scientists of the eighteenth and early nineteenth century, the living machine was a kind of furnace in which foods were burned to liberate heat. The heat was necessary for animal activities in somewhat the same manner that heat is necessary to generate the steam utilized by the steam engine. The scientists of the twentieth century have shown that this concept is entirely incorrect and that the heat produced is really a by-product of the essential energy-releasing chemical reactions of life.

All animals, whether warm-blooded or cold-blooded, produce heat. It is a necessary accompaniment of the transformation of energy. In some cases the heat produced is lost directly to the environment. In other cases it is conserved in one way or another to control the temperature of the microclimate or the animal itself. In the course of evolution animals have utilized this by-product of their metabolism to permit greater independence of the variable environmental temperature. These adaptations are considered in Chapter 10.

In the thermodynamic sense the heat produced in metabolism is wasted free energy. The more inefficient the process, the more heat is produced. In the hexokinase reaction, already described (page 201), the glucose molecule is phosphorylated through a reaction involving the hydrolysis of ATP to ADP. This glucose priming reaction requires about 3000 cal per mole. The conversion of ATP to ADP is associated with a fall of free energy of the order of 8500 cal. In the thermodynamic sense the difference represents wasted energy or the inefficiency of the reaction, but so far as life processes are concerned this is an almost universal reaction, and glucose cannot be metabolized without it. Heat production can be used as a measure of the rate of metabolism, as Lavoisier discovered almost 200 years ago, but it is related to the fuel of the system in a complex manner through the many enzymatic reactions of intermediary metabolism.

The conversion of food into the active metabolites of the body requires energy. Thus, following the intake of food, there is a heat production in excess of that associated with the operation of the machinery in the post-absorptive condition. Rubner discovered this in his pioneer studies of the metabolism of dogs and named it the SPECIFIC DYNAMIC ACTION (SDA). It is also called the CALORIGENIC EFFECT or the HEAT INCREMENT of the ration. Rubner's early work and many subsequent studies are discussed by Brody (1945). Precise values of the SDA vary with the diet, the plane of nutrition and a number of physiological and environmental conditions. The ingestion of protein may elevate the basal energy expenditure of a bird or mammal by 15 to 40 per cent. The SDA for fat is about 12 per cent and that of carbohydrate about 5 per cent. Warm-blooded animals may utilize this heat increment of the ration to maintain body temperatures, but in the thermoneutral environment or in the poikilotherm it is waste heat. The SDA is not attributed to processes of digestion but to the metabolic interconversions and storage of food molecules. Deamination and the formation of nitrogenous wastes (urea) are thought to account for the high SDA of protein. Several of the amino acids (phenylalanine, tyrosine and leucine) have particularly marked calorigenic effects, and it has been suggested that their metabolism is less efficient than some of the others. Excess of fat or sugar, following a meal, must be stored or otherwise metabolized before the animal machinery returns again to the basal conditions. Explanations of this type are usually advanced for the calorigenic effect, but the matter is still not well understood.

DIRECT AND INDIRECT CALORIMETRY

Lavoisier's crude ice calorimeter has been succeeded by many highly refined instruments which permit the measurement of heat production even in the larger mammals (Benedict, 1938; Brody, 1945; Kleiber, 1961). Energy content of food and waste products have also been determined. Rubner, about 1895, first compared heat production in animals with the heat liberated when corresponding samples of food were oxidized in a bomb calorimeter. He found that carbohydrate and fat formed approximately the same amount of heat under the two conditions of "burning" (9.3 kcal per g of fat and 4.1 kcal per g of carbohydrate) but that protein produced less heat in the animal (4.1 in comparison with 5.3 kcal). The protein nitrogen is incompletely oxidized and is excreted in various combinations with hydrogen and carbon. Since Rubner's time, precise relationships have been established between the energy values of the foods consumed, the oxygen used, the nitrogen excreted and the energy released. Living machines, like inanimate ones, are now known to be governed by the first law of thermodynamics or the law of conservation of energy.

Direct measurements of heat production require elaborate equipment. Nowadays indirect techniques, based on the constants determined in earlier days, are commonly employed. Heat production can be calculated from respiratory exchange and nitrogen excretion using well established metabolic constants (Brody, 1945; King and Farner, 1961; Kleiber, 1961). These are the methods of INDIRECT CALORIMETRY. They are much more convenient and, under many conditions, more reliable than the direct methods. In actual practice, oxygen consumption alone is commonly used by comparative physiologists. For most purposes it is entirely adequate. Its merits and limitations are discussed in several of the above publications.

It is obvious from the earlier discussion of intermediary metabolism, that respiratory exchange and nitrogen excretion will depend on the type of fuel and what is happening to it in the organism. The RESPIRATORY QUOTIENT or ratio of carbon dioxide produced to oxygen consumed is 1.0 for carbohydrate, about 0.7 for fat and 0.8 for protein. In the carbohydrate molecule, hydrogen and oxygen are present in the proportions to form water, and the ratio of CO_2 formed to O_2 consumed will obviously be 1:1. In the other foods, however, there is relatively much less oxygen and this is reflected in a lower R.Q. The R.Q. will also be affected by metabolic interconversions such as the formation of fat from carbohydrate (lipogenesis) or carbohydrate from protein (gluconeogenesis). Values as high as 1.49 have been recorded for force-fed geese where compounds are being formed with much higher ratios of hydrogen to oxygen (Benedict and Lee, 1937). Thus, respiratory exchange and nitrogen excretion will vary with lipogenesis, gluconeogenesis, growth and starvation as well as with the composition of the food. These factors must be controlled or evaluated in establishing reliable base lines.

STANDARD AND ACTIVE METABOLISM

Valid comparisons of the metabolism of animals can only be made under carefully controlled conditions. Most frequently an attempt is made to minimize muscular movement as well as the effects of food ingestion and related metabolic activities, by comparing metabolism of animals during periods of fasting and inactivity but not sleep. The term BASAL METABOLISM is used in mammalian studies. It is "the resting energy metabolism in a thermoneutral environment in post-absorptive condition, uncomplicated by heat increments incident to food utilization or to low or high environmental temperatures" (Brody, 1945). Krogh (1914) used STANDARD METABOLIC RATE for the comparable condition of minimal activity in lower animals, and this is the preferred term of comparative physiologists.

Fry and his associates (Chapter 12) recognize three levels of oxygen consumption in fish. The ACTIVE RATE will permit the highest continued level of activity; the ROUTINE RATE is the rate of utilization by fish when all movements are apparently spontaneous; the STANDARD RATE is the nearest attainable approximation to metabolism when all organs are at minimal activity. Many of the recorded measurements of standard metabolism are, in fact, routine metabolism according to these definitions. Some workers have attempted to measure the minimal level by using narcotized fish; others have measured oxygen consumption at several levels of activity and then extrapolated back to zero activity in order to obtain a standard rate (Fig. 7.14). The latter is the approved method, and with refinement of techniques the measurements of standard metabolism have given smaller and smaller values.

Although the minimum rates are the most reliable parameters for comparing the effects of different factors on metabolic demands, the maximum rates (active metabolism) also have physiological significance. The magnitude of the difference between active and standard metabolism varies markedly in different species of animals; in any one species it may change with temperature and other variables. Flying insects show some of the greatest differences between resting and active metabolism. Krogh (1941) reports an almost 170-fold increase for butterflies during flight. The metabolic rate of mammals is increased 10 to 20 times during activity, but the difference is much less in some animals. Fry (1957) found only a fourfold maximum difference in fish. Differences are related to the efficiency of mechanisms which deliver oxygen to the tissues and the ability of the organism to carry on anaerobically and contract oxygen debts. The maximum rate in fish may be primarily limited by the respiratory surface (Fry, 1957), while that of mammals may be limited more by the creatine phosphate stores, the quantity of myoglobin and the ability to accumulate lactic acid. Both groups of factors are involved in fish as well as in mammals; Black's investigations have clearly demonstrated the limiting effects of accumulating lactic acid on the activities of fish (Black *et al.*, 1961).

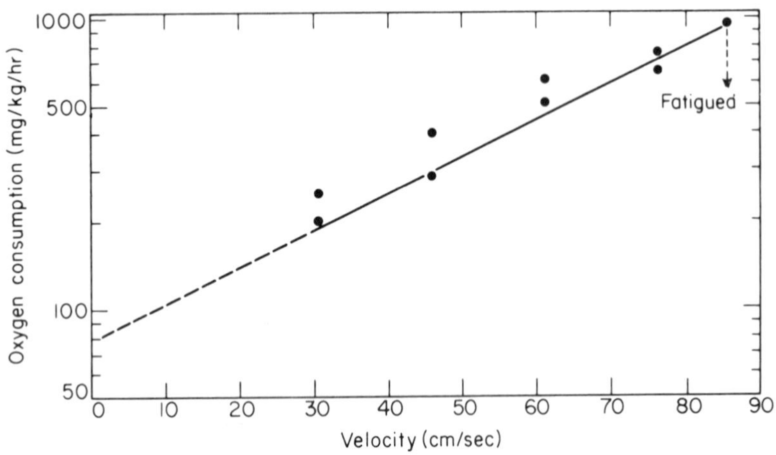

Fig. 7.14. Oxygen consumption in relation to swimming speed of an 88 g sockeye salmon (*Oncorhynchus nerka*) at 15°C (acclimation and test temperature). Projection of line to zero activity gives STANDARD METABOLISM. Line fitted to lower points; higher points due to excitability. Respirometer was a water tunnel through which the flow could be precisely controlled, and measurements were made in duplicate for a series of increasing velocities in which the fish maintained steady swimming for 75 min. [Courtesy J.R. Brett (1963).]

Fry (1947, 1957) argues that the difference between standard and active metabolism represents the extent of respiration available for activity. He terms this "the scope for activity" and finds a good correlation between the maximum steady rate of swimming of a fish and the square root of its scope for activity. Fig. 7.15 shows how the scope for activity of salmon, as measured by differences between active and standard metabolism, depends on the acclimation temperature. In several species of

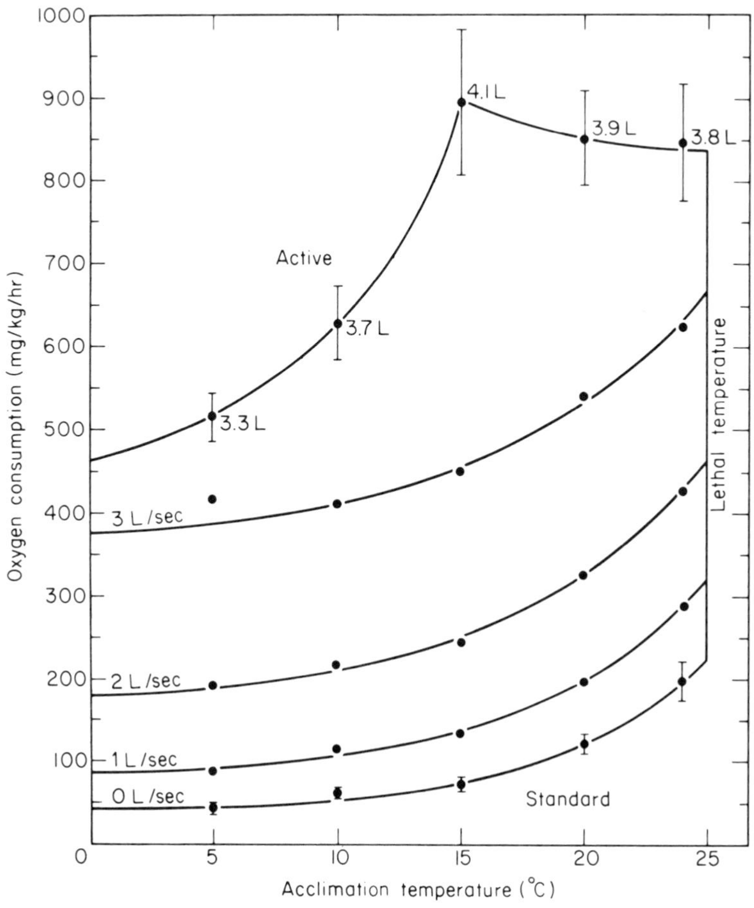

Fig. 7.15. Metabolism of yearling sockeye salmon in relation to acclimation temperature and activity expressed as swimming speeds in lengths per sec (L/sec). Limits include ±2 S.E. Active metabolism shows maximum sustained speeds for 60 min. See also legend for Fig. 7.14. Difference between ACTIVE and STANDARD is the SCOPE FOR ACTIVITY. [Courtesy J.R. Brett (1963).]

fish, maximum differences have been recorded at intermediate temperatures as illustrated for salmon at 15°C in Fig. 7.15. Fry (1957) and Brett (1963) have discussed the implications of these relationships in fishes.

VARIATIONS IN THE RATE OF METABOLISM

There are two kinds of factors which modify metabolic rate: those related to an ever-changing environment, and those related to the physiological or genetical constitution of the animals. The former category includes oscillating diurnal variations, the cyclical seasonal changes in temperature and photoperiod and the effects of different environmental concentrations of respiratory gases, humidity and salinity. These will be considered in later chapters devoted particularly to environmental relationships. Variations associated more directly with the physiology of the animal are summarized here.

THE RELATIONSHIP TO BODY SIZE

The rate of metabolism is proportional to the size of the animal. This is often true of the metabolism of isolated organs and tissues as well as the intact animal, and valid comparisons must usually be based on animals of equal size. Sometimes rates of tissue metabolism are constant over a range of sizes, but until this has been established both the tissue metabolism and that of the whole animal should be measured in a series of individuals of different sizes. Comparisons can then be based on the regression lines as shown in Fig. 7.16, either through the statistical methods for linear regression or by "picking off" equal-sized animals from appropriately fitted lines.

The relationship between size and metabolism is not a direct one. Rather, it seems universally true that the smaller animals have relatively greater rates than the larger ones. Rubner (1883) made the first extensive study of this phenomenon by comparing the metabolism in dogs and other mammals of different sizes, ranging from an 18 g mouse to a 128 kg hog. He found an inverse relationship between metabolism and the body weight but noted a rather constant relation between metabolism and surface area, as expressed by the two-thirds power of the weight. Temperature regulation and heat loss, which are obviously related to surface area, were once thought to be the determinants. However, it is now evident that the situation is more complex, since the same general relationship holds for the poikilotherms (even those of small size) as well as for the homeotherms and often also for isolated tissues from both groups (Fig. 7.16).

The relationship between size and metabolism is an exponential one of the type which characterizes the relationships between body size and growth rate of many individual body parts (allometric growth of Huxley, 1932). It is expressed as: metabolism = $k \times$ body weight^n or $M = k\,W^n$. The logarithmic transformation of the equation is that of a straight line ($\log M = \log k + n \log W$). Thus, in Fig. 7.14 the constant k is the intercept on the y axis of the line with slope n. Rubner equated n to 0.67 (the surface area) but many measurements on all sizes of animals and on some plants show that the best overall value for this constant is about 0.75, with a k which varies for different major groups (Fig. 7.17). It should be noted that this slope, established by Hemmingsen (1960),

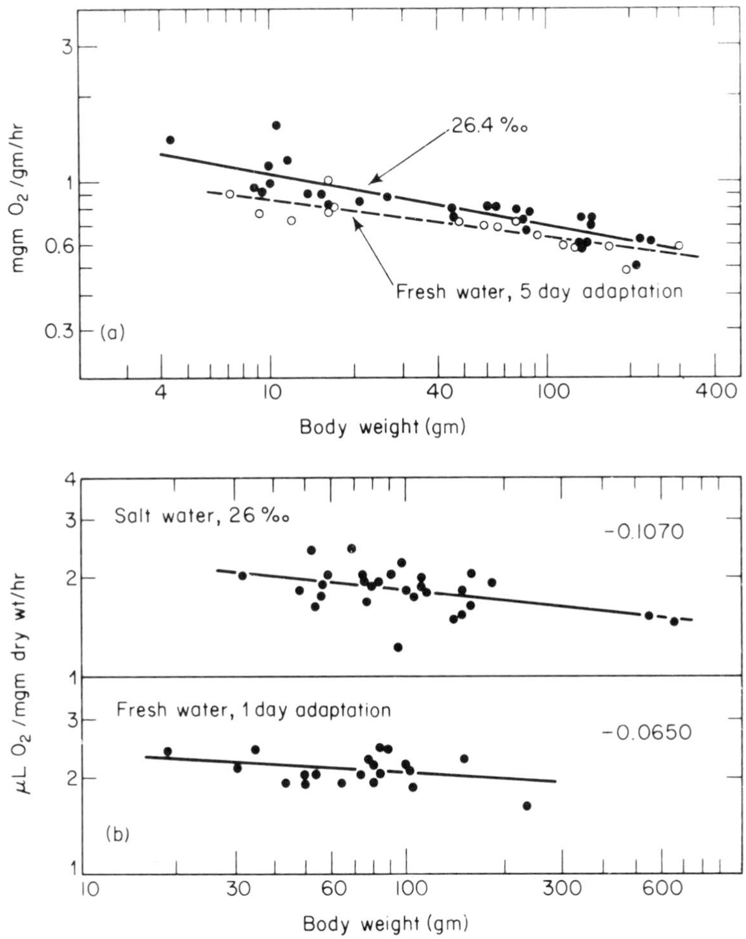

Fig. 7.16. Oxygen consumption of the starry flounder *Platichthys stellatus*. Top, Standard metabolic rate in fresh water and in sea water measured at 14.8°C; regression lines significantly different at the 1% probability level. [Hickman (1959).] Bottom, Metabolism of excised gill lamellae measured by standard Warburg manometric methods at 15.0°C (unpublished data of C.P. Hickman, Jr. and W.S. Hoar).

is based on a smoothed line for a great many values and hides some of the smaller variations to be described in subsequent sections.

The significance of the 0.75 constant has not been established, although many different considerations have been advanced. Several of the arguments are based on the idea that there has been an evolutionary tendency toward increasing size in animal phylogeny and that an impossible situation would develop if certain structures were to grow and if certain processes were to operate in direct relation to body size. Thus, Hemmingsen (1950, 1960) argues that if metabolism increased in proportion to body size from a rat to a rhinoceros, the latter would have to endure surface temperatures of boiling water in order to dissipate the heat. The energy required for such high rates of metabolism would also tax the digesting and absorptive surfaces of the gut. The extent of respiratory epithelium necessary to exchange the gases has also been considered, and similar arguments could be advanced for a number of physiological processes which are directly dependent upon surfaces available for respiration and metabolism. A somewhat different but equally important consideration arises from the variable rates of tissue metabolism. There is relatively more skeletal and connective tissue in a massive organism.

Thus, it is not difficult to argue that the constant n in the weight-metabolism equation should be less than unity. It is also reasonable to argue against any consistent relation to the surface area ($n = 0.67$ in the vertebrates). It has not, however, been possible to explain just why the overall constant should be what it is and why it should be relatively constant for all kinds of organisms so far investigated. Hemmingsen (1960, p. 94) summarizes his discussions by suggesting that "metabolism-body-weight-allometries with identical n have evolved by orthoselection, resulting perhaps from a struggle between proportionality of metabolism to body weight and proportionality to surface functions."

VARIATIONS IN THE SLOPE OF THE WEIGHT-METABOLISM LINE

The foregoing discussion might seem to indicate that differences between metabolic rates of animals of equal size are entirely due to variations in the constant k. Thus, in Fig. 7.17, unicellular organisms display lower Qo_2 values than multicellular poikilotherms of the same size at the same temperature, although the constant n is the same in both groups. Likewise, active metabolism is much greater than standard metabolism, but the difference may be due to the position of the log weight-log metabolism line and not to its slope. However, it may be quite misleading to emphasize the extreme constancy of the value n. Within limited ranges values of n may vary from about 0.5 to 1.0, and the points shown in Fig. 7.17 represent means for a whole family of lines of differing slopes. Fry (1957), for example, finds that most species of fish show $n = 0.8$ (approximately), but for some species values of 0.5 to 0.7 have been recorded.

Many different factors can affect the rate of metabolism, and these differences may alter n as well as k. The genetical constitution of the animal may be reflected in the slope of the weight-metabolism line, as indicated by differences in races, closely related species and different sexes. Changes in physiological condition associated with different stages in development and growth, the state of nutrition and a variety of other factors have also been shown to alter the slope or the position of the line. Several reviews of the literature are available (Hemmingsen, 1950, 1960; Zeuthen, 1953, 1955; Prosser and Brown, 1961).

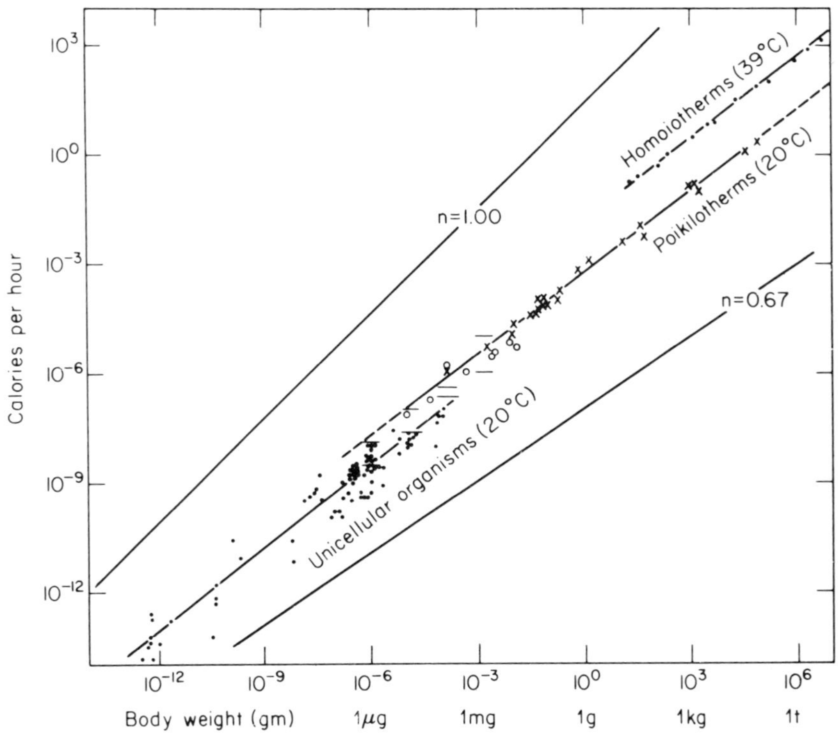

Fig. 7.17. Relation between standard metabolism and body weight in unicellular organisms including marine animal eggs and in many different poikilotherms and homeotherms. Lines fitted by method of least squares assuming n to be identical in the three groups. The slope corresponds to $n = 0.751 \pm 0.015$. [Hemmingsen (1960).]

Endocrine Regulation of Metabolism

This chapter has outlined some of the important enzymatic processes which generate metabolic energy in accordance with the demands of animals. The description started with the monosaccharides, amino acids and simple fats which arise from the digestion of foods or from the storage depots; it ended with the conversion of these into energy in the form of ATP. In the mammal, many of these processes are now known to be regulated by a group of endocrine glands which produce the METABOLIC HORMONES. Evidence of comparable hormones in the arthropods is now accumulating, but there is virtually no information about other groups of invertebrates.

Theoretically, an endocrine regulation of metabolism seems a logical requirement of the physiology of multicellular organization; at the same time, there is probably much less rigidity in the controls of the lower phylogenetic groups. These two hypotheses are supported by the phylogenetic antiquity of the endocrine regulation of reproduction and growth and by the more primitive organization of homeostatic mechanisms in the poikilotherms.

Evidence that the first hormones were probably neurosecretory substances, which timed reproduction and regulated growth, was presented in Chapter 2. Both of these processes depend on a complex interaction of metabolic events. The maturation of ova calls for the mobilization of food and its storage in yolk; growth accentuates anabolic phases of metabolism with the construction of protein and the storage of fats and carbohydrates. Among the crustaceans, metabolic controls based on neurosecretory substances have now been demonstrated in connection with molting and growth (Scheer, 1960). Most invertebrate studies have been restricted to carbohydrate metabolism; they seem to justify these general conclusions concerning endocrine controls, but there have been very few investigations of the more primitive groups.

Although metabolic hormones may be expected in multicellular animals, the controls are probably much less exact in the lower forms. Physiological constants are more variable and a rigid homeostasis seemingly less important among the poikilotherms. In theory, a chemical regulation of the timing of events may be required; but the rates may depend more on environmental temperatures than on hormones. At present, this remains a largely unexplored field of comparative endocrinology. In view of the many contrasts already demonstrated between the mammals and the lower vertebrates with respect to thyroid and adrenal function, this should prove to be a rewarding field for research.

CARBOHYDRATE METABOLISM

The hormone glucagon is a hyperglycemic factor (HGF) which activates mammalian liver phosphorylase and thus produces a rise in blood sugar through the breakdown of glycogen (Fig. 7.3). In some mammals (the cat, for example) the hyperglycemic effect is particularly marked; one microgram per kg may raise the blood sugar by about 20 mg per 100 ml, while an infusion of glucagon for about four hours can deplete the entire glycogen store of the liver. The hormone has no effect on the extrahepatic tissues but seems to be specific for the liver phosphorylase system. Its action at the molecular level is better known than that of many other hormones.

A comparable hormone in the cockroach activates a phosphorylase system in the fat body to produce a parallel hyperglycemic effect (Steele, 1963). In the mammalian liver, the glucose-6-phosphate formed from glycogen is dephosphorylated and passed into the blood as glucose; in the fat body of the insect, an enzyme system converts the glucose-6-phosphate into trehalose which is the circulating blood sugar (Candy and Kilby, 1961; Clegg and Evans, 1961). Trehalose concentrations are high in the hemolymph (about twelve times as high as glucose in mammalian blood) and are the source of energy for activity. The mechanism of transfer of trehalose to muscle is not yet understood; but it has been shown that the Embden-Meyerhof pathway is active in insect muscle, and a conversion of trehalose to glucose-6-phosphate at some point is indicated. Anaerobically the E-M pathway of the insect seems to end with glycerophosphate rather than lactate, but the other enzyme systems are the familiar ones described in Fig. 7.3 (Chefurka, 1958*b*). Thus, in the insect, this hyperglycemic hormone, produced in the corpora cardiaca, plays an important role in mobilizing blood trehalose for active muscles. Like glucagon, it acts only in the carbohydrate storage organ (liver or fat body) and is inactive on phosphorylases of other tissues. Biochemically, the insect hyperglycemic factor is a polypeptide like glucagon; but the two factors are not physiologically the same, and glucagon cannot replace the hormone of the insect fat body (Steele, 1963).

Many years ago a hyperglycemic factor was demonstrated in the sinus gland of crustaceans (Florkin, 1960; Scheer, 1960). It may play a parallel role to mammalian glucagon or the hyperglycemic factor of the cockroach. It may, on the other hand, be more like adrenaline or some of the other hormones concerned with carbohydrate metabolism. Its physiology remains obscure. A hyperglycemic factor has also been reported in the albumen gland of the snail *Helix* but again its mode of action is speculative (Goddard *et al.*, 1964).

Adrenaline (epinephrine) also has a hyperglycemic action in the higher vertebrates. At the molecular level its action on carbohydrate metabolism is like that of glucagon and accelerates glycolysis through a phosphorylase activation. Unlike glucagon, adrenaline acts on extrahepatic as well as on liver tissues. In the liver glucose is formed from glycogen, while in the muscle the end-product is lactic acid, which then escapes into the blood and is carried to the liver to be converted into glycogen or glucose (Levine, 1957; Williams, 1962). In addition to these effects on the carbohydrate stores of liver and muscle, adrenaline releases ACTH which stimulates the adrenal cortex to secrete glucocorticoids. The glucocorticoids in turn promote gluconeogenesis or the formation of glucose from noncarbohydrate sources, particularly protein.

Insulin is a hypoglycemic factor; when injected into a mammal it promptly depresses the blood sugar level, with an increased utilization of glucose by the tissues and a storage of glycogen. In the absence of insulin the blood sugar rises, and a condition of diabetes develops. Although the action of insulin is more evident in the homeotherms, these effects can also be demonstrated in poikilotherms; the insulin control system evidently operates throughout the vertebrates. Several theories for the action of insulin were outlined in Chapter 2; present evidence largely supports the view that insulin, at the molecular level, stimulates the transfer of sugar through the cell membrane (Levine, 1957; Turner, 1960). The action is marked in the carbohydrate storage organs (liver and muscle), while organs which use glucose at a steady rate, such as the brain, are relatively insensitive. Other effects of insulin may be largely indirect, depending on this primary action of glucose transport. These theories, based on studies of mammalian tissues, may be quite inappropriate for some other vertebrates (Chapter 2), but there is still very little comparative information.

Several other metabolic hormones also have definite effects on the carbohydrate metabolism of mammals. The hypophysectomized dog survives pancreatectomy without the fatal symptoms of diabetes. The dog with both pituitary and pancreas removed is named a "Houssay dog" after the celebrated Argentine physiologist who did the pioneer work with the "diabetogenic hormone" of the pituitary. This factor is now known to be the growth hormone, somatotropin, which has an insulin-like or hypoglycemic action, although its primary effects may be on lipid mobilization and protein synthesis (Knobil, 1961). The gluconeogenetic action of the adrenal steroids has been mentioned. The gonadal steroids also have metabolic effects which are reflected in the altered metabolism of carbohydrates (Turner, 1960). Thyroid hormone, in the homeotherms, stimulates many phases of carbohydrate metabolism, from the absorption of sugars to their utilization in the tissues. Although these physiological effects of the metabolic hormones on carbohydrate metabolism are carefully documented, the actions of the hormones at the cellular level are not understood in the same way as those of the pancreatic hormones and adrenaline (Turner, 1960; Williams, 1962).

OTHER EFFECTS OF HORMONES ON TISSUE METABOLISM

In the living animal, mechanisms concerned with the metabolism of carbohydrate, fat and protein are interlocked (Fig. 7.2) and do not operate as independent units. It is not then surprising that each of the metabolic hormones acts on several different aspects of metabolism. Although insulin and glucagon are primarily concerned with carbohydrate metabolism, the pancreatectomized animal shows increased utilization of fat and protein, an impairment of lipogenesis, and a decreased ability to synthesize protein from amino acids. It follows that the effects of any of the metabolic hormones may be expected to act at several points in the biochemical sequences of tissue metabolism. There is a voluminous literature on the endocrinology of metabolism, but most of it pertains to the mammal, and a large part of it is clinical in nature. The relatively meager research on the lower vertebrates has already shown many interesting differences between their metabolic controls and the familiar ones in the mammals (Pickford and Atz, 1957; Hoar, 1965*a*), although many of these apparent differences may disappear when the molecular functions of the hormones are explained.

The comparative data are not adequate to warrant further discussion here. Present knowledge has been comprehensively discussed in several recent textbooks already listed (Chapter 2). Current interest in comparative endocrinology is high, and a rapid extension of our knowledge of the chemical regulation of metabolism can be confidently expected. Tracer techniques and other microanalytical methods now permit critical investigations of smaller animals from the lower phyla. This should prove to be one of the most rewarding fields for immediate research.

8 *Excretion*

Metabolism produces a variety of by-products. Some must be removed (excreted); others perform useful metabolic chores. A single substance may sometimes be an excretion product and, at other times, an indispensable metabolite. Water is a by-product of metabolism and must often be excreted in large amounts to avoid a serious condition of edema; on the other hand, the only source of water available to some animals is metabolic water and this must be rigorously conserved. Carbon dioxide, although a metabolic by-product, is also an important component in the synthetic and regulatory machinery of animals and plants. The same is true of ammonia. Similarly, urea, a prominent constituent of the urine in many animals, sometimes discharges useful physiological functions. If the blood urea in man rises above about 0.05 per cent (normal values 0.01 to 0.03) a pathological condition of uremia develops; but the elasmobranch fishes actively retain urea for purposes of osmotic regulation and have normal blood urea values of 2.0 to 2.5 per cent (Smith, 1953). In some mammals too, urea may perform useful functions. In the ruminant it is secreted in the saliva, passes back into the stomach and is a source of nitrogen for the microflora of the rumen. Thus, in one animal or another, almost all of these metabolic products which are commonly considered excretory, have found a use. Conversely, some compounds, not usually classed as waste, must be removed just as regularly as carbon dioxide or ammonia. Many marine vertebrates drink sea water, and by excreting large amounts of salt (extrarenally through gills or special salt glands) they are able to obtain fresh water for their metabolism. Salt in this case is a by-product from water metabolism—as is ammonia from the metabolism of protein. No concise definition of excretion can be based solely on the chemical nature of the material removed and it is better to define excretion in a very general way as the separation and ejection of the metabolic wastes, usually in aqueous solution.

In the highly organized animals (both invertebrate and vertebrate) there are three well-defined physiological processes included under excretion: FILTRATION, REABSORPTION and SECRETION. In filtration, noncolloidal solutions are moved by hydrostatic differences through a semi-permeable membrane from the body fluids into a space connected with the outside. This filtered material then passes through a tube or other space lined with cells capable of actively transporting molecules from it back into the body fluids (reabsorption), or of secreting additional substances into the filtered fluid. Obviously, at the cellular level there are but two processes, diffusion and active transport. Understanding of the machinery in the phylogenetically lower invertebrates such as protozoa, hydroids and flatworms is less complete than in many of the higher animals; but it seems likely that the processes are similar at the cellular level. Accordingly, although it is very unsatisfactory to attempt a definition of excretion based on the nature of the compounds removed, there is much less ambiguity concerned with the general processes of urine formation.

Nitrogenous Wastes

Removal of ammonia (the most conspicuous by-product of the nitrogen-containing compounds) is one of the major tasks of excretion. Whereas other metabolic residues, such as carbon dioxide and water, are relatively innocuous and can often be removed as gases, ammonia is highly toxic and is always removed in solution—frequently in some detoxified form. Animals, in their phylogeny, have tried several different devices for the removal of excess ammonia and some other nitrogenous wastes, such as the purines arising from nucleoprotein. This story has been told in many places but never more concisely and interestingly than in Baldwin's *Dynamic Aspects of Biochemistry* (1963). Baldwin's arguments will be followed in this summary.

AMMONIA

The metabolism of ammonia was discussed in Chapter 7, and at that point its lability and importance in biochemical syntheses was emphasized. Its removal as a waste product is considered here.

Free ammonia is extremely toxic and never accumulates in living cells or their surrounding media. Simple diffusion experiments show how readily this ion penetrates cell membranes (Heilbrunn, 1952); at the cellular level this may be the basis of its toxicity. Only traces (0.1 to 0.2 mg per 100 ml) are found in human blood. Several simple experiments have demonstrated the toxicity of ammonium ions in mammals and birds. When crystalline urease, which liberates ammonia from urea, was injected into rabbits the animals died, with ammonia blood levels at about 1 part in 20,000. At this point there was no change in the pH of the blood, and death was attributed to the ammonium ion. Similar injections into a normal hen had no effect, presumably because bird blood normally contains only traces of urea which, in the rabbit, served as a precursor for the free ammonia. When the hen was injected with both urea and urease it died. The theory of ammonia toxicity, arrived at much earlier through phylogenetic speculations (Needham, 1931), was thus confirmed (Baldwin, 1963; Sumner, 1951).

Ammonia is excreted as such only when there is an abundance of water for its rapid removal. This happens in the marine invertebrates and in all freshwater animals, whether vertebrate or invertebrate. The marine invertebrates are in osmotic equilibrium with their surroundings and, bathed as they are with osmotically equivalent saline, readily lose the freely soluble ammonia by simple diffusion. The freshwater animals, on the other hand, live in a decidedly hypotonic solution and are continually flooded with fresh water because of osmotic differences. This is steadily pumped out and the same pumping machinery serves as a flushing system for the soluble wastes, of which the most important is ammonia. Animals which excrete ammonia as the main end-product of amino nitrogen metabolism are said to be AMMONIOTELIC. Water, however, is often at a premium, not only in the terrestrial environment but in the environment of many marine fishes which maintain hypo-osmotic body fluids and, in consequence, face a constant osmotic desiccation. In these dry environments ammonia is turned into less toxic forms such as urea (UREOTELIC animals) or uric acid (URICOTELIC animals).

These are broad generalizations as small amounts of urea, uric acid and other nitrogen-containing compounds appear regularly in the urine of both freshwater animals and marine invertebrates (Prosser and Brown, 1961). Amino acids are also secreted as such in the lower forms, but whether this is true excretion or simply leakage is uncertain. The main point is that the excess ammonia arising in metabolism seems to require no further treatment if it can diffuse promptly into the surrounding water, but when water must be conserved, ammonia must be detoxified.

UREA

In some animals, urea is a physiologically important compound and occurs in considerable amounts in the tissues. The situation in the elasmobranchs has been mentioned. The aestivating lungfish is another animal whose tissues tolerate very high levels of urea (Smith, 1953). Since active lungfishes excrete ammonia directly like most other fresh-water fish, Baldwin considers the change to ureotelism during aestivation further evidence for a phylogeny of urea biosynthesis in situations where the water supply is restricted. The evolutionary arguments will be reviewed later. Here, it is noted that the presence of urea at high concentrations in some animals shows that its presence, unlike that of ammonia, presents no insurmountable problems in cellular metabolism.

Chemically, urea consists of two molecules of ammonia united to one of carbon dioxide. On paper, the combination can be simply made as follows:

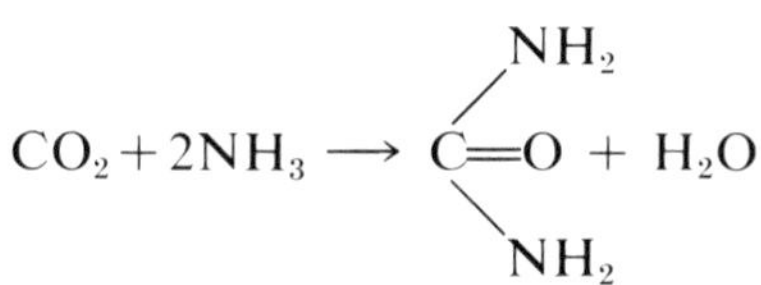

Synthesis in living tissues is not so simple.

The history of urea in biochemical literature is an interesting one (Fruton and Simmonds, 1958). Urea was discovered in 1773. In 1828 Wöhler synthesized it and, in so doing, dealt a shattering blow to the proponents of vitalism. It could no longer be argued that only living tissues formed organic compounds. In 1904 the amino acid arginine was identified as a precursor of urea in mammals, and the enzyme arginase was shown to be essential for the reaction which follows:

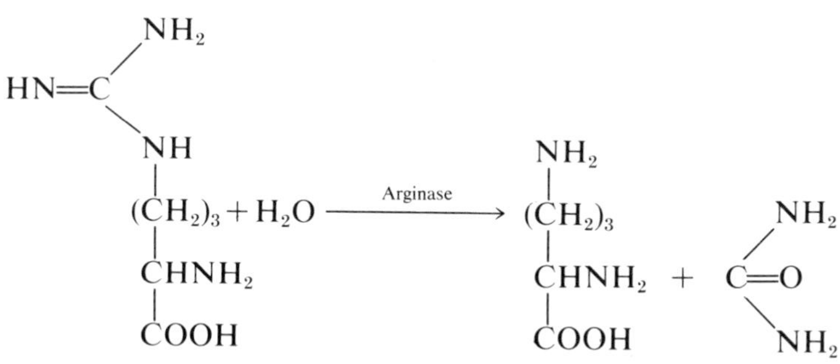

ARGININE ORNITHINE UREA

The reaction suggests that the building blocks of urea (carbon dioxide and ammonia) are in some way added onto the ornithine molecule and then split off as urea by the enzyme arginase. The precise biochemical steps by which this is accomplished eluded biochemists for more than half a century.

The skeleton of the synthetic machinery was suggested by Krebs, following intensive studies of the metabolism of rat liver slices and the identification of citrulline as an intermediary between ornithine and arginine (Krebs and Henseleit, 1932). Krebs' "ornithine cycle" (Fig. 8.1)

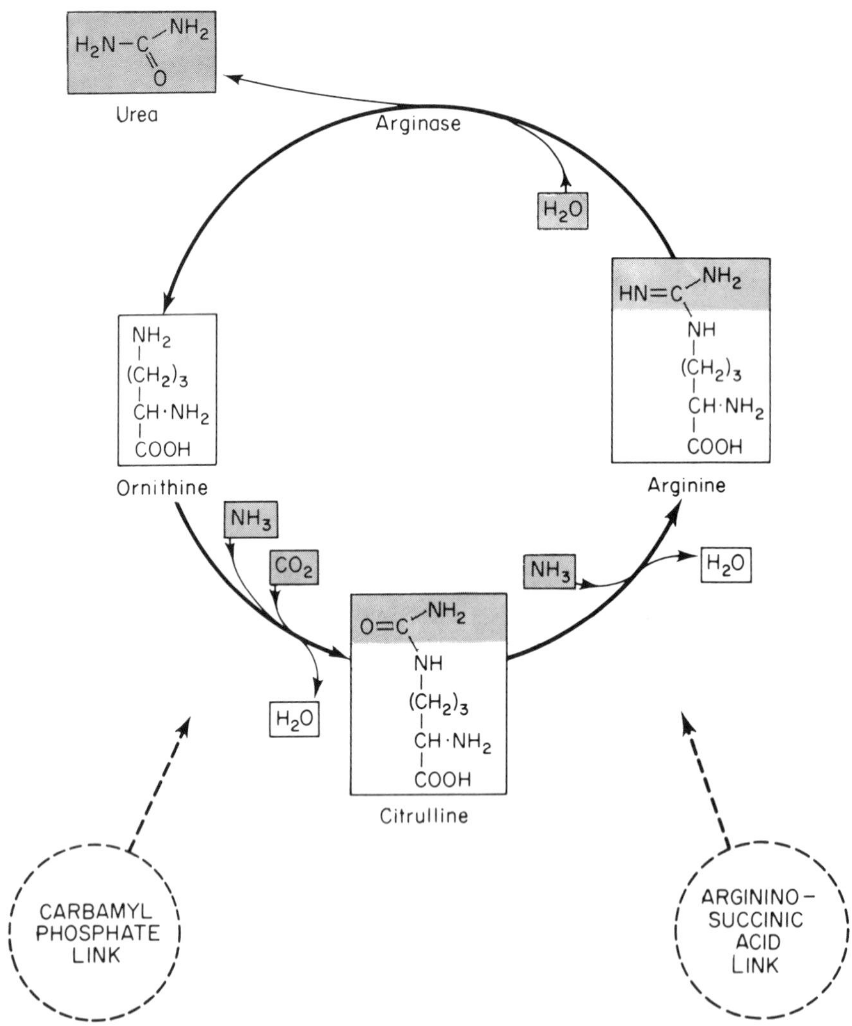

Fig. 8.1. Urea biosynthesis by the Krebs ornithine cycle. Lower circles show links added subsequently and detailed in Figs. 8.2 and 8.3.

remained the recognizedly incomplete explanation of urea biosynthesis for more than twenty years. Modern tracer and microchemical techniques have now added two additional links: The CARBAMYL-PHOSPHATE (CARBAMYL-ASPARTATE) LINK through which one unit each of CO_2 and NH_3 are added between ornithine and citrulline, and the ARGININOSUCCINIC ACID LINK which adds the second amino group to the cycle (Figs. 8.2 and 8.3).

A study of the distribution of these compounds and their associated enzymes suggests that the basic components of urea biosynthesis were present in living organisms long before they were organized into the appropriate chains for the detoxification of ammonia in the formation of urea (Cohen and Brown, 1960). They are widely distributed in bacteria, plants and animals. An additional interesting point is the association of the ornithine cycle with the Krebs citric acid cycle. The molecules which transfer the amino groups and carbon dioxide to the ornithine cycle arise in the citric acid enzyme pool (Fig. 7.2).

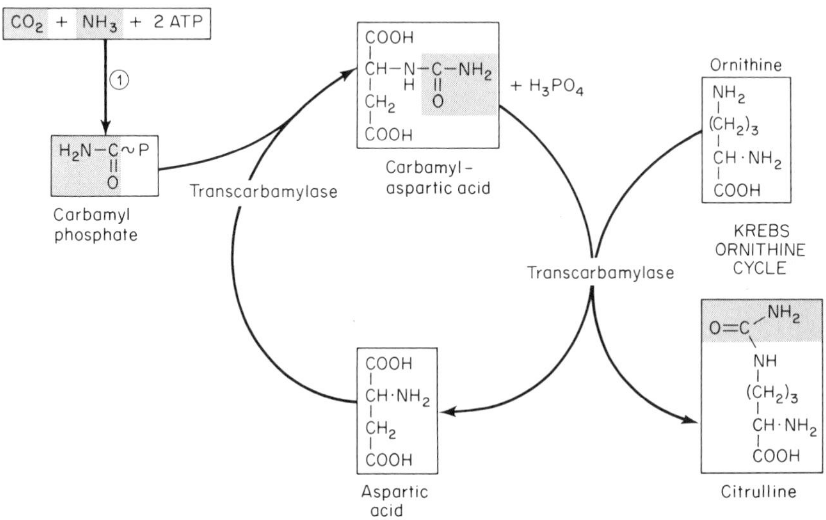

Fig. 8.2. The carbamyl phosphate link in the ornithine cycle. Enzyme 1, carbamyl phosphate synthetase and Mg^{++}.

Carbamyl phosphate. This may have been a key compound in biochemical evolution. In its formation there is a primary fixation of both CO_2 and NH_3 with an associated high-energy phosphate bond. The carbamyl group so formed is readily transferred in several organic syntheses; its widespread distribution in bacteria, plants and animals, along with the obvious importance of adding inorganic carbon and nitrogen into organic systems, suggests a key role in evolution (Cohen and Brown, 1960). In animals, carbamyl phosphate is synthesized in two steps and requires two molecules of ATP along with the enzyme carbamyl phosphate synthetase and certain co-factors, including Mg^{++}. Bacteria can make the combination with one molecule of ATP. The overall reaction for animals is represented as follows:

$$NH_3 + CO_2 + H_2O + 2ATP \longrightarrow H_2N{-}\overset{\overset{\displaystyle O}{\|}}{C}\sim P + 2ADP + P_i$$

In urea formation (also in the biosynthesis of the pyrimidines) carbamyl groups are first transferred to aspartate by the transcarbamylase enzyme system. They may then be transferred to ornithine, thus forming citrulline in the Krebs ornithine cycle (Fig. 8.2). The link through aspartic acid joins the citric acid cycle with the ornithine cycle by the oxaloacetic acid link of the former. The formation of aspartic from oxaloacetic acid through amination or transamination has been described (Figs. 7.2 and 7.11). These two important metabolic cycles are likewise interconnected at the argininosuccinic acid link.

Argininosuccinic acid. This link is also made through aspartic acid (Fig. 8.3). In this case, however, aspartic acid (arising through the amination of oxaloacetic acid) couples with citrulline to form argininosuccinic acid which then splits to form arginine for the ornithine cycle and releases fumaric acid for the citric acid cycle and subsequently the formation of more oxaloacetic acid. One unit of ATP is required for linking of aspartic acid and citrulline. Thus, in terms of metabolic energy, three molecules of ATP are required to make one of urea (Figs. 8.2 and 8.3). This is the cost of detoxifying the ammonia.

There is scant evidence for the ornithine cycle in some animal groups (see below) and also no conclusive demonstration of alternative synthetic pathways for urea formation from CO_2 and NH_3 (Needham, 1942; Cohen and Brown, 1960; Gilmour, 1961). Obviously dietary arginine can lead to urea in the presence of arginase, and this may account for the small amounts of urea excreted by some animals. Urea is also a by-product of purine metabolism in a few animals. The ornithine cycle, however, remains as the only known route for its synthesis from NH_3 and CO_2.

URIC ACID

The third conspicuous nitrogenous waste is uric acid. This too is formed to detoxify ammonia and has the advantage of being highly insoluble and easily precipitated from a supersaturated colloidal solution.

With a few minor exceptions, such as the closely related guanine in arachnids, uric acid is the only nitrogenous excretory product which can be removed in solid form; it thus permits nitrogen excretion without loss of water. All of the successful groups of arid living animals (the pulmonate snails, insects, and birds and saurian reptiles) are uricotelic. A convergence in biochemical evolution has produced the uricotelic habit at least three times.

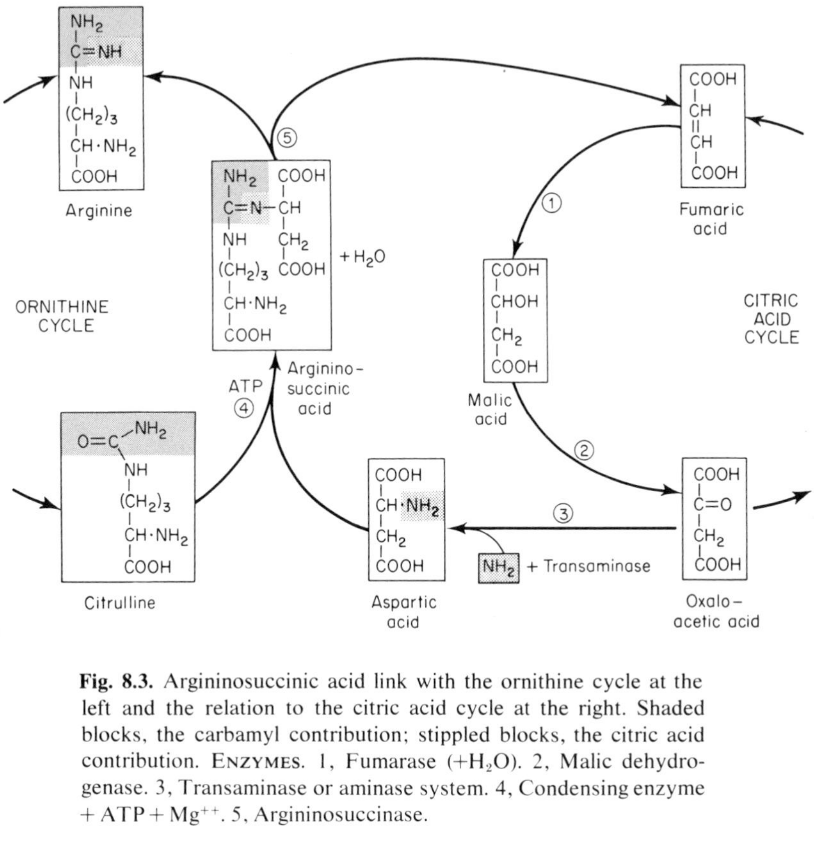

Fig. 8.3. Argininosuccinic acid link with the ornithine cycle at the left and the relation to the citric acid cycle at the right. Shaded blocks, the carbamyl contribution; stippled blocks, the citric acid contribution. ENZYMES. 1, Fumarase ($+H_2O$). 2, Malic dehydrogenase. 3, Transaminase or aminase system. 4, Condensing enzyme + ATP + Mg^{++}. 5, Argininosuccinase.

Uric acid is a member of the purines. The general structure of the purine molecule and that of several chemical arrangements which appear as excretion products are shown in Fig. 8.4. Studies of liver slices from birds which excrete between 70 and 80 per cent of their nitrogen in the form of uric acid, have shown that the hen and the goose form uric acid from added ammonia, while the pigeon forms an intermediate hypoxanthine which is subsequently oxidized to uric acid in the kidney. For

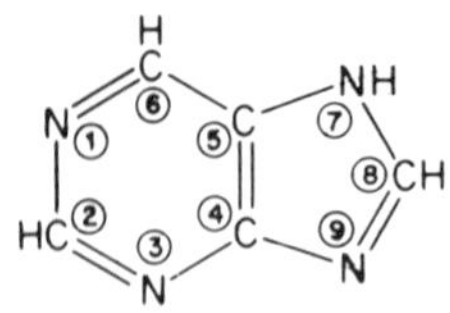

PURINE
(general structure)

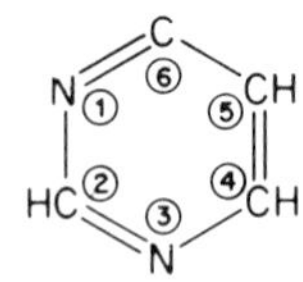

PYRIMIDINE
(general structure)

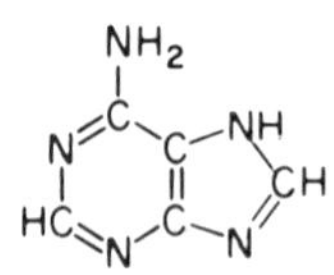

ADENINE
(6-amino purine)

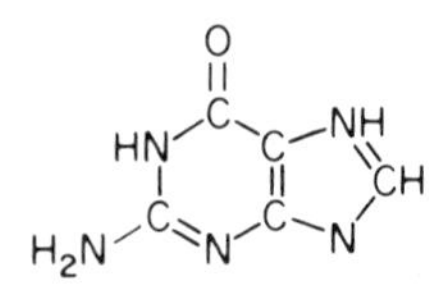

GUANINE
(2-amino-6-oxypurine)

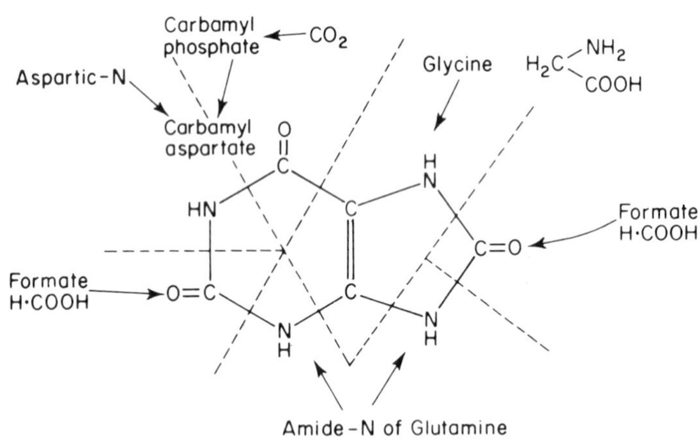

URIC ACID
(2, 6, 8-trioxypurine)

Fig. 8.4. Purines and pyrimidines. General structures for these compounds with the specific structures for adenine, guanine, and uric acid. Broken lines divide the uric acid molecule into the building blocks from which its biosynthesis takes place.

some reason pigeon liver lacks xanthine oxidase. Experiments such as these established the locus of uric acid formation and the purine intermediates; but the compounds involved in the synthesis of the purine molecule itself were only identified after isotopically labelled compounds became available for research.

The different fragments from which the uric acid molecule is assembled are shown in Fig. 8.4. Most of the biosynthetic steps have now been established and are described in recent textbooks of biochemistry (Karlson, 1963). The indications are that the processes are the same in insects and vertebrates (Gilmour, 1961); purine biosyntheses will probably be found to follow similar patterns throughout the living world.

PRODUCTS OF NUCLEOPROTEIN METABOLISM

The nucleic acid component of nucleoprotein contains nitrogen in combinations which, during catabolism in some animals, leads to additional nitrogenous wastes. The constituents of the nucleoprotein molecule are shown in Fig. 8.5 and Fig. 22.1. Nucleic acids are polynucleotides. The structure of adenylic acid, one of the nucleotides, is shown in Fig. 7.1. Removal of the phosphoric acid portion of the nucleotide molecule produces a nucleoside which is, in turn, composed of a nitrogenous base and a pentose. There are two major groups of nucleic acids: the ribose nucleic acids (RNA), which are characteristic of the cytoplasm, and the deoxyribose nucleic acids (DNA), which are characteristic of the nucleus. They differ in their pentose; RNA pentose has one more oxygen than DNA pentose. Ribose may be associated with either of the purines (adenine or guanine) or with the pyrimidines (cytosine or uracil). Thus, there are four possible kinds of ribose nucleosides or nucleotides. The same number of combinations occur with deoxyribose, but thymine substitutes for uracil (Fig. 22.1). Each type of nucleic acid is, then, built up of multiples of four kinds of nucleotides. The importance of these compounds in the coding of biological information will be discussed elsewhere. In this section only their excretory products are considered. The nitrogen portion of the purine or pyrimidine molecule, like that of the amino acid, is removed in solution.

The pyrimidine molecule, during its catabolism, is completely dismantled into its building blocks of CO_2, H_2O and NH_3. The further utilization of these, or their excretion, has been discussed. The catabolism of the purines, on the other hand, rarely leads to these elemental building blocks. Only a few animal groups (sipunculids, crustaceans, some bivalves) possess all the enzymes for complete deamination and oxidation of purines. In a few cases the purines are excreted unchanged. This is true in flatworms, annelids and in the cyclostome *Lampetra fluviatilis*

(Prosser and Brown, 1961). In most animals the excretion product is some intermediate compound between the purine and its simple building blocks, with a phylogenetic trend toward a reduction in the number of required enzymes (uricolytic) in the more advanced phylogenetic groups.

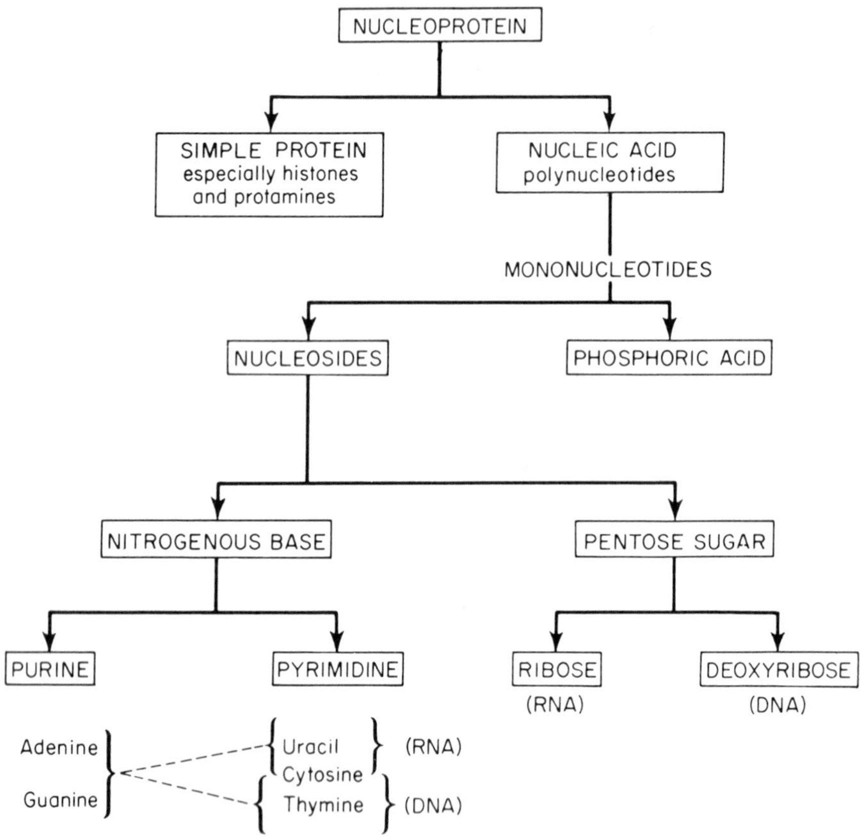

Fig. 8.5. Components of the nucleoproteins.

The literature is summarized in several places (Florkin, 1949; Baldwin, 1963; Prosser and Brown, 1961). The excretory products identified in different animals are shown in Fig. 8.6. The purine molecules are first deaminated and oxidized to form the oxypurines. After this, first one and then the other of the two ring components of the molecule is opened. From the resulting compound (allantoic acid) two molecules of urea are split from glyoxylic acid, and the urea is then separated into CO_2 and

NH_3. At each major step some groups of animals have been shown to lack the enzymes for subsequent steps and consequently excrete the product formed at that stage.

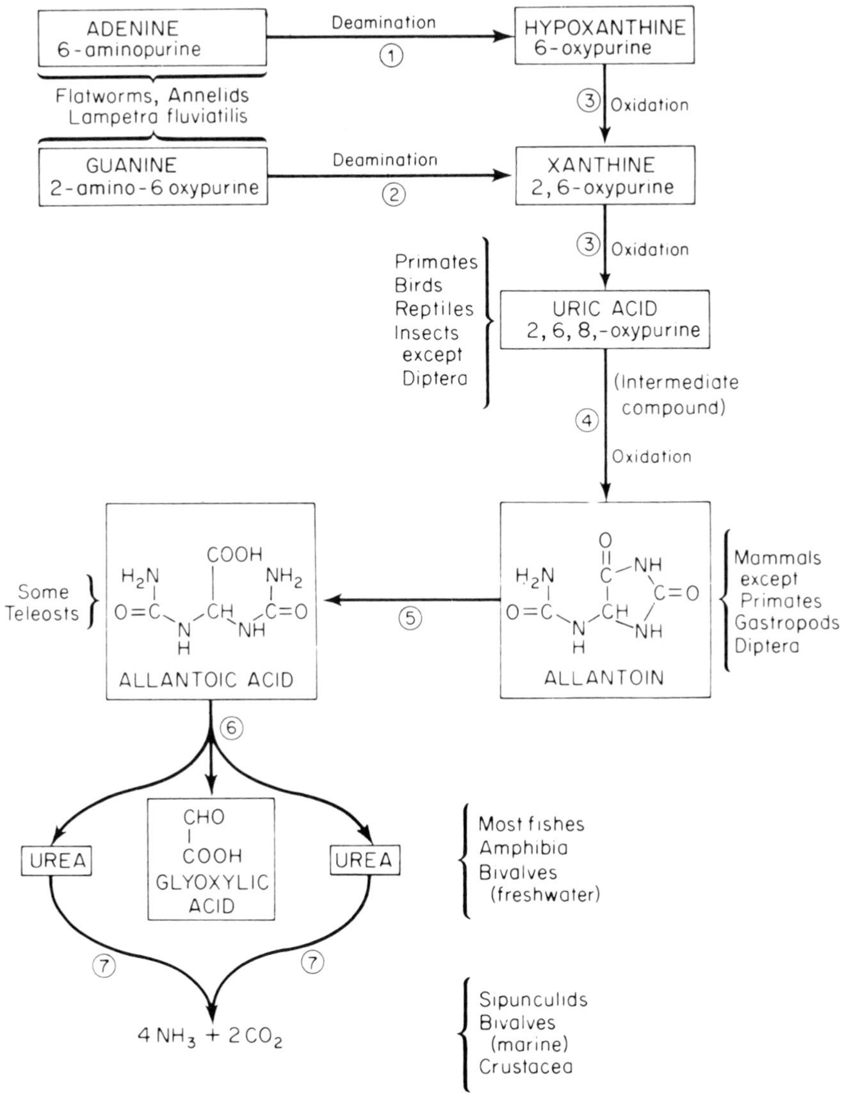

Fig. 8.6. Purine catabolism based on Florkin (1949) and Baldwin (1963). The different animals are grouped with the compounds which they excrete. ENZYMES. 1, Adenase. 2, Guanase. 3, Xanthine oxidase. 4, Uricase (urico-oxidase)- two-step reaction. 5, Allantoinase. 6, Allantoicase. 7, Urease.

MISCELLANEOUS END-PRODUCTS OF NITROGEN METABOLISM

Several additional nitrogen-containing compounds are normally found in the urine. FREE AMINO ACIDS have frequently been identified. They were long ago shown to form 15 per cent or more of the excreted nitrogen in some invertebrates (Nicol, 1960*a*; Baldwin, 1964). Through the development of chromatographic techniques and the identification of trace amounts it has been shown that normal adult humans may excrete slightly over one gram of free amino acids per day, or about 1.2 per cent of the total urinary nitrogen (Fruton and Simmonds, 1958). It is now evident that all groups of animals are liable to excrete some free amino acid, but it is questionable whether this is a true excretion of waste material or whether it represents an unavoidable leakage of relatively small molecules; proteins of low molecular weight (less than about 68,000) as well as amino acids are regularly filtered through the mammalian glomerulus but subsequently recovered by the tubules (Bard, 1961; Forster, 1961).

AMINO ACID CONJUGATES formed in several different detoxification processes may also account for a small part of the nitrogen excreted. Benzoic acid, for example, is toxic. It is formed in small amounts during the metabolism of fat and may also occur in foods. In the mammal it is detoxified through conjugation with glycine to form hippuric acid:

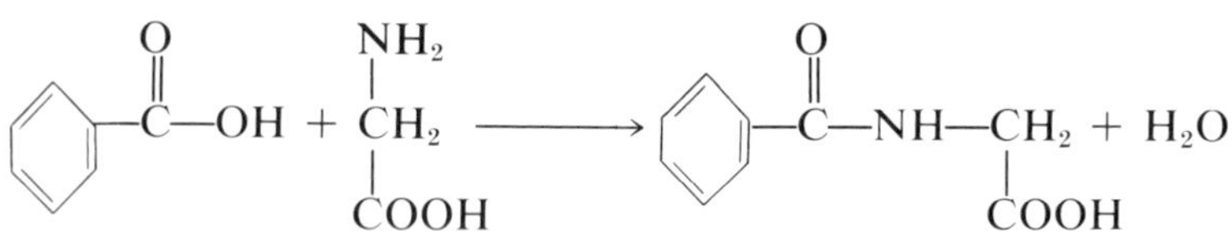

BENZOIC ACID　　GLYCINE　　HIPPURIC ACID

In birds the benzoic acid conjugation occurs with ornithine and forms ornithuric acid.

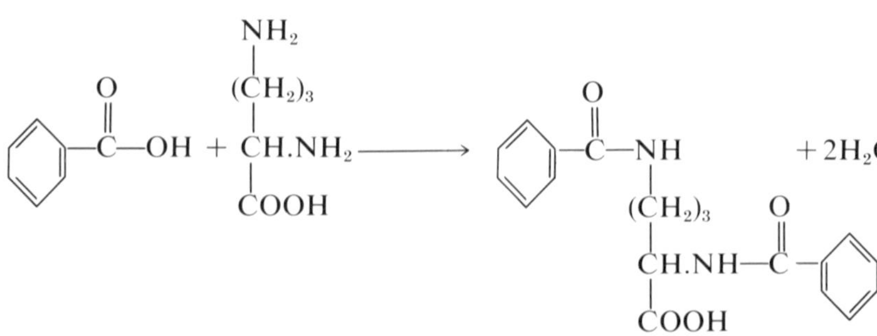

BENZOIC ACID　　ORNITHINE　　ORNITHURIC ACID

Both of these syntheses require ATP which can be considered the necessary price for safe removal of toxic materials. Cysteine may also be involved in conjugation reactions (with bromobenzene, for example), and there are several additional reactions, involving compounds other than amino acids, which produce detoxification products that appear in the urine (Harper, 1963).

CREATINE AND/OR CREATININE have been identified in the urine of different classes of vertebrates and in several of the invertebrates. Creatine plays an important role in the energy transformations of vertebrate muscles. In combination with phosphate (creatine phosphate, one of the phosphagens) it provides a ready store of high-energy phosphate during muscle contraction (Chapter 7). Arginine plays a comparable role among many of the invertebrates. Creatine is a very special amino acid—not one of the alpha group which enter into the composition of proteins but an end-product of the metabolism of glycine, arginine and methionine (Fruton and Simmonds, 1958) found predominantly in muscle. If present in amounts in excess of the requirements, it is excreted chiefly in the anhydride form, creatinine.

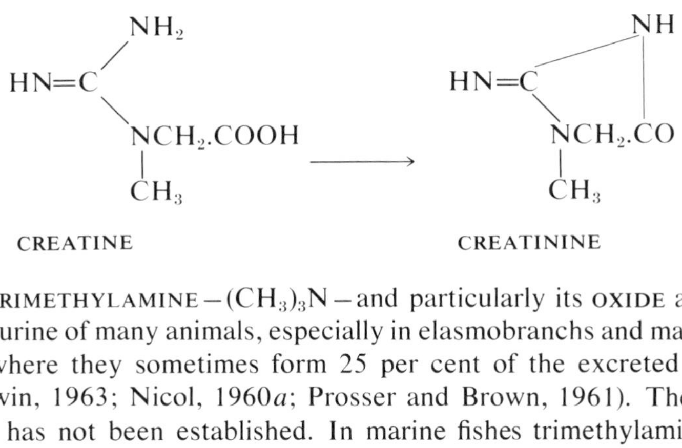

CREATINE CREATININE

TRIMETHYLAMINE—$(CH_3)_3N$—and particularly its OXIDE are found in the urine of many animals, especially in elasmobranchs and marine teleosts where they sometimes form 25 per cent of the excreted nitrogen (Baldwin, 1963; Nicol, 1960*a*; Prosser and Brown, 1961). The biosynthesis has not been established. In marine fishes trimethylamine oxide was at one time thought to be formed as a detoxification product of ammonia and retained to bring the osmotic content of the blood closer to that of the surrounding sea water. This view is now questioned, and TMO is considered to be mainly of exogenous origin in fishes (Fruton and Simmonds, 1958; Wood, 1958).

PHYLOGENETIC INTERPRETATIONS

The catabolism of protein accounts for 90 per cent or more of the excreted nitrogen. With relatively few exceptions this is predominantly in the form of ammonia or urea or uric acid. The significance of the dominant excretion product was first discussed in relation to animal phylogeny and water economy by Joseph Needham (1931, 1942). From his examination of a voluminous literature (mostly on embryonic tissues and excretion products) he concluded that "the main nitrogenous excretory product of an animal depends on the conditions under which its embryos live, ammonia and urea being associated with aquatic pre-natal life, and uric acid being associated with terrestrial pre-natal life." In particular, his studies of the problems of embryonic life in the three highly successful terrestrial groups of animals, the pulmonates, insects and vertebrates, convinced him that the terrestrial oviparous way of life would have been impossible without the uricotelic metabolism.

The disposal of metabolic wastes is as acute a problem in the embryo as in the adult and, from this angle, Needham sees three major avenues for the evolution of terrestrial forms: VIVIPARITY in which the embryo is, in fact as aquatic as its phylogenetic ancestors; a SEMI-AQUATIC EXISTENCE where the young are incubated in water or extremely moist places, as is true of modern amphibia and some reptiles (chelonia); and the CLEIDOIC egg, an impermeable box which must be provided with sufficient stored water to operate the metabolic machinery and dispose of the noncombustible wastes. The success of the pulmonates, the insects and the birds attests the feasibility of the last arrangement.

The cleidoic egg starts its development with some free water held in the highly retentive colloids of the egg albumen and some metabolic water, primarily in the fats. This meager water supply is used with the greatest economy.

If it were possible to avoid the catabolism of protein very much less water would be required, but amino acids must be turned over if cells are to live, differentiate and grow. The embryo, like the adult, is highly susceptible to an accumulation of the toxic ammonium ion which is the primary by-product of amino acid catabolism. Highly insoluble uric acid which precipitates from saturated solution and can be retained in the solid form until hatching, provides the solution to this problem. In a sense it is not an economical solution since uric acid synthesis depletes the carbon stores and requires ATP energy. However, it does solve the water problem and is a highly successful compromise, as the egg-laying land animals demonstrate.

Needham's arguments concerning uricotelism are acceptable to zoologists. The hypothesis fits many curious facts into an orderly pattern. One of these is the variety of materials used as sources of energy in different kinds of embryos. The cleidoic egg uses less protein and more fat, thus reducing the ammonia and increasing the water by-products. A chick during incubation obtains about 6 per cent of its energy from protein and 80 per cent of it from fat, while a frog or fish during this period obtains over 70 per cent of its energy from protein and only 30 per cent from fat (Needham, 1942). The terrestrial invertebrates follow similar patterns, and in several groups the degree of uricotelism follows closely the availability of water in the environment. The gastropods provide excellent examples since this group, like the vertebrates, has mastered all the habitats from the sea shores to the dry hill tops. Patterns established in the embryo, when carried into adult life, permit some of the gastropods, the insects and a few vertebrate species to live in extremely arid habitats. The mammals are their only real competitors, and they are able to perfuse the developing young with maternal water while operating a greatly refined machinery for its conservation.

Needham emphasized the phylogenetic significance of uricotelism in the cleidoic egg. Baldwin (1963; 1964 and earlier) has considered more particularly the advantages of urea as an end-product in habitats where water is restricted but not actually absent. In general, ammonia predominates in the excreta of the aquatic invertebrates, whether marine or freshwater; in the first habitat their blood is isotonic with the sea water; in neither case is there a restriction in tissue water and, it is argued, the ammonia by-product of amino acid metabolism diffuses or is carried away in a copious urine. The freshwater vertebrates also excrete large amounts of ammonia, but the marine vertebrates produce more urea (perhaps also trimethylamine oxide). This is attributed to the hypotonicity of their body fluids which creates a constant osmotic desiccation, so that the tissues are really operating in a dry environment. Thus, ammonia predominates as an excretion product when water is abundant throughout life; but when water is restricted, the ammonia is turned into the less toxic form of urea, again at the expense of ATP.

There are many biochemical data supporting this view. Some of the most significant have been found among the amphibians. The wholly aquatic amphibian *Xenopus* excretes large amounts of ammonia throughout its life; the toad *Bufo* turns out 80 per cent ammonia as an aquatic larva but only 15 per cent as a terrestrial adult. Moreover, the nature of the nitrogenous excretion product is sometimes altered in relation to the availability of water. When *Xenopus* is retained out of water, under experimental conditions, for periods of one to three weeks, the nitrogen excretion (ammonia) declines sharply; on return to the aquatic habitat the ammonia excretion is again normal, but there is a large additional urea nitrogen fraction which accounts for the nitrogen retained during the experimental period out of water. Urea is formed but not excreted, and Balinsky *et al.* (1961) argue that in phylogeny the capacity to store urea preceded the ability to excrete it. Urea biosynthesis in the emerging vertebrates was probably an emergency device for the first tentative journeys onto the land. In the more terrestrial of the amphibians, the capacity to excrete large amounts of nitrogen as ammonia is not apparent even when the animals are held in water; there is a change in the patterns of nitrogen excretion as well as in morphology during amphibian metamorphosis (Frieden, 1961; Bennett and Frieden, 1962).

Homer Smith (1953) challenges Baldwin's argument concerning ammoniotelic patterns of excretion and suggests that urea is always the main end-product of amino acid catabolism (at least in the aquatic vertebrates), and that the ammonia which is so abundant in the urine of freshwater fishes arises peripherally in the regulation of acid-base balance and the conservation of cations. In support of this view it is emphasized that the ammonia in human urine arises in this manner—largely from the stored amino groups of glutamine. The mechanisms by which sodium ions are exchanged for hydrogen or ammonia ions are shown in Fig. 8.7. An exchange in the proximal tubules working against $NaHCO_3$ parallels that illustrated in Fig. 8.7*a* for Na_2HPO_4 and produces CO_2 and H_2O, the former passing back to the kidney tubule and resulting in no pH change in the urine (Harper, 1963). The important point here is that the ammonia in the mammalian urine is of peripheral formation; Smith (1953) suggests that this may be a widespread phenomenon.

The relative merits of these opposing views will be clearer when there are more biochemical data for the lower forms. At the moment there is no evidence for the ornithine cycle in some of the lower animals; the traces of urea which they excrete seem to come from arginine. Likewise, there is no good evidence for major biosynthesis of urea by routes other than the ornithine cycle (Cohen and Brown, 1960). It should be emphasized, however, that the enzymes involved in urea biosynthesis are found in plants and microorganisms. They are evidently phylogenetically very old, and the ornithine cycle is based on particular arrangements of molecules which have been available throughout animal phylogeny. It might be expected to appear rather easily or to disappear in the course of natural selection.

Organs of Excretion and the Formation of Urine

The anatomical unit of the excretory system is most often a minute tubule. Only a few groups of animals, usually of small size, lack excretory tubules and dispose of their wastes through the general body surface or through contractile vacuoles or by phagocytosis. Excreting tubules may occur singly or segmentally in pairs, or they may be collected together into compact organs, often referred to by the non-specific term of KIDNEY. Their function is to move water and dissolved metabolic wastes from a tissue space, body cavity or vascular fluid to the exterior.

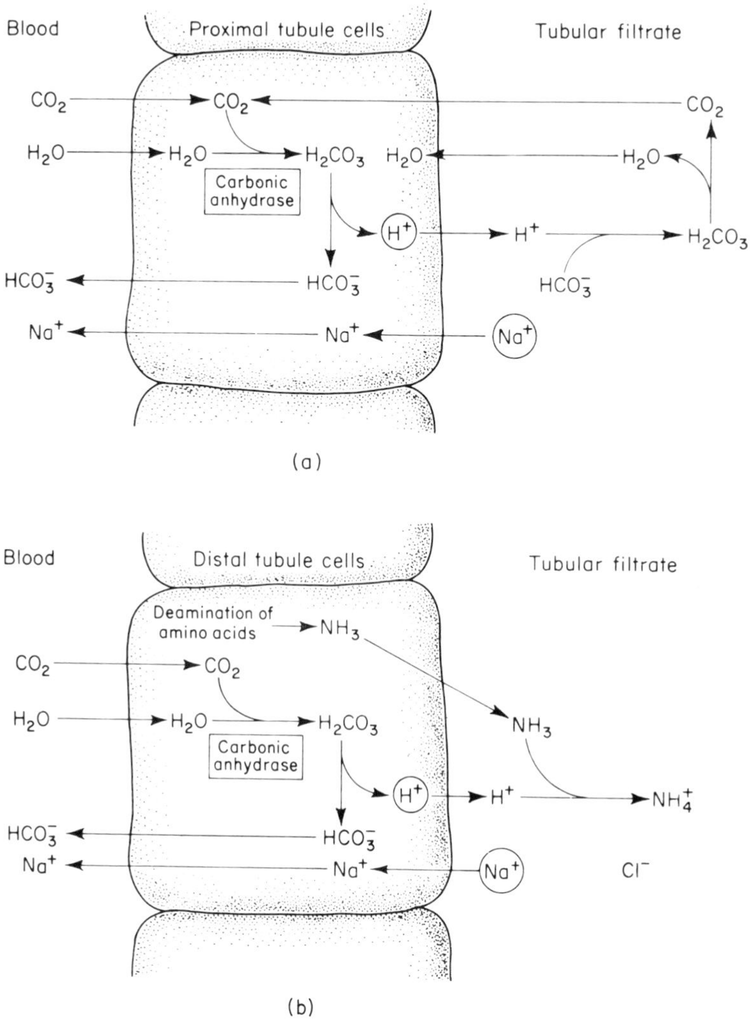

Fig. 8.7. Acid-base regulatory mechanisms in the vertebrate kidney by which hydrogen ions are eliminated and cations are conserved. *a*, In the proximal tubule the exchange first proceeds against sodium bicarbonate while in the distal tubule a similar exchange takes place against Na_2HPO_4 (after all the bicarbonate has been reabsorbed). *b*, Ammonia from the deamination of amino acids forms ammonium ions which replace sodium of the sodium chloride to conserve this cation. [Harper (1963).]

The collection of the excretory fluids (urine) is by FILTRATION under hydrostatic and osmotic pressure differences, or by CILIARY MOVEMENT of fluids from body spaces into open ciliated funnels, or by ACTIVE CELLULAR TRANSPORT from vascular fluids into the lumina of the tubules.

WITHOUT SPECIAL EXCRETORY TUBULES

No special organs of excretion have been identified in many of the Protozoa, in the Coelenterata, in most of the Porifera and in the invertebrate Deuterostomata as a group (Hyman, 1951). Some of the Protozoa and Porifera have contractile vacuoles concerned primarily with water balance, and many of the deuterostomes, especially the larger ones, support an extensive system of phagocytic cells for the removal of wastes. However, a large part of the regulation in all these groups is by way of the body surfaces.

Cell membranes. All living cells are capable of maintaining some concentration differences between the interior and the exterior. This is, in fact, the basis of the bioelectric potential which is a constant cellular characteristic depending on the unequal distribution of potassium and sodium ions across the cell membrane (Chapter 15). Active transport of ions is always involved; in some organisms this capacity, operating over the exposed body surfaces, seems to be the only means of osmotic or ionic regulation and excretion.

ACTIVE TRANSPORT involves the movement of substances from regions of lower concentration to regions of higher concentration at the expense of metabolic energy. Anderson and Ussing (1960) define the process in negative terms, stating that "a substance can be regarded as actively transported only if the transfer of the substance across a membrane cannot be accounted for by the action of the forces of diffusion, electric potential gradient, solvent drag, or these forces in any combination." There is no entirely satisfactory definition (Beament, 1964). The energy requirement of the process is, however, always emphasized since the transport is "uphill" and the inhibiting effects of respiratory poisons are often cited as evidence of its active nature. In no case is the process fully explained. Current theories postulate an active carrier molecule (probably a phosphatide) which combines with the transported material through an enzyme reaction on one side of the cell membrane and then passes through the membrane, to be released from the combination by another enzyme. The transported material then diffuses from this side of the cell membrane while the carrier molecule is reactivated and passes back to transport more molecules across (Giese, 1962).

Although the transport of ions is recognized and forms the basis of processes of osmotic and ionic regulation at all levels of phylogeny

(Chapter 11), the active transport of water has frequently been questioned (Anderson and Ussing, 1960; Robinson, 1960). In many cases the "uphill" flow of water has been shown to be secondary to the active transport of a solute. In the gall bladder, for example, the movement of water is quantitatively linked to the transport of sodium chloride (Diamond, 1964) and although the molecular details with respect to the membranes have not been worked out, many investigators argue that water movement against a gradient is usually a solute-linked phenomenon. However, active transport of water has now been convincingly demonstrated in the rectum of the insect (Beament, 1964; Phillips, 1964) and, consequently, it is hazardous to generalize until the processes are more completely understood in the insects and a wider search has been made for comparable mechanisms in other forms.

Cell membranes have been shown to differ markedly in their water permeability. This variable feature of membrane architecture is a significant factor in water balance and excretion at all levels in animal phylogeny. Some are almost or completely watertight. Both marine and freshwater teleost eggs, for example, maintain an osmotic independence after fertilization; this evidently is due to the impermeability of the vitelline membrane. This membrane, although impermeable to water and solutes, permits the ready diffusion of respiratory gases and ammonia. Varying degrees of membrane permeability have been measured in different tissues and in animals ranging from the Protozoa to the Vertebrata. When it is impossible to analyze the solutions on the two sides of a membrane, indirect measurements of permeability have been made by using heavy water or by osmotic diffusion methods. Representative values are tabulated in Prosser and Brown, (1961).

Contractile vacuoles. These are organs of water balance found in many Protozoa and in some of the freshwater sponges. Because of their minute size it has so far been impossible to analyze the vacuolar fluids. Indirect evidence suggests that it is water or a very dilute solution (Kitching, 1952), and there is now general agreement that these organs operate as pumps to remove osmotic and metabolic water. The usual arguments for an osmoregulatory function are based on the tonicity of the habitats of the animals which contain vacuoles, on the effects of experimentally changing the tonicity and on the action of metabolic poisons on vacuolar activity. Vacuoles are common in freshwater Protozoa and frequently absent from marine and brackish water species; in freshwater species, vacuolar activity is decreased in proportion to increases in the tonicity of the culture medium (consequently in proportion to the reduction in osmotic flooding); in marine species, vacuolar output increases with dilution of the sea water. Cyanide, which inhibits the cytochrome system and prevents oxidative phosphorylation, stops vacuolar activity and leads to rapid swelling of the cell. These observations are consistent with the hypothesis that the main function of the vacuole is to eliminate osmotic water and that this process demands metabolic energy. Quantitative support for this concept has been obtained by measuring the water permeability of the cell membranes and relating this to the volume output of the vacuole. Satisfactory agreement between the two values has been obtained in several species, for example, in *Amoeba* and *Pelomyxa* (Shaw, 1960). Any excretory role which the contractile vacuole may play in the removal of nitrogenous wastes is probably secondary. Ammonia, the end-product of nitrogen metabolism in the Protozoa, diffuses readily into the surrounding water through the cell membrane. The vacuole is essentially an organ of water balance.

There is much less certainty regarding the mechanisms of filling (diastole) and discharge (systole). It is clear that the processes require metabolic energy, probably in the form of ATP. Dilute cyanide suppresses vacuolar activity; cytological studies have revealed rich concentrations of mitochondria or osmiophil substance in close proximity to the vacuolar membrane. Evidently, processes of active transport are involved, but it has thus far been impossible to show just what is being transported. In the absence of direct evidence from analyses of vacuolar fluids, many theories have been advanced. These include an active transport (secretion) of water into the vacuole, an active secretion of solute with water diffusing osmotically, and the formation of vacuolar membranes around cytoplasmic fluid with subsequent transport of solutes back into the cytoplasm. Many physiologists are not convinced that active transport of water is ever possible and, consequently, a mechanism based on the transport of solute or its enclosure in cytoplasmic membranes with a secondary diffusion of water is favored. Electron microscopy has provided evidence that vacuoles in *Amoeba proteus* are formed by coalescence of minute vesicles whose membranes may be derived from the endoplasmic reticulum. These vesicles (0.03 to 0.1 μ in diameter) contribute their membranes (about 60 Å thick) and their contents to the vacuole (Mercer, 1959).

Attempts have been made to draw a parallel between the diastolic filling of the contractile vacuole and the formation of urine in the kidney tubule. In the latter there is a hydrostatic filtration followed by active transport of solutes. Many protozoans are surrounded by stiff layers of ectoplasm as well as the cell membranes, and a hydrostatic turgor pressure can be measured in the endoplasm. This is small (about 4 cm H_2O in *Spirostomum*) but in excess of the colloid osmotic pressure (about 2 cm H_2O in the same species). However, it has been difficult to see how this could squeeze water into an enclosed space, and turgor pressure theories are not popular (Kitching, 1938; 1952; 1954).

The systolic mechanism is also uncertain. Theoretically, the contractile force might reside either in the vacuolar membrane or in the cytoplasm of the cell. Kitching (1954) favors the former view. Electron micrographs of the *Paramecium* vacuole provide support for the theory of a contractile wall. *Paramecium*, like many other ciliates, has a highly organized vacuolar apparatus with a series of canals feeding into a pulsating sac which discharges at a specific point on the surface. Delicate contractile fibrils are present in the wall of the vacuole (Fig. 8.8). On

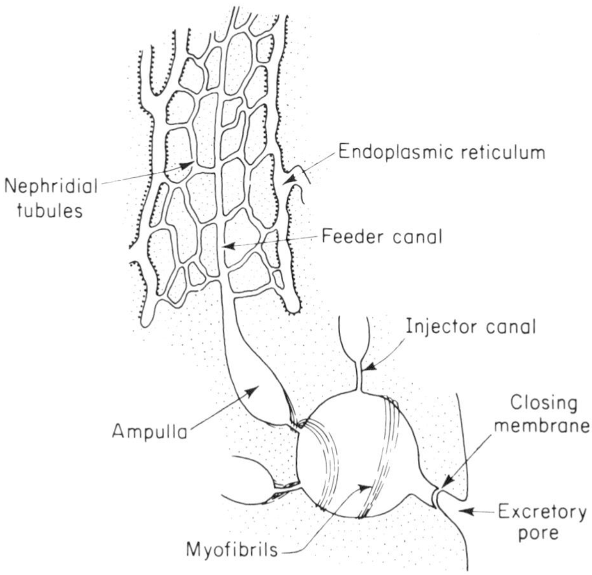

Fig. 8.8. The excretory apparatus of *Paramecium* as shown by the electron microscope. [Gray (1961) based on Schneider (1960).]

contraction, the contents are expelled through the pore while the filler canals close off; on relaxation, the filler canals open and fluid is drawn into the expanding vacuole (Schneider, 1960). A felt-like system of delicate fibrils has also been described in the middle of three layers which form the wall of the contractile vacuole of *Amoeba proteus;* the suggestion has been made that these are responsible for the rapid discharge of the organelle (Bairata and Lehmann, 1956). However, the presence of this special contractile layer in *Amoeba* has been questioned (Mercer, 1959), and there seems to be no good evidence that it is a universal component of all vacuole walls (Rudzinska, 1958). Active contraction of the membranous wall could be independent of specialized fibrils, but this remains to be demonstrated.

Finally, it should be noted that some freshwater Protozoa lack contractile vacuoles. In these, as in *Hydra* and a number of other small freshwater animals, the role of water and electrolyte balance must reside in the cell membrane. Small size in itself confers no advantage against osmotic flooding. As linear measurements change, the surface per unit volume alters in the inverse order. Thus, surface areas are relatively greater in smaller forms, and unless appropriate changes in permeability take place the small freshwater animals have relatively more water to bail out than the large ones. Evidently the plasma membrane alone, either through limited permeability or active transport mechanisms, can cope with this problem; Kitching (1954) suggests that the evolution of the contractile vacuole became necessary with the specialization of the cuticle. The vacuolar membrane probably has essentially the same properties as the plasma membrane. It may be considered an internal plasma membrane which takes care of secretion and possibly excretion. The highly specialized cuticle of many Protozoa made its evolution a necessity.

STORAGE EXCRETION.

A system of cells for the temporary or permanent storage of wastes is a rather constant feature of all multi-cellular animals. These either pick up particulate matter phagocytically or elaborate excretory compounds such as guanate and urate granules. The phagocytic (reticulo-endothelial) system was described in Chapter 5; it was noted there that both wandering ameboid cells and fixed tissues operate to remove foreign material.

Wandering phagocytic cells concerned with the removal of particulate wastes are universal, and in some animals this seems to be the only component of the phagocytic system. This is true of the tunicates and echinoderms. These animals are unusual among the more bulky species in that they lack special excretory organs and depend only on the surface epithelium and a colony of wandering phagocytes. Since they have not penetrated fresh waters, their physiology has never demanded a pump to take care of osmotic flooding. Without terrestrial tendencies the problems of salt balance and the disposal of nitrogenous wastes are adequately handled by permeable body surfaces without specialized areas of excreting epithelia.

Most groups of animals have fixed tissues concerned with storage excretion as well as the wandering ameboid cells. In a number of the Turbellaria, for example, ATHROCYTES or PARANEPHROCYTES are found singly or in clusters near to, or wrapped around, the nephridial tubes (Hyman, 1951). They take up dyes and are assumed to be excretory. The "urate cells" of insects are similarly fixed and seem to elaborate the materials which they accumulate. They are often conspicuous in the fat body and, in some insects, the granules gradually accumulate as the animal grows and seem never to be discharged (Wigglesworth, 1942). Malpighian tubules are absent in some insects; but even when present, the urate cells may play an important part in the disposal of nitrogenous wastes. Spiders have a well-organized system for storage excretion in addition to the Malpighian tubules. Certain intestinal cells in the region of the hypodermis fill with guanates which are later discharged in liquid form into the lumen of the gut and pass into a cloacal pocket where the water is again removed and the guanates are eliminated as crystals (Kerkut, 1958).

EXCRETORY TUBULES

Comparative anatomists have encountered some of their most perplexing problems in studies of the structure and phylogeny of the excretory tubules (Goodrich, 1945). Not only are the tubular channels varied, but they are often intimately associated with the genital ducts, both structurally and functionally. The simultaneous evolution of these two discharge systems has produced many anatomical variations and compromises. It seems likely that the functional arrangements differ less than the anatomical details. For present purposes, the many morphological types will be disregarded and the tubules will be discussed in three groups as follows:

a. *Nephridia*—primitive excretory tubules characteristic of most of the Protostomia and subdivided into *protonephridia* and *metanephridia*.
b. *Malpighian tubules*—found in the Myriapoda, Insecta (except Collembola, some Thysanura and Aphidae) and Arachnida other than *Limulus*.
c. *Vertebrate Nephron*—phylogenetically distinct from the invertebrate nephridial tubes.

Nephridia. The nephridial tubule or the nephridium is the excretory organ of most of the invertebrates. These tubules are found as many separate units throughout the body (as in the flatworms), or serially as a pair of tubes in each segment (as in the annelids), or as a single pair of tubes (as in the crustaceans and molluscs); but they are never gathered together to form compact organs like the vertebrate kidneys. Their walls are single-layered epithelia which often show evidence of being capable of active transport. They may be assumed to secrete materials into the tubular fluids or extract materials from them. Tubules which are closed at the inner end are called PROTONEPHRIDIA, while those which open into the coelom by a ciliated funnel, called the nephridiostome or the nephrostome, are termed METANEPHRIDIA. Both types of tubule open to the outside through nephridiopores and frequently enlarge into a storage (urinary) bladder just before they discharge.

Protonephridia are considered more primitive. In the acoelomate and pseudocoelomate groups, FLAME BULBS form the proximal ends of the system of branching tubules in the parenchyma. These bulbs (sometimes single cells, sometimes multinucleate or multicellular structures) are cup-shaped terminations containing tufts of cilia which are assumed to propel fluids through the minute tubules and perhaps also aid in filtering solutions from the surrounding lymph (Fig. 8.9). In coelomate invertebrates which utilize protonephridia (trochophore and related larvae, some adult polychaetes and *Amphioxus*), the flame bulb is replaced by a SOLENOCYTE. Transitional forms between the two types of termination are found in gastrotrichs, and the solenocyte is evidently a variation of the flame bulbs (Hyman, 1951). The solenocyte cell has a rounded body with a single very long flagellum beating in an exceedingly minute and thin-walled tubule which is attached to the main nephridial system (Fig. 8.9). Solenocytes are usually grouped in packets, sometimes called glomeruli, around the ends of the major nephridial tubes. Further, the bulb-shaped cells are exposed to coelomic fluid and sometimes also applied to the thin wall of a blood vessel. This is obviously an ideal arrangement for filtration or active transport from body fluids, and the possible functional significance of this intimate association of solenocytes and vascular fluids is emphasized. Flame bulbs are similarly bathed in fluid; in the Nemertea they also are closely applied to the blood vessels. Thus, in some of the most primitive animals which possess a distinct system of blood channels there is the possibility of associated excretory filtration. It has not yet been possible to test theories of protonephridial filtration, but the morphology suggests filtration at the solenocyte, propulsion by the flagella with secretion and reabsorption by the epithelia of the nephridial tubules. More refined techniques are required to test these speculations.

Whereas a coelom is only sometimes an adjunct to the protonephridial apparatus, it always forms a physiologically essential partner of the metanephridium. Metanephridial tubes are open at both ends, and the collecting funnel is in the coelom where waste products collect and from where they are wafted by the ciliated nephrostomes into the nephridial tubes. In annelids the coelom is extensive, and there is typically a pair of nephridial tubes in each of its segmental compartments. In molluscs the coelom is represented only by the pericardial cavity and the cavities of the kidneys and gonads. The pericardial coelom communicates with the renal coelom (renal tube) through the renopericardial canal, and the associated structure forms the kidney of the mollusc. In those arthropods which depend on nephridial tubes (segmental tubes in the Onychophora, antennary and maxillary glands in the Crustacea and coxal glands in the Arachnida), the coelom is reduced to a small thin-walled sac attached to the proximal end of the excreting tubule (Fig. 11.6). In all cases, solutions first formed in the coelom move slowly through a long tubule to the point of discharge, and both coelom and tubule are involved in regulating the composition of the urine.

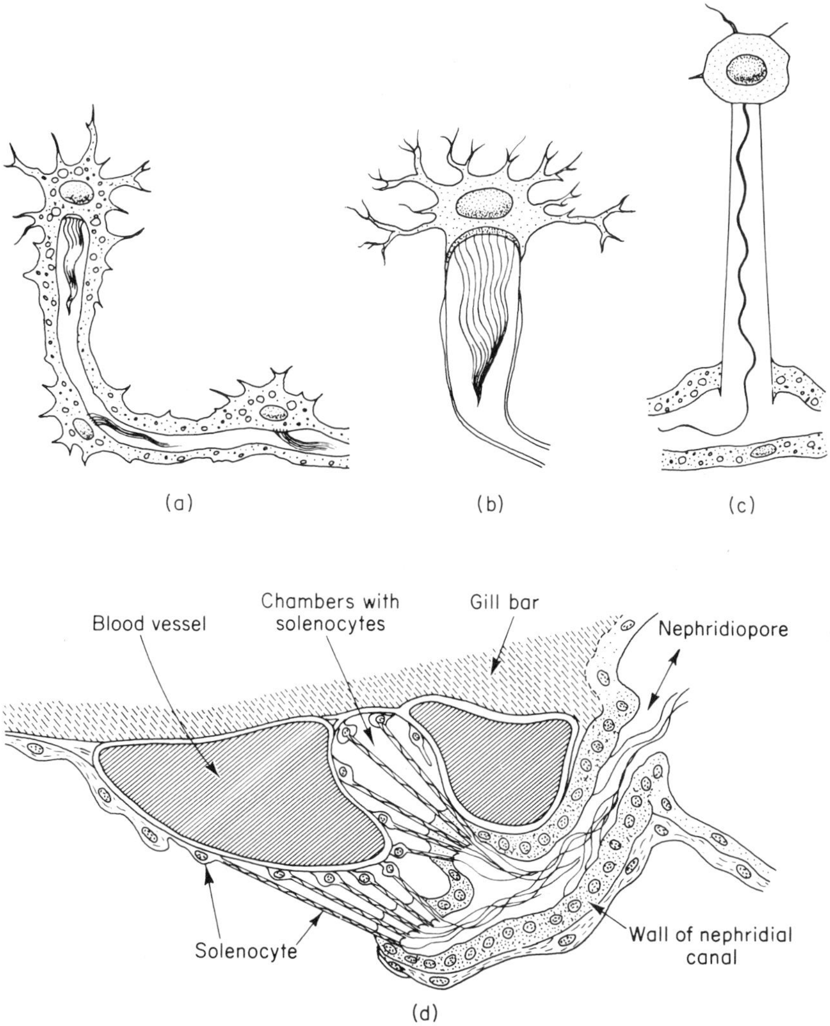

Fig. 8.9. Protonephridial apparatus. *a*, Flame bulb of a polyclad turbellarian. *b*, Flame bulb of a cestode. *c*, Solenocyte of a polychaete. *d*, Transverse section through nephridium of *Amphioxus* showing solenocytes in close proximity to blood vessels and the glandular wall of nephridial canal. Further description in text. [Goodrich (1945).]

These are broad generalizations, and some adult animals have a highly modified metanephridial apparatus with secondary closure of nephrostomes and internal openings of the nephridiopores. In the Oligochaeta, for example, Bahl (1947) describes a series of modifications associated with dry terrestrial habitats. Nephrostomes are lost, and the tubules must operate only by secretion and osmotic differences like Malpighian tubules of insects and aglomerular kidneys of teleosts. In some oligochaetes, secondary openings drain the tubules into the gut (enteronephric) where water is reabsorbed. Annelids with intestinal enteronephric systems live in hot, dry climates, and the arrangement forms one of their special adaptations for water economy (Bahl, 1947).

Urine formation in the metanephridial apparatus has been investigated in a number of the larger invertebrates. Both filtration and active transport are involved (Martin, 1957). The physiological techniques are those first used with such success in studies of vertebrate urine formation. With delicate cannulae fluids are removed from different areas of the tubular apparatus, and the composition and osmotic pressure are compared with blood or other body fluids. Sometimes the hydrostatic pressures in these different compartments can also be measured by micropuncture.

Considerable information concerning the nature of the kidney processes can be adduced from the relative concentrations of different substances in urine and blood. If the ratio of the concentrations (U/B ratio) is unity, then the substance is being excreted in direct proportion to its concentration in the body fluids, and the kidney shows no evidence of actively regulating the output either by secretion (U/B ratio greater than unity) or by reabsorption (U/B ratio less than unity). This is well illustrated with U/B ratios for several electrolytes in a small shore crab, *Hemigrapsus oregonensis,* maintained in waters of different salinities (Fig. 8.10). Sodium, potassium and calcium values are almost the same in urine and blood, indicating a lack of regulatory activity with respect to these ions. Magnesium, however, becomes more and more concentrated in the urine as the salinity of the environment (hence also the hemolymph concentration) increases (Dehnel and Carefoot, 1965). Clearly, the kidney of *Hemigrapsus* excretes magnesium actively to regulate the blood level of this ion but has little control over the levels of the other three electrolytes.

Such techniques can demonstrate the nature of the excreting mechanisms but do not provide quantitative data for the various rates of filtration, reabsorption and secretion. For this, renal physiologists often use the "plasma clearance" test. A nontoxic chemical is injected into the blood and subsequently the amount of this substance is determined simultaneously in blood and urine.

Plasma clearance may be defined as the volume of plasma cleared of a given substance per minute OR the volume of blood or plasma which contains the amount of a particular substance excreted by the kidney in a minute. If P is the plasma concentration, U the urine concentration and V the rate of urine flow in ml/min, then:

$$\text{Clearance (ml/min)} = \frac{U \times V}{P}$$

Thus, if urine is being formed at the rate of 100 ml/hr and found to contain 5 mg/ml of the injected material while the plasma contained 0.2 mg/ml, then the clearance is 42 ml/min, and this means that 42 ml of plasma would have to be completely filtered or cleared of the substance every minute to provide the quantity of the substance found in the urine.

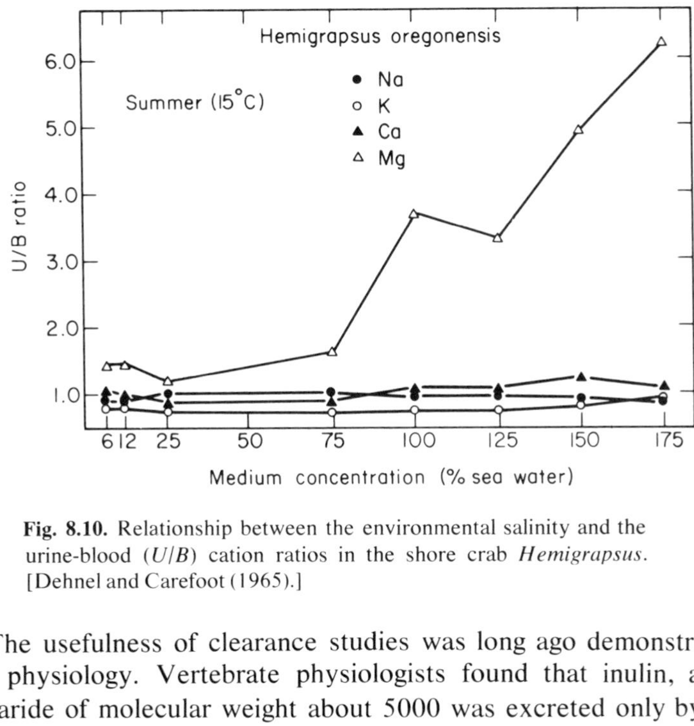

Fig. 8.10. Relationship between the environmental salinity and the urine-blood (U/B) cation ratios in the shore crab *Hemigrapsus*. [Dehnel and Carefoot (1965).]

The usefulness of clearance studies was long ago demonstrated in renal physiology. Vertebrate physiologists found that inulin, a polysaccharide of molecular weight about 5000 was excreted only by filtration. The evidence was based on comparisons of its concentration in the plasma and glomerular filtrate of the frog, its inability to pass into the urine of aglomerular fishes and, more directly, from experiments where tubules were blocked with oil droplets or where tagged inulin was used. In the vertebrates, at any rate, inulin clearance is a good measure of glomerular filtration and substances which are secreted as well as filtered will have correspondingly higher clearance rates, while substances which are reabsorbed will have lower ones. Different rates can thus be quantitatively evaluated.

The techniques of micropuncture and clearance have demonstrated both filtration and active transport in the metanephridial tubule as well as in the vertebrate nephron. For example, inulin has been successfully used to demonstrate filtration in the end sac of the antennal gland of the crayfish (Riegel and Kirschner, 1960), while microanalyses of fluids from different parts of the tubule of the gland show that chloride is reabsorbed as the urine passes along it, resulting in a hypotonic urine and the conservation of salt (Fig. 11.6). Again, Martin (1957) and his coworkers perfused the closed vascular system of the octopus with inulin and later found urine-to-blood ratios of approximately one, indicating a filtration of this material in the octopus. This theory was confirmed when poisons (such as phlorizin and dinitrophenol), known to inhibit active transport, had no effect on the inulin clearance, although they did alter the clearance of other materials. Reabsorption of materials such as glucose and the secretion of compounds such as phenol red were also shown in the octopus by the classical methods of renal physiology; these same techniques have proved fruitful in studies of other molluscs and the larger crustaceans (Harrison, 1962).

The main source of the filtration pressure in the molluscs and arthropods is the hydrostatic pressure of the blood. This will be counteracted to a small degree by osmotic pressure differences between the blood and the coelomic fluids as well as by the hydrostatic pressure in the nephridial apparatus. The wall of the coelomic sac is highly vascular in the crustacean (Parry, 1960), while in the mollusc the heart actually passes through the filtration cavity or pericardial sac (Morton, 1958). The filtering membranes differ in various groups but, in general, blood pressure forms the driving force, and the coelomic space is located near the heart or in a region of high blood pressure. Active transport is dependent on the tubules which drain the coelomic space. The mechanisms have been less satisfactorily demonstrated in the annelids because of their small size and the problem of collecting samples of blood and urine. However, filtration seems possible through the nephridial capillary network or through the vascular wall of the coelom; the tubules are certainly capable of active transport (Laverack, 1963; Martin, 1957).

Malpighian tubules. In the most successful of the terrestrial arthropods, the duties of excretion have been taken over by the gut and the tubular glands of Malpighi which discharge into the posterior portion of it. Usually no vestige remains of the nephridial system, characteristic of the aquatic invertebrates (Goodrich, 1945). Rather, it is replaced by a system which requires neither the forces of blood pressure for filtration nor the coelom for the collection of fluid wastes. The relegation of excretion to the alimentary tract is associated with the novel mode of gas exchange in the terrestrial arthropods; the evolution of the Malpighian tubules may have been a response to the reduced importance of their circulatory system. When gas exchange depends on efficient fluid transport, then the excretory machinery seems always to be coupled to it and to operate, at least in part, by the pressures set up in the contraction of the heart. In the tracheates, an active circulation of blood is absent and thus one of the major forces for urine production in many other groups of animals is lost. The glandular lining of the hind-gut takes over the responsibilities for removal of metabolic wastes and the conservation of essential electrolytes. Tubular glands collect and transport solutions (isosmotic) from the hemolymph into the hind-gut where water and physiologically important compounds are absorbed by the specialized hind-gut epithelium. Malpighian tubules and hind-gut operate together to remove the wastes and, sometimes, to conserve water. The dynamics of this system have been beautifully demonstrated in mosquito larvae and the stick insect, *Dixippus*, by Ramsay (1958 and earlier) who developed novel micromethods for collecting tubular and gut fluids and for determining their osmotic pressures and chemical constituents (Craig, 1960).

Ramsay found that the tubules accumulate potassium from the hemolymph with which they are bathed (Fig. 8.11). This active cellular transport of potassium (against an electro-chemical gradient) is probably a fundamental feature of tubular activity and represents the major metabolic work of their epithelia. In the stick insect, the concentration of potassium in the tubular liquid may be ten times greater than in the hemolymph (Ramsay, 1955). This secretory process seems to be the prime mover in generating the flow of urine. It leads to the diffusion of water and low molecular weight solutes such as inorganic salts, sugar and urea, into the tubules (Ramsay, 1956). By means of tracer techniques Ramsay followed the movements of ions and organic molecules into isolated tubules from drops of fluid which bathed them.

In general, then, the mechanism of excretion by Malpighian tubules depends on the steady movement of an isosmotic solution of soluble low molecular weight substances from the hemolymph into the hind-gut where there is a recovery of essential compounds and an elimination of the wastes. This is an active circulation of fluids; the tubular contents are steadily flushed into the hind-gut where the appropriate amount of water and physiologically important substances are reabsorbed before discharge. Minute intrinsic muscles are often present in the tubules, and these agitate them in the hemolymph to improve the collection of solutes and perhaps also to facilitate circulation of the solutions within them (Roeder, 1953). The reabsorption process has a parallel in the vertebrate nephron, where filtration under hydrostatic blood pressure at the glomerulus produces an isotonic filtrate which is appropriately altered as the filtrate flows along the nephron. In the Malpighian tubule filtration under hydrostatic pressure is absent, and active transport takes its place.

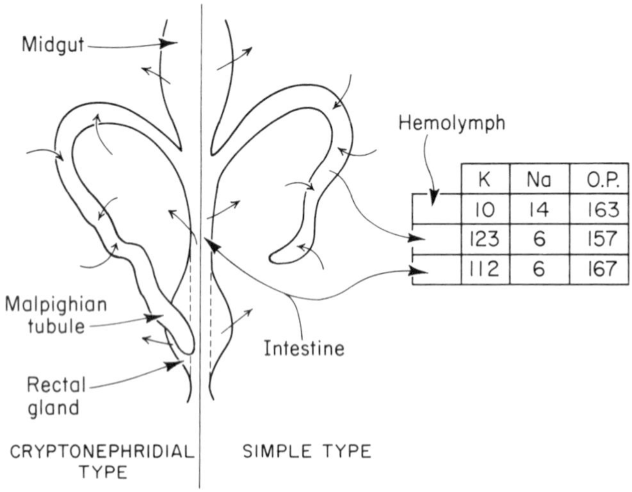

Fig. 8.11. Malpighian apparatus of an insect. Small arrows show direction of liquid flow. Values for potassium and sodium in m equiv/liter and osmotic content (O.P.) in mM/liter NaCl. [Data for *Dixippus* from Ramsay (1955).]

The hind-gut of the insect has the remarkable capacity of concentrating the urine by actively transporting water from the lumen of the gut to the hemolymph. At present this is one of the few clearly demonstrated situations where active movement of water is independent of solute transport (Beament, 1964). Phillips (1964) ligated the rectum of the desert locust *Schistocerca gregaria* so as to isolate it from the hind-gut, rinsed the organ with distilled water and filled it with various experimental solutions, which could be sampled at intervals to follow changes in composition brought about by movements of substances through the rectal wall. Volume changes were measured by means of a reference substance (iodinated human serum albumin) which was shown not to pass through the wall. Sodium, potassium and chloride can be absorbed against concentration differences of up to 100-fold; the movement of the chloride was shown to be an active transport and the sodium and potassium may be active as well. These are processes recognized in many other animal tissues. Phillips' results go beyond this in demonstrating the movement of water independent of net solute transport. Isosmotic trehalose solutions are concentrated in the lumen without significant absorption of the sugar or net flux of ions into the lumen. This capacity for active transport of water is so far recognized only in certain insect tissues. Cellular mechanisms are still speculative.

Several modifications of the general pattern of urine formation have been described, and still others may be revealed when more insects have been studied. In *Rhodnius,* a bloodsucking insect, Wigglesworth (1942) found reabsorption of solutes in the lower portion of the tubules. Associated with this there is a sharp histological distinction between the distal and the proximal tubular epithelia; the process of reabsorption, which in most insects seems to be localized in the hind-gut, is transferred to the attached end of the Malpighian tubule. This may be an adaptation for the production of large volumes of urine after a meal of blood (Ramsay, 1956). Another interesting modification, found in lepidopterous larvae, Coleoptera and several other insects, is associated with water conservation and life in dry habitats. In this, the distal ends of the Malpighian tubules are intimately attached to the wall of the gut, so that the lumina of the gut and tubules are separated by only thin membranes and the hind-gut is clothed with a plexus of tubules, the cryptonephridial tubes (Wigglesworth, 1942). The masses of enteronephric (closed) tubules which open into the gut in some of the dry habitat oligochaetes (Bahl, 1947) may be an evolutionary convergence.

The vertebrate nephron. The vertebrate nephron begins with a PRESSURE FILTER, the renal corpuscle, and extends as a tube of variable length and structure which carries the filtrate to the outside while REABSORBING useful substances from it and SECRETING additional wastes into it. These three basic mechanisms of urine formation are the same as those of the metanephridium, although the anatomy and phylogeny of vertebrate nephron and invertebrate nephridium are quite different.

Comparative anatomists have agreed that there is no phylogenetic connection between these two types of excretory tubule (Goodrich, 1945), even though the more primitive nephric units of both show several physiological parallels. In many embryos and some adult lower vertebrates, the tubules open into the coelom by a ciliated funnel (coelomostome); it has often been suggested that this represents an ancestral condition. In the most primitive situation, a tangle of blood vessels, the glomus, is found in the neighboring wall of the coelom, and this serves to increase filtration of fluids into the body cavity, whence they can be wafted into the ciliated funnels (Fig. 8.12*a*). In the larval *Petromyzon,* for example, there are four segmental funnels; close to each there is a glomus which disappears in the adult *Petromyzon* but persists in the

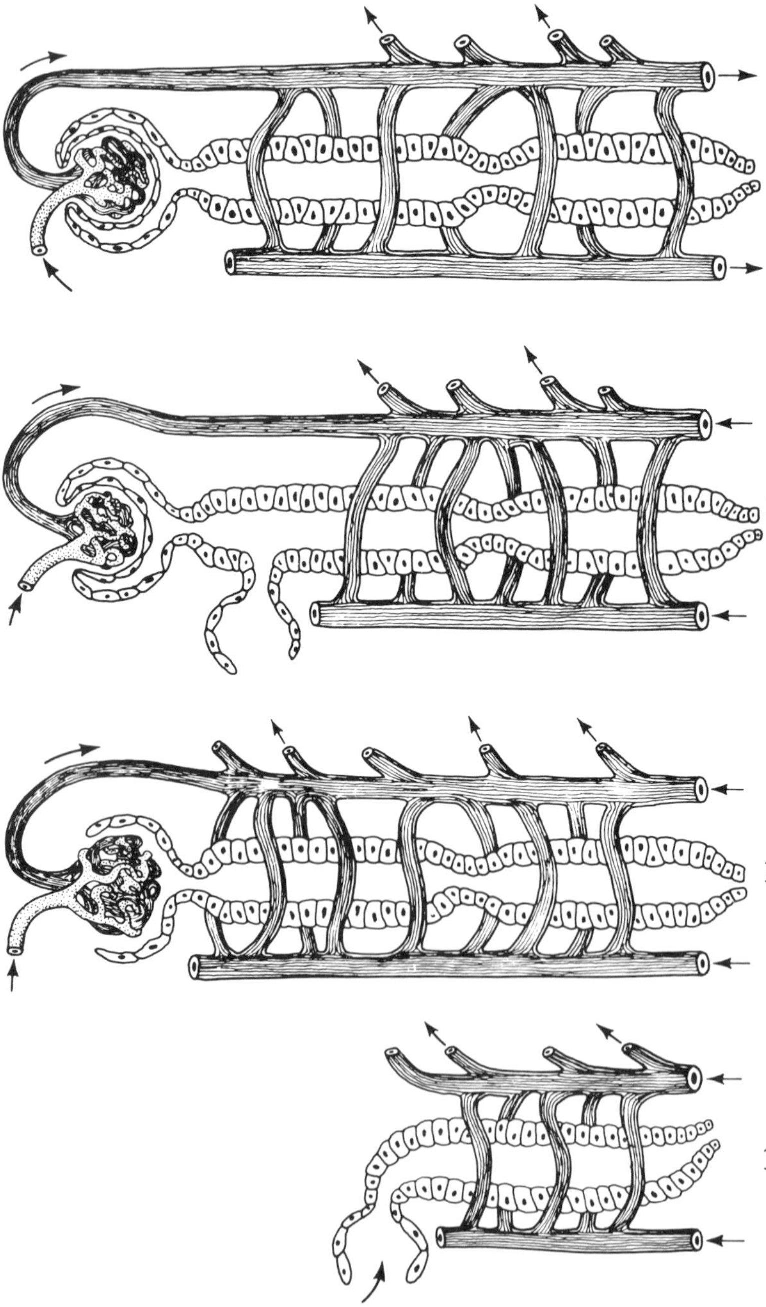

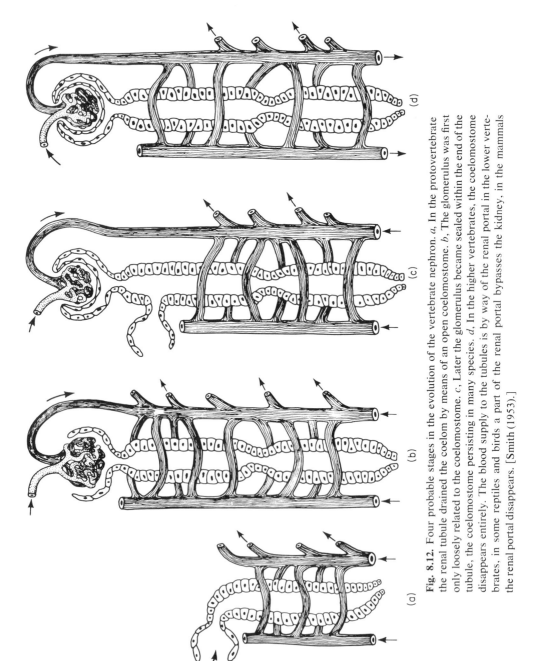

Fig. 8.12. Four probable stages in the evolution of the vertebrate nephron. *a*, In the protovertebrate the renal tubule drained the coelom by means of an open coelomostome. *b*, The glomerulus was first only loosely related to the coelomostome. *c*, Later the glomerulus became sealed within the end of the tubule, the coelomostome persisting in many species. *d*, In the higher vertebrates, the coelomostome disappears entirely. The blood supply to the tubules is by way of the renal portal in the lower vertebrates, in some reptiles and birds a part of the renal portal bypasses the kidney, in the mammals the renal portal disappears. [Smith (1953).]

closely related hagfish *Myxine*. In most vertebrates this primitive vascular arrangement is superseded by one in which the glomus is pushed into the wall of the tubule as a glomerulus and thus forms the renal corpuscle (Fig. 8.12*c*,*d*). The coelomostome usually disappears (or is not even formed embryologically), although it is found in some adult sharks, in *Amia* and in a few amphibians (Smith, 1953). These physiological associations between excretory organs and coelom are similar to but not phylogenetically related to those of the annelids. Excretion in both cases is originally a drainage of coelomic fluids. In vertebrate evolution the nephric tubules are grafted onto the closed circulatory system which, through its very high blood pressures, provides a potent force for filtration. The happy marriage of these two systems required several rearrangements by both partners. The union is completed in the mammalian kidney.

The nephron is a highly adaptable structure. With the exception of the excretory pore there is really only one portion of it—the proximal convoluted or "brush border" segment—which is constant throughout all the vertebrates. Two major variations occur: the suppression of the glomerulus, and the elaboration of the median and the distal ends of the tube. Both of these modifications are associated with life in dry habitats and the problems of water conservation. Since water balance and osmoregulation are discussed in Chapter 11, only an outline is given here.

The aglomerular condition (found in some marine teleosts, a few amphibians and reptiles) reduces the unit to a secretory tubule which is comparable to the Malpighian tubule of many terrestrial arthropods. Marine teleosts are subjected to constant osmotic desiccation because of the hypotonic condition of their body fluids, and thus they experience a water shortage comparable to that of arid dwelling amphibians and reptiles. Reduction or elimination of glomerular filtration was a part of the evolutionary response.

The difficulty was met in quite a different manner by the mammals and some of the birds. In these, the active glomerular filter remains, and a special unit is added for the recovery of the water used in filtration. The loop of Henle and the distal convoluted tubule are so effective in water conservation that mammals such as the kangaroo rats (*Dipodomys* has been intensively studied) can meet all their water demands without drinking and rely entirely on metabolic water (Smith, 1953; Prosser and Brown, 1961).

The physiology of the tubule cannot be divorced from the circulatory system at any point along its length. An active tubule requires a good blood supply; when tubules are numerous, closely packed and no longer bathed in coelomic fluid a rich peritubular capillary network is essential. This was first obtained from the renal portal vein (gnathostomous poikilotherms) while the efferent glomerular artery had no direct connection with it. In birds and mammals the renal portal disappears, and the efferent glomerular artery is spliced into the proximal portion of the peritubular capillary network. Blood filtered in the glomerulus then passes directly through the capillaries around the tubules where its constituents are brought to proper physiological levels before passing into the general circulation.

These two patterns of blood supply (Fig. 8.12) are associated with two quite different lines of physiological specialization in the tubule. The renal portal vein drains a large area of active tissue in the tail and posterior appendages and, as the returning blood circulates through the peritubular capillaries, wastes can be actively transported or can readily diffuse into the tubules. If water is limited, glomerular filtration can be reduced or eliminated without restricting the secretory activities of the nephric units; this trend reached an extreme with the development of aglomerular kidneys in some species. It is, however, no longer possible when the tubular capillaries receive their blood direct from the glomerular artery. The kidney is then committed to continuous glomerular activity, and mechanisms for water conservation are transferred to the distal end of the tube. Constant high pressure filtration at the glomerulus is imperative. The efficiency of this arrangement is dependent upon the relatively high blood pressures of birds and mammals, and this in turn on the evolution of the double heart which supplies constant high pressure filtration at the glomerulus.

Urine formation in the vertebrates. Marcello Malpighi first saw the renal corpuscles in the middle of the seventeenth century and described them hanging from the small arterioles "like apples on the branch of a tree" (Houssay, 1951). He rightly surmised that they were concerned with urine formation, but 200 years elapsed before Bowman in 1842 published his classical description and demonstrated their anatomical relationships with the rest of the tubule. Precise functions have gradually been assigned to the different regions of the nephron in some of the most impressive physiological research of the past century. There are still unanswered questions, but the basic mechanisms are now evident. The history is described in several places, and detailed citations for the following summary can be readily checked in standard texts (Smith, 1951; Bard, 1961).

Bowman noted the glandular nature of the tubular epithelium and thought that the glomerulus produced fluid to wash the secretions of the tubules into the ureter. Ludwig, about the same time, correlated urine flow with changes in the blood pressure and proposed a mechanical theory of urine formation by hydrostatic filtration from the glomerular arteries. Such mechanistic concepts were violently opposed in the latter part of the nineteenth and early twentieth century. The proof of filtration came only in 1924 when Richards and his associates published the results of their micropuncture experiments. With delicate needles Richards withdrew fluid from the renal capsule of the frog and mudpuppy and showed that it contained glucose and chloride in about the same concentration as the plasma but was normally free of protein. In succeeding years, pressures were measured and the dynamics of the corpuscle were established in physical terms of blood pressure, osmotic pressure and pressures of the capsular fluid (Fig. 8.13).

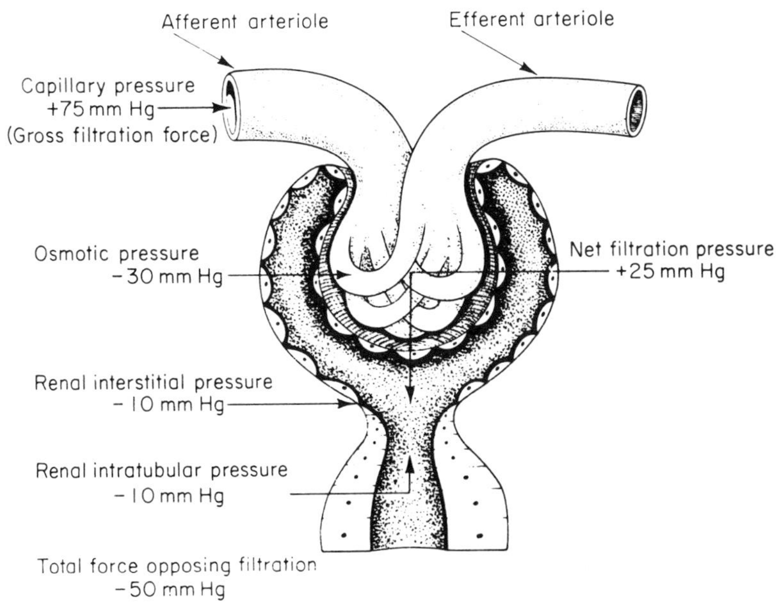

Fig. 8.13. The renal corpuscle showing the pressures which operate to produce a net filtration pressure of about 25 mm Hg. [Sharp and Dohme (1947).]

A few years later Bayliss determined the limits of the permeability of the mammalian glomerular membrane at about 68,000 mol wt dimensions by following the excretion of a series of proteins ranging in size from gelatin (mol wt 35,000) to *Helix* hemocyanin (mol wt 5,000,000). Thus, glomerular filtration was shown to be the first step in urine formation. The fluid formed contains all the low molecular weight solutes of the plasma and is isosmotic with it. Large volumes of fluid are constantly pushed through these small filters. The human kidney with its million or more corpuscles, each containing about 50 capillary loops, filters approximately 120 ml per min or some 40 gallons of fluid per day. But this is only part of the story, for it is actually the tubular epithelium which does the real work in the kidney. In the human, a cellular surface of about six square meters is assigned to this job.

One of the functions of the tubular epithelium is the reabsorption of physiologically important solutes such as glucose, low molecular weight proteins (Forster, 1961) and chloride. This became apparent when glomerular filtration was demonstrated and concomitant analyses were made on the plasma and urine. The mechanisms, however, whether active transport or passive diffusion, were not immediately clear. Moreover, the quantities of certain substances such as urea and creatinine in the urine could be explained equally well by tubular secretion (excretion) or water absorption, leading to their concentration in the bladder urine.

The first clear answer to some of these questions came in studies of renal function in the aglomerular fishes (*Lophius, Opsanus*) where only the tubular epithelium can be involved in urine formation. In a series of studies the aglomerular kidney was shown to excrete water, creatine, creatinine, urea, uric acid, magnesium sulphate, potassium, chloride and a variety of foreign substances such as thiosulphate and phenol red; but glucose, inulin and a number of other materials never appeared in the urine. Active secretion was thus demonstrated in a vertebrate nephron which is considered homologous with the proximal tubule of higher forms. Many analyses of fluids obtained in micropuncture of renal tubules of amphibians and mammals have proved that the tubules secrete as well as reabsorb. The *Necturus* tubule has been particularly useful for studies of this sort.

Another extremely productive technique for the study of tubular activity was also developed in studies of comparative physiology. Forster (1948 and subsequently, Black, 1957) first demonstrated active accumulation of phenol red in isolated pieces of flounder mesonephros. Tubules were observed microscopically, and the dye was seen to concentrate gradually within the tubules. Photometric measurements of the changing dye concentration in the suspension media also showed that it was actually passed into the tubules. These tests have also been performed on tadpole and fetal human kidney tubules. The transport of phenol red evidently depends on active cellular transport since it is readily inhibited by such enzyme inhibitors and poisons as iodoacetate, cyanide and dinitrophenol.

Tracer techniques have also provided valuable evidence for the active transport abilities of the nephron (Solomon, 1962). Perfusion fluids containing radioactive materials have been trapped between two oil droplets in the relatively large tubules from *Necturus* by first injecting a drop of oil into the capsular space and then following this with perfusion fluid and another drop of oil. As the droplets move along the tubules, changes in their composition leave little doubt that substances such as sodium are being actively transported. Quantitative estimations of filtration, reabsorption and secretion are based on the renal clearance studies already discussed (page 277 and Smith, 1956).

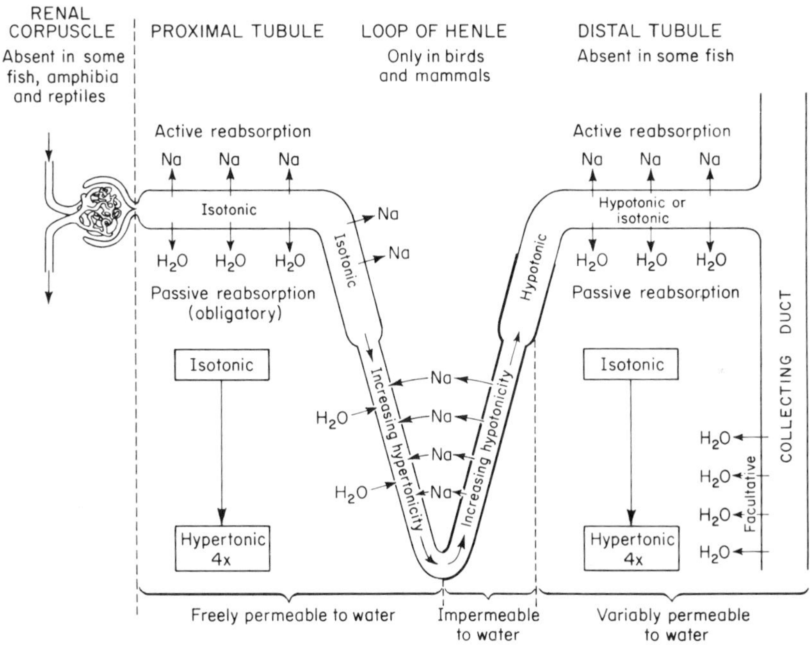

Fig. 8.14. Mechanism of urine formation in the mammal. [After Pitts (1959).]

Mammals produce a hypertonic urine; the locus and mechanism of the water recovery has only recently been satisfactorily explained. The nephron of mammals, and of some birds is unique among the vertebrates in having a long "hairpin" tube, the loop of Henle, which extends deep into the medulla of the kidney. The association of this anatomical feature with the production of hypertonic urine suggests a locus for water recovery but provides no evidence for the mechanism. Analyses of fluids obtained through microcatheter and puncture and the direct cryoscopy of kidney slices have shown that the urine remains isotonic in the proximal tubule but becomes progressively more hypertonic as it slowly descends the loop of Henle. Within the ascending limb of this loop it becomes gradually less hypertonic. Within the distal tubule it is either hypotonic or once more isotonic to the surrounding tissue fluids (Fig. 8.14). As the urine passes through the collecting tubule in the medulla it again becomes hypertonic. It is suggested that the medullary tubules constitute a counter-current multiplier (Gottschalk, 1960; Wirz, 1961) and that the active mechanism is a cellular transport of sodium from the urine in the thick portion of the ascending limb of Henle's loop. The thin portions of the loop are freely permeable to sodium (or may actively absorb it), and thus an increasing hypertonicity develops in the lower part of the loop and in the surrounding tissue spaces (Fig. 8.14). Fluids move very slowly through these passages. This active transport of sodium from the ascending limb produces a concentrated brine bath (about four times as concentrated as the fluids of the cortex) which withdraws water osmotically as it flows through the delicate thin-walled collecting tubules. The microscopic anatomy of the medulla, with its thousands of closely packed parallel tubules, supports such a concept (Smith, 1956; Bard, 1961). The actual length of the loop of Henle shows considerable variation in different mammalian species and is correlated with their ability to concentrate the urine (O' Dell and Schmidt-Nielsen, 1960).

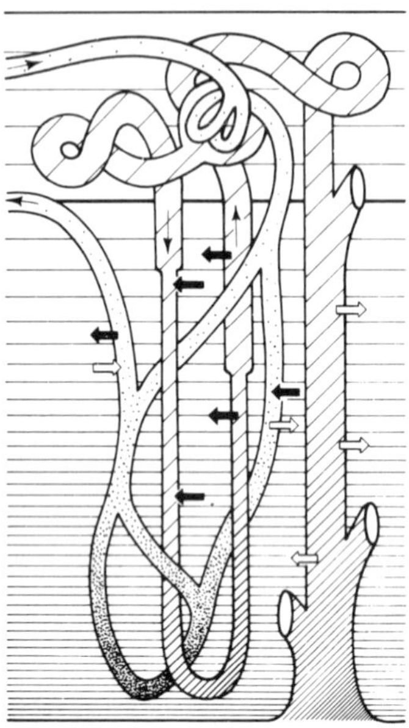

Fig. 8.15. The blood supply (stippled) to the mammalian nephron. Angled lines, renal tubule; horizontal lines, interstitial fluids; intensity of shading indicates stratification of osmotic concentration; white arrows, water transfer (passive); black arrows, transfer of crystalloids (active and passive). [Wirz (1953).]

The arrangement of the blood vessels in the medulla (vasa recta) is also important to the operation of this system (Fig. 8.15). They form a plexus of hairpin loops parallel to the loops of Henle and operate as another counter-current system. The vascular loops do not form a multiplier system like the loops of Henle but are passive exchangers which irrigate the renal medulla without interfering with its osmotic stratification (Wirz, 1961).

Regulatory mechanisms. Clearly, a filtering and partitioning machine such as the kidney must be geared to variable metabolic demands. Theoretically, regulation might occur either at the filter by altering the blood pressure or in the tubules by controlling the movements of substances through the cells.

It has often been experimentally demonstrated that variations in blood pressure alter the filtration rate and that urine production is subject to the autonomic nervous system. Under normal conditions, however, this factor is of minor significance in the regulation of filtration and apparently without any effect on tubular activities (Bard, 1961). The adjustments are primarily hormonal. Two endocrine glands, the adrenal cortex and the neurohypophysis, control tubular activity—particularly sodium-potassium transfer and the permeability of membranes to water.

Several of the adrenal steroids modify electrolyte balance in mammals, but aldosterone is the most potent and seems to be the physiologically important mineralocorticoid. In mammals its action is on the distal tubule where it depresses the Na : K ratio by promoting the absorption of sodium and favoring the excretion of potassium. It has a similar action on some other mammalian tissues such as salivary gland cells and the epithelium of the gut, and this may indicate a more generalized action on the electrolytes of cells. Aldosterone also has dramatic effects on the electrolyte balance of lower vertebrates (Chapter 11), but its effect on urine formation and the localization of its action in the nephron has been carefully investigated only in the mammal. Its significance in osmotic regulation and salt balance is discussed in Chapter 11. The regulation of aldosterone secretion by the changing levels of blood electrolytes was described in Chapter 2.

Antidiuretic hormone (ADH) is the second factor regulating renal tubular activity. Several slightly different octapeptides from the vertebrate hypothalamus are stored in the neurohypopysis and released on demand to perform several different functions, one of which is the absorption of water by the kidney tubule (Chapter 2). Arginine vasotocin is the antidiuretic hormone of amphibians, reptiles and birds, while the mammals rely on vasopressin. In amphibians, ADH affects water permeability of the skin, bladder and distal renal tubule (Sawyer *et al.*, 1960; Maetz, 1963). In the other terrestrial vertebrates its only effect appears to be on the kidney tubule. Osmoreceptors in the hypothalamus control ADH release in response to changes in the osmotic pressure of the plasma circulating through it. ADH acts by increasing water permeability (perhaps by enlarging pores in the membranes) and hence will promote the removal of water from the tubular urine (Bard, 1961; Shaw, 1960). Thus, it is an important factor in the production of hypertonic urine by mammals and is always found as a part of the water-regulating machinery of terrestrial vertebrates. The physiological effects of ADH, as well as those of the adrenocortical hormones are primarily extrarenal among the aquatic vertebrates (Bentley and Follett, 1963; Maetz, 1963). The renal tissues may have come gradually under endocrine control of these hormones during the evolution of terrestrial life.

Environmental

Relations

9

Physiological Compensation for Environmental Variation

An animal rarely lives under constant conditions. Some habitats, such as the depths of the ocean or the interior of a warm-blooded animal which houses its parasites, provide relatively constant conditions. Yet even in the depths of the ocean supplies of food may be uncertain, while the habitat of the parasite can change with the health and nutrition of its host. Most animals face not only nutritional uncertainties but also marked diurnal and seasonal oscillations which alter rates of metabolism and activity; sudden extremes may tax the physiological machinery to the limit. An animal does not exist apart from its environment; the comparative physiologist recognizes this association and attempts to describe and explain the varied mechanisms by which animals compensate for all sorts of environmental alterations and stresses.

It follows that some comparative physiologists study the habitat as well as the animals which live there. In this they share common interests with ecologists. Both measure the environmental parameters and record their normal ranges and extremes; but they study the animals in rather different ways. Both ecologist and physiologist may record the magnitude of the environmental variations found in a tidal estuary with its wide range of salinity and its shores which are sometimes stagnant and always prone to marked temperature alterations. The ecologist examines these factors as they affect the distribution of animals and regulate their population dynamics; he is also interested in the behavioral responses of the animals and their orientations to temperature and salinity gradients or any of the other features of the estuarial habitat.

The physiologist examines the same environmental variables, and he may describe them in the same terms; but his interest is primarily in the physiological machinery and the manner in which this compensates for the environmental alterations. He is much less interested in the way in which salinity affects the distribution, abundance and success of the animals than he is in processes which enable the animal to acquire salts from low salinity waters or to remove excesses of electrolytes when the water is excessively salty. He describes the respiratory problems of the aquatic organism stranded in the air by the ebbing tide, and he attempts to understand the acclimatization which occurs seasonally and the lethal processes associated with extremes.

There is, of course, much common ground, and it is pointless to attempt a sharp division of interests. Ecologists have become increasingly interested in the physiological mechanisms basic to an understanding of the animal-habitat interrelationships; the physiologist has become much more aware of the curious adaptive mechanisms associated with different and peculiar habitats. These studies of the physiological compensations for environmental oscillations and stresses are often considered together as a subdivision of comparative physiology—environmental or ecological physiology.

Nature of the Interaction with the Environment

TOLERANCE AND RESISTANCE

As a part of its genetic endowment, every animal has a capacity to compensate for environmental change. It can live within a certain range of variations, whether the variable is temperature, humidity, oxygen supply or any one of the other environmental factors. This is its TOLERANCE, and it will not be killed or damaged by any particular environmental factor, provided this does not exceed the tolerance limits. Beyond these limits, however, the organism is damaged. Although it may RESIST the change for a longer or shorter period, it will eventually succumb as a result of the change. Thus, an organism has a certain capacity for both TOLERANCE and RESISTANCE. Under appropriate conditions a catfish may live at temperatures ranging from 1°C to 35°C. This is its RANGE OF TOLERANCE, with a lower and an upper INCIPIENT LETHAL LEVEL (Fry, 1947); exposure to temperatures less than the lower or greater than the upper lethal level will kill the animal after a resistance time which depends on the magnitude of the temperature differences.

ACCLIMATION AND ACCLIMATIZATION

An animal has not only a capacity for tolerance and resistance but also one for ACCLIMATION and ACCLIMATIZATION. This means that its previous history with respect to any factor may modify its subsequent tolerance and resistance to changing conditions of this factor. Again, explanations are easiest in terms of familiar temperature effects, but it should be noted that the same principles apply to many of the other variables. If a catfish is maintained for a week or more at 30°C instead of 25°C, then its upper and lower incipient lethal levels are elevated by 2 to 3°C as shown in Fig. 9.1. In short, there is a whole family of upper and lower incipient lethal levels, and the range of tolerance is really a ZONE OF TOLERANCE bounded by a zone or REALM OF RESISTANCE.

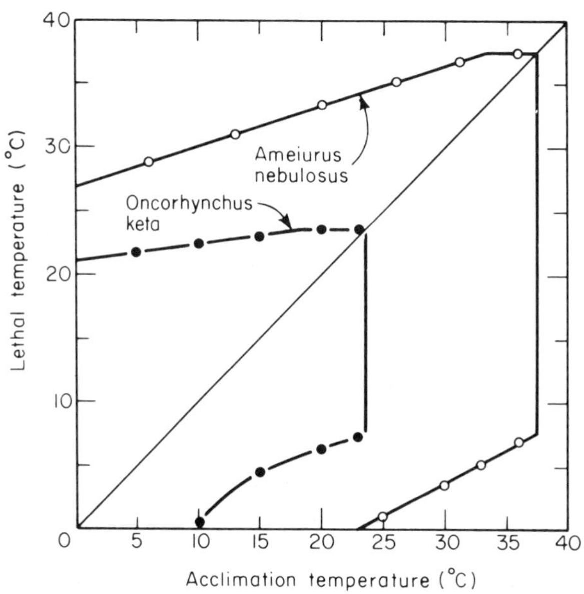

Fig. 9.1. Relation between the acclimation temperature and the upper and lower lethal temperatures for the catfish, *Ameiurus nebulosus* and for the chum salmon, *Oncorhynchus keta*. [Brett (1956).]

Many of the vital functions change in response to altered environmental conditions, whether the environmental changes fall within the zone of tolerance or the zone of resistance. These zones should not be thought of as static physiological areas. Temperature acclimation has, for example, been shown to alter the nature of the body fats of goldfish, the oxygen-binding of the blood of frogs, the heat resistance of the proteolytic enzymes in the stomach juices of snails (*Helix*) and the excitability of the isolated foot of the gastropod (*Limnaea*). Precht (1958 and earlier) has documented these and many other physiological responses to temperature change. Similar examples of responses to other environmental factors will be discussed in subsequent sections. An animal makes a dynamic physiological response, whether the environmental change is within its normal range (zone of tolerance) or more extreme (zone of resistance). In temperature work, Precht (1958) uses the term CAPACITY ADAPTATION for the compensations which take place within the range of normal temperatures (Fig. 10.3) and RESISTANCE ADAPTATION (cold and heat resistance) for compensations to extremes which alter the lethal level of the environmental factor.

Although the terms ACCLIMATION and ACCLIMATIZATION have essentially the same meaning in the English language and are frequently used interchangeably in biological literature, there is a tendency on the part of environmental physiologists to restrict their usage to somewhat different compensatory changes (Prosser and Brown, 1961). In the current terminology, "acclimation" is the descriptive term applied to compensatory changes which occur in the laboratory where the animals are maintained under controlled conditions of the factor in question, while "acclimatization" refers to the more complex situation in nature. With reference to temperature, the catfishes described in Fig. 9.1 were acclimated in the laboratory by holding them in aquaria at different constant temperatures. In nature, these animals also show seasonal changes in their temperature tolerance. These are partly due to the seasonal temperature cycle but may also be associated with photoperiod and other seasonally changing conditions. The term acclimatization is reserved for compensatory changes occurring under such natural conditions. It is the sum of the adjustments which follow repeated and prolonged exposure to natural environmental change.

There is also a third level (the species level) on which temperature compensation is possible. Zones of tolerance may be altered by natural or artificial selection through changes in genotypes. This is not the particular concern of the comparative physiologist.

INTERACTION OF ENVIRONMENTAL FACTORS

The best descriptive term in the English language for the environmental pressures which require physiological compensation is STRESS. The word is used here in this general sense and without any connotation of its specialized medical usage in the "stress syndrome" popularized by

Selye (1949). Unlike the single stress laboratory test by which the zones of tolerance are established, the natural environment is liable to create several different stresses simultaneously. Adverse humidity and temperature often occur at the same time; the salinity and temperature in the tide pool may rise, and the oxygen may be depleted during the intertidal period. There is thus an interaction of stresses. The experimental analysis of such an interacting set of stresses has not often been attempted. McLeese (1956), however, studied the interaction of temperature, salinity and oxygen in the survival of the American lobster. He found that an acclimation to any two of these factors produced a marked alteration in the incipient lethal levels of the third and that acclimation could be readily demonstrated for each factor singly.

At the physiological level these different stresses are operating in several different ways. Low oxygen, for example, restricts metabolism because of the reduction in an essential metabolite required for the production of ATP. Lack of nutrients, vitamins or trace elements would act in the same manner. These factors have been described as LIMITING. Poisons, narcotics and extremely low temperature act in a different way by suppressing the rates of metabolism. They have been called INHIBITING. Factors such as increased salinity, high temperature, or excessive muscular exercise may produce a stress through their excessive demands on metabolism. There may be little or no surplus energy for normal physiological processes. Brett (1958) refers to these factors as LOADING. It is thus evident that the interaction which McLeese described in his studies of the lobster is exceedingly complex physiologically and, further, that the natural environment may produce even more complicated interacting stresses.

MEASUREMENT OF THE LETHAL LEVEL

The precise boundaries of the apparent zone of tolerance will depend on the method of determining the lethal levels. Two techniques have been commonly used. In one, the level of the environmental variable is gradually altered until the animal succumbs; in the other, separate animals (in practice, groups of animals) are placed in a series of constant but lethal environments and the time to death is noted. Certain arbitrary decisions are required in each case. In the first, it is the RATE OF CHANGE which must be standardized. Huntsman and Sparks (1924), for example, raised the temperature of the sea water by 1°C every five minutes until the animals died; Tsukuda (1960) raises or lowers the temperature at a steady rate of 0.5°C per minute until temperature coma is observed. The second type of test involving an exposure to one lethal level presents no problem when the majority of the animals are soon killed by the lethal agent. However, if by definition the lethal level is the level which kills after an indefinite exposure, then, obviously, the experimenter must decide how long the lethal tests are to last. In practice, it is usually possible to determine from the course of the mortality curve whether the lethal agent is continuing to operate and to adjust the experimental procedures accordingly. In lethal temperature work tests have been continued for 12 to 14 hours or even as long as seven days because various species react so differently (Brett, 1956). In general, tests involving sudden exposure to the lethal environment are preferred since there is less chance of acclimation during the test and since the data are more readily susceptible to standard statistical methods of analysis. Most determinations of lethal levels follow this technique.

The analytical techniques have been carefully studied by toxicologists and are described in many places (Bliss, 1952; Burn *et al.*, 1950). They will not be detailed here, but several points are mentioned to facilitate understanding of the physiological literature. The analyses are based on the normal variability which every population shows with respect to its morphological and physiological characteristics. There are giants and dwarfs; there are also individuals which are extremely resistant and others which are particularly susceptible. In between there are the average individuals that make up most of the population. In short, we are usually dealing with a normal distribution curve, and its pattern is the same whether the measurements are sizes of animals or their incipient lethal levels.

The pioneer work was carried out by pharmacologists in their attempts to standardize drugs by bioassay techniques (Burn *et al.*, 1950). In one of the earliest studies the lethal dose of digitalis was determined for each of 573 cats; the lethal doses were distributed around a mean value in the pattern of the normal distribution curve. In another very precise early investigation, 146 frogs were slowly infused with *k*-strophanthin until they died. When the frequency of deaths at different lethal doses was plotted a distribution of the same type was obtained. These pioneer data are shown in Fig. 9.2.

The average individual is represented by the peak of the curve, and this dose (the median lethal dose or LD_{50}) is the best representation of the lethal dose for the sample. In actual practice it is not determined from data such as those shown in Fig. 9.2. On the contrary, relatively small samples are used; different samples are exposed to a single lethal dose, and a graded series of doses is used; the one which kills 50 per cent of the animals in the test period is recorded as the LD_{50}. Usually five or six dose levels are sufficient to estimate the 50 per cent level when these are appropriately analyzed (Fig. 9.3). The mathematics has been carefully studied, and easy graphical methods are now available for the ready determination of lethal levels. These methods are based on the fact that the bell-shaped dose mortality curve becomes a sigmoid when cumulated deaths (or per cent dead) are plotted against the dose or the log dose, as was evident in the very early studies of cats and frogs (Fig. 9.2). A close approximation to the LD_{50} can often be obtained directly from such a sigmoid; for precise comparisons it is rectified through the probit transformation which converts it into a straight line (Fig. 9.3). The LD_{50} values can be obtained from these curves, or the lines can be compared by standard methods of linear regression analysis.

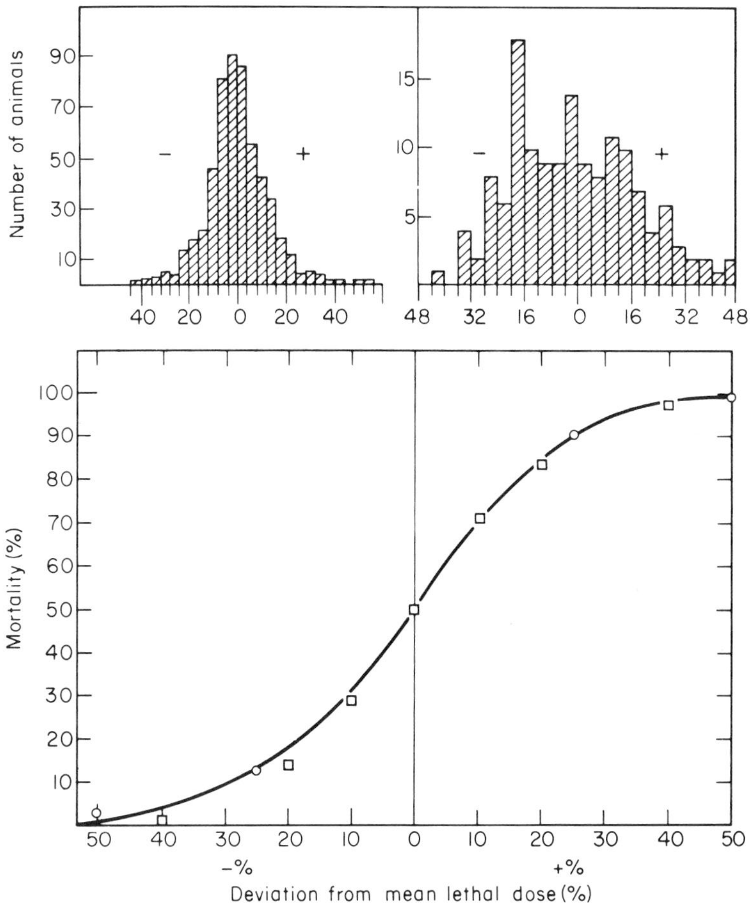

Fig. 9.2. Dose-mortality relationships. Upper left panel, distribution about mean value of the lethal dose of digitalis for different cats. The abcissa *O* represents the mean with lethal doses given in percentages below and above the mean. Upper right panel, same for lethal doses of strophanthin for frogs. Lower graph, frog data plotted as percent mortality (ordinate) with circles for digitalis and squares for strophanthin. [After Burn, Finney and Goodwin (1950).]

The zone of tolerance illustrated in Fig. 9.1 is bounded by points representing temperatures at which 50 per cent of the sample died in tests lasting 14 hours. This provides the best representation of the way in which the population may be expected to respond to a single lethal

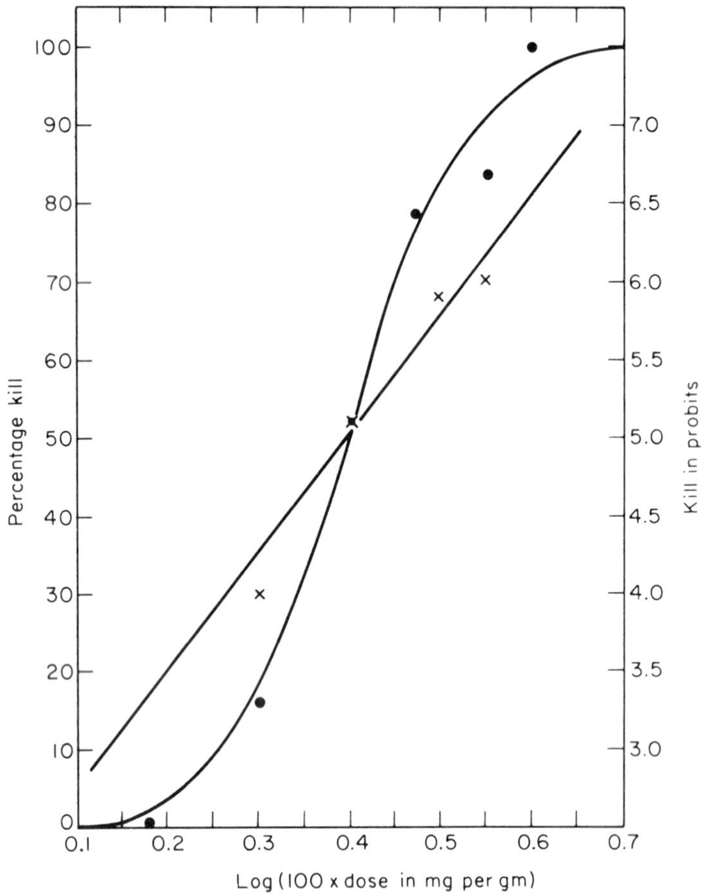

Fig. 9.3. Toxicity of cocaine hydrochloride to mice plotted as percent kill (sigmoid curve) and as probits (straight line) against log dose. [Burn, Finney and Goodwin (1950).]

factor. It is, in a sense, the mean reaction for a sample. However, there are times when the experimentalist may wish to evaluate the level which will kill all of the population or, alternatively, permit them all to survive. The trapezoid could just as well have been drawn for 5 per cent deaths and 95 per cent survival or any other level. The area would vary accordingly.

It should also be emphasized that the trapezoid (Fig. 9.1) is a zone of survival in the face of environmental change. It does not describe, in any way, the effects of this change on various vital processes such as growth, activity or reproduction. It is known, for example, that young salmon fail to grow at temperatures slightly above the lower lethal level and slightly below the upper lethal level. Thus a trapezoid representing tolerance levels for growth would be considerably smaller. Environmental limits for reproduction may be even narrower. Additional areas could be marked off to show the environmental variation compatible with each of several different activities.

PHYSIOLOGICAL COMPENSATION IN THE ZONE OF TOLERANCE

There are two different kinds of physiological compensation for successful living in altered environments. Many animals have tissues with the capacity to operate over wide ranges. In these the internal environment reflects the external environment, and changes in the latter are followed by corresponding alterations in the former. The temperature of a spider crab fluctuates with that of its surroundings; it is said to be POIKILOTHERMIC (poikilos = manifold). The osmotic content of the body fluids of the polychaete worm *Arenicola* almost matches that of the sea water over a range of dilutions down to about 12 per cent; it is said to be POIKILOSMOTIC. The physiological processes of these animals operate well at a series of different temperatures or under varying osmotic conditions. They exemplify an environmental compensation referred to as CONFORMITY or ADJUSTMENT (Fig. 9.4).

In contrast to the conformers, many animals preserve relatively constant conditions in their tissues. They control or regulate their internal environment and are killed if this fluctuates beyond rather narrow limits. Temperature variations or fluctuations in osmotic and other environmental conditions activate the regulatory homeostatic machinery which preserves the constancy of the internal environment. Excess heat is dissipated or heat is generated to make good the losses; water taken in osmotically from a dilute solution is excreted, and ions are absorbed to compensate for those lost through excessive water removal. The homeothermic or the homeosmotic condition is maintained. The animal is said to show REGULATION as opposed to the CONFORMITY (or adjustment) displayed by the first examples (Fig. 9.4).

At least two different types of regulation are frequently observed. The type already mentioned depends on the homeostatic machinery of the animal – primarily the integrated responses of the autonomic nervous system and the hormones. In addition, many animals show behavioral responses which likewise compensate for environmental change. Terrestrial isopods, for example, become active when the humidity falls and crawl at random (kinesis) until they once more find a humid habitat where they become quiet. Many animals in a gradient of an environmental variable such as temperature, humidity or salinity will move about while they are in less favorable areas and remain quiet when they arrive in the more favorable ones. The environment in this case is acting as a DIRECTIVE FACTOR, and the preferendum response results in a behavioral regulation as opposed to the physiological regulation associated with homeostasis.

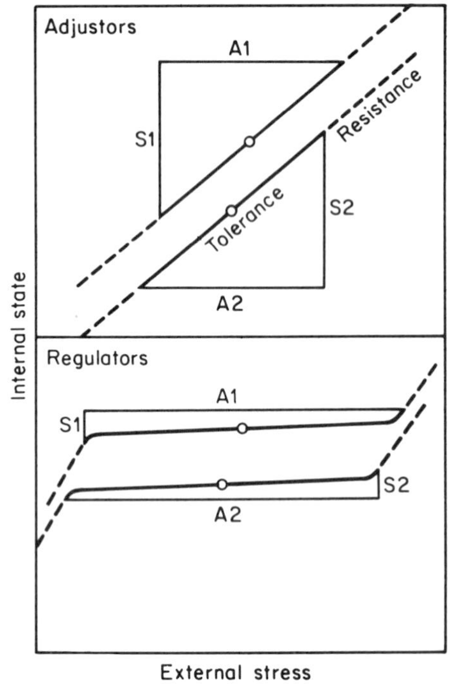

Fig. 9.4. Diagram illustrating the relation between external stress and internal state for the physiological adjustors or conformers (above) and the physiological regulators (below) at two levels of acclimation (*A*1 and *A*2). Note the difference in change of internal states (*S*1 and *S*2) for the two types. [Brett (1958) based on Prosser (1955).]

Prosser (1955) refers to these functional properties of animals which favor their continued successful living in altered environments as PHYSIOLOGICAL ADAPTATION. However, the term adaptation has several different usages in biology, and for this reason the term COMPENSATION will be used here.

RESISTANCE TO EXTREME CONDITIONS

Within the zone of resistance, the physiological mechanisms are taxed so heavily that they eventually collapse. If the lethal factor is not far beyond its incipient level, the deterioration will be slow; if conditions are extreme, death will be sudden. Consequently, the changes which might be traced in an organism while it continues to exist in this zone will vary, and no description can satisfy all the cases. The ultimate failure may occur at any level from the enzyme system to the morphological or chemical organization of the cells, from the particularly susceptible organs or tissues—such as the mammalian cerebrum in anoxia—to the complex homeostatic machinery of the higher vertebrate. All levels may be affected simultaneously, but there is probably one particularly vulnerable link which finally breaks. Extreme heat will quickly coagulate proteins; but less excessive temperatures may merely alter adversely the rates of enzyme activity. Either change can kill the cell, although the temporal relations and cytological alterations will be very different.

The mammalian physiologists have accumulated an impressive body of literature on the harmful effects of extreme conditions on the autonomic nervous and endocrine systems. In many cases the collapse of the pituitary-adrenal system seems to be ultimately responsible for death. Selye (1949, 1961) has emphasized this in his concept of "stress." Any one of a variety of damaging agents such as trauma, extreme temperatures, poisons, infections or social stimulation, can produce a series of stereotyped physiological responses in a mammal. These are essentially the same for all "stressors." When, for example, rats or other laboratory animals have been exposed to prolonged low temperatures, or subjected to trauma, or injected many times with small amounts of formalin, or repeatedly damaged in any one of a variety of ways, there are characteristic changes in the blood constants, in the circulatory machinery and in the lymphatic tissues. In particular, there is an excessive activation of the adrenal cortex; this seems to be a very fundamental response to "stress." Stimulation of the hypothalamus, directly by way of neural pathways or indirectly through the sympathetic nervous release of adrenaline, increases the production of ACTH (often at the expense of other pituitary hormones such as the gonadotropins or growth hormone) and hence the activation of the adrenal cortex. The corticoids mobilize glucose and in other ways meet the demands produced when homeostasis is drastically altered. Resistance is maintained for a time, but eventually the pituitary-adrenal mechanisms fail, and a condition of adrenal insufficiency develops which produces circulatory collapse and other systemic changes found in "stress." The medical physiologist has accumulated convincing evidence for this sequence of changes through his studies of adrenalectomized animals and the effects of injected steroids and ACTH, as well as comparisons of animals maintained under many kinds of altered environments. The higher vertebrates, with their more precise homeostatic controls, are most susceptible; but a similar, although less extreme, picture also develops in many of the lower vertebrates under comparable conditions (Hoar, 1965*a*). It is conceivable that the more complex invertebrates respond to environmental extremes in a comparable way.

Temperature 10

Within an animal's zone of tolerance, temperature change frequently produces a prompt, direct and proportional alteration in the rate of its physiological processes, although the range of temperature for which these relationships hold is usually not more than 10° to 20°C. At temperatures not far outside the normal range biological processes are retarded or completely inhibited. Thus, for many phenomena there is a TEMPERATURE OPTIMUM; this has been demonstrated many times in such diverse processes as the growth rates of fish, the luminescence of bacteria and the movements of animals (Fig. 10.1). Enzyme-catalyzed reactions follow the same pattern, and the obvious explanations are in terms of the chemical reactants.

This line of argument was at one time extended to the concept of a MASTER OR CONTROLLING REACTION for each of the many different physiological processes. It was postulated that the dominant enzyme reaction for complex activities like heart-beat or breathing might be identified by studying the temperature relations and comparing them with different enzyme reactions. This concept was never fully satisfactory and has now been largely discarded, even though it is recognized that some physiological processes may be dominated by one important enzymatic activity or another. Biological phenomena are exceedingly complex and involve temperature-dependent physical (diffusion, absorption) as well as chemical phenomena. Whether chemical or physical, they depend on molecular activities, and their bases should be sought in physico-chemical terms. The fact that there is no simple or single description for temperature effects on physiological activities should not discredit the approach nor lead to its discard in favor of purely empirical relationships such as those proposed by Bělehrádek and others (Bělehrádek, 1930; Johnson *et al.*, 1954).

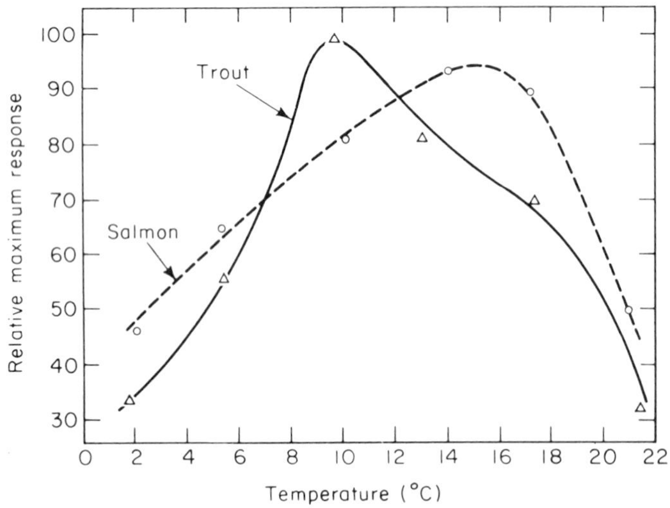

Fig. 10.1. Maximum distance moved by salmon and trout in response to an electrical stimulus at different temperatures. [Fisher and Elson (1950).]

Temperature and the Rates of Biological Activities

Arrhenius, in the latter part of the nineteenth and early twentieth century, first deduced the relationships which are used by both chemists and biologists to describe the effects of temperature on reaction velocity. From a study of the rate of hydrolysis of sucrose he formulated the empirical relationship:

$$\frac{d \ln k}{dT} = \frac{A}{RT^2}$$

where k is the reaction velocity constant, T is the absolute temperature, R is the gas constant (1.987 cal per degree per mole) and A is a constant, the significance of which remained to be demonstrated. The integrated form of the equation between temperatures T_1 and T_2 corresponding to reaction velocities k_1 and k_2 is:

$$\ln \frac{k_2}{k_1} = \frac{A}{R}\left[\frac{1}{T_1} - \frac{1}{T_2}\right]$$

Hence, a straight line relationship may be expected when the ln k is plotted against the reciprocal of the absolute temperature, $1/T$ as shown in Fig. 10.2. The slope of the line is equal to A/R or approximately $A/2$ if natural logarithms are used ($A/2.303R$ if the rate was plotted as $\log_{10}$ reaction velocity). The value of the constant A for a great many enzymatic reactions and biological processes falls between 1000 and 25,000 cal. In some of his later studies of complicated biological reactions, Arrhenius used the term μ instead of A for the constant, and this symbol is now universally used by biologists and referred to as the "critical thermal increment," the "apparent activation energy" or the "temperature characteristic." Its significance was not apparent when the formula was first deduced, and a quarter of a century or more passed before the constant A or μ secured a firm theoretical and experimental basis. A historical account of physical chemistry with theoretical discussions of the constant will be found in texts of cell physiology and molecular biology (Johnson *et al.*, 1954). Only a brief comment is given here.

Chemical reactions depend on molecular collisions and interactions at the electronic level. Thus, temperature change may be expected to alter reaction rates through its effects on molecular activity and the kinetic energy of the reaction system The physical chemists of the nineteenth century noted, however, that the temperature effect was much greater than would be expected on this basis, and thus Arrhenius introduced the hypothesis of an activated state. According to this theory all elementary rate processes (diffusion, solubility, oxidation, hydrolysis) can be considered unstable equilibria between reactants or molecules in the normal state and those in an activated condition (Johnson *et al.*, 1954). In short, of the numerous molecular collisions which occur in a reaction system, only that small fraction which involves active molecules will result in chemical change. These active complexes are very rapidly formed with rising temperatures, so that reaction rates go up by about 12 per cent per degree, in contrast to less than 1 per cent which would be the case if only the increase in average kinetic energy of the molecules in the system were considered.

Experimental evidence in physical chemistry is in full agreement with this theory. Subsequent developments have provided formulae for the calculation of the changes in activation energy associated with temperature alterations (Maxwell-Boltzmann distribution law). The precise meaning of this activated state can only be obtained from an understanding of advanced quantum and statistical mechanics; but the Arrhenius constant A or μ can be appreciated from these brief comments. For our purposes, this constant represents the energy which molecules in their initial state must acquire before they can participate in a chemical reaction. It is the energy of activation for the particular chemical reaction of biological process and remains constant at least over a limited temperature range. Thus, the hydrolysis of β-glycerophosphate by bone phosphatase has a μ value of 9940 cal over the range of 10° to 40°C; the rate of creeping of ants, the chirping of crickets and the flashing of fireflies have μ values in the neighborhood of 12,200 cal; respiratory and cardiac rhythms show higher μ values of about 16,700 cal (Fruton and Simmonds, 1957).

In many cases the value of μ does not remain constant over the temperature range compatible with the particular activity. Marked changes are common in simple enzyme-catalyzed reactions as well as in complex physiological processes (Fig. 10.2). Crozier (1924–25 and later) interpreted these changes in terms of master or controlling reactions which governed the overall rate of complex physiological processes. According to the Crozier theory, a physiological process depends on a catenary series of reactions, each with its characteristic critical thermal increment; the rate of the entire process is governed by the slowest reaction in the series, and this is the master reaction. The μ value for a complex physiological activity is the μ value of the slowest step.

In a general way, this much of the theory is probably true since temperature may have a much more significant influence on one type of process than it has on another. Photochemical reactions, for example, have much lower μ values than thermochemical ones. A process such as photosynthesis which involves both photochemical and thermochemical processes, may show very different μ values over a range of temperatures. At lower temperatures, the limiting factor is the rate at which light quanta can be absorbed (a photochemical process); this is characterized by a much lower μ value than the thermochemical or enzymatic reactions which control the rate of photosynthesis at higher temperatures where the chlorophyll machinery is saturated with radiant energy (Giese, 1962). This concept of the limiting or master reaction which was developed earlier (Blackman–Pütter principle) has remained a part of the thinking of the general physiologist and has found a place in the discussions of the environmental physiologist (Chapter 9; Fry, 1947; Johnson *et al.*, 1954).

Crozier went further, however, and argued that the sharp changes in the slope of the Arrhenius plot (Fig. 10.2) represented a change from one master reaction to another and that it should be possible to identify the master reactions from their μ values. This is an appealing hypothesis and was the basis of considerable research during the early years of the present century. The hope of identifying precise master reactions, however, was never realized, and the expectation of this now seems somewhat

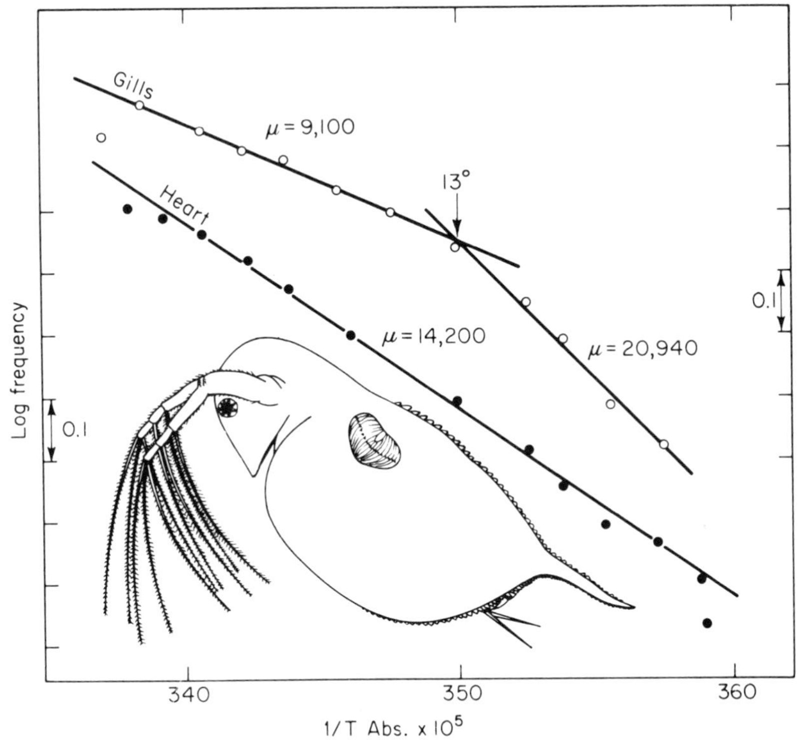

Fig. 10.2. Temperature characteristics for heart rate and respiratory movements in *Daphnia*. [Data from Stier and Wolf (1932) after Barnes (1937).]

illogical. Activities such as the creeping of ants, the breathing of frogs or any one of the many other phenomena examined are as liable to be limited by physical phenomena such as diffusion, viscosity or protein denaturation as they are by the enzyme-catalyzed processes emphasized by Crozier. There must often be an interaction of several potentially limiting processes, physical as well as chemical, and it is not surprising that the relationship between velocity and temperature can sometimes be better represented by a curve than by a series of straight lines with sharp breaks (Fig. 10.2). Excellent discussions of these theories are available.

The critical thermal increment, even though its significance in terms of specific physiological reactions is uncertain, remains the most realistic of the several temperature characteristics which biologists have used to describe temperature effects on reaction rates. It is not the simplest, however; the familiar Q_{10} value (calculated readily from the same data used in determining μ) is frequently as useful as the critical thermal increment for descriptive purposes. Q_{10} is the increase in reaction velocity caused by a 10°C rise in temperature. Thus:

$$Q_{10} = \frac{k_{t+10}}{k_t}$$

where k_t is the velocity constant at temperature t and k_{t+10} the velocity constant at 10°C higher. The value is easily calculated with data obtained over any temperature range from the general formula:

$$Q_{10} = \left(\frac{k_1}{k_2}\right)^{10/(t_1-t_2)} \quad \text{or} \quad \log Q_{10} = \frac{10\,(\log k_1 - \log k_2)}{t_1 - t_2}$$

where k_1 and k_2 are the velocities at t_1 and t_2 respectively.

Numerous Q_{10} values have been tabulated. Like μ values, they vary somewhat with temperature range and the conditions of the material. In general, however, Q_{10} values associated with physical processes such as diffusion or conductivity and those associated with photochemical reactions are less than 1.5, while thermochemical (enzymatic) reactions range from 2 to 3. Values for protein coagulation and heat death are much higher; the Q_{10} for coagulation of egg albumen is 635 and of hemoglobin, 13.8 (Giese, 1962). Similar ranges have been recorded for heat death of protozoans (891–1000) and of rabbit leucocytes (28.8).

PHYSIOLOGICAL COMPENSATION FOR RATE-LIMITING TEMPERATURE EFFECTS

These, then are the rules which govern the effects of temperature on reaction rates. At the molecular level, the varied life processes are governed by a logarithmic law relating velocity of reaction to the temperature.

Free life has escaped the rigidity of this Arrhenius relationship, and some of the most significant steps in organic evolution were made in exploring these escape routes. Among the poikilothermic animals, physiological compensations adjust rates and activities to seasonally changing temperatures and to latitudes. A study of cardiac or respiratory rhythm at a series of temperatures during the summer may indicate that these processes would be almost suspended during the winter. This is not the case. On the contrary, acclimatization may lead to similar rates at both seasons. Likewise, the same animal species in different latitudes may show similar or identical rates even though the temperatures vary greatly. The species has escaped "from the tyranny of a simple application of the Arrhenius equation" (Barcroft, 1934). Among homeothermic animals temperature compensation, which in the poikilotherm occurs at the cellular and biochemical level, depends more particularly on a specialized thermostat in the brain; this controls the body's regulating machinery so that the internal environment is temperature-constant.

Homeothermism was one of the most progressive steps in animal phylogeny. It took place in the evolution of the brain; perhaps its greatest significance has to do with the constant rates and the continuous high level of activity provided for nervous coordination. Barcroft (1934) was the first to discuss these matters in a lucid way. In his words "Here then is a very fine issue—the cold-blooded animal successfully adopting ingenious mechanisms, first biochemical, then physiological, in order to adapt its heart to the variations of its environment; the warm-blooded animal discarding what its cold-blooded predecessor has laboriously beaten out, invoking the nervous system to reverse the normal biochemical relationship and gaining a new freedom by adapting, not itself to the internal environment, but the internal environment to itself." The mechanisms associated with temperature compensation are so radically different in these two animal groups that their physiology will be discussed separately in the following sections.

Temperature Compensation in Poikilotherms

The theoretical consequences of the temperature-variable environment are shown in Fig. 10.3. As indicated by the solid line, raising or lowering the temperature by 10°C will alter the rates of the physiological processes according to the Q_{10} coefficient of about 2. In the laboratory such effects are readily demonstrated. It is obvious that a strict adherence to the van't Hoff--Arrhenius relationships in life processes would result in markedly different seasonal rates and latitudinal differences. As a matter of fact, this is the exception rather than the rule. The immediate consequences of a temperature change such as that shown in Fig. 10.3 are usually followed by gradual compensations (capacity adaptation) which often bring the altered rate back to the original rate or somewhere near it. Following the terminology of Precht (1958) and Prosser (1958), the compensation is referred to as "perfect" if the original rate is attained, or "partial" if an intermediate condition occurs. Examples of "over" and "under" compensation have also been described (Prosser and Brown, 1961).

This type of description can be extended by measuring the velocity of a physiological process at a series of temperatures. The velocity-temperature curves thus obtained may show rather different patterns in

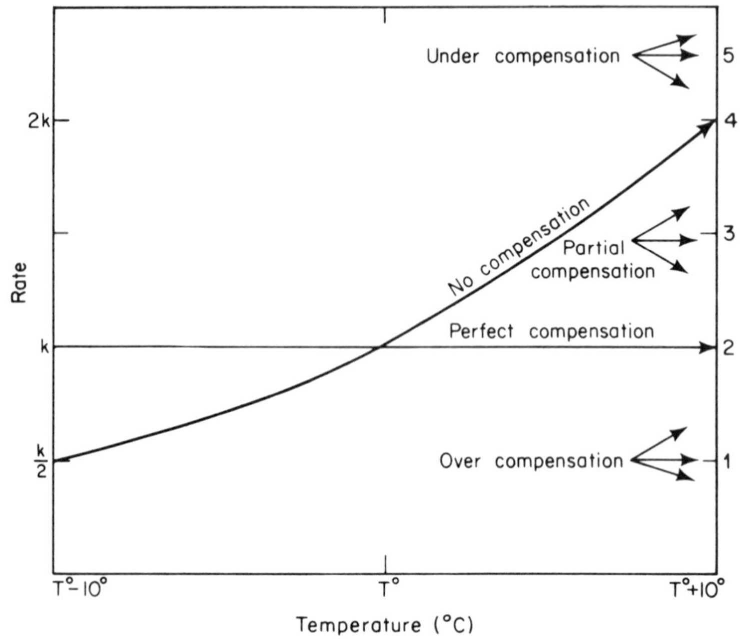

Fig. 10.3. Effect of temperature change on the rate of a biological process. The "No compensation" line shows the immediate effect, based on a Q_{10} of 2.0. Other lines and points show various degrees of compensation which have been recognized. Numbers at the right are the numerical types described by Precht (see text).

relation to the thermal history of the organism. If, for example, metabolic rates of "winter" and "summer" animals are compared at a series of temperatures, the velocity-temperature curves will be expected to fall along one line if no temperature compensation has taken place between winter and summer (Fig. 10.4) but show different positions if the basic biochemical controls have been altered. Several different patterns have been described. The curves are said to show "translation" (Fig. 10.5) if the winter and summer lines are parallel and "rotation" if they are crossed (Fig. 10.6). Prosser and Brown (1961) give many examples.

These changes in position indicate alterations at the molecular level during the seasonal adjustments. Probable physiological mechanisms are suggested below, but the molecular basis is not completely understood for any of the examples.

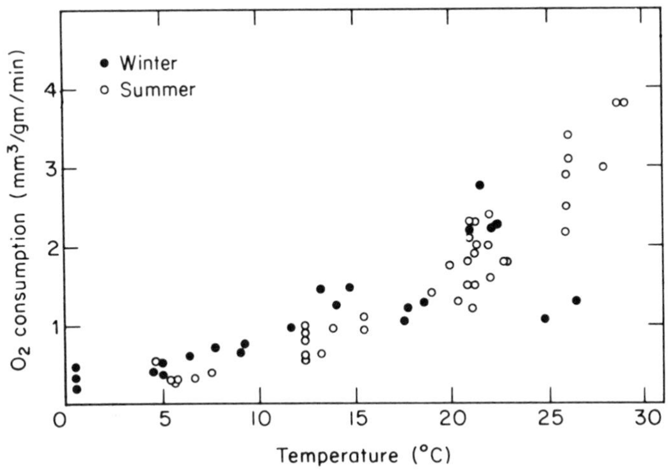

Fig. 10.4 The metabolism of a teleost fish *Tautogolabrus adspersus* during the winter and summer showing little or no seasonal temperature compensation in the rate of function. [Data from Haugaard and Irving (1943).]

The environmental physiologist has made excellent progress in describing the different patterns of temperature compensation. In addition to the type of description suggested in Figs. 10.3 to 10.5, instructive graphical representations of temperature relations may be based on the models of Fry and his students (Fry, 1947; Brett, 1956). The explanation of the physiology is much less satisfactory. It is usual to recognize three levels at which temperature compensation may occur; acclimation, acclimatization and phylogenetic adaptation. The terms were defined in the preceding chapter. However, even though temperature relations can be altered experimentally or naturally in these three ways, it does not follow that three different physiological processes are involved. At the cellular or molecular level there may be a single critical mechanism susceptible to thermal compensation, although it seems more likely that several processes respond during temperature adjustment or deteriorate under lethal conditions.

MECHANISMS FOR TEMPERATURE COMPENSATION

The action of temperature on biological processes may be modified by alterations in the enzymes, their substrates or the reaction media. At this level, temperature compensation is a BIOCHEMICAL AND CELLULAR PROCESS; it represents the most primitive level of adjustment

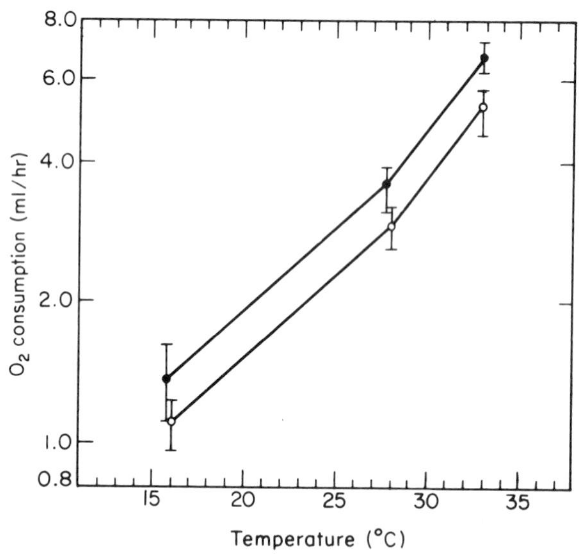

Fig. 10.5. Oxygen consumption of the lizard *Sceloporus occidentalis* maintained for 5 weeks at 16°C (black symbols) and at 33°C (open symbols). Vertical bars, + and − two standard deviations of the mean. This shows a TRANSLATION of the rate-function curve with temperature acclimation. [Based on data in Dawson and Bartholomew (1956).]

(Chapter 2). At the organ-system level of the multicellular animal, temperature effects may be more critical in one tissue or organ system than in another, even though all physiological processes are based on enzyme-catalyzed reactions. In the higher vertebrates the NEUROENDOCRINE system attains the ultimate control by regulating the temperature of the entire organism; even among lower forms a measure of neuroendocrine adjustment of physiological processes occurs. In addition, BEHAVIORAL responses may assist in the adaptation to changing thermal environments. The mechanisms for thermal compensation in the poikilotherms can thus be conveniently considered as biochemical, neuroendocrine and behavioral.

Biochemical and cellular adjustments. Here the adjustments involve enzymes, substrates and reaction media. Extensive research on the biochemistry of temperature compensation and thermal death has focussed attention on adjustments in the water content of the tissues, the temperature relations of the enzyme reactions, the structure of the proteins, the

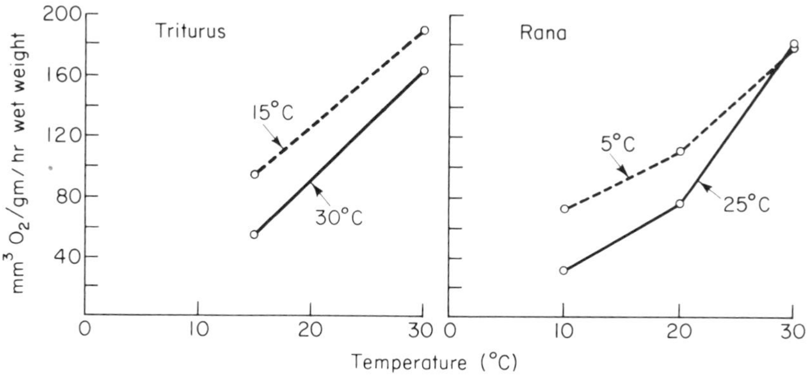

Fig. 10.6. Total oxygen consumption for the amphibians *Triturus viridescens* and *Rana pipiens* acclimated to the two temperatures shown on the graph and measured at a series of ambient temperatures as shown on the horizontal axis. The lines for *Triturus* show TRANSLATION and those for *Rana* show a clockwise ROTATION combined with translation. [Based on Rieck *et al.* (1960).]

organization of the lipids (especially those of the protoplasmic membranes) and the formation of toxic by-products.

Metabolism takes place in an aqueous solution, and consequently life is only possible while water is in the liquid state. The actual biokinetic range is narrower than the temperature range for liquid water (0° to 100°C) and rarely exceeds 10° to 45°C. Temperatures outside these limits either inhibit vital enzyme reactions or bring about irreversible changes in proteins and lipids.

In very cold environments, several adjustments are known to prevent water crystallization which damages cells either through a mechanical disruption of their organization or merely by removing the solvent (water) from the reaction medium, leading to excessively high concentrations of solutes. The latter effect is probably the more damaging since it usually occurs first in the interstitial spaces and leads to osmotic desiccation of the cells. The tissues of some intertidal animals have been shown to tolerate considerable ice formation. Mussels and periwinkles have been found to survive at −22°C for months in the Arctic, with about 75 per cent of their body water frozen and their tissue fluids four times the normal concentration. These forms are evidently able to tolerate dehydration and high salinity as well as quantities of ice (Smith, 1958). This tolerance of high salinity must require very real compensations at the molecular level; it is well known that strong salt solutions denature proteins and dissolve lipoproteins (Smith, 1954).

It is important to note that low-temperature death may occur at temperatures well above freezing (10° to 15°C in warm-acclimated fishes, Fig. 9.1) and that heat death occurs well below the boiling point of water. It is likewise known that a gradual temperature change is much less damaging than a sudden one. Bacteria (*B. coli*, for example) are killed if cooled suddenly from 37°C to 0°C, but they may be gradually cooled to this same temperature without damage even though the cooling period is only 30 minutes (Smith, 1954). There are many similar examples in species ranging from the protozoans to the vertebrates. The hazards of EXTREME temperatures (ice formation, for example) cannot be denied, but thermal death may be expected at temperatures well above the freezing and far below the vaporization of water.

In a test tube, ice formation at temperatures below zero can be avoided by rapid cooling which either leads to the formation of minute crystals or to an amorphous solidification (vitrification); a number of lower organisms have been experimentally taken to very low temperatures in this way and shown to survive. Ice formation can also be avoided by supercooling, a phenomenon easily demonstrated by cooling water or a solution while avoiding agitation. In this way, temperatures considerably below zero develop without ice formation; crystallization occurs rapidly when these supercooled fluids are agitated or "seeded" with an ice crystal or other particulate matter.

This phenomenon has been recognized in nature where fish living in the deep waters off Labrador were shown to have body fluids with freezing points of −0.95°C in waters at −1.75°C. Thus, they are swimming about in a supercooled state with body temperatures about 0.8°C below the freezing point of their blood; they freeze when their bodies are seeded with ice, even though they are surrounded by fluid (Smith, 1958). Insects may also be supercooled to temperatures as low as −30° to −40°C. Unlike the Arctic fishes studied by Scholander, some insects (the European corn borer, for example) can survive freezing subsequent to supercooling (Smith, 1958). Studies of the European corn borer showed that the physiology was subject to seasonal acclimatization, since summer and autumn insects, in contrast to the winter and spring ones, could not tolerate freezing.

Finally, the damaging effects of low temperature may be avoided by altering the freezing points. The freezing point of any solution is lower than that of the pure solvent; a molal solution of any non-electrolyte has a freezing point of −1.86°C. Thus, an increase in the osmotic content of the body fluids will lower the freezing point and, other things being equal, protect the organism from the damage of ice formation. This phenomenon is well recognized both in insects and in fishes. Winter "hardened" insects may show a fantastic increase in the osmotic content of the hemolymph and this, coupled with their capacities for supercooling (down to −47.2°C in overwintering larvae of *Bracon cephi*, a parasite of the wheat stem sawfly), produces the lowest temperature tolerances yet recorded in multicellular animals.

Salt (1959, 1961) showed that glycerol was the solute mainly responsible for this remarkable phenomenon. In *Bracon* the concentrations may rise to 5 molal at the time of hibernation. This depresses the freezing point of the hemolymph to −17.5°C. Glycerol has several properties which make it a particularly useful metabolite in low-temperature resistance (Smith, 1954). It has a strong tendency to supercool, partly due to its high viscosity. Although its melting point is +18.0°C, it is seldom seen in the crystalline state. Small amounts of water depress its freezing point and, conversely, it depresses the freezing point of aqueous solutions. Its utility as an "antifreeze" is well known to the layman, while biologists find it a most useful medium for the low-temperature storage of sperm and blood cells. The literature is discussed in textbooks of cell physiology.

Scholander and associates (1957) found that shallow-water fishes in the fjords of northern Labrador are swimming about in ice water at −1.7° to −1.8°C protected by an unidentified solute (not chloride) which develops with the onset of winter and doubles the osmoconcentration of their body fluids. The invertebrates remain isosmotic both summer and winter and hence cannot freeze as long as they remain in the water. Intertidal forms were mentioned above.

The proportions of "bound" and "free" water can also change. Metabolism occurs only in the "free" water; the "bound" water is loosely held through hydrogen bonding of water dipoles to the polar groups of the proteins and thus becomes an integral part of protoplasmic structure. It is free of solutes and unavailable as a reaction medium or as a reactant. About 4.5 per cent of the water is said to be in this form (Giese, 1962). Changes in the proportions of "bound" and "free" water have been recorded during thermal acclimation, and there are several ways in which this might be of significance in temperature compensation, although attempts to develop a general hypothesis of thermal adjustment based on it have not been convincing (Smith, 1954; Fry, 1958; Allen, 1960*a*).

Effects of temperature on enzyme reaction rates were discussed earlier in this chapter and also in Chapter 2. The significant point to be added here is that changes in the nature of the enzyme systems occur during thermal compensation and are assumed to form a part of the adjustment. In goldfish acclimated to low temperatures, for example, the metabolic pathways for carbohydrate metabolism are partially shifted from the usual Embden–Meyerhof route (Chapter 7) to the hexose-monophosphate or pentose path (Hochachka and Hayes, 1962). The significance of the shift has not been explained. Other enzyme shifts have also been noted during temperature compensation (Precht, 1958), and although their full significance is not yet understood, they are evidence of major adjustments at the enzyme level. At high temperatures, the enzymes as well as other proteins are denatured, and this may sometimes be the ultimate cause of death. Denaturation is a process in which molecular bonds (particularly the secondary and tertiary bonds) are broken so that a disordered arrangement of the molecules results (Anfinsen, 1959). The denatured protein is so altered that its metabolic or structural potentialities are ruined.

Many years ago it was suggested that a disorganization of the lipids might be as significant as the changes in the proteins and further, that temperature compensation depended on adjustments in the nature of these fatty materials, particularly those of the cell membrane. It was noted that animals of the same species from different latitudes often show characteristic differences in tissue fats. Salmon from northern Pacific waters, for example, have fats with lower melting points than those from more southern areas, and similar differences were recorded in several other groups of animals (Heilbrunn, 1952). The character of the body lipids seems to be correlated with environmental temperatures.

Experimental evidence is in agreement. At the very beginning of the present century, Swedish scientists dressed pigs in sheepskin coats and, after two months, compared their body fats with those of controls maintained at about 0°C and about 35°C; the findings were consistent with the theory that an elevated temperature (through insulation) will increase the melting point of the body fats. Similar results were obtained by acclimating fishes and tadpoles to different temperatures. Heilbrunn (1952), who discusses these and many other examples, developed a hypothesis for thermal death based on the disorganization of the cell membrane through the melting of the lipids. He argued that calcium ions were released in this way from the cell membrane and outer cortex of the cell where they are particularly significant in stabilizing these more gelatinous layers. However, the melting point is only one of the lipid characters which changes during temperature compensation; alterations in cholesterol and phospholipids have also been recorded. Although temperature relations of poikilotherms can be altered in a predictable manner by changing the tissue lipids, a general theory for temperature compensation based on the lipids has proved no more satisfactory than those based on the "bound" and "free" water (Fisher, 1958; Fry, 1958). This does not mean that compensatory changes are not taking place in the lipids; they are probably occurring in many of the cellular constituents (fats, proteins, water) which operate in an integrated way during normal metabolism.

Finally, various metabolites may appear in excess at extreme temperatures, and these may alter protoplasm and contribute to the lethal process. Toxic substances, such as histamine which increases cell permeability, or thromboplastic materials which coagulate protein, have often been identified in injured tissues. Within the ZONE OF TOLERANCE adjustments occur in the enzymes, the substrates and the reaction media; within the ZONE OF RESISTANCE denaturation of the proteins, disorganization of the lipids, changes in the distribution of water and electrolytes and the development of toxic materials are some of the factors which lead to cellular death.

Neuroendocrine mechanisms. It has been suggested that heat death in larger organisms is ultimately due to some failure in the nervous system, with a loss of indispensable reflexes such as cardiac or respiratory rhythm. Many years ago Battle (1926, 1929) tested the responsiveness of different tissues at a series of progressively rising temperatures and found that such processes as the automaticity of the heart, myoneural junctions and peristaltic movements in the gut were much more sensitive than tissues such as somatic muscle. Synapses were found to fail at or below the lethal temperature, while some other tissues remained responsive after the animal's death. There are some confirmatory data for other species (Fisher, 1958). Battle also found distinct differences between the resistances of synaptic processes in closely related species of *Raja* and even between small and large individuals of a single species of flounder (*Pseudopleuronectes americanus*). These data suggested a specific locus for failure of vital processes in thermal death.

More recently, Roots and Prosser (1962) have examined the effects of low temperature on caudal reflexes, peripheral nerve conduction, conditioned responses and activity of goldfish (*Carassius auratus*) and bluegills (*Lepomis macrochirus*) acclimated to a series of temperatures. Peripheral nerve conduction continued at temperatures lower than those required to block the caudal reflexes; the reflexes were, in turn, still evident at temperatures lower than those required to block conditioned reflexes. These data indicate that the locus most sensitive to cold is in the central nervous system. Konishi and Hickman (1964) have recorded midbrain potentials of trout at different temperatures in response to optic nerve stimulation. The response pattern is substantially prolonged when fish acclimated to 10°C are transferred to 4°C. With acclimation to the lower temperature, however, there is a progressive decrease in the potential duration at 4°C showing significant compensation. A comparable change was not observed with acclimation to higher temperatures (16°C) and these workers argue that acclimation to low temperatures involves changes in biophysical properties of nervous tissues while high temperature acclimation depends more on metabolic compensation. Further attempts to identify temperature-sensitive loci in the nervous system should prove fruitful.

The endocrine system is also involved in thermal compensation. Seasonal cycles in the endocrine activity of poikilotherms are well documented and may be basic to the temperature acclimatization processes. Goldfish maintained under constant laboratory conditions of temperature show relatively greater resistance to heat during the summer and a relatively greater resistance to cold during the winter (Hoar, 1955*a*). Temperature acclimation is not responsible for the compensation. Since the phenomenon can be partially regulated by altering the photoperiods, it is assumed that the neuroendocrine system (the usual link between the vertebrate photoreceptors and metabolism) is responsible for this compensation (Hoar, 1959). However, many of the details necessary to support the hypothesis have not yet been recorded (Hoar and Eales, 1963).

These examples indicate that in the more complex poikilotherms compensatory changes in the neuroendocrine system play a significant role in temperature compensation. They may have marked the first phylogenetic steps in the evolution of the neuroendocrine controls of the homeothermic animals, but there is at present little pertinent research (Fry, 1958).

Behavioral regulation. This line of argument may be extended to the behavioral regulation shown by several poikilotherms, both invertebrate and vertebrate. Some make use of solar energy, while others utilize metabolic heat to raise their body temperatures. Many different species of animals, when placed in a temperature gradient, have been shown to "prefer" one particular temperature area (Fig. 10.7). They are less active at the PREFERRED TEMPERATURE and thus arrive there by a THERMOKINESIS (Chapter 21).

The terrestrial environment is more prone than the aquatic to sudden temperature changes. The most successful of the terrestrial poikilotherms (insects and reptiles) have made good use of behavioral responses to avoid temperature extremes or to elevate temperatures sufficiently for certain activities. Some of the reptiles have particularly well-developed sensory organs for this purpose. Bullock and his associates (1956, 1957) describe the physiology and anatomy of infrared sense organs in the facial pit of the rattlesnake. These receptors can detect temperature difference of the order of 0.001 to 0.005°C—a sensitivity which is highly valuable in detecting warm-blooded or cool (moist) prey, as well as in orienting the animals to warm or cool environments.

The entomological literature gives many examples of insects which use solar or metabolic energy to warm up before flight. Furthermore, the social insects such as ants, termites and bees may regulate temperatures in their nests or hives through varied activities (Scherba, 1962). Prosser and Brown (1961) cite numerous references to the original literature.

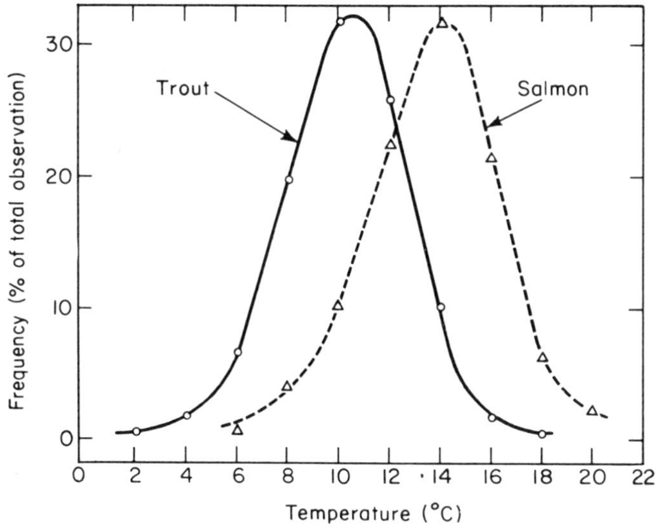

Fig. 10.7. Preferred temperatures of trout and salmon expressed as relative frequencies with which the individuals were observed in different regions of a temperature gradient. [Fisher and Elson (1950).]

Temperature Compensation in Homeotherms

In most mammals the body temperature lies somewhere between 36° and 38°C; in birds it is slightly higher, between 39° and 42°C (King and Farner, 1961). This stabilization of body temperature removes one of the variables of the internal environment and permits a steady high level of activity, both metabolic and locomotory. The advantages (at the metabolic level) are somewhat speculative but very obvious in behavioral, social and cultural evolution demanding continuous associations of individuals. Increasing complexity of organization (especially behavioral organization) makes homeothermy a necessity; or conversely, one may argue that complexity, both physiological and behavioral, becomes progressively more feasible as the internal environmental temperature, especially that of the nervous system, is stabilized. It is none the less curious that all species of mammals or birds should have fixed on about the same body temperature and that this should be of the order of 35° to 40°C rather than, let us say, 10° higher or lower. It may represent a particularly economical level for cellular activity in the environment where the homeotherms first evolved (Dawson, 1962), but again this is speculative (Burton and Edholm, 1955; Young, 1957).

Maintenance of a constant body temperature is a neat balance between heat production and heat loss. It demands a sensitive thermostat in the brain, a capacity not only to use the heat formed as a by-product of metabolism but also to increase the output of metabolic energy in accordance with demands. In addition, it requires several anatomical correlates such as appropriate insulation and special heat exchangers. In extreme conditions the metabolic price of a regulated body temperature may be impossibly high, so that some species temporarily suspend temperature control (torpidity and hibernation) or migrate to more favorable climates. In man, there is a behavioral evasion of extremes with the development of clothing, air conditioning and other technological devices.

PHYLOGENY AND ONTOGENY

Among the homeotherms there is a good general correlation between the precision of temperature control and the complexity of behavioral organization. This is true both phylogenetically and ontogenetically. The variations in body temperature of a series of mammals measured after a two-hour exposure to temperatures ranging from 5° to 35°C are shown in Fig. 10.8. There is a graded series from the poikilothermic reptiles through the primitive mammals (Monotremata and Marsupialia) to the Eutheria.

Likewise, there is variation within the Eutheria; many of them are virtually poikilothermic at birth. Full temperature control is not attained in the newborn rat for seventy-three days (Adolph, 1957). A similar situation is found in many birds (Kendeigh, 1939). Species of homeotherms which are born or hatch in a helpless condition depend for some time on their parents for heat as well as food and shelter; but there are other species which are quite independent at birth and well able to regulate body temperature. The caribou calf is a good example; it can take care of its own heat production even though it is born into an extremely rigorous environment (Hart *et al.*, 1961).

Different species of birds and mammals vary greatly in their temperature-regulating capacity. Some breeds of dogs (also ducks) can withstand an environmental temperature of −100°C FOR ONE HOUR before there is a depression in the "core" temperature of the body. This LOWER CRITICAL TEMPERATURE, as it has been called (Davson, 1959), is by contrast −1°C in naked man, −15° in a porpoise, −30° in a sparrow, −45°

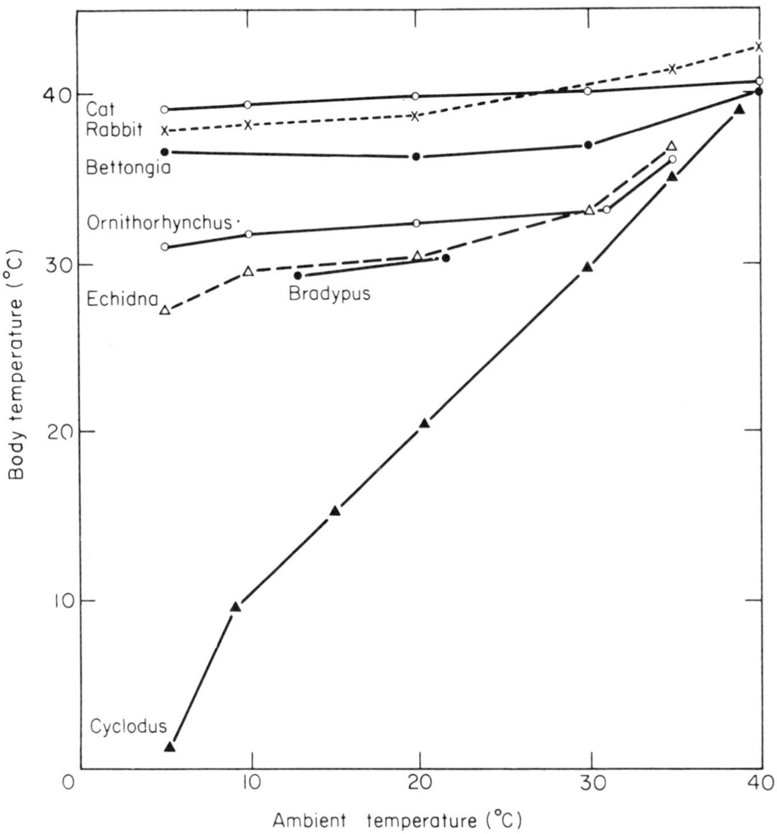

Fig. 10.8. Relationship between body temperature and the ambient temperature for the lizard (*Cyclodus*), the monotremes (*Ornithorhynchus* and *Echidna*), the marsupial (*Bettongia*), the sloth (*Bradypus*, an imperfect homeotherm), and the true homeotherms (cat and rabbit). [Johansen (1962).]

in a rabbit and −90° in a goose (Precht *et al.*, 1955). Several other comparative measurements of temperature resistance are on record. Scholander (1955) defined the CRITICAL TEMPERATURE as the lowest air temperature at which the animal can maintain a resting or basal metabolic rate without losing body temperature. By this criterion, most tropical mammals, including naked man, have critical temperatures between 25° and 27°C while larger arctic mammals such as the fox range from −30° to −40°C. In smaller species such as the lemming it is considerably higher (about +15°C). The variability in metabolic rate which appears long before alterations in the core temperature is shown in Fig. 10.9. The critical temperature is a most useful index of the temperature-regulating and insulating properties of an animal. In Fig. 10.9 it is shown as the point where metabolism diverges from the standard value.

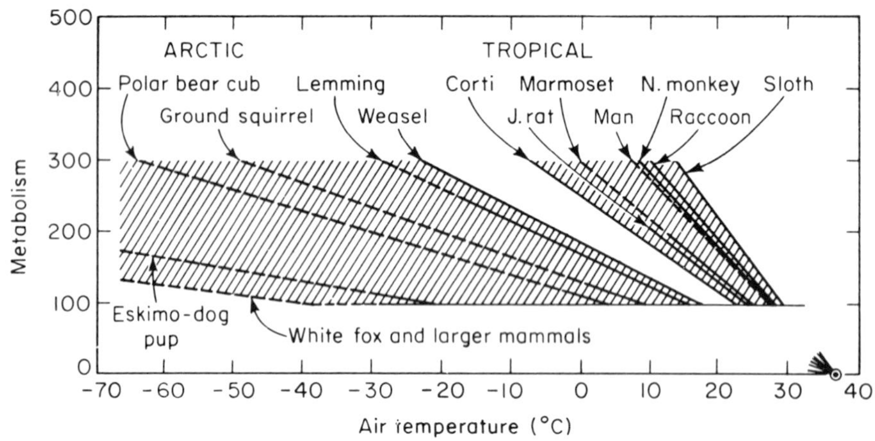

Fig. 10.9. Metabolism of resting mammals in relation to environmental temperature. The base line (100) is the standard or basal metabolism. Solid lines, observed values. Broken lines, extrapolated values. [Based on Scholander *et al.* (1950).]

The ability of birds and mammals to face elevated temperatures is just as variable and again reflects a genetic capacity related to the thermal conditions in the animal's natural environment. The fur seal may actually die of overheating on a warm day in the Arctic at 10°C while an essentially tropical animal like man can tolerate four times this temperature without damage, even though his cooling machinery may be strongly activated under such conditions. Within the same species (men or cattle, for example), marked racial differences in thermal tolerance are known. Prosser and Brown (1961) cite these and many other interesting examples.

REGULATION OF BODY TEMPERATURE

The "Du Bois temperature balance" has been shown in many textbooks of physiology during the past twenty-five years and is still worth careful study (Fig. 10.10). It shows graphically how the physiological and metabolic reactions which produce heat must be matched against those which radiate or conduct it away in order to provide a constant body temperature. Except in a very narrow THERMALLY NEUTRAL ZONE, the maintenance of a constant body temperature makes a steady demand either on the chemical processes of heat production or on the physical devices for heat loss.

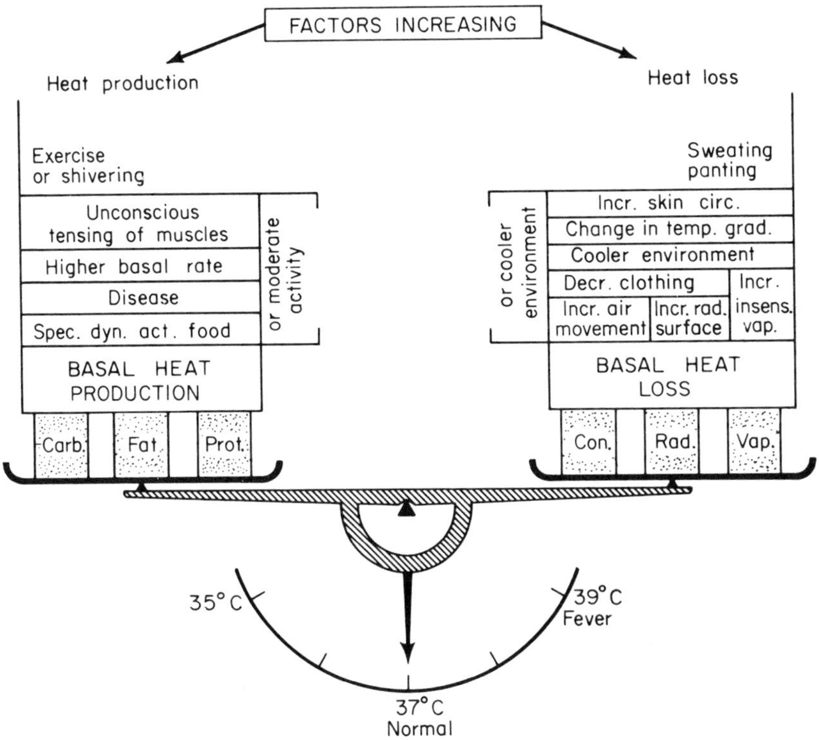

Fig. 10.10. The DU BOIS TEMPERATURE BALANCE. [Du Bois (1937).]

Heat production. A man, when appropriately acclimated, may show an eighteen-fold increase in heat production within twelve minutes if suddenly immersed in a bath at 4°C. In contrast, moderate exercise such as walking at the rate of three miles per hour increases the total heat production by only three times. The eighteen-fold increase is comparable to that observed in maximum physical activity. This phenomenal heat production (of the order of 16,000 kcal/m^2/24 hr) is associated with violent shivering; even under much less extreme conditions this is the familiar response to the cooling of the body surfaces.

In some animals an increased muscle tone can be measured before overt shivering or piloerection is evident. The muscular response, referred to as PHYSICAL THERMOGENESIS, generates a large amount of heat

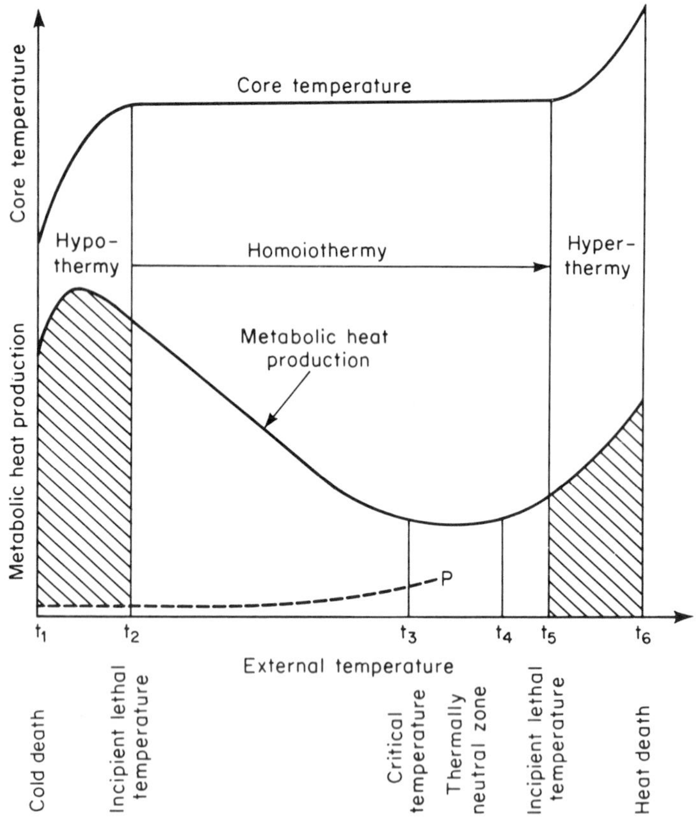

Fig. 10.11. Pattern of heat production and variations in body temperature of homeotherms exposed to various external temperatures. The broken line *P* shows, for comparison, the heat production of a poikilotherm. [Allen (1960*a*) after Precht *et al.* (1955).]

but is by no means responsible for the total. All metabolizing tissues produce some heat, and in the development of homeothermy such active tissues as liver and brain are almost as greatly involved as are the muscles. The contributions of various organs have been carefully studied in some mammals; the literature is found in textbooks of medical physiology.

Approximately 60 per cent of the total heat is usually attributed to physical thermogenesis while the largest part of the remainder comes from liver and brain (CHEMICAL THERMOGENESIS). Both mechanisms are strongly activated in cold stress (Davson, 1959).

Animals vary greatly in their capacity to generate heat. Measured on the basis of calories per kilogram per day, the energy output of a canary is 1000 times that of a sturgeon. One of the greatest contrasts between poikilotherm and homeotherm is in the heat production curves over a series of environmental temperatures (Fig. 10.11). Even among the different species of homeotherms the capacity shows a twenty-fold variation in terms of energy output per kilogram per day (Table 10.1).

TABLE 10.1

ENERGY PRODUCTION UNDER BASAL OR STANDARD CONDITIONS FOR REPRESENTATIVE VERTEBRATES
(Data from Spector, 1956)

Animal	*Body weight kg*	*Body surface m^2*	*Energy output per day kcal/kg*	*kcal/m^2*
Man	56 - 65	1.65–1.83	23.2–25.5	790–910
Beef Cattle	400 -500	3.2 -4.7	15.2	1635
Sheep	42.7- 49.5	0.95–1.1	25.7–26.3	1160–1180
Dog	11.7- 15.5	0.58–0.65	33.5–38.5	770–800
Cat	3.0	0.2	50	750
Rat	0.2	0.03	130	830
Marmot	2.6	0.18	28.3	420
Elephant	3670	23.8	13.3	2060
Duck	0.93	0.1	90	855
Pigeon	0.28	0.04	100	670
Canary	0.016	0.006	310	760
Lizard	1.2	0.11	2.5	29
Frog	0.05	—	—	130
Sturgeon	1400	11.8	0.3	31

Such temperature-metabolism comparisons might suggest that adjustments in heat production would provide important avenues for climatic adaptation to temperature. This is not the case. Metabolism is roughly proportional to body surface, and when comparisons are made on this basis, the differences between various species of true homeotherms are less evident. There is no consistent difference between the heat generating capacities of tropical and arctic species (Table 10.1). The evolution of homeothermic living in the extreme environments was primarily by way of physical regulation of heat dissipation rather than by chemical processes involving heat production.

During the phylogeny of homeothermism, however, the evolving mammals probably depended primarily on variations in heat production and not on physical mechanisms for the maintenance of body temperature (Fig. 10.12). Recent investigations have confirmed many of Martin's

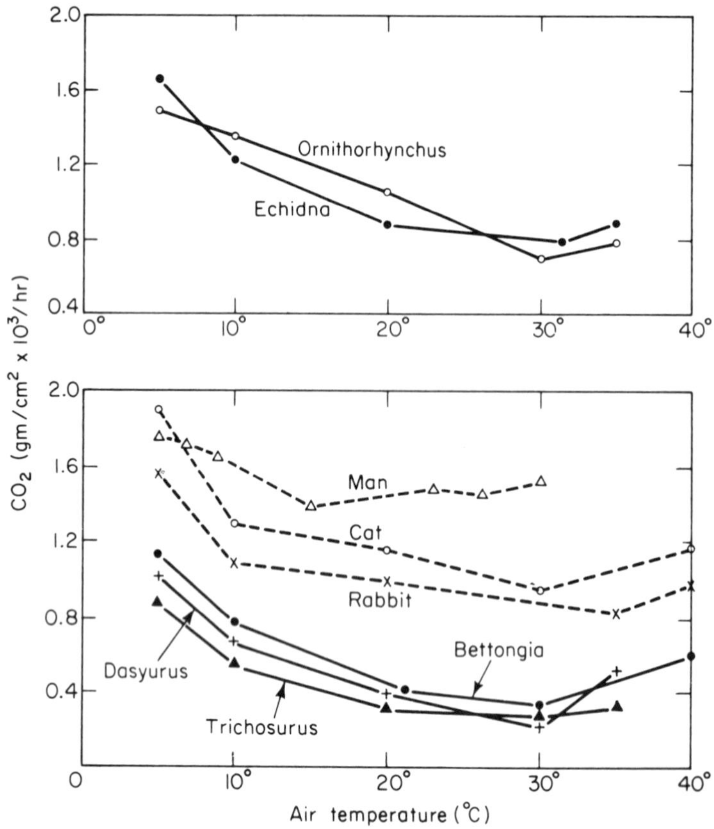

Fig. 10.12. Metabolism of various mammals in relation to ambient temperature based on Martin's (1903) data. Upper panel, monotremes. Lower panel: bottom group, marsupials; top group, placental mammals. [Johansen (1962).]

(1903) early findings on monotremes which indicated a lack of sweat glands and the vasomotor adjustments which are concerned with temperature regulation in higher mammals. It is likely that metabolic and behavioral responses were responsible for temperature regulation in the most primitive mammals. Johansen (1962) has reviewed the recent work.

Heat loss. Temperature regulation would be extremely uneconomical if it depended solely on variations in metabolism. The rapid generation of heat can mean survival in a crisis, such as that which man would face if suddenly immersed in water at 4°C. However, the energy requirements in such a situation are comparable to those of vigorous muscular exercise; they could only be met by increased fuel consumption, and this during seasons and in environments where food is liable to be minimal. Among the warm-blooded animals, temperature adaptation in the genetic sense has been a refinement of the mechanisms for heat conservation or dissipation. Many different anatomical and behavioral correlates have appeared—particularly in connection with body insulation, vascular heat exchangers and economical body forms (Scholander, 1955).

Three weights (conduction, radiation and vaporization) are shown on the right side of the DuBois temperature balance (Fig. 10.10). Convection need not be listed as a separate factor since it only contributes to conduction or radiation. The relative significance of the three different weights varies with the environmental conditions and the structure of the integument. In an aquatic environment conduction will account for the entire transfer. In the terrestrial habitat, on the other hand, only relatively small amounts of heat are exchanged in this way. Most of the homeotherms are terrestrial. In man radiation usually accounts for 55 per cent or more of the heat lost and evaporation for 40 per cent or less—the amounts depending on the environmental temperature and humidity (Ruch and Fulton, 1960; King and Farner, 1961; Hardy, 1961). Transfer of heat by radiation and conduction is only effective in a cool environment. It is obvious that, at high temperatures, the animal will actually take on heat by these routes. Evaporation, on the other hand, is always a negative factor. About 0.6 kcal is required to vaporize 1 g of water from the moist surfaces of the skin or respiratory epithelia. This technique for cooling has been exploited in quite different ways by the birds and mammals.

Birds have a dry skin with no special integumentary organs to increase cooling by vaporization. The respiratory tract serves as the most important avenue for the evaporation of water (Salt,1964). The respiratory rate increases sharply with rising temperatures; the rate of a pigeon at 41.7°C is 46 per minute with a tidal volume of 4 ml and a minute volume of 185 ml. At a body temperature of 43.6°C the corresponding values were 51 per minute for respiratory rate, 1.2 ml for tidal volume and 610 ml for minute volume (Salt and Zeuthen, 1960). At high temperatures 100 per cent of the heat loss in the bird may be by evaporation. The air sacs are of particular significance. Inactivation of the abdominal and thoracic sacs in the pigeon reduces the water loss by 50 to 65 per cent; at high air temperatures such an animal is no longer able to maintain its normal temperature. Several anatomical adaptations regulate air sac evaporation under particular conditions (Salt and Zeuthen, 1960). Some birds increase their cooling by urinating on their legs. The wood stork will excrete as often as once per minute when placed in a very warm environment, and the evaporation of water on the vascular appendages has a significant effect in lowering body temperature (Kahl, 1963).

A mammal, such as a panting dog, may also dissipate considerable heat through evaporation from respiratory surfaces. However, the integument forms the specialized route for water vaporization in most mammals. Mammalian skin is provided with sweat glands, and these seem to be a direct evolutionary response to the pressures of temperature regulation. At any rate, there are many obvious correlations between the cooling problems of the species and the development of these skin glands. Aquatic mammals, for example, lack skin glands and do not depend on vaporization for cooling; man, on the other hand, has sweat glands all over his body and can maintain a steady temperature in a warm environment.

It should be noted that considerable evaporation takes place from the skin even in the absence of sweat glands. As a matter of fact, the integument probably played an important part in temperature compensation long before the development of homeothermy. Cowles (1958) has speculated on the origin of dermal temperature regulation and emphasized the phylogenetic significance of the highly vascular dermal layers of the skin in many amphibians and reptiles. In the poikilothermous amphibian it often serves as a supplementary respiratory organ; in some of the reptiles it is a valuable collector and dispenser of heat (Bartholomew and Tucker, 1963); and finally, in the mammals, it becomes a major organ of temperature regulation. In each case there is a system of dermal blood vessels which dilate in the heat and constrict in the cold to alter the peripheral blood flow. This physiological response in the poikilotherms is a nice preadaptation for the refined temperature regulation of the homeotherm.

Scholander (1955) discusses two major lines of adaptation in the control of heat dissipation: "one is the increase in body insulation as we go toward colder climates; another is an adaptation of extremities and other peripheral parts to tolerate, and remain functional at, low tissue temperatures, sometimes even approaching zero degrees." A third might be an adaptation of the body form (Bergmann's and Allen's rules), but Scholander considers this of little or no significance. Several good discussions of the last point will be found in the literature (Wilber, 1957; King and Farner, 1961; Dobzhansky, 1962).

Insulation by fur and feathers has been compared in many species of mammals and birds, and a good relationship has been established between this capacity of the integument and the natural environment of the animal. In general, tropical species are less well insulated than the arctic species. In addition, there is usually a well-marked seasonal change in the insulative quality.

Animals which lack fur can achieve insulation with a layer of cold superficial tissue. Pigs as well as aquatic mammals have been studied (Irving and Hart, 1957). This protection is somewhat akin to that afforded the skin diver inside his neoprene suit. It differs, however, in that the cold skin is vascular and can be quickly changed from an insulator to a radiator or a conductor through circulatory adjustments. In the seal, sharp temperature gradients have been measured from the skin surface at about 0°C (with animals in ice water) to a skin depth of about 5 cm where the normal mammalian body temperature is found (Irving and Hart, 1957). These cold tissues are sensitive and vascular, although about 35°C cooler than the body proper. Even more astonishing, they can warm quickly if the animal exercises or comes into warm air. Such abrupt thermal changes cannot be tolerated in most animals, even in aquatic poikilotherms. Presumably the surface tissues of the cold-skinned mammal have achieved a rather unique biochemical organization.

Special insulative qualities have been claimed for fat. The fatty layer tends to be thicker in animals acclimatized to cold and particularly so in bare-skinned animals. A comparison has shown that fatter men (body fat about 20 per cent of the body weight) are 30 per cent better insulated than lean individuals with fat about 2 per cent of the body weight (Fry, 1958). The increased thickness provides better insulation, but it is questionable whether fat has peculiar qualities in this regard. Dead fat is admittedly a better insulator than dead skin or muscle (the ratios of thermal conductance for the three are of the order of 3 : 2 : 1), but living fat is reasonably vascular and an active tissue.

There are, however, other properties of fat which may be as significant as its insulative capacities for homeotherms in the cold. The selective deposition of more fluid fats (lower melting point) in colder environments and in more exposed tissues such as those in the extremities of the arctic animal (Heilbrunn, 1952; Irving *et al.*, 1957) may be important in preserving the flexibility of the tissues at low temperatures. Again, fat has significant advantages as a metabolic source of energy (Chapter 7). The heat combustion of animal fats is approximately 9.3 kcal per g in comparison with about 4.1 for the carbohydrates and proteins in the human body (Ruch and Fulton, 1960). Thus, the fat diet or the storage and metabolism of fats is particularly advantageous for the homeotherm in a cold climate (Pagé, 1957).

The Arctic fox can sleep in snow at −40°C and preserve his resting metabolic rate because of his heavy body insulation. The skin surface remains warm like that of a well-clothed man. This same insulation, however, poses a problem when the animal becomes active and generates excess heat associated with the rise in metabolism which may be twenty to thirty times the resting level. The compromise has been an uneven covering with poorly insulated extremities which serve as avenues for heat dissipation. To be useful these extremities must be resistant to cold and capable of rapid changes in temperature. Although they can be kept warm by fur (or feathers) when the animal curls up to sleep, they are fully exposed during activity. The web in a gull's foot may be at 0°C and its leg at 7°C while the "drum stick" is 30°C and the core temperature of the body 41°C. The reindeer's leg may be at 8° to 10°C with a core body temperature of about 37°C. Nerves remain sensitive and cells uninjured in these cold tissues.

The anatomical correlate for this interesting specialization is the counter-current heat exchanger (Scholander, 1955). The principle has already been discussed (Chapter 4). The major arteries to the appendage are located centrally and surrounded by numerous thin-walled veins. When heat must be conserved the peripheral circulation is restricted, and the warm blood flowing into the appendage passes heat to the cool blood of the nearby veins; there may be little more than 1°C between the temperatures of the arterial and venous blood in the proximal areas. When the animal faces the reverse problem of heat dissipation more blood returns through the peripheral vessels, and cool blood rather than warmed blood returns to the body. In many birds and mammals (both from the tropics and the frigid regions) this vascular arrangement is elaborated into a multichannelled RETE made up of bundles of hundreds of intermingled arteries and veins. The tail, as well as the legs, often forms the site for these specialized vascular bundles.

Regulatory mechanisms. The immediate responses to acute temperature change are mediated through the nervous system. The physiological thermostat has been localized in the hypothalamus. Through appropriate surgical procedures and electrical and temperature stimulation it has been shown that the anterior hypothalamus of the mammal is responsible for protection against heat while the posterior hypothalamus confers resistance to cold (Burton and Edholm, 1955; Ruch and Fulton, 1960).

These centers are reflexly activated by the temperature receptors of the skin or mucous membranes and directly through changes in the temperature of the hypothalamus or the blood circulating through it. The efferent nerve fibers are both somatic to the muscles controlling respiration (panting) and voluntary activities (shivering) and visceral to the autonomic system which regulates the cutaneous blood vessels, the sweat glands and the piloerector muscles. Destruction of the autonomic fibers does not entirely eliminate vascular responses to temperature change, indicating, in addition, a direct effect of temperature on the blood vessels.

These are the acute responses to temperature change. If the exposure is more prolonged the endocrine system enters the picture and metabolism is altered, particularly by way of the thyroid and the adrenal glands. These adjustments are considered below.

HOMEOTHERMS IN EXTREME ENVIRONMENTS

The homeotherm has the same general avenues for temperature compensation as the poikilotherm. Several well-marked changes have been described during laboratory ACCLIMATION; the seasonal and latitudinal differences due to ACCLIMATIZATION are recognized both in tropical and frigid regions. The homeotherms, even more than the poikilotherms, have achieved **BEHAVIORAL COMPENSATION** through migration, social cooperation and the development of favorable microhabitats. Finally, at the genetic level a specialized physiology permits some homeotherms to retreat periodically to the poikilothermic state through TORPIDITY or HIBERNATION.

Compensation through acclimation and acclimatization. Many homeotherms retain the capacity for marked compensation to extremes of heat and cold (Fry, 1958; Prosser and Brown, 1961). Although the body temperature remains the same, a lowered perspiration threshold, increased production of dilute sweat and improved vascular responses have been measured when man is exposed to heat for prolonged periods. White men moving to a tropical desert climate may show a slight initial rise in body temperature with an elevated pulse rate; but within a few weeks the physiological constants are back to normal, and there is less and less discomfort with increased moisture production and improved cardiovascular responses (Adolph, 1947).

The literature on compensatory changes in the cold is particularly voluminous. In experimental animals, such as the rat, acclimation increases cold resistance, improves the ability to be active at low temperatures and to maintain the temperature of more exposed parts. The metabolism rises and, with the increased production of heat, there is a change from shivering to nonshivering thermogenesis; the release of noradrenaline may be particularly significant in the latter response (Depocas, 1961). This ability to produce and maintain high rates of heat production in cold climates is the most significant response in acclimation. The body insulation of some homeotherms may actually decrease (by as much as 75 per cent) during cold-acclimation, evidently due to greater peripheral circulation and heat flow (Hart, 1957). However, in the acclimatization which occurs seasonally (under the influence of photoperiod as well as temperature) there is a significant increase in insulation and this reduces the demands for thermogenesis. The thickening of fur or feathers, which may increase insulation by 10 to 50 per cent, is associated with changes in the biochemistry of some of the peripheral tissues permitting them to operate when very cold. These processes of acclimatization extend the low-temperature limits of a red fox by at least 38°C, a porcupine by 33°C, and a lemming by 17°C (Hart, 1957). Man's capacities are much more limited but nevertheless real (Scholander, 1958).

Cold narcosis and hibernation. If the body temperature of a typical homeothermic animal such as man is appropriately lowered, cold narcosis develops. This form of anaesthesia has been extremely valuable in certain types of surgery. In clinical work, temperatures down to about 28°C can be readily produced in several ways—for example, by immersion in a water bath at 6° to 10°C while lightly anaesthetized to prevent shivering (McMillan and Machell, 1961). Temperatures considerably below this (15° to 18°C) can also be produced with impunity if an artificial heart and respiration are combined with the hypothermia (Drew, 1961). Experimental animals, such as dogs and rats, have been cooled to about 0°C, but recovery from this deep hypothermia requires artificial respiration and an external source of heat during re-warming. The hibernator does not require any such assistance while resuming the homeothermic state, and this points to major differences between cold narcosis and physiological hibernation.

These differences are evident at every stage in the process (Lyman and Dawe, 1960). Cold narcosis develops only as a response to a rather sharp lowering of the body temperature. In contrast, although the onset of hibernation comes during cold weather, it is seasonally controlled by internal (endocrine) factors and regularly appears in species such as *Citellus* at ambient temperatures of 30° to 35°C. Heat production falls precipitously with the onset of hibernation. In the marmot, at very low temperatures, it is reduced to less than 2 per cent of the resting value prior to hibernation (Davson, 1959).

Just as striking are the differences during the resumption of the homeothermic condition. The cold narcotized homeotherm requires an external source of heat; the hibernator warms spontaneously with an explosive burst of energy which amounts to as much as 3000 kcal/m^2/24 hr in the marmot and a temperature rise of 20°C in an hour.

A third important difference is found in the functioning of the nervous tissues. The true homeotherm shows respiratory arrest at about 19°C while the hibernator continues to breathe at 5°C or less. Isolated nerves of the rat (a nonhibernator) fail to conduct at 9°C while the hamster (a hibernator) shows nerve conduction down to 3·4°C. Likewise, the isolated auricle of the hedgehog maintains its spontaneous rhythm down to 5°C while that of the rat ceases at 16° to 18°C (Lyman and Chatfield, 1955). These observations attest a special adaptation of rhythmic and nervous tissues for activity at low temperatures. This is also evident in the physiological vigilance which the hibernator retains at low temperatures. Even though the animal is, at that stage, almost poikilothermic, its thermoregulatory machinery is not completely suppressed; the body temperature does not follow the ambient temperature when the latter comes dangerously close to freezing. At this point the hibernator awakes and becomes homeothermic.

Hibernation is then a specialized physiological state associated with the evolution of homeotherms in certain extreme habitats. Several steps between the true homeotherm and the hibernator may be expected. Pearson (1960) groups the birds and mammals into three categories: OBLIGATE HOMEOTHERMS, STUBBORN HOMEOTHERMS and INDIFFERENT HOMEOTHERMS. Most of them belong to the first group and mobilize all their metabolic resources when the body temperature falls; they hold the temperature line just as long as possible and then die. Less common are the stubborn homeotherms which maintain a warm body over a wide range but become torpid when cold, especially if short of food. Deer mice (*Peromyscus*) resort to this expediency. Likewise, swifts, poor-wills and nighthawks which feed on flying insects are able to survive in a torpid state when the weather is cold and there are no airborne insects. Normally they do not show this torpidity if there is adequate food, even though their resting body temperatures may be somewhat below normal. The hummingbird, on the other hand, may maintain its body temperature for a period without food but quickly becomes torpid even at mild temperatures after dark. It is an indifferent homeotherm like most of the North Temperate bats whose body temperatures, even in moderately warm environments drop almost to those of the surroundings whenever they fall asleep. Some members of either the stubborn or the indifferent homeotherms will truly hibernate—that is, show a seasonally regulated fall in temperature associated with winter conditions.

The biological significance of overnight or unfavorable weather torpidity is just as great as that of hibernation. Pearson calculates that a hummingbird, which has a high energy demand because of its small size (Chapter 7), would use 10.3 kcal per 24 hr if it sleeps at night without becoming torpid but only 7.6 if it lowers the thermostat in the evening. This daily reduction in metabolism is only economical in small animals which can quickly cool and warm. A hummingbird may warm at the rate of 1°C per minute. A massive animal such as a bear could not do this; the equivalent of the 24 hr heat budget is required to warm a 200 kg bear from 10° to 37°C (Pearson, 1960). It is much more profitable for the bear to carry a reserve of high energy foods and keep the metabolic fires burning during the night. However, even the bear may sometimes find it economical to lower the temperature, and this has become a part of the normal physiology of species living in northern latitudes whose body temperatures, even in moderately warm environments, drop almost to those of the surroundings whenever they fall asleep. The physiological difference between the short-term torpidity which is diurnal in such animals as bats and hummingbirds and the seasonal torpidity of the animals which hibernate or aestivate, are probably differences in degree rather than kind (Harrison, 1961).

Physiological parameters have been recorded for many hibernating animals. Numerous reviews of the literature are available (Harrison, 1961; Lyman and Dawe, 1960; Prosser and Brown, 1961). The hibernator is essentially poikilothermic down to almost freezing. At low environmental temperatures the body cools rapidly on entering hibernation (in the ground squirrel from about 32°C to 8°C in ten hours) and can warm even more rapidly on arousal (4° to 35°C in four hours).

The metabolic rate declines to between 1/30 and 1/100 of the "resting" level with a very low respiratory quotient which indicates fat utilization. The R.Q. is greater than 1 during the preparation for winter sleep when fat is being stored from the carbohydrate or other foods; but it is only about 0.3 to 0.4 during hibernation while energy is being drawn from the stored fats. The rate of breathing declines (in the ground squirrel from 100–200/min to about 4/min) and is markedly periodic (Cheyne–Stokes respiration).

Circulatory and vascular changes are equally spectacular. Again, in the ground squirrel the normal cardiac rate of 200–300/min falls to 10–20/min; there may also be an initial fall in blood pressure, but later this rises due to vasoconstriction and increased blood viscosity. In some species a pooling of the blood has been noted in the spleen, with this organ several times its normal size during hibernation. An associated prolonged clotting time avoids the hazards of thrombosis during this period of stasis. Increases in the erythrocyte count and hemoglobin levels have also been reported.

The changes in fat metabolism, electrolyte balance and endocrinology have most frequently been examined for causative roles. There may be as much as a 100 per cent weight increase due to rapid lipogenesis just prior to hibernation—at the rate of about 2 g per day in the meadow jumping mouse *Zapus hudsonius* (Morrison and Ryser, 1962). An unsaturation of the body fats occurs with localized developments of "brown fat," sometimes called the hibernating gland. Although the structure and special biochemical characteristics of this tissue have been recorded (richer in phospholipids and carbohydrates, more highly unsaturated lipids, greater vascularity), its special significance still is not clear; it may be especially important in the rapid generation of heat during arousal (Smalley and Dryer, 1963).

There is a similar lack of understanding of the causative mechanisms for the electrolyte changes. Here, the major alteration is an elevation of magnesium. This increases by as much as 25 per cent in the golden hamster, 65 per cent in the ground squirrel, some bats and woodchuck, to a maximum of 92 per cent recorded by Suomalainen in the hedgehog (Riedesel, 1960). High magnesium levels are evidently universal during hibernation and have been of particular interest because of the well-known anaesthetic action of this ion (Heilbrunn, 1952). However, it has never been shown that magnesium actually causes the winter sleep; it has been noted in some species that the levels rise somewhat later than the first depression of the temperature and do not return to normal until after arousal. Riedesel (1960) considers the most likely action of magnesium to be an additive one.

The endocrinology of the thyroid, the islets of Langerhans, the adrenals and the pituitary-hypothalamic neurosecretory system have been frequently investigated. In general, thyroid activity is low during hibernation; there may be an increase in the adrenaline:noradrenaline ratio; the cortical tissues fail to show the usual response to low temperature "stress"; there may be hypertrophy of the pancreatic islet tissues, and well-marked changes have been followed in the hypothalamic neurosecretory system and in the pituitary.

The seasonal nature of hibernation makes it tempting to assign a regulatory role to the endocrine system. Many physiological processes are triggered seasonally by hormone action which is in turn regulated through the hypothalamus by the seasonal cycles of photoperiod and temperature. This may also be true of hibernation, but in some species, at least, the phenomenon seems to depend on an "internal seasonal clock." Pengelley and Fisher (1963) kept ground squirrels (*Citellus*) for two years under constant conditions of low environmental temperature and twelve-hour photoperiods and found seasonal periods of activity and hibernation which corresponded to the normal cycles in nature. However, the fact remains that hibernation is associated with a specialized endocrine physiology, whatever may be the role of hormones in the onset or the arousal from it. Its evolution has probably included adjustments in all the endocrine tissues, most frequently resulting in their involution prior to the winter sleep (Lyman and Chatfield, 1955). As some writers intimated, the physiology of hibernation may have been, in an evolutionary sense, built upon the "general adaptation syndrome" (Selye, 1949), which is the characteristic response of most mammals to extremes of temperature.

Behavioral regulation and migration. Many of the homeotherms avoid extreme temperatures by seeking or constructing more favorable microclimates; others migrate seasonally to less rigorous climates. The physiology of migration has been intensively studied, and some of the more pertinent data will be considered in a later section.

Ionic and Osmotic Balance 11

The tissue fluids are dilute saline solutions with sodium chloride as the predominant electrolyte. Small changes in composition are always permissible, but in most cases the variation compatible with life is extremely limited. The maintenance of this constancy is a major physiological task.

The marked similarity between these dilute salt solutions in tissues and the saline waters of the ocean has long intrigued physiologists. All evidence—both geological and biological—points to the marine habitat as the ancestral home of primitive animal cells, and some phylogenetic relationship between the sea water and body fluids is a seemingly logical postulate. Macallum (1926), one of the first scientists to think seriously about this, saw in it evidence of a gradually changing composition of the oceans during animal evolution. He assumed that the oceans were much less salty when life made its appearance and that some portion of this ancestral sea became enclosed within the cells and tissues of primitive organisms; the body fluids of present-day animals would thus reflect the composition of the sea during the period when their ancestral lines were established. This hypothesis may be traced through the literature for more than a quarter of a century, but neither biologists nor geologists have ever found a shred of evidence for it. The palaeochemistry of sea water has now been carefully studied, and the indications are that the waters of the ocean have changed little in composition during the long period of animal evolution (Rubey, 1951; Robertson, 1957*a*). The salinity of the Palaeozoic seas was probably not unlike that of the present oceans.

However, the fact remains that life originated in sea water and that the body fluids are like sea water in their general composition. These facts may well be connected, even though it is not possible to adduce from them any evidence as to the nature of the ancient oceans. It seems likely that the marine habitat, in contrast to all others, provided conditions which were most suitable for the organization of protoplasm and the metabolism of cells. In all the animal phyla, from protozoa to vertebrates, there are representatives with body fluids of the same osmotic content as sea water; further, many more of the species in primitive phylogenetic groups are isosmotic with sea water. Perhaps the problem of water balance did not exist at the beginning of animal phylogeny. It might first have appeared when animals spread from the oceans into the estuaries, up the rivers, into the ponds and marshes and onto the land.

The problem of electrolyte balance, on the contrary, has certainly existed since the organization of the first cell. Unless primitive cells were very differently organized from those of today, their lives depended on the maintenance of a transmembrane potential brought about by an unequal distribution of ions (particularly sodium and potassium) across the cell membrane (Chapter 15). This bioelectric potential, characteristic of all living cells, depends on active transport of ions; the organization of the first cell demanded efficient machinery for the regulation of its electrolytes and the transport of ions. IONIC REGULATION BY CELLS IN ISOSMOTIC SOLUTIONS is a part of the life of all cells in a multicellular animal as well as in the single-celled organism living in sea water; it is the first physiological topic for consideration in this chapter.

Most of the major phyla met the challenge of adapting their physiology to life in brackish and fresh waters. Some groups were more successful than others; the coelenterates and the echinoderms have been notably unsuccessful. The brackish water environment created a new water balance problem and accentuated the original difficulties of maintaining the balance of electrolytes. The osmotic flooding of water, which is inevitable in a less saline medium, requires a good water pump unless extreme dilution can be tolerated. The removal of this osmotic water leaches out the soluble salts. One of the first physiological challenges in spreading from the marine habitat was the PROBLEM OF MAINTAINING A HYPEROSMOTIC STATE. The opposite difficulty was encountered when phylogenetic lines, which had stabilized their body fluids at osmotically lower levels than the sea water, reinvaded the marine habitat. There are several examples of this; the teleost fishes provide a particularly successful one. Here the difficulty is that of MAINTAINING A STABLE HYPOOSMOTIC STATE in the face of continuous osmotic desiccation. Organisms which live in highly saline ponds and lakes must face the same stress.

In TERRESTRIAL LIVING neither water nor electrolytes can be obtained directly from the ambient medium but are acquired through food and drink. In the most arid of terrestrial environments there may be absolutely no drinking water for long periods, and the animal must produce all of its body water through metabolism. Similarly, the land animal, with its relatively dilute body fluids, faces essentially desert conditions when it

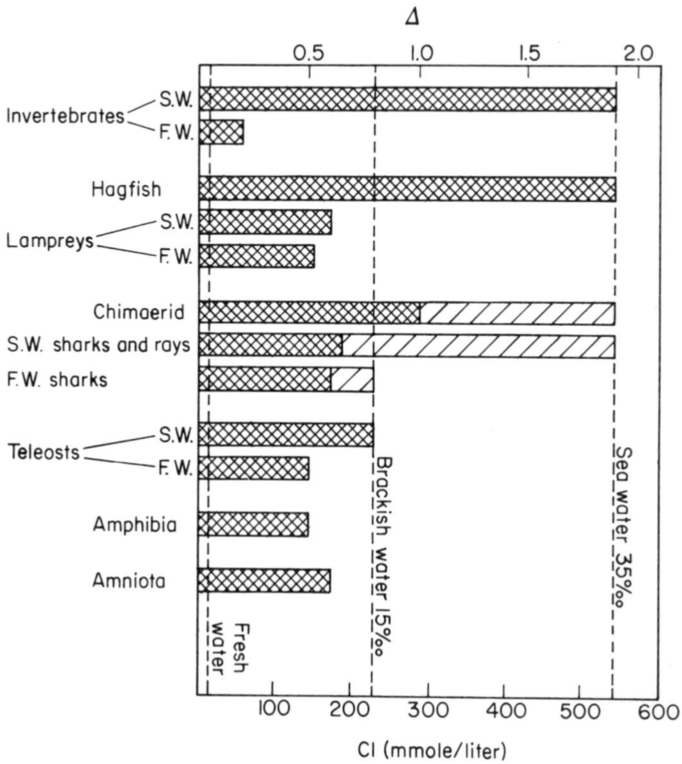

Fig. 11.1 Osmotic content of different groups of animals in relation to the tonicity of their environments. [Data from Robertson (1957), Schlieper (1958), Fänge and Fugelli (1962).]

returns more or less permanently to the ocean and lives in a hyperosmotic environment.

Thus, there are four major problems in the regulation of the electrolytes and water of the tissues (Fig. 11.1): 1, ionic regulation in isosmotic media; 2, maintenance of a hyperosmotic state; 3, maintenance of a hypoosmotic state; and 4, terrestrial living. Before discussing these, the range in electrolyte and water content of the various habitats will be considered.

The Environmental Parameters

The concentration of sea water varies slightly in different geographic regions, but the percentage composition of its different electrolytes is remarkably constant. Surface waters of the open oceans contain about 3.4 to 3.6 per cent salt, with the highest concentrations at the equator where evaporation is greatest. The salinity of the deep waters is almost constant between 3.48 and 3.49 per cent. The major constituents are chlorides (about 55 per cent) of which sodium is the most abundant (about 31 per cent). Because of the chemical constancy in proportions of the inorganic compounds, the total salt content can be readily determined by measuring any one of the constituents. Chlorine, because of its abundance and ease of determination, is the element of choice. The classical technique is a silver nitrate titration which in reality determines the total halides; chlorinity by definition is:

> *The total amount of chlorine, bromine, and iodine in grams contained in one kilogram of sea water, assuming that the bromine and iodine had been replaced by chlorine* (Sverdrup *et al.*, 1942).

To avoid apparent changes in chlorinity which can be brought about by more precise determinations of atomic weights of the elements, an International Commission in 1902 prepared a primary standard of "normal water" at the Hydrographical Laboratories in Copenhagen. Chlorinities are now related to this standard or subsequent standards based on it. A new primary standard prepared in 1937 has a chlorinity of 19.381 parts per thousand (‰). The CHLOROSITY of a sample is the chlorinity expressed as grams per 20°C-liter; it is obtained by multiplying the chlorinity of the sample by its density at 20°C. A chlorinity of 15.00‰ corresponds to a chlorosity of 15.28 g/liter.

Sea water is also described in terms of the total dissolved solids or the SALINITY defined as:

> *The total amount of solid material in grams contained in one kilogram of sea water when all the carbonate has been converted to oxide, the bromine and iodine replaced by chlorine, and all organic matter completely oxidized* (Sverdrup *et al.*, 1942).

It is readily calculated from the empirical formula:

$$\text{Salinity} = 0.03 + 1.805 \times \text{Chlorinity}$$

These relationships are shown in Table 11.1.

Physiologists frequently describe the salinity of the environment as a percentage of sea water. This is quite satisfactory, but the implication must always be that it is a percentage of "normal water" (chlorinity 19.381‰) unless otherwise defined.

Near the shores, where the fresh water from the land meets and mixes with the waters of the ocean, there is every gradation in salinity of habitats. Lakes and rivers are even more variable. Unlike the ocean, they differ not only in salinity but also in the composition of the dissolved

TABLE 11.1

PHYSICOCHEMICAL VALUES FOR BRACKISH AND SEA WATER. SPECIFIC GRAVITY MEASURED AT 0°C IN RELATION TO DISTILLED WATER AT 4°C. SALT CONTENT BASED ON STANDARD OF 293 mmole Cl/liter = Δ1.00°C. From Schlieper (1958).

Salinity ‰	*Chlorinity* ‰	*Specific gravity*	*Freezing point-Δ°C*	*mmole/l*
5.0	2.76	1.0040	0.266	79
10.0	5.56	1.0080	0.533	156
15.0	8.38	1.0121	0.795	233
20.0	11.21	1.0161	1.077	317
25.0	14.08	1.0201	1.350	396
30.0	16.95	1.0241	1.628	477
35.0	19.86	1.0281	1.907	559

salts. Clarke (1924) has summarized a wealth of information on the analyses of waters from all over the world. Waters considered "fresh" range from approximately 15 to 500 parts per million (ppm) of dissolved solids, corresponding to salinity values of 0.015 and 0.5‰. Hutchinson's (1957) mean salinity values for lakes and rivers the world over is 100 ppm. The actual composition depends on the geological formation and the amount of precipitation. It is not unusual to find saline rivers in the interiors of the continents with salinities over 1000 ppm while the salt lakes may be more than 100 times this (10 to 30 per cent).

There are two very different kinds of salt lakes. Both develop in isolated basins from which the drainage never reaches the sea; but in one group (represented by the Great Salt Lake and the Bonneville Basin in North America) the salts have been leached from sedimentary rocks or salt deposits of ancient seas, while in the other they come from volcanic rocks. Lakes of the first group are chloride waters derived directly as remnants or indirectly through leaching from the ancient oceans; they often have the same general composition as sea water. The waters of Great Salt Lake, for example, are like sea water, although the salinity is four to seven times greater, depending on the precipitation. Lakes of the second group, such as the Lahontan Basin in northwestern Nevada, are alkaline and more variable in composition (Clarke, 1924).

The saltern or salt-works provides another interesting habitat of high salinity. Sea water is admitted into a series of ponds through which it slowly circulates as it evaporates. In this process the water not only becomes progressively more saline but shows a changing salt composition with, first, a precipitation of calcium carbonate and traces of iron oxide at a specific gravity of 1.050, followed by the calcium sulfate with further evaporation at a specific gravity of 1.264. As long as calcium is present, such ponds contain a characteristic bacterial and algal flora and a sparse fauna of protozoans (for example, the autotroph *Dunaliella*), crustaceans (particularly *Artemia salina*) and insects (especially *Ephydra millbrae*); this ecological community disappears with the precipitation of the calcium and the rising magnesium concentration (Baas Becking, 1928; Boone and Baas Becking, 1931).

In studies of osmotic regulation the environmental physiologist is often more concerned with the relative osmotic properties of the internal with respect to the external environment than he is in the precise chemical constitution of the two media. When the environment displays the same osmotic pressure as the body fluids it may be either ISOSMOTIC or ISOTONIC, but the two terms do not mean the same thing since the latter is a function of the cell membrane while the former is not.

This can be most easily explained with an example. A sea urchin egg in a 0.53 molar solution of sodium chloride does not swell or shrink; the osmotic content is evidently the same on both sides of the cell membrane. Now, on the basis of theoretical calculations, a 0.37 molar solution of calcium chloride should have the same osmotic pressure, and the size of an egg immersed in it should likewise show no change. Experimentally, however, the 0.37 molar calcium chloride will shrink the egg; it remains unchanged in a more dilute solution of 0.30 molar concentration. It is evident that these salt solutions have in some way modified the permeability properties of the sea urchin egg membrane so that it is not responding like an ideal semipermeable membrane. Determinations of osmotic pressure by physical techniques depend on the number of solute particles and are calculated for an ideal membrane permeable only to the solvent (water). The different response of the sea urchin egg to isosmotic solutions of sodium and calcium chloride illustrates one of the differences between an isotonic and an isosmotic solution. Solutions which produce no osmotic stress are isotonic; those which are theoretically of the same osmotic pressure are isosmotic. Solutions may or may not be both isotonic and isosmotic at the same time.

This argument indicates that the terms HYPEROSMOTIC and HYPOOSMOTIC are preferable to hypertonic and hypotonic for the osmotically more concentrated and dilute solutions in discussions of environmental physiology (Potts and Parry, 1964*a*).

Ionic Regulation in Isosmotic Media

It has been argued that the evolution of an active ion transport system was one of the prime requisites for the organization of primitive cells (Brown and Stein, 1960). According to this hypothesis, primordial cells —evolving in a marine environment—encountered osmotic problems which were solved by a regulated permeability of the plasma membrane and the active transport of cations.

The inevitable organic metabolites of protoplasm are assumed to be the basis of the transmembrane osmotic gradient. An impermeability of the membrane to these organic molecules is a necessity since they are the valuable coinage of life; however, their presence inside the cell creates an excess of osmotically active materials. Organic ANIONS (amino acids and metabolites such as pyruvate, lactate and acetate) are especially significant. Water may be expected to flow into the cell because of this increased osmotic content and, even in an isosmotic environment, osmoregulation becomes essential for the preservation of a constant cell volume. If this concept is correct, the osmotic problem existed even in the ancestral (isosmotic) cell environment.

There are several theoretical ways in which primitive cells might have adapted their physiology to counteract this flooding. The permeability of the cell membrane might have been reduced until the organism was watertight. Alternatively, a water pump might constantly discharge the excess osmotic water, or a salt pump might be used to reduce the electrolytes and maintain an osmotic balance. The latter mechanism seems to be universal, although it is often assisted by the other two. Ion pumps are a part of the physiology of all cells, and they may have evolved first to maintain a constant cell volume in an isosmotic medium.

It follows that the structure and physiology of the plasma membrane should be considered first in any discussion of osmotic and ionic regulation. The metabolic processes of active transport, the physical forces of diffusion and the dynamics of the living membrane which modifies these forces are discussed in several excellent texts of cell physiology (Davson, 1959; Giese, 1962) and will not be detailed here. It is, however, important for the comparative physiologist to remember that cell membranes may be organized so that they are freely permeable to water, to other small molecules or to ions; but they may also be extremely tight and practically impermeable. Thus, the penetration of materials which involve the physical forces of diffusion, electric potential gradient and solvent drag, depends very greatly on the character of the plasma membrane. It is also noted that the environment can markedly alter the permeability of cells; divalent ions, such as calcium, tend to reduce permeability while the monovalent ones, such as sodium, increase it. A proper balance is essential, and the lack of anions, such as calcium, in the environment may greatly reduce the survival time in otherwise innocuous habitats.

Many marine (and parasitic) animals at all levels in phylogeny live in isosmotic environments. Although their total osmotic content matches that of their environment, the ionic composition of the body fluids is never the same as that of the ambient media. Often the potassium is much higher and the sulfate lower, but no sweeping generalizations are possible; the significant point is the continuous regulation of electrolytes which is an essential part of life in all habitats. In the complex multicellular animals many mechanisms for the regulation of water and electrolytes come into play, but active ion transport is the key to them all. Surface areas permeable to water and ions are regularly reduced to a minimum, water pumps in the form of contractile vacuoles, nephridial tubes and kidneys are often present, but the active transport of salts remains a part of the machinery of every cell. In certain organs (the gills of fishes or crustaceans) cells exploit this capacity by forming highly specialized tissues for the excretion of large amounts of salt.

The transfer of regulatory responsibilities from relatively undifferentiated cells to specialized tissues is nicely shown during the ontogeny of such organisms as the marine teleosts (Blaxter and Holliday, 1963). Herring (*Clupea*) eggs tolerate a wide range of salinities and are essentially isosmotic from 5 to 50‰ during the early stages of development. They swell and shrink in relation to changing tonicity of the environment, with only the chorion of the egg mechanically restricting the size increase in salinities lower than 5‰. After gastrulation, however, when the egg is first completely enclosed in the expanding cellular layers of endoderm and ectoderm, the egg contents are regulated at a tonicity equivalent to a salinity of about 12‰ ($\Delta = 0.72$). The relatively undifferentiated surface cells are apparently responsible for this regulatory capacity, and this is probably also the case throughout the larval stages. The newly hatched larvae tolerate salinities ranging from 2.5 to 52.5‰, with the most likely site of regulation in the epidermis. In older fish, however, osmotic and ionic regulation become the responsibilities of other tissues (kidneys and gills) as the skin takes on its protective functions and develops its scaly layers. The mesonephros of the herring has a high glomerular count and serves as a good water pump in the dilute habitats; the gills are the locus of salt transfer and regulation. This sequence of physiological changes during ontogeny probably parallels changes during phylogeny from the first single-celled organisms to the complex multicellular forms.

Living in a Hypoosmotic Environment

Aquatic animals which are able to live within only a narrow range of outside salinities are said to be STENOHALINE; there are many examples both in fresh waters and in the ocean. The familiar freshwater invertebrates such as planarians, mussels and crayfish are in this class, as well as the majority of the marine invertebrates ranging from protozoans to protochordates. Both freshwater and marine fishes provide numerous

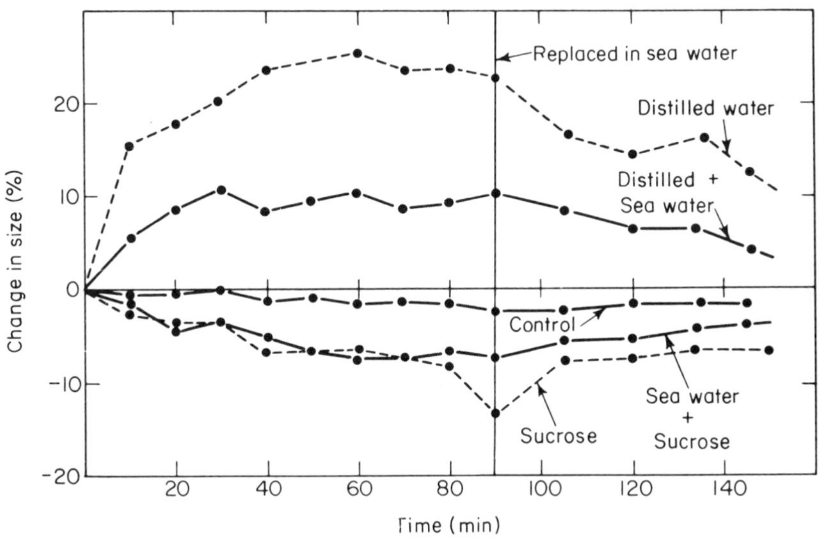

Fig. 11.2. Change in weight or volume of *Eudistylia vancouveri* as per cent difference from the initial values determined in sea water at about 28‰. Sucrose was isosmotic with sea water; mixtures were 50:50 by volume. Each value is an average for 50 worms measured individually in an introductory physiology class.

examples. In contrast to the stenohaline animals, the EURYHALINE forms are able to withstand a wide range of salinities either by conformity or regulation. Again, there are many examples in most of the phyla, although coelenterates and echinoderms are notably inconspicuous in the estuarial habitats where euryhaline species abound.

This section deals with the physiological problems of animals which maintain a hyperosmotic condition in their body fluids. These are the animals of fresh and brackish waters; they may be either stenohaline or euryhaline. They share the characteristic of living in environments which are osmotically less concentrated (hypoosmotic) than their body fluids and are consequently faced with continual flooding of water and a leaching of their salts. During phylogeny the estuary must have been their ancestral home, with the stenohaline freshwater species making their way to rivers and lakes through progressively less brackish habitats.

The electrolyte and water problems of these ancestral lines can be appreciated from simple experiments in which marine or estuarial animals are placed in heterotonic seawater solutions and subsequent measurements are made of the body volume and the composition of the fluids. The two major hazards of living in a hypoosmotic environment are indicated in Fig. 11.2. These data were obtained by simply measuring the weight or volume of a marine polychaete (*Eudistylia vancouveri*) in dilute sea water and in isosmotic sugar solutions. The amount of swelling is proportional to the dilution of the medium; it is roughly twice as great in fresh water as it is in 50 per cent sea water. Although the swelling reached a peak in 60 minutes, recovery did not occur so quickly on return

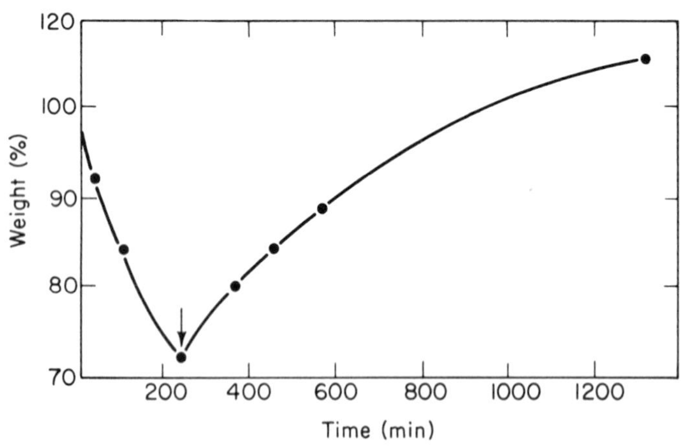

Fig. 11.3. Loss of weight of *Aplysia* in one part of isosmotic cane sugar and three parts of sea water. Vertical arrow, return to full strength sea water. [Krogh (1939) after Bethe.]

to sea water. This could be due to a leaching of the salts with a resultant decrease in the amount of osmotically active material; the sucrose experiments support this suggestion. Loss of weight in isosmotic sucrose must be due to the loss of ions and electrolytes. A similar experiment is summarized in Fig. 11.3, but in this case recovery was followed for a much longer period. It was then evident that the weight, on return to the natural habitat, actually exceeded the original—indicating that the surfaces were not quite impermeable to sucrose but that some of this sugar entered to give an added osmotic component in the body fluids.

Figure 11.2 also illustrates the presence of regulatory mechanisms in *Eudistylia*. The rapid initial swelling is followed by a period of more gradual weight increase; then a static condition or a slight decrease in size occurs even before the animals are returned to their natural environment. The initial flooding is apparently stemmed by regulatory mechanisms which not only prevent further flooding but pump out some of the osmotic water.

Data for another annelid, *Nereis diversicolor*, shown in Fig. 11.4, show a much greater regulatory response and also emphasize the importance of calcium. Cell physiologists have often measured plasma membrane permeability in relation to electrolyte changes in the environment;

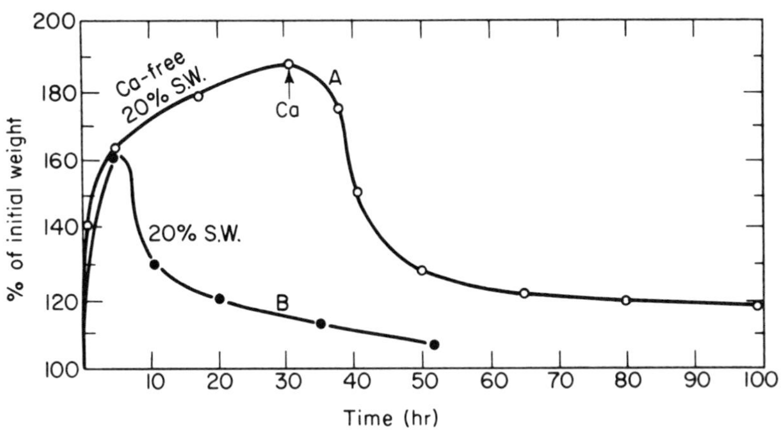

Fig. 11.4. Weight change as per cent of initial weight of *Nereis diversicolor* when transferred from 100% sea water to 20% sea water (curve *B*) or to 20% sea water lacking calcium (curve *A*). Calcium added to 20% sea water at the arrow. [Prosser *et al.* (1950) after Ellis (1937).]

the necessity of an appropriate balance of monovalent and divalent ions has been stressed repeatedly. In general, calcium and certain other divalent ions tend to decrease membrane permeability while the monovalents such as sodium and potassium have the reverse effect. In this particular experiment (Fig. 11.4) the impaired ability to regulate might be traced to several specific changes, but at the cellular level it is probably due to the changed permeability of plasma membranes.

These simple experiments underline the major problems of life in a hypoosmotic habitat—the flooding with osmotic water and the loss of the electrolytes. There are three obvious solutions to the osmotic flooding. The body of the animal might be encased in a rigid box which would balance the osmotic pressure and prevent the flux of water into the cell. The cellulose wall plays this role for plant cells in hypoosmotic environments. Animals may also counteract some swelling in dilute solutions

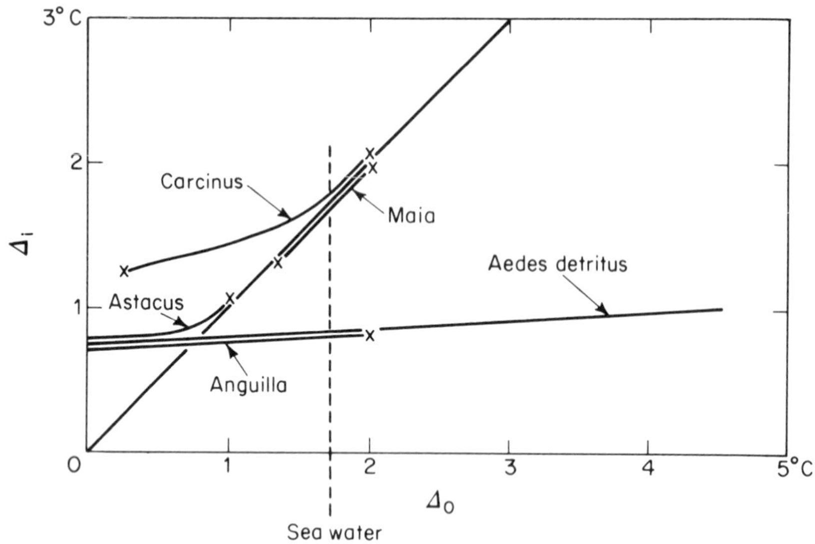

Fig. 11.5. Osmotic regulation in various animals shown by plotting the freezing point depression Δ_i of the blood (vertical axis) against the freezing point depression Δ_o of the external medium (horizontal axis). [Ramsay (1952).]

through their elastic or rigid body coverings, but this mechanism cannot provide a completely satisfactory answer since it is incompatible with animal mobility and the holozoic methods of nutrition which demand a constant flow of the external materials into the body.

Animals living in hypoosmotic environments have then two major avenues for specialization. One of these is to tolerate a dilution and the other is to pump out the water. Limitations on the first of these possibilities are obvious, and the strictly freshwater habitats could never have been attained without water pumps. Only the relatively unspecialized membranes such as the egg membranes of freshwater teleost eggs, some protozoans and perhaps *Hydra* are sufficiently impermeable to maintain a water balance without some special mechanism to expel water. The animals which live in brackish and fresh waters vary remarkably in their abilities to tolerate dilute body fluids. Some representative values for animals living in media of different concentrations are shown in Fig. 11.5. The freshwater mussel *Anodonta* lives successfully with body fluids equivalent to a freezing point of −0.078°C while a marine bivalve has a corresponding value of almost −2.0°C.

Some of the osmotic conformers can live comfortably over a wide range of osmotic concentrations. In at least one species of flatworm, *Procerodes* (=*Gunda*) *ulvae* which has been carefully studied at Plymouth, England, some of the osmotic water is temporarily stored in special tissues (Beadle, 1931; Nicol, 1960*a*). This animal lives in estuaries where it is periodically exposed to fresh water, and by experiment it has been shown that considerable osmotic flooding, with volume increase, occurs after the ebbing of the tide. Provided, however, that there is sufficient calcium in the environment (down to 0.5 mg/liter) an equilibrium is soon attained with some subsequent decline in weight. Evidently the animal has a capacity to remove or exclude water but, in addition, there is the interesting fact that large amounts of this osmotic water pass through the tissues and are stored in large vesicles of the endoderm. When the animals return to sea water these vesicles shrink and the volume of the worm decreases.

Water pumps are almost always present in organisms which live in hypoosmotic environments. Contractile vacuoles, flame cells and other protonephridial tubules, metanephridia and the nephron of the vertebrate are all capable of removing large amounts of fluid (usually by filtration); it may be argued that their primary function was water balance rather than excretion of nitrogenous wastes. Even the closed units such as Malpighian tubules (in mosquito larvae) or the aglomerular kidney (in a freshwater pipefish, *Microphis boaja*) may discharge large volumes of water (Shaw, 1960). Some of the mechanisms are not at all clear (Chapter 8). In a few animals there are no special organs for the removal of water. *Hydra* is the most familiar example. Its ability to regulate ions is well known, but osmotic regulation is problematic. Besides very low water permeability, which has already been mentioned, animals such as *Hydra,* without obvious water pumps, might be capable of removing water by active transport of the water molecules. This process has now been demonstrated in some insect tissues (pages 269 and 280); it may occur more widely (Beament, 1964; Shaw and Stobbart, 1963).

THE ABSORPTION OF SALTS

Another physiological requisite in a hypoosmotic habitat is that of retaining or acquiring essential electrolytes. In general, the marine and estuarial invertebrates produce an isosmotic urine. In the marine environment where these species—with the exception of some of the crustaceans—are in osmotic equilibrium with their environment, urine formation might not be expected to create any ionic imbalance. However, even in the isosmotic habitat the electrolyte composition of the tissues differs from that of sea water; ionic fluxes always occur at the permeable surfaces, and mechanisms are essential to preserve the equilibrium. In brackish water these problems are greatly magnified; the body fluids are hyperosmotic, and the production of an isosmotic urine may soon deplete the electrolytes. The loss will be particularly rapid during periods of fasting. Nevertheless, the invertebrates have not only penetrated the dilute waters of estuaries but have moved on into the rivers and met the hazards of osmotic flooding by pumping out large amounts of isosmotic urine.

One of the classical examples is the mitten crab, *Eriocheir sinensis*. This small crab is indigenous to Asia but has spread widely in Europe during the past 50 years; it has been carefully studied because of its marked euryhalinity. Spawning takes place in the sea, but the growing individuals make their way into rivers where they spend most of their lives until it is time to return to the sea and spawn. Body fluids of this crab are considerably more dilute while in fresh water, but the blood and urine are isosmotic in both the sea and the river (Krogh, 1939). The animal is continually losing its salts, and it has many times been demonstrated that the loss is made good by the active absorption of ions from the ambient water by the epithelial cells of the gills. Even isolated gills take up salts (Robertson, 1957*b*), and such preparations have been used to study some problems of active ion transport. *Eriocheir* has such an efficient mechanism for the accumulation of ions that its blood is actually osmotically more concentrated than that of the crayfish, a strictly stenohaline freshwater species ($\Delta = 1.2°C$ in contrast to 0.8°C, Schlieper, 1958).

Using radioactive isotopes, the active accumulation of sodium ions may be demonstrated with the gills of *Eriocheir*. The chloride seems to move passively. Sodium uptake is highly specific; an ion as similar as lithium is not accumulated and actually inhibits the sodium trapping. The molecular mechanisms are not yet known; but it has been shown that substances which act as anticholinesterases inhibit the process when added to the solutions bathing the gills. The literature is summarized by Lockwood (1962).

The brackish water prawn, *Palaemonetes varians*, is another crustacean with remarkable capacities for exploiting a great range of saline habitats, in spite of a urine isosmotic with the blood. Potts and Parry (1964*b*) have studied its salt-regulating machinery and found the animal to be isosmotic with somewhat dilute sea water (about 65 per cent). At this point of osmotic neutrality, there is no electrical potential difference (EMF) across the body surfaces and the exchange of sodium and chloride ions takes place by passive diffusion. However, when in more dilute or in concentrated sea water, the interior of the prawn's body became negative with an EMF difference up to 30 or 40 mv. By the use of tagged ions the animals were shown to be actively accumulating bromide (CHLORIDE) when in dilute solutions and actively extruding SODIUM in concentrated ones. Although the anion was being actively transported in one case and the cation in the other, the effects on the electrical potential were similar, and in both cases there was a rapid flux of sodium chloride; the oppositely charged ion must closely follow the actively transported one. The body surfaces of *Palaemonetes* are extremely permeable, and this animal has proved most valuable for the analysis of ionic regulation. The studies of ionic fluxes in teleost fishes (House, 1963) as well as in crustaceans have clearly shown that either the chlo-ide *or* the sodium may be the actively transported ion. The movement of a single ion, however, cannot take place from a sodium chloride solution unless an appropriate exchange of other ions occurs to preserve electrical neutrality (Lockwood, 1962).

Active ion absorption at the body surfaces can, then, make good the entire loss of electrolyte even in fresh waters. However, the majority of the more highly organized freshwater aquatics have additional machinery for ion absorption located in the excretory tubules; ion absorption from the environment is associated with ion absorption from the excretory tubule. In this way the tonicity of the urine is lowered and dependence on ion trapping from the environment is greatly reduced. It is never entirely eliminated since a hypoosmotic urine still contains electrolytes (Fig. 11.6), and some leaching of salts may also be expected at permeable surfaces such as the gills.

FORMATION OF A DILUTE URINE

Production of a dilute urine has now been demonstrated in some representatives of all the more advanced phyla. Findings, summarized in Fig. 11.6 for the crayfish, show the magnitude of this ion-concentrating capacity. Comparable data have been obtained for the earthworm and for mosquito larvae by using some of the most delicate microtechniques (Ramsay, 1949; Shaw and Stobbart, 1963). Freshwater fishes and amphibians have likewise been shown to produce hypoosmotic urine. The experimental proof of such mechanisms can be visualized from Fig. 11.6. Isotonicity of blood and glomerular urine is readily demonstrated in *Necturus* by analysis of fluids obtained by micropuncture; since these

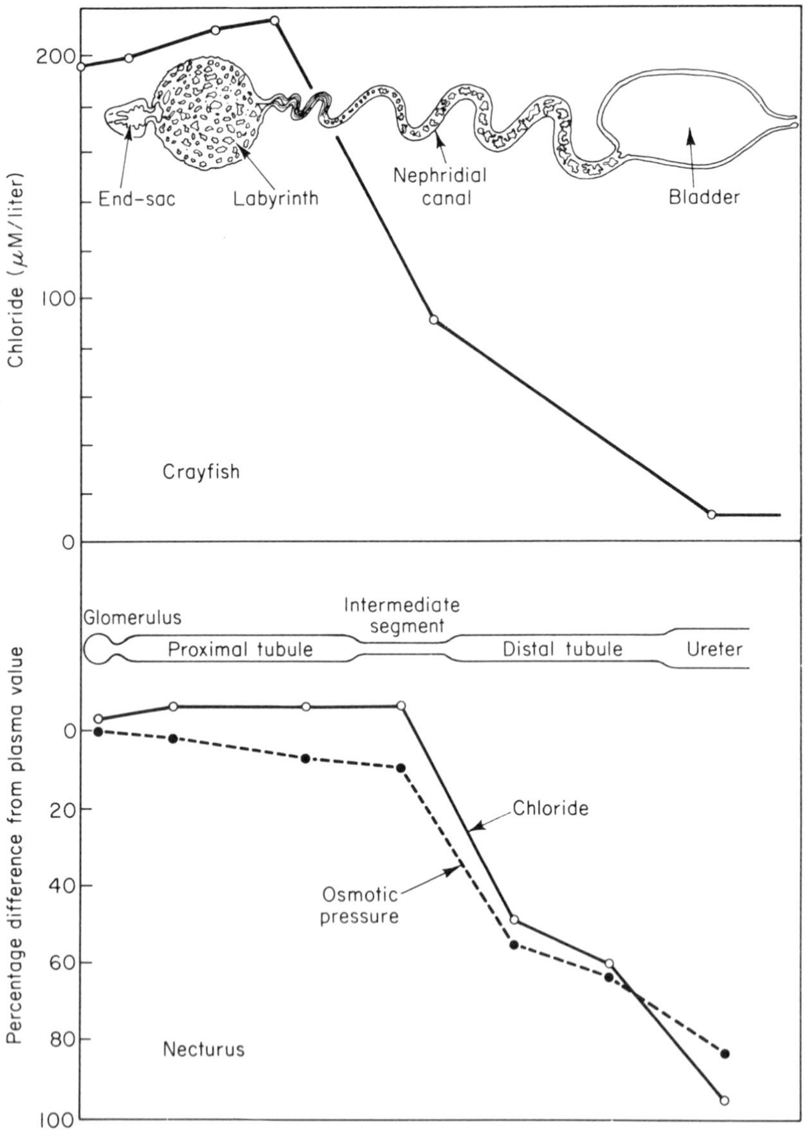

Fig. 11.6. The formation of a hypoosmotic urine in the crayfish and in the mudpuppy (*Necturus*). [Parry (1960) and Shaw (1960).]

tubules are relatively large, the tonicity can readily be followed from segment to segment. The observed dilution of the urine in the distal tubule and ureter might be theoretically attributed to the addition of water or to the extraction of the salts. However, the techniques of renal clearance (described in Chapter 8) as well as the use of metabolic poisons (which prevent active transport) have clearly demonstrated that it is due to an absorption of materials rather than the addition of water (Solomon, 1962).

In summary, the colonization of fresh waters depended on the gradual improvement of less permeable cuticles (Fig. 11.7) and the restriction of semi-permeable boundary membranes to relatively small

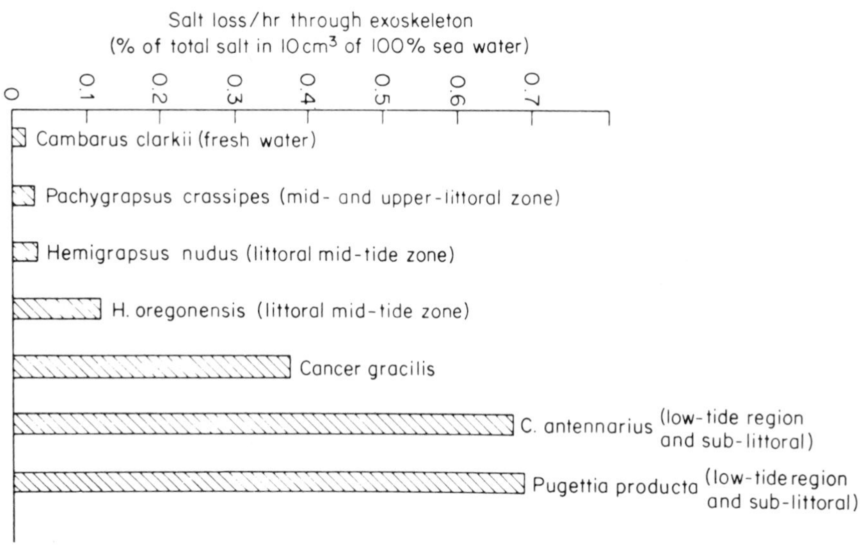

Fig. 11.7. Permeability of the exoskeleton of crustaceans from different environments, showing the tendency for lower permeability in animals from more dilute or semiterrestrial habitats. [Lockwood (1962) after Gross (1957).]

areas; concurrently excretory organs acquired the capacity to form hypoosmotic urines, and special cells appeared for the trapping of ions from the ambient fluid. The metabolic price of this regulation is considerable. It requires energy to transport ions and perhaps also to operate filters; tolerance of dilute body fluids thus becomes metabolically advantageous for animals living in hypoosmotic environments, and this may also have been a vital factor in the colonization of fresh waters (Lockwood, 1962).

Living in Hyperosmotic Environments

Marine fishes provide the outstanding example of aquatic animals living in hyperosmotic habitats (Fig. 11.1). Only the myxinoid cyclostomes among the vertebrates have an electrolyte concentration comparable to that of sea water; their osmotic problems are thus minimal or absent, although ionic regulation is essential. Elasmobranchs, through the retention of osmotically active nitrogenous wastes (particularly urea) also have minimal osmotic gradients. In contrast, the marine lampreys and teleosts are continually dehydrated through the osmotic loss of water at their permeable surfaces. A few of the arthropods live under comparable conditions of osmotic stress. Some of the grapsoid crabs and palaemonid shrimps are hypoosmotic (about 86 per cent of sea water), although the osmotic gradient is considerably less than that of the marine teleosts where body fluids are less than half the concentration of sea water (Fig. 11.1). *Pachygrapsus crassipes* and *Hemigrapsus oregonensis* thrive in hypersaline lagoons where the salinities reach 50 to 55‰ (Gross, 1961). The best invertebrate examples are found among insects (larvae of the mosquito *Aedes detritus*) and the primitive crustacean *Artemia salina* living in salt lakes and brine ponds.

DRINKING SALT WATER AND EXCRETING EXCESS ELECTROLYTES

Pioneer investigations of the physiology of regulating in a hyperosmotic habitat were carried out on the marine teleosts. These early experiments (Krogh, 1939) showed that water lost osmotically was recovered by drinking sea water and excreting the salts extrarenally. Drinking was first demonstrated by placing fish in sea water containing phenol red and later measuring the amount of dye in the gut. From these experiments it was calculated that the sculpin and the eel drink from 50 to 200 ml of sea water per kg body weight per day and extract from it 60 to 80 per cent of the water (Krogh, 1939; Shaw, 1960). In other experiments, balloons were inflated in the esophagus of the eel to block water ingestion. Such animals were able to regulate in fresh water, indicating that the drinking of fresh water was not a necessary part of their osmoregulatory response; but in sea water they lost weight continually and could never achieve a steady state.

Extrarenal excretion of salt was first shown in the classical experiments of Keys (1931) who perfused a heart-gill preparation from the eel. When analyses of the balanced saline solutions used to perfuse the gills were compared with analyses of the solutions bathing the branchial cavities it was evident that chloride was actively passed through the gills from the internal to the external medium. Acidophilic cells, the "chloride secreting cells," at the base of the gills were considered responsible for the salt transfer, although these studies did not actually demonstrate which cells were responsible or whether the active processes involved the chloride or the sodium ion or both. The fine structure of the "chloride cells" has recently been described with the aid of the electron microscope (Threadgold and Houston, 1964).

These experiments, performed many years ago, have now been substantiated by the use of much more refined techniques. The marine bony fishes and cyclostomes (Petromyzontia) compensate for the loss of osmotic water by drinking sea water and eliminating the salts; it is comparable to living in a desert and distilling sea water to make good the water lost by desiccation. In this process the monovalent ions and a part of the water are absorbed from the gut; most of the divalent ions such as Mg^{++}, Ca^{++}, SO_4^{--} and PO_4^{--} remain behind. Their elimination requires part of the ingested water since this intestinal residue is essentially isotonic with the blood (Smith, 1953). Actually, some of the divalents are absorbed, and this is one of the factors which make urine formation a necessity, even though monovalent salts and a large part of the nitrogenous wastes are excreted through the gills. Urine production is scanty in marine teleosts (only about 1 to 2 per cent of that in corresponding freshwater species) but continuous; the magnesium content is sometimes very high.

Several anatomical adaptations are associated with the scanty urine production of the marine teleosts. With reduced demands for filtration, the glomeruli are often partially or entirely eliminated. All mesonephroi possess glomeruli during early stages of development, but the adults of some species are actually aglomerular. Even when glomeruli are present, the constriction or closure of the neck segment of the tubule (Edwards, 1928–35) indicates a minor role for filtration in urine formation. In aglomerular species such as the toadfish, *Opsanus tau,* the nephron is essentially a proximal (brush border) convoluted unit. These kidneys have been of unusual interest to physiologists since they obviously function only by secretion; some of the first evidence for secretion by the vertebrate nephron was adduced from the aglomerular kidneys of teleosts.

In general, the physiological mechanisms for hypoosmotic regulation among the arthropods are comparable to those described for the marine teleosts. They have been beautifully demonstrated by Croghan (1958*a,b*) in *Artemia salina,* an animal which weighs only about 8 mg as a large adult and hence requires the nicest of microtechniques for its study. *Artemia* is able to regulate over an unusually wide range of salinities.

It can survive as long as 24 hours in glass-distilled water but requires an environment of at least 10 per cent sea water for normal life and activities. Its body fluids are hyperosmotic in media more dilute than 25 per cent sea water; they remain relatively constant (equivalent to 1 to 2 per cent NaCl) in habitats of increasing salinity up to about 10 times sea water. In nature the animals may be found in crystallizing brine.

Like the marine teleosts, *Artemia* is able to accomplish this remarkable feat by constantly drinking water, absorbing it together with NaCl through the gut epithelium and actively excreting the salt. The first ten branchiae are the organs of active sodium excretion; the transfer has been shown to be extremely fast. Sodium efflux figures for *Artemia* may be in excess of 150 mmole/liter hemolymph/hr in contrast to 11 mmole for *Daphnia* and 1.4 mmole for the guppy *Lebistes* (Croghan, 1958*c*). These animals are permeable both to water and to salt and have achieved an environmental independence by improving their abilities to transfer salts rapidly away from the tissues.

ADJUSTMENT OF OSMOLARITY WITH AMINO ACIDS AND UREA

An entirely different physiological mechanism for osmotic compensation depends on the adjustment of the osmolarity of the tissues to match that of the environment by the formation or retention of low molecular weight organic molecules. The elasmobranch fishes provide the best known example with urea retention which raises the osmotic content of the tissues to that of sea water (Fig. 11.1). This phenomenon, however, is part of a widespread capacity to compensate for osmotic differences with small size organic molecules. Among the invertebrates, the tissues of worms, molluscs, arthropods and echinoderms often contain free amino acids or products of their metabolism such as taurine (probably derived from cysteine) and glyoxylic acid (from glycine). A part of the intracellular osmotic regulation which some members of these phyla show is due to the presence of these substances (Jeuniaux *et al.*, 1962; Duchâteau-Bosson and Florkin, 1962; Simpson *et al.*, 1959). Figure 11.8 shows the correlation between osmotic content of the environment and the amount of intracellular amino acids and other ninhydrin positive substances (NPS) in the mussel *Mytilus*. Relatively greater concentrations of taurine at the higher salinities are thought to be important in sparing essential amino acids (Lange, 1963).

Both the fishes and the amphibia have exploited this means of avoiding osmotic desiccation (Fig. 11.1). In the myxinoid cyclostomes, the osmotic equivalence of plasma and sea water is due to the high salt concentration of their blood while that of the muscles depends on low molecular weight organic compounds—particularly amino acids (Robertson, 1960); in the elasmobranchs, the total salt concentration of the plasma is not very different from that of the teleosts, but the tonicity is raised to that of the environment by the addition of urea and trimethylamine oxide. The retention of low molecular weight nitrogenous compounds removes the osmotic imbalance, but the electrolyte concentrations of the environment and the body fluids remain very different. Elasmobranchs still face problems of ionic regulation and evidently rely heavily on the rectal gland for the extrarenal elimination of salt which would otherwise accumulate because of the high external salinity (Burger, 1962; Doyle, 1962). This hypothesis finds support in comparative studies of the functional morphology of the gland; rectal glands of marine species are considerably larger and cytologically more active than freshwater species (Oguri, 1964).

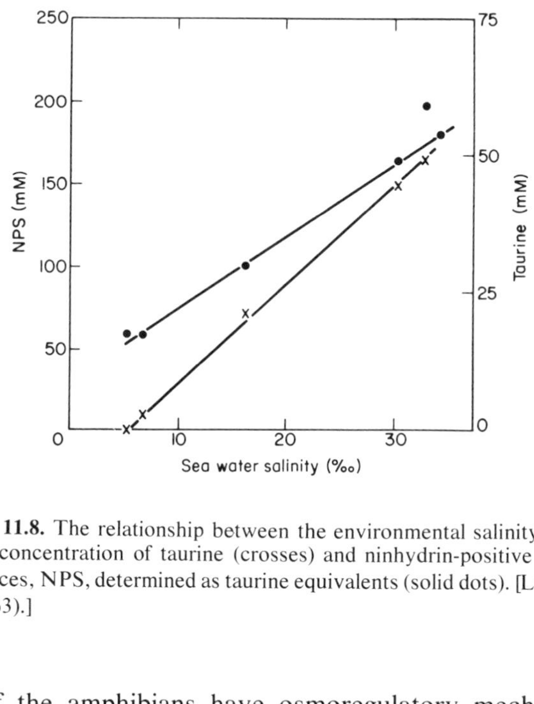

Fig. 11.8. The relationship between the environmental salinity and the concentration of taurine (crosses) and ninhydrin-positive substances, NPS, determined as taurine equivalents (solid dots). [Lange (1963).]

Some of the amphibians have osmoregulatory mechanisms comparable to those of the elasmobranchs (Gordon *et al.*, 1961; Gordon, 1962). This group of vertebrates, unlike the fishes, has not exploited the marine habitat, but there are a few representatives with marked euryhalinity and the ability to live in brackish or marine coastal areas. The green toad (*Bufo viridis*) of Europe and the Middle East can tolerate environmental salinities as high as 19‰ by matching its plasma to that of its surroundings, primarily by increasing its NaCl content (about 84 per cent) but to a small extent by accumulating urea (about 5 to 10 per cent).

The crab-eating frog (*Rana cancrivora*) of Southeast Asia is also able to exploit saline habitats and can tolerate salinities as high as 28‰ at 30°C. Tadpoles are even more tolerant (39‰ at the same temperature). Unlike the green toad, urea retention plays a major role (about 60 per cent) in the crab-eating frog and together with sodium chloride raises the plasma to slightly hyperosmotic levels. The urea concentrations may reach 2.9 per cent.

The skin permeability of these amphibians is the same as that of other anurans and does not account for any part of their exceptional abilities to live in salt water; further, they do not drink water nor put out large amounts of extrarenal salt. Their significant physiological achievement is that of tolerating a uremia or a very high salt content in their tissues. They share the former in common with the elasmobranchs and the lungfish and the latter with the marine invertebrates and the hagfishes. This may be a major biochemical achievement; urea concentrations comparable to those found in the crab-eating frog would denature certain enzymes and affect oxygen transport in many vertebrates (Gordon *et al.*, 1961). In terms of evolutionary potentialities, the distillation of sea water may have been a simpler solution to the problem.

Animals which live in a hyperosmotic environment have probably evolved from freshwater ancestors. Biologists generally agree that this has been the case with the marine teleosts, brine shrimps and mosquito larvae, all of which drink salt water and excrete salts extrarenally. The main controversy centers around the home of the ancestral vertebrates and the position of the myxinoid cyclostomes. Homer Smith (1953), on the basis of kidney structure, and Romer (1946) from palaeontological evidence, argued for the freshwater origin; the opposing view has been just as vigorously maintained by both biologists (Robertson, 1957*a*) and palaeontologists (Denison, 1956). In some of the more recent discussions the hagfish with its isosmotic plasma has been used as evidence for the marine ancestry because of the primitive position of the Cyclostomata and the similarity of their osmotic mechanisms to those of the marine invertebrates which, everyone agrees, evolved in the sea. Gordon's demonstration that certain amphibians – a group which in phylogeny probably crawled onto the land from stagnant freshwater pools – may live in concentrated sea water by physiological adaptations comparable to those of the myxinoids and the elasmobranchs, has reduced the force of some of these arguments. At present, neither the physiological nor the palaeontological evidence seems adequate to settle the matter.

The Water and Electrolyte Problems of Terrestrial Living

The land animals have made good the water deficits of their environment through special modifications of many of the mechanisms discovered by their aquatic ancestors and by evolving a few new ones of their own. In the first category, there is the tightening up of water-permeable coverings, the drinking of water, the extrarenal excretion of salts, the reduction of glomerular filtration and the ability of protoplasm to function efficiently with different relative amounts of electrolytes and water. In the second category, that of evolutionary innovations, are the capacity to recover large amounts of water from the urine (hypertonic urine), uricotelism (Chapter 8), the capacity to absorb significant amounts of water at the surfaces, the ability to depend largely on metabolic water and the behavioral responses of avoiding desiccating microhabitats. These varied mechanisms can be conveniently divided into anatomical, biochemical, physiological and behavioral. There are many excellent reviews (Edney, 1957; Chew, 1961) and only a summary is given here.

ANATOMICAL SPECIALIZATIONS

The waxy chitin of insects or the impervious layers of epidermal keratin which cover the terrestrial vertebrates may reduce evaporation to a minimum. There are as many degrees of water tightness between the emerging terrestrial arthropods (land isopods) and certain insects which live entirely on metabolic water (*Tenebrio*) as there are between the semiterrestrial amphibians and the desert-dwelling amniotes (Fig. 11.9). Detailed comment would be superfluous.

Water conservation in the face of excretory demands for the removal of soluble wastes is met in one of two ways. The phylogenetically lower classes of terrestrial vertebrates followed the pattern of the marine teleosts and reduced filtration. Unlike the teleosts, they seem never to have dispensed entirely with the glomeruli—according to Smith (1953)—because they have no other route for the elimination of chloride. A reduction of the filtering machinery, however, is found in some amphibians, reptiles and birds. The desert-living frog, *Chiroleptes (Cyclorana)*, from Australia is the classical example among the amphibians (Dawson, 1951), while this anatomical trend is quite general among reptiles and birds (Marshall and Smith, 1930; Marshall, 1934). In the latter groups there are relatively few glomeruli, and those present show reduced capillary development with two or three short loops sometimes associated with a syncytial core of non-vascular tissue. The glomerular surface is considerably smaller among the arid-dwelling snakes and lizards than it is among semi-aquatic reptiles such as turtles and crocodiles; the glomeruli of the birds' kidneys are the smallest known (Marshall and Smith, 1930). However, minimal filtration seems to be unavoidable in these groups, either because of the absence of alternative routes for the removal of chlorides, as Smith (1953) suggested, or because of the reduction of the renal portal system (Chapter 8).

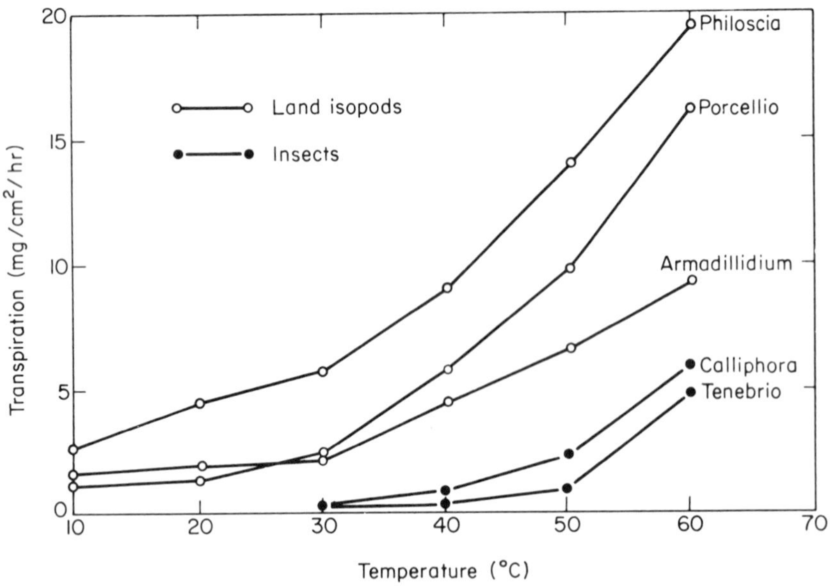

Fig. 11.9. The effect of temperature on the rate of transpiration into dry air from land isopods (open circles) and insects (solid circles). [Edney (1960).]

The other technique for the conservation of urinary water depends on an innovation in renal anatomy, the appearance of the loop of Henle. This seems to operate by actively pumping salt into the intercellular spaces about the tubules of the medulla and recovering water osmotically from the collecting tubules into the saline fluid thus formed (Chapter 8). There is a telling association between the length of the loop of Henle and the water available to the particular species. The beaver has short-looped nephrons which produce a maximum urinary concentration of 600 milliosmolal (mOsM), the rabbit with a mixture of short and long-looped tubules can produce a urine which is two and one-half times this concentration, while the African desert rodent *Psammomys obesus* with only long-looped units produces urine of 6000 mOsM (Prosser and Brown, 1961). Some birds show the reptilian pattern of renal structure with reduced glomerular development while others show the mammalian type with loops of Henle.

A few land vertebrates have taken to the marine habitat and thus excluded themselves from fresh water for drinking and from foods which contain isotonic or hypotonic fluids. Reptiles such as the sea turtles and the marine iguana, as well as many of the aquatic birds, possess orbital glands which secrete watery fluids containing sodium and potassium chlorides. Thus, like the marine teleosts, they can drink sea water and "distil" it. The extrarenal saline excretions may be more concentrated than sea water, and the glands which produce them show a morphological development which is well correlated with the demands for salt elimination (Holmes *et al.*, 1961, 1963; Potts and Parry, 1964*a*).

BIOCHEMICAL AND PHYSIOLOGICAL ADAPTATIONS

Some animals can safely tolerate a significant reduction in their body water. This is well illustrated by the group of amphibians listed in Table 11.2. Although each of them contains about 80 per cent water when in a moist environment, the amount of evaporation which can be safely tolerated varies greatly and is associated with the habitat conditions. The Florida spadefoot, a terrestrial species, can lose an amount of water equivalent to 60 per cent of its body weight while an aquatic frog, such as *Rana grylio,* is killed with a loss of less than 40 per cent.

TABLE 11.2

CORRELATIONS OF THE HABITATS OF DIFFERENT ANURANS WITH THEIR ABILITY TO SURVIVE THE LOSS OF BODY WATER (Thorson and Svihla, 1943).

	Habitat	*Body water per cent weight*	*Vital limits of water loss as per cent*	
			Body weight	*Body water*
Scaphiopus holbrookii	Terrestro-fossorial	79.5	47.9	60.2
hammondii	Terrestro-fossorial	80.0	47.6	59.5
Bufo boreas	Terrestrial	79.8	44.6	55.8
terrestris	Terrestrial	78.8	43.3	54.9
Hyla regilla	Terrestrial	79.4	40.0	50.3
cinerea	Terrestro-arboreal	80.1	39.3	49.0
Rana pipiens	Terrestro-semi-aquatic	78.9	35.5	44.9
aurora	Semi-aquatic	79.7	34.3	43.0
grylio	Aquatic	77.5	29.5	38.0

Similar comparisons have been made with several other terrestrial groups. Man's capacity to tolerate dehydration is relatively limited. In the desert he cannot tolerate a loss of body water equivalent to more than 12 per cent of his weight, but the camel may lose twice this amount (about one-third of the water in its system) without being seriously weakened (Schmidt-Nielsen, 1959). The blood volume of the camel shows no serious reduction under these conditions, indicating a withdrawal of tissue water. It is evident that the cells of vertebrate animals may function at very different tissue water levels. However, one of the major differences between the water demands of man and the camel is the remarkable contrast in their temperature-regulating mechanisms. The camel does not sweat freely until the body temperature rises to about 40.5°C (Schmidt-Nielsen, 1959). The camel can tolerate a temperature fluctuation of 6.5°C (34 to 40.5°C) without taxing its regulatory machinery while man cannot withstand more than 1°C.

This capacity for tissue dehydration may be associated with the ability to absorb large amounts of water rapidly from the surroundings. The Australian desert frog can be desiccated until lean and dry but within two minutes it will take up enough water to be as round as a "knobly tennis-ball" (Buxton, 1923). Its absorptive capacity is so great that the aborigines are said to use water-loaded animals as a source of drinking water. The desert frog is by no means the only amphibian capable of absorbing water from its environment. As a matter of fact, this may be the only route open to them. Water absorption through the anuran skin has been frequently measured, and since these animals are not known to drink water, all environmental water must be acquired in this way (Chew, 1961). Immersion is not essential; contact with moist filter paper or moss is sufficient. Reabsorption of water from the urinary bladder has also been demonstrated in several anurans and is physiologically significant during water shortage (Ruibal, 1962). Absorption of water from the cloaca of reptiles and birds may also occur but has been questioned recently (Chew, 1961). Schmidt-Nielsen (1963) suggests that a reabsorption of solutions from the cloaca coupled with extrarenal salt excretion through the nasal salt glands would provide an efficient mechanism for the conservation of water; the suggestion is based on the demonstration of nasal salt secretion in several desert reptiles and birds.

Some of the terrestrial arthropods can also withstand desiccation and absorb water rapidly when the conditions are suitable (Edney, 1957; 1960). Dry environment insects, such as *Tenebrio* larvae, for example, can absorb moisture from unsaturated air as dry as 50 per cent relative humidity. The capacity of the terrestrial isopods is much more limited; one of the wood lice, *Armadillidium*, can take up water in still air at 98 per cent relative humidity but other species can do this only when the air is saturated (Edney, 1954). There may be special areas of cuticle for water absorption. Both oral and anal drinking have been observed; in the latter process anal papillae extend rhythmically to take up moisture. As much as 50 per cent of the body weight may be absorbed after a period of desiccation.

Water is a by-product of tissue respiration (Chapter 7) and, in some species, this metabolic water takes care of the animal's entire requirements. Foods vary in their water potential. One gram of carbohydrate, when metabolized, produces 0.6 g of water, in contrast to 0.4 g from an equivalent amount of protein and 1.07 g from fat (Schmidt-Nielsen and Schmidt-Nielsen, 1952). Consequently an emphasis on fat metabolism will go far toward alleviating water shortage; on the other hand, the metabolism of protein not only produces relatively small amounts of metabolic water but forms nitrogenous wastes as a by-product which must be removed in solution. There are many examples of dependence on metabolic water. Some of the best are found in chemical embryology; an embryonic chick with its cleidoic egg developing in a dry environment obtains 90 per cent of its energy from fat while a fish or amphibian in contrast metabolizes 90 per cent protein. In this way, the chick forms much more water and much less of the nitrogenous wastes which demand energy or water for their removal (Chapter 8). Some of the desert rodents find the same metabolic advantages in eating large amounts of fatty seeds; when this is coupled with an efficient renal mechanism for the reabsorption of water and a behavior of avoiding the extreme desert heat by seeking moister microclimates, they can dispense entirely with the drinking of water (Schmidt-Nielsen and Schmidt-Nielsen, 1952; Chew, 1961). The urine of the kangaroo rat is about twice as concentrated as the laboratory rat and three times as concentrated as that of the dog. This remarkable ability permits the animal to actually drink sea water under experimental conditions.

It has often been pointed out that the potential benefit of metabolic water to an active land animal is much less than might be expected since the oxidation of the hydrogen requires ventilation with the attendant evaporation of additional water from the respiratory surfaces. This is indeed true, but animals such as the kangaroo rat, *Dipodomys*, which rely on metabolic water, avoid this hazard by remaining underground during the heat of the day where the air is cooler (30°C or less) and the humidity higher (30 per cent relative humidity or greater). Again, one of the most significant differences between the water demands of the desert mammal and that of its near-relatives living in moister environments is associated with their different demands for temperature regulation (Chew, 1961).

A certain amount of water is always required for the excretion of nitrogen. One of the major events in biochemical evolution was the phylogeny of metabolic pathways which reduce these demands to a minimum when water is in short supply. The varied end-products of nitrogen metabolism have already been described, with the phylogenetic implications of the conversion of the primary end-product, ammonia, into less toxic nitrogen compounds (Chapter 8). "The nature of the predominant end-product in any particular case seems to be conditioned by the nature of the habitual environment of the particular organisms, and the known facts are best explained on the supposition that the conversion of ammonia to other products is an indispensable adaptation to limitation of the availability of water" (Baldwin, 1963).

BEHAVIORAL ADAPTATIONS

The first experiments with terrestrial living were probably based on behavioral rather than physiological adaptations. Primitive land animals, both invertebrate and vertebrate, are limited in their capacities to acquire water or to resist dehydration. Their major achievement is an ability to select an appropriate microclimate. The shore crab *Pachygrapsus* prefers 100 per cent sea water when given a choice between this and 50, 75, 125 or 150 per cent sea water (Gross, 1957*b*); the littoral isopod, *Ligia baudiniana*, prefers distilled water to normal sea water (Barnes, 1940); *Birgus*, an air breathing land crab, selects drinking water of an appropriate salinity to maintain its ionic balance (Gross, 1955); terrestrial isopods (wood lice) are active in dry air and show random movement until they find themselves in a moist place where they become quiet again (Fraenkel and Gunn, 1940). Each species thus relates itself to an appropriate habitat and a suitable supply of water and electrolytes.

Similar examples are found among the vertebrates. The stickleback (*Gasterosteus aculeatus*) and the various species of Pacific salmon (genus *Oncorhynchus*) relate themselves to an environmental salinity appropriate to their physiological condition, and this changes at different times in their life cycle (Baggerman, 1957; McInerney, 1964); local distributions of the plethodontid salamander (*Aeneides lugubris*) are nicely correlated with the moisture conditions of the habitat (Rosenthal, 1957); a freshwater race of the snake *Natrix sipedon* is killed in sea water because it drinks the water, but a race which lives in salt marshes, although still preferring fresh waters, tolerates salinities up to 73 per cent of sea water because it avoids drinking (Pettus, 1958). The terrestrial vertebrates may also adjust their ionic balance by making appropriate behavioral responses. The green turtle *Chelonia mydas mydas* drinks sea water, probably to obtain the necessary sodium to balance the excretion of large amounts of potassium obtained in its natural foods (Holmes and McBean, 1964). Some constancy in the ratios of these two ions is maintained in their metabolism and excretion; if the intake of potassium is exceptionally high, additional sodium is required in the diet. Some herbivorous mammals may travel long distances to "salt-licks" for this reason.

Regulatory Mechanisms

Since the permissible variation in tissue water and electrolytes is usually small, it would be surprising if animals did not possess a refined machinery for osmotic and ionic regulation. A chemical rather than a nervous integration might also be anticipated, since the necessary adjustments often follow gradually modified environments associated with seasonal periods of rainfall, tidal cycles or migration.

There is little precise knowledge of these regulating devices in the invertebrates. This is true even in a group under as active study as the crustaceans with their precision machinery for osmotic and ionic balance (Lockwood, 1962). At present, theories for the hormonal control of water and electrolyte balance among the invertebrates rest largely on morphological correlations between neurosecretory granules and the conditions of osmotic or ionic stress.

It seems likely, however, that hormones are responsible for water and electrolyte balance in those invertebrates which regulate in accordance with environmental demands. Lever and his associates (1961*a,b*) have provided evidence for this in the freshwater pulmonate snail *Limnaea stagnalis*. In unoperated animals the granulation of the pleural ganglia changes with water or electrolyte demands in a manner suggestive of neurosecretory regulation; the classical techniques of the endocrinologist have supported this hypothesis. Removal of the pleural glands from adult snails results in body swelling due to increased body water; injection of homogenates of fresh pleural glands causes a rapid decline in the body weight. Evidence of a similar nature points to the brain as a locus of neurosecretory regulation of water and electrolytes in the earthworm (Kamemoto, 1964).

In all groups of vertebrates the hormonal regulation of water and electrolyte balance has been clearly demonstrated and many of the details have been established. It operates at the level of the surface membranes (gills, integument, urinary bladder), at the level of the kidney and also on the special glands of extrarenal salt excretion (gills, orbital glands, rectal glands) and depends primarily on the hormones of the neurohypophysis and the adrenal cortex.

WATER BALANCE AND THE PARS NERVOSA

The neurohypophyseal hormones were introduced in Chapter 2. This family of octapeptides (Fig. 2.10) is secreted by neurons of the hypothalamus and carried by axon transport to the pituitary where they may be stored in a neural lobe. Arginine vasotocin and vasopressin are the potent water balance factors in land vertebrates; because of their action in reducing the flow of urine they are usually called the antidiuretic hormone (ADH).

The first demonstrations of ADH activity were made on mammals. Early in studies of the pituitary hormones, it was evident that extracts of the neurohypophysis often altered urine flow. In 1925, the true nature of this observation was shown by perfusing isolated dog kidneys and recording a reduced urine volume on the addition of small amounts of posterior pituitary extract to the perfusate (Gorbman and Bern, 1962). This antidiuretic effect has now been demonstrated in all groups of land vertebrates. It has never been recorded in the fishes and, interestingly, does not occur in aquatic salamanders nor in purely aquatic anurans such as *Xenopus* (Maetz, 1963; Bentley, 1963).

The physiology of the antidiuretic hormones in fishes is still speculative, although their presence in fish pituitaries has been demonstrated many times. Both Heller (1963) and Maetz (1963) conclude, after comprehensive surveys of the literature, that these are primarily concerned with electrolyte balance and that effects on water balance (such as the diuretic action in the goldfish) are secondary. The evidence is based on the marked action of these peptides on the electrolyte fluxes of the gills of both freshwater and marine teleosts (Meier and Fleming, 1962; Maetz, 1963) and on changes in the amount of neurosecretory materials of the hypothalamic and neurohypophyseal area of euryhaline species such as the migratory salmonids when maintained in heterotonic media (Carlson and Holmes, 1962). These changes have been followed both histochemically and by bioassay.

Increased water absorption by the anuran skin was noted in some of the pioneer studies of the neurohypophyseal factors. A frog or toad swells rapidly when injected with these octapeptides and immersed in water. This response, called the "Brunn effect," has now been shown to be due to the action of ADH (especially arginine vasotocin) on the "pore size" of the skin. It may be demonstrated with isolated pieces of skin as well as with intact animals (Whittembury, 1962). The transfer of water takes place only from the outside towards the inside; the fact that this occurs only when the inside of the skin is hypertonic to the outside medium argues for increased porosity rather than an active transport of water. ADH has a similar action on the urinary bladder of the anurans. Recovery of water from this organ during periods of water shortage has already been mentioned. In this case it has also been shown that the fundamental action of the hormone is to regulate pore size (Peachey and Rasmussen, 1961).

The urodele amphibians, unlike the anurans, are unable to absorb water through the skin or urinary bladder to improve their water economy. Retention of water in *Necturus, Ambystoma* and *Triturus* is exclusively due to renal action; arginine vasotocin and arginine vasopressin were the most effective of the octapeptides tested for an antidiuretic action (Bentley and Heller 1964). The "Brunn effect" seems to be present only in the anurans and may have been an important physiological asset in their mastery of the land habitat.

Osmoreceptors in the hypothalamus regulate secretion of ADH by controlling the activity of the neurosecretory centers in the preoptic nuclei of the lower vertebrates and the supraoptic and paraventricular nuclei of the higher vertebrates. In all cases (anuran skin and bladder, distal tubule of the nephron) the hormone seems to exert its action on water balance by regulating pore size of permeable membranes.

THE ADRENOCORTICAL STEROIDS

The adrenal cortex, or its homologue in the lower vertebrates, is the dominant chemical regulator of electrolytes in the vertebrates. This gland is relatively easy to remove from laboratory mammals and the sequelae have often been recorded: a loss of sodium and chloride through the kidneys, a lowered serum sodium, an elevated serum potassium, a decreased urinary potassium and a decreased plasma volume. Death is inevitable if the animals are not provided with the appropriate cortical steroids (Chapter 2).

In mammals, aldosterone is recognized as the most potent of the adrenal steroids concerned with the electrolyte balance. Its action at the level of the organism is to increase the tubular reabsorption of sodium and to promote the renal excretion of potassium. Actually it has a general regulatory action on all cells of the body increasing the intracellular sodium and decreasing the concentration of potassium; but in this chapter the primary concern is with the regulation of electrolytes between the animal and its environment, and the general action of aldosterone on cell membranes is not discussed. Changes in the electrolyte levels of the blood flowing through the kidney and the brain regulate aldosterone secretion (Fig. 11.10) to control sodium absorption and potassium output through the nephric tubules and, to a lesser extent, through the sweat glands and some of the gastrointestinal glands.

In mammals, the kidney is the organ of significance in a balance of electrolytes. In the lower vertebrates, on the contrary, several other structures may play a part or even the dominant role in maintaining the salt balance. In fishes, the gills are often active either in the absorption of salt (freshwater teleosts) or in its elimination (marine forms). The gastrointestinal epithelium may also be involved in fish which drink sea

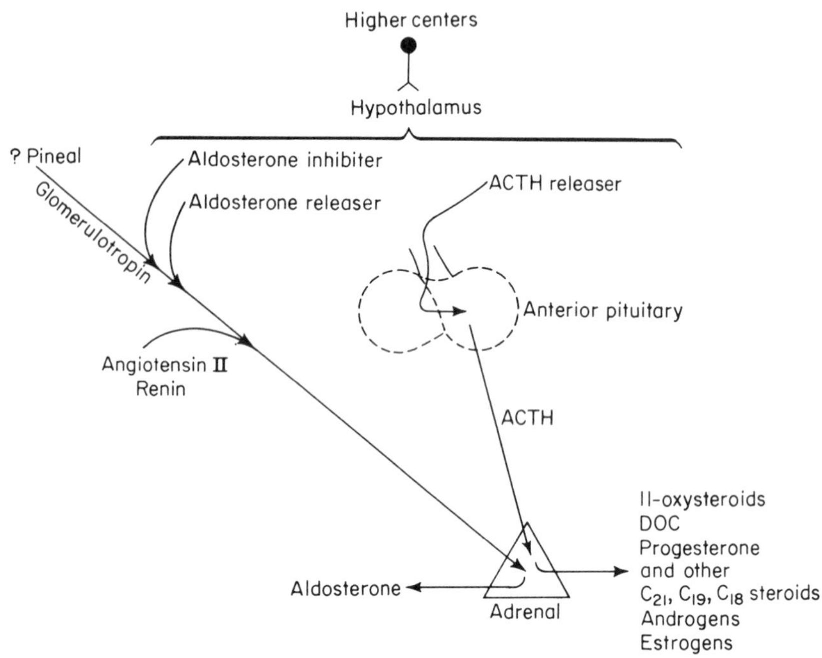

Fig. 11.10. Regulation of adrenocortical activity. [Danowski (1962).]

water to keep up their water supply; in the elasmobranchs there is a special rectal gland concerned with extrarenal salt excretion (Burger, 1962). Amphibian skin controls the passage of electrolytes as well as water (Bentley, 1963; Bentley and Heller, 1964). Marine reptiles and birds can discharge large amounts of salt in a mucous secretion from specialized NASAL or SALT GLANDS located in the supraorbital region (Schmidt-Nielsen, 1960; Holmes *et al.*, 1963; Potts and Party, 1964*a*). These specialized tissues for the extrarenal removal of salt permit their possessors to drink sea water, a feat which only a very few of the mammals have been able to achieve through the refinement of the water reabsorption in the kidney (for example, the desert rat).

All of these extrarenal salt-regulating tissues have now been shown to respond to cortical steroids. The effects of adrenalectomy and salt-loading experiments have clearly demonstrated that both extrarenal and renal tissues are under comparable controls. Several recent reviews are available (Holmes *et al.*, 1963). It is only possible to generalize in a very broad way because the direction of the facilitated ion flux is not constant with respect to corresponding organs in different species; nor is the mammalian distinction between the "glucocorticoids" and the "mineralocorticoids" faithfully maintained in the other phyla.

At this stage in comparative endocrinology it seems logical to follow the arguments of Romer (1949) and Chester Jones (Chapter 2) and to look upon the adrenal cortex as a regulating tissue which evolved along with the primitive kidney or holonephros. The latter has probably been concerned, from the beginning, with ionic as well as osmotic balance, and the cortical tissues which arise from adjacent regions of embryonic mesoderm produce a variety of regulatory steroids; the dominant hormone is aldosterone in the mammal but may be something quite different in some of the lower forms. The reviews cited give many examples of the recorded variations.

Even the nephron may not show the same sensitivity in all groups. In the frog, for example, aldosterone treatment increases urinary sodium and decreases urinary potassium. This renal effect is completely opposite to that found in mammals, but in the frog the sodium is recovered from the bladder urine (Crabbe, 1961), so that for sodium balance the end result is the same. Again, with respect to extrarenal excretion, aldosterone facilitates the sodium and potassium secretion by the salt glands of the duck but reduces the renal sodium and potassium output. In the same animal, corticosterone increases renal potassium excretion while aldosterone decreases it (Holmes *et al.*, 1963). At present the most useful generalization is that the cortical steroids are associated throughout vertebrate phylogeny with the regulation of water and electrolyte balance and that they act at both renal and extrarenal sites in a direction dictated by the needs of the body to maintain homeostasis.

OTHER FACTORS REGULATING WATER AND ELECTROLYTE BALANCE

The hormonal regulation of water and electrolytes is an integrated process dependent on the cooperative action of several chemicals. Although the neurohypophyseal and cortical hormones were considered separately, their action is frequently a cooperative one. Amphibian skin, for example, is said to be responsive to the former only in the presence of the latter (Chester Jones, 1957); likewise, water and electrolytes are regulated by the vertebrate nephron through the interaction of both (Chapter 8).

In addition, some of the metabolic hormones, like thyroxine, have indirect effects on ionic and osmotic balance (Hickman, 1959; Matty and Green, 1963). There are also factors other than the neurohypophyseal and adrenocortical hormones which are specifically concerned with the regulation of electrolytes. The parathyroid hormones which control calcium and phosphorus balance are active throughout the tetrapods and may also be of significance in the fishes (Chapter 2). A caudal neurosecretory system in some fishes (urohypophysis) can probably be added to the list of osmotic and electrolyte regulating organs. Although many details have not yet been described, an impressive array of both histochemical and experimental data can best be interpreted to mean that active neurosecretions are produced here (Enami, 1959; Takasugi and Bern, 1962; Maetz *et al.*, 1964). The pineal apparatus may also be implicated in the regulation of mineral metabolism (Gorbman and Bern, 1962). A complexity of interacting chemicals maintains the balance of water and electrolytes, with the hypothalamus and the adrenal cortex playing dominant roles in the vertebrates.

The Gaseous Environment 12

Joseph Priestley, in the mid-eighteenth century, seems to have been the first to demonstrate scientifically a similarity between life and fire (Kleiber, 1961). By simple experiments he showed that either a mouse or a flame in an enclosed space would change the air so that neither the life of the mouse nor the flame was any longer possible, and that the conditions in the enclosed space were about the same when either of these processes came to an end. Priestley's explanations, in terms of PHLOGISTON, have now been relegated to the curiosities of scientific history; but the similarity between life and fire remains. Both are combustion processes which require oxygen as Lavoisier, a contemporary of Priestley, recognized. Priestley prepared oxygen in 1777 by heating mercuric oxide and showed that it would support the life of animals; but he fitted his facts into the wrong theory, and it remained for Lavoisier to break new ground with the assumption that both fire and animals make the air unfit for their existence, not by producing phlogiston but by removing oxygen to form carbonic acid.

The call for oxygen is almost continuous throughout the life of active animals. As Lavoisier realized, life is a combustion, but the similarities between life and a fire do not really go more deeply than the science of Lavoisier's century. Our century has shown the far greater complexity of metabolic fires and established in some detail the molecular changes through which potential energy in the fuel is channelled into the high energy phosphate bonds of ATP; these, in final analysis, are the source of power for animal living (Chapter 7). The production of large amounts of ATP requires a continuous supply of oxygen. The rate of supply can be limited by certain anatomical and physiological characteristics of the organs of respiration and the transport pigments. These were considered in Chapters 4–6. In addition, the actual oxygen content of the environment may be a limiting factor while other environmental variables such as temperature, carbon dioxide or salinity may impose extra demands for oxygen or affect the rates of exchange. These environmental restrictions in the availability of oxygen and some of the interrelated effects of the environment on metabolism will now be considered.

Oxygen Resources of the Environment

From sea level to the tops of the highest mountains, the earth's atmosphere is everywhere about 21 per cent oxygen. Thus, each liter of air which circulates over the respiratory epithelia contains 210 ml of oxygen. The exchanges of gas between the animal and its environment, however, depend on concentration gradients, and it is the actual number of oxygen molecules in any volume of gas rather than its volume which is important. As Robert Boyle discovered many years ago, the volume occupied by any mass of gas varies inversely with the pressure. At sea level and 0° C a mole of oxygen occupies a volume of 22.4 liters, but at a height of about 18,000 feet where the pressure is reduced to half an atmosphere the volume occupied by the same amount of gas is doubled. The respiratory epithelia of an air breathing animal living at this altitude will then be exposed to only half the number of oxygen molecules in each volume of gas circulated over them. Pressure, rather than volume, is the meaningful parameter for an air breather.

In a mixture of gases, such as the atmosphere (Table 12.1), the pressure exerted by each gas depends on its percentage in the mixture (Dalton's Law of Partial Pressure). Thus, at sea level, where the atmospheric pressure is 760 mm mercury, the oxygen partial pressure (also referred to as the TENSION) is 20.948 per cent of 760 mm or 159.20 mm Hg. On the top of Mt. Everest, although the percentage composition of the air is the same as at sea level, the oxygen partial pressure is only about 45 mm Hg, and this is much too low to maintain the necessary gradients for oxygen exchange.

Temperature also changes the volume of oxygen in a unit volume of air at any pressure (Gay-Lussac's or Charles' Law), but this effect is of little physiological significance; at 0°C a gram-mole of gas occupies 22.4 liters under atmospheric pressure, and this becomes 25.4 liters at the mammalian body temperature of 37°C (an increase of only about 13 per cent). As indicated below, the temperature effects for aquatic organisms are much greater.

Each of the atmospheric gases dissolves in water according to its partial pressure, its solubility coefficient and the temperature. The solubility coefficient is characteristic for each gas. Oxygen is a little

TABLE 12.1.

COMPOSITION OF THE ATMOSPHERE
(Krogh, 1941)

	Per cent	*Partial Pressure (mm Hg)*
Oxygen	20.948	159.20
Carbon dioxide	0.030[1]	0.23
Nitrogen	78.00	592.8
Argon	0.94	7.15
Other	0.082	0.62

[1]May rise to about 0.04 per cent in streets of large cities and is increasing significantly during this century due to burning of fossil fuels and greater agricultural activities (Plass, 1959).

more than twice as soluble as nitrogen, and carbon dioxide is more than three times as soluble as oxygen. Thus, the proportions of the various atmospheric gases are very different in air and in water (Tables 12.1 and 12.2).

TABLE 12.2

OXYGEN (ML/LITER) IN WATER AT DIFFERENT TEMPERATURES AND CHLORINITIES WHEN SATURATED WITH ATMOSPHERIC AIR
(Krogh, 1941)

	Chlorinity (‰)		
Temperature	*0*	*10*	*20*
0°C	10.29	9.13	7.97
10°C	8.02	7.19	6.35
15°C	7.22	6.50	5.79
20°C	6.57	5.95	5.31
30°C	5.57	5.01	4.46

Rising temperature reduces the solubility of gases, and the magnitude of the effect is also characteristic for each different gas. This may be readily calculated from the solubility coefficient, defined as the volume of gas dissolved in one volume of water exposed to the gas at 1 atmosphere pressure. At 0°C the coefficient for oxygen is 0.0486, for nitrogen 0.0235, for carbon dioxide 1.704; the corresponding values at 20°C are 0.0326, 0.0163 and 0.921. Consequently, at sea level and 0°C, water exposed to the atmosphere will dissolve 20.948 per cent of 0.0486 (= 0.0102) ml O_2 per ml water or about 10.2 ml/liter; at 20°C the value becomes about 6.6, a reduction of about 40 per cent. The temperature effect on oxygen availability is thus much greater in water than in air.

The solubility of gases is also reduced by the presence of dissolved solids, and in consequence sea water contains considerably less oxygen than the fresh waters (Table 12.2). The importance of dissolved solids and the magnitude of the temperature effect on the solubility of gases are so great that a measure of partial pressure alone has little meaning as a useful parameter for the availability of oxygen to the aquatic animal. It is more useful and meaningful to record the quantities of dissolved respiratory gases in milligrams or milliliters per liter of water; the former is preferred for the expression of oxygen supply and consumption of aquatic animals.

Still another physical limitation on the availability of oxygen to aquatic organisms is the rate of diffusion. This is very much slower in water than in air and, in many habitats, does not keep pace with the rate at which oxygen is being used. It would require thousands of years for the waters of deep lakes to become saturated with oxygen if they were calm and if only diffusion were involved in gas transport.

Textbooks of oceanography and limnology provide details and generalizations concerning the oxygen-rich and the oxygen-poor habitats of the fresh waters and the ocean. They range from the anaerobic to the supersaturated. The former condition is not uncommon in deep lakes at certain seasons and is characteristic of certain sea waters (Black Sea, Gulf of California). Supersaturation may develop in ponds where there is active photosynthesis, and it is also found in torrents at the base of waterfalls where atmospheric air is carried deep enough to be dissolved in large amounts under the increased pressures. Supersaturation may be sufficiently great to kill fish (Harvey and Smith, 1961). Bishai (1960) summarizes the literature.

Oxygen as a Limiting Factor in the Environment

Life commenced in an oxygen-less world (Chapter 1); but animal evolution was built on the abundance of oxygen required for bulk production of ATP in the mitochondrial processes of oxidative phosphorylation

(Chapter 7). Secondarily, however, many animals have acquired the capacity for life with little or no oxygen. In a few habitats (bottom of water basins, certain soils and the intestines of larger animals) the oxygen levels are continuously low; in others, this condition develops occasionally or seasonally (von Brand, 1946).

Animals may also resort temporarily to anaerobic metabolism during periods of maximum activity when the demands for oxygen exceed the immediate rate of delivery. In this case, an OXYGEN DEBT is incurred which must later be paid for through increased aerobic respiration. For this reason, it is not a true anaerobiosis which permits continuing life without either immediate or subsequent increased oxygen demands.

ANAEROBIOSIS

The anaerobic pathways of metabolism are phylogenetically older but yield only a fraction of the ATP-energy which is generated by the aerobic ones. Consequently, it is logical to look for the major examples of anaerobiosis among the invertebrate animals which are, in general, less specialized and less active. Von Brand's (1946) monograph on the subject lists numerous species and describes tests which have been used to demonstrate their anaerobic capacities. Some vertebrates have also adapted their metabolism to an absolutely oxygen-free world. Blažka (1958) has shown how important and efficient this process may be in the Crucian carp (*Carassius carassius*).

Two somewhat different metabolic specializations seem to be present among the anaerobic animals. The Crucian carp, at low temperature, utilizes the more efficient one. Blažka (1958) found that this animal could live for longer than five months with absolutely no oxygen at temperatures of about 5°C. Carbon dioxide was regularly eliminated, but no fatty acids or other metabolites accumulated in the tissues, and the animals actually synthesized fat. These anaerobic reactions provide some or all of the energy below a critical environmental oxygen level of about 1.7 ml O_2/liter at 5°C. The pathways have not been established, but it seems likely that they are extramitochondrial and depend on a channelling of the triosephosphate and acetate residues from the Embden-Meyerhof pathway into fat (Figs. 7.2, 7.5 and 7.7). Blažka reviews the literature and finds evidence for similar adaptations in some developing fish eggs during periods of anoxia. This may be a primitive and efficient way of escaping both the dangers of anoxia and the hazards of accumulating nonvolatile acid metabolites. The energy yield is meager, and a vertebrate may be expected to resort to it only when inactive and at low temperatures. Fish, such as trout, which have higher rates of metabolism and are more active during winter, lack this capacity for anaerobiosis;

they develop acid metabolites during oxygen deficiencies and contract oxygen debts (Black *et al.*, 1961). This is not a true anaerobiosis.

True anaerobiosis can also be developed through specializations of the mitochondrial system and the cytochrome-dependent metabolic pathways. Many of the parasitic worms have now been studied (Read, 1961). Carbohydrate seems to be the major energy source. The Embden-Meyerhof path, the hexosemonophosphate cycle and the Krebs tricarboxylic acid cycle evidently operate in many forms, but there is ample evidence of specialization in their enzyme systems; the electron transport machinery seems to be highly modified. Cytochromes are present, but hydrogen acceptors other than oxygen are widespread, and a variety of organic acids (acetic, lactic, succinic, propionic, butyric, valeric) are produced. These are readily passed into the surrounding medium.

It is, of course, unnecessary to have specialized anaerobic enzyme machinery to form acids such as acetic, lactic and succinic acids since these are familiar links in the extramitochondrial systems of fermentation. Some of the facultative anaerobic organisms such as worms and molluscs living on stagnant lake bottoms probably depend only on these. The acids diffuse away into the surrounding water, or they may be neutralized by calcareous shells. Dugal (1939), for example, kept clams under anaerobic conditions and showed that the lactic acid, which they continued to produce as long as there was a supply of glycogen, was neutralized by the calcareous shell. This was eroded in the process, and the carbon dioxide content of the mantle cavity fluids increased markedly as a result. Further literature is discussed by von Brand (1946) and Martin (1961).

In summary, animal phylogeny is based on the aerobic way of life even though life itself evolved in an anaerobic world. Active animals can only meet their enormous demands for ATP through the mitochondrial processes of oxidative phosphorylation. Nevertheless, animals at all levels of phylogeny have some capacity for anaerobic living. This may be merely the ability to accumulate a very temporary oxygen debt and form acid metabolites which are removed as soon as the cytochrome system has oxygen to work with; or this restricted metabolism may continue for long periods if ATP demands are minimal and the acid metabolites can diffuse easily away or can be neutralized. On the other hand, true adaptations in the enzyme systems may occur. In these cases animals can evidently bypass the mitochondrial system and turn the residues of the extramitochondrial systems into fat; or they may modify the electron transport system involving the citric acid cycle and oxidative phosphorylation to use hydrogen acceptors other than oxygen. The latter situation, which has been most carefully studied in the parasitic worms, has sometimes been considered an inefficient compromise possible only in an animal surrounded by abundant food. Read (1961) argues that with a reduction in the energy requirements for food gathering it is more economical to reduce the number of enzymatic processes and that there has, in fact, been a positive selection pressure for incomplete oxidation.

OXYGEN CONSUMPTION IN RELATION TO OXYGEN AVAILABILITY

The meaningful relationships are shown diagrammatically in Fig. 12.1. At minimum levels of metabolism (standard or basal metabolism shown by the lower horizontal line in this figure), the animal's oxygen require-

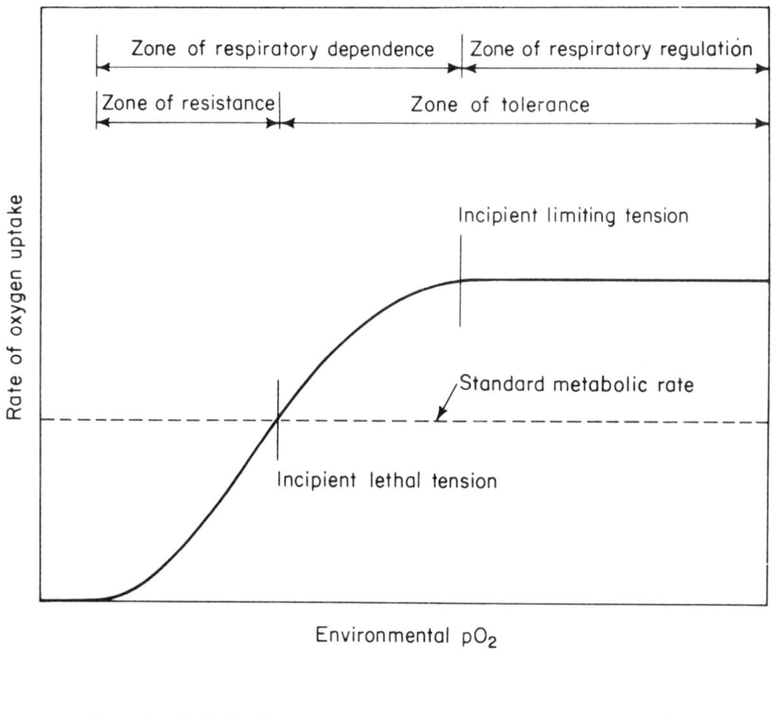

Fig. 12.1. Relation between standard and active (maximum) rates of oxygen uptake at different environmental oxygen concentrations. [After Shepard (1955).]

ments are at their lowest point. This is the INCIPIENT LETHAL LEVEL. An environment which supplies this much oxygen is adequate, but at any lower level a condition of anoxia may be expected, and sooner or later the animal will die (below the incipient lethal level, an animal is living in a ZONE OF RESISTANCE). The upper horizontal level shown in Fig. 12.1 is the INCIPIENT LIMITING LEVEL or the critical pressure (*Pc*) of Prosser and Brown (1961). This is the demand level for active metabolism. At higher oxygen tensions, most animals (regulators) will maintain a steady, independent rate until toxic levels develop (RESPIRATORY INDEPENDENCE or REGULATION). Between these incipient lethal and limiting levels, metabolism or oxygen consumption is dependent on the availability of oxygen (RESPIRATORY DEPENDENCE or CONFORMITY); the organism can tolerate the situation, but the operation of its machinery must be adjusted in accordance with the supply. In a poikilotherm this dependence is markedly affected by temperature (Fig. 12.2).

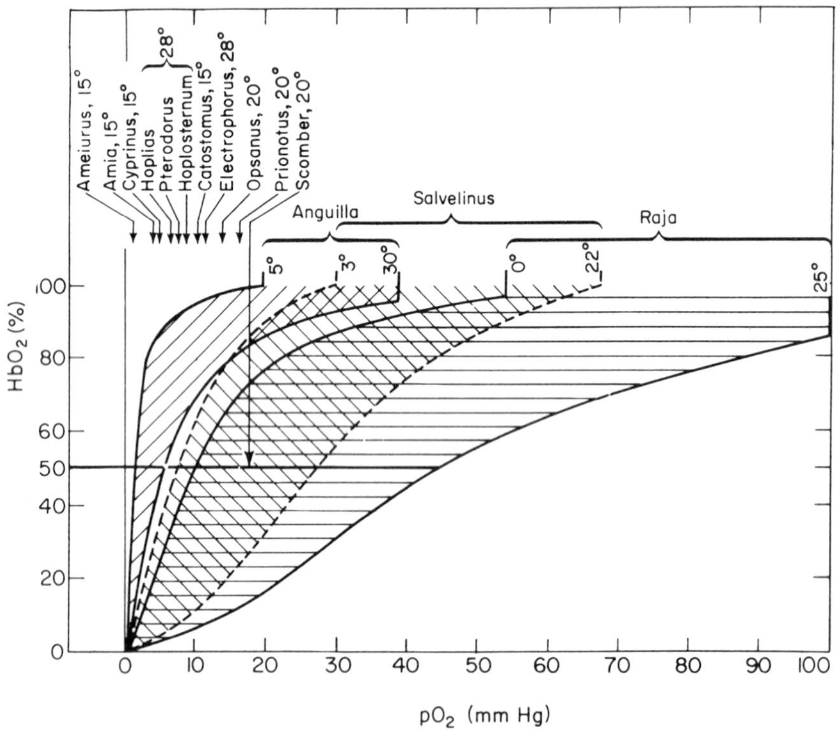

Fig. 12.2. Oxygen equilibrium curves for the bloods of three species of fish in relation to temperature together with the positions of the half-saturation points of the bloods of various other species determined at single temperatures. [Brown (1957).]

Species differences in oxygen requirements. The actual values of the lethal and limiting levels are characteristic of the animal species; they have become established in its phylogeny in response to the oxygen conditions of its environment and its way of life. This genetic or species level of compensation depends on variable capacities of the ventilating system, the transport pigments and the enzymatic machinery of the individual cells. In fishes, for example, the number of gill lamellae show a good relationship to the metabolic demands of the animal and the kind of environment where it lives. Active fish such as mackerel have about

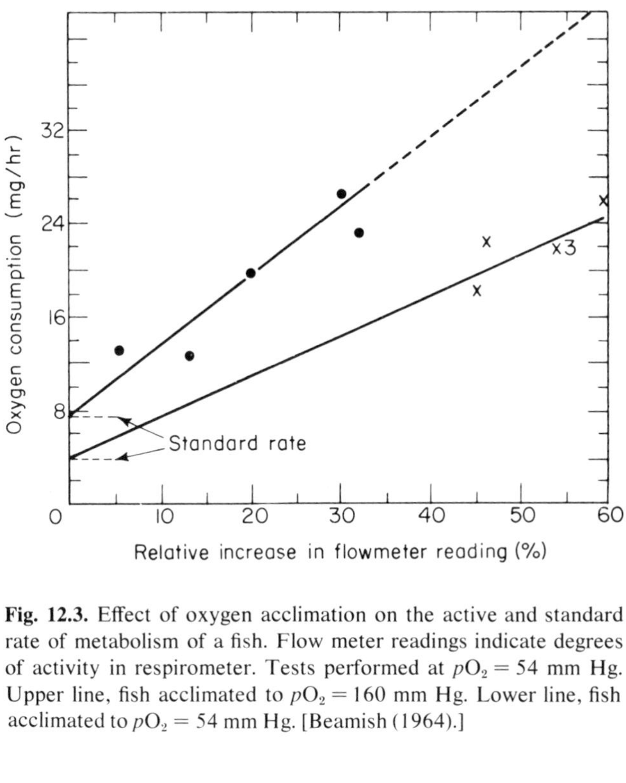

Fig. 12.3. Effect of oxygen acclimation on the active and standard rate of metabolism of a fish. Flow meter readings indicate degrees of activity in respirometer. Tests performed at $pO_2 = 54$ mm Hg. Upper line, fish acclimated to $pO_2 = 160$ mm Hg. Lower line, fish acclimated to $pO_2 = 54$ mm Hg. [Beamish (1964).]

31 lamellae per mm of gill filament and a gill area of 1158 mm^2 per gram of body weight while a toadfish, at the other extreme, shows corresponding values of 11 and 197 (Fry, 1957; Hughes and Shelton, 1962). Similar measurements have been made for the respiratory surfaces of crabs (Gray, 1957). The magnitude of the species difference in hemoglobin transport capacity is indicated by Fig. 12.2. The quantity of oxygen which any hemoglobin can pick up is definitely limited and varies with the species.

Acclimation and acclimatization. Compensation, through acclimation and acclimatization, may also alter an animal's critical oxygen demands. Beamish (1964) found that both the standard and active oxygen consumption of fish could be altered through acclimation (Fig. 12.3); the capacity to take up oxygen in low levels of environmental oxygen could also be changed.

Shepard (1955) studied the lethal levels of oxygen for trout acclimated to different environmental levels of this factor; he concluded that the increased resistance to low environmental oxygen was due to improved gas transport and that changes in the oxygen capacity of the blood, similar to those known to occur in mammals (page 385), were unlikely. Prosser *et al.*, (1957), in comparable experiments with goldfish, however, recorded increased hemoglobin and red cell counts in acclimated fish; they also noted altered rates of metabolism in liver, brain and muscle brei. The independent metabolism of the goldfish changed from 0.239 ml O_2/gm/hr to 0.163 ml O_2/gm/hr when acclimated for several days to environmental oxygen concentrations of 0.7 to 2.0 ml/liter. These authors conclude that this acclimation increased the oxygen capacity of the blood and also lowered the oxidative demands of some of the tissues, presumably through enzymatic adjustments.

Several of the invertebrates are also known to respond to partial anoxia by synthesizing hemoglobin (Fox, 1955). *Daphnia, Artemia, Chironomus* larvae and *Planorbis* are the most familiar examples. The phenomenon can be easily demonstrated by comparing *Daphnia* cultured in oxygen-saturated water with those maintained in water at about 20 per cent oxygen saturation. The animals become conspicuously red in the latter environment and have been shown to survive much better than the pale ones when tested at low oxygen tensions; they can also take up more oxygen. It can be shown that the hemoglobin synthesized under these conditions may be actually necessary for their survival; for example, carbon monoxide treatment is lethal to these red individuals in their partially anoxic habitat but has no effect on either the pale or the red animals when living in oxygen-saturated waters (Fox and Phear, 1953).

The brine shrimp *Artemia salina* shows a similar response (Gilchrist, 1954). Under experimental conditions, the gain or loss of hemoglobin may be demonstrated in a conspicuous way within two or three weeks. Natural populations of *Artemia* become redder as the salinity of their habitat increases since, of course, the oxygen content of the water gradually declines.

Compensation in metabolism through acclimatization is also well documented. Several species of fish have been shown to use more oxygen in the summer than they do in the winter, even though they are maintained at a constant temperature (Wells, 1935; Beamish, 1964).

The photoperiod is probably the dominant environmental regulator of the seasonally changing metabolism of the poikilotherm (Hoar, 1959; Roberts, 1960).

Living at high altitudes. The highest human settlement is a mining camp in the Chilean Andes at 17,500 feet. The Indian miners who live there work in a sulfur mine at 18,800 feet but return to their homes each night to sleep and recover. They know, and it has recently been proven scientifically (Bishop, 1962), that man gradually deteriorates at altitudes of 19,000 feet even when acclimatized as completely as possible. Unacclimatized man is seriously incapacitated at much lower altitudes (9000 to 10,000 feet); fully acclimatized man can spend short periods at much higher levels without supplements of oxygen. Hillary and Tenzing, in the greatest of all mountain climbing epics, removed their oxygen masks on the summit of Everest at 29,002 feet where the partial pressure of oxygen is about 47 mm Hg. They slept for a time without oxygen masks at 27,900 feet (P_{O_2} about 50 mm Hg). but when three French scientists in 1875 ascended directly in a balloon to 26,000 feet, two of them died and the other lost consciousness at about 25,000 feet. These experiences underline two major problems: the physiological limitations at high altitudes and the acclimatization processes which enable men to extend their range of high-altitude living in such a spectacular way.

The limitations of life at high altitudes are not due to the reduced pressures, unless the ascent has been very rapid (Chapter 13), but rather to the lack of oxygen. Figure 12.4 shows atmospheric pressures with corresponding oxygen partial pressures at different altitudes. An oxygen tension of about 80 mm is required to load human hemoglobin (Fig. 6.2), and it can be seen that this is just possible at 18,000 feet. At 36,000 to 37,000 feet even pure oxygen delivered at the pressure of the atmosphere would barely suffice for human needs since there is always a vapor pressure of about 47 mm Hg in the alveoli of the lungs; when this is added to the alveolar CO_2 pressure (ranging from 40 mm to 24 mm, depending on the extent of acclimatization) and the necessary oxygen tension of 80 mm, the total $(47+40+80)$ just about matches the atmospheric pressure (Fig. 12.4). At 63,000 feet the atmospheric pressure is about 47 mm Hg and beyond this altitude human blood would boil. It has been calculated that a man suddenly decompressed to an elevation of 70,000 feet would boil away 4 pounds of water from his lungs before dying in about 3 minutes (Guyton, 1961).

Many terrestrial animals probably experience similar limitations at high altitudes, and life is sparse beyond 18,000 feet (Swan, 1961). However, some primitive insects and spiders live permanently above 19,500 feet, and many birds travel through these altitudes. The bar-headed geese are known to fly from sea level in India on a non-stop flight over the Himalayas to the lakes of Tibet. The comparative physiology of life at high altitudes has not really been studied.

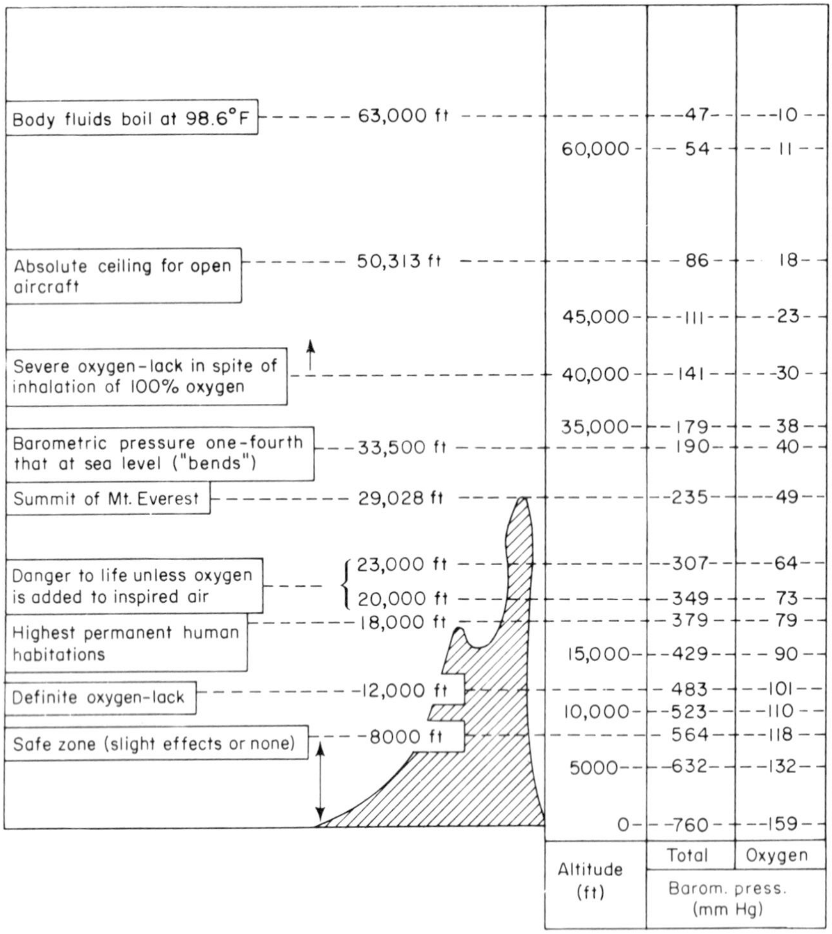

Fig. 12.4. Barometric pressure and oxygen tension in relation to altitude. [Data from Bard (1961).]

Barcroft, who led one of the most famous of the early scientific mountain climbing expeditions into the Peruvian Andes in 1921-22, recorded all the symptoms of progressive anoxia in his men—an increased rate of breathing (hyperventilation), rapid heart beat (tachycardia), cyanosis, fatigue, insomnia. At altitudes where the supply of oxygen to the cortical layers of the brain is inadequate the symptoms become those of anaesthesia or alcoholism: lack of discipline, quarrelling and laughing, poor judgment and loss of memory, nausea and vomiting. The manifestations of anoxia recede after two to four days and gradually disappear with acclimatization (Best and Taylor, 1961). There are detailed discussions of the process in many excellent textbooks of medical physiology; only a summary is appropriate here.

The acclimatization process is one of improving the efficiency of ventilation and accelerating the delivery of oxygen to the tissues. There seems to be no evidence of tissue enzyme changes; the cellular demands are unaltered in the face of prolonged anoxia. The first response to an oxygen deficit is an intensified pulmonary ventilation. This appears when the oxygen falls to about 15 per cent of the sea level pressure; first the depth and then the frequency of breathing increases. The response is a direct one resulting from stimulation of the chemoreceptors of the aortic and carotid bodies (Chapter 4). There is an improved flow of oxygen through the lungs but, at the same time, there is an excessive elimination of carbon dioxide with a resultant increase in blood pH. This disturbed acid-base equilibrium is later adjusted by the kidneys, but before this takes place, oxygen transport by the hemoglobin is somewhat decreased since oxy-hemoglobin dissociates less readily in alkaline solutions (Chapter 6). Further, the respiratory center, which is first strongly activated by carbon dioxide, is inhibited with the elevated pH in opposition to its stimulation by way of the O_2-sensitive chemoreceptors. Alveolar tensions of CO_2 are about 40 mm at sea level and gradually adjust to about 26 mm after 35 days at 14,000 feet; at this altitude the respiratory minute volume is about 50 per cent above the sea level value. The thoracic dimensions actually change if residence at high altitudes is prolonged for many years; Barcroft found the high Andes inhabitants to have chests of larger volumes with the ribs placed more horizontally.

It is worth noting that the metabolic costs of the increased ventilation are considerable. The oxygen demands of the respiratory muscles and heart are greater since they work harder. In addition, the loss of heat due to evaporation of water in the breath creates an added metabolic demand for a homeothermic animal. Beyond a certain altitude the operation of the ventilating machinery requires more oxygen than the air can supply.

The transport of oxygen also becomes more and more efficient during acclimatization. Anoxia produces a prompt elevation in the number of circulating erythrocytes due to contraction of the spleen. This is followed by an accelerated multiplication of red cells and a stimulation of hemoglobin synthesis as the bone marrow is activated by the anoxia. At sea level human blood contains 4 to 5 million erythrocytes per mm^3 but the number rises to about 8.3 million at 18,000 feet. In rats, studied experimentally, the maximum changes occurred at pressures equivalent to 6000 feet when the hemoglobin had increased to 2.2 gm/100 gm body weight from a sea level value of 0.75 gm; the hematocrit, at the same oxygen tension, had altered by 85 per cent (Tribukait, 1963). When these changes are coupled with an increase in blood volume the circulating hemoglobin may rise by as much as 90 per cent. There is little evidence that the oxygen capacity of the hemoglobin is improved, even though the amount is so greatly increased.

Finally, the blood circulating machinery also shows its capacity to respond to prolonged stresses of anoxia. Greater cardiac output (by as much as 20 to 50 per cent) is transient, and the heart rate of the acclimatized person is near normal. There is, however, a very real improvement in the vascularity of tissues such as muscle, heart and brain. The number of capillaries is actually greater in men living at high altitudes and this, together with the enrichment of the blood and the improved ventilation, permits man to make maximum use of the scanty oxygen in these environments.

Air breathing animals under water. All the major groups of terrestrial animals have representatives capable of living under water. Insects, spiders, water mites and each of the classes of land vertebrates are familiar residents of the aquatic habitat. Life in water is easily possible for a tiny animal like a water mite which can get sufficient oxygen by diffusion alone, or for larger animals such as earthworms and amphibians with highly vascular and permeable skins. Simple diffusion and cutaneous respiration, however, are not possible for most terrestrial animals under water, since they retain their highly impervious coverings of chitin or keratin. Usually, they depend on oxygen which is obtained periodically at the surface and used most economically while under water. Their capacity to make efficient use of these oxygen stores is astonishing; the sperm whale and the bottle nose whale are said to go as deep as 900 meters and remain under water for 1 to 2 hours without showing evidence of anoxia. The ability to remain under water varies greatly in different groups; Nicol (1960*a*) has tabulated some of the records.

In general, the major hazard of living under water is the danger of anoxia—essentially the same difficulty encountered at high altitudes. It is obvious, however, that the problem required quite a different solution in the two habitats. In the water, specialization has been in the direction of temporary oxygen storage, with very economical usage and the capacity to deal with oxygen debts, while the adaptations for life at high altitudes have been improvements in the rates of delivery of oxygen to the tissues. The best general discussion of these matters is still Krogh's (1941) monograph published almost a quarter of a century ago.

The tracheates show the most varied arrangements. During submergence, a mosquito larva depends entirely on the oxygen in its tracheal system and, to replenish the oxygen supply, must come to the surface and hang there by hydrophobic hairs grouped around the functional spiracles at the posterior end of the body. Replacement depends entirely on diffusion; a *Culex* larva with a tracheal volume of about 1.5 mm^3 obtains enough oxygen in this way to stay under water for 5 to 10 minutes.

With a relatively larger tracheal volume and by actively ventilating the system when at the surface, some of the larger insects have extended their periods of submergence for as long as 30 minutes—for example, the water scorpion, *Nepa* (Hemiptera). The period of submergence can be further increased by trapping atmospheric air on the outside of the body beneath the modified forewings (elytra) or in a pubescence of hydrofuge hairs. In this way, the predacious diving beetle, *Dytiscus*, extends the period of submergence up to 36 hours (Roeder, 1953). The water bugs (Hemiptera) provide other good examples. Air stores act in a curious way as a gill, since the oxygen dissolved in the water gradually replaces that which the insect uses in its respiration; the respiratory carbon dioxide diffuses away readily. It has been calculated that the air supply lasts 10 to 30 times as long because of this replacement of oxygen in the trapped bubbles (Krogh, 1941).

Aquatic plants may also supply oxygen to insects. Some species can capture the bubbles released in photosynthesis; others (some of the beetles and Diptera larvae) have especially developed hard cutting edges on their spiracles which enable them to puncture into intercellular spaces of the plants.

In all of the examples so far mentioned the peculiar adaptations are for the acquisition of atmospheric air. In addition, however, many of the insects (unlike the air breathing vertebrates) have adapted their respiratory organs for the extraction of oxygen from water. These tracheal gills, which are characteristic of many aquatic insect larvae, permit the animal to live continuously under water and avoid the hazards of journeying to the surface to replenish the air supply. Dragonfly and damselfly nymphs (Odonata) are good examples, with their feathery rectal gills or abdominal gill plates consisting of a rich system of tracheal tubes beneath thin cuticle (Roeder, 1953). The rigidity of the tubes is important in preventing their collapse from the dissolving of the gases into the water. Exchange of gas depends entirely on diffusion; this is improved by moving the gills in the water or by creating water currents over them.

On the whole, terrestrial vertebrates have been more conservative than insects in the variety of their underwater breathing methods. Some of the turtles (family Trionychidae) are said to ventilate the mouth and richly vascularized pharynx when submerged, but absorption of oxygen from the water is most exceptional among the diving amniotes. Reptiles, birds and mammals under water use stores of atmospheric oxygen which must be regularly replenished by surfacing. The physiology of the submerged alligator illustrates several of the basic adaptations (Andersen, 1961). The resting oxygen consumption of a 3 kg alligator is about 4 ml/min at laboratory temperatures of 22° to 27°C. This animal has a lung volume of 250 to 300 ml and this, under optimal conditions, will contain 51 ml of oxygen. The blood volume of the alligator is just over 5 per cent of its body weight or about 150 ml for this animal. A fair estimate of the amount of oxygen in this volume of alligator blood is 8 ml (Andersen, 1961) and this means that the total supply of oxygen on submergence is not more than 60 ml. At a consumption rate of 4 ml/min this store would be completely exhausted in 15 minutes, and yet these animals may stay under water for as long as 2 hours without difficulty. Physiologists have shown that the alligator and other diving amniotes accomplish such remarkable feats not through anaerobiosis but by special oxygen-saving mechanisms.

The most important of these mechanisms is the slowing of the heart rate (bradycardia) and the restriction of the circulation to the most essential of the vascular beds—especially the brain and heart. In the alligator, the heart rate may decline from a pre-diving value of 41/min to 2–3/min after 10 minutes of submergence. Lactic acid increases only slightly in the arterial blood during the dive but rises ten times or more on emerging; this indicates that the circulation to the muscles is shut off during the dive. Reflexes, which in most mammals lead to vasodilation with anoxia in these tissues, no longer operate but the details have not yet been completely explained. The carbon dioxide rises only slightly because of the small amounts of stored oxygen for its production and the efficient buffering in the tissues (Andersen, 1961).

Muscle ischemia during periods of anoxia is not peculiar to the amniotes. Some of the fishes have also discovered this trick. The grunion (*Leuresthes tenuis*) is a teleost with the peculiar habit of spawning on the land. The animals show considerable activity while out of the water; physiological responses include bradycardia and a sharp rise in the muscle lactate with little change in the lactate of the blood until the animal returns to water. During the early phases of recovery, lactic acid in the blood rises acutely as it is released into the circulation from the muscles (Scholander *et al.*, 1962). These physiological adjustments have many parallels in the diving terrestrial vertebrates.

The diving abilities of the birds and mammals are based on adaptations similar to those found in the alligator. Several refinements have, however, been described. The classical work was reviewed by Irving, (1939), Scholander (1940) and Krogh (1941). An abundance of muscle hemoglobin (myoglobin) increases the oxygen capacity of muscles and hence their ability to tolerate oxygen deficits. When Scholander calculated the oxygen balance sheet for a 20 kg seal (*Cystophora*) he rated the muscle oxygen store at about 18 per cent of the total.

The diving mammals (Pinnipedia) have muscular sphincters on some of the great veins which operate reflexly during diving and close off or restrict the circulation from large areas of the muscle and viscera while maintaining the supply to the brain and heart. Such a sphincter is a constant feature of the inferior vena cava in the region of the diaphragm; in some species the hepatic veins may likewise be controlled by muscular valves (Slijper, 1962). Another strange specialization of the vascular system is the widespread presence of numerous, complex and extensive *retia mirabilia*. These intricate nets of small twisted blood vessels form spectacular thick, spongy masses on either side of the vertebral column in the cervical and lumbar regions, in the head and, less conspicuously, in several other regions. They are undoubtedly associated with the redistribution of the blood and the pressure changes which occur during diving, but their precise role has not yet been established (Slijper, 1962).

Another important feature is the insensitivity of the respiratory center to lowered pH (Irving *et al.*, 1941). The carbon dioxide-sensitive ventilation reflexes have been described (Chapter 4); their operation in the diving mammal would be disastrous. A reflex inhibition of breathing occurs when the nostrils of the bird or mammal go under water, and the respiratory center remains quite insensitive to the gradually falling pH during the dive.

In general, the diving mammals show no consistent superiority over other homeotherms in oxygen capacity of their blood, in the rates of basal metabolism or in lung volumes. Their advantages are in circulatory adjustments, the capacity of muscles to tolerate high oxygen debts and the insensitivity of the respiratory center to carbon dioxide and lactic acid. Neural centers responsible for these special reflexes in the duck are apparently located both in the mesencephalon (inhibition of ventilation on diving) and in the diencephalon (cardiovascular responses) (Fiegl and Folkow, 1963).

The human diver is liable to experience decompression sickness (the "bends") if he surfaces too suddenly from a great depth. In this case, the gases dissolved under increased pressures come out of solution rapidly enough to form bubbles which block small blood vessels with disastrous results (Chapter 13). The problem in human diving is created by the necessity of breathing compressed air, maintaining a full lung volume, continuously oxygenating the blood and perfusing all of the tissues. In contrast to this, some of the pinnipedes (grey seals and sea elephants) actually exhale before submerging. Cetaceans, however, fill their lungs to capacity before the dive; but since air is not renewed during the dive, the actual volume of oxygen or nitrogen which might dissolve in the tissues is relatively small. In addition, there are several anatomical specializations which reduce the potential hazard and permit the animal to utilize more fully the alveolar oxygen (Slijper, 1962). The cartilaginous supporting rings of the upper respiratory passages extend farther down into the lung than they do in terrestrial mammals, thus preventing the collapse of these passages under pressure. Besides this there is a special system of sphincters or valves around the respiratory bronchioles which presumably close off the alveoli to prevent air flowing back into the larger passages when the volume is reduced under pressure. Thus, the lungs are prevented from collapse, although the epithelium probably thickens (even though the alveoli may not collapse) and the capillary circulation is restricted so that excessive amounts of gas are not dissolved. Only a slight supersaturation of the body fluids has been found even after dives to great depths (Krogh, 1941).

Oxygen toxicity. Paul Bert (1878) recorded the toxicity of molecular oxygen in one of the early classics of environmental physiology. In our century, both medical and cellular physiologists have intensively studied these effects in aviation and space medicine and in deep-sea diving. More recently, because the damage from excess oxygen resembles that from ionizing radiation, there has been even more widespread investigation.

At atmospheric pressure, man cannot breathe pure oxygen safely for longer than 12 hours. Under increased barometric pressure of diving the hazards are much greater, but at high altitudes equivalent to 35,000 feet with P_{O_2} of only 179 mm Hg, man has been exposed to pure oxygen for longer than two weeks without damage (Bard, 1961).

Lower organisms are less sensitive but, as Bert noted in his early study, invertebrates as well as vertebrates and plants as well as animals are prone to oxygen poisoning. The phylogenetically older groups seem to be more resistant; ferns stand molecular oxygen better than the angiosperms; the poikilotherms better than the homeotherms. Fundamentally, this seems to be related to the rates of tissue metabolism since cells with higher rates of metabolism are evidently more sensitive. Nervous tissue is extremely sensitive; convulsions and paralysis are common symptoms of oxygen poisoning in both vertebrates and invertebrates. Clark and Cristofalo (1961) cite some of the pertinent investigations.

The mechanisms are less well understood than the symptoms. It is evident, however, that rates of cellular metabolism are altered and, in particular, oxygen consumption is reduced at high oxygen tensions. There is probably a blocking of metabolic pathways concerned with oxidative phosphorylation. The steps concerned with the early stages of electron transfer seem to be involved; cytochrome oxidase is not affected but dehydrogenases containing sulfhydryl (SH) groups may be (Dickens, 1955; Bard, 1961).

Effects of the Environment on the Oxygen Demand

Available oxygen as a factor which regulates oxygen consumption or metabolic rate has just been discussed. This, in Fry's (1947) terminology, is a LIMITING FACTOR or one that acts by virtue of its operating in the metabolic chain. Oxygen is indispensable to oxidative phosphorylation (Chapter 7), and below certain minimal levels the production of ATP must be curtailed; the metabolism and activities of the animal are restricted or limited in accordance.

There are other ways in which metabolism is environmentally regulated. The environment may, for example, control oxygen consumption by altering the medium in which the enzymatic processes of metabolism operate. Environmental factors which operate in this way are CONTROLLING FACTORS (Fry, 1947); they govern both the maximum and minimum rates of metabolism while the limiting factor acts only on the active metabolism.

TEMPERATURE, SALINITY AND PHOTOPERIOD

Temperature is a good example of a controlling factor in metabolism; salinity and photoperiod probably operate in the same manner. The action of temperature on cellular metabolism is direct with Q_{10} values of about 2 to 3; its effect on the total metabolism of both poikilotherms and homeotherms has been considered (Chapter 10).

It is more difficult to generalize concerning salinity effects. Hickman (1959) found that the standard metabolic rate of the starry flounder adapted to fresh water was consistently and significantly less than the marine flounder; the rate was highest in supranormal salinities (Fig. 7.16). He suggested that the metabolic demands for salt excretion (a constant process in the marine habitat) were greater than those of water filtration and ion absorption which take place in fresh water. It may also be significant that the osmotic gradient between the body fluids and the environment is usually greater in the marine habitat. Thus, in Hickman's study flounders in sea water of osmotic content $\Delta = -1.35$ had a blood concentration of $\Delta = -0.70$ (a difference of $\Delta = 0.65$) while for the freshwater fish the osmotic content was $\Delta = -0.57$. Several studies of euryhaline fish are in agreement with Hickman's findings (Brett, 1962). For a number of invertebrate species oxygen uptake is greater in the more dilute media (Prosser and Brown, 1961). Dehnel (1960), in a comprehensive study of *Hemigrapsus,* found this to be true for crabs acclimated to 25 and 75 per cent sea water and temperatures of 5° and 20°C (Fig. 12.5); the relationships are complicated by marked seasonal changes and a definite size dependence. Until the physiological mechanisms and the energetics of ion transport are better known, it is difficult to evaluate these species differences.

Photoperiod is also an environmental factor which may alter oxygen consumption by controlling the rate of metabolism. The effect is probably mediated through neurosecretory centers and seasonally changing levels of metabolic hormones.

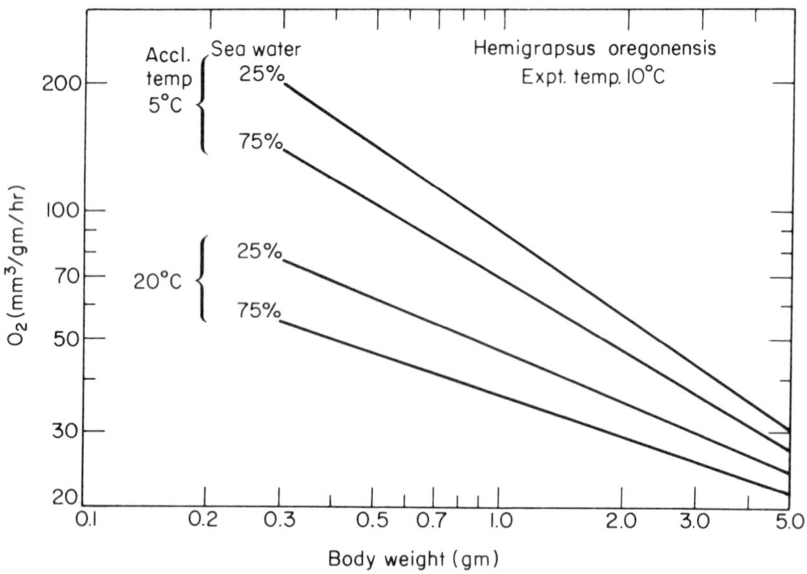

Fig. 12.5. Effect of salinity and temperature acclimation on the oxygen consumption of a crab *Hemigrapsus oregonensis* measured at 10°C. [Dehnel (1960).]

CARBON DIOXIDE

Carbon dioxide is a vital physiological constituent and may act in several different ways to modify oxygen consumption. Although it is formed as a waste product in the internal environment, it performs several well-marked regulatory activities. It modifies the rate of ventilation through its direct action on the centers of respiratory control; it alters the oxygen-combining properties of hemoglobin through Bohr or Root effects (Chapter 6); it acts directly on the vasomotor centers and is thus a factor in the regulation of blood pressure. In general, carbon dioxide, along with other metabolites, serves as a delicate signal for the oxygen demands of the tissues; as the pH falls the ventilation, circulation and delivery of oxygen are often improved.

As a factor in the external environment, carbon dioxide (whether dissolved in the water that flows over the respiratory surfaces or in the air) will enter the tissues and act the same as it does when produced as a metabolite. Its action on ventilation rates in many groups of animals has been mentioned (Chapter 4); the magnitude of its Bohr or Root effect may limit the transport capacity of the hemoglobin. At very high environmental levels, carbon dioxide becomes toxic through a depressing action on the nervous tissues; it is a useful anaesthetic in insect physiology.

This complexity of carbon dioxide effects has been nicely demonstrated in the physiology of fish respiration (Hughes and Shelton, 1962). When the metabolism of a fish is minimal (STANDARD conditions), oxygen uptake is unaffected by carbon dioxide unless this reaches unnaturally high levels; the ACTIVE metabolic rate, on the other hand, may diminish exponentially with any increase in carbon dioxide (Fig. 12.6).

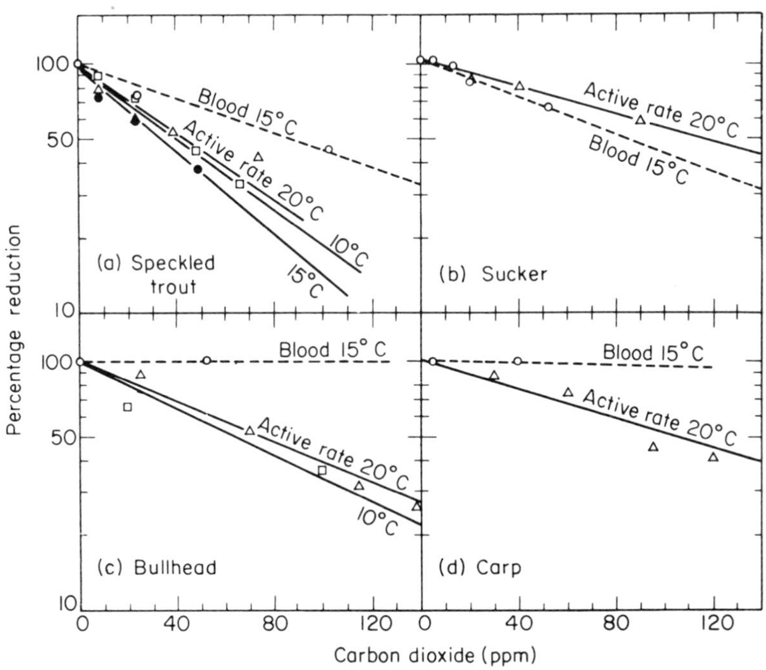

Fig. 12.6. Comparison of the effects of carbon dioxide on the oxygen capacity of the blood and on the active respiration of fishes. Value of 100 on vertical axis is for blood in equilibrium with oxygen at air saturation and minimal amounts of CO_2 or for the rate of oxygen consumption of active fish under the same conditions; percentage reduction are percentages of these maximum values found at the CO_2 tensions of the horizontal axis. [Basu (1959).]

This decline in the oxygen utilization by an active fish may be attributed to the CO_2 effects on both ventilation and transport systems. In fish, as in other animals, elevated carbon dioxide accelerates the rate of ventilation. This in turn, through increased activity of the respiratory muscles, creates greater demands for oxygen. The augmented ventilation volume might be thought to satisfy these demands by an elevation

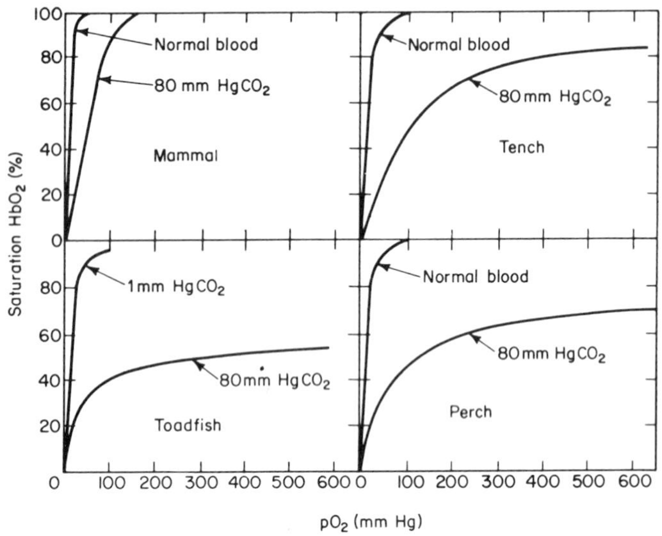

Fig. 12.7. The effect of carbon dioxide on the oxygen equilibrium curves of mammalian and fish bloods. In each case the left curve is for blood exposed to minimal amounts of carbon dioxide (1 mm Hg or less) and the right curve for blood at 80 mm Hg carbon dioxide. Dog blood shows a typical Bohr effect; toadfish blood shows the typical Root effect; in the presence of CO_2 it cannot be saturated with oxygen even at the highest of oxygen pressures. [Based on Jones and Marshall (1953).]

in the utilization of oxygen. This, however, does not happen, since hyperventilation results in less intimate contact between water and blood; in final analysis, this contact is the important factor because the exchange is a diffusion phenomenon. As already noted (Chapter 4), the tips of the gill lamellae move apart in hyperventilation; the more rapidly flowing water is in less intimate contact with the lamellae and in contact for a briefer period. Both of these factors operate against the efficiency of exchange.

The transport pigments are also modified by carbon dioxide and usually carry progressively less oxygen as the CO_2 tension rises (Figs.

6.4 and 12.7). However, there does not seem to be any simple relationship between the loading capacity of the blood and the ability of fish to utilize oxygen in the presence of carbon dioxide. In some species, such as the sucker, this relationship is reasonably direct; but in others, such as the carp or the bullhead, it is nonexistent (Fig. 12.6). These species differences are not yet understood. Explanations must apparently be sought in terms of cardiac output, circulation efficiency and utilization of oxygen in the tissues as well as in the ability of hemoglobin to capture oxygen from the environment (Black, 1940; Basu, 1959).

Species differences in carbon dioxide sensitivity of fishes may be simply demonstrated by asphyxiating animals in closed containers with sufficient oxygen but varying amounts of carbon dioxide and measuring the levels of the two gases at the time of death. Partial pressures of CO_2 must be well over 200 mm Hg to produce respiratory stress in the bullhead, *Ameiurus nebulosus*, but salmonids, bass and many other species are limited at tensions of 50 to 80 mm Hg (Black *et al.*, 1954). These are, of course, unusually high tensions for natural waters where carbon dioxide in the form of carbonic acid quickly combines with cations to form carbonates and bicarbonates. The free CO_2 in sea water is only about 0.25 mm Hg (Krogh, 1941) and, in fresh waters, varies up to a usual maximum of about 5 mm. A significant depression in respiratory metabolism is unlikely until the CO_2 of natural waters rises some tenfold (Brett, 1962) although the effect varies considerably with the temperature.

13

Pressure and Buoyancy

The aquatic habitat, because of its density, creates several special physiological challenges for the animals which live there. Two of these will now be discussed: the forces of hydrostatic pressure and the problems of maintaining a neutral buoyancy.

At sea level, a terrestrial animal experiences a maximum pressure of 14.7 pounds per square inch (760 mm Hg). Under natural conditions this can increase only if the animal descends into a deep cave or a mine shaft; the decrease in barometric pressure with altitude has been considered (Fig. 12.4). These pressures of the terrestrial habitat are, in themselves, of no physiological significance, although they do exert profound effects on the exchange of gases (Chapter 12).

The aquatic animal, however, must withstand not only the atmospheric pressure prevailing at sea level but also the additional weight of water at that level. This hydrostatic pressure increases by about one atmosphere for every 10 meters or 33 feet, and yet life exists in the very deepest marine trenches (almost 11,000 meters) where pressures exceed 1000 atmospheres. From these extreme depths, the *Galathea* brought up sea anemones attached to stones and caught fish at 7000 meters, more than three-and-a-half miles beneath the surface of the sea (Marshall, 1954). The pressures which exist at these depths, when applied experimentally to protoplasm at the earth surface, will alter its constituents (particularly the proteins) and disturb the normal organization and physiology of cells; it seems reasonable to assume that barophilic organisms have, in their evolution, acquired special adaptations for life under these great hydrostatic pressures.

The different species of aquatic animals are ecologically adapted to particular depths. Some are narrowly restricted; others move freely up and down, but none is able to survive and flourish outside a normal range which is a small part of the vertical distribution of life. The specific gravity of protoplasm (exclusive of such dense materials as mollusc shells or echinoderm tests) lies between 1.02 and 1.10, while sea water has a maximum value of about 1.028 (Nicol, 1960*a*; Marshall, 1954). Hence, without specializations to counteract gravity, aquatic organisms will sink or continually expend energy to maintain their normal depth. In terms of energy requirements, there are obvious advantages in maintaining the same density as the aquatic habitat or a NEUTRAL BUOYANCY as it is called. The metabolic economy is considerable (Denton and Marshall, 1958); the mechanisms are curious and varied (Denton, 1963).

The Effects of Hydrostatic Pressure

The *Talisman* dredging expedition of 1882–83 sparked the first scientific research on the effects of hydrostatic pressure. The French scientist Regnard, in particular, was stimulated by the discovery of animals living beneath 12,000 meters of sea water at pressures of about 1000 atm. He designed an apparatus which permitted him to test, and sometimes observe, the effects of hydrostatic pressures up to 1000 atm on many different organisms. His findings were described in a classical monograph which appeared in 1891; they have been summarized in several modern reviews (Cattell, 1936; Heilbrunn, 1952; Johnson *et al.*, 1954).

Perhaps the most surprising of the early observations was that modest pressures, up to at least 100 atm, had little or no effect on many organisms and that the changes observed at pressures up to 1000 atm were often reversible. At pressures of about 500 atm bacteria, yeasts, algal cells, salmon eggs, tadpoles, skeletal muscle and many other tissues or processes often showed depressed activity or retarded growth but no permanent injury following moderate exposure times. Some larger organisms such as echinoderms and coelenterates slowly recovered after an hour at pressures as high as 1000 atm while others (for example, molluscs, crustaceans and fishes) were much more sensitive and could be killed at pressures in the 500 atm range. Precise effects are a function of time; when Regnard watched small aquatic organisms such as *Daphnia, Cyclops* or *Gammarus* through the quartz window of his experimental chamber, he observed their agitation at pressures of about 100 atm. At somewhat higher pressures they stopped swimming and fell to the bottom. If soon released from the pressure they recovered, but longer application led to progressive paralysis or coma and then death. The nervous system seemed to be particularly sensitive.

Technical advances since Regnard's day now permit the use of experimental pressures up to 10,000 atm (in some experiments even 100,000 atm), and it is apparent that a sharp physiological distinction is to be drawn between the moderate pressure effects of 100 to 1000 atm and the excessive pressures between 1000 and 5000 atm or more. The excessive pressures accelerate protein denaturation and produce irreversible changes; the moderate pressure effects are often reversible and retard denaturation or stabilize proteins in situations which denature them, as for example, at high temperatures.

At the cellular or molecular level the action of pressure seems to be primarily on the proteins. Recent studies of enzyme reactions, luminescent bacteria, muscle contraction, protoplasmic viscosity as seen in ameboid movement and the cell division of echinoderm eggs have focussed attention on the denaturation of proteins. At least one of the effects of pressure is to disorder or alter their molecular arrangements, particularly the primary and tertiary bonding of the molecules. This work is, however, beyond the realm of environmental and comparative physiology (Giese, 1962; Johnson *et al.*, 1954). The environmental physiologist has not yet been able to investigate this factor as it applies to truly barophilic organisms. The technical difficulties of obtaining animals from great depths and studying them under relatively normal conditions are very great.

MAN AS A DEEP-SEA DIVER

Man has no specialized physiological machinery for life under water and must continue to ventilate his lungs and perfuse all his tissues with oxygenated blood. His capacity to incur an oxygen debt is very limited. Thus, when he goes beneath water for more than a few minutes, some device must be used to deliver air to the lungs under the pressures which exist at that level. Unless this is done, the lungs collapse as the pressure increases in accordance with Boyle's Law. The relationship is shown in Fig. 13.1. At a depth of 33 feet the lung volume would be halved with a doubling of the pressure from 1 atm at sea level. Caisson workers in deep tunnels, men in diving bells and the thousands of underwater explorers with their SCUBA diving equipment (SELF-CONTAINED UNDERWATER BREATHING APPARATUS) are maintaining a full lung volume with air at whatever pressure exists in their immediate environment. This creates two serious hazards. The first of these is due to the toxicity of the excessive quantities of gases which dissolve in the tissues under pressure and the second develops if the diver ascends so rapidly that these gases come quickly out of solution or the air expands too rapidly in the lungs.

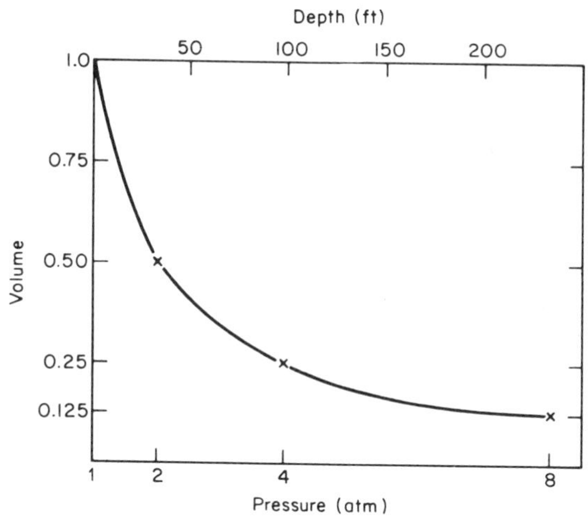

Fig. 13.1. The effect of hydrostatic pressure (depth) on the volume of a gas in an enclosed space.

Oxygen and nitrogen are the dangerous gases under these conditions. Although carbon dioxide is toxic in high quantities (above 10 per cent), it occurs in only small amounts in atmospheric air and does not usually accumulate dangerously in most of the devices used for diving. Oxygen toxicity was mentioned in the previous chapter. Dangerous amounts can dissolve in the tissues within half an hour at 33 feet (increased pressure of 1 atm) if the breathing apparatus provides pure oxygen and the individual is active.

In breathing compressed air the hazards are primarily from nitrogen which accounts for about four-fifths of the volume of the air and is particularly soluble in tissues. At sea level, a man has about 1 liter of nitrogen dissolved in his tissues, with less than half of this in the body water and somewhat more than half of it in the lipids (Guyton, 1961). Although only about 15 per cent of the body is fat, the dissolved nitrogen is largely in this fatty tissue. At sea level this is innocuous but, in deep water, large amounts in solution under pressure are extremely toxic and produce a nitrogen narcosis ("raptures of the depths"). The nitrogen dissolves slowly, and it requires an hour or more at any pressure to produce an equilibrium. If, however, nitrogen saturation is permitted, a mild narcosis may be expected at 130 feet where the pressure is about 5 atm; the diver will become quite helpless at 300 feet with about 10 atm pressure.

The physiology of nitrogen narcosis is not well understood; at least superficially it is similar to that of other anaesthetics. Nitrogen solubility in plasma membranes, particularly in the neurons, depresses the excitability of the cells in general and the nervous system in particular. Theories and discussions of these matters will be found in textbooks of pharmacology and medical physiology. Because of its highly toxic nature, nitrogen is often replaced by helium in the gas mixtures prepared for divers. Helium is less soluble than nitrogen, lacks the narcotic effect and, because of its low molecular weight, diffuses much more quickly from the tissues.

The second major hazard is the expansion of the gas and its release from solution if the pressure is too quickly reduced. If the diver ascends rapidly, air can expand suddenly enough in the lungs to rupture membranes and capillaries and permit gas to enter the circulatory system (air embolism). Gases dissolved throughout the tissues may also be released as air bubbles with symptoms and damage which vary with the location of the gas. The dangers depend both on the depth and the length of the dive: a diver can stay 5 hours or more at a depth of 35 feet without fear of injury upon sudden decompression, while little more than 10 minutes at 130 feet make a sudden decompression hazardous. Clinical symptoms seen in aviation medicine and deep-sea diving, safe limits of decompression, types of diving gear and many other details are discussed in several recent texts of medical physiology.

Man is not the only animal that runs the risk of sudden decompression. Similar damage has been described in fish which have come through the turbines of a power dam and were suddenly released into shallow water after their residence in a deep reservoir behind the power dam (Hamilton and Andrew, 1954).

Buoyancy

In theory, an organism might adjust its weight and counteract gravity either by excluding some of the heavier elements or by including lighter materials which operate as floats or buoyancy tanks. There are many examples (both in the plant and animal kingdom) of organisms which have solved the buoyancy problem in one or the other of these ways. In addition, or as an alternative, it is possible to improve flotation by altering the surface-to-volume relationships. Some of the radiolarians (*Acanthometra*), for example, possess a system of symmetrically radiating spicules on which contractile threads of protoplasm (the myomeres) are anchored. The myomeres arise in the extracapsular protoplasm of the cell and are inserted on the tips of the spicules; when they contract the gelatinous surface layer is so greatly expanded that the animal rises in the sea; with relaxation of the myomeres and a shrinking of the protoplasmic mass, the animal sinks once more toward the bottom. The *Nautilus,* an immensely larger and more complex animal, also improves its buoyancy by greatly extending the soft parts of the body. In this case a large part of the animal can be extended from or withdrawn into the beautifully coiled shell. Other curious examples are described in books by Jacobs (1954) and Marshall (1954).

EXCLUSION OF HEAVIER ELEMENTS

Sea water has a specific gravity of about 1.026. A hypothetical animal from one of the lower phyla, containing body fluids isosmotic with sea water, would obtain a lift of 26 mg per ml of fluid if its salts were replaced by fresh water. This is, of course, biologically impossible, but a measure of hypotonicity is sometimes permissible, and the pelagic egg of the marine teleost owes a portion of its buoyancy to its lowered tonicity (Kanoh, 1954; Denton, 1963). Fertilized eggs become impermeable to sea water and retain the tonicity characteristic of adult fish; unfertilized eggs take on sea water rapidly and sink. It has been suggested that one of the major advantages of hypotonicity in the marine teleost is its contribution to the formation of pelagic eggs.

A lift can also be obtained by replacing the heavier ions with lighter ones. Our hypothetical animal could retain its isotonicity and achieve a lift of 3.5 mg per ml if pure sodium chloride replaced the other sea salts (Denton, 1961). A complete replacement is physiologically impossible, but some of the algae and protozoans, the gelatinous planktonic ctenophores, medusae, nudibranchs and tunicates have reduced amounts of the heavier ions such as Ca^{++}, Mg^{++} and $S0_4^{--}$. Exclusion of the latter ion seems to be particularly important in these gelatinous forms where the proportions of water are relatively great (about 95 per cent in a jellyfish). A partial replacement of sodium chloride with ammonium chloride is said to account for the buoyancy of the luminescent protozoan *Noctiluca miliaris* (Krogh, 1939; Denton, 1963). The feeble ossification and reduction in the caudal and trunk musculature of many bathypelagic fishes contribute markedly to their buoyancy (protein has a density of about 1.33). The density of some of these forms may be within 0.5 per cent of sea water, with a body containing less than 5 per cent protein in comparison with 17 per cent in coastal fishes (Denton, 1961) They have become floating traps through the loss of the swimming muscles and the retention of heavily muscled jaws.

By far the most elegant buoyancy machine based on these principles is the cuttlebone of the cuttlefish, *Sepia officinialis*. This operates as a

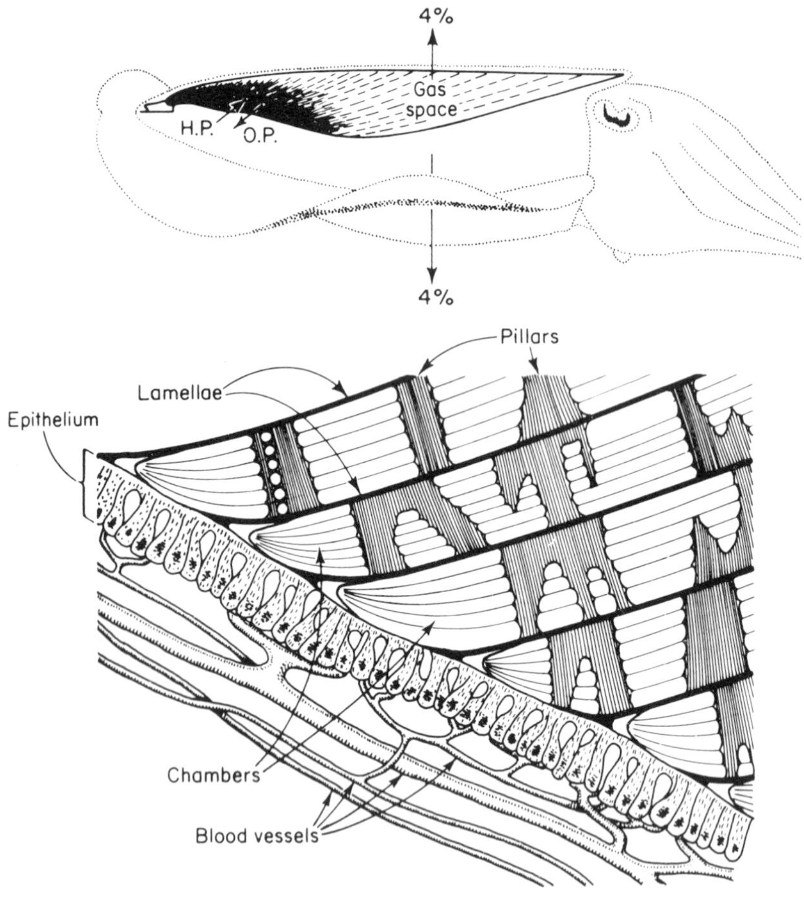

Fig. 13.2. The cuttlebone of the cuttlefish *Sepia officinalis* (outlined above) has a gas space and a liquid-filled area (shown in black). Below, section of cuttlebone showing the epithelium lying along the posterior ventral surface. *H.P.*, hydrostatic pressure of the sea is balanced by an osmotic pressure (*O.P.*) between the cuttlebone liquid and the blood. In sea water the cuttlebone gives a net lift of 4% of the animal's weight in air and thus balances the excess weight of the rest of the animal. [After Denton (1961).]

buoyancy tank in which the amount of liquid can be varied by a "desalting apparatus"; removal of the salt from the liquid in the tank lowers its tonicity and, in consequence, water moves out osmotically. This buoyancy tank (the cuttlebone) contains only a small amount of gas, mostly nitrogen; the effective changes are due to the osmotic flow of water.

The cuttlefish may range to depths of more than 600 feet where the pressures are 20 atm. Its cuttlebone is beautifully built to withstand these pressures. About 100 plates or lamellae of calcified chitin are placed one above the other and held apart by sturdy vertical pillars. The chambers thus formed are further divided by thin membranes parallel to the lamellae (Fig. 13.2). The whole structure is sealed off along the dorsal, lateral and anterior-ventral surfaces by a tough calcified membrane, but the posterior-ventral or siphuncular surface is covered with a vascular layer of epithelial cells. This is the ion pump or salt extractor. Denton (1961) and his associates have shown that the animal can use it to alter buoyancy rather quickly in accordance with behavior. Cuttlefish lie on the bottom during the day and hunt in the surface waters at night (Fig. 13.3). The density of the cuttlebone varies from about 0.5 (containing 10 per cent liquid) to almost 0.7 (containing 30 per cent liquid). At a

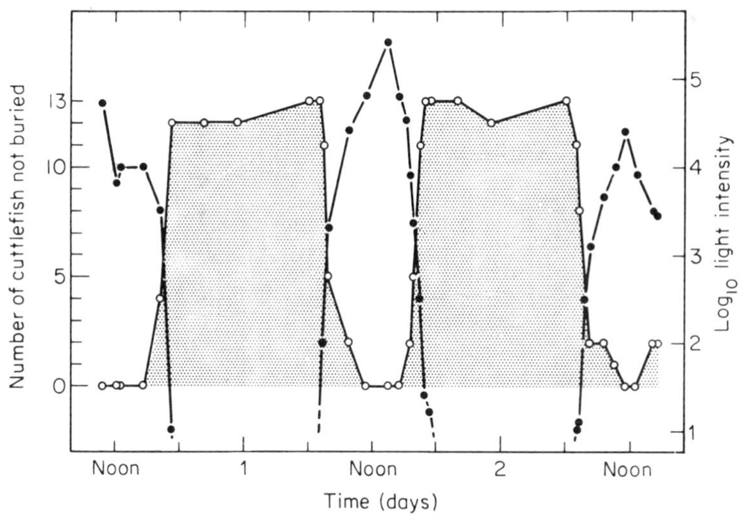

Fig. 13.3. Diurnal changes in the behavior of cuttlefishes. Open circles, number of animals not buried (total number of animals, 13). Solid circles, light intensity on a logarithmic scale. Light corresponds approximately to that found in the sea at about 125 ft. [Denton and Gilpin-Brown (1961).]

density of 0.6, an animal of 1000 gm would achieve an upthrust of 40 gm, and this will just about balance the excess weight of the animal in sea water (Denton, 1961).

INCLUSION OF LIGHTER MATERIALS

In addition to exchanging heavy for lighter ions, animals may actually accumulate or secrete low specific gravity materials such as fats, ammonium salts or gases and thus attain a neutral buoyancy.

Oil droplets and fat depots. The specific gravity of fish oil is about 0.93. Oil droplets in pelagic fish eggs and diatoms add to the lift achieved by excluding heavy ions. Some of the larger vertebrates, such as sharks and whales, have exploited fats as their major buoyancy device. Sharks (Family Squalidae) have extremely fatty livers making up about 25 per cent of their body volume and containing a special fatty hydrocarbon, squalene, with a specific gravity of 0.86 (Denton, 1963). Per gram, squalene has 70 per cent greater lifting power than fish oils. Whales also have generous amounts of low density fats—in this case, esters of long chain aliphatic alcohols with fatty acids.

Accumulations of ammonium salts. Like Piccard's bathyscaphe with its gasoline-filled buoyancy tank, the deep-sea squids (Cranchiidae) attain a neutral buoyancy with a float of low density liquid—in this case, a solution of ammonium chloride. Again, the cephalopods have shown their originality for, like the cuttlebone, this large buoyancy tank is without parallel in the animal world.

Although bulky, the buoyancy tank has a definite advantage over cuttlebone for an animal exploiting the depths of the ocean. If the water in the cuttlebone were completely desalted the osmotic difference could not act against hydrostatic pressures of more than 20 to 25 atm (about 800 feet); cuttlefish are most frequently found between 100 and 250 feet. Since water is virtually incompressible, the major limitation on the use of a fluid-filled buoyancy tank is one of bulk.

The ammonium chloride solution is accumulated in the large coelomic cavity which forms about two-thirds of the total volume of the squid. Denton (1961) has measured its density at 1.010 to 1.012 and found that it contains 480 mM of ammonium and only about 90 mM of sodium. In contrast, the body fluids of *Sepia* contain approximately 465 mM of sodium (Nicol, 1960*a*). The pH of the fluid in *Cranchia is* around 5, and this acidity accounts for the retention of the ammonia in the form of ammonium salts. Molecular ammonia diffuses quickly through tissues and is extremely toxic. The efficiency of this fluid as a buoyancy device is easily demonstrated by draining the coelomic cavity and watching the animal sink; the success of the group as bathypelagic animals is attested by their range of form and size. Some of them are the largest of the invertebrates; *Architeuthis* exceeds 50 feet in total body length (Morton, 1958).

Floats containing gas. If the technical problems can be solved, a tank of compressed air (density 0.00125 at sea level) is by far the most efficient device for flotation. The air bladder of a teleost fish forms about 5 per cent of its body volume, the cuttlebone about 10 per cent of *Sepia* and the coelomic fluid of the cranchid squid approximately 65 per cent.

Gas-filled spaces are common in floating plants and in animals at many levels in phylogeny. Active processes are often involved in the accumulation of this gas, as evidenced by unique constituents and the tremendous pressures which can be maintained. For example, the pneumatocysts of some of the giant kelps may contain 5 to 10 per cent carbon monoxide (Rigg and Swain, 1941), and this may also contribute significantly (0.5 to 13 per cent) to the float of the Portuguese man-of-war (*Physalia*) where it is evidently formed from a substrate of L-serine (Wittenberg, 1960). The gas pressures are just as astonishing as the strange constituents; teleosts with air bladders have been caught at 4500 meters where the pressures in the bladder must be in the region of 450 atmospheres (Denton, 1961). This is an extreme example, however, and most of the animals with gas-filled spaces are above 1000 meters. In deeper waters the swim bladder is either lost or its gas is replaced by oil (Jones and Marshall, 1953).

Jacobs (1954) and Marshall (1954) describe many curious examples of animals with gas floats. The minute rhizopod protozoan *Arcella,* not more than 1.1 mm in diameter, adjusts its buoyancy with bubbles of oxygen (Bles, 1929); the giant coelenterate *Physalia* with trailing tentacles that may be 30 feet in length, operates a float or pneumatophore of up to one liter capacity with a gas-generating layer of cells and a pore through which gas can be emitted to adjust the volume. This gas mixture is about 20 per cent oxygen, with the remainder carbon dioxide, nitrogen, argon and carbon monoxide (Wittenberg, 1960). The cephalopods (nautiloids and fossil ammonoids and belemnoids of the Palaeozoic and Mesozoic seas) also experimented successfully with buoyancy tanks of compressed air, but the teleost fishes provide the best of all examples (Denton, 1961).

In phylogeny, the air or swim bladder of fishes probably served first as an accessory organ for the exchange of gases (Chapter 4). It has assumed several different functions in the evolution of the teleosts (Jones and Marshall, 1953), but its role as a hydrostatic organ dominates. Because of pressure-volume relationships (Fig. 13.1), a gas float is only useful over a range of depths if the quantity of gas can be readily altered. In short, when the fish descends 33 feet the volume of its swim-bladder gas will be halved; this must be recovered by acquiring gas and retaining it at a pressure of 2 atm to achieve the same buoyancy as it had at sea level. The formation of gas and its removal are the major physiological problems concerned with the function of this structure as a hydrostatic organ. Only these aspects of its physiology are summarized here. A detailed discussion and comprehensive bibliography of the literature will be found in reviews by Jones and Marshall (1953) and Denton (1961).

The teleostean swim bladder develops from the esophageal region of the gut. This connection (the pneumatic duct) is retained in the more generalized groups (Physostomi), and air can be readily passed in either direction through it. In the least specialized examples (salmon, for example) there are no other arrangements for gassing or degassing. The pneumatic duct is under the autonomic nervous control characteristic of this region of the gut, and a well-defined series of reflexes operates to adjust the volume, but the organ can only be filled if the animal comes to the surface and gulps air (Tait, 1960). In the more specialized teleosts, and particularly those that live in deep water, the pneumatic duct is lost during ontogeny (Physoclisti) and the gas supply depends on the blood transport system. Intermediate conditions also occur, and many fish (for example, the Atlantic eel) have both a pneumatic duct and a specialized gas gland.

It is the closed or physoclistus bladder which presents the major physiological problems; there are still many questions concerning the details of gas flow through it. In general, however, the organ is a gas-tight sac in the physoclist, with thick elastic walls through which gases dissolve slowly or not at all. Exchanges depend on two specialized areas: the RESORBENT PART (oval or posterior chamber), concerned with the removal of gas, and the SECRETORY PART, an organ of gas production, consisting of a gas gland with adjacent rete mirabile.

The oval is a vascular pouch on the dorsal wall of the bladder. It is surrounded by a ring of muscle which can be relaxed to expose its vascular surface to the gases in the main bladder or constricted to separate the two areas. The removal of gas from the physoclist bladder depends on its resorption by the blood in the vascular net of the oval. The significant factors are pressure differences, blood flow and the transport capacities of the hemoglobin; the principles are not different from those which operate at other places in the animal. Instead of an oval some of the physoclists have a special resorptive posterior chamber separated by a partial diaphragm (Fänge, 1953; Marshall, 1960), but the physiology of gas removal is the same.

The production of gas cannot be so readily explained in terms of familiar physiological principles. The process is often termed SECRETION, but it is still not clear whether the liberation of the gas depends on a metabolic production of gas molecules or whether the mechanisms involve only the dissociation of the gases from hemoglobin and their diffusion or active transport from solution in the plasma. At present, secretion of swim-bladder gases implies only that the gases accumulate at partial pressures higher than those in the blood.

The problem can be readily demonstrated in an elementary physiology laboratory equipped with simple pipettes for gas analysis (Hoar, 1960). Gas secretion is stimulated by removing some of the bladder gas with a small hypodermic needle or by altering the buoyancy (adding a weight to the fish, increasing the depth of water above it or diluting the medium if it is a marine species). A stickleback or a *Fundulus* is suitable and demonstrates that the gas secreted in response to this stimulus is largely oxygen. If the process is followed over an extended period, the oxygen is gradually replaced by other gases in proportions which vary somewhat with the species and the depth at which they live. The nitrogen content, for example, increases with the depth at which hake (*Urophycis*) and ratfish (*Macrurus*) are caught (Scholander, 1954). Easy experiments of this sort were first performed by Moreau in the nineteenth century (Denton, 1961).

The elegant tracer techniques of our century have shown that the oxygen is derived from the ambient water. When fish swim in water containing only O^{18} dissolved oxygen, the gas which turns up in the swim bladder is entirely labelled and is deposited as molecular oxygen without a preliminary split into oxygen atoms (Wittenberg, 1961). These experiments argue for a direct transport of oxygen by the hemoglobin from the gills to the swim bladder. Its gradual replacement by other gases might, in theory, be due to active metabolic processes or physical replacement of oxygen by the other gases in the plasma. The latter hypothesis is favored.

The two anatomical structures responsible for gas liberation are the epithelium of the gas gland and the associated rete mirabile. The former is somehow concerned with the release of gas; the latter seems to act as a COUNTER-CURRENT MULTIPLIER which concentrates oxygen and permits an active flow of blood to the gland without marked loss of gas in the venous return.

The epithelium of the gas gland is clearly not a simple diffusion membrane. In some species its surface becomes a foamy liquid film during activity; increased glycolysis, elevated production of carbon dioxide and lactic acid as well as several changes in enzyme activity (carbonic anhydrase, for example) have been measured during stimulated gas production (Fänge, 1953 and reviews cited). The processes seem to require energy or the formation of special metabolites such as carbonic and lactic acid. The lowered pH which results from these acid metabolites has been the basis for several theories of gas secretion since Haldane (1927) emphasized the theoretical possibility of oxygen release from hemoglobin through a Bohr or Root effect. Reference to Fig. 12.7, shows how oxyhemoglobin might be unloaded and remain in this condition at very high tensions of oxygen if the blood has a marked Bohr or Root effect. This must be a factor in many species, but there are deep-sea fishes which maintain high gas tensions in the swim bladder and show virtually no Root effect (Denton, 1961).

Several workers have speculated on the significance of the marked carbonic anhydrase activity in the tissues of the gas gland. This might provide an active mechanism for charging the blood with carbon dioxide and thus promoting the dissociation of oxygen. In support of this hypothesis, Fänge noted that inhibitors of this enzyme system prevented gas secretion while Copeland (1951) reported a 50 per cent reduction in the gas regeneration capacity of the swim bladder after removal of the PSEUDOBRANCH, an organ of uncertain function which produces very large amounts of carbonic anhydrase.

In theory, the solubility of the blood gases might also be lowered by the addition of salt (Table 12.2). Many physiological processes depend on the active transport of salt; one of the most spectacular was described in the hairpin loops of the mammalian nephron which operate as counter-current multipliers for the concentration of the urine (Chapter 11.). Kuhn *et al.* (1963) argue for the importance of a "salting out effect." This, together with the Bohr and Root effects, provides the theoretical possibilities of releasing large amounts of gases from the blood in the region of the gas gland.

Haldane (1927) seems to have been the first to emphasize the probable importance of the rete mirabile in gas retention. Its capillaries seem to be the longest in the animal kingdom. In some species they measure 4 mm in comparison with the very long skeletal muscle capillaries which are only about 0.5 mm (Denton, 1961). They are numerous. It has been estimated that the rete of the eel contains 88,000 venous and 116,000 arterial channels. They are closely packed (Fig. 13.4) and ideally arranged for a counter-current exchange system. Haldane (1927) visualized a COUNTER-CURRENT DIFFUSION PROCESS with the release of oxygen from oxyhemoglobin by acid. Figure 13.4 suggests that such a process could be extremely efficient in reducing the loss of gas from the bladder.

A moment's reflection, however, shows that this by itself can operate only as a retention system. Something more is required to accumulate gases in the bladder at high pressures. If, for example, oxygen is to be steadily delivered from the blood to the swim bladder, its concentration must obviously be higher at the entrance of the capillary loop than it is in the exit channel. Active production at some point within the gland is essential.

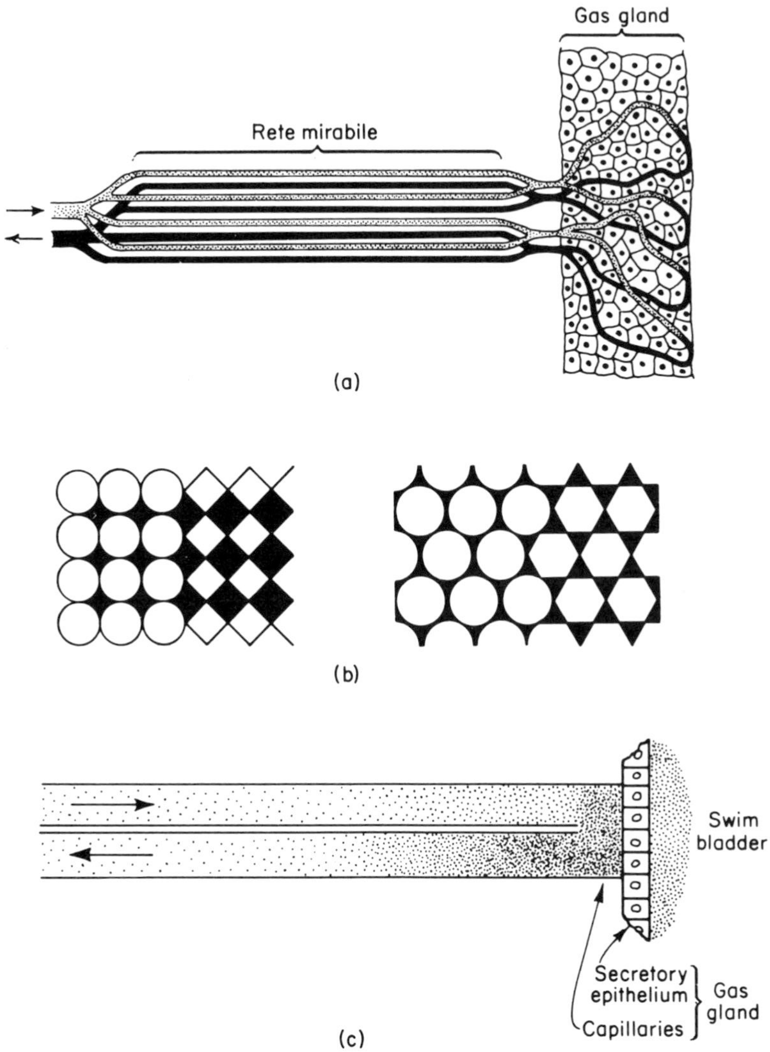

Fig. 13.4. Diagrams of parts of the gas gland and rete mirabile of the teleost swim bladder. *a*, Arterio-venous loop to gas gland. [Marshall (1954).] *b*, Cross section through the loops showing some possible arrangements of venous (open) and arterial (black) capillaries. [Scholander (1954).] *c*, To show how the counter-current diffusion system could reduce the loss of gas once this gas had been secreted.

Denton (1961) and Kuhn *et al.* (1963) have emphasized the theoretical advantages of a COUNTER-CURRENT MULTIPLIER similar to that described in the mammalian kidney. A carrier molecule which could transport oxygen actively from the venous to the arterial capillaries would provide an excellent concentrating mechanism for the development of the astonishing oxygen tensions known to develop in this system. This mechanism would parallel the sodium transport in the loop of Henle. Wittenberg (1961) and Wittenberg and Wittenberg (1961) have provided some evidence for such a transport system and suggested further that the epithelium of the gas gland itself transports the oxygen to the lumen of the bladder while preventing its backward diffusion. Minute intracellular gas bubbles form at the base of the gas gland cells, adjacent to the capillary wall, and pass from there into the swim bladder, but backward diffusion is impossible because of the impermeability of the cell membrane. The arguments are based on the analyses of swim-bladder gases of toadfish (*Opsanus tau*) maintained in sea water equilibrated with gas mixtures and containing fixed amounts of oxygen and varying proportions of carbon monoxide. After emptying the swim bladder, both gases were found to accumulate at higher than ambient tensions. Studies of the proportions of oxyhemoglobin to carboxyhemoglobin in the blood and of oxygen to carbon monoxide in the bladder indicate that the swim-bladder gases are not evolved directly from the blood hemoglobin and suggest the presence of a special intracellular oxygen transport system. These studies suggest that nitrogen and other inert gases diffuse into the actively transported oxygen and are thus carried into the swim bladder.

Kuhn *et al.* (1963, 1964) have criticized the Wittenbergs' interpretations and argue that the salting out of gases, together with the Bohr and Root effects, are adequate to explain the release of both oxygen and nitrogen from the blood. Kuhn's arguments are based on established physiological and physicochemical principles while the oxygen pump postulates an unidentified carrier.

The swim-bladder reflexes concerned with inflation and deflation have been investigated in several species (Fänge, 1953). The autonomic supply is well developed, with parasympathetics of the intestinal vagi and sympathetics from the coeliac ganglia. Fibers pass both to the smooth muscle of the bladder wall and to the gas gland. Tension receptors in the wall of the bladder initiate reflexes appropriate to the volume changes required for an efficient buoyancy device (Fänge, 1953; Qutob, 1962).

Light

14

Solar radiation is the ultimate source of energy for all life. When a photon (the packet or quantum of radiant energy) strikes and interacts with particles of matter, it sends an electron into a higher energy level or an excited state. These electrons drop back to the ground state after little more than 10^{-7} seconds, but during this brief interval they provide the electronic energy which powers the machinery of life. Highly efficient biochemical substances capture the excited electrons, uncouple them from their partners and permit them to return to the ground state through a sequence of energy-yielding reactions. In photosynthesis this electronic energy is channelled into the pyrophosphate bonds of ATP and the reduced pyridine nucleotides; in turn, these are used to synthesize the complex organic molecules which are the fuels of metabolism. These events have been sketched in Chapter 1. Emphasis, in the present chapter, is not on radiant energy as the source of power for life but on light as an environmental factor which limits, controls and orients animal processes.

Twentieth-century theories of quantum mechanics provide a unified concept for the properties of light and matter. Details are beyond the scope of this book, but the principles are pertinent to the present discussion. According to theory, light can be accurately characterized in two very different ways. On the one hand, it has the properties of particles or corpuscles as Newton argued in the seventeenth century while, on the other hand, it exhibits wavelike properties just as his contemporary Huygens so vigorously insisted. Modern theory not only shows that both particle and wave concepts are to be used in certain contexts but also gives the precise quantitative relationships between them. Each packet of light or photon has an energy content which can be calculated from its wavelength by Planck's formula. $E = hc/\lambda$ where h is Planck's universal constant (1.58×10^{-34} calorie seconds), c is the velocity of light (3×10^{10} cm per second) and λ is the wavelength. Einstein's law of photochemical equivalence teaches that photochemical reactions occur only when a molecule absorbs a photon. Hence a mole of substance (containing 6.02×10^{23} particles) can be expected to absorb a mole of photons in a photochemical reaction. The energy of this number of photons is the EINSTEIN, equivalent to 2.854×10^{7} gram-calories. Thus, the physicist is able to calculate the energy associated with light of different wavelengths or, conversely, wavelengths or radiation which correspond to energies of activation for chemical reactions (Chapter 10). Figure 14.1 shows broad bands for the energies of activation of ordinary chemical reactions and for photochemistry, with much narrower bands for several important photobiological processes.

Photobiological Processes

SIGNIFICANCE OF THE TERM "LIGHT"

Life exists in and operates on a relatively narrow band of the electromagnetic spectrum (Fig. 14.1). The entire spectrum extends from the cosmic and gamma rays with wavelengths of only a ten billionth of a centimeter to the radio waves which may be miles in length. Within this broad expanse of radiant energy, there is a narrow band which we call LIGHT because of the sensation which it creates when it falls on the retina of the human eye. Its wavelengths extend from 380 to 760 millimicrons (mμ), with extreme limits of 310 to 1050 mμ in very intense artificial sources. This is our range of conscious vision, and we justly attach great significance to it. However, the comparative physiologist could scarcely confine attention to this particular band unless its action had a much broader basis in animal physiology. This is indeed the case, and the particular band of radiant energy, which we recognize as LIGHT, controls all of the important photobiological processes; the action spectrum for photosynthesis extends from about 400 to 760 mμ, photoperiodism in plants from about 500 to 800 mμ, while photoreception in all animals is almost covered by the extreme human range. For this reason alone the phenomena discussed here are more appropriately grouped under the heading of LIGHT rather than under the broader term of RADIANT ENERGY. There are, however, more cogent reasons for this distinction in photophysiology.

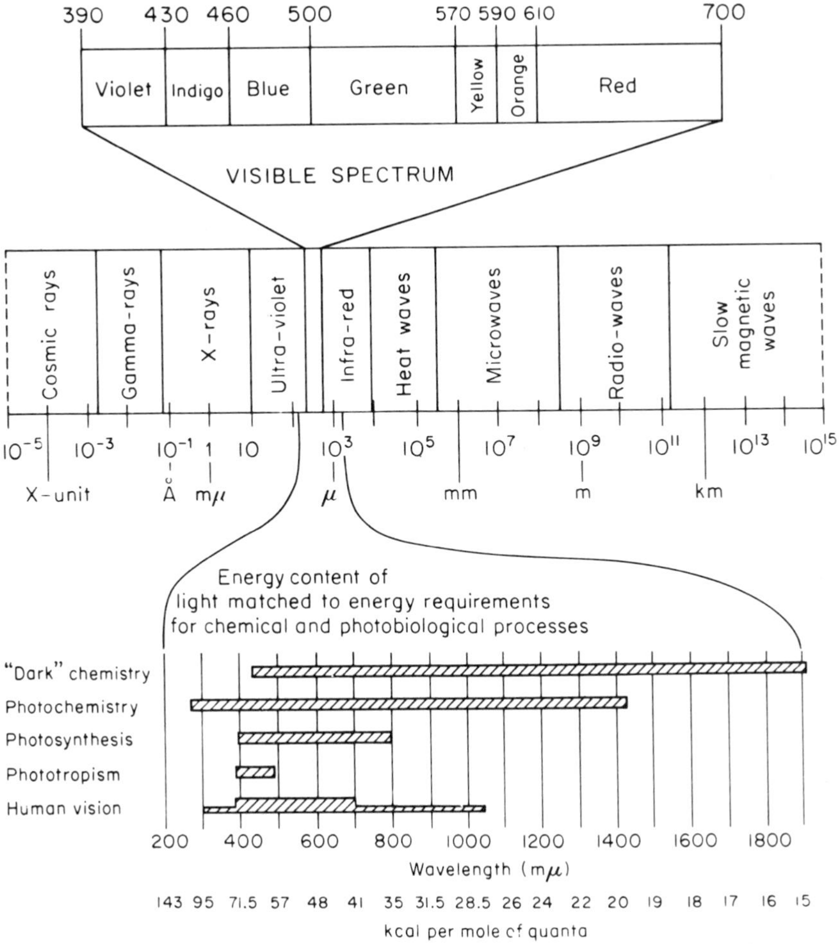

Fig. 14.1. The electromagnetic spectrum with wavelengths in millimicrons at center. Visual spectrum enlarged above and (at the bottom) the energy content of light matched to the energy requirements of chemistry and photobiological processes and to the absorption spectra of photoreactive substances. [Based on values from Ditchburn (1952) and Wald (1959).]

The environmental physiologist might reasonably restrict his attention to this band of the spectrum because it encompasses almost all the solar energy which actually reaches the earth's surface (Fig. 14.2). The ultraviolet is cut off sharply at wavelengths shorter than about 300 mμ by the blanket of ozone which surrounds the earth in its upper atmosphere;

in the aquatic habitat the spectral band is still further restricted as the sunlight penetrates deeper and deeper (Fig. 14.2). The biologist's attention can also be focussed on this band because only this portion of the spectrum is primarily active in photochemical reactions. Wald, in many stimulating papers, has argued that biological processes, no matter where they exist, (on this planet or elsewhere) must be confined to the same range of wavelengths because of the physical nature of the action of radiant energy in chemical processes.

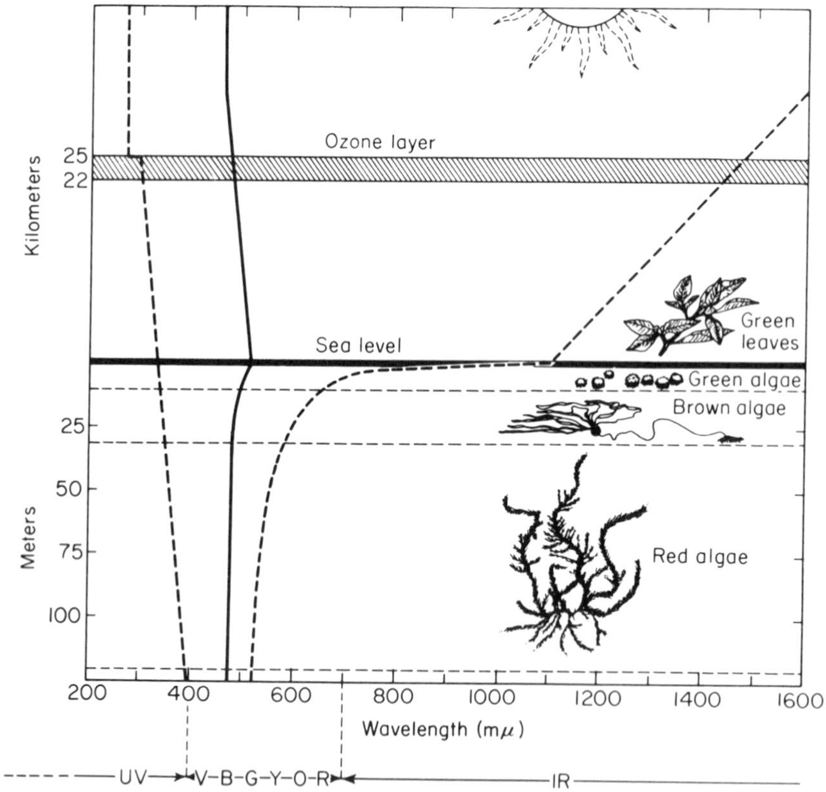

Fig. 14.2. The narrowing of the spectrum of sunlight by atmospheric absorption and by absorption in sea water. The heavy solid line from top to bottom locates the wavelengths of maximum intensity. Broken lines from top to bottom limit the wavelength boundaries within which 90% of the solar energy is concentrated at each level in the atmosphere and ocean. *UV*, Ultraviolet. *V*, Violet. *B*, Blue. *G*, Green. *Y*, Yellow. *O*, Orange. *R*, Red. *IR*, Infrared. [After Wald (1959).]

Because of the complex and delicate nature of many organic compounds, the radiant energy compatible with photobiological reactions is considerably more restricted than that which is concerned with many other photochemical processes. The delicate secondary and tertiary bondings which give the proteins and nucleic acids their highly specific properties are destroyed by radiation shorter than 300 mμ (95 kilocalories per mole). Proteins are denatured and nucleic acids are depolymerized; the living cell is destroyed. This sets a lower limit on the radiation compatible with life. There are other limits associated with particular reactions. Energies required to break single covalent bonds fall between about 40 and 90 kcal per mole (710 to 310 mμ); those which excite valence electrons to higher orbital levels involve energies of 20 to 100 kcal per mole (1430 to 280 mμ). These are the important photochemical reactions of life, and they all fall approximately in the solar spectrum which reaches the earth's surface and drives the indispensable photobiological reactions. On these bases, Wald (1959) argues that only the radiant energy which we call LIGHT is a suitable source of power for living machines.

PHOTOBIOLOGICAL EFFECTS

Three different effects follow the irradiation of protoplasm by various components of the electromagnetic spectrum. The more energetic wavelengths associated with the gamma rays, X rays and the extreme ultraviolet (shorter than about 300 mμ) shatter the molecules by displacing electrons and producing IONIZATION; disintegration of the atomic nucleus may also occur with very high energy radiation. Inorganic as well as organic cellular constituents are altered; the ionized products of water are particularly reactive. It is the chemical changes which follow ionization which are even more destructive than the ionization itself. The literature on ionizing radiation is extensive, for it is now a subject of great medical and biological importance (Lea, 1962; Giese, 1962). Strictly speaking, however, it is not part of the environmental physiology of animals, for the curtain of ozone in our upper atmosphere screens life from most of the ionizing effects.

In the visible portion of the spectrum, from the ultraviolet to the infrared, radiant energy has a PHOTOCHEMICAL and a THERMAL ACTION. The thermal effects extend beyond the visible, but as the wavelengths become longer and longer protoplasm gradually becomes transparent to the radiant energy and is quite unaffected by long waves such as radio waves.

Both the photochemical and thermal effects are due to the activation of molecules. The necessary energy of activation for a chemical reaction may be acquired through thermal agitation or the collision of a photon. In both cases, chemical reactivity is increased through the activation of molecules. Electrons may be raised to higher energy levels, but this is a much less drastic effect than the ejection of an electron which takes place in ionizing radiation. However, even though the molecular alterations are less drastic in photochemical and thermal reactions, the effects can still be damaging or lethal.

The significant photochemical processes of life depend on a few different pigmented molecules which absorb radiant energy and thus initiate indispensable biochemical and physiological processes. These colored molecules may provide the mechanisms which generate electronic power for the operation of photosynthesis (as in the case of chlorophyll), or they may trigger the release of energy in some entirely different biochemical system; the visual pigments do this through a molecular rearrangement which initiates a nerve impulse.

Most, and perhaps all, of these special pigmented molecules are synthesized only by plants from which the animals must acquire them in order to capitalize on this process. In plants the chlorophylls operate photosynthesis; the carotenoids are involved in phototropism; the phytochromes regulate photoperiodism. In animals one set of pigments, the visual pigments, is concerned not only with reactions to light but, indirectly, also with phototaxis and photoperiodism. These are the carotenoid pigments and the animal must obtain them or their important building blocks from the plants. Insect photoperiodism may provide an exception to this broad generalization. Suggestive evidence points to the pterins in the regulation of seasonally changing endocrine activity of some insects (L'Helias, 1961, 1962). The biosynthetic pathways of these pigments are not yet fully described (Forrest, 1962), and it is not known what precursors the insects must acquire from the plants in order to manufacture them.

ABSORPTION AND ACTION SPECTRA

When white light is passed through a colored solution the colored solute molecules absorb photons of particular energy values in accordance with the atomic structure of the molecules. A solution of chlorophyll appears green to us because only light of wavelengths in the vicinity of 520 mμ (green) is transmitted through it. The chlorophyll molecules absorb photons associated with the other wavelengths, but the band of green light is transmitted and gives rise to green sensations when it, in turn, is absorbed by the photosensitive pigments of our eyes.

A characteristic curve is obtained when the percentage of light transmitted through a solution is graphed as a function of different wavelengths (Fig. 14.3). Such a curve is called an absorption curve if the "peaks" correspond to high absorption, or a transmittancy curve if the "valleys" correspond to high absorption. The ABSORPTION MAXIMUM of the former corresponds to the energy required to boost an electron into a higher orbit or to EXCITE a molecule of the particular solute. The absorption spectra for chlorophyll and the visual pigments of the human eye are compared in Fig. 14.3; it is evident that the point of maximum transmission for the former is the point of maximum absorption for the latter.

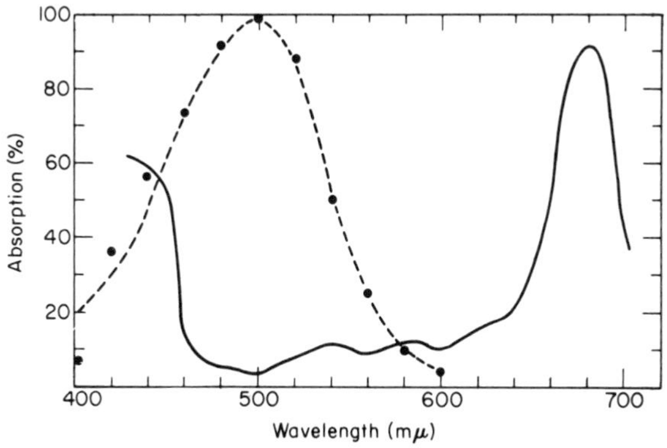

Fig. 14.3. Absorption spectra for human rhodopsin (broken line) and for a group of chlorophylls (solid line). The rhodopsin curve represents the absorption spectrum while the plotted points represent human scotopic sensitivity plotted as percentage of maxima. [Rhodopsin based on data from Crescitelli and Dartnall (1953). Chlorophyll based on data from Emerson and Lewis (1942).]

One might logically postulate some correlation between the absorption spectrum of a substance such as chlorophyll or visual purple and the rate of its biochemical or physiological action in light of different wavelengths. The rates of photobiological processes have often been measured under light of different wavelengths, and the data have been recorded in the form of ACTION SPECTRA. The postulated correlation between absorption and action spectra is evident (Fig. 14.3). Thus, the action spectrum has become a useful tool for the identification of compounds associated with different photobiological processes. The spectral sensitivity curve for human twilight vision (scotopic vision) has a peak at 500 mμ which corresponds to the absorption spectrum of rhodopsin or visual purple, the rod pigment concerned with vision in dim light. The spectral sensitivity for daylight or photopic (cone) vision is centered around 550 mμ, and it has been possible to identify three pigments in the fovea or color-sensitive area of the human retina (Chapter 17) with absorption maxima at 450 mμ, 525 mμ and 555 mμ (Brown and Wald, 1964).

Injurious Effects of Sunlight

Sunburning is a familiar experience which leaves little doubt that the radiant energy at the earth's surface can be damaging to protoplasm. From 1 to 5 per cent of the total solar radiation which reaches the earth is in the ultraviolet (between 300 to 390 mμ). This not only creates sunburn in the lightly pigmented human skin but can also injure or kill other naked animals such as earthworms, planarians or protozoans in shallow water. This band produces rather nonspecific photochemical effects on the cell proteins in contrast to the shorter ultraviolet band with its distinct nuclear and genetic effects. The shorter ultraviolet range, particularly between 200 and 300 mμ, has been intensively used in cell physiology since Müller's discovery of the mutagenic action of X rays on *Drosophila*; (induction of *Drosophila* mutants with ultraviolet came a few years later). The literature is reviewed by Giese (1950), Hollaender (1955) and texts already cited but is not considered here since animals do not experience the effects of the short or far ultraviolet in their natural habitats. There are, however, several interesting physiological effects of sunlight on exposed organisms which are not mediated through the specialized photoreceptor pigments; these will now be discussed.

PHOTODYNAMIC ACTION

Not only ultraviolet but visible radiation up into the red region of the spectrum may be damaging under certain conditions. Raab discovered this accidentally, near the end of the nineteenth century, while studying the toxic effects of acridine on paramecia. Cultures were killed in 6 minutes with acridine concentrations at 1 : 20,000 in bright sunlight but survived 1 hour in diffuse sunlight; identical cultures in the dark were uninjured. In 1900, he performed another experiment which demonstrated that effects of this sort were not peculiar to protozoan cultures. Mice, which had been injected with eosin, were obviously uncomfortable and irritated when in the light. They scratched their skins and sought the shade. In a short time, sores appeared on exposed areas, the tissues became necrotic and the animals died. Another scientist, Meyer-Betz, in 1913 boldly injected himself with 0.2 gm of hematoporphyrin and carefully described the symptoms which followed irradiation of a small area of his arm: erythema (red coloration), edema, pain, hemorrhagic sore, followed by a scab in about three weeks and eventually a deep scar. Like the mice, he experienced intense discomfort in the light and was forced to seek total darkness during a period of photosensitization which lasted several weeks. All of the symptoms did not disappear for about 6 months. Laurens (1933) gives an account of these pioneer experiments.

Several of the plant pigments are now known to cause photosensitization under natural conditions. White pigs which feed on the roots of *Lachnanthes* or white sheep eating the St. John's-wort, *Hypericum crispum*, may become ill and die while the black members of the species are uninjured. Buckwheat (*Fagopyrum esculentum*) may poison cattle, swine and sheep in the same way. Photosensitization can be readily demonstrated by feeding fresh buckwheat plants to guinea pigs for about 4 days. Giese (1962) has studied a photosensitizing pigment which develops in the protozoan, *Blepharisma*, when cultured in darkness; only the pigmented individuals are killed when exposed to strong light.

This PHOTODYNAMIC ACTION, as it is called, is the result of a nonspecific photosensitized oxidation (Davson, 1959). The molecules of a photodynamic dye, which are more or less fluorescent, hold or trap quanta of absorbed radiant energy for a brief period of about 10^{-7} or 10^{-8} seconds before passing it on to EXCITE other molecules which then become oxidized while in this reactive state. Light of wavelengths up to 800 mμ may be effective. It is now thought that the structural proteins are activated and that it is their oxidation which forms toxic by-products that damage cells. The presence of a reducing agent or the exclusion of oxygen interferes with the reaction. Photodynamic action may be demonstrated in the laboratory by adding small amounts of Rose Bengal or eosin to suspensions of erythrocytes or cultures of protozoans and exposing them to the light, with adequate controls in darkness.

SUNBURN AND SUNTAN

Most land animals possess special coverings which protect them from the action of ultraviolet rays and at the same time provide moisture-proofing and, in some cases, temperature regulation. Arthropods achieve this protection with a heavily chitinized, noncellular, waxy cuticle produced by the underlying epidermis; in the land vertebrates, the superficial epidermal cells are modified into scaly plates through the loss of their nuclei and the development of keratohyalin granules of highly insoluble protein. Even thin layers of keratin absorb or reflect a large part of the ultraviolet, while specialized epidermal appendages (scales, feathers, fur) increase this screening and cut off all ultraviolet from the actively dividing layers of the epidermis (stratum germinativum) and the nutritive layers of the dermis. For the most part, man lacks these specialized appendages and depends on thickening of the stratum corneum and on epidermal pigmentation for his protection.

The action of sunlight on human skin has been studied many times since the pioneer experiments of Finsen at the end of the nineteenth century (Blum, 1945, 1961). The reactions may be systemic as well as cutaneous and are due both to heat and ultraviolet radiation; only the effects of the ultraviolet on the skin are considered here.

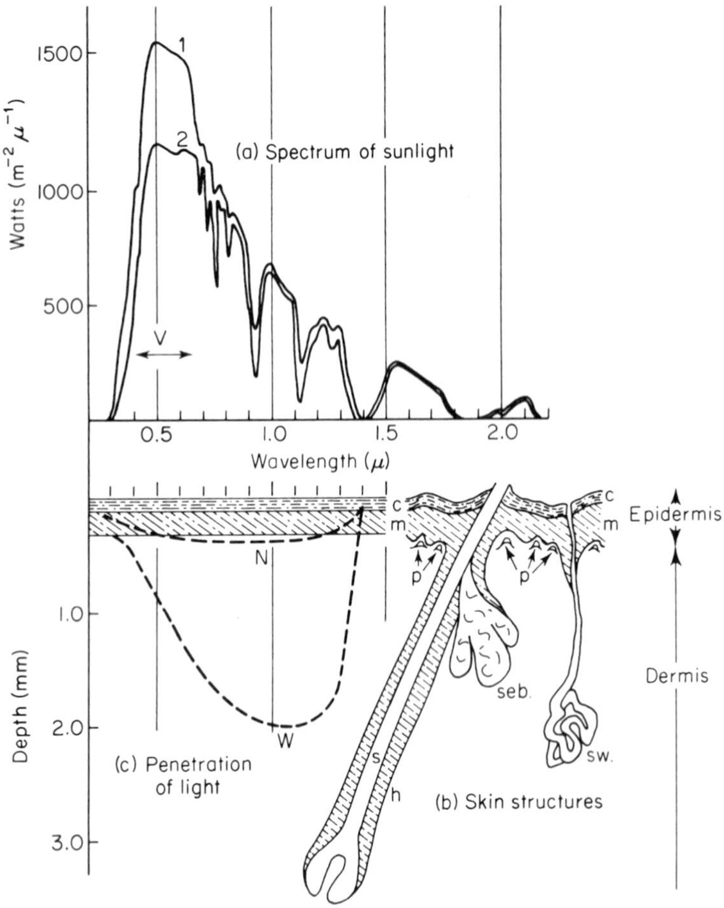

Fig. 14.4. Penetration of light into human skin. Upper figure, spectral distribution of sunlight at the surface of the earth. Curve 1, Sun at zenith. Curve 2, Sun at 60° (4 hr) from zenith. V, Spectral limits of human vision. Lower figure, section of human skin and distance of penetration of different wave lengths into Negro (N) and White (W) skins. *c*, Corneum. *m*, Malpighian layer. *sw*, Sweat gland. *seb.*, Sebaceous gland. *p*, The most superficial blood vessels. *h* and *s*, Hair follicle and shaft. [After Blum (1961).]

The marked erythema or red coloration of sunburn appears an hour or more after exposure, is usually confined to the irradiated area and persists for several days. The action spectrum for erythema is a narrow one with a peak at about 300 mμ; studies of the transmission of this spectral band through pieces of human skin show that it is almost entirely reflected or absorbed before it penetrates to the dermal layers where all of the blood vessels are found (Fig. 14.4). In other words, the light must be acting in the epidermis; only secondarily is it producing the vascular reactions which are responsible for erythema. An active vasodilator is almost certainly produced through the photochemical decomposition of nucleoproteins (perhaps also simple proteins) in the deeper layers of the epidermis (Blum, 1955, 1961). This evidently diffuses from the non-vascular epidermis and produces an enlargement and engorgement of the minute vessels of the dermis, with an accompanying intracellular edema and migration of leucocytes into the surrounding tissues. The vasodilator has not been identified. In the pioneer studies, these ultraviolet effects were compared with reactions induced by pricking histamine under the skin or with mild cutaneous damage, such as scratching, which elicits a TRIPLE RESPONSE in the form of a local RED REACTION, a spreading FLUSH or FLARE and a local EDEMA or WHEAL (Best and Taylor, 1961). At present, it is by no means clear that these parallels are justified or that histamine is the active vasodilator (Blum, 1955).

In lighter colored skins increased pigmentation (suntan) follows the erythema with a very gradual change from red to brown. This does not prove, however, that the erythema and pigmentation are causally related. In fact, there are actually two processes involved in the suntanning itself; one of these, directly related to the erythemal spectrum, depends on the formation of additional melanin in the deeper layers of the epidermis while the other, produced by a different spectral band, is a photo-oxidation of bleached or leuko-melanin to a black form. This latter reaction is called "pigment darkening" and has a much wider action spectrum (maximum near 340 mμ) than the erythemal band. Common window glass cuts out all wavelengths below 320 mμ, and this excludes the entire erythemal band and most of the pigment darkening band (Blum, 1955).

Many of the links in melanogenesis have not yet been fully described. In general, however, it is clear that melanin is formed from the amino acid tyrosine through a series of intermediates (Thomson, 1962; Fig. 2.13) and that its production depends on a special dendritic cell, the melanocyte. During ontogeny, melanocytes arise from the neural crest and migrate into the epidermis where they occur in varying numbers up to about 4000 per mm^2 among the cells of the Malpighian layer. In some manner, not yet clearly explained, the melanin is transferred from the dendrites of the melanocytes to the epidermal cells (Montagna, 1961).

In blond individuals, this black or brown pigment is confined to the deep epidermal layers, but in dark-skinned people it extends into the outer cornified layers.

Biological significance of pigmentation. The physiological advantages of pigmentation have been debated for a very long time (Blum, 1961). In the pioneer studies, Finsen recorded protection from sunburning on areas of his arms which were coated heavily with India ink. It was assumed that melanin, like India ink, was opaque to ultraviolet and in this way protected the living cells of the Malpighian layers. Indeed, the histology of the skin seems to support this hypothesis since the black granules normally form supra-nuclear caps in this layer and are thus advantageously placed for the screening of the sensitive nucleoproteins.

This, however, is now known to be only a partial explanation. Albino skins and areas of vitiliginous (non-pigmented) skin show acclimatization to sunburning. It is also recognized that protection from sunburn is more transient than the pigmentation of suntanning. Exposure to ultraviolet produces a marked increase in the thickness of the stratum corneum, and this probably provides more protection than the increased pigmentation. Racial as well as acclimatization differences in the thickness of the stratum corneum have been recorded. This is now considered the major factor in excluding ultraviolet from the deeper layers, although pigmentation may also have some action (Blum, 1961).

Blum (1961) and Dobzhansky (1962) summarize the hypotheses and rather speculative evidence for an adaptive significance of skin color in racial evolution. Since the darkest races usually live in the hottest climates, an association between skin color and the amount of sunlight seems obvious. There is, however, no very satisfactory evidence to support the hypothesis. Physiological studies indicate that the thickening of the corneum is more critical than melanization in excluding the ultraviolet; further, a white skin actually reflects about 30 per cent more sunlight than a black one (Blum, 1945). Thus, the black body has an increased heat load; this could be an advantage if the cooling machinery were activated at a lower temperature or if it operated more efficiently. Other suggested advantages of a dark skin in the sunnier lands have been protection from skin cancer (Blum, 1961) and camouflage (Cowles, 1959). The statistics support the cancer theory, but there is no evidence of its significance in evolution.

The possible advantages of the non-pigmented skin have also been emphasized. The arguments here are based on the importance of vitamin D in the development of bones and the prevention of rickets. Ultraviolet wavelengths shorter than 320 mμ are responsible for the photochemical production of this vitamin from sterols in the outer layers of the epidermis (Blum, 1945). There is no question of the importance of vitamin D during growth and of the limited amount of effective sunlight for this purpose in the more frigid regions of the earth. It should be noted, however, that the requirements depend on the type of diet and that rickets may be quite unknown among the Eskimo who are at the greatest disadvantage as far as sunlight is concerned. More significant is the absence of evidence that a white skin is able to synthesize more vitamin D than a dark one. Thus, the antirachitic argument is no more satisfactory than the others and, at present, there is a general lack of convincing evidence that any of these factors is sufficiently critical to provide a selection pressure in evolution.

Photoreceptor Pigments

The carotenoid pigments are the most widespread of all the colored compounds in the living world; their importance in animal evolution seems to rank with that of the chlorophylls. It is pointless to argue that any one of life's indispensable compounds is more important than another; but it seems safe to maintain that the chlorophylls and the carotenoids are members of a family of very special molecules which were required to launch animal evolution. The chlorophyll molecule is the primary link in trapping radiant energy which indirectly operates animal machinery; the carotenoid pigments play their indispensable role in the orienting and directing mechanisms which coordinate feeding activities as well as much of the animal's general behavior and social organization. In both cases there is a complete dependence on the plant world. Animals, with the exception of a few of the protozoans (Protista), are unable to synthesize either chlorophyll or carotenoids. The latter are universal dietary requirements for animals. Even the beautifully colored sea anemone becomes colorless if fed on white fish muscle devoid of carotene (Fox and Vevers, 1960).

CHEMISTRY OF THE CAROTENOIDS

The carotenoids take their name from carotene, the yellow pigment of carrots, which was first isolated in 1831 (Fruton and Simmonds, 1958). It is one of a group of fat-soluble substances characterized by a long skeletal chain of carbon and hydrogen with alternating single and double bonds between the carbon atoms. The color which is attributed to this alternating arrangement of bonds varies from yellow through orange and red to violet, depending on the increasing number of double bonds and the presence of certain radicals.

The formula at the top of Fig. 14.5 represents a molecule of β-carotene, one of the most important plant pigments in animal nutrition. The molecule is built of eight 5-carbon isoprenoid units, linked to form a long chain of 40 carbon atoms with an ionone ring at each end. Halfway along its length the molecule is turned on itself and, at this point, may be broken

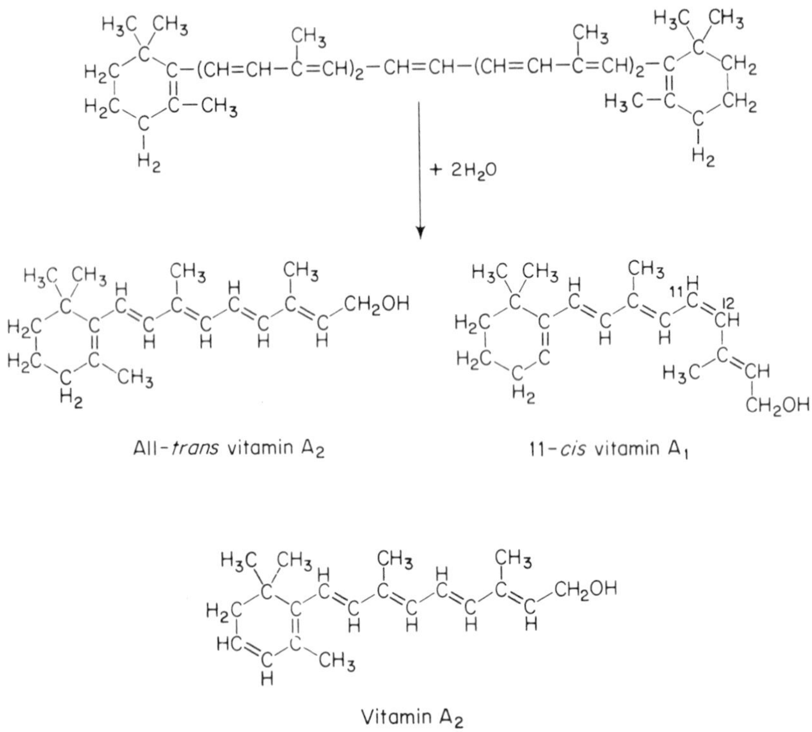

Fig. 14.5. A molecule of β-carotene (upper) and the important physiological isomers of Vitamin A which develop from it. The isoprene units are enclosed by brackets and the arrow shows where the carotene molecule is hydrolyzed to form Vitamin A.

hydrolytically to yield two molecules of vitamin A. The latter exists in two forms which differ only in a pair of hydrogens (presence or absence of a double bond) in the terminal ring (Fig. 14.5). This formula typifies the carotenoids; the ends of the different kinds of carotenoid pigments differ with incomplete terminal rings or a ring at only one end (Goodwin, 1962).

Cis-trans isomerism. A family of differing molecular configurations is possible. By changing the position of either the —H or the —CH_3

attached to the carbons of the double bond, these groups may appear on the same (CIS) or on opposite (TRANS) sides of the chain. The result is that the CIS-isomers are kinked molecules while the all-TRANS forms are straight (Fig. 14.5). Most of the naturally occurring carotenoid molecules have their double bonds in the all-TRANS configuration. Irradiation of the natural pigments with ultraviolet will produce a variety of CIS-isomers. There are, also, some naturally occurring CIS-isomers. One of these, the 11-CIS or NEO-B isomer of vitamin A, which has the two hydrogens on the same side of the double bond between carbons 11 and 12, is particularly significant in visual processes. The excitation of the photoreceptor seems to depend on the straightening out of the kinked molecule (CIS to TRANS isomer). This, in some way, triggers an impulse in the optic nerve (Wald, 1961). Further details are considered in Chapter 17.

Carotenoproteins. The carotenoid pigments of animals are either dissolved in the tissue fats or chemically combined with specific proteins; in either form, they play a part in animal coloration (Fox and Vevers, 1960). As prosthetic groups of proteins, two of them can form the highly specialized molecular machines which are the basis of photoreception.

Visual pigments have now been investigated in representatives of each of the major phyla with highly specialized eyes. In all cases, the active pigment is an aldehyde of Vitamin A, known as RETINENE, combined with a protein called OPSIN. Relationships between the two forms of vitamin A and their associated pigments are as follows:

Vitamin A_1 (alcohol with one double bond in ring) —OXIDATION→ Retinene$_1$ (aldehyde with one double bond in ring)

Retinene$_1$ —OXIDATION (IN VITRO)→ Retinene$_2$

Vitamin A_2 (alcohol with two double bonds in ring) —OXIDATION→ Retinene$_2$ (aldehyde with two double bonds in ring)

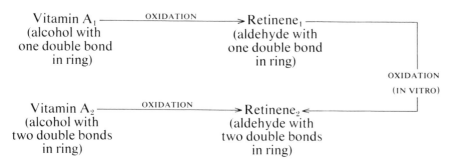

Although there are only two known retinenes, many different visual pigments have been categorized on the basis of their absorption and action spectra; the absorption maxima of the known pigments range from 430 to 562 mμ in the A_1 series and from 510 to 620 in the A_2 series (Dartnall and Tansley, 1963). These differences are presumably due to the opsin component of the molecule (either the species specific nature of the proteins or differences in the manner of coupling the prosthetic groups). A completely satisfactory explanation of the differences has not yet been found (Wald, 1960; Dartnall and Tansley, 1963).

Visual pigments in biochemical evolution. The phylogeny of the two major groups of visual pigments is still one of the interesting problems of biochemical evolution. Wald (1960*a*) has summarized the very extensive literature and provided a critical evaluation of its significance (Fig. 14.6).

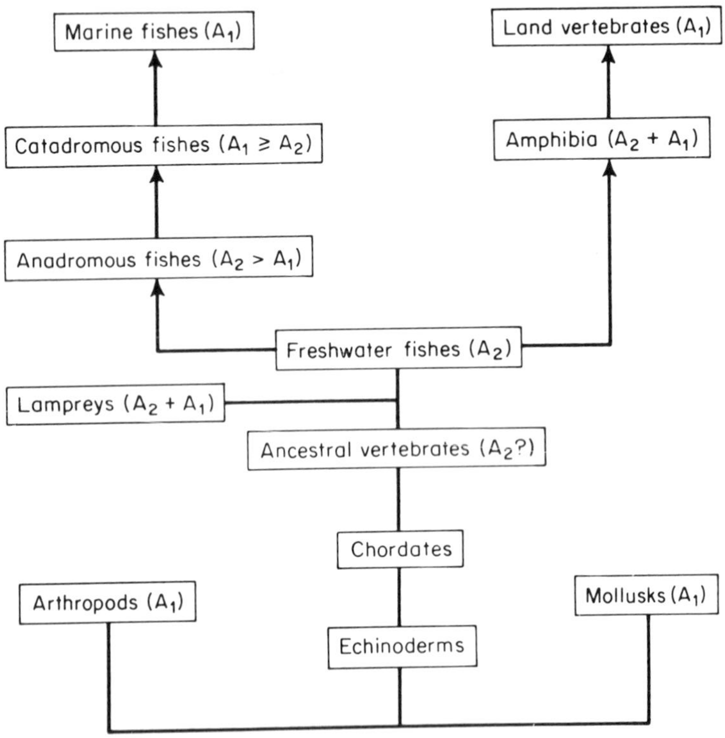

Fig. 14.6. Phylogeny of the visual pigments. [After Wald (1960).]

The first visual pigment to be examined came from a frog. It was called RHODOPSIN or visual purple, and its bleaching to a yellow color in the light was noted as early as 1876 (Fox and Vevers, 1960). Its relationship to vitamin A_1 and retinene$_1$ was subsequently established. Somewhat later it became apparent that the freshwater fishes possessed visual pigments based on vitamin A_2 and retinene$_2$. The first of these was named PORPHYROPSIN. Even though a multiplicity of pigments has now been identified, the terms rhodopsin and porphyropsin may still be usefully retained to refer to the two major groups of pigments; the rhodopsin series with absorption maxima near 500 mμ is based on retinene$_1$, and the porphyropsin series with maxima near 525 mμ is based on retinene$_2$.

There are several generalizations concerning the distribution of these chromophores. The visual pigments of all invertebrates so far investigated belong to the A_1 or rhodopsin series. The mammals and birds and the marine fishes, with some few exceptions among the Labridae and the Coridae, likewise have rhodopsin systems. The strictly freshwater teleosts, on the contrary, have pigments of the porphyropsin series. Phylogenetic interest is centered on the transitional groups, on the amphibia and the reptiles which form a bridge between the aquatic and terrestrial vertebrates, on the euryhaline, the anadromous and catadromous fishes which exploit both the fresh waters and the oceans, and on the cyclostomes which are at the base of the entire vertebrate series.

Species which show a metamorphosis have proved particularly instructive. Amphibians which change from an aquatic to a terrestrial mode of life (tadpole to frog) possess a predominantly porphyropsin system before metamorphosis but a rhodopsin system during adult life; a newt such as *Diemyctilus*, which shows a second metamorphosis before returning to water at spawning time, alters its pigments in the reverse direction at this stage of life. The teleost fishes likewise maintain a good relationship between the type of visual pigment and the habitat. Euryhaline forms have a mixture of porphyropsin and rhodopsin; this is also true of the anadromous and the catadromous species, but in these the dominant pigment is characteristic of the habitat where the fish spawns. Cyclostomes, the most primitive of the vertebrates, possess both pigments; in some species changes have been described at metamorphosis.

Wald emphasizes that three times in animal phylogeny there have evolved highly organized, image-forming photoreceptors; in each case the pigments of the more advanced species are based on vitamin A_1. He believes that the evidence fits best a theory that the ancestral vertebrates started out with an A_2 system (presumably in freshwater ancestors) and that this was altered to an A_1 system through transitional forms which had mixtures of the two. The suggestion is that this is the most efficient chromoprotein that animals could produce with the materials available for their evolution.

The opsin portion of the visual pigment molecule seems also to have been susceptible to natural selection. Studies of the retinae of deep-sea fishes reveal a definite correlation between depth of habitat and the color of the visual pigment, with the absorption maxima of the pigments decreasing from just over 500 mμ to about 480 mμ, with habitat-depths increasing up to over 200 fathoms. Since the blue light of wavelengths around 480 mμ penetrates farthest into the clear ocean waters, this change in absorption maxima may well be of adaptive value. The literature has been summarized (Wald, 1960*a*; Dartnall and Tansley, 1963).

Both portions of the chromoprotein, the carotenoid and the protein, have been useful in the biochemical evolution of efficient visual pigments.

VISUAL CYCLES

Little is known about carotene metabolism in the lower animals. In the mammal, dietary carotene is converted to vitamin A in the wall of the gut while the liver serves as a storehouse. Even though liver is rich in vitamin A, this compound is evidently synthesized elsewhere; when rats

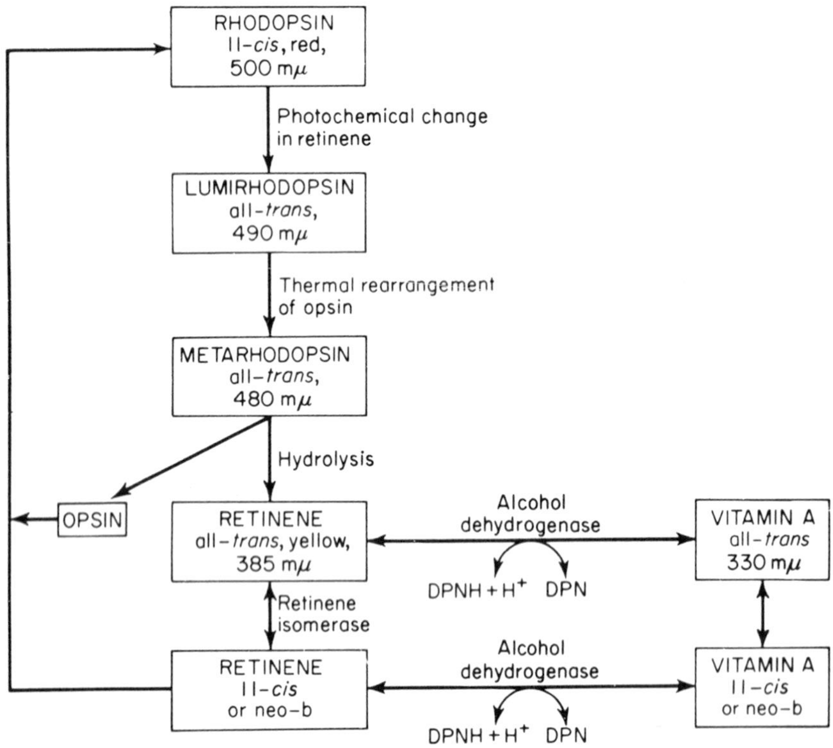

Fig. 14.7. Chemical events in the visual cycle of rhodopsin. Values for absorption maxima are approximate.

were maintained on a vitamin A-deficient diet and given carotene intravenously, they stored large amounts of the carotene in their livers but synthesized no vitamin from it and showed the symptoms of A deficiency. Livers of some mammals (polar bear, for example) store such tremendous amounts of vitamin A under natural conditions that they are toxic in human diets (Heilbrunn, 1952). From these liver stores, or directly from the wall of the gut, this vitamin passes by way of the blood to replenish the wastage which occurs through the visual processes in the retina. It circulates only in the all-TRANS form and must be converted to the 11-CIS isomer in the retina before it is available for rhodopsin synthesis (Fig. 14.7).

Most of the biochemical studies of photoreception have been confined to rhodopsin (Wald, 1961). A series of chemical transformations follows exposure to light, but only one of these is entirely dependent on the radiant energy. When rhodopsin absorbs a quantum of light, the 11-CIS retinene of the molecule is isomerized to all-TRANS retinene, and in some way the photoreceptor is stimulated to fire the nerve impulse. The succeeding events, outlined in Fig. 14.7, are enzymatic thermal reactions which do not require radiant energy. Small amounts (30 per cent or less) of the 11-CIS retinene may be regenerated directly from the all-TRANS retinene with the enzyme retinene isomerase; this reaction is stimulated by light of short wavelengths (blue) but can occur in darkness. Most of the 11-CIS retinene is resynthesized by the oxidation of 11-CIS vitamin A; this, in turn, comes from the all-TRANS form of the vitamin by steps which are not yet established. Retinal tissue has a high content of DPN and this, with the enzyme alcohol dehydrogenase, is responsible for the oxidation-reduction reactions which take place between retinene and vitamin A.

Phototactic Responses

Practically all living organisms are light-sensitive. A variety of orientation responses are characteristic of both primitive plants and animals. In phylogeny, these simple adaptive movements must have preceded the complex activities associated with the visual systems just considered. Both are based on the carotenoids, but unfortunately there is not nearly enough precise knowledge of the biochemical mechanisms responsible for phototaxis in the primitive animals to reveal any definite trail of biochemical evolution. Only a brief comment on phototaxis is appended here.

Over a period of almost 300 years scientists have frequently recorded their observations on the growth of plants toward the light. The phenomenon was first called PHOTOTROPISM in the middle of the nineteenth century. This term is now reserved for fungi, higher plants and sessile animals such as hydroids which are anchored at one end and develop a curvature in response to light; the comparable reaction in motile organisms is called PHOTOTAXIS. In this, there is a free movement of the entire organism, with the light acting either directly or indirectly on organs of locomotion such as muscles and flagella. Thimann and Curry (1960) review the literature.

At the biochemical level, the analysis of phototropism has gone much farther than that of phototaxis. The growing shoots of oats (*Avena*) and of the fungus *Phycomyces*, have been favored subjects. In the former it is clear that the ultimate effector is an asymmetric distribution of a plant growth hormone, auxin; in the latter this does not seem to be the case, but in both, the photic control is through the medium of the carotenoid pigments. In fact, the action spectrum for phototropism in higher plants was demonstrated in the nineteenth century when a worker placed a flask of port wine between a plant and the light and noted that the plant continued to grow but no longer turned toward the light (Wald, 1959). The red wavelengths which are most effective in photosynthesis are ineffective in phototropism; this depends on wavelengths shorter than 550mμ.

In general, phototaxis also depends on the carotenoids. There are exceptions among the photosynthetic bacteria and some algae where changes in the photosynthetic rate seem to govern the response, but the carotenoids are clearly involved in primitive animals such as the flagellates. Two pigments sometimes appear to be active, but these may be different carotenoids. The analysis of phototaxis in primitive animals has not been as rewarding as that of the *Avena* coleoptiles; no biochemical effector comparable to that of auxin which regulates cell elongation has been found. The carotenoid may act directly to trigger motile organs such as flagella, but the mechanisms remain to be demonstrated. The responses of higher animals which depend on special photoreceptors and the coordinated activities of nervous system and effector organs are discussed in Chapters 17 and 21.

Biological Clocks

Life is strongly rhythmical. In our own species there are rapid oscillations in the muscles of the heart and in the neurons of the breathing centers, diurnal rhythms of sleep and activity, lunar periodicity in reproduction and seasonal changes in physiology as well as in social activities. The longer oscillations measured in periods of days, months or years are environmentally determined. Even though they sometimes persist stubbornly under constant experimental conditions, the oscillations usually change or disappear sooner or later unless reinforced or "corrected" by environmental change.

The biological advantages of activities geared in an adaptive way to changes in the surroundings are obviously great. Light is the most likely force in regulating such cycles with its persistent and constant differences from day to night and from summer to winter. Tidal oscillations, temperature cycles and the seasonal variations in the quality and quantity of food are additional but indirect forces which trace their rhythms back to the rotation of the earth and its changing exposure to the sun.

CIRCADIAN RHYTHMS

Phylogenetically, the most primitive of these light-induced rhythms were probably diurnal and tied to the cycles in energy production through photosynthesis. In the existing plants, not only photosynthesis and respiration but many other physiological processes such as growth, spore discharge and flowering are markedly diurnal (Bünning, 1964).

The photosynthetic dinoflagellate, *Gonyaulax polyedra*, displays an interesting daily rhythm (Sweeney, 1960; Giese, 1962). This organism, which can be claimed by both botanists and zoologists, shows regular oscillations in cell division and luminescence as well as photosynthesis. Its rhythm of luminescence has been carefully studied. When stimulated by agitation, *Gonyaulax* produces a brief flash of light (about 90 milliseconds duration) which is much more intense during the night. The major point of interest is that the rhythm of flash intensity is not rigidly tied to the cyclical supply of photosynthetic energy but will persist for long periods when the organisms are grown in darkness or in dim light. In short, the rhythm is ENDOGENOUS; there are many such rhythms in both plants and animals. They were called CIRCADIAN by Halberg in 1959 to indicate that the period length is about (*circa*) one day (*diem*). Frequently the rhythm is short of 24 hours; it may vary with the temperature and can be altered by the light exposure. This type of biological clock comes closest to our familiar timepiece. The literature, both descriptive and theoretical, is now extensive (Aschoff, 1960; Bruce, 1960; Pittendrigh, 1960), but the endogenous mechanisms are not yet clarified. In the present context, it is of interest that diurnal light cycles have imposed an activity rhythm on animal life and this, in phylogeny, has strong tendencies to become endogenous. Some examples have already been given (Fig. 13.3).

LUNAR PERIODICITY

As the moon travels around the earth on a cycle of about 29½ days it reflects the maximum amount of solar illumination to the earth at the time of the "full moon"; its "size" progressively increases before the "full moon" while it gradually decreases from night to night until it "disappears" thereafter. This lunar cycle is also of potential significance in the evolution of cyclical natural phenomena. Many half-lunar or full-lunar cycles have been recorded (Korringa, 1957), as well as physiological events which occur only once or a few times during the year but always in association with some particular phase of the moon, (Brown, 1957*a*). One of the classical examples is the Palolo worm (*Leodice*) which is a tube-dweller in coral reefs. The West Indian species, *L. fucata*, spawns only during the third quarter of the June-July moon. The anterior part of the animal remains in its burrow beneath the sea, but the posterior ends, distended with ripe gametes, break off and wriggle to the surface in such vast numbers that the waters are milky for an hour or two with the eggs and sperms. This swarming occurs at dawn and thus is precisely timed both to sun and moon. Another spectacular example is the beach spawning of the Pacific grunion, *Leuresthes tenus*, which swims up on the beaches, spawns and then flips back into the water just after the turn of the tide on the second, third and fourth nights after the full moon in the months of March, April, May and June. Precision of this sort greatly increases the chances of successful reproduction and may also synchronize the hatching of larvae with suitable plankton blooms.

The type of lunar rhythm which occurs throughout the year in association with the tidal cycle has also been carefully documented. Brown (1957*a*) analyzed the daily changes in chromatophore appearance and oxygen consumption of the fiddler crab, *Uca,* and found a tidal as well as a diurnal cycle. Both are endogenous and persist for long periods under constant light conditions; they also show a measure of temperature independence. The tidal cycle could be altered by appropriate manipulation of the illumination, thus indicating that the light from the moon played a direct part in its establishment. This could, of course, be reinforced by the changing tidal amplitude, but the principle remains that the moon may serve as a potential cue for the establishment of biologically useful rhythms.

PHOTOPERIODISM

The success of a species often depends on a life cycle which is precisely timed to take full advantage of the changing seasonal conditions. In temperate and frigid regions, young animals are most likely to survive if their birth coincides with the onset of warm weather and unlimited supplies of food; in the tropics, the rainy season may be equally important for both aquatic and terrestrial life. Animals may prepare for the rigors of winter by storing fat, by hibernating or by migrating; diadromous migrations are often timed to take advantage of the flooding rivers in the spring or autumn. The examples could be multiplied. Plants as well as animals show seasonal rhythms which maintain advantageous relations between the major physiological demands and the seasonal environmental cycles. They are examples of a different type of physiological chronometer. In this case, the mechanism has its parallel in the interval marker or the hourglass rather than our familiar timepiece; something starts the mechanism and it terminates after a definite interval.

The length of the day (PHOTOPERIOD) is the most dependable cue for this seasonal timing; it most frequently SETS the biological clock. At any point on the earth's surface, the length of the day depends only on the latitude and the time of the year. Temperature, annual rainfall, and the availability of food also show orderly seasonal changes, but these tend to fluctuate more from year to year than the photoperiod. In many animals, seasonal physiological rhythms have evidently become independent of the environmental controls and are endogenously regulated; they persist under constant conditions or may depend on the environment only for the "correction" of the endogenous clock. This type of rhythm has been mentioned in the hibernating ground squirrel (Chapter 10).

Photoperiodism was first recognized about 1920 as an environmental regulator of flower development in many plants. It was shown experimentally that certain plants failed to flower unless the days were of the "right" length; in some cases flowering was induced by short days, and in other cases long days provided the effective stimulus. The extensive studies on animal photoperiodism were initiated by Rowan's studies of bird migration in 1925 and Kogure's experiments with silkworms in 1933. The voluminous literature is reviewed in several places (Withrow, 1959; Farner, 1961), and there are popular accounts of the classical experiments mentioned above (Butler and Downes, 1960; Beck, 1960).

What is the mechanism for this biological clock? It appears, in each case, to depend on some photosensitive pigment. Unlike the photoreceptors which are all based on the carotenoids, photoperiodism is regulated by biochemically-different colored molecules in plants and animals; further, it now seems probable that the animals have utilized more than one group of pigments. In 1959, plant physiologists isolated a pigment, *phytochrome,* which is the active principle in plant photoperiodism. This pigment exists in two forms, an inactive form (P_{660}) with an absorption maximum at 660 mμ and an active form (P_{735}) with a maximum at 735 mμ. During the photoperiod response the pigment is changed from the inactive to the active form, and this then stimulates the growth phenomena. The reaction is reversible, with P_{735} changing to P_{660} in darkness at a rate and to a degree which depends primarily on the genetics of the plant; thus, there are "short day" plants, such as chrysanthemums, which flower in the autumn and "long day" plants, such as petunias, which require long summer days and short nights to maintain the necessary supplies of P_{735}. Not only flowering, but fruiting and many growth processes are regulated in this manner. Phytochrome is evidently an enzyme (protein) which catalyzes a critical reaction; it has been suggested that it may regulate the supply of acetyl coenzyme A (Butler and Downes, 1960).

Animal photoperiodicity is more complex. For one thing, it may depend on more than one biochemical group of photosensitive pigments; for another, the photochemical reaction is linked to the regulated physiological effect by a complex endocrinology and further, a much more varied group of processes is photoperiodically controlled. These include, in addition to diversified growth processes, such phenomena as coat color in the snow-shoe hare, salinity preference and temperature resistance in fish and the behavior associated with migration and reproduction in several different groups of animals.

Among the vertebrates, the visual receptors usually form the first link in the chain of photoperiod control. This strongly suggests an involvement of the carotenoid pigments, although the action spectrum in some species is farther to the red (maximum 600 to 750 mμ in ducks) than that for photopic vision. Moreover, the classical experiments of Benoit and his associates in France have shown that light of the entire visual spectrum can act directly on the hypothalamic centers. In some of Benoit's experiments on ducks the light was conducted straight to the brain through fine quartz rods and the possibilities of extra-ocular pathways were conclusively demonstrated (Benoit, 1962; Farner, 1961). The link between the radiant energy and the stimulation of neurosecretion has not been demonstrated but, presumably, there is some photosensitive substance in the nervous centers so that the endocrine system can be activated directly as well as indirectly by way of the retina and the visual pathways.

Among the arthropods, there is no evidence that the light pathways ever involve the visual receptors (Lees, 1960, 1964). Eyes of potato beetles and aphids have been cauterized or covered with opaque paint without destroying the photoperiodicity. By shielding different parts of the body, the most probable site for the photoreceptors was found to be the dorsum of the brain. Some suggestive correlations between the photoperiod and the quantity of pterins in the eyes and the endocrine complex of aphids suggest that these compounds may form a photosensitive link (L'Helias, 1962). The pterins are widespread compounds which include a group of pigments in arthropods and lower vertebrates (Chapter 20). Their absorption maxima are in the ultraviolet at 340 and 370 mμ. It may be significant that the short wavelengths have been found to be more active in arthropods (mites) while longer wavelengths are more active in vertebrates (ducks).

In animal species, the relative lengths of day and night seem to operate in at least three different ways to activate the photosensitive pigments or processes (Farner, 1961). In some birds, the duration of the light period is all-important, and there is no dark requirement *per se*. In this case the activity of the neurosecretory cells continues as long as the animal is in the light, with a short "carry-over" period at the beginning of the dark period before the secretory processes cease. Either "long" or "short" days might operate in this manner, depending on the associated endocrine links. However, in some of the arthropods the dark period seems to have real meaning in photoperiodicity. In both insects and mites the dark as well as light periods must sometimes be of a certain minimum duration in order to trigger the physiological process (Lees, 1960; Farner, 1961). Still another type of control is indicated in diapause regulation of some insects where the gradually CHANGING LENGTH of the photoperiod is basic to the response. Sexual maturation in the domestic fowl may provide another example of this type of regulation. In theory, at any rate, there is no reason why any one of the seasonally changing components of daily light duration (the light period, the dark period, or their changing ratios) might not serve as a reliable cue and, as more examples are investigated, it appears that the evolutionary process has selected the one which best meets the demands of the animal's physiology, behavior and habitat. A measure of expediency seems to be common in the workings of organic evolution.

Nervous Integration and Animal Activity

Irritability 15

Animal life usually depends on a capacity to move about and encounter food, to respond in a purposive way to the food and to react in an adaptive manner to a varied habitat as well as to the different living organisms encountered in the search for food. This activity is one of the most obviously distinctive features which separate the animals from the plants. It has been a dominant force in phylogeny and the basis for many of the refinements in neurosensory structures and in the feeding and digesting machinery. This capacity for the active and effective exploitation of the varied resources of the environment is expressed in many different ways but stems from a single fundamental property of all living cells—their IRRITABILITY or EXCITABILITY.

The concept of irritability as a general attribute of living matter can be traced back to Francis Glisson in the seventeenth century (Heilbrunn, 1952). Verworn (1899 and earlier) in his classical textbooks of general physiology defined it clearly in a modern form and discussed it at length as one of the distinctive properties of the living in contrast to lifeless substances. According to Verworn's definition, the irritability of protoplasm is its "capacity of reacting to changes in its environment by changes in the equilibrium of its matter and its energy." Claude Bernard also discussed irritability as a universal property of protoplasm, stressing the excitation or activity which follows environmental change (Bayliss, 1960). It is interesting that Verworn's definition covers inhibition as well as excitation. He emphasizes in several places that the significant feature of irritability is the CHANGE IN VITAL PHENOMENON—sometimes excitation, sometimes depression or inhibition. The effective environmental change is the STIMULUS; the resulting protoplasmic reaction is the RESPONSE. That irritability need not necessarily be expressed in activity but that inhibition might be the normal response to stimulation, has been recognized for more than 100 years; the brothers Weber demonstrated cardiac inhibition following stimulation of the vagus nerve of the frog in 1845 (Bayliss, 1960).

The pioneer physiologists also recognized CONDUCTION (the progressive spread of excitation) as a fundamental property of living cells and one which is inseparably connected with irritability. Although the most familiar examples of irritability and conduction are found in nervous and muscular tissues, these properties can be readily demonstrated in many other types of cells, both plant and animal. Verworn (1913) and Heilbrunn (1952) cite many examples of protoplasmic conduction in the rhizopod protozoa, elongated algal cells, such as *Nitella*, and in higher plants such as *Elodea*.

Molecular Basis of Cellular Irritability

At the molecular or ionic level, cellular irritability is related to minute differences in electrical potential across the surface membrane of every cell. In the so-called "resting cell," this transmembrane potential is of the order of 30 to 100 millivolts (mv) and, with but few exceptions (Giese, 1962), the inside of the membrane is negative with respect to the outside. The classical materials for the demonstration of these bioelectric potentials were the giant axon of the squid, with a diameter of about 1 mm, and some of the large algal cells such as *Halicystis*. The RESTING POTENTIAL in the former is about 50 to 75 mv and in the latter 70 to 80 mv. Today it is possible to explore some of the smallest cells with microelectrodes and highly sensitive recorders. The principle is the same, however: one electrode is placed inside the cell and the other on its surface. The response which follows stimulation is always associated with a change in this membrane potential; it is this potential change (ACTION POTENTIAL) which is the most fundamental cellular attribute of irritability and the one on which the phylogeny of integrated animal activity has been founded.

At the level of the organism the receptor organs, such as eye or ear, act as transducers altering the stimulus energy (light or sound waves) into the minute EMF of the activated cell, and this then passes as a wave along the nerves to activate related neurons, muscles, glands, chromatophores or other effector organs. The responses of these effector organs are again often associated with action potentials.

Knowledge concerning the coupling of the stimulated receptor with the conducted impulse and the latter in turn with the characteristic activity of the effector organ is still incomplete. However, it now seems clear that, fundamentally, cellular irritability is based on changes in these membrane potentials. The variety in cellular activity (conduction, contraction), is a specialized and peculiar feature of each kind of cell; it generally appears in association with an action potential (Hagiwara and Naka, 1964).

THE IONIC BASIS OF THE RESTING POTENTIAL

As long as a cell is alive its surface membrane separates solutions of different chemical composition. The osmolarity of the external solution equals that of the internal solution (except for the surface cells of fresh-water and some marine organisms), but the ionic species are very different; it is this difference which produces the resting membrane potential. In a vertebrate, for example, more than 90 per cent of the osmotic content of the extracellular medium is made up of sodium and chloride ions while these ions account for less than 10 per cent of the solutes inside the cell. In the intracellular fluid, potassium takes the place of sodium, and the organic anions produced during metabolism (aspartate, glutamate, phosphate esters) replace the chloride to produce AN ELECTRICALLY BALANCED SOLUTION.

This latter point should be emphasized: the bioelectric potentials under discussion are membrane potentials. At the plasma membrane, where the internal and external fluids would tend to mix by diffusion, there are localized accumulations of positive and negative charges separated by this bimolecular layer. This is a purely localized phenomenon with ionic diffusion fronts of K^+ pressing toward the outside and Na^+ pressing toward the inside. Exchanges of ions between the cell and its surroundings are restricted but not entirely prevented by the permeability properties of the cell membrane; the balance is maintained by cellular processes of active ionic transport (sodium pump). Thus, electrical neutrality is preserved both in the extra- and the intracellular fluids, but the diffusion fronts result in sufficient separation to create the transmembrane bioelectric potential.

The magnitude of difference in ionic distribution between the extra- and intracellular fluids is shown in Table 15.1. These values are typical of most tissues although there are some notable variations (Brown and Stein, 1960; Giese, 1962). Physiological evidence points to the K^+ as the principal basis of the "resting" potential; its diffusion front toward the extracellular fluid creates the transmembrane potential with the inside of the membrane negative. Experimentally, the membrane potential of a squid giant axon or a frog muscle may be changed quantitatively by altering the K^+ of the bathing fluid. The system behaves as though the cell membrane were impermeable to all cations other than potassium, and calculations show that the resting potential is approximately what might be expected from the potassium concentrations (Bayliss, 1960). Textbooks of cellular physiology and biophysics discuss the theoretical background and quantitative details (Davson, 1959; Oncley, 1959; Giese, 1962).

TABLE 15.1.

IONIC GRADIENTS ACROSS CELL MEMBRANES EXPRESSED AS RATIO OF INTRACELLULAR TO EXTRACELLULAR CONCENTRATIONS FOR THE CATIONS AND THE RECIPROCAL OF THIS FOR Cl. EXTERNAL FLUIDS ARE PLASMA EXCEPT FOR SEA URCHIN EGG AND SQUID NERVE WHICH WERE IN SEA WATER.
Values selected from Brown and Stein (1960).

Organism	*Cell*	Na^+	K^+	Ca^{++}	Mg^{++}	Cl^-
Sea urchin – *Paracentrotus*	Egg Unfertilized	0.11	21	0.36	0.2	7
Squid – *Loligo*	Nerve Resting	0.09	31			7.9
	Stimulated	0.3	23			6.4
Crab – *Carcinus*	Muscle	0.09	9.2		0.7	9.9
Frog	Muscle	0.03	58	2.5	12	50
Turtle	Erythrocyte	0.15	13.6			
Rat	Muscle	0.02	24	0.61	11	24
	Erythrocyte	0.18	23			1.44

Bernstein (1902) developed a hypothesis for nervous excitation which was, for many years, the cornerstone of physiological thinking on cellular irritability. He postulated a membrane which was selectively permeable to potassium ions and impermeable to sodium, chloride and the cellular organic anions. Excitation, according to Bernstein, was due to a sharp increase in permeability to the extracellular ions so that the membrane was rapidly depolarized and the potential dropped toward zero.

This theory served as a workable hypothesis for about fifty years until modern electronic recording instruments and radioactive tracer techniques demonstrated two major deficiencies. First, the membrane is usually not simply depolarized during excitation; the potential is often substantially reversed (40 to 50 mv with the inside positive in nerve) and, moreover, there are many cases where membranes are actually hyperpolarized on stimulation. Second, the use of radioactive isotopes has clearly shown that the membrane is permeable to sodium and chloride as well as to potassium.

Consequently, it has been necessary to modify Bernstein's hypothesis; the present theories place a "cation pump" in the membrane to do the job which Bernstein attributed merely to membrane properties of selective permeability. Although Bernstein's detailed postulates are no longer tenable, his generalized concepts of the importance of the plasma membrane, its selectivity and variable permeability, remain basic to all modern theories (Katz, 1959*a*, 1961). The membrane is considered to be differentially permeable with potassium entering much more readily than sodium; the slow leakage of sodium into the cell is controlled by the "sodium pump" (Fig. 15.1).

There are several lines of evidence for active ion transport mechanisms in the maintenance of the membrane potential. When, for example, an axon is treated with metabolic inhibitors such as dinitrophenol, azide or cyanide, the active efflux of tracer sodium ceases but not its leakage into the cell; significantly also, the "pumping" is temporarily resumed when ATP or arginine phosphate is injected into the axoplasm of the cyanide-inhibited squid fiber (Katz, 1959*a*). Thus, it is evident that the pyrophosphate bond supplies the energy for the cation pump and that the "resting" cell is not really resting but continually expending energy to maintain a balance. In fact, cellular metabolism is involved in two ways: (*a*) in the synthesis of the organic anions which cannot diffuse through the plasma membrane and (*b*) in operating the ion exchange mechanism.

The selectivity of the plasma membrane remains a significant part of the hypothesis, both in its impermeability to the organic anions and in its differential permeability with respect to sodium and potassium. Sodium leaks through very slowly, potassium much more rapidly so that the potential difference across the resting membrane approximates that of a potassium-concentration cell. Moreover, potassium seems to be actively transported into the cell as well as diffusing in "passively." The cation pump evidently accumulates potassium within the cell at the same time that it eliminates sodium (Fig. 15.1). In the nerve axon again the rate of tracer sodium efflux falls when potassium is withdrawn from the bath solution. In general, rates of sodium efflux and potassium influx change simultaneously and in a parallel manner, although not in one-for-one proportions (Brown & Stein, 1960; Katz, 1959*a*). There is evidently a linking of the movements of these two ions through the pump, but the mechanism is not understood.

Thus, in general terms, cellular irritability depends on this delicate balance of ions at the surface of the cell; responses are usually triggered through sudden increases in permeability which permit a flood of Na^+ into the cell. Measurements of membrane potentials during excitation have become one of the most useful tools for the study of cellular irritability and stimulus-response mechanisms.

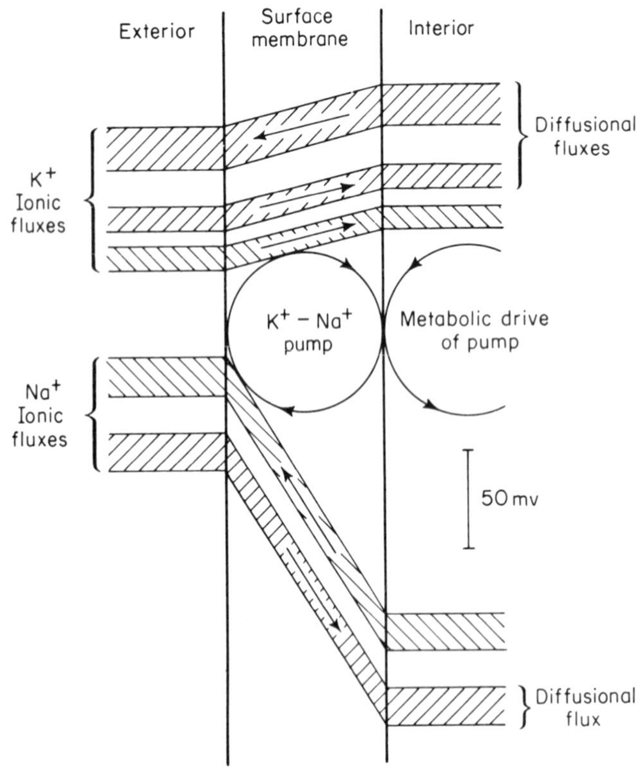

Fig. 15.1. Diagrammatic representation of K^+ and Na^+ fluxes through the surface membrane in the resting state. The slopes in the flux channels across the membrane represent the respective electrochemical gradients. At the resting membrane potential (–70 mv) the electrochemical gradients, as drawn for the K^+ and Na^+ ions, correspond respectively to potentials which are 20 mv more positive and about 130 mv more negative than the equilibrium potentials (note the potential scale). The fluxes due to diffusion and the operation of the pump are distinguished by the direction of hatching. The outward diffusional flux of Na^+ ions would be less than 1 per cent of the inward and so is too insignificant to be indicated as a separate channel in this diagram, because the magnitudes of the fluxes are indicated by the widths of the respective channels. [Eccles (1957).]

PHYLOGENY IN PROTOPLASMIC IRRITABILITY

It can scarcely be argued that the membrane potential evolved to meet the demands for animal activity. It must certainly have been one of those pre-adaptations which served as a springboard for protoplasmic specializations ranging from simple cellular movements to the integrated and complex behavior of modern man. A seemingly logical argument for this delicately balanced condition of ions at the plasma membrane has already been presented in a discussion of ionic regulation (Chapter 11). The hypothesis enunciated was that VOLUME REGULATION formed the first step in the evolution of the ion pumps characteristic of living cells (Brown and Stein, 1960).

The organic anions (pyruvate, acetate) produced during the metabolism of the cell are essential by-products. They must be retained since they are links in the production of energy. Cell membranes are impermeable to them, and their presence imposes a Donnan distribution on the diffusible ions. Even at equilibrium, however, there is a net excess of osmotically active material within the cell (Brown and Stein, 1960). A primitive cell in its marine environment might maintain its volume in the face of osmotic flooding by pumping out the water or by pumping out some of the diffusible ions. The cation pump is the most economical measure since membranes, in general, are far more permeable to water than to ions. Thus it is suggested that volume regulation was the first evolutionary pressure for the development of the cation pump. Plant cells, under similar conditions, avoid the hazards of volume increase by living in rigid cellulose boxes. There will still, however, be an unequal distribution of diffusible ions between the extra- and intracellular fluids because of the presence of the organic anions.

Some Morphological Correlates

If the above arguments are sound, the organization of the very first cell produced a transmembrane potential due to an unequal distribution of ion species; the steady state or resting potential depended on the properties of the cell membrane and the presence of the cation pump. This has remained a universal attribute of living cells at all stages in their phylogeny. In addition, it can be assumed that the most primitive cell encountered a variety of alterations in its environment (stimuli) which were of sufficient magnitude to disturb this delicate balance of ions and change the value of the resting potential, in other words, to cause ELECTROGENESIS. This constitutes a stimulus-response situation and, at the risk of some oversimplification, the capacity for electrogenesis may also be listed with the universal attributes of cells. In any case, it is the cornerstone in the evolution of the diverse and complex tissues and processes concerned with excitability and the phylogeny of animal activity.

The discharge of electricity as a terminal physiological activity occurs only in the electric organs of some fishes. Usually, cellular electrogenesis is coupled with some other process to effect such characteristic responses as locomotion or color change. It follows that the primitive response of electrogenesis required the evolution of a battery of specialized effector organs to achieve the complexities of animal physiology and behavior. Likewise, at the point of the stimulus, the evolutionary process has produced delicate transducers with specialized sensitivity for particular categories of environmental change; electrogenesis is the fundamental response, but it may be triggered in many different ways and it, in turn, may trigger several different kinds of activities. Both receptors and effectors have been built onto the primitive electrogenic activity of cells.

INDEPENDENT EFFECTORS

When receptor and effector functions are confined to a single cell, this is called an INDEPENDENT EFFECTOR. Parker (1919), in his classic book *The Elementary Nervous System*, selected the porocyte of the asconoid sponges as an example of such a cell. A porocyte is a conical cell pierced by a tube which actually forms one of the numerous pores or ostia through which water streams into the body of the animal. The water currents are created by the flagella of the choanocytes which line the cavities of the sponge, but this flow can be interrupted in unfavorable situations through the closure of the ostia by a slow contraction of the porocyte. Prosser *et al.* (1962) found that the oscula of a number of marine and freshwater sponges exhibit local, graded responses to mechanical stimuli but are not responsive to electrical stimulaton. Oscula are the openings of the exhalant canals and contain fusiform contractile elements resembling smooth muscle and called myocytes. In Prosser's studies there was no evidence of propagated excitation from one part of the osculum to another. These contractile systems of sponges seem to fulfil the requirements of independent effectors.

Far more complex receptor-effector systems exist in single cells. The cnidoblast or nematocyte of the coelenterate is a highly specialized example. These cells produce bubble-like intracellular capsules (nematocysts) which possess an introverted and coiled hollow thread. The capsule contains a toxic substance, and on stimulation the thread is explosively everted with sufficient force to penetrate cuticle or epidermis. Descriptions of the physiology and anatomy are given elsewhere (Autrum,

1959; Prosser and Brown, 1961). The interesting point for the present discussion is that the cells respond to mechanical stimuli, that the nature of the mechanical stimulus necessary to elicit a response may be modified in an appropriate way by chemicals (for example, it is reduced by dissolved food substances), and that the response is an elaborate one involving the release of a toxic product of cell metabolism. These intricate cells are double sense organs as well as effectors (Autrum, 1959).

RECEPTOR-EFFECTOR SYSTEMS

Parker selected the epitheliomuscular cell of the coelenterate epidermis as an example of a phylogenetically primitive receptor-effector system. This cell has a receptor surface exposed on the outside of the animal and an expanded specialized base containing a myoneme or contractile fibril; excitation spreads from the receptor surface to the effector base. Although it is by no means certain that these cells always operate independently of nerves, the cell still seems to provide a useful example of a simple system which combines the properties of receptor, conductor and effector. It seems reasonable to argue with Parker that the parcelling out of these three activities into different kinds of cells and tissues was a necessary step in the evolution of large animals with their complexity of integrated activities.

In the first hypothetical step visualized by Parker, the effector action is allocated to a specialized effector cell and the receptor and conductor functions remain associated; in the second stage the main responsibility for conduction is transferred to an intermediate nerve cell. Systems exemplifying each of these theoretical steps in phylogeny can be found in the coelenterates (Hyman, 1940), but these particular cell types were not discarded during later stages in animal evolution. The olfactory cells of a mammal are receptors with delicate hairlike projections making contact with the external environment, and elongated axonic basal filaments which conduct excitation to the olfactory tract (Fig. 16.1).

Each of the three components of this primitive neuro-effector apparatus (the receptor, the conductor and the effector) has become elaborated during phylogeny. It is, however, the intermediate component, serving first as link between the receptor surface and the effector organ, which assumes the great responsibilities for integration. Some of these capacities appear in the coelenterate (Chapter 21), but they only reach their full expression with the development of elaborate concentrations of neurons which decode the electrogenic input from receptors and transmit appropriate pulses to effector organs. Two phylogenetic steps are suggested in comparing a coelenterate nerve net with a central nervous system of one of the higher invertebrates or a vertebrate. In the first, the interconnecting neurons serve primarily as stations for the switching of signals from the receptor line to the effector line; in the second, the interconnecting neurons modify the input from receptors so that the output may bear no simple relation to it. The elaborate types of animal behavior are obviously based on the latter.

Physiological Properties of Excitable Tissues

ELECTROGENESIS

The excitation of receptor organs, transmitting cells and effector tissues can be most satisfactorily explained in terms of the ionic permeability theory of electrogenesis. This has been stated in a modern form by Grundfest (1961), Katz (1959*a, b*) and others; only a brief summary is given here. Comprehensive discussions may be found in textbooks of neurophysiology and particularly in the *Handbook of Physiology* (American Physiological Society).

The ionic permeability theory of electrogenesis can be most easily visualized by reference to Eccles' (1957) diagram of the cell membrane shown in Fig. 15.1, with the addition of channels for the flux of chloride as well as Na^+ and K^+. The cation pump functions in the maintenance of stability and in the recovery processes which follow excitation; it may be neglected for the moment. The membrane itself appears to be a barrier perforated with pores which are capable of passing specific ions. Many of the facts fit a concept of "valved" openings which operate on an all-or-none principle to admit or exclude specific ions (Boettiger, 1961). Three types of valves have been distinguished (Na^+, K^+ and Cl^-) but there may also be Ca^{++} and/or Mg^{++} valves (Hagiwara and Naka, 1964). Excitation, according to this hypothesis, involves a change in the number of open valves rather than an increased flow of ions through channels which remain continuously open. In some membranes, the valves are operated only electrically (ELECTRICALLY EXCITABLE VALVES), while in others specific chemicals or a mechanical stretching of the membrane provides the stimulus (ELECTRICALLY INEXCITABLE VALVES); frequently both types of valves occur in the same membrane.

Propagated potentials. Electrogenesis was first investigated in the giant axons of cephalopods. The most familiar examples are still those described for nerves and muscles, even though several other types of electrogenic cells (receptors, glands) are probably phylogenetically simpler.

In the resting muscle fiber or nerve axon, the Na^+ valves are mainly closed; the K^+ and Cl^- valves are open only in sufficient numbers to balance the electrochemical forces and establish the resting potential. These cells are usually excited physiologically by the release of a transmitter substance such as acetylcholine which combines with a receptor molecule to open the ion valves. The transmitter is quickly destroyed by an enzyme (cholinesterase for acetylcholine), but if a sufficient number of valves are opened the redistribution of ions at this point shifts the potential sufficiently (electrogenesis) to excite neighboring ELECTRICALLY EXCITABLE VALVES, and a short-circuiting produces a wave of depolarization which spreads along the axon or muscle cell. This TRANSDUCER ACTION, which starts a wave of depolarization along the cell, is thus initiated by a chemical but depends on the presence of electrically excitable valves in the surface membrane. Experimentally, electric currents are often used to study the excitation of nerves and muscles; the electrical stimulus acts by redistributing ions and altering their concentrations so that the valves are electrically excited.

When one electrode is placed inside and another on the outside of an excitable cell, as was first done with the giant squid axon, electrogenesis is recorded as a sharp SPIKE (Keynes, 1958 and Fig. 15.2). These spikes are all-or-none responses of an electrically excitable membrane and at their peak usually reverse the membrane potential to an inside positivity. They are capable of propagating without decrement and have a form and duration which is characteristic for different types of cells (cf. Fig. 15.2 and 19.16).

The movements of the ions can be followed by radioactive tracers. Only minute numbers pass across the membrane during any single electrogenic response. It has been calculated that, even in the absence of the cation pump, a squid axon could be stimulated thousands of times before its ion store was exhausted (Katz, 1959*a*). The relative contributions of ion pumps and valves to the electrogenic response can also be evaluated. Metabolic poisons such as cyanide will eliminate the pump without altering the valves. Likewise, there are chemical agents which alter ion permeability in a selective manner. For example, in certain neurons the entrance of Na^+ (Na-activation) can be diminished by poisoning with urethane. This eliminates the spike but leaves a small GRADED RESPONSE indicating that the spike associated with all-or-none conduction is primarily due to flooding with Na^+. The small graded response, which has been shown to be associated with the outward flux of K^+ (K-activation), is unaffected by urethane but diminished by tetramethylammonium ion (Grundfest, 1961). Experiments such as these demonstrate the different types of valves and the significance of the movements of specific ions in the electrogenic response. Although a Na-activation is characteristic of many electrically excitable cells, it is by no means universal (Grundfest, 1961); the electrically excitable plant cell, *Chara,* produces a spike as a result of Cl-activation; divalent ions (especially Ca^{++}) rather than Na ions play the major role in production of action potentials in crustacean muscle fibers (Hagiwara and Naka, 1964).

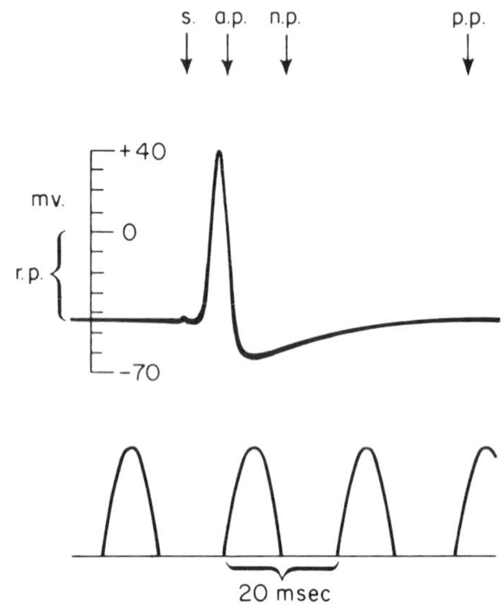

Fig. 15.2. Resting and action potentials reached between an electrode within the giant axon and one outside. The vertical scale indicates the potential of the internal electrode (in millivolts) relative to the sea water outside. At rest the inside of the fiber is negative (*r.p.*). When the fiber is excited to conduct an action potential the inside becomes positive to the outside. The stimulus artefact shows as a small kink, *s.* The action potential (*a.p.*) is followed by negative after potential (*n.p.*). The positive after potential (*p.p.*) is beginning to show at the end of the record. [Young (1957) after A. L. Hodgkin and A. F. Huxley (1945).]

Graded responses. The propagated action potential is a highly specialized cellular attribute. In many membranes the transducer action which follows stimulation produces only local responses in which the electrogenesis varies in amplitude with the stimulus strength and is decrementally propagated (GRADED RESPONSES). This type of response is phylogenetically older and considered to be the basis for the evolution of the all-or-none propagated activity required for long-distance transmission of excitation in multicellular animals (Grundfest, 1959*a*). Graded local responses in crustacean muscle fibers are shown in Fig. 19.21. Another example of local nonpropagated excitation will be described in the discussion of the Pacinian corpuscle (Chapter 18).

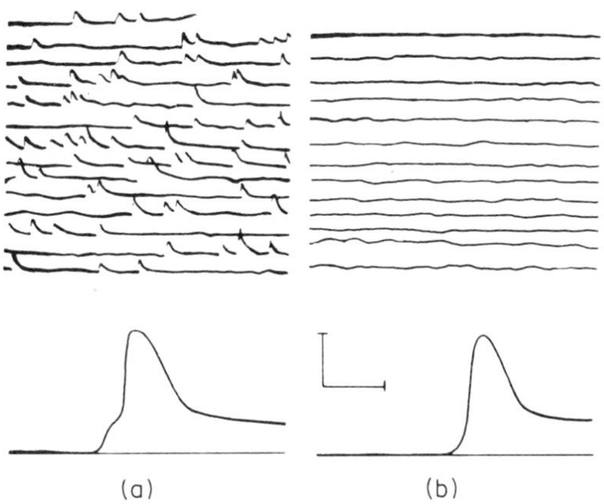

Fig. 15.3. Intracellular recordings of electrical potentials in frog skeletal muscle. *a* was recorded at the end-plate and *b* at a distance of 2 mm from the end-plate in the same muscle fiber. The upper recordings, taken at low speed and high amplification, show the spontaneous activity confined to the end-plate; the lower recordings, made at high speed and low amplification, show the response to the nerve stimulus (shock applied at the beginning of the sweep); *a* shows the step-like initial end-plate potential which leads to the propagated wave; *b* shows only the propagated action potential delayed by conduction over a distance of 2 mm. Voltage and time scales: 3.6 mv and 47 msec for the upper part; 50 mv and 2 msec for the lower part. [Fatt and Katz, 1952.]

The myoneural junction (on the frog sartorius, for example) is another useful preparation for the study of graded responses (Fig. 19.15 and 15.3). These junctions are electrically inexcitable, although the neighboring parts of the membrane contain electrically excitable valves as described above. Transmission at the myoneural junction is chemically mediated. The application of different drugs provides a most useful technique for sorting out the events associated with this functional activity. Curare (an arrow poison used by South American Indians), seems to compete with acetylcholine for the receptor substance in the membrane. When applied to the junction, it reduces the potentials in accordance with its concentration. When the junction potential is reduced to about 30 per cent of the maximum the neighboring electrically excitable valves are no longer activated, and the spike, the all-or-none response, does not appear in the muscle (Fig. 15.4).

Physostigmine (a plant alkaloid used by native peoples of West Africa in ordeal trials) or its synthetic counterpart neostigmine, on the other hand, competes with acetylcholine for the enzyme cholinesterase. Hence, acetylcholine is not rapidly destroyed in the presence of neostigmine and the junctional potential is greatly prolonged (Fig. 15.5).

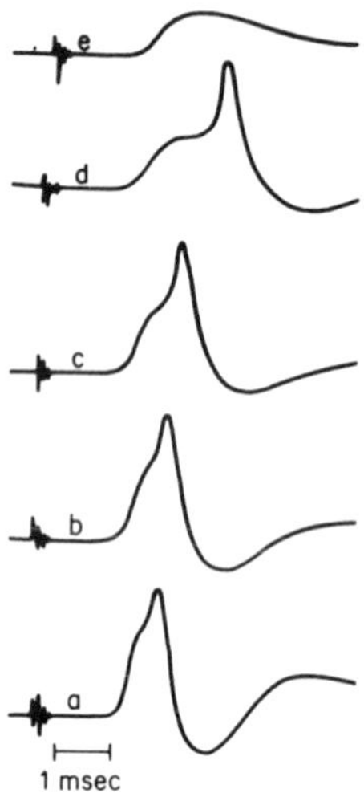

Fig. 15.4. Action potentials from the region of the end-plate in frog sartorius. *a*, Before curarization. *b* to *d*, Increasing degrees of curarization. *e*, Curarization complete. Propagated spike arises from junction potential in *a* to *d*. [Based on Kuffler (1942).]

Only the myoneural junction of nerve-muscle preparation from adult frogs shows this sensitivity to acetylcholine. Embryonic frog muscles or the fetal muscles of rats, on the other hand, show a general chemosensitivity; the entire cell membrane can be excited by applying acetylcholine at any point. After the innervation has been established, only the end-plate responds to acetylcholine; chemo-sensitivity has been lost over the surface of the fiber (Thesleff, 1961). If the nerves to the adult muscle are cut, the general chemosensitivity gradually returns. In some way the motor nerve can control the size of the chemoreceptor surface.

Inhibition. An integrating nervous system could never have been perfected with excitatory responses only. Inhibitory activity is an essential component of both the central nervous system and the peripheral control. As Sherrington (1947) demonstrated more than half a century ago, integrative action depends on an interplay of both excitation and inhibition.

The nerve-muscle preparations of crustaceans have been most useful in the study of nervous inhibition (Furshpan, 1959 and Chapter 19). The skeletal muscles of crustaceans receive separate nerve fibers for excitation and inhibition. Recordings with intracellular electrodes show greatly reduced end-plate potentials following a stimulation of the inhibitory fibers. When only the inhibitory fibers are stimulated, there will be little change in the membrane potential if this is at or near the resting level at the moment of stimulation; if, however, it be displaced somewhat (as can be done experimentally) then muscle potentials develop as transient hyperpolarizations or depolarizations depending on the direction of displacement. In short, the membrane potential tends to be stabilized by the stimulation of the inhibitory fiber; these fibers counteract changes in the resting potential. This is at least in part due to increased K^+ permeability (K-conductance) or outward movement of K^+ which tends to neutralize depolarizing effects. However, this does not provide a complete explanation. Separate transmitter substances are thought to be produced by the two types of fibers and to antagonize each other or compete for active sites on the postsynaptic membrane (Davson, 1959; Furshpan, 1959; Grundfest, 1961).

Unlike the crustaceans, inhibition of vertebrate somatic muscles is a central phenomenon. Mauthner's axons in teleosts may be exceptions to this rule or exemplify some special synaptic arrangement in the central

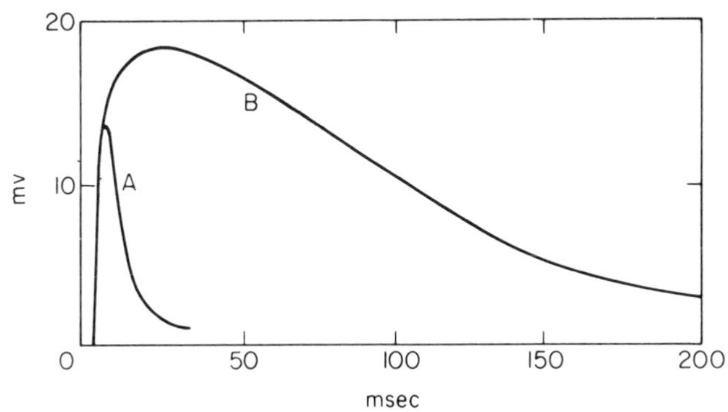

Fig. 15.5 Effects of an anticholinesterase drug on end-plate potential of single muscle fiber produced by stimulation of motor nerve. *A*, when neuromuscular transmission is blocked after reduction of sodium concentration in bathing medium. *B*, from same fiber after addition of neostigmine to the sodium deficient bathing medium. [Ruch and Fulton (1960) after Fatt and Katz (1951).]

nervous system (Retzlaff, 1957; Wiersma, 1961). In general, peripheral inhibition is confined to the visceral nervous system among the vertebrates. The cardiac arrest which follows stimulation of the vagus is the most familiar example in the elementary physiology laboratory. This was shown to depend on the release of a chemical substance (since shown to be acetylcholine) in classical experiments by Otto Loewi, published in 1921 (Heilbrunn, 1952). It is now known that acetylcholine produces hyperpolarization or stabilization of the resting potentials of heart muscle, an activity which is entirely opposite to its effect on the myoneural junction. In the membrane of the cardiac muscle cell it increases only K^+ ion conductance, and the membrane tends to move toward, or be held at, the potassium equilibrium potential (Katz, 1959*b*). In the myoneural junction, on the other hand, Na-conductance is also increased and general depolarization is initiated.

Integrative action. In summary, Grundfest (1959*a*) argues that the generalized excitable cell exhibits three distinct physiological capacities. These appeared at different times in evolution and have been exploited to different degrees by various types of excitable cells to produce highly integrative animal systems. Receptor cells which are not electrically excitable and which show a graded electrogenesis (either depolarizing or hyperpolarizing) in accordance with the strength of the stimulus must be closest to the more primitive excitable cells. The spike-generating membrane structure which transmits coded messages from the receptor to the effector is phylogenetically more recent. The coded messages flow from receptors to effectors in all-or-none pulses which vary only in number and frequency. Finally, the hyperpolarizing, inhibitory type of synaptic electrogenesis provides a control on excitatory activities; the interaction of excitation and inhibition is the physiological basis of integrated animal activity.

GENERAL CHARACTERISTICS OF STIMULUS AND RESPONSE

Many of the classical exercises in the physiology laboratory have been built around quantitative descriptions of tissue responses to carefully measured stimuli. The electric current has been the favored type of stimulus because its intensity, duration and rate of rise to peak value can be precisely controlled and because of its effectiveness in eliciting responses in readily available tissues such as the heart and nerve-muscle preparations from the frog. These relationships are detailed in textbooks of vertebrate physiology and will not be described here. It is, however, important to note that most of them find a ready explanation in terms of the ionic permeability theory of electrogenesis.

An effective stimulus must obviously be of a certain THRESHOLD or minimal value if it is going to open sufficient numbers of valves to produce the transmitted type of electrogenic response. The subthreshold, subminimal or subliminal stimulus, however, may be expected to produce some electrogenesis (LOCAL EXCITATORY STATE) which, under certain conditions, can be added to and results in the SUMMATION OF INADEQUATE STIMULI. As noted in the last section, any change in the membrane potential will initiate recovery processes which involve both the action of the cation pump and the valves; it follows then that the stimulus must rise to peak value within a certain period of time, or the recovery processes will counteract those which tend toward depolarization. A stimulus must also last long enough (MINIMAL EFFECTIVE DURATION) to open a sufficient number of valves to trigger a response. Thus, the effective stimulus is characterized by its STRENGTH, DURATION and RATE OF RISE to peak value. Strength-duration relationships for several activated organs are shown in Fig. 15.6.

Responses measured in the effector organs are characterized by time relationships which also find a ready explanation in terms of membrane electrogenesis. The time required for an action current to develop at a myoneural junction or to move along a muscle or nerve fiber creates a measurable LATENT PERIOD between stimulus and observed response; the depolarization of the membrane leaves it in a refractory state from

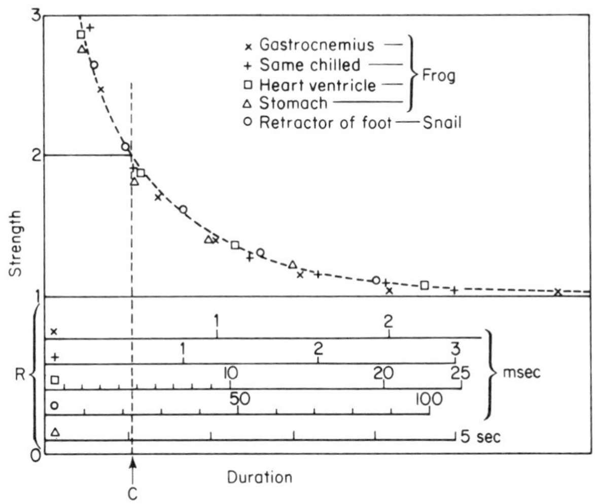

Fig. 15.6. Five strength-duration curves superimposed by adjusting the time scale. Stimulus strength 1 is the strength which just fails to excite in an infinitely long time; it is called the RHEOBASE. The duration required to stimulate when the strength is twice the rheobase (stimulus 2 on the ordinate) was termed the CHRONAXIE by Lapicque and is shown at the broken line C. [Heilbrunn (1952) based on Lapicque.]

which it gradually recovers through stages which are first ABSOLUTE REFRACTORY PERIODS and then RELATIVE REFRACTORY PERIODS.

Intercellular transmission often requires more than one stimulus. Several stimuli in rapid succession may be necessary to activate certain synapses or the myoneural junctions of crustaceans, or vertebrate junctions which have been treated with curare. This SUMMATION results in FACILITATION and is probably evidence that a single stimulus, no matter how intense, is incapable of releasing sufficient neurohumor to produce a depolarization at these junctions. FATIGUE and SENSORY ADAPTATION or ACCOMMODATION, in which repeated stimulation leads to reduced responsiveness, may also be explained by the membrane hypothesis; cation pumps require a steady supply of metabolites, neurohumors gradually become exhausted, and the responsive membrane can only tolerate limited changes in the distribution of ions. The present membrane theories of cellular irritability provide a satisfactory explanation for many of the classical demonstrations of the physiology laboratory.

Receptor Mechanisms and Chemoreception 16

"Man doth not live by bread only." The free life of an animal depends on a constant flow of information from its environment, the computation and integration of this into meaningful and purposive instructions for the effectors and the relay of the instructions to the appropriate glands, muscles, chromatophores and other organs concerned with animal activities. This flow of information pertaining to the environment is every whit as important as the energy-yielding foods which must also be acquired from the outside. The first link which unites an animal with its habitat is the sensory receptor system, specialized to transform chemical, radiant, electrical or mechanical energy into a train of membrane potentials which are the only data received in the computing centers of the brain or coordinating ganglia.

It has already been argued that the ancestral animal cells were endowed with protoplasmic irritability. It can be assumed that these simple cells took advantage of this capacity to avoid some of the environmental hazards. Like the familiar *Amoeba*, they probably showed protoplasmic responses to a shift in environmental temperature, to changing light conditions, to vibrations and to foreign chemicals. With nothing more than simple avoiding reactions, a measure of contact with the more suitable parts of the habitat is possible. With the evolution of specialized receptors and the associated integrating machinery, animals have been able to exploit the world in a much more positive manner: to locate and utilize particular foods, to find mates and care for their young, to establish territories and orient their travels.

In the higher animals, these capacities were further enlarged with the specialization of cells and tissues for the production of distinctive animal signals and the gradual incorporation of these into systems for communication. These "languages" are as often based on odors as they are on sounds and sometimes incorporate light or electrical fields. As the range and variety of environmental stimuli have gradually changed during animal evolution, the receptor organs have made use of more and more of the potential information. Primitive animal reactions are positive or negative movements with respect to broad bands of the stimulus spectrum; the delicate transducers of the more advanced phyla discriminate among different wavelengths or the planes of polarization of light; they permit responses to specific frequencies and amplitudes of vibratory stimuli and detect complex organic chemicals which may have meaning for only one sex or one species out of a multitude of animal species.

The receptor system of a complex multicellular animal must collect information from the internal as well as the external environment. Coordinated activities depend on a delicate balance between the movements of the different parts. Receptors in muscles, tendons and joints (PROPRIOCEPTORS) provide the basic information for these adjustments. Signals from the visceral receptors (INTEROCEPTORS) are concerned with much of the internal regulation of visceral functions (for example, the cardiovascular pressoreceptors or the osmoreceptors of the hypothalamus); they may also modify the overt activity of an animal (visceral pain, for example). These parts of the receptor system which signal changes from within the organism, although superficially inconspicuous, would rank in bulk with the distance receptors if they were collected together in one place.

Physiologists interested in the sense organs have acquired most of their information from two different lines of investigation—behavioral and electrophysiological. In the behavioral type of analysis, some obvious activity of the animal is related to a measured change in environmental energy. A change in light intensity or sound, the exposure to a chemical or the change in an electric field may modify an animal's activities in a real and obvious manner. Through appropriate conditioning experiments it is possible to evaluate an animal's ability to discriminate extremely small differences. Bull (1957), for example, found that some species of fish can perceive differences of only 0.06‰ salinity or 0.03°C temperature. In the electrophysiological studies, the generator currents of the receptor cells or the action potentials of the associated neurons are measured during exposure of the cells to controlled environmental stimuli. The capacity of the transducer can be accurately evaluated;

infrared detectors in rattlesnakes, for example, respond to temperature changes of the order of 0.001°C (Bullock, 1959*a*).

The recorded information on the structure and function of the receptor organs forms a large segment of the physiological literature. The present discussion will be restricted to a brief comment on the transducer mechanisms, an attempt to discover some phylogenetic trends in the functional anatomy and an emphasis on the receptors as links between the different animals and between the animals and their habitats. This seems to be the logical course in an endeavor to trace a phylogeny in physiological mechanisms. Comprehensive surveys of the literature can be found in Prosser and Brown (1961), in the *Handbook of Physiology* (American Physiological Society) and in physiological monographs devoted to the various animal groups. Chemoreception will be considered in this chapter; receptors concerned with light, vibrations and temperature are discussed in the two subsequent chapters, while comment on reception of electrical stimuli is reserved for the description of electrical organs in Chapter 20.

Chemoreception

This category of receptor screens a broad spectrum of chemicals ranging from hydrogen ions and simple inorganic compounds, such as water and sodium chloride, to complex organic molecules of many different kinds (Moncrieff, 1951).

MORPHOLOGY

There are two types of cell concerned with chemical reception. One of these is a bipolar nerve cell in which the membrane of the dendrite is specialized and highly excitable in the presence of specific chemicals. The other is a columnar epithelial cell in which the excitable and exposed apex of the cell is extended in a hairlike process while the base is in contact with a dendritic arborization of an associated neuron (Fig. 16.1). These are sometimes called PRIMARY and SECONDARY sense cells respectively. The former are assumed to be phylogenetically older since only the neurosensory type of receptor cell occurs among the invertebrate animals (Hyman, 1951; Hodgson, 1955; Autrum, 1959). Although the non-nervous chemoreceptor seems to be phylogenetically more recent, it is not a more acute receptor. In fact, the taste buds which are secondary sense cells are intermediate in receptor capacity between the free nerve terminals which subserve the relatively crude common chemical sense and the olfactory cells which detect extremely complex organic molecules in trace quantities.

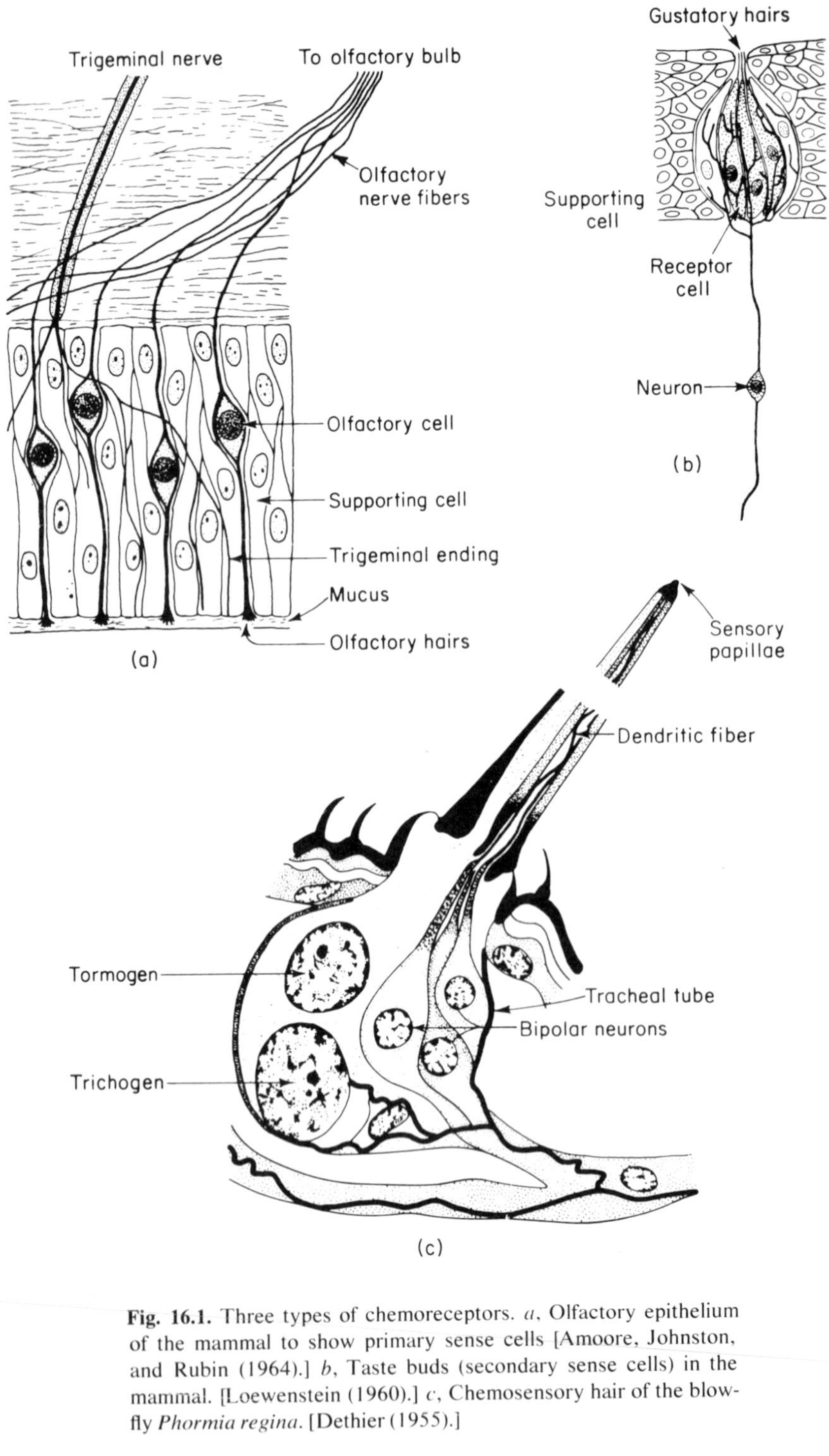

Fig. 16.1. Three types of chemoreceptors. *a*, Olfactory epithelium of the mammal to show primary sense cells [Amoore, Johnston, and Rubin (1964).] *b*, Taste buds (secondary sense cells) in the mammal. [Loewenstein (1960).] *c*, Chemosensory hair of the blowfly *Phormia regina*. [Dethier (1955).]

Three different chemoreceptors are shown in Fig. 16.1. The exposed portions of the dendrites of the vertebrate olfactory epithelium are delicate filaments of the surface membrane extending into the mucus which covers the surface of the organ. The filaments presumably form the transducing membranes. The olfactory cells of insects are morphologically more complex, probably because of the dry covering with which they are associated; often they are just as specialized in chemical sensitivity.

Some of the most productive research in chemoreception has been based on insects. Structural details of the organs vary (Dethier, 1955) but, in general, several neurons are grouped together near the body surface, and each sends a long dendritic filament into a chitin-protected space. This space may take the form of a pit, a peg or a hairlike papilla. The covering cuticle is extremely thin (thickness less than 1 μ) and probably specialized in its permeability. It usually seems to seal the space from the outside world, but in some cases minute pores permit direct access of air to the dendritic tips (Slifer, 1961). Only the tips of the filaments are chemically excitable; they may be subdivided into elements of about 0.02 μ diameter. Associated with the cell bodies of the neurons are non-nervous cells (*trichogen* and *tormogen* in Fig. 16.1*C*) which produce the hair and its socket. In this structure, as in all other chemoreceptors, the activating chemicals pass into solution before reaching the receptor membranes.

A chemosensory hair on the labium of the blowfly (Fig. 16.1) consists of three neurons, only two of which send filaments into the "hair." This organ has been particularly useful for the analysis of the transducer mechanism since action currents can be recorded directly from the dendrites. The evidence indicates that one of the neurons responds only to sugars while the other is activated by monovalent salts; the neuron which terminates at the base of the hair is a mechanoreceptor; a fourth neuron (not localized histologically) is excited by water (Dethier, 1962). This preparation has intriguing possibilities for the student of animal behavior. The stimulation of a single sensory neuron will initiate complete behavior responses of proboscis extension in response to sugar or proboscis retraction or inhibition when the non-sugar receptor is activated (Dethier, 1955, 1962).

Morphologically unspecialized dendrites or naked nerve endings may also serve as chemoreceptors. In the carotid sinus and aortic bodies of vertebrates the dendrites arborize in highly vascular tissues, sense changes in CO_2 or pH, and initiate impulses which bring about appropriate cardiovascular responses. The COMMON CHEMICAL SENSE of vertebrates also depends on naked nerve endings. This is the least discriminating of the chemical senses and is only stimulated at relatively high concentrations of acids, alkalis and various irritating compounds. Moncrieff (1951) regards it as a distinct sense and not merely a reflection of tissue irritation or damage. The evidence is based on responses to acids and various irritants after destruction of the nerves concerned with taste and smell, or after treatment with anaesthetics which eliminate responses from tactile stimulation and nonirritating chemicals. The aquatic vertebrates as well as the mammals have been studied in this manner. A similar sense is claimed for the insects (Roeder, 1953).

Chemoreceptors which are secondary sense cells are represented by the taste buds (Fig. 16.1). These are confined to the oral regions of the land vertebrates but are widely distributed over the head, fins and flanks of some fishes where their distribution follows the VII, IX and X cranial nerves (Hasler, 1957).

GENERAL PHYSIOLOGY OF RECEPTOR CELLS

The chemoreceptors will serve to illustrate several physiological properties which are characteristic of receptors generally. These are in addition to the general principles of stimulus and response referred to at the end of the last chapter.

The highly SPECIFIC NATURE OF THE EFFECTIVE STIMULUS is well illustrated in chemoreception. The two morphologically similar dendrites in the labellar hairs of the blowfly provide an excellent example; one of these responds to sugar and the other to salts. Moncrieff (1951) cites numerous examples based on human responses. For instance in the following series of three nitrotoluidines, the first one is very slightly bitter, the second is tasteless and the third sweet.

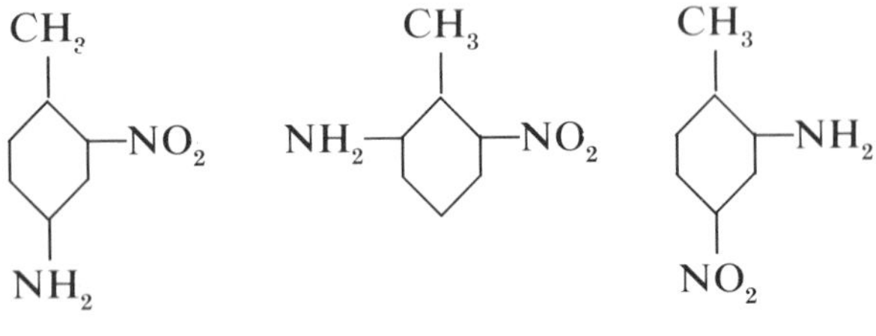

This display of differential sensitivity is akin to the concept of the ADEQUATE STIMULUS in human sensory physiology. Each receptor is especially sensitive to one form of energy. The classical example is the retina, the cells of which normally respond to radiant energy of wavelengths between about 400 and 650 mμ. Although they can also be stimulated mechanically they are much more sensitive to radiant energy; light is their adequate stimulus.

Müller introduced the concept of SPECIFIC NERVE ENERGIES to human physiologists many years ago (Heilbrunn, 1952). He pointed out that a sense organ could be stimulated by other than the adequate stimulus, but the subjective response is always the same and not influenced by the KIND of energy. Stimulation of the retina gives the sensation of light, whether the cells are stimulated by radiant energy or mechanically. Physiologists now understand that this must be the case since the only functional activity of a nerve fiber is the membrane potential. The same general principle can be illustrated from comparative physiology. The chemically sensitive hair-fibers of the blowfly can also be activated by bending or mechanical stimulation, but the resulting movement of the proboscis is the characteristic response in both cases (Hodgson and Roeder, 1956).

ADAPTATION is particularly fast in some chemoreceptors, a familiar human experience when we try to detect a delicate odor. In contrast, some receptors such as the proprioceptors of muscles, tendons and joints adapt scarcely at all. The biological significance of these physiological differences is obvious. Rates of adaptation for the two labellar hairs of the blowfly are shown in Fig. 16.2 and indicate that morphologically

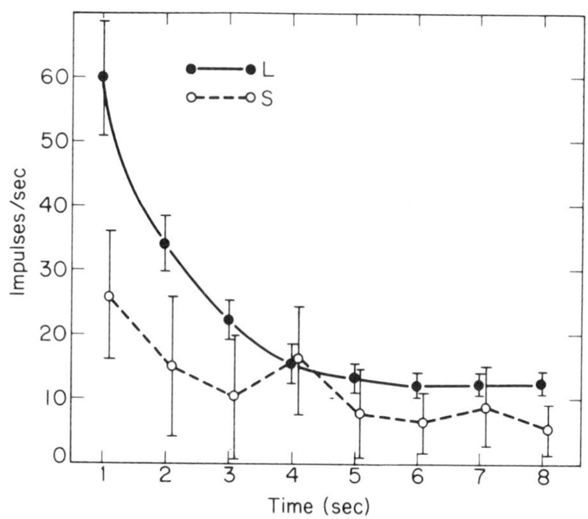

Fig. 16.2. Progressive adaptation in the two different fibers (*L* and *S*) of the chemosensory hair of the blowfly. Average values with six repetitions for the application of 0.5 molar NaCl to the tip of the same labellar hair. Variations are 2*X* standard errors of means. Electrical responses on the vertical axis, and time after application of salt on the horizontal axis. [Hodgson and Roeder (1956).]

similar and spatially close receptors of the same sort may show somewhat different patterns of adaptation.

The relationship between receptor activity and intensity of stimulus is often semilogarithmic. This may also be illustrated with some of the blowfly data (Fig. 16.3). The relation between logarithm of stimulus intensity and response is extremely important in sensory physiology since it so greatly extends the range of responsiveness. The intensity of sunlight is about 30,000 times greater than that of moonlight, and yet we can see moderately well in both. The range in capacity of nerve fibers to conduct waves of excitation is not more than several hundredfold; the logarithmic relation permits responsiveness of receptors over vastly greater ranges. This phenomenon is discussed in books of general and sensory physiology and is sometimes given the dignity of a law ("Weber-Fechner Law") named after the men who first emphasized its importance. It is not an invariable law but frequently applies over certain ranges of intensities (Schmitt, 1959).

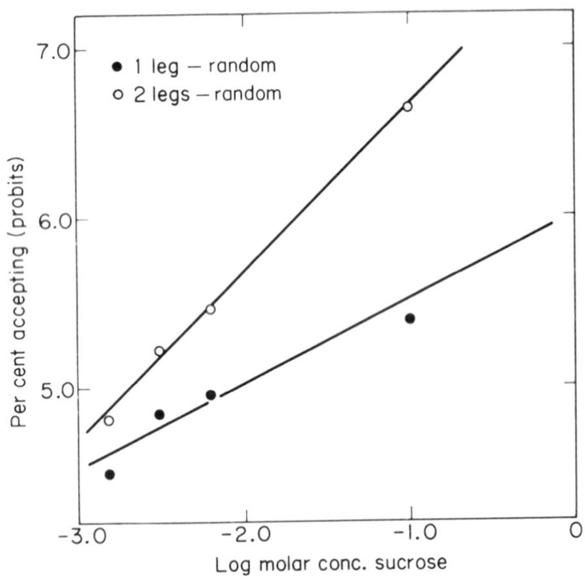

Fig. 16.3. Relationship between receptor activity and stimulus intensity. Acceptance thresholds by blowflies for sucrose when stimulated unilaterally (solid circles) or bilaterally (open circles). [Dethier (1963).]

Some of these general properties of receptors can be more aptly illustrated with one receptor than another, but they are all characteristic of sensory phenomena and apply to some degree in each receptor process.

TRANSDUCER MECHANISMS IN CHEMORECEPTION

Little evidence concerning the nature of the transducing mechanism was possible before the development of micro-electrophysiological techniques. With these it is possible to record from single receptor cells and nerve fibers and to study responses in relation to chemical constitution, molecular concentrations, enzyme inhibitors and temperature.

The valves in the cell membrane are chemically excitable and, in theory, depolarization might be initiated by a simple ionic imbalance—especially by acids and salts; alternatively, some more specific combination of a stimulating chemical and a special receptor compound or site in the cell membrane might be required. Evidence points toward the latter phenomenon. The process may be likened to that which occurs in synaptic or myoneural transmission. This complexing or adsorption of the stimulating chemical then leads to an opening of valves and a depolarization of the membrane. However, these theories must still be formulated in very general terms, and no entirely satisfactory explanation of the molecular mechanisms has yet been found (Davies, 1962; Dethier, 1962).

More purely mechanical theories based on low-frequency molecular vibrations or rotations have been proposed (Wright, 1963). The active molecules might initiate nerve impulses through their vibrations or they might in turn excite pigment molecules which are conspicuous in many olfactory cells. The suggestions are purely hypothetical but are in strong contrast to chemical reactions which might depend on the presence of specific enzymes (Baradi and Bourne, 1953). In general, the reactions seem to be more nearly biophysical than biochemical, but the explanations are still unsatisfactory (Dethier, 1956; Davies, 1962).

THE CHEMICAL SENSE AND ANIMAL ORIENTATION

At the base of the phylogenetic tree chemoreception depends on relatively high concentrations of chemicals and the resultant behavior is largely trial-and-error. At the peak in animal specialization, the receptors sample chemicals from great distances, serve to guide animals through their territories and play a major part in their social behavior. Thus, the more primitive groups possess only a CONTACT CHEMICAL SENSE while the more advanced ones have specialized DISTANCE RECEPTORS as well.

In human experience these two capacities are associated with TASTE and SMELL respectively; the distinction is a very real one. Taste and smell are subserved by distinct groups of cells which appear to have had different phylogenetic histories. In addition, olfactory receptors have much lower thresholds for excitation; they receive their stimulation from airborne sources while the taste receptors are activated by direct contact. Finally, gustatory stimulation leads to acceptance (usually, feeding responses) or to direct rejection of the source of stimulation; olfactory stimulation often results in locomotion and more complex behavioral responses.

Two separate receptor systems (olfactory and gustatory) can be most easily distinguished in the mammals. The distinctions can still be maintained in the aquatic vertebrates on the basis of homologous anatomical parts, although some of the other criteria are lacking. In the insects a nice separation can be made on the basis of behavioral responses and the source of stimulation—whether direct contact or from airborne sources. In the aquatic invertebrates, however, most of the criteria for a separation can no longer be found. Chemoreception is always due to direct contact with dissolved materials, and separate receptors for different kinds of chemicals have not yet been described. Nevertheless, the more specialized of the aquatic invertebrates do rely on chemoreception in many behavioral situations other than feeding and seem to differentiate a variety of chemicals (Carthy, 1958; Barber, 1961). Only the lower phylogenetic groups show a generalized chemical reception and response, and in these the sense is more allied to tasting than to smelling.

The most valid interpretation is probably the phylogenetic one. Very generalized reactions to the contact of chemicals have, during evolution, differentiated into acute distance receptors, with separate anatomical parts for testing foods about to enter the body and for sampling distant odorous materials. The comparative physiologist can throughout most of the animal kingdom retain a useful distinction between the contact chemical sense—which is often localized in the mouth region, depends on relatively high concentrations of chemicals and elicits feeding or avoiding reactions—and the distance receptors which are sensitive to very low concentrations of chemicals and usually lead to locomotion and complex behavioral responses.

The contact chemical sense. Fraenkel and Gunn (1940) depict trails of protozoans, flatworms, insects and other invertebrates in the presence of food attractants or repellent chemicals. The animals always position themselves through indirect routes. The reactions are classed as kineses and klinotaxes. At low concentrations only the speed or frequency of locomotion may be altered (ORTHOKINESIS); at somewhat higher concentrations there may be an increase in the amount or frequency of turning per unit time (KLINOKINESIS). Orientation becomes more precise in close proximity to the chemical and is then a DIRECTED REACTION either toward the chemical or away from it (TAXIS). In chemotaxis, however, movements with respect to the stimulus are not straight-line orientations (TROPOTAXIS), but the goal is attained as the animal moves its body from side to side testing the environment during its progression (KLINOTAXIS).

This sort of classification is adequate to describe the movements of planarians, leeches or mites toward bait or their avoidance of acids but does not exhaust the capacities of animals to exploit the contact chemical senses. The honeybee which informs its companions of a source of honey by the form of its dance also tells them how sweet the honey is by the vigor of the dance (von Frisch, 1950). Spiders sample the insects caught in their webs and treat a fly very differently from a wasp. The wasp is bundled up in a web without being "tasted," and a fly will be treated in the same way if it is first soaked in turpentine (Carthy, 1958). Pacific salmon show a preference for water of a certain specific salinity, a preference which changes seasonally in a progressive manner and seems to lead the fish through estuaries into the ocean (McInerney, 1964). Many other examples might be given to show that complex behavior has often become associated with the contact chemical sense to relate animals to foods and mates and habitats in elaborate ways. Examples of chemotaxis, uncomplicated by other reactions, are found only in the primitive groups and cells—especially in some of the gametes, leucocytes, bacteria and protozoans (Rosen, 1962).

Sensing of distant chemicals. Several evolutionary advances were possible as animals extended their range for detection of elaborate organic molecules. One of the most significant is the production of species-specific odors. This may be thought of as the positive approach to the development of a language based on the chemical senses. These species-peculiar scents are elaborated by different epithelial glands in the epidermis, the oro-anal and the urinogenital regions. Chemically, they belong to diverse groups of compounds (amino acids, alcohols, organic acids, lipids). Attempts have been made to demonstrate biochemical similarities or mechanical (molecular vibrational) properties which might explain their action on the receptor cell (Moncrieff, 1951; Wright, 1963), but no completely satisfactory correlations are apparent.

The full exploitation of the chemical sense in animal integration depends on a storage of information pertaining to the particular molecule. This becomes a progressively more important aspect of the exploitation of chemosensitivity. In the lower forms, both invertebrate and vertebrate, there is a considerable capacity for the inheritance of odor-dependent reactions. Complex interactions between the sexes, between predator and prey or between different members of a species often depend on innate behavior patterns which are released by odors. In the higher groups these relationships are more frequently built up through learning and experience. This is a very real evolutionary trend in all behavior. With increasing encephalization there is a progressively later differentiation of reactions in accordance with the experiences of the animal in its environment.

Some examples of chemoreceptor-dependent behavior. Only a few examples have been selected to illustrate the range of behavior which has become odor-dependent. The extensive literature is reviewed in many places (Carthy, 1958; Wright, 1964).

Chemoreception associated with feeding has sometimes been elaborated into complex food-finding behavior and communication of information concerning the source or nature of the food. Von Frisch's (1950) study of the honeybee provides a classical example. Through simple conditioning experiments he first showed the capacity of the bee to detect and to discriminate many different odors. He then demonstrated that bees which had located a rich source of scented honey or sugar water carried this odor back to the hive and passed it on to their companions both directly from the outside of their bodies and by regurgitating some of the scented material. In addition, special scent glands are used to mark flowers which are rich in honey and these odors also guide the searchers in their hunt for the food. The odors of both the plants and the bees are woven into a language of communication associated with food-finding.

In some insects the location and selection of a mate seems to depend entirely on the chemical sense. The attractions which females of certain species of moth show for their males have long excited the wonder of naturalists. Females of the common silk moth *Bombyx mori* produce a scent which is attractive to males in concentrations of 0.01γ. This material (a complex alcohol) has been isolated and its chemical structure established in one of the great feats of microchemistry (Karlson, 1960). It is a representative of a biological class of materials known as the PHEROMONES. These are special gland secretions which are active in minute amounts and are discharged not into the blood (as is the case with hormones) but into the environment where they act on another individual of the same species to regulate a behavior or a developmental process. They are messenger substances between individuals.

Parasitism and commensalism often depend on chemoreception. The larvae of the ichneumon wasp, *Ephialtes ruficollis*, parasitize the caterpillar of the pine shoot moth *Rhyacionia buoliana*. The adult parasite is repelled by pine oil when it emerges from its host in the pine woods. It leaves the pines for three or four weeks, but as it becomes sexually mature the pine oil becomes strongly attractive, and it then returns to the woods to parasitize the caterpillars of the pine shoot moth (Carthy, 1958).

A curious story in the evolution of epidermal glands in one group of teleost fishes (Ostariophysi) has been selected for the final example (Pfeiffer, 1962, 1963). Specialized epidermal cells (CLUB CELLS) elaborate a chemical which is another of the pheromones; this substance, when released from the fish, initiates a fright reaction in the same or closely related species. These special glandular cells have no ducts or openings to the exterior and, in histological sections, look like tiny sacs or bubbles of homogeneous staining material. When the skin is injured their contents are liberated into the water. Although the skin contains active cells at hatching, the fright reaction cannot be elicited until the fish are considerably older (50 days in *Phoxinus*). Thus the very young fish when injured will frighten the adults but will not themselves be alarmed; this reaction provides important insurance against cannibalism. The behavior is innate but is intensified through experience.

Like other groups of fish the Ostariophysi can be conditioned rapidly to odors, and the innate fright reaction (*Schreckreaktion*) can be elaborated and intensified through conditioning. For example, when a pike attacks and alarms a school of minnows, the odor of the pike also becomes associated with the fright reaction; pike odor then takes on a meaning which it did not have before the encounter. Reactions to pike odor are not innate although the *Schreckreaktion* is. Likewise, visual stimuli may become associated with the fright reaction to give it added emphasis in certain situations. This fright reaction is confined to the Ostariophysi and has considerable biological importance for the schooling species. It does not protect the individual under attack but operates to the benefit of the group.

17 Photoreception

Many of the complex organic molecules of protoplasm are easily altered by radiant energy. Proteins are denatured, nucleotides are depolymerized and isomeric arrangements in carotenoid pigments are changed. This reactivity of protoplasm to radiant energy of wavelengths between about 350 to 700 mμ is the basis of a receptor system which permits the animal to exploit the advantages and avoid the disadvantages of radiant energy and especially to relate its activities to the objects in its environment through the light which is reflected from them.

Light as an environmental factor was considered in Chapter 14. The effects described there were generalized photochemical reactions and the long-range physiological consequences of a diurnal and seasonal nature. The photochemical mechanisms considered in this chapter relate the animal quickly and adaptively to its environment. This is a chemical sense as far as the transducer action is concerned. It is, however, a highly specialized one in which the active chemicals are produced endogenously and altered photochemically to generate nerve action potentials. Like all functioning receptor systems, this one becomes progressively more useful with increasing capacities of the integrating nervous system and specialization of the effector organs.

During phylogeny more and more of the potentialities of the radiant energy were utilized. Responses which first depended only on the presence or absence of light became directional and permitted precise orientations when the receptor cells were grouped and the light only reached them from certain angles. Modifications in the morphology of the receptor cells and in their sensitive pigments permitted utilization of different wavelengths and the exploitation of the plane of polarization; the associated evolution of central nervous mechanisms opened the possiblities for analysis of images, detection of movement or the appreciation of distances and form.

The Dermal Light Sense

Steven (1963), in a helpful review of this subject, has compiled the evidence for a dermal light sense in all the major phyla of animals. Diffuse photosensitivity over a large part of the body is extremely common; it is found in many animals with localized photoreceptors as well as in those without them. It is rare in the terrestrial arthropods and may not occur in cephalopods and amniote vertebrates with the possible exception of direct chromatophore responses. The soft, moist coverings of aquatic animals are more likely to contain dermal light receptors than the dry integuments of the terrestrial animals.

THE DERMAL PHOTORECEPTORS

In many cases, the cells actually responsible for the dermal light reactions have not been satisfactorily localized. A direct action of light on protoplasm is recognized, and this can be demonstrated not only in many protozoans but also in certain cells and tissues from multicellular animals, such as the isolated mesenteries of *Metridium* or the isolated iris of the eel where the muscle fibers are thought to be stimulated directly (Steven, 1963). Light-induced responses have also been established in several other cells and tissues which are not recognized as receptors. Chromatophores sometimes operate as independent effectors and show changes in pigment distribution associated with light and darkness. It has also been shown that some parts of the nervous system can be activated directly by light and, as a consequence, initiate adaptive behavioral reactions. In studies with blinded minnows, von Frisch (1911) found evidence for photosensitivity of the diencephalon associated with color changes; Young (1935) obtained photokinetic responses in ammocoetes by illuminating the spinal cord; Prosser (1933) and Welsh (1934) monitored changes in the action potentials of the ventral nerve of the crayfish when the last abdominal ganglion was illuminated and noted that these animals continued to avoid light after both eyes were destroyed but only so long as the ganglion was intact. Steven (1963) gives other examples.

The evidence for specialized photoreceptor cells associated with the diffuse sensitivity of the integument is less satisfactory. A photoreceptor system is clearly operating since complex reactions involving central nervous mechanisms are initiated through the action of light on the integument. Cells assumed to be the photoreceptors have been described in earthworms, clams and other animals, but the evidence is based on morphology, and the functions of these cells have not yet been experimentally examined. Steven (1963) concludes that there is no single type of receptor which can account for the dermal light reactions of all animals.

DERMAL LIGHT REACTIONS

Reactions which follow stimulation of the dermal receptors are varied, sometimes elaborate and complex. In addition to the direct responses of the stimulated cells, such as the chromatophores already mentioned, there are three major types of activity initiated through this sense: (1) the photokinetic locomotion of free moving animals, (2) the bending of the body of a sessile animal such as a hydroid or the local movements of tentacles, tube feet and spines and (3) the shadow reflexes or withdrawals of exposed parts in response to sudden illumination.

When light operates through the dermal photoreceptor system to control the direction of locomotion, the response is a KINESIS. A TAXIS, the other major category of orienting response (Fraenkel and Gunn, 1940), is precluded in the absence of eyes which are localized receptors organized to admit light only from certain angles. Most of these photo-orientations are orthokineses, although the movements of blinded planarians and ammocoetes are klinokinetic (Steven, 1963 and Chapter 16).

Shadow reflexes are common in many of the invertebrates and lower vertebrates. The adaptive value is obvious. Usually the response is most marked when the light intensity decreases, but sometimes the reverse is the case. The retraction of the siphon of the bivalve *Mya* is a carefully investigated example of the shadow reaction in response to suddenly increased illumination.

One example will serve to illustrate the complexity of behavior which may depend on dermal light sensitivity. Millott (1960) and others have studied the responses of the spines of the sea urchin, *Diadema*. The reaction to a change in illumination is a sharp swinging movement of the spines which may be repeated several times depending on the intensity of the stimulus. The shadow reaction, following a decrease in light ("off" reaction) is much easier to elicit than the "on" reaction which follows sudden illumination. The urchins are eyeless, and the responses depend on the dermal sense and associated nervous system. The radial nerve is indispensable, indicating the reflex nature of the reaction. Like the crayfish ganglion mentioned above, the radial nerve of the sea urchin can be stimulated directly by light; shading a spot of radial nerve not more than 10μ in diameter will elicit a movement of spines, but no reaction is obtained from shading a spot of equal size just outside the margin of the nerve. No receptors have been located, and Millott (1960) concludes that the nerve elements themselves must be excited by the light. The photosensitive pigment has not been identified, but its action spectrum shows a peak between 455 and 460 mμ.

These shadow reflexes of sea urchins have been built into rather complex behavior. When *Diadema* is placed under a checkerboard of electric lamps it will rapidly adjust the angle of its spines and point them at any lamp which is suddenly turned off. Another urchin (*Lytechinus*) which inhabits coral reefs in the Caribbean, responds to a narrow beam of light directed at its aboral surface by picking up opaque objects such as seaweed with its tube feet and pedicellariae and placing them in the beam of light, like a parasol (Milne and Milne, 1959). Thus, it is evident that complex behavior can be built onto responses mediated through the dermal light sense and that they probably depend on reflexes set up in "naked" nerves.

SOME PHYSIOLOGICAL PARAMETERS

Several of the general properties of receptor systems can be very nicely demonstrated with the dermal light response. Reaction times are slow in contrast to comparable periods for responses mediated through eyes, and instructive measurements are possible with simple techniques. For example, the minimum time for the retraction of the siphon of *Mya* is about 1 second and for movements of *Myxine* about 20 seconds. The strength-duration relationships (Fig. 17.1) show clearly that similar reactions may be expected with a series of flashes of increasing intensity but constant duration, or with a series of progressively longer flashes at constant intensity. A minimum dose of light is necessary to elicit a response. It has also been found unnecessary to illuminate the receptors for the entire latent period; the minimal exposure time is only a part of the total reaction time (Fig. 17.1).

Extensive experiments of this type were first carried out by Hecht almost half a century ago. Steven (1963) summarizes his findings. From studies of the retraction of the siphon in *Mya,* Hecht (1937 and earlier) proposed a photochemically controlled mechanism which proved basic in the development of physiological thinking on photoreception. This represents one of the many fundamental contributions which comparative studies have made in the history of physiology. Hecht found that the first part of the reaction which depended on the light was independent of temperature, but the "dark" process was temperature-dependent. He assumed that the retraction of the siphon was a coupled reaction with an initial photochemical phase followed by a thermochemical reaction. With *Mya*, his facts fitted the theory remarkably well; the fit of the equations

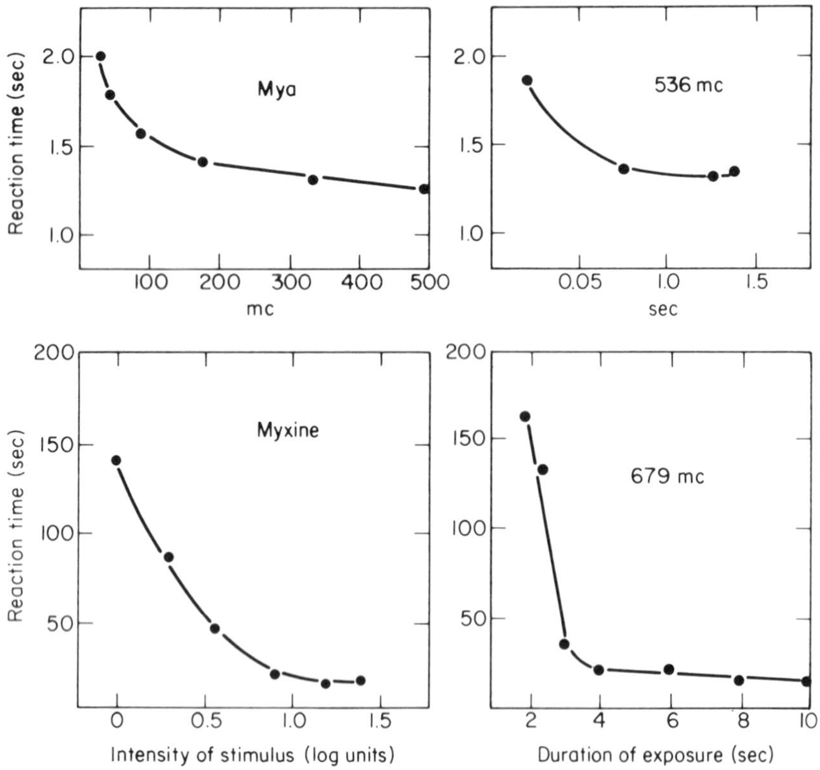

Fig. 17.1. The reaction times of the mud clam *Mya* and the hagfish *Myxine*. Left, intensity measured in metric candles (mc) was varied while duration remained constant. Right, duration was varied while intensity was constant, [Steven (1963). *Mya* data from Hecht and *Myxine* data from Steven.]

is less satisfactory with several other animals such as *Myxine*, and later workers have pointed out that the two phases or reactions probably overlap or proceed simultaneously (Newth and Ross, 1955).

Rates of adaptation, action spectra and the Weber-Fechner law (intensity discrimination) can also be effectively demonstrated with the dermal light responses of many invertebrates and lower vertebrates. Steven (1963) cites several examples, and many others will be found in Hecht's original papers.

Localized Photoreceptors or Eyes

The advantages of precise orientation probably provided the evolutionary force toward a localization of photoreceptors. When light can only strike the receptor cells from certain definite angles, movements with respect to it become directional. It can be assumed that the change from a photokinesis to a phototaxis would often confer a sizable advantage on the ancestral species. The flat retina, which is presumably the first step, is found in primitive representatives of all the major animal phyla (Fig. 17.2). The stigmata or eyespot of the protozoan *Euglena* exemplifies this step within a single mass of protoplasm. This light-sensitive bit of protoplasm is a swelling at one side of the flagellum and is shaded from one direction by a curtain of orange-red pigment (Wolken, 1960). The photoreceptor and the flagellar machinery are intimately linked, and this may have been basic in the evolution of some other types of visual receptors such as the vertebrate rod cell (Porter, 1957).

The directions from which light reaches the receptors can be further limited through the formation of cups and vesicles with progressively narrower apertures or with lenses in the apertures to focus the light on the retina. Cup-shaped and vesicular retinae are also found in each of the major phyletic groups. A lens is usually, but not always, present. The frequency with which these basic structural patterns recur in distantly related groups of animals is suggestive of both the evolutionary trail and the limited directions possible with the biological materials available (Novikoff, 1953).

The fourth structural pattern shown in Fig. 17.2 is the convex retina found in many of the annelids, molluscs and arthropods. In this, groups of simple eyes or ocelli are arranged in a radiating pattern on some eminence or knob-like development of the body surface. In some ways this is a radical departure from the vesicular type of eye. However, it should be noted that the sensory cells are still located in a vesicle. The photoreceptor cells of each simple eye are surrounded by a curtain of pigment so that they are actually at the base of a deep cone (Fig. 17.6). Just as in the vesicular eye, light enters the unit from only one direction (at least when the pigment is dispersed), and the unit has capacities for directional orientation which are similar to those of the vesicular eye. The convex retina, like the other patterns, has been tried many times in evolution

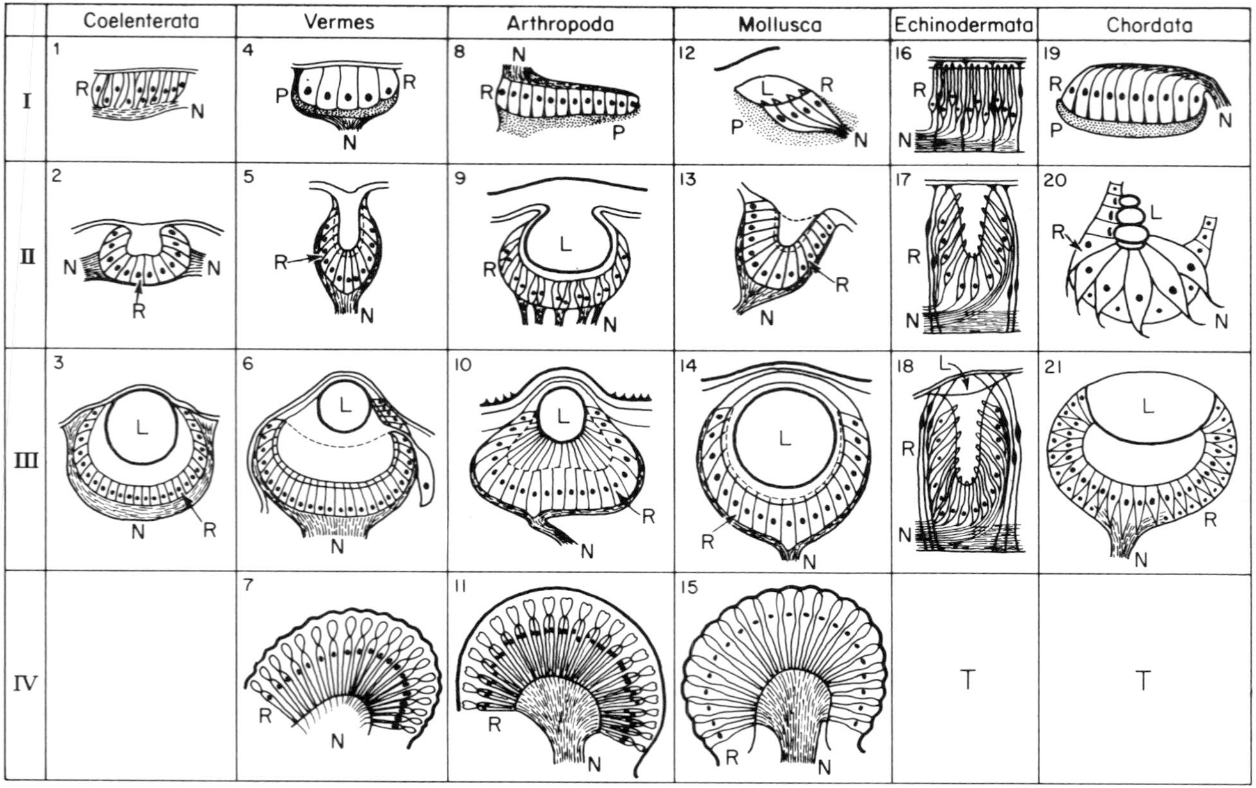

Fig. 17.2 Diagrams showing the four general patterns of photoreceptor organs. I, Flat eyes. II, Cup-shaped eyes. III, Vesicular eyes. IV, Convex (compound) eyes. *T*, Tendency towards the formation of a compound eye. *L*, Lens. *N*, Optic nerve. *P*, Pigment. *R*, Retina. ANIMALS REPRESENTED. 1, *Aurelia aurita*. 2, *Sarsia mirabilis*. 3, *Charybdea marsupialis*. 4, *Nais proboscidea*. 5, *Ranzania sagittaria*. 6, *Vanadis formosa*. 7, *Sabella reniformis*. 8, *Limnadia lenticularis* (one ocellus of the median eye). 9, *Limulus polyphemus*. 10, *Peripatus edwardsii*. 11, *Limnadia lenticularis* (compound eye). 12, *Chiton subfuscus*. 13, *Patella* sp. . 14, *Murex* sp. . 15, *Arca noae*. 16, *Astropecten mülleri*. 17, *Astropsis pulvillus*. 18, *Asteria tenuispina*. 19, *Salpa pinnata* (one ocellus of the complex photoreceptive organ). 20, *Amaroucium constellatum* (larva). 21, *Lacerta agilis* (embryo-pineal eye). [Novikoff (1953).]

(Milne and Milne, 1959). In its most specialized form, as found in the insects, it has proved capable of almost as many capacities as the camera eye. Differences between the visual abilities of insects and vertebrates are often differences in central nervous mechanisms rather than in the capacities of the photoreceptor cells.

These structural patterns have been variously modified to serve animals in many kinds of habitats and to meet diverse behavioral requirements. The literature is well summarized by Prosser and Brown (1961) and will not be detailed here.

FUNCTIONAL ANATOMY OF PHOTORECEPTOR CELLS

A photoreceptor cell must do several rather different things. In the first place it has certain metabolic functions. In addition to the main-

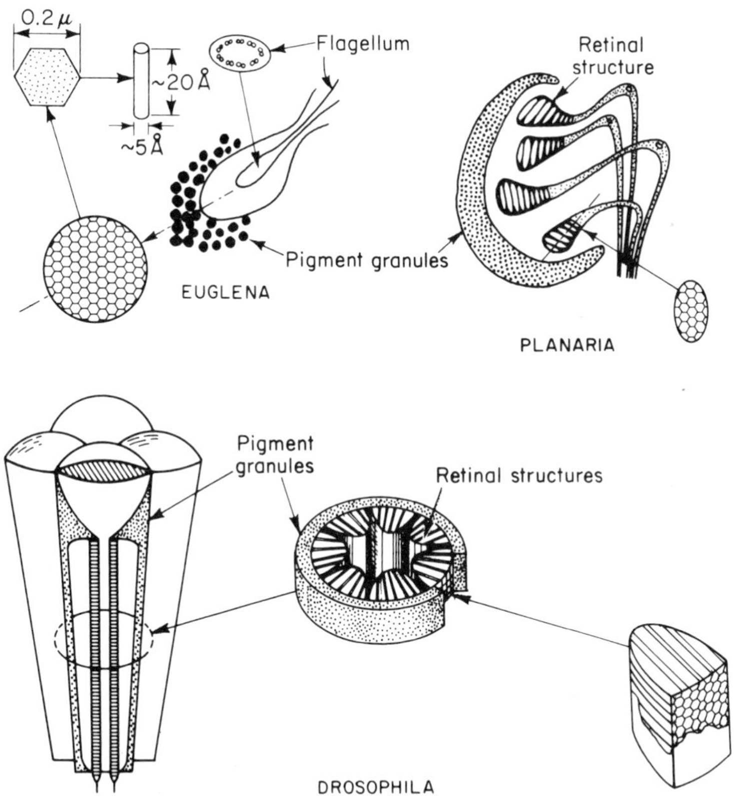

Fig. 17.3. Submicroscopic structure of three invertebrate photoreceptors. [Wolken (1958).]

tenance metabolism, chemical machinery must be operated to assemble or generate the chromoproteins and perhaps the transmitter substance which effects the synapse. In a cell such as the mammalian rod there is a well-marked metabolic area containing an abundance of mitochondria (Fig. 17.4). The chromoproteins, which through a photochemical change set up the generator potential, were considered in Chapter 14.

In addition to its metabolic machinery, a photoreceptor also contains a light-trapping apparatus. Light traps are a part of the photosynthetic as well as the photoreceptor cell; it has already been noted (Chapter 1) that the chloroplast which does this job in photosynthesis is a layered or laminated structure. This seems to be true also of photoreceptors. Electron microscopy of a wide spectrum of photoreceptors, ranging from the stigmata of the *Euglena* and the simple eyes of *Planaria* to the rods and cones of man, have revealed an orderly array of lamellae or rods in the most exposed portion of the receptor (Wolken, 1958, 1960). The eyespot of *Euglena gracilis*, about $2 \times 3\mu$, is made up of 40 to 50 rod-like granules (diameters 100 to 300 mμ) embedded in a matrix. The free end of the photoreceptor of a flatworm (Fig. 17.3) is not unlike that of the rod cells of a vertebrate. In *Planaria* each receptor cell has 8 to 10 double-layered plates, each about 10 mμ thick. A model of the vertebrate retinal rod which has many more layers is shown in Fig. 17.4. Plates of protein alternate with bimolecular layers of lipoprotein, the visual pigment, like stacks of coins. In detail, the lipoprotein layers are closely packed macromolecules arranged vertically in the plates. This outer segment of the vertebrate rod containing the visual pigment is joined to the inner metabolic segment by a narrow connecting piece which is a modified cilium as shown by its embryology and submicroscopic structure (DeRobertis *et al.,* 1960; Cohen, 1963). During the histogenesis of the vertebrate photoreceptor, a bulge containing the structural elements of a cilium differentiates into the outer segment of a rod or a cone. Photoreceptors in several groups of animals (coelenterates, chaetognaths, molluscs) are found to be elaborations of cilia (Miller, 1958; Horridge, 1964); many photoreceptors may have evolved from photosensitive cilia.

The detailed arrangement of the lipoprotein rods is different in arthropod and mollusc eyes, but the orderly pattern and basic structure remain the same (Wolken, 1958, 1960). The essential morphology of the structural units of the compound eye of the insect is shown in Figs. 17.3 and 17.6. The unit or OMMATIDIUM contains several RETINULA CELLS, the primary receptor cells concerned with photoreception. These are elongated unipolar sense cells arranged radially to form a cylinder. The number of retinulae in any one ommatidium varies from as few as two in the dorsal ocellus of the cockroach to eight in the bees (Ruck, 1962; Dethier, 1963). The compound eye of *Drosophila* consists of about 700 ommatidia, each

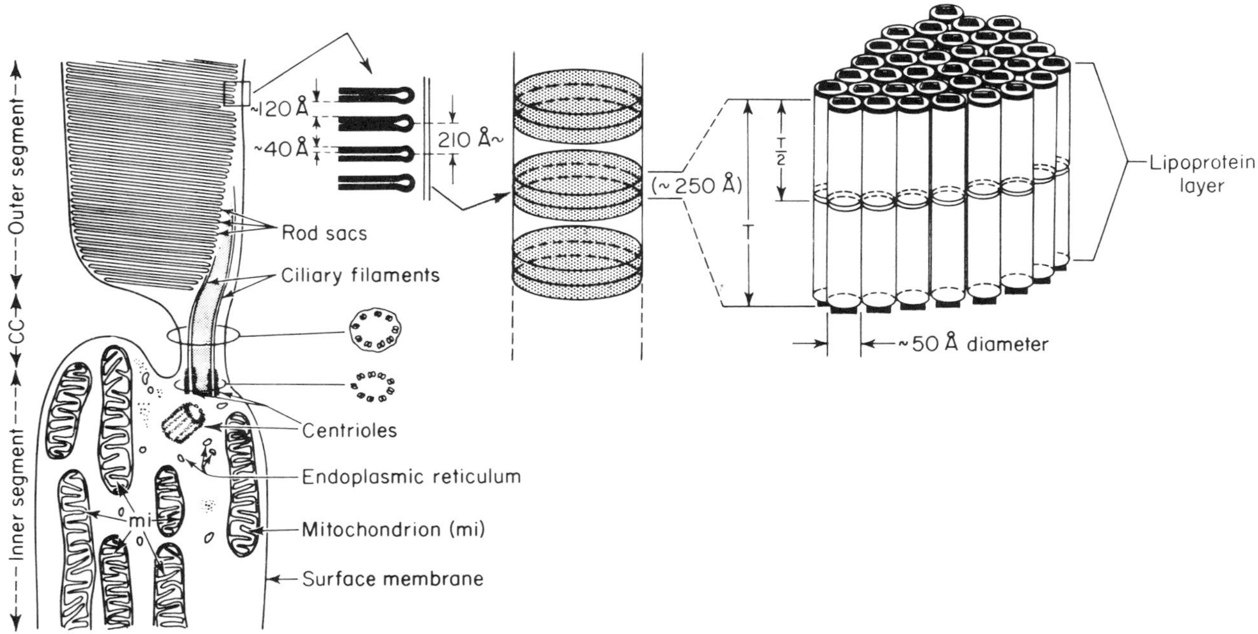

Fig. 17.4 Diagram of the retinal rod of a mammal. [Left, Giese (1962) after De Robertis *et al.* (1960). Right, Wolken (1958).]

with seven retinula cells which measure about 17μ in diameter and 70 to 125μ in length (Wolken, 1958).

The inner border (RHABDOMERE) of the elongated retinula cell probably forms the light trap. It is made up of closely packed rods or tubes of lipoprotein which are actually microvilli (about 12 mμ diameter) differentiated from this region of the retinular cell membrane (Fig. 17.3). The several rhabdomeres of an ommatidium jointly form a rod, the RHABDOM, (Fig. 17.6). The ommatidia of *Limulus* differ from all others by the presence of an ECCENTRIC CELL with an elongated dendrite located in the center of the group of retinular cells (Miller *et al.*, 1961; Ruck, 1962). The eccentric cell has no rhabdomere. This arrangement is thought to be primitive.

Photoreceptor cells, no matter how they may differ morphologically, operate as transducers of light energy into membrane potentials or nervous action. Many facts concerning the chemistry of vision have now been established, but it is still not known how the photochemical change induces generator potentials. One of the visual pigments, rhodopsin, seems to be an ATPase (McConnell and Scarpelli, 1963). The *Limulus* eye and some of the simple eyes of insects have been particularly valuable in studies of the membrane potentials, but the connection between photochemistry and electrogenesis remains theoretical (Hartline, 1959; Ruck, 1962).

Specialized Visual Functions

Just what does an animal see? Shadow reactions, kineses and taxes are found at all levels in phylogeny. The light-dependent behavior becomes more varied in the advanced animal phyla as the visual apparatus acquires the capacity to form images, discriminate color and brightness, detect movements, appreciate distances and operate over a wide range of intensities. These refinements confer expanding potentialities in relating the animal to its habitat and the other forms of life. Again, as with the other sense organs, the understanding of visual capacities is based on observations of behavior in relation to light or on the recording of action potentials in the visual apparatus.

PERCEPTION OF FORM AND MOVEMENT

A few of the molluscs, some of the arthropods and most of the vertebrates have the necessary visual machinery to distinguish shapes and to utilize, in an adaptive manner, the different patterns of light which are reflected to their eyes from various objects in their surroundings. This is a matter of observation in some of the cephalopods, crustaceans, insects and many of the lower vertebrates. It has also been often demonstrated with conditioning experiments. There are many summaries of the pertinent literature (Thorpe, 1956; Carthy, 1958); only a few examples will be given here.

An octopus, for instance, will learn to attack a crab when it sees a square of one particular size if this has been associated with a food reward; but it will avoid or fail to attack a somewhat different-sized square if this presentation has been associated with an electric shock. Experiments of this sort show that the octopus can discriminate a variety of different figures: a horizontal stripe from a vertical stripe, a square from a diamond (Boycott and Young, 1950). In comparable experiments bees may be trained to locate sugar-water in a cardboard box with a certain pattern pasted around the entrance (von Frisch, 1950). A sphere is easily separated from a cross, but other shapes, such as a sphere and a square or a triangle (which are quite distinct to us) are not distinguished. Bees also show spontaneous preferences for certain patterns and use the markings on flowers to guide them to sources of honey. There are many other examples of pattern perception by insects. The classical experiments of Tinbergen (1951) with the bee-killer wasp, *Philanthus*, clearly demonstrate a visual orientation by this insect when it returns to the nest where it is storing bees. These bees are stored in preparation for the grub which develops from the wasp's egg, laid on its final journey to the nest. Although these findings clearly indicate abilities to utilize light patterns in orientation, they do not require any precise analysis of the details, and most of the evidence indicates that the insect eye is highly adapted for the detection of motion but has limited capacities for the analysis of pictorial details (Burtt and Catton, 1962).

Fish also recognize the spatial relations of their environment and can be trained to discriminate among a variety of patterns. The three-spine stickleback, *Gasterosteus aculeatus*, builds a nest in a particular part of its environment and relates its activities to this through vision; other male sticklebacks are attacked while females are courted; the differences between the two sexes are recognized visually by body form, its position and characteristic movements (Tinbergen, 1951). Movement becomes an integral part of the visual stimulus in many of these more complex behavioral responses.

The ability to detect changing light patterns or movement in a light source is a more primitive and widespread capacity than form perception. It probably stems from the shadow reaction through temporal specializations of response and movement in relation to changing light. Buddenbrock (1953), for example, showed that the scallop, *Pecten*, reacted in a predictable manner to certain speeds of movement. This animal has a row of rather complex eyes along the mantle; when white stripes on a black background are moved past its eyes, responses of the tentacles and shell valves are often evident. If the movements are of the order of 0.66 mm/sec the animal shows no reaction, but at about 1.7 mm/sec the tentacles are markedly extended from the shell. At 7.7 mm/sec the tentacles are extended and then the shell partially closes; at speeds of movement between 11.6 and 29.4 mm/sec the tentacles are withdrawn and the valves of the shell close. These visual reactions are associated with chemosensory responses, and the extended tentacles are sampling the water for odors from starfish and whelks—the natural predators of the scallop. The significant point for the present discussion is that the speed of movement controls the reaction and, in nature, this reaction time is adapted to the speed of the enemies (Carthy, 1958).

Physiological comparisons of the capacities of different animals to detect movements are based on tests such as those just described for *Pecten* with a series of moving stripes (or flashing lights). As the stripes pass the eye at slow speeds an optomotor reaction (for example, turning the head or moving the eyes) can often be observed; at higher speeds the reaction disappears (critical flicker fusion frequency); as our eyes see it, the pattern disappears or the light ceases to flicker. The reaction can also be followed by recording action potentials in the retina or optic nerves. Eyes vary greatly in their ability to resolve the temporal features of the stimulus; some values for maximum flicker fusion frequencies in flashes per sec, tabulated by Waterman (1961), follow: frog 5, pigeon 143, cricket 5, bee, hornet and fly 200, crab and crayfish about 55. The critical flicker fusion frequency depends on the intensity of illumination and the temperature (Hanyu and Ali, 1963).

These few examples, selected from the many now recorded, attest the capacities of different types of eyes to form images and detect movements. Two lines of specialization in the functional morphology of the receptor organs have been particularly significant: the increasing number of interconnected sensory neurons and the dioptric apparatus or the lens system. A good photograph depends both on the emulsion of the film and the lens system of the camera; pictures will be poor if either of these is inferior.

The vertebrate retina. By analogy with the photographic camera, the retina is often likened to the emulsion and the photosensitive cells to the "grain" of the film. The likeness, however, is only superficial and the comparison rather deceptive. A picture is never fixed in the retina but sets up a continuous series of impulse patterns more akin to the television camera than the photographic camera. Only a few types of receptor cells (proprioceptors in muscles, for example) fire impulses steadily in response to a constant stimulus. Most sense cells adapt rather quickly, and this is the case with the photoreceptors. When constantly stimulated by a fixed light they cease to respond. The picture which is apparently stable to the human eye is really dancing over a multitude of photosensitive cells; the "steady" eye is rarely motionless. This dynamic feature, related to the excitatory processes of sensory cells, is one of the

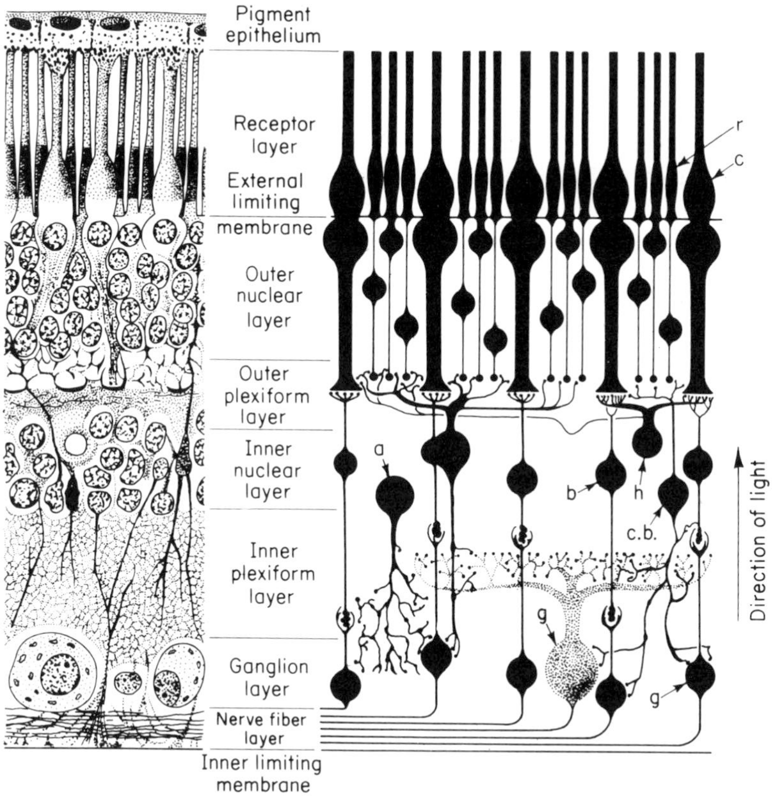

Fig. 17.5. The human retina showing the arrangement of cells and a schematic "wiring diagram" of the connections. *a*, Amacrine cell. *b*, Bipolar nerve cell. *c*, Cone. *c.b.*, Centripetal bipolar cell. *g*, Ganglion cell. *h*, Horizontal cell. *r*, Rod. [Young (1957) based on Walls (1942) and Polyak (1941).]

two factors which preclude the functioning of individual retinal units in isolation to form steady or fixed images (Rushton, 1962). The second factor is static and depends on the cytological arrangements of the neurosensory fibers and the interconnecting neurons between them and the visual centers in the brain.

The human retina has been calculated to contain over 100 million rods, six million cones and only about one million optic nerve fibers (Guyton, 1961; Ham and Leeson, 1961). Thus there are over 100 times as many rods and six times as many cones as there are conducting fibers to the visual centers. Unless the rods and cones were divided evenly into clusters associated with different optic fibers, the concept of a photographic "grain" in the retina would largely disappear. As indicated in Fig. 17.5, there is no such orderly arrangement. On the contrary, the interconnections appear to be varied and elaborate. There is, however, one area of the human retina where each cone cell connects with a single bipolar nerve. This is the FOVEA CENTRALIS and, anatomically, it most nearly satisfies the requirements for isolated transmission lines from visual receptors to brain.

The fovea centralis is a highly specialized depression on which the light passing through the lens comes to a sharp focus. It is, in fact, the only point in the human retina where this occurs and is the region where we see objects clearly. The area is small, measuring only about 1500 μ in diameter; in its densest portion it contains approximately 150,000 closely packed cones per square millimeter and no rods (Bard, 1961). There are no blood vessels in this tiny spot, and the ganglionic nerve fibers diverge to admit the light directly to the cones. In short, this much of the anatomy suggests direct transmission lines. However, there are other facts which fail to support such a theory. For one thing, the small branching AMACRINE CELLS which associate bipolar and ganglionic nerve cells (Fig. 17.5) show that cross circuiting is possible, even though the functions of these cells are not well understood. In addition, studies of the resolving power of the human eye indicate that more than two cones must be activated to distinguish two points in a picture. This resolving power or visual acuity is a measure of the ability to resolve two lines in close proximity, usually in terms of the visual angle which they subtend. This may be measured experimentally and calculated from the optics of the eye. The results imply that more than two cone cells, which measure about 3.2 μ across, are being stimulated and that these retinal units do not function in isolation (Bayliss, 1960; Young, 1957). Much of the analysis is evidently dependent on the ganglionic connections and the central nervous system.

This, however, is not the whole story, and the characteristics of the photoreceptors themselves confer certain properties on the visual system. These characteristics might be likened to the "kind of film" and include both the variety in pigments and the morphology of the cells. More than one pigment is common in many retinae; this feature will be considered with color vision in a later section.

For more than 100 years the two morphological types of vertebrate photoreceptor have been credited with different visual capacities

(Rushton, 1962). Rods are the cells of twilight vision while the cones operate in bright light. The physiology of this distinction is still not fully understood. It is known that the cells contain different pigments, and this is one factor in the explanation. In addition, it is evident (Fig. 17.5) that the axons from the rods are elaborately interconnected in the ganglionic layer so that summation becomes particularly significant; minimal amounts of light falling on many rods can excite an optic nerve fiber. A single quantum of radiant energy can evidently produce electrogenesis in one human rod, but six rods must be excited to produce a detectable visual response (Hecht *et al.*, 1942). This, however, does not explain the significance of the two cell types – one long and thin, the other short and thick. It is thought that the thicker cone with its refractile ELLIPSOID (sometimes also an oil droplet) may be important in converging the rays on the photosensitive pigments of the outer segment of the cone (Fig. 17.5). It seems as though the cones are designed for efficient capture of radiant energy coming from a particular direction – along the focal plane. Walls (1942) looks on the rod as a special adaptation of the cone in which the outer segment has become an elongated cylindrical container of rhodopsin organized in almost crystalline regularity. This thin bristle of rhodopsin captures minimal amounts of light falling on it diffusely from different angles.

The arthropod retina. The long tubular ommatidia, which are the visual units of the compound eye, seem to be ideal machines for the detection of separate points of a picture and their direct translation to the central nervous system. Two types of the arthropod compound eye are distinguished. In the diurnal insects such as flies, bees and butterflies, each separate ommatidium is surrounded by a curtain of pigment and thus appears to operate as a separate unit. Moreover, the light-sensitive retinulae abut directly onto the cone of the lens and receive light parallel to the ommatidial axis. This is the APPOSITION EYE (Fig. 17.6). In the SUPERPOSITION EYE, characteristic of nocturnal insects and many crustaceans, the ommatidia are much elongated and the pigment is confined to the outer area while the retinulae are separated from the cone of the lens by a considerable space filled with a non-refractile transparent medium (Wigglesworth, 1942). In this eye, the retinulae can be excited by light from neighboring lenses as well as from their own (Fig. 17.6). This, like the rod vision of the vertebrate eye, is ideal for dim light and summation phenomena but unsuited for a good resolution of the picture.

Because of their morphology, the ommatidia of the apposition eye have long been thought to operate by receiving light from very restricted angles and projecting a pattern or mosaic of luminous points varying in brightness; hence the "mosaic theory" of insect vision. This theory was based mainly on behavioral responses. It has now been more critically tested with electrophysiological techniques and by precise measurements of the capacities of the dioptric system; these studies do not give any substantial support to the mosaic theory (Burtt and Catton, 1962; Kuiper, 1962).

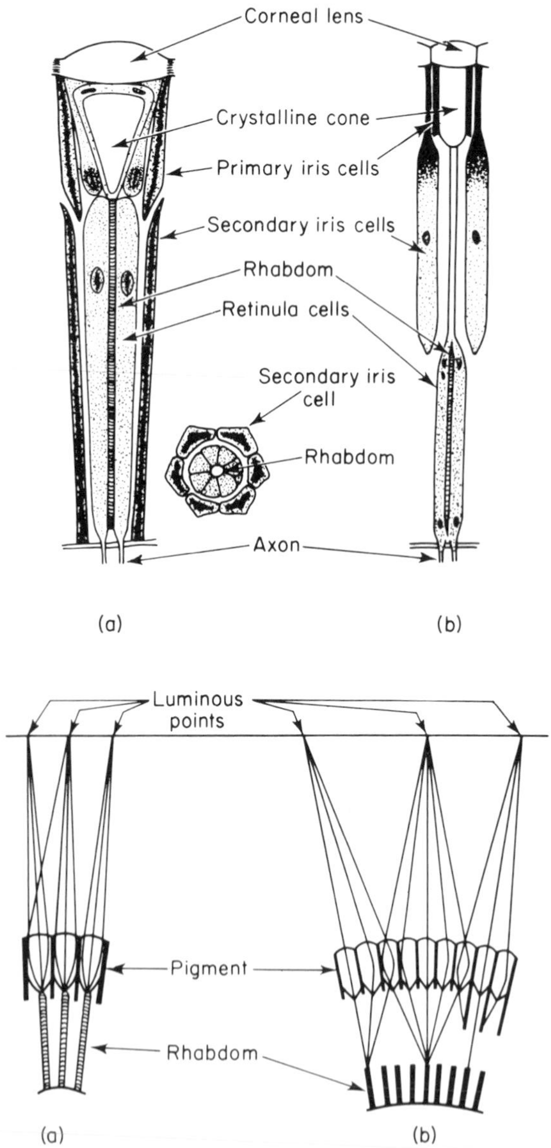

Fig. 17.6. Diagrams of the two chief types of ommatidium in insects. *a*, Apposition eye. *b*, Superposition eye. [Wigglesworth (1942).]

The field of vision of a single ommatidium is much wider than was generally assumed. By covering parts of the locust eye and exposing only a limited number of ommatidia, it was discovered that a single ommatidium apparently has a relatively large angle of acceptance of about 20°; consequently, a single point source must illuminate many ommatidia (Burtt and Catton, 1962). It is also possible to make slices of an insect eye, such as that of the locust, and to study the images which the lenslets form. As is to be expected from the wide angle of acceptance, the images formed beyond the crystalline cone by adjacent ommatidia cover overlapping parts of the visual field. Moreover, such a section of an insect eye forms not one but a succession of images along the length of the ommatidium as one focusses at successively deeper levels in the slice. Thus, in reality, an eye such as that of the locust also forms superposition images, contrary to the usual understanding of the apposition eye. These studies indicate that the resolving power depends on the deeper images produced by groups of ommatidia. Images cannot be very distinct, and the whole optic system suggests an eye specialized to detect movement rather than to resolve images (Burtt and Catton, 1962).

From electrophysiological studies, Kuiper (1962) also concludes that the field of view of one ommatidium is much larger than is generally assumed and that the concept of the ommatidium as a functional unit is incorrect. As in the vertebrate retina, nerve fibers from individual retinulae cross and join the fibers of adjacent ommatidia so that pattern recognition depends on ganglionic connections and central nervous system as well as on the receptor cells. The mechanisms are still speculative, but discussions of some of the possibilities will be found in the literature cited.

The dioptric apparatus. Some of the cup-like eyes are broadly open with only a transparent lining over the photosensitive cells (the limpet *Patella*) and some of the vesicular eyes (the *Nautilus*) operate as pin-hole cameras. Most eyes, however, have a lens or dioptric apparatus of transparent tissue which serves to concentrate the light on the receptor cells.

A lens is found in the eyespot of some dinoflagellates and in certain hydroid medusae such as *Sarsia* (Fig. 17.2). It is evidently a phylogenetically ancient device for the convergence of light rays on the photoreceptors. In most of the cup-like or vesicular eyes of invertebrates the lens almost or completely fills the cavity and is quite immobile. The focus is fixed like that of an inexpensive camera. The same is true of the aggregate or compound eyes (Fig. 17.6). On the other hand, the eyes of all the vertebrates and a few of the invertebrates (cephalopod and heteropod molluscs and alciopid polychaete worms) possess a dioptric apparatus which can be changed to focus the eye. This capacity is referred to as

ACCOMMODATION and, like a fine camera, permits the lens to form a sharp image on the retina for objects both near and far.

In focussing a camera, the position of the lens is altered with respect to the photographic film by moving the lens forward for near objects. Invertebrates and lower vertebrates also accommodate by altering the lens/retinal distance. Several devices have been described. In the polychaete worm, *Alciopa*, the lens/retinal distance seems to be adjusted by changing the fluid volume in one of the two regions of the optic cup. In the heteropod and cephalopod molluscs the distance is altered by squeezing the optic cup or moving the lens forward (Carthy, 1958; Nicol, 1960*a*). The lower vertebrates also accommodate by changing the position of the lens. In lampreys and teleosts the lens is said to be moved backward to focus on distant objects (Brett, 1957, notes several exceptions) while elasmobranchs, amphibians and snakes move the lens forward to adjust for near objects (Prosser and Brown, 1961). These adjustments are like those of the camera or microscope.

The mammals, birds and reptiles other than snakes went one step further. In their visual systems a soft, pliable lens in a transparent capsule can be squeezed by altering the tension on the tough ligaments attached to it. The "camera" is focussed by changing the shape of the lens. The action is rapid and under autonomic control. Parasympathetic stimulation contracts the circular fibers of the ciliary muscle, and this relaxes the ligaments of the lens which then bulges and increases its refractive power to permit focussing on objects near at hand. Contraction of the radial fibers innervated by the sympathetic system as well as a relaxation of the circular fibers takes place during accommodation for far vision. Thus, in many amniotes, accommodation is quick and precise; it is probably rather crude in the invertebrates and lower vertebrates.

There are several curious devices which make accommodation unnecessary. Certain bats, for example, have a corrugated or folded retina which brings many rods into focus at different distances; in the ray, the horse and probably some other vertebrates the retina is arranged on a "ramp", with the axial length of the eyeball changing continuously in the vertical meridian (Walls, 1942). Such devices serve well when visual acuity is less important than sensitivity.

PHOTOPIC AND SCOTOPIC EYES

The world is alive with animal life both night and day, but quite different species are often abroad and active at these times. Both the arthropods and the vertebrates show several distinctive retinal specializations associated with daily activity rhythms. Some of the differences are morphological; others are physiological. The monographs by Walls (1942) and Detwiler (1943) contain a wealth of details; only a brief summary is given here.

Some of the morphological specializations have already been mentioned. In the arthropods, the retinulae of the superposition eye are placed to capture light from the lenses of many different ommatidia (Fig. 17.6). These eyes are characteristic of nocturnal species whereas the apposition eye, which receives light from only one lens system, is found in diurnal forms.

Vertebrate specializations for photopic (light) and scotopic (dark) vision are based on two morphologically different photoreceptors—the cones and the rods. Some strictly nocturnal vertebrates such as bats, armadillos and guinea pigs have no cones whatever while others, such as the rat, have relatively few. Some purely diurnal creatures like the squirrel, certain birds and reptiles have only cones. Arhythmic species, which are active either during the day or night, have a good development of both rods and cones, usually with the cones concentrated in the AREA CENTRALIS.

The area centralis is a specialization of the diurnal eye. A well-marked series of changes during its evolution have greatly improved the resolving power of this tiny retinal spot which lies in the focal plane of the optic lens system. In the more primitive situation, the area centralis is a retinal THICKENING caused by a concentration of cones, each ideally with its own bipolar and ganglion cells. In animals with more precise diurnal vision, the area becomes very THIN since the tangled nerve fibers diverge from the cones on all sides to form a FOVEA where light falls directly on the photoreceptors. Some foveae (higher primates) contain an abundance of yellow pigment which corrects for chromatic aberration. The area centralis is then referred to as a MACULA LUTEA.

The retina reaches its climax as a diurnal photoreceptor in some of the birds. In water birds and species which live in open plains the fovea may be greatly extended into a horizontal band, and cone density may reach 1 million/mm^2 in contrast to about 140,000/mm^2 in the human fovea (Pumphrey, 1961; Detwiler, 1943). A temporal as well as a central fovea is common in birds which depend on accurate distance judgement (hawks, swallows, hummingbirds or kingfishers). These eyes are capable of resolution over a large part of the visual field. Increasing cone density is associated with a decrease in the general vascularity and the development of a special organ, the PECTEN, which protrudes from the back of the optic cup and assists in the diffusion of metabolites into the vitreous humor. The pecten is a sizable comb-like structure of folded vascular tissue which, in its phylogeny, may have acquired an optic function in addition to its trophic one. The evidence (reviewed by Pumphrey, 1961) comes from morphological correlations between the habits of different species of birds and the development of their pectines. In these studies, Menner (1938) concluded that this organ could enhance the sensitivity of the eye to movements by producing shadows on the retina.

Scotopic eyes are specialized for maximum dim light sensitivity at the expense of the resolving power of the retina. Batteries of elongated rods connect in groups to single bipolar nerve cells and thus effect a maximum summation. Bats may have as many as 1000 rods connected to one nerve cell (Young, 1957). Moreover, the retinae of many nocturnal animals contain reflecting tissue (the TAPETUM LUCIDUM) which acts as a mirror to reflect the light back through the photosensitive layers and double its effect on the rods. A tapetum lucidum is characteristic of many nocturnal arthropods as well as vertebrates from fish to mammals. The nature of the reflecting material and its distribution varies in different species. Guanine crystals are common, but some insects rely on shiny tracheal tubes, and some mammals (the musk ox, for example) achieve the same advantages with glistening white collagenous fibers. The tapetum lucidum of the bush baby (lemuroid *Galago*) is a layer of golden yellow crystals of riboflavin (Fox and Vevers, 1960).

There are also good correlations between the shape of the optic cup and the daily activity rhythms. In general, the lens/retinal distance is greater in the diurnal forms, permitting the projection of larger images on the retina and the possibility of greater resolution of details (Walls, 1942; Young, 1957). The use of color filters may also increase visual acuity as well as correct for chromatic aberration. The macula lutea has already been mentioned. In addition, many diurnal animals have a yellowish lens or cornea, and in some birds and reptiles there are yellowish oil droplets in the photosensitive cells. Walls (1942) describes these filters and discusses their probable significance.

Color vision. Wavelength discrimination is a special capacity of the diurnal eye and its associated neural centers. Although relatively few groups of animals have acquired the ability, it seems to be potentially present in all of the more highly organized optical systems and is capable of expression under evolutionary pressures for high visual acuity. Von Frisch, more than half a century ago, demonstrated color vision in the honeybee (von Frisch, 1950; Burkhardt, 1962, and since that time it has been found in several orders of insects (Coleoptera, Diptera, Hymenoptera, Lepidoptera). It may also occur in other invertebrate groups (crustaceans, cephalopods), but the evidence is largely circumstantial (Buddenbrock, 1952; Prosser and Brown, 1961).

Among the vertebrates, hue discrimination has been demonstrated with certainty in primates, birds, lizards, turtles, frogs, and teleost fishes. It is associated with bright-light vision, foveae with rich areas of cones and eyes with good mechanisms for accommodation. These associations are obviously linked with high visual acuity and pictorial analysis rather than with taxonomic position. Electrophysiological studies (Granit, 1955) indicate that the retinal factors essential for color perception are sometimes present even when the animal behaves as though it were color blind (cats, for example). The importance of the analytical centers in the brain is apparent.

The first acceptable theory of color vision was formulated by Thomas Young in 1801 (literature reviews by Walls, 1942; Granit, 1955). This is based on the well-known fact that a proper mixing of three "primary colors" (blue, yellow and red for pigments or blue, green and red for lights), will produce white or any of the colors recognized by the human eye. Young made three fundamental assumptions: that color reception is organized by the retina, that the number of color-sensitive elements in the retina is limited and that they represent widely different regions of the spectrum. These basic assumptions remain fundamentally correct (Granit, 1955), although the detailed nineteenth-century theory proposed by Helmholtz has been extensively modified by later investigations. The YOUNG-HELMHOLTZ or TRICHROMATIC THEORY ascribed color perception to the interaction of three specific types of retinal element (sensitive to red, green and violet respectively) with zonal representation of the colors in the cortex. It has now been possible to test the theory by studying the retinal action potentials (electroretinograms) associated with the stimulation of areas of the retina with monochromatic light and also to measure the absorption spectra of pigments in the vertebrate fovea. In addition, the examination of the insect retina has been particularly valuable because electrodes can be inserted into individual retinula cells; the most refined techniques for the vertebrate retina only permit the recording from individual ganglion cells which are connected with several rods and/or cones. The insect work will be summarized first.

Burkhardt (1962) summarizes studies of the spectral sensitivity of the fly *Calliphora erythrocephala*. Recordings were made from individual retinula cells while the eye was stimulated with flashes of monochromatic light (wavelengths separated by about 20 mμ). The duration of the flash was $\frac{1}{10}$ or $\frac{1}{50}$ sec, and the intensity was adjusted so that the quantal energy was always the same. In *Calliphora* the resting potentials are between -50 and -70 mv, but when stimulated the potential may rise to a maximum of about 50 mv, indicating an almost total depolarization during strong stimulation.

When the response is plotted against the wavelength of stimulus the majority of the retinula cells show two peaks, one with a maximum at about 350 mμ and the other at about 490 mμ. These are called the green-type receptors and, on a statistical basis, there are about five of these in every seven of the retinula cells which make up the ommatidium of *Calliphora.* The remaining cells are of two types, each making up about one seventh of the total retinular elements: one of these is a blue-type with a maximum sensitivity below 470 mμ and the other is a yellow-green-type with a maximum above 520 mμ. In both cases there is a second maximum which, like the green-type, comes at 350 mμ. Actually these three types of cells occur only in the ventral portion of the eye; the dorsal part contains only green-type cells.

These spectral efficiency curves might indicate four pigments associated with the four distinct peaks; but Burkhardt (1962) has shown with the green-type receptor that only one photosensitive substance is responsible for both the 350 and the 490 mμ peak. It thus seems that *Calliphora* has three visual substances distributed in a rather precise manner in the ommatidia. *Calliphora's* information about wavelength appears to depend on the distribution of excitation among these three cell types. The peak at 350 mμ is associated with the ultraviolet sensitivity which marks one of the striking differences between insect and vertebrate eyes. In comparison with the vertebrates, the insect spectral sensitivity is shifted about 100 mμ toward the shorter wavelengths.

Granit (1955 and earlier) pioneered the electrophysiology of the vertebrate retina; his theory (Dominator-Modulator Theory) is now a basic concept in the interpretation of color vision. It is not yet possible to record potentials from individual rods and cones. At best, a microelectrode is placed on a single ganglion cell or nerve fiber, and thus the records are for composite responses of a group of rods and/or cones associated with the fiber. The data may be more comparable to what an insect physiologist would record from an individual ommatidium rather than from a retinula cell.

Two visual systems are readily demonstrated in a retina such as that of man. If one determines the threshold intensity for a series of wavelengths when in dim light (scotopic vision), a luminosity curve can be developed with a peak (minimum intensity to stimulate) at 505 mμ. At night this wavelength (green) is most effective in stimulating the human eye. A comparable experiment can be carried out in bright light (photopic vision) by determining the intensity required to match a moderately bright standard light with lights of different wavelengths. This luminosity curve has a peak at 562 mμ. This shift in relative brightness of colored objects as the intensity drops below the cone threshold or rises above it is called the PURKINJE PHENOMENON after the man who first described it. There is abundant evidence that the scotopic system depends on rhodopsin (or porphyropsin) since both their absorption spectra and their spectral sensitivities measured electrophysiologically in dim light match the action spectra for the dark-adapted eyes (Fig. 17.7). The photopic curve, on the other hand, does not correspond with any single pigment and seems to be a composite.

In the light-adapted eye the electroretinograms recorded by Granit and others often resemble the photopic visibility curve, but sometimes, when narrow spectral bands are used as stimuli, the responses from different units (ganglion cells) vary. The sensitivities of these individual

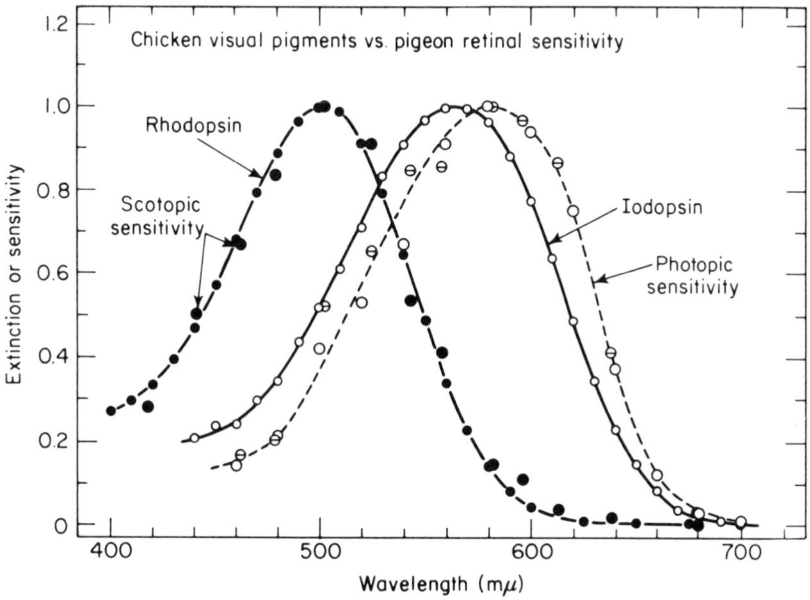

Fig. 17.7. Scotopic and photopic sensitivities of the pigeon compared with the absorption spectra of chicken rhodopsin and iodopsin in digitonin solution. Spectral sensitivities measured electrophysiologically and plotted in terms of the reciprocals of the numbers of quanta needed to produce a constant response. [Granit (1955) based on data from Wald and associates (absorption spectra), Donner (scotopic and photopic sensitivity–barred circles) and Granit (photopic sensitivity-open circles).]

units are rather broad but cluster in three groups; red-yellow (580 to 600 mμ), green (520 to 540 mμ), and blue (450 to 470 mμ). Thus, there are two dominator responses, named by Granit the SCOTOPIC AND PHOTOPIC DOMINATOR RESPONSES, and three MODULATOR RESPONSES. Color analysis appears to be based on the distribution of excitation among the scotopic dominator and the three modulators, and the Helmholtz concept is true only in a statistical fashion (Ruch and Fulton, 1960). If it were possible to record from single cone cells the results might be like those found for the insect eye. Rushton's (1962) experiments extend this line of thinking to the actual visual pigments.

Rushton's technique depends on measurements of light reflected from the fovea in living subjects. The principle is easily visualized by anyone who has noted the brilliant green "eye-shine" of a cat or skunk in the headlights of an automobile. In this case the light is being reflected from a green-colored tapetum lucidum. In Rushton's tests with the human fovea the amount of reflected light is extremely small since there is no tapetum; very sensitive instruments are required for its measurement. Now, when the fovea is exposed to a series of different wavelengths, the reflected densities will be maximal in the region of the spectrum corresponding to the color of the pigment in the cones. The presence of different pigments is shown by bleaching the retina with different colored lights and comparing the retinal sensitivity to the series of wavelengths before and after bleaching. Thus, bleaching with a deep red light might be expected to remove red pigment and leave pigments of other colors. Tests of this sort have provided good evidence for a green-catching pigment (chlorolabe) and a red-catching pigment (erythrolabe) in the fovea of normal eyes. The retinae of color-blind individuals, who lack one or another of these pigments, have been particularly useful in this analysis.

Even more precise information has been obtained recently by Wald and his associates who study the absorption characteristics of individual receptor cells (Brown and Wald, 1964). Human retinae are removed and mounted on the stage of a microscope, with the visual cells pointing upward and the light passing through them axially in the direction of incidence in the living eye. Absorption maxima of the rods occur at 505 mμ. Three types of cones have been convincingly separated with maxima at 450 mμ (blue receptors), 525 mμ (green receptors) and 555 mμ (red receptors), as shown in Fig. 17.8. Clearly, there is a firm biochemical basis for the kind of theory which Helmholtz developed in the nineteenth century.

Several different color receptor systems are probably present in the animal kingdom, and some may be much simpler than that of the human retina. The retina of the frog evidently contains three visual pigments, two in the rods and one in the cones (Muntz, 1964). The peak sensitivity of the green rods is at 440 mμ and of the red rods at 502 mμ; the cone pigment shows peak sensitivity at about 560 mμ. Both behavior and action potential recordings from the optic nerves show that frogs are especially sensitive to blue, although this is not due to any single pigment in the retina. The frog's preference for blue and the tendency to jump towards it or towards the light when startled seems to be adaptive and favors escape towards the aquatic habitat.

Polarized light sensitivity. In addition to its intensity and wavelength, the light which reaches the earth has an important quality associated with the DIRECTION OF ITS WAVE MOTION. The wave motion of white light radiated from the sun is considered to be in all directions perpendicular

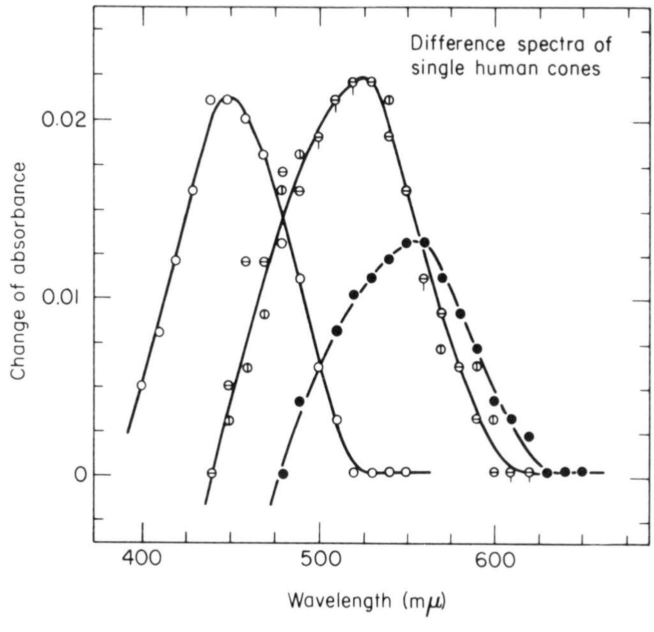

Fig. 17.8. Difference spectra of visual pigments in single cones of the parafoveal region of the human retina. In each case the absorption spectrum was recorded in the dark from 650 to 380 mμ, then again after bleaching with a flash of yellow light. The differences between these spectra are shown. One of these cones, apparently a blue receptor, has λ max about 450 mμ; two cones, apparently green receptors, have λ max about 525 mμ; and one, apparently a red receptor, has λ max about 555 mμ. In making these measurements light passed through the cones axially in the direction of incidence normal in the living eye. [Brown and Wald (1964).]

to the direction of transmission. If, for any reason, this vibration is restricted to one plane, the light is said to be PLANE POLARIZED. Certain types of glass, plastic or crystals will polarize light passing through them because their orderly molecular arrangement permits vibrations only in one plane. Light may also be polarized by reflection and, in nature, this occurs in the upper atmosphere when the short wavelengths (blue) are scattered by molecules of air (especially the inert gases and nitrogen) to produce the blue sky in what is often spoken of as "Tyndall scattering." The "azure vault of heaven" is in reality a layer of reflected short wavelengths of light about twelve miles above the earth.

Both the extent and the angle of polarization in any patch of sky depend on the relative position of the patch of sky with respect to the sun (Fig. 17.9). The effect is most pronounced at right angles to the sun's

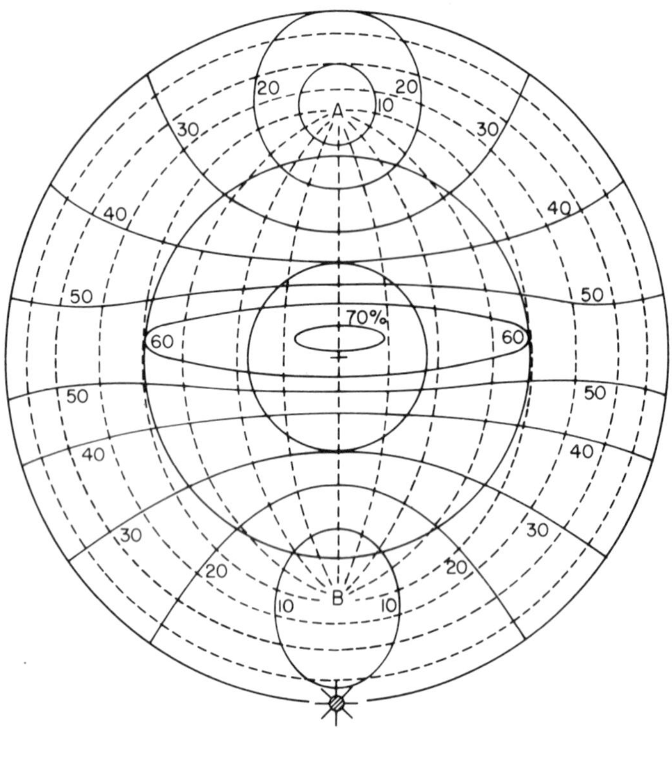

Fig. 17.9. Distribution of polarized light in the sky when the sun is on the horizon. Solid lines indicate the points of equal percentage of polarization and the broken lines, points where the angle of polarization is the same. *A* and *B* are the two points where the light is unpolarized. The diagram represents the hemisphere of the sky, + being the highest point and the two rings concentric with + being the lines subtending angles of 30° and 60° with the horizontal. [Carthy (1958).]

rays; if one looks straight up at sunrise or sunset with a suitable detecting instrument (called an ANALYZER OR POLARIZER) the blue sky becomes a distinct and predictable map.

Von Frisch (1950) was the first to demonstrate clearly that the blue sky is being used in animal navigation. In addition, he constructed a polaroid analyzer which produced precise light patterns when aimed at specific patches of sky at particular times in the day. He pointed out that his model had certain counterparts in the rhabdomeres of the eye of the honeybee and postulated that the rhabdome might be serving as an analyzer. Since von Frisch's classical studies of the honeybee, it has been shown that many different terrestrial arthropods are capable of orienting themselves with respect to polarized light (Carthy, 1958; Prosser and Brown, 1961). It is also recognized that light penetrating the aquatic environment often becomes polarized and that several different crustaceans and cephalopods are capable of orienting themselves to it (Waterman, 1960*a*; Jander *et al.*, 1963). The occurrence of this ability in separate phyla with different kinds of eyes indicates that the basic visual machinery (probably the orderly arrangement of lipoprotein rods or plates) has the capacity to acquire sensitivity to the plane of polarization if this confers an evolutionary advantage.

The physiological mechanisms of polarized light sensitivity have not been satisfactorily explained. It seems likely that the orderly arrangement of tubes or microvilli in the visual cells is important. Their structure, as revealed by the electron microscope, appears suitable for forming light intensity patterns of the sort postulated by von Frisch. A characteristic distribution of excitation in the group of retinula cells of an ommatidium may be associated with the planes of polarization and may also be responsible for the relay of necessary information. There are several theoretical possibilities; these are considered in detail by Waterman (1960, 1961) and the investigators whom he cites.

PHOTOMECHANICAL RESPONSES AND THE ARHYTHMIC EYE

The arhythmic eye, which performs well over a wide range of light intensities, has several adaptive mechanisms associated with activity during both night and day. These are primarily devices for controlling the amount of illumination which reaches the photosensitive cells. The maximum available light should impinge on the receptors during the night but during the day, when illumination is adequate, the significant problem is the resolution of pictures. In other words, the retinal elements or small groups of the cells must be excited separately by different points from the picture during the day; but at night acuity is sacrificed for sensitivity, and light is collected from many angles to excite the receptor cells. The human eye works well over a 30,000-fold intensity range of illumination (sunlight to moonlight), and moderately well over about three times this intensity range; it can detect changes in intensity of the order of 2 to 5 per cent. Comparable capacities are found in several groups of animals. This twenty-four-hour habit depends on several different photomechanical responses involving rapid changes in the distribution of pigment and the action of contractile elements in the iris and/or the retina.

Pigment migration. Photomechanical responses in the arthropods are confined to pigment migration. The apposition eye has been described as photopic and the superposition eye as scotopic. Pigment migrations occur in both but are more striking in the superpositional organ, and this is the visual system which is best adapted to arhythmic behavior. Pigment occurs both in the retinulæ and in the envelope or iris cells surrounding each ommatidium (Fig. 17.6). Among the crustaceans, pigment migration occurs in both kinds of cells (Kleinholz, 1961); among the insects it is confined to the iris cells (Wigglesworth, 1942). It should be noted that pigment distribution may be altered, but the cells in which it is found do not change their shapes.

In dim light the pigment concentrates in a small area of the cell, and the eye behaves like the superposition organ described earlier; in bright light the pigment is dispersed to screen the delicate rhabdomeres, and the eye becomes appositional. In many species of arthropods marked diurnal rhythms of changing pigment distribution have been observed, and these may persist for a long time under constant light conditions. The phenomena appear to be under nervous regulation in insects but under hormonal control in the crustaceans (Roeder, 1953; Kleinholz, 1961; Prosser and Brown, 1961).

Retinal pigment migration also occurs in many vertebrates. It is said to be rapid and extensive in the teleosts, anurans and birds; it is slow and less marked or slight in turtles and crocodilians; it is absent in snakes and mammals (Walls, 1942). In darkness, the pigment granules within the epithelial cells surrounding the rods and cones move to the back of the retina; in the light they are dispersed through the receptor layer and the outer layers of the retina (Fig. 17.10).

A most curious example of pigment migration was described many years ago in the elasmobranch eye. The epithelial cells associated with the rods and cones are devoid of pigment in these fishes, but the choroid contains chromatophores which are said to spread like curtains over a series of slanted guanine plates of the choroidal tapetum (Fig. 17.11). Walls's (1942) monograph contains a beautiful illustration showing fully exposed tapetal plates at night when the pigment is concentrated and a black surface during the day when the pigment is dispersed. The original investigation was carried out by Franz on *Mustelus laevis* (reviews by Walls, 1942, and Nicol, 1963).

Nicol (1961, 1963) has extended the observations to several species of elasmobranchs and finds support for Franz's arguments in some of the pelagic sharks such as *Mustelus* and *Squalus;* in benthic species such as

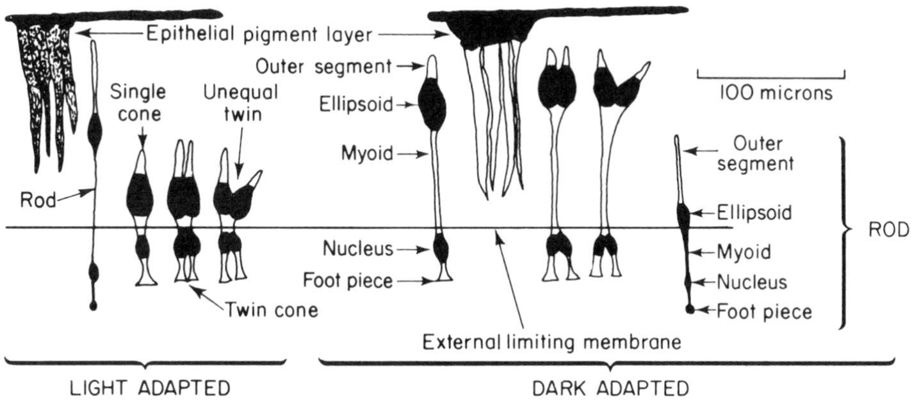

Fig. 17.10. Photomechanical responses in the retina of a salmon. Extreme right, diagram to show the parts of a typical rod. Left, LIGHT ADAPTED ELEMENTS showing dispersion of melanin granules in pigment cells, movement of the rods into the pigment cell layer and contraction of the cones towards the light which strikes the retina from the bottom of the diagram. Middle, DARK ADAPTED ELEMENTS showing the concentration of pigment granules away from the photosensitive cells, movement of outer segment of rod towards light and cones away from the light. [Courtesy of M.A. Ali.]

Raja and *Scyliorhinus,* however, the tapetum is fixed and nonocclusible. Species with a nonocclusible tapetum lucidum show rapid and extensive pupillary movements in contrast to forms with a fixed tapetum. The mechanism of the pigment movements on the tapetal plates and the functional significance of these differences in occlusibility are still not clear (Nicol, 1963).

Visual cell movements. In those vertebrates which show pigment migration there is usually an associated photomechanical change in the position of the receptor cells. The few exceptions include some of the fishes where only the pigment moves and others where the activity is largely confined to the rods or cones (Walls, 1942; Nicol, 1963).

Movements of the photosensitive cells depend on the MYOID, the highly contractile inner stalk-like portion of the rod or cone between the nucleus and the ellipsoid (Fig. 17.10). These associated movements of the pigment granules and receptor cells are not rapid and can be easily traced by histological techniques in which eyes are fixed after intervals of exposure to different intensities of illumination (Ali, 1959; Nicol, 1963). In teleost fishes, where this type of retinomotor response is conspicuous, as much as an hour may be required for complete change from light-adaptation to dark-adaptation (Ali, 1959). However, this is quite adequate to keep pace with the changing daily light conditions and provides an effective means of adjusting the retina to the external illumination.

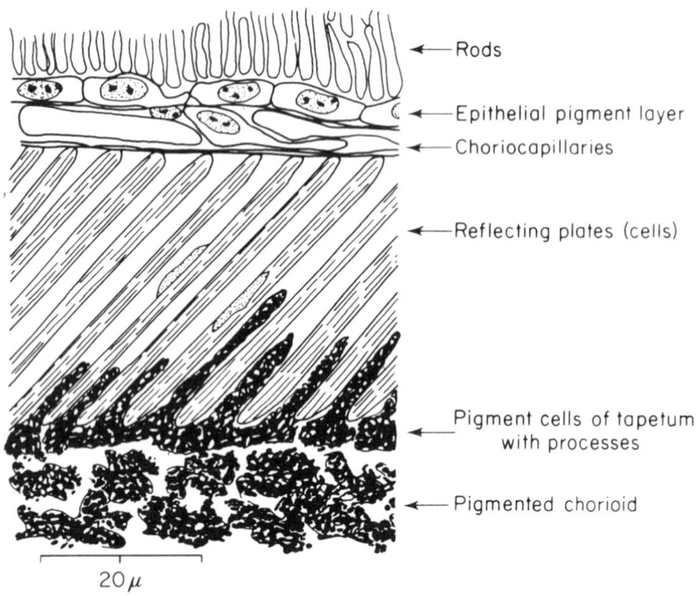

Fig. 17.11. Section through the tapetum lucidum of the dorsal region of the eye of *Scyliorhinus canicula*. [Denton and Nicol (1964).]

Pupillary responses. A mobile iris which, like the diaphragm of a microscope or camera, rapidly alters the aperture to the camera-like eye is the most efficient of the light-regulating adaptations for the arhythmic habit. It reaches its climax in the mammals where its smooth muscle is under rapid autonomic control. The shape of the aperture varies from a circle in some species to a slit in others, depending on the demands of the animal for light at low intensities. The cat, with its reasonably good twenty-four-hour vision, provides a familiar example of the slit pupil. Like a pair of curtains, this can be drawn apart to permit a full view of the stage.

The mammals have no particular monopoly on pupillary responses. They occur in the cephalopod eye where they are under nervous control (Nicol, 1960*a*) and in all classes of vertebrates except the cyclostomes (Walls, 1942). Only a few of the teleosts (the eel, for example) have a mobile iris, but the elasmobranchs show extensive, although slow, pupillary responses. Other fishes (ganoids, dipnoans) and the terrestrial vertebrates have some pupillary control. It is slight in the lower forms, becoming progressively more rapid and extensive as the retinomotor responses decrease in significance through the amniotes. The birds are unique in preserving rapid and extensive retinomotor responses and at the same time possessing a highly mobile iris.

In the lower forms the smooth muscle of the iris is directly but very slowly activated by light (Walls, 1942; Barr and Alpern, 1963). A nervous control is absent; the pupil may require two or three minutes to close in bright light and as long as an hour to reopen in the darkness. A measure of autonomic control is achieved in the amphibians; the pupillary responses become much more rapid and extensive in some reptiles, birds and mammals where there is not only improved nervous regulation but also an increased development of the iris musculature. In general, phylogeny among the vertebrates has seen a gradual reduction and disappearance of retinomotor responses with a progressive development of iris mobility and pupillary control.

ADAPTATIONS TO SPACE, MOTION AND UNUSUAL HABITATS

The basic physiology of the photoreceptor system has been described. This has been adapted in many different ways to meet varied habits and habitats. The morphology of the eye may be curiously altered in association with the habitat, as in deep-sea fishes. Through learning and the specialization of visual centers in the brain, depth and distance may be accurately evaluated. The position of the eye and its mobility may greatly enlarge the fields of vision. Special coverings of tissue may form "spectacles" or "goggles" for protection in swift swimming or burrowing. These and many other curious devices are based on the machinery already considered; the visual system is one of the most versatile in the variety of evolutionary adaptations.

Like many phylogenetic trails, that which has led to the most specialized of photoreceptors shows numerous diverging paths. Sometimes a more primitive mechanism is preserved by a more advanced group, as the birds, which retain the photomechanical activities of the visual units along with a mobile iris. The reverse may also be true; lower groups may acquire certain devices which are usually associated with the higher forms. Pupillary responses occur among some of the invertebrates and lower vertebrates, although they are most characteristic of the birds and mammals. Darwinian evolution works with a strictly limited number of building materials and weaves these into patterns which frequently show clearly marked trends of specialization but, at the same time, display random elements of the potential variation.

Reception of Mechanical and Thermal Stimuli 18

Mechanoreception

Many cells are excited by contact stimuli which stretch or wrinkle their surface membranes. This is easily demonstrated with protozoa and some other cells not particularly specialized as receptor organs. Avoiding responses to contact stimuli were probably the phylogenetic bases of this highly important system of receptors which, in more advanced groups, collects information from distant sources as well as local contacts and informs the central nervous system of both the internal body pressures and those which arise in the external environment.

The proprioceptors in the organs of locomotion transmit steadily to the central nervous centers so that tensions are properly adjusted and body equilibrium is maintained. There is also a constant monitoring of the position of the body with respect to gravity and angular acceleration. Pressure receptors in the viscera may function with respect to such diverse phenomena as the sensing of hydrostatic pressure or visceral disturbances which produce pain. Distant vibrations often provide information concerning dangers, mates and foods while the actual production of vibrations becomes the basis of a special language and orientation in a manner parallel to that considered in Chapter 16 for the chemical receptor system.

EXCITATION OF MECHANORECEPTORS

In 1950, Bernard Katz made the remarkable discovery that the electrogenic properties of the muscle spindle were quite different from those of the nerve associated with it. The muscle spindle is a mechanoreceptor concerned with the adjustment of tensions in skeletal muscle. Katz (1950) found that a modest stretching generates a very weak and purely localized electric current while more vigorous stretching gives a greater response until a point is reached where an impulse is triggered in the associated nerve. These localized potential changes, referred to as GENERATOR POTENTIALS, are graded responses in direct relation to the energy of stimulation; the nerve impulse which they generate is an all-or-none propagated wave of depolarization. Within the muscle spindle, the relationship between input and output is like that found in a carbon microphone where the mechanical deformations of the disk of carbon by the sound waves reduce the electrical resistance so that an electrical current flows through it, and the strength is proportional to the sound (Loewenstein, 1960).

Physiologists have now investigated several different mechanoreceptors, and it is apparent that Katz discovered the fundamental transducing mechanism in his work with the muscle spindle. The crustacean stretch receptor (Kuffler, 1958) and the Pacinian corpuscle (Loewenstein, 1961) have been most useful in developing the current ideas. The latter will be described to illustrate several of these.

Pacinian corpuscles (Fig. 18.1) are pressure receptors found in the deeper layers of the skin, in the connective tissues around the tendons, muscles and joints and in the serous membranes and mesenteries of the viscera. They are extremely large, reaching almost 1 mm in length and 0.6 mm in diameter. These are primary sense cells in which the terminal portion of the nerve fiber is surrounded by a relatively thin granular mass and covered by concentric layers of connective tissue like the many coats of an onion. The spaces between these layers contain fluid which may be important in transmitting the superficial pressure changes to the delicate nerve ending within. However, the coverings are not essential to the generation of electric potentials; it has been possible to dissect away 99.9 per cent of this structure without destroying its capacity to transduce mechanical stimuli. The myelin sheath of the associated nerve extends for about one-third of its distance within the corpuscle, but the terminal part is unmyelinated. As indicated in Fig. 18.1, there is an important node of Ranvier inside the corpuscle.

In studies of the Pacinian corpuscle, most of the connective tissue lamellae are removed and the almost naked nerve ending is stimulated with a minute glass stilus. This is made to vibrate very precisely at one point by a controlled electric current operating through a piezoelectric crystal which converts the electrical energy into mechanical vibrations of the stilus (Loewenstein, 1960, 1961). At rest the membrane potential is steady. When a mechanical pulse is applied at one point and the generator current measured at varying distances from the point of stimulation,

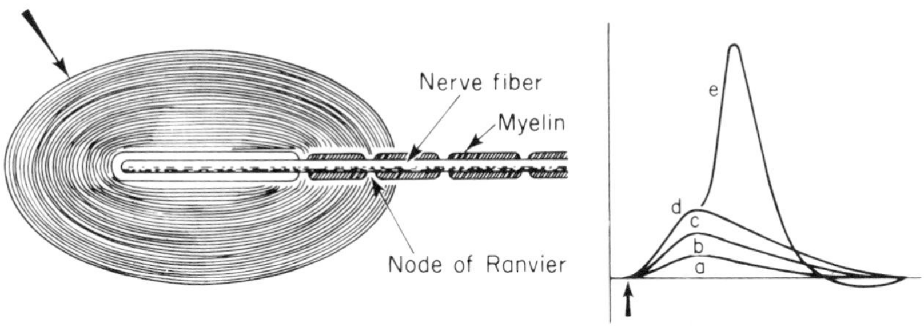

Fig. 18.1. Diagram of the Pacinian corpuscle (left) and the electrical potentials (right) which follow progressively stronger stimulation applied at the point of the arrow. A weak stimulus produces a weak generator current (*a*). Progressively stronger stimuli produce correspondingly stronger generator currents (*b* and *c*). The threshold stimulus (*d*) fires an all-or-none nerve impulse (*e*). If the first node of Ranvier is blocked the all-or-none impulse cannot be induced. [Loewenstein (1960).]

the potentials are found to decrease with distance (Fig. 18.2). Clearly, the excitation is restricted to the region of stimulation, and the signals fade rapidly in the surrounding regions of the membrane.

When the almost naked fiber is stimulated at two regions separated by about 0.5 mm, the generator currents are added to produce a single large generator potential (Fig. 18.3). It is evident that the flow of current increases in proportion to the area of the membrane deformed (spatial summation). In the terminology of Chapter 15, wrinkling of the cell membrane opens valves (mechanically operated valves) which permit the flow of ions and produce electrogenesis. The facts are consistent with the view that the mechanical operation of valves or the opening of holes is in direct relation to the amount of wrinkling and that, when this reaches a point where the excitation passes the first node of Ranvier, an all-or-none depolarization of the nerve fiber occurs. The local generator currents increase until they initiate a "spike" (Fig. 18.1).

SOME ANATOMICAL VARIATIONS

The transducing membrane which sets up the train of nerve impulses in mechanoreception may be a dendritic filament of a primary sense cell such as the Pacinian corpuscle, or it may be an area of a secondary sense cell as, for example, in the crustacean stretch receptor or the organ of Corti. These secondary sense receptor cells trigger an adjacent nerve through a synapse. Although the transducing events seem to be rather stereotyped, the structures concerned with the process are most varied

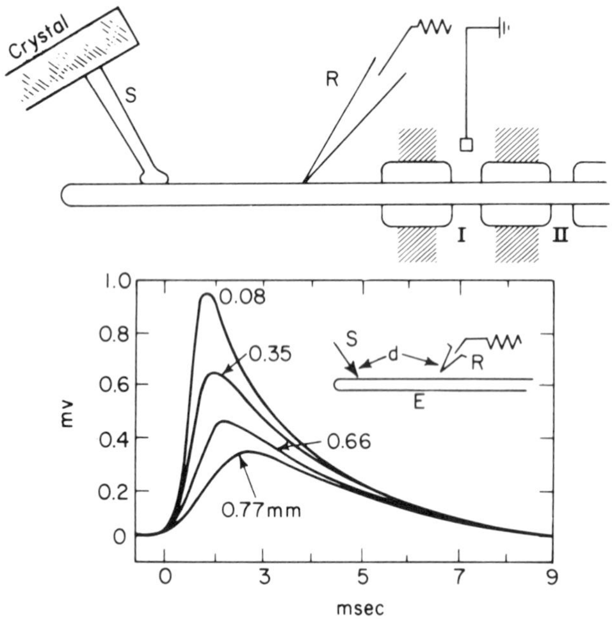

Fig. 18.2. Spread of excitation from the point of stimulus (*S*) along the nerve ending of a Pacinian corpuscle. *Upper*, diagram of apparatus. The lamellae of the corpuscle have been removed. The mechanical pulses of a piezoelectric crystal are applied by a glass stylus (*S*). The resulting generator potentials are recorded with a microelectrode (*R*) from the surface of the receptor membrane or, alternatively, between the first (I) and second (II) nodes of Ranvier by electronic spread. *Lower*, a small region of the receptor membrane (*E*) is stimulated with equal mechanical pulses while the surface of the receptor membrane is scanned with a microelectrode (*R*). Four selected samples of generator potential recorded at the distances indicated (*d*) have been superimposed. [Loewenstein (1961).]

and specialized. There are few physiological machines that exist in so many different models. The examples described in this chapter illustrate the variety but do not exhaust the anatomical types.

STATOCYSTS, concerned with reactions to gravity, are very old types of a specialized mechanoreceptor. The one illustrated in Fig. 18.4 is from the scallop *Pecten*. It is a closed sac lined with sensory cells and containing a hardened concretion, the STATOLITH. The sensory cells possess delicate hairlike filaments (the transducing membranes) which are activated by the statolith. As this falls on different groups of these hairs or filaments the impulses are relayed to the nervous system to

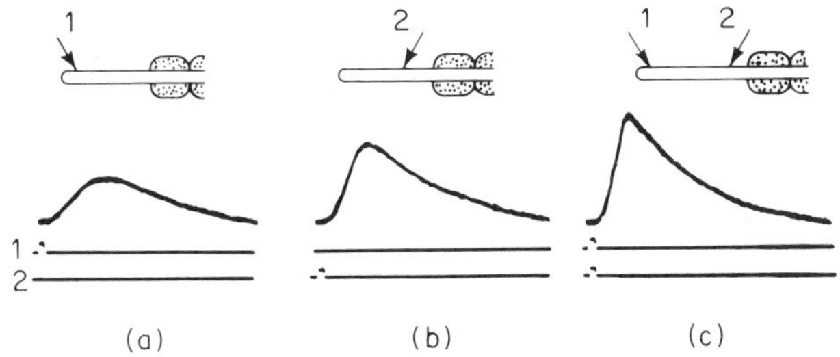

Fig. 18.3. Spatial summation in the receptor membrane. Styli 1 (about 30 μ diameter) and 2 (about 20 μ diameter) belong to independent crystals that stimulate two membrane spots about 400 μ apart. Generator potentials (*upper beam*) in response to a mechanical pulse applied in *a*, to spot 1; in *b*, to spot 2; and in *c*, to both spots simultaneously. *Lower beams* signal pulses of styli. Calibration: 1 msec.; 50 μv. [Loewenstein (1961).]

provide information concerning the position of the animal with respect to gravity. Organs of this type are present in the coelenterates and flatworms (Hyman, 1940, 1951); they are very old phylogenetically. In some cases the space containing the statolith is partially open on the

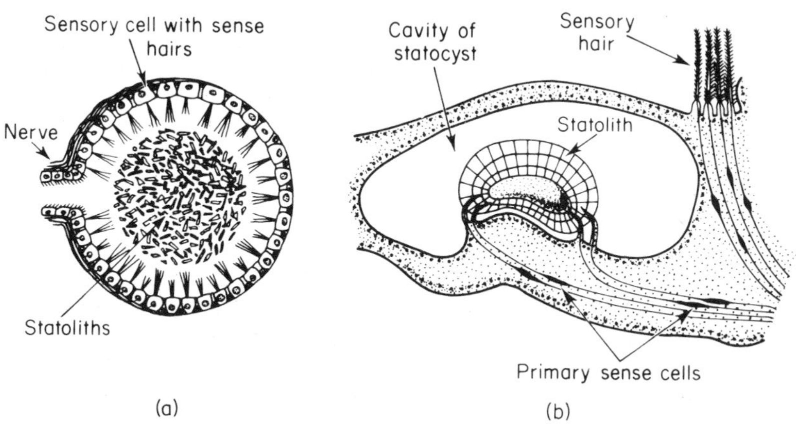

Fig. 18.4. Statocysts of invertebrate animals. *a*, *Pecten* with a free statolith. *b*, *Leptomysis* with dendritic hairs attached to the statolith. Free sensory hairs with attached dendrites are also shown in *b*. [Heidermanns (1957) after Wurmbach.]

surface of the animal; in evolution, surface vesicles probably preceded closed sacs. The type illustrated from *Leptomysis*, a crustacean, is a variant in which a few sensory neurons are anchored in a sac containing the statolith (Fig. 18.4*b*).

Tactile and chordotonal sensillae of insects. Two forms of tactile hairs from insects are shown in Fig. 18.5 When these are moved they pull on the attached dendrites. Receptors of this type are also found in the most primitive groups (Hyman, 1951). The hair sensillae of insects are sufficiently specialized to act as simple acoustic organs when they vibrate in a tiny socket and pull on a nerve cell (Fig. 18.5). The SCOLOPHOROUS SENSE CELL (SCOLOPIDIUM) of insects is basically similar, but the entire

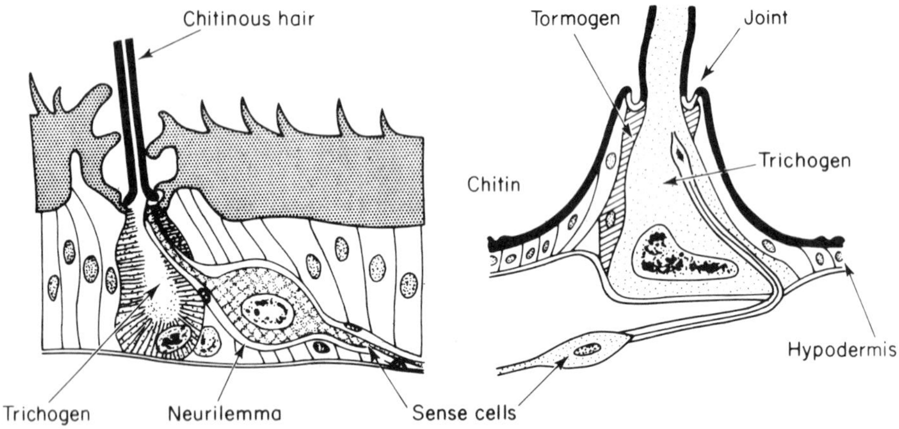

Fig. 18.5. Hair sensillae of insects. Left, from the cercus of the cricket *Liogryllus*. Right, from the caterpillar *Pieris*. The trichogen is the hair-forming cell; the tormogen cell secretes the chitinous joint membrane. [Weber (1933).]

machine is internal and depends on the movement of an area of pliable cuticle to which a fiber, the terminal dendritic strand, is anchored. There are many varieties of scolopoid sensilla; they have been utilized by insects to form delicate organs for the sensing of tactile stimuli and vibrations from both near and far.

A group of scolopidia forms a CHORDOTONAL ORGAN. These organs may stretch across a fluid-filled space as in the subgenual organs in the legs or Johnston's organ in the second antennal segment. The former serves as a tactile organ or pickup for low-frequency vibrations (200 to 6000 cycles per second) from the ground or substratum where the animal lives; the latter are probably "statical organs" (Autrum, 1959; Dethier, 1963). Chordotonal organs may also stretch across an air sac or tracheal space and form auditory organs of many different patterns and varying complexity. The TYMPANAL ORGANS are specialized acoustic organs in which the scolopidia (as many as 1500 or more in a cicada) are associated with a thin membrane (the tympanum), either by a direct attachment to it or to the surrounding tracheal structures. The membrane improves the pickup of distant vibrations. Electrophysiological and behavioral studies show that these hearing organs of insects are sensitive to changes in the rhythm of vibrations (an analysis of temporal patterns) but do not discriminate differences in the frequency of the sound waves themselves, i.e., pitch and harmonics (see below). Many of the insect sounds are supersonic to the human ear. Sounds produced by insects range up to 63,000 cps (Roeder, 1953) while the human ear has its maximum sensitivity between 800 and 2500 cps with an upper limit of about 20,000 cps.

Rheoreceptors. Receptors for the detection of water currents (rheoreceptors) are found at all levels in phylogeny and seem to have been the basis for an evolution of the most specialized distance receptor, the auditory organ of the higher vertebrate. The rheoreceptors of the turbellarian, *Mesostoma,* are large neurons with several rather long filamentous dendrites protruding beyond the cilia which cover the animal's body (Hyman, 1951). The lateral line organs of the aquatic vertebrates are structurally similar and operate in a like manner, although these vertebrate receptors are secondary sense cells while all invertebrate receptors are primary.

THE ACOUSTICO-LATERALIS SYSTEM

The neuromasts or sensory hillocks of the aquatic vertebrates proved to be the most versatile of all mechanoreceptors in the evolution of specialized transducers for vibratory stimuli. Basically, they are organs of touch and monitor water currents at short distances. In phylogeny they have been turned to the detection of gravitational forces, accelerations, and the precise analysis of sounds from distant sources. Dijkgraaf (1963) has carefully reviewed the physiological literature of more than half a century.

A neuromast or sensory hillock of a fish consists of a cluster of pear-shaped secondary sense cells supported in a basket-like arrangement of tall epithelial cells (Fig. 18.6). Elongated sense hairs project from these receptors into the gelatinous material forming the cupula, a product of the neuromasts. Movements of the cupula activate these delicate sense hairs. In the aquatic amphibians, the cyclostomes and some of the more advanced groups of fishes, all of the sensory hillocks are free and exposed on the body surface, but in many of the fishes some or all of them are located in canals or tunnels beneath the epidermis. The canal organs have evidently evolved from surface neuromasts through the development of pits and grooves, and there is a good correlation between the behavior of the fish and the degree of protection of its neuromasts;

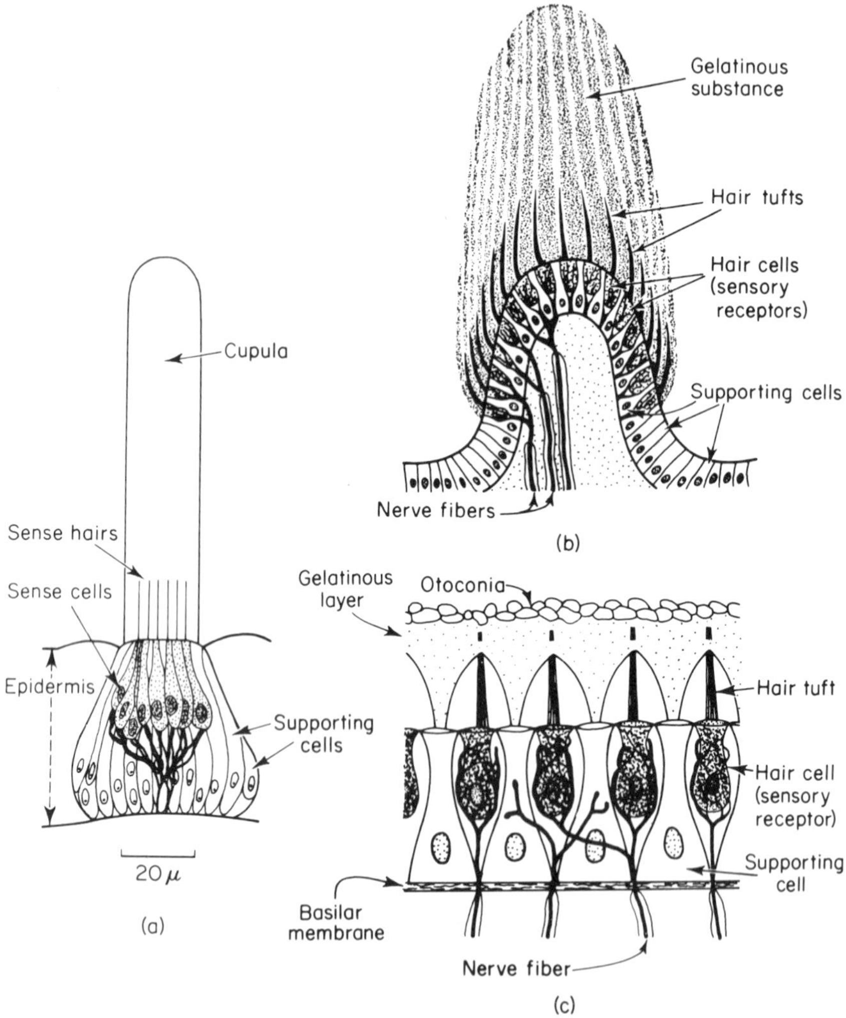

Fig. 18.6. Some receptors of the acoustico-lateralis system. *a*, Superficial neuromast of a bony fish such as the minnow *Phoxinus*. [After Dijkgraaf (1963).] *b*, The mammalian crista. [Netter, F. H. The Ciba Collection of Medical Illustrations. Vol. 1, Nervous System. Ciba Co., Ltd., Montreal. (1953).] *c*, The mammalian macula. [Netter (1953).]

the canals are better developed in the more active forms. Lateral line canals usually open to the surface through regularly spaced pores and contain a fluid, the canal endolymph. A cupula is a consistent feature of the neuromast, whether it is exposed or hidden in a canal.

The evolution of the membranous labyrinth or internal ear from an anterior portion of this canal system is a familiar story in comparative anatomy and will not be detailed here. In brief, the embryonic ectodermal

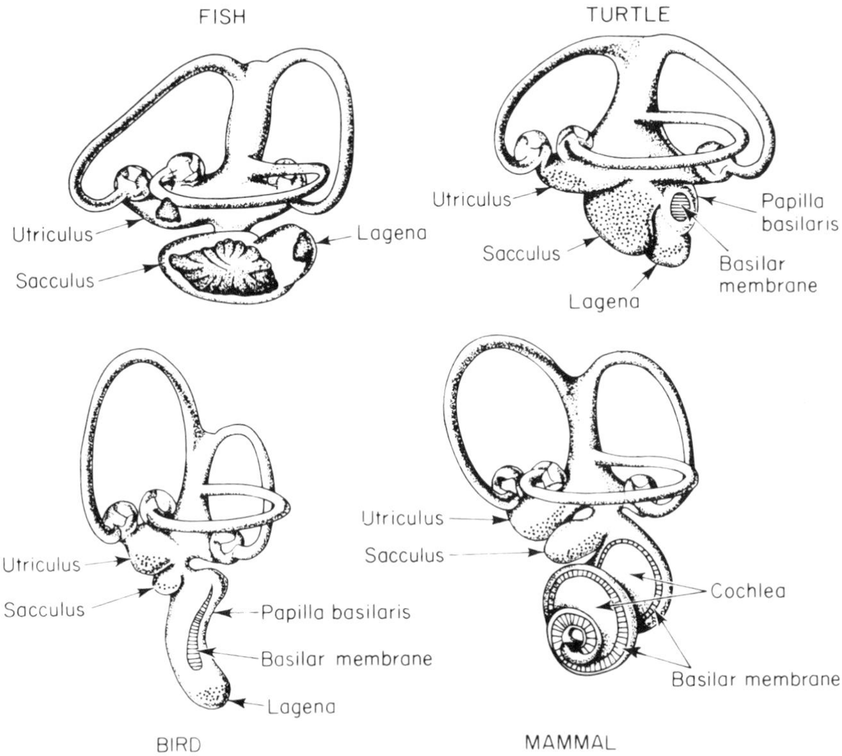

Fig. 18.7. Membranous labyrinth of various vertebrates. [von Frisch (1936).]

sac (OTIC VESICLE) can be thought of as an enlarged anterior portion of the lateral canal system. In the gnathostomes, this differentiates into two sacs, a ventral SACCULUS (the more primitive portion) and a dorsal UTRICULUS. Three semicircular canals, set at right angles to one another, open into the vestibule, an expanded portion of the utriculus; one end of each canal is expanded into a bulb-like AMPULLA. A ventral lobe of the sacculus is extended into a structure (the LAGENA) which varies from a tiny flap in the fishes to an elongated coiled duct in the mammals (COCHLEA). This system of sacs and ducts (Fig. 18.7) is filled with a fluid, the ENDOLYMPH, and housed in a bony or connective tissue space filled with PERILYMPH.

Within the membranous labyrinth, the receptor cells are grouped in six or seven (reptiles and birds only) distinct patches—one in each of the three ampullae and one in each of the chambers, the utriculus, the sacculus, the lagena and the cochlea. Since only the reptiles and birds have both a lagena and a cochlea (Pumphrey, 1961), their internal ears have seven instead of six sensory areas.

Physiologically, the receptors of the ampullae, called the CRISTAE (Fig. 18.6), are most like the sensory hillocks on the skin of a fish. Because of their position in the fluid-filled canals set in three different planes, their cupulae are very liable to displacement during angular acceleration or rotation of the head. Rotational movements provide the adequate stimuli; they are probably not influenced by linear acceleration (Gernandt, 1959).

The patches of sense cells in the utriculus, sacculus and lagena (the MACULAE) are excited by the movements of heavy mineralized concretions, the ear stones (OTOLITHS or OTOCONIA). Hence, these three maculae are sometimes grouped as the otolith organs. The utricular macula (PARS SUPERIOR) is concerned with gravitational stimuli and throughout the vertebrates is an organ of major importance in postural reflexes. The PARS INFERIOR, including both the sacculus and its appendage, the lagena, has had a much more varied history; the role of the sacculus in the higher vertebrates is still somewhat obscure (Gernandt, 1959). In the lower vertebrates the pars inferior (both sacculus and lagena) is concerned with hearing. As the lagena elongated the cochlear duct which developed as a consequence, became a delicate organ for the analysis of sound (ORGAN OF CORTI). In the mammals the lagena (which is at the end of this duct in the reptiles and birds) does not occur.

Thus the membranous labyrinth consists of three receptor systems which analyze three different kinds of movements—those produced by gravitational forces, rotational stimuli and distant vibrations. The phylogenetic sequence in the differentiation of these systems is debatable (Pumphrey, 1950; Dijkgraaf, 1963). It seems clear, however, that the lateral line from which they have evolved was basically concerned with the detection of shearing forces induced by movements of fluids at close quarters and that otolith organs which pick up distant vibrations came later. Rheoreceptors evidently preceded organs of hearing. In phylogeny, the localization of distant vibrations in water might first have been greatly improved by adding calcareous material to a portion of the neuromast system, thus forming a primitive otic sac (Pumphrey, 1950). The membranous labyrinth may thus have started as an otolith organ associated with hearing, and the semicircular canals and cochlear duct developed later as specializations.

Physiology of the ordinary lateral line organs. The role of the neuromasts of fishes has remained controversial since the pioneer studies at the beginning of the twentieth century. Claims have been made for a short-distance auditory function, a temperature receptor and a chemical sense. Dijkgraaf (1963) does not find the evidence for any of these at all convincing. From both classical behavioral studies and modern electrophysiological recording there is strong evidence that local water displacements provide the normal stimulus. It is obvious that disturbances of many kinds in the surroundings of a fish can activate the neuromasts, but the adequate stimulus is moving water on the surface of the body. The patterns of electrogenesis are interesting. Hoagland (1932) was the first to record a continuous "resting" discharge of action potentials in the lateral line nerves of fish. This has been many times confirmed, and it is now recognized that these organs, unlike many other receptors, send a steady spontaneous train of bioelectric potentials along their nerves and that the rhythm of the pulses changes during stimulation (Fig. 18.8). The basis for this steady state of rhythmic electrogenesis is unknown.

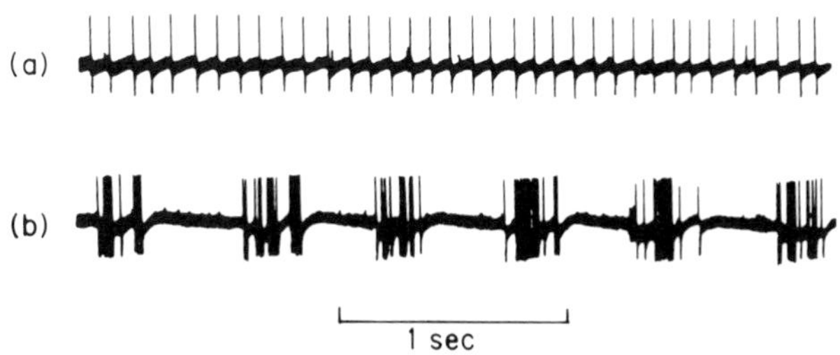

Fig. 18.8. Impulses in the lateral nerve fibers of *Xenopus*. Upper, spontaneous activity. Lower, responses of sensory unit when surrounding body of water was made to swing to and fro. Periods of activity correspond to headward current. [Dijkgraaf (1963).]

The message of the neuromast is not merely "disturbance in the water nearby" but "water moving from head to tail" or "water moving from tail to head." This discrimination is based on an asymmetry in the distribution of the filaments within the sense hairs (Dijkgraaf, 1963). There are two types differentially activated by water currents from two main directions. Potentials measured in the associated nerves of *Xenopus* show that when one system is activated the other is inhibited (Fig. 18.9).

The information received by an animal with such a system might, at least in theory, be of use in rheotaxis; in reality, this is probably of minor importance since vision seems to play the dominant role in rheotaxis of fish. More important functions of the lateral line organs are probably concerned with detecting and locating moving animals (predators, prey, and social partners).

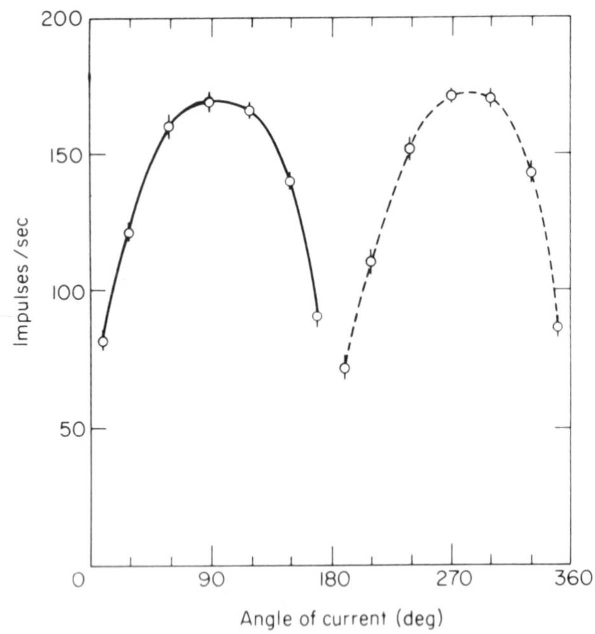

Fig. 18.9. Responses of two lateralis fibers (one shown as a solid line and the other as a broken line) innervating one row of neuromasts in *Xenopus*. The stimulus was a current parallel to the skin from different directions with respect to the long axis of the row. Maximum response occurs to currents at right angles to the row. Note opposite response of both fibers. Spontaneous discharge frequency was about 25 per sec. [Dijkgraaf (1963).]

The Organ of Corti. This is the most specialized of all biological systems for the analysis of distant vibrations.

Sound has three main physical properties: its LOUDNESS which depends on the amplitude of the vibration, its PITCH which depends on the frequency or speed of vibration and its TONE, a quality which varies with the number and strength of the OVERTONES. In birds and mammals all these can be sorted out by the Organ of Corti and its associated nervous

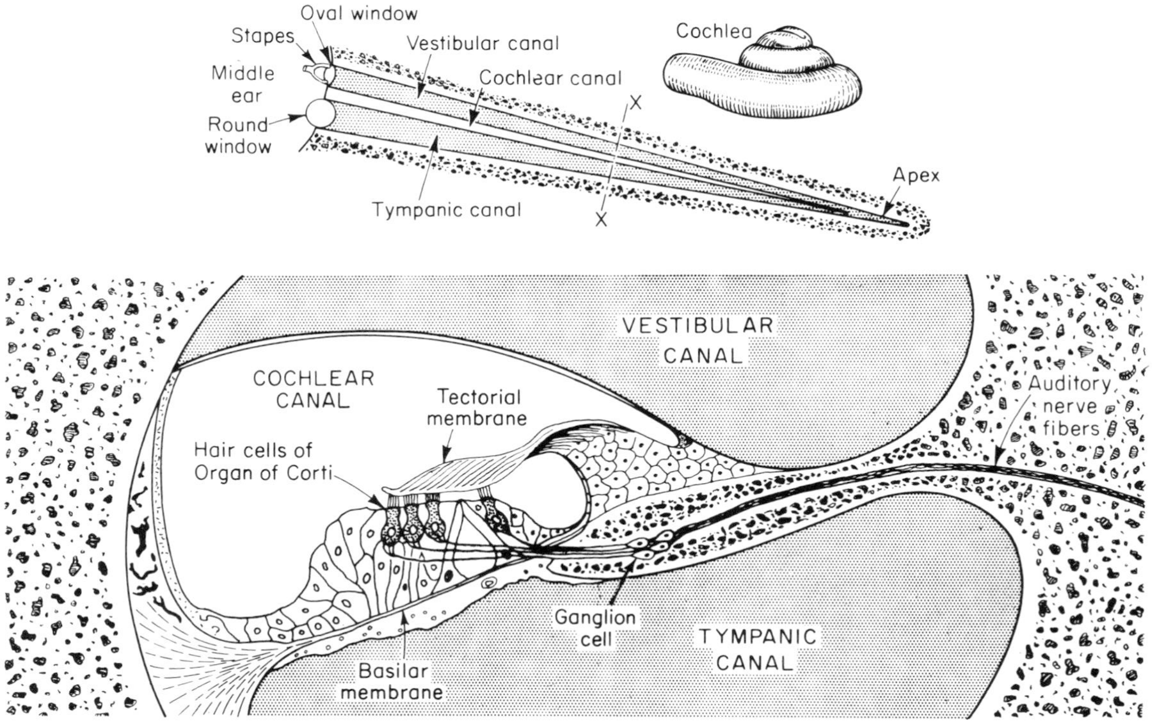

Fig. 18.10. Diagrams of the mammalian cochlea. Above, the spiralled cochlea has been uncoiled and split open to show the relationships of its three canals. Below, a cross-section through *X–X* to show the Organ of Corti sitting on the basilar membrane. The receptor cells for hearing (hair cells) are secondary sense cells innervated by fibres of the auditory nerve. The cochlea is embedded in bone.

centers; the insect is unable to analyze any of these properties but depends only on the rhythm of sound pulses; the lower vertebrates have intermediate capacities (Lanyon and Tavolga, 1960).

During life the cochlea, like a tiny beautifully spiralled snail, is housed in a bony case. When uncoiled and examined in cross section (Fig. 18.10), it is found to consist of three fluid-filled canals, the central COCHLEAR canal containing the Organ of Corti and the two peripheral TYMPANIC and VESTIBULAR canals which communicate at the apex and have movable membranes or WINDOWS at their base. In contrast, the base of the cochlear canal is solid bone, and this is important in transducer action.

The long ridge of receptor cells which make up the Organ of Corti sits on a dense mat of connective tissue, the BASILAR MEMBRANE. Helmholtz, in the mid-nineteenth century, was the first scientist to develop a workable theory of hearing. He noted that this membrane became gradually wider toward the apex of the spiral and argued that fibers of different lengths resonated in accordance with the frequency of the sound; this membrane with its fibers under some tension and of different lengths (like the strings of a piano) was assumed to be the basis of hearing (Ackerman, 1962, and texts of medical physiology). The resonator theory has now been disproved, although a shadow of it remains since the varying width of the basilar membrane is still considered important.

Present thinking is based on the careful studies of von Békésy (1956 and earlier) who explored the physical properties of the fluids and membranes and made direct microscopic observations of their movements in preparations from fresh cadavers. A traveling wave theory seems to fit the facts best. This wave is first generated in the vestibular fluids by the movement of the ear bones on the oval window. It travels varying distances along the canals in accordance with the diameter of the canal and the width of the basilar membrane. Above about 60 cps the basilar membrane begins to vibrate unequally over its area. Short wavelengths die out more quickly than the longer ones. In other words, maximal vibrations of different areas of the membrane are related to the different tones, with the higher frequencies operating closest to the oval window. Finer aspects of discrimination depend on the central nervous system; the analysis at the level of the basilar membrane is a rough, mechanical frequency analysis. The nervous system sharpens the analysis in some manner not yet understood (von Békésy, 1957).

The transducer action in the receptor cell probably depends on mechanically operated valves. The fluids within the cochlear duct are about 80 mv electrically positive relative to the surrounding tissues while the receptor cells themselves are about 70 mv electrically negative inside. In short, there is a potential difference of about 150 mv across their membranes, and the movements of the sense hairs initiate electrogenesis. The receptor cells show an orderly arrangement within the Organ of Corti, with a single inner row and three or four outer rows separated by a supporting arch or pillar. The sense hairs are anchored in the tectorial membrane, and the whole system is delicately balanced to move with the waves in the fluids of the vestibular canal. Many additional details will be found in textbooks of medical and sensory physiology.

COMMUNICATION BASED ON MECHANORECEPTORS

Twentieth-century recording instruments have revealed a much "noisier" world than man's receptor capacities would lead him to suspect (Lanyon and Tavolga, 1960). The human ear is limited to an extreme range of about 20 to 20,000 cps, with a maximum sensitivity at about 2000 cps. Insects, in contrast, make much use of supersonics up to more than 45,000 cps while the frequency range of hearing in some bats extends out to 150,000 cps (150 kc). Thus, there are many sounds of which we are unaware; these are, however accessible to analysis by appropriate instruments, and careful studies have shown that the majority of the invertebrates and many of the lower vertebrates make no use of this modality in communication. Hearing is much more widespread than the ability to communicate. Some animals may show alarm or avoidance reactions to distant mechanical vibrations but lack the capacity to produce sounds. Communication by sound involves the reception of meaningful vibrations produced by another animal at some distance.

Among the invertebrates, only relatively few insects (particularly the Orthoptera and the Cicadidae) have well-developed systems of communication based on sound. Although many of the decapods produce sound, it has not been conclusively shown that they have mechanisms for its reception and analysis (Carthy, 1958; Cohen and Dijkgraaf, 1961). Phonoreception is universal among the major groups of vertebrates but communication based on it is far less common. Some of the teleosts, the anurans and a few representatives of each of the surviving orders of reptiles produce meaningful sounds. The remaining groups of poikilotherms seem to be silent (Lanyon and Tavolga, 1960). The homeotherms, on the other hand, have refined this means of communication in many different ways.

Insect sounds are usually produced by rubbing together two different parts of the hardened integument. Frequently a ribbed or toothed file is moved rapidly across a fixed surface to produce a shrill stridulation. This may be called the file-and-peg technique and has numerous variations in detail (Pumphrey, 1940; Pringle, 1956). The cicadas use quite a different method; they produce sounds by buckling modified areas of the exoskeleton. Insect sounds are often of very high frequency, perhaps because of the small surfaces concerned with their reception. The evidence is that insects with tympanal organs are able to localize sounds but that their capacities for analysis are extremely limited. Many different patterns of vibration are produced, and these often form meaningful phrases in the language of one species (Faber distinguished 12 in the grasshopper), but it seems that only one of the characteristics of the sound, viz., its pulse rhythm, has significance (Pumphrey, 1940, 1950); insects cannot analyze for pitch and tone quality but rely only on the pattern of pulses (Roeder, 1953).

Many of the teleost fishes also produce sounds by drumming or stridulation of hard body parts. In the black bass (*Centropristes striatus*), for example, the pounding of the opercula against the cleithra and other supporting pectoral bones creates a series of drumming thumps; in the sea catfish (*Galeichthys felis*), there is a high-pitched creaking sound when a tuberosity at the base of the first dorsal is rubbed against the inside of its socket formed by the cleithrum (Tavolga, 1960). There are many variations of this drumming, rasping and creaking.

Some teleosts also make use of the air bladder, either as an auxiliary to the skeletal machinery or as an independent sound producer. Specializations of this organ have been incorporated into refinements of sound reception as well as sound production. Members of the Ostariophysi, which show the greatest acuity among fishes, have a series of modified vertebral elements between the swim bladder and the internal ear (Weberian apparatus); these transmit vibrations from the wall of the swim bladder to the auditory apparatus. Fish protoplasm is essentially transparent to sound, and the detection of distant vibrations in water became feasible through the incorporation of materials of different density into the system – the ear stones and sometimes sacs of air as in the Ostariophysi. Fish sounds are of low frequency, generally below about 800 cps, although some whistles and grunts have been recorded in the 2000 to 4000 cps range. The communicative value of many of the recorded sounds is as yet unknown. It seems clear, however, that fish do use sound as "warnings" and in reproductive behavior and intraspecific communication; this remains a potentially productive field for research both in physiology and ethology.

The organs of ventilation provide the basic machinery for sound production in the terrestrial vertebrates. With few exceptions, such as the warning "rattle" of the rattlesnake, the sounds of tetrapods are due to the controlled movements of air through respiratory passages. There are many anatomical modifications: the larynx and vocal cords, the resonating vocal sacs of the anurans, the syrinx and certain air sacs of birds and the lips of man. The most primitive communicating noise may have been the hiss which is common in tetrapods with and without a specialized voice.

In any case, during evolution, this system has expressed many of the potentialities of the woodwind instruments of an orchestra. With a refined motor control for the organs of breathing, the development of the Organ of Corti and the associated neural centers for the discrimination of pitch and tone, a vastly more elaborate system of communication was available to the birds and the mammals.

Sound reception as well as sound production are based on quite different principles in the insects and the terrestrial vertebrates. Pumphrey (1940) classes the insect receptors as DISPLACEMENT RECEIVERS and points out that even the tympanum, which looks superficially like an ear drum, has air at atmospheric pressure on both of its sides; as far as the receptor cells are concerned, the action of its movement is the same as that of the moving bristle. The inner ear of the vertebrate, on the other hand, is a PRESSURE RECEIVER with the distant vibrations creating a system of waves in a fluid-filled space.

Echo orientation. Several groups of animals make use of reflected sound in orientation. The bat is the best known example. The series of researches which led to the discovery of this highly specialized capacity is one of the really great classics in zoological research. Griffin, who wrote one of the later chapters in this classic, tells the history in his books (Griffin, 1958, 1959). Lazzaro Spallanzani of Pavia, in 1793, became much interested in animals which can navigate in the dark. He soon showed that the owl could not really find its way about in complete darkness and was evidently using its eyes at low light intensities. The bat, however, posed a different problem. Spallanzani carried out many experiments. Blinded bats easily found their way back to the bell tower of the cathedral where he had captured them earlier. What was even more surprising, their stomachs were filled with freshly caught insects, proving that they could capture insects as well as navigate in the dark. He and others who became interested in the problem during the eighteenth century showed that the senses of vision, touch, smell and taste were of no significance but that the ears were indispensable. The problem was insoluble since everyone agreed that bats produced no sounds whatever, and by 1800 Spallanzani's findings were dismissed as ridiculous and soon were almost forgotten.

Just about a century and a half elapsed before Griffin brought the first bats into range of equipment capable of recording ultrasonic vibrations and started a chain of research which has shown that bats and several other animals are operating in a world of sounds which is completely inaccessible to the human ear. Griffin and his associates showed that covering the mouth was just as effective as excluding the ears in disorienting the bat.

It is now known that the bats (Chiroptera) vary in their capacity for echo orientation with many differences in the organs for the transmission and reception of sound (Griffin, 1958; 1962). The old-world fruit-eating bats (Megachiroptera) all have large eyes and orient visually as would seem to be necessary in animals which feed on fruit, pollen and nectar. With the exception of one genus, *Rousettus*, the Megachiroptera evidently rely solely on vision. *Rousettus* also has good eyes and can orient visually in the light; but when flying in dark caves, it emits clicks which are clearly audible to human ears. These animals will start clicking as soon as the lights in the laboratory are extinguished, and the sounds become much more pronounced as the problems of orientation are increased. Many experiments show that *Rousettus* echo-orients in the dark but not in the light.

There are two suborders of bats, and the Microchiroptera, in contrast to the Megachiroptera, all emit high-frequency and short wavelength sounds which are used in orientation. Most of these bats feed on flying insects and, as Spallanzani discovered, these are regularly captured in the darkness. The sounds are characteristic of the different groups and are emitted in short pulses ranging in length from a tenth of a second (100 msc) to less than one millisecond. Most of the frequencies are beyond the range of human ears; they vary in different species from about 10 kc/sec (wavelength 34 mm) to over 130 kc/sec (wavelength 2.5 mm). The intensity of the sound is considerably higher in species which hunt insects on the wing, and the pulse repetition rate increases with the difficulties of orientation.

In comparing the sounds of four families of Microchiroptera, Griffin (1962) found some representatives which emit sounds of almost constant frequency throughout the duration of the pulse (Rhinolophidae). But in most the pulse is frequency-modulated (Vespertilionidae, Mollossidae and Noctilionidae) with a downward sweep by about one octave during the pulse. The Rhinolophidae or horseshoe bats also differ from the other groups in their techniques of sound transmission; their faces are modified into trumpet-like structures (hence the name "horseshoe bats") which confine their calls to narrow beams (Moehres, 1960). These the animals direct in accordance with their problems of navigation. In other groups the sound spreads around the animal in all directions. There are no sharp lines between the vocabularies of the four families mentioned; the species form a continuum in frequency patterns. The pulse patterns have been adapted to the navigation problems of the particular species.

Since some insects are known to create and respond to high-frequency vibrations, it is not surprising to find a behavioral interaction between the predatory bats and their flying insect prey. Roeder and Treat (1957) recorded responses in the tympanic nerves of several species of noctuid moths; these responses were closely related to the cries of bats. Electrogenesis followed the bat's cry immediately and persisted for some time after it ceased. These moths are known to respond to sound in the range of 3 to 240 kc, with peak sensitivity between 15 and 60 kc. The reactions of some of these moths in the presence of bats substantiates the theory that they can actively evade their predators (Griffin, 1958; Roeder, 1964).

Bats are not alone in the use of echolocation. In 1953, Griffin showed by experiments similar to some of the classical ones carried out earlier on bats, that *Steatornis*, the oilbird of Caripe (Venezuela), flies swiftly and safely in completely dark caves emitting clicks (6000 to 10,000 cps) which are well within the range of human ears. Swifts of the genus *Collocalia,* famous for the production of the salivary glue used in bird's nest soup, likewise orient themselves in caves with low-frequency clicks (Novick, 1959). Nor is the capacity confined to bats among mammals. Marine species are well equipped for echolocation (Kellogg, 1961) as are also the tiny shrews (Gould *et al.*, 1964). This ability may also be utilized by such insects as the noctuid moths and certain other groups of animals. It seems to appear in habitats or situations where it may be presumed to confer a biological advantage. A rich literature on the biological uses of echoes is now available (Griffin, 1958, 1959; Milne and Milne, 1962).

Temperature Receptors

A potentiality for response mechanisms based on temperature change is to be anticipated from the universal action of temperature on both physical and chemical processes. This maxim may be coupled with another; the lethal effects of extreme temperatures and the advantages of constant body temperatures place a high premium on behavior which relates an animal reliably to suitable temperatures. This potentiality and the strong biological advantage associated with its expression have been basic to the phylogeny of a delicate system of thermal reception as well as to many curious and intricate animal activities. Several examples have already been described (Chapter 10). Both poikilotherms and homeotherms avoid extremes and "select" a favorable temperature when placed in a gradient; warm-blooded animals regulate their body temperature through metabolic adjustments which are controlled by temperature receptors in the hypothalamus; many cold-blooded animals regulate their temperature through behavioral responses which are triggered by the cutaneous receptors; blood-sucking arthropods (mosquitos, lice) often locate their warm-blooded prey by delicate receptors sensitive to a gradient as narrow as 0.5°C; the rattlesnake, with the most acute temperature receptors known, is able to detect a rat-sized object 10°C warmer than its environment at a distance of 40 cm after only 0.5 sec (corresponding to a threshold of 0.001° to 0.002°C). Behavior based on temperature reception may be extremely intricate. This is well illustrated by the curious activities of a family of birds, the Megapodidae in Australia, which incubate their eggs in mounds of rotting vegetation and adjust the temperature of the nest almost continually throughout the day by changing the amount of insulating or fermenting material which covers the eggs. *Leipoa* males may be busy for three to seven hours each day from September to March. They evidently obtain their cues from thermal receptors on the face or inside the mouth; the animals show a characteristic probing behavior, repeatedly thrusting their heads into the sand beside the eggs with mouth open and then proceeding to adjust the blanket which covers the eggs. These and other interesting examples of behavior which depend on temperature receptors are reviewed by Murray (1962).

Although human experience, as well as these observations of temperature-dependent behavior at all levels in phylogeny, leave no doubt of the existence of temperature receptors, there are still many uncertainties about the detailed mechanisms. Murray (1962) has reviewed the literature and emphasized the unsatisfactory state of present knowledge concerning the nature of the receptor organs and their mode of excitation.

MORPHOLOGY

At one time textbooks of mammalian physiology showed two distinct nerve endings associated respectively with the sensations of heat and cold. Among the lower vertebrates, the lateral line was considered to play a dominant part in temperature reception because of the marked effect of temperature on the electric potentials which can always be monitored in its nerves; evidence for thermal reception by the ampullae of Lorenzini in elasmobranchs seemed even more convincing. Among the arthropods, thermosensitive hairs have been described on the antennae or legs of several different species. In each case investigators attributed temperature reception to morphologically distinct receptor organs. The evidence, however, was circumstantial and is now considered inadequate. On the contrary, temperature reception probably depends on the branching processes of free nerve endings. This at least is true of the two situations most carefully analyzed by electrophysiological methods, viz., the thermal receptors in the cat's tongue (Zotterman, 1953, 1959) and the facial pits of the crotalid snakes (Bullock, 1959*a*). In the latter, nerve fibers end freely in palmate expansions with numerous fine branching processes; from 500 to 1500 of these expanded endings are found in one square millimeter of the pit-membrane of the rattlesnake.

TRANSDUCER MECHANISM

Concepts of the physiology of thermal reception have had a history which is somewhat parallel to that of the morphology. Earlier hypotheses assumed some indirect action of temperature on the dendrites concerned with electrogenesis. Temperature-sensitive mechanical or thermal processes were postulated as steps in the excitation of nerves. Thermal expansion of materials in the ampullae of Lorenzini, changes in volume of gases or liquids in thermal sensillae of insects and changes in tension of elastic elements were some of the suggested physical means of exciting cell membranes; chemical theories were based on temperature coefficients of reactants involved in the syntheses of transmitter substances (acetylcholine) or of the enzymes concerned with their destruction. These hypotheses seem to be disappearing with those which attribute the receptor action to special morphological cell types.

It now seems likely that the temperature effect is directly on the processes concerned with electrogenesis in the free nerve endings which serve as receptors. After a careful review of the available information, Murray (1962) concludes that "enough is now known or will soon be known of the physical and chemical basis of nerve activity and of the way in which the various processes are affected by temperature, for a plausible explanation of thermoreceptor transduction to be made without invoking any other special mechanisms." An understanding of the details is still very inadequate, but there are temperature-sensitive processes in electrogenesis which are associated both with membrane permeability and the operation of the cation pump; understanding of temperature reception will probably be in terms of its action on these processes and not by indirect mechanical or chemical transducer mechanisms.

19

Effector Organs and The Physiology of Movement

It is by the effector organs that animals express their unique characteristics. Specialized structures for locomotion, the production of electricity, bioluminescence and rapid changes in color are virtually absent from the plant world. It is true that plants may show movements, but these are usually based on growth or turgor and not on a specialization of contractile proteins as is the case with animals. Only the amoeba-like slime molds, the flagellated algal cells or the sex cells of a few higher plants possess this kind of motile cell. All of the multicellular animals, on the other hand, depend on muscular movements for the activity of visceral organs and usually for locomotion as well. Glands also are universal effector organs among multicellular animals. Electric organs, luminescent structures and the activities of chromatophores occur in many different animals, although they do not play as general a role as the organs of locomotion and secretion. There are also several unusual effectors of very limited distribution such as the nematocysts or stinging hairs of coelenterates and the colloblasts or adhesive cells of the ctenophores; their physiology is not considered here since it has little bearing on the story of animal phylogeny. Furthermore, secretion will not be separately treated but mentioned only with the physiology of the organs and systems which depend on this process. The present discussion is confined to the mechanisms which produce movement, to the electric organs, the luminescent structures and the chromatophores. Motility is considered in this chapter; the other three processes are dealt with in Chapter 20.

Mechanisms Producing Movement

Animal locomotion and complex visceral activities, such as the propulsion of materials through ciliated or muscled tubes, may have evolved from the changing shapes shown by some of the enzyme and protein molecules which participate in the fundamental energy exchanges of life. Mitochondria, both *in vitro* and *in vivo,* may very slowly swell and contract, sometimes with oscillating regularity (Lehninger, 1962*a,b*). These changes, which are due to the NON-OSMOTIC uptake and extrusion of water, are directly linked to cellular respiration. Several different substances (phosphate, calcium ions, thyroxine) will induce swelling, but only in the presence of endogenous respiration or added substrates; phosphorylating respiration or ATP ALONE will cause contraction.

Lehninger postulates that the enzymes of the respiratory chain are "mechanoenzymes." They convert the oxidation-reduction energy not only into phosphate-bond energy of ATP but also into mechanical energy by changing their molecular arrangement in the mitochondrial membranes. It is of interest that a number of other important protein molecules change their configuration with their functional state; the change from oxygenated to deoxygenated hemoglobin and the change of cytochrome *c* from the oxidized to the reduced form are characterized by significant alterations in protein structure (Lehninger, 1962*a*; Perutz, 1964). In the present context, the most significant observations are the striking similarities between the enzymatic and mechanochemical properties of the muscle protein actomyosin and the energy-coupling mechanisms in the mitochondrial membranes. Lehninger finds similarities in pH optima, in the effects of heavy metals and azide, in stimulation of ATPase by DNP, involvement of divalent cations and other biochemical characteristics as well as the changes in shape.

Mitosis is another universal cellular activity which may be based on a physiology similar to that of the motile proteins of cilia and muscle. The slow movements of the elements in the mitotic spindle show several suggestive similarities to the more rapid ones of cilia and muscle fibrils (Inoué, 1959). Fundamental principles common to all motile phenomena were postulated almost one hundred years ago (Weber, 1958), and it now seems that the molecular biologists of the twentieth century may provide the evidence to support such a hypothesis.

THE BASIC MECHANISMS INVOLVED IN THE MOVEMENTS OF CELLS

Movement depends on special protein structures which actively change their form or position to produce an elongation or a contraction.

The ancestral unicellular or acellular animals probably experimented with several different arrangements before muscles and cilia were selected as the most satisfactory structures for locomotion.

Present-day protozoans support such a hypothesis. An *Amoeba* rounds up when stimulated and then lengthens markedly (without any pull from the outside) as it spreads out and "crawls away." Some ciliates possess TRICHOCYSTS and others have MYONEMES in addition to their rhythmically beating cilia. Trichocysts are small bodies in the outer layers of the cytoplasm which may explode either spontaneously or when stimulated. In exploding they discharge elongated threads some 6 to 7 times their original length; myonemes are contractile fibrils in the pellicle which contract to alter the body of the animal. The myoneme in the stalk of *Vorticella* has attracted considerable physiological interest because of its accessibility and superficial resemblance to a muscle fibril. *Vorticella* is shaped like an inverted bell with a long stalk resembling the handle on the bell. The stalk which attaches the animal to the substrate consists of a central contractile myoneme within a flexible sheath. When stimulated, the contraction of the myoneme bends the sheath into a tight spiral and the animal rapidly withdraws. As the myoneme relaxes the stalk straightens out because of the elasticity of the sheath.

Thus, the protozoans have realized three different kinds of movement: elongation, contraction and rhythmic vibration (cilia). Studies of the biochemistry and cellular physiology of these systems, however, have shown the superficiality of such a classification of fundamental mechanisms. The contraction of the muscle fiber and the stalk of *Vorticella*, although apparently alike, are based on somewhat different biochemical systems.

Contractile models. Dead cell models have proved most valuable in the analysis of the basically different processes involved in movement. The first of these was prepared from vertebrate skeletal muscle by Szent-Györgyi (1949) who used 50 per cent aqueous glycerol to extract pieces of the psoas muscle from rabbits. This extraction removes the soluble constituents of the sarcoplasm (proteins, enzymes, substrates) and leaves little more than the fibrous contractile elements. Cellular metabolism is no longer possible, but the models still contract when ATP is added under appropriate conditions, and in doing so they exhibit many of the characteristics of intact contracting muscle. This isolation of the power-plant from the contractile machinery has permitted a much more precise analysis of the activities of both. Hoffman-Berling (1960) has applied the same technique to other motile cells such as flagella, trichocysts, *Vorticella* stalks, amoebae and fibroblasts.

By means of strong salt solutions it is possible to dissolve the contractile proteins of muscle. When these solutions are squirted through a fine orifice, well-organized threads of actomyosin are formed, and these also will shorten and perform work under conditions comparable to those which initiate muscle contraction. Such threads were first produced by Weber in 1934 (see reviews by Weber, 1958, 1960). Contractile protein systems of this kind have also been prepared from slime molds and sarcoma cells, but several other motile systems have not yet been successfully dissolved and reorganized (Hoffman-Berling, 1960).

Studies of cell models and contractile protein threads reveal four physiological types of motile systems (Weber, 1958): (1) the stretching and (2) contraction of organelles by Ca^{++} (these are prevented or reversed by ATP), (3) the stretching movements induced by ATP and other polyphosphates and (4) the contraction produced exclusively by ATP and related nucleoside triphosphates. All of these movements are either initiated by ATP or reversed and inhibited by ATP, and in each case this is evidently the ultimate source of energy.

Movements inhibited or reversed by ATP. All motile systems which have been examined from the multicellular animals are driven by ATP. Among the protozoans, however, two are known to be induced by ATP-free reactions (Hoffman-Berling, 1960). One of these, the trichocyst, is an elongation; the other, *Vorticella's* myoneme, is a contraction.

Although the myoneme of the *Vorticella* stalk is like a minute muscle, models of the stalk do not contract on the addition of ATP. On the contrary, their contraction seems to be physiologically triggered by calcium ions. Several other substances may produce a similar effect. Sr^{++} and the ions of the quaternary ammonium bases are very effective; Ba^{++} has a weak action while Mg^{++} and Be^{++} are inactive. Removal of the calcium by the chelating agent EDTA (ethylenediaminetetraacetate) reverses the contraction and relaxes the stalk. Under natural conditions calcium is assumed to be the active agent. Since the preparations used in these studies are cell models and lack the capacities to generate energy, it can be argued that the calcium is acting directly on the contractile proteins.

Even though ATP does not initiate contraction in the stalk, it is assumed that the energy of the system is ultimately derived from its high energy bonds. The details are not yet clear, but if ATP is added to the contracted model the system relaxes; under certain conditions ATP will induce a rhythm of spontaneous contractions and relaxations. The relaxation is quite different from that produced by EDTA which is a permanent condition due to the removal of Ca^{++}. The evidence summarized by Hoffman-Berling (1960) indicates that the ATP effect is on the contractile proteins rather than on the calcium. In the *Vorticella* stalk, the chemical energy of ATP is apparently utilized in the relaxation phase and stored in the contractile system.

Isolated trichocysts elongate explosively in a manner comparable to living trichocysts when Ca^{++}, Sr^{++} or certain other ions (but not Mg^{++}) are added. Again Ca^{++} is probably the physiologically active agent. This system is also inhibited by ATP; in the presence of ATP the isolated trichocysts fail to elongate when Ca^{++} is added. In this case, also, the ATP inhibition is not due to Ca^{++} binding but seems to depend on a complexing with the contractile proteins. These interesting models are not yet completely understood, but they show very clearly that there are motile systems in the animal world which operate very differently from those present in muscles and cilia.

ATP-driven movements. At all levels in animal phylogeny some motile cells are activated by ATP. The two ATP-inhibited systems just described are exceptional even among the protozoans.

Active contractions are readily induced by ATP in glycerol-extracted amoebae and amniotic fibroblasts as well as in muscle cells. This activity also depends on the presence of Mg^{++}, a suitable pH and definite ionic concentrations. The other nucleoside triphosphates may replace ATP but are neither as powerful nor as effective; adenosine monophosphate (AMP), creatine phosphate, other organic phosphates and the inorganic polyphosphates are inactive. Conditions required for contraction of the amoeboid and muscle cell models are similar in every respect; differences are quantitative, and the indications are that comparable machinery is responsible in both cases.

ATP is also required for the relaxation of muscle and fibroblast models. Its action, however, is quite different in the processes of contraction and relaxation. In the shortening process, the pyrophosphate bond is hydrolyzed by the muscle ATPase; relaxation, on the contrary, takes place in preparations poisoned by Mersalyl, a substance which prevents the splitting of ATP by poisoning the enzyme ATPase. Although the cleavage of ATP is not required for muscle relaxation, its presence is essential. Contracted models fail to relax if all the ATP is removed; they enter a condition of rigor. The binding of ATP to the contractile protein without subsequent splitting has a plasticizing effect; in this action it may be replaced not only by the other nucleoside triphosphates but also by any of the inorganic polyphosphates (Weber, 1960). All conditions for relaxation are comparable in the models of amoebae, fibroblasts and muscle cells.

Hoffman-Berling (1960) summarizes the biochemical studies on the movements of the mitotic apparatus; these involve active elongations as well as contractions. Both are ATP-driven systems with biochemical requirements similar to those of the muscle and fibroblastic models. The inescapable conclusion seems to be that mechanisms responsible for the motility of such highly specialized structures as muscle cells are both phylogenetically and ontogenetically older than the muscle cells themselves.

Amoeboid Movement

The elusive *Amoeba* has provided generations of students with their first great challenge in zoology. Ever since these minute masses of protoplasm were first described by Rösel von Rosenhof in 1755 (Allen, 1961) microscopists have attempted to explain their gentle agitations and delicate gliding movements, for it is felt that these activities may be fundamentally primitive and might provide clues to the general physiology of locomotion by cells.

The functional morphology of amoeboid cells is detailed in many familiar zoological texts and will not be repeated here. Excellent bibliographies are available (Allen, 1961; Prosser and Brown, 1961). The present discussion is confined to current hypotheses of the mechanics of the movement.

The first half of the twentieth century saw the formulation, experimental examination and eventual discard of hypotheses which attempted to localize the motive forces in changing surface tensions or in sol-gel transformations of colloidal cytoplasm (De Bruyn, 1947). At present there is a return to the much earlier theory of protoplasmic contraction. In detail, the current theories of contraction bear little similarity to the early ones proposed by Dujardin (Allen, 1961), but the general concept is the same since both postulate forces which depend on the contraction of the cellular proteins.

Allen (1961, 1962), one of the active students of amoeboid movement describes the recent work. On the basis of optical studies and measurements of the cytoplasmic consistency and the endoplasmic velocity in different parts of the cell he advocates the terminology shown in Fig. 19.1; this involves an abandonment of the terms "plasmagel" and "plasmasol" and the theories associated with these terms. Instead, an active contraction of the cytoplasm is postulated either in the fountain zone or in the tail process (uroid). If this contraction is in the fountain zone, then the animal is being pulled along; but if it occurs in the uroid the animal is being pushed forward. Allen regards the former theory as the more likely; he also finds it applicable to a wider variety of amoeboid forms (slime molds and foraminiferans as well as amoebae) and suggests a possible parallel with muscular movement.

The evidence for contraction in the fountain zone is still indirect. In part, it depends on the fact that amoebae continue to stream after rupture of the plasmalemma. Since this would presumably lower any internal tension associated with squeezing at the tail end, movement should cease if it depended on tail end pressures. Further, a two-way streaming of the cytoplasm is sometimes observed in intact amoebae and regularly seen in the fine pseudopodia (reticulopodia) of foraminiferans (Jahn and Rinaldi, 1959). A localized pressure due to posterior contraction could not create a two-way stream, while a shortening of proteins at a sharp bend in the cytoplasm such as the fountain zone or the tip of a reticulopodium might do just this.

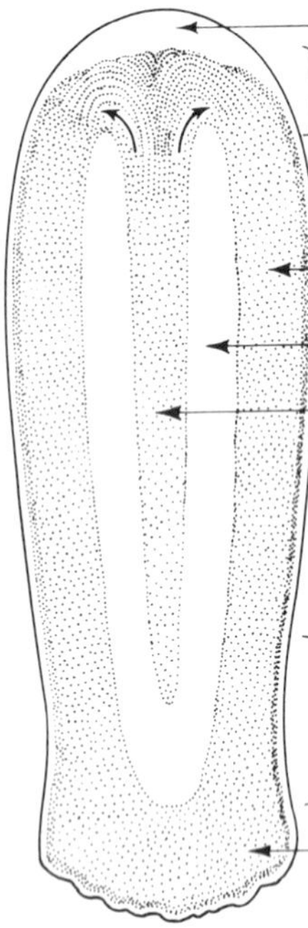

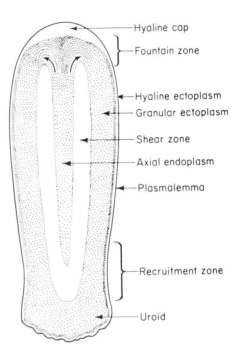

Fig. 19.1. Structure of an *Amoeba* as described by Allen (1960*b*).

The endoplasm is evidently not homogeneous but contains a central core or plug of more rigid material separated from the ectoplasmic tube by a fluid mantle, the shear zone. Allen postulates a shortening or movement of the molecules in the front end which pulls this axial endoplasm toward the forward end of the ectoplasmic tube. The hyaline cap or watery area at the front end of an advancing *Amoeba* is presumably due to SYNERESIS or the squeezing of liquid from the contracting gel. The fluid of the hyaline cap appears to move posteriorly between the plasmalemma and the ectoplasmic tube, to be reabsorbed in the recruitment zone as the ectoplasmic material softens and relaxes to join the endoplasmic stream (Allen, 1962).

Movements of Cilia and Flagella

Cilia and flagella are vibratile extensions of the cell surface which permit mechanical work without any marked change in the form of the effector cell. All the major groups of animals, except the nematodes and the arthropods, make use of them to propel either individual cells, such as protozoans and spermatozoa, or entire multicellular animals such as planarians and ctenophores, or to move fluids and adherent materials over the lining surfaces of tubular organs. In some places they have been remarkably modified to produce such varied structures as undulating membranes or the sensory processes of photoreceptor cells.

Gray (1928), in a classical study of cilia and flagella, described their comparative morphology in different organisms and classified the several different forms of movement as revealed by the light microscope. His book remains a rich source of information on their mechanical performance and capacity to do work under varying loads and at different temperatures, pH, ionic equilibria or in the presence of narcotics.

Several ingenious theories for ciliary locomotion were proposed by the earlier workers (Gray, 1928). However, with only the light microscope to reveal their micromorphology, these hypotheses were scarcely more satisfactory than Leeuwenhoek's concept of "diverse incredibly thin feet, or little legs, which were moved very nimbly" (Satir, 1961). Here again the electron microscope has probably provided a clue which will lead to a true understanding of these delicate machines. Although the mechanism is still not understood, the revelation of a constant fibrillar pattern suggests a common basis for ciliary movement and muscular contraction; current theories are based on contractions of these fibrils.

Cilia may range in length from several microns to several hundred microns, but their diameter is surprisingly constant—ranging from about 0.1 to 0.5 μ. This uniformity in diameter is a reflection of the regular pattern of internal fibrils (Fig. 19.2). The covering membrane of a cilium is continuous with the plasma membrane. Just inside the plasma membrane, around the periphery, are nine fibrils (sometimes a multiple of nine) about 0.028μ in diameter with two additional fibrils of smaller size in the center of the organelle. The nine peripheral filaments seem to merge at the base into a hollow tube which forms the basal granule; the two central fibrils do not seem to reach the basal granule, but all the fibrils appear to merge at the outer tip of the cilium. This uniform fibrillar pattern suggests very strongly that the motility depends on these fibrils and that the arrangement is significant for their action.

Several hypotheses have now been based on the contraction of the fibrils. Bradfield's (1955) theory typifies present lines of reasoning. He suggests that the effective stroke is due to the simultaneous contraction of five of the peripheral fibrils along their entire length; the other four fibrils remain idle during the effective stroke but then slowly contract, beginning at the base, to produce the recovery stroke. It is assumed that the

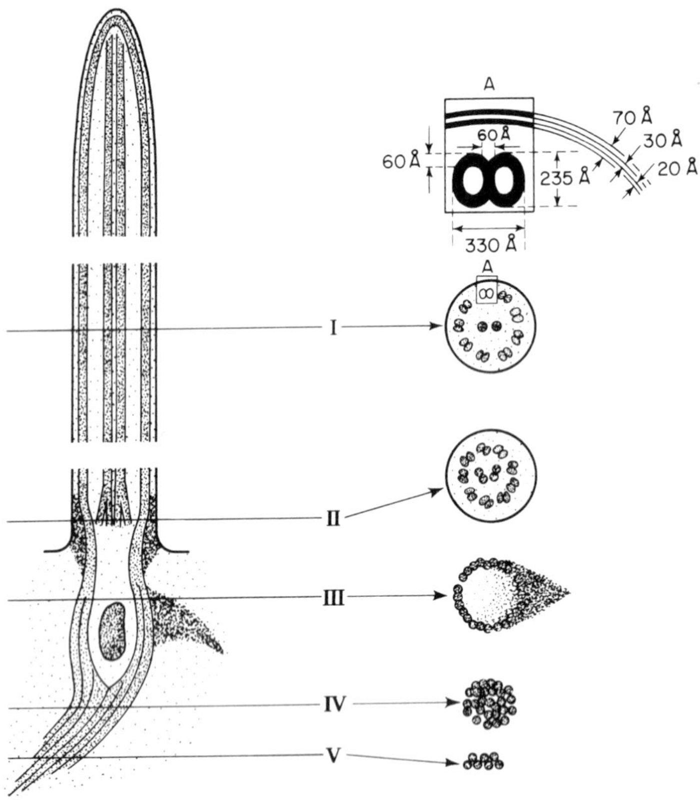

Fig. 19.2. Structure of the cilium as revealed by electron microscopy. [Rhodin and Dalhman (1956).]

timing or triggering mechanism resides in the basal body and that the central fibrils serve as transmission lines to provide rapid conduction up the cilium. Fibrils shorten simultaneously and rapidly throughout most of their length during the effective stroke; the cilium bends sharply forward as a stiff rod because of an internal fluid pressure. This group of fibrils then relaxes during the recovery phase, and the impulse spreads around the basal granule to initiate local contractions in the other fibrils; these bend more gently since the impulse passes along them slowly from the base. The result is a series of gentle curves starting from the base and bringing the cilium from the horizontal to the vertical position (Fig. 19.3). There are several different forms of ciliary and flagellar movement (Fig. 19.3), and Bradfield (1955) suggests modifications of the theory which might explain the two-dimensional and corkscrew-like waves of flagella. Fawcett (1961) and Sleigh (1962) discuss this and other theories which depend on fibrillar contractions.

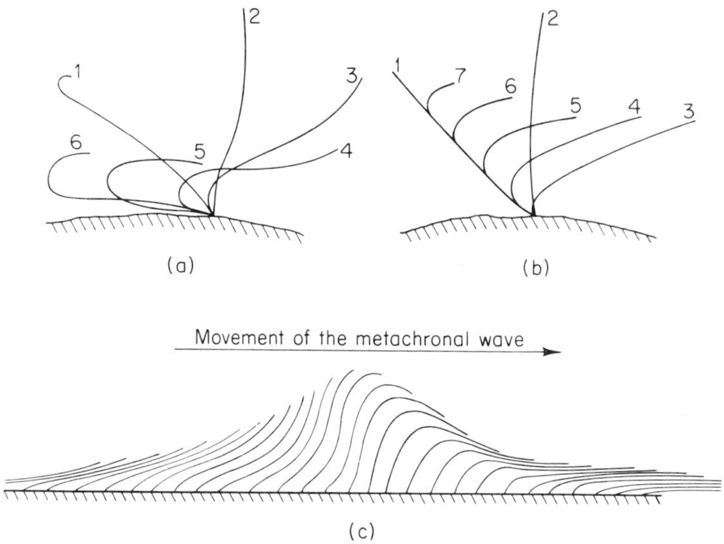

Fig. 19.3. Diagram of sequence of movements by cilia of *a*, *Sabellaria* and *b*, *Paramecium*, *c*, diagram of metachronal wave of *Opalina* showing the component cilia. The plane of the beat is approximately in the plane of the paper, and successive movements of a cilium can be followed by moving along the row from right to left. The animal is moving towards the left. [Sleigh (1962).]

A coordination of activities is apparent in the rhythmic waves which move constantly over a ciliated epithelium. This rhythm is said to be ISOCHRONAL when all of the cilia beat together, and METACHRONAL when the successive cilia in each row beat in sequence to form a regular series of waves (Fig. 19.3). The latter is characteristic of most ciliated surfaces. It seems necessary to postulate a special mechanism for such a precise coordination, and two theories, advanced in the latter part of the nineteenth century, are still current. The neuroid theory postulates nerve-like impulses conducted through the protoplasm at the bases of the cilia; the mechanical theories hold that the movement of one cilium mechanically stimulates the next to action (Fawcett, 1961). Neither theory seems entirely satisfactory.

Different types of fibers are associated with the basal bodies in the cortical cytoplasm of protozoans, in the ciliated epithelia of molluscs and elsewhere. The "silver-line" system of the ciliate protozoan may be demonstrated with silver staining as a very regular lattice, and this morphology long ago suggested a neuromotor function for it. Other evidence for a neuroid transmission system at the base of the cilia has been adduced from the incoordination of movements which often follows microsurgery. Appropriate incisions in ciliates and in the gut or gill epithelia of molluscs have been shown to alter the rhythm on the two sides of the cut. However, the electron microscope fails to demonstrate any morphological connections between the fibrils and the basal bodies of cilia, and it seems necessary to reject a simple neuroid theory (Fawcett, 1961). The arguments which led Gray (1930) to discard this theory more than thirty years ago are still valid. He found the rates of conduction slower than in any known nerve transmission, an absence of centers where stimuli might arise and no serious disturbance in physiological polarity when ciliated cells were isolated from one another.

Although the concept of a system of fibers with nerve-like transmission is no longer tenable, there is adequate evidence, both of a biochemical and physiological nature, for conduction as well as contraction in ciliary movement. Glycerin-extracted models of cilia and flagella may be preserved for weeks and then activated by ATP. When such preparations are treated with surface-active agents (digitonin or saponin) the models of flagella still show rhythmic activity in response to ATP, but the ciliated cells lose their coordinated beat. It is assumed that the surface-active agents remove a lipid or lipoprotein which is essential for the coordination of the beat; this indicates the presence of elements responsible for coordination as well as contraction.

Further, physiologists find that nervous stimulation sometimes alters the activity in ciliated epithelia, and this too suggests a coordination under central control. Prosser and Brown (1961) review the literature. Responses to nerve stimulation have been clearly demonstrated in ciliary systems of ctenophores, turbellarians, annelids, molluscs and frogs; both excitatory and inhibitory effects have been noted. Cilia on the pharyngeal epithelia of the frog beat more rapidly with waves of greater amplitude when certain of the cranial nerves are stimulated; they appear to be under autonomic control. Both adrenaline and acetylcholine have been tested and, although some of the recorded data are debatable, the acetylcholine response seems incontestable in a number of preparations. Serotonin (5-HT) has also been used and has an extremely potent cilioexcitatory action on the lateral gill cilia of *Mytilus* (Gosselin, 1961). These pharmacological effects may or may not reflect a physiological action by transmitter substances. In any case, it seems clear that some ciliated epithelia have come under the control of the nervous system.

In general, it is concluded that neither a simple mechanical theory nor one of neuroid transmission satisfactorily accounts for the control and coordination observed in ciliary movement. Clearly there is a marked automaticity, but a complete explanation seems to demand a pacemaker susceptible to nervous and other influences. It also requires a mechanism in which the action of one cilium can modify others. In short, an INTRAciliary excitation process as well as INTERciliary conduction seems to operate (Fawcett, 1961). There are still many challenging problems for physiologists interested in cilia.

Muscular Movement

Studies of muscle have formed a large segment of physiology—particularly in the laboratory—ever since the beginning of experimental work in animal biology. Almost two centuries ago, Galvani (1737–98) was fascinated by the twitchings of skinned frog legs in response to electrical stimuli; these preparations still pose some unanswered questions (Wilkie, 1956) and never fail to provide interest for the beginner in zoology.

An appreciation of the structural basis of contractile tissues stems from Bowman's classical description of its fibrillar nature in 1840. Details, insofar as they could be revealed by the light microscope, were gradually established during the latter half of the nineteenth century, and the mechanical properties were carefully described within the limits of the recording instruments available. Familiar experiments with the frog gastrocnemius, loops of intestine and the hearts of turtles and frogs were introduced into physiology during this period (Verworn, 1899; Bayliss, 1920).

The basic biochemistry of muscle was established during the first half of the twentieth century. This period opened with Fletcher and Hopkins' description of lactic acid production in 1907—to be followed by an elucidation of the glycolytic changes during the next 25 years. Lohmann's scheme for the ATP-creatine phosphate source of triggering energy was postulated in the middle thirties (Chapter 7). This was largely the biochemistry of the sarcoplasm; the studies of the muscle proteins (although initiated by Kühne in 1859) came somewhat later. Some of the most exciting discoveries in muscle biochemistry took place between 1940 and 1950 with the recognition that myosin was an ATPase enzyme, with its crystallization and with the descriptions of actomyosin, tropomyosin and paramyosin.

The second half of this century has been marked by an extension of the morphological analysis with the electron microscope and persistent attempts to associate the biochemical with the mechanical events. Many of the pertinent details have probably now been recorded, but there is still a great uncertainty regarding the linking of the chemical reactions which surround the binding and splitting of ATP with the contraction, relaxation or movement of the fibrillar proteins.

Although the pioneer physiologists devoted considerable attention to a variety of contractile systems such as cilia, flagella, protoplasmic streaming, amoebae and *Vorticella* (Verworn, 1899), interest in the comparative physiology of muscular tissues is recent. Especially since 1950, details of micromorphology in many different species have been recorded, and an intensive examination has been made of the neuromuscular physiology of animals from all phyletic levels. The functioning of intact muscles depends on the manner in which they are activated and also on such passive elements as connective tissue. Studies of neuromuscular physiology are basic to an understanding of muscular movement.

Literature on the physiology of muscle is now abundant. Monographs edited by Bourne (1960) are most comprehensive. The comparative physiologist will also find much of value in Ritchie (1928) and in the recent discussions by Hoyle (1957, 1962). The historical notes just mentioned can be readily checked and amplified from these books.

FIBRILLAR SYSTEM

Like other types of animal cells, the muscle cell contains an elaborate system of enzymes for the production of ATP. Power production and cell movement operate as a unified system. The sources of ATP were described in Chapter 7, and the channels by which it reaches the contractile elements are shown in Fig. 19.4. This shows that the glycolytic enzymes concerned with the formation of lactic acid from glycogen or glucose are found in the structureless areas of the cytoplasm (sarcoplasm in muscle), while the carbon fragments which they form are utilized to produce large amounts of ATP within the mitochondria (sometimes called sarcosomes in muscle).

These enzyme systems probably show many functional correlations with muscle physiology, although there is relatively little information on the comparative aspects. It has, however, been noted that vertebrate skeletal muscle, which can accumulate a considerable oxygen debt, has relatively small mitochondria in comparison with cardiac muscle where the mitochondria are both larger and more numerous. The sarcosomes of insect flight muscle are the most numerous and the largest observed in any animal cells and attain as much as 40 per cent of the weight of the muscle in *Phormia*. Likewise the very active mantle muscle fibers of the cephalopods have a much more conspicuous mitochondrial system than the tonic fibers of the lamellibranch adductors. Similar correlations between activity and the development of the mitochondrial system have been made in some other groups, but relatively few forms have been examined (Hanson and Lowy, 1960).

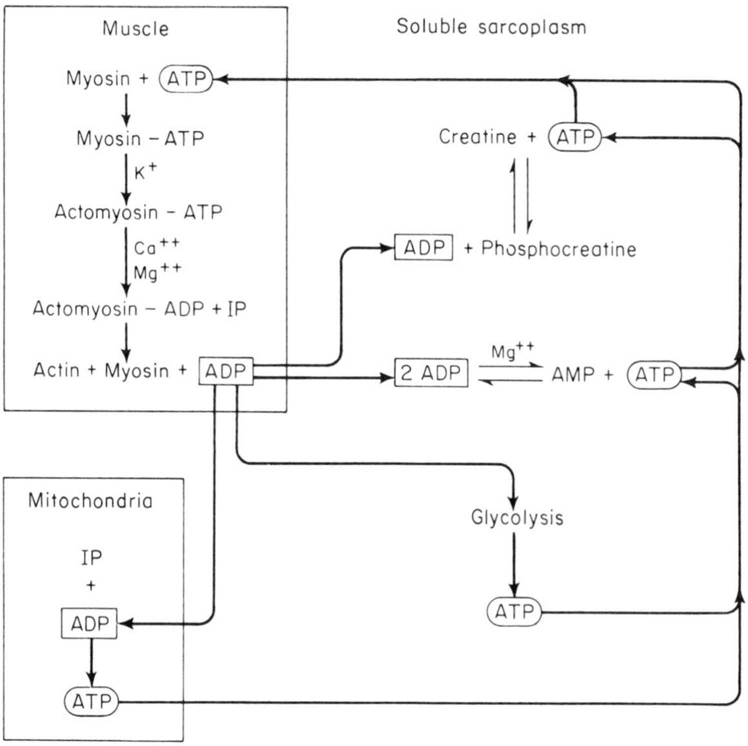

Fig. 19.4. The production of ATP and its utilization within the contractile elements of the muscle cell. [Siekevitz (1959).]

Muscle cells are called fibers because of their elongated form. They all contain longitudinally arranged, submicroscopic elements, the MYOFILAMENTS, composed of long protein molecules concerned with the motility of the cells. These myofilaments may be organized into MYOFIBRILS.

It is customary to distinguish two histological types of muscle on the basis of the presence or absence of distinct transverse striations under the light microscope. These were first described for vertebrate muscles. The striated fibers are characterized by alternating light ISOTROPIC (weakly birefringent) and dark ANISOTROPIC (strongly birefringent) transverse bands. Two types of striated fiber are found in the vertebrates. In the skeletal muscles large multinucleate cells are arranged in parallel bundles; in cardiac muscles, smaller uninucleate cells are separated by intercalated discs and connected in a sheet to form a net with an irregular arrangement of longitudinal slits between the fibers. The smooth or non-striated fiber of vertebrates is uninucleate and spindle-shaped and varies in length from about 20 μ in small blood vessels to about 500 μ in the pregnant uterus.

Although these two morphological types are also characteristic of the invertebrate animals, there are several variations of the smooth type and such a range in size and form, with heterogeneity in the same muscle, that it is more logical to think of a broad spectrum rather than of two types of muscle cells. No clear phylogenetic trends have been detected. The range among primitive multicellular animals is almost as great as it is in the entire animal kingdom. Some coelenterates contain classic smooth muscle fibers, and others have evenly striated fibers (swimming muscles of some of the medusae); there are, moreover, many curious types of the musculo-epithelial cells which combine the functions of motility with those of digestion or protection. Coelenterate contractile elements range from epithelial cells with mere tails containing contractile threads to highly specialized fibers with cross-striations superficially similar to those of vertebrate skeletal muscle (Hyman, 1940; Horridge, 1954; Hoyle, 1957). The latter specialization is evidently associated with the rapid rhythmic swimming movements of the medusae; there seems to be a similar trend toward cross-striations associated with more rapid movements throughout the animal world, but the correlation is by no means perfect (Prosser and Brown, 1961).

Invertebrate muscles vary greatly in fiber size and in the form and distribution of the myofilaments. Striated fibers up to 2 cm long have been described in the anterior byssal retractor of *Mytilus;* in general, smooth muscle cells whether vertebrate or invertebrate, are rarely more than 10 to 15 μ in diameter, but those of *Ascaris* measure as much as 1 mm $\times$ 0.2 mm in cross section. Some of the thickest striated muscle cells are found among the arthropods; those in the flight muscles of the Diptera or the shell muscles of the giant barnacle *Balanus nubilus* reach about 2 mm in diameter (Hoyle and Smyth, 1963).

The myofilaments form the functional elements in the cytoplasm of the muscle fiber, and it is their development which provides the most characteristic features of the muscle types. In some CLASSIC SMOOTH MUSCLES (retractors of the pharynx and penis of *Helix*, retractors of *Phascolosoma*, vertebrate smooth muscle) the myofilaments are not grouped into myofibrils but scattered through the cell parallel to its long axis. Thus, the sarcoplasm appears homogeneous with the light microscope and displays little or no evidence of its fibrillar nature.

In the HELICAL SMOOTH MUSCLES of many invertebrates (locomotor muscles of annelids, cephalopods, intervertebral muscles of ophiuroids) the myofibrils or bundles of myofilaments follow a regular spiral course around the fiber. In other words, each fiber has a core of sarcoplasm about which are wound ribbon-like myofibrils (bundles of myofilaments). Examined under the light microscope, such muscles may display a diagonal striation or a diamond pattern ("double-oblique striation") as different parts of the spiral come into focus; this apparent striation is not comparable to the cross-banding of striated muscles which depends on the organization of two kinds of the myofilaments. The wide distribution of helical smooth muscle in invertebrate organs of locomotion suggests some special functional significance, but there is at present no satisfactory explanation of the physiology of the spiral arrangement (Hanson and Lowy, 1960; Hoyle, 1962).

The PARAMYOSIN SMOOTH MUSCLE is known only in the molluscs where it apparently serves a tonic function associated with the prolonged and continuous contractions of adductor muscles. The tenacity with which a bivalve can maintain tightly closed shells is evidence of its capacity in this regard. Structurally these fibers contain two types of filaments: (1) the paramyosin filaments which are extremely large, ranging up to 1500 Å in diameter; each filament is composed of a number of ribbon-like elements of paramyosin (a special water-insoluble form of tropomyosin) stacked side by side to form the filaments; (2) a few small (50 Å) filaments of actomyosin. The mitochondria occur only in small numbers. The prolonged tension which persists long after the active state may be related to the activities of these thick paramyosin filaments, although the evidence is only circumstantial (Hodge, 1959).

Striated muscle owes its appearance to the orderly arrangement of the myofilaments within the myofibrils. High magnifications provided by the electron microscope, together with X-ray diffraction and phase contrast or interference microscope studies of fresh preparations, indicate that the alternating light and dark bands (Fig. 19.5) are produced by the arrangement of two types of protein filaments. The thick filaments (about 110 Å in fixed vertebrate muscles) lie parallel to one another about 450 Å apart and form the anisotropic band; they probably consist of the protein myosin. The thin filaments of actin (about 50 Å in vertebrate muscle) are disposed in an orderly array between the thick ones as shown in

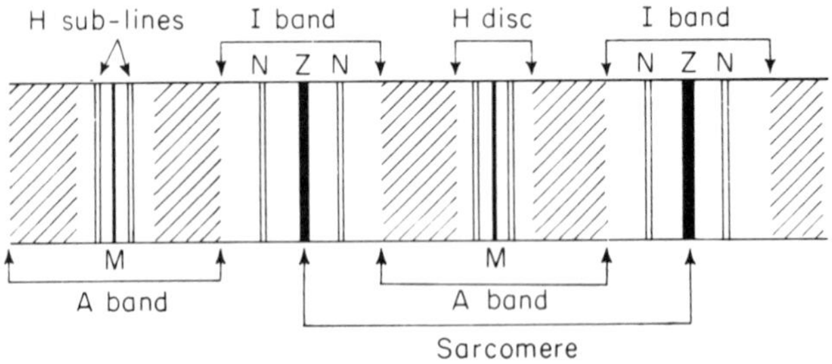

Fig. 19.5. Diagrammatic representation of cross bands and lines of the striated myofibril. The *M*, *N*, and *H* sub-lines are not always evident. [Perry (1960).]

Fig. 19.6. They are bisected by the *Z* membranes (delimiting the myofibril units or sarcomeres) and almost meet in the middle of the anisotropic band when the muscle is relaxed. The space between the ends of these thin actin filaments forms the *H* zone of the fiber (Fig. 19.5). A pattern of large and small dots (shown in the lower part of Fig. 19.6) is evident in electron micrographs of muscle cross sections and has been important in establishing the arrangement of the myofilaments. Large numbers of regularly-spaced lateral projections from the thick filaments have been described. These appear to touch the thin filaments and are thought to be significant in the sliding or ratchet-like action of the filaments which, according to a popular theory of contraction, is the significant event in the shortening of the muscle (Fig. 19.7; Huxley, 1958, 1960; Huxley and Hanson, 1960).

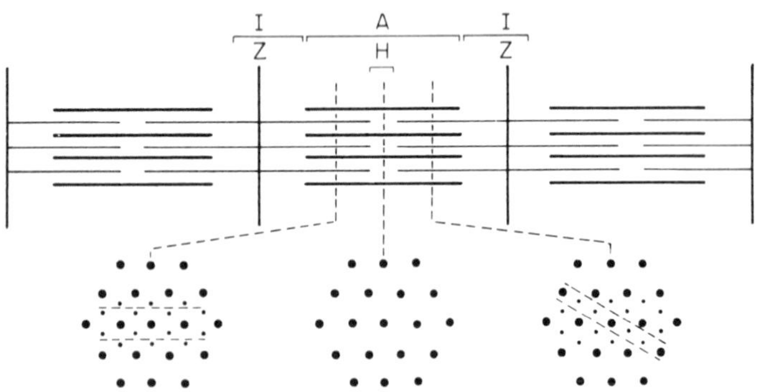

Fig. 19.6. Diagram illustrating the arrangement of the two kinds of protein filaments in a myofibril. At top are three sarcomeres in longitudinal section. Below are transverse sections through the filaments in the regions indicated. [Huxley and Hanson (1960).]

The first detailed descriptions of the myofilaments of striated muscle were based on studies of rabbit muscles; but muscles of representatives from all other vertebrate classes as well as several invertebrates (insects, crustaceans and molluscs) have now been examined (Perry, 1960; Hanson and Lowy, 1960). It is agreed that the striations in all cases are due to a comparable arrangement of myofilaments; these probably vary considerably in size and length, but the orderly disposition of the filaments of myosin and actin is basically the same.

The banding of striated muscle sometimes shows an *M* line (due to a slight thickening in the middle of the myosin filaments) in the central area of the *H* disc. Less frequently, *N* lines of unknown significance appear in the *I* band on either side of the *Z* membrane (Perry, 1960).

THE CONTRACTILE PROTEINS

There are three major classes of fibrous proteins associated with the contractile machinery of muscle—the MYOSINS (mol wt about 450,000), the ACTINS (mol wt about 60,000) and TROPOMYOSIN (mol wt about 53,000). The latter, although always present, occurs in relatively small amounts. In addition some invertebrate muscles contain PARAMYOSIN (mol wt about 134,000) with distinctive solubility and other properties. These proteins have been intensively studied by many biochemists since Kühne first prepared extracts of muscle which he called myosin in 1859. Their properties are described in the monographs and reviews already cited and also summarized in many places (Bailey, 1956; Hodge, 1959; Mommaerts, 1960). They will not be detailed here.

There are, however, several points of comparative physiological interest. One of these is the conservative nature of the actomyosin system. Actin and myosin with very similar properties have been extracted from many animals. Although the relative amounts of the two proteins vary and although there are indications of slight biochemical differences, no systematic patterns which might indicate phyletic trends have been established; the indications are that the actomyosin system appeared early in animal phylogeny and has remained virtually unchanged. A species specificity of proteins is expected but is not yet established with certainty for purified myosins and actins (Perry, 1960). Uncertainties are due to the variable combinations of the two components to form actomyosin, the effects of ATP level and ionic concentrations on this complex and on the characteristics of the two molecules.

Tropomyosin is also a universal component of the contractile system of fibrous proteins. Like actomyosin it seems to be of uniform character wherever found. Its localization in the myofibril (perhaps in the *Z* disc or the lateral projections on the myofilaments) suggests some contractile role or an essential structural component of the contractile system, but both its functions and location are still speculative (Perry, 1960).

Paramyosin is also called "insoluble tropomyosin" or tropomyosin *A*, but Hodge (1959) considers it sufficiently distinct chemically to justify the separate term. Paramyosin is known only among invertebrates, particularly in the adductor muscles of the molluscs, where it may play a vital role in the maintenance of tension that is characteristic of these muscles. This theory requires confirmation. From the comparative angle, this variant of the contractile proteins suggests some caution in emphasizing the uniformity of these compounds; there are still many animals whose muscles have not been studied by the biochemist.

Several other myofibrillar proteins occur in lesser amounts, but little or nothing is known of their physiology (Perry, 1960). In addition, there are numerous proteins other than the fibrous proteins in muscle cells (myoglobins, enzymes, foı example); the emphasis of uniformity in the actomyosin system should not obscure the fact that these other proteins vary markedly in different organs and different species of animals. Muscle proteins, like the plasma proteins discussed in Chapter 6, show distinct species specificity and have been used in systematic studies to investigate phylogenetic relationships (Tsuyuki *et al.*, 1962).

MECHANISMS OF CONTRACTION

The really significant question in the cellular physiology of muscle is the manner in which the protein molecules operate to produce muscular contraction and relaxation. Two hypotheses are currently under investigation. The older of these, and perhaps the simpler to visualize, postulates a folding (during contraction) and an unfolding (during relaxation) of the fibrous protein threads. It has been proposed in several forms, but all variants assume that the contractile elements remain extended while there is mutual repulsion of like charges along the molecule; the changes associated with contraction (hydrolysis of ATP and activity of Mg^{++}) produce equal numbers of positive charges among the negative ones causing the contractile element to fold or coil, thereby shortening the muscle. Many facts have been marshalled to support these FOLDING MECHANISMS, but they now seem less popular than the more recently suggested SLIDING MECHANISMS.

The sliding filament hypothesis was most strongly supported by the arrangements of myofilaments in glycerine-extracted vertebrate striated muscle as revealed in electron micrographs by Huxley and his associates (reviews cited). Figure 19.7 shows how the cross bridges on the thick filaments might pull the thin filaments in a kind of ratchet action. This requires the presence of active sites on the actin filaments into which the cross bridges temporarily hook to pull the filament a short distance and then release it and hook onto the next site. Thus, the hooks on the myosin filaments are oscillating bridges. Weber (1958, 1960) has postulated a series of chemical reactions which might lead to simultaneous ATP hydrolysis and a shifting of the molecules of the actin filaments alongside

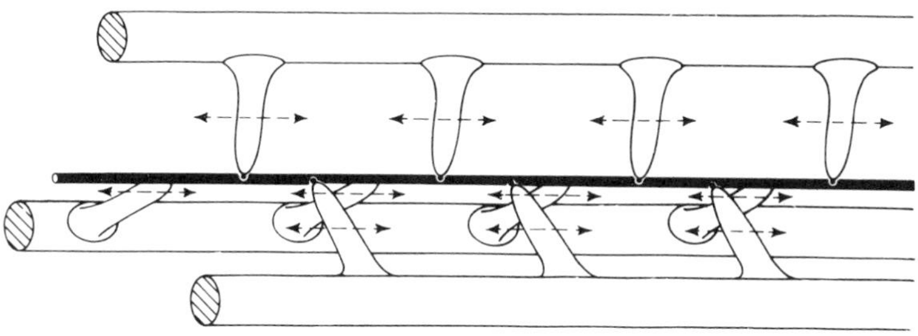

Fig. 19.7. Theory for action of sliding filaments in skeletal muscle. Cross-bridges or hooks on the thick (myosin) filaments are able to hook onto the thin black filament (actin) at the specific active sites. The arrows indicate that the bridges oscillate and thus produce muscular contraction by hooking onto an active site, pulling the thin filament a short distance, releasing it and then hooking onto the next active site. [Giese (1962) after Huxley (1958).]

those of myosin. In this, the ATP is supposed to activate a site on the actin by binding phosphate to an acid group; this then forms a succession of links with –SH groups, phenolic and alcoholic –OH groups.

The sliding filament theory was first advanced as an explanation for the contraction mechanism in vertebrate striated muscle; Lowy and Millman (1962, 1963) find it adequate to explain the contractions of paramyosin smooth muscles in the *Mytilus* byssus retractor and the cephalopod helical muscles of the mantle and funnel retractor, both of which contain two types of myofilaments. However, it has not been possible to demonstrate two types of filaments in some other types of smooth muscles, such as those of vertebrates. Even in vertebrate striated muscle it has been claimed that the filament lengths change during contraction (Sonnenblick *et al.*, 1963). There are other difficulties with the sliding filament theories (Morales, 1959), and the explanations may be considerably altered when the molecular details of muscular contraction (and relaxation) are fully understood.

MECHANICAL PROPERTIES OF MUSCLE

An emphasis on the homogeneity of the contractile proteins throughout the animal kingdom should not obscure the fact that the muscular organs are among the most versatile physiological machines (Pantin, 1956; Prosser, 1960). Contraction times range from those of the flight muscles of certain insects which have been clocked at less than a millisecond to those of the circular muscles in the column of sea anemones where a single contraction-relaxation sequence may require five or six minutes. Insect flight muscles are striated while those of the sea anemone are smooth, and, in general, striations are associated with the more rapidly contracting muscles. The correlation is not perfect, however; striated muscles in the jellyfish *Aurelia* have contraction times of about 1 second while the unstriated ones in the chromatophores of the squid *Loligo* operate in half this time. Speed of relaxation is just as variable (see Table 50 in Prosser and Brown, 1961). There may also be significant differences between contraction and relaxation times of a single muscle; both the slow and the rapidly operating fibers are often present within the same muscular organ.

Extent as well as speed of contraction is variable. In visceral organs such as the urinary bladder, which shows regular and remarkable changes in size, the smooth muscle may be passively extended to many different resting lengths. Striated muscles usually operate through the production of tension and do not change their length by more than about 20 to 30 per cent (Morales, 1959); the smooth muscle of the retractor of the snail *Helix* can shorten by 80 per cent of its extended length.

The responses of muscles also depend on the manner in which they are activated. Some, such as the skeletal muscles of vertebrates, respond to a single stimulus with a maximal twitch while others, such as crustacean skeletal muscles, fail to respond to a single stimulus no matter how intense; they require a rapid sequence of stimuli for excitation.

This versatility in the action of the muscular organs depends on three factors: (1) the organization of the myofilaments within the fibers as previously discussed, (2) the arrangement of the muscle cells and the non-contractile connective tissues and (3) the nervous control. Some of the mechanical properties of muscle, which depend on the first two of these, will now be considered. Nervous control is discussed in the final section on the contractile tissues.

Types of muscle contraction. If an isolated skeletal muscle such as a frog gastrocnemius (also a single muscle fiber) is momentarily stimulated, it changes from a flaccid organ into a much firmer structure which then more slowly becomes soft as it relaxes. If allowed to do so, it will shorten and then lengthen during the process. This is the familiar muscle TWITCH, a characteristic response to a single stimulus of threshold or greater intensity. By appropriate recording devices a graphic representation of the phenomenon (Fig. 19.8) is readily obtained; the time relationships and form of the contraction curve varies with the load.

If a muscle is stimulated a second time before it has relaxed it is again activated and responds to a somewhat greater degree, the precise response depending on the interval between successive stimuli. With a rapid series of stimuli (about 30/sec for frog muscles at 0° C) there is a complete fusion, individual responses are no longer evident, and the muscle shows the smooth maintained contraction called a TETANUS (Fig. 19.8).

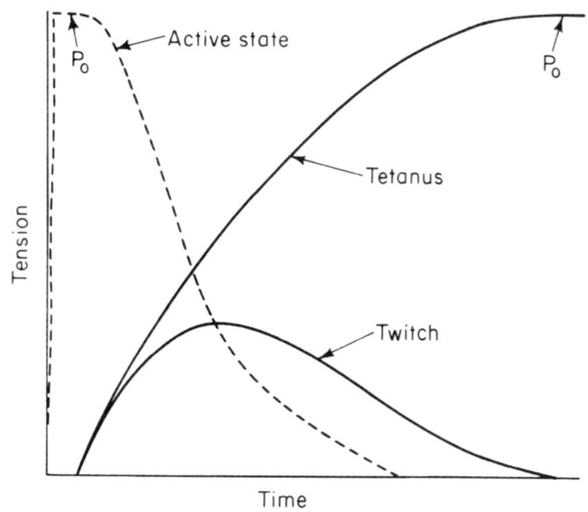

Fig. 19.8. Diagram showing the relation between tension and time for a twitch, a tetanus and the active state in vertebrate striated muscle. P_o is the maximum tension of which the fiber is capable. Stimulus begins at zero time. [Bard (1961).]

Muscles may do work by changing their lengths and moving weights for variable distances as in lifting or moving a heavy object. They may, on the other hand, develop tension and exert a force without any perceptible shortening as is the case when one attempts to lift an object which is impossibly heavy. Physiologists refer to the first kind of muscular activity as ISOTONIC (equal tension or constant load) and the second as ISOMETRIC (equal or fixed length). In either case, the time sequence of changes depends on the load lifted or the tension exerted as well as on the temperature, the physiological condition of the muscle, the species of animal and the type of muscle.

In the older techniques, isometric contractions were recorded mechanically with muscles lifting weights or operating against almost, but not quite, immovable springs or metal strips to produce movements of levers which recorded on moving papers. Suitable transducers are now available, and recordings obtained in this way permit a much more precise analysis of the contraction and relaxation phenomena.

The elastic elements in muscle. Physiological evidence for the existence and importance of the elastic components of muscle will be considered first.

If the length of an isolated muscle is recorded at rest in relation to a series of weights, the length-tension or stress-strain curve for the resting muscle is curvilinear as shown in the lower right area of Fig. 19.11. Tension begins to develop when the muscle is slightly longer than its normal *in situ* length and is a function of length up to the breaking point.

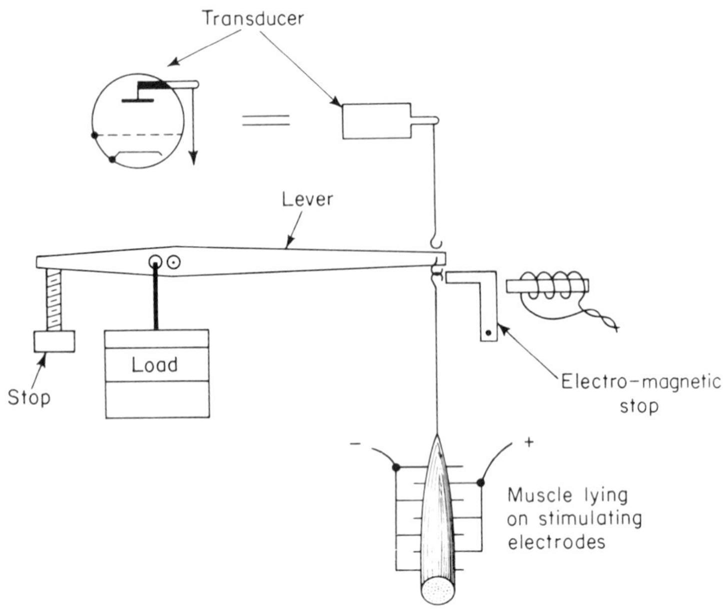

Fig. 19.9. Diagram of apparatus used by Wilkie to examine the mechanical properties of muscle. [After Wilkie (1956).]

This elasticity is sometimes said to be due to the PARALLEL ELASTIC ELEMENT (Prosser and Brown, 1961) and is attributed not only to the elasticity of the muscle fibers themselves but also to the sarcolemma and the connective tissues. These noncontractile elements are important in smoothing out rapid changes in tension. Length-tension relationships of resting muscles vary considerably (Fig. 19.10, and Hanson and Lowy, 1960).

The presence of elastic components can also be inferred from many experiments with active muscle. For example (Wilkie, 1956), a muscle is arranged to pull on a lever and lift a weight, but its movement is prevented by an adjustable stop so that it develops tension isometrically when stimulated (Fig. 19.9). The stop can be suddenly removed so that the muscle shortens as it pulls on the weight; the weight can be varied; the muscle can be released at various intervals (measured in msec) after the stimulus. In such an experiment the muscle shows a sudden shortening at the moment of release, with the tension falling to zero and then rising rapidly as the muscle takes the load. This is interpreted as a sudden adjustment of a SERIES ELASTIC COMPONENT. It is like an undamped spring which adjusts quickly under changing tensions; the muscle fibers contract and relax more slowly. The extent of the adjustment in the elastic elements is a function of the load or tension on the

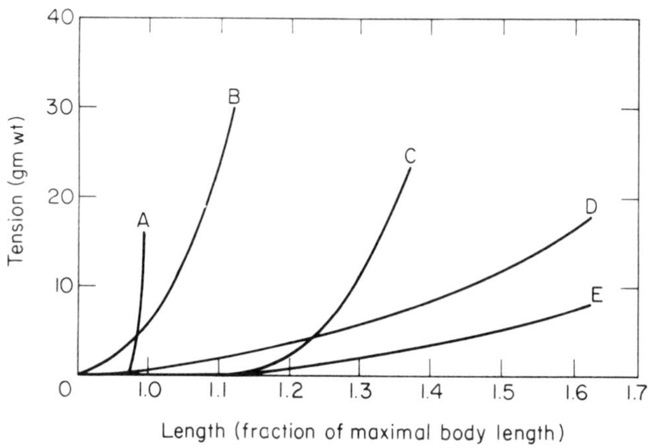

Fig. 19.10. Tension-length curves for resting muscles from *A*, bumblebee flight muscle; *B*, locust flight muscle at 11°C; *C*, frog sartorius muscle at 0°C; *D*, anterior byssal retractor of *Mytilus* at 14°C; and *E*, the pharynx retractor of *Helix* at 14°C. [Hanson and Lowy (1960).]

system, but the time of release after stimulus (varying from 100 to 600 msec in frog experiments) has no effect. This argues that the elastic component is an inert element and not one called into action by the stimulus (Wilkie, 1956; Davson, 1959).

This quick-release-recovery effect has been studied in many types of muscle (both striated and smooth) as well as in glycerol-extracted fibers. It is always present, although expressed to different degrees in various species and muscles. In part it reflects differences in the amount of connective tissue, in part the properties of the sarcolemma and sarcoplasm. The elasticity of insect flight muscles is much less than that of vertebrate skeletal muscle, probably because the former possess little connective tissue; smooth muscle is in general more extensible than striated muscle (Fig. 19.10).

In summary, muscle behaves as though two different elastic components were involved in its dynamics. The parallel elastic elements are especially manifest in muscle stretched beyond its resting length; the series elastic elements operate with the contractile elements during the mechanical events. The force of the contraction is exerted through the series elastic components. The morphological distinction of these different elastic elements is not yet established (Mommaerts *et al.*, 1961).

Properties of isolated muscles. The physiological activities of isolated muscles have most often been examined in relation to (1) the latency, contraction and relaxation phases of isotonic twitches (2) summation and the development of tetanus (3) length of the muscle in relation to the tension which it can develop (LENGTH-TENSION CURVES) (4) the speed of shortening (FORCE-VELOCITY CURVES and LENGTH-VELOCITY CURVES) and (5) duration and magnitude of the "active state" (ACTIVE-STATE CURVES). These various parameters are described for vertebrate skeletal muscle in many textbooks of medical physiology (see also Wilkie, 1956, and Davson, 1959), for vertebrate smooth muscle by Csapo (1960) and for several invertebrate muscles by Hanson and Lowy (1960) and Lowy and Millman (1962, 1963). Prosser and Brown (1961) compare several vertebrate and invertebrate muscles.

In general, the response patterns are similar for all kinds of muscles, but the quantitative relationships vary considerably. Selected examples such as those illustrated for the length-tension relationships of resting muscle (Fig. 19.10) show a spectrum of responses varying in magnitude and time relationships but all basically alike. In the present context, the similarities are more significant than the differences since they argue for essentially similar contractile mechanisms in all muscles. Detailed comparisons will not be attempted here. Selected examples of curves illustrating the parameters are, however, given as an aid to understanding the literature.

A typical LENGTH-TENSION CURVE for frog skeletal muscle is shown in Fig. 19.11. Very similar curves have been published for rabbit uterine smooth muscle (Csapo, 1960), for the anterior byssus retractor of *Mytilus* (Lowy and Millman, 1963), for the funnel retractor muscle of the *Octopus* (Lowy and Millman, 1962) and for many others, covering the range of important muscle types and illustrating the general nature of the observed responses. If the resting muscle is set at various lengths before tetanic stimulation, maximum tension develops when the muscle is at about its normal body length. When stretched longer than this the active tension levels off, then falls or sometimes rises slightly. These changes in the stretched muscle are, however, partly due to the parallel elastic components already described. When the lower right curve of Fig. 19.11, which represents the tension in the resting muscle, is subtracted from the upper curve, the pattern for the contractile elements

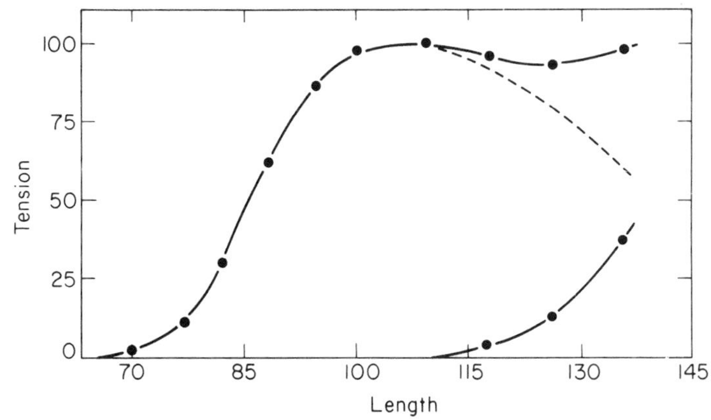

Fig. 19.11. Tension-length relations in vertebrate striated muscle. Curve at right, stress-strain curve for resting muscle. Curve at left, tension-length curve for active muscle. Broken line, difference between stress-strain and tension-length curves. 100 is the resting *in situ* length and the length of maximum tension. [Bard (1961).]

(which is the difference between the two, represented by the broken line) is always downward. Similar curves can be obtained by relating the length at maximum contraction in isotonic tetanus to the load lifted.

The velocity of shortening is plotted against the load to give a FORCE-VELOCITY DIAGRAM for the funnel retractor of the *Octopus* in Fig. 19.12. The actual velocity of shortening varies greatly in different types of muscle, but the patterns of the force-velocity curves are the same. Many examples will be found in the literature cited. Hill (1938) developed an empirical equation which describes this relationship and is frequently used in studies of this sort.

$$V = \frac{(P_o - P)\,b}{(P + a)}$$

where V is the velocity, P_0 is the isometric maximum tension which the muscle can develop, P is the actual tension developed during shortening or, in other words, the experimental force imposed, b is a constant with the dimensions of velocity and a is a constant with the dimensions of force. Thus, the velocity of shortening is proportional to the difference between the applied force P and the maximum tension the muscle can develop (the isometric tension, P_0) and inversely proportional to the applied force. In short, force-velocity curves are hyperbolic (Bard, 1961; Davson, 1959).

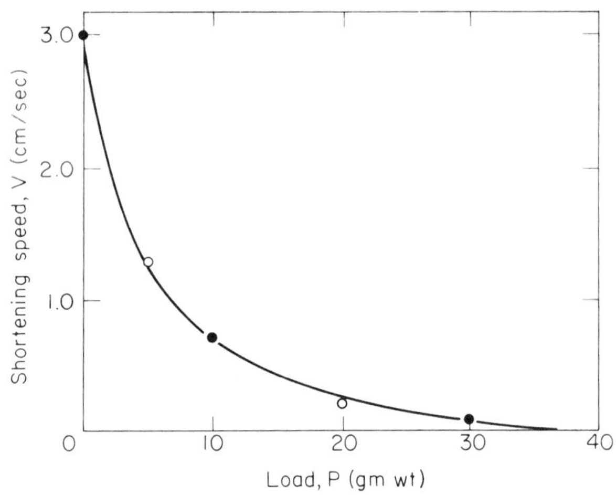

Fig. 19.12. Relationship between shortening speed and load in the funnel retractor of *Octopus* at 18°C. The curve was fitted by means of Hill's equation (see text) using the three solid points. [Lowy and Millman (1962).]

Length and force are interdependent, and since velocity is a function of force, relationships between length and velocity may likewise be anticipated; these have also been examined (Bard, 1961).

Wilkie (1956) defines the ACTIVE STATE as "the isometric tension which the contractile component can develop (or just bear without lengthening) at that instant." It is the tension which depends on the contractile elements alone without the intervening series elasticity. There are several different experimental approaches to its evaluation (Mommaerts *et al.*, 1961). The active state develops very rapidly in the excited muscles; the tension in the whole muscle rises more slowly (Fig. 19.8) because the contractile elements operate through the series elastic components. In frog sartorius at 0°C the active state is manifest 3 msec after the beginning of stimulation and reaches full intensity within 20 msec (Csapo, 1960). Muscles vary greatly in the rapidity of response; uterine muscle at 37°C reaches a peak about 4 seconds after stimulation. Hanson and Lowy (1960) illustrate the development of the active state in a number of different invertebrate muscles.

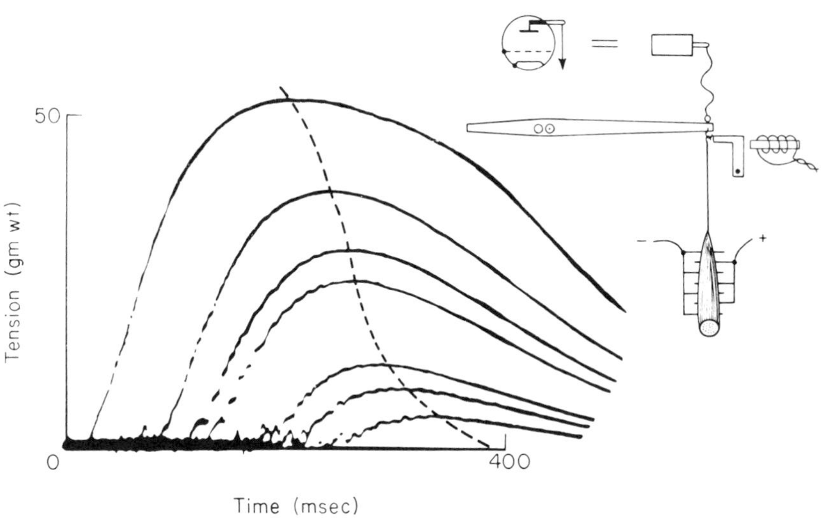

Fig. 19.13. Series of tension curves recorded at various intervals after stimulation (see text). The broken line shows the decline in the active state. Arrangement of recording apparatus is shown at the right. [Wilkie (1956).]

The decay in the active state may be determined with the experimental arrangements described previously (Fig. 19.9). The apparatus is first adjusted by removing the load and loosening the connection between the transducer and the lever as shown in the inset of Fig. 19.13. The muscle is now stimulated and develops tension isometrically against the electromagnetic stop. The series elastic components will be stretched during this development of tension. When the stop is suddenly removed the elastic elements shorten, but this is not recorded because of the slack between the lever and the transducer; the adjustment of the slack however, is such that when the contractile element shortens, tension is then recorded as a truncated twitch. The peak of the twitch represents the active state since neither the contractile component nor the series elastic component is shortening or lengthening at that instant.

The series of twitches shown in Fig. 19.13 is obtained by removing the electromagnetic stop at intervals after stimulation. The greatest and most rapid rise in recorded tension occurs at zero time; tension develops later and later and is progressively less as the interval of release after stimulation becomes longer. A curve drawn through the peaks of these plateaus gives a picture of the decline in active state. In frog muscle this reaches zero in about 400 msec as shown in Fig. 19.13; in the anterior byssus retractor muscle of *Mytilus* it is about 6 sec under the conditions of the experiment illustrated in Fig. 19.14. Thus, the capacity of the muscle to initiate further contraction gradually declines; these rates of decay in the active state depend not only on the types of muscle but also on environmental conditions such as temperature and various ions; they may also be altered by certain drugs. Examples are given in the literature already cited. Abbott and Lowy (1958) show curves for *Mytilus* pedal retractor comparable to those in Fig. 19.13.

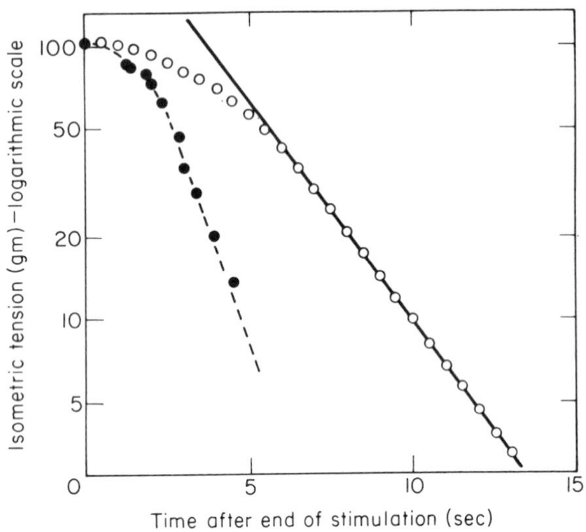

Fig. 19.14. Decay in isometric tension (right curve of open circles) and active state (left curve of closed circles) in the anterior byssus retractor muscle of *Mytilus* after repetitive stimulation at 10 shocks per sec and temperature at 20°C. [Lowy and Millman (1963).]

Both the development and the decay of the active state are much more rapid than that of the corresponding changes in the tension of the whole muscle. This, as previously noted, is due to the noncontractile, series elastic elements. The rapid rise in active state of frog muscle is shown in Fig. 19.8; in Fig. 19.14, the decay in the active state of *Mytilus* muscle is contrasted with its decline in isometric tension. In all kinds of muscle the latter falls slowly and exponentially, but the temporal relations vary with the type of muscle (about 0.4 sec for frog sartorius at 0°C, about 4 sec for the *Mytilus* pedal retractor at 14°C).

Two highly specialized muscles. Two kinds of invertebrate muscle, the adductor or holding muscles of lamellibranchs and the flight muscles of insects, are so highly specialized in their mechanical properties as to require an additional comment.

The lamellibranch muscles (paramyosin smooth muscles) are able to maintain high levels of tension for long periods without signs of fatigue. Two hypotheses have been considered. The older theories postulated a "set" or "catch" of certain elements while the muscle is in the shortened state and a prolonged maintenance of tension without expenditure of energy. Postulates of a "catch mechanism" with tension maintained passively have existed in one form or another for more than fifty years. However, it is now known from electrical recordings that these muscles are not continuously passive during prolonged contraction; they must be periodically activated or the tension will decline to zero (Abbott and Lowy, 1958). This finding weakens but does not entirely exclude some sort of "catch mechanism."

According to the other hypothesis, tension is maintained due to a continuous activity comparable to tetanus in vertebrate skeletal muscle. Evidence for "spontaneous" bursts of activity has been found in some of these muscles, suggesting an INTERMITTENT ACTIVATION MECHANISM (Lowy and Millman, 1963). According to this concept, the physiological differences in the contractile mechanisms of the holding muscles and familiar skeletal muscles are quantitative rather than qualitative (Hanson and Lowy, 1960). It is argued further that the sliding filament hypothesis first proposed for vertebrate skeletal muscle also satisfactorily explains the contractile mechanisms of paramyosin smooth muscles.

INSECT FLIGHT MUSCLE has the peculiar ability to oscillate rapidly—sometimes at frequencies as great as 1000 cps (Hanson and Lowy, 1960). Structurally, this is also a highly specialized muscle with anatomical differences which are as markedly in contrast to other muscle types as are the physiological attributes. In the rapidly oscillating muscles of insects the sarcomeres are extremely large and numerous; mitochondria are particularly abundant and probably reduce or eliminate the tendency to develop oxygen debts during activity. The muscles are sometimes called "fibrillar" because of the ease with which fibrils (Tiegs, 1955) separate, but again the differences are in degree rather than in kind and, like other skeletal muscles, the fibers (cells) of these muscles also contain fibrils consisting of groups of myofilaments separated from each other by nonfibrillar sarcoplasm.

The physiological peculiarities of these insect muscles are not as simply described as the anatomical ones. There is much evidence, however, for a myogenic rhythm of contractions maintained by some structural arrangement that is associated with an area of the exoskeleton which yields or buckles under tension. Pringle's (1957) studies of the "tymbal" (sound producing) muscles of the cicadas were significant in developing this concept. Pringle was able to make isolated nerve-muscle preparations with their associated connections and found that a single stimulus excited the muscle to contract almost isometrically against the elastic resistance of the tymbal cuticle; at a certain tension the cuticle buckles and clicks to the IN position thus producing the sound. The tension is reduced, and the myofibrils are deactivated by this sudden release in tension. The exoskeleton then rebounds to its former OUT position; the original condition is restored in the system and the muscle contracts once more.

A single stimulus applied to the motor nerve at 30°C elicits four sound pulses; at stimulus frequency of 50 per sec there is a rapid oscillation of 320 per sec. Larger insects such as the locust with relatively low wing beats (18 per sec) show a 1 : 1 relationship between the electrical and the mechanical events in the muscles, while rapidly oscillating muscles such as the "tymbal" muscles of the cicadas or the flight muscles of flies and bees (with usual frequencies from 100 to 300 per sec) show no such direct relationship. On the contrary, there are many muscular oscillations for one action potential. In the blowfly, for example, 3 action potentials per sec were recorded when the wing beat frequency was 120 per sec.

Although the initiation of a myogenic rhythm seems to explain best the activities of these specialized muscles, it is by no means clear that a click mechanism operates in all cases or offers a complete explanation of the phenomenon. Boettiger (1957) emphasizes the probable importance of stretching the muscles on their reexcitation. His studies have included examination of glycerol-extracted fibers from the flight muscles of bees; these, like mammalian skeletal muscle fibers, will oscillate spontaneously under certain conditions in the complete absence of a click mechanism (Hanson and Lowy, 1960).

NERVOUS CONTROL OF MUSCLES

During animal phylogeny contractile cells have been adapted in several different ways to effect a considerable range of motor capacities. Contrasts between the skeletal and smooth muscles of vertebrates, the oscillating flight muscles of insects and the tonic holding muscles of molluscs have been described; they owe many of their special properties to the structural nature of the myofibrils and their arrangements with respect to sarcoplasm and connective tissues. This, however, is only one line of specialization toward the versatility of movement manifest in the activities of animal life. Muscles are activated by nervous impulses, and the myoneural arrangements have also been adapted in several different ways to provide additional plasticity. The same muscle may act very differently (quick in contrast to slow contractions, for example), depending on the nature of the excitation processes.

Myoneural junctions. In most cases the nerves subdivide to form minute branching ramifications which come into close contact with the muscle cell. The naked cell membranes of the nerve endings are in direct contact with the sarcolemma of the muscle fiber, but the nerves do not actually penetrate the muscle cells, except in the highly specialized dipteran fibrillar muscles (Tiegs, 1955). Specialized motor end-plates have long been known in vertebrate skeletal muscle but are not recognized in vertebrate smooth or cardiac muscle, nor in the slow-fiber junctions of the lower vertebrates. Among the invertebrates motor end-plates have been recognized in only a few insect skeletal muscles (Hoyle, 1955; Tiegs, 1955) and in the segmental muscles of nereid polychaetes (Dorsett, 1964).

The vertebrate motor end-plates vary in detail (Couteaux, 1960; Prosser and Brown, 1961) but are similar in that the myelin sheath of the axon ends near the muscle while the nerve ending, covered only by its plasma membrane, expands into an irregular area that sits in synaptic gutters or troughs formed as depressions in the muscle fiber (Fig. 19.15).

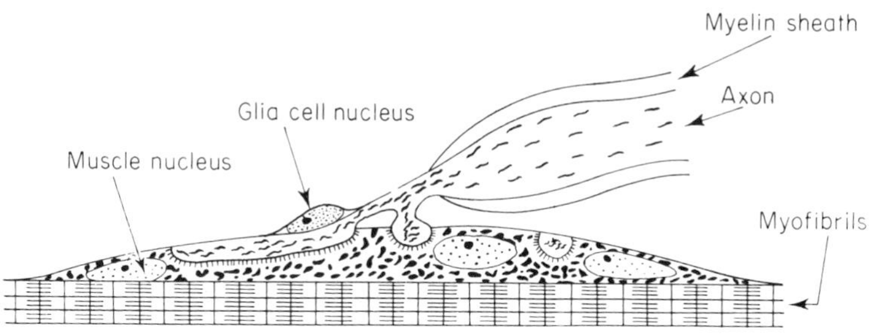

Fig. 19.15. Diagram of the structure of the motor end-plate of mammalian skeletal muscle. [Couteaux (1960).]

The sarcolemma lining the troughs or gutters is thrown into a series of folds which, in vertical sections, look like tiny perpendicular rods (the PALISADES). The plasma membranes of muscle and nerve seem to be in direct contact. Both the axoplasm and the sarcoplasm of the end-plate contain numerous mitochondria, indicating a region of high metabolic activity.

Excitation of muscle by nerve. It has already been noted (Chapter 15) that the spread of excitation from nerve to muscle at the vertebrate motor end-plate is effected through the release of acetylcholine. In some manner not clearly understood this chemical leads to an increase in the ionic permeability of the plasma membrane; a wave of depolarization spreads from the end-plate along the surface of the muscle cell. Although the transmitter substance is certainly not the same in all groups of animals nor in all muscles from the same animal, the principle of a chemical mediation of the events at the neuromuscular junction is generally accepted as applying to most of them.

At rest, the permeability properties of muscle cells are such that an electrical potential of 30 to 100 mv is maintained across their plasma membranes. In nervous excitation transmitter substances, released at the nerve endings, increase ionic permeability and lead to a junctional

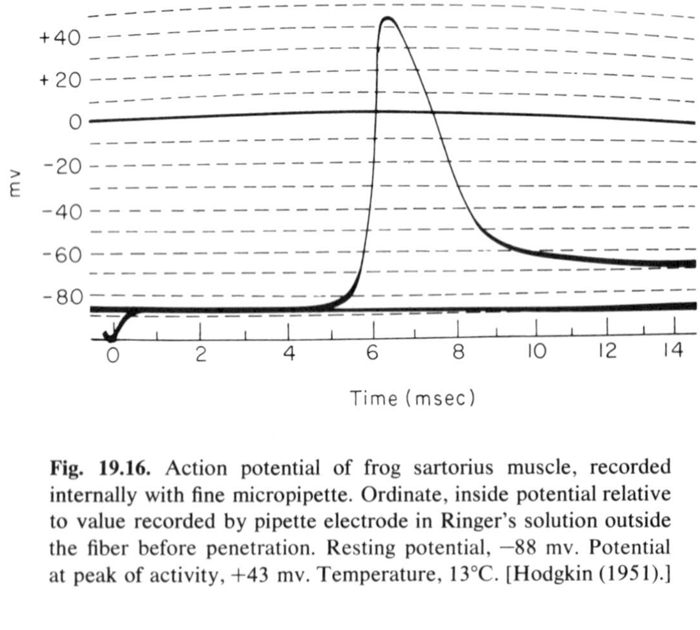

Fig. 19.16. Action potential of frog sartorius muscle, recorded internally with fine micropipette. Ordinate, inside potential relative to value recorded by pipette electrode in Ringer's solution outside the fiber before penetration. Resting potential, −88 mv. Potential at peak of activity, +43 mv. Temperature, 13°C. [Hodgkin (1951).]

end-plate potential which then spreads along the surface of the muscle fiber (Fig. 19.16).

It is clear that the activities of the myofilaments must be linked to the membrane potential in such a way that the reduction in potential leads to muscular contraction. The coupling mechanism, however, is not understood. Several hypotheses have been considered: the development of longitudinal electrical fields, the entrance of Ca^{++}, the direct action of the transmitter substance, the release and action of some entirely different chemical. Hoyle (1962) favors a theory based on the influx of Ca^{++}. This ion will cause contractures when injected into muscle cells in small amounts; its influx, as measured by radiocalcium, increases some thirty times in frog sartorius muscle during activity; it has a decisive action on general muscular excitability in many different animals as well as in isolated muscle preparations. Thus, several lines of evidence argue for some special significance of Ca^{++} in the coupling of the electrical with the mechanical events. If this proves to be truly fundamental, then the analysis has been carried another step, but there are still other questions to be resolved before the molecular details which link calcium penetration with the movements of the myofilaments are clearly understood.

Quick and slow contractions. The most primitive multicellular animals probably experimented with different kinds of neuromuscular controls as well as with various arrangements and types of myofibrils. It has already been noted that the coelenterates possess a morphological range of contractile elements varying from epitheliomuscular cells to typical smooth and characteristically cross-striated fibers. The early phylogeny of different functional systems is now emphasized. Two types of response to nervous stimulation are evident in this group, and the indications are that they were established early and have remained basic to the evolution of variety in neuromuscular activities. These are the QUICK and the SLOW form of contraction, now known to occur throughout the major animal phyla from coelenterates to vertebrates. The same muscle fibers or groups of fibers may be activated either rapidly or very slowly, depending on the excitation of their nerves (Chapman *et al.*, 1962).

Pantin (1935) did the classical studies on the quick withdrawal movements and the slow changes in shape and position associated with feeding and pumping activities in sea anemones. Entire animals and strips of various muscles have been frequently studied since that time (Hoyle, 1957); Ross (1957) examined both quick and slow contractions in a preparation of the isolated marginal sphincter of the anemone *Calliactis parasitica.* The rhythmic swimming movements of the medusae have also excited the interest of many physiologists—particularly Horridge (1956).

The range of neuromuscular response is illustrated in Figs. 19.17 and 19.18. When strips of jellyfish such as *Aurelia* or *Rhopilema* containing the subumbrellar muscles are stimulated electrically, the muscle contracts in a 1 : 1 relationship to the stimulus (Fig. 19.17). The single twitch is followed by a long refractory period (about 0.7 sec at 18°C). This is an "all-or-nothing" reaction independent of stimulus strength; a train of stimuli produces responses of increasing magnitude. This FACILITATION

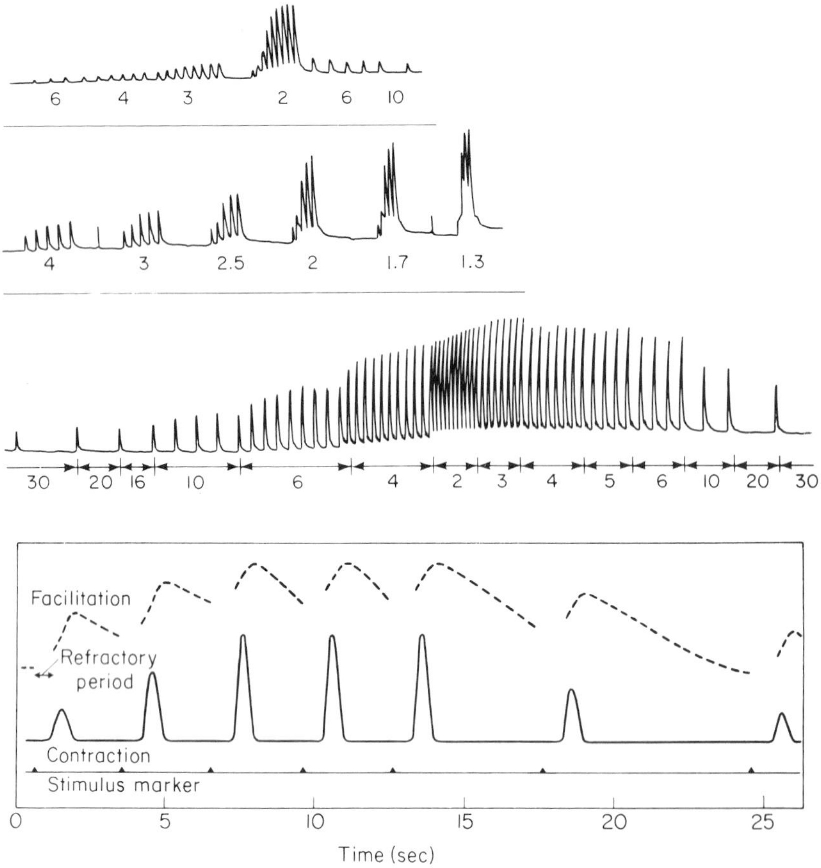

Fig. 19.17. Facilitation in a strip preparation of *Rhopilema* without marginal bodies. Upper, recording with constant stimulus at intervals in sec as indicated by the numbers. Lower, hypothetical curve of the development and decay of facilitation in Scyphomedusae. [Bullock (1943).]

(improvement in action with repeated stimulation) is not fully explained (Hoyle, 1957). Its locus might be neuromuscular, intramuscular or intermuscular.

In contrast to the jellyfish, an actinian such as *Calliactis* or *Metridium* always requires more than one stimulus to effect a response. This is true for the isolated sphincter as well as for preparations from the mesenteries or body wall (Ross, 1957). In Fig. 19.18*a* the quick responses are

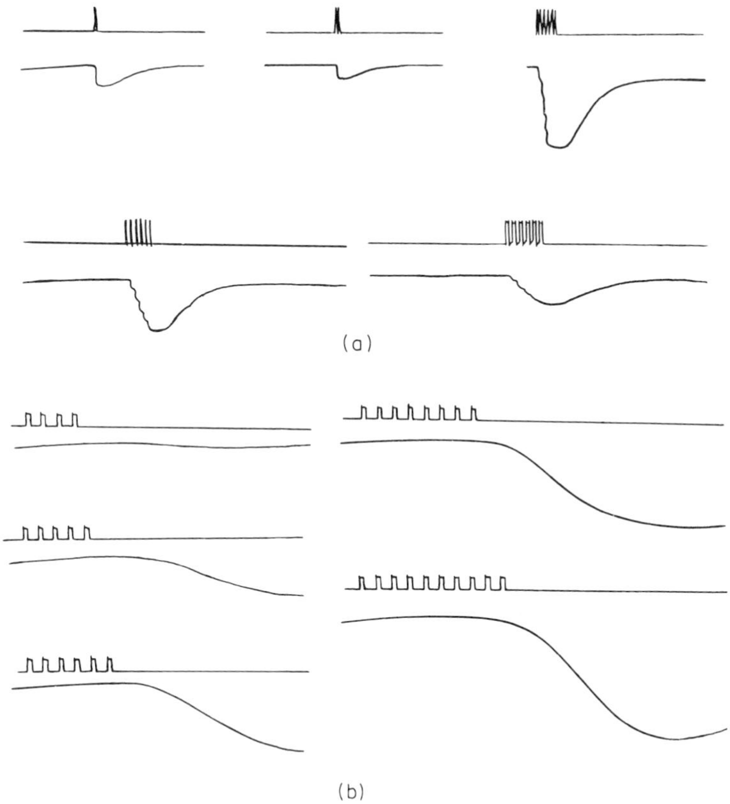

Fig. 19.18. Quick and slow responses of the sphincter muscle of *Calliactis*. *a*, Facilitated quick responses to two stimuli at separations of 0.5 and 1.0 sec and to 6 stimuli at 1.0, 1.5 and 2.0 sec intervals. *b*, Slow responses to 4, 5, 6, 8, and 10 stimuli at frequencies of 1/sec. Contraction recorded downward. [Ross (1957).]

seen to appear on the second stimulus and show marked facilitation with additional stimuli. Slow responses, on the other hand, do not coincide with the arrival of a stimulus and may begin as long as two minutes after stimulation (Fig. 19.18*b*).

The magnitude of these responses depends on temperature and ionic environment; they can also be modified by certain drugs such as tyramine, tryptamine and adrenaline. Ross (1960) argues that the similarity in response of quick and slow systems to K^+ excess (excitation probably by general depolarization action) and to Mg^{++} excess and Ca^{++} lack (excitability depressed or abolished) indicates a similarity in conditions of membrane excitability. The contractile machinery, however, may be operating somewhat differently in the two muscle types. Excess Ca^{++} and tyramine do not directly excite the muscle but cause an enhancement of the quick responses to stimulation without affecting the slow responses. Excess Mg^{++} abolishes both quick and slow contractions. Ross finds evidence in these ion and drug effects for a difference in the contractile mechanisms of the muscle cells or in the mechanisms which initiate contraction. These conclusions are in line with the generalized nature of membrane excitability and are evidence for specializations in contractile elements and neuromuscular connections.

In general, the coelenterates illustrate a spectrum of neuromuscular controls. These range from the direct "all-or-nothing" (non-facilitated) twitches to very highly facilitated contractions. The facilitated types include quick contractions which are set in action only by two or more stimuli (perhaps a two-stage excitation) and slow responses requiring several stimuli and showing no direct relationship to the stimulus sequence. Facilitation is markedly characteristic of these systems and is developed to varying degrees in different forms.

Although these findings indicate that varied processes of neuromuscular control are phylogenetically old, there are many aspects of the analysis which cannot be resolved with coelenterates because of the difficulties of recording from individual cells. The annelids are the most primitive of the invertebrates which permit a study of individual nerves and muscles by electrophysiological techniques. Both quick and slow contraction mechanisms are common. Two groups of nerves have been identified in the retractor of the proboscis of the sipunculid *Phascolosoma*. One group is made up of nerves with large fibers (approximately 2μ in diameter) and the other of smaller fibers (about 1μ in diameter); these can be separately stimulated to activate the quick and the slow responses respectively. The quick twitches show neither summation nor facilitation; the slow ones show both of these phenomena. These and other experiments have demonstrated that the quick and the slow contractions of certain annelid muscles are associated with two sets of nerve fibers, but it still is not clear whether there are two types of muscle fibers corresponding to these nerves (Hoyle, 1957; Dorsett, 1964).

The arthropods have been popular for studies of neuromuscular physiology and have demonstrated several additional specializations in nervous control. Particularly in the decapods and insects individual nerves can be readily stimulated, and action potentials may be recorded from both muscles and nerves. Quick and slow contractions have been definitely associated with different nerves. The two actions are distinct in recording the contractions of the closer muscle of the crayfish (Fig. 19. 19). There is no evidence that these two types of nerve are associated with different muscle fibers; the quick and the slow contractions evidently depend on the innervation rather than on physiological differences in muscle cells.

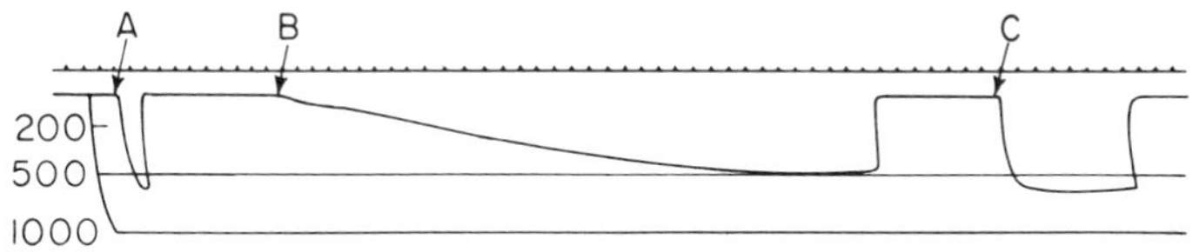

Fig. 19.19. Fast and slow isometric contractions (recorded downward) at the same stimulus frequency (approximately 50/sec) of the closing muscle of *Pacifastacus trowbridgii*. *a* and *c* on fast fibers, *b* on slow fibers. Tension in grams, time in sec. [Wiersma (1961) after van Harreveld and Wiersma (1936).]

The decapod crustaceans often have still another type of nerve in their leg muscles. This is an inhibitor, and its presence marks one of the distinctive contrasts in the neurophysiology of crustaceans and vertebrates. Inhibition following stimulation of nerves occurs in the vertebrate autonomic system (vagal inhibition of the heart, for example) but is not found in the somatic musculature. Inhibition in the organs of locomotion of a vertebrate or an insect is a centrally controlled phenomenon; in the crustacean it is controlled peripherally. The leg muscles of the decapods are innervated by relatively few fibers—usually not more than four or five. An entire muscle may be innervated by only two motor axons, one excitatory and one inhibitory. Frequently there are two types of excitatory fibers (the thick ones which elicit fast contractions and the thin ones which bring about slow contractions), but there is only one kind of inhibitor. The precise number and arrangement of fibers is characteristic of the species (Wiersma, 1961).

Contrasts between the vertebrates and the crustaceans. Several of the differences are indicated in Fig. 19.20. The functional unit of the vertebrate muscle is not the muscle itself nor the individual muscle cell but the MOTOR UNIT; this consists of a single motor neuron and the group of muscle cells which its single axon innervates (Ruch and Fulton, 1960).

The number of muscle cells comprising the unit varies from as few as two to six in some of the eye muscles to as many as several hundred in the limb muscles of the mammal. The units are smaller where the movements are delicate and finely graded. It has been estimated that the

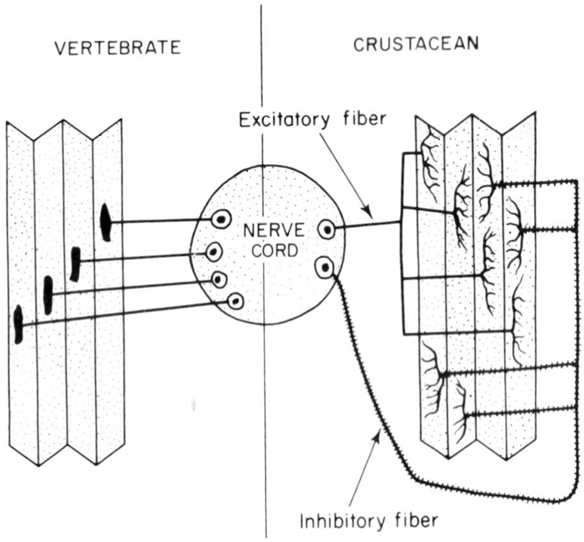

Fig. 19.20. Diagrammatic comparison of the neuromuscular connections in the appendages of vertebrates and crustaceans. For simplicity only one muscle fiber is shown in association with each vertebrate motor axon, whereas in reality it is a group of fibers forming a motor unit; further, only one end-plate is shown on a fiber whereas there are occasionally two or three. In the diagram for the crustacean only one excitatory fiber is shown, but this is the minimum number. In some muscles there are as many as five (some slow and others fast); further, each axon may not have a branch to every muscle fiber.

mammal may contain about a quarter of a billion individual muscle cells but only about 450,000 myelinated nerve fibers, and it is thus evident that most of the motor axons are associated with a great many muscle cells. The individual fibers belonging to a motor unit are scattered throughout the muscle, and hence the action of the unit is on the muscle as a whole and not in a localized muscle area. In summary, a vertebrate muscle receives a large number of axons while the individual muscle cells are innervated by very few motor end-plates (usually only one).

In contrast, crustacean muscles are innervated by a small number of axons (two to five usually), and each of these divides and subdivides to supply a significant percentage of all the cells which comprise the muscle. Motor units are absent. Moreover, each of the axonal branches to a muscle fiber is subdivided into numerous fine twiglets which contact the muscle cell at many points.

The physiological contrasts are as striking as the anatomical differences (Welsh and Schallek, 1946). In the vertebrate, fast and slow contractions and the gradation in muscular control are achieved by varying the activity of the motor units. There are two factors involved: the number of motor neurons discharging and the rate of discharge in the motor neurons. A muscle cell, when excited, shows a membrane potential which is all-or-nothing, but the contractile elements, which are coupled to the electrical potentials, show summation and the development of tetanus with increasing frequencies of membrane potentials (i.e., stimuli). Thus, by recruiting motor units in varying numbers at different times and at different rates, a very delicate control with smooth contractions is possible in the whole muscle.

In the crustacean, fast and slow contractions are achieved through the excitation of different nerves while gradation in response depends on localized excitation in the muscle fibers and on facilitation. This localized peripheral excitation and facilitation, like the inhibition, are in striking contrast to the situation in vertebrate skeletal muscle; in the vertebrates, variable control of motor units, facilitation and inhibition are central phenomena. Both physiologically and behaviorally, the crustaceans are a most versatile and varied group; the many physiological differences in detailed neuromuscular physiology permit only very broad generalizations (Hoyle, 1957; Wiersma, 1961).

The slow motor system owes many of its special properties to a definite and long-lasting facilitation. Single nerve impulses are never effective, but beginning with two stimuli smooth tetani develop; the magnitude of contraction increases with frequency of stimuli, but always gradually and with a very slow steady rise in tension. No action potential is usually recorded on the first stimulus to the slow axon; repeated stimuli elicit small LOCALIZED junctional potentials which facilitate markedly. The slow response is based on localized contractions associated with these junctional potentials; there is no propagated spike and no all-or-nothing wave of depolarization of the type described for vertebrate muscle (Fig. 19.16).

The physiology of the fast motor system is more variable. In some preparations a single nerve impulse elicits a muscle twitch, but more frequently at least two stimuli are required; the fast system like the slow system requires facilitation. However, the facilitation is much less. Characteristically, the fast system shows a shorter latent period, a more rapid contraction (with twitches which are almost as great as tetani), the development of higher tensions and quicker onset of fatigue. Localized junctional potentials summate to produce spikes; if the stimulus frequency is great enough these may result in the all-or-none type of depolarization spike, but usually the spikes are abortive (Fig. 19.21). Spikes may be recorded in one part of the fiber while small junctional potentials are recorded in another. The neuromuscular excitatory processes are localized; the differences between the slow and the fast systems are quantitative rather than qualitative.

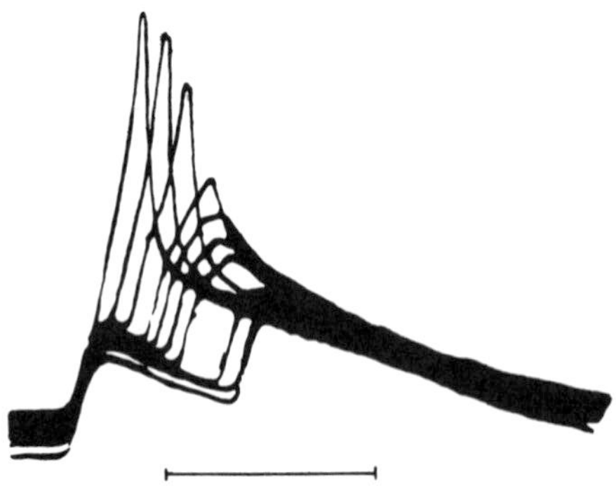

Fig. 19.21. Summation of fast junctional potentials and genesis of spikes in a muscle fiber of the main flexor in *Panulirus interruptus*. The "fastest" motor axon was stimulated with successive pairs of shocks separated by continually decreasing intervals. Note summation as the two responses (represented by two distinct notches for longer stimulus intervals) come closer together, with gradual increase of abortive spikes and absence of all-or-none relation even when true spiking occurs. Time unit 20 msec. [Wiersma (1961) after Furshpan (1955).]

The inhibitor is usually the smallest of the three types of axons in the crustacean muscle. Its stimulation either produces no change in the muscle or reduces the tonus when present—usually after a definite latent period. If inhibitory and excitatory neurons are stimulated together the excitatory activity will be reduced or completely suppressed; the slow system is more sensitive to inhibition than the fast. Membrane potentials likewise vary in accordance with the state of the muscle at the time of stimulus. If the potential is near its normal resting value, the effect of inhibitory stimulation is inconspicuous. If, on the other hand, the potential has been displaced from the resting value, then inhibitory stimulation tends to return the potential to the resting value. It is assumed, although the evidence is far from complete, that different transmitter substances are involved in excitation and inhibition.

The delicately controlled mobility of skeletal muscles is regulated peripherally in the crustaceans but centrally in the vertebrates. In the former group versatility depends on the interaction of three types of neurons which produce different degrees of excitation at many points in the muscle fiber. In the vertebrates motor units are activated by varied patterns and frequencies of impulses from the central nervous system. Somatic motor nerves producing peripheral inhibition are unknown among the vertebrates.

The slow fiber system of vertebrate skeletal muscle was first studied in the frog but has now been identified in other groups of vertebrates – cat, chick, garter snake (Hess, 1963) and hagfishes (Andersen *et al.*, 1963). The axons of the slow fibers are only about 5μ in diameter in contrast to about 12μ in diameter for the fast ones. They also differ in their myoneural associations; slow fibers do not terminate on motor end-plates but, like the crustacean fibers, arborize to form a multiple innervation of delicate twigs on the muscle fiber. Resting potentials are lower in the slow fibers, and stimulation is followed by localized junctional potentials of small amplitude and long duration but without the propagated spikes. The muscle fibers, particularly those of the postural muscles, contract slowly in association with these alterations in potential. There are many similarities between this slow system of the frog and the skeletal muscles of the decapod crustaceans, but it is of interest that the latter have achieved both the fast and the slow control with similar nerve endings while the frog has two distinct types (those associated with motor end-plates and those with multiple arborizations). In the hagfish the slow muscle fibers are histologically distinct, with a much greater lipid content than the fast fibers (Flood and Mathisen, 1962).

Retrospect. Animal activity is based on ATP-driven systems of protein molecules which shorten or change their positions to effect the movements of cells. This system seems to be a conservative one in the homogeneity of the contractile proteins and in the activation by ATP. It has expressed its versatility in the many cell types concerned with movement and in the varied ways in which they are governed by nerves. Cell types range from amoeboid masses of protoplasm and cells with ciliated surfaces to many kinds of muscle fibers. Variety in myofibrillar arrangement ranges from simple myonemes in the epitheliomuscular cells of coelenterates to irregularly arranged masses of myofilaments in classical smooth muscle types and the orderly arrangement of spiralled myofilaments in helical smooth muscles or the cross-banded filaments of the striated types. The trend toward orderliness in the myofilaments seems to be associated with speed of movement. Precision and versatility in muscular control depend largely on the manner in which the muscles are activated by the nerves. Separate neuron types are associated with quick and slow contractions in all multicellular phyla while some groups have inhibitor fibers as well. A precision of control is possible through a grading of activities at the myoneural junctions. Among the vertebrates, however, this control is largely taken over by the central nervous system.

Contractile systems still offer many challenging areas for investigation. This is particularly true in the field of neuromuscular physiology. It is agreed that muscular activity is mediated through transmitter substances released at nerve endings, but the nature of these substances remains speculative in many systems. The association of electrical events with the mechanical events in the muscle cell is still not well understood. Only a few examples have been carefully studied out of the great variety of animal forms, and although the picture may now be essentially correct in its outline, many of the details may be quite different when fully understood.

Electrical Discharge, Light Production and Color Changes

20

Electric Organs

Although electrogenesis occurs in all receptor-effector systems, the discharge of electricity as an effector action has been described only in some of the fishes. There are well-known representatives among both the elasmobranchs and the teleosts; the elasmobranch species are marine while the teleost species, with one exception (the stargazer *Astrocopus*) live in tropical fresh waters (Keynes, 1957; Grundfest, 1960). Several of the families of electric fishes are quite unrelated; apparently these organs evolved independently in at least six different groups.

Electric fishes have long excited man's curiosity. The writings of the ancients record astonishing experiences with these strange animals while Charles Darwin, in his classic *On the Origin of Species*, wrote that "the electric organs of fishes offer another case of special difficulty." His dilemma in this instance was to explain the evolution of specialized and unique structures, such as the powerful electric organs, by natural selection when there was apparently no conceivable function for them in ancestral species lacking an ability to deliver paralyzing electrical discharges. Darwin's faith, however, that "we are far too ignorant to argue that no transition of any kind is possible" was vindicated almost exactly a century later when Lissmann (1958) demonstrated the usefulness of low voltages in some species of fish which depend on regular pulsating discharges for their orientation; these fishes are able to sense changes in their electrical fields and thus avoid objects or react to other animals. Since electric organs develop from the myoneural apparatus during ontogeny, it can be assumed that their physiological phylogeny has been built onto the electrogenesis associated with the activities of skeletal muscle. Electrogenesis was thus a preadaptation which became useful in the evolution of electric organs for orientation, communication and interaction between certain aquatic animals. The extent to which electrocommunication enters into the behavior of fishes is currently under active investigation.

MORPHOLOGY

Electric organs develop from muscle, some directly from the fibers and others from their motor end-plates. The morphological details vary, but all are similarly constructed of units, the ELECTROPLAXES or ELECTROPLATES which are the modified muscle cells. These are thin, wafer-like, flattened units arranged in an orderly manner with one surface (relatively smooth) a specialized nervous layer and the other a papilliform nutritive layer; like surfaces all face in the same direction. In some species the nervous layer is directly supplied with a dense net of nerve fibers; in others, the nerve supply is indirect to one or several sturdy stalks emerging from this surface (Fig. 20.1). Electroplates are embedded in a jelly-like material and individually housed in a series of connective tissue compartments.

The arrangement and number of the electroplates are as variable as their cytology but show many obvious adaptations to the special requirements of the species. In the giant ray *Torpedo nobiliana* they are horizontal, piled up from ventral to dorsal surface in columns like stacks of coins; there are over 1000 "coins" in a column and approximately 2000 columns. In the electric eel *Electrophorus electricus* the electroplaxes are vertical in longitudinal columns parallel to the spinal cord. This animal has from 6000 to 10,000 units in each column with about 60 columns on each side of the body (Grundfest, 1960; Keynes, 1961). About 40 per cent of the eel's total bulk is devoted to this specialized tissue which forms the most powerful bioelectric generator known, with the capacity to discharge something more than 500 volts. The electric eel inhabits fresh waters and thus requires a large number of electroplaxes in series to overcome the resistance; *Torpedo,* on the other hand, generates a lower voltage in salt water with lower resistance, but by having 2000 columns in parallel it achieves an extraordinary amperage. The electric catfish *Malapterurus* exhibits still another arrangement with a jacket of electric tissue which surrounds the body in a thick layer extending from the gills to the tail. This organ was at one time thought to be exceptional in arising from skin glands rather than muscles; but it is now known to arise from myoblasts in a manner comparable to other electric organs (Johnels, 1956*b*).

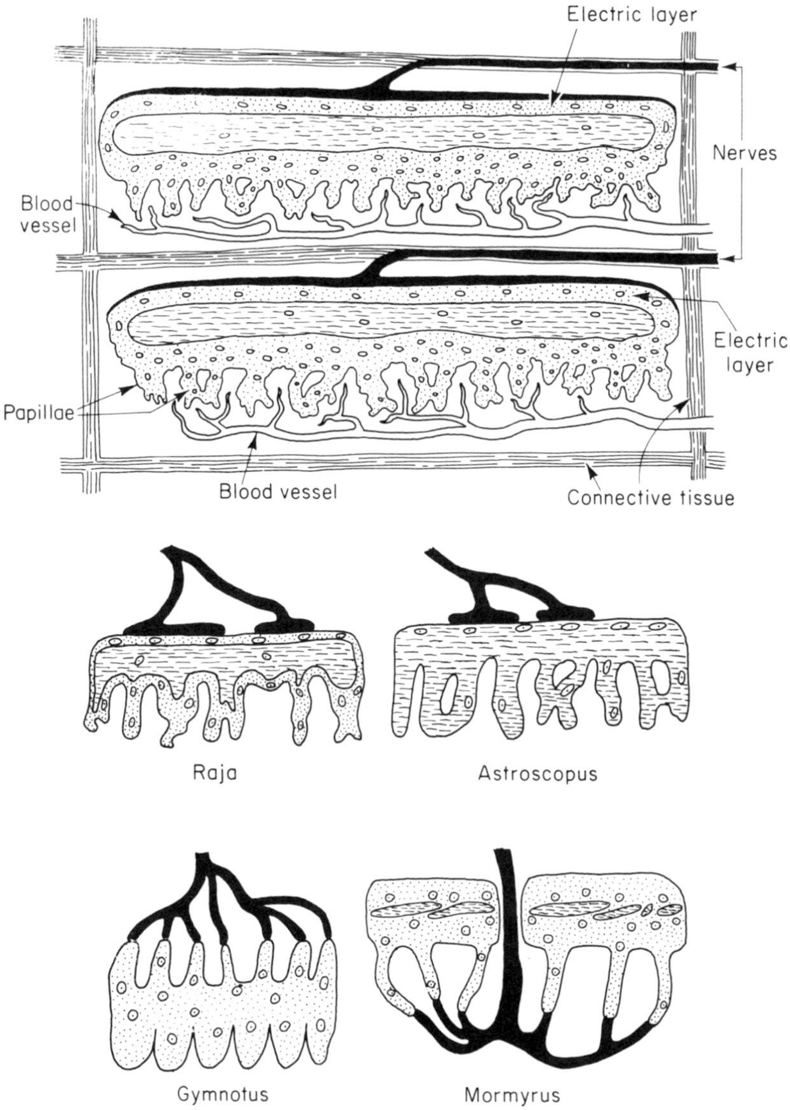

Fig. 20.1. Structure of an electroplate. Above, arrangement of two neighboring plates; below, four kinds of electroplates; cross-hatching, modified muscle. [Above based on Ihle *et al.* (1927); below, based on Dahlgren and Kepner (1908).]

PHYSIOLOGY

The scientists of the nineteenth century appreciated the significance of the arrangement of the electroplates. Their hook-up in series adds the output of the units to build up the voltage; the arrangement of the columns in parallel builds up the amperage. The pioneer workers noted that the nervous face of the electroplax became negative to the non-nervous layer during the discharge, but they had neither the theoretical knowledge nor the delicate instruments necessary to carry the analysis further. The first significant theoretical discussions of the mechanism responsible for the potential differences are those of Bernstein and his associates (Keynes, 1957).

Bernstein's classical concepts of cell permeability and ion fluxes during excitation were described in Chapter 15. These theories, applied to the electric organs, postulated a selective cell membrane permeability for potassium with an impermeability to sodium (as in muscle and nerve) but, in addition, assumed a difference in the response of the two faces of the electroplate during activity. Bernstein argued that the nervous face became depolarized during stimulation while the non-nervous face retained its resting potential and thus, the non-nervous membranes, lying parallel to one another with their resting potentials of about 85 mv (in *Electrophorus*) are suddenly connected in series like an electric battery. This hypothesis could not be experimentally tested until microelectrodes and suitable amplifiers became available almost fifty years later. The recordings with intracellular electrodes quickly demonstrated that Bernstein's basic assumption of differences in the permeability of the two membranes was correct but incomplete. During excitation the nervous layer is not merely depolarized but shows a reversal in polarity (to about 67 mv in *Electrophorus*) as described earlier for muscle (Chapter 15). In this way the nervous face develops a potential difference in the same direction as that of the non-nervous face, and when these become connected in series both faces of the electroplax contribute to the charge of "the battery" (Fig. 20.2).

The electric eel uses this discharge system to deliver high-voltage paralyzing electric shocks. Subsequent studies show that this is only one of several discharge systems used by fishes and emphasize once more the remarkable opportunism in the evolutionary process (Grundfest and Bennett, 1961). The greatest diversity occurs among the weakly electric fishes which use pulses of electricity for electro-echo orientation. Some of the knife fishes (*Gymnotus*) and some of the mormyrids (*Gnathonemus*) produce diphasic or triphasic rather than monophasic pulses. Both faces of the electroplate show changing permeability (potentials) but not simultaneously, so that the alternating activity of nervous and non-nervous faces produces very rapid diphasic pulses (0.3 msec in *Gnathonemus*).

The duration of the spikes may vary so greatly that the resulting pulse can be almost monophasic; in the mormyrid *Mormyrus rume* and the African catfish *Malapterurus* the rostral spike is very long and the caudal spike extremely short. Representative examples of the spikes from the two surfaces and the resulting external discharge are shown in Fig. 20.3.

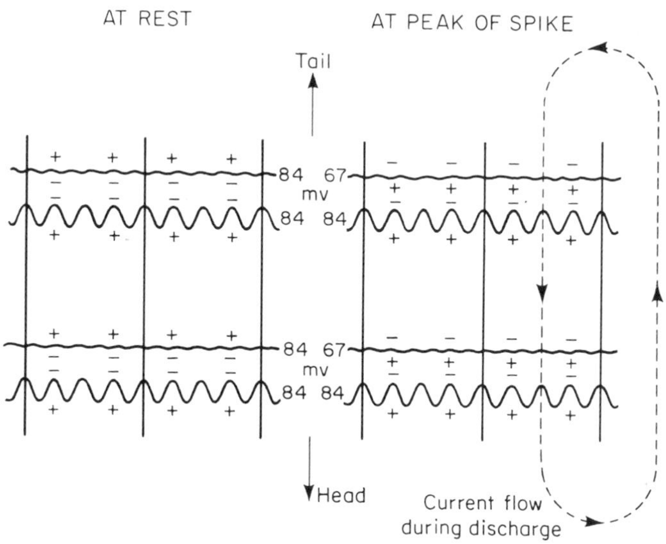

Fig. 20.2. Mechanism of additive discharge in the electroplates of the Organ of Sachs in *Electrophorus*. *a*, At rest there is no net potential across the electroplates. *b*, At the peak of the spike, all the potentials are in series, and the head of the eel becomes positive with respect to its tail. [Keynes (1957).]

Vertebrate skeletal muscle cells are normally activated through motor nerves by way of the motor end-plate. It will be recalled (Chapters 15 and 19) that the motor nerve initiates junctional potentials in the end-plate (through release of acetylcholine) which rise to a certain peak value and then trigger the all-or-none action potential in the muscle cell. Thus, in vertebrate skeletal muscle there are two major bioelectric events—the end-plate potentials and the action potentials of muscle. During the phylogeny of electric organs from muscle some fishes have capitalized on the end-plate potentials (elasmobranchs), and others have utilized muscle action potentials (freshwater teleosts). This interesting variation in physiological phylogeny was also discovered after the advent of electrophysiological recording instruments, although the findings were based on observations made more than eighty years ago (Grundfest and

Bennett, 1961). At that time it was noted that the electric organs of the ray *Torpedo* could not be stimulated electrically while those of the eel *Electrophorus* could. When *Electrophorus* has been forced to discharge its electric organs to the point of exhaustion the organs can still be excited

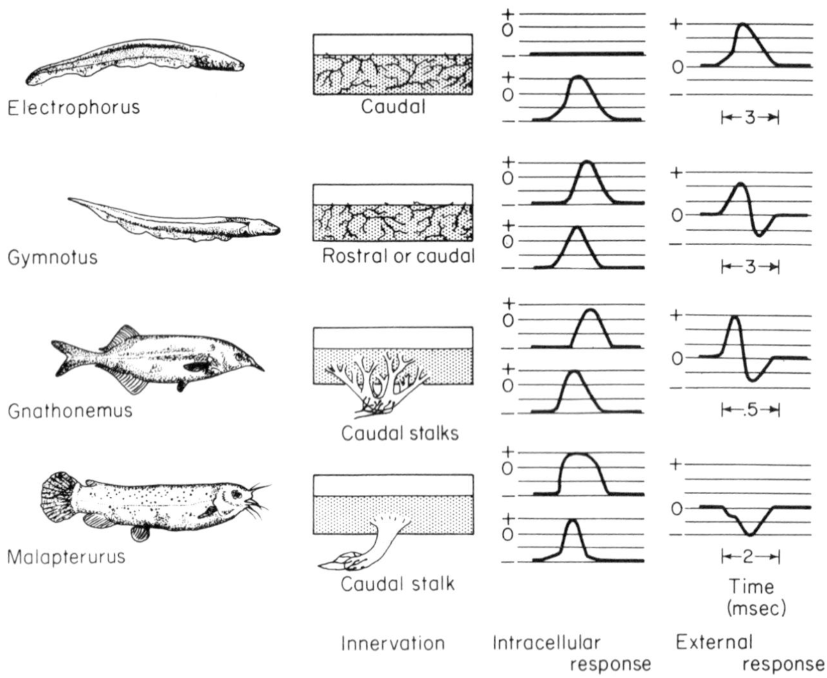

Fig. 20.3. Discharges of different electric fishes. Shaded area of the electroplates (SECOND SERIES OF DIAGRAMS) shows the innervated membranes. Top curve of each pair (THIRD COLUMN) shows intracellular potential across uninnervated membrane during a response. Bottom curve, response of innervated membrane. External response (RIGHT CURVES) is algebraic summation of oppositely directed potentials of the two membranes. [Grundfest (1960).]

by direct electric or mechanical stimuli; *Torpedo*, in a similar test, is completely unresponsive to direct stimulation. The fatigued organs of *Torpedo* will, however, respond to a direct application of acetylcholine.

The solution to this puzzle was evident when it was found that the myoneural junction is an electrically inexcitable membrane, while the muscle cell itself can be directly excited by electrical stimuli (electrically excitable membrane) as well as indirectly through its nerves and, further, that the end-plate potentials develop at the myoneural junction in accordance with the release and accumulation of acetylcholine. Thus, the electric organs of the rays are specialized synaptic membranes (electrically inexcitable) while those of the freshwater teleosts are specialized muscle membranes and are electrically excitable—although normally activated through nerves. The marine teleost *Astroscopus*, in contrast to all freshwater teleosts, has an electrically inexcitable system suggesting opportunism rather than sequential phylogeny.

NERVOUS CONTROL

Like all effectors, the electric organs are only useful physiological machines when they respond appropriately to meet the exigencies of a complex environment. As a means of stunning prey or discouraging predators these organs act in response to information gathered by the visual and tactile receptors; as a system for detecting objects in the environment and orienting in dark habitats they require a battery of specialized electroreceptors. In any case, sensory information must be received and coordinated in the computing centers of the brain, and these neural centers must discharge the appropriate motor impulses to the electric organs. Certain areas of the brain (particularly the cerebellum and parts associated with the lateral line system) are almost as highly specialized as are the muscles which give rise to the electric organs; the phylogeny of a specialized electric discharge system has modified these fishes in many curious ways (Grundfest, 1960; Lissmann, 1963).

Some of the problems of coordination can be readily appreciated in *Electrophorus*. An electric eel may reach a length of six to eight feet, and yet the electric organs which stretch all along its sides discharge in a matter of about 3.0 msec; this is only slightly longer than the discharge time of a single electroplate. Clearly, there is some very precise system for synchronizing the discharges from several thousand electroplates. In part this is due to a difference in the morphology of the nerves to the anterior and posterior parts of the organs; the electric nerves which run from the vertebral column to the electroplates become progressively shorter from cephalic to caudal segments. In part, also, the synchronization depends on the physiology of synapses with a progressive decrease in the spinal synaptic delay from head to tail. The impulse rate from the neural centers is the same at all points along the spinal cord, but the synapses to the motor neurons can stall the delivery to the electroplates, and this delay varies from head to tail (Keynes, 1957). What seems to be true for *Electrophorus* is not necessarily true for other electric fishes; in *Torpedo* the most significant factor in synchronization seems to be a hyperpolarizing effect of the starting discharge on the late electroplates (Fessard, 1961). A variety of arrangements—both morphological and physiological—will probably be revealed as more species are carefully studied.

Another interesting problem in physiological control is exemplified by those electric fishes which produce continuous streams of electric pulses for the purpose of sensing their environment. The different species show characteristic discharge frequencies ranging from 50 to as high as 1600 per sec; the rate may be astonishingly steady to within 0.5 per cent in some of the knife fishes even when stimulated. In sensing unfamiliar objects some species vary only the amplitude of the pulses (*Gymnarchus*) while others can vary frequency of discharge as well as the amplitude (Mormyridae). These two systems have evidently evolved in parallel in unrelated families both in Africa and South America (Lissmann, 1961, 1963).

Lissmann did the pioneer work with *Gymnarchus niloticus,* an African fish which lives in turbid waters of very low visibility and orients by sensing changes in the pattern of discharges from the small electric organs at the end of its long pointed tail. This animal sends out a steady stream of pulses at the rate of about 300 per sec; these vary only in amplitude, waxing and waning as the fish approaches an unfamiliar object. The animal swims with its beautifully undulating fins but maintains a relatively rigid vertebral column. At each electric discharge the tip of the tail becomes momentarily negative to the head so that the animal is surrounded by an electric field, the configuration of which depends on the conductivity of the water and the presence of objects of variable electric conductivity. The characteristic swimming with rigid body is no accident, for the configuration of the field is the main sensing device in dark and turbid waters; the animal can operate as easily in reverse as in forward swimming.

The ability of *Gymnarchus* to use this system in electro-orientation has been carefully established through classical conditioning experiments (Lissmann and Machin, 1958). *Gymnarchus* is sensitive to potential differences as small as 0.03 mv/cm. The reactions of the fish to electric currents, magnets, conductors and nonconductors when introduced into their surroundings prove their sensitivity to any change in electric fields; they detect the presence of magnets and can distinguish conductors and nonconductors. They can obviously detect the presence of another fish by this system, but it is evident that their prey (species lacking this system) are unaffected by the discharges.

The neural centers and nerves which control this complex system are large, with cerebellar lobes which cover half of the entire brain in *Gymnarchus*. Cerebellar development reaches a climax in some of the mormyrids where other parts of the brain are completely covered by these extensive lobes—a development which is superficially similar to the cerebral hemispheres of the mammals.

The detection of the electric pulses requires a specialized type of receptor organ. This probably depends on the AMPULLARY LATERAL LINE ORGANS. Dijkgraaf (1963) divides lateral line organs into two groups: the ordinary lateral line organs (discussed in Chapter 18) and the ampullary lateral line organs which are apparently specialized electroreceptors. These ampullary organs have been derived from superficial neuromasts, but during development the sensory cells sink into a very deep vesicle or ampulla, lose their cupula and become embedded in a jelly-like substance which completely fills the vesicle. A tube-like duct of varying length opens on the surface. This group of organs includes the AMPULLAE OF LORENZINI on the heads of elasmobranchs, the small PIT-ORGANS of silurids and the MORMYROMASTS of the mormyrids. Several other functions have been suggested, but the present consensus is that they are specialized lateral line organs in which electrical potential changes have replaced mechanical forces as the adequate stimuli. This may not have been such a great evolutionary step since ordinary neuromasts show constant rhythmic potential changes which are normally altered by deformation of the hair cells (Machin and Lissmann, 1960; Dijkgraaf, 1963).

Luminescent Organs

In some chemical reactions the changes in free energy lead to an emission of light. Electrons of reactant molecules are hoisted to a higher energy level (excited) and, in returning to the ground state, give off their excess energy as quanta of light or photons. Many examples of chemiluminescence have now been studied both in physical and biological systems (Johnson *et al.*, 1954; McElroy and Glass, 1961). The release of radiant energy as a consequence of metabolism occurs in some of the bacteria and fungi and in certain representatives of all the major phyla (Harvey, 1952, 1960). Although widespread, the distribution is sporadic and does not seem to follow any definite evolutionary pattern from one phylum to another. In some organisms the role of bioluminescence is clearly defined; in others its function is obscure, and its presence may be a fortuitous consequence of tissue metabolism.

Bioluminescence, like bioelectricity and animal heat, seems to have evolved as a by-product of tissue metabolism. Its scattered distribution among the lower forms, the varied and curious functions of luminescent organs and the emission of light without obvious function, suggest a phylogeny based on widespread biological processes. Some of the best evidence for this concept comes from studies of the luminescent bacteria. Many different species are recognized, and several of these (particularly representatives of the genera *Photobacterium* and *Achromobacter*) have been isolated and grown in cultures for many years. They are common on dead fish or spoiling meat. The importance of oxygen to their luminescence was recognized by Robert Boyle about 300 years ago, long before the metabolic basis of living light was appreciated. Boyle noted that very small amounts of "air" were required to maintain the glow of "shining meat," and we now know that the important constituent of the air is oxygen and the reaction an oxidative one requiring in addition flavin mononucleotide, a long-chain aldehyde and a specific enzyme or luciferase (Harvey, 1960; McElroy and Seliger, 1962). The biochemical steps in bacterial luminescence are thought to be linked to the electron transport chain of oxidative phosphorylation as indicated in Fig. 20.4.

The metabolic significance of these reactions is unknown, and the value of the light to the bacteria is questionable. It has been suggested, however, that such a reaction may have been important in the removal of free oxygen during the early stages of biochemical evolution (McElroy and Seliger, 1962). It will be recalled (Chapters 1 and 7) that life evolved under anaerobic conditions and that the first energy-yielding pathways were anaerobic. Oxygen, liberated in small amounts as a metabolic by-product, may have been toxic during these stages, and reactions such as those illustrated in Fig. 20.4 may have effectively removed it. The biochemical sequence involves several of the universal components of respiratory metabolism (reduced pyridine nucleotide and riboflavin phosphate) together with a specific enzyme and an aldehyde. If this speculation is valid, the light emission of present-day bacteria is probably a vestigial process since oxygen removal now serves no useful purpose. In support of this concept, mutant strains of some of these bacteria have been shown to lack one or the other of the constituents required for luminescence without obvious disadvantages to their growth and metabolism (Harvey, 1960). There are distinct "bright," "dim" and "dark" mutants. One of the dim strains becomes bright on the addition of a flavin to the culture fluid; another particularly interesting dark mutant seems to lack only the long-chain aldehyde and glows brightly when minute amounts of dodecaldehyde are supplied. The enzyme (luciferase) is evidently present, but a part of its substrate is absent. These bacterial studies support the theory of an evolution associated with oxidative cellular processes but quite divorced from any significance with respect to the emission of light.

It would be bold to argue that the phylogeny of animal bioluminescence had any direct connection with the processes of bacterial metabolism just described. The biochemistry is different in its specific details, and it seems more logical to assume an independent evolution in many different phyla, with the initial stages derived from the by-products of different metabolic processes. Luminescent earthworms of the genus *Eisenia*

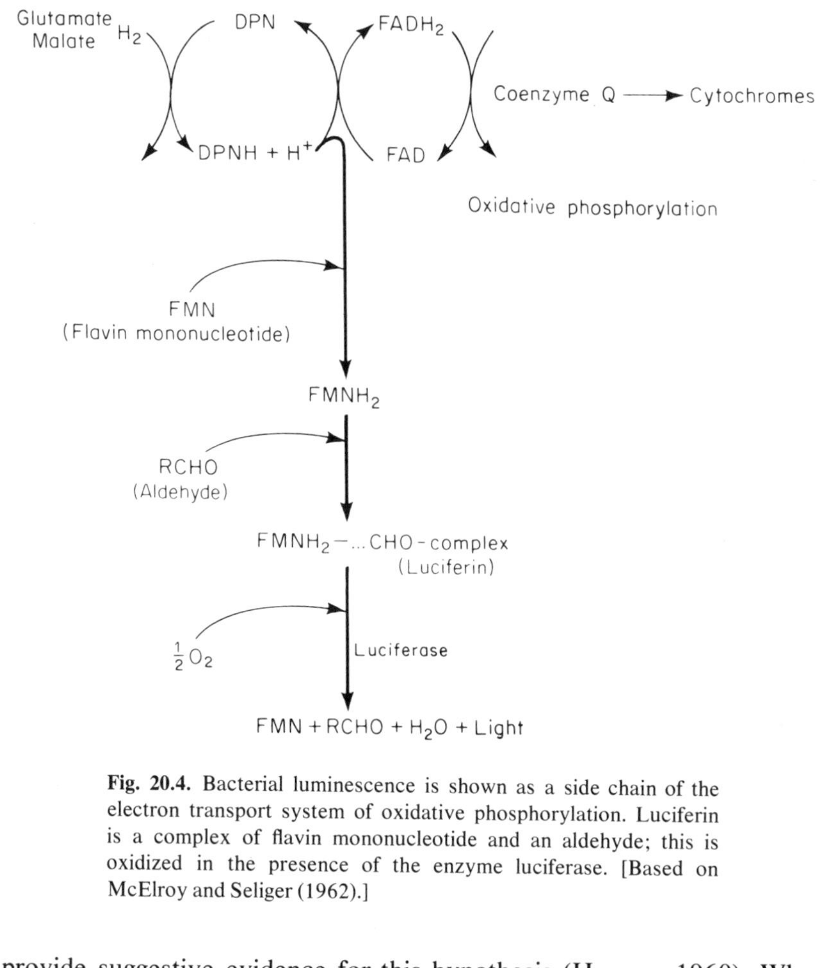

Fig. 20.4. Bacterial luminescence is shown as a side chain of the electron transport system of oxidative phosphorylation. Luciferin is a complex of flavin mononucleotide and an aldehyde; this is oxidized in the presence of the enzyme luciferase. [Based on McElroy and Seliger (1962).]

provide suggestive evidence for this hypothesis (Harvey, 1960). When disturbed, *E. submontana* exudes a yellowish slime from dorsal pores which open from its body cavity; on contact with the air this glows with a yellowish-green light. The pigment appears to be riboflavin. The significant point is that a closely allied species of worm (*E. foetida*) releases a yellowish fluid of similar biochemical nature when disturbed, but this is nonluminous. It seems likely that the fluid plays an adaptive role in the biology of these animals but that the light-emitting reaction is coincidental.

DISTRIBUTION OF BIOLUMINESCENCE

Biologists owe a great debt to E. Newton Harvey and his associates who, for more than half a century, accumulated information on the distribution of luminescent organisms, studied the biochemistry of light emission and gathered evidence concerning its biological significance and probable phylogeny. His monograph, published in 1952, contains a wealth of information on the distribution and biology of animals which emit light. In summary, most of the phyla of free-living animals have luminescent representatives, and these are particularly numerous among the larger phyla—protozoa, coelenterates, annelids, molluscs, arthropods and vertebrates. In all, some forty to fifty different groups emit light (Harvey, 1960). The majority are marine animals, ranging in habitat from the surface to the depths where only animal light flashes in the abyssal blackness. In contrast, the fresh waters are devoid of bioluminescence except for certain bacteria and a limpet, *Latia neritoides,* in the lakes and streams of New Zealand. In some parts of the world the terrestrial habitat is brightened at night by the flashing of fireflies, glowworms and lightning bugs (all members of the Coleoptera—beetles); in addition there are several other orders of insects, centipedes, millipedes, earthworms and one land snail capable of producing light. However, this is a relatively small array in contrast to the marine species; there are no luminescent organs among the terrestrial vertebrates or plants (other than bacteria and fungi).

BIOCHEMISTRY OF LUMINESCENCE

The pioneer experiments were performed by the French physiologist Raphaël Dubois (1885, 1887). He used the photogenic organs of the West Indian elaterid beetle *Pyrophorus* for the first of these. When brightly luminescent organs were plunged into boiling water the lights were extinguished, but the water, if quickly cooled, contained something which produced light when mixed with an extract prepared from similar organs by triturating them in cold water and letting the mixture stand until the luminescence had disappeared. These classical experiments were followed by comparable and much more detailed studies of the bivalve mollusc *Pholas dactylus*. This animal has the habit of boring in soft rock and thus creating the tunnels where it lives; its luminescence has excited the interest of naturalists since the days of Pliny (Harvey, 1952). Dubois' investigations of *Pholas* extended over a period of more than forty years. They have been summarized many times; Harvey (1952) has provided an extended bibliography.

Dubois coined the term LUCIFERIN for the principle in his hot water extracts and LUCIFERASE for that in the cold extracts. Very early in these studies he concluded that light production took place when luciferin was oxidized by molecular oxygen in the presence of a catalyst (luciferase). Subsequent research has shown that he was correct. Bioluminescence is an instance of chemiluminescence in which complex organic molecules (luciferins) are oxidized in the presence of specific enzymes (luciferases); molecular oxygen is almost always required for the reactions (Harvey, 1960). More than sixty years work since these

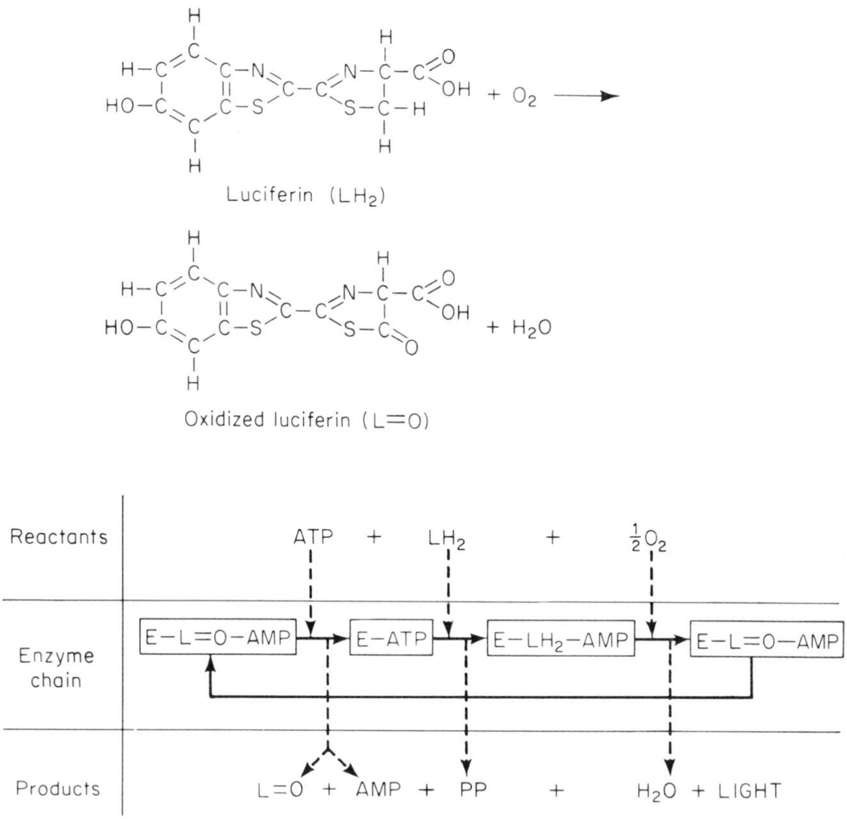

Fig. 20.5. Structural formula of firefly luciferin (above) with the suggested chemical sequence of luminescence below. *E*, luciferase enzyme; reactions also require Mg^{++}. [Based on McElroy and Seliger (1962).]

early studies of Dubois has demonstrated the varied nature of the organic molecules involved but confirmed the universality of a generalized luciferin-luciferase reaction. The three groups of organisms most carefully investigated biochemically are the luminescent bacteria (described above), the fireflies and the marine crustacean *Cyprinidia*.

The structural formula of firefly luciferin (Fig. 20.5) was established after almost half a century of continuous research (Harvey, 1914; McElroy and Seliger, 1961, 1962). Its chemical structure has now been confirmed by synthesis, and the associated luciferase has been purified and shown to contain about 1000 amino acid residues. The reaction requires magnesium ions and phosphate bond energy; ATP is split to form adenosine monophosphate and inorganic pyrophosphate as summarized at the bottom of Fig. 20.5. The reaction occurs in an aqueous medium; dried lanterns from fireflies which have been dead for many years will luminesce brightly when broken and moistened. This is also true of many other bioluminescent tissues. During wartime, the Japanese soldiers turned the reaction to practical use by pulverizing dried bodies of tiny crustaceans (*Cyprinidia*) in their hands and moistening them to provide sufficient light for map reading (Harvey, 1952).

Cyprinidia hilgondorfii, a small (2 to 3 mm long) ostracod from Japan, has long been a favored object for the investigation of the luciferin-luciferase reaction. Harvey who first introduced it to research workers in 1916, describes the biology of this interesting little animal together with a history of the biochemical studies (Harvey, 1952, 1960). The suggested formula for ostracod luciferin is as follows (Johnson *et al.*, 1961):

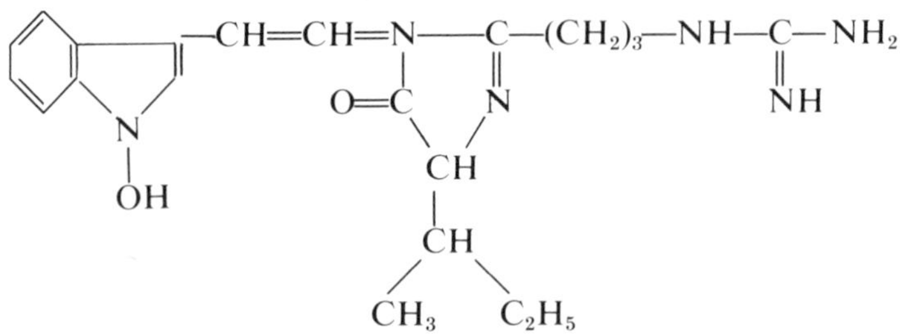

The oxidation of this material also requires molecular oxygen but does not depend on the presence of Mg^{++} and ATP. Many other luciferins are now under active investigation, and it is apparent that the oxidizable compounds and reactants are as different as the groups of animals which produce them. Light emission in some of the Hydromedusae (*Aequorea, Halistaura*) depends on a single protein instead of the usual enzyme substrate ("luciferin-luciferase") system. This protein luminesces with Ca^{++}; the reaction is independent of the oxygen tension. *Balanoglossus* luciferase seems to be a peroxidase with peroxide rather than oxygen required for the emission of light. These curious exceptions to the usual type of reaction, first described by Dubois, emphasize an opportunism in the evolution of luminescent processes and suggest that there may still be many surprises for the biochemist who studies them. Recent work is summarized in the monographs edited by Giese (1964).

PHYSICAL PROPERTIES

The colors of living lights vary all the way from blues, ranging from 410 mμ in some of the bacteria, polychaetes and teleosts, to the reds of some of the beetles which extend from 650 mμ through orange and yellow to yellow-greens. Bioluminescence is most frequently blue, blue-green or white; green and yellow are less common; orange and red are comparatively rare (Nicol, 1962). A few animals possess two kinds of luminous organs, each emitting its particular color of light. The "railroad worm" (larval stages of *Phixothrix*) from Central and South America emits a greenish-yellow light from 11 pairs of luminous spots on the posterior lateral margins of the second thoracic to the ninth abdominal segments of the body, and a bright red glow from paired organs on the head. The two sets of lamps operate independently, and when only the headlights are on, the organism looks like a glowing cigarette; when disturbed and crawling, the green lights also flash on to suggest a moving train with red head lamps (Harvey, 1962; McElroy and Seliger, 1962).

Spectral emission curves are usually rather narrow and sharply peaked; occasionally they are broad and sometimes bimodal in form (Fig. 20.6). The light is always of low intensity, although the brilliant flashes of the ctenophore *Mnemiopsis* may be one to two million times brighter than the dim flashes of the dinoflagellate *Noctiluca*, when comparisons are made on the basis of comparable areas of receptor surface

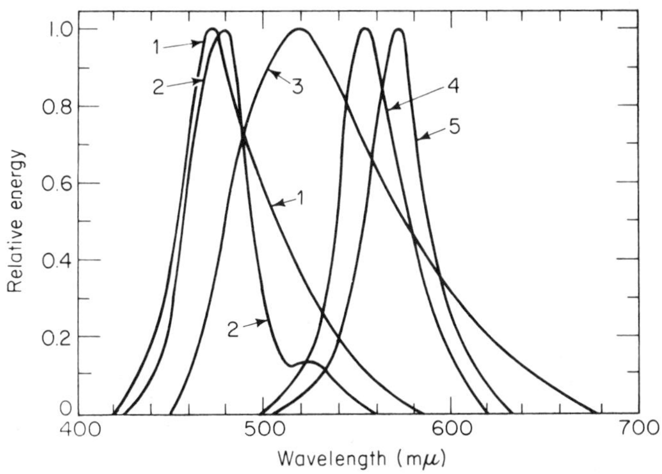

Fig. 20.6. Some relative spectral emission curves. 1, *Noctiluca miliaris*. 2, *Euphausia pacifica*. 3, polynoid worms. 4, *Photuris pennsylvanica*. 5, *Photinus pyralis*. [Nicol (1962).]

and distance. For the multicellular animals this range can be reduced by a factor of 10 to 100 times. Nicol (1960*a,b*, 1962) has summarized data on spectral quality, brightness of illumination and various temporal characteristics of the flashes.

MORPHOLOGICAL CORRELATES

"There are always two aspects to any evolutionary problem: (1) the first beginnings of a new organ, in this case the appearance of chemical reactions which emit light; (2) the further evolution of accessory structures, in this case the development of lenses, reflectors, and pigment screens" (Harvey, 1960). In no system is this more completely illustrated than in the bioluminescent organs which have achieved considerable variety and great complexity in most of the phyla where luminescent organs occur. Many of these beautiful lanterns have been described in detail and are well illustrated in books by Harvey (1952) and Nicol (1960*a*). There are three fundamentally different patterns: SPECIAL TISSUES OR ORGANS UTILIZING SYMBIOTIC BACTERIA, the discharge of luminous secretions (EXTRACELLULAR LUMINESCENCE) and the presence of light-emitting cells (INTRACELLULAR LUMINESCENCE). A few animals possess both types of intrinsic luminescent tissue.

Use of symbiotic bacteria. Some ot the myopsid squids and a few families of deep-sea teleosts depend on symbiotic bacteria which grow in special tissue sacs; these sacs may be provided with reflectors, lenses and pigment curtains to control the emission of the light. Fishes of the family Anomalopidae have a conspicuous elongated organ just below the eye. This is formed of long glandular tubes filled with luminous bacteria. Numerous blood vessels supply the tubes. The organ has pores to the outside and a reflector layer at the rear. The bacteria luminesce continuously, but the light can be intermittently concealed in some species by turning the organ downward until its light surface is covered by a pocket of black pigmented tissue, while in others a fold of black tissue can be drawn up over the light surface like an eyelid.

Extracellular luminescence. Luminous secretion has been described in representatives of all the major groups of light-emitting animals, from coelenterates and nemerteans to the balanoglossids and fishes (Nicol, 1962). It is common among the marine invertebrates but rare among the terrestrial invertebrates and the fishes. Exceptions among the latter groups include some of the myriapods and oligochaetes and a single group of fishes, the alepocephalid genus *Searsia*. Secretions may appear as a luminous slime over the surface of the body as in balanoglossids, or as discrete scintillating points of light in the beautiful little transparent nudibranch *Phyllirrhoe bucephala*; often these exudates are suddenly released in a brilliant luminescent cloud as in some of the pelagic shrimps, in the boring bivalve *Pholas dactylus*, in the polychaete *Chaetopterus* or in the fireworm *Odontosyllis*.

The photocytes are elongated flask or club-shaped cells. They usually occur as patches of unicellular glands interspersed with mucus cells (Fig. 20.7). Sometimes they are grouped into compact masses which open through a common duct like an alveolar or tubulo-alveolar gland. The epithelial area concerned may be epidermal as in *Chaetopterus* and *Pholas*, or it may be coelomic as in the earthworms or pelagic shrimps (green gland secretion).

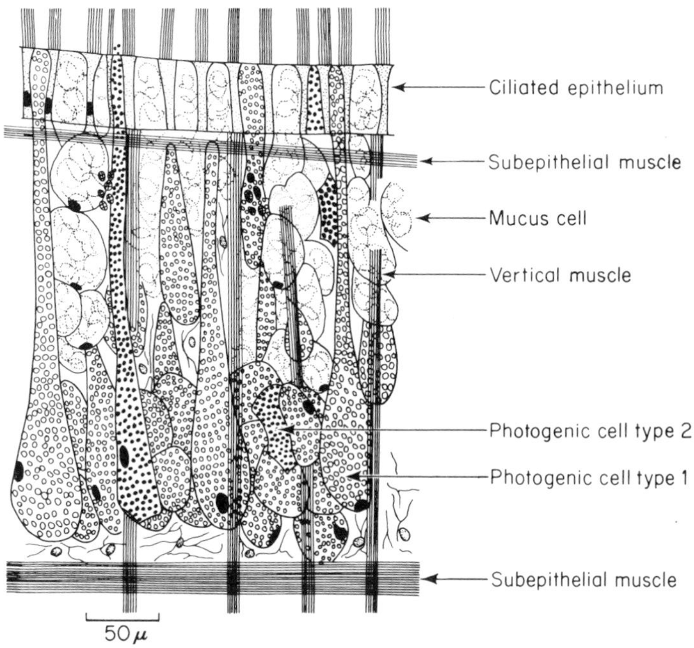

Fig. 20.7. Cross section through tissue responsible for extracellular luminescence in *Pholas dactylus*. [Nicol (1962).]

Most of the details of extracellular luminescence remain unsolved. The biochemistry and morphology have been described in relatively few forms; physiological controls are understood in only general terms. Extrusion could be dependent on associated muscle fibers as illustrated in Fig. 20.7, but the photocyte itself may be responsible since nerve endings have been traced directly to it in some forms (Nicol, 1962). Extracellular luminescence is usually intermittent, and nervous control has been satisfactorily demonstrated in certain forms from coelenterates throughout the phylogenetic series (Nicol, 1960*b*, 1962); but details of receptors, pathways and transmitter substances remain to be elucidated. In some animals such as *Cyprinidia* two types of granular cells are evident, and it is presumed that luciferin and luciferase are separately discharged and mixed in water; in many forms no such morphological separation of cell types is apparent, and the manner in which enzyme and substrate are brought together remains obscure.

Intracellular luminescence. The greatest structural complexities occur in photophores where light is produced intracellularly. In many cases the light from groups of photocytes is concentrated by an arrangement of mirrors and lenses to sparkle like a brilliantly lighted jewel in the darkness. Some of these organs (photophores) look very much like eyes in which the receptor surface or retina has been replaced by a photogenic light-transmitting surface (Fig. 20.8).

Luminescence is almost always intracellular in the more advanced groups such as the fishes, terrestrial arthropods and cephalopods. It also occurs in some of the more primitive groups where there are no specialized photophores (Nicol, 1962). Several species of protozoans luminesce when stimulated. In the dinoflagellate *Noctiluca miliaris* photogenic granules of two sizes are arranged along strands of protoplasm which radiate from a concentrated area of granules near the oral groove; these join together around the periphery so that the cell, in surface view, looks like a shimmering fan (Harvey, 1952). The granules seem to be permanently located, but the flashing is intermittent and passes over the cell in waves which originate near the oral groove.

The luminous polynoid worm *Acholoë astericola* is another carefully described example in which intracellular photogenic tissues are diffuse rather than concentrated in photophores. Luminescence is confined to elytra or scale-like plates which cover the body segmentally. The photocytes occur in a single layer just above the cuticle of the lower surface of the scale and are well supplied by branches of the elytral nerve. When the animal is irritated a flash of light runs along the scales, passing from segment to segment; sometimes elytra are detached, and the animal swims away leaving its glowing scales behind it. Characteristically, the luminous polynoids have easily detached scales and swim with rapid movements (Harvey, 1952).

Intracellular luminescence is no better understood than extracellular luminescence; problems associated with the physiological control are similar in both. Intracellular light is always intermittent. In the multicellular forms, control by nerves is well documented at all levels in phylogeny, and there is no evidence of hormonal influence (Nicol, 1960*b*).

The physiological regulation has been most carefully studied in the fireflies where flashing lights form a complex signalling system between

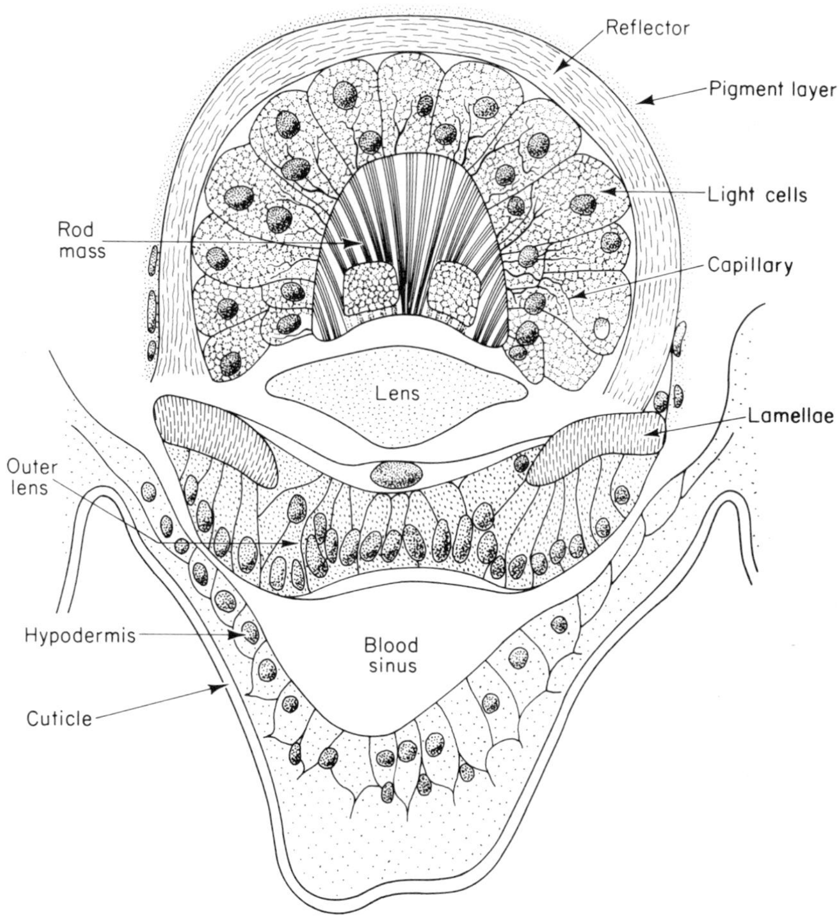

Fig. 20.8. Photophore of the euphausid *Nyctiphanes norvegica*. Light emitting surface at bottom. [Based on Harvey (1952) after Dahlgren (1916).]

the males and females. The precise timing of the flashes and their relation to an intricate mating sequence indicate a nervous control, but the details of its organization are still somewhat speculative. Two morphological characters have long figured prominently in the theories. One of these is the tracheolar system which in most species provides the photocytes with numerous closely applied air capillaries (Buck, 1948); the other is the innervation which is well developed and often parallels the tracheolar tubules. Two different theories have been current for a long time (Buck, 1948; Nicol, 1962). According to one of these, nervous excitation leads to a sudden release of air, and this puff of oxygen to the chemical reactants produces a flash; according to the other theory, adequate oxygen is normally present, but release of the transmitter substance acetylcholine triggers the chemical reaction. McElroy and Seliger (1962) favor the latter view as indicated in Fig. 20.5.

Physiological controls of other complex photophores have not been at all well investigated. Among the fishes, only the midshipman *Porichthys* has been carefully studied. Nicol (1960*b*, 1962) reviews the older work and his own more recent findings. There is morphological as well as physiological evidence for a nervous control from centers in the spinal cord – probably mediated through sympathetic nerves. Although a hormonal regulation by adrenaline has been suggested, the evidence is largely against it.

FUNCTIONAL SIGNIFICANCE OF BIOLUMINESCENCE

Bioluminescence has been woven into the lives of many animals in ways that affect the survival of individuals or the reproductive success of the species. Sometimes it seems as though there may be no functional significance but, although this was suggested in the earlier section on phylogeny, the concept is never completely acceptable; the lack of apparent functional significance for the light may be due to limitations in knowledge concerning the species. The literature already cited contains abundant evidence for the biological importance of living light. A few examples have been selected to indicate the various ways in which this occurs.

One of the most striking examples of the use of BIOLUMINESCENCE IN FOOD GATHERING is provided by the glowworms of the famous caves at Waitomo about 200 miles north of Wellington, New Zealand (Harvey, 1952). These glowworms are dipteran larvae (Bolitophilidae) which live in vast numbers on the ceilings of the caves. Each spins a long, sticky, glistening thread which hangs down 15 to 60 cm and serves as a trap for other insects. The glowworms are carnivorous, and this unique method of trapping their food probably depends on attraction of prey by the lights as well as the air currents which move through the caves. The lights are rapidly extinguished if there is any unusual disturbance in the cave.

A number of the marine invertebrates emit light in ways which suggest a significant role in FACILITATING ESCAPE FROM PREDATORS. Some, such as the deep-sea shrimp *Systellaspis* or the squid *Heteroteuthis*, suddenly discharge a cloud of luminous secretion when irritated, and this might confuse a predator and permit an escape into the darkness. Easily detachable luminous scales of the polynoid worms might serve in a similar manner to distract a predator while the remainder of the animal swims away. These possibilities have never been tested experimentally.

There are several well-known instances of bioluminescence during sexual behavior; in some cases the light plays a part in the TIMING OF REPRODUCTION and in synchronizing the activities of the males and females; in other cases, well-defined photophore patterns or specific timing of flashes seem to serve as INTRASPECIFIC RECOGNITION SIGNALS. The swarming of fireworms, *Odontosyllis* (Polychaeta), is timed by lunar and diurnal light rhythms (Chapter 17), but the mating sequence seems to be controlled by the flashing of living lights. The much larger females commence swimming in the surface waters at a precise time in the evening; they suddenly become brilliantly phosphorescent as they swim rapidly in small circles two to three inches in diameter, discharging eggs and luminous secretions to form halos into which the males, emerging from deeper waters, dart to discharge their sperms (Harvey, 1952).

The mating of fireflies often depends on a very accurate signalling system. Females of the common Eastern North American species (*Photinus pyralis*) do not fly about but crawl onto a blade of grass in the evening and wait in the darkness for a proper signal. The males flash their lanterns as they fly approximately 50 cm above the ground; if a female sees one of these flashes within three to four meters, she may be expected to flash back after an exact interval (2 sec at 25°C). This attracts the male in her direction. After four or five exchanges of signals the male reaches the female and mating occurs. In this species, recognition evidently depends on the flash interval. Other species have somewhat different signalling systems; females of the European glowworm *Lampyris noctiluca* are flightless and emit a long-lasting light which attracts the much less brilliantly luminous males; in some species the males lack luminescent organs. These signalling systems of the fireflies have reached a high level of specialization. Other groups of animals may have equally complex light-emitting behavior, but there is at present no accurate information. The teleost fishes, which are assumed to make use of their highly complex lanterns, are deep-sea animals rarely seen by man. Sexual differences in the patterns of the photophores and in the colors of their lights are suggestive of sex recognition structures, but no experimental work has been done, nor are there any satisfactory observations of mating behavior. The significance of the light to most of the luminescent animals is still an unexplored field of animal behavior.

Pigment Effector Cells

Pigmented compounds are found in animals at all levels in phylogeny. The carotenoids capture radiant energy in the photoreceptors and through photochemical changes excite nerves; metalloporphyrins and metalloproteins as blood pigments combine with oxygen and store or transport it to serve aerobic respiration; the body coverings of multicellular animals are usually pigmented, and it is a matter of general observation as well as careful experiment that such colorations are frequently cryptic and often provide recognition marks of importance in behavior. In contrast to the visual and respiratory pigments, the integumentary pigments are extremely varied biochemically, ranging from the almost ubiquitous melanins and carotenoids to the less common quinones, pterins and flavins (Fox and Vevers, 1960).

Most of the multicellular animals are characterized by a distinct color and often by a particular color pattern. These pigmented patterns are static or change only slowly from juvenile to adult stage, or with sexual maturation, or seasonally in accordance with the formation or destruction of pigment (MORPHOLOGICAL COLOR CHANGES). They may also change gradually under selection pressures, as in the slow replacement of the typical light-colored Pepper Moth *Biston betularia* by a black melanotic variety in the industrial areas of Britain (Kettlewell, 1961).

In addition to these fixed or very slowly changing colors, several groups of animals have a specialized system of effector organs which can rapidly alter the amount of exposed pigment in the integument so that the animal appears darker or lighter or assumes a matching background pattern. These are PHYSIOLOGICAL COLOR CHANGES and depend on specialized effector cells (chromatophores) in which the pigment is moved about in response to specific stimuli. This capacity is most highly developed among the cepalopods, the crustaceans and the poikilothermous vertebrates—especially the teleost fishes and the lizards. Some of the annelids and echinoderms become lighter during the day and darker at night, while a few of the insects adapt to the color of their background. But these groups are not characterized by species which habitually alter their colors to match their surroundings. Chromatophores as activated effectors are not found among birds and mammals.

MORPHOLOGY OF CHROMATOPHORES

Two types of effector are concerned with physiological color change. One of these, evidently confined to the molluscs, is a minute organ consisting of a sac-like cell containing pigment granules and surrounded by a stellate series of radial muscle fibers. These are attached to the elastic membrane of the cell and quickly contract or relax to change the shape of the pigment mass and hence the color of the animal. (Fig. 20.9). The scintillating colors which characterize some of the cephalopods depend on these small organs. A similar but much more slowly operating structure has been described in some of the nudibranchs (Nicol, 1964).

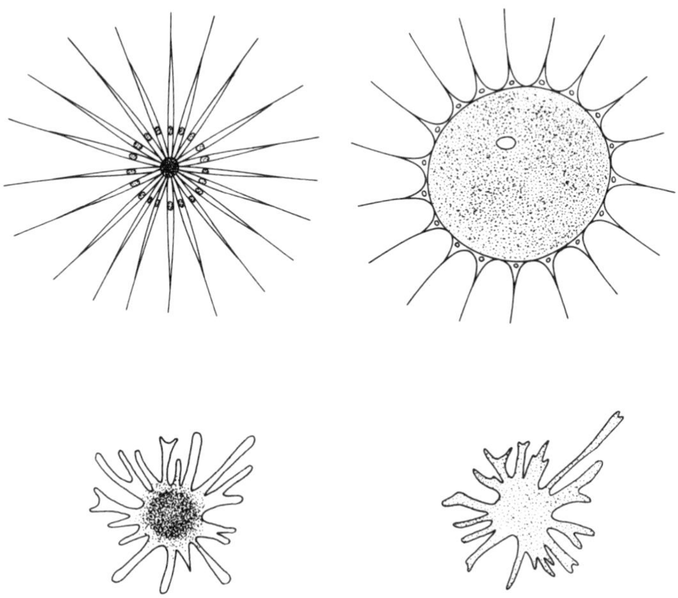

Fig. 20.9. Chromatophores with pigment aggregated on the left and expanded on the right. Upper, *Loligo* chromatophore with attached muscle cells [based on Parker (1948) after Bozler (1928).] Lower, melanophores of *Fundulus* [based on Matthews (1931)].

The other type of pigment effector is a single, irregularly shaped cell (sometimes an intermingled group of similar cells) containing pigment granules which can be concentrated in a small area or dispersed throughout the protoplasm. Only one kind of tissue is present in the second type of effector, and movement of the pigment does not depend on extracellular contractile elements. The cell boundaries are indistinct, and special techniques are required to make them visible. Shapes of chromatophores vary from lenticular or plate-like forms to intricate arborizing and stellate structures. As indicated in Figs. 20.9 and 20.10, pigment granules move out of the processes or away from the periphery to concentrate in a small area in the central part of the cytoplasm. Rapidity of movement and degree of concentration depend on the type of chromatophore and the nature of its physiological controls. Much of the quantitative work has been based on a five point MELANOPHORE INDEX (Fig. 20.10), first used by Hogben and Slome (1931) for amphibian chromatophores but subsequently adapted to other groups. The chromatophore index remains a reliable method of describing pigment changes (Waring, 1963).

Vertebrate chromatophores are clearly uninucleate cells containing one biochemical type of pigment (monochromatic). The chromatophores of crustaceans are sometimes described as syncytial or multinucleate masses of protoplasm (Kleinholz, 1961) which may contain as many as four different kinds of pigment. They are consequently dichromatic, trichromatic or polychromatic, depending on the number of colors which

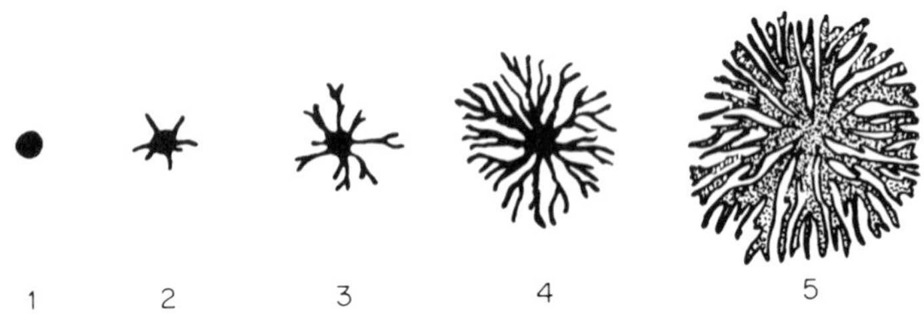

Fig. 20.10. The five-point melanophore index as used by Healey (1951) in his studies of *Phoxinus phoxinus*. 1, Punctate. 2, Puncto-stellate. 3, Stellate. 4, Reticulostellate. 5, Reticulate.

they display. These multicolored structures are sometimes called CHROMATOSOMES. Parker (1948) considered the chromatosome to be a group of unicellular chromatophores so closely united as to constitute a single color unit. All workers agree that each different kind of pigment moves independently within these structures, and many writers follow Parker in describing chromatosomes as intimately associated groups of chromatophores. Some of the complex pigment areas of amphibians and teleosts are clearly organized in this way with closely associated melanophores, xanthophores and guanophores (Fig. 20.11).

Four kinds of chromatophores have long been distinguished on the basis of color and the biochemical nature of their pigments. The distinctions were first made when it was thought that all black and brown pigments were melanins while the reds and yellows were carotenoids and the silvery deposits were guanine. On this basis, brown and black pigment cells were called MELANOPHORES; the red chromatophores were called **ERYTHROPHORES**; the yellow ones **XANTHOPHORES** and the silvery ones **GUANOPHORES** or **IRIDIOPHORES**. These terms are still prevalent, but their usage is changing since it is now clear that chromatophore color may depend on several pigments other than the melanins and the carotenoids. The beautiful colors of the cephalopod, for example, are neither

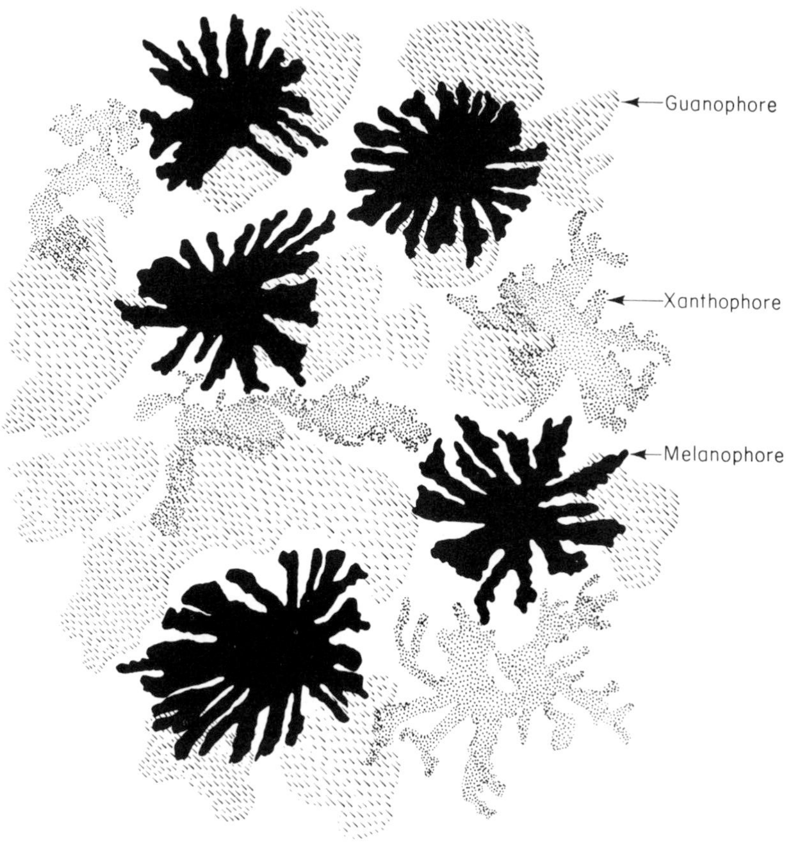

Fig. 20.11. Chromatophores just beneath the epidermis of the flounder *Paralichthys albiguttus*. [Based on Kuntz (1915).]

melanins nor carotenoids but ommochromes. This is a varied group of pigments which may appear black, brown, red, orange or yellow. The iris pigments of insects and crustaceans are ommochromes, as are also some of their body colors. Pterins form another group of pigmented substances which may be responsible for the yellow, orange and red tints. These are common in fishes and amphibians; they have also been found in crustaceans and insects.

The particular terms applied to chromatophores may now be defined somewhat differently but more precisely. The term melanophore should be restricted to the black or brown pigment effector cell containing melanin. This pigment also occurs in cells (melanocytes) which are not concerned with physiological color change; these are discussed below. The terms xanthophore and erythrophore may be applied to yellow and red chromatophores without any implications of the biochemical nature of their pigments. Guanophore is the preferred term for the effector cell which contains silvery guanine crystals or deposits. The terms leucophore and iridiophore (iridiocyte) have also been used for these guanine-containing cells. Sometimes iridiophore is used in a more restricted sense to describe rather large cells of constant shape which provide a silvery background for the chromatophores (cephalopods, for example), or the small aggregates of guanine crystals which look like brilliantly sparkling jewels in close association with the chromatophores, as in some teleosts. Although formed inside modified connective tissue cells, these masses of guanine may come to lie in the extracellular spaces (Parker, 1948).

MECHANISM OF PIGMENT MIGRATION

Chromatophores, except for the contractile pigment cells of molluscs, are of fixed form. This was not appreciated by early workers who attempted to explain their apparent changes in shape by theories of amoeboid movement and muscular contraction. The older literature is summarized by Lerner and Takahashi (1956).

Matthews (1931) made the first significant contribution when he demonstrated conclusively that the melanophores of *Fundulus* have an almost constant size during all phases of activity. He observed the cells in tissue culture and proved that the pigment distribution changes but the shape of the cell is not altered; these pigment movements may be observed in isolated cell processes as well as in intact melanophores. Micromanipulations led Matthews to conclude that granule dispersion was associated with decreased protoplasmic viscosity while the protoplasm became more viscous when the granules were clumping. Marsland's (1944) investigations of the action of hydrostatic pressure on *Fundulus* melanophores also linked granule movement with changes in protoplasmic viscosity. High pressure which is known to increase fluidity of protoplasm (sol condition) inhibits the clumping of granules; the effect is proportional to the pressure applied up to 7000 pounds per square inch. Low temperature (6°C) which has a similar action to high pressure on protoplasmic viscosity likewise inhibits clumping; high temperature (30°C) has the reverse effect. These responses are independent of nerves. Marsland was convinced that the movement of granules was a physical rather than a chemical process and depended on the capacity of protoplasm to undergo sol-gel transformations. Some observers have described contractile elements in the protoplasm of melanophores and suggest that these may move attached granules either by their own contractions or in association with viscosity changes. The work is cited in the above references.

Kinosita (1963) postulates an electrophoretic migration of pigment granules in the melanophores of *Oryzias*. His studies, like those of Matthews, were made on isolated melanophore processes as well as on intact cells. Evidence is based on measurements of melanophore potentials; these vary in a predictable manner with cellular activity and in accordance with the position of the inserted electrode. The granules appear to be negatively charged since they move toward the anode. In the dispersed state the central part of the pigment cell is electrically more negative than the cell processes; consequently the granules move out into the processes. Kinosita also finds a change from the sol condition in the dispersed phase to the gel condition in the clumped phase; these colloidal changes are coupled with the electrophoretic movement. Agents such as KCl and adrenaline, which clump melanin granules, alter the cell potentials in accordance with a theory of electrophoretic migration. Kinosita has also investigated *Oryzias* guanophores. The pigment granules are likewise negative but the chromatophore potential is reversed with the processes electrically more negative that the center of the cell. In accordance with theory, KCl has an opposite effect on the movements of melanophore and guanophore pigment granules.

There is now a rich literature on the effects of ions and drugs on the movement of pigment granules (Novales *et al.*, 1962; Novales, 1963). The clumping action of potassium ions has been mentioned; sodium ions have the reverse effect. MSH which disperses melanin granules (page 606) acts only in the presence of sodium ions and it is evidently the influx of Na^+ rather than the MSH which changes the distribution of the granules. This is currently an active area of investigation; the present findings indicate that the ultimate explanations will be in terms of membrane permeability and potentials.

CHROMATOPHORE PIGMENTS

The chromatophore pigments are the melanins, the ommochromes, the carotenoids, the pterins or pteridines and guanine. Several other groups of chemicals are also involved in the varied color displays of animals (Fox, 1953; Fox and Vevers, 1960), but the present description is confined to those which are common in chromatophores.

Melanins. Melanin is formed through the oxidative metabolism of the aromatic amino acid tyrosine. A copper-containing enzyme, tyrosinase (also called phenol or polyphenol oxidase) catalyzes the initial oxidation to 3, 4-dihydroxyphenylalanine (DOPA). Several of the subsequent steps are outlined in Fig. 20.12, but some of the details are still uncertain. It should be realized that melanin is not a single compound but a group of polymers of different sizes (Thomson, 1962). Their colors are as variable as those of human hair. In chromatophores, the melanin granules may be linked to protein.

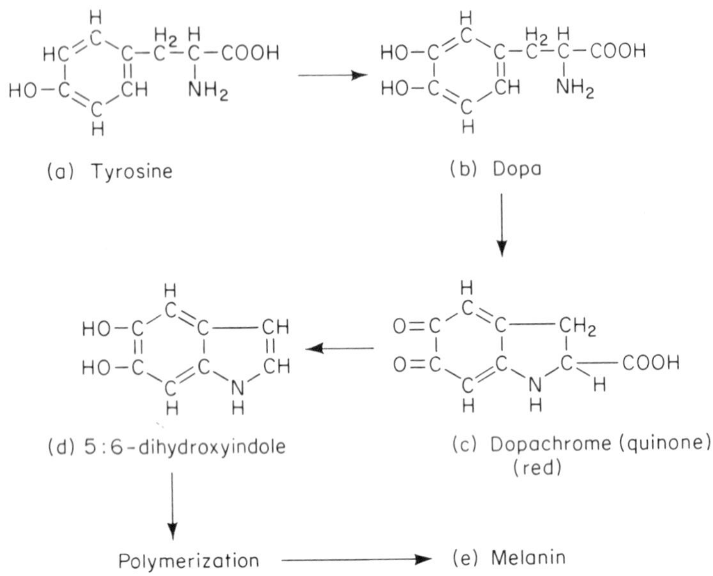

Fig. 20.12. Several steps in melanogenesis. See also Fig. 2.13.

The metabolism of tyrosine and phenylalanine was already mentioned in connection with the biosynthesis of noradrenaline and adrenaline (Chapter 2, Fig. 2.13). These hormones or transmitter substances, like melanin, arise from tyrosine by way of "DOPA"; it is of interest that the cells concerned with melanogenesis in vertebrates, as well as the tissues of the adrenal medulla, develop from the neural crests. Embryonic cells with the capacity to synthesize melanin are called MELANOBLASTS; both the MELANOPHORES (pigment effector cells) and the MELANOCYTES are their direct descendants. The latter are also responsible for melanogenesis but do not show pigment movement (Gordon, 1959). They are found in various tissues throughout the vertebrates and were identified in Chapter 14 as responsible for melanogenesis in human skin. The melanocytes of mammalian skin occur at the dermo-epidermal junction, with dendritic processes extending into the stratum germinativum to which they pass melanin as described in Chapter 14. They are usually colorless cells, but their biosynthetic characteristics may be easily revealed histochemically by the "DOPA" reaction (Ham and Leeson, 1961).

Melanogenesis is not confined to the descendants of melanoblasts from the neural crests of vertebrates. It probably occurs in plants (some mushrooms and bacteria) and in at least a few animals at all levels in phylogeny (the anemone *Metridium senile,* the echinoderm *Diadema,* the polychaete *Chaetopterus* and the gastropod *Limnaea*). However, among the invertebrates melanin probably is less common than some of the other black or brown pigments (Fox and Vevers, 1960; Thomson, 1962). One of the most active melanin-producing tissues is the ink gland of cephalopods. With the exception of *Nautilus,* these molluscs secrete melanin from a glandular mass in the region of the digestive tract and store it in the ink sac. When the animal is excited, ink can be squirted through the anus in a black cloud to serve as a smoke screen behind which the animal escapes. As evidence of the chemical stability of melanin, fossil ink sacs have yielded melanin which was stored in the fossil form for as long as 150 million years.

Ommochromes. Until about 1940 all the black or brown pigments were considered to be melanin. First, the brown tanned protein SCLEROTIN was identified in the cuticle of insects and, at almost the same time, ommochromes and not melanins were shown to form the iris pigments of insects and crustaceans. Ommochromes can be readily separated from melanins on the basis of solubility and colors in certain specific reagents (Fox and Vevers, 1960). They are common in molluscs and arthropods and responsible for fixed colors as well as the pigments of chromatophores. Ommochromes have also been identified in the eggs of *Urechis*; they are unknown in the vertebrates.

The ommatins are derivatives of the heterocyclic amino acid tryptophan. The metabolic breakdown of this essential amino acid involves an oxidation with the opening of the pyrrole ring (enzyme, tryptophan pyrrolase) followed by a hydrolysis to form kynurenine. Several of the subsequent steps in the biosynthesis of the yellow pigment xanthommatin are shown in Fig. 20.13. In the higher animals, the products of tryptophan metabolism are excreted as kynurenine, 3-hydroxykynurenine or derivatives (Henderson *et al.*, 1962); in some of the lower forms (particularly the molluscs and arthropods) these substances are converted into integumentary and chromatophore pigments. Information on the comparative biochemistry is still sketchy. The basis of the color differences, ranging from yellow to black, is unknown; the genetics of the enzyme systems has been investigated only in some of the fruit flies (*Drosophila*).

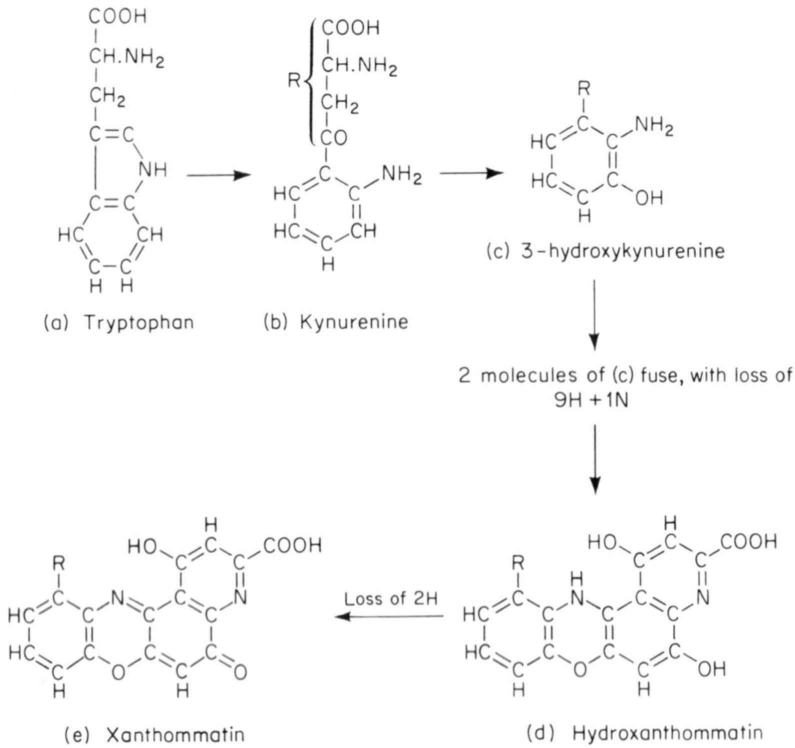

Fig. 20.13. Biosynthesis of xanthommatin.

Carotenoids. Knowledge of the carotenoids is much more extensive and of much longer standing than that of the ommatins. Perhaps because of their ubiquitous distribution and their prominence in plants they have been studied by chemists for well over a hundred years (Chapter 14). No animal is known to synthesize carotenoids; they are obtained directly or indirectly from the plants, and yet at all levels in animal phylogeny they play an essential role in visual processes and in integumentary pigmentation; in some animals they also function in color changes and probably in other processes. The orange, brown and red colors of coelenterates and sponges are often carotenoids, as are also the bright colors in the exoskeleton of crustaceans like the lobster and the crayfish (astaxanthin), or the dermis of the goldfish or the feathers of the canary. In the crustaceans the carotenoids share with the ommatins the responsibility for a range of colors from yellow to black; in the vertebrates they function in a similar manner with the melanins and the pterins. The diversity of carotenoid colors may be due to differences in the proteins with which they combine to form carotenoproteins as well as to variations in the carotenoid part of the molecule. Carotenoids may not be present in mollusc chromatophores (Goodwin, 1962). The chemistry of carotenoid pigments was considered in Chapter 14.

Pterins. The pterins or pteridines were discovered during the early part of the present century in the wings of butterflies. The first of these was a yellow pigment XANTHOPTERIN. Its name comes from the Greek roots for yellow and wing. Thus it records the history of the first biochemical isolation of these substances from lepidopteran wings, almost a quarter of a million of which were used in one of the pioneer studies (Fox and Vevers, 1960).

The pterins became much more than a biochemical curiosity when it was discovered in 1945 that an important vitamin, folic acid (pteroyl-L-glutamic acid) is a pterin-containing compound (Fruton and Simmonds, 1958). Another essential vitamin, riboflavin (Fig. 7.9) seems to be closely related to the pteridines in its biosynthesis (Forrest, 1962). These substances are described here because of their presence in chromatophores. They are often associated with carotenoids in determining the yellow, orange and red colors of fishes and amphibians. They may also occur in some of the chromatophores of crustaceans (Fox and Vevers, 1960). Their role in chromatophore physiology seems to be subsidiary to that of the carotenoids and the ommochromes.

The pterins are related to the purines from which they may be derived in their biosynthesis. F. G. Hopkins who discovered them in the latter part of the nineteenth century, thought that he was dealing with a derivative of uric acid (2, 6, 8-trioxypurine) which is present along with isoguanine (2-oxy-6-aminopurine) in butterfly wings. However, the biosynthetic pathways of the pterins are still uncertain (Forrest, 1962). The structures of xanthopterin, biopterin (found in normal human urine, in fruit flies, etc.) and folic acid are shown in Fig. 20.14. The pteridine nucleus which is characteristic of this class of compounds seems to be of universal occurrence, from bacteria through all living organisms to the higher plants and animals. As a constituent of vital enzyme systems it probably occurs in all cells. There is no evidence that animals are able to synthesize pteridines; they may always obtain them indirectly from the plants as they do their carotenoids (Forrest, 1962).

Guanine. As a constituent of the nucleic acids, guanine (2-amino-6-hydroxypurine) is ubiquitous in both plant and animal cells. In addition to its position as an essential building block of the genetic code (Chapter 22), the comparative physiologist knows it as an excretion product in the spiders (Chapter 8) and as an important component of some of the most beautiful animal colors.

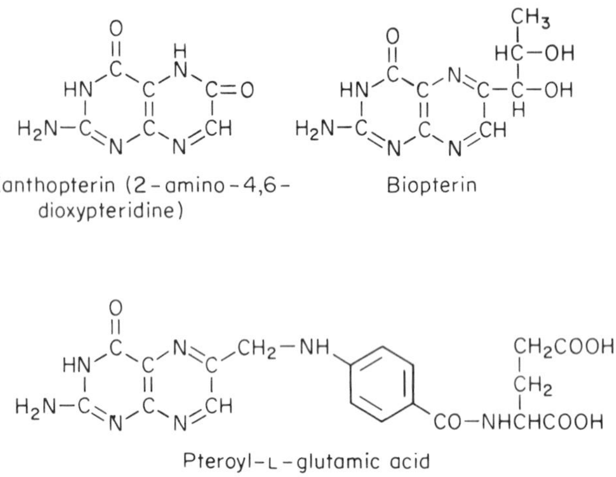

Fig. 20.14. Some pteridine compounds.

Purine biosynthesis occurs widely in animal tissues, and the phylogenetic adaptation of guanine to the problems of animal coloration may have been based on its tendency to form relatively insoluble deposits with the capacity to reflect light. On the other hand, its use in integumentary colors may have been built on a process of storage excretion. The storage excretion of urates and guanates in the terrestrial arthropods was noted in Chapter 8. A system of special cells takes up these highly insoluble nitrogenous wastes and stores them either permanently or temporarily, and it seems reasonable to assume that such cells might be adapted to other purposes. It may be significant that guanine occurs abundantly in the connective tissues of internal organs like the swim bladder as well as in the integument of some of the marine teleosts, a group of animals in which the supplies of water for removal of soluble nitrogenous wastes is very limited.

Guanine operates in several different ways to affect the colors of animals. In some of the cephalopods it occurs as myriads of orderly arranged crystals in large connective tissue cells or iridiophores; the crystals are static, and the sheets of iridiophores form a mirror-like background for the chromatophores. In some of the teleosts the guanine particles are so minute that the incident light undergoes a Tyndall scattering which, against a background of melanophores, appears blue. The visual effects may be silvery or white, depending on the size and distribution of the particles, while associated chromatophores may produce a varied iridescence and different metallic hues.

Pigment effector cells containing guanine (guanophores) have been described in the teleosts and amphibians. Their activities are controlled by neurohumors in a manner comparable to those of other chromatophores (Parker, 1948; Bagnara, 1958). The white pigment in some crustacean chromatophores may be guanine, but this has not yet been established (Carlisle and Knowles, 1959; Kleinholz, 1961).

FACTORS REGULATING THE MOVEMENT OF PIGMENT

Chromatophore responses are described as PRIMARY if they are evoked by nonvisual stimuli, and SECONDARY if the visual pathways are involved. This distinction was first drawn in studies of larval salamanders where the earliest responses of the pigment effector cells are often independent of the eyes (Parker, 1948). Larval *Ambystoma* of several different species, ranging in length from about 1.5 cm to 5.0 cm, are light in color when in complete darkness but become dark when in bright light; animals which are larger than about 5 cm show almost the reverse reaction. Moreover, the older ones will revert to the early larval type of chromatic behavior if they are blinded. A similar sequence of primary, followed by a secondary response has been noted in many but not all fishes and amphibians during early life. The secondary color response, characteristic of late larval and adult life, depends on the nature of the background, more particularly on the ratio of the incident to reflected light reaching the retina.

In many adult animals pigment effector cells are activated in several ways which do not involve the eyes. Light, temperature and humidity may alter the distribution of pigment in certain blinded animals, and these responses are also usually called PRIMARY. Sometimes the pigment cells respond as independent effectors, as they evidently do in the larval primary responses: in other cases, nerve reflexes and the hormones are definitely involved. This classification in terms of primary or secondary responses is not entirely satisfactory in view of the varied physiology involved in both types of coordination (Fingerman, 1959; Waring, 1963).

Chromatophores act as independent effectors in relatively few cases. Waring (1963) lists only *Xenopus* and *Phrynosoma* as unquestionably showing chromatophore changes after both denervation of the skin and removal of the pituitary; usually, pigment movement is controlled either by hormones or through nerves. The hormonally regulated changes are relatively slow; those mediated by direct innervation may be exceedingly rapid. The latter appears to be more specialized and more recent phylogenetically. Waring (1963) tabulates data suggesting that the more ancient animals had a hormonal control of chromatophores while those of recent origin may be controlled only by reflexes. The more ancient fishes (cyclostomes and elasmobranchs) and the primitive tetrapods (amphibians) show relatively slow chromatophore responses which are hormonally regulated; some of the teleosts and reptiles depend only on nerves. The teleost fishes as a group present the most convincing picture, with a completely humoral control in the Anguillidae, a group which can be traced back into the early Eocene, a mixed nervous and endocrine coordination in families such as the Siluridae and Pleuronectidae which seem to have evolved in the late Eocene, and an entirely nervous regulation in families of very recent origin such as the Gasterosteidae and Cyprinodontidae—evolving sometime in the Pleistocene. Waring presents the picture tentatively, for there is much that is speculative and many blanks still exist. The concept, however, finds further support in the two groups of invertebrates which show marked physiological color changes. Chromatophores of the decapod crustaceans, with a probable origin in the Triassic, are entirely controlled by hormones while the highly specialized reflexly-controlled pigment cells of the dibranchiate cephalopods belong to animals of Pleistocene or Recent origin.

Nervous control in cephalopods. The chromatophores of cephalopods are the most highly specialized structures concerned with color change. They are in reality pigment effector ORGANS rather than cells, and the movement of the pigment mass depends on the stretching of the cell membrane by radiating extrinsic muscle cells. Contractions may be extremely rapid (0.14 to 0.5 sec in *Loligo* and about 1 sec in *Sepia*) and can produce waves of varied hues which sweep swiftly over the animal to assist in camouflage by breaking up the body outline. These oscillating colors may produce definite patterns which are precisely associated with different aspects of the animal's behavior (Nicol, 1960).

The innervation of the chromatophore muscles has been described and the coordination has been shown to depend on color centers in the subesophageal ganglia of the brain. The pathways from the neurons of these ganglia are direct to the muscles of the chromatophores. Most of the experimental work was carried out many years ago. It was summarized by Parker in 1948. The more recent contributions are discussed by Fingerman (1963) and Nicol (1964).

The minute muscles in *Sepia officinalis* will respond to electrical stimuli without fatigue for as long as 30 minutes at frequencies of about

30 per sec. Single twitches can be elicited by direct stimulation of the skin at frequencies just less than 1 per sec; partial summation occurs at about 1.5 per sec and complete summation or tetanus at about 10 per sec. The exact values will vary with the temperature and, because of the direct nature of the stimulation, it is not known whether the action is on the muscle itself or indirectly through the nerves. These experiments, however, do demonstrate properties of a typical nerve-muscle preparation.

Denervation results in an initial blanching of the area involved, but after several days the region becomes permanently darker than the rest of the animal. These denervated areas fail to show the changes which are characteristic of the remainder of the animal, and the technique has proved useful in tracing the distribution of nerves. An interesting series of reactions is also observed in sections of skin which have been isolated and maintained under physiological conditions. Initially, the excised integument is pale, but after a few hours it may show waves of varied dark and light tints which pass to and fro over the sections until death. These curious reactions, frequently observed, have been studied with respect to different ions and many drugs. The peculiar properties of the muscles responsible for the changes are still not understood (Nicol, 1964).

The earlier literature records the effects of numerous drugs, either injected into animals or applied to pieces of skin. Some of the findings suggest a humoral control in addition to the neural regulation. The classical experiments of Sereni (1930 and earlier) are reviewed by Parker (1948). One of his most convincing demonstrations involved the parabiotic union of the circulatory systems of two octopuses. The two animals then change color as a single individual, and even when two different species with quite distinct coloration are used, a change induced in one of the partners leads to a parallel change in the other. Sereni also identified tyramine as an important secretion of the posterior salivary glands of cephalopods and noted that removal of these glands led to lighter skin colors while injection of tyramine produced darkening. Tyramine, like adrenaline, increases the muscular tone and thus expands the chromatophores. Betaine, also known to be present in cephalopod blood, has the reverse reaction and shares this with acetylcholine, pilocarpine and related substances. These results are suggestive but by no means conclusive evidence for an endocrine control of the cephalopod chromatophore. The regulation is predominantly nervous, and the above effects may be those of the transmitter substances.

Hormonal control in crustaceans. Physiological color changes in arthropods depend on hormonally-regulated movements of pigment granules within chromatophores. There is no innervation of the effector cells; there are no extrinsic contractile elements; pigment movement is probably by protoplasmic streaming. Thus, the system is built on mechanisms which seem to be phylogenetically most ancient. The extent of specialization within this framework, however, is such that some of the arthropods are capable of remarkably varied and beautiful color patterns which change adaptively in relation to environmental factors, both visual and nonvisual. It is not known when pigment effector cells first appeared in phylogeny, but the present-day crustaceans with a fossil record extending back almost 300 million years show some of the most notable color reactions in the animal world. This ability seems to have been achieved through the variety of different pigments within chromatosome complexes, or polychromatic syncytial cells, and through the specialization of different hormones to regulate the independent movements of these varied pigments.

The arthropods as a group show a considerable range in chromatic abilities. Although the capacity for morphological change in color is widespread, physiological change is restricted to a few of the insects and to several orders of the Malacostraca among the crustaceans (Isopoda, Stomatopoda, Decapoda). By far the largest number of species showing color change are decapod crustaceans which have the greatest variety of pigments and the most elaborate system of endocrines for their regulation. The least specialized condition is shown by some of the isopods which change from darker to lighter phases under environmental conditions but have no real capacity to alter their colors or color patterns because of the limited variety of chromatophores present. The chromatophores of isopods are monochromatic and usually contain a reddish brown pigment which is probably an ommochrome. Relatively small numbers of white and yellow pigment cells may be present, but the dark ones dominate. From this simple situation, some of the brachyuran (true) crabs *(Uca, Hemigrapsus, Callinectes, Eriocheir)* represent an intermediate condition between the isopods and the natantian decapods (shrimps). The brachyurans have three (occasionally four) kinds of monochromatic chromatophores (black, red and white) scattered throughout the hypodermis but not arranged so as to produce striking color patterns; many of the shrimps (Natantia) have an elaborate system of chromatosomes or polychromatic chromatophores which may contain as many as four different pigments within one complex and as many as eight differently responding chromatophore types in the genus *Crago (Crangon)*. These are often arranged in such a way that changes in color pattern as well as shade and tint of color are possible (Prosser and Brown, 1961).

The literature of the nineteenth and early twentieth century records many attempts to associate the nervous system with the activities of the pigment effector cells. It is now agreed that the control is entirely hormonal. The classical experiments were performed by Koller (1929) who adapted shrimps *(Crangon)* to black or to white or to yellow backgrounds and showed that the blood from black-background animals would disperse the black chromatophore pigments when injected into shrimps on white background, while the blood from animals adapted to a yellow background would disperse the pigment of the xanthophores in similar white-adapted animals. Perkins (1928), at about the same time, showed that although cutting of nerves had no effect, the occlusion of the blood supply to certain regions prevented color changes which were restored when the circulation returned to these areas. Perkins went further and localized the source of the hormones in the eyestalks by injecting sea-water extracts of different tissues. Parker (1948) summarizes these significant pioneer experiments.

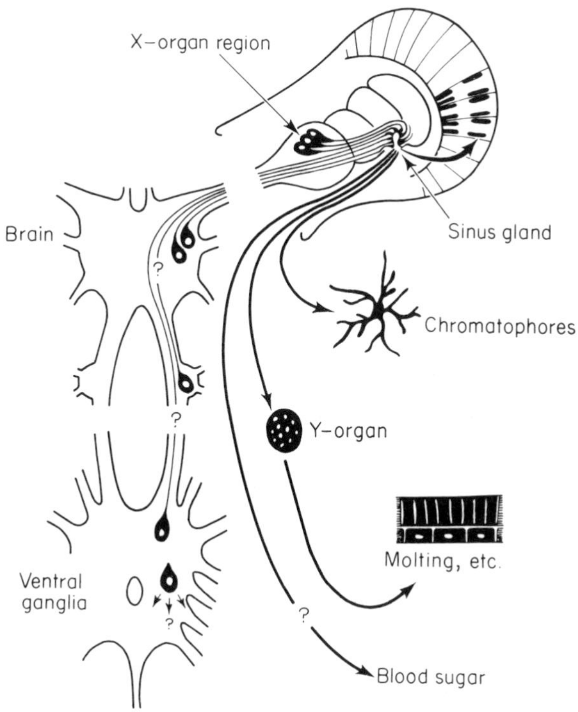

Fig. 20.15. Diagram of brachyuran sinus gland neurosecretory system. [Welsh (1961).]

The sinus gland is the immediate source of chromatophorotropins in the crustaceans. As indicated in Fig. 20.15, the secretions which are stored in this neurohemal organ may arise from the neurons of the *X*-organ, the brain or certain ventral ganglia. Although the *X*-organ is known to be a major source of chromeactivating factors, it is probable that, at least in some species, these substances are also secreted by neurons arising in other areas. At any rate, it has been experimentally demonstrated that extracts of ganglia other than those of the *X*-organ sometimes activate chromatophores and, further, that distinct color changes may follow electrical stimulation of the central surfaces exposed by removal of the *X*-organ-sinus-gland complex. The primary source of these neurosecretory materials probably varies in different groups. In the few insects which show physiological color change (the stick insect *Carausius mormosus,* for example), the brain and the corpora cardiaca probably function in a manner comparable to the *X*-organ and sinus gland in the crustaceans (Fingerman, 1959, 1963).

The chromeactivating hormones of arthropods are probably polypeptides of relatively small molecular weight, but they have not yet been satisfactorily characterized (Fingerman, 1963; Kleinholz, 1961). In theory, a single hormone might be responsible. Its presence might actively concentrate or disperse the pigment while the reverse effect might take place in its absence; further, reactions of different kinds of chromatophores might be caused by their differential sensitivity to a single chemical or by the interaction between hormone and photochemically sensitized pigments of several kinds. The experimental findings are contrary to such theories, and most workers agree that there are several distinct hormones; some of these actively disperse while others actively concentrate the pigment granules. Moreover, there appear to be different hormones for specific types of pigment cell. It is unlikely that there is a distinct hormone for each type of cell. Carlisle and Knowles (1959) suggest that the present knowledge of arthropod color changes could be explained on the basis of four hormones; Prosser and Brown (1961) suggest three or four. There may be considerable variation in different species, but much more work is required before one can generalize, beyond the statement that distinct hormones are probably associated with concentrating and dispersing effects and that there are different factors involved in the control of certain types of chromatophores.

Pigment movements in arthropod chromatophores are environmentally regulated by several different factors and may show persistent rhythmical changes under "constant" conditions (Carlisle and Knowles, 1959; Fingerman, 1963). Greater TOTAL ILLUMINATION often increases the dispersal of chromatophore pigments; at higher TEMPERATURES the dark pigments are sometimes concentrated and the white pigments dispersed so that reflection is greater, and a measure of body temperature regulation may be achieved. In the stick insect *Carausius* changes in the HUMIDITY alter the distribution of the chromatophore pigments. The animals become darker at higher humidities; the reaction is mediated through the neurosecretory system. Background or ALBEDO RESPONSES are also characteristic of crustaceans. These depend on the ratio of incident to reflected light, so that the dark pigments disperse and the light pigments concentrate on dark backgrounds while the reverse happens on white backgrounds. The principles are similar to those found among the vertebrates and will be discussed in the next section. Finally, some of the crustaceans show rhythmic diurnal changes in the pigments of the chromatophores and the eyes, which may be in phase with solar and lunar changes (Chapter 14) but persist for a considerable period when animals are maintained under constant conditions of temperature and illumination. These PERSISTENT RHYTHMS have been extensively studied by Brown and his associates (Prosser and Brown, 1961).

Neurohumoral regulation in vertebrates. Hormones and nervous reflexes, either separately or in combination, provide the lower vertebrates with a highly varied and rapid control of their pigment effector cells. Although there are still many puzzling details, the major components of the regulatory machinery are now known (Waring, 1963). Some of the most distinguished biologists of the past century have been associated with its investigation. Parker (1948) provides a comprehensive bibliography, and the historical notes which follow can be amplified from his monograph and that of Waring (1963).

Joseph Lister of antisepsis fame reported the first experimental work on vertebrate color changes in 1858. He noted that blinded frogs were light in color and failed to show pigmentary responses to altered background. This he interpreted in terms of a nervous regulation and concluded that the cerebrospinal axis was essential to color changes and that the regulation of chromatophores was "chiefly, if not exclusively" dependent on the central nervous system.

A neural control was further emphasized by the distinguished French scientist Pouchet (1871–76) who found that sectioning the peripheral nerves of the flatfish resulted in a darkening of the denervated areas while electrical stimulation resulted in a pallor. It seemed obvious that autonomic nervous stimulation excited the chromatophores and led to a concentration of pigment while the pigment dispersed in the absence of nervous excitation. Von Frisch (1910–12) confirmed Pouchet's findings. Using the minnow *Phoxinus*, he was the first to trace the distribution of the chromatophore nerves from their origin in the medulla. Although these early studies focused attention on the autonomic nervous system, there were at the same time, indications of regulatory factors apart from the nerves. Injections of extracts of the adrenal gland or adrenaline were shown to cause blanching in frogs; application of adrenaline to the melanophores in isolated fish scales concentrated their melanin granules; decapitated amphibian larvae became light in color and failed to respond to changes in background; hypophysectomized tadpoles and adult frogs behaved in the same way.

The full significance of these many experimental observations was not appreciated until the publication of a series of papers by Hogben and Winton in 1922 and 1923 (see Waring, 1963). These workers demonstrated that hypophysectomized frogs were permanently pale even when on a dark background and that the frog pituitary contains a factor which, when injected into the hypophysectomized or normal animal, will produce a jet black frog. A single pituitary gland was shown to be sufficiently potent to cause melanin dispersal in 50 hypophysectomized animals. Hormone production was localized in the pars intermedia and the factor was termed INTERMEDIN. This term is still used, although MELANOPHORE STIMULATING HORMONE MSH is now more common. Hogben and Winton demonstrated further that stimulation of nerves or sectioning of nerves to the skin did not produce color changes. Thus, the frog was shown to be unlike the turbot or the minnow in its chromatic responses, and although Lister's experimental results with blinded frogs were sound, his interpretation was not supported by the later work.

Somewhat later, Hogben and Slome (1936) and Hogben (1942), using the African clawed toad *Xenopus,* explained the ocular responses in a series of classical experiments which have been summarized by Waring (1963). In brief, the position and anatomy of the frog's eye is such that the ventral portions of the retina are only stimulated by direct, transmitted light from above while the dorsal segment of the retina is stimulated by light reflected from the background (Fig. 20.16). When only the ventral segment of the retina is excited (black background and absence of reflected light) the animal becomes dark, and for this reason the ventral part of the retina is called the *B* (black) area. Likewise, when the dorsal area of the retina is strongly stimulated (white background and reflected light) the animal assumes a lighter color, and the associated area of the retina is called *W* (white). This, in essence, is the basis of the secondary or background responses of the lower vertebrates (also called albedo responses). Some workers refer only to the black background response as SECONDARY and call the white background response a TERTIARY ocular response (Waring, 1963).

The experiments outlined in the last few paragraphs are only a few of the many performed during the first quarter of the present century (Parker, 1948). A generalized picture of the machinery concerned with the background responses has grown out of them. This, as summarized in Fig. 20.16, indicates two major systems of control, one operating through the hypothalamic-pituitary hormones and the other by way of the autonomic nervous system. The cyclostomes, most of the elasmobranchs and the amphibians probably depend entirely on hormonal integration.

The teleosts depend on an interplay of endocrine and nervous control; in some, such as the eel *Anguilla*, hormones dominate, while in others, such as *Fundulus*, the autonomic nervous system can override the hormones. A parallel situation is found among the reptiles. In the Iguanidae (*Anolis*), chromatophore control is predominantly humoral while the autonomic system holds sway among the Chameleonidae.

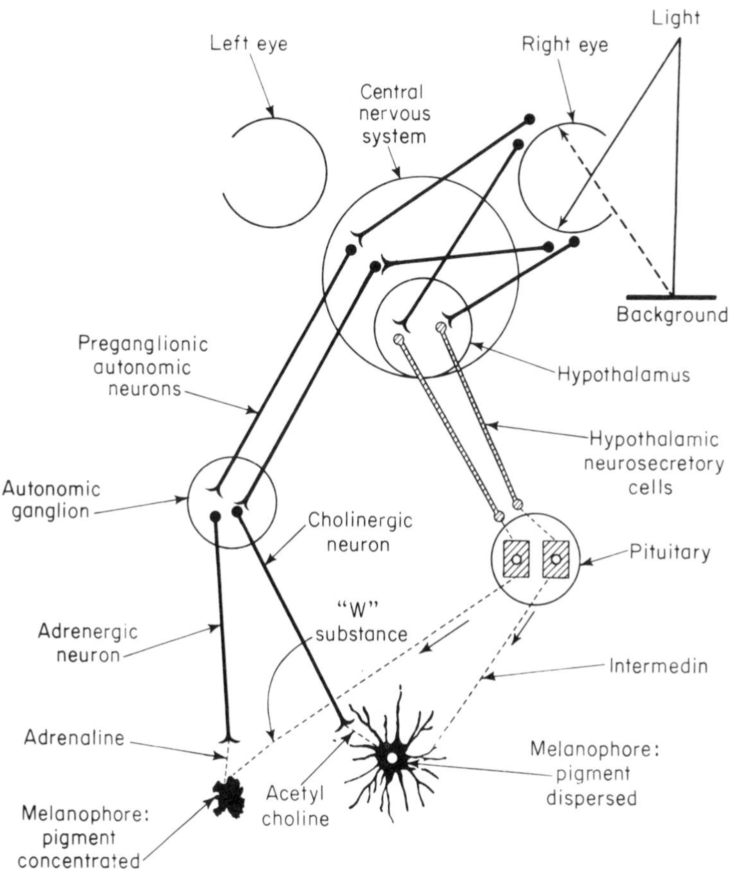

Fig. 20.16. Diagram for the regulatory machinery of the chromatophores of the eel, *Anguilla*. [Scharrer and Scharrer (1963).]

It is not necessary to postulate two hormones or two kinds of nerves, since excitation might produce a color change and the absence of excitation might have the reverse effect. An extended series of research indicates generic and specific differences in this respect. The best classical physiological evidence for a melanophore-concentrating or aggregating hormone (MCH or MAH), as distinct from a melanophore-dispersing or melanophore-stimulating hormone, (MDH or MSH) comes from comparative work on frogs and *Xenopus* (Hogben and Slome, 1936). Hogben and his associates compared the amount of MSH required to produce a certain degree of melanin dispersal in hypophysectomized and intact white background animals. *Xenopus* is more sensitive (i.e., requires relatively less hormone) when completely hypophysectomized; the reverse is true of the frog. Intact animals would be expected to be more sensitive since they should have some small reserve of their own MSH even on a white background, and this is evidently the case in the frog. The fact that the intact *Xenopus* is less sensitive than the hypophysectomized counterpart (i.e., requires more hormone to produce the same effect) has been interpreted to mean that its pituitary normally produces a second hormone which concentrates melanin (MCH). Removing different parts of the pituitary, it was concluded that MSH came from the pars intermedia (posterior lobe) and MCH from the pars tuberalis. Waring (1963) reviews these experiments and gives a critical discussion of the one- and the two-hormone hypotheses. It is indicated but not yet proven that *Xenopus* and the teleosts synthesize two similar polypeptides, one concerned with melanin dispersal and the other with melanin aggregation. The latter hormone has no effect on frog melanophores, and the frog evidently produces no MCH. These interesting experiments are summarized in Fig. 20.17. The normal *Xenopus* is intermediate in responses between the totally hypophysectomized animals and those with intact pars tuberalis only.

Chromeactivating hormones may also be derived from tissues other than the pituitary gland. The catechol amines, adrenaline or noradrenaline, often have pronounced concentrating effects on melanin. Melatonin (*N*-acetyl-5-methoxytryptamine) is 100,000 times more potent than noradrenaline in paling frog skin (Fingerman, 1963; Waring, 1963). This substance has been isolated from the pineal gland and, although its physiology has not yet been clearly established, there are indications that the pineal is also involved in the color responses of some of the lower vertebrates. Bagnara (1960, 1963) found that removal of the pineal abolished pigment aggregation in the body melanophores of *Xenopus* tadpoles kept in the dark and that melatonin at concentrations of 0.01 mg/ml aquarium water would induce blanching in the pinealectomized animals. It is of current interest that Wyman (1924), many years ago, noted that desiccated pineals (added to the ambient water) induced a blanching in *Fundulus* embryos.

Among the teleosts both components of the autonomic nervous system are probably active in the control of chromatophores (Waring,

1963). The sympathetic has a pigment-concentrating effect; parasympathetic stimulation or acetylcholine injections usually disperse the pigment. This control is said to be DINEURONIC. A dineuronic control is probably also present in the lizards, although the evidence is less satisfactory than in teleosts like *Fundulus* (Waring, 1963). In contrast, the innervation of the chromatophores of the elasmobranchs *Mustelus* and *Squalus* is MONONEURONIC with a pigment-concentrating action. Several other elasmobranchs (*Raja* and *Scyllium*) have been shown to be ANEURONIC and to have chromatophores which are subject only to hormonal regulation. These facts were carefully established by Parker and his associates (Parker, 1948) by stimulating nerves and, more particularly, by cutting nerves to certain areas of the skin and noting the color changes (CAUDAL BANDS) which are confined to the distribution of the severed nerves.

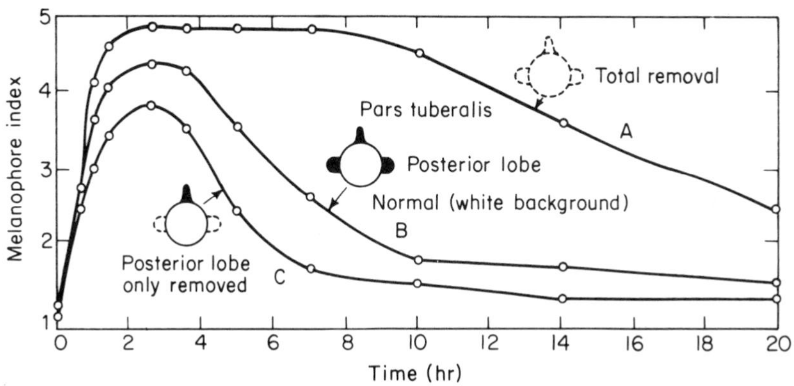

Fig. 20.17. Tolerances of three groups of *Xenopus* to extracts containing MSH. All animals were the same weight and received equal injections. *A*, Completely hypophysectomized. *B*, Intact animals. *C*, Posterior lobe only removed. White background. Temperature 14°C. [Hogben and Slome (1936).

Figure 20.16 does not provide a complete picture of the potential mechanisms for vertebrate color responses. A series of nonvisual or primary responses has been described in adult as well as embryonic animals. Hogben and Slome (1931), for example, found that blinded *Xenopus* showed dispersion of melanin in the light and its aggregation in darkness. The response persisted after the complete destruction of the spinal cord, and it seems reasonable to class this as an UNCOORDINATED

NONVISUAL RESPONSE in which chromatophores must behave as independent effectors (Waring, 1963). COORDINATED NONVISUAL RESPONSES have also been studied in *Xenopus*, but these are more completely analyzed in some of the reptiles.

The presence of dermal photoreceptors was shown by Zoond and Eyre (1934) in an ingenious series of experiments on the chameleon *Chamaeleo pumilus*. Blinded animals usually become darker in bright light. If an area of the skin of such an animal is covered with an opaque object, the precise pattern of the shaded area becomes lighter than the exposed regions in about two minutes. This does not happen if the skin is denervated or removed, although the melanophores may still be active as evidenced by their responses to electrical stimulation. These experiments show that the chameleon melanophores do not behave as independent effectors. Reflex control through integumentary receptors was demonstrated by decapitating animals and eviscerating them, so that the spinal cord and peripheral nerve trunks were intact but the circulatory system (hence the possibility of endocrine regulation) was removed. The light and dark reactions remained in such preparations. When, however, the nerves were cut on one side of the body, the color of that side was permanently dark while the opposite (intact) side responded to light and darkness as before. These experiments demonstrate a coordinated nonvisual response which can be activated by dermal photoreceptors. High temperature (37° to 40° C) overrides the darkening reactions in response to light and induces a pallor. Zoond and Eyre (1934) discuss these changes in relation to temperature regulation. Waring (1963) reviews this and other pertinent literature on the nonvisual responses to background illumination.

Nervous Integration 21

The diversified activities of a complex animal depend on a steady flow of information from the receptors to the effectors. Pertinent environmental stimuli are coded by the receptor cells as a series of electrogenic pulses; these are transmitted through the nervous system to activate muscles, glands, chromatophores and other effector structures. The nervous system is the indispensable link between the receptors and effectors and serves the dual functions of transmission and integration. Physiologically, it is much more than a telegraphic or telephonic system of communication where there is a one-to-one correspondence between input and output. No such simple relationships are usually found in animal responses. Activities such as nest building, fighting or courtship may follow a relatively simple visual stimulus as an extended sequence of highly varied muscular movements. In the lower forms, vertebrate as well as invertebrate, such behavior is innate and expressed in full measure without prior experience. In the phylogenetically higher vertebrates the relationships between input and output are regularly modified through learning. Thus, in its most specialized form, the nervous system permits the complexity of action which a musician displays when he appears with his instrument before an audience or the organizational abilities of the construction engineer who directs an intricate operation from a sheaf of blueprints.

The phylogeny of this integrating system depended on the evolution of highly specialized transmitting cells (the NEURONS) and their associations in coordinating ganglia and in a central nervous system. The neuron is an evolutionary product of three lines of cellular specialization: an INPUT or receptor surface, a conducting fiber or TRANSMITTING area of cell membrane and an OUTPUT region concerned with the release of a specific secretion or transmitter substance (Fig. 21.1).

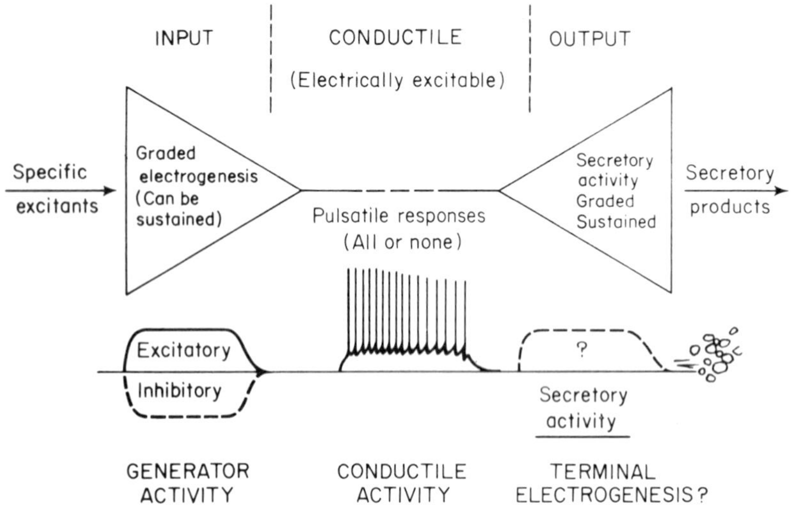

Fig. 21.1. The different responsive components of an excitable cell. The conductile portion is often absent (glands, muscle fibers, electroplax). The types of electrogenesis are shown on the lower line of the diagram, the possibility of inhibitory, hyper. polarizing responses being indicated by the broken lines. [Grundfest (1957).]

Excitability as a general property of cells was considered in Chapter 15. Primitive organisms and cells were probably responsive to a wide variety of stimuli, but in receptor cells and neurons the input areas are only excited by specific environmental changes, such as a wrinkling of the cell membrane or the application of some particular chemical. An electrogenesis is the characteristic consequence of this excitation. Phylogenetically, the input area may be considered the oldest portion of the excitable cell; its many specializations in the receptor organs have been discussed in previous chapters. Whatever the nature of the specific excitant, the consequence at the input is a series of electrogenic pulses, graded in frequency according to the strength of stimulus (Fig. 21.2).

Electrogenesis, initiated at one point on the cell membrane, spreads as a wave of depolarization (sometimes hyperpolarization) over the cell. The extension of nerve cell membranes as slender fibers or filaments provides for the distant transmission of this electrical activity. These nerve fibers are electrically excitable, spike-generating structures which

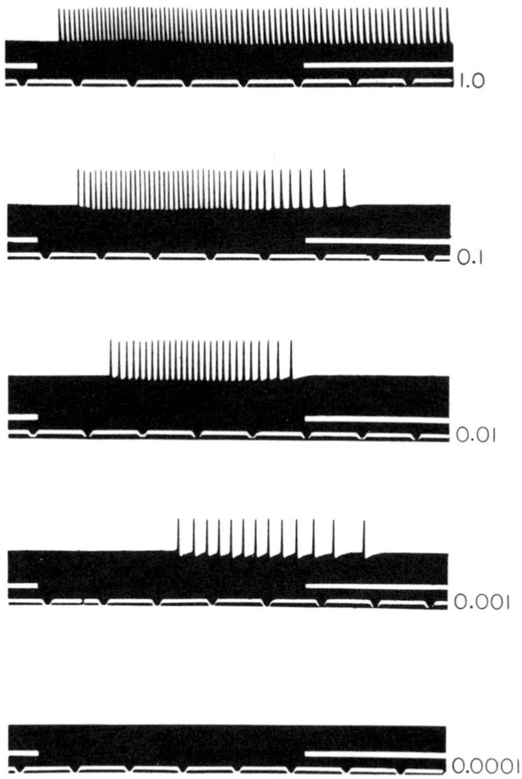

Fig. 21.2. Coding of impulses in a single optic nerve fiber of *Limulus* by a one-second flash of light of relative intensities shown at the right. Oscillograph records of action potentials. The lower white line marks 0.2 sec intervals and the gap in the upper white line gives the period for which the eye was illuminated. [Hodgkin (1964) after Hartline (1934).]

transmit faithfully and rapidly the information coded at the receptor surface. They become progressively more numerous and extend much farther in the larger multicellular animals where the problems of coordination are greater and the distances between receptors and effectors are longer. A single afferent nerve fiber in man may be as long as two meters. Increasing speed of transmission is the evident phylogenetic trend in the physiology of this conductile component of excitable cells.

The terminal part of the excitable cell is concerned with the release of a specific transmitter. This, in turn, excites another nerve cell or an effector organ. The concept of chemical transmission has been considered (Chapter 15), and the recognized transmitter substances were described (Chapter 2). An understanding of formation, storage and release of these substances is still incomplete. Acetylcholine has been most intensively investigated since it is the recognized transmitter in vertebrate myoneural junctions and synapses (McLennan, 1963). The enzyme choline acetylase, required for its synthesis, is manufactured in the soma of the nerve cells and transferred through the axoplasm to the ends of the fibers. The formation of acetylcholine itself seems to occur in relation to the mitochondria throughout the cells and their fibers; it accumulates in special vesicles just inside the membrane of the output region. Most of the acetylcholine is present in a bound form so that it is physiologically inert and protected from the hydrolytic action of the enzyme cholinesterase. In some manner, not yet understood, the electrical events in the conductile portion of the cell free the acetylcholine from this bound form and trigger its release from the cell in quantal fashion.

Explanations of the coding of stimuli and the transmission of this information to another cell are based on these three components of excitable cells. The integrative properties of the nervous system, however, depend on the intricate synaptic associations of these units into nervous tissues. Architecturally, these arrangements vary from diffuse nerve nets to massive aggregations of cells in centralized nervous systems with distinct areas devoted to particular functions. Explanations of the higher capacities of the nervous system, such as instinctive behavior patterns, learning and memory, are almost completely speculative, but many of the elements of neurophysiology can be understood in terms of established properties of synapses and the anatomical arrangements of the neurons. The present discussion is confined to neurons, synapses, the physiological properties of several different arrangements of nerve cells and some of the simple functional units of animal behavior.

Nerve Cells

Although the cell theory was clearly enunciated during the first half of the nineteenth century, its application to the central nervous system remained controversial for another fifty years (Bullock, 1959*b*). Routine histological preparations often reveal only a tangle of delicate fibers with scattered cells and provide scant basis for understanding the physiological complexity of this system. Many of the scientists of the past century believed in a continuity between the processes of neighboring neurons, and this concept was staunchly supported by Camillo Golgi

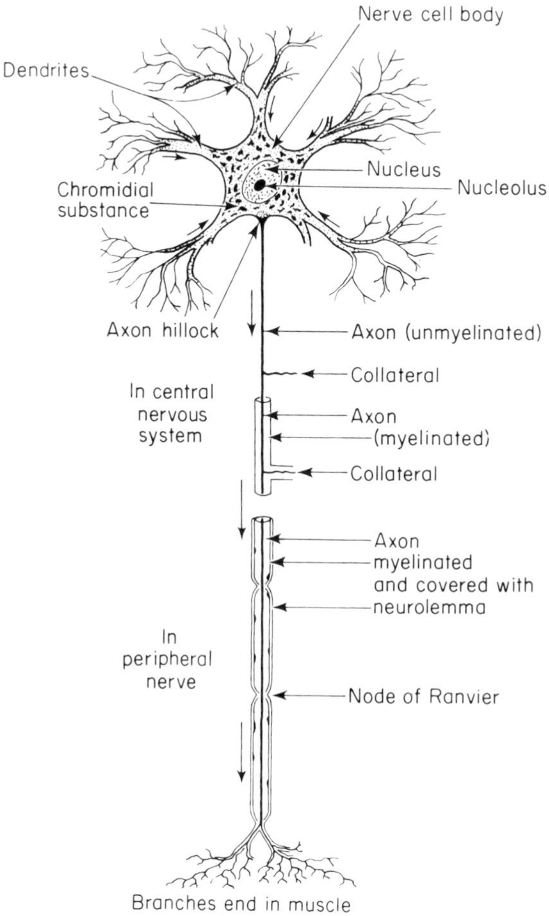

Fig. 21.3. Diagram of a multipolar neuron. [Ham and Leeson (1961).]

of the University of Pavia who, in 1873, developed the classical silver-staining methods for the differentiation of nerve fibers. His beautiful preparations served only to strengthen his faith in the reticular organization of nervous tissues. It was the Spanish investigator Ramon y Cajal, using improved Golgi techniques, who was primarily responsible for demonstrating that neurons are the functional units of the nervous system, that there is no direct continuity between the protoplasm of one cell and the next and that definite points of contact between nerve fibers can be recognized. This concept, sometimes known as the NEURON DOCTRINE, is applicable to the nervous tissues of all animals. A syncytial organization is recognized only in some of the giant fibers of invertebrates, the enteric plexus of the leech, and perhaps at certain points in nerve nets (Bullock, 1959*b*; Mackie, 1960). In 1906, Golgi and Cajal shared the Nobel prize for their contributions to our knowledge of the structure of nervous tissues.

MORPHOLOGICAL TYPES OF NEURONS

The vertebrate motor neuron from the ventral horn of the spinal cord is most often selected to illustrate a typical nerve cell (Fig. 21.3). This is a multipolar cell with numerous short fibers (DENDRITES) associated with the input or reception, and one long fiber (AXON) which transmits to the muscle. Characteristically, the soma or cell body contains a central spherical nucleus with prominent nucleolus and fine chromatin granules while the cytoplasm is filled with prominent granules, flakes or clumps of chromidial material, the Nissl bodies. These are composed of ribose nucleoproteins and thought to be responsible for the synthesis of proteins —possibly the enzymes concerned with acetylcholine synthesis. With appropriate techniques, fine neurofibrils can be shown to course through the cytoplasm and to extend into the dendrites and axon.

This multipolar cell is only one of many forms of neurons. Several different types from the mammalian brain, including monopolar and bipolar cells, are shown in Fig. 21.4. Most of the invertebrate neurons lack dendrites. They are monopolar with axo-axonal synapses. Frequently, the nerve cell body or soma is spatially distant from the conducting fiber (Fig. 21.4).

NERVE FIBERS

The membrane theory of nerve conduction is illustrated diagrammatically in Fig. 21.5. It is based on the transmembrane electric potential, with the outside positive in "resting" cells (Chapter 15). Excitation produces an altered permeability of the cell membrane, with a flood of Na^+ into the cell; the membrane potential is momentarily reversed and an internal positivity results. Thus, the inside of the membrane is positive when active, and negative when resting, and the reverse is true for the outside. A local circuit develops between resting and active nerve; first one point on the membrane and then another is excited, and the wave of internal positivity and of increased permeability spreads along the fiber. The valves (Chapter 15) are electrically excitable; the propagating agent is the electric current generated by the change in permeability.

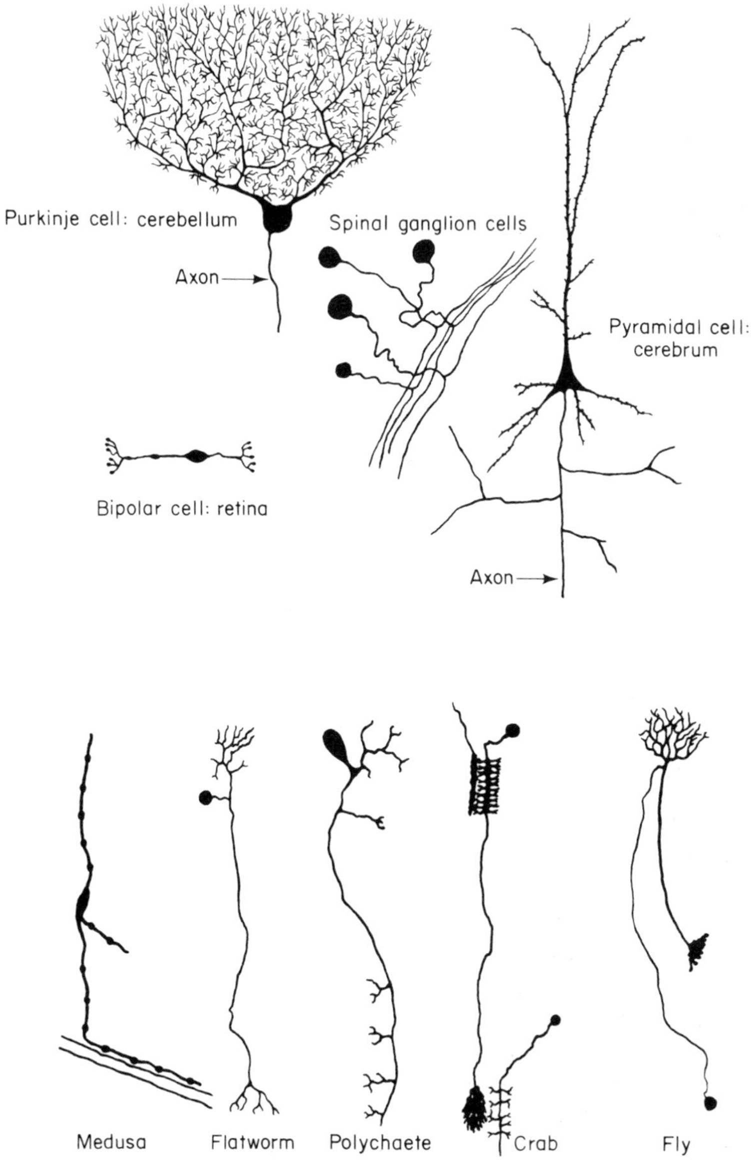

Fig. 21.4. Different morphological types of neurons. Upper series, vertebrate; lower series, invertebrate types. [Le Gros Clark (1958) and Bullock (1952).]

Recovery processes are rapidly initiated; the action potential lasts only about 1/1000 sec or 1 msec (Fig. 15.2) and travels at a velocity of 1 to 100 meters per sec, depending on the kind of nerve and the temperature (Table 21.1).

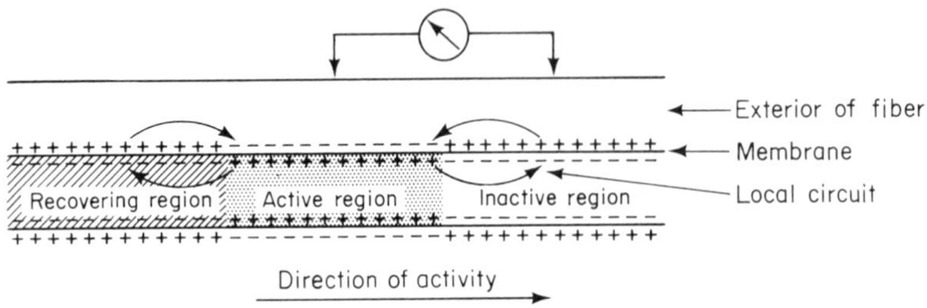

Fig. 21.5. Local circuit excitation as the mechanism for the propagation in an electrically excitable membrane.

Experiments with the giant axons of the squid *Loligo* have provided particularly convincing evidence for this theory. Membrane potentials can be readily measured with microelectrodes since these fibers often reach 1 mm diameter. Conduction velocity in these fibers can be altered in a predictable manner by changing the electrical resistance of the fluid outside the nerve; conduction time in giant axons of *Loligo* can be increased by as much as 100 per cent when measurements are made in moist air rather than in sea water. It is also possible to squeeze the axoplasm from a giant squid axon and replace it with artificial solutions varying in ionic content. Using isotonic solutions, an increase in the internal Na^+ or a reduction in the internal K^+ reduces the membrane potential in accordance with the membrane theory. Hodgkin (1964) summarizes these interesting experiments and other evidence for the membrane theory of nerve conduction.

The transmitting properties of a nerve fiber depend not only on the nature of its semifluid protoplasm but also on its diameter and its insulation. Although the electrical conductivity of protoplasm is high, the small diameter of the fiber creates an extremely great longitudinal resistance. The axis cylinders of human nerves vary from about 0.1 μ to 10 μ; Hodgkin (1964) calculates a resistance of about 10^{10} ohms per cm for a nerve fiber of about 1 μ diameter containing axoplasm with resistivity of approximately 100 ohm/cm. The resistance in a meter length of such a small nerve is comparable to that in 10^{10} miles of 22-gauge copper wire—a distance roughly ten times that between the earth and the planet Saturn. This formidable problem was solved during animal evolution by enlarging the diameter of nerves (other things being equal, conduction is proportional to the cross-sectional area) and/or by increasing the insulation. The former solution is most characteristic of the invertebrates and the latter of the vertebrates. Representative conduction rates are given in Table 21.1, and more detailed comparative tables may be found in Nicol (1960*a*) and Prosser and Brown (1961).

TABLE 21.1

CONDUCTION VELOCITIES OF REPRESENTATIVE NERVES, *A* FIBERS ARE MYELINATED SOMATIC; *B* FIBERS, MYELINATED AUTONOMIC; *C* FIBERS, NON-MYELINATED; TEMPERATURES FOR POIKILOTHERMS, ABOUT 21°C; HOMEOTHERMS, BODY TEMPERATURE. DATA FROM SPECTOR (1956)

Nerve	*Conduction Velocity m/sec*	*Fiber Diameter μ*
Calliactis nerve net		
mesentery, longit.	1.2	
column, longit.	0.1	
circular	0.15	
radial	0.04	
Myxicola giant fiber	6–20	100–1000
Lumbricus		
lateral giant	7.5–15	40–60
Median giant	15–45	50–90
Loligo giant fibers	18	260
	35	520
Homarus leg nerves	2–10	35–70
Ameiurus Mauthner's fiber	50–60	22–43
Esox Olfactory n.	16–24	
Rana motor n.	20–30	10–15
Dog *A* fibers	100	
B fibers	4.5	3
C fibers	0.6	1–5
Man sciatic	65	1–30

Giant nerve fibers. Giant fibers occur in many of the more complex invertebrate groups (particularly the annelids, the crustaceans and the decapod cephalopods) and in the anamniote vertebrates. They are characterized anatomically by their large size which is usually greater than that of ordinary fibers and, physiologically, by their role in the coordination of quick withdrawal movements of a startled animal.

Some of the giant fibers are the enlarged processes of single neurons. These are assumed to be more specialized than the multicellular types which are formed through a fusion of neurons during their development. There is, however, no clear phylogenetic trend of decreasing multicellularity. Within a single closely related group of animals such as the polychaete worms, some of the species have a few long unicellular fibers

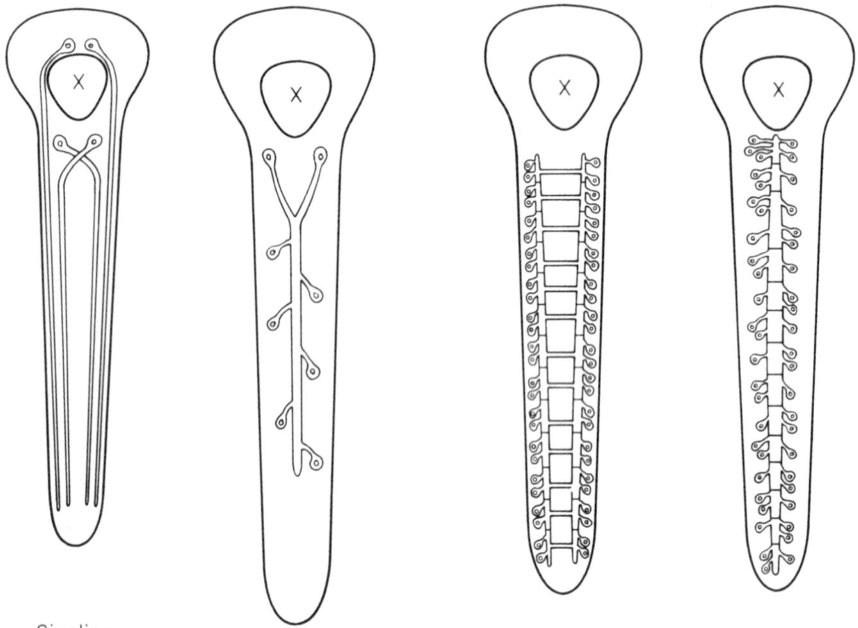

Fig. 21.6. Representative giant axons from annelids. From left: Unicellular giant axons arising in the supraesophageal ganglion (upper) and the anterior nerve cord of *Sigalion squamatum*. Multicellular giant axons of *Clymene*. Paired lateral and single median giant axons of *Lumbricus* illustrating the multicellular septate variety; the lateral giants are connected by cross anastomoses Wilson (1961). *X*, Esophagus. [Based on Nicol (1948).]

while others have highly complex multicellular types formed through the fusion of hundreds of neurons (Nicol, 1948). The giant axon of vertebrates (MAUTHNER FIBER), at the top of the phylogenetic series, is the development of a single cell, except in a few fishes such as the lungfish *Epiceratodus*, where it develops through the fusion of five or six axons (Kappers *et al.*, 1936). Thus, it appears that giant fibers have evolved independently on many occasions where there was evolutionary pressure for the rapid coordination of responses in different parts of the animal.

Giant fibers of the multicellular variety are organized in many superficially different ways. In annelids, such as the earthworms, several neurons in each segment contribute to the large longitudinal fibers; these are divided segmentally by oblique septa or partitions (synapses) which are indicative of their segmental origin (Fig. 21.6). Interconnections between these longitudinal fibers are often recognized (Nicol, 1948, 1960*a*; Wilson, 1961). A similar arrangement occurs in some of the crustaceans. In animals without marked segmentation, the nerve cell bodies may be concentrated in ganglia with the fusion of hundreds of emerging axons into a giant conducting cable (Fig. 21.7). The third-order giant fibers of the squid *Loligo* represent one of the most highly organized

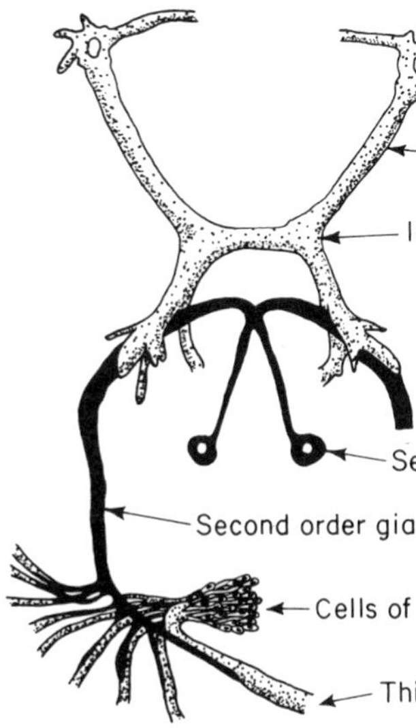

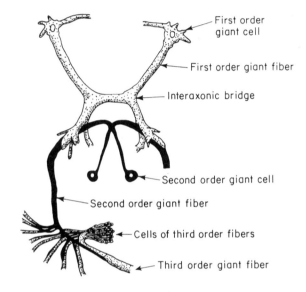

Fig. 21.7. Giant nerve system of the squid *Loligo pealii.* Cells of third order fibers form stellate ganglion. [McLennan (1963) based on Young (1939).]

examples of this type with axons which receive contributions from as many as 1500 nerve cells (Young, 1939). This nonseptate variety is also found among some annelids where the cell bodies occur along the length of the fiber and are not concentrated in a ganglion (Fig. 21.6). The syncytial connections found in some of the coelenterate nerve nets (*Velella*) seem to represent this tendency towards a fusion of nerve fibers at the most primitive levels of multicellularity (Mackie, 1960).

Nerves which are classed as "giant" vary in diameter from about 20 μ to something over 1500 μ in the very large multicellular fibers of the squid *Loligo* or the tubicolous polychaete *Myxicola*. Some of the ordinary nerves reach this lower limit. Lateral line nerves of a teleost fish often measure 20 to 60 μ in diameter; the Mauthner fibers in the same group also fall within this range (Prosser and Brown, 1961). Although the mammals do not have giant fibers, some of their nerves may attain a diameter of 20 μ.

The distinction between giant and ordinary nerves is only partially based on size. There is a fundamental physiological difference. The giant fiber system serves the rapid coordination of large groups of muscles in quick escape or withdrawal responses. Three examples will illustrate this. *Myxicola* dwells in a mucoid tube from which it extends the anterior part of its body to feed and carry on other activities; it can withdraw into the tube with lightning rapidity when disturbed. This capacity rests on a highly organized giant fiber system where a single giant axon forms a final common path to all the longitudinal muscles concerned with the withdrawal reflex, and excitation can occur at all levels (Nicol, 1960*a*). The squid represents the climax in the evolution of a swimming mollusc. The quick and simultaneous contraction of a number of different mantle muscles operates a jet propulsion system. These muscles are supplied by third-order giant axons arising in the stellate ganglion (Fig. 21.7). Since the axons to the different groups of muscles vary in diameter with their length and since transmission velocity is proportional to the size of the fiber, the many muscles can thus be operated in a unified manner. Finally, in the lower vertebrates, two large neurons (Mauthner's cells) with enormous cell bodies in the floor of the medulla send out axons which extend to the tip of the spinal cord. Fibers from neurons in the cerebellum, the sensory nucleus of the trigeminal, the vestibular nerve and the optic tectum form synapses with Mauthner's cells. The system serves as a final common path for the speedy coordination of complex swimming movements. It is well developed in fishes and amphibians with functional lateral line systems and a pronounced tail musculature but reduced or absent in some forms which live on the bottom and in tailless species (Healy, 1957; Kappers *et al.*, 1936).

Medullated nerves. Although the velocity of the nerve impulse increases with the size of the conducting fiber, the most rapidly conducting nerves are not the giant axons but the much smaller medullated fibers of vertebrates. Some mammalian nerves (cat *B* fibers) conduct at rates of 80 to 100 m/sec while the median axon of the earthworm *Lumbricus*, one of the most rapidly conducting giant axons of invertebrates, transmits at about 30 m/sec. Mauthner's fibers in teleosts are also rapidly conducting giant fibers, but the conduction rates are only about half those recorded for cat *B* fibers (Prosser and Brown, 1961). Bullock (1952) emphasizes the unsatisfactory correlation between size *per se* and conduction velocity in giant axons of invertebrates. Species differences in axoplasm and the nature of the insulation are presumed to be responsible for this variation.

Nerve fibers, invertebrate as well as vertebrate, are often covered by cells which provide insulation (in an electrical sense) and support or protection (in a mechanical sense). The cells responsible are of two sorts: those which arise like the neurons from neurectoderm (Schwann cells from the neural crests or neural tube in vertebrates) and connective tissues of mesodermal origin. In the vertebrates Schwann cells frequently expand and spiral around the nerve fibers to form thick layers of myelin. This substance is composed largely of lipids (cholesterol, phospholipids, glycolipids) with smaller amounts of protein and is similar biochemically to the cell membranes from which it arises. In mammals, all nerves greater than 1 μ in diameter are covered with myelin (medullated nerves) which may reach a thickness of about 2.5 μ on larger fibers. Myelin sheaths are also found in some invertebrate nerves, as in the polychaete *Clymene* and the crustaceans *Mysis* and *Palaemon* (Nicol, 1960*a*). They are, however, relatively rare below the vertebrates; even when they are present they usually lack the organization in nodes and internodes which is so important in the physiology of vertebrate medullated fibers (Andrew, 1959; Wiersma, 1961; Narahashi, 1963).

Seen with the ordinary light microscope, the myelin sheath of a vertebrate medullated nerve is a homogeneous osmophilic layer closely surrounding the axoplasm and neatly covered with the cytoplasm of Schwann cells (Causey, 1960). Outside this again are the connective tissues (Fig. 21.8) which will be omitted from further discussion. Deep constrictions in the myelin sheath (nodes of Ranvier) occur at intervals of about 1 mm. At these points the myelin is interrupted, and the axoplasm is covered only by the neighboring Schwann cell. A single Schwann cell nucleus is found in each internodal segment and this is, in fact, the nucleus of the cell responsible for the myelin of this region. One of the very remarkable achievements of electron microscopy has been the demonstration that myelin is a laminated material with regularly arranged layers of lipid molecules alternating with thinner layers of protein; these lipid-protein "sandwiches" measure about 18 mμ perpendicular to the planes of the layers. The Schwann cells produce these layers, wrapping themselves around the axon by continuous infolding of the outer Schwann cell membrane as indicated in the classical diagrams of Geren (Fig. 21.8).

The physiological importance of the insulating myelin sheath is well established. Its significance in transmission might be argued from comparative measurements of conduction velocities. Thus, in a shrimp, a giant axon measuring 50 μ diameter, with the myelin sheath forming about 20 per cent of the fiber thickness, conducts with the same velocity (about 25 m/sec) as a squid giant axon of 650 μ lacking this insulation (Nicol, 1960*a*). The physiological studies of vertebrate medullated nerves have, however, given much more concrete evidence concerning the insulating capacities of myelin and the part which it plays in the conduction of the nerve impulse. Hodgkin (1964) summarizes the evidence. Much of it is based on the application of microphysiological techniques to single myelinated nerve fibers of frogs. Internodal distances may be as great as 1 mm, and this permits precise application of stimuli with respect to nodes and internodal regions.

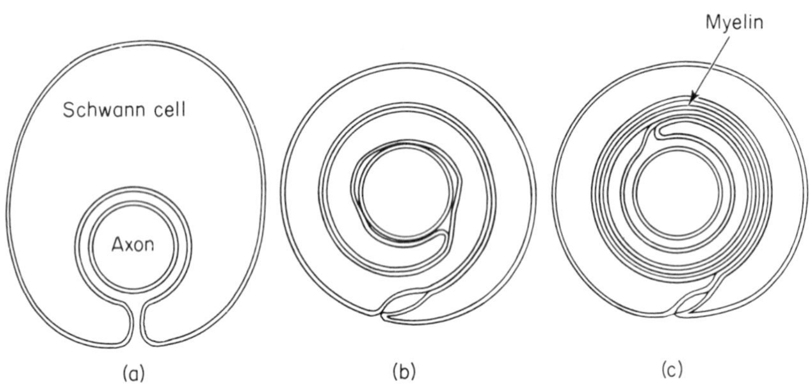

Fig. 21.8. Diagram of the structure of the medullated nerve fiber based on Geren's theory for the origin of myelin sheath. [Young (1957) after Geren (1924).]

The threshold of an electrical stimulus, applied at various points along such a fiber, is lowest when the cathode is opposite the node and highest when it is at the middle of the internode. When the current is confined to the internode the threshold is virtually infinite, but if the cathode and anode are at different internodes, the spread of current along the fiber will act at an intermediate node. Many different experiments have shown that the effective stimulating current acts at the node. Moreover, temperature changes or blocking agents such as cocaine and urethane act at the nodes but have no effect on the internodes. These experiments are in good agreement with the theory that, during excitation, depolarizing permeability changes associated with the flood of Na^+ and loss of K^+ occur only at the nodes and that a "cable conduction" takes place through the internodal areas. If this is true, measurements of action currents over different areas of nerve during the passage of an impulse should show the typical diphasic potential change at the node but only a leakage or outward current along the internodes. This again has been convincingly supported by several ingenious experiments. One of these

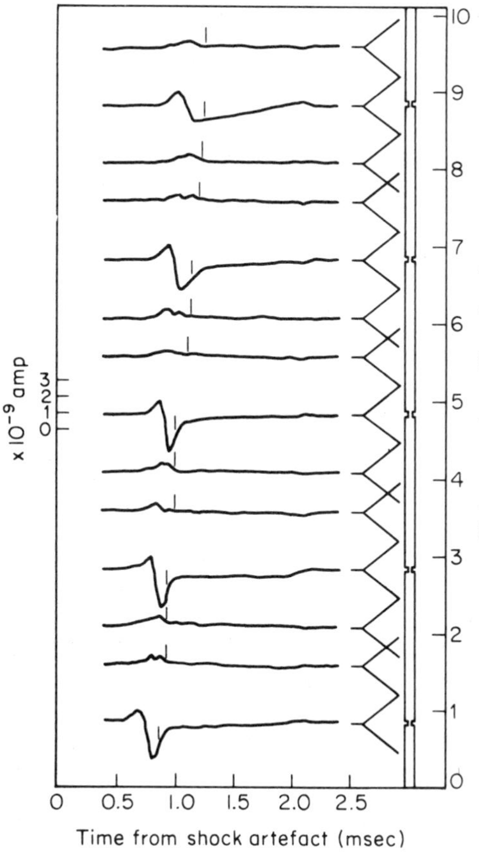

Fig. 21.9. Distribution and time course of membrane current in frog's myelinated nerve fiber. Each curve shows the difference between the longitudinal currents at two points 0.75 mm apart; the position of these two points relative to the nodes is indicated on the right. Vertical marks show the time of peak membrane potential. Outward current is plotted upward. [Huxley and Stämpfli (1949).]

is illustrated in Fig. 21.9; further details are summarized by Hodgkin (1964) and many textbooks of medical physiology.

In summary, myelin provides electrical insulation; the generation of the membrane potentials associated with the passage of the nerve impulse takes place only at the nodes of Ranvier. In nonmedullated nerve and muscle the spread of depolarization is continuous along the plasma membrane and conduction is a uniform process; in medullated nerves, the active generation of current is confined to the nodes of Ranvier, and the impulse behaves as though it jumped from one node to the next (SALTATORY CONDUCTION). Actually, it does not "skip from node to node" but spreads along the internodal regions at a finite rate by cable conduction from amplifier to amplifier. Saltatory conduction is an evolutionary achievement of the vertebrates and possibly of some higher invertebrates. Although nodes are present in myelin sheaths of a few of the higher invertebrates (crustaceans), these are irregularly arranged and conduction has not yet been shown to have the saltatory features which have been demonstrated in vertebrate nerves. This type of transmission confers two distinct advantages. The first of these is high conduction velocity; a frog's medullated fiber of 20 μ diameter conducts at the same rate (20 m/sec) as a squid's giant axon of 500 μ diameter. The second advantage is one of metabolic economy. If only the nodes are depolarized there is relatively less movement of ions across the membranes and appreciably fewer demands on the "ion pumps."

Interneuronal Transmission

SYNAPSES

Sir Charles Sherrington (1861–1954) who spent a long and productive life studying the integrative action of the nervous system first applied the term "synapsis" to the point of contact between two nerve cells. He and the pioneer physiologists of the late nineteenth century established several of the important properties of synaptic transmission long before there was any concrete supporting morphological evidence for the phenomena which they described (McLennan, 1963). In particular, they noted that there was a certain delay in the passage of an impulse over a synapse, a susceptibility to fatigue and a definite polarity or one-way transmission not found in nerve fibers. Moreover, synaptic phenomena were found to be less stereotyped than those in nerve fibers and permitted a SUMMATION and AFTER DISCHARGE which was very different from the all-or-nothing action found in nerves. The first electron microscope studies of the synapse, made about 1953, revealed a very real morphological basis for the delay, polarity, fatigue and potentialities for summation and after discharge.

Several different synaptic arrangements are shown in Fig. 21.10. Axons may be applied to dendrites, to other axons or to cell bodies; they may branch profusely, ending in numerous tiny swellings (*boutons terminaux*, END-BULBS, END-FEET), or they may divide only a few times to form a basket-like system which contains the postsynaptic cell. The

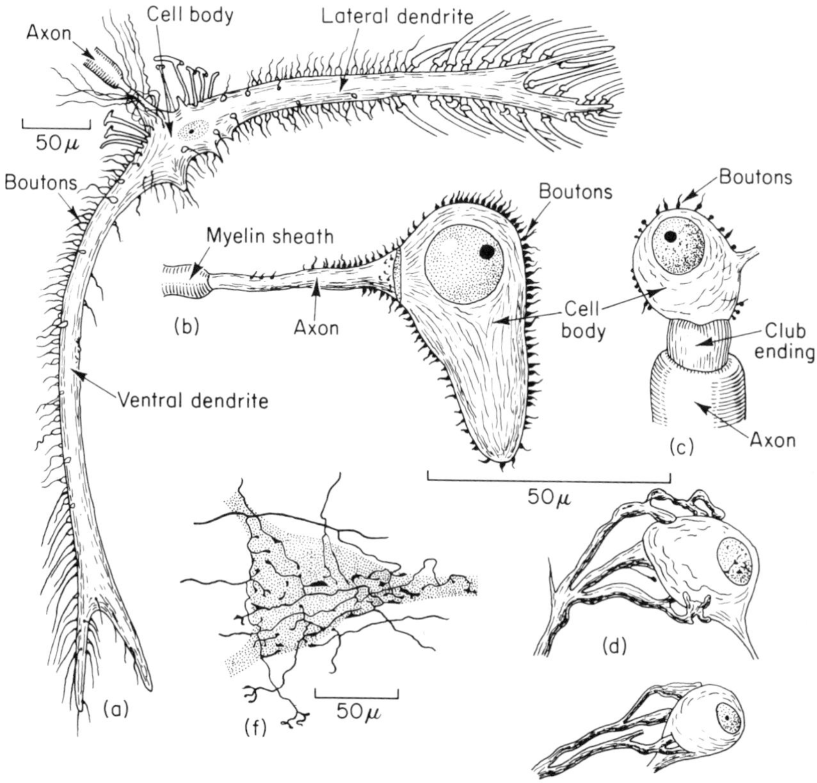

Fig. 21.10. Several different types of synapse. *a*, Semischematic representation of the synaptic apparatus found on Mauthner's cell in the goldfish. The endings on the lateral dendrite are all of vestibular origin while those on the ventral dendrite and cell body come from other sources. *b*, Large motor cell from the reticular formation of the goldfish showing relatively uniform distribution of homogeneous boutons on the cell body and proximal part of the axon. *c*, Cell from the reticular formation of the goldfish showing a single large club ending as well as small boutons. *d* and *e*, Two cells from the oculomotor nucleus of the goldfish showing a basket-like system of club endings derived from a single large branching axon. *f*, Large interneuron from the spinal cord of a young cat. [Young (1957) after Bodain (1942).]

molecular organization responsible for transmission is probably less variable. This has been most carefully examined in the end-feet on the vertebrate motor neuron, but there seems no reason to suppose that it is basically different in other synapses (McLennan, 1963).

A typical motoneuronal bouton is shown in Fig. 21.11. There may be as many as 2000 of these small bulbs (1 to 5 μ, diameter) applied to a single motor neuron of the mammalian spinal cord, sufficient to cover

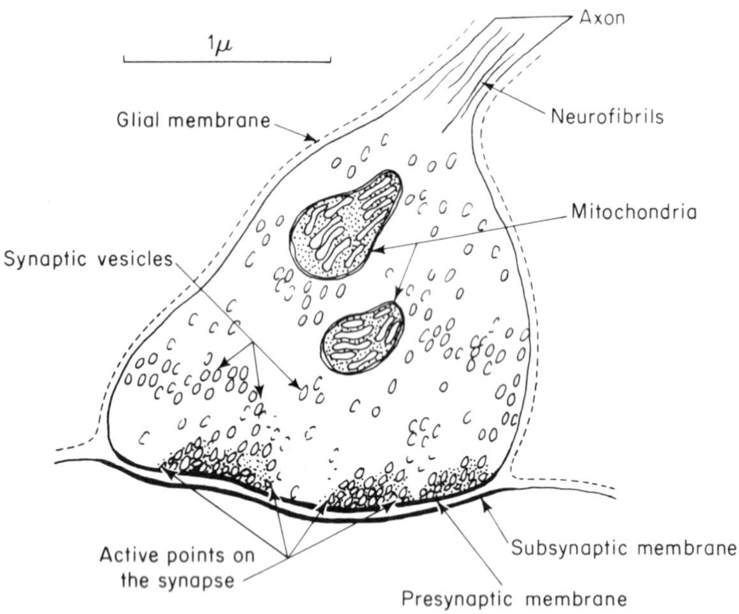

Fig. 21.11. Diagram of the fine structure of a typical motoneuronal bouton as revealed by the electron microscope. [De Robertis *et al.* (1960).]

about four-fifths of its surface area. Each terminal swelling contains many mitochondria and numerous clear spheres or tubes, the SYNAPTIC VESICLES (diameter 20 to 60 mμ), which presumably contain the transmitter substance. Vesicles are often clustered near the PRESYNAPTIC MEMBRANE which covers the bouton in the region of the postsynaptic cell. The delicate neurofibrils of the nerve fiber may be evident where the axon swells out into the bouton. Presynaptic and subsynaptic membranes (about 6 mμ thick) are separated by a narrow SYNAPTIC CLEFT (average width about 20 mμ) which is continuous with the extracellular spaces and fluids.

There is an obvious anatomical similarity between the synaptic junction of the bouton and the end-plate of mammalian skeletal muscle (Fig. 19.15). The physiological mechanisms are likewise comparable; these have already been discussed with the general properties of excitable tissues in Chapter 15 and with particular reference to muscle stimulation in Chapter 19. Evidence for the synaptic events in motoneurons of vertebrates has been carefully reviewed (McLennan, 1963; Eccles, 1965). In summary, the release of synaptic transmitter through the presynaptic membrane alters the ionic permeability of the subsynaptic membrane (chemically excitable valves). The resulting changes in electrical potential can be recorded with intracellular microelectrodes. During excitation there is an increased permeability to all ions, resulting particularly in a flood of Na^+ and a depolarization of the membrane, the EXCITATORY POSTSYNAPTIC POTENTIAL (EPSP). During inhibition the increased permeability involves only Cl^- and/or K^+, and stimulation is followed by hyperpolarization (INHIBITORY POSTSYNAPTIC POTENTIALS—IPSP). These potentials rise to a peak in from 1 to 2 msec and then decline exponentially with a time constant of about 5 msec. Like the potentials at the motor end-plate, synaptic potentials are graded in relation to the intensity of stimulus (quantity of transmitter released) and are thus very different from the all-or-nothing action currents of the axon or skeletal muscle cell.

It will be recalled that the motoneuron may have as much as four-fifths of its surface covered with terminal boutons; the potentialities for SPATIAL SUMMATION, through the release of transmitter substance from many different boutons, are considerable, and the electrical events recorded with microelectrodes are fully in accord with such a concept. TEMPORAL SUMMATION is also recognized. Successive stimuli from the same presynaptic terminal add to the amounts of transmitter already there. A second subliminal stimulus, applied before the complete restoration of the membrane (up to about 15 msec), will produce a further permeability change; two or more such stimuli may thus summate to raise the potential to the critical value (about 20 mv for vertebrate motoneurons) where excitation occurs in the postsynaptic neuron. In theory, excitation and inhibition might be due either to different synaptic transmitters or to differences in the synaptic membranes. Both possibilities have been considered (Florey, 1962*b*; McLennan, 1963). At present, only two transmitters have been identified with certainty (acetylcholine and noradrenaline), but there is suggestive evidence for several others, in particular, 5-hydroxytryptamine (serotonin), substance or factor *I* and a vertebrate sensory transmitter (Florey, 1962*b*; McLennan, 1963).

Much less is known about the synapses of the invertebrates and the lower vertebrates. If, however, the synapse is defined as a point of contact between two neurons, then there must obviously be some differences physiologically and probably also morphologically. For example, transmission in the multicellular segmental giant axons of annelids and crustaceans is nonpolarized and occurs with minimum delay in either direction (about 0.2 msec in crayfish giant axons). It is equally clear from electron microscopy and physiological investigations of synapses in the higher invertebrate phyla that many are typical in the sense that they are polarized and show an accumulation of synaptic vesicles and mitochondria in the presynaptic endings. The subsynaptic valves are certainly chemically excitable, although the time constants may be very different from those of the vertebrate motoneuron described above.

Some writers would not classify the septal divisions in giant axons as synapses. The spread of excitation from one segment to another seems to be electrical without the intervention of a chemical transmitter. The action potential in one unit initiates the potential change in the next by an electronic current flow. In short, the valves are electrically excitable; the transmission is EPHAPTIC. The fact that an appreciable delay can be measured at these junctions argues for an active excitatory synaptic process rather than an uninterrupted wave of depolarization from one segment to the next along the membranes. Ephaptic transmission at synapses and ephaptic interaction between neighboring neurons has been considered in a number of different preparations, but the number of recognized examples are few and confined to some invertebrate ganglia and giant fibers (Grundfest, 1959*b*; McLennan, 1963).

Integrating Systems of Neurons

Animal behavior depends on the integrative properties of the nervous system as a whole. The complexity increases phylogenetically from very simple movements such as the feeding reactions of a hydroid or the phototactic responses of a planarian to the intricate social behavior of the higher vertebrates. Even at the very primitive multicellular level of the coelenterates, which depend only on diffuse nerve nets, curious and prolonged sequences of precisely coordinated movements may follow rather simple stimuli .The swimming anemone *Stomphia* rocks to and fro, tugs itself loose and swims away when stimulated by small amounts of secretion from the starfish *Dermasterias* (Ross and Sutton, 1964); the anemone *Calliactis* hoists itself onto the shells of the hermit crab *Pagurus* in a series of seemingly deliberate movements; these are unrelated to any stimuli provided by the hermit crab but depend on a factor present in the periostracum of the empty mollusc shell occupied by the crab (Ross and

Sutton, 1961). This is integrative action at a high level and, it must be admitted, at a level which has defied satisfactory descriptions in physiological terms. The physiologist has, however, had some success in describing the integrative properties of smaller systems of neurons, and some examples of integration at this level will now be considered.

Integration is said to occur when the output from a cell, a group of cells or an organism bears no direct relation to the input (Bullock, 1957; Horridge, 1963). Understanding of the physiological mechanisms is largely restricted to those properties of cell membranes which have already been described. Neurons are regularly excited to fire their own messages when stimulated by several neighboring neurons or by temporally separated stimuli from one neuron; such properties as facilitation and spatial and temporal summation are integrative properties at this level of organization. The descriptions which follow are in terms of cellular excitation and synaptic transmission as found in several different anatomical arrangements of neurons. The examples are not selected to show a phylogenetic sequence, but they do illustrate several different integrative properties of groups of neurons which are involved in animal behavior. Neurophysiologists in many places are searching for additional properties of neurons in groups and masses, for there is a conviction that complex behavior, memory and mind can be explained in such terms (Bullock, 1958).

COELENTERATE NERVE NETS

The nerve net represents the most primitive organization of neurons into a system for the integration of the behavior of an entire animal. It is the nervous system of coelenterates and, with modest ganglionic additions, remains the basis of the nervous system in several other primitive invertebrate phyla. Further, in phylogenetically more advanced groups the integration of autonomic and vegetative processes often depend on nerve nets. Hence, it is not surprising that zoologists have looked so carefully at the coelenterate nervous system for clues to the evolution of neurological mechanisms.

Parker's (1919) concept of the origin of the nervous system proved acceptable to most physiologists for half a century. He argued that independent effectors, in the form of separate contractile muscle cells, preceded the nervous system. An epithelial receptor or sense cell was postulated as the most primitive nervous unit; this, by an extension of its basal processes, activated the effector cells. Subsequently, protoneurons linked receptor and effector and were organized into the integrating nerve net.

Pantin (1956) finds serious difficulties with this theory. He considers it unlikely that the primitive nervous system evolved to control single cells and argues that the evolutionary demand was for the integration of groups of cells—more specifically, for the integration of activities which depend on sheets of muscle. The independent effector may have preceded the nervous system, but it was the increasing size of animals with the organization of special tissues such as the contractile sheets of muscle which required nervous coordination.

Passano (1963) goes a step further to speculate on the origin of the nerve net itself. He argues that the association of myocytes into assemblages of contractile cells came first and that pacemakers localized in these synchronized their contractions to permit useful movements. There is suggestive evidence for localized pacemakers controlling separate spontaneous movements in different areas of simple coelenterates such as *Hydra* and *Corymorpha* polyps; the linking of these to synchronize the rhythmically spontaneous movements of a more massive animal such as a sea anemone may have provided the basis for the evolution of the nerve net. Passano's argument has considerable force. Nonnervous conduction from cell to cell occurs in several embryonic contractile tissues (myotomes of fish embryos, chick amnion); embryonic cardiac muscle is rhythmically active before its innervation, and the specialized conducting system in the heart of higher vertebrates has its origin in the cardiac muscle (Chapter 5). Moreover, rhythmic bursts of activity have been recorded in many different neurons, groups of neurons, receptor cells and muscle cells such as the pacemakers of the heart. The primitive nerve net may have evolved from the primitive muscle net (in the first instance for the coordination of the muscle), and only later came under the influence of sensory cells and stimuli from the external environment.

Morphological arrangement of neurons. The coelenterate nervous system is basically a plexus of relatively short-fibered bipolar and multipolar nerve cells, together with neurites from sensory cells (Fig. 21.12). There is a main plexus between the epidermis and the musculature, with a second less highly developed network associated with the gastrodermis and connected at various points with the epidermal plexus. Ever since the classical work of Schafer and the Hertwigs in the seventies of the past century, the nerve net has been recognized as a synaptic association of neurons in which fibers make contact but do not fuse (Hyman, 1940; Pantin, 1952). Schafer was much impressed by the histological resemblances between this system and the autonomic plexuses of higher forms.

The coelenterates are a highly successful and extremely diversified phylum of animals, and it is not surprising that this basic pattern of the nerve net (as seen in a simple form like *Hydra*) is considerably modified in the larger representatives with their complex reactions. In *Hydra* the neurons are only slightly more concentrated in the hypostome and the pedal disc, where the plexus has a circular arrangement suggesting a nerve ring, but in the scyphozoans (jellyfishes) the neurons are concentrated and the fibers aligned to form a thick "through conducting" nerve

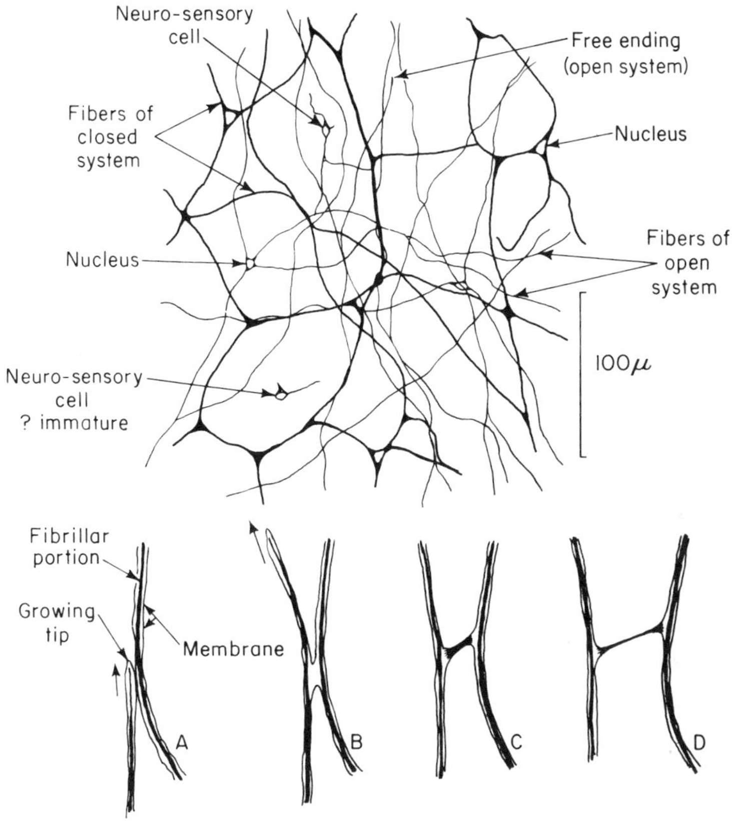

Fig. 21.12. Camera lucida drawing of a portion of the ectodermal nerve nets of *Velella* (above) and Mackie's concept of the formation of adhesion bridges in the closed system (below). Based on silver staining. [Mackie (1960).]

ring at the margin of the bell (Fig. 21.13). Special transmission lines often occur also along the radial canals, and in some groups there are radially arranged marginal sensory bodies (RHOPALIA) which contain ganglionic concentrations of neurons. In the mesenteries of an actinozoan such as the sea anemone *Metridium* some of the fibers are greatly elongated (up to 7 or 8 mm), and the net is stretched out to form an irregular ladder or lattice. These long bipolar nerve cells form a THROUGH CONDUCTION SYSTEM for rapid transmission and are comparable to the giant fiber systems of the higher invertebrates (Pantin, 1952).

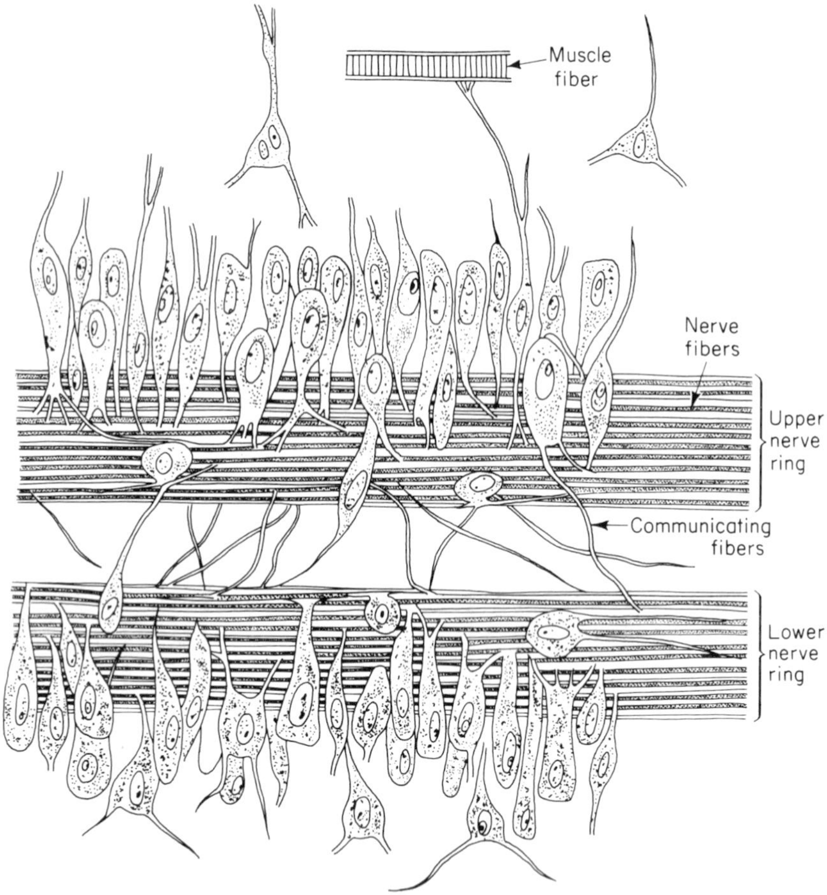

Fig. 21.13. Nerve ring of *Gonionemus*. [After Hyman (1940) based on Hyde (1902).]

Mackie (1960) describes two distinct components in the ectodermal nervous system of *Velella*, a colonial, free-swimming hydrozoan (Siphonophora). The fibers of THE CLOSED SYSTEM are relatively large (diameters 1 μ to 5 μ and much more conspicuous than those of THE OPEN SYSTEM (fiber diameters 0.25 μ to 0.5 μ). The closed system is characterized by a continuity between neighboring fibers so that the neurons form a syncytium of the type visualized for all coelenterate nerve nets by the early anatomists. Mackie suggests that these connections between neurons are secondarily established through adhesion bridges formed during development (Fig. 21.12), and that this is, in fact, a giant fiber system comparable to that of the annelids. In the open system the fibers are not continuous but run independently, frequently coming close together to form synapses of the type described as *en passant*. Clearly the coelenterates have adapted the nerve net to the processes of rapid transmission in their through conducting or giant fiber types of nerves and have achieved some measure of centralized control in sensory ganglionic masses.

Physiological properties of nerve nets. Several of the physiological properties of nerve nets are understandable in terms of the large number of synapses and the nature of the synaptic transmission. Transmission in the nerve net, by comparison with other nervous systems, is slow (Table 21.1); the nerve processes are relatively short and the large number of junctions decreases the rate of conduction. The actual synaptic delay, as calculated by Pantin (1952), is of the order of a few milliseconds (2.5 msec in the mesenteries of *Metridium*) and comparable to that of synapses in higher animals (squid stellate ganglion, 1 to 2 msec at 9°C and 0.5 msec at 20°C; cat spinal cord, 0.5 msec). Thus, the slow rate of conduction is due to the number of synapses rather than to differences in the rate of synaptic transmission.

The synaptic junctions are usually not polarized. Excitation spreads in all directions over the net from the point of stimulation; the process seems to be the unpolarized ephaptic type (Grundfest, 1959*b*) found in the septate giant fibers of the earthworm and the crayfish. Morphologically, the synaptic clefts are narrow (about 20 mμ) and have synaptic vesicles on both sides. In these features they are similar to other synapses where electrical transmission takes place and differ from chemically transmitting synapses which have wider clefts, up to 50 mμ, with vesicles only on the presynaptic side (Horridge, 1963).

Although morphological polarity may be absent at the synapses, impulses often pass more easily across some parts of the nerve net than others. This is in part structural, due to varying lengths of nerve fibers and their distribution; it is in part also due to greater interneural facilitation in certain directions. In the coelenterate nervous system facilitation is marked, and repeated stimulation is normally required to elicit a response. Examples of neuromuscular facilitation in the coelenterates have already been discussed (Chapter 19). The interneural facilitation has similar properties.

Interneural facilitation is also responsible for a "decrement" evident in the nervous conduction of some coelenterates (Carter, 1961; Pantin,

1935). If the disc of a sea anemone is touched lightly, the edge of the disc will frequently bend inward; the bending is marked near the point of stimulation and gradually fades around the disc but extends progressively farther with stronger stimuli. The stimulus evidently becomes weaker as it passes over the net, seemingly in contradiction to the principle of an all-or-nothing response in nerves. Actually, this decrement

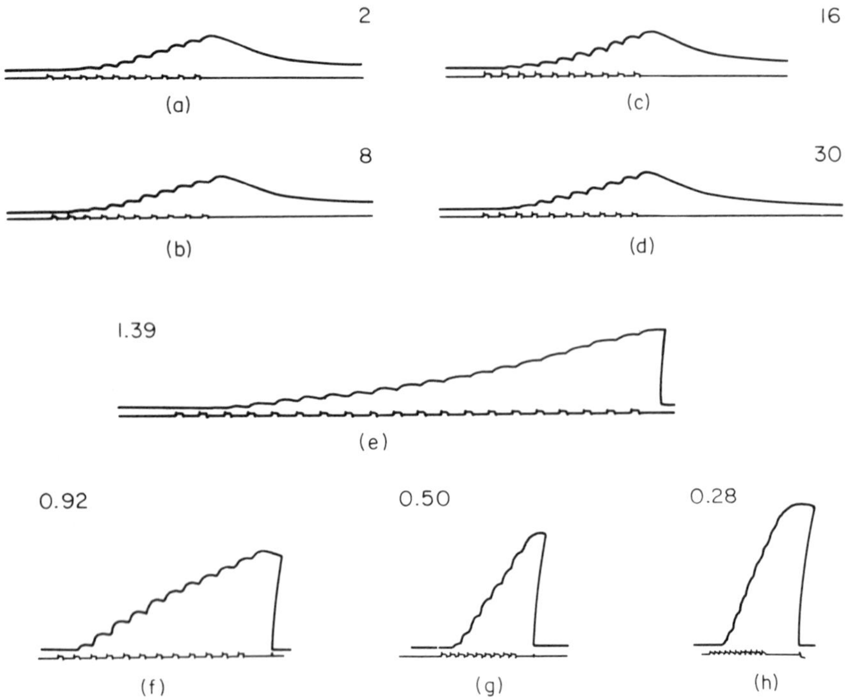

Fig. 21.14. Response of the sphincter muscle of *Calliactis*. *a*, *b*, *c*, and *d*, Responses of the sphincter to stimuli of different strengths but constant frequency (1 stimulus/sec). The threshold was 1.8 and the intensity was increased as shown by the numbers on the right of each trace. *e*, *f*, *g*, and *h*, Responses to a series of increasing frequencies of stimulation. Numbers on these traces are intervals (in seconds) between the stimuli. [Pantin (1935).]

is observed only in response to repeated stimuli such as a tactile (pressure) stimulus or a series of electric shocks; a single electric shock either sets up no disturbance or one that disappears suddenly. In a strongly facilitated system of neurons the first of a series of repetitive stimuli will only facilitate the receiving neuron while the second stimulus may excite it to transmit to the next neuron which will in turn be facilitated. The third stimulus will thus excite the second neuron and so on. The response will depend on the number of stimuli rather than on their intensity (Fig. 21.14). Studies of different regions of the nerve net of the sea anemone show a variation from areas which show little or no interneural facilitation to the highly facilitated condition just described.

Coelenterate nerve nets are also characterized by long refractory periods. In the *Metridium* net refractory periods are 50 to 100 times longer than those of crustacean nerves which are, in turn, about three times longer than those of mammalian nerve (Pantin, 1935). These, however, like other properties, differ from those of other animals in degree rather than in kind. The same is true of inhibitory processes and spontaneous (pacemaker) activity. The former was at one time denied, but some of the evidence for it seems incontestable (Ross and Sutton, 1964); the latter has been demonstrated in many well-controlled experiments (Pantin, 1952).

One of the most significant facts revealed by many studies of coelenterate nets is their dependence on the same basic physiology of excitation and transmission known in higher forms. In other words, the molecular basis of excitation and transmission was established in the primitive multicellular forms. It has been refined, but the mechanisms are similar at all levels in phylogeny.

PACEMAKER NEURONS

An unexpected feature to emerge from some of Pantin's later work on the sea anemone was the discovery of spontaneous and periodically active pacemaker systems (Pantin, 1952). A slow rhythmic activity may be recorded in an apparently resting actinian such as *Metridium* (Fig. 21.15). A coordinated series of rhythmic movements continues for hours under constant environmental conditions and in the absence of vibrations. The conclusion is that these movements are inherent, spontaneous and timed by some, as yet unidentified, cell or group of cells within the animal. More complex movements may also arise spontaneously; a starved anemone sometimes goes through the entire series of feeding activities "as though starvation has so lowered the threshold that the complex machinery started to operate spontaneously." The rhythmic pulsations of a swimming jellyfish are much more obvious.

Pacemaker systems have now been identified in several different tissues and in many animals at all levels in phylogeny. Embryonic limbs may show coordinated movements before the reflex arcs are formed; a pacemaker of myogenic origin sets the rhythm in the vertebrate heart; ciliated epithelia often show a metachronal rhythm; tube-dwelling, polychaete worms show spontaneous activity cycles associated with life in a burrow. Bullock (1961) cites these and other examples. The point of interest in the present discussion is that certain neurons may fire spontaneously and in a rhythmic manner. This capacity of nerve cells to generate activity independent of external stimulation seems to have evolved early in animal phylogeny and plays an important part in regulating behavior as well as in visceral functions. Many of these systems have not yet been systematically investigated. Two which have been analyzed in considerable detail will be described briefly.

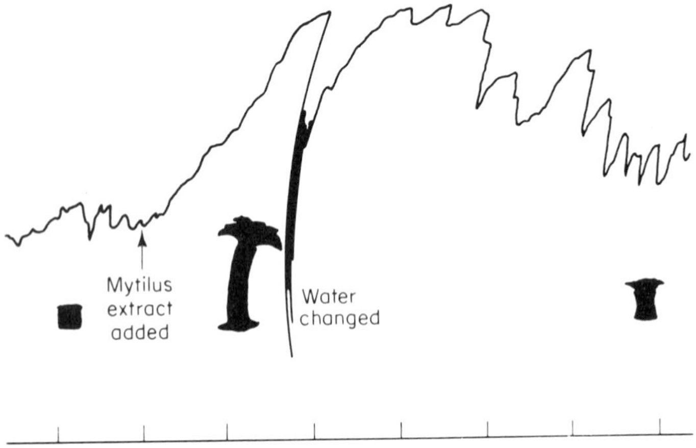

Fig. 21.15. Inherent activity of *Metridium* shown at the left and right sides of the figure with the feeding movements (induced by the addition of *Mytilus* extract) in the central part of the trace. The partially rhythmic contractions (registering downwards) and extensions are recorded isotonically with the record running from the left. [Pantin (1950).]

The first of these is a FIXED-FREQUENCY ALARM CLOCK concerned with the production of characteristic sounds in the cicada *Graptosaltria nigrofuscata* (Hagiwara and Watanabe, 1956; Bullock, 1961). The duration of the sound varies with external stimulation, but the frequency of the buzzer is constant at about 100/sec. The sound depends on the rapid oscillation of certain muscles which are controlled on either side by a motor nerve arising in the mesothoracic ganglion. The triggering of the sound depends on sensory nerves from certain of the hair sensillae. The pacemaker is a single interneuron which fires impulses at a fixed frequency of 200/sec. This pacemaker interneuron excites the motoneuron controlling the sound producing muscles. These muscles, left and right, are alternatively active; there is evidently a reciprocal inhibition of the two sides. Every other interneuron impulse fires the motoneurons to produce the muscle activity of 100/sec. Sensory stimulation changes only the duration of the burst; its oscillation frequency is fixed. This interesting system can be isolated experimentally; recordings have been made with microelectrodes placed on sensory or motor nerves or penetrating the pacemaker neuron in the ganglionic center. In this preparation nervous integration may be studied in a nervous pathway involving only a few neurons.

The second example is the pacemaker system of the crustacean heart. In this case a group of nine neurons (the cardiac ganglion) maintains rhythmic activity but permits a variable rate. Lobster hearts (*Homarus americanus* and *Panulirus interruptus*) were used in many of the classical experiments (Maynard, 1955, 1960; Bullock, 1957, 1961). There is now convincing experimental evidence that the cardiac ganglion is the pacemaker of the decapod heart (Maynard, 1960). The heart (or any isolated part of it) displays spontaneous contractions only as long as the ganglion or some part of it is present. Moveover, the ganglion may continue to show electrical activity even after it has been isolated from the heart. In the intact heart electrical activity of the ganglion precedes by about 10 to 14 msec both the electrical and mechanical events in the cardiac muscle. The rhythm of the decapod heart depends on a neurogenic pacemaker; the timing of the cardiac cycle can be readily modified experimentally and varies under physiological conditions in response to a variety of factors such as stretching, inorganic environment or drugs, as well as special cardiac-accelerating and inhibiting nerves (Maynard, 1960; Chapter 5).

The arrangement of neurons in the cardiac ganglion of the spiny lobster is shown diagrammatically in Fig. 21.16. The five anterior cells are considerably larger than the four posterior ones. Their arrangement is such that the individual neurons can be successfully penetrated with microelectrodes and their activities recorded. The ganglion is clearly a spontaneously active integrating system in which the neurons fire in a coordinated burst at the beginning of each systole and then remain quiet for the remainder of the cycle; this discharge pattern may remain constant for long periods.

The organization of the system is intricate, and the details of the interaction of its nine neurons have not yet been established. It has, however, been demonstrated that any particular burst of activity involves several impulses from each neuron and that no individual neuron fires at the burst frequency. Evidently, this is an integrating system in which the ouput bears no direct relation to the input.

The primary pacemaker resides in the posterior group of smaller cells and is probably a single cell—at least insofar as an individual patterned burst is concerned (Bullock, 1961). The five larger anterior nerve cells are the major motoneurons to the cardiac muscle; they are sometimes called the follower neurons. Not only does the excitability and

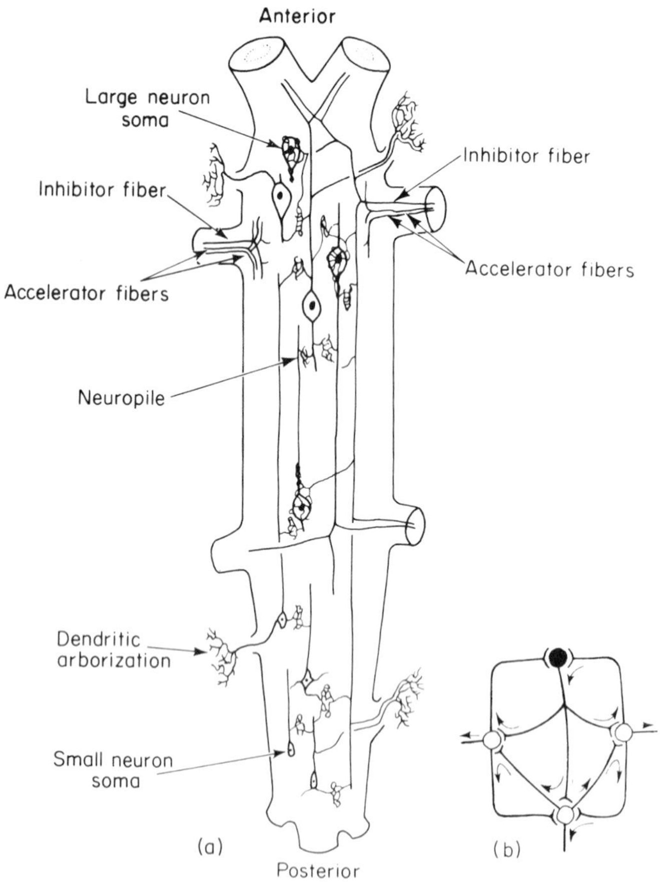

Fig. 21.16. *a*. Diagram of the heart of the spiny lobster *Panulirus interruptus* showing the cardiac ganglion. The ganglion is about 12 mm long and the largest cells about 50 μ. *b*. A possible connection of cardiac ganglion cells to produce patterned bursts. Small cell at top acts as pacemaker, but there is feedback and the patterned burst depends on the properties of this interaction. [Bullock (1957).]

responsiveness vary in the different neurons, but there is feedback of information among them. Several possible connections of neurons have been suggested; the one shown at the right of Fig. 21.16 satisfies many of the physiological findings. The morphological arrangement of the neuropile is intricate and could satisfy this theoretical organization.

SYNAPTIC TRANSMISSION IN THE STELLATE GANGLION OF THE SQUID

The axo-axonic junction between the second- and third-order neurons of the squid stellate ganglion serves as a most convenient system for the analysis of simple synaptic events. Young (1939) has detailed the morphology of this giant fiber system (Fig. 21.7). The nine to eleven third-order giant fibers innervate the mantle musculature which is concerned with swimming and ventilation of the mantle cavity. All the third-order giant fibers are excited simultaneously at the synapse. However, because they are graded in size, with the largest going to the most distant muscles, and because the rate of transmission is proportional to size, the different parts of the musculature are also excited simultaneously to produce the coordinated movements involved in the jet propulsion. Microelectrodes can be inserted into the presynaptic and postsynaptic elements to permit recordings of the electrical activity following stimulation of the various nerves. A number of the important principles of synaptic transmission have been demonstrated with this preparation.

One-way conduction. This is a typical polarized synapse and conducts in only one direction. Stimulation of the second-order giant fibers elicits activity in the third-order fibers, but the reverse is not true. A direct stimulation of the third-order fibers excites a conducted impulse in them, but this does not cross the synapse to activate the second-order giants.

Obligatory transmission. The unfatigued preparation is a non-integrating system. Threshold or greater stimuli to the presynaptic fiber invariably evoke conducted impulses in the postsynaptic fiber; the transfer is a one-to-one phenomenon, and the synapse can be driven at rates up to 400/sec for short periods. This is a direct axo-axonic connection, and there is no evidence of facilitation.

Synaptic delay. Recordings of the postsynaptic activity show an initial small decrease in membrane potential followed directly by the conducted action potential. The SYNAPTIC DELAY between the arrival of the presynaptic impulse and the local postsynaptic response is of the order of 0.5 to 1 msec (Fig. 21.17). The time interval is somewhat longer when measured to the point of the conducted action potential in the postsynaptic (POSTSYNAPTIC RESPONSE TIME).

Fatigue and temporal summation. With repeated stimulation of the presynaptic fiber, the activity develops more and more slowly in the postsynaptic fiber and eventually fails to appear (Fig. 21.17). At this point of failure local postsynaptic responses spread electrotonically for a short distance around the synapse but do not result in a conducted impulse. The system may now show integrative capacities since these local

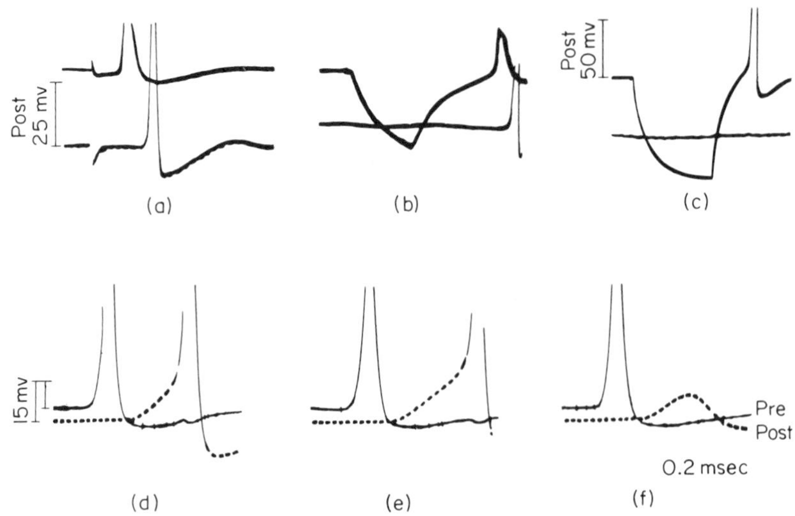

Fig. 21.17. Simultaneous recording of the action potentials in the presynaptic and postsynaptic fibers of the synapse of giant fibers in the stellate ganglion of the squid *Loligo pealii*. *a*, Stimulus to the presynaptic (upper trace) excites the postsynaptic (lower trace) after a synaptic delay. *b*, A hyperpolarizing pulse was applied to the presynaptic without effect on the postsynaptic (traces in same position). *c*, Hyperpolarizing pulse applied to the postsynaptic (upper trace) without effect on the presynaptic (lower trace). *d*, *e*, and *f*. Simultaneous records in the presynaptic (continuous line) and postsynaptic fibers (broken lines) taken just as transmission begins to fail, during prolonged high-frequency presynaptic stimulation. [Hagiwara and Tasaki (1958).]

postsynaptic responses can be summed, and two presynaptic impulses arriving at a short interval will excite a postsynaptic. Under these conditions the synapse is not obligatory and shows TEMPORAL SUMMATION, a characteristic of integrative action. These synaptic events are best understood in terms of the release of transmitter substance at the presynaptic membrane, and although the chemical has not yet been identified the evidence for its existence is strong.

REFLEX ACTION

A reflex is a stereotyped response to a stimulus. The term implies a REFLECTION of stimulus excitation by the central nervous system to the effectors. The spinal frog has long been the classical preparation for its demonstration. Generations of students have now watched the suspended pithed frog respond to a stimulus of dilute acid applied to one of its toes. It is not difficult to devise experiments which will show that this simple FLEXION REFLEX depends on sensory nerves from the pain receptors of the toe and motor nerves to the muscles of the leg, with an area of spinal cord connecting them in between. The simplest of spinal reflexes (for example, the knee jerk) involves only two neurons, the dorsal sensory and ventral motor neuron with a direct synapse in the spinal cord (Fig. 21.18). Most reflexes, however, are considerably more complex,

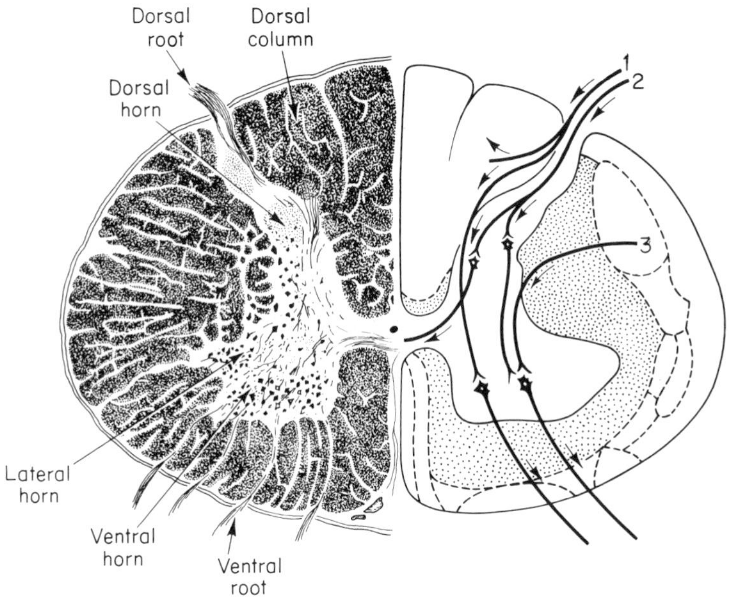

Fig. 21.18. Transverse section of the human spinal cord in the cervical region showing on the left the histological appearance with the medullated nerve fibers and cells stained. On the right, a diagrammatic representation of some fiber connections and pathways. 1, A monosynaptic pathway involving only two neurons as in the stretch or myotactic reflex. 2, Flexor and crossed extensor reflexes involving connector neurons and a crossing of fibers from one side of the cord to the other. 3, The corticospinal pathway by which impulses from the higher centers of the brain may modify the response. Areas surrounded by broken lines on right are nerve tracts running from brain through spinal cord. [Young (1957).]

and this may also be demonstrated with the spinal frog by placing the acid on a different part of the animal. If the acid is placed under the arms, for example, the animal will wipe the spot with its leg or legs and "attempt" to remove the irritation. This is a complex reaction involving several different groups of muscles, some of which must be inhibited while others are excited. Obviously, many different connector neurons must be concerned with the integration since it requires responses on both sides of the body and in several segments of the spinal cord. Many familiar reflexes also depend on the special sense organs as receptors and the higher centers of the brain as parts of the connector system. Detailed discussions are given in texts of medical and vertebrate physiology. The term reflex is also applied to those homeostatic mechanisms which depend on the autonomic nervous system. Several of these—such as the cardiac and the vasomotor reflexes—have already been described.

Many physiologists have come to regard the reflex as the functional unit of the nervous system and to look upon an animal's behavior as a complex chain of reflexes. Parker's (1919) classical arguments have usually been followed by comparative physiologists in attempting to sketch the phylogeny. A two-unit system consisting of a neurosensory cell and an effector cell represents the primitive situation. From this, through the coelenterate-like animals, the phylogeny is assumed to depend on the appearance of a connector neuron, the organization of a nerve net, the development of through conducting pathways within the net, the appearance of ganglionic integrating centers and, finally, their consolidation in the brain (encephalization). Functionally, it is postulated that increasingly complex reflexes became organized into a hierarchy of movements through the integrating nervous system and, further, that an animal's repertoire of reflexes can often be modified through experience. An obvious distinction is made between the innate or unlearned reflexes and those which are learned through conditioning or other processes (Thorpe, 1950).

There are several unsatisfactory features in these descriptions of behavior in terms of reflexes. The most obvious is the failure to recognize the spontaneous activities which depend on pacemaker systems of the sort already described. A sea anemone displays a characteristic sequence of movements in response to food (Fig. 21.15), but the starved animal may spontaneously show a similar pattern of activity without apparent stimulation from the outside world. Bullock (1961) lists several rhythmic behavior movements which may occur in the absence of peripheral stimulation: the motoneurons to a swimmeret of a crayfish continue to discharge rhythmically after isolation of the abdominal cord from the periphery; the swimming movements of a medusa, the peristaltic creeping of the earthworm, the swimming of a leech and the rhythmic flying movements of the locust depend on a neurogenic rhythm rather than a phasic input from the periphery. There is evidently a central automatism which persists in the absence of peripheral stimulation, although feedback from the periphery may alter or modify it. Bullock (1961) considers several theoretical possibilities and emphasizes the importance of pacemakers, neurogenic rhythms and the feedback of information in the organization of animal behavior.

The student of animal behavior, as well as the physiologist, finds the reflex a very inadequate unit of animal behavior (Tinbergen, 1951). Classical reflexes occur as relatively direct responses to stimulation, while many of the instinctive movements or innate behavior patterns identified by the ethologist follow the releaser situation by relatively long intervals and continue as intricate patterns of movements for extended periods. Several examples are given in the final section of this chapter. Here, it is emphasized that the reflex, either innate or conditioned, is only one of the components of animal behavior. Unless the definition is substantially altered, the reflex should not be termed THE functional unit of the nervous system.

PRINCIPLES OF CONVERGENCE AND DIVERGENCE

Many of the properties of the integrating nervous system are due to the multiplicity of presynaptic endings applied to a postsynaptic cell. Several motoneurons, beset with numerous terminal boutons, are illustrated in Fig. 21.10. The dendrites and basal portions of the axon, as well as the soma of the cell, may serve as synaptic points. It is estimated that the soma of a motoneuron in the vertebrate spinal cord may receive 15 to 30 boutons and may have up to 40 per cent of its surface covered with these synapses. A comparable architecture occurs widely in the larger nerve centers of invertebrate as well as vertebrate animals.

Sherrington (1929) described several of the physiological consequences of this architecture in his pioneer studies of the spinal reflexes of vertebrates. He noted that the result of a simultaneous stimulation of two or more afferents might be very different from the total effect of their separate stimulation. If the stimulation is of high intensity the simultaneous effect is less (OCCLUSION); if the stimulation is of low intensity the simultaneous effect may be greater (FACILITATION or SPATIAL SUMMATION). These integrative properties of neurons in groups find their explanation in terms of the arborizing presynaptic terminals. Any particular presynaptic makes contact at many points with several postsynaptic cells (PRINCIPLE OF DIVERGENCE). It follows that any postsynaptic serves as a FINAL COMMON PATH for several presynaptics (PRINCIPLE OF CONVERGENCE) as shown in Fig. 21.19.

Suppose that two boutons of either *A* or *B* must be activated to excite any one of the fibers on the right of Fig. 21.19. If *A* is separately stimulated it will only excite fibers 1 and 2; likewise, *B* will excite 5 and 6, but neither 3 nor 4 will be excited under these conditions. If, however, *A* and *B* are simultaneously stimulated, then all six fibers will be excited because of the overlap or convergence on the central fibers leading to a summation or facilitation with respect to fibers 3 and 4. On the other hand, if only one active bouton is required to excite the fibers on the right, then either *A* or *B* stimulated by itself will excite four fibers but, stimulated simultaneously, they excite only six fibers, and there is an OCCLUSION of two fibers because of the overlap. The diagram is oversimplified and, in point of fact, several presynaptics are probably always required to excite a postsynaptic, but the principle is the same.

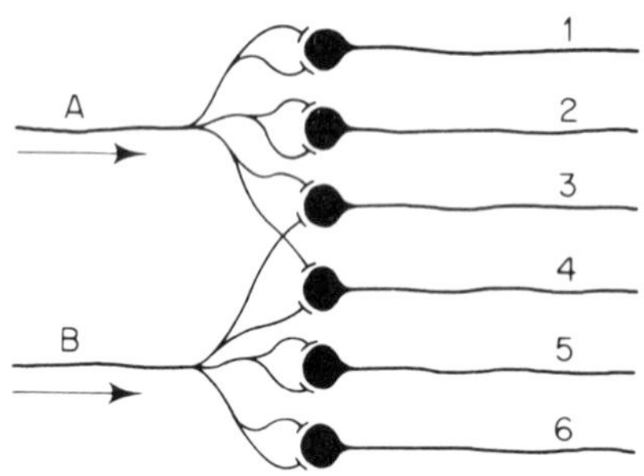

Fig. 21.19. Diagram to show occlusion and spatial summation. Explanation in text.

This divergence of presynaptic terminals to several postsynaptic neurons leads to the facilitation and occlusion which Sherrington noted when afferents were separately or simultaneously stimulated at different intensities. Each presynaptic may be expected to have a large number of terminals on some neurons and a smaller number on others. A weak stimulus to an afferent may excite only those neurons on which it makes many synapses but may set up a local excitatory state on the neighboring ones where it has relatively few junctions. However, if two neighboring afferents are simultaneously stimulated with relatively weak stimuli, then the neurons in their overlap areas or subliminal fringes will be excited, and the total effect will be greater than the separate effects (facilitation or spatial summation). With intense stimulation the neurons in the overlap area are excited in either case, and the simultaneous stimulation leads to an occlusion. Sherrington's classical diagrams of these phenomena are shown in Fig. 21.20.

ACTION OF INTERNEURONS

Sometimes, as in the myotactic or stretch reflex, there is a direct linking of sensory input to motor output with only two neurons involved. These monosynaptic pathways, however, are rare. More frequently, masses of interconnecting neurons provide integrating connections between receptors and effectors. In the centralized ganglia of invertebrates and in the brains of vertebrates these internuncial cells have short fibers

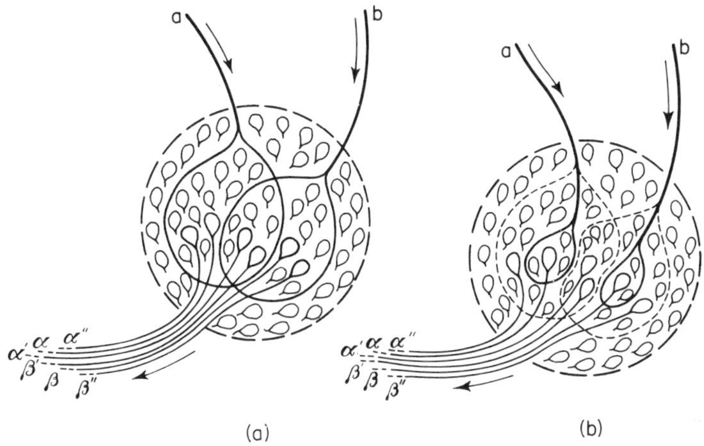

Fig. 21.20. Sherrington's classical diagrams of: (a), occlusion and (b), summation. (a), Two excitatory afferents, *a* and *b*, with their fields of supraliminal effect in the motoneurone pool of a muscle. *a* activates by itself 4 units (α', α, α'' and β'); *b* by itself, 4 (β', β, β'' and α'). Concurrently they activate not 8, but 6, i.e., give a deficit by occlusion of α' and β' (b), Weaker stimulation of *a* and *b* restricting their supraliminal fields of effect in the pool as shown by the continuous-line limit. *a* by itself activates 1 unit; *b* similarly; concurrently they activate 4 units (α', α, β', and β) owing to summation of subliminal fields outlined by dots. (Subliminal fields of effect are not indicated in diagram (a).) [Sherrington (1929).]

which appear to form a disorganized "felt" in routine preparations. Actually, the interneurons are probably always highly organized anatomically as well as physiologically. Lorente de Nó (1938), from a study of Golgi silver preparations and from a careful physiological investigation, described two patterns of interneurons in the mammalian brain: the MULTIPLE CHAIN and the CLOSED CHAIN (Fig. 21.21). Similar patterns are probably found at other levels in animal phylogeny.

It is evident that in either of these patterns an excitation of the main transmitter will generate extended activity in its postsynaptic area. In the multiple chain a parallel series of neurons is connected through collateral branches, and the postsynaptic bombardment is prolonged (perhaps also rhythmic) in accordance with the number of synapses along the connecting route. In the closed chain the collaterals are interconnected to reexcite neurons and set up a reverberation of impulses with continued prolonged postsynaptic effects. Either of these architectural arrangements provides for a sustained action or after-discharge. Large areas of the central nervous system are made up of these chains of interneurons with their many synapses; in these the properties of occlusion and summation, described in the previous section, may also be expected to operate.

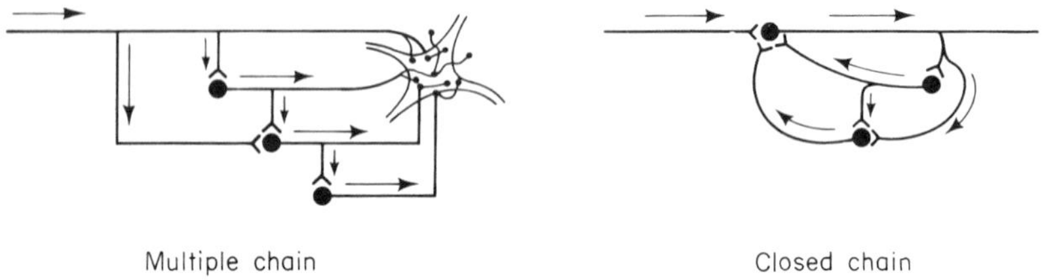

Fig. 21.21. Diagrams of the two types of chains formed by internuncial cells, as described by Lorente de Nó (1938).

CEPHALIZATION AND A HIERARCHY OF NERVOUS CENTERS

These integrative properties of neurons and small groups of neurons provide a certain physiological understanding of nervous action but are quite inadequate to explain many of its capacities in higher forms. Bullock (1958) speculates that "the main factor in evolutionary advance is not just numbers of cells and connections" and that a satisfactory explanation of complex behavioral sequences, learning and memory must probably await "the discovery of new parameters of neuronal systems." At present, descriptions of the phylogeny of higher nervous systems are largely morphological; experimental work has been essentially an exercise in the localization of functions. An excellent recent example on a little-known nervous system is a study of the brain and behavior of the *Octopus* (Wells, 1962). The capacities of these animals for sensory perception and learning were first established through many careful conditioning experiments; lesions were then placed in different areas of the brain and their effects on behavior were noted. Comparable studies have also been made on the effects of brain lesions on the instinctive behavior of fishes (Segaar and Nieuwenhuys, 1963). Various experiments of a similar nature, extending over many years, have localized motor and sensory areas of higher forms while numerous rather fruitless attempts have been made to find the "memory trace" in mammals (Lashley, 1950). Valuable information of this type has come also from the association of pathological disturbances with morphological changes and from electrical stimulation of different areas of the brain. The fact remains, however, that these are LOCALIZATIONS OF FUNCTIONS and do not provide a satisfactory explanation of how the nervous system controls behavior.

The central nervous systems of higher forms are made up of many functionally distinct but interrelated areas. This differentiation of functional parts is also characteristic of the nervous systems of the most primitive multicellular animals. Although the functional organization is vastly more intricate and depends on many more centers in forms with compact brains and a cephalic concentration of sense organs, the principle is equally well emphasized at the primitive level of the coelenterate nerve net. Pantin (1952) discusses this division of the excitation system in the elementary nervous system of the sea anemone; he provides evidence for independent effectors, a local reflex system in the disc, a through conducting reflex system and a spontaneously active semi-independent system in the column. These different systems are tied together to provide for behavior of considerable complexity as described earlier in this chapter. In higher forms, the neurons associated with different functions are localized in ganglia or nuclei of the brain, but it is of interest that comparable functional separations may occur in nerve nets.

The departure from a nerve net and the localization of different functions in ganglia appear to be related to cephalization (the differentiation of the anterior or oral end into a head with its battery of special sensory organs), to the one-way passage of food through the gut, to metamerism or segmentation and to the requirements for individual control of specific areas.

Initially, ganglia seem to appear at strategic locations, either where the sensory input is high or where the motor controls must be refined. Thus, the supraesophageal or cerebral ganglia at the anterior end, dorsal to the gut and the subesophageal ganglia below the gut, appear early in phylogeny with the differentiation of a head, its complex feeding structures and sensory instruments. The anus, genital organs and other anatomical parts may have separate ganglia for their control. The molluscs illustrate nicely this strategic location of ganglia in areas associated with structures which require individual controls: the cerebral ganglia of the head, the pedal ganglia of the foot, the pleural, visceral and parietal ganglia of different parts of the visceral mass. Comparative histological studies of ganglia in the different phyla indicate an evolution from

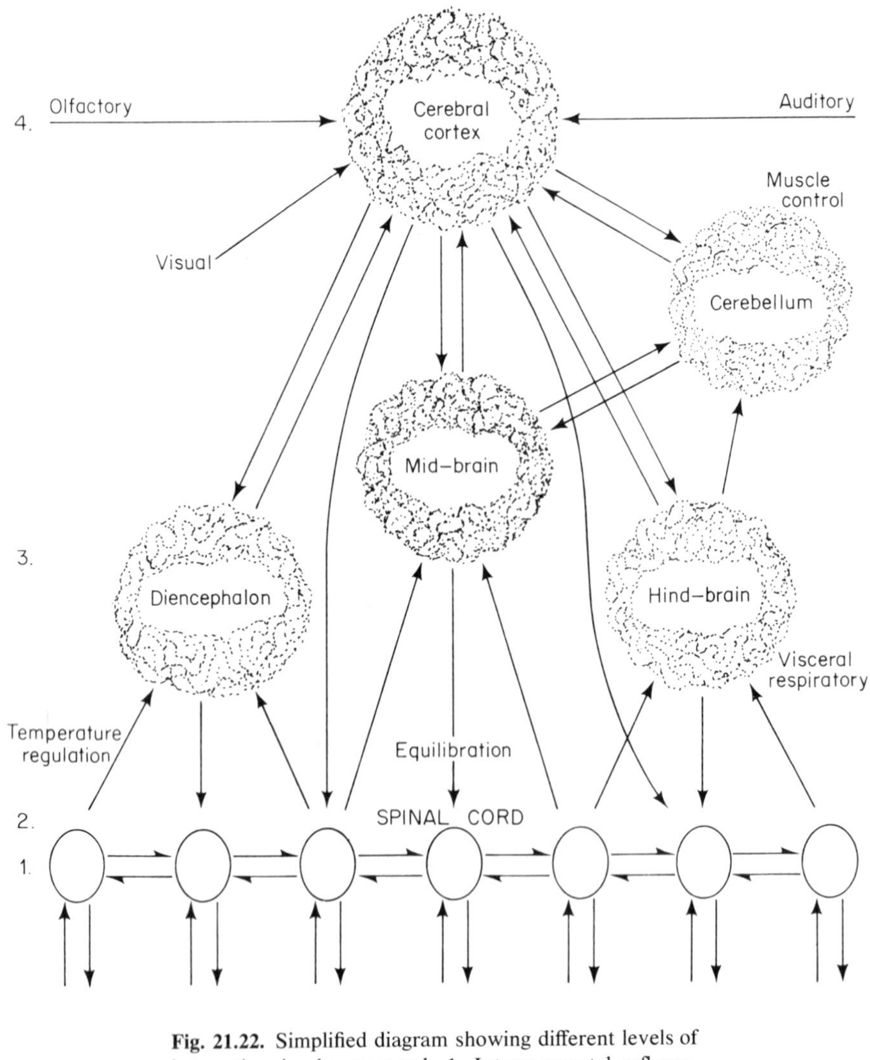

Fig. 21.22. Simplified diagram showing different levels of integration in the mammal. 1, Intrasegmental reflexes. 2, Intersegmental reflexes. 3, Functional centers for more complex activity. 4, Principal association areas for integration of 3 and for input from special senses.

relay stations to complex centers for integration (Dethier and Stellar, 1964). The brain of a flatworm contains relatively few cells but many fiber tracts relaying information from the eyes and other sensory structures of the head to the ladder-like nerve net; the segmental ganglia of the earthworm are monosynaptic junctional areas between the sensory and motor neurons. On the other hand, the cerebral ganglia of higher invertebrates (polychaetes, molluscs, insects) contain many short, interconnecting neurons; presumably, the more complex nervous integration which these forms display is related to them.

A hierarchical organization of controls is also apparent, both from morphological studies of the interconnections between nerve centers and from the experimental localization of functions. Purposeful behavior demands an integrating system of controls for the many separate ganglia or nerve centers, and this develops in the head region which receives the main input of sensory information from the environment. This process of encephalization is illustrated in the morphology of several different groups of animals. The vertebrates provide the most familiar example. In fishes and amphibians the tectum (dorsal area of the midbrain) receives information from all other areas of the brain and serves as the highest level for overall integration of behavior. In amniotes the forebrain which develops first as an olfactory area becomes progressively more dominant. Among reptiles forebrain and midbrain are about equally significant as the dominant regulating centers. In birds the basal ganglia assume this function, while in mammals the roof of the cerebral hemispheres (neopallium) receives sensory information from all parts of the body and transmits impulses to the motor centers which control the effector organs (Fig. 21.22). These relationships are detailed in textbooks of comparative anatomy (Brewer, 1961; Romer, 1955).

Physiology of Behavior

There is now a rapidly growing interest in the PHYSIOLOGY OF BEHAVIOR (Tinbergen, 1963). Both physiologists and zoologists have been active in the development of this exciting field. Physiologists, for their part, have extended the analysis of movements from nerve muscle preparations to simple reflexes, complex reflexes and conditioned reflexes; in doing so, they have become more and more convinced of the inadequacy of the reflex as the sole unit of behavior and increasingly aware of the existence of spontaneous movements and rhythmic activities arising in the central nervous system. The ethologist, on the other hand, has extended his investigations from the descriptive to the analytical and, in his attempts to understand the immediate causation of behavior, has adopted many of the techniques of the physiologist. The two are meeting more and more frequently on common ground.

Many components of animal behavior have now been described in physiological terms. The sensory physiologists have been particularly successful in demonstrating the environmental cues which orient animal activities. Von Frisch (1962), in one of the outstanding classics of modern zoology, has shown that honeybees depend on their eyes and a keen sense of smell to locate nectar, and that they use a stereotyped dance pattern associated with characteristic sounds (Wenner, 1964) to inform their fellow colony members of the location and direction of rich sources of food. Creutzberg (1961) finds that the shoreward movement of young eels, *Anguilla anguilla,* is determined by a tidal mechanism coupled with positive reaction to odors in the waters from the land. Numerous interesting demonstrations of this sort have now been made; several were described in Chapters 16 to 18, devoted to sensory physiology.

Sensory physiology is only one aspect of the physiology of behavior. Neurophysiologists are actively seeking areas of the brain and integrative mechanisms responsible for complex behavior patterns. Current work on brain stimulation has been particularly successful in providing an insight into the neural basis of intricate activities (von Holst and von Saint-Paul, 1962). Some of the earliest work was carried out on cats. By stimulating appropriate areas of the brain through implanted electrodes the animals could be induced to eat, attack or flee. Von Holst and his associates have used chickens. The animals continue in good health while the implanted electrodes remain "permanently" in place; the leads may be attached to the electrical circuit for any particular experiment. Progressively increased stimulation of one particular area leads to a gradual arousal of escape behavior; in another area the stimulation provokes an attack on an object which would normally arouse no such response. Many clearly distinct behavior patterns can be elicited in this way. Curiously, the simultaneous stimulation of two areas may provoke quite a different response. One particularly interesting one is the THREAT which may appear with the simultaneous arousal of ESCAPE and ATTACK. This neurophysiological demonstration provided an interesting confirmation of a relationship which ethologists had predicted from observational data.

A further line of study in the neurophysiological field is based on chemical rather than electrical stimulation of areas of the brain (Fisher, 1964). Implantation of gonadal steroids in localized areas of the rat's brain may elicit specific patterns of sexual behavior. With appropriate hormones male animals display female behavior and vice versa. The work again demonstrates the localized nature of the brain centers controlling complex motor acts but goes further in showing that specific chemicals applied to groups of neurons facilitate a particular behavior pattern in a predictable manner. Both the electrical and chemical stimulation experiments are pushing the analysis beyond a mere localization of neurons and showing something of their interactions and the significance of the internal chemical environment in controlling their activities. Endocrine studies are by no means confined to the stimulation of brain centers with hormones. The role of hormones in social behavior (pheromones) and in the regulation of seasonally changing patterns of behavior are subjects of lively research.

Physiological understanding of behavior must be in terms of recognizable movements or coordinated groups of movements which combine to form the animal's complete repertoire. The biologists, rather than the physiologists, have been responsible for the dissection of behavior into discrete sequences of movements, and for demonstrating that these are predictable and stereotyped elements of extremely complex activities. This anatomy of behavior must obviously precede the physiology.

Jacques Loeb (1859–1924) made the first attempt to describe the total behavior of lower forms in purely mechanistic terms. His thinking was strongly influenced by the plant physiologists of the late nineteenth century who had introduced the concepts of TROPISM to describe the growth movements of plants. Loeb (1918), whose work in this field started about 1888, did a great service to biology by so forcefully rejecting the prevailing anthropomorphic and subjective explanations of animal activities and by substituting hypotheses which were susceptible to experimental analysis and explicable in terms of known physical and chemical laws. According to the thinking of the nineteenth century, a moth flies towards the light because it is curious about this bright and shining object; according to Loeb there are certain energy forces which compel the oriented flight of the moth to the light; the light is controlling the response through the animal's eyes. It is a forced movement of the whole organism towards or away from the stimulus and determined by internal and external forces. The term tropism is now used for the growth movements of plants and sessile animals while the locomotory orientations of mobile animals are called TAXES. Loeb, in his analysis, emphasized a physiological as well as a morphological bilateral symmetry in animals and argued that the processes inducing forward locomotion are equal in both halves of the central nervous system, in the symmetrical muscles and in the peripheral receptors. The animal normally moves in a straight line. If, however, the velocity of reactions are changed in one half of the animal as happens when a light falls on one eye, then the physiological symmetry is disturbed; the animal changes direction and turns until the two sides are again in equilibrium. A unilaterally blinded moth flies in circles. This is a forced response of the whole organism in accordance with the strength of stimulus.

Fraenkel and Gunn (1940), Tinbergen (1951), Thorpe (1958) and others have described the opposition of biologists to Loeb's extreme views. Some of the earliest and most telling criticisms came from work on protozoans which might be presumed, from their lowly phylogenetic position, to support these theories best. Jennings (1923), who made many classical observations, found that numerous activities of the invertebrates were trial-and-error orientations; during the early part of the twentieth century more and more examples were found which did not fit well into the concept of tropisms or taxes. In 1919, Kühn published a classification of behavior which incorporated the concepts of undirected locomotory reactions as well as the directed orientation reaction or taxis. A modification and elaboration of this classification is given by Fraenkel and Gunn (1940). The term KINESIS is introduced for the undirected locomotory reactions, in which the speed of movement or the frequency of turning depends on the intensity of stimulation.

This period during which biologists attempted to categorize behavior in terms of taxes and kineses of several different varieties was the period in which the physiologists saw the intact animal as a reflex machine. Pavlov was born in 1849, ten years earlier than Loeb, and was awarded the Nobel prize in 1904 for his concepts of the conditioned reflex. According to the Pavlovian analysis, the instinctive act was an inherited reflex, and learning was synonymous with conditioning.

The mid-twentieth century witnessed the rise of a new branch of biology devoted to the causal analysis of animal behavior and known as ETHOLOGY (Thorpe, 1958, Tinbergen, 1963). It stems from the observations of naturalists with a genuine interest in what animals are doing and from the penetrating analysis of innate behavior patterns by Konrad Lorenz. Changes in thinking have taken place since Lorenz published his classical paper in 1935, but the broad principles on which his analysis was based have remained the same. The outline which follows is based on the writings of Tinbergen and Thorpe, already mentioned, and on a paper by Baerends (1957); it attempts to summarize current concepts insofar as they provide a useful framework for the study of a physiology of behavior.

BEHAVIOR AS A SERIES OF STEREOTYPED MOVEMENTS

Lorenz saw dissectable components in the behavior of the birds and fishes which he studied. He regarded these elements or patterns of behavior as ORGANS or attributes with special functions. Tinbergen (1963) considers this emphasis on the FIXED ACTION PATTERNS of the species as the first of Lorenz's three important original concepts. The second was that these patterns are vastly more complex than the reflexes usually studied by physiologists, and the third was that internal factors played a much larger part than neurophysiologists of that period believed.

These patterns of movement are innate, stereotyped and performed under standard conditions by all members of the species in essentially the same way; they are as characteristic and fixed in their form as are the anatomical parts of the animal. Any particular behavior pattern occurs in relation to a specific internal physiological state (food requirement, sexual maturity, rhythmic activity in neural centers) and usually in response to definite RELEASING SITUATIONS in the external environment (presence of food, a potential mate). Both the internal and the external contributions to behavior are susceptible to analysis.

The releasing situations are as predictable as are the behavior patterns with which they are associated. The relationship is comparable to the key and the lock. A male stickleback (*Gasterosteus aculeatus*) fights in response to a visual releaser in the form of a red stripe on the underside of another male or in response to a crude model of another fish with the appropriate color contrast. A female stickleback spawns in response to a mechanical releaser created when the male nudges her body while she is in the nest; the same reaction may be induced by probing with a glass rod. The male sheds his sperm partly in response to a chemical releaser diffusing from the recently laid eggs, and fans these eggs during incubation at an intensity which is related to the carbon dioxide content of the environment. Thus, a small part of the total sensory information which the animal receives sets in motion a complex group of stereotyped muscular movements. This information may be received through any of the sense organs, and the activity, unlike a simple reflex, often continues for some time after the presentation of the releaser. Further, the intensity of the response is usually related to the amount of information received. The effectiveness of many different releasing situations varies with the intensity of color or the structural relationships of different parts in a complex visual releaser. Moreover, the releasing information for a particular behavioral pattern is sometimes received through more than one sensory channel. Spawning of the pike is triggered by a rising temperature (thermal receptors) when the fish are in the presence of a particular type of vegetation (visual receptors). What actually happens in such a case seems to depend on the way in which these stimuli are summed in the central nervous system (HETEROGENEOUS SUMMATION). Under normal circumstances a certain amount of information comes through each sensory channel, but the response may also occur when one of the sensory channels receives little or no information. provided that the other is strongly stimulated. Pike may spawn if the temperature is high even though the vegetation is sparse (Fabricius, 1953).

One additional feature is characteristic of simple instinctive behavior. There is not only the fixed pattern of movement, but there is normally also a steering or orienting component to the movement. The male stickleback, in fanning his eggs, uses definite groups of muscles and performs stereotyped activities; but the location of the activity is governed by the entrance of the nest and certain other features in the geography of its environment. This orienting factor may be quite distinct from the releasing situation.

APPETITIVE BEHAVIOR

Behavior, then, consists of a limited number of innate, stereotyped patterns of movement which are released by specific stimuli and guided or oriented by definite features of the environment of the animal. Many of the things which an animal does can be thought of in terms of this simple framework. Such activities as escaping enemies, maintaining the relation to other members of the species or to a territory, feeding when food is abundant and numerous other patterns may be linked very directly with the releasing situation. However, this is not always the case. The animal may lose its position with respect to the group or territory; food may not be immediately available when required; the animal may be in an environment where temperature, salinity or some other factor is unfavorable. In such cases much activity may be necessary before the animal encounters an appropriate releasing situation.

The term "APPETITIVE BEHAVIOR" is used by the ethologist to describe the extended activity which frequently precedes the goal situation and which—in subjective terms—may be described as an urge or an appetite for some particular activity such as feeding, drinking or reproducing and which results in an increased locomotion. The movement may be random (kinesis) or directed (taxis) with respect to environmental gradients such as temperature, current, chemicals or light. This is a much more variable component of the animal's behavior, and predictions of it will have correspondingly broader limits of confidence.

A complicated behavior pattern such as reproduction which occurs seasonally, or perhaps only once in the animal's life, is associated with a series of physiological changes (endocrine activity and maturation of gonads) and may require months of varied activity for consummation. In this case the many activities are evidently organized as a rigid series of behavior patterns released in a predictable sequence. Each pattern may be preceded by a phase of appetitive behavior—lasting many weeks in the case of migration—before the goal situation is reached. The behavior pattern of the goal situation has been referred to as the CONSUMMATORY ACT.

The matter is perhaps more easily visualized by thinking of three major levels of organization: the drive, the appetitive behavior and the consummatory act. When an animal reaches a particular size or age, internal physiological changes prepare it for reproduction which may occur several months later. In some cases these changes have been related to endocrine activity which is regulated by photoperiod or temperature. Admittedly there is little detailed information, but it is abundantly evident that something is happening within the organism which makes it progressively more likely to express the behavior patterns associated with reproduction. This has given rise to the concept of "drive," broadly defined as "the complex of internal and external states and stimuli leading to a given behavior" (Thorpe, 1951; Baerends, 1957). Neither the anatomical nor physiological nature of this "drive" is known, but the fact that something is happening which makes a specific pattern of action more likely cannot be doubted. Its development is associated with appetitive behavior which may be prolonged. This culminates in the goal situation and the consummatory act.

This then is the ethologist's general concept of the anatomy of behavior. A series of innate movements are set in motion by specific releasing situations and guided by conditions or factors in the environment. They may be preceded by considerable locomotion (appetitive behavior) before the appropriate releasing situation is encountered. Complex activities such as reproduction are organized as a rigid (hierarchical) series of such movements. The immediate causation of the varied components of this framework is susceptible to physiological analysis.

COMPLEXITY AND VERSATILITY IN BEHAVIOR

The implicit suggestion of rigidity in the foregoing statements is at variance with the obvious versatility of animals and their abilities to adjust their activities to the problems of living. The ethologist is well aware of this, and his analysis has shown several of the factors involved. The spontaneous or pacemaker type of activity (Roeder, 1955) has already been mentioned several times in this book; the effect of varying amounts of releasing-information on the intensity of some behavioral movements (heterogeneous summation) is another source of diversity. Three other important causes will be briefly mentioned: internal motivation, displacement phenomena and learning.

Internal motivation. This may be defined as that "state of the animal responsible for its readiness to perform the behavior pattern of one instinct in preference to all other behavior patterns" (Thorpe, 1959). This variability may depend on hormones, changing blood sugar levels, proprioceptive or central nervous impulses. Using the stickleback again as an example, sexual behavior in the male has been shown to occur only in animals of a certain minimal size or greater, under the influence of gonadal hormones. It fails to appear in gonadectomized animals unless they are treated with an androgen. This means that the effectiveness of a given quantity of releasing information will vary with the degree of internal motivation. In captive animals the internal motivation may develop to such an intensity that the behavior pattern appears in the absence of the normal releasing situation (vacuum activity).

Displacement and "fall back" phenomena. Under ordinary conditions the hierarchy of movements occurs in an orderly and logical sequence. Under some other conditions, however, the sequence may be quite inappropriate and seemingly illogical. One of the most important contributions of the ethologist has been the establishment of a general principle with respect to these illogical movements and the demonstration that they, too, are predictable. Some excellent examples are to be found in Tinbergen's (1951) studies of the stickleback.

When the male stickleback has prepared a nest and is ready to spawn he will lead a female to the nest in the so-called zig-zag dance and show her the entrance, or he will fight another male if one intrudes into his territory. If, at this time, a female appears and does not respond to him or is removed before he can show her the nest, he will carry out some quite inappropriate movements. Usually he will perform the "fanning" movements normally associated with the incubation of the eggs but at this time inappropriate since the eggs have not been laid. Less frequently he will glue the nest—a movement which is also quite inappropriate since the nest has already been glued when it was built. If another male stickleback appears and suddenly flees or is removed the inappropriate responses are the same, but in this case gluing behavior is more common.

These inappropriate behavior patterns have been termed "displacement activities." They are very similar to the normal appropriate movements, although they may be less intense or may become ritualized (Baerends, 1957). They occur when two incompatible instincts are simultaneously aroused or when the normal releasing situation disappears before the completion of the behavior pattern.

Under certain conditions a similar sort of behavior may be observed when a fish is strongly disturbed. In these cases the behavior has been observed to "fall back" to an earlier stage of the hierarchical organization. If a male stickleback, in more advanced reproductive stages, is frightened or subjected to an abnormal lowering of temperature, the behavior falls back to preliminary phases—first to nest building, and, if strongly disturbed, farther back to migration. The activities, although inappropriate, are predictable and can be analyzed.

Learning. A variety of different processes by which an animal's behavior may be adaptively changed as a result of experience are referred to as learning. All groups of animals show some ability to learn by experience. Thorpe (1951) has provided for the zoologist a useful classification of learning processes, and his organization will be followed here.

Animals readily learn not to respond to stimuli which are without significance for them (HABITUATION). Some type of orientation reflex is to be expected when an animal encounters a sudden stimulus such as a noise or change in illumination. If, however, such stimuli are repeated without any evidence of harm to the animal, the orientation reflex wanes and disappears. The matter of habituation may be described in another way by saying that an animal readily becomes tame.

Animals also learn quickly to associate environmental changes with reward or punishment (CONDITIONING). They may be trained to respond in either a positive or a negative manner to changes in chemical, thermal, photic or mechanical stimuli. In this type of conditioning the releasing stimuli are modified by experience, but the motor patterns remain the same. It involves essentially a substitution of stimuli. This simple (Pavlovian) conditioning probably plays a fundamental part in the development of the highly adaptive behavior which many animals show in nature. In the laboratory, Pavlovian conditioning experiments have been responsible for the establishment and evaluation of the acuity of the different sensory mechanisms.

An apprehension of spatial relations of the environment (INSIGHT) is a part of the complex behavior of most animals. Territorial species may move freely over an area and always return to some definite point. Such behavior shows a detailed knowledge of rather intricate geography. Aronson (1951) found *Bathygobius soporator* so well oriented that it will jump from pool to pool at low tide—even though it is unable to see the neighboring pools—and rarely or never jumps onto the land. It may pass through a series of six or more pools to the open water, jumping over the ledges and rocks which separate the pools. Laboratory experiments with different types of mazes likewise show that animals quickly learn the spatial relationships of their environment and make appropriate responses on the basis of this apprehension (LATENT LEARNING and INSIGHT LEARNING).

There may also be sudden and permanent changes in behavior associated with some very brief experience at a particular time in the animal's life. IMPRINTING, as this is called, was first systematically studied in young geese by Lorenz and other students of bird behavior. The animals, when reared from eggs in isolation, will react to the first relatively large moving object (probably their keeper) as they would to their normal parent. The association, once formed, is permanent and persists throughout life. Comparable learning is known to exist in other groups of lower animals (Thorpe, 1956).

Many animals may also be trained to do rather different and unusual things, such as manipulating a lever in order to secure food (TRIAL AND ERROR LEARNING). Thorpe (1956) gives many examples. In this type of learning the motor action is a new and different response, not one of the inherited patterns which form the normal repertoire. In other types of learning different stimuli or releasers have been substituted for the more usual ones, or a pattern has been suppressed because the stimulus became meaningless. In such examples the plasticity resides in the sensory part of the behavior situation. In trial and error learning the adaptive change is in the motor response, and this is an uncommon adaptation of behavior for invertebrates and lower vertebrates.

These examples will suffice to show that behavior may be variously modified by experience. They do not, however, contradict the basic argument that the normal activities are a collection of fixed stereotyped movements which are released in a predictable manner by definite releasers. Under natural conditions habituation, conditioning, and imprinting are not fundamentally different from changes which occur during development as an inevitable result of the gradual ontogeny of structures and functions in the organism. The complete understanding of behavior, so that useful predictions can be made, is still possible in spite of the variables imposed by these elementary learning processes.

Reproduction and Development

Reproduction 22

The structures and processes described in this chapter are concerned with the survival of the species rather than the individual. The physiology of reproduction depends on the same metabolic machinery and is served by the same sensory, motor and neural mechanisms as the other organ systems but is not essential to the functioning of any of them. Animals, both primitive and advanced, may develop, grow and live a normal life span without reproducing. However, the continuance of the species and all evolutionary changes would quickly come to an end without this constant replacement of the old with similar but somewhat variable offspring. Depending on one's philosophy, the events concerned with reproduction may be considered the ultimate objective of all other life processes or they may be considered "a privilege which may or may not be indulged" (Hisaw, 1959).

The Genetic Material

Even the layman with only a casual interest in living phenomena is now aware that his biological inheritance depends on genes which are arranged on chromosomes and that the actual code of the hereditary information is in the deoxyribonucleic acids (DNA) of the genes. The current spate of literature on genetic coding in both popular and scientific journals is probably greater than that on any other single topic. The evidence linking genes and DNA with the genetic code will not be repeated here. Excellent summaries are available (Anfinsen, 1959; Drysdale and Peacocke, 1961; Crick, 1962; Barry, 1964). There are, however, several considerations which are pertinent to the concepts of a phylogeny of living processes, and these will be summarized before discussing the physiology of reproductive organs and systems.

DEOXYRIBONUCLEIC ACID (DNA)

The probable significance of DNA in the coding of genetic information was recognized many years ago, and this is its most frequently emphasized role in introductory courses and in popular writings. Much more recently, the broad outlines of its activities in directing the synthesis of proteins have been established (Nirenberg, 1963). These two interrelated functions must have evolved together since the replication of entire animals is probably an extension of the capacities to replicate their most characteristic building blocks (the proteins) and the enzymes which control metabolism. Different forms of life owe their peculiar characteristics to their proteins; the continuation of life requires a faithful duplication of these units and of the organism which houses them; the evolution of new species depends on the chance appearance of small variations (mutations) which are in some way superior to the existing arrangements. The point to be emphasized here is that the DNA machinery responsible for these processes seems to have remained basically the same throughout evolution. Only minor variations (mentioned below) have been noted in the base composition of the nucleic acids. Moreover, it appears that identical "code letters" are used to assemble particular amino acids in the synthesis of proteins from bacterial systems to men (Nirenberg, 1963).

Nucleic acids, like proteins, are long-chain polymers of high molecular weight which can be split chemically into repeating units. About two dozen amino acids form the repeating units of proteins; only four different NUCLEOTIDES are joined in varied sequences to form the nucleic acids. A nucleotide was defined in Chapter 7 as a substance composed of a nitrogenous base (either a purine or a pyrimidine), a pentose and phosphoric acid. Adenosine monophosphate (Fig. 7.1) is a mononucleotide which, together with two additional phosphate units, forms the important high-energy phosphate compound ATP. The same nucleotide is found in several vitamins and enzymes (riboflavin, DPN, coenzyme A). The other nucleotides also play a part in metabolism as well as in the coding of genetic information. Uridine triphosphate, for example, is a high-energy compound involved in glycogen synthesis, while protein synthesis seems to require the polyphosphates of all four nucleoside constituents of the nucleic acids. Thus, the essential building blocks of the nucleic acids are by no means unique to them but are also constituents of important energy-transferring compounds of metabolism. Again, the ubiquity of a relatively few indispensable biochemical combinations is apparent.

There are two kinds of nucleic acids (Fig. 22.1). In animal cells *deoxyribonucleic acid* (DNA) is found primarily in the chromosomes of the nucleus; *ribonucleic acid* (RNA) is also found in the nucleus, but the amount there is relatively small and much larger quantities are present in the cytoplasm (particularly in the ribosomes). The chemical differences between these two compounds are shown in Fig. 22.1. In DNA the sugar is 2-deoxy-D-ribose; in RNA the sugar is D-ribose. There is also a difference in one of the pyrimidines; the irregular member of the pair is thymine in DNA but uracil in RNA. Small variations occur in the base composition of DNA in some plants and microorganisms (Anfinsen, 1959), but amongst animals, only the crustaceans have as yet shown a departure from the usual pattern and here the differences are quantitative differences in the proportions of the bases rather than qualitative (Smith, 1964).

One of the most remarkable biochemical achievements of our century has been the demonstration of the order and significance of the arrangement of nucleotides in the DNA molecule. The Watson-Crick model, proposed in 1953, shows two chains coiled together in a double helix (Fig. 22.3) The two ribbons of the helix are composed of a series of sugar-phosphate units joined through 3′–5′ phosphate diester bridges. The two ribbons are cross-linked through a hydrogen bonding formed between the oxygen and nitrogen atoms on the adjacent bases of paired nucleotide molecules. This is only possible between specific base pairs as shown in Fig. 22.2, so that thymine is ALWAYS joined to adenine and cytosine to guanine. It is also to be noted that the molecules in each pair run in opposite directions and that the four nucleotides can be arranged in an almost infinite number of sequences, thus providing for the existence of many different kinds of DNA (Fig. 22.3).

The evidence for this model was based on both chemical and physical data. The chemical analyses showed that the sum of the purines always equals the sum of the pyrimidines and further, that the adenine content equals the thymine content, the cytosine equals the guanine, but the total amount of adenine and thymine rarely or never equals the total amount of guanine and cytosine. Hydrogen bonding was also evident from the chemical analyses while X-ray diffraction studies clearly showed a regular and uniform molecular pattern. The historical events leading up to the Watson-Crick model of DNA are summarized in reviews already cited. This model is now supported by convincing evidence from many sources and has provided a most fruitful impetus to the studies of inheritance and protein synthesis. Watson, Crick and Wilkins were awarded the Nobel prize in 1962 for their discoveries.

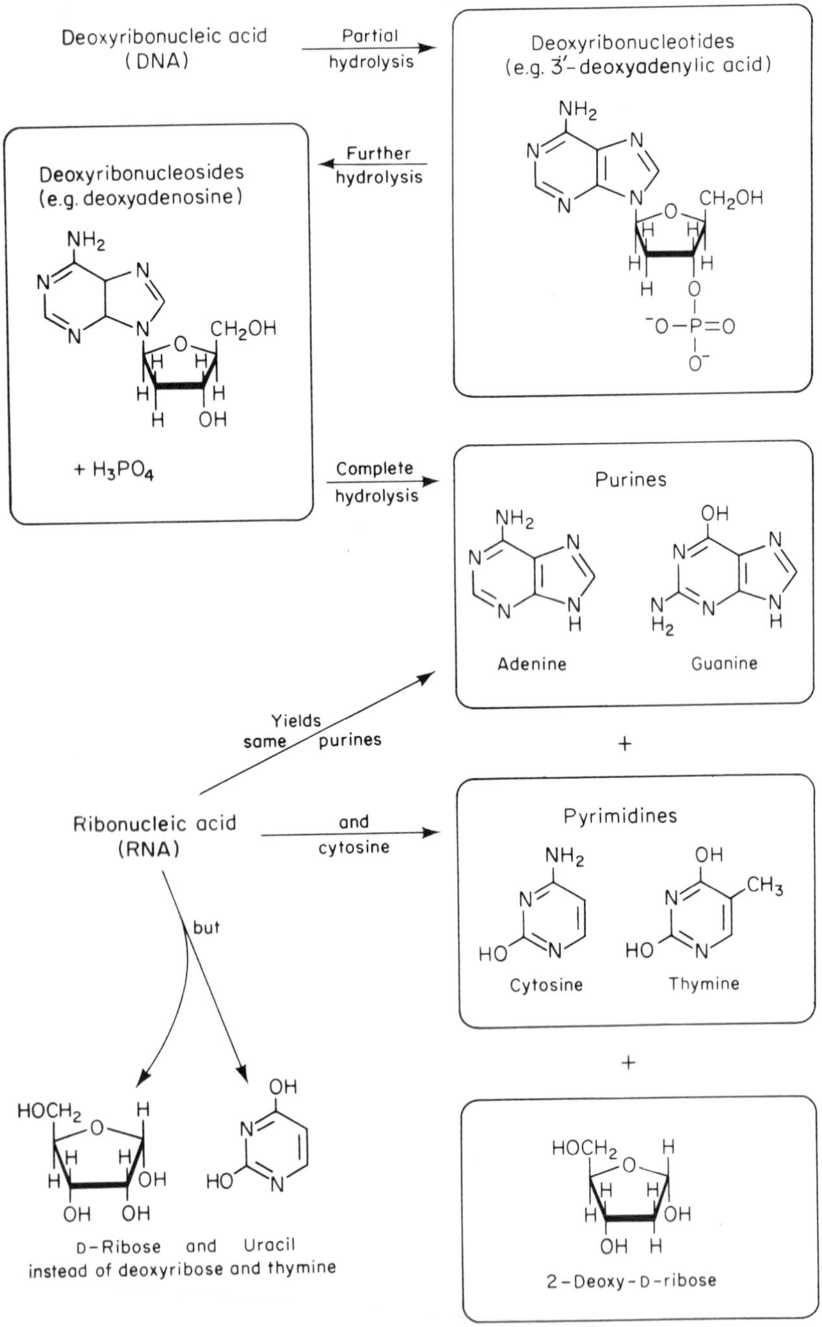

Fig. 22.1. The products of hydrolysis of deoxyribonucleic acid (DNA) and ribonucleic acid (RNA). [Based on Anfinsen (1959).]

Many elegant experiments have demonstrated that DNA can make copies of itself (Barry, 1964). According to the Watson-Crick hypothesis the strands of the double helix separate and serve as templates for the assembling of matching nucleotide chains. Kornberg was awarded a

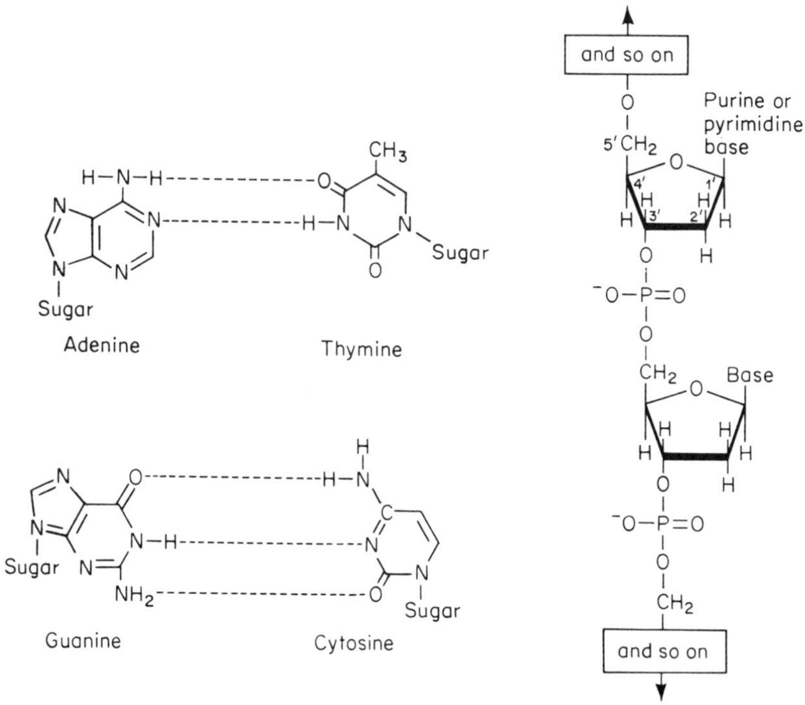

Fig. 22.2. Linkages in the DNA molecule. Left, hydrogen bonding between adenine and thymine, and guanine and cytosine. Right, linkage of nucleotides through 3′–5′ phosphate diester bridges.

Nobel prize in 1959 for convincing *in vitro* experiments demonstrating this. The recent work goes much further and shows how the DNA of the nucleus transfers its code to RNA which passes into the cytoplasm, and how the RNA system of the cytoplasm assembles amino acids into specific proteins. It is now accepted that the genetic alphabet, consisting of four letters (adenine, guanine, thymine and cytosine) is used to spell three-letter words which are quite specific for the different amino acids. Some of the words are now known (Nirenberg, 1963), and it will not be long before the code words for each of the amino acids are identified. The first of these to be recognized was the code for phenylalanine which is uracil-uracil-uracil or UUU.

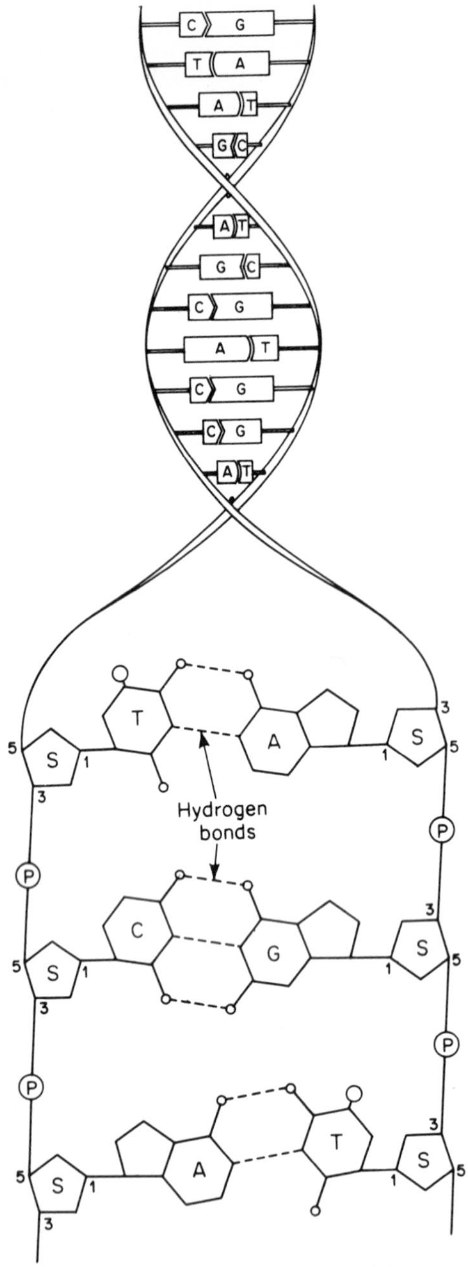

Fig. 22.3. Schematic diagram of the DNA molecule showing the base pairing and the helical structure. A, adenine; C, cytosine; G, guanine; P, phosphate; S, pentose; T, thymine. [McElroy (1964).] For a discussion of single-stranded DNA see Sinsheimer (1962).

DIPLOIDY AND SEX

The units of heredity were named "genes" by Johanssen in 1911. Their presence was adduced from genetical studies starting with those of Gregor Mendel (1822–84) on garden peas. Only in recent years has it been generally recognized that all genes are DNA, with the exception of some of the viral genes which are RNA. A gene is a functional unit, an area of DNA in a chromosome which contains directions for the synthesis of messenger RNA (mRNA) and hence of the proteins (STRUCTURAL GENES), or the information required to regulate the function of the structural genes (REGULATOR GENES). A gene is, in short, a center of specific enzymatic activity.

It was also apparent from breeding experiments, carried out long before the significance of DNA was appreciated, that almost every gene in animal cells has an identical partner and that the expression of any unit character depends on the combined action of two genes. Animals are diploid organisms, and this is a point of particular significance in their evolution and in the development of sexually reproducing mechanisms. Since their observable characteristics (phenotypic) depend on the existence and interaction of two partners, a stability can be expected in the processes of vegetative reproduction. In ordinary cell division (MITOSIS) the genes are duplicated so that the diploid number appears in each of the daughter cells. Unless the same alterations (mutations) occur simultaneously in both members of a genic pair, the phenotype will not be altered during vegetative reproduction or mitosis. In haploid organisms such as molds and bacteria with one set of genes, mutations can lead to a rapid phenotypic expression of the mutant allele. In diploid organisms there is only a remote chance that two members of a gene pair will mutate in the same way at the same time. The significance of diploidy in conferring genetic stability during growth and vegetative reproduction is emphasized. Animals which reproduce by budding or parthenogenetically, self-fertilizing hermaphrodites or gynogenetic clones are genetically rigid and unadaptable in the face of change. They may be highly successful in the environment where they are found but lack the plasticity necessary to meet gradual changes in their environment or to penetrate different environments; they may be quickly eliminated.

While diploidy confers stability, sex provides for diversity. The two fundamental processes of sexual reproduction are MEIOSIS and FERTILIZATION. In meiosis or reduction division the members of the homologous pairs of chromosomes separate at some stage, and the two haploid germ cells resulting from this division each contain half of the DNA of the diploid cells. Actually, meiosis is not a single nuclear division but a double division with only one duplication of the chromosomes. The significant point for present arguments is that the diploid cells containing two of each kind of chromosome give rise to haploid gametes containing one of each kind of chromosome. In fertilization two haploid cells combine to form a new diploid which then divides mitotically during the growth and development of the individual. Now, the geneticist has shown that the paired chromosomes of the diploid cell are RANDOMLY ASSORTED into the haploid cells or gametes. This is true for all sorts of organisms from bread molds to men and is the source of genetic recombination which produces new varieties. Meiosis followed by fertilization is a process which maintains a constancy in the chromosome content of the species and, at the same time, continually generates new individuals with random assortments of parental characters. Organic evolution is based on this steady flow of new varieties into the population. Within the limitations of the DNA of the species, there is thus the possibility that the population will contain individuals which can take advantage of new environments or survive in the face of environmental changes. "Sex arose in organic evolution as a master adaptation which makes all other evolutionary adaptations more readily accessible. Perhaps no other biological function appears in such a bewildering diversity of forms in different organisms as does sexual reproduction. Yet, despite its diversity, sex everywhere serves the same basic function—production of genetic variability by gene segregation and recombination" (Dobzhansky, 1955).

The evolution of sex itself has played a key role in the diversification of animals. Many curious morphological parts, intricate physiological controls and complex behavioral adaptations are the direct consequences of the fundamental importance of sex in organic evolution. Presumably the first sexual processes involved the combination of similar cells of different mating types. In some of the primitive algae and protozoans the partners are morphologically indistinguishable, and if either is grown by itself it will produce only asexual progenies (CLONES) without any fusion of individuals; when cells from different clones are mixed a pairing of individuals takes place. Even among the Protozoa, however, a morphological differentiation of male and female individuals is not uncommon. This can range from small differences in cell size, as in some species of *Paramecium,* to the development of distinctly different male and female forms. In extreme cases sexual union takes place between a large, passive, nonmotile, food-filled female macrogamete and a minute, motile flagellated male microgamete (Hyman, 1940). These are, in fact, eggs and sperm. Sporozoans, such as the malarial parasite *Plasmodium*, provide the most familiar examples of eggs and sperms in the protozoans. The formation of two types of gametes is general throughout all the multicellular groups. In many of the primitive representatives and some of the most advanced, the two types of gonad-producing structures are housed in the same individual (monoecious or hermaphroditic condition), but even in the most primitive groups these may develop in separate animals (dioecious condition). Many complex features of physiology and behavior are associated with this separation of male and female individuals and the necessity of bringing their sex products together at the time of reproduction.

Reproductive Mechanisms

SOME ALTERNATIVES TO SEX

Many protozoans divide mitotically to form clones of like individuals. Some are not known to reproduce in any other way, and their evolution is tied to the slow mutational changes of diploid cells. A reduction division occurs in sexually reproducing forms, and their sexual processes confer the same genetic advantages as those of multicellular animals.

Sexual reproduction is the rule in all multicellular phyla—including the sponges. Many of the more primitive groups, however, have marked capacities for extensive regeneration and often reproduce asexually for longer or shorter periods in their life. Some sponges will regenerate after being reduced to small masses of cells by squeezing them through a filter; many of the sponges reproduce by budding; all freshwater and some marine species, form special asexual bodies called GEMMULES; these consist of hard, round balls containing masses of food-laden cells which are released when the sponge disintegrates. Budding and fragmentation occur in several different phyla—particularly among the coelenterates, the platyhelminths, the nemertines, a few of the annelids and tunicates. Sometimes lateral buds are formed as in *Hydra;* sometimes the animal multiplies by a series of transverse divisions as in the scyphistoma of *Aurelia*, in many of the flatworms, both free-living and parasitic, and in some of the nemertines and oligochaetes; sometimes the fragmentation takes a less regular course and results in variously shaped pieces as in some of the platyhelminths. Many examples are given in Hyman's monographs and in the book by Vorontsova and Liosner (1960). In general, however, these are NOT alternatives to sexual reproduction but an adjunct to it. The asexual multiplication alternates with a sexual stage and provides for a rapid increase in numbers of individuals through vegetative processes without a loss of the evolutionary advantages of sexual reproduction.

Strictly parthenogenetic species, gynogenetic forms, and self-fertilizing hermaphrodites, on the other hand, form clones of genetically identical individuals. These are closed genetic systems which have lost the advantages of producing new varieties through reshuffling the old.

PARTHENOGENESIS is the development of a new individual from an egg or a spermatozoan without the participation of a germ cell from the opposite sex. Among animals only the maternal germ cells are known to give rise to parthenogenetic individuals, but certain algae arise in this manner from paternal cells (Parkes, 1960). Although many examples of artificial parthenogenesis have been recorded, the natural process is restricted to some groups of invertebrates (particularly the insects) and to a few lizards (several subspecies of *Lacerta saxicola* and possibly the genus *Cnemidophorus*) among the vertebrates (Maslin, 1962; Kallman and Harrington, 1964). In some platyhelminths and rotifers and certain wasps and sawflies (Hymenoptera) parthenogenesis is the only known method of reproduction. This also seems to be the case in the earthworm *Eisenilla tetraedra* which has male reproductive organs but never forms mature sperm (Cain, 1954). In many parthenogenetic invertebrates there is a cyclical alternation of asexual with bisexual reproduction. Parthenogenesis may be seasonal and related to temperature or food supply, or it may appear at irregular intervals. In several insects (honeybees, some wasps and sawflies) unfertilized eggs develop into haploid males while fertilized eggs give rise to diploid females. Suomalainen (1962) discusses the evolutionary implications. The nuclear changes associated with the formation of gametes vary considerably in different parthenogenetic species, and textbooks of cytology should be consulted for details.

In GYNOGENESIS, a spermatozoan activates an egg but does not contribute any genetic material to it. The resulting embryo carries only maternal chromosomes. The reverse condition, where the chromosome contribution comes exclusively from the male, is called ANDROGENESIS, but in animals this is known only experimentally. Naturally-occurring gynogenesis is recognized in a few nonsegmented worms, a ptinid beetle and two species of teleost fishes (Parkes, 1960; Kallman, 1962*a*). *Poecilia* (*Mollienesia*) *formosa*, a poeciliid teleost, has been more carefully examined than other gynogenetic animals and is particularly interesting in that it borrows sperm from a different species to effect the fertilization of its eggs; in some flatworms gynogenesis is of the racial type, with eggs of the gynogenetic race activated by sperm of a bisexual race. *Poecilia formosa* maintains itself in nature by mating with *P. sphenops* or *P. latipinna*. The offspring are exclusively females. The homozygosity of different clones was demonstrated by tissue transplant techniques; tissue grafts among members of the same clone always survive whereas grafts between members of different clones are rejected (Kallman, 1962*a*, *b*).

HERMAPHRODITISM, or the monoecious condition, is one in which both male and female gametes are formed in the same individual. It is common among primitive animals, and all the major groups, including the vertebrates, have their hermaphroditic representatives. Cross-fertilization is usual, and under these conditions the significance of reproduction in evolutionary processes is the same as that of dioecious species. Self-fertilizing hermaphrodites, on the other hand, form clones of identical individuals. The teleost fishes provide interesting examples. Some species of Sparidae and Serranidae are invariably hermaphroditic, producing eggs and sperm in different areas of the same gonad; they may be self-fertilizing (D'Ancona, 1949). However, self-fertilization is not obligatory. In *Serranellus subligarius* a single individual may shed both eggs and sperm in an aquarium, and these produce normal offspring. In nature, however, there is an elaborate sexual play, with paired individuals in different color phases playing distinct roles. Curiously enough, an animal may show a change of color phase and behavior during any mating sequence (Clark, 1959). Cross-fertilization is probably the usual outcome.

The cyprinodont *Rivulus marmoratus*, on the other hand, is a self-fertilizing hermaphrodite (Harrington, 1963). The homozygous nature of the genotypes in clones of *Rivulus* has been established by tissue transplantation (Kallman and Harrington, 1964). Thus, the teleost fishes show many curious reproductive specializations; parthenogenesis seems to occur only sporadically, but gynogenesis and obligatory self-fertilization are established beyond doubt. Both evidently represent a secondary loss of the potential for genetic variability through sexual processes.

MORPHOLOGY OF THE REPRODUCTIVE ORGANS

Some of the most heated discussions of classical embryology have centered around the origin, segregation and lineage of the germ cells, the source of nongerminal gonadal tissues and the differentiation of the gonad (Nelsen, 1953). These topics are reviewed in textbooks of embryology and in monographs devoted to the reproductive organs. The present discussion will start with the mature gonads containing a stock of germ cells, from whatever source, and will consider them as organs for the production of gametes and the integration of reproductive processes.

In some primitive animals the gamete-producing tissues are diffuse, consisting of numerous scattered loci for the proliferation of the sex cells. In all the more advanced animals the gonads are localized, and in the bilaterally symmetrical forms they arise as paired structures. Sometimes one of the gonads degenerates secondarily. The birds provide a familiar example with paired testes in the male and a single left ovary in most females.

Primordial germ cells which have set out on the path of female development are called OOGONIA; those which are on the male path are SPERMATOGONIA. Oogonia and spermatogonia, like the somatic cells, are diploid and may divide many times mitotically. However, when they commence their maturation divisions and undergo meiosis to form haploid cells, they are called OOCYTES and SPERMATOCYTES respectively. A PRIMARY OOCYTE or a PRIMARY SPERMATOCYTE is undergoing its first reduction division; the stage referred to as SECONDARY is associated with the second maturation division, and the various transformations beyond this produce the mature eggs and sperms. Vitellogenesis or the storage of yolk is usually initiated after the early stages of the first meiotic division. The number of mitotic divisions and the timing of meiosis varies in different groups. In certain representatives of advanced phyla the processes of vitellogenesis and the initiation of meiosis have been shown to be hormonally regulated.

The ovary. The primary and universal function of the ovary is to generate the female sex cells or eggs. A second function which is an almost universal adjunct to this is the elaboration of a store of nutritive materials (yolk) for the early stages of embryonic development. The synthesis of hormones for the chemical coordination of reproductive functions is also an ovarian responsibility in the vertebrates and in some of the more advanced invertebrates; information on this point is lacking for many of the lower forms. A fourth ovarian function, present in some of the specialized viviparous animals, is the housing and nourishment of developing young (FOLLICULAR GESTATION). There are many radical differences in ovarian morphology (Raven, 1961; Zuckerman, 1962). The examples which follow have been selected to illustrate these four functions.

The first examples, drawn from the turbellarians, illustrate some of the most unusual and highly specialized methods for the storage of reserve food (Hyman, 1951). In the Acoela, Polycladida and some of the Rhabdocoela, there are no special follicle or nurse cells; but the developing ovum draws its nourishment from surrounding maternal tissues (SOLITARY EGG FORMATION). In some rhabdocoels and in the Alloeocoela, however, egg formation is ALIMENTARY as in most animals (Raven, 1961) with groups of specialized yolk-synthesizing cells associated with the developing eggs. The follicle of *Prorhynchus,* illustrated in Fig. 22.4*b*, shows the more primitive condition where one of the ovocytes becomes an egg and others are arranged around it as follicle cells which supply it with food. In the elongated ovary these follicles become progressively more differentiated toward the gonopore (Fig. 22.4). This follicular organization of a developing ovum within a ball of epitheloid cells is a characteristic one, from the primitive to the most advanced animals (Fig. 22.7). In a more specialized condition of many turbellarians groups of cells are set aside as a special yolk-producing gland or vitellarium. These animals are hermaphroditic but cross-fertilizing, and after copulation the sperm fertilize the ova in the oviduct; eggs then receive the products of the yolk glands as they move towards the genital atrium where a cocoon or shell is added. The details vary; the important point

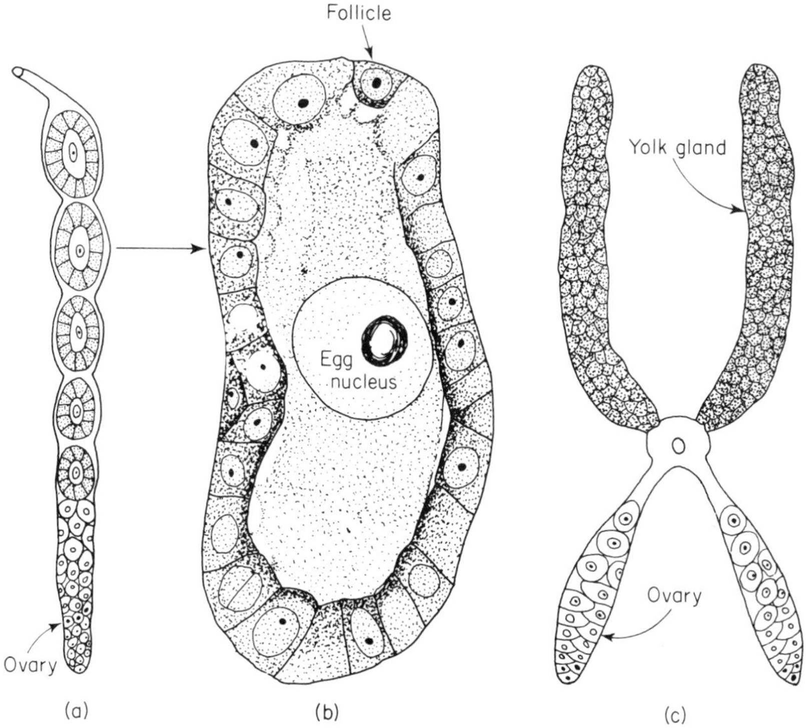

Fig. 22.4. Reproductive glands of female turbellarians. *a*, A germovitellarium composed of maturing follicles in the Prorhynchidae, *b*, A follicle of *Prorhynchus*, *c*, The condition found in most rhabdocoels and alloeocoels with two yolk glands and one or two ovaries. [Hyman (1951).]

is that nutritive functions have become separated and that these primitive animals show highly specialized methods of provisioning their eggs.

An example of solitary egg formation is illustrated in the section of the gonad of the bivalve *Sphaerium* (Fig. 22.5). This is a hollow structure formed of columnar epithelial cells, some of which give rise to oocytes. The developing oocytes bulge into the lumen but remain attached by a stalk with elongated germinal epithelial cells arranged around it. These elongated cells are assumed to supply nourishment to the developing egg; sometimes they seem to be ingested by the ovum (Woods, 1931; Raven, 1961).

The insects show several types of alimentary egg formation, one of them comparable to the vitellarium of the turbellarians (Bonhag, 1958).

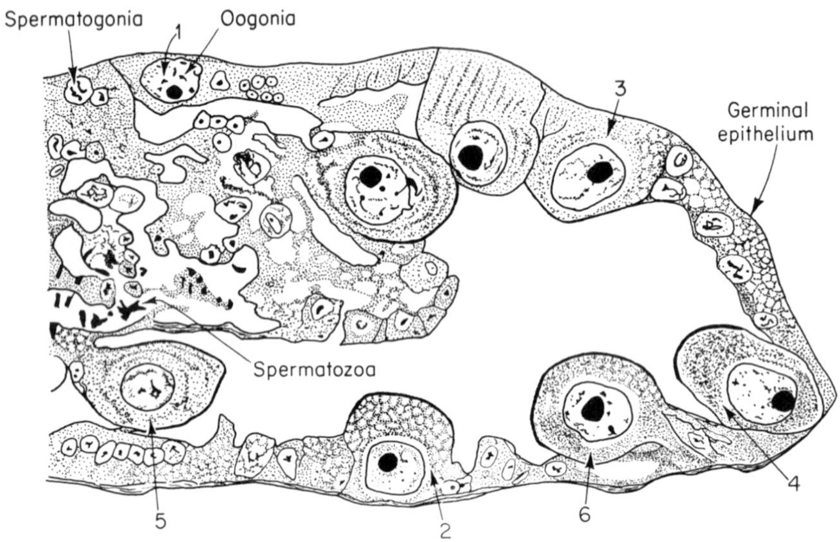

Fig. 22.5. Section through a maturing gonad of *Sphaerium striatinum*. Numerals indicate successive stages in the growth of the oocytes. [Based on Woods (1931).]

The ovary consists of a series of egg tubes or ovarioles varying in number from one in the viviparous dipteran *Glossina* to more than 2000 in certain termites (Wigglesworth, 1942). Three different situations are illustrated in Fig. 22.6. In each case the elongated ovariole gradually widens from its terminal filament to the broad base which opens into the oviduct, and the developing eggs become progressively larger and more mature from pointed apex to base. The apex consists of densely packed cells and is called the germarium. Some of its cells are primordial germ cells and differentiate into oocytes while others take on a nutritive function. In the most primitive type (PANOISTIC) the nurse cells become arranged around the oocyte in a follicle (Ephemeroptera, Orthoptera); in the most specialized form (TELOTROPHIC) the nutritive cells form specialized TROPHOCYTES and are localized in the apex and connected to the developing ova by long nutritive cords (Hemiptera, some Coleoptera). In the

Diptera, Hymenoptera, Lepidoptera and some others there is an intermediate condition (POLYTROPHIC) in which each oocyte has a number of trophocytes enclosed with it in its follicle. Further details with descriptions of the lineage of these cells will be found in textbooks of insect

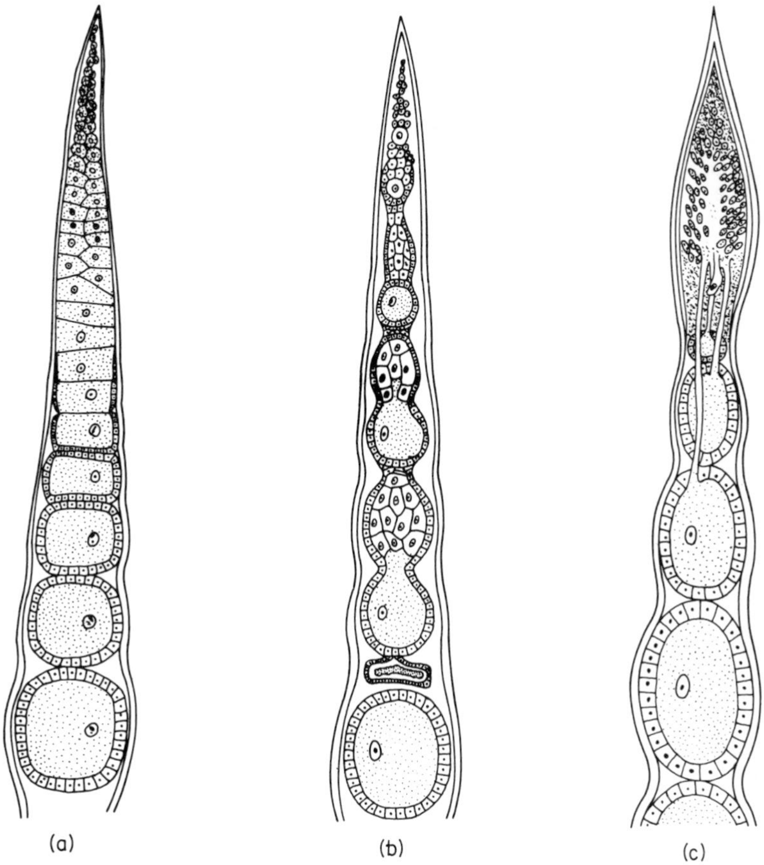

Fig. 22.6. Histology of the insect ovary. *a.* PANOISTIC TYPE represented by the firebrat *Thermobia domestica, b,* POLYTROPHIC TYPE represented by the queen honeybee. *c,* TELOTROPHIC TYPE represented by the milkweed bug *Oncopeltus fasciatus.* [De Wilde (1964).]

anatomy (Snodgrass, 1935) and physiology (Wigglesworth, 1942; De Wilde, 1964). Endocrine production by the insect ovary is questionable Gorbman and Bern, 1962). It is well known, however, that gestation takes place in the ovaries of some of the viviparous species.

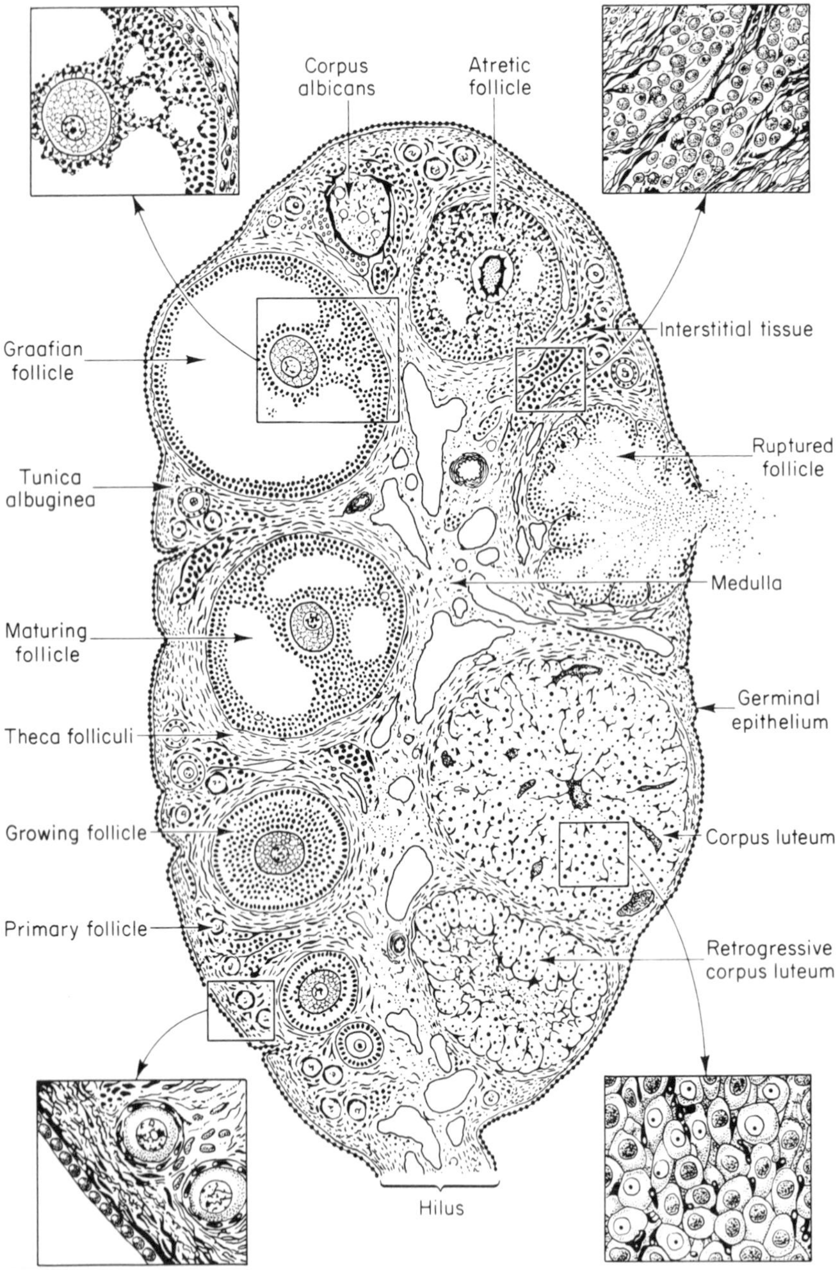

Fig. 22.7. Diagram of a mammalian ovary. A mature follicle may become atretic (upper right) or ovulate and undergo luteinization (lower right). [Turner (1960).]

The physiologically important features of the vertebrate ovary are illustrated in Fig. 22.7. Within the cortex of the gland single oocytes differentiate inside a ball of follicular cells which are epithelial in nature and vary in number from a single layer in some forms to numerous layers in others. This is the FOLLICULAR EPITHELIUM or GRANULOSA, and its primary function was probably that of providing materials for the synthesis of yolk and the growth of the ovum. The stroma of the ovary surrounding the granulosa becomes organized into connective tissue layers called the theca. In higher forms, the THECA INTERNA becomes a glandular and vascular estrogen-synthesizing layer which is distinct from the theca externa. In vertebrates the mature eggs are usually shed into the peritoneal cavity where they pass into the open ends of the oviducts (most species) or from the body through abdominal pores (some fishes). In some teleost fishes the mature eggs are discharged into the ovarian lumen which is continuous with a short oviduct (Hoar, 1957). It is within this type of ovary that follicular gestation occurs in viviparous species.

The follicular epithelium or granulosa discharges several different functions in vertebrate animals. As previously mentioned, its primary role seems to be nutritive. In all vertebrates, however, it also plays a phagocytic role when the ovum finishes its development. The ovary, like many other organs, operates with a considerable margin of safety, and many follicles never produce a mature egg. Variable numbers, depending on physiological conditions, degenerate, and the granulosa cells are concerned with the removal of the yolk and other substances. They perform the same function in removing blood clots and other debris following ovulation. This phagocytic activity is often evident in ovaries and can be demonstrated experimentally by removing the pituitary gland; vitellogenesis ceases without the gonadotropic hormones and the developing follicles are cleared of yolk by the granulosa.

In addition to its nutritive and phagocytic activities, the granulosa may take on the functions of an endocrine gland. Following ovulation in the mammal there is a proliferation of the granulosa and theca interna to form the CORPUS LUTEUM concerned with the synthesis of progesterone. Comparable morphological bodies are formed in the ovaries of many vertebrates, ranging from the cyclostomes to the mammals; they may arise during follicular atresia (pre-ovulatory corpora lutea) or after ovulation (post-ovulatory corpora lutea). There is no conclusive evidence of an endocrine function in corpora lutea of lower forms. For this reason, some writers refer to them as CORPORA ATRETICA and reserve the term corpus luteum for the endocrine structure of the mammalian ovary, known to produce progesterone and to be under the gonadotropic control of the pituitary. The controversy has been reviewed (Hoar, 1957,

1965*b*; Hisaw, 1963). Further studies will be required to solve this problem; in some fishes and reptiles the evidence for an endocrine function is strongly suggestive. During the evolution of the vertebrates the ovarian follicle has assumed the duties of providing two different hormones (estrogen and progesterone) as well as the generation of female gametes.

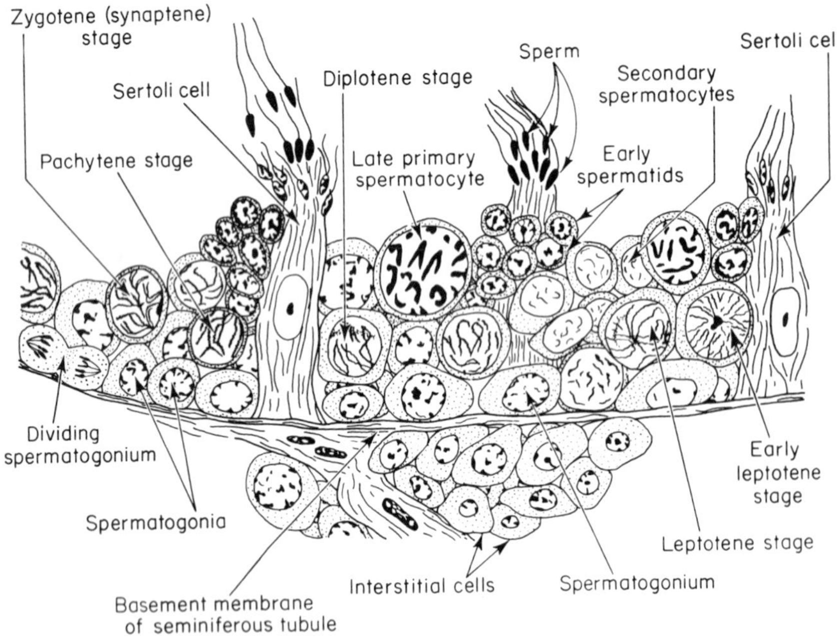

Fig. 22.8. Diagram of a part of the seminiferous tubule of the cat testis. [Nelsen (1953).]

The testis. The gonad of the male has a less varied role to play and for that reason is structurally simpler. The complexity of the male reproductive system is associated with its accessory structures rather than the testes since the male animal usually plays the more active part in bringing the two sexes together and in the transfer of gametes, but the spermatozoa of the various species are structurally similar.

When the spermatogenetic tissue is organized into compact testes, as it is in the more advanced phyla, the organ is made up of a series of elongated follicles or seminiferous tubules. The form of these units varies greatly as does also the organization of the seminiferous epithelium within them. Often all stages in spermatogenesis are evident at any level in cross-sections of the tubules (Fig. 22.8); spermatogonia are located just inside the basement membrane of the tubule, and the series of maturing stages occur toward the lumen where the mature sperm are released. This arrangement is characteristic of most of the vertebrates. In the elasmobranchs, however, the testes are made up of ampullae which contain only one stage of developing germ cells. This feature proved most useful in localizing the source and action of the pituitary gonadotropins of these fishes, since the removal of the ventral lobe of the pituitary and no other part affected one particular stage of development (Dodd *et al.*, 1960). Testes of insects are also zonated structures, comparable in histological arrangement with the ovary in this group (Fig. 22.6). Testicular follicles contain a succession of zones, each composed of cells in one particular stage of development; progressively more mature stages in differentiation occur from the apical area of spermatogonia to the basal area of spermatozoa.

Androgen-producing endocrine tissue is recognized within the testes of all vertebrate animals. It may be identified histochemically by its staining reactions. Small groups of relatively large polyhedral cells with granular cytoplasm and large nuclei are situated in the spaces between the seminiferous tubules (CELLS OF LEYDIG, INTERSTITIAL TISSUE) or are arranged as LOBULE BOUNDARY-CELLS in the walls of the seminiferous tubules. The lobule boundary-cell arrangement is known only in some of the teleost fishes and may be a secondary development (Hoar, 1965*b*). The staining properties of these two types of androgen-producing tissue are similar, and they probably elaborate similar hormones. Endocrine-producing tissues have not been identified in the gonads of most invertebrates (Chapter 23).

INTERSEXUAL RELATIONSHIPS

The mechanisms which bring sperm into contact with eggs and the subsequent processes of fertilization must be absolutely reliable or the species will perish. This requirement of life has been satisfied through a host of special adaptations; some of these are cellular, others occur at the tissue or organ level, and still others at the species and interspecies level of social organization.

At the cellular level there are the egg secretions which influence sperm (FERTILIZIN) and sperm secretions which influence eggs (ANTIFERTILIZIN). Although primitive multicellular animals are usually hermaphroditic, they are normally cross-fertilizing and, even though sperm from a different animal have been injected into oviducts or other egg-holding spaces, they must still make contact with and penetrate the egg. These interacting chemicals produced by the gametes form the chemical basis of fertilization. The bisexual condition of higher forms in which ovaries and testes are housed in separate individuals, eliminates the possibility of self-fertilization but increases the importance of the chemical system of attraction between eggs and sperm. Animals, from the most primitive to the most advanced, display a range of specializations which, on the one hand, insure cross-fertilization through a separation of the sexes and, on the other, magnify the opportunities for union between the eggs and sperm from different individuals. Cross-fertilizing hermaphrodites with internal fertilization have many curious morphological arrangements to reduce the chances of self-fertilization; both hermaphrodites and bisexual species which broadcast their gametes into the ambient water have timing devices (some chemical and based on egg and sperm substances and others neuroendocrine) which often induce mass spawning and thus increase the chances of cross-fertilization by the sheer concentration of cells. Internal fertilization of bisexual individuals is also based on chemical reactions between the gametes as well as on a host of morphological specializations and behavioral adaptations to insure that sperm are deposited in the right place at an appropriate time.

Fertilization. Research extending over more than half a century has now established the presence of interacting egg and sperm chemicals which hold the cells together once contact has been made and, in some cases, stimulate mass spawning (Nelsen, 1953; Rothschild, 1956; Bonner, 1958). Many of the pioneer studies were carried out with sea urchins. A specific chemotaxis whereby an egg attracts sperm to its surface is unlikely among animals (Rothschild, 1956). However, once the sperm, through its motility or otherwise, makes contact with the egg a definite reaction occurs. If sperm are added to "egg-water" (water in which ripe eggs of the same species were retained for a period of time) they are first activated and then agglutinated or clumped. The sperm-activating and agglutinating material was named FERTILIZIN by F. R. Lillie who worked on sea urchin eggs. Comparable materials have been demonstrated in many animals, vertebrate as well as invertebrate; they are usually species-specific and probably form a complex of materials in any one species rather than a single substance. In sea urchin eggs fertilizin is localized in the gelatinous coat; it is an acid mucopolysaccharide in which the carbohydrate component differs among the various species (Raven, 1959). Sperm contain a chemical or chemicals called ANTIFERTILIZIN which unites with the fertilizin of the egg so that the spermatozoon is trapped on the surface layer of the egg. This is an acidic protein which seems to be located on the sperm head. The fertilizing reaction also depends on the presence of lytic substances produced by the sperm which must penetrate the egg as well as attach itself to the egg surface. In mammals the substance HYALURONIDASE, an enzyme found in sperm and certain other places, brings about the disintegration of the follicular cells associated with the mammalian egg at ovulation. Several other sperm compounds with lytic properties have been studied (Rothschild, 1956). Reactions between eggs and sperm are species-specific and bear many resemblances to immunological reactions. Comparable reactions occur on the surfaces of conjugating protozoans. The different mating types "stick together;" the reacting substances seem to be associated with the cilia in *Paramecium*, but this is not true of some other ciliated forms (Wichterman, 1953; Bonner, 1958).

Reciprocal induction of spawning. Egg and sperm secretions have been shown to induce spawning in some of the marine invertebrates (Nelsen, 1953; Rothschild, 1956). This phenomenon was observed in the spawning of oysters *Ostrea virginica* many years ago (Galtsoff, 1938, 1940, 1961). The presence of oyster sperm stimulates spawning of female oysters; the presence of oyster eggs stimulates the males to release sperm. The reactions are specific, and foreign eggs or sperm are quite ineffective. A mass spawning is triggered in this way, and the chances of successful fertilization are increased. Similar reactions have been demonstrated in some other invertebrate species and are probably of wide occurrence—particularly in sessile or sedentary forms. They may also be important in some of the more advanced aquatic animals such as the fishes, but the coordination at this level is more apt to depend on neuroendocrine and behavioral mechanisms.

The associations of males with females. The evolution of the bisexual or dioecious condition can be considered one of the most significant phylogenetic advances. The localization of ovaries and testes in different individuals removed all chances of self-fertilization and insured the advantages which come through the shuffling of two sets of genes. Moreover, the bisexual species has freedom, both to specialize in gamete production and to divide the labors of protecting and nourishing the young. It is obvious that at the top of the phylogenetic tree man's peculiar evolution, which has attained a certain freedom from the germ plasm, owes much of its rich variety and interest to the existence of separate male and female personalities.

Many biologists have noted the marked diversity in reproductive structures, physiology and behavior. It seems to exceed that of any other system. In part, this may be attributed to the existence of two kinds of individuals, the males and females. In part, however, it is due to the freedom of reproductive structures and processes from the demands of other organs and systems. There is a definite autonomy of the reproductive system; it exists for the future of the species and not for the individual which houses it. This autonomy seems to have been responsible for the frequent appearance of highly specialized processes such as viviparity in groups widely separated phylogenetically (Dodd, 1960;

Hoar, 1965*a, b*). The relative advantages of many different processes must have been frequently weighed during animal phylogeny—many eggs or a few well-nourished ones, internal or external fertilization, oviparity or ovoviviparity or viviparity, monogamy or polygamy.

The array of reproductive devices is too vast for detailed consideration in this survey. Rather, one group of animals, the teleost fishes, has been chosen to illustrate the potentialities of evolutionary processes. Within a closely related group of animals, living in one type of habitat, there is an almost complete range of techniques for bisexual reproduction including a few which are unique. Some other classes of animals might equally well have been chosen as examples; the insects and gastropods show almost as sweeping a range of modifications.

The varied physiology of teleost reproduction is indicated in Table 22.1. Within each of the major categories shown for the dioecious species there is further profusion of minor variations on the central theme. In fact, this table does not include all the types of curious activities of this group of animals. The very loose embryo-maternal relations of ovoviviparous species may not be very different physiologically from oral incubation practised by the cichlids. In some species of oral incubators the fertilized eggs are picked up by the female and in some cases by the male. Again, the effect of oral incubation on the embryo may not differ physiologically from embryonic development in a nest such as that of *Gasterosteus* or within the body of a different species of animal; the developing bitterling *Rhodeus amarus* is incubated within a freshwater mussel. The nest, the oral cavity and the urogenital cavity are very different kinds of protecting habitat but may all be without particular physiological effects on the developing young. In the urogenital cavity, however, some teleosts have taken the step from ovoviviparity to true viviparity where the developing embryo or fetus draws nourishment from the maternal sources for extended periods. Here, again, there is considerable diversity in the different groups with a complete range of what seems possible (Hoar, 1955*b*, 1957; Amoroso, 1960).

In most viviparous vertebrates fertilization follows ovulation, but this is the exception among the teleosts (Turner, 1947). Only in *Zoarces* is ovulation said to precede fertilization. In other viviparous teleosts sperm penetrate the ovarian tissue and may be stored and nourished there for considerable periods before entering the follicle to fertilize the egg. Within the follicle, fertilized ova may develop until parturition at an advanced stage, or they may pass into the ovarian cavity during early cleavage. Intimate and curious maternal-embryonic connections are

TABLE 22.1.

REPRODUCTIVE BEHAVIOR IN SOME TELEOST FISHES

CONDITIONS		ACTIVITIES									EXAMPLES
						Courtship					
							Copulation				
		Aggregation–Migration	*Territoriality*	*Nest building* ♂	*Nest building* ♀	*Bisexual play*	*Sperm to female*	*Eggs to male*	*Parental care* ♂	*Parental care* ♀	
Parthenogenetic											
Natural (?)											*Lebistes*
Artificial											*Salmo*[1]
Gynogenetic		−	−			+	*				*Mollienesia*[2]
Hermaphroditic											
self-fertilizing											
a. facultative		−	+			−					*Serranellus*
b. obligatory		−	−								*Rivulus*[3]
cross-fertilizing		−	+			+					*Serranellus*
parasitic		?	−			−					*Ceratias*[4]
Dioecious	No Pair formation	+	−		−	−		−	−	−	*Richardsonius*, *Roccus*
Dioecious	Pair formation	+	−	−	−	+	−	−	−	−	*Mugil*, *Notropis*
Dioecious	Pair formation	+	+	−	+	+	−	−	−	−	*Salmo*
Dioecious	Pair formation	+	−	−		+	+	−	−	−	*Lebistes*
Dioecious	Pair formation	+	+	+	−	+	−	−	+	−	*Gasterosteus*
Dioecious	Pair formation	+	−		−	+	−	+	+	−	*Syngnathus*[4]
Dioecious	Pair formation	+	+	+	+	+	−	−	+	−	*Tilapia*
Dioecious	Pair formation	+	+	+	+	+	−	−	+	+	*Geophagus*

*Sperm of related species transferred to female.
[1]Parkes (1960)
[2]Kallman (1962).
[3]Harrington (1963).
[4]Greenwood (1963). Other references in Hoar (1963).

established either within the cavity of the ovary (OVARIAN GESTATION) or inside the follicle (FOLLICULAR GESTATION). In ovarian gestation, glandular folds or villi of the epithelium of the ovary may grow into the gill cavities and mouth of the embryo (Jenynsiidae) to provide nourish-

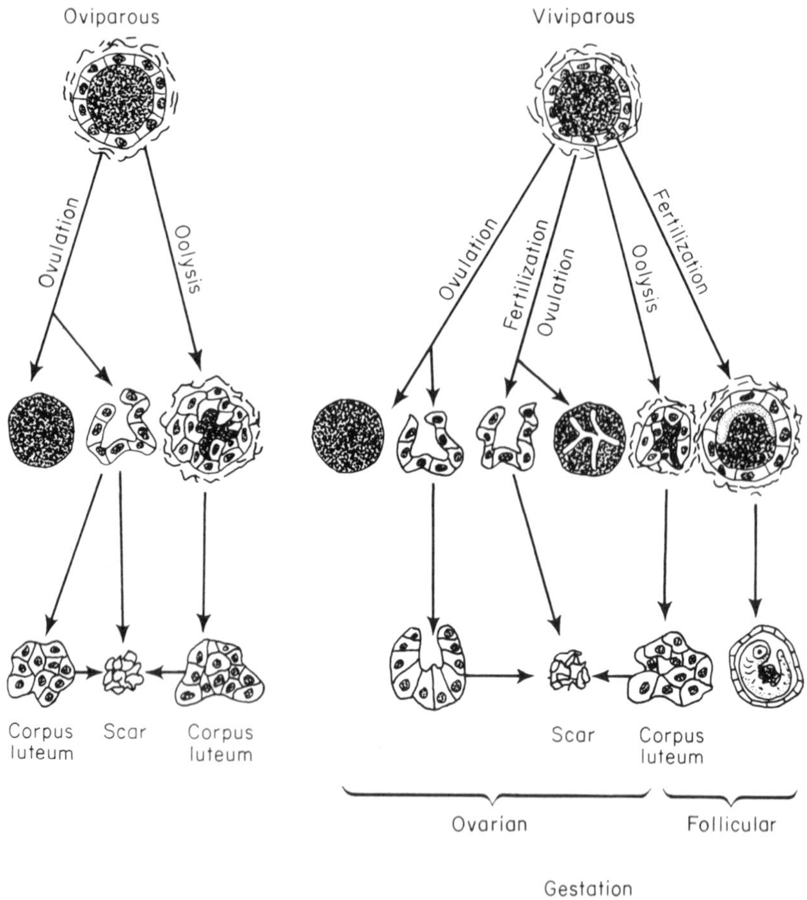

Fig. 22.9. History of the ovarian follicle in different teleost fishes.

ment; specialized ribbon-like extensions (trophotaeniae) of the anal or urinogenital region (Goodeidae) or vascular extensions of the vertical fins (*Cymatogaster*) may become intimately associated with the ovigerous folds. In follicular gestation similar outgrowths of the embryo from the pericardial or petitoneal sacs or urinary bladder establish a placental type of interconnection with the vascular and folded wall of the follicle. Superfetation, the simultaneous development of several broods of young, is common in a number of the Poeciliidae. *Heterandria formosa* seems to exemplify the climax in this specialization with as many as nine broods developing simultaneously in one female (Turner, 1937). A single insemination may be effective for as long as ten months with the immobilized sperm embedded and nourished in the epithelium of the ovary; young are produced at intervals of about 5 days. The teleost fishes illustrate in a dramatic fashion the three main avenues of follicular specialization among animals (Fig. 22.9). The universal and primary function of egg formation is variously modified to produce ova of many different sizes and capacities for subsequent development. In addition, the follicle is probably always the source of steroid hormones whether or not a corpus luteum is formed for this purpose. Finally, the follicle sometimes serves as an incubation chamber in which the developing young remain for several months until ready to lead a completely independent existence. This latter role is relatively rare but occurs among insects as well as in some teleost fishes.

23 Endocrine Regulation of Reproduction

Reproduction is usually a seasonal or cyclical activity. A sockeye salmon *Oncorhynchus nerka* lives for about four years, attains a weight of five to ten pounds, travels many hundreds of miles into the ocean and returns to the headwaters of a river where it spawns and dies. At the same time, one of its internal nematode parasites *Philonema oncorhynchi,* acquired from the food (*Cyclops,* a copepod) during the salmon's freshwater juvenile existence, rides along during these migrations and matures and reproduces in the peritoneal cavity of the female salmon. When the salmon spawns, the nematodes, now filled with thousands of larvae, pass with the eggs into the water where they swell and burst, releasing the larvae to infect the copepods (Platzer, 1964). In this example both the salmon and its parasite have a single period of reproduction at the end of their lives, and this is timed seasonally in accordance with the requirements for the success of the next generation.

Sometimes the most advantageous period occurs rarely, and reproduction only takes place at irregular intervals. This is the case with some tropical birds where the gonads may remain quiescent for several seasons of drought but respond quickly to rainfall or its effects (Barrington, 1963; Lehrman, 1959). Often reproduction is cyclical as in many female mammals with regular estrous cycles; occasionally sexual activity may be continuous as in males of some higher vertebrates. However, in the animal kingdom as a whole, continuous reproduction is the exception and seasonal or cyclical reproduction the rule.

If reproduction is seasonal or occurs only once in the animal's life cycle, it must be precisely timed so that young appear when food is abundant and other conditions are optimal for survival. Seasonal changes in temperature, photoperiod, moisture, food or chemicals may serve as triggers for the timing of the associated physiological changes. In each case it seems that the most reliable environmental change has been utilized. In the stickleback *Gasterosteus aculeatus*, the physiological changes can be experimentally manipulated by photoperiod, with temperature playing a subsidiary role (Baggerman, 1957). The sexual cycle in the minnow *Couesius plumbeus*, on the other hand, shows only a slight photoperiod effect under experimental conditions but a marked response to temperature change (Ahsan, 1964). Sexual maturation of the nematode parasite of the sockeye salmon, mentioned previously, is probably timed by the gonadal hormones of the female salmon and this in turn by photoperiod and/or temperature.

In the majority of animals neurosecretory cells form the first link between the environmental trigger and the physiological machinery concerned with reproduction (Scharrer and Scharrer, 1963). Neurosecretory cells have been recognized for many years in some of the primitive worms and more recently have been described in a coelenterate, *Hydra* (Gilbert, 1963; Gabe *et al.*, 1964). Functions of these cells are unknown in the lower forms, but it is probable that very early in animal phylogeny nerve cells acquired the capacity to secrete substances into the tissues or blood for the regulation of reproduction.

Sometimes the neurosecretory materials act directly on effectors, but in the higher forms there are often intermediate links; the nerve cells pass their more specific responsibilities on to other parts of a complex endocrine system. In many animals the gonads also attain a glandular status and secrete substances which act directly on the effectors; the interrelationships between trigger, neurosecretory center, intermediate endocrine gland and effector may be complex (Fig. 23.1) and very nicely balanced through a feedback of information (Chapter 2).

Invertebrate Hormones of Reproduction

Endocrine regulation of reproduction in the most primitive animals is still questionable; but in all the more advanced groups (annelids, molluscs, arthropods and vertebrates) the evidence is now conclusive with many of the details carefully documented (Gilbert, 1963).

ANNELIDS

Hormonal regulation of reproduction and growth of annelids is indicated by seasonal changes in the histology of neurosecretory cells

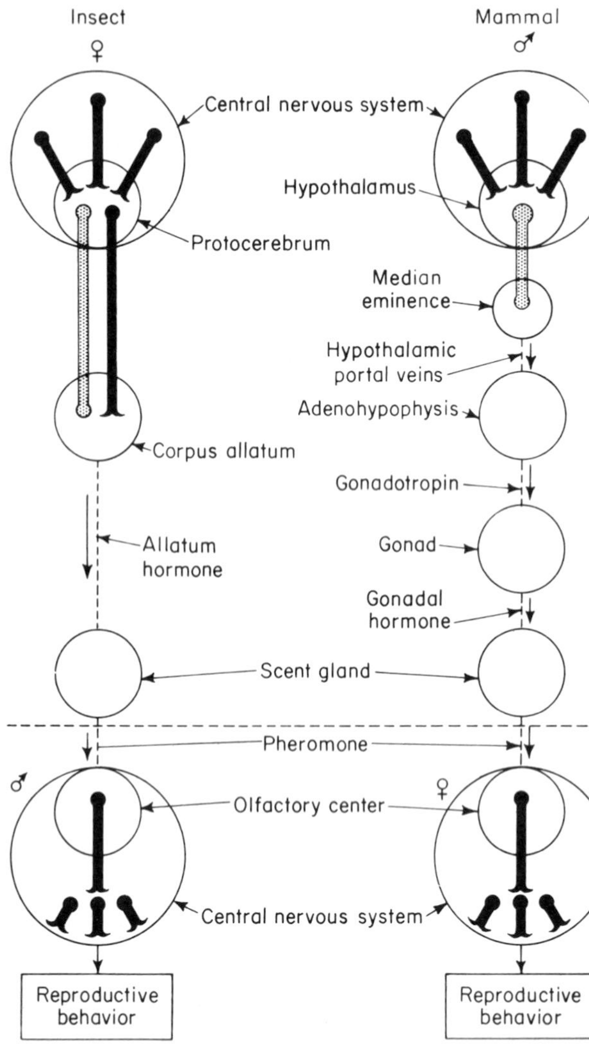

Fig. 23.1. Comparison of pheromone systems in an insect and a mammal. In the insect, the corpus allatum is supplied by ordinary and neurosecretory fibers from the central nervous system. In *Byrsotia fumigata*, for example, a corpus allatum hormone activates a scent gland in the female whose secretion attracts males. In the mammal, e.g., the male guinea pig, the supracaudal gland requires gonadal hormone for its maintenance; the availability of this hormone depends on a series of neural and endocrine glands. [Scharrer and Scharrer (1963).]

in the cerebral ganglia. Moreover, surgical manipulations, including transections of the nerve chain, removal of various ganglia and implantation of cerebral ganglia into decerebrate individuals, have predictable effects on reproductive processes. In general, the facts argue for the existence of a hormone of cerebral origin. Marked species differences are indicated. In the nereids the hormone seems to inhibit the development of germ cells and associated somatic structures; in the oligochaetes it appears only to stimulate the somatic sexual characters (Durchon, 1962; Gilbert, 1963). Thus, regulation is sometimes by inhibition and sometimes by excitation. The nature of the hormone(s) is unknown; the presence of intermediate endocrine glands linking neurosecretory centers to effectors has not been demonstrated; the action of environmental triggers is speculative. Comparative endocrinologists are currently devoting considerable attention to the annelids.

MOLLUSCS

Reproduction in the molluscs is also mainly dependent on neurosecretions. Removal of the tentacles from the slug *Arion* is followed by an increase in the number of eggs in the ovotestis; further, growth of the ovotestis is inhibited in young animals by injections of homogenized tentacles. Homogenates of the brain stimulate egg production. Seasonal changes in the cytology have been documented, and Pelluet and Lane (1961) postulate a dual hormonal control, with tentacle hormone regulating production of sperm, followed by egg production under control of the brain hormone.

Wells (1959, 1960) describes the role of the optic glands in regulating the onset of sexual maturity in the female *Octopus*. Indications are that the male is under a similar control and that the pattern is general for the dibranchiate cephalopods. The optic glands are small spherical bodies lying on the optic stalks, close to the optic lobes on either side of the brain. Correlations of the anatomical changes associated with sexual maturity and experiments involving removal of the glands, replacement therapy and the effects of destroying the optic nerves or the eyes, have demonstrated the presence of a gonad-regulating hormone in the optic gland. The optic glands in turn are under inhibitory nervous control from the higher centers of the brain. These controls have their parallel in the hypothalamic-pituitary system of the vertebrates. In the *Octopus*, however, there is no evidence for an ovarian hormone, although a testicular one has been suggested (Wells, 1960).

CRUSTACEANS

The major components of the crustacean endocrine system are shown in Fig. 2.6. Removal of the eyestalks in juvenile or nonbreeding females leads to a rapid increase in ovarian weight through the stimulation of vitellogenesis (Fig. 23.2). The neurosecretory cells in the eyestalk complex secrete a gonad-inhibiting hormone, and when the eyestalks are removed surgically or when the activities of the cells are suppressed, yolk production is initiated. Under natural conditions the changing photoperiod seems to regulate the activity. A high titer of sinus gland extract also inhibits molting in egg-bearing females. In crayfishes, for example, the spring molt is postponed in females while they are carrying developing

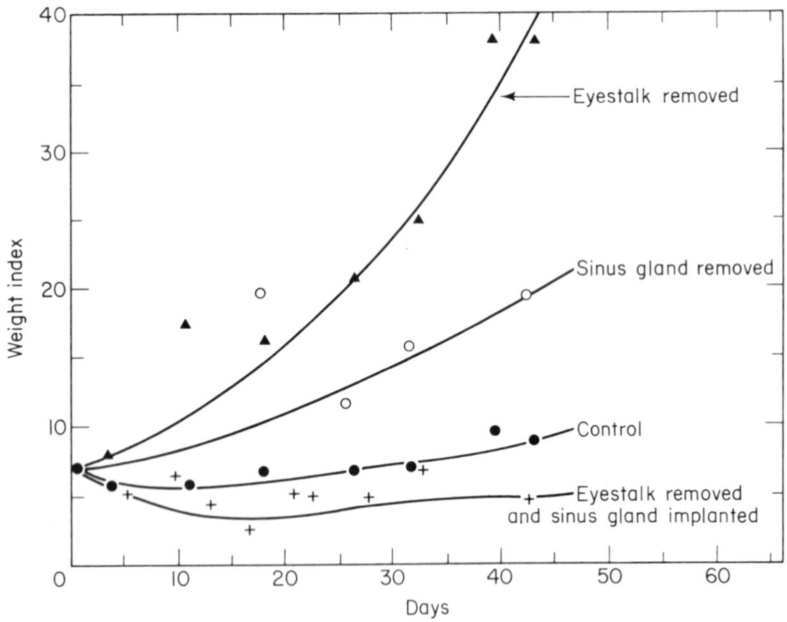

Fig. 23.2. Rate of increase in ovarian weight of the shrimp *Leander*. Weight index determined by dividing the wet weight of the ovaries by the body length cubed. [Data from Panouse (1944).]

eggs attached to their pleopods. If their sinus glands are removed they molt at the same time as the males or nonbreeding females. Thus, the sinus gland hormone first inhibits vitellogenesis; then, as its secretion is gradually suppressed under changing environmental conditions (photoperiod), the ovary increases rapidly in weight and accumulates the food supply for the future embryos; following mating and egg-laying, the eyestalk hormone(s) is again secreted in sufficient amounts to inhibit vitellogenesis and to prevent molting while the eggs are attached to the female.

Once vitellogenesis has been initiated, the ovary takes over several of the endocrine functions associated with reproduction. It is particularly responsible for certain secondary sex characters (ovigerous hairs, brood pouches) and brooding behavior.

The testes of juveniles may also be restrained by a gonadotropic hormone from the eyestalk, but the sexual cycle is less marked in many male crustaceans where the animals tend to be ripe throughout the year (Carlisle and Knowles, 1959). The dominant endocrine gland of the male is the VAS DEFERENS or ANDROGENIC GLAND. This is a small mass of cells attached to the distal end of the vas deferens. Its removal is followed by failure of testicular development and the appearance of female characters in the operated males. Further, transplantation of vas deferens glands into females will convert their ovaries into testes and cause them to assume male sexual behavior (Scheer, 1960; Gilbert, 1963). The vas deferens gland is clearly the source of a potent male hormone and seems to be the major (sometimes the only) endocrine gland concerned with reproduction in male crustaceans. In some species of isopods the testis itself, rather than this gland, is the source of the male hormone (Scheer, 1960; Carlisle and Knowles, 1959). The vas deferens gland may have arisen phylogenetically from interstitial cells of the testis.

In addition to sinus gland and gonadal hormones there is evidence for an involvement of the *Y*-organ in reproductive controls. Removal of this gland before sexual maturity is followed by degeneration of the gonads and sex failure in both sexes. Since a similar operation on adults has little or no effect on sex functions, its action may be on the general maturation of juveniles rather than specifically on the reproductive processes.

INSECTS

Insect reproduction is remarkable among higher groups of animals in its relative freedom from endocrine regulation. As against the crustacean (and vertebrate) regulation, there is an absence of gonadal hormones directly influencing reproductive structures, functions and behavior. Experiments involving gonad removal or transplantation in several species have been done without effect on secondary sex characters and behavior. Males often seem to be independent of any hormonal control of reproduction while, in females, the most prominent endocrine effect has to do with vitellogenesis. Maturation of gametes, secondary sex characters and behavior usually appear to be autonomous (Scheer, 1960; Gilbert, 1963). It is hazardous to generalize concerning the physiology of a class of animals as diversified as the insects but, with some few exceptions, their reproductive hormones are metabolic rather than morphogenetic.

The corpus allatum (Chapter 2 and Fig. 24.2) is the main link between the neural centers and the reproductive glands. Wigglesworth (1936) performed the pioneer experiments on the bug *Rhodnius*, a bloodsucker of mammals. If the corpora allata are removed from this animal, egg development ceases at the point where yolk deposition should begin. Testicular development was unaffected by the operation, but the secretory activity of the accessory glands of the male (as well as the female)

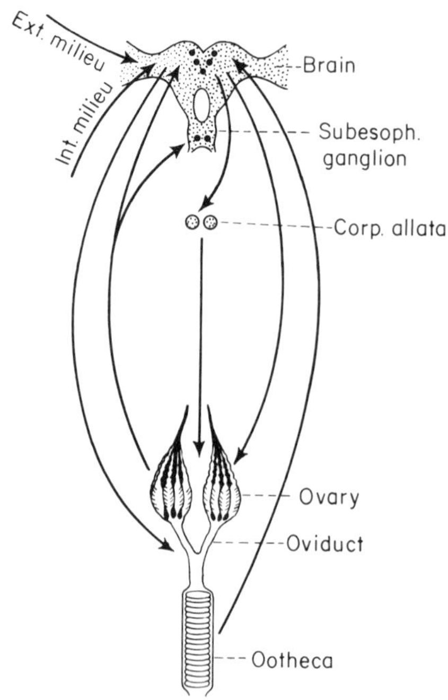

Fig. 23.3. Diagram of reproductive controls in female insects. The activity of the corpora allata (source of gonadotropins) is governed by afferent stimuli from the ovary and ootheca which are routed through the central nervous system. These and other modifying influences from internal and external milieu are integrated in the brain by means of neurosecretory cells (black circles). [Scharrer in Gorbman (1959).]

Rhodnius was impaired. Allatectomies have been performed on many species of insects since these early studies; evidently vitellogenesis depends on the presence of the corpus allatum and can only continue in allatectomized animals which have received implants or extracts of corpora allata.

The activity of the corpus allatum is controlled by neurosecretory centers in the pars intercerebralis of the brain (Fig. 23.3). In different species of insects reproduction is timed in relation to seasonal environmental changes and food supply, so that the production of young occurs with maximum opportunities for survival and success; a feedback of information from the genital tract suppresses the neurosecretory centers as the developing eggs reach an appropriate size (Fig. 23.3). Thus, there is an interrelated cycle of controls which regulates hormone production in accordance with physiological demands. This system has its counterpart in the reproductive endocrinology of vertebrates, discussed in the next section.

Many of the insects live in a world dominated by odors, and some of the best known examples of pheromones are associated with insect reproductive behavior. The female gypsy moth *Porthetria dispar* cannot fly and depends on a sex attractant to lure the winged males. Scientists who isolated and identified the pure substances used 500,000 female gypsy moths to obtain 20 milligrams; they found that male gypsy moths would curve their bodies and make copulatory motions when exposed to as little as a trillionth of a microgram (1×10^{-12} μg) of this chemical. Only molecular amounts are required to attract males from some distance; traps baited with this chemical are proving an effective weapon in controlling the moth (Jacobson and Beroza, 1964). Several other insect pests are now being controlled by the use of their specific sex attractants; the organic chemist has been able to synthesize many of them so that the applied entomologist is not dependent on the natural source of supply.

The "queen substance" provides another interesting example of a specific sex substance used in the social life of insects. The mandibular glands of the queen honeybee produce a substance which inhibits ovarian growth in the worker bees as long as they are obtaining it by occasionally licking her body. If an accident happens to the queen or if she is removed from the hive, the ovaries of the workers (neuter-type females) commence developing. Details of the endocrinology have not been worked out, but it is clear that the spread of a chemical through the hive by contact with the queen inhibits ovarian development in the workers. The "queen substance" has been isolated and synthesized (Gilbert, 1963).

Vertebrate Controls

In the vertebrates the adenohypophysis, through its gonadotropic hormones, links the neurosecretory centers of the brain to the endocrine tissues of the gonads. The neurosecretory centers, gonadotropins and gonadal hormones form a delicately balanced system for the timing of reproduction, the development of the gonads and the differentiation of the secondary sexual characters; these various hormones together with the nervous system itself regulate the behavior associated with reproduction (Fig. 23. 4).

The neurosecretory link between the external environment and reproductive processes is evidently primitive and was probably established early in animal evolution (Chapter 2). It seems probable that the adenohypophyseal link between brain and target organs was also present in the

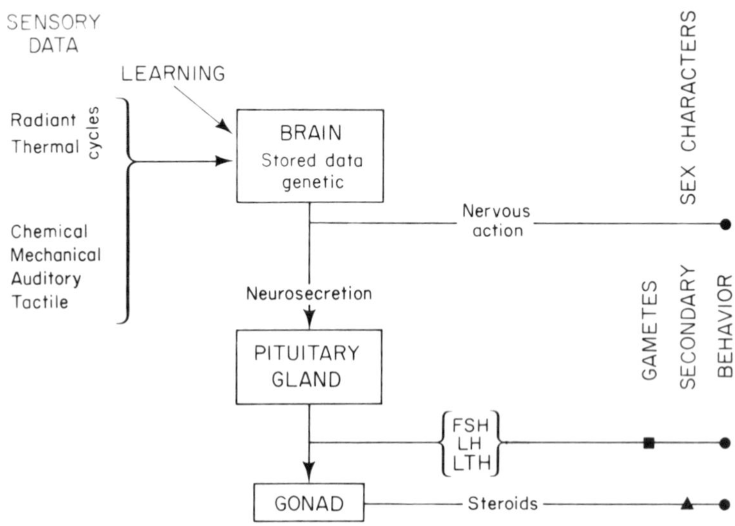

Fig. 23.4. Generalized scheme of the reproductive controls in the vertebrates.

most primitive vertebrates. Studies of existing vertebrates indicate that its significance in the regulation of reproduction has increased during phylogeny. In some primitive jawless forms (Agnatha: Petromyzontia), hypophysectomy has a much less drastic effect on reproduction than it has in the gnathostomes. In the male lamprey this operation delays, but does not eliminate, the production of sperm; in the female, ovarian growth ceases but the developing oocytes do not degenerate (Evennett and Dodd, 1963). In all higher vertebrates, removal of the pituitary leads to cessation of spermatogenesis and atrophy of developing ova (Hoar, 1965*a*, *b*). Throughout the gnathostomes the pituitary is in complete command of gametogenesis. The studies of hypophysectomized lampreys suggest that during vertebrate phylogeny the anterior pituitary first exerted a metabolic effect on the gonads (vitellogenesis) and that its gametogenetic activities were secondary, as they evidently are in the insects.

Endocrine tissues are found in the gonads of all vertebrates. From the most primitive to the most advanced forms they produce a series of steroid hormones whose synthesis has evidently been pituitary-regulated from a very early stage in vertebrate phylogeny. This concert of hormones from pituitary and gonads perform together to regulate reproductive processes, and, while the pituitary gonadotropins stimulate the gonadal tissues, the gonadal steroids through a feedback mechanism serve to check the activity of the gonadotropic cells of the pituitary.

THE GONADOTROPINS

Hypophysectomy is always followed by a regression of reproductive functions. In all classes, except the cyclostomes, gametogenesis is blocked at the spermatogonial or oogonial stages. The gametogenetic cells may continue to divide by mitosis, but the maturation stages of meiotic division do not take place. Spermatocytes and oocytes are not formed and vitellogenesis ceases or is not initiated. Yolk-filled ova degenerate and the yolk is removed, often with the formation of a corpus luteum-like structure. Further, the secondary sex characters fail to develop in hypophysectomized animals of all classes, including the cyclostomes. Since these characters are known to be under the influence of the endocrine tissues of the gonads, it is apparent that the gonadotropins control hormone production of the gonad.

Two separate gonadotropic factors are recognized in the higher vertebrates. One of these, the FOLLICLE STIMULATING HORMONE FSH, regulates gametogenesis while the other, the LUTEINIZING HORMONE LH, controls the production of the gonadal steroids. These factors were first identified in mammals where FSH controls the growth and maturation of ovarian follicles in the female and spermatogenesis in the male. LH, in the female mammal, acts synergistically with FSH to further the development of the ovarian follicle and stimulate the secretion of the ovarian hormones; in the male (where it is also called INTERSTITIAL CELL STIMULATING HORMONE ICSH), it stimulates the Cells of Leydig to produce androgenic hormone, an activity which may require the synergistic action of FSH. Like all other pituitary hormones, the gonadotropins are proteins. The fractions are known to vary somewhat in different mammalian species; molecular weights are of the order of 50,000 to 100,000 (Geschwind, 1959; Gorbman and Bern, 1962).

The evidence for two gonadotropic hormones is satisfactory in all the tetrapods, but a distinct FSH is not yet recognized in fishes (Hoar, 1965*a, b*). Many different workers have failed to demonstrate any effects of purified mammalian FSH on the reproductive processes of fish but have noted that mammalian LH has a stimulatory action on both the gametogenetic and the endocrine tissues of fish gonads. In short, mammalian

LH, when injected into fish, appears to initiate activities which are attributed to two distinct hormones in the higher vertebrates. Among the more recent studies, Ahsan (1964) found mammalian LH to be just as effective as a combination of FSH and LH or purified fish gonadotropins when injected into the hypophysectomized minnow *Couesius plumbeus*. These results strongly suggest that fish gonadotropin is like mammalian LH and that a separate FSH appeared in the tetrapods. The situation, however, is not this simple. When extracts of fish pituitaries are injected into higher vertebrates they often show effects usually attributed to FSH as well as LH-like action. Bioassays, using pituitaries from several different teleosts, have been performed on amphibians, birds and mammals; the FSH activity is relatively low but always present along with a stronger LH action. Further, it has been possible to achieve a biochemical separation of the two distinct factors from pituitaries of salmon; moreover, the histochemist now has associated two types of pituitary cell with gonadotropin production in fish as in higher vertebrates. Further work on the biochemistry of the fish gonadotropins is required before these data can be evaluated. It seems possible, however, that both factors (either as separate entities or in some kind of combination) were present at an early stage in vertebrate phylogeny but that the FSH-like action first became physiologically distinct in the amphibians.

A third factor, the lactogenic hormone PROLACTIN, is also a gonadotropin in some vertebrates. Astwood (1941) who did the pioneer work, found it to be essential for the maintenance of corpora lutea in the rat, and for this reason it has been named LUTEOTROPIN LTH. Luteotropic activity has not been found in several other mammals (rabbit, monkey, man) nor in any of the lower vertebrates (Everett, 1961; Hoar, 1965*a*). An international committee has recently recommended that this pituitary factor be named the LACTOTROPIC HORMONE (Van Oordt, 1965). A more detailed discussion of lactotropin is reserved for a later section.

THE GONADAL STEROIDS

Representatives from all classes of living vertebrates have now been successfully gonadectomized (Dodd, 1960; Dodd *et al.*, 1960). The data are consistent; the operation is followed not only by a cessation of gamete production but also by a regression of secondary sex characters or a failure to develop them. There are only a few recorded exceptions. In weaver finches (*Euplectes* spp) development of the dimorphic plumage is directly controlled by the pituitary gonadotropins rather than the gonadal hormones which the gonadotropins dominate (Witschi, 1961). This, however, is an exception; among all classes of vertebrates the control of secondary sex characters is normally the direct responsibility of the gonadal hormones. This was probably their first function in phylogeny. In many animals the performance of normal sexual behavior also depends on the gonads but this, and certain other functions associated with reproduction, are much more variable from species to species.

The gonadal hormones are steroid compounds. Several members of this biologically important group of chemicals were identified in Chapter 2 as adrenocortical hormones (Fig. 2.12). Those concerned with vertebrate reproduction are the ANDROGENS from the interstitial tissues of the testis, the ESTROGENS from the ovarian follicle and PROGESTERONE (GESTOGENS) from the corpus luteum and certain other structures in the mammal (Velle, 1963). These compounds are all interrelated. Many of the steps in their biosynthesis have been established. Cholesterol, synthesized from acetate, is the parent substance. Through several intermediate steps this gives rise to progesterone and thence to the androgens of which testosterone is physiologically the most important. In turn, the biogenesis of the estrogens is from the androgens with testosterone the major link and estradiol-17β the first step. The adrenocortical steroids are linked to the same chains. These reactions are reversible; the interrelationships are indicated in Fig. 23.5.

An understanding of the biochemical relationships of these substances is essential to the interpretation of many of the physiological findings. The identification of a particular steroid in the blood or tissues of an animal is no evidence that it acts as a hormone in this species; it may be present as a step in the biogenesis of the active endocrine. Moreover, animals may be treated with exogenous steroids which are quickly metabolized to something rather different. Considerable caution is required in interpreting physiological data both from steroid hormone treatments and from chemical assays of hormone levels. Androgens are believed to be the active male hormones in fish as in higher vertebrates, and yet the level of testosterone is sometimes higher in the spawning female salmon than in the male. In the male it may be serving as a physiological androgen; in the female as a precursor of the estrogens (Hoar, 1965*b*).

It now appears that the metabolic chains leading to estrogens and androgens are phylogenetically very ancient. Both progesterone, at the beginning of the chain, and the estrogens at the end of the chain have been identified in several of the invertebrates (echinoderms, lamellibranchs) as well as in the lower vertebrates. Estrogens are well known in the plant world (Bickoff, 1963). The gonads of many animals, both male and female, contain several androgens, estrogens and gestogens. Differences in secretion are probably quantitative rather than qualitative.

Androgens. The androgens are steroids, characterized biochemically by the presence of methyl groups at C-10 and C-13; they lack a side

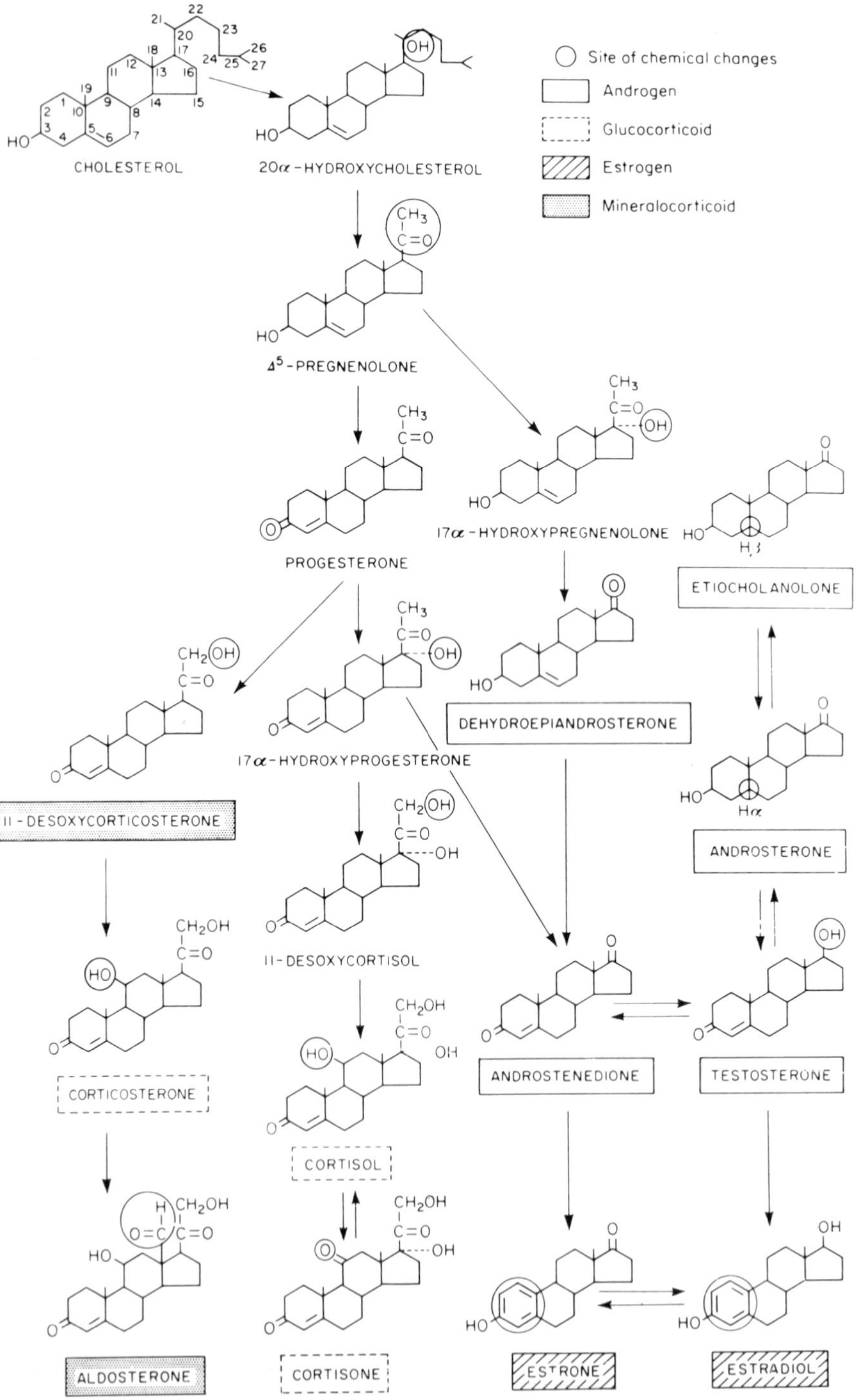

Fig. 23.5. Biogenesis of some important gonadal steroids. [By Permission of the Ciba Company.]

chain at C-17 and have oxygen substitutions at C-3 and C-17. They are sometimes referred to as the C-19 steroids because of the methyl group in the C-10 position (Fig. 2.14); this is lacking in the estrogens.

One example will suffice to illustrate the type of evidence adduced for a testicular control of secondary sex characters by androgens. The male stickleback *Gasterosteus aculeatus* builds a nest of algae or plant fragments. The strands of building material are piled neatly together at one spot and glued there with a mucous secretion which the fish presses onto the edges of the nest from his urogenital opening as he passes over it in a characteristic motion. The source of this secretion is the kidney which acquires this capacity only during the breeding season. The brush

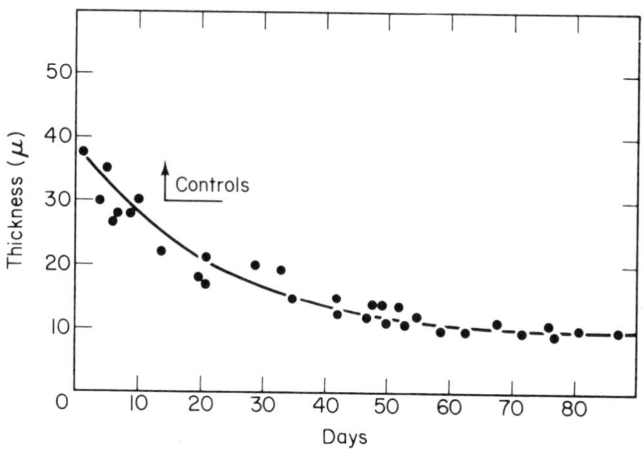

Fig. 23.6. Effect of castration on the thickness of mucus-secreting mesonephric tubules (a secondary sex character) of the stickleback. Values for mature male controls ranged from 20 to 40 micra. [Hoar (1962).]

border segments of the kidney tubules increase in height and become packed with secretory granules at the onset of the breeding season. Immature males, adult males in the nonbreeding condition and females at all times have brush border tubules which measure about 10 μ in height, while the cells lining these tubules in the breeding males range from 35 to 40 μ. Figure 23.6 shows the effects of castration on the kidney tubules of the mature male. Over a period of about 30 days the tubules gradually return to the resting condition, and at the same time the animals lose their brilliant breeding colors and cease to build nests (Hoar, 1962). This is a secondary sex character which can be precisely quantified, and the gonad is obviously essential for its expression.

When gonadectomized adult sticklebacks are treated with an androgen the brush border tubules again assume their glandular characteristics. The reaction can be elicited in females as readily as in males and in juveniles of both sexes (Fig. 23.7). The data are in accordance with the hypothesis that this secondary sex character is dependent on the testis

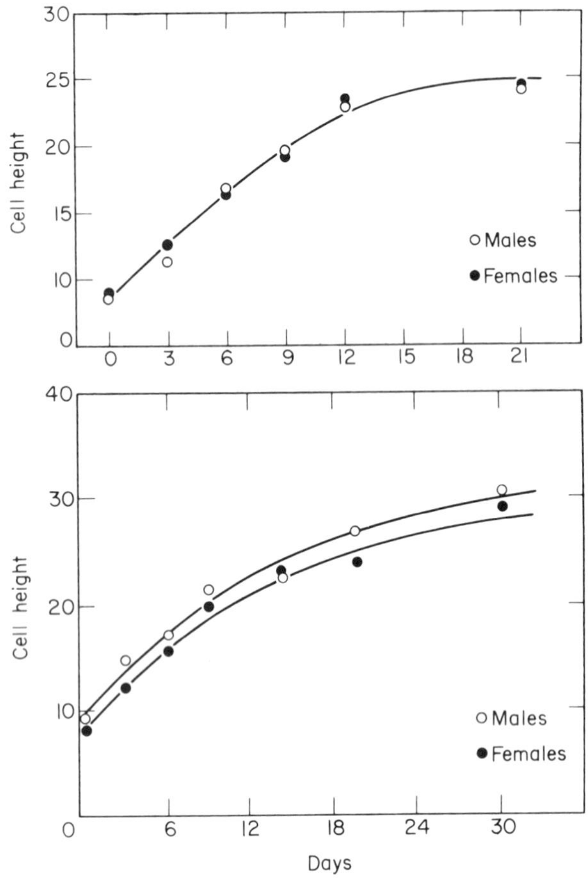

Fig. 23.7. Effects of methyl testosterone on the brush border segment of the mesonephric tubules (secondary sex character) in juvenile (above) and gonadectomized (below) sticklebacks. Mean cell heights in micra.

and that the endocrine factor is an androgen. The literature records many similar examples from all classes of vertebrates (Van Oordt, 1963). Testosterone is considered to be biologically the most important androgen, but comparative studies are not yet sufficiently extensive to generalize for all groups (Hoar, 1965*b*).

Estrogens. The estrogens are C-18 steroids which differ from the androgens in that they lack the C-19 carbon. They are also characterized by the presence of an aromatic ring (*A* or *I*). Two steroids, equilin and equilenin, found in mare's urine also have the *B* ring partially or totally converted to the aromatic form (Fig. 23.8). Their estrogenic activity is relatively weak. Estradiol-17β, estrone and estriol (Fig. 23.5) are most frequently isolated from animal sources. Estradiol-17β is the most potent of the group and is usually assumed to be the physiologically active substance. It has been found in several invertebrates as well as in all groups of vertebrates (Hisaw, 1963; Hoar, 1965*b*) and is evidently an ancient biological substance. Several of the estrogens usually associated with animal tissues are also found in plants. Several others which are not known to be present in animals are also of regular occurrence in certain plants. Structurally, they may vary considerably from the animal steroids (Fig. 23.8). Their presence is sometimes of physiological significance in animal nutrition (Bickoff, 1963).

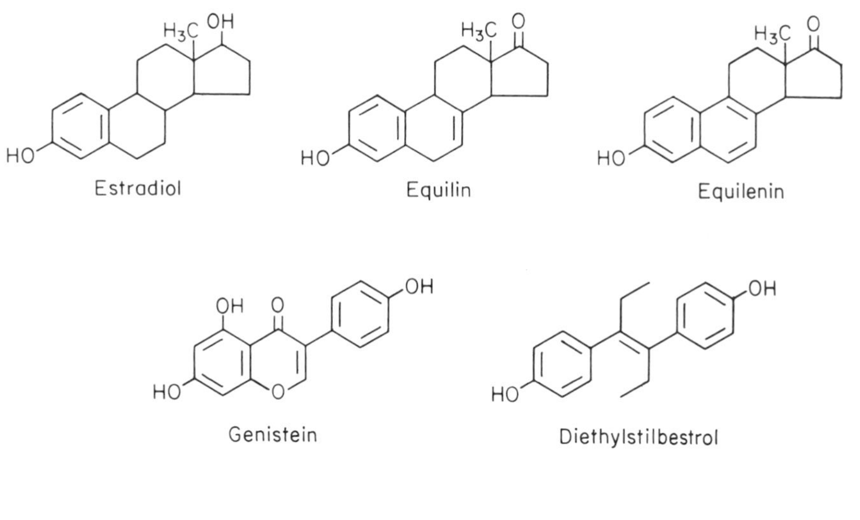

Fig. 23.8. Structure of estradiol and two unusual animal estrogens found in mare's urine (*equilin* and *equilenin*), a plant estrogen *genistein* and a synthetic estrogen *diethylstilbestrol.* Stilbestrol is the most active of the group.

Progesterone. Progesterone and certain biologically related substances (gestogens) are similar to the androgens in containing both the C-18 and the C-19 positions; in addition, they have an oxy- or hydroxy group on C-20 while the terminal carbon (C-21) is a methyl group.

The key position of progesterone in steroid biogenesis is shown in Fig. 23.5. Since it is an early step in the sequence which leads both to the cortical steroids and to the gonadal steroids, it is not surprising to find it in many animals where no endocrine activity has yet been ascribed to it. There is not yet sufficient evidence to decide just where it achieved an endocrine status in animal evolution (Hoar, 1965*b*). Hisaw (1959, 1963) maintains that the corpus luteum was added to the endocrine system in the mammals and that there is no convincing evidence for hormonal activities of progesterone in the submammalian groups. Further studies are required, for it is recognized that both preovulatory and postovulatory "corpora lutea" are common in many of the lower vertebrates, that our knowledge of the endocrinology of the reptiles (obviously a key group in these arguments) is fragmentary and that progesterone, in association with estrogen, does have a marked effect on the avian oviduct (Velle, 1963).

Nevertheless, there is considerable force in Hisaw's arguments. Estrogens are the female hormones produced during the follicular phase of ovarian activity; they control the development of secondary sex characters and prepare the animal for ovulation and fertilization. Viviparity in many of the lower forms is of the ovoviviparous type in which yolky eggs are merely housed within the mother and do not depend on extensive elaboration of maternal tissues. In some forms ovarian or oviducal secretions are a source of nourishment for the young, but there is no evidence that they develop in response to progesterone; if a hormone is involved it may be estrogenic in nature. In the mammals, on the other hand, the ovarian follicle enters a distinct luteal phase following ovulation, and many classical experiments have shown that the corpus luteum so formed is essential to the proliferation of the uterine tissues and the establishment of the maternal-fetal connections and the continuance of gestation. In some mammals (rat, opossum, rabbit, goat, cow) the ovary (corpus luteum) must be present throughout the greater part of pregnancy, and its removal is followed by abortion; in others (mare, monkey, human) the ovary may be removed once pregnancy is under way, without any serious effects. In the latter groups, the placenta gradually takes over the functions of endocrine production (estrogens, progesterone and gonadotropins) and serves as its own chemical regulator (Barrington, 1963).

REGULATION OF BREEDING CYCLES

It is not usually valid to attribute a single function to any one of the several hormones just described. They very often act in a cooperative manner. Sometimes their action is that of an antagonist, sometimes that of a synergist; an independent action in isolation from other factors is much less frequent. Several examples will illustrate this point.

Differentiation of the secondary sex characters often appears to be entirely controlled by gonadal steroids. The male accessory glands of a castrated and hypophysectomized rat regress to the juvenile condition but can be fully restored with androgen (Turner, 1960); within limits, the response to the androgen is proportional to the dose. The secondary sex characters of the male stickleback, described previously, provide another example of an endocrine regulation which is androgen-dependent; although the experimental animals (Figs. 23.6 and 23.7) were not hypophysectomized, the responses to androgen treatment were equally marked in fish with low and high gonadotropic activity (controlled by regulation of the photoperiod). In some cases, however, pituitary gonadotropins and not gonadal steroids control the differentiation of secondary sex characters (plumage of weaver finches); in a few instances their development seems to be regulated genetically rather than hormonally (claspers of the elasmobranchs).

Numerous reproductive phenomena have been shown to depend on an interaction of pituitary and gonadal hormones. In the male stickleback (Hoar, 1962), the nest building and sexual behavior appeared much sooner and more regularly when castrates were treated with androgens and maintained under photoperiod regimes known to stimulate gonadotropic activity. Presumably gonadotropin is acting syngergistically with the androgen in regulating the breeding behavior of the fish. The inhibitory action of gonadal steroids on the pituitary has been demonstrated in many ways. It is, for example, apparent in the histological changes of the gonadotropic cells and areas of the pituitary following castration or treatment with exogenous steroids. In the first type of experiment the gonadotropic area enlarges; in the second, it decreases in size.

The mammalian endocrinologist has recorded many instances of synergistic and inhibitory interaction of gonadal and gonadotropic hormones. Although FSH initiates the differentiation of the ovarian follicle, a concerted action of FSH and LH is required for its full maturation and the secretion of estrogen; small amounts of estrogen may also have a stimulatory effect on the follicle. This is true also for the male. Although the sole action of FSH seems to be on the germinal epithelium, the normal production of sperm often seems to require some LH and androgen as well as the FSH. Again, progesterone production is largelyLH-controlled, but in at least a few mammals its secretion depends also on prolactin (LTH). In the mammal a rising tide of estrogen from the developing follicle inhibits FSH production but stimulates LH to the point where the follicle ruptures (ovulation is usually under the influence of LH), and LH stimulates the production of a corpus luteum; the progesterone secretion of the corpus luteum then inhibits LH synthesis. Further details of these interrelations are recorded in many recent texts (Turner, 1960; Knobil and Sandler, 1963). They are noted here as a warning in the examination of several of the simplified diagrams which follow.

Figure 23.9 summarizes the hormonal regulation of reproductive processes in the vertebrates. In some species (Pacific salmon *Oncorhynchus*, for example), gametogenesis occurs only once in the life of the animal, and the single period of reproduction culminates in death. Usually, however, vertebrate reproductive processes are reoccurring and cyclical. If the cycle is a seasonal one, environmental changes trigger the neurosecretory centers at the most advantageous seasons for the development and growth of the young. If reproductive activity is continuously cyclical or almost so, as is the case with many homeothermic animals and some of the tropical poikilotherms, then the controls are usually endogenous and depend on feedback mechanisms to the neurosecretory centers and perhaps also on neural pacemakers.

There is an evident parallel between the ovarian and testicular controls in the submammalian groups where the ovary shows only the follicular phase (Fig. 23.9). A true luteal phase is present only in the mammals. It is associated with viviparity and has been built onto the ovarian follicular phase with the development of a new endocrine gland (corpus luteum) which synthesizes progesterone in large amounts, under the control of the pituitary. A concomitant responsiveness of uterine and associated tissues to progesterone is a necessary part of the functional system. In some mammals the placenta also acquires endocrine responsibilities and takes over from both pituitary and gonads the production of hormones concerned with gestation.

These endocrine modifications associated with viviparity and parental care in the mammals form a significant part of the many evolutionary adaptations required for this mode of life (Amoroso, 1960). Successful fertilization, implantation and subsequent nourishment of the developing embryo, the birth of the young at an appropriate stage and its sustenance by secretions of the mammary glands depend on a precisely timed sequence of cyclical endocrine changes and tissue responses.

The sexual cycles of vertebrates are extremely variable (Asdell, 1946; Parkes, 1960; Barrington, 1963). Usually the female will only receive the male during a relatively brief period of ESTRUS or heat, but in our own species receptivity may occur throughout the cycle. Again, ovulation is normally spontaneous and occurs during estrus (Fig. 23.10), but in some animals, such as the rabbit, ferret and mink which are INDUCED OVULATORS, the stimulation of coitus acting through the hypothalamo-hypophyseal pathways with the release of LH is required for the discharge of the ovum from the ovary. Fertilization usually takes place within a few hours of coitus, but in certain bats copulation occurs in the autumn and fertilization is delayed until the spring. Implantation

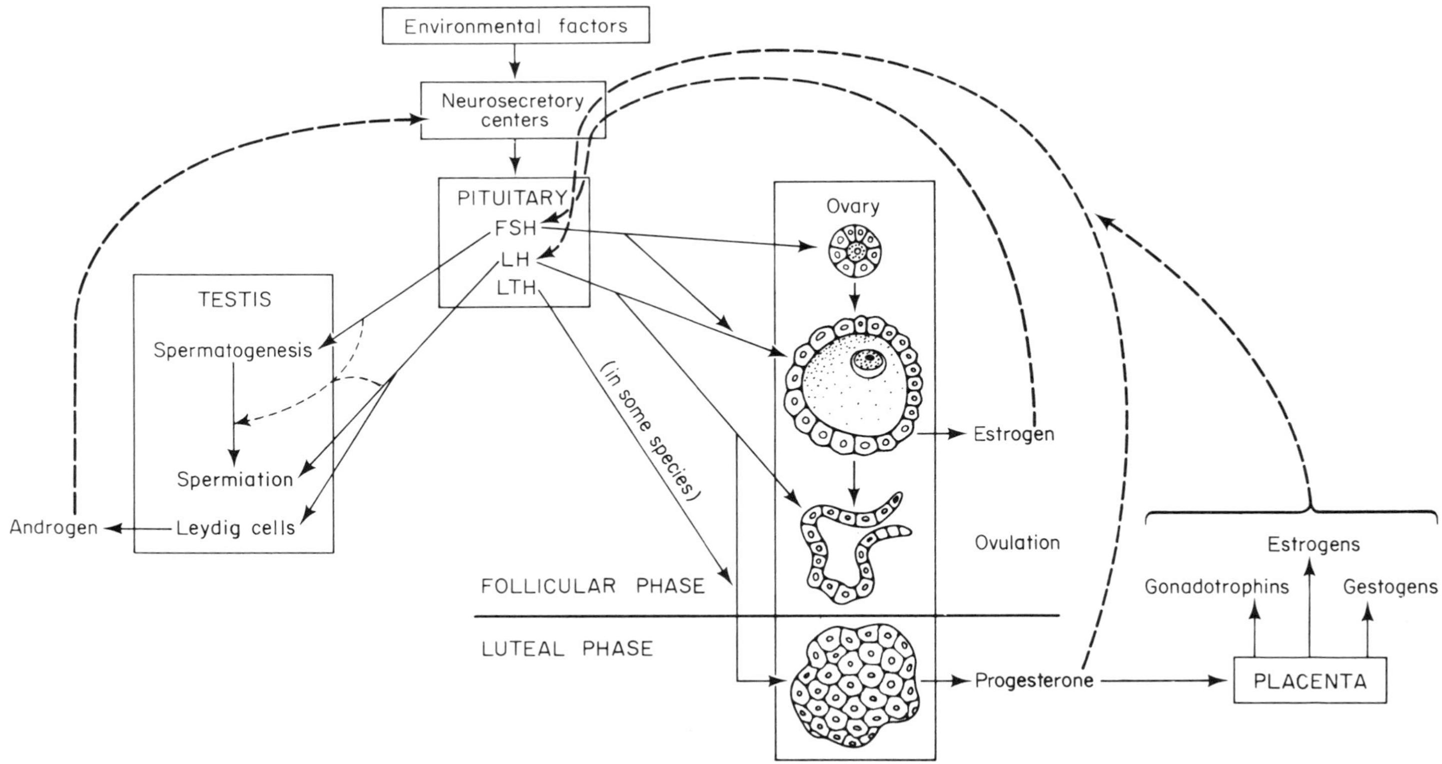

Fig. 239. Endocrine regulation of gonadal maturation in vertebrates. Continuous lines, stimulation. Heavy broken lines, inhibition. Light broken lines, probable interaction of FSH and LH. The luteal phase is present only in mammals. FSH may be absent in fishes, and the entire regulation may depend on LH.

occurs after about one week of development in human, rabbit, mouse and some other mammals when the dividing mass of cells has attained the status of a BLASTOCYST. In the pig, dog and cat implantation is delayed for about two weeks, while in the marten, weasel and badger mating takes place during the summer but implantation of the blastocyst

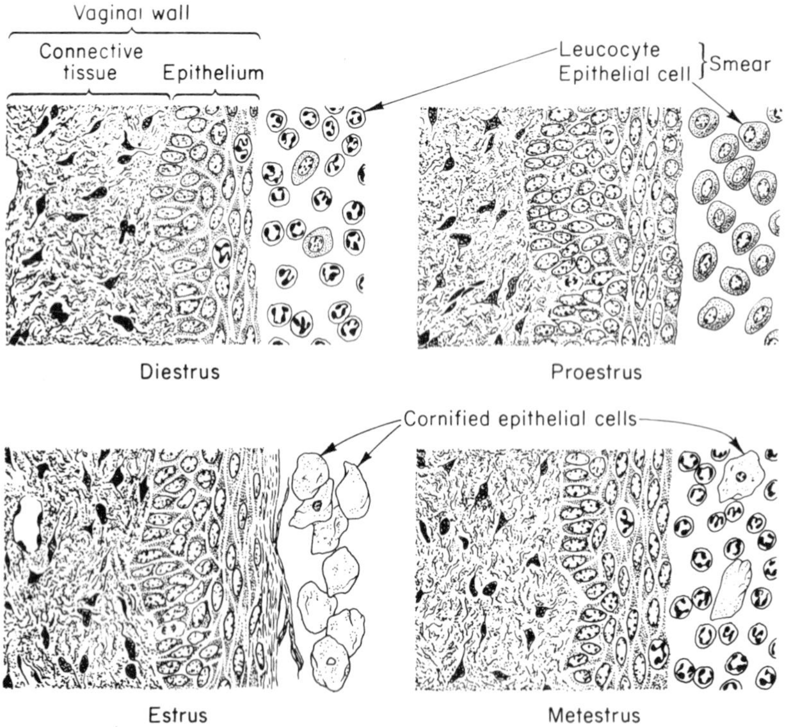

Fig. 23.10. Sections through the rat's vaginal wall during different stages of the estrous cycle with the cells (at right) which characterize vaginal smears during each of the corresponding stages. [Turner (1960).]

occurs late in the winter (DELAYED IMPLANTATION). These and several other variations in the timing of reproductive processes are discussed by Barrington (1963). This diversity emphasizes the plasticity of organisms in adjusting reproductive processes to the conditions of the environment and the limitations of the species. Wherever the processes have been carefully studied, they have been found to be highly adaptive in the evolutionary sense.

Details of the mammalian sexual cycle are best known in the laboratory rodents and in the human. Rats and mice have a cycle of four to five days. Ovulation occurs during the period of heat (estrus) lasting 9 to 15 hours: estrus is under the influence of FSH. Since the female will only receive the male during this period, ovulation and fertilization are well coordinated. During estrus, the uterus becomes enlarged and edematous in preparation for implantation; the vaginal mucosa proliferates and the superficial epithelial layers are squamous and cornified in preparation for copulation. Vaginal smears made at this time contain characteristic squamous cells and serve as a means for ready diagnosis of the stage in the estrous cycle. Such smears are used regularly in studies of reproductive biology, and detailed descriptions with illustrations are available in many places (Turner, 1960).

Subsequent events depend on sexual contact with a male. In the absence of copulation the cycle is almost completely follicular. During METESTRUS (10 to 14 hours), however, a small corpus luteum forms and some progesterone is secreted. This stage is characterized by a diminished vascularity of the uterus, while the vaginal smears show leucocytes along with cornified cells indicating a thinning of the mucosa and migration of leucocytes through it. The corpora lutea regress during DIESTRUS (60 to 70 hour period), the uteri are relatively small and anemic; cells in the vaginal smears are almost entirely leucocytes. PROESTRUS, lasting about 12 hours, is a preparation for the next estrus. Degeneration of the old corpora lutea continues, but new follicles are growing rapidly, and the uterus is again becoming distended with fluid; vaginal smears contain nucleated (not cornified) epithelial cells which may be detached singly or in sheets. The changes are shown diagrammatically in Fig. 23.10. The classical description for the rat is that of Long and Evans (1922). Rats and mice are POLYESTROUS, and this cycle of events occurs in unmated animals every four to six days. Many animals have only one estrous cycle during the year, and a prolonged period of ANESTRUS (diestrous period) occurs between the metestrus and proestrus. The silver fox, for example has a single period of heat lasting about 5 days during late winter; it is said to be MONESTROUS. Sheep and cattle are seasonally polyestrous with several periods of heat during one season of the year; several interesting variations seem to have appeared during domestication (Barrington, 1963).

In unmated rats and mice the luteal phase does not produce the progestational changes usually associated with progesterone. These may, however, be artificially induced in the absence of pregnancy by mating females with sterile males or by stimulating the cervix uteri with various mechanical or electrical means. The response is called PSEUDOPREGNANCY and evidently depends on afferent stimuli to the hypothalamic-pituitary axis, as indicated by the failure of such experiments in anaesthetized animals or in animals following destruction of the uterine nerves. Pseudopregnancy lasts for about 13 days in the rat (pregnancy is of about 21 days duration), and during this period the corpora lutea remain active and the uteri undergo changes similar to those seen in pregnancy. Hormone changes and the associated proliferation of the mammary glands are similar to those of the pregnant animal. This pseudopregnant phase occurs as a normal part of the cycle in many unmated animals (guinea pigs) and is not affected by sterile matings or similar stimulation of the reproductive tract.

In man, apes and monkeys the progestational phase is terminated by MENSTRUATION during which the inner portion of the endometrium or mucous membrane of the uterus collapses and is discharged with a certain amount of bleeding. As indicated in Fig. 23.11 this occurs at a time of rapid decline in levels of hormones which were responsible for the proliferation of the endometrium, the development of its glands and highly vascular condition. In some other animals (dogs, for example) there may be some bleeding from the hyperemic uterus during estrus,

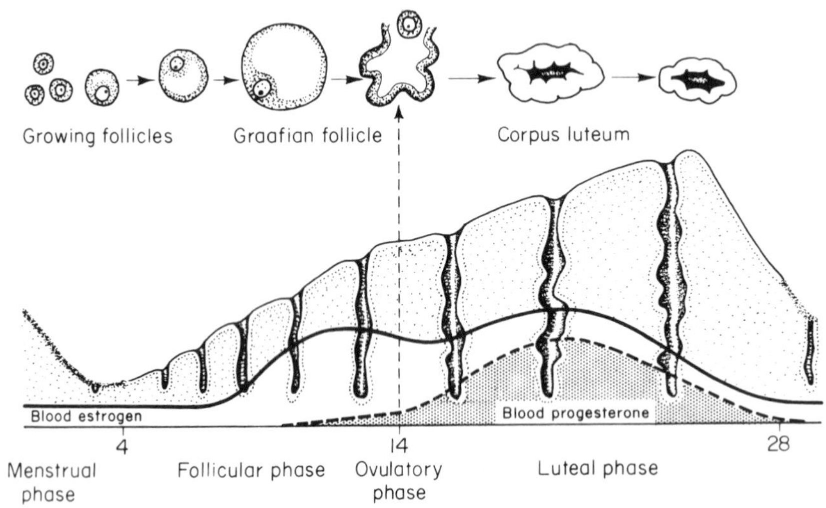

Fig. 23.11. Diagram showing changes in the endometrium, the ovaries and the circulating ovarian hormones during the menstrual cycle. [Turner (1960).]

but this is not comparable to menstruation (a terminal event), and no sloughing of the endometrium takes place; the menstrual cycle is characteristic of the higher primates—particularly the Old World monkeys (Asdell, 1946).

OTHER HORMONES CONCERNED WITH VERTEBRATE REPRODUCTION

The placental hormones. In many mammals the placenta is not only an organ of embryonic attachment, nourishment, respiration and excretion but also an endocrine gland which produces a variety of hormones concerned with gestation and parturition. The extent to which the placenta assumes responsibilities for steroid and gonadotropic synthesis varies greatly in different animal species. In rats, mice, rabbits and hamsters removal of the ovaries at any time during pregnancy results in abortion, and it is evident that the ovary is the major source of the steroid hormones of pregnancy. In the guinea pig, cat, dog and ewe, on the other hand, ovaries may be removed (without causing abortion) after mid-pregnancy; in humans, monkeys and mares they may be removed at an even earlier stage. Progesterone will usually maintain pregnancy in ovariectomized animals which characteristically abort their embryos after ovariectomy. However, the situation is somewhat variable (Gorbman and Bern, 1962), and it is recognized that the placenta is sometimes a major source of estrogen (mouse and rabbit) and sometimes a source of both estrogen and progesterone (man, some monkeys, mare). On the basis of the earlier discussion of steroid synthesis, it is not surprising to find that a number of different steroids have been isolated from placental tissues.

Mammals also vary greatly in their dependence on the pituitary gonadotropins. Although the hypophysis is always essential for ovulation and implantation, its secretions can evidently be dispensed with during the latter part of pregnancy in several different species (mouse, rat, guinea pig, monkey). In others (rabbit, cat, dog) hypophysectomy leads to abortion at any time during pregnancy. The presence of placental gonadotropins in several animals has been demonstrated with appropriate endocrinological techniques.

The two placental gonadotropins most familiar to the endocrinologist are HUMAN CHORIONIC GONADOTROPIN (HCG) isolated from pregnancy urine of women, and PREGNANT MARE SERUM (PMS) obtained from the blood serum of the pregnant mare. These have often proved useful in experimental work because they can be readily isolated in quantity and have been commercially available for many years. Since they are used frequently as substitutes for the pituitary fractions, it should be noted that they are not the same biochemically, even though both types are glycoproteins. They mimic the pituitary gonadotropins, but their actions are somewhat different.

HCG is secreted by the chorionic villi of the placenta (embryonic origin) and appears in large quantities in the urine during the first two months of pregnancy; it continues to be secreted in lesser amounts until parturition. Experimentally, its action in the mammal is usually similar to that of LH. PMS is of uterine (endometrial) origin and often has an action similar to a mixture of FSH and LH, with the predominant effect depending on dosage. This factor is not excreted (unlike HCG, FSH and LH) but remains in the blood; the amounts are particularly high from the fortieth to the hundred-and-twentieth day of pregnancy (Turner, 1960).

Relaxin. Mammals must enter the outer world through a relatively narrow bony ring, the pelvis. This requirement of mammalian anatomy has imposed certain restrictions and compromises during the evolution of viviparity. In all mammals the size of the pelvis sets an upper limit on the growth of the young in the uterus. In some habitats, such as those exploited by burrowing and flying species, there may be definite advantages in restricting the size of the pelvis, but any tendency in this direction imposes a disadvantage which must be compensated for at parturition.

In 1926, Hisaw isolated a substance with a pronounced effect on the connective tissues of the symphysis pubis and the sacroiliac joints and ligaments of the estrogen-primed guinea pig. He named the substance RELAXIN because of its apparent function in relaxing the pelvis and softening the cervical mucosa in preparation for parturition. Hormonally-induced tissue changes which facilitate stretching of the cervix and pelvis are now recognized in many mammals (cow, pig, human, rat). Relaxin has not been completely characterized, but it is known to be a polypeptide which acts in association with estrogen (Velle, 1963). It has been isolated from the blood and reproductive tissues (ovary, placenta) of several mammals and has also been identified in some birds and fish. Several functions have been ascribed to it, in addition to those involving a splitting and softening of collagenous fibers and associated tissues, but its comparative physiology is not well known (Steinetz *et al.*, 1959).

The comparative physiologist rarely finds that evolutionary processes have provided a single solution to any problem. This is certainly true of the pelvic adaptations of mammals. The mole represents an extreme situation in which the cartilaginous pubic arch is resorbed during early life; the two halves then grow together dorsal to the digestive and reproductive tracts to form a secondary symphysis. Thus, the adult reproductive tract is entirely outside and ventral to the pelvis. This solution seems to be independent of the endocrine system and has been acquired through genetic changes. In the pocket gopher there are also drastic changes in the morphology of the pelvis, but these occur only in the female and are under the control of estrogen. The juvenile pelvis is complete in both sexes, but at the time of the first estrus there is a resorption of pubic bone leaving the pelvis open ventrally. It remains intact in the male.

Prolactin (*lactotropic hormone*). Prolactin is a member of the family of adenohypophyseal hormones. Highly purified fractions from beef and sheep (mol wt from about 24,000 to 26,000) are proteins consisting of a single peptide chain which, unlike the gonadotropins FSH and LH, is not bound to carbohydrate. As the name suggests, this hormone is concerned with lactation in mammals; its first demonstrated action was that of initiating lactation in fully developed mammary glands. At about the same time (1932), it was also shown to stimulate the pigeon's crop glands which produce a cheesy secretion by desquamation of the epithelium; this material, called pigeon's "milk" serves as nourishment for the young squabs (Knobil and Sandler, 1963; Beams and Meyer, 1931). Since that time, prolactin-like substances have been identified in the pituitaries of many different animals at all levels in vertebrate phylogeny, male as well as female. Moreover, studies of the endocrinology of lactation have shown that prolactin is only one of several hormonal factors involved in milk production. These two important considerations, the complexity of hormones which regulate lactation and the comparative endocrinology of prolactin can be conveniently separated in the following discussion.

Three different processes are involved in the production and delivery of milk to suckling animals. The first of these is the development of the mammary glands at the time of puberty or sexual maturity; the second involves their further proliferation and the secretion of milk, while the third is the evacuation or delivery of milk to the nursing young. The complex of interacting hormones concerned with these processes is shown diagrammatically in Fig. 23.12.

Mammary gland development at puberty, like other secondary sex characters of the female, is under the control of estrogen with some cooperation from the growth hormone somatotropin. The further proliferation of the glands during gestation, with the subsequent production of milk, is a highly complex process which requires the simultaneous activation of metabolic pathways concerned with protein, carbohydrate and fat synthesis, the mobilization of calcium and phosphorus and the regulation of specific levels of electrolytes and water. It is not then surprising to find that lactogenesis is regulated to some extent by all the metabolic hormones as well as the reproductive hormones. The research of the past quarter of a century has displaced prolactin from its position as the central regulator of lactation to a membership in a complex endocrine committee. Detailed discussion will be left to textbooks of mammalian endocrinology (Turner, 1960; Cowie and Folley, 1961).

The third process involved in milk production depends on nervous as well as on endocrine factors. Milk removal requires afferent stimuli from the nipple. An anaesthetized mother can only supply the milk stored in the cistern and major ducts. Release of milk from the main portions of the mammary apparatus depends on contractions of the myoepithelial or "basket cells" which surround the alveoli. Their contractions are normally initiated by the hormones of the posterior pituitary. Suckling provides afferent stimuli to the supraoptic and paraventricular nuclei of the brain; these lead to the release of oxytocin which, in turn, brings about contraction of the myoepithelial cells surrounding the alveoli. The same afferent stimuli acting through the hypothalamo-hypophyseal

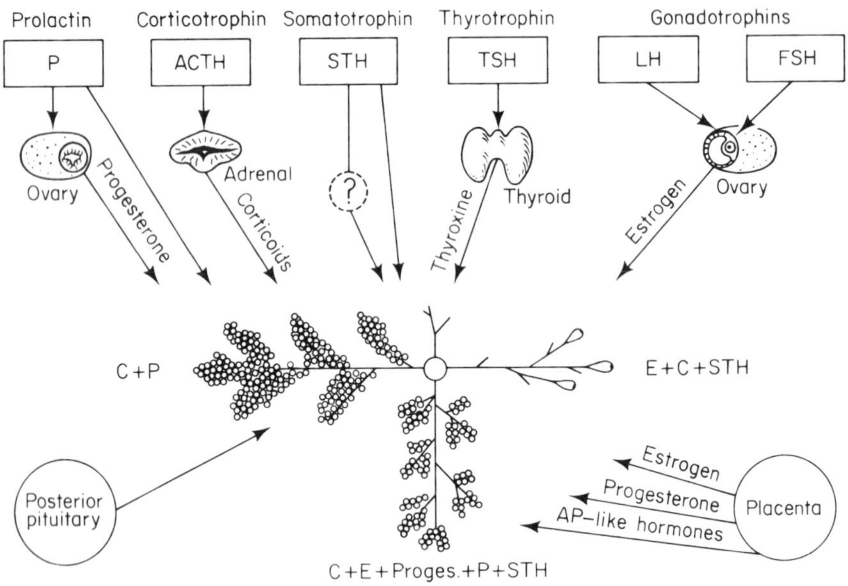

Fig. 23.12. Diagram showing the action of hormones on the growth of the mammary glands and lactation. In the diagram of the gland: upper, rudimentary gland; right, prepuberal and puberal gland; lower, prolactational gland of pregnancy; left, lactating gland; *c*, corticosteroids; *E*, estrogens. [Turner (1960) based on Lyons, Li, and Johnson (1958).]

pathways trigger release of prolactin to stimulate milk secretion by the gland cells. Thus, prolactin stimulates milk secretion (lactogenesis), a process which also requires the regulatory activities of different metabolic hormones; oxytocin is responsible for milk ejection.

The varied and curious functions attributed to prolactin form one of the most interesting chapters of comparative vertebrate endocrinology. A logical evaluation of the details must await further studies of its comparative biochemistry and physiology. At present, the identification of the hormone is usually based on one of three different methods of bioassay (Zarrow *et al.*, 1964): (a) the increase in interducal hydrostatic pressure following introduction of the hormone into the major mammary duct of the estrogen- and progesterone-primed rabbit, (b) stimulation of the crop glands of the pigeon and (c) the behavioral response of the hypophysectomized newt *Diemictylus viridescens*. The latter test is based on the fact that the prespawning migrations of these animals are prolactin-controlled. Hypophysectomized animals fail to make the usual migration from land to water unless they are injected with prolactin; the gonadal hormones play no part in the response. Prolactin is evidently a specific trigger for this behavior as well as for the metabolic changes of the associated metamorphosis (Grant, 1961). Using sometimes one, sometimes another of these three tests, a substance with prolactin-like activity has now been demonstrated in the pituitaries of many animals ranging from fish to men. It is not surprising that extracts from the lower vertebrates are not always positive in bioassays involving higher forms, since the lactotropic hormone, like other proteins, may be expected to have some species specificity.

Hisaw (1963) has noted that in the physiology of most vertebrates prolactin controls processes related to the nourishment, comfort or care of the young. Thus, in the rat, prolactin as well as LH is required for the production of progesterone on which gestation depends. The corpus luteum appears normal in the absence of prolactin but fails to secrete; its activities can be restored with purified prolactin, and for this reason prolactin is also called luteotropin (LTH). This function of prolactin may not be widespread among other mammals. Among some birds, prolactin has been associated with the development of incubation or brood patches, incubating behavior and parental care, functions which may also be related to estrogens and progesterone (Eisner, 1960). Among the amphibians, prolactin plays a part in preparing the immature *Diemictylus* for its aquatic life and may also be involved in regulating the secretory activity of the oviducal glands in *Bufo arenarum*. In the discus fish *Symphysodon discus* prolactin is claimed to stimulate the formation of epidermal secretions which serve to nourish the young and to stimulate fanning in a closely related species and in the wrasse *Crenilabrus ocellatus*. The literature on its effects in lower vertebrates has been reviewed (Hoar, 1965*a*, *b*). These several examples provide support for Hisaw's observation of a widespread action of prolactin in processes which pertain to the well-being of young animals. There are, however, several other functions which show no such obvious relationship.

Pickford's classical studies on the hypophysectomized *Fundulus heteroclitus* revealed two actions of prolactin, neither of which is related to reproduction (Pickford and Atz, 1957; Pickford, 1959; Hoar, 1965*a*).

Hypophysectomized animals cannot survive in fresh waters with a low content of dissolved solids but live for prolonged periods in dilute sea water. Death is associated with a marked loss of chloride and can be prevented by injections of prolactin. A persistent attempt to implicate other hormones in this reaction has failed; the missing factor is likely to be prolactin or a substance closely related to it. Several other euryhaline teleosts live satisfactorily in fresh water after hypophysectomy, but *Fundulus heteroclitus* is not alone in requiring prolactin. Another function of prolactin, also demonstrated with the hypophysectomized *Fundulus,* is its action in melanogenesis. Hypophysectomized animals gradually become less deeply pigmented due to the disappearance of melanin and not due to changes in its distribution within the melanophores. Prolactin seems to be specific in the restoration of melanin to the ghosts of the depigmented melanophores (Kosto *et al.,* 1959).

There are two obvious explanations for the diversity of activities which prolactin displays. It is possible that the same substance has been used during evolution in many different processes. This possibility is in no way contrary to the principles of comparative endocrinology or evolution. Expressed in a much-quoted aphorism, "it is not hormones which have evolved but the uses to which they are put." It is also possible that the prolactin molecule may be structurally similar to other pituitary hormones, such as STH and ACTH, so that some of the effects which follow its injection (often in relatively high doses) are normally elicited by other factors under physiological conditions. A satisfactory solution to this puzzle must await further research.

RETROSPECT

In summary, comparative endocrinology has now progressed to the point where it can be confidently stated that reproductive processes are integrated in a similar manner throughout all vertebrate classes. From the Agnatha to the primates, neurosecretory centers in the brain trigger a release of gonadotropins from the adenohypophysis while the gonadotropins, in their turn, regulate the steroid-secreting tissues of the gonads. It seems probable that this basic machinery has remained substantially unchanged since the origin of the vertebrates, some 500 million years ago.

Generalizations can only be cautiously extended from this broad statement. It is probable that pituitary hormones always start the changes associated with the reproductive cycle. This is true of gametogenesis (except perhaps in the cyclostomes) and perhaps also of some aspects of presexual behavior. Subsequently, the pituitary delegates some or all of its responsibilities to the gonadal hormones or, in some of the mammals, to the extragonadal tissues of the placenta. Thus, the gonads are often concerned with the later events of reproduction (such as the differentiation of secondary sex characters and sexual behavior) while the pituary is more directly involved in the earlier phases (such as gametogenesis and pre-breeding migrations). It should be noted, however, that a strictly independent action of pituitary and gonadal hormones is unlikely in the intact animal. Secretion of the gonadal hormones is stimulated by the pituitary; secretion of the pituitary gonadotropins is inhibited by the gonadal hormones. Within this broad framework of reproductive controls interrelationships of the hormones and their actions on specific target organs are almost as variable as the animals themselves. The evolutionary processes have made use of these chemicals in ways which are just as curious and diversified as the morphological correlates of sex and reproduction. Students of reproductive endocrinology may confidently expect many variants of the general rule as the investigations are extended to include more and more species.

24 Growth and Development

The analysis of early stages of growth and differentiation is traditionally the prerogative of the embryologist. Mechanisms regulating postembryonic development come under the purview of the physiologist. Experimental biologists in many areas of research have analyzed the mathematics of growth and described it graphically. Mammalian physiologists and biochemists have been particularly active in studies of the pituitary growth hormone, somatotropin, and the growth effects of thyroxine, corticosteroids, insulin and diet. General and cell physiologists have analyzed cell division, measured growth, studied effects of various stimulants and inhibitors on regeneration and tissue differentiation and probed into the cytological details of protein synthesis and tissue organization. The comparative physiologist has made his major contribution in studies of metamorphosis. There is now a rich literature on these many different aspects of growth (Needham, 1964): only two topics (regeneration and metamorphosis) will be considered here.

Regeneration

All animals have some capacity to restore tissues or body parts which have been lost through normal physiological processes or destroyed accidentally. A complete *Amoeba* may grow from a fragment representing $\frac{1}{80}$th of the original animal provided that the nucleus is included in the fragment. Only $\frac{1}{200}$th of a *Hydra* or $\frac{1}{280}$th of a planarian is necessary to regenerate a completely new animal. Some of the primitive oligochaete worms can regenerate from a single segment. This potential for extensive regeneration from very small fragments is common in other lower phyla. Sometimes, under unfavorable conditions certain sponges are reduced to an amorphous mass which then acquires its original structure when conditions improve. Many protozoans reproduce asexually by binary fission; hydroids and planarians may also reproduce by fission and regenerate the missing parts. In the more advanced phyla, missing appendages are often regenerated and the outer coverings of cuticle, chitin or cornified epidermis are periodically replaced. In man, the germinal layers of the epidermis and the mucous membranes of the digestive tract are continuously proliferating to replace cells which are always being rubbed off. Holocrine glands such as the sebaceous glands secrete by accumulating a load of secretory materials in the cytoplasm and then disintegrating.

These varied examples are all expressions of the capacities of animal tissues to restore lost parts. In their monograph Vorontsova and Liosner (1960) divide them into three general categories: PHYSIOLOGICAL REGENERATION which is a part of the normal and regular functioning of some organs such as sebaceous glands, mucous membranes and the outer layers of the skin; REPARATIVE REGENERATION which is provoked by wounding or traumatic destruction and ASEXUAL REPRODUCTION which is a natural process involving the isolation of a part of the animal and its transformation into a daughter organism. The distinction is useful since the functional significance of the three processes is quite different. It should be noted, however, that all three are, in reality, "physiological," that CELL RENEWAL (Leblond and Walker, 1956) is probably a more appropriate term than physiological regeneration and that the word REGENERATION is usually reserved for reparative and post-traumatic processes. It is this latter phenomenon which is considered here; the discussion is based on Needham (1952), Raven (1959) and Vorontsova and Liosner (1960).

REPARATIVE PROCESSES

The recorded descriptions of regeneration in all groups of animals are now voluminous. The literature has been compiled in a systematic way by Vorontsova and Liosner (1960).

The sequence of events. Needham (1952) describes six morphological events which can be conveniently separated for descriptive purposes. The first of these is WOUND CLOSURE which in lower forms involves only a contraction of neighboring tissues and a stretching of the surrounding cells over the wound; in higher forms the vascular fluids clot (Chapter

6) and thus form a basis for the later processes of repair. Wound closure is followed by DEMOLITION and DEFENCE which, in the higher vertebrates, begins with a triple response (page 421) caused by the release of toxic substances from injured tissues and expressed as increased dilatation of blood vessels, collection of fluid and eventually the removal of the damaged tissues through autolysis and phagocytosis. The vascular reactions are observed only in the molluscs, arthropods and vertebrates; lower forms probably depend entirely on phagocytosis.

Several different processes are associated with the healing which follows demolition and defence. The first of these is often a DEDIFFERENTIATION of tissues to provide indifferent cells for subsequent regenerative processes. Although dedifferentiation has been described in lower forms and may occur to some degree in all cases, it is most characteristic of the vertebrates and has been extensively studied in regenerating amphibian appendages. In lower forms it is believed that nondifferentiated or pluripotent cells (NEOBLASTS) are always present and that these migrate into the area of injury from nearby tissues. Needham suggests that the development of the highly efficient vertebrate circulatory system reduced the importance of maintaining a stock of undifferentiated migrant cells. The process of dedifferentiation brings to an end the regressive phase of regeneration; this is followed by the progressive phases: formation of the BLASTEMA or regeneration bud, its GROWTH and subsequent DIFFERENTIATION into the regenerated structure. The blastema or regeneration bud is composed of a mass of dedifferentiated or immigrant cells; in the amphibians, the blastema is fully established prior to a sudden initiation of mitotic activity which heralds the new growth. The intense cellular proliferation which follows produces a mass of relatively small cells which subsequently increase in size and become somewhat separated as intercellular spaces appear during differentiation. The mitotic rate declines as the regenerating structure continues to differentiate and becomes functional.

These then are the morphological events which characterize regeneration. Explanations of the causal mechanisms have been persistently sought for more than half a century. Experimental embryologists have been particularly active in the search for factors which induce regeneration, the determination of events within the differentiating blastema, gradients in regenerative capacity and metabolism in organisms or parts of organisms and the inductive action of different tissue transplants (Needham, 1952; Raven, 1959). Medical physiologists have investigated the posttraumatic blood clotting, vascular responses and inflammatory reactions which precede repair. Comparative physiologists have recently demonstrated a commanding position of the neurosecretory system in the regulation of regeneration among some of the lower forms.

The regenerative capacities of the marine polychaete *Nereis diversicolor* have been carefully studied by Clark and his associates (Clark and Ruston, 1963; Clark and Sully, 1964; Sully, 1964). *Nereis* grows by adding new segments until it has produced 40 or 50 of them; thereafter new segments are only added slowly and growth is mostly due to increase in segment size. When the worms have about 90 segments, growth by either means ceases. Segment proliferation is regulated by hormones produced in the supraesophageal ganglia. If these ganglia are removed in young individuals, segment proliferation ceases but is resumed following implantation of ganglia from other young worms. Moreover, old worms which have ceased to grow can be induced to grow by implanting ganglia from young, growing worms but the brains of old worms do not stimulate segmentation in other old worms.

Worms less than 60 segments in length have remarkable capacities for regeneration and this, like normal growth, depends on the supraesophageal ganglia. Amputation of a part of the worm stimulates the neurosecretory cells to elaborate a substance or substances which provoke segment proliferation. The potency of ganglia to stimulate regeneration has been shown to reach a maximum about three days after the trauma and thereafter to decline. Regeneration capacity is gradually lost as the animals become older so that worms longer than about 60 segments show little tendency to grow additional segments following injury. However, old, sexually mature worms which normally do not regenerate can be induced to proliferate segments by implanting ganglia from young regenerating worms. It is not yet known whether the GROWTH-PROMOTING and the REGENERATION-PROMOTING HORMONES are identical or distinct.

These studies have implicated the neuroendocrine system in the control of regeneration in *Nereis*. Needham (1964) summarizes the literature which points toward comparable controls in several other groups ranging from planarians to vertebrates. Injury acting directly on nerves or through the release of cellular products presumably stimulates neurosecretory cells to produce hormones which trigger the regeneration processes. This may be a universal component of the regulatory mechanisms concerned with regeneration in multicellular animals. Even if this proves to be the case, there are still many unanswered questions in the analysis of regeneration.

Biological significance of regeneration. Many workers have noted that the capacity to regenerate is primitive in both the phylogenetic and the ontogenetic sense. Representatives of the lower animal phyla regenerate completely after the loss of large portions of their bodies and younger individuals usually respond much more readily than the older mature ones. These principles apply widely throughout the animal world and numerous examples will be found in the monographs already cited.

If it is true that the ability to regenerate lost parts is primitive, then it seems curious that such an important capacity should have been partially lost during the evolution of the higher forms.

Needham (1952) suggests that the advantages of extensive regeneration are less significant in the larger, more complex and more active animals. Whereas a substantial portion of an annelid worm may be sacrificed to a predator while the remainder escapes to regenerate the missing parts, a vertebrate usually escapes with relatively minor injuries or is captured and killed. The more active life of the vertebrates and some of the higher invertebrates reduces their chances of major injury; at the same time, relatively minor damage such as wounds and broken bones are readily repaired. It has also been suggested that the extensive dedifferentiation required for blastema formation in a large vertebrate animal might impose both metabolic and physical disadvantages which would outweigh the advantages. Needham argues in this way that the ability to regenerate lost parts is both pristine and adaptive in the evolutionary sense. The concept has been challenged (Vorontsova and Liosner, 1960) but the arguments will not be detailed here.

Metamorphosis

Metamorphosis is a profound postembryonic reorganization of tissues and processes which usually prepares an animal for life in a different habitat. In many animals (lamellibranchs, barnacles, echinoderms) the larval stages are highly motile or planktonic while the adults are either sessile or have a restricted distribution in relation to specialized habitats and food requirements. Planktonic larvae of fishes often drift from the spawning areas to distant feeding grounds, while the adults actively migrate back to the spawning grounds at sexual maturity. Larval forms of many insects are relatively sedentary and feed actively where they hatch; the adults often exploit a different source of food and may fly about to mate and disperse the species. Amphibian metamorphosis permits escape from a habitat essential for reproduction and early development but, at the same time quite unsuitable for the adult and liable to be radically changed at certain seasons.

These larval stages and the consequent problems of metamorphosis hold a justifiably important place in biological thought and theory. They form the basis of the distribution of many species and are just as significant to their survival and success as are the adult forms. In some cases larval forms may have provided the evolutionary material for radically new phylogenetic lines. Sexual maturity sometimes occurs in larval forms (NEOTENY), and it seems not unreasonable to assume that certain groups of animals have evolved through the omission of highly specialized adult stages and the adaptation of the more youthful and generalized larval features to new and different ways of life (PAEDOMORPHOSIS). This line of argument has been particularly helpful in speculation concerning the ancestry of insects and vertebrates (De Beer, 1958)—to quote Garstang (1951):

Now look at Ammocoetes *there, reclining in the mud,*
Preparing thyroid-extract to secure his tiny food:
If just a touch of sunshine more should make his gonads grow,
The Lancelet's claims to ancestry would get a nasty blow!

The primitive endocrine system probably assumed responsibilities for the regulation of growth, tissue regeneration and metamorphosis at and early stage in phylogeny. However, at present, the established factual information is almost completely restricted to polychaetes, crustaceans, insects and vertebrates. The present discussion is confined to some aspects of the endocrinology of growth and metamorphosis in the arthropods and vertebrates.

Arthropod Growth and Metamorphosis

The "growth" of an arthropod is not a continuous process but occurs in a series of disjunct steps. The rigid exoskeleton is an excellent solution to the problem of protection but precludes a continuous increase in size. In arthropods, this depends on the periodic discarding of the old shell (MOLT or ECDYSIS) with a decided expansion of the body before the hardening of a new one. This size increase is due to the rapid uptake of water (crustaceans) or air (insects), and actual growth, which in the strict sense involves synthesis of new protoplasm, occurs throughout the intermolt. The metabolism of an arthropod is markedly cyclical as a consequence of this sequence of changes associated with molting. Metamorphosis, where it occurs, is regulated in the same general way as molting, and the two phenomena may be considered together.

MOLTING IN CRUSTACEANS

Metamorphic changes in crustaceans are less dramatic than those of insects and have not yet been studied physiologically (Passano, 1960). Molting, on the other hand, has been scientifically investigated for almost half a century, and its endocrinology, together with the associated metabolism of growth, is now known in considerable detail.

The molt or ecdysis during which a crustacean withdraws from its old shell and acquires a new one is a conspicuous event which seems to divide the animal's life neatly into periods of molt and intermolt. Studies of metabolism, however, show that the cycle is one of almost continuous activity during which structures such as the integument and the hepatopancreas are constantly showing gradual but measurable changes. It is customary to divide the cycle into the PREMOLT (proecdysis), MOLT (ecdysis), POSTMOLT (metecdysis) and INTERMOLT; the latter is referred to as DIECDYSIS if it is very short or imperceptible as in animals which molt regularly throughout the year, or ANECDYSIS if the intermolt is prolonged as in the crayfish which molts seasonally. There are several different variants of the molting cycle (Carlisle and Knowles, 1959).

The premolt is a period of active metabolism during which calcium is withdrawn from the exoskeleton and stored in the hepatopancreas, blood or gastroliths (concretions formed in the anterior wall of the cardiac stomach of some crustaceans such as the crayfish). Glycogen accumulates in the hepatopancreas, the epithelial and subepithelial connective tissues, and the new exoskeleton starts to form near the end of proecdysis. Concomitant changes also occur in the lipids and proteins, with the net result that organic and mineral reserves are withdrawn from the old exoskeleton and mobilized for the development of a new one. The extent of the resorption varies with species and the conditions of the molt; as much as 79 per cent of the organic and 18 per cent of the inorganic matter may be withdrawn from the carapace of the crab *Carcinus,* although the values are often considerably lower than this (Passano, 1960). During the later stages of premolt in the crayfish, there is a marked decline in the activity of hepatopancreatic enzymes involved in the pentose oxidative cycle (McWhinnie and Corkill, 1964). This pathway is strongly active during intermolt and the cyclical changes which it shows are again evidence of profound alterations in physiological chemistry during the different stages of molting (Chapter 7).

During the molt there is a rapid uptake of water, amounting to about 70 per cent of the premolt body weight in *Carcinus.* The influx of water is largely through the lining of the digestive tract and is dependent on both osmotic and hydrostatic factors (Passano, 1960). The osmotic pressure of the blood rises to about 105 per cent of the sea water at the beginning of the molt; the gastric lining breaks down and becomes permeable, the animal drinks water and thus increases the hydrostatic pressure in the gut. Swelling produced by the influx of water breaks the old carapace and molt or exuviation follows. The water uptake continues for a time after the animal emerges from its shell.

During the postmolt period the shell hardens and the true tissue growth of the organism commences. The latter may continue through the period of intermolt, or there may be a period of relative metabolic equilibrium if this period is an anecdysis.

Hormonal regulation of the molt cycle depends on the eyestalks (*X*-organ, sinus gland) and the *Y*-organ. This endocrine complex has already been described (Chapter 2) and illustrated (Figs. 2.6 and 20.15). It has been known for more than 50 years that removal of the eyestalks during the intermolt will initiate a molt. Recently (1959) it was demonstrated that removal of the *Y*-organs completely eliminates the molting processes, while implants of *Y*-organs frequently stimulate a molt. Figure 24.1 illustrates the results of experiments of this type. The eyestalks contain a neurohemal organ (sinus gland) which receives neurosecretory fibers from the *X*-organ (medulla terminalis *X*-organ or MTGX).

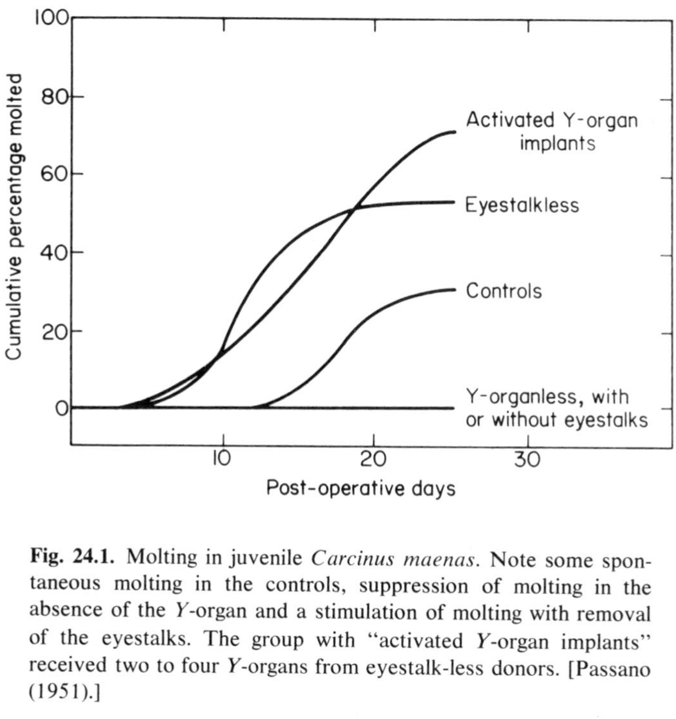

Fig. 24.1. Molting in juvenile *Carcinus maenas*. Note some spontaneous molting in the controls, suppression of molting in the absence of the *Y*-organ and a stimulation of molting with removal of the eyestalks. The group with "activated *Y*-organ implants" received two to four *Y*-organs from eyestalk-less donors. [Passano (1951).]

It is now agreed that the *X*-organ produces a MOLT-INHIBITING HORMONE which is stored in the sinus gland and passes to the *Y*-organ to inhibit its activity. When the level of molt-inhibiting hormone falls the *Y*-organ becomes fully active and secretes crustacean ECDYSONE (the molting hormone) which stimulates the molt. A MOLT-ACCELERATING HORMONE has also been described (Carlisle and Knowles, 1959), but its existence is questioned by some workers (Passano, 1960). The interesting experiments leading to the elucidation of this system of molting controls have been summarized (Carlisle and Knowles, 1959; Passano, 1960). The regulatory mechanisms are shown diagrammatically in Fig. 2.6.

In some crustaceans (*Homarus, Cancer pagurus*) molting cycles are continuous until death, and the animals may reach a very large size. In other species (*Maia, Carcinus, Callinectes, Pachygrapsus*) a definite adult size is fixed at the final molt, and the animals continue to live for some time thereafter. Mechanisms determining the final molt seem to vary; in *Maia* it is said to be due to a degeneration of the *Y*-gland; in *Carcinus* the *X*-organ-sinus-gland complex seems to produce excessive amounts of molt-inhibiting hormone (Carlisle and Knowles, 1959). It appears that, in this as in many other phenomena, the available mechanisms have been used in different ways during evolution to attain the same ends.

It is obvious that the mechanisms which regulate reproduction must be related to those concerned with molting. Females do not molt while they are carrying developing young. Moreover, in most of the Malacostraca, copulation is only possible between a freshly molted female and a male with hard integument (Carlisle and Knowles, 1959). These integrating mechanisms have not yet been worked out in detail.

INSECT METAMORPHOSIS AND DIAPAUSE

Several lines of endocrine research have originated from the investigations of insect physiologists. When the Polish scientist Kopeć found evidence for chemical regulation of metamorphosis in caterpillars of the moth *Porthetria* (*Lymantria*), he not only initiated work on the endocrinology of invertebrates but also implicated the nervous tissues in processes of chemical integration. Much of the basic work on neurosecretion stems from these pioneer studies of insect brain hormones. The presence of pheromones may also be cited as an important area of endocrinology which was first explored by students of insect physiology.

Insects are such hardy experimental animals that they are extremely useful in endocrine research. Kopeć (1922 and earlier) found that his animals lived for a considerable period after the removal of the brain but that the caterpillars failed to pupate unless the brain had been present for a period of about 10 days following the final larval molt. If the extirpation was carried out before this "critical period" had elapsed, pupation never occurred; if, on the contrary, the brain was removed 10 days or more after this molt, then pupation was normal although the animals were brainless. He also noted that a tight ligature posterior to the thorax had no effect on pupation if 10 days had elapsed since the final molt; but if the ligature was applied before 10 days, only the portions of the body anterior to the ligature would pupate. He concluded from these and many other convincing experiments that the brain was the source of a factor responsible for pupation and that within 10 days after the final larval molt enough of this material had diffused from the brain into the tissues to effect their transformation. His conclusions are now supported by comparable experiments on many species of insects. Several other experiments are cited in the following sections. The history of insect endocrinology has been traced in some recent reviews (Gilbert, 1964; Gabe *et al.*, 1964) and will not be detailed here.

Patterns of insect metamorphosis. There are three general patterns of metamorphosis in insects. The **Ametabola**, a primitive group represented by the springtails (Collembola), undergo a series of postembryonic molts without any particular change in general appearance; they lack a proper metamorphosis. The **Hemimetabola** are said to show an incomplete or gradual metamorphosis since the young or NYMPHS have the same general appearance as the adults but lack wings which gradually appear in a series of nymphal molts. The developmental stages are called INSTARS; the full expression of adult characters appears with the final molt. Familiar examples are grasshoppers and cockroaches (Orthoptera), bugs such as *Rhodnius* (Hemiptera), dragonflies (Odonata) and earwigs (Dermaptera). In the third group (**Holometabola**) development is said to show a complete metamorphosis; the larvae are very different in appearance from the adult, and pupation occurs between the last larval instar and the adult stage. Familiar examples are the true flies (Diptera), the moths and butterflies (Lepidoptera), the ants, wasps and bees (Hymenoptera) and the beetles (Coleoptera). Larval stages are commonly called maggots, caterpillars and grubs. In each case this series of wormlike stages, which bear no resemblance to the adult, is followed by a molt in which the last instar is transformed into a PUPA or CHRYSALIS, a superficially quiescent, nonfeeding stage, during which there is an active transformation of tissues leading to the emergence of the adult at final molting.

Diapause. This is a period of suspended animation and arrested growth characteristic of the life histories of many insects and mites. It is a physiological mechanism for survival during adverse conditions and confers the same biological advantages as comparable states of dormancy found in other groups of animals: encystment in the protozoans, drought resistant eggs of the brine shrimp *Artemia,* aestivation in the lungfish, delayed implantation in some mammals and hibernation in the homeotherms. In each case, the rate of metabolism is depressed and growth is either completely arrested or very slow. Both onset of dormancy and resumption of growth or activity are usually abrupt; the diapause is followed by metamorphosis, rapid growth or reproductive activity. The monograph by Lees (1955) discusses the physiology and describes many examples. The notes which follow are drawn from Lees.

Like so many biological phenomena, diapause is a spectrum of similar conditions rather than a single well-defined state. In a relatively constant environment, such as that of the laboratory, some species (the blowfly *Lucilia sericata*, the red spider mite *Metatetranychus ulmi*) have been reared for years and found to enter diapause only when the environment is appropriately altered. Their diapause is said to be FACULTATIVE. In other species, diapause is OBLIGATORY and occurs as a regular event at a specific time in the annual life cycle. Even in closely related species and subspecies or in different populations of the same species, both facultative and obligatory diapause may occur as well as non-diapausing forms. The European corn borer *Ostrinia nubilalis* spends the winter in diapause – as adults in more northern latitudes where only one generation occurs each year (UNIVOLTINE life cycle) but as full grown caterpillars inside old corn stalks in more southern regions where a second generation reaches the prepupal larval stage by late summer or autumn. The mosquito *Aedes canadensis* also has a univoltine life cycle but in this case diapause occurs in the eggs which are laid in the autumn. *Aedes dorsalis* produces several generations during the year (MULTIVOLTINE species) but only the eggs laid in the fall enter diapause. In the first species of mosquito, diapause is obligatory; in the second it is facultative. In Quebec, the spruce sawfly *Gilpinia polytoma* has one generation per year with an obligatory diapause but in Connecticut, several hundred miles to the south, there are three generations per year with a predominantly facultative diapause; an intermediate condition occurs in areas between these two extremes. Subspecies of migratory locust *Locusta migratoria* develop without diapause in the tropics but show diapause in the northerly limits of their range. Lees gives many other examples.

Thus, the stage in the life cycle at which diapause takes place varies in different species; it may be characteristic of egg, larva, pupa or adult. In adults there is typically a failure in development of reproductive organs and a hypertrophy of fat bodies and storage structures, while in the earlier stages, growth is arrested. Occasionally diapause may occur during more than one stage in a life cycle. The grasshopper *Pardalophora apiculata* has a two-year life cycle and spends the first winter as a diapause egg and the second as a late nymph. In some insects there is a QUIESCENCE characterized by slow growth and irregular development rather than a true diapause. These conditions have their parallels in the states of torpor or narcosis and true hibernation among the homeotherms. Lees cites several examples: the alder fly *Sialis lutaria* and the dragonfly *Anax imperator*, which have two-year life cycles, spend the first winter in quiescence as half-grown larvae and the second in the true diapause of the last larval stadium.

This spectrum of conditions found in closely related insect species suggests that diapause has evolved many times and emphasizes once more the opportunism of phylogenetic processes.

The phenomenon is hormonally regulated. In species with facultative diapause, activity of the endocrine organs is environmentally triggered; when the diapause is obligatory, genetically established endogenous rhythms may play a dominant role. As in many other environmentally-controlled physiological processes, photoperiod provides the most universal and reliable cue; in northern latitudes where winter diapause is common, short days frequently initiate the change. Temperature, moisture, available oxygen, quality and quantity of food may also be involved. Temperature, in particular, often modifies the photoperiod effect and, in some cases, completely overrides it. The literature now contains numerous examples of the way in which several environmental cues have been woven together to form reliable controls which meet the survival requirements of different species (Beck, 1963; Clements, 1963; Farner, 1961).

Endocrine controls. It has now been abundantly demonstrated that the brain produces only one of several substances concerned with the regulation of metamorphosis in insects. The several links in this regulatory chain are shown in Fig. 24.2. They are basically the same in all groups, whether the metamorphosis is complete or incomplete.

The neurosecretory cells in the pars intercerebralis of the brain produce a tropic substance (ECDYSIOTROPIN or PROTHORACOTROPIN) which passes by axon transport to a neurohemal organ, the CORPUS CARDIACUM (CORPORA CARDIACA), located in close proximity to the brain. Under appropriate stimulation the ecdysiotropic hormone is released into the blood and activates the ECDYSIAL or PROTHORACIC GLAND to secrete ECDYSONE (also called the molting hormone, the prothoracic gland hormone PGH and the growth and differentiation hormone GD). Ecdysone is presumed to have a direct effect on the chromosomal mechanisms concerned with molting. During larval stages, the action of ecdysone is checked by the juvenile hormone JH secreted by the CORPORA ALLATA. What actually happens seems to depend on the ratio of these two substances, for when the juvenile hormone is completely withdrawn adult transformation occurs.

Evidence for this chain of controls has been found in many different experiments involving several groups of insects. Wigglesworth's (1936, 1964) experiments on *Rhodnius* will serve as a single example, but many others are summarized in the literature already cited. The molt-initiating stimulus differs in various species of insects. In *Rhodnius* the

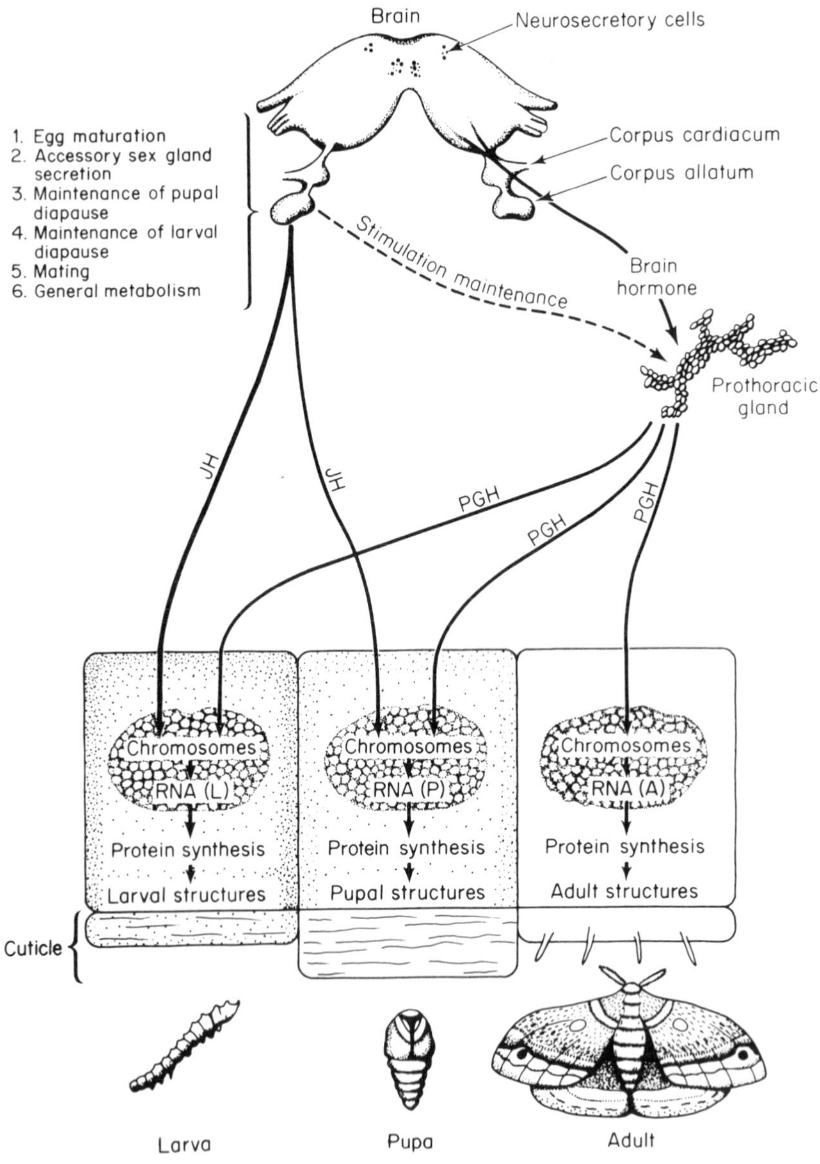

Fig. 24.2. Endocrine control of growth and development in a moth. It is assumed that a critical titer of ecdysone (PGH) and a specific concentration of juvenile hormone leads to the transfer of appropriate nuclear information to the cytoplasm via messenger compounds indicated as RNA "*L*", "*P*", or "*A*" for the formation of larval, pupal or adult structures respectively. The corpora allata may stimulate and maintain the prothoracic glands as well as regulate the synthesis of larval structures. [Gilbert (1964).]

mechanical distension of the body resulting from a full meal of blood activates the neurosecretory centers of the brain and triggers the chain of hormonal activity. *Rhodnius* fails to molt if given only small meals of blood; a large meal with body distension is requisite to growth. Further, the neurosecretory cells require a certain period of time to elaborate enough hormone to initiate a molt. If the brain (source of ecdysiotropic hormone) is removed very shortly after the meal of blood, the animal

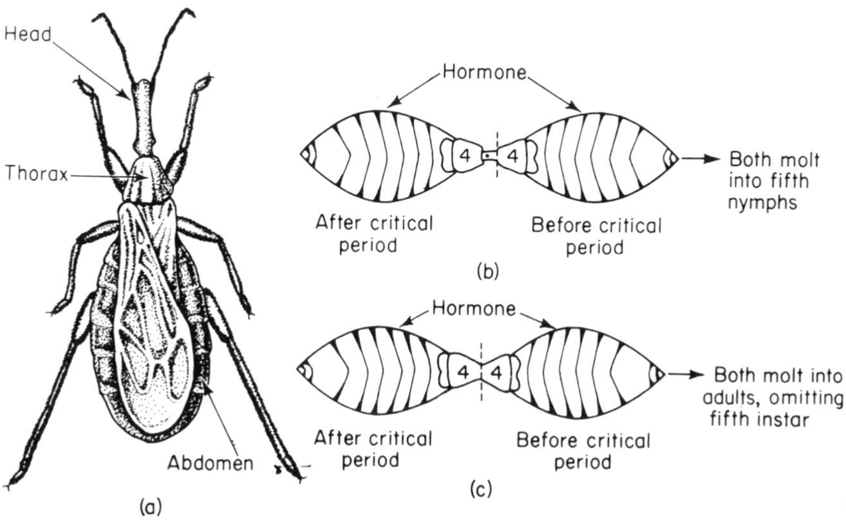

Fig. 24.3. The bloodsucking bug *Rhodnius prolixus* on the left with two diagrams on the right illustrating some of Wigglesworth's (1936) endocrinological experiments outlined in the text. Broken line, the level of decapitation. Black dot, the presence of the corpus allatum.

will never molt, although it may continue to live for more than a year. If, however, a week or more has elapsed since the engorgement with blood, removal of the brain and corpora cardiaca has no effect on the subsequent molt. In this case, sufficient hormone has diffused into the tissues to effect transformation.

The long head of *Rhodnius* is singularly convenient for surgical work. Animals may be decapitated somewhat anteriorly to remove only the protocerebrum (source of the ecdysiotropic hormone), while a more posterior section will also remove the corpora allata (source of juvenile hormone). Decapitated animals have been joined with capillary tubes or fused together parabiotically as indicated in Fig. 24.3 to demonstrate several features of their endocrinology. When a fourth-instar nymph is decapitated immediately after feeding and combined with a nymph which has been decapitated ANTERIORLY several days after feeding (Fig. 24.3*b*), both molt together to form the next nymphal stage, since the anterior decapitation did not injure the corpora allata which is the source of the juvenile hormone. If, however, the experiment is done in the same way except for a more POSTERIOR decapitation of the second individual, both nymphs molt into adults, thus omitting further larval stages because the source of juvenile hormone was removed (Fig. 24.3*c*). Comparable experiments can produce supernumerary nymphal stages or a reversion of adults to nymph-like forms. The importance of the corpora allata may also be shown by direct extirpation of the glands (leading to premature adult molts) or implantation of allata (producing extra nymphal instars).

This pattern of controls has been described in several groups of insects. However, it is not universal. Variations in both morphological and physiological details have been described (Gilbert, 1964) and are to be expected, for evolutionary processes have very often attained similar ends by somewhat devious routes. Comparative endocrinology is replete with examples of variable usage of a group of hormones to achieve some specific regulatory function.

Diapause is a special stage in the hormonally regulated growth sequence of some insects and mites. Environmental changes are responsible for both the cessation of growth and the reactivation of development but these changes always operate through the neuroendocrine system. No peculiar organs have been associated with the production of diapause hormones; on the contrary, diapause is regulated through an adaptation of the endocrine controls already described for other metamorphic processes. Additional complexity is found in both the environmental cues which trigger the processes and in the varied nature of the stages and processes which are temporarily suspended. Diapause is frequently triggered by one environmental change and "broken" by another. In many lepidopterans such as the giant Cecropia silkworm *Hyalaphora cecropia* (Williams, 1952) and the European corn borer *Ostrinia nubilalis* (Beck, 1963), diapause is initiated in the autumn by decreasing photoperiods and comes to an end only after an exposure to the chilling winter temperatures. The Cecropia silkworms have a pupal diapause. Williams performed many interesting experiments with their isolated abdomens after sealing them off anteriorly with coverslips. The prothoracic glands are removed by this operation and the abdomens may remain in diapause for a very long time. If, however, they are implanted with glands from active pupae, or if a diapausing abdomen is joined parabiotically to an activated (chilled) pupa, metamorphosis of the isolated abdomen occurs and, in some cases, these preparations may lay eggs. Regulation by chemicals produced in the anterior parts of the body and triggered by low temperature was thus established. An exposure to temperatures of 3° to 5°C for a period of one to two months is required for activation of diapausing Cecropia pupae. The aedine mosquitoes have an egg diapause and also require chilling temperatures for reactivation—as long as six months in *Aedes stimulans*. In this case there is an additional factor since the eggs will not hatch until they have been submerged in deoxygenated water (Clements, 1963). Many other examples are given in the literature previously cited and in a recent review by Wigglesworth (1964).

A complexity in diapause endocrinology can be anticipated from the varied nature of the processes regulated. Larval and pupal diapause have been traced to an interruption in the cyclical events responsible for the production and action of ecdysone. Thus, the primary links in regulation are the brain, corpora cardiaca and prothoracic glands. Diapause in adult insects (imaginal diapause) is marked by reproductive dormancy and probably controlled through the neurosecretory centers and corpora allata. Egg and embryo diapause have posed some of the most puzzling physiological problems. These processes are maternally regulated. The endocrine system of the female, in response to environmental cues, produces substances which act in the ovary and hence regulate developmental processes which operate in eggs or embryos many months later. Details are different in various insects. The oriental silkworm *Bombyx mori* has been intensively studied by Japanese workers (bibliography in Wigglesworth, 1964). A special "diapause hormone" has been extracted from the subesophageal ganglion of *Bombyx* pupae; this when injected into female pupae leads to the production of diapause eggs by the resulting moth even in insects which would normally produce non-diapausing eggs. Details of the regulation are being actively investigated but are, at present, incompletely explained.

P. Karlson and his associates have been responsible for the chemical isolation and identification of ecdysone (review by Gilbert, 1964). This is one of the great achievements of twentieth-century biochemistry since such fantastically small amounts of the hormone are present in a single insect. The first sample of 25 mg of crystalline material came from 500 kg of silkworm (*Bombyx*) pupae. In a later isolation a somewhat greater yield of 250 mg was obtained from four tons (wet weight) of animals. There is evidence for at least two slightly different ecdysone molecules. Karlson reports a molecular weight of 464 with the empirical formula $C_{27}H_{44}O_6$.

The suggested structural formula, which still requires confirmation, is as follows:

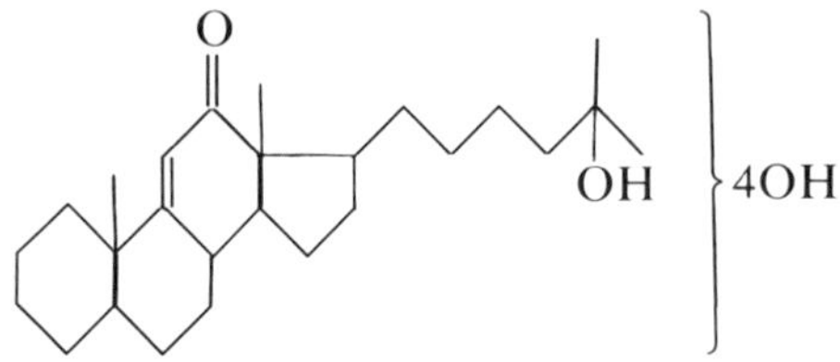

A substance very similar to insect ecdysone has been isolated from the shrimp *Crago vulgaria*, and this suggests that there may be a similarity in the molting hormones throughout the arthropods. Although the juvenile hormone has been partially purified, its chemical nature is not yet known (Gilbert, 1963, 1964). Williams (1961) describes it as a relatively small, apolar, heat-stable lactone.

Karlson has also developed much of the impressive evidence for a direct interaction between ecdysone and the genetic material (Gilbert, 1963; Karlson and Sekeris, 1964). This evidence is based on studies of the giant chromosomes of the Diptera (Beermann, and Clever, 1964). Characteristic PUFFING in specific regions of the chromosomes is associated with active RNA formation at these sites; the RNA, in turn, is the key link in protein synthesis. In *Chironomus* specific chromosomal puffs (genes) are activated during pupation, and these same genes have been induced to puff by injecting ecdysone. A significant body of evidence now links ecdysone with the chromosomal puffing characteristic of molting, and the implications are that this hormone is directly concerned with the activation of specific genes. Certain other hormones, including some of those of vertebrates, may also operate by a direct action on specific genes (Callan and Lloyd, 1960).

Growth, Molting and Metamorphosis in the Vertebrates

GROWTH HORMONE

The significance of the vertebrate pituitary in the regulation of growth was convincingly demonstrated during the first two decades of the twentieth century. Aschner (1912) first described arrested growth in the hypophysectomized dog; his studies were soon followed by a classical series of experiments on the white rat (Smith, 1930). Since that time, growth hormone (somatotropin, STH) has been highly purified, studied biochemically and used in many physiological experiments; but in spite of half a century of active research, the underlying mechanisms at the molecular level are still obscure (Knobil, 1961). Its general metabolic effects, on the other hand, are well known and include increased deposition of protein, mobilization of fat to the liver, increased ketogenesis, rise in the circulating free fatty acids and several effects on carbohydrate metabolism. This remains an active field of mammalian endocrinology.

Comparative studies indicate that a pituitary regulation of growth processes was established at an early stage in phylogeny. Retardation or complete cessation of growth following hypophysectomy has been recorded in elasmobranchs, teleosts and amphibians. Some of the first observations of growth arrest following pituitary ablation were made on tadpoles, while one of the most detailed of all studies in this field is that of Pickford (1953 and later) on the teleost fish *Fundulus heteroclitus*. It has not, however, been demonstrated that growth in the cyclostomes is pituitary-regulated, and there are several other indications that the dominant growth-regulating effects of somatotropin may be absent at a very early stage in phylogeny as well as ontogeny. Hypophysectomized elasmobranchs may grow normally if force-fed; axolotls likewise grow normally after the removal of the pituitary; larval amphibians frequently show retardation rather than cessation of growth after this operation; the pituitary appears to exert little effect during mammalian fetal life. The literature has been reviewed (Pickford and Atz, 1957; Knobil, 1961; Hoar, 1965*a*), but there is not yet sufficient information to trace a story in the phylogeny. There is, however, abundant evidence of species variations, both in physiological controls and in the biochemistry of the hormone.

It should be emphasized again that endocrine regulation usually depends on the integrated action of several hormones, and to single out one particular factor is rather misleading. Even though the pituitary has a commanding position and growth is arrested in its absence, growth processes depend on many different synthetic pathways and most of the hormones are involved in their control. Thyroidectomy depresses growth in higher animals, probably because of the stimulating effect of thyroid hormone on general metabolism. Insulin, ACTH, and the corticosteroids will also play their part, since the metabolism of the body fuels is greatly dependent on their activities.

MOLTING IN VERTEBRATES

Molting processes are characteristic of many of the terrestrial vertebrates. Epidermal structures are involved. Amphibians and reptiles periodically shed the outer layers of their skin while birds and mammals often alter their plumage or pelage with the season. Concomitant color changes are characteristic of some species. The correlation of molt with season, often also with reproduction, suggests an involvement of the endocrine system. In many cases where the molt is associated with reproduction, pituitary gonadotropins and/or gonadal steroids have been definitely implicated (Gorbman and Bern, 1962). Seasonal color changes (morphological color changes) of some of the northern birds and mammals are pituitary-regulated and can be modified by an appropriate manipulation of the photoperiod. In the varying hare *Lepus*, for example, the pituitary gonadotropins are said to induce shedding of white winter fur and the growth of a brown coat. Only the gonadotropins seem to be involved since the reaction can be induced in both castrated and thyroidectomized animals (Lyman, 1963; Prosser and Brown 1961).

In general, molting or changes in the pigmentation of plumage and pelage are regulated by endocrines but, as in other physiological processes, the precise role of the specific hormones is often different in the various groups. In some birds (domestic fowl, pigeon) thyroidectomy inhibits molting while thyroxine stimulates it; in others (crows, jackdaws), the epidermis is relatively insensitive to thyroid manipulation (Gorbman and Bern, 1962). Thyroid hormone, perhaps more than any other factor, is frequently associated with morphogenetic and epidermal changes in the lower vertebrates. In the control of breeding plumage and color changes associated with reproduction the gonadotropins and gonadal steroids are often associated with the metabolic hormones.

Details of molting endocrinology in the vertebrates are best understood in some of the Amphibia. A relationship between thyroid state and skin structure was noted many years ago, and more recently the corticosteroids have also been associated with these processes (Gorbman, 1964). The Amphibia show two distinct stages in molting, and these seem to be subject to different endocrinological controls. There is first an epidermal proliferation with a cornification of the outer layers; this is followed by the secretion of mucus and the shedding and eating of the detached outer layers of skin (slough). Hypophysectomy inhibits both processes. The second process, involving shedding or sloughing, is inhibited or completely suppressed by thyroidectomy in several species and can be regularly stimulated in intact animals by thyroxine, whether or not it is inhibited by thyroidectomy. The first process (proliferation and cornification) seems independent of thyroid hormone and may continue in thyroidectomized individuals to produce layers of unusually thick epidermis. Evidently this process is regulated by ACTH and the corticosteroids. Hypophysectomized toads *Bufo bufo* show the proliferation and cornification reaction with formation of a slough when treated with ACTH or corticosteroids. Corticosterone is more active than aldosterone, while cortisol is relatively inactive. Factors such as thyroxine, somatotropin, prolactin and the neurohypophyseal octapeptides have no effect on this particular response of the hypophysectomized toad (Jorgensen and Larsen, 1964).

VERTEBRATE METAMORPHOSIS

The amphibians provide the best-known examples of metamorphosis among the vertebrates. The young usually hatch as fish-like tadpoles in fresh water and, after a period of aquatic life, metamorphose into terrestrial adults which use lungs instead of gills for respiration and show several profound biochemical changes, associated with a change of diet and restrictions in the availability of water (Frieden, 1961, 1963). Some of these changes are reversed when the adults return again to the aquatic habitat at the time of spawning.

Some fishes show equally significant metamorphic changes (Barrington, 1961). The ammocoete larvae of the lamprey live a sedentary life in the mud of freshwater streams, feeding on small food particles which they trap in a sticky ciliated pharyngeal groove; the sticky mucus is secreted by the subpharyngeal gland (endostyle) and discharged into the pharynx. This feeding technique is similar to that of the protochordates. After some years there is a metamorphosis which includes the formation of eyes, the loss of the endostyle and the development of a rasping circular mouth. The lamprey then swims forth to feed on other fishes and sometimes to migrate into the ocean, a habitat which makes very different physiological demands on mechanisms concerned with water and electrolyte balance. Several species of teleost likewise change from a freshwater to a marine habitat at a specific time and in association with definite biochemical and metabolic changes. The smolt transformation of salmonids is the most familiar example. However, in the salmonids, as in most teleosts, the post-embryonic changes in morphology are slight compared with those of the cyclostomes. Metamorphic changes are also characteristic of the Atlantic eel *Anguilla* which, as larvae or leptocephali, are carried by ocean currents from the spawning grounds of the Sargasso sea into the fresh waters from rivers in the North Atlantic. There is a distinct metamorphosis from the leptocephalus to the elver which enters the rivers and again, after a number of years when fully grown, from the yellow stage to the silver stage, which migrates to the ocean on the spawning journey. The examples could be multiplied; the flatfish (Heterosomata) changes from a symmetrical larva to the laterally compressed adult form with both eyes on one side; the mudskipper *Periophthalmus* adopts a semiterrestrial life at metamorphosis.

Wald (1960*b*) argues that every metamorphosis invites a second metamorphosis. The juveniles which undergo changes necessary for life in an entirely different habitat (such as the change from water to land, or from fresh to salt water) must often show an equally radical transformation when they return to their original habitat at spawning time. Several of these physiological and biochemical changes have already been described (visual pigments, hemoglobins and the transport capacity of the blood, electrophoretic mobility of plasma proteins, excretion and electrolyte balance, alterations in digestive enzymes and in several of the metabolic pathways). They will not be detailed further; in general, the change is appropriate to the physiological demands of the altered habitat and these demands were considered at length in Part II. Excellent reviews of the biochemistry of vertebrate metamorphosis are available (Wald, 1960*b*; Barrington, 1961; Frieden, 1961, 1963; Etkin, 1964).

The endocrinology of vertebrate metamorphosis has been studied for more than half a century. In one of the pioneer studies of thyroid physiology, Gudernatsch (1912) showed the acceleration of tadpole development which follows thyroid feeding. Since that time the thyroid has been most frequently implicated in the endocrinological control of metamorphosis. Among fishes, it has been noted that some of the cells of the endostyle are transformed into thyroid follicles when the ammocoete changes to the form of an adult lamprey and that the thyroid shows evidence of increased activity at certain critical stages in the transformation of the eel, in the metamorphosis of flatfishes and in the smoltification of salmonids. In many cases, however, it is not yet clear whether the thyroid is regulating the metamorphic processes. Attempts to hasten the metamorphosis of the ammocoete, to induce the assumption of semiterrestrial life in *Periophthalmus* or to increase the salinity resistance of young salmonids have been uniformly unsuccessful (Barrington, 1961; Gorbman and Bern, 1962). The thyroid may be only one of several metabolic hormones activated during these critical periods; thyroid changes may be associated with the metamorphosis rather than cause it. In any case, the pituitary which regulates the thyroid must form the first link between environmental triggers and the growth and metamorphic processes.

As already indicated, correlations between thyroid activity and amphibian metamorphosis are long-standing and convincing. Metamorphosis from tadpole to adult is always associated with a surge of pituitary thyrotropic and thyroid activity. Some of the findings for *Xenopus* are summarized in Fig. 24.4.

Amphibians occupy a key position in the phylogeny of terrestrial vertebrates. Their endocrinology is of particular significance in considerations of biochemical evolution. There are always two distinct parts to an endocrine mechanism since the responsiveness of the target organs is just as significant as the hormone itself. The tailed amphibians show a curiously interesting variety in tissue responsiveness to thyroid stimulation. Metamorphosis in many of the Caudata, as in the Anura, may be accelerated with thyroid hormone. Some of the salamanders, however,

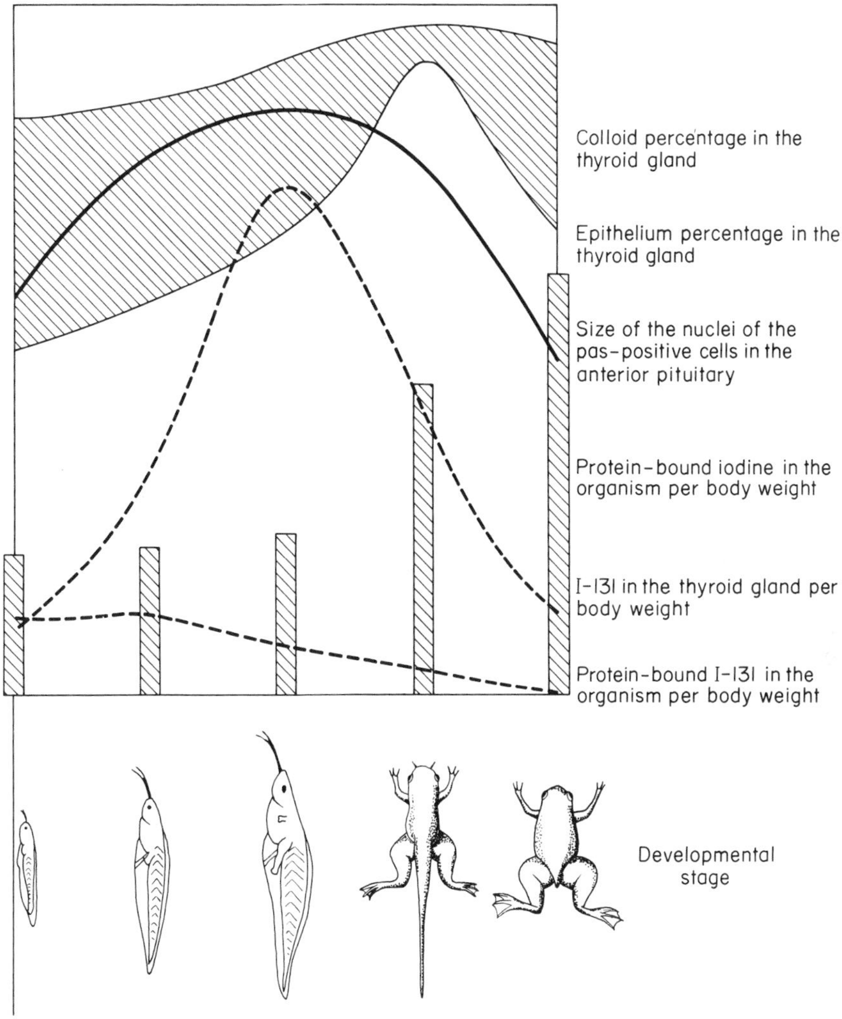

Fig. 24.4. Pituitary-thyroid function during metamorphosis of the African clawed toad *Xenopus laevis*. [Saxén *et al.* (1957).]

have a facultative metamorphosis. Axolotls, *Ambystoma tigrinum*, in many localities metamorphose regularly, losing their external gills and assuming a terrestrial existence. In certain regions (some of the high lakes of the Rocky Mountains), however, the larval characteristics are retained throughout life and the animals become sexually mature as neotenous adults. "They cling to youth perpetual and rear a tadpole brood" (Garstang, 1951). Thyroid hormone stimulates metamorphosis in these neotenous races. In nature *Ambystoma tigrinum* can have the best of two worlds.

The pituitary-thyroid control is not the only endocrine mechanism concerned with amphibian metamorphosis. The second metamorphosis of *Diemictylus* (*Triturus*) *viridescens* is triggered by prolactin (Grant, 1961). The experimental evidence was considered in the previous chapter. At this point it is of interest to note that migration and the alteration of skin texture, induced by prolactin or prolactin-like substances, represent only the first stage of the transformation. Although gills do not appear, there is a functional restoration of the lateral line, development of a keeled, swimming tail, changes in pigmentation, and biochemical changes in visual pigments, nitrogen excretion and electrolyte balance. Indications are that the pituitary-thyroid machinery, melanophore-stimulating hormones and neurohypophyseal factors are involved in these later phases (Grant, 1961). Prolactin induces only water drive and pigmentary responses.

Some of the urodeles (the perennibranchs *Proteus* and *Necturus*) are genetically incapable of losing their external gills and assuming the terrestrial form. Aquatic life is obligatory. During phylogeny, genetic changes in the responsiveness of tissues must have preceded or must have been associated with the development of endocrine controls. Only negative results have been obtained with thyroid treatment of the perennibranchs—to use Garstang's words once more:

> *They do not even contemplate a change to suit the weather,*
> *But live as tadpoles, breed as tadpoles, tadpoles altogether!*

References

Aaes-Jorgensen, E. 1961. Essential fatty acids. Physiol. Rev. 41: 1–51.

Abbott, B. C., and J. Lowy. 1958. Contraction in molluscan smooth muscle. J. Physiol. 141: 385–397.

Ackerman, E. 1962. Biophysical science. Prentice-Hall, Englewood Cliffs, N.J. 626 p.

Adams, E. 1959. Poisons. Sci. Am. 201 (5): 76–84.

Adams, W. E. 1958. The comparative morphology of the carotid body and carotid sinus. Thomas, C. C. Springfield, Ill. 272 p.

Adolph, E. F. 1947. Physiology of man in the desert. Interscience, New York. 357 p.

Adolph, E. F. 1957. Ontogeny of physiological regulations in the rat. Quart. Rev. Biol. 32: 89–137.

Adolph, E. F. 1961. Early concepts of physiological regulations. Physiol. Rev. 41: 737–770.

Adrian, E. D., and F. J. J. Buytendijk. 1931. Potential changes in the isolated brain stem of the goldfish. J. Physiol. 71: 121–135.

Ahsan, S. N. 1964. The control of cyclical changes in the testicular activity of the lake chub *Couesius plumbeus* (Agassiz). Ph.D. thesis. Univ. British Columbia. 132 p.

Ali, M. A. 1959. The ocular structure, retinomotor and photobehavioral responses of juvenile Pacific salmon. Can. J. Zool. 37: 965–996.

Allee, W. C., *et al.* 1949. Principles of animal ecology. Saunders, Philadelphia. 837 p.

Allen, M. B. 1960*a*. Utilization of thermal energy by living organisms. *In* Florkin and Mason, 1: 487–514.

Allen, R. D. 1960*b*. The consistency of ameba cytoplasm and its bearing on the mechanism of ameboid movement. J. Biophys. Biochem. Cytol. 8: 379–397.

Allen, R. D. 1961. Ameboid movement. *In* Brachet and Mirsky, 2: 135–216.

Allen, R. D. 1962. Amoeboid movement. Sci. Am. 206 (2): 112–122.

Amoore, J. E., J. W. Johnston, Jr., and M. Rubin. 1964. A stereochemical theory of odor. Sci. Am. 210(2): 42–49.

Amoroso, E. C. 1952. Placentation. *In* A. S. Parkes (ed.), Marshall's physiology of reproduction. 2: 127–311.

Amoroso, E. C. 1960. Viviparity in fishes. Symp. Zool. Soc. London 1: 153–181.

Andersen, B., and H. H. Ussing. 1960. Active transport. *In* Florkin and Mason, 2: 371–402.

Andersen, H. T. 1961. Physiological adjustments to prolonged diving in the American alligator *Alligator mississippiensis*. Acta Physiol., Scand. 53: 23–45.

Andersen, P., J. K. S. Jansen, and Y. Lyning. 1963. Slow and fast muscle fibers in the Atlantic hagfish (*Myxine glutinosa*). Acta Physiol., Scand. 57: 167–179.

Andrew, W. 1959. Textbook of comparative histology. Oxford U.P., New York. 652 p.

Anfinsen, C. B. 1959. The molecular basis of evolution. Wiley, New York. 228 p.

Annison, E. F., and D. Lewis. 1959. Metabolism in the rumen. Methuen, London. 184 p.

Anthony, E. H. 1961. Survival of goldfish in presence of carbon monoxide. J. Exp. Biol. 38: 109–125.

Arnon, D. I. 1960. The role of light in photosynthesis. Sci. Am. 203 (5): 105–118.

Arnon, D. I. 1962. Photosynthetic phosphorylation and a unified concept of photosynthesis. Comp. Biochem. Physiol. 4: 253–279.

Aronson, L. R. 1951. Orientation and jumping behavior in the gobiid fish *Bathygobius soporator*. Am. Mus. Novitates 1486: 1–22.

Aschner, B. 1912. Über die Funktion der Hypophyse. Pflüger's Arch. 146: 1–146.

Aschoff, J. 1960. Exogenous and endogenous components in circadian rhythms. Cold Spring Harbor Symp. 25: 11–28.

Asdell, S. A. 1946. Patterns of mammalian reproduction. Comstock, Ithaca, N.Y. 437 p.

Astwood, E. B. 1941. The regulation of corpus luteum function by hypophysial luteotrophin. Endocrinology 28: 309–320.

Autrum, H. 1959. Nonphotic receptors in lower forms. Handbook of Physiology 1 (1): 369–385.

Baas-Becking, L. G. M. 1928. On organisms living in concentrated brine. Tijdschr. der Ned. Dierkundige Ver. Ser. 3, 1: 6–9.

Baerends, G. P. 1957. The ethological analysis of fish behavior. *In* M. E. Brown, 2: 229–269.

Baggerman, B. 1957. An experimental study on the timing of breeding and migration in the three-spined stickleback *Gasterosteus aculeatus* L. Arch. Néerl. Zool. 12: 105–317.

Bagnara, J. T. 1958. Hypophyseal control of guanophores in anuran larvae. J. Exp. Zool. 137: 265–283.

Bagnara, J. T. 1960. Pineal regulation of the body lightening reaction in amphibian larvae. Science 132: 1481–1483.

Bagnara, J. T. 1963. The pineal and the body lightening reaction of larval amphibians. Gen. Comp. Endocrinol. 3: 86–100.

Bahl, K. N. 1947. Excretion in the Oligochaeta. Biol. Rev. 22: 109–147.

Bailey, K. 1956. Muscle proteins. Brit. Med. Bull. 12: 183–187.

Bairati, A., and F. E. Lehmann. 1956. Structural and chemical properties of the contractile vacuole of *Amoeba proteus*. Protoplasma 45: 525–539.

Baldwin, E. 1963. Dynamic aspects of biochemistry. 4th ed. Cambridge U.P., London. 554 p.

Baldwin, E. 1964. An introduction to comparative biochemistry. 4th ed. Cambridge U.P., London. 179 p.

Balinsky, J. B., M. M. Cragg, and E. Baldwin. 1961. The adaptation of amphibian waste nitrogen excretion to dehydration. Comp. Biochem. Physiol. 3: 236–244.

Bang, F. B. 1962. Serological aspects of immunity in invertebrates. Nature 196: 88–89.

Baradi, A. F., and G. H. Bourne. 1953. Gustatory and olfactory epithelia. Int. Rev. Cytol. 2: 289–330.

Barber, S. B. 1961. Chemoreception and thermoreception. *In* Waterman, 2: 109–131.

Barcroft, J. 1914. The respiratory function of the blood. Cambridge U.P., London. 320 p.

Bard, P. (ed.) 1961. Medical physiology. 11th ed. Mosby, St. Louis, Mo. 1339 p.

Barnes, T. C. 1937. Textbook of general physiology. Blakiston, Philadelphia. 554 p.

Barnes, T. C. 1940. Experiments on *Ligia* in Bermuda. VII. Further effects of sodium, ammonium and magnesium. Biol. Bull. 78: 35–41.

Barnett, A. J. G., and R. L. Reid. 1961. Reactions in the rumen. E. Arnold & Co., London. 252 p.

Barr, L., and M. Alpern. 1963. Photosensitivity of the frog iris. J. Gen. Physiol. 46: 1249–1265.

Barrington, E. J. W. 1942. Blood sugar and the follicles of Langerhans in the ammocoete larva. J. Exp. Biol. 19: 45–55.

Barrington, E. J. W. 1959. Some endocrinological aspects of the protochordata.

Barrington, E. J. W. 1957. The alimentary canal and digestion. *In* M. E. Brown, 1: 109–161.

In Gorbman (1959): 250–265.

Barrington, E. J. W. 1961. Metamorphic processes in fishes and lampreys. Am. Zoologist 1: 97–106.

Barrington, E. J. W. 1962. Digestive enzymes. Adv. Comp. Physiol. Biochem. 1: 1–65.

Barrington, E. J. W. 1963. An introduction to general and comparative endocrinology. Clarendon Press, Oxford. 387 p.

Barry, J. M. 1964. Molecular biology: Genes and the chemical control of living cells. Prentice-Hall, Englewood Cliffs, N.J. 139 p.

Bartholomew, G. A., and V. A. Tucker. 1963. Control of changes in body temperature, metabolism, and circulation by the agamid lizard, *Amphibolurus barbatus*. Physiol. Zool. 36: 199–218.

Bass, A. D. 1959. Evolution of nervous control from primitive organisms to man. A. A. A. S. Pub. 52, Washington, D.C. 231 p.

Basu, S. P. 1959. Active respiration of fish in relation to ambient concentrations of oxygen and carbon dioxide. J. Fish. Res. Bd. Canada 16: 175–212.

Battle, H. I. 1926. Effects of extreme temperatures on muscle and nerve tissue in marine fishes. Trans. Roy. Soc. Canada 20: 127–143.

Battle, H. I. 1929. A note on lethal temperature in connection with skate reflexes. Contrib. Can. Biol. and Fisheries, N. S. 4: 497–500.

Bayliss, L. E. 1960. Principles of general physiology. Vol. 2. Longmans, Ltd., London. 848 p.

Bayliss, W. M. 1920. Principles of general physiology. 3rd ed. Longmans, Ltd., London. 862 p.

Bayliss, W. M., and E. H. Starling. 1902. The mechanism of pancreatic secretion. J. Physiol. 28: 325–353.

Bayliss, W. M., and E. H. Starling. 1903. On the uniformity of the pancreatic mechanism in vertebrata. J. Physiol. 29: 174–180.

Beadle, G. W. 1948. The genes of men and molds. Sci. Am. 179 (3): 30–39.

Beadle, G. W., and E. L. Tatum. 1941. Genetic control of biochemical reactions in *Neurospora*. Proc. Nat. Acad. Sci. 27: 499–506.

Beadle, L. C. 1931. The effect of salinity changes on the water content and respiration of marine invertebrates. J. Exp. Biol. 8: 211–227.

Beadle, L. C. 1957. Osmotic and ionic regulation in aquatic animals. Ann. Rev. Physiol. 19: 329–358.

Beament, J. W. L. 1964. The active transport and passive movement of water in insects. Adv. Insect Physiol. 2: 67–129.

Beamish, F. W. H. 1964. Respiration of fishes with special emphasis on standard oxygen consumption. Can. J. Zool. 42: 161–175, 177–188, 189–194, 355–366.

Beams, H. W., and R. K. Meyer. 1931. The formation of pigeon 'milk.' Physiol. Zool. 4: 486–500.

Beck, S. D. 1960. Insects and the length of the day. Sci. Am. 202 (2): 109–118.

Beck, S. D. 1963. Animal photoperiodism. Holt, Rinehart & Winston, New York. 124 p.

Beermann, W., and U. Clever. 1964. Chromosome puffs. Sci. Am. 210 (4): 50–58.

Békésy, G. von. 1956. Current status of theories of hearing. Science 123: 779–783.

Békésy, G. von. 1957. The ear. Sci. Am. 197 (2): 66–78.

Bělehrádek, J. 1930. Temperature coefficients in biology. Biol. Rev. 5: 30–58.

Benedict, F. G. 1938. Vital energetics. Carnegie Inst., Washington, D.C. 215 p.

Benedict, F. G., and R. C. Lee. 1937. Lipogenesis in the animal body, with special reference to the physiology of the goose. Carnegie Inst., Wash. Publ. No. 489: 1–232.

Bennett, T. P., and E. Frieden. 1962. Metamorphosis and biochemical adaptation in amphibia. *In* Florkin and Mason, 4: 483–556.

Benoit, J. 1962. Hypothalamo-hypophyseal control of the sexual activity in birds. Gen. Comp. Endocrinol. Supp. 1: 254–274.

Bentley, P. J. 1963. Neurohypophysial function in amphibians, reptiles and birds. Symp. Zool. Soc. London 9: 141–152.

Bentley, P. J., and B. K. Follett. 1963. Kidney function in a primitive vertebrate, the cyclostome *Lampetra fluviatilis*. J. Physiol. 169: 902–918.

Bentley, P. J., and H. Heller. 1964. The action of neurohypophysial hormones on the water and sodium metabolism of urodele amphibians. J. Physiol. 171: 434–453.

Bernard, C. 1957. An introduction to the study of experimental medicine. (Trans. H. C. Greene) Dover, New York. 226 p.

Bernfeld, P. 1962. Polysaccharidases. *In* Florkin and Mason, 3: 355–425.

Bernstein, J. 1902. Untersuchungen zur Thermodynamik der bioelektrischen Ströme. I. Pflüger's Arch. 92: 521–562.

Berrill, N. J. 1929. Digestion in ascidians and the influence of temperature. J. Exp. Biol. 6: 275–292.

Bert, P. 1943. Barometric pressure. (La pression barometrique, 1878.) (Trans. M. A. Hitchcock) College Book Co., Columbus, Ohio. 1055 p.

Best, C. H. 1959. A Canadian trail of medical research. J. Endocrinol. 19: i-xvii.

Best, C. H., and N. B. Taylor. 1961. The physiological basis of medical practice. 7th ed. Williams & Wilkins, Baltimore. 1554 p.

Bickoff, E. M. 1963. Estrogen-like substances in plants. Proc. 22nd Ann. Biol. Colloq., Oregon State Univ. (Corvallis) 1961: 93–118.

Bijtel, J. H. 1949. The structure and the mechanism of movement of the gill-filaments in Teleostei. Arch. Néerl. Zool. 8: 267–288.

Bishai, H. M. 1960. The effect of gas content of water on larval and young fish. Z. Wiss. Zool. 163: 37–64.

Bishop, B. C. 1962. Wintering on the roof of the world. Nat. Geogr. 122: 503–547.

Black, E. C. 1940. The transport of oxygen by the blood of fresh-water fish. Biol. Bull. 79: 215–229.

Black, E. C. 1951. Respiration in fishes. Univ. Toronto Stud. Biol. Ser. (Publ. Ont. Fish. Res. Lab.) 71 (59): 91–111.

Black, E. C., F. E. J. Fry, and V. S. Black. 1954. The influence of carbon dioxide on the utilization of oxygen by some fresh-water fish. Can. J. Zool. 32: 408–420.

Black, E. C., A. C. Robertson, and R. R. Parker. 1961. Some aspects of carbohydrate metabolism in fish. *In* Martin (1961): 89–124.

Black, V. S. 1957. Excretion and osmoregulation. *In* M. E. Brown, 1: 163–205.

Blaxter, J. H. S., and F. G. T. Holliday. 1963. The behaviour and physiology of herring and other clupeids. Adv. Marine Biol. 1: 261–393.

Blažka, P. 1958. The anaerobic metabolism of fish. Physiol. Zool. 31: 117–128.

Bles, E. J. 1929. Arcella. A study in cell physiology. Quart. J. Microscop. Sci. 72: 527–648.

Bliss, C. I. 1952. The statistics of bioassay. Academic Press, New York. 628 p.

Blum, H. F. 1945. The physiological effects of sunlight on man. Physiol. Rev. 25: 483–530.

Blum. H. F. 1955. Sunburn. *In* A. Hollaender (ed.), Radiation biology 2: 487–528. McGraw, New York.

Blum, H. F. 1961. Does the melanin pigment of human skin have adaptive value? Quart. Rev. Biol. 36: 50–63.

Boettiger, E. G. 1957. The machinery of insect flight. *In* Scheer (1957): 117–142.

Boettiger, E. G. 1961. Cellular processes in transmission and reception. Bull. Inst. Cellular Biol., Univ. Connecticut (mimeogr.) 3(7): 1–8.

Bohr, C. 1909. Blutgase und respiratorische Gaswechsel. Nagel's Handbuch der Physiol. 1: 54–222.

Bonhag, P. F. 1958. Ovarian structure and vitellogenesis in insects. Ann. Rev. Entomol. 3: 137–160.

Bonner, J. T. 1958. The evolution of development. Cambridge U.P., London. 103 p.

Boolootian, R. A., and A. C. Giese. 1959. Clotting of echinoderm coelomic fluid. J. Exp. Zool. 140: 207–229.

Boone, E., and L. G. M. Baas-Becking. 1931. Salt effects on eggs and nauplii of *Artemia salina*. L. J. Gen. Physiol. 14: 753–763.

Bourne, G. H. (ed.) 1960. The structure and function of muscle. Vols. 1–3. Academic Press. New York.

Boycott, B. B., and J. Z. Young. 1950. The comparative study of learning. Symp. Soc. Exp. Biol. 4: 432–453.

Boyd, W. C. 1950. Genetics and the races of man. Little, Boston. 453 p.

Boyden, A. 1942. Systematic serology: a critical appreciation. Physiol. Zool. 15: 109–145.

Boyden, A. 1963. Precipitin testing and classification. Systematic Zool. 12: 1–7.

Boyer, S. H. 1963. Papers on human genetics. Prentice-Hall, Englewood Cliffs, N. J. 305 p.

Brachet, J., and A. E. Mirsky. 1961. The cell. Vols. I–V. Academic Press, New York.

Bradfield, J. R. G. 1955. Fibre patterns in animal flagella and cilia. Symp. Soc. Exp. Biol. 9: 306–334.

Brand, T. von. 1946. Anaerobiosis in invertebrates. Biodynamica, Normandy, Missouri. 328 p.

Brett, J. R. 1956. Some principles in the thermal requirements of fishes. Quart. Rev. Biol. 31: 75–87.

Brett, J. R. 1957. The sense organs: the eye. *In* M. E. Brown, 2: 121–154.

Brett, J. R. 1958. Implications and assessments of environmental stress. *In* P. A. Larkin [ed.], The investigation of fish-power problems. pp. 69–83. H. R. MacMillan Lectures in Fisheries. Univ. British Columbia, Vancouver.

Brett, J. R. 1962. Some considerations in the study of respiratory metabolism in fish, particularly salmon. J. Fish. Res. Bd. Canada 19: 1025--1038.

Brett, J. R. 1963. The energy required for swimming by young sockeye salmon with a comparison of the drag force on a dead fish. Trans. Roy. Soc. Canada IV, 1: 441–457.

Brewer, C. V. 1961. The organization of the central nervous system. Heinemann, London. 166 p.

Brodal, A., and R. Fänge. 1963. The biology of *Myxine*. Universitetsforlaget, Oslo, Norway. 588 p.

Brody, S. 1945. Bioenergetics and growth. Reinhold, New York. 1023 p.

Brown, F. A. 1957*a*. The rhythmic nature of life. *In* Scheer (1957): 287–304.

Brown, F., and W. D. Stein. 1960. Balance of water, electrolytes, and nonelectrolytes. *In* Florkin and Mason, 2: 403–470.

Brown, M. E. (ed.) 1957*b*. The physiology of fishes. Vols. 1 & 2. Academic Press, New York.

Brown, P. K., and G. Wald. 1964. Visual pigments in single rods and cones of the human retina. Science 144: 45–52.

Bruce, V. G. 1960. Environmental entrainment of circadian rhythms. Cold Spring Harbor Symp. 25: 29–48.

Buck, J. B. 1948. The anatomy and physiology of the light organ in fireflies. Ann. N.Y. Acad. Sci. 49: 397–482.

Buckley, E. E., and N. Porges. 1956. Venoms. Amer. Assoc. Adv. Sci., 44, Washington, D.C. 467 p.

Buddenbrock, W. von. 1952. Vergleichende Physiologie. Birkhäuser, Basel. I. Sinnesphysiologie. 504 p.

Buddenbrock, W. von, and E. Moller-Racke. 1953. Über den Lichtsinn von *Pecten*. Pubbl. Staz. Zool. (Napoli) 24: 217–245.

Bueding, E. 1962. Comparative biochemistry of parasitic helminths. Comp. Biochem. Physiol. 4: 343–351.

Bull, H. O. 1957. Behavior: conditioned responses. *In* M. E. Brown, 2: 211–228.

Bullock, T. H. 1943. Neuromuscular facilitation in Scyphomedusae. J. Cell. Comp. Physiol. 22: 251–272.

Bullock, T. H. 1952. The invertebrate neuron junction. Symp Quant. Biol. 17: 267–273.

Bullock, T. H. 1957. Neuronal integrative mechanisms. *In* Scheer (1957): 1–20.

Bullock, T. H. 1958. Evolution of neurophysiological mechanisms. *In* Behavior and Evolution (A. Roe and G. G. Simpson, eds.). pp. 165–177.

Bullock, T. H. 1959*a*. Initiation of nerve impulses in receptor and central neurons. *In* Oncley (1959): 504–514.

Bullock, T. H. 1959*b*. Neuron doctrine and electrophysiology. Science 129: 997–1002.

Bullock, T. H. 1961. The origins of patterned nervous discharge. Behavior 17: 48–59.

Bullock, T. H., and F. P. J. Diecke. 1956. Properties of an infra-red receptor. J. Physiol. 134: 47–87.

Bullock, T. H., and W. Fox. 1957. The anatomy of the infra-red sense organ in the facial pit of the pit vipers. Quart. J. Microscop. Sci. 98: 219–234.

Bünning, E. 1964. The physiological clock. Academic Press, New York. 145 p.

Burger, J. W. 1962. Further studies on the function of the rectal gland in the spiny dogfish. Physiol. Zool. 35: 205–217.

Burkhardt, D. 1962. Spectral sensitivity and other response characteristics of single visual cells in the arthropod eye. Symp. Soc. Exp. Biol. 16: 86–109.

Burn, J. H., D. J. Finney, and L. G. Goodwin. 1950. Biological standardization. 2nd ed. Oxford,London. 440 p.

Burnet, M. 1959. The clonal selection theory of acquired immunity. Vanderbilt U. P., Nashville. Tenn. 208 p.

Burton, A. C., and O. G. Edholm. 1955. Man in a cold environment. E. Arnold & Co., London. 273 p.

Burtt, E. T., and W. T. Catton. 1962. Resolving power of the compound eye. Symp. Soc. Exp. Biol. 16: 72–85.

Butler, W. L., and R. J. Downes. 1960. Light and plant development. Sci. Am. 203 (6): 56–63.

Buxton, P. A. 1923. Animal life in deserts. E. Arnold & Co, London. 176 p.

Cain, A. J. 1954. Animal species and their evolution. Hutchinson's University Library, London. 190 p.

Callan, H. G., and L. Lloyd. 1960. Lampbrush chromosomes of crested newts *Triturus cristatus* (Laurenti). Phil. Trans. Roy. Soc. London B, 243: 135–219.

Calvin, M. 1962. Evolution of photosynthetic mechanisms. Perspectives in Biol. and Med. 5: 147–172.

Candy, D. J., and B. A. Kilby. 1961. The biosynthesis of trehalose in the locust fat body. Biochem. J. 78: 531–536.

Cannon, W. B. 1929. Organization for physiological homeostasis. Physiol. Rev. 9: 399–431.

Cannon, W. B. 1939. The wisdom of the body. Norton, New York. 312 p.

Carlisle, D. B., and F. Knowles. 1959. Endocrine control in crustaceans. Cambridge U.P., London. 120 p.

Carlson, I. H., and W. N. Holmes. 1962. Changes in the hormone content of the hypothalamo-hypophysial system of the rainbow trout (*Salmo gairdneri*). J. Endocrinol. 24: 23–32

Carter, G. S. 1931. Aquatic and aerial respiration in animals. Biol. Rev. 6: 1–35.

Carter, G. S. 1957. Air breathing. *In* M. E. Brown, 1: 65–79.

Carter, G. S. 1961. A general zoology of the invertebrates. 4th ed. Sidgwick and Jackson, London. 421 p.

Carthy, J. D. 1958. An introduction to the behaviour of invertebrates. G. Allen, London. 380 p.

Cattell, McK. 1936. The physiological effects of pressure. Biol. Rev. 11: 441–476.

Causey, G. 1960. The cell of Schwann. E. & S. Livingstone Ltd., Edinburgh and London. 120 p.

Chagas, C., and A. Paes de Carvalho (eds.) 1961. Bioelectrogenesis. Elsevier, Amsterdam. 413 p.

Chapman, D. M., C. F. A. Pantin, and E. A. Robson. 1962. Muscle in coelenterates. Rev. Can. Biol. 21: 267–278.

Chapman, G. 1958. The hydrostatic skeleton in the invertebrates. Biol. Rev. 33: 338–371.

Chefurka, W. 1958*a*. Oxidative metabolism of carbohydrates in insects. Can. J. Biochem. Physiol. 36: 83–102.

Chefurka, W. 1958*b*. On the importance of a-glycerophosphate dehydrogenase in glycolysing insect muscle. Biochem. Biophys. Acta 28: 660–661.

Chester Jones, I. 1957. The adrenal cortex. Cambridge U.P., London. 316 p.

Chester Jones, I., and J. G. Phillips. 1960 Adrenocorticosteroids in fish. Symp. Zool. Soc. London 1: 17–32.

Chester Jones, I., J. G. Phillips, and D. Bellamy. 1962. Studies on water and electrolytes in cyclostomes and teleosts. Gen. Comp. Endocrinol. Supp. 1: 36–47.

Chew, R. M. 1961. Water metabolism of desert-inhabiting vertebrates. Biol. Rev. 36: 1–31.

Chuang, S. H. 1963. Digestive enzymes of the echiuroid, *Ochetostoma erythrogrammon*. Biol. Bull. 125: 464–469.

Clark, A. M., and V. J. Cristofalo. 1961. Some effects of oxygen on the insects *Anagasta kuehniella* and *Tenebrio molitor*. Physiol. Zool. 34: 55–61.

Clark, E. 1959. Functional hermaphroditism and self-fertilization in a Serranid fish. Science 129: 215–216.

Clark, R. B., and R. F. G. Ruston. 1963. Time of release and action of a hormone influencing regeneration in the polychaete *Nereis diversicolor*. Gen. Comp. Endocrinol. 3: 542–553.

Clark, R. B., and U. Scully. 1964. Hormonal control of growth in *Nereis diversicolor*. Gen. Comp. Endocrinol. 4: 82–90.

Clarke, F. W. 1924. The data of geochemistry. 5th ed. U.S. Geol. Survey Bull. 770: 1–841.

Clegg, J. S., and D. R. Evans. 1961. The physiology of blood trehalose and its function during flight in the blowfly. J. Exp. Biol. 38: 771–792.

Clements, A. N. 1963. The physiology of mosquitoes. Pergamon, Oxford. 393 p.

Cohen, A. I. 1963. Vertebrate retinal cells and their organization. Biol. Rev. 38: 427–459.

Cohen, M. J., and S. Dijkgraaf. 1961. Mechanoreception. *In* Waterman, 2: 65–108.

Cohen, P. P., and G. W. Brown, Jr. 1960. Ammonia metabolism and urea biosynthesis. *In* Florkin and Mason, 2: 161–244.

Collip, J. B. 1925. The extraction of a parathyroid hormone which will prevent or control parathyroid tetany and which regulates the level of blood calcium. J. Biol. Chem. 63: 395–438.

Copeland, D. E. 1951. Function of glandular pseudobranch of teleosts. Am. J. Physiol. 167: 775.

Copp, D. H. 1964. Parathyroids, calcitonin and control of calcium.Recent. Prog. Hormone Res. 20: 59–88.

Couteaux, R. 1960. Motor end-plate structure. *In* Bourne, 1: 337–380.

Cowdry, E. V. 1950. A textbook of histology. 4th ed. Lea & F., Philadelphia. 640 p.

Cowie, A. T., and S. J. Folley. 1961. The mammary gland and lactation. *In* Young, 1: 590–642.

Cowles, R. B. 1958. Possible origin of dermal temperature regulation. Evolution 12: 347–357.

Cowles, R. B. 1959. Some ecological factors bearing on the origin and evolution of pigment in the human skin. Am. Naturalist 93: 283–293.

Crabbé, J. 1961. Stimulation of active sodium transport across the isolated toad bladder after injection of aldosterone to the animal. Endocrinology 69: 673–682.

Craig. R. 1960. The physiology of excretion in the insect. Ann. Rev. Entomol. 5: 53–68.

Crane, R. K. 1960. Intestinal absorption of sugars. Physiol. Rev. 40: 789–825.

Crescitelli, F., and H. J. A. Dartnall. 1953. Human visual purple. Nature 172: 195–197.

Creutzberg, F. 1961. On the orientation of migrating elvers (*Anguilla anguilla* Turt.) in a tidal area. Netherl. J. Sea Res. 1: 257–338.

Crick, F. H. C. 1962. The genetic code. Sci. Am. 207 (4): 66–74.

Croghan, P. C. 1958*a*. The osmotic and ionic regulation of *Artemia salina* (L.). J. Exp. Biol. 35: 219–233.

Croghan, P. C. 1958*b*. The mechanism of osmotic regulation in *Artemia salina* (L.). J. Exp. Biol. 35: 234–242 and 243–249.

Croghan, P. C. 1958*c*. Ionic fluxes in *Artemia salina* (L.). J. Exp. Biol. 35: 425–436.

Crozier, W. J. 1924–25. On biological oxidations as function of temperature. J. Gen. Physiol. 7: 189–216 and 571–579.

Csapo, A. 1960. Molecular structure and function of smooth muscle. *In* Bourne, 1: 229–264.

Cushing, J. Z., (Chmn.) 1962. Symposium on immunogenetic concepts in marine population research. Am. Naturalist 96: 193–246.

Dahlgren, U., and W. A. Kepner. 1928. A textbook of the principles of animal histology. Macmillan, New York. 515 p.

D'Ancona, U. 1949. Ermafroditismo ed intersessualità nei Teleostei. Experientia 5: 381–389.

Danowski, T. S. 1962. Clinical endocrinology. Vol. 4. Williams and Wilkins Co., Baltimore. 494 p.

Dartnall, H. J. A. 1957. The visual pigments. Methuen, London. 216 p.

Dartnall, H. J. A., and K. Tansley. 1963. Physiology of vision: retinal structure and visual pigments. Ann. Rev. Physiol. 25: 433–458.

Davenport, H. W. 1958. The ABC of acid-base chemistry. 4th ed. U. of Chicago, Chicago. 86 p.

Davies, F., and E. T. B. Francis. 1946. The conducting system of the vertebrate heart. Biol. Rev. 21: 173–188.

Davies, F. 1930. The conducting system of the bird's heart. J. Anat. 64: 129–146.

Davies, J. T. 1962. The mechanism of olfaction. Symp. Soc. Exp. Biol. 16: 170–179.

Davis, B. C. 1961*a*. The teleonomic significance of biosynthetic control mechanisms. Cold Spring Harbor Symp. 26: 1–10.

Davis, D. D. 1961*b*. Origin of the mammalian feeding mechanism. Am. Zoologist 1: 229–234.

Davson, H. 1959. A textbook of general physiology. 2nd ed. Churchill, London. 846 p.

Dawson, A. B. 1951. Functional and degenerate or rudimentary glomeruli in the kidney of two species of Australian frog. Anat. Record 109: 417–429.

Dawson, W. R. 1962. Evolution of temperature regulation in birds. *In* Hannon and Viereck, 1: 45–71.

Dawson, W. R., and G. A. Bartholomew. 1956. Relation of oxygen consumption to body weight, temperature, and temperature acclimation in lizards, *Uta stansburiana* and *Sceloporus occidentalis*. Physiol. Zool. 29: 40–51.

De Beer, G. 1958. Embryos and ancestors. 3rd ed. Clarendon Press, Oxford. 197 p.

De Bruyn, P. P. H. 1947. Theories of amoeboid movement. Quart. Rev. Biol. 22: 1–24.

Dehnel, P. A. 1960. Effect of temperature and salinity on the oxygen consumption of two intertidal crabs. Biol. Bull. 118: 215–249.

Dehnel, P. A., and T. H. Carefoot. 1965. Ion regulation in two species of intertidal crabs. Comp. Biochem. Physiol. 15: 377–397.

Denison, R. H. 1956. A review of the habitat of the earliest vertebrates. Fieldiana: Geol. (Chicago Nat. Hist. Mus.) 11: 359–457.

Denton, E. J. 1961. The bouyancy of fish and cephalopods. Progr. Biophys. 11: 177–234.

Denton, E. J. 1963. Buoyancy mechanisms of sea creatures. Endeavour 22: 3–8.

Denton, E. J., and J. B. Gilpin-Brown. 1961. The effect of light on the buoyancy of the cuttlefish. J. Marine Biol. Assoc. U. K. 41: 343–350.

Denton, E. J., and N. B. Marshall. 1958. The buoyancy of bathypelagic fishes without a gas-filled swimbladder. J. Marine Biol. Assoc. U.K. 37: 753–767.

Denton, E. J., and J. A. C. Nicol. 1964. The chorioidal tapeta of some cartilaginous fishes (Chondrichthyes). J. Marine Biol. Assoc. U.K. 44: 219–258.

Depocas, F. 1961. Biochemical changes in exposure and acclimation to cold environments. Brit. Med. Bull. 17: 25–31.

De Robertis, E. D. P., W. W. Nowinski, and F. A. Saez. 1960. General cytology. 3rd ed. Saunders, Philadelphia. 555 p.

Dethier, V. G. 1955. The physiology and the histology of the contact chemoreceptors of the blowfly. Quart. Rev. Biol. 30: 348–371.

Dethier, V. G. 1956. Chemoreceptor mechanisms. *In* Grenell and Mullins (1956): 1–33.

Dethier, V. G. 1962. Chemoreceptor mechanisms in insects. Symp. Soc. Exp. Biol. 16: 180–196.

Dethier, V. G. 1963. The physiology of insect senses. Methuen, London. 266 p.

Dethier, V. G., and E. Stellar. 1964. Animal Behavior. 2nd ed. Prentice-Hall, Englewood Cliffs, N.J. 118 p.

Detwiler, S. R. 1943. Vertebrate photoreceptors. Macmillan, New York. 184 p.

De Wilde, J. 1964. Reproduction. *In* Rockstein, 1: 9–90.

Diamond, J. M. 1964. The mechanism of isotonic water transport. J. Gen. Physiol. 48: 15–42.

Dickens, F. 1955. The toxic effect of oxygen on nervous tissue. *In* K. A. C. Elliott (ed.), Neurochemistry. Thomas, C. C., Springfield, Ill. 1035 p.

Dijkgraaf, S. 1963. The functioning and significance of the lateral-line organs. Biol. Rev. 38: 51–105.

Ditchburn, R. W. 1952. Light. Blackie, Glasgow. 680 p.

Dobzhansky, T. 1955. Evolution, genetics and man. Wiley, New York. 398 p.

Dobzhansky, T. 1962. Mankind evolving. Yale U.P., New Haven, Conn. 381 p.

Dodd, J. M. 1960. Gonadal and gonadotrophic hormones in lower vertebrates. *In* Parkes, 1 (2): 417–582.

Dodd, J. M., P. J. Evennett, and C. K. Goddard. 1960. Reproductive endocrinology in cyclostomes and elasmobranchs. Symp. Zool. Soc. London 1: 77–103.

Dodd, J. M., and T. Kerr. 1963. Comparative morphology and histology of the hypothalamo-neurohypophysial system. Symp. Zool. Soc. London 9: 5–27.

Doi, Y. 1920. Studies on muscular contraction. J. Physiol. 54: 218–226.

Doolittle, R. F., and D. M. Surgenor. 1962. Blood coagulation in fish. Am. J. Physiol. 203: 964–970.

Dorfman, R. I. 1959. Comparative biochemistry of adreno-cortical hormones. *In* Gorbman (1959): 613–623.

Dorsett, D. A. 1964. The sensory and motor innervation of *Nereis*. Proc. Roy. Soc. London B, 159: 652–667.

Doyle, W. L. 1962. Tubule cells of the rectal salt-gland of *Urolophus*. Am. J. Anat. 111: 223–238.

Drew, C. E. 1961. Profound hypothermia in cardiac surgery. Brit. Med. Bull. 17: 37–42.

Dreyer, N. B., and J. W. King. 1948. Anaphylaxis in the fish. J. Immunol. 60: 277–282.

Drummond, J. C., and A. Wilbraham. 1939. The Englishman's food. J. Cape, London. 574 p.

Drysdale, R. B., and A. R. Peacocke. 1961. The molecular basis of heredity. Biol. Rev. 36: 537–598.

Du Bois, E. F. 1937. Lane medical lectures: the mechanism of heat loss and temperature regulation. S.U.P., Stanford, Calif. 95 p.

Dubois, R. 1885. Fonction photogénique des pyrophores. C. R. Soc. Biol. (Paris) 37: 559–562.

Dubois, R. 1887. Note sur la fonction photogénique chez les Pholades. C. R. Soc. Biol. (Paris) 39: 564–566.

Duchâteau-Bosson, G., and M. Florkin. 1962. Adaptation à l'eau de mer de crabes Chinois (*Eriocheir sinensis*) présentant, dans l'eau douce, une valeur élevée de la composante aminoacide des muscles. Arch. Int. Physiol. Bioch. 70: 345–355.

Ducrocq, A. 1957. The origins of life. (Trans. A. Brown) Elek Books, London. 213 p.

Dugal, L.-P. 1939. The use of calcareous shell to buffer the product of anaerobic glycolysis in *Venus mercenaria*. J. Cellular Comp. Physiol. 13: 235–251.

Dukes, H. H. 1955. The physiology of domestic animals. 7th ed. Comstock, Ithaca, N.Y. 1020 p.

Durchon, M. 1962. Neurosecretion and hormonal control of reproduction in Annelida. Gen. Comp. Endocrinol. Supp. 1: 227–240.

Duve, C. de. 1963. The lysosome. Sci. Am. 208(5): 64–72.

Eccles, J. C. 1957. The physiology of nerve cells. Johns Hopkins, Baltimore. 270 p.

Eccles, J. C. 1965. The synapse. Sci. Am. 212(1): 56–66.

Edkins, J. S. 1906. The chemical mechanism of gastric secretion. J. Physiol. 34: 133–144.

Edney, E. B. 1954. Woodlice and the land habitat. Biol. Rev. 29: 185–219.

Edney, E. B. 1957. The water relations of terrestrial arthropods. Cambridge U. P., London. 109 p.

Edney, E. B. 1960. Terrestrial adaptations. *In* Waterman, 1: 367–388.

Edwards, J. G. 1928. Studies on aglomerular and glomerular kidneys. I. Anatomical. Am. J. Anat. 42: 75–108.

Edwards, J. G., and L. Condorelli. 1928. Studies on aglomerular and glomerular kidneys. II. Physiological. Am. J. Physiol. 86: 383–398.

Eisner, E. 1960. The relationship of hormones to the reproductive behaviour of birds. Behaviour 8: 155–179.

Elek, S. D., T. A. Rees, and N. F. C. Gowing. 1962. Studies on the immune response in a poikilothermic species (*Xenopus laevis*, Daudin). Comp. Biochem. Physiol. 7: 255–267.

Ellis, W. F. 1937. The water and electrolyte exchange of *Nereis diversicolor* (Müller). J. Exp. Biol. 14: 340–350.

Ells, H. A., and C. P. Read. 1961. Physiology of the vinegar eel, *Turbatrix aceti* (Nematoda) I. Observations on respiratory metabolism. Biol. Bull. 120: 326–336.

Emerson, R., and C. H. Lewis. 1942. The photosynthetic efficiency of phycocyanin in *Chroococcus*, and the problem of carotenoid participation in photosynthesis. J. Gen. Physiol. 25: 579–595.

Enami, M. 1959. The morphology and functional significance of the caudal neurosecretory system of fishes. *In* Gorbman (1959): 697–724.

Etkin, W. 1964. Metamorphosis. *In* Moore (1964): 427–468.

Euler, U. S. von, and H. Heller. 1963. Comparative endocrinology. Vols. 1 & 2. Academic Press, New York.

Evans, C. L. 1956. Principles of human physiology, 12th ed. Churchill, London. 1233 p.

Evennett, P. J., and J. M. Dodd. 1963. Endocrinology of reproduction in the river lamprey. Nature 197: 715–716.

Everett, J. W. 1961. The mammalian female reproductive cycle and its controlling mechanisms. *In* Young, 1: 497–555.

Fabricius, E. 1950. Heterogenous stimulus summation in the release of spawning activities in fish. Rept. Inst. Freshwater Res. Drottningholm 31: 57–99.

Fairbairn, D. 1957. The biochemistry of *Ascaris*. Exp. Parasitol. 6: 491–554.

Fänge, R. 1953. The mechanisms of gas transport in the euphysoclist swimbladder. Acta Physiol. (Scand.) 30 (110): 1–133.

Fänge, R., and K. Fugelli. 1962. Osmoregulation in Chimaeroid fishes. Nature 196: 689.

Fänge, R., A. G. Johnels, and P. S. Enger. 1963. The autonomic nervous system. *In* Brodal and Fänge (1963): 124–136.

Fantl, P. 1961. A comparative study of blood coagulation in vertebrates. Austral. J. Exp. Biol. 39: 403–412.

Farner, D. S. 1961. Comparative physiology: photoperiodicity. Ann. Rev. Physiol. 23: 71–96.

Fatt, P., and B. Katz. 1952. Spontaneous subthreshold activity at motor nerve endings. J. Physiol. 117: 109–128.

Fawcett, D. 1961. Cilia and flagella. *In* Brachet and Mirsky, 2: 217–297.

Fessard, A. 1961. La synchronisation des activités élémentaires dans les organes des poissons électriques. *In* Chagas and Paes de Carvalho (1961): 202–211.

Fiegl, E., and B. Folkow. 1963. Cardiovascular responses in "diving" and during brain stimulation in ducks. Act Physiol. (Scand.) 57: 90–110.

Fingerman, M. 1959. The physiology of chromatophores. Int. Rev. Cytol. 8: 175–210.

Fingerman, M. 1963. The control of chromatophores. Pergamon, London. 184 p.

Fisher, A. E. 1964. Chemical stimulation of the brain. Sci. Am. 210 (6): 60–68.

Fisher, K. C. 1958. An approach to the organ and cellular physiology of adaptation of temperature in fish and small mammals. *In* Prosser (1958): 3–49.

Fisher, K. C., and P. F. Elson. 1950. The selected temperature of Atlantic salmon and speckled trout and the effect of temperature on the response of an electrical stimulus. Physiol. Zool. 23: 27–34.

Flood, P. R., and J. S. Mathisen. 1962. A third type of muscle fibre in the parietal muscle of the Atlantic hagfish *Myxine glutinosa* (L.) Zeit. Zellforschung 58: 638–640.

Florey, E. 1962*a*. Neurohormones. The Physiologist 5: 285–292.

Florey, E. 1962*b*. Recent studies on synaptic transmitters. Am. Zoologist 2: 45–54.

Florey, E. 1963. Acetylcholine in invertebrate nervous systems. Can. J. Biochem. Physiol. 41: 2619–2626.

Florkin, M. 1934. La fonction respiratoire du "milieu intérieur" dans la série animale. Ann. Physiol. Physicochim. Biol. 10: 599–684.

Florkin, M. 1949. Biochemical evolution. Academic Press, New York. 157 p.

Florkin, M. 1952. Comparative biochemistry. Ann. Rev. Biochem. 21: 459–472.

Florkin, M. 1960. Blood chemistry. *In* Waterman, 1: 141–159.

Florkin, M., and H. S. Mason. 1960–64. Comparative biochemistry. Vols. 1–6. Academic Press, New York.

Forrest, H. S. 1962. Pteridines: structure and metabolism. *In* Florkin and Mason, 4: 615–641.

Forster, R. P. 1948. Use of thin kidney slices and isolated renal tubules for direct study of cellular transport kinetics. Science 108: 65–67.

Forster, R. P. 1961. Kidney cells. *In* Brachet and Mirsky, 5: 89–161.

Fox, D. L. 1953. Animal biochromes and structural colours. Cambridge U. P., London. 379 p.

Fox, H. M. 1948. Haemoglobin of *Daphnia*. Proc. Roy. Soc. London B, 135: 195–212.

Fox, H. M. 1955. The effect of oxygen on the concentration of haem in invertebrates. Proc. Roy. Soc. London B, 143: 203–214.

Fox, H. M., and E. A. Phear, 1953. Factors influencing haemoglobin synthesis by *Daphnia*. Proc. Roy. Soc. London B, 141: 179–189.

Fox, H. M., and G. Vevers. 1960. The nature of animal colours. Sidgwick and Jackson, London. 246 p.

Fox, S. W. 1960. How did life begin? Science 132: 200–208.

Foxon, G. E. H. 1955. Problems of the double circulation in vertebrates. Biol. Rev. 30: 196–228.

Foxon, G. E. H. 1964. Blood and respiration. *In* Moore (1964): 151–209.

Fraenkel, G. S., and D. L. Gunn. 1940. The orientation of animals. Clarendon Press, Oxford. 352 p.

Frieden, E. 1961. Biochemical adaptation and anuran metamorphosis. Am. Zoologist 1: 115–149.

Frieden, E. 1963. The chemistry of amphibian metamorphosis. Sci. Am. 209(5): 110–118.

Friedmann, H., and J. Kern. 1956. The problem of cerophagy or wax-eating in the honey-guides. Quart. Rev. Biol. 31: 19–30.

Frisch, K. von. 1911. Beiträge zur Physiologie der Pigmentzellen in der Fischhaut. Pflüger's Arch. Ges. Physiol. 138: 318–387.

Frisch, K. von. 1936. Über den Gehörsinn der Fische. Biol. Rev. 11: 210–246.

Frisch, K. von. 1950. Bees—their vision, chemical senses and language. Cornell U. P., Ithaca, N.Y. 119 p.

Frisch, K. von. 1962. Dialectics in the language of the bees. Sci. Am. 207 (2): 79–87.

Fromageot, C., and J. C. Senez. 1960. Aerobic and anaerobic reactions of inorganic substances. *In* Florkin and Mason, 1: 347–409.

Fruton, J. S., and S. Simmonds. 1958. General biochemistry. 2nd ed. Wiley, New York. 1077 p.

Fry, F. E. J. 1947. Effects of the environment on animal activity. Univ. Toronto Stud. Biol. 55 (Pub. Ontario Fish. Res. Lab.) 68: 1–62.

Fry, F. E. J. 1957. The aquatic respiration of fish. *In* M. E. Brown, 1: 1–63.

Fry, F. E. J. 1958. Temperature compensation. Ann. Rev. Physiol. 20: 207–224.

Fry, F. E. J., V. S. Black, and E. C. Black. 1947. Influence of temperature on the asphyxiation of young goldfish (*Carassius auratus* L.) under various tensions of oxygen and carbon dioxide. Biol. Bull. 92: 217–224.

Fulton, J. F. (ed.) 1955. A textbook of physiology. 17th ed. Saunders, Philadelphia. 1275 p.

Furshpan, E. J. 1959. Neuromuscular transmission in invertebrates. Handbook of Physiology 1(1): 239–254.

Gabe, M., P. Karlson, and J. Roche. 1964. Hormones in invertebrates. *In* Florkin and Mason, 6: 245–298.

Gabriel, M. L., and S. Fogel. 1955. Great experiments in biology. Prentice-Hall. Englewood Cliffs, N. J. 317 p.

Gaffron, H. 1960*a*. The origin of life. Perspectives in Biol. and Med. 3: 163–212.

Gaffron, H. 1960*b*. The origin of life. *In* S. Tax (ed.), Evolution after Darwin. Vol. 1. U. of Chicago, Chicago 629 p.

Galtsoff, P. S. 1938. Physiology of reproduction of *Ostrea virginica*. II. Stimulation of spawning in the female oyster. Biol. Bull. 75: 286–307.

Galtsoff, P. S. 1940. Physiology of reproduction of *Ostrea virginica*. III. Stimulation of spawning in the male oyster. Biol. Bull. 78: 117–135.

Galtsoff, P. S. 1961. Physiology of reproduction in molluscs. Am. Zoologist 1: 273–289.

Garstang, W. 1951. Larval forms with other zoological verses. Blackwell, Oxford. 76 p.

Gernandt, B. E. 1959. Vestibular mechanisms. Handbook of Physiology 1(1): 549–564.

Geschwind, I. I. 1959. Species variation in protein and polypeptide hormones. *In* Gorbman (1959): 421–443.

Giese, A. C. 1950. Action of ultraviolet radiation on protoplasm. Physiol. Rev. 30: 431–458.

Giese, A. C. 1962. Cell physiology. 2nd ed. Saunders, Philadelphia. 592 p.

Giese, A. C. (ed.) 1964. Photophysiology. Vol. 2: Academic Press, New York. 441 p.

Gilbert, L. I. 1963. Hormones controlling reproduction and molting in invertebrates. *In* von Euler and Heller, 2: 1–46.

Gilbert, L. I. 1964. Physiology of growth and development. *In* Rockstein, 1: 149–225.

Gilchrist, B. M. 1954. Haemoglobin in *Artemia*. Proc. Roy. Soc. London B, 143: 136–146.

Gilmour, D. 1961. The biochemistry of insects. Academic Press, New York. 343 p.

Goddard, C. K., P. J. Nicol, and J. F. Williams. 1964. The effect of albumen gland homogenate on the blood sugar of *Helix aspersa* Müller. Comp. Biochem. Physiol. 11: 351–366.

Goodrich, E. S. 1945. The study of nephridia and genital ducts since 1895. Quart. J. Microscop. Sci. 86: 113–392.

Goodwin, T. W. 1962. Carotenoids: structure, distribution and function. *In* Florkin and Mason, 4: 643–675.

Gorbman, A. (ed.) 1959. Comparative endocrinology. Wiley, New York. 746 p.

Gorbman, A. 1964. Endocrinology of the amphibia. *In* Moore (1964): 371–325.

Gorbman, A., and H. A. Bern. 1962. A textbook of comparative endocrinology. Wiley, New York. 468 p.

Gordon, M. (ed.) 1959. Pigment cell biology. Academic Press, New York. 647 p.

Gordon, M. S. 1962. Osmotic regulation in the green toad (*Bufo viridis*). J. Exp. Biol. 39: 261–270.

Gordon, M. S., K. Schmidt-Nielsen, and H. M. Kelly. 1961. Osmotic regulation in the crab-eating frog (*Rana cancrivora*). J. Exp. Biol. 38: 659–678.

Gosselin, R. E. 1961. The cilioexcitatory activity of serotonin. J. Cell. Comp. Physiol. 58: 17–26.

Gottschalk, C. W. 1960. Osmotic concentration and dilution in the mammalian nephron. Circulation 21: 861–868.

Gould, E., N. C. Negus, and A. Novick. 1964. Evidence for echolocation in shrews. J. Exp. Zool. 156: 19–38.

Granit, R. 1955. Receptors and sensory perception. Yale U. P., New Haven, Conn. 369 p.

Grant, W. C., Jr. 1961. Special aspects of the metamorphic process: second metamorphosis. Am. Zoologist 1: 163–171.

Gratzer, W. B., and A. C. Allison. 1960. Multiple haemoglobins. Biol. Rev. 35: 459–506.

Gray, I. E. 1957. A comparative study of the gill area of crabs. Biol. Bull. 112: 34–42.

Gray, J. 1928. Ciliary movement. Cambridge U.P., London. 162 p.

Gray, J. 1930. The mechanism of ciliary movement. VI. Photographic and stroboscopic analysis of ciliary movement. Proc. Roy. Soc. London B, 107: 313–332.

Green, D. E. 1962. Structure and function of subcellular particles. Comp. Biochem. Physiol. 4: 81–122.

Greene, C. W. 1926. The physiology of the spawning migration. Physiol. Rev. 6: 201–241.

Greenwood, P. H. 1963. A history of fishes (revision of J. R. Norman). Benn, London. 398 p.

Greep, R. O. 1963. Parathyroid glands. *In* von Euler and Heller, 1: 325–370.

Grégoire, C., and H. J. Tagnon. 1962. Blood coagulation. *In* Florkin and Mason, 4: 435–482.

Grenell, R. G., and L. J. Mullins. 1956. Molecular structure and functional activity of nerve cells. Am. Inst. Biol. Sci. Washington, D. C. 1: 1–169.

Griffin, D. R. 1958. Listening in the dark. Yale U. P., New Haven, Conn. 413 p.

Griffin, D. R. 1959. Echoes of bats and men. Anchor Books, Garden City, N.Y. 156 p.

Griffin, D. R. 1962. Comparative studies of the orientation sounds of bats. Symp. Zool. Soc. London 7: 61–72.

Gross, W. J. 1955. Aspects of osmotic regulation in crabs showing the terrestrial habit. Am. Naturalist 89: 205–222.

Gross, W. J. 1957*a*. An analysis of response to osmotic stress in selected decapod Crustacea. Biol. Bull. 112: 43–62.

Gross, W. J. 1957*b*. A behavioral mechanism for osmotic regulation in a semi-terrestrial crab. Biol. Bull. 113: 268–274.

Gross, W. J. 1961. Osmotic tolerance and regulation in crabs from a hypersaline lagoon. Biol. Bull. 121: 290–301.

Grossman, M. I. 1950. Gastrointestinal hormones. Physiol. Rev. 30: 33–90.

Grundfest, H. 1957. Electrical inexcitability of synapses and some consequences in the central nervous system. Physiol. Rev. 37: 337–361.

Grundfest, H. 1959*a*. Evolution of conduction in the nervous system. *In* Bass (1959): 43–86.

Grundfest, H. 1959*b*. Synaptic and ephaptic transmission. Handbook of Physiology 1 (1): 147–197.

Grundfest, H. 1960. Electric fishes. Sci. Am. 203 (4): 115–124.

Grundfest, H. 1961. Ionic mechanisms in electrogenesis. Ann. N.Y. Acad. Sci. 94: 405–457.

Grundfest, H., and M. V. L. Bennett, 1961. Electrophysiology of marine electric fishes. *In* Chagas and Paes de Carvalho (1961): 57–101.

Gudernatsch, J. F. 1912. Feeding experiments on tadpoles. Arch. Entwicklungsmech. Organ. 35: 457–483.

Gunter, G., L. L. Sulya, and B. E. Box. 1961. Some evolutionary patterns in fishes' blood. Biol. Bull. 121: 302–306.

Guyton, A. C. 1961. Textbook of medical physiology. 2nd ed. Saunders, Philadelphia. 1181 p.

Hagiwara, S., and K. Naka. 1964. The initiation of spike potential in barnacle muscle fibers under low intracellular Ca^{++}. J. Gen. Physiol. 48: 141–162 and 163–179.

Hagiwara, S., and I. Tasaki. 1958. A study on the mechanism of impulse transmission across the giant synapse of the squid. J. Physiol. 143: 114–137.

Hagiwara, S., and A. Watanabe. 1956. Discharges of motoneurons of cicada. J. Cell. Comp. Physiol. 47: 415–428.

Halberg, F., E. Halberg, C. P. Barnum, and J. J. Bittner. 1959. Physiologic 24-hour periodicity in human beings and mice, the lighting regimen and daily routine. *In* Withrow (1959) : 803–878.

Haldane, J. S. 1927. Respiration. Yale U.P., New Haven, Conn. 427 p.

Haldane, J. S., and J. G. Priestley. 1935. Respiration. Oxford U.P., London. 493 p.

Hall, F. G. 1929. The influence of varying oxygen tensions upon the rate of oxygen consumption in marine fishes. Am. J. Physiol. 88: 212–218.

Hall, R. P. 1953. Protozoology. Prentice-Hall, Englewood Cliffs, N. J. 682 p.

Ham, A. W., and T. S. Leeson. 1961. Histology. 4th ed. Lippincott, Philadelphia. 924 p.

Hamilton, J. A. R., and F. J. Andrew. 1954. An investigation of the effect of

Baker dam on downstream-migrant salmon. Bull. Int. Pacific Salmon Fish. Comm. 6: 1–73.

Hannon, J. P., and E. Viereck (eds.) 1962. Comparative physiology of temperature regulation. Arctic Aeromedical Laboratory, Fort Wainwright, Alaska. 455 p.

Hanson, J., and J. Lowy. 1960. Structure and function of the contractile apparatus in the muscles of invertebrate animals. *In* Bourne, 1: 265–335.

Hanyu, I., and M. A. Ali. 1963. Flicker fusion frequency of electroretinogram in light-adapted goldfish at various temperatures. Science 140: 662–663.

Hardy, J. D. 1961. Physiology of temperature regulation. Physiol. Rev. 41: 521–606.

Harper, H. A. 1963. Review of physiological chemistry. 9th ed. Lange Medical Pub., Los Altos, California. 437 p.

Harrington, R. W., Jr. 1963. Twenty-four-hour rhythms of internal self-fertilization and of oviposition by hermaphrodites of *Rivulus marmoratus*. Physiol. Zool. 36: 325–341.

Harrison, F. M. 1962. Some excretory processes in the abalone, *Haliotis rufescens*. J. Exp. Biol. 39: 179–192.

Harrison, L. H. 1961. Hibernation in mammals and birds. Brit. Med. Bull. 17: 9–13.

Hart, J. S. 1957. Climatic and temperature induced changes in the energetics of homeotherms. Rev. Can. Biol. 16: 133–174.

Hart, J. S., O. Heroux, W. H. Cottle, and C. A. Mills. 1961. The influence of climate on metabolic and thermal responses of infant caribou. Can. J. Zool. 39: 845–856.

Hartline, H. K. 1934. Intensity and duration in the excitation of single photoreceptor units. J. Cell. Comp. Physiol. 5: 229–247.

Hartline, H. K. 1959. Receptor mechanisms and the integration of sensory information in the eye. *In* Oncley (1959): 515–523.

Harvey, E. N. 1914. On the chemical nature of the luminous material of the firefly. Science 40: 33–34.

Harvey, E. N. 1952. Bioluminescence. Academic Press, New York. 649 p.

Harvey, E. N. 1960. Bioluminescence. *In* Florkin and Mason, 2: 545–591.

Harvey, H. H., and S. B. Smith. 1961. Supersaturation of the water supply and occurrence of gas bubble disease at Cultus Lake Trout Hatchery. Can. Fish Culturist 30: 39–47.

Hasler, A. D. 1957. Olfactory and gustatory senses of fishes. *In* M. E. Brown, 2: 187–209.

Haugaard, N., and L. Irving. 1943. The influence of temperature upon the oxygen consumption of the cunner (*Tautogolabrus adspersus* Walbaum). J. Cell. Comp. Physiol. 21: 19–26.

Hawk, P. B., B. L. Oser, and W. H. Summerson. 1954. Practical physiological chemistry. 13th ed. McGraw, New York. 1439 p.

Healey, E. G. 1951. The colour change of the minnow (*Phoxinus laevis* Ag.) J. Exp. Biol. 28: 298–319.

Healey, E. G. 1957. The nervous system. *In* M. E. Brown, 2: 1–119.

Hecht, S. 1937. Rods, cones, and the chemical basis of vision. Physiol. Rev. 17: 239–290.

Hecht, S., S. Shlaer, and M. H. Pirenne. 1942. Energy, quanta, and vision. J. Gen. Physiol. 25: 819–840.

Heidermanns, C. 1957. Grundzüge der Tierphysiologie. Gustav Fischer Verlag, Stuttgart. 427 p.

Heilbrunn, L. V. 1952. An outline of general physiology. 3rd ed. Saunders, Philadelphia. 818 p.

Heller, H. 1963. Neurohypophyseal hormones. *In* von Euler and Heller, 1: 25–80.

Heller, H., and R. B. Clark (eds.) 1962. Neurosecretion. Mem. Soc. Endocrinol. 12: 1–455.

Hemmingsen, A. M. 1950. The relation of standard (basal) energy metabolism to total fresh weight of living organisms. Rep. Steno. Hosp. Copenhagen 4: 1–58.

Hemmingsen, A. M. 1960. Energy metabolism as related to body size and respiratory surfaces, and its evolution. Rep. Steno. Hosp. Copenhagen 9 (pt. 2): 1–110.

Henderson, L. M., R. K. Gholson, and C. E. Dalgliesh. 1962. Metabolism of aromatic amino acids. *In* Florkin and Mason, 4: 245–342.

Henriques, V., and C. Hansen. 1901. Vergleichende Untersuchungen über die chemische Zusammensetzung des thierischen Fettes. Skand. Arch. Physiol. 11: 151–156.

Herter, K. 1947. Vergleichende Physiologie der Tiere. I. Stoff-und Energiewechsel. Gruyter, Berlin. 148 p.

Hess, A. 1963. Two kinds of extrafusal muscle fibers and their nerve endings in the garter snake. Am. J. Anat. 113: 347–364.

Heymans, C., and E. Neil. 1958. Reflexogenic areas of the cardiovascular system. Churchill, London. 271 p.

Hickman, C. P. 1959. The osmoregulatory role of the thyroid gland in the starry flounder, *Platichthys stellatus*. Can. J. Zool. 37: 997–1060.

Hill, A. V. 1938. The heat of shortening and the dynamic constants of muscle. Proc. Roy. Soc. London B, 126: 136–195.

Hill, R. 1936. The oxygen dissociation curves of muscle haemoglobin. Proc. Roy. Soc. London B, 120: 472–483.

Hill, R., and C. P. Whittingham. 1957. Photosynthesis. 2nd ed. Methuen, London. 175 p.

Hisaw, F. L. 1926. Experimental relaxation of the public ligament of the guinea pig. Proc. Soc. Exp. Biol. Med. 23: 661–663.

Hisaw, F. L. 1959. Endocrine adaptations of the mammalian estrous cycle and gestation. *In* Gorbman (1959): 533–552.

Hisaw, F. L. 1963*a*. The evolution of endocrine adaptations of the ovarian follicle. Proc. 22nd Ann. Biol. Colloq., Oregon State Univ. (Corvallis) 1961: 1–16.

Hisaw, F. L. 1963*b*. Endocrines and the evolution of viviparity among the vertebrates. Proc. 22nd Ann. Biol. Colloq., Oregon State Univ. (Corvallis) 1961: 119–138.

Hoagland, H. 1932. Impulses from sensory nerves of catfish. Proc. Nat. Acad. Sci. (U.S.) 18: 701–705.

Hoar, W. S. 1955*a*. Seasonal variations in the resistance of goldfish to temperature. Trans. Roy. Soc. Canada 49: 25–34.

Hoar, W. S. 1955*b*. Reproduction in teleost fish. Mem. Soc. Endocrinol. 4: 5–24.

Hoar, W. S. 1957. Endocrine organs. *Also* The gonads and reproduction. *In* M. E. Brown, 1: 245–285, 287–321.

Hoar, W. S. 1959. Endocrine factors in the ecological adaptation of fishes. *In* Gorbman (1959): 1–23.

Hoar, W. S. 1960. The environmental physiology of animals. 2nd ed. Scholar's Library, New York. 98 p.

Hoar, W. S. 1962. Hormones and the reproductive behaviour of the male three-spined stickleback, (*Gasterosteus aculeatus*). Animal Behaviour 10: 247–266.

Hoar, W. S. 1963. Hormones and reproductive behavior of the poikilothermous vertebrates. Proc. 22nd Ann. Biol. Colloq., Oregon State Univ. (Corvallis) 1961: 17–35.

Hoar, W. S. 1965*a*. Hormonal activities of the pars distalis in cyclostomes, fish and amphibians. *In* G. W. Harris and B. T. Donovan (eds.), The pituitary gland. Butterworth and Co., London.

Hoar, W. S. 1965*b*. Comparative physiology: hormones and reproduction in fishes. Ann. Rev. Physiol. 27: 51–70.

Hoar, W. S., and J. G. Eales. 1963. The thyroid gland and low-temperature resistance of goldfish. Can. J. Zool. 41: 653–669.

Hochachka, P. W., and F. R. Hayes. 1962. The effect of temperature acclimation on pathways of glucose metabolism in the trout. Can. J. Zool. 40: 261–270.

Hodge, A. J. 1959. Fibrous proteins of muscle. *In* Oncley (1959): 409–425.

Hodgkin, A. L. 1951. The ionic basis of electrical activity in nerve and muscle. Biol. Rev. 26: 339–409.

Hodgkin, A. L. 1964. The conduction of the nerve impulse. Liverpool U.P. 108 p.

Hodgson, E. S. 1955. Problems in invertebrate chemoreception. Quart. Rev. Biol. 30: 331–347.

Hodgson, E. S., and K. D. Roeder. 1956. Electrophysiological studies of arthropod chemoreception. J. Cellular Comp. Physiol. 48: 51–75.

Hoffmann-Berling, H. 1960. Other mechanisms producing movement. *In* Florkin and Mason, 2: 341–370.

Hogben, L. 1942. Chromatic Behaviour. Proc. Roy. Soc. London B, 131: 111–136.

Hogben, L., and D. Slome. 1931. The pigmentary effector system. VI. The dual character of endocrine co-ordination in amphibian colour change. Proc. Roy. Soc. London B, 108: 10–53.

Hogben, L. and D. Slome, 1936. The pigmentary effector system. VIII. The dual receptive mechanism of the amphibian background response. Proc. Roy. Soc. London B, 120: 158–173.

Hogness, D. S. 1959. Induced enzyme synthesis. *In* Oncley (1959): 256–268.

Hollaender, A. (ed.) 1954–56. Radiation biology. Vol. 3. McGraw, New York. 765 p.

Holmes, W. N., D. G. Butler, and J. G. Phillips. 1961. Observations on the effect of maintaining glaucous-winged gulls (*Larus glaucescens*) on fresh water and sea water for long periods. J. Endocrinol. 23: 53–61.

Holmes, W. N., and R. L. McBean. 1964. Some aspects of electrolyte excretion in the green turtle, *Chelonia mydas mydas*. J. Exp. Biol. 41: 81–90.

Holmes, W. N., J. G. Phillips, and I. Chester Jones. 1963. Adrenocortical factors associated with adaptation of vertebrates to marine environments. Recent Progr. Hormone Res. 19: 619–672.

Holst, E. von, and U. von Saint-Paul. 1962. Electrically controlled behavior. Sci. Am. 206 (3): 50–59.

Holter, H. 1961. How things get into cells. Sci. Am. 205 (3): 167–180.

Horecker, B. L. 1962. Alternative pathways of carbohydrate metabolism in relation to evolutionary development. Comp. Biochem. Physiol. 4: 363–369.

Horridge, G. A. 1954. Observations on the nerve fibres of *Aurellia aurita*. Quart. J. Microscop. Sci. 95: 85–92.

Horridge, G. A. 1956. The nerves and muscles of medusae. V. Double innervation in Scyphozoa. J. Exp. Biol. 33: 366–383.

Horridge, G. A. 1963. Integrative action of the nervous system. Ann. Rev. Physiol. 25: 523–544.

Horridge, G. A. 1964. Presumed photoreceptive cilia in a ctenophore. Quart. J. Microscop. Sci. 105: 311–317.

House, C. R. 1963. Osmotic regulation in the brackish water teleost, *Blennius pholis*. J. Exp. Biol. 40: 87–104.

Houssay, B. A. 1951. Human physiology. McGraw, New York. 1118 p.

Houssay, B. A. 1959. Comparative physiology of the endocrine pancreas. *In* Gorbman (1959): 639–667.

Hoyle, G. 1955. The anatomy and innervation of locust skeletal muscle. Proc. Roy. Soc. London B, 143: 281–292.

Hoyle, G. 1957. Comparative physiology of the nervous control of muscular contraction. Cambridge U.P., London. 147 p.

Hoyle, G. 1962. Neuromuscular physiology. Adv. Comp. Physiol. Biochem. 1: 177–216.

Hoyle, G., and T. Smyth. 1963. Neuromuscular physiology of giant muscle fibers of a barnacle, *Balanus nubilus* Darwin. Comp. Biochem. Physiol. 10: 291–314.

Huennekens, F. M., and H. R. Whiteley. 1960. Phosphoric acid anhydrides and other energy-rich compounds. *In* Florkin and Mason, 1: 107–180.

Huff, C. G. 1940. Immunity in invertebrates. Physiol. Rev. 20: 68–88.

Hughes, G. M. 1963. Comparative physiology of vertebrate respiration. Heinemann, London. 145 p.

Hughes, G. M., and G. Shelton. 1962. Respiratory mechanisms and their nervous control in fish. Adv. Comp. Physiol. Biochem. 1: 275–364.

Huntsman, A. G., and M. I. Sparks. 1924. Limiting factors for marine animals. 3. Relative resistance to high temperatures. Contr. Can. Biol. N. S. 2: 95–114.

Hutchinson, G. E. 1957. A treatise on limnology. Vol. 1. Wiley, New York. 1015 p.

Hutner, S. H., and A. Lwoff (eds.) 1955. Biochemistry and physiology of protozoa. Vol. 2. Academic Press, New York. 388 p.

Huxley, A. F. and R. Stämpfli. 1949. Evidence for saltatory conduction in peripheral myelinated nerve fibres. J. Physiol. 108: 315–339.

Huxley, H. E. 1958. The contraction of muscle. Sci. Am. 199 (5): 66–86.

Huxley, H. E. 1960. The structure of striated muscle. *In* Nachmansohn (1960): 1–16.

Huxley, H. E., and J. Hanson. 1960. The molecular basis of contraction in cross-striated muscle. *In* Bourne, 1: 183–227.

Huxley, J. S. 1932. Problems of relative growth. Methuen, London. 276 p.

Hyman, L. H. 1940–59. The invertebrates. Vols. 1–5. McGraw, New York.

Ichikawa, M. 1962. Brain and metamorphosis of Lepidoptera. Gen. Comp. Endocrinol. Supp. 1: 331–336.

Ihle, J. E., P. N. v. Kampen, *et al.* 1927. Vergleichende Anatomie der Wirbeltiere. Chap. 4. Springer. Berlin. 906 p.

Ingram, U. M. 1961. Gene evolution and the haemoglobins. Nature 189: 704–708.

Inoué, S. 1959. Motility of cilia and the mechanism of mitosis. *In* Oncley (1959): 402–408.

Irving, L. 1939. Respiration in diving mammals. Physiol. Rev. 19: 112–134.

Irving, L. 1956. Physiological insulation of swine as bare-skinned animals. J. Appl. Physiol. 9: 414–420.

Irving, L., and J. S. Hart. 1957. The metabolism and insulation of seals as bare-skinned mammals in cold water. Can. J. Zool. 35: 497–511.

Irving, L., K. Schmidt-Nielsen, and N. S. B. Abrahamsen. 1957. On the melting points of animal fats in cold climates. Physiol. Zool. 30: 93–105.

Irving, L., P. F. Scholander, and S. W. Grinnell. 1941. The respiration of the porpoise, *Tursiops truncatus*. J. Cell. Comp. Physiol. 17: 145–168.

Jacobs, M.H., H.N. Glassman, and A.K. Parpart. 1950. Hemolysis and zoological relationship. J. Exp. Zool. 113: 227–300.

Jacobs, W. 1954. Fliegen. Schwimmen. Schweben. Springer–Verlag, Berlin. 136 p.

Jacobson, M., and M. Beroza. 1964. Insect attractants. Sci. Am. 211 (2): 20–27.

Jahn, T. L., and R. A. Rinaldi. 1959. Protoplasmic movement in the foraminiferan, *Allogromia laticollaris;* and a theory of its mechanism. Biol. Bull. 117: 100–118.

Jander, R., K. Daumer, and T. H. Waterman. 1963. Polarized light orientation by two Hawaiian decapod cephalopods. Z. Vergl. Physiol. 46: 383–394.

Jenkin, P. M. 1962. Animal hormones. Pergamon, London. 310 p.

Jennings, H. S. 1923. The behavior of lower organisms. Columbia U. P., New York. 366 p.

Jennings, J. B. 1962. Further studies on feeding and digestion in triclad Turbellaria. Biol. Bull. 123: 571–581.

Jeuniaux, C. 1961. Chitinase: an addition to the list of hydrolases in the digestive tract of vertebrates. Nature 192: 131–136.

Jeuniaux, C., S. Bricteux-Grégoire, and M. Florkin. 1962. Régulation osmotique intracellulaire chez *Asterias rubens*. Rôle du glycocolle et de la taurine. Cahiers Biol. Marine 3: 107–113.

Jimenez-Porras, J. M. 1961. Biochemical studies on venom of the rattlesnake, *Crotalus atrox atrox*. J. Exp. Zool. 148: 251–258.

Johansen, K. 1960. Circulation in the hagfish, *Myxine glutinosa* L. Biol. Bull. 118: 289–295.

Johansen, K. 1962. Evolution of temperature regulation in mammals. *In* Hannon and Viereck, 1: 73–131.

Johansen, K. 1963. The cardiovascular system of *Myxine glutinosa* L. *In* Brodal and Fänge (1963): 289–316.

Johansen, K., and A. W. Martin. 1962. Circulation in the cephalopod, *Octopus dofleini*. Comp. Biochem. Physiol. 5: 161–176.

Johnels, A. G. 1956*a*. On the peripheral autonomic nervous system of the trunk region of *Lampetra planeri*. Acta Zool. 37: 251–286.

Johnels, A. G. 1956*b*. On the origin of the electric organs in *Malapterurus*. Quart. J. Microscop. Sci. 97: 455–464.

Johnson, F. H., H. Eyring, and M. J. Polissar. 1954. The kinetic basis of molecular biology. Wiley, New York. 874 p.

Johnson, F. H., E. H.-C. Sie, and Y. Haneda. 1961. The luciferin-luciferase reaction. *In* McElroy and Glass (1961): 206–218.

Jones, F. R. H., and N. B. Marshall. 1953. The structure and functions of the teleostean swimbladder. Biol. Rev. 28: 16–83.

Jørgensen, C. B., and L. O. Larsen. 1963. Neuro-hypophysial relationships. Symp. Zool. Soc. London 9: 59–82.

Jørgensen, C. B., and L. O. Larsen. 1964. Further observations on molting and its hormonal control in *Bufo bufo* (L.). Gen. Comp. Endocrinol. 4: 389–400.

Kahl, M. P. 1963. Thermoregulation in the wood stork, with special reference to the role of the legs. Physiol. Zool. 36: 141–151.

Kallman, K. D. 1962*a*. Gynogenesis in the teleost, *Mollienesia formosa* (Girard), with a discussion of the detection of parthenogenesis in vertebrates by tissue transplantation. J. Genetics 58: 7–24.

Kallman, K. D. 1962*b*. Population genetics of the gynogenetic teleost, *Mollienesia formosa* (Girard). Evolution 16: 497–504.

Kallman, K. D., and R. W. Harrington, Jr. 1964. Evidence for the existence of homozygous clones in the self-fertilizing hermaphroditic teleost *Rivulus marmoratus* (Poey). Biol. Bull. 126: 101–114.

Kamemoto, F. I. 1964. The influence of the brain on osmotic and ionic regulation in earthworms. Gen. Comp. Endocrinol. 4: 420–426.

Kanoh, Y. 1954. On the buoyancy of the eggs of Alaska pollack, *Theragra chalcogramma*. Jap. J. Ichthyol. 3: 238–246.

Kappers, C. U. A., G. C. Huber, and E. C. Crosby. 1936. The comparative anatomy of the nervous system of vertebrates including man. Vol. 2. Macmillan, New York. 1845 p.

Karlson, P. 1960. Pheromones. Ergeb. Biol. 22: 212–225.

Karlson, P. 1962. Chemistry and mode of action of insect hormones. Gen. Comp. Endocrinol. Supp. 1: 1–7.

Karlson, P. 1963. Introduction to modern biochemistry. Academic Press, New York. 433 p.

Karlson, P., and C. E. Sekeris. 1964. Biochemistry of insect metamorphosis. *In* Florkin and Mason, 6: 221–243.

Katz, B. 1950. Depolarization of sensory terminals and the initiation of impulses in the muscle spindle. J. Physiol. 111: 261–282.

Katz, B. 1959*a*. Nature of the nerve impulse. *In* Oncley (1959): 466–474.

Katz, B. 1959*b*. Mechanisms of synaptic transmission. *In* Oncley (1959): 524–531.

Katz, B. 1961. How cells communicate. Sci. Am. 205 (3): 209–220.

Kellogg. W. N. 1961. Porpoises and sonar. U. of Chicago, Chicago. 177 p.

Kendeigh, S. C. 1939. The relation of metabolism to the development of temperature regulation in birds. J. Exp. Zool. 82: 419–438.

Kerkut, G. A. 1958. The invertebrata. 3rd ed. of Borradaile, L. A. *et al.* Cambridge. U.P., London. 795 p.

Kettlewell, H. B. D. 1961. The phenomenon of industrial melanism in the Lepidoptera. Ann. Rev. Entomol. 6: 245–262.

Keynes, R. D. 1957. Electric organs. *In* M. E. Brown, 2: 323–343.

Keynes, R. D. 1958. The nerve impulse and the squid. Sci. Am. 199 (6): 83–90.

Keynes, R. D. 1961. The development of the electric organ in *Electrophorus electricus* (L.). *In* Chagas and Paes de Carvalho (1961): 14–19.

Keys, A. B. 1931. The heart-gill preparation of the eel and its perfusion for the study of a natural membrane *in situ*. Z. vergl. Physiol. 15: 352–388.

Kikuchi, G., J. Ramirez, and E. S. G. Barron. 1959. Electron transport system in *Ascaris lumbricoides*. Biochem. Biophys. Acta 36: 335–342.

King, J. R., and D. S. Farner. 1961. Energy metabolism, thermoregulation and body temperature. *In* Marshall, 2: 215–288.

Kinosita, H. 1963. Electrophoretic theory of pigment migration within fish melanophore. Ann. N. Y. Acad. Sci. 100: 992–1004.

Kitching, J. A. 1938. Contractile vacuoles. Biol. Rev. 13: 403–444.

Kitching, J. A. 1952. Contractile vacuoles. Symp. Soc. Exp. Biol. 6: 145–165.

Kitching, J. A. 1954. Osmoregulation and ionic regulation in animals without kidneys. Symp. Soc. Exp. Biol. 8: 63–75.

Kleiber, M. 1961. The fire of life. Wiley, New York. 454 p.

Kleinholz, L. H. 1961. Pigmentary effectors. *In* Waterman, 2: 133–169.

Knobil, E. 1961. The pituitary growth hormone: some physiological considerations. *In* M. X. Zarrow (ed.), Growth in living systems. pp. 353–381. Basic Books, New York. 759 p.

Knobil, E., and R. Sandler. 1963. The physiology of the adenohypophyseal hormones. *In* von Euler and Heller, 1: 447–491.

Knowles, F. G. W. 1963. The structure of neurosecretory systems in invertebrates. *In* von Euler and Heller, 2: 47–62.

Knox, W. E. 1951. Two mechanisms which increase *in vivo* the liver tryptophan peroxidase activity: specific enzyme adaptation and stimulation of the pituitary-adrenal system. Brit. J. Exp. Path. 32: 462–469.

Köhler, K., and C. B. Metz. 1960. Antigens of the sea urchin sperm surface. Biol. Bull. 118: 96–110.

Koller, G. 1929. Die innere Sekretion bei wirbellosen Tieren. Biol. Rev. 4: 269–306.

Konishi, J., and C. P. Hickman, Jr. 1964. Temperature acclimation in the central nervous system of the rainbow trout (*Salmo gairdnerii*). Comp. Biochem. Physiol. 13: 433–442.

Kopéc, S. 1922. Studies on the necessity of the brain for the inception of insect metamorphosis. Biol. Bull. 42: 323–342.

Korringa, P. 1957. Lunar periodicity. Mem. Geol. Soc. Am. 67 (1): 917–934.

Kosto, B., G. E. Pickford, and M. Foster. 1959. Further studies of the hormonal induction of melanogenesis in the killifish, *Fundulus heteroclitus*. Endocrinology 65: 860–881.

Krebs, H. A. 1935. Metabolism of amino-acids. III. Deamination of amino-acids. Biochem. J. 29: 1620–1644.

Krebs, H. A., and K. Henseleit. 1932. Untersuchungen über die Harnstoffbildung im Tierkörper. Z. Physiol. Chem. 210: 33–66.

Krebs, H. A., and H. L. Kornberg. 1957. Energy transformations in living matter. Ergeb. Physiol. 49: 212–298.

Krijgsman, B. J. 1952. Contractile and pacemaker mechanisms in the heart of arthropods. Biol. Rev. 27: 320–346.

Krijgsman, B. J. 1956. Contractile and pacemaker mechanisms of the heart of tunicates. Biol. Rev. 31: 288–312.

Krijgsman, B. J., and G. A. Divaris. 1955. Contractile and pacemaker mechanisms of the heart of molluscs. Biol. Rev. 30: 1–39.

Krijgsman, B. J., and N. E. Krijgsman. 1957. Some features of the physiology of the tunicate heart. *In* Scheer (1957): 277–286.

Krogh. A. 1914. The quantitative relation between temperature and standard metabolism in animals. Int. Z. physik.-chem. Biol. 1: 491–508.

Krogh, A. 1939. Osmotic regulation in aquatic animals. Cambridge U. P., London. 242 p.

Krogh, A. 1941. The comparative physiology of respiratory mechanisms. U. of Pa., Philadelphia. 172 p.

Kuffler, S. W. 1942. Electric potential changes at an isolated nerve-muscle junction. J. Neurophysiol. 5: 18–26.

Kuffler, S. W. 1958. Synaptic inhibitory mechanisms. Properties of dendrites and problems of excitation in isolated sensory nerve cells. Exp. Cell. Res. Suppl. 5: 493–519.

Kuhn, W., A. Ramel, H. J. Kuhn, and E. Marti. 1963. The filling mechanism of the swimbladder. Experientia 19: 497–511.

Kuhn, W., E. Marti, H. J. Kuhn, and P. Moser. 1964. Analogieversuch zur Füllung der Schwimmblase von Fischen. Pflügers Archiv. 280: 337–351.

Kuiper, J. W. 1962. The optics of the compound eye. Symp. Soc. Exp. Biol. 16: 58–71.

Kuntz, A. 1915. The histological basis of adaptive shades and colors in the flounder, *Paralichthys albiguttus*. Bull. U.S. Bur. Fish. 35: 1–30.

Lange, R. 1963. The osmotic functions of amino acids and taurine in the mussel, *Mytilus edulis*. Comp. Biochem. Physiol. 10: 173–179.

Langley, J. N. 1921. The autonomic nervous system. Heffer, Cambridge. 80 p.

Lanyon, W. E., and W. N. Tavolga. 1960. Animal sounds and communication. Am. Inst. Biol. Sci. Vol. 7, Washington, D.C. 443 p.

Larimer, J. L., and A. F. Riggs. 1964. Properties of hemocyanins – I. The effect of calcium ions on the oxygen equilibrium of crayfish hemocyanin. Comp. Biochem. Physiol. 13: 35–46.

Lashley, K. S. 1950. In search of the engram. Symp. Soc. Exp. Biol. 4: 454–482.

Laurens, H. 1933. The physiological effects of radiant energy. The Chemical Catalog Co., Inc., New York. 610 p.

Laverack, M. S. 1963. The physiology of earthworms. Pergamon, London. 206 p.

Lawler, S. D., and L. J. Lawler. 1957. Human blood groups and inheritance. 2nd ed. Heinemann, London. 103 p.

Lea, D. E. 1962. Actions of radiations on living cells. 2nd ed. Cambridge U. P., London. 416 p.

Leblond, C. P., and B. E. Walker. 1956. Renewal of cell populations. Physiol. Rev. 36: 255–276.

Lees, A. D. 1955. The physiology of diapause in insects. Cambridge U. P., London. 151 p.

Lees, A. D. 1960. Some aspects of animal photo-periodism. Cold Spring Harbor Symp. 25: 216–268.

Lees, A. D. 1964. The location of the photoperiodic receptors in the aphid *Megoura viciae* Buckton. J. Exp. Biol. 41: 119–133.

Le Gros Clark, W. E. 1958. The tissues of the body. 4th ed. Oxford U.P., London. 415 p.

Lehninger, A. L. 1960. Energy transformation in the cell. Sci. Am. 202 (5): 102–114.

Lehninger, A. L. 1962*a*. Water uptake and extrusion by mitochondria in relation to oxidative phosphorylation. Physiol. Rev. 42: 467–517.

Lehninger, A. L. 1962*b*. Intermediate enzymatic factors in the coupling of phosphorylation to electron transport. Comp. Biochem. Physiol. 4: 217–228.

Lehrman, D. S. 1959. Hormonal responses to external stimuli in birds. Ibis 101: 478–496.

Lenhoff, H. M. 1961. Activation of the feeding reflex in *Hydra littoralis*. I. Role played by reduced glutathione, and quantitative assay of the feeding reflex. J. Gen. Physiol. 45: 331–344.

Lerner, A. B., and Y. Takahashi. 1956. Hormonal control of melanin pigmentation. Recent. Prog. Hormone Res. 12: 303–320.

Lever, J., J. Jansen, and T. A. DeVlieger. 1960. Pleural ganglia and water balance in the fresh water pulmonate *Limnaea stagnalis*. Koninkl. Ned. Akad. Wetenschap. Proc. C, 64: 531–542.

Lever, J., and J. Joose, 1961. On the influence of the salt content of the medium on some special neurosecretory cells in the lateral lobes of cerebral ganglia of *Lymnaea stagnalis*. Koninkl. Ned. Akad. Wetenschap. Proc. C, 64: 630–639.

Levine, R. 1957. On the mechanisms of action of hormones on cells. Survey of Biol. Progr. 3: 185–213.

L'Helias, C. 1961. Le rôle des ptérines, intermédiares photosensibles et thermosensibles dans la genèse des hormones du complexe endocrinien le l'insecte. Année Biol. 37: 367–392.

L'Helias, C. 1962. Corrélations entre les ptérines et le photopériodisme dans la régulation du cycle sexual chez les pucerons. Bull. Biol. France et Belgique 96: 187–198.

Lipmann, F. 1941. Metabolic generation and utilization of phosphate bond energy. Adv. Enzymol. 1: 99–162.

Lissmann, H. W. 1958. On the function and evolution of electric organs in fish. J. Exp. Biol. 35: 156–191.

Lissmann, H. W. 1961. Ecological studies on gymnotids. *In* Chagas and Paes de Carvalho (1961): 215–226.

Lissmann, H. W. 1963. Electric location by fishes. Sci. Am. 208 (3): 50–59.

Lissmann, H. W., and K. E. Machin. 1958. The mechanism of object location in *Gymnarchus niloticus* and similar fish. J. Exp. Biol. 35: 451–493.

Lockwood, A. P. M. 1962. The osmoregulation of Crustacea. Biol. Rev. 37: 257–305.

Loeb, J. 1918. Forced movements, tropisms, and animal conduct. Lippincott, Philadelphia. 209 p.

Loewenstein, W. R. 1960. Biological transducers. Sci. Am. 203 (2): 98–108.

Loewenstein, W. R. 1961. Excitation and inactivation in a receptor membrane. Ann. N.Y. Acad. Sci. 94: 510–534.

Long, J. A., and H. M. Evans. 1922. The estrous cycle of the rat and its associated phenomena. Mem. Univ. Calif. 6: 1–148.

Lorente De Nó, R. 1938. Analysis of the activity of the chains of internuncial neurons. J. Neurophysiol. 1: 207.–244.

Lorenz, K. Z. 1935. Der Kumpan in der Umwelt des Vogels. J. Ornithol. 83: 137–213 and 289–413. See also Symp. Soc. Exp. Biol. 4: 221–268, 1950.

Lowy, J., and B. M. Millman. 1962. Mechanical properties of smooth muscles of cephalopod molluscs. J. Physiol. 160: 353–363.

Lowy, J., and B. M. Millman. 1963. The contractile mechanism of the anterior byssus retractor muscle of *Mytilus edulis*. Phil. Trans. Roy. Soc. London B, 246: 105–148.

Lwoff, A. (ed.) 1951. Biochemistry and physiology of protozoa. Academic Press, New York. 434 p.

Lyman, C. P. 1943. Control of coat color in the varying hare *Lepus americanus* Erxleben. Bull. Mus. Comp. Zool. (Harvard) 93: 393–461.

Lyman, C. P., and P. O. Chatfield. 1955. Physiology of hibernation in mammals. Physiol. Rev. 35: 403–425.

Lyman, C. P., and A. R. Dawe (eds.) 1960. Mammalian hibernation. Bull. Mus. Comp. Zool. (Harvard) 124: 1–549.

Macallum, A. B. 1926. The palaeochemistry of the body fluids and tissues. Physiol. Rev. 6: 316–357.

Machin, K. E., and H. W. Lissmann. 1960. The mode of operation of the electric receptors in *Gymnarchus niloticus*. J. Exp. Biol. 37: 801–811.

Mackie, G. O. 1960. The structure of the nervous system in *Velella*. Quart. J. Microscop. Sci. 101: 119–131.

Maetz, J. 1963. Physiological aspects of neurohypophysial function in fishes with some reference to the amphibia. Symp. Zool. Soc. London 9: 107–140.

Maetz, J., J. Bourguet et B. Lahlouh. 1964. Urophyse et osmorégulation chez *Carassius auratus*. Gen. Comp. Endocrinol. 4: 401–414.

Manwell, C. 1960. Comparative physiology: blood pigments. Ann. Rev. Physiol. 22: 191–244.

Marshall, A. J. (ed.) 1961. Biology and comparative physiology of birds. Vols. 1 & 2. Academic Press, New York.

Marshall, E. K. 1934. The comparative physiology of the kidney in relation to theories of renal secretion. Physiol. Rev. 14: 133–159.

Marshall, E. K. and H. W. Smith. 1930. The glomerular development of the vertebrate kidney in relation to habitat. Biol. Bull. 59: 135–153.

Marshall, N. B. 1954. Aspects of deep sea biology. Hutchinson, London. 380 p.

Marshall, N. B. 1960. Swimbladder structure of deep-sea fishes in relation to their systematics and biology. Discovery Rep. 31: 1–122.

Marsland, D. A. 1944. Mechanism of pigment displacement in unicellular chromatophores. Biol. Bull. 87: 252–261.

Martin, A. W. 1957. Recent advances in knowledge of invertebrate renal function. *In* Scheer (1957): 247–276.

Martin, A. W. 1958. Comparative physiology (excretion). Ann. Rev. Physiol. 20: 225–242.

Martin, A. W. (ed.) 1961. Comparative physiology of carbohydrate metabolism in heterothermic animals. Univ. Washington Press, Seattle. 144 p.

Martin, C. J. 1903. Thermal adjustment and respiratory exchange in monotremes and marsupials. A study in the development of homeothermism. Phil. Trans. Roy. Soc. London B, 195: 1–37.

Maslin, T. P. 1962. All-female species of the lizard genus *Cnemidophorus*. Teiidae. Science 135: 212–213.

Matthews, S. A. 1931. Observations on pigment migration within the fish melanophore. J. Exp. Zool. 58: 471–486.

Matty, A. J., and K. Green. 1963. Permeability and respiration effects of thyroidal hormones on the isolated bladder of the toad *Bufo bufo*. J. Endocrinol. 25: 411–425.

Maynard, D. M. 1955. Activity in a crustacean ganglion. II. Pattern and interaction in burst formation. Biol. Bull. 109: 420–436.

Maynard, D. M. 1960. Circulation and heart function. *In* Waterman, 1: 161–226.

McConnell, D. G., and D. G. Scarpelli. 1963. Rhodopsin: an enzyme. Science 139: 848.

McCutcheon, F. H. 1940. The respiratory mechanism in the grasshopper. Ann. Ent. Soc. (Am.) 33: 35–55.

McElroy, W. D. 1964. Cell physiology and biochemistry. 2nd ed. Prentice-Hall, Englewood Cliffs, N.J. 120 p.

McElroy, W. D., and B. Glass (eds.) 1961. A symposium on light and life. Johns Hopkins, Baltimore. 924 p.

McElroy, W. D., and H. H. Seliger. 1961. Mechanisms of bioluminescent reactions. *In* McElroy and Glass (1961): 219–257.

McElroy, W. D., and H. H. Seliger. 1962. Biological luminescence. Sci. Am. 207(6): 76–89.

McInerney, J. E. 1964. Salinity preference: an orientation mechanism in salmon migration. J. Fish. Res. Bd. Canada 21: 995–1018.

McLeese, D. W. 1956. Effects of temperature, salinity and oxygen on the survival of the American lobster. J. Fish, Res. Board Canada 13: 247–272.

McLennan, H. 1963. Synaptic transmission. Saunders, Philadelphia. 134 p.

McMillan, I. K. R., and E. S. Machell. 1961. The technique of induced hypothermia. Brit. Med. Bull. 17: 32–36.

McWhinnie, M. A., and A. J. Corkill. 1964. The hexosemonophosphate pathway and its variation in the intermolt cycle in crayfish. Comp. Biochem. Physiol. 12: 81–93.

Meier, A. H., and W. R. Fleming. 1962. The effects of pitocin and pitressin on water and sodium movements in the euryhaline killifish. *Fundulus kansae*. Comp. Biochem. Physiol. 6: 215–231.

Menner, E. 1938. Die Bedeutung des Pecten im Auge des Vogels für die Wahnehmung von Bewegungen. Zool. Jahrb. Abt. allg. Zool. Physiol. 58: 481–538.

Mercer, E. H. 1959. An electron microscopic study of *Amoeba proteus*. Proc. Roy. Soc. London B, 150: 216–232.

Merck, Sharp and Dohme. 1947. Seminar, 9(3) Sharp and Dohme.

Meschia, G., A. Hellegers, J. N. Blechner, A. S. Wolkoff, and D. H. Barron. 1961. A comparison of the oxygen dissociation curves of the bloods of maternal, fetal and newborn sheep at various points. Quart. J. Exp. Physiol. 46: 95–100.

Metz, C. B. 1957. Mechanisms in fertilization. *In* T. H. Bullock (ed.), Physiological triggers. pp. 17–45. American Physiol. Soc., Washington, D.C.

Metz, C. B., and K. Köhler. 1960. Antigen of arbacia sperm extracts. Biol. Bull. 119: 202–209.

Miller, P. L. 1964. Respiration-aerial gas transport. *In* Rockstein, 3: 557–615.

Miller, W. H. 1958. Fine structure of some invertebrate photoreceptors. Ann. N.Y. Acad. Sci. 74: 204–209.

Miller, W. H., F. Ratliff, and H. K. Hartline. 1961. How cells receive stimuli. Sci. Am. 205 (3): 233–238.

Millott, N. 1960. The photosensitivity of sea urchins. Symp. Comp. Biol. Academic Press, New York. 1: 279–293.

Milne, L. J., and M. Milne. 1959. Photosensitivity of invertebrates. Handbook of Physiology 1 (1): 621–645.

Milne, L. J., and M. Milne. 1962. The senses of animals and men. Atheneum, New York. 305 p.

Moehres, F. P. 1960. Sonic orientation of bats and other animals. Symp. Zool. Soc. London 3: 57–66.

Mommaerts, W. F. H. M. 1960. Contractile protein system of heart and muscle. Modern Concepts of Cardiovascular Disease 29 (3): 581–584.

Mommaerts, W. F. H. M., A. J. Brady, and B. C. Abbott. 1961. Major problems in muscle physiology. Ann. Rev. Physiol. 23: 529–576.

Moncrieff, R. W. 1951. The chemical senses. 2nd ed. Leonard Hill, Ltd., London. 538 p.

Montagna, W. 1961. Skin and integument and pigment cells. *In* Brachet and Mirsky, 5: 267–322.

Moore, J. A. (ed.) 1964. Physiology of the amphibia. Academic Press, New York. 654 p.

Morales, M. F. 1959. Mechanisms of muscle contraction. *In* Oncley (1959): 426–432.

Morrison, P., and F. A. Ryser. 1962. Metabolism and body temperature in a small hibernator, the meadow jumping mouse. *Zapus hudsonius*. J. Cell. Comp. Physiol. 60: 169–180.

Morton, J. E. 1958. Molluscs. Hutchinson Univ. Library, London. 232 p.

Morton, J. E. 1960. The functions of the gut in ciliary feeders. Biol. Rev. 35: 92–140.

Mott, J. C. 1957. The cardiovascular system. *In* M. E. Brown, 1: 81–108.

Muntz, W. R. A. 1964. Vision in frogs. Sci. Am. 210 (3): 111–119.

Murray, R. W. 1962. Temperature receptors. Adv. Comp. Physiol. Biochem. 1: 117–175.

Murray, R. W. 1962. Temperature receptors in animals. Symp. Soc. Exp. Biol. 16: 245–266.

Myers, V. C., and A. H. Free. 1943. Clinical enzyme studies. Am. J. Clin. Path. 13: 42–56.

Nachmansohn, D. (ed.) 1960. Molecular biology. Academic Press, New York. 177 p.

Najjar, V. A. 1963. Some aspects of antibody-antigen reactions and theoretical considerations of the immunologic response. Physiol. Rev. 43: 243–262.

Narahashi, T. 1963. The properties of insect axons. Adv. Insect Physiol., 1: 175–256.

Needham, A. E. 1952. Regeneration and wound-healing. Methuen, London. 152 p.

Needham, A. E. 1964. The growth process in animals. Pitman, London. 522 p.

Needham, J. 1931. Chemical embryology, 2: 615–1253. Cambridge U. P., London.

Needham, J. 1942. Biochemistry and morphogenesis. Cambridge U. P., London. 785 p.

Nelsen, O. E. 1953. Comparative embryology of the vertebrates. McGraw, New York. 982 p.

Newth, D. R., and D. M. Ross. 1955. On the reaction to light of *Myxine glutinosa* L. J. Exp. Biol. 32: 4–21.

Nicol, J. A. C. 1948. The giant axons of annelids. Quart. Rev. Biol. 23: 291–323. 291–323.

Nicol, J. A. C. 1952. Autonomic nervous systems in lower chordates. Biol. Rev. 27: 1–49.

Nicol, J. A. C. 1960*a*. The biology of marine animals. Pitman, London. 707 p.

Nicol, J. A. C. 1960*b*. The regulation of light emission in animals. Biol. Rev. 35: 1–42.

Nicol, J. A. C. 1961. The tapetum in *Scyliorhinus canicula*. J. Mar. Biol. Assoc. U.K. 41: 271–277.

Nicol, J. A. C. 1962. Animal luminescence. Adv. Comp. Physiol. 1: 217–273.

Nicol, J. A. C. 1963. Some aspects of photoreception and vision in fishes. Advances in Marine Biology 1: 171–208.

Nicol, J. A. C. 1964. Special effectors. *In* Wilbur and Yonge, 1: 353–381.

Niel, C. B., van. 1935. Photosynthesis of bacteria. Cold Spring Harbor Symp. 3: 138–150.

Niel, C. B. van. 1943. Biochemical problems of the chemo-autotrophic bacteria. Physiol. Rev. 23: 338–354.

Nirenberg, M. W. 1963. The genetic code. II. Sci. Am. 208 (3): 80–94.

Novales, R. R. 1963. Responses of cultured melanophores to the synthetic hormones—MSH, melatonin, and epinephrine. Ann. N.Y. Acad. Sci. 100: 1035–1047.

Novales, R. R., B. J. Novales, S. H. Zinner, and J. A. Stoner. 1962. The effect of sodium, chloride, and calcium concentration on the response of melanophores to melanocyte-stimulating hormone (MSH). Gen. Comp. Endocrinol. 2: 286–295.

Novick, A. 1959. Acoustic orientation in the cave swiftlet. Biol. Bull. 117: 497–503.

Novikoff, M. M. 1953. Regularity of form in organisms. Systematic Zool. 2: 57–62.

O'Dell, R., and B. Schmidt-Nielsen. 1960. Concentrating ability and kidney structure. Fed. Proc. 19: 366.

Oguri, M. 1964. Rectal glands of marine and fresh-water sharks: comparative histology. Science 144: 1151–1152.

Olsson, R. 1963. Endostyles and endostylar secretions: a comparative histochemical study. Acta Zool. 44: 299–328.

Oncley, J. L. (ed.) 1959. Biophysical science—a study program. Wiley, New York. 568 p.

Oord, A. van den. 1964. The absence of cholesterol synthesis in the crab, *Cancer pagurus* L. Comp. Biochem. Physiol. 13: 461–467.

Oordt, G. J. van. 1963. Male gonadal hormones. *In* von Euler and Heller 1: 154–207.

Oordt, P. G. W. J. van. 1965. Nomenclature of the hormone-producing cells in the adenohypophysis. Gen. Comp. Endocrinol. 5: 131–134.

Oparin, A. I. 1953. The origin of life. Dover Pub., New York. 270 p.

Overbeeke, A. P. van. 1960. Histological studies on the interrenal and the phaeochromic tissue in Teleostei. Thesis, Univ. Amsterdam. Van Munster's Drukkerijen N. V., Amsterdam. 102 p.

Owen, G. 1955–1956. Observations on the stomach and digestive diverticula of the Lamellibranchia. Quart. J. Microscop. Sci. 96: 517–537 and 97: 541–567.

Pagé, E. 1957. Body composition and fat deposition in rats acclimated to cold. Rev. Can. Biol. 16: 269–278.

Panouse, M. J. 1944. L'action de la glande du sinus sur l'ovaire chez la Crevette *Leander*. C. R. Acad. Sci. 218: 293–294.

Pantin, C. F. A. 1935. The nerve net of the Actinozoa. J. Exp. Biol. 12: 119–164.

Pantin, C. F. A. 1950. Behaviour patterns in lower invertebrates. Symp. Soc. Exp. Biol. 4: 175–195.

Pantin, C. F. A. 1952. The elementary nervous system. Proc. Roy. Soc. London B, 140: 147–168.

Pantin, C. F. A. 1956. Comparative physiology of muscle. Brit. Med. Bull. 12: 199–202.

Pantin, C. F. A. 1956. The origin of the nervous system. Pubbl. Staz. Zool. (Napoli) 28: 171–181.

Parker, G. H. 1919. The elementary nervous system. Lippincott, Philadelphia. 229 p.

Parker, G. H. 1948. Animal colour changes and their neurohumors. Cambridge U. P., London. 377 p.

Parkes, A. S. (ed.) 1960. Marshall's physiology of reproduction Vol. 1, (2), 3rd ed. Longmans, Ltd., London. 877 p.

Parry, G. 1960. Excretion. *In* Waterman, 1: 341–366.

Parsons, T. R., and W. Parsons. 1923. Observations on the transport of carbon dioxide in the blood of some marine invertebrates. J. Gen. Physiol. 6: 153–166.

Passano, L. M. 1960. Molting and its control. *In* Waterman, 1: 473–536.

Passano, L. M. 1961. The regulation of crustacean metamorphosis. Am. Zoologist 1: 89–95.

Passano, L. M. 1963. Primitive nervous systems. Proc. Nat. Acad. Sci. (U.S.) 50: 306–313.

Peachey, L. D., and H. Rasmussen. 1961. Structure of the toad's urinary bladder as related to its physiology. J. Biophys. Biochem. Cytol. 10: 529–553.

Pearson, O. P. 1960. Torpidity in birds. Bull. Mus. Comp. Zool. (Harvard) 124: 93–103.

Pelluet, D., and N. J. Lane. 1961. The relation between neurosecretion and cell differentiation in the ovotestis of slugs (Gasteropoda: Pulmonata). Can. J. Zool. 39: 789–805.

Pengelley, E. T., and K. C. Fisher. 1963. The effect of temperature and photoperiod on the yearly hibernating behavior of captive golden-mantled ground squirrels (*Citellus lateralis tescorum*). Can. J. Zool. 41: 1103–1120.

Perkins, E. B. 1928. Color changes in crustaceans, especially in *Palaemonetes*. J. Exp. Zool. 50: 71–105.

Perks, A. M., and M. H. I. Dodd. 1963. Evidence for a neurohypophyseal principle in the pituitary gland of certain Elasmobranch species. Gen. Comp. Endocrinol. 3: 286–299 and 184–195.

Perks, A. M., and W. H. Sawyer. 1965. A new neurohypophyseal principle in an elasmobranch, *Raia ocellata*. Nature 205: 154–156.

Perry, S. V. 1960. Muscular contraction. *In* Florkin and Mason, 2: 245–340.

Perutz, M. F. 1964. The hemoglobin molecule. Sci. Am. 211 (5): 64–76.

Pettus, D. 1958. Water relationships in *Natrix sipedon*. Copeia (1958) 3: 207–211.

Pfeiffer, W. 1962. The fright reaction of fish. Biol. Rev. 37: 495–511.

Pfeiffer, W. 1963. Alarm substances. Experientia 19: 113–123.

Phillips, J. E. 1964. Rectal absorption in the desert locust, *Schistocerca gregaria* Forskål. J. Exp. Biol. 41: 15–80.

Pickford, G. E. 1953. A study of the hypophysectomized male killifish, *Fundulus heteroclitus* (Linn.) Bull. Bingham Oceanogr. Coll. 14 (2): 5–41 and 46–68.

Pickford, G. E. 1959. The nature and physiology of the pituitary hormones of fishes. *In* Gorbman (1959): 404–420.

Pickford, G. E., and J. W. Atz. 1957. The physiology of the pituitary gland of fishes. N.Y. Zoological Society, New York. 613 p.

Pittendrigh, C. S. 1960. Circadian rhythms and the circadian organization of living systems. Cold Spring Harbor Symp. 25: 159–184.

Pitt-Rivers, R., and J. R. Tata, 1959. The thyroid hormones. Pergamon, New York, 247 p.

Pitts, R. F. 1959. The physiological basis of diuretic therapy. Thomas, C. C. Springfield, Ill. 332 p.

Plass, G. N. 1959. Carbon dioxide and climate. Sci. Am. 201 (1): 41–47.

Platzer, E. G. 1964. The life history of *Philonema oncorhynchi* in sockeye salmon from Cultus lake and the morphometric variation of the adult nematodes. M.Sc. thesis. University of British Columbia. 91 p.

Ponnamperuma, C., R. M. Lemmon, R. Mariner, and M. Calvin. 1963. Formation of adenine by electron irradiation of methane, ammonia, and water. Proc. Nat. Acad. Sci. (U.S.) 49: 737–740.

Porter, K. R. 1957. The submicroscopic morphology of protoplasm. Harvey Lectures 51: 175–239.

Potts, W. T. W., and G. Parry. 1964*a*. Osmotic and ionic regulation in animals. Pergamon, London. 423 p.

Potts, W. T. W., and G. Parry. 1964*b*. Sodium and chloride balance in the prawn, *Palaemonetes varians*. J. Exp. Biol. 41: 591–601.

Prakash, R. 1957. Structure, development and phylogeny of the impulse conducting (connecting) tissue of the vertebrate heart. J. Anat. Soc. (India) 6: 30–39.

Precht, H. 1958. Concepts of the temperature adaptation of unchanging reaction systems of cold-blooded animals. *In* Prosser (1958): 50–78.

Precht, H., J. Christophersen, and H. Hensel. 1955. Temperatur und Leben. Springer-Verlag, Berlin, 514 p.

Pringle, J. W. S. 1956. Insect song. Endeavour 15: 68–72.

Pringle, J. W. S. 1957. Insect flight. Cambridge U. P., London. 132 p.

Prosser, C. L. 1933. Action potentials in the nervous system of the crayfish. II. Responses to illumination of the eye and caudal ganglion. J. Cellular Comp. Physiol. 4: 363–377.

Prosser, C. L. 1955. Physiological variation in animals. Biol. Rev. 30: 229–262.

Prosser, C. L. 1958. Physiological adaptation. American Physiological Society, Washington, D.C. 185 p.

Prosser, C. L. 1960. The comparative physiology of activation of muscles, with particular attention to smooth muscles. *In* Bourne, 2: 387–434.

Prosser, C. L., L. M. Barr, R. D. Pinc, and C. Y. Lauer. 1957. Acclimation of goldfish to low concentrations of oxygen. Physiol. Zool. 30: 137–141.

Prosser, C. L., and F. A. Brown. 1961. Comparative animal physiology. 2nd ed. Saunders, Philadelphia. 688 p.

Prosser, C. L., T. Nagai, and R. A. Nystrom. 1962. Oscular contractions in sponges. Comp. Biochem. Physiol. 6: 69–74.

Pumphrey, R. J. 1940. Hearing in insects. Biol. Rev. 15: 107–132.

Pumphrey, R. J. 1950. Hearing. Symp. Soc. Exp. Biol. 4: 3–18.

Pumphrey, R. J. 1961. Sensory organs: Hearing. *In* Marshall, 2: 69–86.

Qutob, Z. 1962. The swimbladder of fishes as a pressure receptor. Arch. Néerl. Zool. 15: 1–67.

Rabinowitch, E. I. 1948. Photosynthesis. Sci. Am. 179 (2): 25–35.

Ramsay, J. A. 1949. The osmotic relations of the earthworm. J. Exp. Biol. 26: 46–56 and 65–75.

Ramsay, J. A. 1952. A physiological approach to the lower animals. Cambridge U.P., London. 148 p.

Ramsay, J. A. 1955. The excretory system of the stick insect, *Dixippus morosus* (Orthoptera, Phasmidae). J. Exp. Biol. 32: 183–199.

Ramsay, J. A. 1956. Excretion by the Malpighian tubules of the stick insect, *Dixippus morosus* (Orthoptera, Phasmidae): calcium, magnesium, chloride, phosphate, and hydrogen ions. J. Exp. Biol. 33: 697–708.

Ramsay, J. A. 1958. Excretion by the Malpighian tubules of the stick insect, *Dixippus morosus* (Orthoptera, Phasmidae): amino acids, sugars and urea. J. Exp. Biol. 35: 871–891.

Randall, D. J., and G. Shelton. 1963. The effects of changes in environmental gas concentrations on the breathing and heart rate of a teleost fish. Comp. Biochem. Physiol. 9: 229–239.

Raven, C. P. 1959. An outline of developmental physiology. 2nd ed. Pergamon, London. 224 p.

Raven, C. P. 1961. Oogenesis: the storage of developmental information. Pergamon, London. 274 p.

Read, C. P. 1961. The carbohydrate metabolism of worms. *In* Martin (1961): 3–34.

Redfield, A. C. 1934. The haemocyanins. Biol. Rev. 9: 175–212.

Retzlaff, E. 1957. A mechanism for excitation and inhibition of the Mauthner's cells in teleost. J. Comp. Neurol. 107: 209–225.

Rhodin, J., and T. Dalhamn. 1956. Electron microscopy of the tracheal ciliated mucosa in rat. Z. Zellforsch. 44: 345–412.

Richards, A. N. 1924. Methods and results of direct investigations of the function of the kidney. Beaumont Foundation Lectures, Series 8. Williams & Wilkins, Baltimore.

Ridgway, G. J., and G. W. Klontz. 1960. Blood types in Pacific salmon. U.S. Fish Wildlife Service, Spec. Sci. Rep. Fish. 324: 1–9.

Rieck, A. F., J. A. Belli, and M. E. Blaskovics. 1960. Oxygen consumption of whole animal and tissues in temperature acclimated amphibians. Proc. Soc. Exp. Biol. Med. 103: 436–439.

Riedesel, M. L. 1960. The internal environment during hibernation. Bull. Mus. Comp. Zool. (Harvard) 124: 421–435.

Riegel J. A., and L. B. Kirschner. 1960. The excretion of inulin and glucose by the crayfish antennal gland. Biol. Bull. 118: 296–307.

Rigg, G. B., and L. A. Swain. 1941. Pressure-composition relationships of the gas in the marine brown alga, *Nereocystis luetkeana.* Plant Physiol. 16: 361–371.

Ritchie, A. D. 1928. The comparative physiology of muscular tissue. Cambridge U.P., London 1928. 111 p.

Roberts, J. L. 1960. The influence of photoperiod upon thermal acclimation by Crucian carp, *Carassius carassius,* L. Verhandl. Deut. Zool. Ges. (Bonn/Rhein), (1960): 73–78.

Robertson, J. D. 1957*a*. The habitat of the early vertebrates. Biol. Rev. 32: 156–187.

Robertson, J. D. 1957*b*. Osmotic and ionic regulation in aquatic invertebrates. *In* Scheer (1957): 229–246.

Robertson, J. D. 1960. Studies of the chemical composition of muscle tissue. J. Exp. Biol. 37: 879–888.

Robinson, J. R. 1960. Metabolism of intracellular water. Physiol. Rev. 40: 112–149.

Rockstein, M. 1964. The physiology of Insecta. Vols. 1 & 3. Academic Press, New York.

Roeder, K. D. (ed.) 1953. Insect physiology. Wiley, New York. 1100 p.

Roeder, K. D. 1955. Spontaneous activity and behavior. Sci. Month. 80: 362–370.

Roeder, K. D. 1964. Aspects of the noctuid tympanic nerve response having significance in the avoidance of bats. J. Insect Physiol. 10: 529–546.

Roeder, K. D., and A. E. Treat. 1957. Ultrasonic reception by the tympanic organ of noctuid moths. J. Exp. Zool. 134: 127–157.

Romer, A. S. 1946. The early evolution of fishes. Quart. Rev. Biol. 21: 33–69.

Romer, A. S. 1955. The vertebrate body. 2nd ed. Saunders, Philadelphia. 644 p.

Roots, B. I., and C. L. Prosser. 1962. Temperature acclimation and the nervous system of fish. J. Exp. Biol. 39: 617–629.

Rose, W. C. 1938. The nutritive significance of the amino acids. Physiol. Rev. 18: 109–136.

Rose, W. C. 1949. Amino acid requirements of man. Federation Proc. 8: 546–552.

Rosen, W. G. 1962. Cellular chemotropism and chemotaxis. Quart. Rev. Biol. 37: 242–259.

Rosenthal, G. M. 1957. The role of moisture temperature in the local distribution of the plethodontid salamander *Aneides lugubris.* Univ. Calif. Pub. Zool. 54: 371–420.

Ross, D. M. 1957. Quick and slow contractions in the isolated sphincter of the sea anemone, *Calliactis parasitica*. J. Exp. Biol. 34: 11–28.

Ross, D. M. 1960. The effects of ions and drugs on neuromuscular preparations of sea anemones. J. Exp. Biol. 37: 732–752 and 753–774.

Ross, D. M., and L. Sutton. 1961. The response of the sea anemone *Calliactis parasitica* to shells of the hermit crab *Pagurus bernhardus*. Proc. Roy. Soc. London B, 155: 266–281.

Ross, D. M., and L. Sutton. 1964. The swimming response of the sea anemone *Stomphia coccinea* to electrical stimulation. J. Exp. Biol. 41: 735–749.

Ross, D. M., and L. Sutton. 1964. Inhibition of the swimming response by food and of nematocyst discharge during swimming in sea anemone *Stomphia coccinea*. J. Exp. Biol. 41: 751–757.

Rothschild, Lord. 1956. Fertilization. Methuen, London. 170 p.

Rothschild, M., and B. Ford. 1964. Breeding of the rabbit flea *Spilopsyllus cuniculi* (Dale) controlled by the reproductive hormones of the host. Nature 201: 103–104.

Rubey, W. W. 1951. Geologic history of sea water. Bull. Geol. Soc. Am. 62: 1111–1148.

Ruch, T. C., and J. F. Fulton (eds.) 1960. Medical physiology and biophysics. 18th ed. Saunders, Philadelphia. 1232 p.

Ruck, P. 1962. On photoreceptor mechanisms of retinula cells. Biol. Bull. 123: 618–634.

Rudzinska, M. A. 1958. An electron microscope study of the contractile vacuole in *Tokophrya infusionum*. J. Biophys. Biochem. Cytol. 4: 195–202.

Ruibal, R. 1962. The adaptive value of bladder water in the toad, *Bufo cognatus*. Physiol. Zool. 35: 218–223.

Rushton, W. A. H. 1962. Visual pigments in man. Liverpool U. P., Liverpool. 38 p.; and Sci. Am. 207(5): 120–132.

Ruud, J. T. 1954. Vertebrates without erythrocytes and blood pigment. Nature 173: 848–850.

Sallach, H. J., and R. W. McGilvery. 1963. Intermediary metabolism (charts). Gilson Medical Electronics, Middleton, Wisconsin.

Salt, G. W. 1964. Respiratory evaporation in birds. Biol. Rev. 39: 113–136.

Salt, G. W., and E. Zeuthen. 1961. The respiratory system. *In* Marshall, 1: 363–409.

Salt, R. W. 1959. Role of glycerol in the cold-hardening of *Bracon cephi* (Gahan). Can. J. Zool. 37: 59–69.

Salt, R. W. 1961. Resistance of poikilothermic animals to cold. Brit. Med. Bull. 17: 5–8.

Satchell, G. H. 1959. Respiratory reflexes in the dogfish. J. Exp. Biol. 36: 62–71.

Satchell, G. H. 1960. The reflex co-ordination of the heart beat with respiration in the dogfish. J. Exp. Biol. 37: 719–731.

Satchell, G. H., and H. K. Way. 1962. Pharyngeal proprioceptors in the dogfish *Squalus acanthias* L. J. Exp. Biol. 39: 243–250.

Satir, P. 1961. Cilia. Sci. Am. 204 (2): 108–116.

Saunders, R. L. 1961–62. The irrigation of the gills in fishes. Can. J. Zool. 39: 637–653, and 40: 817–862.

Sawyer, W. H., R. A. Munsick, and H. B. Van Dyke. 1960. Antidiuretic hormones. Circulation 21: 1027–1037.

Saxén, L., E. Saxén, S. Toivonen, and K. Salimäki. 1957. Quantitative investigation on the anterior pituitary—thyroid mechanism during frog metamorphosis. Endocrinology 61: 35–44.

Scharrer, B. 1955. Hormones in invertebrates. *In* G. Pincus and K. V. Thimann (eds.), The hormones. 3: 57–95. Academic Press, New York.

Scharrer, E. 1959. General and phylogenetic interpretations of neuroendocrine interrelations. *In* Gorbman (1959): 233–249.

Scharrer, E., and B. Scharrer. 1963. Neuroendocrinology. Columbia U.P., New York. 289 p.

Scheer, B. T. 1948. Comparative physiology. Wiley, New York. 563 p.

Scheer, B. T. (ed.) 1957. Recent advances in invertebrate physiology. Univ. Oregon Pub., Eugene, Ore. 304 p.

Scheer, B. T. 1960. The neuroendocrine system of arthropods. Vitamins and Hormones 18: 141–204.

Scheer, B. T. 1963. Animal physiology. Wiley, New York. 409 p.

Scherba, G. 1962. Mound temperature of the ant *Formica ulkei* Emery. Am. Midland. Nat. 67: 373–385.

Schlieper, C. 1958. Physiologie des Brackwassers. Die Binnengewässer 22: 217–330.

Schmidt-Nielsen, K. 1959. The physiology of the camel. Sci. Am. 201 (6): 140–151.

Schmidt-Nielsen, K. 1960. The salt-secreting gland of marine birds. Circulation 21: 955–967.

Schmidt-Nielsen, K., A. Borut, P. Lee, and E. Crawford. 1963. Nasal salt excretion and the possible function of the cloaca in water conservation. Science 142: 1300–1301.

Schmidt-Nielsen, K., and B. Schmidt-Nielsen. 1952. Water metabolism of desert animals. Physiol. Rev. 32: 135–166.

Schmitt, O. H. 1959. Biological transducers and coding. *In* Oncley (1959): 492–503.

Schneider, L. 1960. Elektronenmikroskopische Untersuchungen über das Nephridialsystem von *Paramaecium*. J. Protozool. 7: 75–90.

Scholander, P. F. 1940. Experimental investigations on the respiratory function in diving mammals and birds. Hvalrådets Skr. 22: 1–131.

Scholander, P. F. 1954. Secretion of gases against high pressures in the swimbladder of deep sea fishes. II. The rete mirabile. Biol. Bull. 107: 260–277.

Scholander, P. F. 1955. Evolution of climatic adaptation in homeotherms. Evolution 9: 15–26.

Scholander, P. F. 1958. Studies on man exposed to cold. Federation Proc. 17: 1054–1057.

Scholander, P. F., E. Bradstreet, and W. F. Garey. 1962. Lactic acid response in the grunion. Comp. Biochem. Physiol. 6: 201–203.

Scholander, P. F., W. Flagg, R. J. Hock, and L. Irving. 1953. Studies on the physiology of frozen plants and animals in the Arctic. J. Cell. Comp. Physiol. 42 (Suppl. 1): 1–56.

Scholander, P. F., R. Hock, V. Walters, F. Johnson, and L. Irving. 1950. Heat regulation in some Arctic and tropical mammals and birds. Biol. Bull. 99: 237–258.

Scholander, P. F., L. van Dam, J. W. Kanwisher, H. T. Hammel, and M. S. Gordon. 1957. Supercooling and osmoregulation in Arctic fish. J. Cell. Comp. Physiol. 49: 5–24.

Schwarz, K. (ed.) 1961. Nutritional significance of selenium. Federation Proc. 20 (1): 665–702.

Scully, U. 1964. Factors influencing the secretion of regeneration-promoting hormone in *Nereis diversicolor*. Gen. Comp. Endocrinol. 4: 91–98.

Segaar, J., and R. Nieuwenhuys. 1963. New etho-physiological experiments with male *Gasterosteus aculeatus,* with anatomical comment. Behaviour II: 331–346.

Selye, H. 1949. Textbook of endocrinology. 2nd ed. Acta Endocrinologica, Montreal. 914 p.

Selye, H. 1961. Nonspecific resistance. Ergeb. Pathol. 41: 208–241.

Sereni, E. 1930. The chromatophores of the cephalopods. Biol. Bull. 59: 247–268.

Shaw, J. 1960. The mechanisms of osmoregulation. *In* Florkin and Mason, 2: 471–518.

Shaw, J., and R. H. Stobbart. 1963. Osmotic and ionic regulation in insects. Adv. Insect. Physiol. 1: 315–399.

Shelton, G., and D. J. Randall. 1962. The relationship between heart beat and respiration in teleost fish. Comp. Biochem. Physiol. 7: 237–250.

Shepard, M. P. 1955. Resistance and tolerance of young speckled trout (*Salvelinus fontinalis*) to oxygen lack, with special reference to low oxygen acclimation. J. Fish. Res. Bd. Canada 12: 387–446.

Sherrington, C. 1929. Some functional problems attaching to convergence. Proc. Roy. Soc. London B, 105: 332–362.

Sherrington, C. 1947. The integrative action of the nervous system. 2nd ed. Yale U.P., New Haven, Conn. 413 p.

Shimomura, O., F. H. Johnson, and Y. Saiga. 1963. Further data on the bioluminescent protein, Aequorin. J. Cell. Comp. Physiol. 62: 1–8 and 9–15.

Siekevitz, P. 1959. Oxidative phosphorylation in muscle mitochondria and its possible regulation. Ann. N.Y. Acad. Sci. 72: 500–514.

Simpson, J. W., K. Allen, and J. Awapara. 1959. Free amino acids in some aquatic invertebrates. Biol. Bull. 117: 371–381.

Sindermann, C. J., and D. F. Mairs. 1959. A major blood group system in Atlantic sea herring. Copeia 1959: 228–232.

Sindermann, C. J., and D. F. Mairs. 1961. A blood group system for spiny dogfish, *Squalus acanthias* L. Biol. Bull. 120: 401–410.

Singer, C. A short history of scientific ideas to 1900. Oxford U.P., London. 525 p.

Sinsheimer, R. L. 1962. Single-stranded DNA. Sci. Am. 207 (1): 109–116.

Sleigh, M. A. 1962. The biology of cilia and flagella. Pergamon, Oxford. 242 p.

Slifer, E. H. 1961. The fine structure of insect sense organs. Int. Rev. Cytol. 11: 125–159.

Slijper, E. J. 1962. Whales. Hutchinson, London. 475 p.

Smalley, R. L., and R. L. Dryer. 1963. Brown fat: Thermogenic effect during arousal from hibernation in the bat. Science 140: 1333–1334.

Smith, A. U. 1954. Effects of low temperatures on living cells and tissues. *In* R. J. C. Harris (ed.) Biological applications of freezing and drying. Academic Press, New York. 415 p.

Smith, A. U. 1958. The resistance of animals to cooling and freezing. Biol. Rev. 33: 197–253.

Smith, H. W. 1953. From fish to philosopher. Little, Boston. 264 p.

Smith, H. W. 1956. Principles of renal physiology. Oxford University Press, New York. 237 p.

Smith, M. 1964. Deoxyribonucleic acids of Crustacea. J. Mol. Biol. 9: 17–23.

Smith, P. E. 1930. Hypophysectomy and a replacement therapy in the rat. Am. J. Anat. 45: 205–273.

Snodgrass, R. E. 1935. Principles of insect morphology. McGraw, New York. 667 p.

Solomon, A. K. 1962. Pumps in the living cell. Sci. Am. 207 (2): 100–108.

Sonnenblick, E. H., D. Spiro and T. S. Cottrell. 1963. Fine structural changes in heart muscle in relation to the length-tension curve. Proc. Nat. Acad. Sci. (U.S.) 49: 193–200.

Spector, W. S. 1956. Handbook of biological data. Saunders, Philadelphia. 584 p.

Starkey, R. L. (Convener). 1962. Symposium on autrophy. Bact. Rev. 26: 142–175.

Starling, E. H. 1918. The law of the heart. Longmans, Ltd. London. 27 p.

Steele, J. E. 1963.. The site of action of insect hyperglycemic hormone. Gen. Comp. Endocrinol. 3: 46–52.

Steen, J. B., and A. Kruysse. 1964. The respiratory function of teleostean gills. Comp. Biochem. Physiol. 12: 127–142.

Steinetz, B. G., V. L. Beach, and R. L. Kroc. 1959. The physiology of relaxin in laboratory animals. *In* C. W. Lloyd (ed.), Recent progress in the endocrinology of reproduction. pp. 389–427. Academic Press, New York.

Steven, D. M. 1963. The dermal light sense. Biol. Rev. 38: 204–240.

Sumner, J. B. 1951. Urease. *In* J. B. Sumner and K. Myrback (eds.), The enzymes. 1(2): 873–892. Academic Press, New York.

Suomalainen, E. 1962. Significance of parthenogenesis in the evolution of insects. Ann. Rev. Ent. 7: 349–366.

Sverdrup, H. U., M. W. Johnson, and R. H. Fleming. 1942. The oceans. Prentice-Hall, Englewood Cliffs, N.J. 1087 p.

Swan, L. W. 1961. The ecology of the high Himalayas. Sci. Am. 205 (4): 68–78.

Sweeney, B. M. 1960. The photosynthetic rhythm in single cells of *Gonyaulax polyedra*. Cold Spring Harbor Symp. 25: 145–148.

Swisher, S. N., and L. E. Young. 1961. The blood grouping systems of dogs. Physiol. Rev. 41: 495–520.

Szent-Györgyi, A. 1949. Free-energy relations and contraction of actomyosin. Biol. Bull. 96: 140–161.

Tait, J. S. 1960. The first filling of the swimbladder in salmonids. Can. J. Zool. 38: 179–187.

Takasugi, N., and H. A. Bern. 1962. Experimental studies on the caudal neurosecretory system of *Tilapia mossambica*. Comp. Biochem. Physiol. 6: 289–303.

Tavolga, W. N. 1960. Sound production and underwater communication in fishes. *In* Lanyon and Tavolga (1960): 93–136.

Thesleff, S. 1961. Nervous control of chemosensitivity in muscle. Ann. N.Y. Acad. Sci. 94: 535–546.

Thimann, K. V. 1963. The life of bacteria. 2nd ed. Macmillan, New York. 909 p.

Thimann, K. V., and G. M. Curry. 1960. Phototropism and phototaxis. *In* Florkin and Mason (1960) 1: 243–309.

Thomson, R. H. 1962. Melanins. *In* Florkin and Mason, 3: 727–753.

Thorpe, W. H. 1950. The concepts of learning and their relation to those of instinct. Symp. Soc. Exp. Biol. 4: 387–408.

Thorpe, W. H. 1951. The definition of some terms used in animal behaviour studies. Bull. Animal Behav. 1: 34–40.

Thorpe, W. H. 1956. Learning and instinct in animals. Methuen, London. 493 p.

Thorpe, W. H. 1958. Ethology as a new branch of biology. *In* A. A. Buzzati-Traverso (ed.) Perspectives in marine biology, pp. 411–428. Univ. Calif. Press, Berkeley, Calif.

Thorson, T. B. 1958. Measurement of the fluid compartments of four species of marine chondrichthyes. Physiol. Zool. 31: 16–23.

Thorson, T. B., and A. Svihla. 1943. Correlation of the habitats of amphibians with their ability to survive the loss of body water. Ecology 24: 374–381.

Threadgold, L. T., and A. H. Houston. 1964. An electron microscope study of the "chloride cell" of *Salmo salar* L. Exp. Cell Research 34: 1–23.

Tiegs, O. W. 1955. The flight muscles of insects—their anatomy and histology; with some observations on the structure of skeletal muscle in general. Phil. Trans. Roy. Soc. London B, 238: 221–348.

Tinbergen, N. 1951. The study of instinct. Clarendon Press, Oxford. 228 p.

Tinbergen, N. 1963. On aims and methods of ethology. Z. Tierpsychol. 20: 410–433.

Tribukait, B. 1963. Der Einfluss chronischer Hypoxie entsprechend 1000–8000 m Höhe auf die Erythropoiese der Ratte. Acta Physiol. (Scand.) 57: 1–25.

Tsukuda, H. 1960. Heat and cold tolerance in relation to body size in the guppy, *Lebistes reticulatus*. J. Inst. Polytech. (Osaka City Univ.) D, 11: 55–62.

Tsuyuki, H., E. Roberts, and R. E. A. Gadd. 1962. Muscle proteins of Pacific salmon (*Oncorhynchus*). Can. J. Biochem. Physiol. 40: 929–936.

Turner, C. D. 1960. General endocrinology. 3rd ed. Saunders, Philadelphia. 511 p.

Turner, C. L. 1937. Reproductive cycles and superfetation in poeciliid fishes. Biol. Bull. 72: 145–164.

Turner, C. L. 1947. Viviparity in teleost fishes. Sci. Monthly 65: 508–518.

Underwood, E. J. 1962. Trace elements in human and animal nutrition. 2nd ed. Academic Press, New York. 429 p.

Urey, H. C. 1952. The planets, their origin and development. Yale U.P., New Haven, Conn. 245 p.

Velle, W. 1963. Female gonadal hormones. *In* von Euler and Heller, 1: 111–153.

Verworn, M. 1899. General physiology. Macmillan, London. 615 p.

Verworn, M. 1913. Irritability. Yale U.P., New Haven, Conn. 264 p.

Vonk, H. J. 1937. The specificity and collaboration of digestive enzymes in metazoa. Biol. Rev. 12: 245–284.

Vonk, H. J. 1960. Digestion and metabolism. *In* Waterman, 1: 291–316.

Vonk, H. J. 1962. Emulgators in the digestive fluids of invertebrates. Arch. Int. Physiol. Biochem. 70: 67–85.

Vorontsova, M. A., and L. D. Liosner. 1960. Asexual propagation and regeneration. Pergamon, London. 489 p.

Wagge, L. E. 1955. Amoebocytes. Int. Rev. Cytology 4: 31–78.

Wald, G. 1952. Biochemical evolution. *In* E. S. G. Barron (ed.), Modern trends in physiology and biochemistry. pp. 337–376. Academic Press, New York.

Wald, G. 1959. Life and light. Sci. Am. 201 (4): 92–108.

Wald, G. 1960*a*. The distribution and evolution of visual systems. *In* Florkin and Mason, 1: 311–345.

Wald, G. 1960*b*. The significance of vertebrate metamorphosis. Circulation 21: 916–938.

Wald, G. 1961. The molecular organization of visual systems. *In* McElroy and Glass (1961): 724–753.

Wald, G. 1963. Phylogeny and ontogeny at the molecular level. *In* A. I. Oparin (ed.), Evolutionary Biochemistry. pp. 12–51. Pergamon,London.

Walls, G. L. 1942. The vertebrate eye and its adaptive radiation. Cranbrook Inst. Sci. Bull. 19. Bloomfield Hills, Michigan. 785 p.

Waring, H. 1963. Color change mechanisms of cold-blooded vertebrates. Academic Press, New York. 266 p.

Waterman, T. H. 1960*a*. Interaction of polarized light and turbidity in the orientation of *Daphnia* and *Mysidium*. Z. Vergl. Physiol. 43: 149–172.

Waterman, T. H. 1960–61. The physiology of the crustacea. Vols. 1 and 2. Academic Press, New York.

Weber, H. 1933. Lehrbuch der Entomologie, Gustav Fischer, Jena. 726 p.

Weber, H. H. 1958. The motility of muscle and cells. Harvard U. P., Cambridge, Mass. 69 p.

Weber, H. H. 1960. Chemical reactions during contraction and relaxation. *In* Nachmansohn (1960): 1–16.

Weel, P. B. van. 1961. The comparative physiology of digestion in molluscs. Am. Zoologist 1: 245–252.

Wells, G. P. 1949. Respiratory movements of *Arenicola marina* L.: intermittent irrigation of the tube, and intermittent aerial respiration. J. Mar. Biol. Assoc. U.K. 28: 447–464.

Wells, G. P. 1950. Spontaneous activity cycles in polychaete worms. Symp. Soc. Exp. Biol. 4: 127–142.

Wells, M. J. 1960. Optic glands and the ovary of *Octopus*. Symp. Zool. Soc. London 2: 87–107.

Wells, M. J. 1962. Brain and behaviour of cephalopods. Heinemann, London. 171 p.

Wells, M. J., and J. Wells. 1959. Hormonal control of sexual maturity in *Octopus*. J. Exp. Biol. 36: 1–33.

Wells, N. A. 1935. Variations in the respiratory metabolism of the Pacific killifish *Fundulus parvipinnis* due to size, season and continued constant temperature. Physiol. Zool. 8: 318–336.

Welsh, J. H. 1934. The caudal photoreceptor and responses of the crayfish to light. J. Cell. Comp. Physiol. 4: 379–388.

Welsh, J. H. 1957. Neurohumors or transmitter agents. *In* Scheer (1957): 161–171.

Welsh, J. H. 1959. Neuroendocrine substances. *In* Gorbman (1959): 121–133.

Welsh, J. H. 1961. Neurohumors and neurosecretion. *In* Waterman, 2: 281–311.

Welsh, J. H., and W. Schallek. 1946. Arthropod nervous systems: a review of their structure and function. Physiol. Rev. 26: 447–478.

Wenner, A. M. 1964. Sound communication in honeybees. Sci. Am. 210 (4): 117–124.

Whitford, W. G., and V. H. Hutchinson, 1963. Cutaneous and pulmonary gas exchange in the spotted salamander, *Ambystoma maculatum*. Biol. Bull. 124: 344–354.

Whittembury, G. 1962. Action of antidiuretic hormone on the equivalent pore radius at both surfaces of the epithelium of the isolated toad skin. J. Gen. Physiol. 46: 117–130.

Wichterman, R. 1953. The biology of paramecium. McGraw, New York. 527 p.

Wiersma, C. A. G. 1960. Inhibitory neurons: a survey of the history of their discovery and of their occurrence. *In* Florey, E. (ed.), Nervous inhibition. pp. 1–7. Pergamon, Oxford.

Wiersma, C. A. G. 1961. The neuromuscular system. Reflexes and the central nervous system. *In* Waterman, 2: 191–279.

Wigglesworth, V. B. 1930. A theory of tracheal respiration in insects. Proc. Roy. Soc. London B, 106: 229–250.

Wigglesworth, V. B. 1936. The function of the corpus allatum in the growth and reproduction of *Rhodnius prolixus* (Hemiptera). Quart. J. Microscop. Sci. 79: 91–121.

Wigglesworth, V. B. 1942. The principles of insect physiology. 2nd ed. Methuen, Soc. London B, 106: 229–250.

Wigglesworth, V. B. 1964. The hormonal regulation of growth and reproduction in insects. Adv. Insect Physiol. 2: 247–336.

Wilber, C. G. 1957. Physiological regulations and the origin of human types. Human Biology 29: 329–336.

Wilbur, K. M., and C. M. Yonge. 1964. Physiology of Mollusca. Vol. 1. Academic Press, New York. 473 p.

Wilkie, D. R. 1956. The mechanical properties of muscle. Brit. Med. Bull. 12: 177–182.

Willey, C. H. 1930. Studies on the lymph system of digenetic trematodes. J. Morph. 50: 1–37.

Williams, C. M. 1952. The physiology of insect diapause. Biol. Bull. 103: 120–138.

Williams, C. M. 1961. Insect metamorphosis: an approach to the study of growth. *In* M. X. Zarrow (ed.), Growth in living systems. pp. 313–320. Basic Books, New York. 759 p.

Williams, R. H. (ed.) 1962 Textbook of endocrinology. 3rd ed. Saunders. Philadelphia. 1204 p.

Willmer, E. N. 1934. Some observations on the respiration of certain tropical freshwater fishes. J. Exp. Biol. 11: 283–306.

Wilson, D. M. 1961. The connections between the lateral giant fibers of earthworms. Comp. Biochem. Physiol. 3: 274–284.

Wirz, H. 1953. Der osmotische Druck des Blutes in der Nierenpapille. Helv. Physiol. Acta 11: 20–29.

Wirz, H. 1961. Newer concepts of renal mechanism in relation to water and electrolyte excretion. *In* C. P. Stewart and Th. Stengers (eds.), Water and electrolyte metabolism. pp. 100–108. Elsevier, Amsterdam.

Withrow, R. B. (ed.) 1959. Photoperiodism and related phenomena in plants and animals. Amer. Assoc. Adv. Sci. Publ. 55. Washington, D.C.

Witschi, E. 1961. Sex and secondary sexual characters. *In* Marshall, 2: 115–168.

Wittenberg, J. B. 1960. The source of carbon monoxide in the float of the Portuguese man-of-war, *Physalia physalis*.L. J. Exp. Biol. 37: 698–705.

Wittenberg, J. B. 1961. The secretion of oxygen into the swim-bladder of fish. I. The transport of molecular oxygen. J. Gen. Physiol. 44: 521–526.

Wittenberg, J. B., and B. A. Wittenberg. 1961. The secretion of oxygen into the swim-bladder of fish. II. The simultaneous transport of carbon monoxide and oxygen. J. Gen. Physiol. 44: 527–542.

Wolken, J. J. 1958. Studies of photoreceptor structures. Ann. N.Y. Acad. Sci. 74: 164–181.

Wolken, J. J. 1960. Photoreceptors: comparative studies. Symp. Comp. Biol. Academic Press, New York. 1: 145–167.

Wolverkamp, H. P., and T. H. Waterman. 1960. Respiration. *In* Waterman, 1: 35–100.

Wood, J. D. 1958. Nitrogen excretion in some marine teleosts. Can. J. Biochem. Physiol. 36: 1237–1242.

Woods, F. H. 1931. History of the germ cells in *Sphaerium striatum* (Lam.). J. Morph. 51: 545–595.

Wright, R. H. 1963. Molecular vibration and insect sex attractants. Nature 198: 455–459.

Wright, R. H. 1964. The science of smell. G. Allen,London. 164 p.

Wurtman, R. J., and J. Axelrod. 1965. The pineal gland. Sci. Am. 213(1): 50–60.

Wyatt, G. R. 1961. The biochemistry of insect hemolymph. Ann. Rev. Entomol. 6: 75–102.

Wyman, L. C. 1924. The reactions of melanophores of embryonic and larval *Fundulus* to certain chemical substances. J. Exp. Zool. 40: 161–180.

Yokoe, Y., and I. Yasumasu. 1964. The distribution of cellulase in invertebrates. Comp. Biochem. Physiol. 13: 323–338.

Yonge, C. M. 1928. Feeding mechanisms in the invertebrates. Biol. Rev. 3: 21–76.

Yonge, C. M. 1937. Evolution and adaptation in the digestive system of the metazoa. Biol. Rev. 12:87–115.

Yonge, C. M. 1941. The protobranchiate Mollusca; a functional interpretation of their structure and evolution. Trans. Roy. Soc. London B, 230: 79–148.

Young, J. Z. 1935. The photoreceptors of lampreys. 1. Light-sensitive fibres in the lateral line nerves. J. Exp. Biol. 12: 229–238.

Young, J. Z. 1939. Fused neurons and synaptic contacts in the giant nerve fibres of cephalopods. Phil. Trans. Roy. Soc. London B, 229: 465–505.

Young, J. Z. 1957. The life of mammals. Clarendon Press, Oxford. 820 p.

Young, J. Z. 1962. The life of verbebrates. 2nd ed. Oxford U.P. 820 p.

Young, W. C. (ed.) 1961. Sex and internal secretions. 3rd. ed. Vols. 1 & 2. Williams & Wilkins, Baltimore.

Zarrow, M. X., J. M. Yochim, and J. L. McCarthy. 1964. Experimental endocrinology. Academic Press, New York. 519 p.

Zeuthen, E. 1953. Oxygen uptake as related to body size in organisms. Quart. Rev. Biol. 28: 1–12.

Zeuthen, E. 1955. Comparative physiology (respiration). Ann. Rev. Physiol. 17: 459–482.

Zoond, A., and J. Eyre. 1934. Studies in reptilian colour response. Phil. Trans. Roy. Soc. London B, 223: 27–55.

Zotterman, Y. 1953. Special senses: thermal receptors. Ann. Rev. Physiol. 15: 357–372.

Zotterman, Y. 1959. Thermal sensations. Handbook of Physiology 1(1): 431–458.

Zuckerman, S. 1962. The ovary. Vols. 1 & 2. Academic Press, New York.

Index

B

F

I

N

O

P

Q

R

S